Webster's
Dictionary of
American Women

Webster's Dictionary of American Women

Created in Cooperation with the Editors of

MERRIAM-WEBSTER INC.

This edition published in 1996 by
SMITHMARK Publishers
a division of US Media Holdings Inc.
16 East 32nd Street
New York, NY 10016.

SMITHMARK books are available for bulk purchase for sales promotion and premium use. For details, write or call the manager of special sales, SMITHMARK Publishers, 16 East 32nd Street, New York, NY 10016; (212) 532-6600.

Library of Congress data available upon request.

ISBN: 0-7651-9793-6

Printed in the United States of America.

10 9 8 7 6 5 4 3 2 1

Contents

Introduction

It is the task of biography to help enlarge and enrich the historical record, to turn the details of the lives of individuals into compelling, enlightening, and perhaps most important, entertaining narratives. A look beneath the surface of traditional history reveals a number of remarkable American women who, by struggling against, adapting to, or ignoring the strictures laid on them, compiled striking records of accomplishment and not infrequently made lasting contributions to their times.

Webster's Dictionary of American Women brings together the stories of over 1,100 such women. Chronologically, they range from Virginia Dare, who in 1587 was the first European child to be born in America, to such contemporary figures as Jane Fonda, Susan Sontag, and Hillary Rodham Clinton. They include artists and astronomers, church leaders and criminals, feminists and frontier heroines, poets and politicians.

The biographical sketches in this book (13 of them treating two subjects) average some 400 words in length. Each includes the date and place of birth (unless not known), a brief description of the subject's education and of any special early circumstances that bear on her story, and an account of her career and accomplishments, generally supplemented by an attempt to place her work in historical context and indicate its significance. Each sketch ends with the subject's place and date of death, or, in the case of living subjects, a mention of more recent activities. It may be worth noting, in order to prevent any misunderstanding, that information concerning subjects' marriages and families is also included when a change of name occurred, when a significant impact on her career resulted, or when a marriage partner or child became a notable figure in his or her own right. The sketches are arranged alphabetically by name; to find a subject by occupation or field of endeavor, turn to the index that begins on page 687.

While the biographical sketches in *Webster's Dictionary of American Women* deal with a vast range of endeavors—from mountain climbing to experimental particle physics, from cordon bleu cookery to theology—they are all written in a straightforward narrative style that should welcome the reader with a perfect mix of gentle detail and precise fact. One usage that may not be immediately self-evident is most easily explained by example: In the sketch of Sarah Chauncey Woolsey, the parentheses in the phrase "Through the influence of her close friend Helen Hunt (Jackson)" indicate that Miss Hunt, as she was at the time, is better known by her later married name and is entered under that name in this book.

While the function of biography is to record the history of an individual, the following summaries of the lives of over 1,100 notable American figures do more than serve as a valuable reference tool. They are also fascinating stories which are sure to entertain as well as inform.

Abbott, Berenice 1898–1991 photographer and writer

Born in Springfield, Ohio, on July 17, 1898, Berenice Abbott spent only one and a half semesters at Ohio State University before moving to New York City to study to become a sculptor. After four years of study there, she left for Europe, continuing her studies first at the Kunstschule in Berlin in 1923 and later in Paris. In France, however, her art veered off in a new direction; taking up photography, she let her training in sculpture help to guide her use of the camera. In later years she herself recalled the connection she found between these two disciplines: "Photography is not only drawing with light . . . It is modeling or sculpturing with light, to reproduce the plastic form of natural objects."

From 1923 to 1925 she served as a darkroom assistant to photographer Man Ray, then remained in Paris for four years as owner of a photography studio and as a documentary and portrait photographer. She made photographic portraits of such famous sitters as James Joyce, André Gide, Marcel Duchamp, Jean Cocteau, Max Ernst, Leo Stein, Princesse Marthe Bibesco, Sylvia Beach, Peggy Guggenheim, Violette Murat, Janet Flanner, Edna St. Vincent Millay, and the photographer Eugène Atget. Abbott was so taken with Atget's own work that later in her life, she saved the Atget collection and introduced his photography to a U.S. audience.

Abbott returned to New York in 1929. Continuing to do portraits, she also began documenting the city in photographs. From 1930 through 1939, both during and following the Great Depression in the U.S., she was among the New York City artists hired through the Federal Art Project; her photographs from this period were published under the title *Changing New York*, 1939. From 1935 she shared her expertise for 23 years by teaching photography at the New School for Social Research in New York City. She also wrote several books, including: *Greenwich Village Today and Yesterday*, 1949; *Guide to Better Photography*, 1941 and 1953; *The View Camera Made Simple*, 1948; *The World of Atget*, 1964; *A Portrait of Maine*, 1968; and *Berenice Abbott: Photographs*, 1970.

Turning to scientific photography in 1958, she worked for the Physical Science Study Committee at the Massachusetts Institute of Technology to produce scientific illustrations for the high school textbook *Health*, 1960. In her later years, she received honorary doctorate degrees from the University of Maine, 1971, Smith College, 1973, the New School for Social Research, 1981, Bates College, 1981, and Bowdoin College, 1982. Her last project was similar to *Changing New York*; taking photographs along Route 1 from Maine to Florida, she documented the changing American landscape. In 1968 she settled in Maine, where she concentrated on printing her work. She died at her home in Monson, Maine, on December 9, 1991.

At the time of her death Abbott's work remained on exhibit in numerous galleries and museums, including the Museum of Modern Art, New York; the Metropolitan Museum of Art, N.Y.; the Museum of the City of New York; the International Museum of Photography, George Eastman House, Rochester, N.Y.; the Museum of Fine Arts, Boston; the Smithsonian Institution, Washington, D.C.; the Art Institute of Chicago; the Museum of Fine Arts, Houston; the San Francisco Museum of Art; and the Bibliothèque Nationale, Paris.

Abbott, Grace 1878–1939 social worker

Born in Grand Island, Nebraska, on November 17, 1878, Grace Abbott graduated from Grand Island College in 1898 and for eight years thereafter taught high school in her native town. During that period she undertook graduate studies at the University of Nebraska in 1902 and at the University of Chicago in the summer of 1904. In 1907 she moved to Chicago and the next year became a resident of Jane Addams's Hull-House settlement. She was awarded a Ph.M. degree in political science by the University of Chicago in 1909.

By then she was devoting herself to the work of the Immigrants' Protective League, which she helped Sophonisba Breckinridge and others organize in 1908 and of which she became director at that time. Her work with the League led to her involvement in securing protective legislation; to her studies of conditions at Ellis Island (the main point of entry for immigrants, in New York harbor), in Massachusetts, and in 1911 in eastern Europe; to her testimony before Congress against immigration restrictions; and to numerous published articles, a report on *The Immigrant in Massachusetts*, 1915, and a book *The Immigrant and the Community*, 1917. During 1910–1917 she was also on the faculty of the Chicago School of Civics and Philanthropy (later the University of Chicago's Graduate School of Social Service Administration). In 1917 Abbott joined the staff of the federal Children's Bureau at the invitation of its head, Julia Lathrop. She was responsible for enforcement of the Child Labor Act of 1916 until it was declared unconstitutional in 1918. As an adviser to the War Labor Policies Board during World War I, she succeeded in having clauses prohibiting child labor written into all government war contracts even after the federal law was struck down. In October 1919 she returned to Illinois as director of the new Illinois State Immigrants' Commission.

The commission was allowed to lapse in 1921, and in August of that year she was named by President Warren G. Harding to succeed Lathrop as head of the Children's Bureau. Her major concern during her first years in that post was the administration of the Sheppard-Towner Act, passed in November 1921, which extended federal aid to states for programs in maternal and infant health care. The aid program was ended by Congress in 1929. Following the declaration of a second federal child-labor law as unconstitutional in 1922, she worked for the adoption of a constitutional amendment on the subject. From 1922 to 1934 she was also an unofficial representative of the United States at the League of Nations Advisory Committee on Traffic in Women and Children. In 1934 Abbott resigned from the Children's Bureau and was appointed a professor in the University of Chicago's School of Social Service Administration, of which her sister Edith was dean. In 1934–1935 she helped plan the Social Security system as a member of President Franklin D. Roosevelt's Council on Economic Security, and she was U.S. delegate to the International Labor Organization in 1935 and 1937. During 1934–1939 she was editor of *The Social Service Review*, and in 1938 she published her two-volume work on *The Child and the State*. Grace Abbott died in Chicago on June 19, 1939. A collection of her papers appeared as *From Relief to Social Security* in 1941.

Abzug, Bella 1920– public official

Born in New York City on July 24, 1920, Bella Savitsky attended public schools and graduated from Hunter College in 1942. She then entered the Columbia University Law School, where she was an editor of the *Columbia Law Review*, and from which she took a degree in 1945. In June 1945 she married Martin M. Abzug. She was admitted to the New York bar in 1947.

Over the next 23 years she divided her time between the practice of law — labor law principally, along with a heavy load of civil rights work, much of it on a pro bono publico basis, defending indigent, African-American, and McCarthy-smeared defendants — and work on behalf of various causes, especially those of peace and disarmament. She was a founder of the Women Strike for Peace organization in 1961, and in the later 1960s, as the growing involvement of the United States in the Vietnam war became a focus of public protest, she led in agitating for change through such groups as the Coalition for a Democratic Alternative, which supported Senator Eugene McCarthy's challenge to President Lyndon B. Johnson, the Coalition for an Open Convention, and the New Democratic Coalition. In 1970 she entered the Democratic primary and unseated Leonard Farbstein, a seven-term incumbent, to win the congressional nomination from New York's 19th

Congressional District, a district encompassing a wide cross-section of voters from the upper class to slum dwellers. In November she defeated her Republican-Liberal opponent, and in January 1971 she took her seat in the 92nd Congress. Her campaign had established a national image as a brash, flamboyant, and fearless supporter of the peace movement, the feminist movement, and other liberal-radical causes, and her career in Congress followed that pattern. She broke with House tradition by rising on her first day to offer a resolution, one that called for the immediate withdrawal of all U.S. troops from Indochina. Outspoken in her criticisms of presidents and other figures, she became an established public figure herself as she proved to be reliably exciting copy for national media, and her perennial wide-brimmed hats became a familiar symbol.

In 1971, along with Gloria Steinem and Shirley Chisholm, she co-founded the National Women's Political Caucus, which aimed at increasing the participation of women in government. She retained a seat in Congress, through a redistricting, in the 1972 and 1974 elections. In 1976 she gave it up to run for the Senate, but she was defeated by Daniel P. Moynihan. In September 1977 she lost a primary election for the Democratic nomination for mayor of New York City. In February 1978 she lost a special election held to fill the congressional seat vacated by Mayor Edward Koch.

She played a prominent role at the National Women's Conference held in Houston in November 1977. She was subsequently named cochairman of the National Advisory Committee on Women by President Jimmy Carter, a post she held until January 1979, when Carter dismissed her on grounds that the committee's public criticisms of the administration had been counterproductive.

She returned to the practice of law in 1980, but remained in the public eye as the president of Women USA, a grassroots political action organization, as a contributor to *Ms.* magazine, and as a daily news commentator for the Cable News Network. In 1984 she published *Gender Gap: Bella Abzug's Guide to Political Power for American Women* with Mim Kelber. In 1992 she served as a senior advisor to the United Nations Conference on Environmental Development ("Earth Summit") in Rio de Janeiro, Brazil.

Adams, Abigail Smith 1744–1818 letter writer and First Lady

Born on November 11 (old style), 1744, in Weymouth, Massachusetts, Abigail Smith was a frail child and received no formal schooling. Nevertheless she read widely in English and French and early displayed a lively intelligence. Much of her childhood was passed at the home of her grandparents in Mount Wollaston. In October 1764 she married John Adams of Braintree (now Quincy). The marriage was a happy one, and five children were born in the next ten years. From 1774 until 1784 the couple were mostly separated as Adams's political and diplomatic business kept him in Philadelphia or abroad. From that period date the letters for which Abigail Adams was later famous. Combining reports on her highly successful management of the Adams farm, reflections on people and events, news and gossip of home, and unselfconscious affection, they provide a sprightly and fascinating view of life in those trying times. In March 1776 she wrote her husband, then in Philadelphia attending the Continental Congress: "Remember the Ladies, and be more generous and favourable to them than your ancestors. Do not put such unlimited power into the hands of the Husbands . . . If perticuliar care and attention is not paid to the Laidies we are determined to foment a Rebelion, and will not hold ourselves bound by any Laws in which we have no voice, or Representation."

In 1784 she joined her husband in Europe, where he was U.S. commissioner in Paris and from 1785 the first U.S. minister to Great Britain. Despite suffering social discourtesies Abigail Adams was later to write "England . . . is the country of my greatest partiality." She continued to support warmly her husband's political career after their return to Braintree and to express to him her own thoughts. During his vice-presidency and presidency she alternated residence in Braintree and in the capital (located in turn in New York, Philadelphia, and then Washington, D.C.), and in November 1800 she became the first First Lady to occupy the yet unfinished White House, which she found very uncomfortable. From 1801 the couple lived in quiet retirement in Braintree. Abigail Adams died at home on October 18, 1818. The first of several increasingly complete editions of her letters was published by Charles Francis Adams, her grandson, in 1840.

Adams, Hannah 1755–1831 compiler of historical information

Born on October 2, 1755, in Medfield, Massachusetts, Hannah Adams was the daughter of a notably eccentric bibliophile father whose lack of business acumen kept the large family in poverty. She inherited his love of books and remarkable memory, and although she received no formal schooling she was well tutored by divinity students boarding in the home. One of these showed her the Reverend Thomas Broughton's *Historical Dictionary of All Religions*, which prompted her to read widely and keep voluminous notes in the field of religions. The notes were published in 1784 as *An Alphabetical Compendium of the Various Sects Which Have Appeared from the Beginning of the Christian Era to the Present Day*. The book was well received, saw three more American editions and three in London, and brought its author a modest financial return. Determined to earn her living in this way, she set to work on *A Summary History of New-England*, which appeared in 1799.

By this time her eyesight was affected by her constant work. While preparing an abridged version of her history for schools, she learned that the Reverend Jedidiah Morse was engaged in a similar project. Morse's book appeared first, and hers apparently suffered in sales as a result. A number of Boston liberal intellectuals, motivated both by admiration for her and antipathy to Morse, a staunchly conservative Calvinist, precipitated a public controversy over the matter, in which Morse conducted himself so clumsily as to lose all public support. Hannah Adams took little direct part in the celebrated controversy. Several of her Boston supporters established an annuity for her, and the rest of her days were devoted to the compilation of data. She published *The Truth and Excellence of the Christian Religion Exhibited*, 1804, *History of the Jews*, 1812, and *Letters on the Gospels*, 1824. She died in Brookline, Massachusetts, on December 15, 1831; her *Memoir of Miss Hannah Adams, Written by Herself* appeared the following year.

Adams, Maude 1872–1953 actor

Born on November 11, 1872, in Salt Lake City, Utah, Maude Ewing Adams Kiskadden began her theatrical career at the age of nine months, when she was carried on stage by her mother in a production of *The Lost Child*. She began playing actual roles as soon as she could talk, adopting her actress mother's maiden name (Adams) for the stage. At five she attracted considerable attention in San Francisco in *Fritz*, and at sixteen she joined Edward H. Sothern's company in New York City, making her debut in that city in *The Paymaster* in September 1888. Soon after her appearance in *A Midnight Bell*, 1889, she moved to Charles Frohman's company where, from 1892 to 1897, she regularly played opposite John Drew in such pieces as Clyde Fitch's *Masked Ball* and *Rosemary*. She first won top billing as Lady Babble in James M. Barrie's *The Little Minister* in 1897. Although she played a wide range of roles, including several of Shakespeare's great heroines, it was her portrayals of Barrie characters that brought her acclaim and the lasting devotion of audiences. Her greatest successes were in *Quality Street*, in 1902 and again in 1915–1916, *What Every Woman Knows*, 1908–1909, *A Kiss for Cinderella*, 1916–1918, and especially *Peter Pan*, in which she starred in more than 1500 performances in 1905–1907, 1913, and 1918. Other plays in which she appeared included *Romeo and Juliet*, 1899, Edmond Rostand's *L'Aiglon*, 1900–1901, Schiller's *Joan of Arc (Die Jungfrau von Orleans)*, 1909, and *Chantecler*, 1910–1911.

In 1918, though still a dazzling beauty, she retired from the stage and for a time worked with Charles P. Steinmetz on improving stage lighting. In 1931 she played opposite Otis Skinner in *The Merchant of Venice* and in 1934 made her last appearance, in *Twelfth Night*. From 1937 to 1943 she was chairman of the drama department of Stephens College in Columbia, Missouri. She had always kept her private life from public view, and she lived quietly in retirement until her death in Tannersville, New York, on July 17, 1953.

Addams, Jane 1860–1935 social reformer

Born in Cedarville, Illinois, on September 6, 1860, Jane Addams graduated from Rockford Female Seminary in 1881 and was granted a degree the following year when the institution became Rockford College. The death of her father in 1881, her own health problems, and an unhappy year at the Woman's Medical College of Pennsylvania left her depressed and aimless for some years. She traveled in Europe in 1883–1885, but neither there nor in Baltimore in 1885–1887 did she find a vocation.

In 1887 she returned to Europe with a Rockford classmate, Ellen Gates Starr. On a visit to the Toynbee Hall settlement house in London's East End in 1888 her vague leanings toward reform work crystallized. The two women were soon in Chicago and by September 1889 had begun their work in the decrepit Hull mansion in the midst of a teeming immigrant ward. From the first it was Addams's view that Hull-House, as the settlement was called, was as much or more for the benefit of the overprivileged and inexperienced persons she attracted to the work there as for that of the poor among whom they labored. Within a few years myriad clubs and programs of education, vocational and domestic training, and playground and nursery care had sprouted. Art and craft classes eventually led to a museum and a theater group. The success of the programs rested to a great extent on the quality of the full- and part-time residents of Hull-House, who included Grace and Edith Abbott, Julia Lathrop, Robert Morss Lovett, Gerard Swope, Sophonisba Breckinridge, Florence Kelley, and many others.

Hull-House grew eventually to include 13 buildings around the original site and a summer campground near Lake Geneva, Wisconsin. Directly and through various of her colleagues, Jane Addams worked to relieve and outlaw sweatshop working conditions, to promote organized labor, to investigate and expose social conditions in slum districts, to outlaw child labor, and to secure juvenile court, eight-hour day, tenement regulation, and workmen's compensation legislation. In addition she was the chief fund raiser for Hull-House, a task that brought her into contact with the wealthy of Chicago; and she wrote a steady stream of articles, pamphlets, and books on the work of the institution. Among her early books were *Democracy and Social Ethics*, 1902, *Newer Ideals of Peace*, 1907, and the classic *Twenty Years at Hull-House*, 1910.

In 1909 she was the first woman to be elected president of the National Conference of Charities and Correction (later the National Conference of Social Work), in 1910 she was the first woman to receive an honorary degree from Yale University, and she was head of the National Federation of Settlements from its founding in 1911 until her death. She campaigned vigorously for Theodore Roosevelt's Progressive party candidacy for president in 1912. In 1915 she was elected chairman of the new Woman's Peace party and then president of the International Congress of Women meeting at The Hague. Her dedication to peace lost her much support during World War I, but during and after the war she worked effectively for refugee relief. From 1919 until her death she was president of the Woman's International League for Peace and Freedom, and in 1920 she helped found the American Civil Liberties Union. The postwar period was less interested in social reform, but Hull-House survived. In 1931 Jane Addams shared the Nobel Peace Prize with Nicholas Murray Butler. Among her later books were *Peace and Bread in Time of War*, 1922, *The Second Twenty Years at Hull-House*, 1930, *The Excellent Becomes the Permanent*, 1932, and *My*

Friend, Julia Lathrop, 1935. She died in Chicago on May 21, 1935. Hull-House moved its headquarters in 1963; the original campus was demolished, as part of an urban renewal program, except for the Hull mansion, which was preserved as a memorial.

Adler, Sara 1858–1953 actor

Born in 1858 in Odessa, Russia, Sara Levitzky was of a well-to-do Jewish family. She studied singing at the Odessa Conservatory for a time and then joined a Yiddish theater troupe managed by Maurice Heine, whom she shortly married. The repressions that followed the assassination of Alexander II in 1881 bore heavily on the Jews of Russia, and in September 1883 Yiddish plays were expressly forbidden. Early the next year the Heine troupe emigrated to the United States, where Sara soon gained a following in the Yiddish theater in New York City. In 1890 she divorced Heine and married Jacob Adler, the leading tragic actor on the American Yiddish stage. Adler, together with playwright Jacob Gordin, was undertaking to revitalize the Yiddish theater, then overburdened by outmoded stock material, with modern drama reflecting the urban milieu of Jews in America. Sara and Jacob Adler's productions over the next several decades, mainly at their own theater on the Bowery, were the rebirth of serious Yiddish theater. She played some 300 leading roles, including many from the popular theatrical repertoire of the day. Her greatest role, and the one that established her preeminence on the Yiddish stage, was that of Katusha Maslova in Gordin's dramatization of Tolstoy's *Resurrection*. A close second was her starkly realistic portrayal of the abandoned and unbalanced wife in Gordin's *Homeless*. She performed infrequently after Jacob Adler's death in 1926. In 1939 she recreated her role in *Resurrection* at a tribute to her at the New Yorker Theatre. Not the least of her contributions to the theater were her children Stella Adler, born in 1901, and Luther Adler, born in 1903. Sara Adler died in New York City on April 28, 1953.

Adler, Stella 1901–1992 actor, director and acting teacher

Born in New York City on February 10, probably in 1901, Stella Adler grew up in a theater family. Her father, Jacob P. Adler, often called "the Henry Irving of Yiddish theater," was an actor and manager as was her mother, Sarah Lewis (originally Sara Levitzky). After her parents emigrated to the U.S. from Russia at the turn of the century, they gained prominence as tragedians of the Yiddish stage and formed the organization deemed largely responsible for promoting Yiddish theater in early twentieth-century America, the Adlers' Independent Yiddish Art Company. In addition, all of Adler's seven siblings became actors and actresses in their own right: Frances, Celia, Julia, Luther, Jay, Abe, and Charles. As she said: "In my family, immediately you could barely walk, you were put on the stage."

She made her stage debut at age four at New York's Grand Street Theater in her father's production of *Broken Hearts*. After that, she received little formal schooling, either in the three R's or in the art of acting; instead she studied with her father by watching other actors and actresses, and by performing herself in both boy and girl roles in her parents' company as well as in other theater companies.

In 1919 Adler made her international debut in the role of Naomi in *Elisha Ben Avia* in London at the Pavilion Theatre. Returning to New York the following year, she played feature roles, performed in vaudeville, and toured Europe and South America as the head of a repertory company. Between 1927 and 1931 she performed over a hundred roles.

In 1931, she joined the innovative Group Theater, an organization founded on the principle of artistic unity and comprised of people representing all parts of a production, including actors and actresses, writers, designers and directors. The players were trained by Lee Strasberg in "Method acting," a system propounded by Russian actor and theater director, Konstantin Stanislavsky, based on the idea that actors peform by invoking affective memory or a personal memory of the emotion they are trying to portray.

After studying with Stanislavsky in Russia in 1933, she revised his principles, which she considered too rigid and unhealthy. She returned to the Group Theater to teach acting and completely transformed its acting style, even though her new style challenged Strasberg and even though she was frustrated with the Group Theater for being, in her word, "a man's theater . . . aimed at plays for men." Her last performance there was as Clara in Clifford Odets's *Paradise Lost* in 1935.

In her classes, Adler taught that drawing on personal experience alone was too limited. She believed instead that the actor should use his or her imagination to create characters. She told her students: "Don't use your conscious past. Use your creative imagination to create a past that belongs to your character. I don't want you to be stuck with your own life. It's too little."

In the early 1940s, she began teaching acting at Erwin Piscator's Dramatic Workshop at the New School for Social Research in New York City. In 1949 she left and established the Stella Adler Theater Studio, where young performers could both study and act. In 1960 the school was renamed the Stella Adler Conservatory of Acting. While teaching at her own school, she also taught at Yale University's School of Drama from 1966 to 1967 and headed New York University's drama department in the 1980s. Adler herself performed up until 1961, giving her final performance in London. As a teacher, Adler mentored such personalities as Marlon Brando, Warren Beatty, and Robert De Niro, among scores of other actors and actresses.

In addition to acting and teaching, Adler worked as an associate producer for MGM in the early 1940s, directed commercial theater in New York City throughout the 1940s and 1950s, and published her own book on acting, *The Technique of Acting*, 1988. She was married three times; briefly to Horace Eleascheff, then to Harold Clurman, one of the founding members of the Group Theater, from 1943 to 1960, and finally to Mitchell Wilson, a physicist and novelist, who died in 1973. She had one daughter, Ellen, from her first marriage. Adler died at home in Los Angeles on December 21, 1992.

Agassiz, Elizabeth Cabot Cary 1822–1907 educator

Born in Boston on December 5, 1822, Elizabeth Cary was related to many of the city's leading families. She received no formal schooling but acquired a somewhat haphazard education at home. In April 1850 she was married to the distinguished and recently widowed Swiss naturalist Louis Agassiz. She proved to be invaluable to his career. Her notes on his lectures were the raw material of much of his published work, and she helped organize and manage several of his expeditions into the field, notably the Thayer Expedition to Brazil in 1865–1866 and the Hassler Expedition through the Strait of Magellan in 1871–1872. Her own published work included *A First Lesson in Natural History*, 1859, *Seaside Studies in Natural History*, in collaboration with her stepson Alexander Agassiz, 1865, and *A Journey in Brazil*, jointly with her husband, 1867.

From 1855 to 1863 she conducted in their Cambridge, Massachusetts, home a school for girls that was a pioneering effort in the field, as well as a needed supplement to the family's income. For some years after the death of Louis Agassiz in 1873 she busied herself in the care of her grandchildren and in working on a memoir of her husband, which finally appeared in 1885 as *Louis Agassiz: His Life and Correspondence*. In 1879 she joined in organizing a somewhat informal program of higher education for women conducted at the Harvard Annex from September of that year. In 1882 the program was incorporated as The Society for the Collegiate Instruction of Women with Elizabeth Agassiz as president. In 1894 the college was named Radcliffe in honor of Ann Radcliffe, founder of the first Harvard scholarship (1643), and formally linked to Harvard University. Elizabeth Agassiz remained president until 1899, when she relinquished her duties to the dean of the college, Agnes Irwin, and "honorary president" until 1903, when she was at last allowed to resign. She died in Arlington Heights, Massachusetts, on June 27, 1907.

Albright, Madeleine Korbel 1937– Political scientist and U.S. Representative to the United Nations

Born on May 15, 1937 in Prague, Czechoslovakia, Madeleine Korbel's father was a member of the Czech diplomatic service at the time of her birth and she spent her early years in Belgrade, London, and Prague. At the age of 10, she was sent to boarding school in Switzerland and when she was 12, her family settled in Colorado, where her father worked as a professor of international relations at the University of Denver. He wrote a number of books on foreign affairs and eventually became the dean of the university's Graduate School of International Studies. Throughout her life, she credited her father as a major personal and political influence. As a child she became fluent in both French and English, as well as her native language, Czech. She went on to Wellesley College and studied political science while working on the school's newspaper, thus combining her two major interests, politics and journalism. She graduated from Wellesley College with a B.A. in 1959.

After graduation, she married Joseph Albright, whom she met while they were both interning at the *Denver Post*. The couple settled in Chicago and Joseph Albright began writing for the Chicago *Sun-Times*. In 1961 they moved to Long Island, New York, and by 1967, they had three daughters. She began graduate studies in public law and government at Columbia University, and in 1968 she earned both an M.A. and a certificate in Russian studies. In 1976 she earned a Ph.D. from Columbia as well. In 1968, while still a graduate student, she and her family moved to Washington, D.C., where her husband worked as the Washington bureau chief for *Newsday*. From 1968 through the early 1970s, she held a number of volunteer positions including raising funds for Senator Edmund S. Muskie, who unsuccessfully sought the presidential nomination in 1972. She was dedicated to Muskie, a member of the Senate Foreign Relations Committee, and from 1976 to 1978, she served as his chief legislative assistant.

In 1978 she joined the staff of the National Security Council as a congressional liaison with a focus on foreign policy legislation. In 1981 and 1982, she worked as a senior fellow in Soviet and European affairs at the Center for Strategic and International Studies, and she was awarded a Woodrow Wilson fellowship from the Smithsonian Woodrow Wilson Center for Scholars. As a fellow she wrote the book *Poland: The Role of the Press in Political Change* published in 1983, the same year her marriage to Joseph Albright ended in divorce. In 1982 she began working as a research professor of international affairs and as director of the Women in Foreign Service Program at Georgetown University.

Over the next few years, she became a major player in U.S. politics — working as the foreign policy coordinator for Democratic candidate for president Walter F. Mondale and later working for presidential candidate Michael S. Dukakis. In 1989 she became president of the Center for National Policy, a nonprofit Democratic research institute. In 1992 she worked with Warren Christopher, Anthony Lake, and Samuel R. Berger to develop then-presidential candidate Bill Clinton's platform on foreign policy. After the election, President Clinton made her the U.S. delegate to the United Nations, as well as one of his cabinet officers and a U.S. ambassador. She also became a member of the National Security Council and was a presidential adviser on foreign policy. In her position as United Nations representative she acted not only as spokesperson for the U.S. government, but was instrumental in developing national foreign policy in a number of crisis-burdened countries such as the former Yugoslav republics of Bosnia, Croatia, and Slovenia, the former Soviet republics, and Somalia, Ethiopia, and Mozambique. She was known not only for her passionate, outspoken, and fearless leadership, but also for her fairness and enthusiasm.

Louisa May Alcott

Alcott, Louisa May 1832–1888 novelist

Born in Germantown, Pennsylvania, on November 29, 1832, Louisa May Alcott was the daughter of Amos Bronson Alcott, educator and philosopher. She grew up in Boston and Concord, Massachusetts, and from earliest age was on familiar terms with Ralph Waldo Emerson, Henry David Thoreau (who tutored her for a time), Theodore Parker, and others of the Transcendentalist circle. Her education was largely at the hands of her father, for a time in his innovative Temple School in Boston and later at home. In her youth she began to assume some responsibility for the welfare of her family. To relieve her mother of a portion of the burden of making up for her father's improvidence, she did sewing, worked as a domestic, taught school, and, from 1851, began publishing under pseudonyms poems, stories, and sketches in various periodicals. Many of her stories, notably those signed "A. M. Barnard," were lurid and violent tales of adventure. In 1854 she published her first book, *Flower Fables*. During the winter of 1862–1863 she was briefly a volunteer nurse in the Civil War hospitals of Washington, D.C., and her letters home during that time formed the basis for her first successful book, *Hospital Sketches*, 1863. Her first novel, *Moods*, published in 1864 but written four years earlier, was less successful; but her stories and poems for children continued to appear, and in 1867 she became editor of a children's magazine, *Merry's Museum*.

At the urging of her publisher she reluctantly undertook a novel for young girls. Published in two parts in 1868–1869 under the title *Little Women*, the book was an immediate and phenomenal success, selling 60,000 copies in its first year and assuring the Alcott family's financial security. *Little Women* was patently autobiographical and in its warmth and homely detail captured forever the period's ideal of middle-class domestic life. *An Old-Fashioned Girl* followed in 1870, *Little Men* in 1871, six volumes of stories and sketches under the title *Aunt Jo's Scrap Bag* in 1872–1882, a second adult novel, *Work*, in 1873, *Eight Cousins* in 1875 and a sequel *Rose in Bloom* in 1876, *Silver Pitchers* in 1876, *A Modern Mephistopheles*, an adult novel published anonymously in 1877, *Under the Lilacs* in 1878, *Jack and Jill* in 1880, *Proverb Stories* in 1882, *Spinning-Wheel Stories* in 1884, and three volumes of *Lulu's Library* in 1886–1889. Throughout her last twenty years, except for a European tour in 1870 and a few briefer trips to New York, she lived in Boston and Concord, devoting herself to the care of her mother, who died after a lengthy illness in 1877, and her increasingly helpless father; late in life she also adopted the children of two of her sisters who died prematurely. Her own health, never robust, declined as well. She took some interest in the cause of woman suffrage and in other reforms. The strain of caring for her father in his last illness, added to her exhaustion and constant pain, was too much. She died in Boston two days after he did, on March 6, 1888.

Alden, Cynthia May Westover 1862–1931 social worker and journalist

Born on May 31, 1862, in Afton, Iowa, Cynthia Westover was reared largely by her father, a geologist, in western mining camps. She developed skills with horses and rifles at a young age. She attended and later taught school in Denver, completed a normal course at the University of Colorado, and in 1882 made her way to New York City to seek a career as an opera singer. Failing at that, she won appointment as a U.S. customs inspector in 1887, and in 1890 she became secretary to the New York City commissioner of street cleaning. In the latter capacity she invented and patented an improved street cleaner's handcart and a self-emptying dump cart. In 1892, with C. F. Ober, she published *Manhattan, Historic and Artistic*. In 1894 she secured a position as editor of the women's department of the *New York Recorder*, and in 1896 she published *Bushy, or Child Life in the Far West*, based on her own early life.

In August 1896 she married John Alden, later editor of the *Brooklyn Eagle*. About that time she began the practice of sending Christmas cards to shut-ins; soon she was passing on Christmas gifts as well, and in 1896 a group of fellow journalists organized themselves as the Sunshine Society to carry on the practice. Her column in the *Recorder* brought additional members, and she spread word of the movement when she moved to the New York *Tribune* in 1897 and to the *Ladies Home Journal* in 1899.

On March 9, 1900, the International Sunshine Society was incorporated; Cynthia Westover was to remain president for the rest of her life. In 1902 the society established a sanatorium in Bensonhurst to care for blind children (in 1917 it became Harbor Hospital), and in 1905 a nursery and a kindergarten for blind children were established in Brooklyn. In 1910 the Sunshine Arthur Home for blind babies was established in Summit, New Jersey, and over a period of years the society's efforts led to legislation providing care for blind infants and children in 18 states. She published *Women's Ways of Earning Money*, 1904, and *The Baby Blind*, 1915. She died in Brooklyn, New York, on January 8, 1931. By that time the International Sunshine Society counted 500 local branches in 38 states and 8 foreign nations and operated hospitals and homes for the blind and orphans, summer camps, lodges, facilities for working women, and other services.

Alden, Isabella Macdonald 1841–1930 writer of children's books

Born on November 3, 1841, in Rochester, New York, Isabella Macdonald grew up there and in Johnstown and Gloversville, New York. She was educated at home and at Oneida Seminary, Seneca Collegiate Institute at Ovid, and the Young Ladies Institute at Auburn, all upstate New York boarding schools. She subsequently became a teacher at Oneida Seminary. She is reputed to have published a story in her hometown newspaper at the age of ten.

Her first novel, *Helen Lester*, appeared in 1866, when a friend submitted it without her knowledge to a competition for a book explaining the scheme of Christian salvation to children. In that same year she married the Reverend Gustavus R. Alden, with whom she traveled to a succession of pastorates from New York to Indiana over the next several years. The success of *Helen Lester* led to a steady stream of books, numbering in all more than 75, nearly all for children, mainly on religious themes, and all signed simply "Pansy," a childhood nickname. They bore such titles as *Ester Ried*, 1870, *Four Girls at Chautauqua*, 1876, *Little by Little*, 1879, *Judge Burnham's Daughter*, 1888, *The Prince of Peace*, a child's life of Jesus, 1893, *Yesterday Framed in To-day*, 1899, *A Modern Sacrifice*, 1899, *The Fortunate Calamity*, 1927, and *An Interrupted Night*, 1929. In addition Alden contributed regularly to the Presbyterian Primary *Quarterly* and the *Westminster Teacher*, served on the staffs of *Trained Motherhood* and the *Christian Endeavor World*, and for 30 years published an annual serial in the *Herald and Presbyter*. From 1874 to 1896 she edited her own children's periodical, the *Pansy*. The great popularity of her books — at her peak she sold over 100,000 copies a year, and they were widely circulated by public and especially Sunday School libraries — was due to the wholesome interest and variety of their situations and characters and the clearly moral but not somber lessons of their plots. The Pansy Society, an outgrowth of the magazine, enrolled a great many young members who pledged themselves to self-improvement. Alden was an active supporter of the Chautauqua movement and of the Woman's Christian Temperance Union. She lived in Philadelphia after 1897 and in Palo Alto, California, after 1924. She died there on August 5, 1930. Her unfinished autobiography was completed by her niece, Grace Livingston Hill, and published in 1931 as *Memories of Yesterdays*.

Alden, Priscilla Mullins 1602?–? pilgrim

Born about 1602 in Dorking, Surrey, England, Priscilla Mullins (or Mollins or Molines) came to America aboard the *Mayflower* with her parents and younger brother in 1620. The other three members of the family died during the terrible first winter of the

Plymouth Colony. Probably in 1623 she married John Alden, a cooper. They lived in Plymouth until about 1631, when they were among the first settlers of Duxbury, and they had 11 children. John Alden became a prominent figure in colonial Massachusetts, but virtually nothing is known of Priscilla's later life. The date of her death is unknown, but it may well have occurred before her husband's in 1687. Alone among the women of the Plymouth Colony, Priscilla Alden is remembered, owing to a legend transmitted orally in the family and then published in embellished form by Henry Wadsworth Longfellow in "The Courtship of Miles Standish" in 1858. The tale of the triumph of romantic love is nearly unique in the lore of the Pilgrims and is probably unfounded in fact; nonetheless, the story, and especially the words "Why don't you speak for yourself, John?", remain a part of American folklore.

Aldrich, Bess Genevra Streeter 1881–1954 novelist and short-story writer

Born in Cedar Falls, Iowa, on February 17, 1881, Bess Streeter graduated from Iowa State Teachers College (now the University of Northern Iowa) in 1901 and then taught school for five years, the last in Salt Lake City, Utah. In September 1907 she married Charles S. Aldrich, a banker and lawyer with whom she lived in Tipton, Iowa, and later in Elmwood, Nebraska. From an early age she had been interested in writing, and at the age of fourteen she had sold a story to the *Chicago Record.* She continued to publish occasionally, until 1918 generally under the pen name "Margaret Dean Stevens."

In 1924 she issued her first book, a collection of short stories under the title *Mother Mason.* Her first novel, *The Rim of the Prairie*, appeared in 1925, the year of her husband's death. Thereafter her output sharply increased. For her themes and characters she drew on the life of the Plains settlers of the nineteenth century, including her own forebears. Her depictions of that life were realistic and vivid, while her plots tended to the simple and sentimental. Her more than 160 short stories appeared in such leading magazines as *Woman's Home Companion*, *Saturday Evening Post*, *Century*, *Collier's*, *McCall's*, and *Harper's Weekly*; some were collected in *The Man Who Caught the Weather*, 1936, the title story of which won an O. Henry Prize, *Journey into Christmas*, 1949, and *The Bess Streeter Aldrich Reader*, 1950. Her novels included *The Cutters*, 1926; *A Lantern in Her Hand*, which enjoyed great success in America and in numerous translations abroad, 1928; *A White Bird Flying*, third on the best-seller list for 1931; *Miss Bishop*, also a best seller and later made into a successful motion picture, 1933; *Spring Came On Forever*, 1935; *Song of Years*, 1939; *The Drum Goes Dead*, 1941; and *The Lieutenant's Lady*, 1942. She died in Lincoln, Nebraska, on August 3, 1954.

Alexander, Francesca 1837–1917 illustrator and author

Born in Boston on February 27, 1837, Esther Frances Alexander, as she was christened, was known in childhood as Fanny. When she was sixteen, her prosperous family moved to Europe and settled at length in Florence. She was educated at home, and her extremely protective mother guided her studies and activities closely throughout her life. Young Fanny gained a reputation as a philanthropist among the people of Tuscany, from whom in turn she collected folk songs, tales, and customs. In 1882 she met John Ruskin, who was deeply impressed by a manuscript collection of "Roadside Songs of Tuscany" she had compiled and illustrated with drawings done in a fine and highly personal style. Ruskin bought the manuscript and another, publishing the second in 1883 as *The Story of Ida*, signed simply "Francesca." The volume enjoyed several British and American editions. He edited and published *Roadside Songs* in 1884–1885 and a third collection, *Christ's Folk in the Apennines*, in 1887–1889. An intimate correspondence between Ruskin, Alexander and her mother continued for some years. After his death Francesca herself published *Tuscan Songs*, 1897, and *The Hidden Servants and Other Very Old Stories Told*

Over, 1900. Blindness and ill health plagued her last years. She died in Florence on January 21, 1917.

Alexander, Jane Quigley 1939– actor and chairperson of the National Endowment for the Arts

Born on October 28, 1939, in Boston, Massachusetts, Jane Quigley's father was a surgeon who dabbled in acting when he was younger, and her mother was a nurse. She grew up in Brookline, a suburb of Boston, and by age six was already interested in acting, appearing in school productions every chance she got. In 1957 she enrolled at Sarah Lawrence College as a math major. However, after only two years at Sarah Lawrence, she grew restless and transferred to the University of Edinburgh, in Scotland. There she joined the drama club and began acting in university plays.

In 1961, she moved to New York City to try her luck at becoming a professional actress. She worked as a secretary during the day, and at night, struggled to find acting jobs. Her determination finally paid off when she convinced a stage manager at the Eugene O'Neill Theater to keep her in mind if any understudy positions became available. *A Thousand Clowns* opened there in 1963 and before its closing, she had several opportunities to substitute for Sandy Dennis in the role of social worker Sandra Markowitz. After the play closed she found a few small parts in off-Broadway productions, and in 1964, she moved back to Boston, where she joined the company-in-residence at the Charles Playhouse. Her big break came when she landed a part in the Arena Stage production of *Saint Joan* in Washington D.C. Her performance kept her working for two additional seasons at the Arena Theater, and in 1967, aided by a grant from the National Endowment for the Arts, the Arena Stage produced Howard Sackler's drama *The Great White Hope*, about the career of a black boxing champion played by James Earl Jones. She played the part of his white wife, Eleanor Bachman. The production was so successful, it was revived less than a year later on Broadway, again with Jones and Alexander in the starring roles. She received tremendous critical acclaim for her performance, and was awarded a Tony Award for Best Supporting Actress in 1969. The play was made into a film in 1970 and she recreated her role a second time, once again to critical and popular success.

Her acting career took off from there, and over the next 20 years she appeared in numerous stage, film, and television productions including the Broadway plays *Find Your Way Home* in 1974 and *First Monday in October* in 1978, for which she received Tony Award nominations; and the films *All the President's Men*, 1976, *Kramer vs. Kramer*, 1979, and *Glory*, 1989. Her television credits included *Eleanor and Franklin: The White House Years*, 1974, and *Playing for Time*, 1980, for which she received an Emmy Award. All told, she appeared in more than 40 films and over 100 plays. Her performances earned her six Tony nominations, four Oscar nominations, and five Emmy nominations. In 1983 she appeared in the movie *Testament*, about a small town contending with nuclear holocaust, a subject close to her heart. She was ardently opposed to nuclear weapons and not only gave an outstanding performance in the film, but was instrumental in getting it made in the first place. In 1987 she starred in the film *Square Dance*, and was also the co-producer.

In 1993, while she was appearing on Broadway in Wendy Wasserstein's *The Sister's Rosensweig*, President Bill Clinton nominated her for the position of chairperson of the National Endowment for the Arts, the controversial federal agency that oversees public funding for the arts. She was confirmed without challenge by the Senate in September of 1993. As the first artist to hold the position customarily given to administrators, many believed she brought both credibility and glamour to the high-profile fight for arts funding. Outspoken yet diplomatic, she spent 1994 touring the country — determined to visit every state — promoting arts education. She firmly believed that while art for art's sake is legitimate, art can be a tool for furthering social issues as well.

Allen, Elizabeth Anne Chase Akers 1832–1911 journalist and poet

Born in Strong, Maine, on October 9, 1832, Elizabeth Chase grew up in Farmington, Maine, where she attended Farmington Academy (later Maine State Teachers College). She is said to have had a poem published in the Boston *Olive Branch* at fifteen. In 1851 she was married to Marshall S. M. Taylor, but within a few years they were divorced. She took a job on the *Portland* (Maine) *Transcript* in 1855 and the next year published her first book of poetry, *Forest Buds from the Woods of Maine*, under the pseudonym Florence Percy. On the proceeds of that venture she traveled in Europe in 1859–1860. During that journey she served as a correspondent for the *Transcript* and for the *Boston Evening Gazette*. From Rome she dispatched to the *Saturday Evening Post* of Philadelphia a poem entitled "Rock Me to Sleep," whose opening lines "Backward, turn backward, O Time, in your flight,/And make me a child again, just for to-night!" became universally familiar. That poem remained by far her best known, although she published much superior verse, frequently in the *Atlantic Monthly*.

In August 1860 she married Benjamin Paul Akers, a Maine sculptor whom she had met in Rome; he died the next year. In 1863–1865 she worked as a government clerk in Washington, D.C., and in the latter year she married Elijah M. Allen. In 1866 she published a volume of her collected *Poems* under the name Elizabeth Akers. The volume included "Rock Me to Sleep," and a controversy ensued with one Alexander M. W. Ball of New Jersey, who for some years claimed authorship of the poem. After several years residence in Richmond, Virginia, she returned to Portland, Maine, in 1874 and for seven years was literary editor of the *Daily Advertiser*. After 1881 she and her husband lived in Tuckahoe, New York. Later collections of her verse included *Queen Catherine's Rose*, 1885, *The Silver Bridge*, 1886, *Two Saints, a Tribute to the Memory of Henry Bergh* (founder of the Society for the Prevention of Cruelty to Animals, of which she was a strong supporter), 1888, *The High-Top Sweeting*, 1891, *The Ballad of the Bronx*, 1901, and *The Sunset Song*, 1902. Allen died in Tuckahoe, New York, on August 7, 1911.

Allen, Florence Ellinwood 1884–1966 jurist

Born on March 23, 1884, in Salt Lake City, Florence Allen was a descendant of Ethan Allen and the daughter of a former classics professor and later congressman. She graduated from Western Reserve University's College for Women in 1904 and for two years studied music in Berlin. An injury foreclosed a concert career, and from 1906 to 1909 she was music critic for the *Cleveland Plain Dealer*. In 1908 she received a master's degree in political science from Western Reserve.

Allen then turned to the study of law, first at the University of Chicago and then at New York University, graduating from the latter in 1913. She was admitted to the Ohio bar in 1914. While establishing a law practice in Cleveland, she worked also for the Legal Aid Society and campaigned strenuously for woman suffrage. In 1919 she was appointed assistant prosecutor of Cuyahoga County; in 1920 she was elected a judge of the court of common pleas; and in 1922 she was elected to the Ohio supreme court. In each of those posts she was the first female incumbent, and in the last, to which she was reelected by a large majority in 1928, she was the first woman to sit on any court of last resort in the world. In March 1934 another precedent was set when President Franklin D. Roosevelt named Judge Allen to the U.S. Court of Appeals for the Sixth Circuit; she was the first woman to sit on any federal bench of general jurisdiction. She retained that seat for 25 years, the last as chief judge, until her retirement in October 1959.

Among the thousands of cases she heard was the constitutional testing of the Tennessee Valley Authority in 1938. She was active in numerous international law organizations, was a leader particularly of the human rights section of the International Bar Association, and was the recipient of numerous honorary degrees and other awards. She published *This Constitution of Ours*, 1940, *The Treaty as an Instrument of Legislation*, 1952, and a volume of memoirs, *To Do Justly*, 1965. Judge Allen died on September 12, 1966, in Waite Hill, Ohio.

Allen, Paula Gunn 1939– poet, novelist and scholar

Born in 1939 in Cubero, New Mexico, Paula Gunn Allen's heritage was part Sioux and part Lebanese American. At San Francisco State University she earned three degrees: a B.A. in English, an M.F.A. in creative writing, and a Ph.D. in Native American Studies. In 1970, she was invited to teach in the newly-formed Native American Studies program at the University of New Mexico.

Returning "to the sacred hoop of my grandmother's ways," she began in her writing to focus on the experiences of Native American women. Her first novel, *The Woman Who Owned the Shadows*, 1983, wove traditional tribal songs, rituals and legends into the story of a woman of mixed heritage whose struggle for survival is aided by Spider Grandmother, an ancient figure from tribal mythology. In *The Sacred Hoop: Recovering the Feminine in American Indian Traditions*, 1986, she argued that feminist and Native American perspectives on life are compatible, claiming that traditional tribal lifestyles were never patriarchal and were generally based on "spirit-centered, woman-focused worldviews." An anthology, *Spider Woman's Granddaughters: Traditional Tales & Contemporary Writing by Native American Women*, 1989, presented stories to be read as "tribal women's literature, an old and honored literary tradition in its own right."

Allen has edited several general works on Native American writing, including the pioneering *Studies in American Indian Literature*, 1983, *Grandmothers of the Light: A Medicine Woman's Source Book*, 1991, and *Voice of the Turtle: American Indian Literature, 1900–1970*, 1994. She also published seven collections of poetry, including *The Blind Lion*, 1974, *Coyote's Daylight Trip*, 1978, *Starchild*, 1981, *A Cannon Between My Knees*, 1981, *Shadow Country*, 1982, *Wyrds*, 1987, and *Skins and Bones*, 1988. Much of her poetry reflects her views as an antiwar and antinuclear activist, as well as a feminist and Native American.

Besides teaching Native American studies at the University of New Mexico, Allen has taught in the department of Ethnic Studies at the University of California, Berkeley, and at the University of California at Los Angeles.

Anderson, Helen Eugenie Moore 1909– diplomat

Born on May 26, 1909, in Adair, Iowa, Eugenie Moore grew up in various Iowa towns where her father held Methodist pastorates, and she graduated from high school in Clarinda. She attended Stephens College (Columbia, Missouri) in 1926–1927, Simpson College (Indianola, Iowa) in 1927–1928, and Carleton College (Northfield, Minnesota) in 1929–1930; she took no degree. In September 1930 she married John P. Anderson, an artist, of Red Wing, Minnesota. During two years in New York City she studied piano at the Juilliard School's Institute of Musical Art. She and her husband settled in Red Wing, where she developed a strong interest in foreign affairs and became a leader of and lecturer for the Minnesota League of Women Voters.

In 1944 she became active in state Democratic politics, helping to effect the Democratic-Farmer-Labor fusion and becoming county party chairman. In 1946 she was named to the party's state executive committee and made vice-chairman of the central committee. She was a delegate to the 1948 Democratic national convention and there was named to the party's national committee. Her effective campaigning that year on behalf of President Harry Truman and Senator Hubert H. Humphrey led to her appointment in October 1949 as U.S. ambassador to Denmark. She was the first American woman to hold that rank, her female predecessors in diplomacy having held rank no higher than minister. She held the post until succeeded in July 1953. She remained active in politics and international affairs. She was chairman of the Minnesota Commission for Fair Employment Practices in 1955–1960, a member of the Democratic National Committee's advisory committee on foreign policy in 1957–1961, a member of the American delegation to the Atlantic Conference in London in 1959, and vice-chairman of the Citizens Committee for International Development in 1961–1962. From May 1962 to December 1964, on appointment of President John F. Kennedy, she served as U.S. envoy to Bulgaria. From August 1965 to September 1968 she was the U.S. representative on the United Nations Trusteeship Council, and she also served as an alternate delegate to the UN General Assembly; from September 1967 she was senior adviser to the U.S. delegation to the UN. From 1968 she held the title of special assistant to the secretary of state, and from 1973 she was a member of the Commission on Minnesota's Future.

Anderson, Laurie 1947– performance artist, composer and writer

Born on June 5, 1947, in Wayne, Illinois, the second of eight children, Laurie Anderson began studying classical violin at five years of age and later performed with the Chicago Youth Symphony. In 1966, she moved to New York City, where she earned a Bachelor of Arts in the history of art from Barnard College in 1969 and a Master of Fine Arts in sculpture from Columbia University in 1972. For two years, she taught art history at the City University of New York.

Turning to performance art, Anderson in *Automotive*, 1972, orchestrated car horns at the Town Green in Rochester, Vermont. In *Duets on Ice*, another early piece performed at various public sites, Anderson appeared in ice skates frozen in blocks of ice; she then proceeded to play a duet with herself on an altered violin that she described as like a "ventriloquist's dummy" — she replaced the bow hair with pre-recorded audio tape and the string with a tape head. *Duets on Ice* would end once the ice melted.

To support her performance art early in her career, Anderson worked as a freelance interviewer and art critic for *Artnews* and *Artforum*. By 1974 she had received several grants that gave her more freedom to pursue her artistic explorations. She came to rely on a driving rock beat as a backdrop to many of her pieces; this led to a musical single, "It's Not the Bullet that Kills You — It's the Hole," 1977. Another song, the eight-minute-long "O Superman," 1981, reached the number two spot on England's pop charts.

She was better known as a composer and performer of multimedia exhibits, which combined music, photography, film, drawings, and animation with text. Her most ambitious work, *United States I-IV*, consists of seventy-eight segments organized into four sections: Transportation, Politics, Money, and Love. First performed at the Brooklyn Academy of Music in 1983, it ran for over six hours and employed more than 1,200 photos, cartoons and films. Her first record album, *Big Science*, was composed of excerpts from *United States I-IV*. She used some of the same material again in writing, directing and performing the film *Home of the Brave*, 1986. Anderson collaborated on *Set and Reset* with visual artist Robert Rauschenberg and choreographer Trisha Brown, whose dance company premiered the piece at *The Next Wave* festival in late 1983. In 1989, she premiered *Empty Places: A Performance*, at the Spoleto Arts Festival in Charleston, South Carolina.

Stories from the Nerve Bible, 1993, combines music, comedy, illusion, dance, film, songs, and a tornado simulated on stage. In 1994 she began collaborating with rock musicians Brian Eno and Peter Gabriel on an "experience park," a project to develop new forms of interactive experience. She created and performed many songs and shows, and regularly toured in the U.S. and abroad. Her numerous honors included a grant from the National Endowment for the Arts, 1977, a Guggenheim Fellowship, 1983, and a Grammy Award nomination, 1991.

Anderson, Margaret Caroline 1893?–1973 editor

Born in Indianapolis about 1893, Margaret Anderson grew up in a middle-class atmosphere that she rejected at the earliest possible moment. While still in her teens she traveled to Chicago, determined to make the richest life she could for herself. She found the means in the arts. In 1914 she founded the *Little Review*, a magazine of the arts that announced itself as devoted to "Life for Art's sake" and that succeeded in becoming foremost in its field. With her longtime associate, Jane Heap, Anderson managed to publish the magazine regularly with no ascertainable resources and to attract the best writers in the country, although they were paid nothing. As the organ of the "Chicago school," the *Little Review* published contributions by Carl Sandburg, Maxwell Bodenheim, Ben Hecht, and Sherwood Anderson, among others, and dealt with movements ranging from anarchism to psychoanalysis to feminism and with thinkers from Nietzsche to Bergson to Emma Goldman. Margaret Anderson excelled as a literary impresario, and by a combination of luck, energy, and a fascination with anything novel, she produced a magazine of legendary quality. Once, to protest the temporary lack of exciting new works, she issued 64 blank pages between covers. Other writers who contributed to the *Review* included William Carlos Williams, Amy Lowell, Ford Madox Ford, Wallace Stevens, and Malcolm Cowley. In 1917 Ezra Pound became foreign editor, and through his influence the *Little Review* published works by William Butler Yeats, T. S. Eliot, Hart Crane, and James Joyce, whose *Ulysses* was serialized beginning in 1918, when the magazine moved to New York City. Four issues were seized and burned by postal authorities during the three-year serialization of *Ulysses* and the matter became a cause célèbre when a charge of obscenity was sustained in court. In 1924 Anderson moved to Paris, where the *Little Review* was published until 1929, championing Cubism, Dada, and Surrealism. After the demise of her magazine she published three volumes of autobiography — *My Thirty Years' War*, 1930, *The Fiery Fountains*, 1951, and *The Strange Necessity*, 1970 — and a *Little Review Anthology*, 1953, before her death at Le Cannet, France, on October 18, 1973.

Anderson, Marian 1902–1993 opera singer

Born on February 17, 1902, in Philadelphia, Marian Anderson displayed vocal talent as a child, but her family could not afford to pay for formal training. From the age of six, she was tutored in the choir of the Union Baptist Church, where she sang parts written for bass, alto, tenor, and soprano voices. Members of the congregation raised funds for her to attend a music school for a year. At nineteen she became a pupil of Giuseppe Boghetti, who was so impressed by her talent that he gave her free lessons for a year. In 1925 she entered a contest with 300 competitors and won first prize, a recital at Lewisohn Stadium in New York City with the New York Philharmonic Orchestra. Her appearance in August 1925 was a great success.

Although many concert opportunities were closed to her because of her race, she appeared with the Philadelphia Symphony and toured African-American Southern college campuses. She made her European debut in Berlin in 1930 and made highly successful European tours in 1930–1932, 1933–1934, and 1934–1935. Still relatively unknown in the United States, she received scholarships to study abroad and appeared before the crowned heads of Sweden, Norway, Denmark, and England and sang at the Salzburg music festival in 1935. On hearing her sing, the Finnish composer Jean Sibelius wrote "Solitude" for her. Arturo Toscanini described her voice and artistry of her Salzburg performance saying, "what I heard today one is privileged to hear only in a hundred years." Her pure vocal quality and tremendous range made her, in the opinion of many, the world's greatest contralto.

Her New York concert debut at Town Hall in December 1935 was a personal triumph. She subsequently toured South America and in 1938–1939 Europe again. In 1939, however, she attempted to rent concert facilities in Washington's Constitution Hall, owned by the Daughters of the American Revolution, but was refused because of her race. This sparked widespread protest from many people, including Eleanor Roosevelt, who resigned from the DAR. Arrangements were made for Anderson to appear instead at the Lincoln Memorial on Easter Sunday, and she drew an audience of 75,000. She was awarded the Spingarn Medal for high achievement by a member of her race in 1939, and she received the $10,000 Bok Award in 1940. On January 7, 1955, she became the first African-American singer to perform as a member of the Metropolitan Opera in New York City. Before she began to sing her role of Ulrica in Verdi's *Un ballo in maschera*, she was given a standing ovation by the audience.

In 1957 she made a 12–nation, 35,000–mile tour sponsored by the Department of State, the American National Theatre and Academy, and Edward R. Murrow's television series "See It Now." She refused to compromise her beliefs, and her success in the world of traditional opera did not prevent her from including many African-American spirituals in her performance repertoire.

Her role as a goodwill ambassador for the United States was formalized in September 1958 when she was made a delegate to the United Nations. Anderson was awarded the Presidential Medal of Freedom in 1963 by President Lyndon B. Johnson, and she was the recipient of numerous honorary degrees. She made farewell tours of the world and the United States in 1964–1965. Her 75th birthday in 1977 was marked by a gala concert at Carnegie Hall, at which she received New York City's Handel Medallion and a congressional resolution of congratulations delivered by First Lady Rosalyn Carter. She was honored by the Kennedy Center in 1978. She received the first New York City Human Rights Award in honor of Eleanor Roosevelt in 1984, the National Medal of Arts in 1986, and a Grammy for Lifetime Achievement in 1991.

Andrews, Fannie Fern Phillips 1867–1950 pacifist and writer

Born on September 25, 1867, in Margaretville, Nova Scotia, Fannie Phillips grew up there and, from about 1876, in Lynn, Massachusetts. She graduated from the Salem Normal School (now Salem State College) in 1884 and taught school in Lynn until her marriage to Edwin G. Andrews in July 1890. In 1895 and 1896 she attended summer school at Harvard, and in 1902 she graduated from Radcliffe College. Deeply interested in education and reform, she formed in Boston in 1905 one of the earliest school-affiliated parents' organizations. This was followed in 1907 by the Boston Home and School Association, of which she served as secretary and in 1914–1918 as president.

In 1908 she combined her interests in schools and pacifism in organizing the American School Peace League. Through her remarkable talents for publicizing and enlisting support the League grew rapidly throughout the country. Pacifist literature and study courses produced by the League, much of it written by Andrews, were circulated widely and in 1912 began to be distributed by the U.S. Bureau of Education, with which she was associated until 1921 as a special collaborator. On a trip to Great Britain in 1914 she helped organize the similar School Peace League. The American League changed its name in 1918 to the American School Citizenship League, and Andrews remained secretary until her death. World War I turned her attention to the establishment of international organizations to preserve peace. Through the Central Organization for a Durable Peace, which she helped found at The Hague in 1915, she conducted studies of international problems and published *The Freedom of the Seas*, 1917, while through the School Citizenship League and the League to Enforce Peace she distributed literature on international organization. In 1919 she wrote *A Course in Foreign Relations* for the army's educational commission.

She naturally supported President Woodrow Wilson's League of Nations plan, and she attended the Paris Peace Conference as a representative of the U.S. Bureau of Education and of the New England Women's Press Association. Her plan for a bureau of education in the League of Nations was rejected at the time, but an international Bureau of Education was formed in Geneva in 1927, and she sat thereafter on its advisory board and at its third and fifth international conferences on public instruction in 1934 and 1936 represented the United States officially on appointment by President Franklin D. Roosevelt. In 1923 she was awarded a Ph.D. by Radcliffe for a study of the postwar mandate system, and in 1925 she traveled through the Near East to study the system at first hand. Her two-volume *The Holy Land under Mandate*, 1931, was well regarded by scholars. Andrews was also active in the American Association of University Women, chairing its international relations committee in 1925–1932. In 1948 she published *Memory Pages of My Life*. She died in Somerville, Massachusetts, on January 23, 1950.

JILL KREMENTZ

Maya Angelou

Angelou, Maya 1928– poet, playwright, and actor

Born on April 4, 1928, in St. Louis, Missouri, Marguerite Annie Johnson was given the name Maya by her older brother Bailey Jr. who had been calling her "My" or "Mine." After her parents' divorce she and her brother were sent to Stamps, Arkansas, to be raised by their paternal grandmother, Annie Henderson. At age seven, while visiting her mother in St. Louis, she was raped by her mother's boyfriend. A trial culminated in his conviction, and he was later beaten to death. Vowing not to talk in public again, Maya Johnson was sent back to Stamps and spent the next five years in self-imposed silence, immersed in books.

In 1940 she and her brother moved to San Francisco to be with their mother, who had by then remarried. She took drama and dance lessons. At sixteen years of age, she became a streetcar conductor in San Francisco. She gave birth to her son, Clyde "Guy" Johnson, just a few months after graduating from high school in 1945. At 22, she married Tosh Angelos, a former sailor of Greek descent, but she left her marriage two and a half years later and set out to become a professional dancer.

Moving to New York, she landed a featured role in a State Department-sponsored production of George Gershwin's opera *Porgy and Bess*; with this troupe she toured twenty-two countries in Europe and Africa. She also studied dance with Martha Graham, Pearl Primus and Ann Halprin. In 1961, she performed in *The Blacks*, an Obie-award winning play by the French writer, Jean Genet, next to James Earl Jones, Lou Gosset, Jr. and Cicely Tyson. That same year, she was persuaded by Vusumzi Make, a South African dissident to whom she was briefly married, to move to Cairo, Egypt, where she worked as an associate editor for the *Arab Observer*. She later moved to Ghana, where her son was attending the national university. There she served as feature editor of *The African Review* and performed in a production of *Mother Courage*.

She returned to California in 1966, taking a role in Jean Anouilh's *Medea* and wrote *Black, Blues, Black* (1968), a ten-part television series about the role of African culture in American life. In 1970 she published her first book, the autobiographical *I Know Why the Caged Bird Sings*; released to wide critical acclaim, it won a nomination for the National Book Award. *Just Give Me a Cool Drink of Water 'fore I Diiie*, 1971, a collection of poems, was nominated for a Pulitzer Prize.

When her screenplay *Georgia, Georgia* was produced in 1972, Angelou became the first African-American woman to have a feature film adapted from one of her own stories.

She wrote and directed the film *All Day Long*, 1974. She was nominated both for an Emmy Award (for her portrayal of Kunta Kinte's grandmother in the television miniseries *Roots*, 1977) and for a Tony Award (for her portrayal on Broadway of Mary Todd Lincoln's dressmaker in *Look Away*, 1978). Other volumes of poetry included *Oh Pray My Wings are Gonna Fit Me Well*, 1975, *And Still I Rise*, 1978, and *Shaker, Why Don't You Sing?* 1983.

By 1986 Angelou had published four more autobiographical volumes: *Gather Together in My Name*, 1974; *Singin' and Swingin' and Gettin' Merry Like Christmas*, 1976; *The Heart of a Woman*, 1981, about her work with Martin Luther King, Jr. and Malcolm X; and *All God's Children Need Traveling Shoes*, 1986, about the complexities of life in Ghana. Other non-fiction work from this period included *Lessons in Living*, 1993, a book of short, inspirational messages, and *Wouldn't Take Nothing for My Journey Now*, 1993, a collection of essays. Other volumes of poetry included *Now Sheba Sings the Song*, 1987, *I Shall Not Be Moved*, 1990, and *Life Doesn't Frighten Me*, 1993, a book of poems for children. In 1993, she wrote the poetry for the film *Poetic Justice*; she also appeared briefly in this film.

Angelou's many honors included an American Academy of Achievement Award in 1990 and a Horatio Alger Award in 1992; she also received more than fifty honorary degrees. Named a professor of American studies at Wake Forest University, she also lectured widely elsewhere. Angelou's work reached its largest single audience in January 1993 when she recited her poem "On the Pulse of Morning" at the inauguration of President William Clinton; she was the first poet to receive such an invitation since Robert Frost in 1961.

Anthony, Susan Brownell 1820–1906 reformer and political writer

Susan B. Anthony

Born on February 15, 1820, in Adams, Massachusetts, Susan Anthony grew up there and in Battenville, New York. She was reared in the Quaker tradition, received a good education for her sex and day, and began teaching school to supplement the family's finances. In 1839 she took a position in a Quaker seminary in New Rochelle, New York, and in 1846 she became headmistress of the female department of Canajoharie Academy. In 1849 she returned to the family farm (now near Rochester, New York), where she met many leading Abolitionists, including Frederick Douglass, Parker Pillsbury, Wendell Phillips, William Henry Channing, and William Lloyd Garrison. Soon the cause of temperance enlisted her sympathy and then, after meeting Amelia Bloomer and through her Elizabeth Cady Stanton, so did that of woman suffrage.

The rebuff of her attempt to speak at a temperance meeting in Albany in 1852 prompted her to organize the Woman's New York State Temperance Society, of which Stanton became president, and pushed her farther in the direction of women's rights advocacy. In a short time she became known as one of the cause's most zealous, serious advocates, a dogged and tireless worker whose personality contrasted sharply with that of her friend and coworker, E.C. Stanton. She was also a prime target of public and newspaper abuse. While campaigning for a liberalization of New York's laws regarding married women's property rights, an end attained in 1860, Anthony served from 1856 as chief New York agent of Garrison's American Anti-Slavery Society. Early in the Civil War she helped organize the Women's Loyal National League, which urged the case for emancipation. After the war she campaigned unsuccessfully to have the language of the Fourteenth Amendment altered to allow for woman as well as "Negro" suffrage, and in 1866 she became corresponding secretary of the newly formed American Equal Rights Association. An exhausting speaking and organizing tour of Kansas in 1867 failed to win passage of a state enfranchisement law.

In 1868 she became publisher, and Stanton editor, of a new periodical, *Revolution*, originally financed by the eccentric George Francis Train. In the same year she represented the Working Women's Association of New York, which she had organized recently, at the National Labor Union convention. In January 1869 she organized a woman suffrage convention in Washington, D.C., and in May she and Stanton formed the National Woman Suffrage Association. A portion of the organization deserted later in the year to join Lucy Stone's more conservative American Woman Suffrage Association, but the National remained a large and powerful group and Susan Anthony remained its principal leader and spokeswoman.

In 1870 she relinquished her position on the *Revolution* and embarked on a series of lecture tours to pay off the paper's accumulated debts. As a test of the legality of the suffrage provision of the Fourteenth Amendment, she cast a vote in the 1872 presidential election in Rochester, New York. She was arrested, convicted (the judge's directed verdict of guilty had been written before the trial began), and fined, and although she refused to pay the fine the case was carried no further. She traveled constantly, often with Stanton, in support of efforts in various states to win the franchise for women: California in 1871, Michigan in 1874, Colorado in 1877, and elsewhere. In 1890, after lengthy discussions, the rival suffrage associations were merged into the National American Woman Suffrage Association, and at Stanton's resignation in 1892 Anthony became president. Her principal lieutenant in later years was Carrie Chapman Catt.

By the 1890s she had largely outlived the abuse and sarcasm that attended her early efforts, and she emerged as a national heroine. Visits to the World's Columbian Exposition in Chicago in 1893 and to the Lewis and Clark Exposition in Portland, Oregon, in 1905 were warmly received, as were her trips to London in 1899 and Berlin in 1904 as head of the U.S. delegation to the international Council of Women (which she helped found in 1888). In 1900, at the age of eighty, she retired from the presidency of the National American Woman Suffrage Association, passing it on to Catt. Principal among her written works was the *History of Woman Suffrage*, written with Stanton and Matilda J. Gage and published in four volumes in 1881, 1882, 1886, and 1902. (Ida Husted Harper later added two more volumes in 1922.) Susan Anthony died in Rochester, New York, on March 13, 1906. With the issue of a new dollar coin in 1979 she became the first woman to be depicted on United States currency.

Antin, Mary 1881–1949 writer

Born in Polotsk, Russia, on June 13, 1881, Mary Antin emigrated to the United States with her mother, sisters, and brother in 1894, joining her father, who had preceded them in 1891, in Massachusetts. After learning English she had a brilliant school career. Her plan to attend Radcliffe was dropped after her marriage to Professor Amadeus W. Grabau in October 1901, following which they settled in New York City. She studied at Teachers College and Barnard College of Columbia University from 1901 to 1904. Her first book about her experiences as an immigrant, *From Plotzk* [Polotsk] *to Boston*, was written in Yiddish; it was published in an English translation in 1899. *The Promised Land*, 1912, originally serialized in the *Atlantic Monthly*, was also autobiographical and was a notable success. *They Who Knock at Our Gates*, 1914, also dealt with immigrants and their hopes, characters, and experiences. She lectured for a number of years on the subject of immigration — during 1913–1917 she spoke widely on behalf of the Progressive party at the invitation of Theodore Roosevelt — and campaigned against proposals in Congress to adopt restrictive immigration legislation. She was widely acclaimed for her efforts to secure understanding and the realization of the American promise for the immigrant. She died in Suffern, New York, on May 15, 1949.

Apgar, Virginia 1909–1974 physician

Born on June 7, 1909, in Westfield, New Jersey, Virginia Apgar graduated from Mount

Holyoke College in 1929 and from the Columbia University College of Physicians and Surgeons in 1933. After an internship at Presbyterian Hospital, New York, she held residencies in the relatively new specialty of anesthesiology at the University of Wisconsin and then at Bellevue Hospital, New York, in 1935–1937. In 1936 she was appointed an instructor of anesthesiology at Columbia. She advanced to assistant professor in 1938 and to associate professor in 1942 and in 1949 became the first woman to hold a full professorship on Columbia's medical faculty. From 1938 she was also director of the department of anesthesiology at Columbia-Presbyterian Medical Center.

An interest in obstetric procedure, and particularly in the treatment of the newborn, led her to develop a simple system for quickly evaluating the condition and viability of newly delivered infants. As finally presented in 1952, the Apgar Score system relied on five simple observations to be made by delivery room personnel — nurses or interns — on the infant within one minute of birth, observations designated mnemonically: appearance (color), pulse, grimace (reflexes), activity (muscle tone), and respiration. Numerical scores of 0 to 2 for each category yielded a total that proved to be a reliable guide to the infant's health and to the necessity for immediate attention by the physician. The Apgar Score system soon came into general use throughout the United States and was adopted by several other countries. In 1959 Apgar left Columbia and took a degree in public health from The Johns Hopkins University. She then became head of the division of congenital malformations of the National Foundation–March of Dimes. In 1967 she was promoted to director of basic research of the National Foundation, and in 1968 she became senior vice-president for medical affairs. In 1972 she published *Is My Baby All Right?* She died in New York City on August 7, 1974.

Arbus, Diane Nemerov 1923–1971 photographer

Born in New York City on March 14, 1923, Diane Nemerov was the daughter of Gertrude Russek and David Nemerov, who owned Russeks Fifth Avenue, a fur and women's clothing store. After attending the Ethical Culture School and the Fieldston School, she worked as a fashion artist in her father's store. At age 18 she married fellow employee Allan Arbus; before separating in 1959, they worked collaboratively in commercial fashion photography for *Harper's Bazaar*, *Show*, *Esquire*, *Glamour*, *The New York Times*, and *Vogue*. They had two daughters, Doon and Amy.

After taking a short photography course with Berenice Abbott, Arbus met Lisette Model, an Austrian-born documentary photographer, and studied with her from 1958–1960. With Model's encouragement Arbus decided to give up commercial work to concentrate on fine art photography. In developing a style of her own, she put her subjects first. Often she chose to photograph people on the margins of society: giants, midgets, drag queens, fat ladies, junkies, naturists, and the mentally challenged; she also photographed beauty contestants, twins, couples, children, families, and people wearing masks. As she later told her students, "for me the subject of the picture is always more important than the picture. And more complicated."

She received Guggenheim Fellowships for her work in 1963 and again in 1966. In the later years of her life she taught photography at the Parsons School of Design in New York, from 1965 to 1966; at the Cooper Union in New York, from 1968 to 1969; at the Rhode Island School of Design, from 1970 to 1971; and at Hampshire College, in June 1971. She published *Diane Arbus: Portfolio* in 1971; not long thereafter she committed suicide on or about July 26, 1971.

Her work has since been exhibited in many museums and galleries around the world, including: the Museum of Modern Art, New York; the International Museum of Photography, George Eastman House, Rochester, New York; the Museum of Fine Arts, Boston; the Library of Congress, Washington, D.C.; the Minneapolis Institute of Art; the New

Orleans Museum of Art; the Museum of Fine Arts, Houston; the Center for Creative Photography, the University of Arizona, Tucson; the National Gallery of Canada, Ottawa; and the Bibliothèque Nationale, Paris.

Arden, Elizabeth 1884–1966 businesswoman

Born on December 31, 1884, in Woodbridge, Ontario, Florence Nightingale Graham briefly pursued nurse's training, worked as a secretary, and held various other jobs before moving from Canada to New York City about 1908. She became assistant to a beauty specialist, Eleanor Adair, and in 1910 went into partnership with Elizabeth Hubbard in a beauty salon on Fifth Avenue, investing about $1000 in the venture. The partnership split up, and Graham decided to continue under the corporate name of Elizabeth Arden. In 1914 she hired chemists to produce a fluffy face cream and an astringent lotion, the first products in a cosmetics line which eventually included about 300 items. A pioneer in the advertising of beauty aids, she stressed her products' acceptable, "ladylike" qualities in an age when makeup and beauty aids were still thought of in many circles in connection with "low women." In 1915 she began to market her cosmetics internationally, selling them wholesale to pharmacies and department stores. She opened a Paris salon in 1922, and in later years she operated salons across Europe and in South America and Australia as well. By the time of her death there were 100 Elizabeth Arden beauty salons throughout the world, offering hairdressing, facial treatments, exercise, steam baths, massage, manicures, pedicures, and many other luxury services. She also operated luxurious and exclusive Maine Chance beauty spas in Mount Vernon, Maine, and in Scottsdale, Arizona. Her clientele included socialites, politicians, European royalty, and movie stars. One of the nation's foremost racehorse owners, she operated stables near Lexington, Kentucky, from which came Jet Pilot, winner of the 1947 Kentucky Derby. She bolstered her own image of ageless beauty by successfully concealing her age, which was not divulged until her death on October 18, 1966, in New York City.

PETER STEIN

Hannah Arendt

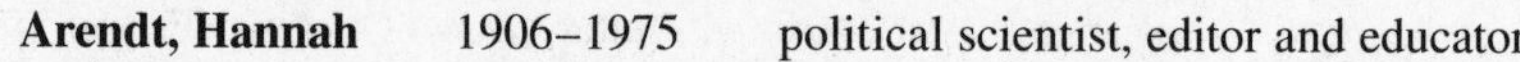

Arendt, Hannah 1906–1975 political scientist, editor and educator

Born on October 14, 1906, in Hannover, Germany, Hannah Arendt grew up there and in Königsberg (now Kaliningrad, Russia). She studied at the universities of Marburg, Freiburg, and Heidelberg, taking her Ph.D. in philosophy at Heidelberg in 1928. With the rise of the Nazi regime in 1933 she left Germany for Paris, where she continued to study and for four years did social work with Jewish orphans. In 1940 she came to the United States, where ten years later she became a citizen. From 1944 to 1946 she served as research director for the Conference on Jewish Relations, and from 1946 to 1948 she was chief editor of Schocken Books. During this period, and while serving as executive secretary of Jewish Cultural Reconstruction, 1949–1952, she published a number of articles that pointed toward her first major book, *The Origins of Totalitarianism*, 1951, in which she closely examined the phenomenon of modern totalitarianism, particularly as manifested in Nazism and Communism. While tracing its roots back to the imperialism and anti-Semitism of the nineteenth century, she held that the totalitarian state was a fundamentally different structure from the traditional nation-state. Arendt was awarded a Guggenheim fellowship in 1952 and lectured at Princeton in 1952–1953. In 1955 she was at the University of California at Berkeley, and in 1956 she delivered the Walgreen Lectures at the University of Chicago. These were later published as *The Human Condition*, 1958. She became the first woman to hold full professorial rank at Princeton when she was appointed visiting professor of political science in 1959. She was visiting professor at Columbia in 1960; from 1963 to 1967 she was professor of political science at the University of Chicago, and in 1967 she became a member of the faculty of the New School for Social Research in New York City. Her other books, in which a strain of pessimism is evident in her penetrating analysis of history and of political man, include

On Revolution, 1963; *Eichmann in Jerusalem*, a highly controversial work in which she charged Jewish community leaders with having cooperated in Nazi actions against Jews, 1963; *Men in Dark Times*, 1968; *On Violence*, 1970; and *Crises of the Republic*, 1972. She died in New York City on December 4, 1975. Her unfinished manuscript on *The Life of the Mind* was edited by Mary McCarthy and published in 1978.

Astor, Caroline Webster Schermerhorn 1830–1908 socialite

Born in New York City on September 22, 1830, Caroline Schermerhorn was the daughter of a wealthy merchant and had colonial Dutch aristocracy on both sides of her family tree. Her marriage to William Astor, son of William Backhouse Astor and grandson of John Jacob Astor, in September 1853 united her fortune with an even greater one. Her social career was unremarkable until the late 1860s, when the social and political turmoil of a rapidly expanding and industrializing economy threw up numbers of nouveaux riches eager for admittance to the upper circles. Astor determined to be the arbiter of society and to maintain the primacy of family and old wealth. In this ambition she had first to unseat her sister-in-law, Mrs. John Jacob Astor III, and to that end she enlisted the support of Ward McAllister, well-known socialite, bon vivant, snob, promoter of Newport, and author of the phrase "the Four Hundred." By dint of lavish entertainments, notably her annual January balls and her more exclusive dinner parties, and sheer force of personality, she succeeded in both ambitions. She was forced to concede somewhat in calling on the parvenu Alva E. S. Vanderbilt (Belmont) in 1883 in order to secure an invitation for her daughter to the great Vanderbilt costume ball, but through the 1880s and 1890s she managed to hold the upper crust together in a semblance of its old self. Her unshakable insistence on being recognized as the head of the family, to be addressed simply as "Mrs. Astor," following the death of John J. III in 1890 was in large degree responsible for the removal of William Waldorf Astor and his wife to England later in that year. Caroline Astor was the owner of a fabulous collection of jewelry, which she was not shy to wear en masse, especially at the Metropolitan Opera. Her stature as the grande dame of American aristocratic society survived in the public estimation even after the inevitable passing of the kind of society that could be so dominated. An invalid in her last two years, she died at her Fifth Avenue home in New York City on October 30, 1908.

Atherton, Gertrude Franklin Horn 1857–1948 novelist

Born in San Francisco on October 30, 1857, Gertrude Horn grew up in a prosperous neighborhood of that city until her parents' divorce and thereafter mainly on the San Jose ranch of her maternal grandfather, under whose stern discipline she was introduced to serious literature. She attended St. Mary's Hall school in Benicia, California, and for a year Sayre Institute in Lexington, Kentucky. In February 1876 she eloped with George H. B. Atherton, who had been courting her now twice-divorced mother. Her life at the Atherton estate, Fair Oaks (now Atherton), California, dominated by her mother-in-law, was an unhappy one. Despite her husband's attempts to stifle her, she managed to write a novel, *The Randolphs of Redwoods*, based on a local society scandal, whose serial publication in the San Francisco *Argonaut* in 1882 outraged the family. (The novel was published in book form as *A Daughter of the Vine* in 1899.) The death of her husband in 1887 released Gertrude Atherton, and she promptly traveled to New York City and thence in 1895 to England and Europe. In rapid succession she produced books set in those locales or in old California, including such titles as *What Dreams May Come*, 1888, *Hermia Suydam*, 1889, *A Question of Time*, 1891, *The Doomswoman*, 1892, *A Whirl Asunder*, 1895, *Patience Sparhawk and Her Times*, 1897, *The Californians*, 1898, *American Wives and English Husbands*, 1898 (later reissued as *Transplanted*, 1919), *The Bell in the Fog*, 1905, *Ancestors*, 1907, *Tower of Ivory*, 1910, *The Living Present*, 1917, and *The White Morning*, 1918, both drawing on her experiences in hospital relief work during

World War I, *The Sister-in-Law*, 1921, *Sleeping Fires*, 1922, *Black Oxen*, the sensational best-seller of 1923, which made a world celebrity of Dr. Eugen Steinach, whose "rejuvenation" treatments Atherton had undergone, *California*, 1927, and *Sophisticates*, 1931. She also wrote a volume of stories, *Before the Gringo Came*, 1894 (later reissued in revised form as *The Splendid Idle Forties*, 1902); three fictionalized biographies, *The Conqueror*, 1902, on Alexander Hamilton, *Rezánov*, 1906, about the Russian entrepreneur in Alaska, and *The Immortal Marriage*, 1927, on Pericles and Aspasia; and a volume of essays entitled *Can Women be Gentlemen?*, 1938. Most of her novels featured strong-willed, independent heroines active in the world at large, and not infrequently their success stemmed from the characters' frank pursuit of sexual as well as other pleasures. As literature they were largely undistinguished. *Adventures of a Novelist*, 1932, was an autobiography, as was in part *My San Francisco: A Wayward Biography*, 1946. Gertrude Atherton died in San Francisco on June 14, 1948.

Austin, Mary Hunter 1868–1934 novelist, short-story writer and playwright

Born on September 9, 1868, in Carlinville, Illinois, Mary Hunter graduated from Blackburn College in 1888 and soon afterward moved with her family to Bakersfield, California. She married Stafford W. Austin in May 1891, and for several years they lived in various towns in the Owens Valley. Austin soon learned to love the desert and the Native Americans who lived in it, and both figured in the sketches that comprised her first book, *The Land of Little Rain*, 1903, which was a great and immediate success. It was followed by a collection of stories, *The Basket Woman*, 1904, a romantic novel, *Isidro*, 1905, and *The Flock*, 1906. In 1905 she separated from her husband and moved to Carmel, California. She later traveled to Italy, France, and England, where meeting H. G. Wells and other intellectuals strengthened her feminist ideas and added a deep commitment to socialism to her own deeply personal and sustaining form of mysticism. Returning to New York City, she became associated with John Reed, Walter Lippmann, and others of the group of writers and artists whose center was Mabel Dodge (Luhan). *The Arrow Maker*, a play, 1911, and her best novel, *A Woman of Genius*, 1912, were the product of those New York years, as were scores of rather didactic articles on socialism, women's rights, and a variety of other topics, and such novels as *The Ford*, 1917, and *No. 26 Jayne Street*, 1920. In 1924 she settled in Santa Fe, New Mexico. She published in that year *The Land of Journeys' Ending* and followed it with, among other books, *Everyman's Genius*, 1925; *The Children Sing in the Far West*, 1928 (like her earlier *The American Rhythm*, 1923, a collection of Native American songs and original poems inspired by them); *Starry Adventure*, 1931; *Experiences Facing Death*, 1931; and an autobiography, *Earth Horizon*, 1932. Her best writing, that which was concerned with nature or Native American life, was reminiscent of Ralph Waldo Emerson and John Muir in its transcendental tone and occasional primitivist leaning. She was active in movements to preserve Native American arts, crafts, and culture. Austin died in Santa Fe on August 13, 1934.

Avery, Byllye 1937– health care activist

Born in 1937 in DeLand, Florida, into the family of a rural schoolteacher, Byllye Avery graduated from Talledega College in Talledega, Alabama, and received an M.A. in special education from the University of Florida in 1969. Early in her work life, she devoted herself to the education of emotionally disturbed children, first as a teacher and then as a consultant to the state of Florida.

Her life changed dramatically when her husband died suddenly at age 33, and she was left alone to parent her young son and daughter. This experience was the catalyst for her commitment to improving the health of the African-American community, particularly women who, like herself, had a high level of stress in their lives. The self-help groups for

African-American women facing poverty, crime, violence, and racism were the cornerstones of her activism.

Not only did these groups serve as models throughout the nation and worldwide, but they would also pave the way for Avery's founding of the National Black Women's Health Project (NBWHP). In 1974 she cofounded the Gainesville, Florida, Women's Health Center, later becoming its president and executive director. Four years later she cofounded Birthplace, an alternative birthing center, also in Gainesville.

In 1981 she moved to Atlanta to pioneer a health project focused on African-American women. That year the NBWHP held its first national conference at Spelman College in Atlanta. As executive director of NBWHP, Avery enabled thousands of African-American women to take charge of their health care. She helped the grassroots advocacy organization grow to an international network of more than 2,000 participants in 22 states and 6 foreign countries, producing not only the first Center for Black Women's Wellness, but also the first documentary film by African-American women exploring their perspectives on sexuality and reproduction. For her proposals and work with NBWHP, Avery was awarded a MacArthur Fellowship in 1989.

In the 1990s she wrote and lectured widely on how race, sex and class affect women's empowerment in the women's health movement. As a Visiting Fellow at the Harvard School of Public Health, she developed the NBWHP's Walking for Wellness Program. She was an international consultant to women's health care groups in Latin America, Africa, and the Caribbean and served as adviser to the Kellogg Foundation for its International Leadership Program on health issues.

Ayres, Anne 1816–1896 religious

Born in London, England, on January 3, 1816, Anne Ayres came to America with her family in 1836 and settled in New York City. Until 1845 she supplemented the family income by teaching daughters of well-to-do families. In the summer of that year she heard Dr. William Augustus Muhlenberg preach on "Jephtha's Vow" at St. Paul's College and determined upon a life of religious service. On All Saints' Day, November 1, she was consecrated Sister Anne by Muhlenberg.

There were at that time no sisterhood orders in the Episcopal Church in America or in the Church of England. The few women who joined Sister Anne in conducting a parish school and doing charitable work among the poor were formally organized in 1852 as the Sisterhood of the Holy Communion, with Sister Anne as "First Sister." The sisters adopted regulation dress but no habits and instead of vows made pledges of service, renewable in three-year terms. In 1853 they opened a small infirmary, and five years later they moved to the new St. Luke's Hospital, built by Muhlenberg's efforts. Sister Anne directed both housekeeping and nursing work at St. Luke's until 1877. In 1865 she joined Muhlenberg in opening St. Johnland on Long Island, a rural refuge for the poor, handicapped, orphaned, and homeless, and she remained there after leaving the superintendency of the hospital. The sisterhood came to be known sometimes as that of St. Luke and St. John. In 1867 she published *Evangelical Sisterhoods*, in 1875–1877 she published *Evangelical Catholic Papers*, an edition of Muhlenberg's writings, and in 1880 she published *The Life and Work of William Augustus Muhlenberg*; she was unwilling throughout her life to have her work appear as more than a part of his. Sister Anne died at St. Luke's Hospital, New York City, on February 9, 1896. The Sisterhood survived until 1940.

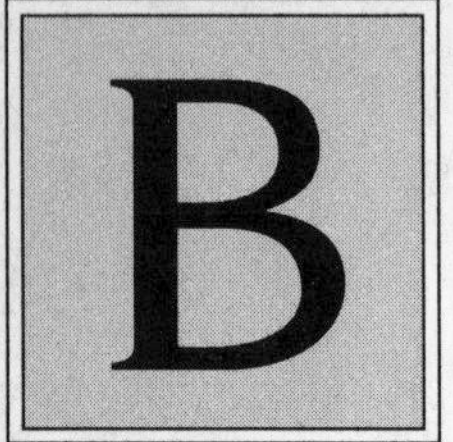

Bacon, Albion Fellows 1865–1933 reformer and writer

Born on April 8, 1865, in Evansville, Indiana, Albion Fellows, daughter of a Methodist minister and younger sister of Annie Fellows (Johnston), grew up in nearby McCutchanville. After graduating from high school in Evansville she worked as a secretary until her marriage to Hilary E. Bacon, a banker and merchant, in October 1888. The next several years were marked by the birth of several children, the publication of a volume of verse, *Songs Ysame*, with her sister in 1897, and a lengthy period of illness.

Almost by chance she discovered one day Evansville's riverfront slums and was moved to become a "friendly visitor" for the city's associated charities. In time she organized the Men's Circle of Friendly Visitors, the Flower Mission for poor working girls, a Working Girls' Association, an Anti-Tuberculosis League, and the Monday Night Club of influential citizens interested in charitable work. Becoming convinced that substandard housing lay at the root of all the social ills she had tried to deal with, Bacon attempted unsuccessfully to have tenement regulation included in a new city building code.

In 1908 she decided to approach the problem at a higher level and drafted a model state law that, after she had directed a year-long public campaign and lobbying effort, was passed by the Indiana legislature in 1909. Amendments had limited the bill's application to Evansville and Indianapolis, however, so in 1911 she helped organize the Indiana Housing Association, which successfully pushed through a new bill of statewide application in 1913. In 1914 she published a record of her campaign, *Beauty for Ashes*. She was also instrumental in the passage in 1917 of a law authorizing the condemnation of unsafe or unsanitary dwellings. In later years she remained active as head of the executive committee of the Indiana Child Welfare Association and with the state Commission on Child Welfare, through which she worked to secure establishment of a juvenile probation system and passage of child labor and school attendance laws.

Bacon also wrote several devotional books, including *The Soldiers' Book of Worship*, 1917, *Consolation: A Spiritual Experience*, 1922, *The Path to God*, 1928, and *The Charm String*, 1929, and a number of pageants, including the Indiana centennial pageant in 1917; *War and Peace*, adopted by the American Legion; and *Citizenship* for the General Federation of Women's Clubs. Bacon died in Evansville, Indiana, on December 10, 1933.

Bacon, Delia Salter 1811–1859 writer

Born on February 2, 1811, in what soon became Tallmadge, Ohio, Delia Bacon grew up there and in Hartford, Connecticut, where she attended Catharine E. Beecher's school for girls. After working as a teacher in various schools from 1826 to 1832 she tried and failed to establish her own school in several places. She then turned to writing — *Tales of the Puritans*, 1831, and a play, *The Bride of Fort Edward*, based on the story of Jane McCrea, 1839 — and also lectured on literary and historical topics. She was successful as a lecturer until about 1850, when as a result of a humiliating relationship with a young minister she withdrew from active life.

Bacon gradually evolved a theory that the works attributed to Shakespeare had in fact been written by a coterie of writers led by Francis Bacon and including Edmund Spenser and Sir Walter Raleigh, and were credited by them to the relatively obscure actor and theater manager William Shakespeare largely for political reasons. Becoming thoroughly convinced of the notion, and with some encouragement from Ralph Waldo Emerson, she traveled to England in 1853, ostensibly to seek proof. She was uninterested in looking for original source material, however, and for three years she lived in poverty while she developed her thesis out of ingenuity and "hidden meanings" found in the plays. In 1856, for unknown reasons, she abandoned her plan of opening Shakespeare's grave to look for certain documents she believed would support her position. Nathaniel Hawthorne, at that time U.S. consul in Liverpool, took pity on her, lent her money, and arranged for the publication of her book, *The Philosophy of the Plays of Shakespeare Unfolded*, 1857. Immediately after the appearance of the book she went insane and never learned that it had met with little but ridicule. She was brought back to the United States in 1858; she died in Hartford, Connecticut, on September 2, 1859. The idea that had obsessed her assumed a life of its own, and the theory continued to have its adherents throughout the years.

Baez, Joan 1941– folk singer

Born on January 9, 1941, on Staten Island in New York City, Joan Baez grew up there and in other Eastern cities and, after graduation from high school, moved with her family to Boston. She attended Boston University briefly and then began singing in coffeehouses in Boston and Cambridge. Her strong, direct renditions of traditional folk songs and ballads, backed by her simple but sure guitar playing, soon attracted a considerable local following, and in 1959, after an appearance in Chicago, she was invited to sing at the Folk Festival in Newport, Rhode Island. The audience there received her enthusiastically, and she returned for the festival in 1960.

A recording contract resulted, and her first album, titled simply *Joan Baez*, was a great success, as were the many that followed. Drawing her repertoire from old English ballads, Southern and country music, and increasingly from the modern canon of protest songs, she made a concert tour in 1961 that evoked high praise from audiences and critics for her clear soprano voice and her straightforward manner. Other tours — of Europe and Japan, and of campuses and concert halls across the United States — increased her popularity, and she soon ranked with Bob Dylan at the top of her field.

Baez became deeply involved in civil rights activities during the early 1960s. In the later 1960s she became involved in the opposition to the Vietnam War and was in particular a supporter of the movement resisting the military draft. In 1964 she refused to pay the sixty percent of her federal taxes destined for defense spending, and in 1965 she founded an institute for the study of nonviolence. In her concert and television appearances she continued to mix performing with pleas for nonviolent opposition to war and injustice, although in later years her music took on more personal concerns as well. She was a member of the National Advisory Council of Amnesty International from 1979 to 1992.

In 1978 she appeared in *Renaldo and Clara*, a film produced by Bob Dylan. Her later recordings include *Diamonds and Rust*, 1975, *Gulf Wind*, her one entirely self-penned album, 1976, *Honest Lullaby*, 1979, *European Tour*, 1981, *Live Europe 83*, 1983, *Very Early Joan*, 1983, *Recently*, 1988, *Diamonds and Rust in the Bullring*, performed live in Spain, 1989, *Speaking of Dreams*, 1989, and *Play Me Backwards*, 1992.

Bagley, Sarah G. ?–1847? labor organizer

Born on a date unknown, probably in Meredith, New Hampshire, Sarah Bagley went to work in 1836 in a cotton mill in Lowell, Massachusetts, then widely considered a model factory town. She was apparently content with her lot for several years, but she shared in the unrest that grew among the factory girls in the early 1840s following a series of speedups and wage cuts. In December 1844 she organized and became president of the Lowell Female Labor Reform Association, whose program called for improved working conditions and a ten-hour day and whose immediate object was to influence an investigation of Lowell conditions by a committee of the Massachusetts legislature. Despite petitions, pamphlets, and other pressures extending over a period of a year, the legislature declined to take any action.

By early 1845 Sarah Bagley had left her mill job, and she soon had organized branches of the Female Labor Reform Association in Waltham and Fall River in Massachusetts and Manchester, Nashua, and Dover in New Hampshire. In May 1845 she was appointed corresponding secretary of the New England Working Men's Association, to whose journal, *Voice of Industry*, which moved to Lowell in October, she was a frequent contributor. She organized an Industrial Reform Lyceum to bring radical speakers to Lowell, wrote a series of pamphlets on labor topics, and by her militant criticism contributed decisively to the demise of the pro-owner *Lowell Offering*, edited by Harriet Farley, in December 1845. The ten-hour movement largely disintegrated in 1846 following the legislature's refusal to act, and Sarah Bagley, her health declining, turned to Fourierism. In February she became superintendent of the Lowell telegraph office; she is credited with being the nation's first female telegraph operator. After her replacement as president of the Lowell Female Labor Reform Association in February 1847 there is no record of her.

Bailey, Ann 1742–1825 scout

Born in 1742 in Liverpool, England, Ann Hennis came to America, probably as an indentured servant, in 1761. Her first husband, Richard Trotter, a Shenandoah Valley settler and survivor of General Edward Braddock's disastrous expedition of 1755, was killed at the battle of Point Pleasant on October 10, 1774. Thereupon his widow adopted male dress, took up rifle and tomahawk, and became a frontier scout, messenger, spy, and Indian fighter. She was the subject of numerous adventures, both true and legendary, and became widely known as the "white squaw of the Kanawha" and more bluntly as "Mad Ann." In 1788 she moved with her second husband, John Bailey, also a scout, to "Clendenin's Settlement" on the site of present-day Charleston, West Virginia. The settlement's principal feature was Fort Lee, and its siege by Native Americans in 1791 provided the occasion for Ann Bailey's most famous exploit. When the defenders' powder ran low she volunteered to ride for help. She dashed from the fort and through the host of besiegers, rode a hundred miles through the forest to Fort Union (present-day Lewisburg), and returned on the third day with powder. After her second husband's death she went to live with her son in Ohio. She died in Gallia County, Ohio, on November 22, 1825.

Bailey, Anna Warner 1758–1851 "Mother Bailey," patriot

Born in Groton, Connecticut, in October (probably the 11th) 1758, Anna Warner was orphaned and reared by an uncle. On September 6, 1781, a large British force under the turncoat General Benedict Arnold landed on the coast near Groton and stormed Fort Griswold. American casualties were very high, and among them was Anna Warner's uncle, Edward Mills. She walked several miles to the scene of battle, found her uncle after much difficulty, and learned that he was mortally wounded. At his request she hurried home, saddled a horse for her aunt, and herself carried her infant cousin back for a last meeting of the family. This feat soon became a favorite tale of the Revolution. Anna Warner later married Captain Elijah Bailey, postmaster of Groton. In 1813, during the second war with Great Britain, Mother Bailey appeared among the Groton soldiers aiding in the defense of New London against a blockading British fleet. On learning of a shortage, she contributed her flannel petticoat — her "martial petticoat," as it came to be known — for use as cartridge wadding. Mother Bailey died in Groton on January 10, 1851.

Bailey, Florence Augusta Merriam 1863–1948 ornithologist and science writer

Born in Locust Grove, Lewis County, New York, on August 8, 1863, Florence Merriam was a younger sister of Clinton Hart Merriam, later first chief of the U.S. Biological Survey. She attended private school in Utica, New York, and during 1882–1886 Smith College; she did not follow a degree course at Smith but was later, in 1921, granted a B.A.

Her interest in bird life was already well developed, and a series of articles she wrote for the *Audubon Magazine* she later collected and developed into her first book, *Birds Through an Opera Glass*, 1889.

Travel and dabblings in social work filled the next few years, but the onset of tuberculosis sent her west to convalesce. Her experiences in Utah, southern California, and Arizona bore fruit in *My Summer in a Mormon Village*, 1894, *A-Birding on a Bronco*, 1896, and *Birds of Village and Field*, 1898. She then took up residence with her brother in Washington, D.C., and in December 1899 married Vernon Bailey, a naturalist with the Biological Survey. Thereafter they shared the life of field naturalists, her energy and enthusiasm enabling her to undertake expeditions on foot or horseback through mountains and across plains. She continued to publish articles regularly and in 1902 produced her *Handbook of Birds of the Western United States*, a counterpart to Frank M. Chapman's *Handbook of Birds of Eastern North America*. She also contributed to several of her husband's books, notably *Wild Animals of Glacier National Park*, 1918, and *Cave Life of Kentucky*, 1933. She was a founding member of the Audubon Society of the District of Columbia and frequently led its classes in basic ornithology. She became the first woman associate member of the American Ornithologists' Union in 1885, its first woman fellow in 1929, and the first woman recipient of its Brewster Medal in 1931, awarded for her comprehensive *Birds of New Mexico*, 1928, which she had begun under the auspices of the U.S. Biological Survey. Her last major written work was *Among the Birds in the Grand Canyon National Park*, published by the National Park Service in 1939. A variety of California mountain chickadee was named *Parus gambeli baileyae* in her honor in 1908. Bailey died in Washington, D.C., on September 22, 1948.

Bailey, Pearl 1918–1990 singer

Born March 29, 1918, in Newport News, Virginia, Pearl Mae Bailey was the daughter of Reverend Joseph James Bailey. Her father's church, the House of Prayer, was a "Holy Roller" style congregation, and Pearlie Mae, as she was known, attributed to her experience there her love of dance, song and rhythm. Her brother, Bill Bailey, enjoyed a career as a tap dancer; he too later became a minister.

In 1933 Bailey's family moved to Philadelphia, and Pearl soon got her start in the entertainment business by winning an amateur-night contest at a local vaudeville house. Her prize was a two-week performance contract at a weekly salary of $30, but the theater closed and she was never paid. Undeterred, she entered and won another amateur contest — this one at the Apollo Theatre in New York — and went on from there to perform at small clubs in the vaudeville circuit in rural Pennsylvania. Despite her complete lack of formal training, she played a number of smaller clubs successfully, including club dates with jazz artists Cootie Williams and Count Basie, with whom she later recorded several albums. After moving to New York, she performed at the Village Vanguard in 1944 and at the Blue Angel, an East-side café.

With the advent of World War II, she left New York for a USO tour of stateside training camps. Her stage debut came in 1946, as Butterfly in the "Negro" musical *St. Louis Woman*, for which she won a Donaldson award as the most promising new performer. During this period, she acted in *Variety Girl*, her first film. She played the part of an escaped Virginia slave in the stage musical *Arms and the Girl*, and in 1950 she was cast in the revue *Bless You All*.

Between 1950 and 1954, Bailey performed in numerous nightclubs: the Latin Quarter in Boston; the Capitol Theatre, the Greenwich Village Inn and La Vie en Rose in New York City; Ciro's in Hollywood and various clubs in London. Known for what critics called a "sexy, throaty drawl," Pearl Bailey often embellished her material through adlibbing and employing chit-chat and asides. She was famous for such songs as "Tired" (her first single); "Birth of the Blues"; "Toot, Toot, Tootsie, Goodbye"; "Takes Two to Tango; Row, Row, Row"; "Bill Bailey, Won't You Please Come Home?" and "St. Louis Blues".

She was briefly married in the 1930s, and again from 1948 to 1952. Her third marriage, to London drummer Louis Bellson, lasted until her death almost 40 years later. With Bellson, she adopted two children, a son, Tony, and a daughter, Dee Dee.

In 1954, she starred opposite Dorothy Dandridge in *Carmen Jones*. Her film career also includes *That Certain Feeling*, with Bob Hope and Eva Marie Saint, 1956, *Porgy and Bess*, 1959, and *All the Fine Young Cannibals*, 1960. From 1967 to 1969, in perhaps the highlight of her career, she played opposite Cab Calloway in the title role of an all-black production of the musical *Hello, Dolly!* Her performance brought New York theater audiences to their feet nightly and won her a special Tony award; she was also named Entertainer of the Year by *Cue* Magazine. In 1968, an original cast recording of the show was released. A popular guest on television programs such as the "The Ed Sullivan Show" and the "The Perry Como Show," she starred in her own show on ABC in 1970–71.

In her later years she wrote several books: *The Raw Pearl*, 1968, *Talking to Myself*, 1971, *Pearl's Kitchen*, 1973, and *Hurry Up America and Spit*, 1976. In 1975 she was appointed special ambassador to the UN by Gerald Ford. She received an honorary doctorate from Georgetown University in 1978; she later enrolled at Georgetown and, at age 67, graduated with a bachelor's degree in theology. Her last book, *Between You and Me*, 1989, detailed her experiences with higher education. In 1988 Bailey received the Presidential Meal of Freedom from Ronald Reagan. She died on August 17, 1990, in Philadelphia, Pennsylvania.

Baker, Josephine 1906–1975 entertainer

PIAZ

Josephine Baker

Born in St. Louis on June 3, 1906, Josephine Baker grew up fatherless and in poverty. Between the ages of eight and ten she was out of school, helping to support her family. She was attracted to things theatrical and as an adolescent danced occasionally in local vaudeville houses. At sixteen she joined a Philadelphia-based traveling dance troupe and shortly afterward, in 1923, won a spot in the chorus line of *Shuffle Along* on Broadway. She next appeared in *Chocolate Dandies* and then at the plush Plantation Club in Harlem.

In 1925 she accepted an offer to appear in the Paris show *La Revue Nègre*. She rose to stardom on the wave of French enthusiasm for jazz and African-American culture and was soon receiving top billing at the Folies Bergère, where she became celebrated across Europe for her G-string ornamented with bananas. She opened her own Paris club in 1926 and became the darling of café society. Given to eccentricities, she created a sensation by walking a leashed leopard on the Champs Élysées. She began to sing professionally in 1930 and thereby added a new and more exciting dimension to her performances. During the 1930s she appeared in several French movies and in *La Créole*, a light opera with music by Jacques Offenbach.

Baker became a naturalized French citizen in 1937. At the outbreak of World War II she did volunteer work with the Red Cross, and when France was invaded in 1940 she joined the Resistance, for which she was later awarded the Legion of Honor. In 1949 she published a volume of *Mémoires*. After the war she starred again at the Folies Bergère and later made a number of world tours. On visits to the United States she performed and took part in civil-rights activities, including the 1963 march on Washington. She maintained a large estate in the south of France, stocking it with all manner of animals and rearing a large "rainbow family" of adopted children of various colors and nationalities. In 1968 the estate was sold to satisfy accumulated debts. She died in Paris on April 12, 1975, during the celebration of the fiftieth anniversary of her Paris debut.

Baker, Sara Josephine 1873–1945 physician and public health administrator

Born on November 15, 1873, in Poughkeepsie, New York, Sara Josephine Baker prepared at private schools for Vassar, but the death of her father put that college out of reach. She decided to study medicine and after a year of private preparation entered the Women's Medical College of the New York Infirmary in New York City. After graduating in 1898 she interned at the New England Hospital for Women and Children and then entered private practice in New York City.

In 1901 she was appointed a medical inspector for the city health department, and in 1907 she became assistant to the commissioner of health. In that post she aided in the apprehension of "Typhoid Mary" Mallon. More importantly, however, she developed from the rudimentary program of inspection for infectious diseases a comprehensive approach to preventive health care for children. In the summer of 1908 she was allowed to test her plan in a slum district on the East Side. A team of 30 nurses under her direction sought out every infant in the district, taught simple hygiene to the mothers — ventilation, bathing, light clothing, breast feeding — and made follow-up visits. At the end of the summer the district had recorded 1200 fewer infant mortalities than the previous summer.

In August 1908 the Division of Child Hygiene was established in the health department and Baker was named director. The division (later raised to bureau) was the first government agency in the world devoted to child health. There Baker evolved a broad program including strict examination and licensing of midwives (and from 1911 free instruction at Bellevue Hospital), appointment of school nurses and doctors, compulsory use of silver nitrate drops in the eyes of all newborns, inspection of schoolchildren for infectious diseases, and numerous methods of distributing information on health and hygiene among the poor.

To deal with the inescapable problem of working mothers, she organized "Little Mothers' Leagues" to provide training to young girls required to care for infants. In 1911 she organized and became president of the Babies Welfare Association; the next year it was reorganized as the Children's Welfare Federation of New York, of which she was president until 1914 and chairman of the executive committee in 1914–1917. As a result of her division's work, the infant mortality rate in New York City fell from 144 per 1000 live births in 1908 to 88 in 1918 and 66 in 1923. By that time the division's health stations were caring for some 60,000 babies a year — half those born in the city. From 1916 to 1930 she lectured on child hygiene at the New York University-Bellevue Hospital Medical School, and in 1917 she was the first woman to receive from it a doctorate in public health. For 16 years from its organization in 1912 she was a staff consultant to the federal Children's Bureau. She retired from the Bureau of Child Hygiene in 1923 but remained active in many national and international organizations; her membership on the Health Committee of the League of Nations in 1922–1924 made her the first woman to serve the League in an official capacity. In 1917–1918 she was president of the American Child Health Association, which she had helped found in 1909.

In addition to over 200 articles in popular and professional journals she published *Healthy Babies*, *Healthy Children*, and *Healthy Mothers*, all 1920, *The Growing Child*, 1923, *Child Hygiene*, 1925, and an autobiography, *Fighting for Life*, 1939. She died in New York City on February 22, 1945.

Balch, Emily Greene 1867–1961 economist, social reformer and essayist

Born on January 8, 1867, in Jamaica Plain (now part of Boston), Massachusetts, Emily Balch was in the first class to graduate from Bryn Mawr College, in 1889. She pursued further studies in Paris and Berlin and at the University of Chicago and received training in social work from followers of Jacob Riis in New York City and in a settlement house in

Boston, where she was associated with Vida Scudder. In 1896 she began her teaching career at Wellesley College, becoming in 1913 professor of political economy and political and social science.

She continued her interest in the settlement house movement, working with Jane Addams's Hull House in Chicago, was active in promoting various child-welfare reforms, and served on Massachusetts commissions on industrial education, 1908–1909, and immigration, 1913–1914, and on the Boston city planning board, 1914–1917. A member of the Society of Friends, Balch became increasingly committed to the cause of peace and, following her attendance at the International Congress of Women at The Hague in 1915, she devoted her major efforts to that cause. Pacifism being an unpopular position in the United States at that time, she was relieved of her post at Wellesley in 1918. She helped Jane Addams found the Women's International League for Peace and Freedom in Zurich the following year and served as its secretary until 1922, when ill health forced her resignation; she resumed the post again briefly in 1934–1935 and in 1936 was elected honorary international president.

In 1926 she was a member of an informal commission organized to study conditions in Haiti, and the committee's report, *Occupied Haiti*, 1927, of which she was the principal author, was credited with hastening the withdrawal of U.S. forces from the country. Her work for peace finally achieved its due recognition in 1946, when she shared the Nobel Peace Prize with John R. Mott. She gave her share of the money award to the W.I.L.P.F. Among her writings are *Outline of Economics*, 1899, *A Study of Conditions of City Life*, 1903, *Our Slavic Fellow-Citizens*, a thorough and sympathetic study of Slavic immigrants, 1910, *Approaches to the Great Settlement*, 1918, *Refugees as Assets*, 1939, *The Miracle of Living*, a volume of verse, 1941, *One Europe*, 1947, *Vignettes in Prose*, 1952, and *Toward Human Unity, or Beyond Nationalism*, 1952. She died in Cambridge, Massachusetts, on January 9, 1961.

Baldwin, Faith 1893–1978 novelist

Born on October 1, 1893, in New Rochelle, New York, Faith Baldwin grew up in New York City. Her well-to-do family sent her to private academies and finishing schools, and in 1914–1916 she lived in Dresden, Germany. She married Hugh H. Cuthrell in 1920. The next year she published her first novel, *Mavis of Green Hill*, and although she often claimed she didn't care for authorship — she had once hoped to be an actress — she turned out a steady stream of books thereafter. Over the next 56 years she published more than 85 books, over 60 of them novels with such titles as *Magic and Mary Rose*, 1924, *Those Difficult Years*, 1925, *Alimony*, 1928, *The Office Wife*, 1930, *Babs and Mary Lou*, 1931, *District Nurse*, 1932, *White-Collar Girl*, 1933, *Honor Bound*, 1934, *Private Duty*, 1936, *Manhattan Nights*, 1937, *Career by Proxy*, 1939, *Temporary Address: Reno*, 1941, *He Married a Doctor*, 1944, and *Marry for Money*, 1948; her last completed novel, *Adam's Eden*, appeared in 1977.

Typically, a Faith Baldwin book presented a highly simplified version of life among the wealthy. No matter what the difficulties, honor and goodness triumphed, and hero and heroine were united. Evil, depravity, poverty, sex, and the like found no place in her work, which she explicitly intended for the housewife and the working girl. The popularity of her writing was enormous. In 1936, in the midst of the Depression, she published five novels in magazine serial form and three earlier serials in volume form and saw four made into motion pictures, for an income that year in excess of $315,000. She also wrote innumerable stories, articles, and newspaper columns, no less ephemeral than the novels. One of the most successful writers of light fiction in the 20th century, she died in Norwalk, Connecticut, on March 18, 1978.

Ball, Lucille 1911–1989 actor

Born on August 6, 1911, in Celoron, a suburb of Jamestown, New York, Lucille Désirée Ball determined at an early age to become an actress and left high school at fifteen to enroll in a drama school in New York City. Her early attempts to find a place in the theater all met with rebuffs, and she took a job as a model under the name Diane Belmont. She was moderately successful as a model, and a poster on which she appeared won her spots in *Broadway Through a Keyhole*, 1933, *Roman Scandals*, 1933, *Blood Money*, 1933, *Kid Millions*, 1934, and other movies.

PHILIPPE HALSMAN/YVONNE HALSMAN

Lucille Ball

She remained in Hollywood to appear in increasingly larger roles in a succession of movies — *Carnival*, 1935, *Roberta*, 1935, *Top Hat*, 1935, *Follow the Fleet*, 1936, *That Girl From Paris*, 1936, *Stage Door*, 1937, *Room Service*, 1938, *The Affairs of Annabel*, 1938, *Five Came Back*, 1939, and in 1940 *Too Many Girls*, in which she starred and which also featured Desi Arnaz, whom she married in November of that year. For ten years they conducted separate careers, he as a band leader who took occasional small parts in movies and she as a movie actress who was usually seen in B-grade comedies. She won major roles in *The Big Street*, 1942, *Du Barry Was a Lady*, 1943, *Without Love*, 1945, *Ziegfeld Follies*, 1946, *Easy to Wed*, 1946, *Her Husband's Affairs*, 1947, *Sorrowful Jones*, 1949, *Fancy Pants*, 1950, and *The Fuller Brush Girl*, 1950, all comedies which were box-office successes, but she was less fortunate in dramatic parts. In 1947–1948 she toured in a production of Elmer Rice's *Dream Girl*.

In 1950 she and her husband formed Desilu Productions which, after experimenting with a radio program, launched in October 1951 a television comedy series entitled "I Love Lucy." Starring the two of them in a comedy version of their real lives, the show was an instant hit, and for the six years (1951–1956 and, under the title "The Lucille Ball-Desi Arnaz Show," 1957–1958) during which fresh episodes were produced, it remained at or near the top of the TV ratings. "I Love Lucy" won an Emmy award in 1956. Released into syndicated distribution, it was still being seen in reruns by viewers around the world at the time of her death. Lucille Ball won many awards for best comedienne on television in 1952 and 1955.

Meanwhile Desilu began producing other shows for television and became one of the major companies in a highly competitive field. Ball and Arnaz were divorced in 1960, and two years later she succeeded him as president of Desilu, becoming the only woman at that time to lead a major Hollywood production company. She starred in the Broadway show *Wildcat* in 1961 and in 1962–1968 returned to television in "The Lucy Show," which won an Emmy in 1968; she personally won Emmys again in 1967 and 1968. She resumed movie work with *Yours, Mine and Ours*, 1968, and *Mame*, 1974.

She sold Desilu in 1967 and formed her own company, Lucille Ball Productions, which in 1968–1974 produced her third television series, "Here's Lucy." She continued to appear thereafter in special productions and as a guest star. In 1985 she played a Manhattan bag lady in the television film "Stone Pillow." Her fourth television series "Life with Lucy" aired for two months in 1986.

In 1977 she became the first woman to receive the Friar's Club Life Achievement Award, and she was inducted into the Television Academy Hall of Fame in 1984. She died in Los Angeles on April 26, 1989.

Bankhead, Tallulah Brockman 1903–1968 actor

Born in Huntsville, Alabama, on January 31, 1903, Tallulah Bankhead was the daughter of William B. Bankhead, congressman and speaker of the House in 1936–1940. She was educated in convent schools and at fifteen, having won a movie-magazine beauty contest, went to New York to become an actress. She made her first Broadway appearance in *Squab Farm* in 1918. During the next four years she played a number of roles, none particularly memorable, in such productions as *Foot-Loose*, 1920, *Nice People*, 1921, and *The Exciters*, 1922, while becoming a member of the "Algonquin set" — a group that included Alexander Woollcott, Dorothy Parker, Robert Benchley, and Harpo and Groucho Marx — and a figure about town.

In 1923 she starred in the London production of *The Dancers*. She remained in London for eight years, appearing in more than a dozen plays — including Michael Arlen's *The Green Hat* in 1925, *Fallen Angels* also in 1925, Sidney Howard's *They Knew What They Wanted* in 1926, *Her Cardboard Lover* in 1928, and *The Lady of the Camelias* in 1930 — and becoming a celebrity's celebrity. Between 1931 and 1933 she made several movies, including *Tarnished Lady*, 1931, *My Sin*, 1931, *The Devil and the Deep*, 1932, and *Faithless*, 1932, and then returned to Broadway in a series of productions that, with the possible exception of a 1935 revival of *Rain*, failed to engage her unique talents. Finally, in 1939, she appeared in Lillian Hellman's *The Little Foxes* and gave a performance as Regina that won the year's top acting award from the New York Drama Critics' Circle. She won the award again three years later for her performance in Thornton Wilder's *The Skin of Our Teeth* and in 1944 took the New York Film Critics' highest award for her role in Alfred Hitchcock's *Lifeboat*.

Such successes established her as a star whose name could underwrite any production; her deep voice, lush beauty, and mysterious manner, to say nothing of her singular name, fascinated millions. She continued to play on Broadway in, among other productions, Philip Barry's *Foolish Notion*, 1945, Noel Coward's *Private Lives*, 1948, *Dear Charles*, 1954, a 1956 revival of Tennessee Williams's *Streetcar Named Desire*, *Eugenia*, 1957, and *Midgie Purvis*, 1961, while appearing occasionally in movies, notably *A Royal Scandal*, 1945, and *Main Street to Broadway*, 1953, and later on television.

In 1950–1952 she conducted a combined variety and talk program on radio. In 1952 she published the frank and witty *Tallulah, My Autobiography*. Her last Broadway appearance was in *The Milk Train Doesn't Stop Here Anymore*, 1964, and in 1965 she was in the motion picture *Die! Die! My Darling*. Tallulah — her last name was entirely superfluous — died in New York City on December 12, 1968.

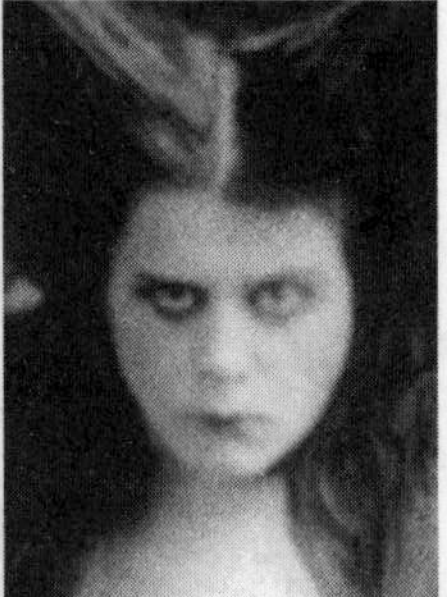

Theda Bara

Bara, Theda 1885?–1955 actor

Born in Cincinnati on July 20, probably in 1885 (although she later claimed 1890), Theodosia Burr Goodman attended the University of Cincinnati in 1903–1905. In New York City she tried briefly for a stage career under the name Theodosia de Coppet before she began her movie career in 1915 with William Fox, who built his motion-picture empire on her films. She appeared first in *A Fool There Was* that year and created a nationwide sensation; this film, together with a huge outpouring of excessively imaginative studio publicity, some of it bordering on the farcical, made her one of the most magnetic stars of the silent-movie era. It was in that silent film that a title card had her delivering the classic line "Kiss me, my fool!" It was also in that film that she created the character of the "vamp" or "vampire," a cold and heartless, but irresistible, woman who leads men to their doom. The role was perfectly suited to her sultry, heavy-lidded manner and often semiclad person. In five years she made some 40 films, including *Carmen*, 1915, *The Serpent*, 1915, *Romeo and Juliet*, 1916, *Under Two Flags*, 1916, *Madame Du Barry*, 1917, *Cleopatra*, 1917, and *Salome*, 1918.

Her screen appearances were of such an arousing nature that on several occasions she was denounced from the pulpit. She had changed her name legally to Theda Bara at the outset of her career, and the Fox publicity department had a field day telling the nation that her first name was an anagram for "death" and her second was "Arab" spelled backward; she was, they suggested darkly, the daughter of a French artist and an Arabian princess and had been born somewhere in the Sahara. Others of her films included *The*

Vixen, *The She Devil*, *The Tiger Woman*, *Forbidden Path*, and *The Rose of Blood*, titles designed to convey the mysterious allure of the star. The brief vogue for her sort of sex appeal having passed, Bara left the movies in 1920. She made one unsuccessful attempt on Broadway in *The Blue Flame* and then retired to live quietly in Los Angeles until her death there on April 7, 1955.

Barnard, Kate 1875–1930 political reformer and labor organizer

Born on May 23, 1875, in Geneva, Nebraska, Kate Barnard lived with relatives in Kansas until 1889, when she rejoined her widowed father in the newly opened Oklahoma Territory. After graduating from high school in Oklahoma City she worked as a teacher and stenographer, became a clerk for the Democratic minority in the territorial legislature, and in 1904 was given a post with the Oklahoma Commission at the Louisiana Purchase Exposition in St. Louis.

In the slums of that city she had her first view of the underside of industrialism and urbanization and determined to prevent such evils from befalling Oklahoma. Letters on these topics to the *Daily Oklahoman* led to her appointment as matron of the Provident Association of Oklahoma City in December 1905, and through that organization she directed the relief of hundreds of poor families and clothed and sent to school hundreds of their children. She also began campaigning for organized labor, forming the Federal Labor Union in the city and securing its affiliation with the American Federation of Labor. At a joint meeting of farmer and labor representatives in 1906 — the "Shawnee Convention" — called to hammer out a common platform to present to the upcoming state constitutional convention, she played a major organizing role and pushed through planks on compulsory education and child labor abolition. Her campaigning helped produce a friendly Democratic majority for the constitutional convention in November, which adopted her planks and established the office of state commissioner of charities and corrections, while it defeated a woman suffrage plank in which she took no interest. She relinquished her post with the Provident Association to run for commissioner, and in the election of 1907 she was elected, leading the Democratic ticket in most districts and winning majorities even in otherwise Republican districts. She was the first woman ever elected to a statewide office in any state. Reelected in 1910, she was for seven years a highly active and effective reform leader. Compulsory education and child labor laws were strengthened, progressive labor legislation was passed, and the care of mental patients and prisoners greatly improved. Her unannounced personal inspection of the Kansas state prison in Lansing exposed atrocious conditions and ended the system under which some 600 Oklahoma convicts were "contracted" out to Kansas institutions; reform in Kansas also resulted, and a similar campaign in Arizona followed in 1911–1912.

Barnard's successes made her a frequent speaker at reform and charity conventions. In 1911 she launched an investigation into widespread fraud in the state-court administered system of guardianship for Native American minors. Her efforts recovered nearly a million dollars for 1,361 Native American children defrauded of oil, gas, timber, and land rights but stirred up such heated opposition that the legislature turned on her. Her staff and budget cut, she declined to seek reelection in 1914. She lived in Oklahoma City until her death there on February 23, 1930.

Barrett, Janie Porter 1865–1948 welfare worker

Born in Athens, Georgia, on August 9, 1865, Janie Porter, the daughter of former slaves, grew up largely in the home of the cultured white family who employed her mother. She graduated from Hampton Institute in Hampton, Virginia, in 1884 and for five years was a teacher, first in a rural school in Dawson, Georgia, then at Lucy Craft Laney's Haines Normal and Industrial Institute in Augusta, and from 1886 until her marriage, in October 1889 to Harris Barrett, at Hampton Institute. Soon after her marriage she was conducting an informal day-care school in her home in Hampton, Virginia, that grew rapidly, and in October 1890 was formally organized as the Locust Street Social Settlement, the nation's first settlement organization for African-American people. In 1902 the Barretts built a separate structure on their property to house the settlement's numerous activities, which included clubs, classes in domestic skills, and recreation. Hampton Institute students and faculty provided assistance and support, and through them several chiefly Northern philanthropists were found to fund the settlement.

In 1908 Barrett led in the founding and became president of the Virginia State Federation of Colored Women's Clubs. Through the federation she labored for several years to raise money for a residential industrial school for the large number of young African-American girls she had been shocked to discover relegated to jails. In 1914 a 147–acre farm at Peake (also known as Peaks Turnout) was purchased, and in January 1915 the Virginia Industrial School for Colored Girls opened with 28 students. With advice from many prominent social workers and especially from the Russell Sage Foundation, a program stressing self-reliance and self-discipline, visible rewards, "big-sister" guidance, close attention to individual needs, and academic and vocational instruction was developed.

Later in 1915 Barrett, now a widow, moved to the school as superintendent. She was deeply involved in every aspect of the school's program and personally conducted the parole system by which girls who demonstrated sufficient responsibility were placed in carefully selected foster homes, given employment, and supported by such follow-up services as ministerial guidance, a newsletter (*The Booster*), and personal letters. In 1920 the state of Virginia assumed financial responsibility for the school. Supervision was shared by the state and the women's club federation until 1942, when it became solely a function of the Virginia Department of Welfare and Institutions. In the early 1920s the Russell Sage Foundation rated the school, whose average enrollment was then about 100, one of the five best of its kind in the country. Barrett retired as superintendent in 1940 and died in Hampton, Virginia, on August 27, 1948. Two years later the school she had built was renamed the Janie Porter Barrett School for Girls.

Barrett, Kate Harwood Waller 1857–1925 social worker

Born on January 24, 1857, in Falmouth, Virginia, Kate Waller spent her childhood, except for the Civil War years, on the family estate and completed her private education with two years at the Arlington Institute for Girls in Alexandria. In July 1876 she married the Reverend Robert S. Barrett. She accompanied him to parishes in Richmond, 1876–1880, Henderson, Kentucky, 1880–1886, and Atlanta, 1886–1894. While still in Richmond, she became interested in the plight of prostitutes and unwed mothers. She first sought a practical education in this field of social work, traveling to London to take the course at the Florence Nightingale Training School and St. Thomas's Hospital and in 1889 entering the Women's Medical College of Georgia, from which she received an M.D. degree in 1892. In that year she contacted Charles N. Crittenton, businessman turned evangelist and missionary to "fallen women," who had opened four homes for such women in California. With a contribution from him she opened a home in Atlanta in 1893, the fifth of the Florence Crittenton chain (named for Crittenton's deceased daughter). In 1894 the Barretts moved to Washington, D.C., where Reverend Barrett died in 1896.

Dr. Barrett continued to work with the National Florence Crittenton Mission, established in 1895, and in 1897 became vice-president and general superintendent of the organization. Crittenton himself held the title of president, but Dr. Barrett was effectively in charge of the nationwide chain of more than 50 semi-autonomous homes. She founded a magazine, a training program, and a conference series for the workers in the missions and in 1903 published *Some Practical Suggestions on the Conduct of a Rescue Home*. In December 1909, following Crittenton's death, she succeeded to the presidency of the national organization, retaining the post of general superintendent as well; she continued both jobs until her death. Under her administration the tenor of care in Florence Crittenton homes gradually changed from evangelism to training in maternal skills and vocational guidance. In 1909 Dr. Barrett was invited to the White House Conference for the Care of Dependent Children, and in 1914 she was a special representative of the Labor Department on a commission investigating the treatment of women deported from the United States on morals grounds. She was also active in the National Council of Women, serving as corresponding secretary in 1899–1903, vice-president at large in 1903–1911, and president in 1911–1916. She served as vice-president of the Virginia Equal Suffrage League from 1909 to 1920 and as president of the National Women's Auxiliary of the American Legion in 1922–1923. She died in Alexandria, Virginia, on February 23, 1925.

Barry, Leonora Marie Kearney 1849–1930 "Mother Lake," labor leader and social reformer

Born on August 13, 1849, in Kearney, County Cork, Ireland, Leonora Kearney emigrated with her family to the United States in 1852, settling in St. Lawrence County, New York. After several years of teaching school she married W. E. Barry in November, 1871. He died ten years later; left with two children to support, she took a menial job in a clothing factory in Amsterdam, New York. Typically for the time, working conditions in the factory were poor and the pay was exceedingly low (Barry's wages for her first week were 65 cents), and in 1884 she joined a women's branch of the Knights of Labor. She rose rapidly to the post of master workman of the local branch, and in 1886, at the national convention of the Knights in Richmond, Virginia, she was elected to take charge of the newly created department of women's work. During four years in that post she worked tirelessly to improve wages and working conditions for women throughout the country, traveling widely to organize, inspire, and investigate. Her annual reports were detailed and vigorous indictments of the effects of the factory system on women and children, and they contributed greatly to the passage of a factory inspection law in Pennsylvania in 1889. She resigned from her position in April 1890 upon her marriage to O. R. Lake, but, from her new home in St. Louis, she continued to travel and speak on behalf of women's suffrage, temperance, and other movements. During this period and later, after moving to Minooka, Illinois, in 1916, she was active in the Woman's Christian Temperance Union and the Catholic Total Abstinence Union of America, and, as a popular lecturer on the Chautauqua and Redpath circuits until 1928, she roused much public support for Prohibition. Barry, sometimes known in later life as Mrs. Barry-Lake or Mother Lake, died in Minooka, Illinois, on July 15, 1930.

Barrymore, Ethel 1879–1959 actor

Born in Philadelphia on August 15, 1879, the daughter of Maurice and Georgiana Drew Barrymore and the sister of Lionel and John Barrymore, Ethel Barrymore attended the Convent of the Sacred Heart in Philadelphia and, after first intending to be a pianist, made her stage debut at fourteen in a Montreal production of Sheridan's *The Rivals*, which also featured Lionel and her grandmother, Louisa Drew. She first appeared in New York with the same production in January 1894. She next appeared with her uncle, John Drew, in *The Bauble Shop* and then went to London, playing in *Secret Service*, *The Bells*, and *Peter the Great* in 1897–1898. Returning to Broadway, she starred in the Charles Frohman production of *Captain Jinks of the Horse Marines* in 1901. Subsequent roles in *A Doll's House* and *Alice-Sit-by-the-Fire*, both 1905, *Sunday*, 1906, *Mid-Channel*, 1910, *Trelawney of the Wells*, 1911, *Déclassée*, 1919, *Rose Bernd*, 1922, *The Second Mrs. Tanqueray*, 1924, *The Kingdom of God*, 1928, in which she opened the Ethel Barrymore

Theatre in New York City, *The Constant Wife*, also 1928, *Scarlet Sister Mary*, 1931, *L'Aiglon*, 1934, *Whiteoaks*, 1938, and *The Corn Is Green*, 1942, won her a great and lasting reputation in the theater. She also played in vaudeville, on radio, on television, and in motion pictures, appearing with both of her brothers in *Rasputin and the Empress*, 1932. Her performance in *None but the Lonely Heart*, 1944, won her an Academy Award for supporting actress. Born a member of the American theater's "royal family," she earned her acknowledged position of first lady of the American stage. She published *Memories* in 1955 and died in Hollywood, California, on June 18, 1959.

Barrymore, Georgiana Emma Drew 1854–1893 actor

Born in Philadelphia on July 11, 1854, Georgiana Drew was the daughter of John Drew and Louisa Lane Drew, both distinguished actors, and the younger sister of John Drew, Jr., later also a great star. She made her theatrical debut in 1872 in *The Ladies' Rattle* at the Arch Street Theatre, Philadelphia, under her mother's management. In 1875 she followed her brother to join Augustin Daly's repertory company at the Fifth Avenue Theatre in New York City; her debut there came on May 6, 1875, in Bulwer-Lytton's *Money*. Over the next year she played in *As You Like It*, *Frou-Frou*, *Divorce*, *The School for Scandal*, and *Pique*. In the cast of the last was the young English actor Maurice Barrymore (originally Herbert Blythe), whom she married in December 1876. Over the next several years she appeared with A. M. Palmer's company, in her husband's short-lived companies, and in support of such stars as Lawrence Barrett, Edwin Booth, John McCullough, and in particular Helena Modjeska, with whom she formed a close friendship. Her successes in such plays as *Diplomacy*, *Moths*, *The Wages of Sin*, *L'Abbé Constantin*, and *Mr. Wilkinson's Widow* were punctuated by the births of three children destined also for the stage: Lionel (1878–1954), Ethel (1879–1959), and John (1882–1942). Her greatest stage success was a comic role opposite W. H. Crane in *The Senator*, which opened in January 1890 and in which she appeared for nearly two years, until ill health forced her to leave the cast in December 1891. Ill health also cut short a San Francisco season with Charles Frohman's company in 1892, and in February 1893 she made her final stage appearance in New York. In May she traveled to Santa Barbara, California, to convalesce, but she died there on July 2, 1893.

Clara Barton

Barton, Clara 1821–1912 founder of the American Red Cross

Born on December 25, 1821, in Oxford, Massachusetts, Clarissa Harlowe Barton was the youngest of five children. She was educated at home and grew up willful and independent, with a love for outdoor sports. She began a career of teaching at the age of fifteen. In 1850–1851 she attended the Liberal Institute at Clinton, New York, and in 1852 she established in Bordentown, New Jersey, a free school that soon became so large that the townsmen would no longer allow a woman to run it. Rather than subordinate herself to a male principal, she resigned. She was employed by the U.S. Patent Office from 1854 to 1857 and again in 1860. In 1861 she showed characteristic initiative in organizing facilities to recover soldiers' lost baggage and in securing medicine and supplies for men wounded in the first battle of Bull Run. She gained permission to pass through the battle lines to distribute supplies, search for the missing, and nurse the wounded. She carried on this work through the remainder of the Civil War, traveling with the army as far south as Charleston in 1863. In June 1864 she was formally appointed superintendent of nurses for the Army of the James. In 1865 she organized a program to investigate the cases of soldiers listed as missing. During 1866–1868 she spoke widely about her Civil War work.

In 1869 she went abroad for her health but soon was busy in relief work in the Franco-Prussian War. Learning of the activities of the international Red Cross recently organized in Geneva, Switzerland, she campaigned and lobbied vigorously, after her return to the United States in 1873 and another period of convalescence, with the result that the United

States became a signatory of the Geneva Convention in March 1882. In 1881 she organized the American Association of the Red Cross, known from 1893 as the American National Red Cross, and served as its president until 1904. She devoted herself entirely to the organization, soliciting contributions and taking to the field with relief workers even as late as the Spanish-American War in Cuba, when she was seventy-seven. She was jealous of any interference, however, and supervised the organization's activities so closely that finally charges of authoritarianism were brought against her by members of her executive council led by Mabel T. Boardman. The Red Cross had been chartered by Congress in 1900, and the rebelling faction used that lever to force her resignation in 1904. Despite the arbitrariness of her administrative methods, her achievements remained — in particular her successful advocacy of the "American amendment" to the Geneva Convention in 1884, a provision that permitted the Red Cross to provide relief in times of natural disasters and calamities as well as in wartime. In addition to many pamphlets and books on the Red Cross she wrote *The Story of My Childhood*, 1907. Clara Barton died in Glen Echo, Maryland, on April 12, 1912.

Bascom, Florence 1862–1945 geologist

Born on July 14, 1862, in Williamstown, Massachusetts, Florence Bascom grew up there and, from 1874, in Madison, Wisconsin, where her father was president of the University of Wisconsin. She graduated from the university with two bachelor's degrees in 1882, took a B.S. in 1884, and received her master's degree in geology in 1887. After teaching for two years at Rockford College, Illinois, she undertook an unofficial program of advanced study in geology at The Johns Hopkins University, and despite her informal status she was awarded a Ph.D. in 1893 for work in the newly developed field of petrography. She was able to demonstrate that the pre-Cambrian formations in South Mountain, Maryland, were of volcanic rather than sedimentary origin. Her doctorate was the first awarded to a woman by Johns Hopkins and the first in geology to a woman in the United States. After two years on the faculty of Ohio State University Bascom joined that of Bryn Mawr College in 1895. Her scientific reputation and her popularity as a teacher were already such that she was soon able to establish geology as a major field at Bryn Mawr and to resist successfully a later attempt by M. Carey Thomas, college president, to reduce it again to elective status. In 1906 she advanced to full professor. Eventually a graduate program in geology was established, after Bascom's strenuous efforts had secured laboratory space, a mineral collection, and equipment for research and instruction, and Bryn Mawr became a major center of American geology.

In 1896 Bascom had accomplished another first in receiving appointment as geological assistant with the U.S. Geological Survey; she advanced to assistant geologist in 1901 and to geologist in 1909. Her investigations for the Survey in the Mid-Atlantic Piedmont area took her regularly into the field, and her findings appeared in several Survey publications: the Philadelphia Folio, 1909, the Trenton Folio, 1909, the Elkton-Wilmington Folio, 1920, and bulletins on Quakertown-Doylestown, 1931, and Honeybrook-Phoenixville, 1938. She retired from Bryn Mawr in 1928 and from the Survey in 1938, but she remained active. The first woman elected a fellow of the Geological Society of America, in 1894, she became a councillor in 1924 and vice-president in 1930. She died in Northampton, Massachusetts, on June 18, 1945.

Bates, Katharine Lee 1859–1929 educator, essayist and poet

Born on August 12, 1859, in Falmouth, Massachusetts, Katharine Bates grew up in Wellesley, Massachusetts. She graduated from Wellesley College in 1880. After a few years of teaching school she returned to Wellesley in 1885 as an instructor in English. She was made a professor and head of the department of English in 1891 and remained with the college for 40 years in all, retiring as professor emeritus in 1925. During her long career as a teacher she also wrote volumes of poetry, travel books, and scholarly works, among them *The College Beautiful and Other Poems*, 1887, *Rose and Thorn*, 1888, *English Religious Drama*, 1893, *Spanish Highways and By-ways*, 1900, *From Gretna Green to Land's End*, 1907, *The Story of Chaucer's Canterbury Tales Re-told for Children*, 1909, *Fairy Gold*, 1916, *The Retinue and Other Poems*, 1918, *Sigurd*, 1919, *Yellow Clover*, 1922, *The Pilgrim Ship*, 1926, and *America the Dream*, published posthumously in 1930. While on a western tour in the summer of 1893 she climbed Pike's Peak and was inspired by the view to write a poem entitled "America the Beautiful." She first published it in the *Congregationalist* in July 1895; it appeared in a revised version in the *Boston Evening Transcript* in November 1904 and in its final form in 1911. Set to the music of Samuel A. Ward's "Materna," the poem became, unofficially but indisputably, the national hymn. Bates died in Wellesley, Massachusetts, on March 28, 1929.

Battle, Kathleen 1948– opera singer

Born on August 13, 1948, in Portsmouth, Ohio, Kathleen Deanne Battle's father was a steelworker and a singer in an African-American gospel quartet, while her mother stayed at home to care for her and her six older siblings. Although she began taking piano lessons at the age of 13 and came from a "musical family," she did not aspire to be a performance musician until she was well into adulthood. She graduated from Portsmouth High School in 1966 and was awarded a Ford Foundation National Achievement Scholarship. She entered the College Conservatory of Music at the University of Cincinnati, majoring in music education rather than performance. She earned both a bachelor's and a master's degree and in 1971 began teaching music education at an inner-city elementary school in Cincinnati.

While teaching she began studying voice with Franklin Bens, who focused on the oratorio literature. In 1972 she auditioned for Thomas Schippers, then director of the Cincinnati Symphony Orchestra. Although she lacked any formal experience, Schippers was so impressed and moved by her voice, he hired her to perform at the Spoleto Festival of Two Worlds in Italy. Singing in the festival was a major turning point, helping her to decide on a career as a professional singer. She continued to study back in the U.S., performing with the Cincinnati Symphony Orchestra. In 1973 Schippers introduced her to the pianist and conductor James Levine who would become a combination mentor, teacher, and friend to her, shaping and influencing her career and encouraging her to develop a repertoire which included sacred music and emphasized Mozart.

Over the next five years, her career flourished. She received a Young Artists Award from the Kennedy Center for the Performing Arts and a Martha Baird Rockefeller Fund for Music Award, and under Levine's tutelage, sang supporting roles in a number of major U.S. opera houses. In 1978, at the age of 30, she made her debut at the Metropolitan Opera in New York City as the Shepherd in a production of Wagner's *Tannhäuser*. She received rave reviews for her performance as well as for the many others that followed, some placing her among the best coloratura sopranos in the world. Her voice has been called "exceptionally pure, retaining its perfection at both ends of her two and a half octave range, from low A, to high E." Throughout her career she continued to refine her skills, performing such roles as Sophie in Jules Massenet's *Werther*, Blonde in Mozart's *Die Entführung aus dem Serail*, the extremely demanding Zerbinetta in Richard Strauss's *Ariadne auf Naxos*, and the two queens in Handel's *Solomon*. She also began giving extremely well-received recitals, expanding her material to include not only traditional opera, but African spirituals and popular music as well.

In February of 1994 the Metropolitan Opera dismissed her for what they called "unprofessional actions," accusing her of mistreating fellow opera personnel from stage hands to fellow cast members. Despite her great talent, she was suddenly considered "difficult" and "a prima donna." By 1996, however, she was regularly touring the world, performing opera, spirituals, and a wide range of other musical selections. Her numerous recordings continued to sell, and in 1995 she released the album, *So Many Stars* which proved to be a major popular success.

Bay, Josephine Holt Perfect 1900–1962 financier

Born on August 10, 1900, in Anamosa, Iowa, Josephine Perfect grew up in Brooklyn, New York. After graduating from Brooklyn Heights Seminary and attending Colorado College for a year, 1918–1919, she became active in various civic groups in Brooklyn, notably the Junior League. With her sister she also operated a successful Christmas card business. In August 1942 she married Charles U. Bay, a senior partner in the brokerage firm of A. M. Kidder & Co. She took an active interest in his business from the start. During 1946–1953 she accompanied her husband to Norway, where he served as U.S. ambassador and she worked in various ways to help relieve the distresses left by World War II. In 1955, when Charles Bay fell ill, Josephine Bay was elected to a limited partnership in A. M. Kidder, and she also succeeded him as a director of the American Export Lines. (Charles Bay died in December 1955.) In 1956 she was chosen chairman of the executive committee of American Export (a passenger and shipping firm then doing $60 million gross annual business), and in December of that year she was elected to the presidency and chairmanship of the board of A. M. Kidder.

Bay was the first woman to head a member firm of the New York Stock Exchange. In February 1959 she moved up to chairman of the board of American Export Lines, a post she held until the next year. She remained at the head of A. M. Kidder until her death in New York City on August 6, 1962. She was succeeded by her second husband, C. Michael Paul, whom she had married in January 1959, and he retained the post until A. M. Kidder went out of business in June 1963.

Beach, Amy Marcy Cheney 1867–1944 composer and pianist

Amy Cheney Beach

Born in Henniker, New Hampshire, on September 5, 1867, Amy Cheney had already demonstrated precocious musical talent when the family moved to Boston in 1870. She began taking piano lessons at six, although she had been composing simple melodies on the keyboard since four, and she studied under such teachers as Ernst Perabo and Carl Baermann. In October 1883 she gave her first public recital at Boston Music Hall. Several more successful recitals followed, and in March 1885 she played the Chopin F-minor concerto with the Boston Symphony Orchestra.

In December 1885 she married Dr. Henry H. A. Beach, an eminent surgeon, Harvard professor, and devoted amateur musician. He encouraged his wife to concentrate on composition. Curtailing her public performing, she undertook a rigorous course of self-instruction in musical theory and composition. Her first efforts were in smaller forms — musical settings of favorite poems and other pieces — but in February 1892, after three years' work, she heard the Boston Symphony and the Handel and Haydn Society perform her Mass in E-flat major, her first major work (numbered Opus 5) and the first by a woman to be performed by those organizations. Subsequent important compositions included "Eilende Wolken," an aria based on Schiller and premiered by Walter Damrosch and the New York Symphony later in 1892; *Festival Jubilate* for the dedication of the Woman's Building at the World's Columbian Exposition in Chicago in 1893; the *Gaelic Symphony*, premiered by the Boston Symphony in October 1896; Sonata in A-minor for violin and piano, first performed in January 1897 by herself and Franz Kneisel; Piano Concerto in C-sharp minor, which she performed with the Boston Symphony in April 1900; a Quintet for piano and strings, completed in 1908; and *Panama Hymn* for the Panama-Pacific Exposition in San Francisco in 1915. Mrs. H. H. A. Beach, as she was known, was by far the preeminent woman composer in America, and her more than 150 numbered works, nearly all of which were published, also included choral works; church music; chamber works; cantatas with such titles as "The Rose of Avontown," "Sylvania," "The Sea-Fairies," "The Chambered Nautilus," and "Canticle of the Sun"; and songs to words of Shakespeare, Burns, and especially Browning, whose "Ah, love, but a day" and "The year's at the spring" inspired two of her best known pieces. Following the death of Dr. Beach in 1910 she spent the years 1911–1914 in Europe, where she was widely acclaimed both for her performing and for her compositions. She died in New York City on December 27, 1944.

Beach, Sylvia Woodbridge 1887–1962 bookseller and publisher

Born in Baltimore on March 14, 1887, Sylvia Beach was educated mainly at home. In 1901 she accompanied her father, a Presbyterian clergyman, to Paris, where he served as pastor of the American Church. She did volunteer relief work in France during World War I and in 1918–1919 served with the American Red Cross in Serbia. In 1919 she opened Shakespeare & Co., a bookshop on the Rue Dupuytren in the St.-Germain-des-Prés quarter of Paris. She specialized in books published in Great Britain and the United States and at the same time operated a lending library. The growing interest in American literature among French students and literati soon made her shop a gathering place for them and for expatriate British and American authors; among those who frequented it were André Gide, Paul Valéry, Jules Romains, Gertrude Stein, Ernest Hemingway, and F. Scott Fitzgerald. In 1922 she undertook to publish James Joyce's monumental *Ulysses*, segments of which had already been judged obscene in England and the United States, and which had been rejected by several established publishers. She worked closely with Joyce in the exceedingly difficult task of reading and correcting proofs. The 1,000–copy first printing was sold exclusively by her shop, and over the next 11 years she sold some 28,000 copies of 14 printings. She also published Joyce's *Pomes Penyeach*, 1927, and Samuel Beckett's *Our Exagmination Round His Factification for Incamination of Work in Progress*, 1929. Her shop remained a literary mecca until it closed in 1941 as a result of the German occupation of Paris. In 1943 Sylvia Beach was interned by the Germans for several months. In 1959 she published a memoir of her life and literary work as *Shakespeare and Company*. She died in Paris on October 5, 1962.

Beaux, Cecilia 1855–1942 painter

Born in Philadelphia on May 1, 1855, Eliza Cecilia Beaux, as she was christened, was left by her widowed father to be reared by relatives in New York City and later West Philadelphia. She was educated at home and for two years at a Philadelphia finishing school and at sixteen took up the study of art. Under the tutelage of her cousin, Catharine Drinker (Janvier), an artist and writer of some note, and later of Adolf van der Whelen and William Sartain, she developed rapidly into a skilled painter. In 1883 she opened a studio in Philadelphia. Her first major work, a full-length portrait of her sister and nephew, was exhibited in 1885 at the Pennsylvania Academy of Fine Arts, where it was awarded the Mary Smith Prize, and in 1886, under the title "Les Derniers Jours d'Enfance," at the Paris Salon. During 1888–1889 she traveled and studied in Europe, taking instruction at the Academie Julian in Paris and from several leading artists.

Returning to her Philadelphia studio, she achieved considerable success over the next several years. She won the Mary Smith Prize again in 1891 and 1892 and in 1896 exhibited six portraits at the Paris Salon — "Rev. Matthew B. Grier," "Ernesta Drinker, with Nurse," "A Lady from Connecticut," "Sita and Sarita," "Cynthia Sherwood," and "The Dreamer." In 1894 she was elected an associate of the National Academy of Design, and she was elevated to full academician in 1902. In 1895 she became the first woman instructor at the Pennsylvania Academy of the Fine Arts, and in 1896, on the strength of her showing at the Paris Salon, she was elected to membership in the Société

Nationale des Beaux-Arts. Cecilia Beaux moved to New York City in 1900. Later major works included commissioned portraits of Mrs. Theodore Roosevelt and her daughter Ethel, Mary Adelaide Nutting (for the Johns Hopkins Hospital), Mrs. Andrew Carnegie, Richard Watson Gilder, and, for the National Art Committee's project on World War I leaders, Admiral Lord David Beatty, Georges Clémenceau, and Cardinal Mercier. Her paintings were placed in such major collections as the National Collection of Fine Arts, the Metropolitan Museum, the Art Institute of Chicago, the Luxembourg Museum of Paris, and the Uffizi Gallery of Florence. Cecilia Beaux was acknowledged as one of the leading portraitists of her day. Her work, while it suggested at times the influence of some of her French Impressionist teachers, and at other times was compared to that of John Singer Sargent, was not imitative of any master. Following an injury in 1924 she painted little. In 1930 she published *Background with Figures*, an autobiography. She was elected to membership in the American Academy of Arts and Letters in 1933, and two years later the Academy presented a retrospective exhibit of some 65 of her canvases. The recipient of numerous other honors, medals, and awards, she died at her summer home in Gloucester, Massachusetts, on September 17, 1942.

Beecher, Catharine Esther 1800–1878 educator

Born in East Hampton, New York, on September 6, 1800, Catharine Beecher was the eldest daughter in one of the nineteenth century's most remarkable families. Daughter of Lyman Beecher and sister of Edward and Henry Ward Beecher and Harriet Beecher Stowe and half-sister of Isabella Beecher (Hooker), to name only the most prominent of her siblings, she grew up in an atmosphere of learning but was hindered by her sex from receiving much formal education. She grew up from 1810 in Litchfield, Connecticut, where she attended schools for young ladies conducted in the fashion of the day while independently studying Latin, philosophy, and mathematics. After the death of her mother in 1816 she had much of the care of the family. In 1821 she became a schoolteacher, and in 1823 she and her sister Mary established a girls' school that four years later became the Hartford Female Seminary in Hartford, Connecticut, an innovative institution in which she introduced calisthenics in a course of physical education.

Moving with her father to Cincinnati in 1832, she opened the Western Female Institute; financial difficulties and her precarious health closed the school five years later. The rest of her life was devoted to the development of educational facilities in the Middle West and to the promotion of equal educational opportunities for women. She worked through the Board of National Popular Education, a private agency headquartered in Cleveland, in 1847–1848 and in 1852 founded the American Woman's Educational Association to recruit and train teachers to staff schools on the frontier. She inspired the founding of several women's colleges in the Midwest, and her writings did much to introduce domestic science into the American school curriculum.

Among her published works were *A Treatise on Domestic Economy*, 1841, *The Duty of American Women to their Country*, 1845, *The Evils Suffered by American Women and American Children*, 1846, *Physiology and Calisthenics for Schools and Families*, 1856, *Woman Suffrage and Woman's Profession*, 1871, and *Educational Reminiscences and Suggestions*, 1874. Though in sympathy with much of the reformist spirit of the century, she stoutly opposed woman suffrage as inimical to the domestic sphere proper to woman. She died on May 12, 1878, in Elmira, New York.

Beers, Ethel Lynn 1827–1879 poet

Born in Goshen, New York, on January 13, 1827, Ethelinda Eliot, a descendant of John Eliot, the "Apostle to the Indians," began at an early age to contribute to periodicals under the name Ethel Lynn. In March 1846 she married William H. Beers, and thereafter she published under the name Ethel Lynn Beers. On November 30, 1861, *Harper's*

Magazine printed her poem entitled "The Picket Guard," which soon became better known by its first line, "All quiet along the Potomac tonight," a familiar newspaper caption of those early months of the Civil War. The poem, often reprinted and later regularly anthologized, was subsequently claimed by several others. In 1863 she published *General Frankie: a Story for Little Folks*. Her poems continued to appear in the periodical press, particularly in the *New York Ledger*, and among the most popular in their day were "Weighing the Baby" and "Which Shall It Be?" For years she confessed to a fear that should her collected verse be published she would soon die; *All Quiet Along the Potomac and Other Poems* appeared on October 10, 1879, and she died the next day in Orange, New Jersey.

Bellanca, Dorothy Jacobs 1894–1946 labor leader

Born on August 10, 1894, in Zemel, Latvia, Dorothy Jacobs came with her family to the United States in 1900 and settled in Baltimore. At thirteen she left school and went to work as a hand buttonhole maker in a clothing factory. The working conditions then prevailing in the industry quickly led her to the cause of organized labor, and about 1908 or 1909 she joined in the formation of Local 170 of the United Garment Workers of America. In 1912 she was prominent in a walkout that rapidly developed into, an industry-wide strike, and by 1914 she was head of her local, which by then had enrolled a majority even of the predominantly male machine buttonhole sewers.

In that year the United Garment Workers split, the older, mainly native, craft-union oriented leadership remaining, while the younger members, predominantly Jewish and Italian immigrants and more radically committed to industrial unionism, left to form the Amalgamated Clothing Workers of America (ACWA). Dorothy Jacobs led her local into the ACWA, serving as a delegate to the organizing convention, becoming a member of the Baltimore joint board, and in 1915 becoming the board's secretary. She was active in organizing campaigns in Chicago in 1915 and in Philadelphia and New York City in 1917, was elected to the general executive board of ACWA in 1916, and was appointed its first full-time woman organizer in 1917. In August 1918 she resigned from her second term on the general board upon her marriage to August Bellanca, also a member of the ACWA board and a well-known organizer among Italian workers.

She nonetheless remained an active organizer and during the 1920s and 1930s was in the field in New York City, New Jersey, Pennsylvania, Connecticut, and Ohio, directing picket lines, organizing relief for strikers, and most importantly bringing thousands of new members into the ACWA. She was especially effective among the mainly rural shirtmakers during the 1932–1934 organizing campaign in that industry, and she later worked with neckwear workers, laundry workers, cleaners and dyers, and other groups. She headed the ACWA's short-lived Women's Bureau in 1924–1926 and throughout her career struggled to win equal recognition of women workers in union affairs. In 1934 she was elected once again to the general board of the ACWA and served as its only female vice-president until her death. In 1937–1938 she was a special organizer for the Textile Workers Organizing Committee of the Committee for Industrial Organization. Reform politics was a natural activity for her. In 1933 she campaigned effectively for Fiorello H. La Guardia for mayor of New York, in 1936 she helped organize the American Labor party, and in 1938 she ran unsuccessfully on the Labor and Republican tickets for a New York congressional seat. She served on a great many governmental and international commissions and boards at the appointment of such as La Guardia, governors Herbert H. Lehman and Thomas E. Dewey of New York, and President Franklin D. Roosevelt. Early in World War II she was an adviser on women workers to the War Manpower Commission and the Department of Labor. Dorothy Bellanca died in New York City on August 16, 1946.

Belmont, Alva Ertskin Smith Vanderbilt 1853–1933 socialite, social reformer and architect

Born in Mobile, Alabama, on January 17, 1853, Alva Smith grew up there and, after the Civil War, in France. She married William K. Vanderbilt, grandson of Cornelius, in April 1875. Although the Vanderbilts were among the very richest people in the world, they were excluded from the "Four Hundred," the cream of New York society, by the arbiters of such matters, Mrs. William B. Astor and Ward McAllister. Vanderbilt undertook an aggressive plan to break in. Richard M. Hunt was commissioned to build a $3 million mansion on Fifth Avenue, a gesture which ended McAllister's resistance; then, in 1883, plans were made for an Olympian masquerade ball for 1200 persons, by far the most opulent entertainment yet seen by New York. At the last moment Astor capitulated, calling on Vanderbilt in order to secure an invitation for young Caroline Astor. As a final touch Vanderbilt had Hunt build a palace — ostentatiously referred to as a "cottage" —at Newport, Rhode Island, that, with its furnishings, cost $9 million on completion in 1892. In 1895 Vanderbilt divorced her husband and, a year later, after arranging the marriage of her daughter Consuelo to the Duke of Marlborough, she married Oliver Hazard Perry Belmont in January 1896.

After Belmont died in 1908 she became deeply interested in the cause of women's rights. She brought the English suffragette Christabel Pankhurst to the United States in 1914 for a speaking tour and opened her houses and her purse to Alice Paul and the militant feminists. With Elsa Maxwell she wrote *Melinda and Her Sisters*, a suffragist operetta, and staged it at the Waldorf-Astoria Hotel in 1916. In 1921 she was elected president of the National Woman's party, a post she held for the rest of her life, and she was the founder of the Political Equality League. She is credited with offering the advice "Pray to God. She will help you." In her later years she became a noted architectural designer and was one of the first women ever elected to the American Institute of Architects. Belmont spent much of her time in her last years in France, where she owned several residences. She died in Paris on January 26, 1933.

Benedict, Ruth Fulton 1887–1948 anthropologist

Born on June 5, 1887, in New York City, Ruth Fulton grew up in Norwich, New York, in St. Joseph, Missouri, in Owatonna, Minnesota, and in Buffalo, New York, as her widowed mother moved from teaching job to job, finally becoming a librarian in Buffalo. She had a difficult childhood that left her with deep psychic scars. She graduated from Vassar College in 1909, lived in Europe for a year, and then settled in California, where she taught in girls' schools. She married Stanley R. Benedict, a biochemist, in June 1914 and returned to New York.

For some years she sought vainly for an occupation. In 1919 she enrolled at the New School for Social Research, where the influence of Elsie Clews Parsons and Alexander Goldenweiser sent her to study anthropology under Franz Boas at Columbia University. Taking her doctorate in 1923 with a dissertation on "The Concept of the Guardian Spirit in North America," she became a Columbia instructor the next year, an associate professor in 1931, and a full professor in 1948, only a few months before her death.

Her first book, *Tales of the Cochiti Indians*, 1931, and her two-volume *Zuñi Mythology*, 1935, were based on 11 years of research into the religion and folklore of Native Americans, predominantly the Pueblo, Apache, Blackfoot, and Serrano peoples. *Patterns of Culture*, 1934, was a major contribution to anthropology. In that book she demonstrated, through a comparison of Zuñi, Dobu, and Kwakiutl cultures, how small a portion of the possible range of human behavior is incorporated into any one culture, and argued that it is the "personality," the particular complex of traits and attitudes, of a culture that defines the individuals within it as successes, misfits, or outcasts. Six years later, with the publication of *Race: Science and Politics*, she showed that the unity of mankind is a simple fact, despite the arrogance of racists. From 1925 to 1940 she edited the *Journal of American Folklore*. During 1943–1945 she was a special adviser to the Office of War Information on dealing with the peoples of occupied territories and enemy lands. A long standing interest in Japanese culture bore fruit in *The Chrysanthemum and the Sword*, 1946. She returned to Columbia in 1946, and in 1947 she was president of the American Anthropological Association. By that time she was acknowledged the outstanding anthropologist in America. In the summer of 1948 she began her most comprehensive research undertaking as director of a study of contemporary European and Asian cultures sponsored by the Office of Naval Research and by Columbia. Upon returning from a trip to Europe she became ill, and she died in New York City on September 17, 1948.

Bennett, Belle Harris 1852–1922 church worker

Born on December 3, 1852, in Whitehall, near Richmond, Kentucky, Isabel (known always as Belle) Bennett was educated privately in Kentucky and Ohio. She became a member of the Southern Methodist Church in 1876 and soon began teaching in a Sunday school. In 1889, having obtained information from the Chicago Training School for City, Home, and Foreign Missions (founded by Lucy R. Meyer for the Northern Methodist Church a few years earlier), she won adoption by the Southern Methodist Woman's Board of Foreign Missions of a plan to establish a similar training school. Appointed agent to collect funds, she traveled and spoke widely throughout the South for that purpose. A major benefaction from Dr. Nathan Scarritt of Kansas City, Missouri, made possible the early realization of the plan, and in September, 1892 the Scarritt Bible and Training School was dedicated in Kansas City. In all, her efforts raised over $130,000 for building and endowing the school. (In 1924 the school was relocated to Nashville, Tennessee, and renamed Scarritt College for Christian Workers.) In 1897 she opened the Sue Bennett Memorial School, named for an older sister, in London, Kentucky. In 1892 Bennett was named to the central committee of the Woman's Parsonage and Home Mission Society; in 1896 she was chosen president of the society, and in 1898 she moved up to the presidency of the newly organized Woman's Board of Home Missions. Under her the board became active in the field of urban missions, and a system of more than 40 "Wesley Community Houses" for white people and "Bethlehem Houses" for African-Americans was established throughout the South. In 1902 she successfully urged the board to set up a program of lay deaconesses to staff the houses and other home mission projects. In 1910 she became president of the unified Woman's Missionary Council, responsible for both home and foreign mission work, and she retained the post until her death. She was particularly active in the establishment of a woman's college (later named for her) in Rio de Janeiro and of the Woman's Christian Medical College in Shanghai. When her campaign of a dozen years finally resulted in the admission of women to full lay status in the Southern Methodist Church in 1919, she became the first woman to be elected a delegate to the church's General Conference. Before the conference convened, however, she died in Richmond, Kentucky, on July 20, 1922.

Berenson, Senda 1868–1954 educator and sportswoman

Born in Butrimonys (or Butrymance or Biturmansk), near Vilnius, Lithuania, on March 19, 1868, Senda Valvrojenski was brought to the United States by her parents in 1875. The family adopted the name Berenson and settled in Boston. Senda's brother Bernard, not quite three years her senior, was destined to become an authority on Italian art and a collector of worldwide note. She was a frail child whose health often interfered with her education. In 1890 she entered the Boston Normal School of Gymnastics, established a year earlier by Mary P. T. Hemenway, and soon found her physical condition much improved. After two years at the school she joined the staff of Smith College as a teacher of physical training. Her teaching emphasized the Swedish gymnastics she had learned at the Boston school and, from 1895, fencing. In 1897 she studied advanced fencing at the Royal Central Institute of Gymnastics in Stockholm. In 1901 she saw to the introduction of field hockey at Smith.

Her major contribution to women's physical education, however, was her devising of women's basketball, a modified version of the men's game that she introduced at Smith in the fall of 1892 after reading of James Naismith's invention of the game in nearby Springfield, Massachusetts. Her version of basketball deemphasized the contest for possession and full court movement in favor of passing and position. Players were allowed to dribble only three times and to hold the ball for no more than three seconds. The game spread quickly among girls' schools. (Clara Baer of Newcomb College, New Orleans, also contributed greatly to the development of the game, notably the three-zone "line basketball" idea.) From 1899 to 1917 Berenson edited the version of the rules accepted as official, and from 1905 to 1917 she was chairman of the Basketball Committee for Women. Her version of basketball remained standard for 70 years.

Berenson left Smith on her marriage in June 1911 to Herbert V. Abbott, a professor of English. She was director of physical education at a private girls' school until 1921. From 1934, by then a widow, she lived in Santa Barbara, California, where she died on February 16, 1954.

Berg, Gertrude 1899–1966 actor, producer and screewriter

Born in New York City on October 3, 1899, Gertrude Edelstein graduated from high school, and in December 1918, while enrolled in a playwriting extension course at Columbia University, she married Lewis Berg. After a few years living in Louisiana the Bergs returned to New York City, and she began writing radio scripts. Success came in 1929 when the National Broadcasting Company accepted her outline for a weekly series called "The Rise of the Goldbergs," a situation comedy featuring the trials and domestic adventures of a Jewish family in the Bronx. The program premiered on November 20, 1929, in a 15-minute format with Gertrude Berg herself playing the inimitable Molly Goldberg, the chatty and philosophical mother in the fictional family. Writer and producer as well as star of the show, she created virtually an entire neighborhood of characters and incidents and won an audience eventually numbering in the millions. By 1931 the show was broadcast five times weekly. In that year she published a book, *The Rise of the Goldbergs*. "The Goldbergs" remained a weekly program until 1934, returned to the air over the Columbia Broadcasting System for a few months in 1936, was on NBC again briefly in 1937, returned to CBS from 1938 to 1945, and had a last run in 1949–1950.

In the meanwhile Gertrude Berg created and wrote "The House of Glass," a second radio series, in 1935, wrote scripts for other shows, appeared in a motion picture *Make a Wish* in 1937, and wrote and starred in a Broadway production, *Me and Molly*, based on "The Goldbergs," in 1948. In 1949–1951 and again in 1952 and 1953 "The Goldbergs" was a highly popular weekly television program; in 1950 she won an Emmy for her television work. In 1951 her perennially popular Jewish family made a sweep of entertainment media with a motion picture entitled simply *Molly*, of which she was co-author. For some years thereafter Berg devoted herself to summer stock theater, but in 1959 she opened on Broadway in a much acclaimed performance in *A Majority of One*, for which she was voted a Tony award. In 1963 she starred in *Dear Me, the Sky is Falling*. She died in New York City on September 14, 1966.

Berg, Patricia Jane 1918– golfer

Born in Minneapolis on February 13, 1918, Patty Berg took up golf at the age of thirteen and soon proved to have a remarkable talent for the game. In 1935 she won the

Minnesota state women's championship at the age of seventeen. Later that year she reached the final round of the national women's amateur championship tournament. In 1936 she repeated as state champion and won several lesser national tournaments. In 1937 she was again defeated after reaching the finals of the national championship, but in 1938 she capped a season of 9 victories in 12 tournaments by winning the national women's amateur title at the age of twenty. She was voted the outstanding woman athlete of the year in an Associated Press poll in 1938, an award she won again in 1943 and 1955. She reduced her tournament schedule on entering the University of Minnesota in 1939, and an appendectomy prevented her defending her national title that year.

In 1940 she gave up her amateur status by taking a promotional position with the Wilson Sporting Goods Company in Chicago. An injury in 1941 kept her out of competition until 1943, when she won the Women's Western Open. Later that year she enlisted in the Women Marines. In 1945 she won the All-American Open, and in 1946 she won the first U.S. Women's Open. In 1948 she staged a remarkable drive to come from behind and defeat Mildred Didrikson Zaharias in the Western Women's Open. She repeated at the Western Open in 1949; won the Eastern Open in 1950; the Western Open again in 1951; the World Open, All-American Open, and Titleholders' in 1953; the World Professional in 1954; the World Open, All-American Open, Titleholders', and Western Open in 1955, the same four in 1957; the American Open and Western Open in 1958; and the American Open in 1960.

In 1954, 1955, and 1957 she was the leading money winner in the Ladies' Professional Golfers Association. One of the game's great shotmakers, Patty Berg won the Bob Jones Award from the US Golf Association in 1963 and the Ben Hogan Award of the Golf Writers Association in 1976. She was inducted into the World Golf Hall of Fame in June 1974, the PGA Hall of Fame in 1978 and the International Women's Sports Hall of Fame in 1980. In 1978 the Ladies' PGA established the Patty Berg Award for outstanding contributions to women's golf, and in 1990 they awarded it to Patty Berg.

She continued to appear occasionally in tournaments in later years, and conducted golf clinics as she toured the country for a manufacturer of sporting-goods.

Bergman, Ingrid 1915–1982 actor

Born in Stockholm, Sweden, on August 29, 1915, Ingrid Bergman suffered multiple early losses. Her mother, Friedel, died when she was just three years old. Her father, Justus, a painter turned photographer, died when she was thirteen. The unmarried aunt with whom she was sent to live died six months later. Finally she was raised by an uncle while she attended a private school for girls until she was eighteen. Despite shyness and the resistance of her relatives, she worked assiduously to pass the difficult exams for admission to the Royal Dramatic Theatre School in Stockholm.

After a year at school, she secured a part in the film *Munkbrogreven*, 1934. As a fledgling actress, she met Petter Lindstrom, a dentist who later became a neuro-surgeon, and they were married in 1937. The couple settled in Stockholm, where their daughter Pia was born. Within three years of her film debut she was a star, and she signed a five-year contract with Gustav Molander, the director of her best-known early film, *Intermezzo*, 1936. Her performance so impressed producer David Selznick that he signed her to do a Hollywood remake of the film. The immediate success of her American debut in *Intermezzo*, 1939, led to a long-term contract with Selznick.

Bergman moved to the U.S. after the outbreak of World War II in Europe. Between 1942 and 1946, she appeared in some of the most popular films in history: *Casablanca*, 1942, *For Whom the Bell Tolls*, 1943, *Gaslight*, 1944, for which she won an Academy Award, *The Bells of St. Mary's*, 1945, *Spellbound*, 1945, and *Notorious*, 1946. In 1946 she became the top money earner of all Hollywood actresses. Also in that year, she was offered the opportunity to play Joan of Arc on Broadway in *Joan of Lorraine*, a role for which she won a Tony Award.

Her marriage foundered and, according to her own account, she had a long affair with the photographer Robert Capa. Impressed with the films of Roberto Rosellini, she wrote to ask him if she might play a part in one. She left for Rome in 1949 and their working relationship blossomed into a love affair — outraging the American public who had become enthralled with the purity she projected on the silver screen.

Her reputation ruined, she was exiled from Hollywood and branded in the U.S. Senate as a "powerful influence for evil." She married Rosellini and turned to family life, giving birth to Robertino in 1950 and to twin daughters in 1952. By the time their marriage had ended, she had made six films with Rosellini, none of them successful.

For her performance in *Anastasia*, which was released in the U.S. in 1956, she won a second Oscar and the New York Film Critics' Award. After eight years abroad, she was welcomed back by cheering crowds and the press, apparently forgiven for earlier indiscretions. She married theatrical producer Lars Schmidt in 1958, divorcing him in 1975.

She made her American television debut in 1959 as a frightened governess in NBC's *Turn of the Screw*, for which she won an Emmy Award. In 1974 she won her third Academy Award for *Murder on the Orient Express*, but most agree that her finest late performance was as the neurotic mother in Ingmar Bergman's *Autumn Sonata*, 1978. By then she had been struggling with cancer for four years and announced that she had made her last film.

In 1980 she published her autobiography *Ingrid Bergman, My Story*. She returned to television to play Golda Meir in "A Woman Called Golda," for which she was posthumously awarded an Emmy in 1982. She died in London on her 67th birthday in 1982.

Bernstein, Aline 1882–1955 theatrical designer

Born in New York City on December 22, 1882, Aline Frankau attended Hunter College and the New York School for Applied Design before her marriage to Theodore Bernstein, a businessman, in November 1902. She developed her artistic talent studying under Robert Henri and abandoned her earlier ambition to be an actress in favor of stage design. It required a two-year fight to win admittance to the United Scenic Art Union, of which she at last became the first woman member. She became involved in experiments in amateur theatrical production at the Henry Street Settlement House, and when Alice and Irene Lewisohn established the Neighborhood Playhouse there in 1915 she became its principal set and costume designer. She remained with the Playhouse through its transition from amateur to professional repertory group in 1920 until its dissolution in 1927.

Among the productions in which her designs won particular praise were *The Little Clay Cart* and *The Miracle* in 1924, *The Dybbuk* in 1925, and several editions of the annual (from 1923) *Grand Street Follies*. During the 1920s and 1930s she worked mainly with the Theatre Guild and the Civic Repertory Theatre. Among her greatest successes in this period were Robert Sherwood's *Reunion in Vienna* in 1931, Eva Le Gallienne's production of *Alison's House* in 1931, Philip Barry's *Animal Kingdom* in 1932, the Alfred Lunt-Lynn Fontanne presentation of *The Seagull* in 1937, and especially her collaborations with Lillian Hellman in the productions of *The Children's Hour*, 1934, *Days to Come*, 1936, and *The Little Foxes*, 1939.

For five years, 1925–1930, she carried on a stormy affair with the young novelist Thomas Wolfe, who dedicated *Look Homeward, Angel* to her in 1929. That relationship was the subject of one of the stories in her collection *Three Blue Suits*, 1933, and of her novel *The Journey Down*, 1938. In 1937 she helped Irene Lewisohn establish the Museum of Costume Art; she served as director of the museum until 1946, when it became the Costume Institute of the Metropolitan Museum of Art, after which she was its president.

Outstanding among her later theatrical designs were those for James Thurber's and Elliott Nugent's *The Male Animal*, 1940, George Balanchine's ballet *The Spellbound Child*, 1946, and *Regina*, Marc Blitzstein's operatic adaptation of *The Little Foxes*, for which she won a Tony award in 1949. Other published works included the autobiographical *An Actor's Daughter*, 1941; *Miss Condon*, a novel, 1947; *The Martha Washington Doll Book*, for children, 1945; and the posthumous *Masterpieces of Women's Costume of the Eighteenth and Nineteenth Centuries*, 1959. Aline Bernstein died in New York City on September 7, 1955.

Berry, Martha McChesney 1866–1942 educator

Born on a plantation near Rome, Georgia, on October 7, 1866, Martha Berry was tutored at home and in 1882–1883 attended a fashionable girls' school in Baltimore. On the death of her father in 1887 she inherited a considerable estate. Her career began largely by chance when, one Sunday in the late 1890s, while reading in a cabin retreat her father had once built her, she was approached by three mountain children. She entertained them with Bible stories, and on succeeding Sundays more and more children appeared. Struck by their lack of educational opportunity, she resolved to open a school for them. A conventional day school, open half the year, proved insufficient to break the bonds of apathy, however, and in January 1902 she opened the Boys' Industrial School. Her plan was to eke out the school's resources, which at first were entirely of her giving, by having the students, who were generally of high school age, contribute labor for two hours a day in a pioneering work-study program; the experience of work would in addition supplement their vocational training.

The school soon had more applicants than space, and Berry began to solicit support elsewhere. She developed great skill in tapping northern philanthropists such as Andrew Carnegie and especially Henry Ford, who over the years gave nearly $4 million. The tours she arranged for visiting benefactors were masterpieces of showmanship — the carefully arranged rustic charm of the school and grounds never failed to impress. In November 1909, having become concerned for the lack of suitable wives for her graduates, she opened the Martha Berry School for Girls on the same work-study basis. Both schools (the boys' later renamed Mount Berry School for Boys) continued to emphasize vocational, agricultural, and domestic training and self-help. In 1916 the school's range was extended downward to include a grammar school, and ten years later a junior college was established that in 1930 became a four-year college. The state of Georgia had been quick to profit from her example, having opened 11 schools modeled on the Berry Schools by 1912, and other states followed. Berry was widely honored for her work. She was named a distinguished citizen of Georgia in 1924, received the Theodore Roosevelt Memorial Medal from President Calvin Coolidge in 1925, was voted one of the 12 greatest living American women in a *Good Housekeeping* readers' poll in 1931, and was voted Southern woman of the year in a farmers' poll in 1939. She died in Atlanta on February 27, 1942. The Berry schools, which by 1929 had already graduated some 7000 students, had by 1942 grown to include some 125 buildings on 35,000 acres of land. By 1960 graduates numbered more than 16,000.

Bethune, Louise Blanchard 1856–1913 architect

Born on July 21, 1856, in Waterloo, New York, Louise Blanchard, christened Jennie Louise, graduated from Buffalo, New York, High School in 1874 and for two years traveled and taught school. In 1876 she abandoned her plan to enter Cornell University and instead took a position as a draftsman in the architectural office of Richard A. Waite of Buffalo. She spent a profitable apprenticeship, and in October 1881 she opened her own architectural office in partnership with Robert A. Bethune, whom she married in December. As the first woman professional architect in America, she purposefully worked on a wide range of building types — chapels, stores, factories, banks, houses, apartment buildings. Among their major commissions were the Lockport High School, begun in 1890, the East Buffalo Live Stock Exchange, and the Hotel Lafayette in Buffalo, completed in 1904. In 1885 she joined the Western Association of Architects, of which she later served a term as vice president. In April 1888 she became the first woman elected to membership in the American Institute of Architects, and the next year she became the first woman fellow of the institute. Her last years were spent in semiretirement. She died in Buffalo, New York, on December 18, 1913.

Bethune, Mary McLeod 1875–1955 educator

Born on July 10, 1875, in Mayesville, South Carolina, Mary McLeod was the daughter of former slaves. She attended a local school, then traveled to Concord, North Carolina, to enter Scotia Seminary (now Barber-Scotia College), from which she graduated in 1893. After graduating from the Moody Bible Institute in Chicago in 1895 she began a teaching career and until 1903 taught in a succession of small Southern schools, including Lucy Laney's Haines Normal and Industrial Institute in Augusta, Georgia, in 1896–1897. She married Albertus L. Bethune in May 1898.

In 1904 she moved to the east coast of Florida, where a large African-American population had grown up at the time of the construction of the Florida East Coast Railway, and in Daytona Beach, in October, she opened a school of her own, the Daytona Normal and Industrial Institute for Negro Girls. Having virtually no tangible assets with which to start, she worked tirelessly to build a schoolhouse, solicit help and contributions, and enlist the goodwill of both the African-American and white communities. In 1923 the school was merged with the Cookman Institute for Men, then in Jacksonville, Florida, to form what was known from 1929 as Bethune-Cookman College in Daytona Beach. Bethune remained president of the college until 1942 and resumed the position in 1946–1947 before retiring as president emeritus. Under her administration the college won full accreditation and grew to an enrollment of over 1000.

Bethune's efforts on behalf of education and of improved racial relations brought her to national prominence. Awarded the Spingarn Medal of the National Association for the Advancement of Colored People in 1935, she was appointed the next year administrative assistant for Negro affairs (a title changed in 1939 to director of the division of Negro affairs) of the National Youth Administration by President Franklin D. Roosevelt, a post she held until 1944. In 1935 she founded the National Council of Negro Women, of which she remained president until 1949, and she was vice-president of the NAACP from 1940 to 1955. She was an adviser on minority affairs to Roosevelt and advised the secretary of war on the selection of officer candidates for the Women's Army Auxiliary Corps (WAAC), established in 1942. In 1945 she went as an observer with the U.S. delegation to the organizational conference of the United Nations in San Francisco. Widely honored for her lifelong dedication to her work, she died in Daytona Beach on May 18, 1955.

Bickerdyke, Mary Ann Ball 1817–1901 hospital worker

Born on July 19, 1817, in Knox County, Ohio, Mary Ann Ball grew up in the houses of various relatives. In Cincinnati in 1847 she married a widower, Robert Bickerdyke; the couple moved in 1856 to Galesburg, Illinois, where Bickerdyke died in 1859. She supported herself by the practice of "botanic" medicine.

Soon after the outbreak of the Civil War she volunteered to accompany and distribute a collection of supplies taken up for the relief of wounded soldiers at a makeshift army hospital in Cairo, Illinois. On her arrival there she found conditions to be primitive in the extreme, and she set to work immediately at cleaning, cooking, and caring for the men. She became matron when a general hospital was organized there in November 1861. Following the fall of Fort Donelson in February 1862 she made a number of forays onto the battlefield to search for wounded, and her exploits began to attract general attention. Her alliance with the U.S. Sanitary Commission began about that time. Bickerdyke soon attached herself to the staff of General Ulysses S. Grant, by whom she was given a pass for free transportation anywhere in his command; she used it unsparingly in order to be at the front, where her services were most needed.

From Shiloh through the campaigning in Tennessee, Kentucky, and Mississippi she worked prodigies of organization, scavenging supplies and equipment, establishing mobile laundries and kitchens, and endearing herself to the wounded and sick as "Mother" Bickerdyke. To incompetent officers and physicians she was brutal, succeeding in having several dismissed, and she retained her position largely through the influence of Grant, General William T. Sherman, and others who properly valued her work. Late in 1862 and again in 1864 she made speaking tours of midwestern and northern cities on behalf of the Sanitary Commission. At other times she remained in the field, with Sherman's Army of the Tennessee from Vicksburg through Tennessee to Georgia and again from Wilmington, North Carolina, to Beaufort, where she was at work at war's end.

During 1866–1867 she worked with the Chicago Home for the Friendless, and in 1867, in connection with a plan to settle veterans on Kansas farmland, she opened a boarding house in Salina with backing from the Kansas Pacific Railroad. The venture failed in 1869, and in 1870 she went to New York City to work for the Protestant Board of City Missions. In 1874 she returned to Kansas, where her sons lived, and made herself conspicuously useful in relieving the victims of locust plague. In 1876 she removed to San Francisco, where she secured through Senator John A. Logan, another wartime patron, a position at the U.S. Mint. She also devoted considerable time to the Salvation Army and similar organizations. She worked tirelessly on behalf of veterans, making numerous trips to Washington to press pension claims, and was herself granted a pension of $25 a month by Congress in 1886. She returned to Kansas in 1887 and died in Bunker Hill on November 8, 1901.

Bingham, Amelia 1869–1927 actor

Born in Hicksville, Ohio, on March 20, 1869, Amelia Smiley left Ohio Wesleyan University in 1890 when her performance in a summer amateur theatrical production attracted the notice of Lloyd Bingham, manager of a traveling professional company, who encouraged her to go on the stage. She made a Pacific Coast tour with the McKee Rankin company and in December 1893 made her New York debut at the People's Theatre in *The Struggle for Life*. By that time she had married Bingham. Subsequent appearances in *The Power of Gold*, *The Shaughraun*, *The Colleen Bawn*, *The Village Postmaster*, *Captain Impudence*, and others brought her great popularity, and in 1897, after winning a newspaper popularity poll over such stars as Lillian Russell, Ada Rehan, Fanny Davenport, and Maude Adams, she came under the management of Charles Frohman. For four years she was Frohman's leading lady in such productions as *The White Heather*, *The Pink Domino*, *The Proper Caper*, *On and Off*, *At the White Horse Tavern*, *The Cuckoo*, *His Excellency the Governor*, and *Hearts are Trumps*.

In 1900 she decided to become a producer. She took over the Bijou Theatre in New York City, assembled a cast, and in January 1901 opened in her own production of Clyde Fitch's *Climbers*. She was apparently the first American actress to succeed as a producer as well. The success of that venture was repeated with *Lady Margaret* in 1902, *The Modern Magdalen* in 1902, and *The Frisky Mrs. Johnson* in 1903. Subsequently she starred in *Olympe*, 1904, and *Mlle. Marni*, 1905, played with various stock companies, toured Great Britain in *Big Moments from Great Plays* in 1909, and at various times appeared in *One of Our Girls*, *A Contented Woman*, *The Eternal City*, *A Modern Lady Godiva*, *My Wife's Husbands*, and *Her Other Self*. In 1913–1914 she starred with Douglas

Fairbanks and William H. Crane in *The New Henrietta*. Following the death of her husband in 1915 (while he was among the party on the Henry Ford Peace Ship) and with her own health declining, she retired from the stage. She returned to appear in *Trelawney of the Wells* in 1925 and *The Pearl of Great Price* in 1926. Amelia Bingham died in New York City on September 1, 1927.

Bishop, Elizabeth 1911–1979 poet

Born on February 8, 1911, in Worcester, Massachusetts, Elizabeth Bishop spent part of her childhood with grand parents in Nova Scotia. She attended Walnut Hill School in Natick, Massachusetts, and in 1934 graduated from Vassar College. A private income enabled her to devote herself to travel and writing. For some years she traveled widely in Europe and North Africa, and from 1938 to 1943 she made her home in Key West, Florida. During the 1930s several of her poems appeared in the *Partisan Review*, and in 1945 a selection of them won her the Houghton Mifflin Poetry Fellowship. The selection was published as *North & South*, 1946, a volume that was widely praised, especially by fellow poets. Her poems, displaying a close attention to physical reality and nature and an almost analytic precision of language, were buoyed by a rapt exploration of subjective experience into realms of speculation, metaphysics, and even fantasy.

JAMES LAUGHLIN

Elizabeth Bishop

After a lengthy stay in Mexico, Elizabeth Bishop returned to the United States for a time. She was a consultant in poetry at the Library of Congress in 1949–1950, and in the latter year she was the recipient of the American Academy of Arts and Letters Award. For several years thereafter she lived mainly in Petrópolis, near Rio de Janeiro. In 1955 she published *North & South: A Cold Spring*, an expanded collection that won a Pulitzer Prize for verse. She translated *The Diary of "Helena Morley"* from Alice Brant's *Minha Vida de Menina* in 1957, contributed a volume on Brazil to the Life World Library Series in 1962, and edited an *Anthology of Contemporary Brazilian Poetry* in 1972. Her own poems continued to appear in periodicals, particularly the *New Yorker*, and in *Questions of Travel*, 1965, *Complete Poems*, which won a National Book Award, 1969, and *Geography III*, which won a National Book Critics' Circle Award for poetry, 1976. In 1967 she returned to the United States, and from 1970 she was a lecturer in English at Harvard University. In 1976 she was elected to the American Academy of Arts and Letters. She died in Boston on October 6, 1979.

Bishop, Hazel Gladys 1906– chemist and businesswoman

Born in Hoboken, New Jersey, on August 17, 1906, Hazel Bishop graduated from Barnard College in 1929 and attended graduate night courses at Columbia University while working as a hospital technician. From 1935 to 1942 she was an assistant in a dermatological laboratory, and in the latter year she took a job as an organic chemist with the Standard Oil Development Company. From 1945 to 1950 she worked in a similar capacity for the Socony Vacuum Oil Company.

In 1949, after a long series of home experiments, she succeeded in perfecting a lipstick that stayed on the lips longer than any then available. In 1950 she formed Hazel Bishop, Inc., to manufacture her "Lasting Lipstick." The lipstick was a great success in the market, and rival manufacturers soon introduced similar "non smear" products. She was president of the firm until November 1951, when she resigned in a dispute with the majority stockholder. A lawsuit was finally settled in 1954, by which time Hazel Bishop, Inc., had annual sales in excess of $10 million, and in selling her interest she severed all connection with the firm.

She then organized Hazel Bishop Laboratories to conduct research into consumer-oriented chemical products. A leather cleaner was developed in 1955 and other personal care and cosmetic products followed, various other companies being formed to manufacture them. In November 1962 she became a registered agent for the brokerage firm of

Bache and Company. She was successful on Wall Street and some years later became a financial analyst for Evans and Company. Hazel Bishop was a member of numerous professional organizations.

Black, Winifred Sweet 1863–1936 journalist

Born in Chilton, Wisconsin, on October 14, 1863, Winifred Sweet grew up from 1869 on a farm near Chicago. She attended private schools in Chicago, in Lake Forest, Illinois, and in Northampton, Massachusetts, and after an unsuccessful attempt to establish herself in the theatre she turned to journalism. On a western trip on family business in 1890 she won a position as reporter for the *San Francisco Examiner*, William Randolph Hearst's first newspaper. The era of yellow journalism was just dawning, and the example of "Nellie Bly" (Elizabeth Seaman) had helped set the style for woman reporters. Taking the pseudonym "Annie Laurie," Winifred Sweet scored a number of exposés, scoops, and circulation building publicity stunts: A "fainting spell" on a downtown street led to an exposé of and reform in San Francisco's receiving hospital and the purchase of a city ambulance; she secured by a ruse an exclusive interview with President Benjamin Harrison aboard his campaign train in 1892; in the same year she investigated the leper colony on Molokai, Hawaiian Islands. She was also active in organizing various charities and public benefactions, using her column in the *Examiner* to mobilize public concern; among these was the California Children's Excursion to the World's Columbian Exposition in Chicago in 1893.

In June 1892 she married a colleague, Orlow Black; they were divorced five years later. In 1895 Hearst sent her to New York to help his newly acquired *New York Journal* battle Joseph Pulitzer's *New York World*, but she found that city uncongenial and in 1897 settled in Denver, where she joined the staff of Harry H. Tammen's and Frederick G. Bonfils's boisterous *Denver Post*. She continued to contribute feature articles to Hearst's chain as well. When Hearst launched a newspaper campaign against Mormon polygamy in 1898, she went to Utah and reported from the scene. In 1900 she disguised herself as a boy and slipped through a police cordon to become the first outside and only woman reporter to enter Galveston, Texas, in the aftermath of the disastrous flood of September 8. She opened a temporary hospital in the city and administered relief funds collected through the Hearst papers. In 1906 she reported from San Francisco following the great earthquake of April 18, and in 1907 she observed the trial of Harry K. Thaw for his June 1906 murder of architect Stanford White. The very favorable coverage accorded by her and other woman reporters to Evelyn Nesbit Thaw, the featured attraction of the case, gave rise to the despised epithet "sob sister." In February 1901 she married Charles A. Bonfils, brother of the *Post's* co-publisher; they were to all intents separated from 1909. She continued to travel widely in her late years, covering World War I and the Versailles peace conference in Europe, the Washington Naval Arms Limitation conference in Washington, D.C., and other stories. She died in San Francisco on May 25, 1936.

Blackwell, Alice Stone 1857–1950 feminist, reformer and translator

Born on September 14, 1857, in Orange, New Jersey, Alice Stone Blackwell was the daughter of Lucy Stone and of Henry B. Blackwell, who in turn was the brother of Elizabeth and brother-in-law of Antoinette Blackwell. Her childhood in Orange and later in Dorchester, Massachusetts, was dominated by the family's involvement in the feminist movement. She graduated with honors from Boston University in 1881 and immediately joined the editorial staff of the *Woman's Journal*, organ of her mother's American Woman Suffrage Association. While becoming the dominant force on the journal she helped urge her mother to effect a reconciliation with the radical wing of the suffrage movement, and on the merging of the American with Susan B. Anthony's National Woman Suffrage Association into the National American Woman Suffrage Association in 1890 she became the organization's recording secretary, a post she held until 1918. She remained chief editor of the *Woman's Journal* until 1917, and during 1887–1905 she edited and distributed the "Woman's Column," a periodical collection of suffrage news articles, to newspapers across the country.

Around the turn of the century she became interested in various other causes, especially those of various oppressed peoples. She translated and published several volumes of verse from such groups, notably *Armenian Poems*, 1896 and 1916, *Songs of Russia*, 1906, *Songs of Grief and Gladness* (Yiddish), 1908, and *Some Spanish-American Poets*, 1929, and she struck against czarist oppression in *The Little Grandmother of the Russian Revolution — Catherine Breshkovsky's Own Story*, 1917. She was also active in the Woman's Christian Temperance Union, the Women's Trade Union League, the National Association for the Advancement of Colored People, the American Peace Society, and the Massachusetts League of Women Voters, of which she was a founder. She supported Senator Robert M. La Follette's Progressive party campaign in 1924, demonstrated for Sacco and Vanzetti in 1927, and remained to the end of her life one of the last exponents of nineteenth century style New England radicalism. In 1930 she published a biography of her mother, *Lucy Stone*. She died in Cambridge, Massachusetts, on March 15, 1950.

Blackwell, Antoinette Louisa Brown 1825–1921 clergyman, social reformer and writer

Born on May 20, 1825, in Henrietta, New York, Antoinette Brown was a precocious child and at an early age began to speak at meetings of the Congregational church to which she belonged. She attended Oberlin College, completing the literary (non-degree) course in 1847 and, after overcoming objections by family, faculty, and friends (even Lucy Stone was taken aback by the idea), completed the theological course in 1850. Although her professors had allowed her to preach, they refused to license or to graduate her. She was an itinerant preacher and lecturer until September 1853, when she was given a permanent appointment as pastor of the Congregational church in South Butler, New York; she became thereby the first formally appointed woman pastor in the country.

Brown was active in numerous reform movements, particularly those for abolition, temperance, and women's rights. Despite her considerable achievements and the fact that she was an accredited delegate, she was barred from addressing the World's Temperance Convention in New York in 1853 on grounds of her sex. Her changing religious convictions led her to resign her pastorate in July 1854, and shortly thereafter she became a Unitarian. In January 1856 she married Samuel C. Blackwell, a brother of Dr. Elizabeth Blackwell, whose other brother Henry had married Lucy Stone a few months earlier. Although she retired then from public activity she carried on a broad and varied program of study in the physical and social sciences and other fields, work that bore fruit in several books: *Studies in General Science*, 1869, *The Sexes throughout Nature*, 1875, *The Physical Basis of Immortality*, 1876, *The Philosophy of Individuality*, 1893, *The Making of the Universe*, 1914, and *The Social Side of Mind and Action*, 1915. She also wrote a novel, *The Island Neighbors*, 1871, and a volume of verse, *Sea Drift*, 1902. In 1879–1880 she briefly resumed lecturing. Before and after her husband's death in 1901 she lived in various towns in New Jersey and in New York City. Her last years were spent in Elizabeth, New Jersey, where she died on November 5, 1921.

Blackwell, Elizabeth 1821–1910 physician and medical writer

Born on February 3, 1821, in Counterslip, near Bristol, England, Elizabeth Blackwell was of a large, prosperous, and cultured family and was well educated by private tutors. Financial reverses and the family's liberal social and religious views prompted them to emigrate to the United States in the summer of 1832. Soon after taking up residence in New York the elder Blackwell, Samuel, became active in abolitionist activities, and

William Lloyd Garrison became a friend of the family. The Blackwells moved to Jersey City, New Jersey, in 1835 and to Cincinnati in 1838. Soon afterward Samuel Blackwell's death left the family in poverty and Elizabeth and two sisters opened a private school. Later she taught school in Henderson, Kentucky, and in 1845–1847 in North and South Carolina.

During the latter period she undertook the study of medicine privately with sympathetic physicians, and in 1847 she began seeking admission to a medical school. All the leading schools rejected her application, but she was at length admitted, almost by fluke, to Geneva Medical College (a forerunner of Hobart College) in Geneva, New York. Her months there were extremely difficult. Townspeople and much of the male student body ostracized and harassed her, and she was at first even barred from classroom demonstration. She persevered, however, and in January 1849, ranked first in her class, became the first woman in the United States to graduate from medical school and the first woman doctor of medicine in modern times.

In April, having become a naturalized U.S. citizen, she traveled to England to seek further training, and in May she went on to Paris, where in June she entered the midwives' course at La Maternité. While there she contracted an infectious eye disease that left her blind in one eye and forced her to abandon hope of becoming a surgeon. In October 1850 she returned to England and worked at St. Bartholomew's Hospital under Dr. (later Sir) James Paget. In the summer of 1851 she returned to New York, where she was refused posts in the city's hospitals and dispensaries and was even unable to rent private consulting quarters. Her private practice was very slow to develop, and in the meantime she wrote a series of lectures, published in 1852 as *The Laws of Life, with Special Reference to the Physical Education of Girls*.

In 1853 she opened a small dispensary in a slum district. Within a few years she was joined by her younger sister, Dr. Emily Blackwell, and by Dr. Marie E. Zakrzewska, and in May 1857 the dispensary, greatly enlarged, was incorporated as the New York Infirmary for Women and Children. In January 1859, during a year-long lecture tour of Great Britain, she became the first woman to have her name placed on the British medical register. At the outbreak of the Civil War she helped organize the Woman's Central Association of Relief and the U.S. Sanitary Commission and worked mainly through the former to select and train nurses for war service.

In November 1868 a plan long in the perfecting, developed in large part in consultation with Florence Nightingale in England, bore fruit in the opening of the Woman's Medical College at the infirmary. She set very high standards for admission, academic and clinical training, and certification for the school, which continued in operation for 31 years, and herself occupied the chair of hygiene. In 1869 Blackwell moved permanently to England. She established a successful private practice, helped organize the National Health Society in 1871, and in 1875 was appointed professor of gynecology in the London School of Medicine for Women, a post she held until an injury in 1907 forced her to retire. Among her other writings were *The Religion of Health*, 1871, *Counsel to Parents on the Moral Education of their Children*, 1878, her autobiographical *Pioneer Work in Opening the Medical Profession to Women*, 1895, *The Human Element in Sex*, 1884, and *Essays in Medical Sociology*, 1902. She died in Hastings, Sussex, England, on May 31, 1910.

Blackwell, Emily 1826–1910 physician and educator

Born in Bristol, England, on October 8, 1826, Emily Blackwell was a younger sister of Elizabeth Blackwell and received a similar upbringing and education. She grew up in New York City, New Jersey, and Cincinnati, and in 1848, following her sister's example, she began reading medicine. She was rejected by several medical schools, including the Geneva Medical College that had accepted Elizabeth. In 1852–1853 she attended Rush

Medical College in Chicago until outside pressures forced the school to dismiss her. At last she gained admittance to the medical college of Western Reserve University in Cleveland, from which she graduated in March 1854. She subsequently pursued further studies in Edinburgh under Sir James Young Simpson, in London under Dr. William Jenner, and in Paris, Berlin, and Dresden.

In 1856 she settled in New York City and took up work in her sister's dispensary, which the next year became the New York Infirmary for Women and Children. From the beginning of that association Emily Blackwell took responsibility for management of the infirmary and in large part for the raising of funds. The infirmary grew steadily. In-home medical social work was subsequently undertaken, followed by a program of nurses training beginning in 1858; a full medical school was in operation by 1868. In 1869 Emily Blackwell became entirely responsible for the operation of the infirmary and the school when her sister removed to England. As dean of the college as well as professor of obstetrics and the diseases of women, she oversaw the growth of the college into a four-year institution (in 1893 — ahead of much of the profession, as it had been in instituting a three-year course in 1876). By 1899 the college had graduated 364 women. In that year she transferred her students to Cornell University Medical College, which had begun accepting men and women students on an equal basis. She continued her work with the infirmary until her death in York Cliffs, Maine, on September 7, 1910.

Blake, Lillie Devereux 1833–1913 novelist, essayist and reformer

Born on August 12, 1833, in Raleigh, North Carolina, Elizabeth Johnson Devereux, known through life as Lillie, grew up there and in New Haven, Connecticut. She was educated in a private school and by tutors and in her youth was a belle of New Haven society. In June 1855 she married Frank G. Q. Umsted, a lawyer, with whom she lived in St. Louis and New York City until his death, an apparent suicide, in May 1859. Left penniless, she turned for support to writing, a field in which she had already made a small beginning with the publication of a story in *Harper's Weekly* in November 1857, followed by other stories and verses and a moderately successful novel, *Southwold*, 1859. She was soon turning out stories and articles by the score under sundry pseudonyms for newspapers and magazines, and she also completed four other novels, two serialized in the *New York Mercury* and two published in book form as *Rockford, or Sunshine and Storm*, 1863, and *Fettered for Life, or Lord and Master* 1874. From May 1866 until his death in 1896 she was married to Grinfill Blake.

About 1869 she became interested in the movement for woman suffrage, and many of her stories after that date reflected that interest, notably those collected in *A Daring Experiment*, 1892. She became a popular lecturer and served as president of the New York State Woman Suffrage Association from 1879 to 1890 and of the New York City Woman Suffrage League from 1886 to 1900. In those posts she led several unsuccessful campaigns for woman suffrage legislation at the state level, while successful campaigns secured the vote for women in school elections (in 1880) and legislation requiring that women physicians be available in mental institutions, that matrons be on hand in police stations, that chairs be provided for saleswomen, that women be employed as census takers, that mothers and fathers be recognized as joint guardians of their children, that Civil War nurses be eligible for pensions, and in 1894 that women be eligible to sit in the state constitutional convention. In 1883 she published *Woman's Place To-day* in reply to the Reverend Morgan Dix's *Lectures on the Calling of a Christian Woman*, 1883. She was active in the National Woman Suffrage Association (after 1890 the National American Suffrage Association), but her energy, ambition, and attractiveness, as well as her interest in reforms other than suffrage, aroused suspicion if not actual hostility on the part of Susan B. Anthony. During 1895–1899 Blake headed a "committee on legislative advice" within the Association until Anthony abolished it. She failed in an attempt to succeed Anthony as president of the Association in 1900, losing to Carrie Chapman Catt, and thereupon withdrew to form her own National Legislative League. Ill health forced her retirement from public activity after 1905, and she died in Englewood, New Jersey, on December 30, 1913.

Blanchfield, Florence A. 1884–1971 nurse and army officer

Born in Shepherdstown, West Virginia, on April 1, 1884, Florence Blanchfield was educated at business college in Pittsburgh and at the University of California and Columbia University. In 1906 she graduated from the South Side Training School for Nurses in Pittsburgh. After additional training at the Johns Hopkins Hospital, she entered upon a succession of posts in Pittsburgh, in the Canal Zone in 1913, at the United States Steel plant in Bessemer, Pennsylvania, and as superintendent of nurses at Suburban General Hospital in Bellevue, Pennsylvania in 1916. In August 1917 she enlisted in the Army Nurse Corps, and she served in France until 1919. Subsequently she was assigned to army hospitals in Michigan, California, the Philippines, Washington, D.C., Georgia, Missouri, and China; she served for a time also in the office of the surgeon general. In March 1942 she was given a commission as lieutenant colonel to serve as assistant to Colonel Julia Flikke, superintendent of the Army Nurse Corps. Because their ranks were found to be without legal basis, they were paid as major and lieutenant colonel, respectively, and when Blanchfield succeeded Flikke as superintendent in 1943, she made it one of her concerns to secure full rank, as opposed to relative rank (which consisted of the formality but not the pay or benefits of full rank), for army nurses. During World War II she supervised the worldwide work of some 60,000 nurses on all fronts. Her case for full rank was won on a temporary basis in 1944, and in April 1947 both the army and navy revised regulations to permit women to hold full rank. Colonel Blanchfield thereupon received from General Dwight D. Eisenhower the first regular army commission to be awarded a woman. She retired in that year, living thereafter in Arlington, Virginia. She died in Washington, D.C., on May 12, 1971.

Blatch, Harriot Eaton Stanton 1856–1940 suffragist and writer

Born in Seneca Falls, New York, on January 20, 1856, Harriot Stanton was a daughter of Elizabeth Cady Stanton and early absorbed a reformer's zeal from her and from her father, Henry B. Stanton, an abolitionist, politician, and journalist. She attended private schools and in 1878 graduated from Vassar College. After a year at the Boston School of Oratory and another traveling in Europe, she assisted her mother and Susan B. Anthony in completing their *History of Woman Suffrage*. Her principal contribution to the work was a hundred-page chapter on Lucy Stone's American Woman Suffrage Association, rival of Stanton's and Anthony's National Woman Suffrage Association.

In November 1882 she married William H. Blatch, an English businessman, with whom she lived in Basingstoke, England, for the next 20 years. During that time she was close to British reform circles, especially the Fabian Society, in which she associated with Beatrice and Sidney Webb, Ramsay MacDonald, and George Bernard Shaw. In 1894 she was awarded an M.A. degree by Vassar for a statistical study of English villages, a project she had done partly in collaboration with British sociologist Charles Booth.

In 1902 the Blatch family moved to the United States, where Blatch soon became involved in the Women's Trade Union League and the National American Woman Suffrage Association. The latter, a coalition of the two old rival groups, she found to be apathetic and too concerned with internal affairs to be effective, and in 1907 she founded the Equality League of Self-Supporting Women. Under her leadership the League enrolled thousands of working women who had never before been sought out by or attracted to suffrage organizations, and new life was quickly injected into the cause. Open-air meetings were organized, and on May 21, 1910, a mass parade down Fifth Avenue publicized the campaign, the first of many such public demonstrations. Older and more conservative suffragist leaders feared a backlash, but the new vigor of the movement produced results. In 1910 the League's name was changed to the Women's Political Union, and in 1916 it was merged with the Congressional Union (later the National Woman's party) under Alice Paul. On the death of her husband in 1915 Blatch regained her American citizenship (lost by marriage to a foreigner, a legal provision she had bitterly protested) by naturalization, and she spent 1915–1917 in England settling his affairs. On her return she became head of the speakers bureau of the wartime Food Administration and a director of the Woman's Land Army.

In 1918 she published *Mobilizing Woman-Power* on the war work of European women and in 1920 *A Woman's Point of View, Some Roads to Peace*. After the war and the successful conclusion of the suffrage campaign she remained active in women's rights and socialist activities. She opposed special protective legislation for women, breaking with several older groups on that question, and worked through the National Woman's party for a federal equal rights amendment. In 1922 she published *Elizabeth Cady Stanton, as Revealed in Her Letters, Diary and Reminiscences* with her brother, Theodore Stanton. After an injury in 1927 she lived in a nursing home. Her autobiographical *Challenging Years*, written with Alma Lutz, appeared in 1940. She died in Greenwich, Connecticut, on November 20, 1940.

Bloomer, Amelia Jenks 1818–1894 social reformer and editor

Born in Homer, New York, on May 27, 1818, Amelia Jenks was educated in a local school and for several years thereafter taught school in Clyde and tutored pupils privately in Waterloo, New York. In April 1840 she married Dexter C. Bloomer, a Quaker newspaper editor of Seneca County, through whom she became interested in public affairs. She began contributing articles to newspapers on various topics and was an early and staunch member of the local ladies' Temperance Society. Bloomer attended but took no part in the Seneca Falls convention organized by Elizabeth Cady Stanton and Lucretia Mott in 1848. In January of the following year, however, she began a newspaper for women — probably the first to be edited entirely by a woman — *The Lily: A Ladies Journal Devoted to Temperance and Literature*, and opened it to women's-rights advocates as well as temperance reformers.

Although she was rather slow to embrace the cause of women's rights, by 1853 she had become quite active, making speaking appearances in New York City and elsewhere. She became involved in a dress-reform movement as well when she began appearing in public wearing full-cut pantaloons, or "Turkish trousers," under a short skirt. She attracted considerable ridicule for appearing in the costume, which came to be called "bloomers." Although she had not originated the costume — among others, Fanny Kemble and Lydia Sayer (Hasbrouck) had worn it as early as 1849, and Elizabeth Smith Miller had actually introduced it to Bloomer and Elizabeth Cady Stanton early in 1851 — Bloomer's defense of it in *The Lily* spread word of it and linked her name with it indissolubly. The episode had the unfortunate effect of distracting attention from her reform efforts, but she continued to publish *The Lily* in Seneca Falls, where she was also deputy postmistress, and later in Mt. Vernon, Ohio, where she assisted her husband on the *Western Home Visitor*. In 1855 she and her husband moved to Council Bluffs, Iowa, and she sold the newspaper. Her interest in reform, expressed in writing and lectures, continued until her death in Council Bluffs on December 30, 1894.

Bloor, Ella Reeve 1862–1951 political organizer and writer

Born on July 8, 1862, near Mariners Harbor, Staten Island, New York, Ella Reeve grew up in Bridgeton, New Jersey. After her marriage to Lucien Ware in 1881 or 1882 (she was divorced from him in the 1890s and later twice remarried), she became involved in a number of reform movements, notably the Woman's Christian Temperance Union and the women's rights movement. She contributed articles on political subjects to various periodicals and also published *Three Little Lovers of Nature*, a textbook, in 1895 and *Talks About Authors and Their Work* in 1899. In 1897 she joined the Social Democratic party, formed that year by Eugene V. Debs and Victor L. Berger. In 1898 she moved to the more radical Socialist Labor party headed by Daniel De Leon, but in 1902 she returned to Socialist orthodoxy in Debs' Socialist party.

For the next 17 years she was a tireless and effective organizer for the party, particularly in Connecticut, where in 1908 she became the first woman to run for state office when she filed for secretary of state, and in Pennsylvania, Michigan, Colorado, Ohio, New York, and elsewhere, where she organized strike and striker-relief activities among miners, hatters, steelworkers, needle workers, and others. In 1905 she helped Upton Sinclair gather information on the Chicago stockyards for his book, *The Jungle*, and at his invitation she served in 1906 on a presidential commission investigating conditions there. In 1910 she joined in forming the National Women's Committee of the Socialist party. She ran for lieutenant governor of New York in 1918. In Chicago she had worked under the assumed name of "Mrs. Richard Bloor," and thenceforward she was known among workers and fellow socialists by the affectionate nickname "Mother Bloor."

In 1919 she was among the radical faction of the Socialist party that was expelled and then organized independently as the Communist Labor party. She continued her ceaseless organizing on behalf of the new party and in 1921 and 1922 was selected to attend the first and second Red International of Labor Union conventions in Moscow. From 1922 to 1948 she sat on the central committee of the Communist party. During the 1930s she was especially active in organizing farmers in the Plains into the United Farmers' League. She also worked to achieve an equal voice for women within the Communist party, serving as chairman of a committee to that end from 1934 to 1940. She campaigned on behalf of the party line first against and then, after the German invasion of the Soviet Union, for American participation in World War II. In 1938 she was the Communist candidate for governor of Pennsylvania, and from 1941 to 1947 she headed the party in that state. In 1940 she published an autobiography, *We Are Many*. She claimed proudly that in her long career as an agitator and organizer of workers and farmers she had been arrested "hundreds" of times, the last in Nebraska in 1936, when she was seventy-four years old. Mother Bloor died in Richlandtown, Pennsylvania, on August 10, 1951. Her son, Harold Ware, also a well known Communist organizer and winner of the Lenin Peace Prize, was said to have introduced Alger Hiss to Whittaker Chambers.

Blow, Susan Elizabeth 1843–1916 educator and writer

Born in Carondelet (now part of St. Louis), Missouri, on June 7, 1843, Susan Blow was the daughter of a prosperous businessman and later congressman. She was educated by tutors and at a private school in New York City. She accompanied her father to Brazil in 1869–1870 and later traveled on her own in Europe. In Germany she learned of the revolutionary kindergarten methods developed by Friedrich Froebel, and back in St. Louis in 1871 she approached William Torrey Harris, superintendent of city schools, on the possibility of opening a kindergarten in the city. Harris, a devotee of German idealist philosophy, was already interested.

After a year of study under Maria Kraus-Boelté in New York, Blow opened the first public kindergarten in America at the Des Peres School in St. Louis in September 1873. The next year she established a training school for kindergarten teachers, and by 1880 kindergartens had been opened in all the public schools of St. Louis. Throughout this period she remained the unofficial and unpaid supervisor of the system. Froebelian doctrine tended to rigidity, and her expression of it, shaped by the influence of Harris and

German idealism, was perhaps more so; consequently she was unsympathetic to innovation in method. When younger kindergarten teachers began nonetheless to experiment in the mid-1880s, at a time when her health was precarious, she soon lost contact with the schools.

In 1889 she moved east and thereafter lived in Cazenovia, New York, in Boston, and then in New York City. She lectured widely on Froebelian thought, of which she remained the leading American exponent (even Madame Kraus-Boelté was less rigidly doctrinaire than she), and published several books on orthodox kindergarten practice, including *Symbolic Education*, 1894, a two-volume translation of Froebel's *Mother Play*, 1895, *Letters to a Mother on the Philosophy of Froebel*, 1899, *Kindergarten Education*, 1900, and *Educational Issues in the Kindergarten*, 1908. In 1905–1909 she was a lecturer at Teachers College, Columbia University, where the kindergarten innovator Patty Smith Hill was also teaching. Susan Blow died in New York City on March 26, 1916.

Bly, Nellie *see* Seaman, Elizabeth Cochran

Boardman, Mabel Thorp 1860–1946 Red Cross leader

Born in Cleveland on October 12, 1860, Mabel Boardman was of a well-to-do family and was educated privately in Cleveland and New York City. For several years in her youth she traveled, spending some time enjoying the German imperial court, where an uncle was U.S. minister. She also devoted time to various social philanthropies, such as the Children's Day Nursery in Cleveland and the Children's Hospital in Washington, D.C. During the Spanish-American War in 1898 she was active in recruiting nurses.

In 1900 her name appeared, apparently without her knowledge, among those of the fifty incorporators on the application of the American Red Cross for a congressional charter. She accepted the involvement, secured a seat on the executive committee of the Red Cross, and began studying its work and that of foreign Red Cross groups. She quickly concluded that the arbitrary administration of the aging and autocratic Clara Barton was largely responsible for the low esteem into which the Red Cross had fallen, and she began to agitate for change. Barton successfully resisted attempts to curb her authority until 1903, when Boardman used her political contacts to influence President Theodore Roosevelt to withdraw governmental support and to call for an investigation into the management of the Red Cross. Complicated maneuvers resulted in Barton's resignation in 1904. By congressional act of January 5, 1905, drafted by Boardman, the Red Cross was rechartered, its president was made an appointee of the president of the United States, and the War Department was given authority to audit the books. Roosevelt appointed William Howard Taft president, but Boardman, resuming the seat on the executive committee from which pro-Barton forces had earlier suspended her, remained the effective executive power. She refused even the chairmanship of the committee, insisting that the occupancy of the conspicuous positions by men was necessary to retain public confidence. To that same end she worked hard to develop support for the Red Cross among the socially prominent. By her indefatigable labors the Red Cross accumulated a large endowment fund, established branches across the country, greatly improved its lifesaving, first aid, and other services, in part through hard-won cooperation with such groups as the American Nursing Association, and developed a readiness to respond quickly to disasters and military needs.

In conscious contrast to Clara Barton, Mabel Boardman refrained from appearing at the scenes of disaster work, remaining instead at her administrative tasks in Washington. A major fund drive made possible the erection of a huge headquarters, dubbed the "Marble Palace," in Washington, D.C., in 1917. In 1915 she published *Under the Red Cross Flag at Home and Abroad*. As the European war required increasing attention from 1914, the resources of the Red Cross were taxed, and by 1916 moves were afoot to reorganize the administration of its work. In April 1917 a Red Cross War Council superseded the regular executive committee, and Boardman was relegated to relatively minor tasks. She failed to win reappointment to the reconstituted executive committee in 1919.

In September 1920 she became, on appointment by President Woodrow Wilson, the first woman member of the Board of Commissioners of the District of Columbia. In 1921 she returned to the Red Cross as central committee member and national secretary. She opposed unsuccessfully the development of permanent social services by the Red Cross under the leadership of professionals, and from 1922 she devoted herself mainly to continuing the tradition of volunteer service. She organized the Volunteer Service (later Volunteer Special Services), including nurses aides, a motor corps, a canteen corps, a home service corps, and the "Gray Ladies," and was director from 1923. Her notion of these corps as the domain of the elite, however, was increasingly at odds with social realities. She resigned as director of the Volunteer Special Services, whose 9 corps then numbered over 2.7 million volunteers, in August 1940, retired from her local chapter in January 1944, and resigned from the central committee of the Red Cross in December 1944. She died in Washington, D.C., on March 17, 1946.

Bogan, Louise 1897–1970 poet and professor

Born in Livermore Falls, Maine, on August 11, 1897, Louise Bogan attended Mount St. Mary's Academy in Manchester, New Hampshire, and the Boston Girls' Latin School. She left Boston University after a year, in 1916, to marry. Four years later she was left a widow with a child.

Her poems were first published in the *New Republic*, and in 1923 her first volume appeared under the title *Body of This Death*. She continued to contribute both verse and criticism to the *New Republic*, the *Nation*, the *New Yorker*, *Poetry*, *Atlantic Monthly*, and other periodicals while publishing *Dark Summer*, 1929, *The Sleeping Fury*, 1937, and *Poems and New Poems*, 1941. Her verse was frequently compared with that of such Metaphysical poets as George Herbert and Henry Vaughan in its exploration of intensely personal experience and its compressed diction and imagery, and she was accounted one of the major American poets of her time.

Poetry magazine awarded her its John Reed Memorial Prize in 1930 and the Helen Haire Levinson Prize in 1938, and in 1933 and 1937 she was given Guggenheim fellowships. In 1944 she was a fellow in American letters at the Library of Congress, and in 1945–1946 she held the chair of poetry there. *Achievement in American Poetry, 1900–1950*, 1951, was a major critical survey. Her *Collected Poems*, 1954, won a share of the Bollingen Prize, and *Selected Criticism*, 1955, was a further major contribution in that area. She won a fellowship from the Academy of American Poets in 1959 and a National Endowment for the Arts award in 1967. In 1968 she was elected to the American Academy of Arts and Letters. She was a frequent lecturer or visiting professor at colleges and universities, including the University of Washington in 1948, the University of Chicago in 1949, and Brandeis University in 1964–1965. Her later works included *The Blue Estuaries: Poems 1923–1968*, 1968, and *A Poet's Alphabet*, 1970, and translations of *The Journal of Jules Renard*, 1964, and of Goethe's *Elective Affinities*, 1964, and *The Sorrows of Young Werther*, 1971. She died on February 4, 1970, in New York City.

Bombeck, Erma 1927–1996 humorist and writer

Born on February 21, 1927, in Dayton, Ohio, Erma Louise Fiste began her writing career on her high school newspaper, and after graduation in 1944 she got a job with the *Dayton Journal-Herald*. A year later she entered the University of Dayton, from which she graduated in 1949. She then went back to the *Journal-Herald*, where she wrote obituaries, radio listings, and finally a housekeeping column for the women's page. In

August 1949 she married William L. Bombeck, also a journalist. She left the newspaper on the birth of her first child in 1953 and for the next 11 years led the life of a suburban housewife.

Her ambition to write surfaced again in 1964, when she persuaded a local weekly newspaper, the *Kettering-Oakwood Times*, to take a weekly humor column from her for $3 a week. The next year she began contributing a twice-weekly column to the *Journal-Herald*, and it was quickly picked up by the Newsday Specials syndicate. By 1968 the column, called "At Wit's End," was appearing in some 200 newspapers around the country. Its rapid success was attributable to Bombeck's ability to capture the trials of modern housewifery and through her own style of satirical, hyperbolic, and often self-deprecatory humor to make them palatable. Cleaning, children, car pools, husbands, meetings, shopping — all the ingredients of everyday life found their way into her column, and her readers identified with her and her misadventures by the millions.

In addition to the column she wrote a number of books, including *At Wit's End*, 1967, *Just Wait Till You Have Children of Your Own*, 1971, *I Lost Everything in the Post-Natal Depression*, 1973, *The Grass Is Always Greener Over the Septic Tank*, a best-seller in 1976, *If Life Is a Bowl of Cherries — What Am I Doing in the Pits?*, also a best-seller, 1978, *Aunt Erma's Cope Book*, 1979, *Motherhood: The Second Oldest Profession* and *Erma Bombeck, Giant Economy Size*, both 1983, *Laugh Along with Erma Bombeck*, 1984, *Family — The Ties that Bind...and Gag!*, 1987, *I Want to Grow Hair, I Want to Grow Up, I Want to Go to Boise: Children Surviving Cancer*, 1989, and *When You Look Like Your Passport Photo, It's Time to Go Home*, 1991. She wrote for several magazines as well and in 1969–1974 had a regular column in *Good Housekeeping*. She was also in demand as a lecturer.

By the late 1970s her thrice-weekly column, which she had moved to the Publishers-Hall syndicate and then the Field Newspaper syndicate in 1970, was distributed to some 800 newspapers, and she was firmly established as the leading woman comic writer of the day. Recognized not only for her contribution as a humorist, she was appointed to the President's National Advisory Committee for Women in 1978.

Bond, Carrie Jacobs 1862–1946 composer

Born in Janesville, Wisconsin, on August 11, 1862, Carrie Jacobs attended local schools and, on her own and occasionally under various teachers, learned to play the piano. In December 1880 she married E. J. Smith, whom she divorced in 1888, and in June 1889 she married Dr. Frank L. Bond, with whom she lived in Iron River in the upper peninsula of Michigan until his death in 1895. By that time she had already begun to write songs and in December 1894 had seen two, "Is My Dolly Dead?" and "Mother's Cradle Song," published in Chicago.

A short time later she moved to Chicago, where she ran a boarding house, painted china, and continued to write songs, most of which remained for many years in manuscript. By giving recitals and concerts in private homes and in public she supplemented her meager income and at the same time gradually built up a ready audience for her songs. Finally, in 1901, with the help of a loan, she published *Seven Songs as Unpretentious as the Wild Rose*, which included two of her most popular songs, "I Love You Truly" and "Just a-Wearyin' for You." The success of that venture allowed her to open the Bond Shop, where she sold sheet music, designed by herself and printed by the Carrie Jacobs Bond and Son company.

An invitation to sing for President Theodore Roosevelt at the White House, a recital in England in which she appeared along with the young Enrico Caruso, and a series of three recitals in New York City in 1906–1907 all buoyed her fame. She was already wealthy by 1910, when she published her most popular song, "The End of a Perfect Day," the ultimate expression of the artlessly sentimental style in which she worked. By the early 1920s "The End of a Perfect Day" had sold 5 million copies in sheet along with uncounted recordings and piano rolls. From 1910 Carrie Bond lived in Hollywood, California. In all she wrote over 400 songs, of which about 170 were published. The rapid social changes of the years of and immediately following World War I dimmed the appeal of her kind of music, however, and she even found herself occasionally being parodied. In 1927 she published *The Roads of Melody*, a memoir, and in 1940 *The End of the Road*, a collection of thoughts and verses. She died in Hollywood, California, on December 28, 1946.

Bonney, Mary Lucinda 1816–1900 educator and reformer

Born in Hamilton, New York, on June 8, 1816, Mary Bonney was educated in a local academy and for two years at Emma Willard's Troy Female Seminary, from which she graduated in 1835. She became a school teacher and held positions in schools in Jersey City and New York City, in South Carolina, in Providence, Rhode Island, in Philadelphia, and elsewhere. She also taught for a time at the Troy Female Seminary. In Philadelphia in 1850 she and a friend opened the Chestnut Street Female Seminary, a successful school of which Mary Bonney remained senior principal for 38 years. In 1883 it was moved to Ogontz, Pennsylvania, as the Ogontz School for Young Ladies. She was active in the home and foreign mission activities of her Baptist church and of the interdenominational Woman's Union Missionary Society of America for Heathen Lands, of which she was an officer.

Congressional proposals in 1879 to abrogate treaties reserving lands in Indian Territory to certain tribes aroused her to action. With help from her missionary circles she mounted a petition campaign that by early 1880 had gathered 13,000 signatures; they presented the petition, calling for the honoring of treaties, to President Rutherford B. Hayes and then to Congress. A second petition with 50,000 signatures was presented to the Senate through Senator Henry L. Dawes in January 1881, by which time Bonney and her colleagues had become known as the Central Indian Committee. Later in 1881 the group organized formally as the Indian Treaty-Keeping and Protective Association, of which Bonney was chosen president. In February Dawes presented to the Senate the group's third petition, this one bearing 100,000 signatures and outlining in detail a proposal (drafted by Bonney's closest associate, Amelia S. Quinton) for the allotment of tribal lands to individual Native Americans. In 1882 the group changed its name to the National Indian Association and in 1883, after the formation of the men's Indian Rights Association, to the Women's National Indian Association. In the latter year Bonney successfully proposed that the organization devote its efforts to missionary work among Native Americans, offering especially training in English and religion and in domestic skills along white patterns. In November 1884 she resigned as president, and in 1888 she retired as principal of the Ogontz school. She remained active in the Indian reform movement, which reached a culmination with the passage of the Dawes Severalty Act of February 1887, embodying the allotment principle. In 1888 Bonney traveled to London to attend a conference of Protestant mission societies, and there she met; and married the Reverend Thomas Rambaut, who died in 1890. She died in Hamilton, New York, on July 24, 1900.

Bonney, Thérèse 1894?–1978 photographer and writer

Born about 1894 in Syracuse, New York, Mabel Thérèse Bonney grew up there and from about 1902 in California. She graduated from the University of California, took a master's degree in Romance languages at Harvard, and after a short time at Columbia completed her doctorate of letters at the Sorbonne in Paris. In 1919 she founded the European branch of the American Red Cross Correspondence Exchange. Later she established the Bonney Service, an illustrated press service supplying feature stories to the press of 33 countries.

M. Thérèse Bonney

In 1929 she and an older sister collaborated on a series of guidebooks to the antiques, shops, and restaurants of Paris and on a French cookbook. During this period she accumulated a magnificent collection of early photographs, and in 1932 an exhibit of a number of them was mounted in Paris, later traveling to several cities in the United States under the title "The Gay Nineties." Many of the items in the show were published in *Remember When?*, 1933. In 1934 she exhibited a collection of daguerreotypes under the title "The Second Empire." In that year she was awarded the Legion of Honor for her work on the centenary observation of the death of the Marquis de Lafayette. In 1935 she moved to New York to become director of the new Maison Française, a gallery in Rockefeller Center dedicated to fostering better U.S.-French cultural understanding. Within a few years, however, she turned to active photography and published *The Vatican*, containing many never before photographed scenes, in 1939 after several of the photos had appeared in *Life* magazine.

In 1939 she traveled to Finland to photograph the preparations for the 1940 Olympic Games and instead found herself the only photojournalist at the scene of the Russian invasion in November. In 1940 she was in France, first helping in refugee relief at the Belgian frontier and later in Paris. She was given carte blanche by General Maxime Weygand, commander of French home forces, and was the only foreign journalist present at the battle of the Meuse in June. She then returned to the United States and prepared an exhibition of photographs that was displayed at the Library of Congress under the title "To Whom the Wars are Done" and around the country as "War Comes to the People."

In 1941 Thérèse Bonney traveled again to Europe, visited and photographed in Spain, Portugal, unoccupied France, England, Finland (where she acted as an agent of the Office of Strategic Services), and elsewhere, and created the collection that was shown in 40 cities and published in 1943 as *Europe's Children*, a moving, even shocking portrayal of the effects of war that was highly praised by critics. In November 1941 she was awarded the Croix de Guerre by the French government. In 1944 her "War Comes to the People" collection was published in book form. After the war she resumed residence in France, where she continued to pursue photography, wrote a column for *Le Figaro*, and translated a number of French plays for Broadway production.

In her eighties she returned to the Sorbonne to study for a second doctorate in gerontology. In the fall of 1976 the Museum of the City of Paris mounted a retrospective exhibition of her work entitled "An American — Witness of Her Time." Not least among her accomplishments was to have been painted six times by Georges Rouault and three times by Raoul Dufy and to have photographed many of the great French artists of the 20th century. She was the recipient of a great many awards and decorations from several nations. She died in Paris on January 15, 1978.

Booth, Evangeline Cory 1865–1950 Salvation Army leader

Born on December 25, 1865, in the South Hackney section of London, Eva Booth was the daughter of William Booth, soon afterward founder of the Salvation Army. She was educated at home and grew up in the work of the Army, assuming a post of responsibility in the Marylebone district of London at seventeen. Her musical talent aided her in mission work among the poor and often hostile residents of her district, as did her striking personal appearance, and she soon became known as the "White Angel of the Slums."

In 1889, still only twenty-three, she was given charge of the Army's International Training College in Clapton and put in command of all Salvation Army forces in the home counties (London and surrounding area). She became the Army's principal trouble-shooter as well, and in 1896, when her older brother Ballington Booth and his wife Maud, commanders of Army forces in the United States, threatened to break away from General Booth's autocratic rule, Evangeline Booth was sent to deal with the situation. She arrived too late to prevent the resignation of Ballington and Maud, but she effectively took over command of the shaken organization and stayed the tide of public opinion against the Army until the arrival of the new commanders, her sister Emma Booth-Tucker and her husband Frederick St. G. Booth Tucker.

It was on her arrival in America that she adopted the name Evangeline as more dignified. She then proceeded to Toronto, where she took command of the Salvation Army in Canada. During her command there she sent Army mission forces into the Yukon during the gold rush and among the Native Americans of Alaska. In 1904, her sister Emma having died and Booth-Tucker unable to carry on alone, Evangeline became commander of the Salvation Army in the United States. In that post her administrative skills flourished. New forms of social service were instituted, including hospitals for unwed mothers, a chain of "Evangeline Residences" for working women, homes for the aged, and during World War I canteens featuring "doughnuts for doughboys." (Her services to the war effort won her a Distinguished Service Medal in 1919.)

Under her personal supervision the Salvation Army quickly developed disaster relief services following the San Francisco earthquake and fire of 1906. She abandoned the Army's tradition of street begging and organized instead an efficient system of fund-raising. She was successful in enlisting the open support of a great many distinguished and wealthy public figures, and the first national drive in 1919 raised $16 million. The rapid growth of the Army and the proliferation of its services and facilities necessitated the establishment of four regional commands, but she remained in clear control from her New York headquarters. Her only political involvement was to throw the weight of the Salvation Army behind the movement for prohibition and against the later movement for repeal. Her popularity was such that in 1922 the general of the Salvation Army, her eldest brother Bramwell Booth, was forced to abandon the policy of rotation and allow her to remain in command in the United States. In April 1923 she became a naturalized citizen. In 1929 the arbitrary rule of Bramwell ended with his deposition. He was succeeded by Edward J. Higgins until November 1934, when Evangeline Booth became the fourth general of the Salvation Army and the last member of the Booth family to hold world command. In October 1939 she retired and returned from London to her home in Hartsdale, New York. Among her published works were *Love is All*, 1908, *The War Romance of the Salvation Army*, with Grace Livingston Hill, 1919, *Songs of the Evangel*, a collection of hymns composed by her, including the popular "The World for God," 1927, *Toward A Better World*, 1928, and *Woman*, 1930. She died in Hartsdale, New York, on July 17, 1950.

Booth, Mary Louise 1831–1889 translator, journalist, and editor

Born in Millville (now Yaphank) on Long Island, New York, on April 19, 1831, Mary Booth supplemented her regular schooling with voracious reading and study of languages. At fourteen she taught for a year in a school of which her father was principal, in what is now a section of Brooklyn. She then moved to Manhattan, where she worked as a vest-maker by day and wrote and studied by night. She contributed to various journals and was a space-rate reporter for the *New York Times*, but gradually translation became her chief labor, beginning with a *Marble-Workers' Manual* from French in 1856. In all she translated some 40 volumes from French, including works of Pascal and Victor Cousin. At the same time she worked assiduously on a large and comprehensive *History of the City of New York*, the first work of its kind, which was published in 1859 and went through four editions.

In 1861, in a week of almost ceaseless labor, she produced a translation of Count

Agénor de Gasparin's *The Uprising of a Great People: The United States in 1861* that was received with great enthusiasm and proved a vital morale builder in the early phase of the Civil War. As the war progressed, she translated Gasparin's *America before Europe*, 1862, Edouard Laboulaye's *Paris in America*, 1863, and Augustin Cochin's *The Results of Slavery*, 1863, and *The Results of Emancipation*, 1863, earning high praise from President Abraham Lincoln and others. In 1864–1866 she translated three volumes of Henri Martin's *History of France*.

In 1867 she was invited to become first editor of Harper & Brothers' new weekly *Harper's Bazar*. Under her direction the magazine was a great success, growing to a circulation of 80,000 in its first decade. *Harper's Bazar* printed information on fashion, interior decoration, and domestic arts and crafts, and fiction and essays by leading popular authors of the day. Mary Booth remained editor until her death in New York City on March 5, 1889.

Booth, Maud Ballington 1865–1948 religious and welfare leader

Born on September 13, 1865, in Limpsfield, Surrey, England, Maud Elizabeth Charlesworth grew up from the age of three in London. The examples of her father, a clergyman, and her mother, who worked with her husband in his slum parish, predisposed Maud to social service, and in 1882 she joined the Salvation Army. Organizing work in France and Switzerland was followed by pioneering social service work in London slums. In September 1886 she married Ballington Booth, son of General William Booth, and adopted both his names.

In April 1887 they took command of the Salvation Army forces in the United States. In their successful efforts to establish the American branch on a firm basis and earn recognition for its work, she was particularly adept at winning the support of persons of position and influence. At the same time she remained personally active in slum mission work in New York City. The Ballington Booths became naturalized citizens in May 1895. In January 1896 a period of growing tension between them and General Booth in England culminated in their being ordered to another post. Instead they resigned from the Salvation Army and in March organized the Volunteers of America, closely patterned on the Army, of which Ballington Booth was repeatedly elected general until his death in 1940.

Maud Ballington Booth devoted her efforts to a subsidiary but largely independent organization, the Volunteer Prison League. Beginning at Sing Sing Prison, New York, in May 1896, the League established rehabilitation missions in prisons across the country. Alongside the work inside prisons were welfare programs for prisoners' families, post-release employment counseling, and halfway houses called "Hope Halls." The League's work was supported by contributions and by the proceeds of her popular lecture tours. She also published a number of books on mission and prison work and others for children, among them *Beneath Two Flags*, 1889, *The Curse of Septic Soul-Treatment*, 1892, *Branded*, 1897, *Did the Pardon Come Too Late?*, 1897, *Sleepy-Time Stories*, 1899, *Lights of Child-Land*, 1901, *After Prison — What?*, 1903, *Little Mother Stories*, 1906, *Twilight Fairy Tales*, 1906, and *Was It Murder? or, The Relentless Current*, 1912. Following the death of her husband in 1940 she was elected general of the Volunteers of America, a post she held for the remainder of her life. She was also a founder of the national Parent-Teachers Association, of which she was honorary vice-president from 1943. She died in Great Neck, Long Island, on August 26, 1948.

Borden, Lizzie Andrew 1860–1927 accused murderer

Born on July 19, 1860, in Fall River, Massachusetts, Lizzie Borden was the daughter of a well-to-do businessman who married for a second time in 1865, three years after Lizzie's mother died. Tension grew between the new Mrs. Borden on the one side and Lizzie and her elder sister on the other, much of it seemingly arising from anxiety on the part of the girls as to the eventual disposition of Mr. Borden's wealth. The marked frugality and sternness of Mr. Borden added to the strain.

While the problem remained unresolved, Lizzie became active in the affairs of her church and the Woman's Christian Temperance Union. By 1892 the family dissension was approaching a breaking point; on one occasion the elder Bordens suspected they were being poisoned, and at the same time Lizzie expressed fears for her father's safety. On the morning of August 4, Mr. Borden left the house for a time. Upon his return Lizzie told him that her step-mother had gone to visit a friend. He fell asleep, and a short time later Lizzie, claiming she had just come in from the barn, awoke the maid and cried that someone had killed her father. His body was terribly mutilated about the head, apparently with an axe, and a subsequent search of the house revealed her step-mother's body upstairs, similarly mutilated. Examination showed her to have been killed more than a hour before her husband. Soon afterward Lizzie was found burning a dress in the kitchen stove. She was arrested and charged with both murders, but despite the burden of circumstantial evidence she was acquitted in a sensational trial in June 1893.

She was nonetheless ostracized thereafter by the people of Fall River, where she continued to live until her death on June 1, 1927. The grisly murders inspired a great many books, both serious studies and fiction, and one immortal, if slightly inaccurate, quatrain: "Lizzie Borden took an axe / And gave her mother forty whacks; / And when she saw what she had done / She gave her father forty-one."

Bottome, Margaret McDonald 1827–1906 columnist and religious organizer

Born in New York City on December 29, 1827, Margaret McDonald grew up and attended school in Brooklyn. In 1850 she married the Reverend Frank Bottome. Her long-standing practice of giving informal talks on the Bible culminated in January 1886, when she and nine other women organized themselves into a permanent study group for self-improvement and Christian service to others, taking the name "King's Daughters." Each of the ten organized a group of ten, as did those, and so on. (The idea for this pattern stemmed from Edward Everett Hale's story "Ten Times One is Ten.") In 1887 men were admitted to the organization, which accordingly became the Order of the King's Daughters and Sons, and within 20 years membership had grown to an estimated half million in the United States and Canada; by that time the word "international" had been added to the name. Bottome was annually elected president of the order. From 1888 she contributed regularly to the order's magazine, *Silver Cross*, and from 1889 to 1905 she conducted a column in the *Ladies' Home Journal* for members. In 1896 she was chosen president of the Medical Missionary Society. Among her published works were *Crumbs from the King's Table*, *A Sunshine Trip: Glimpses of the Orient*, *Death and Life*, *Seven Questions After Easter*, and *The Guest Chamber*. She died in New York City on November 14, 1906.

Bourgeois, Louise 1911– sculptor

Born in Paris on December 25, 1911, Louise Bourgeois spent her early years living on the Boulevard Saint-Germain, in an apartment above her parents' tapestry gallery. In 1919 her family bought property south of Paris and set up a tapestry restoration workshop, where Louise helped her parents by completing the designs for damaged parts of tapestries; many depicted unclothed angels or goddesses, and "it was my job to fill that space" so that the nudity would not offend American collectors. Her most painful childhood memories involved her father, a charming womanizer who startled the family by having an affair with a "tutor" almost as young as his daughter; the episode inspired in her a bitter rage, fueled by betrayal and, she later said, by an almost murderous jealousy.

She attended the Lycée Fénelon in Paris, where she studied mathematics, with a particular interest in geometry, and received her baccalaureate in 1932. She enrolled at the Sorbonne for graduate work in mathematics and philosophy, but she soon turned to art instead. Between 1934 to 1938 she took classes at several art schools, including the Académie des Beaux-Arts. During this time, she met and worked with cubist artist, Fernand Léger, who kindled her interest in sculpture. She married American art historian Robert Goldwater in 1938 and moved with him to New York City, where they had three sons.

Her early work in the U.S. consisted of painting, drawings, and prints influenced by cubism and by her study of geometry. She exhibited in 1939 at the Brooklyn Museum and she had her first solo exhibition of 12 paintings in 1945 at the Bertha Schaefer Gallery. In the 1940s she began producing painted wood sculptures of life-size abstract figures, which she often arranged in groups. She debuted as a sculptor at the Peridot Gallery in 1949, where she showed 17 such pieces, including *The Blind Leading the Blind*, 1947–9. Her enduring interest in environmental sculpture is evidenced in these works and in works depicting abstract plant-like forms such as the *Night Garden*, 1953. In the 1960s she began sculpting in a variety of materials, including bronze, plaster, rubber and stone. Much of this later work was concerned with abstract organic forms that are rich with anatomical references and personal symbolism, as in *Unconscious Landscape*, 1967, and *Partial Revolt*, 1979. To many people such pieces proved profoundly disturbing, for they often employed images which, while abstract, suggested sexuality, violence, or both at once. On the other hand, her work was often seen as brazenly feminist, and in the 1980s her work exercised enormous influence over the development of a new generation of artists, particularly women.

From 1950 until the late 1970s, she had only four solo sculpture shows; then, within three years (1978–1981) she had seven more. A full-scale retrospective was presented at New York's Museum of Modern Art in November 1982, and a traveling exhibit of her work from 1982–93 was mounted in 1994 to appear at the Brooklyn Museum and the Corcoran Gallery of Art.

During the 1970s, she held teaching positions at several schools, including The School of Visual Arts and Columbia University. She received several honorary degrees. During one ceremony, Yale's president Kingman Brewster spoke of her as one who has "not been afraid to disturb our complacency" and as one who "offered us powerful symbols of our experience and of the relations between man and woman." The *New York Times* said "if one of the functions of art is to make trouble for the stuffed shirt, then that function could hardly have been better fulfilled than by Louise Bourgeois."

Bourke-White, Margaret 1906–1971 photographer

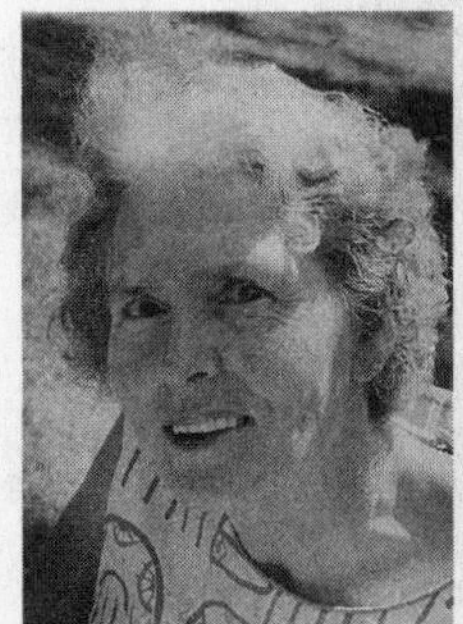

Margaret Bourke-White

Born on June 14, 1906, in New York City, Margaret White studied at Columbia University, the University of Michigan, and Cornell University, graduating from Cornell in 1927. She had already taken up photography, first as a hobby and then on a free-lance professional basis, when, on leaving Cornell, she moved to New York City. There she quickly established herself as an architectural and industrial photographer. For her professional name she combined her own last name with her mother's maiden name (Bourke) to create the hyphenated form by which she was known thereafter. Her command of the camera brought her increasingly important commissions, and from its founding in 1929 to 1933 she was an associate editor of *Fortune* magazine, in which much of her work was published. Several extensive tours of the Soviet Union resulted in the picture-and-text books *Eyes on Russia*, 1931, *Red Republic*, 1934, and *U.S.S.R., a Portfolio of Photographs*, 1934. She also photographed the Krupp Iron Works in Germany and other major installations and for various firms in America created remarkable photomural displays.

In 1936 she became a member of the original staff of *Life* magazine, of which she remained an editor for 33 years and to which she contributed countless photographs and photo-essays, including the magazine's first cover illustration (Fort Peck Dam). With Erskine Caldwell, her husband from 1939 to 1942, she produced *You Have Seen Their Faces*, a study of the rural South, 1937, *North of the Danube*, 1939, and *Say! Is This the U.S.A.?*, 1941. From the outbreak of World War II in 1939 she traveled extensively in Europe, the Near East, and the Soviet Union (where in 1941 she photographed Josef Stalin in the Kremlin), covering political and military events, and in 1942 she became the first woman to be accredited as a war correspondent to the U.S. army. After surviving the torpedoing of her transport ship, she was at the front in the North African and Italian campaigns and at the siege of Moscow. She accompanied General George S. Patton's Third Army into Germany in 1944, where she recorded on film the opening of Buchenwald and other concentration camps.

Later she made photojournalistic studies in India and South Africa and in the 1950s was again a war correspondent during the Korean War. Other books of her photographs and text included *Shooting the Russian War*, 1942, *They Called It Purple Heart Valley*, 1944, *Dear Fatherland, Rest Quietly*, 1946, and *Halfway to Freedom: A Study of the New India*, 1949. In later years she was rendered less active by chronic illness. Later published works included *A Report on the American Jesuits*, 1956, and a volume of autobiography, *Portrait of Myself*, 1963. She retired formally from *Life* magazine in 1969 and died in Stamford, Connecticut, on August 27, 1971.

Bow, Clara 1905–1965 actor

Born on August 6, 1905, in Brooklyn, New York, Clara Bow went to Hollywood by way of a beauty contest while still in high school. A small part in *Beyond the Rainbow*, 1922, brought her considerable attention, and she was soon playing starring roles in such movies as *Down to the Sea in Ships*, 1925, *The Plastic Age*, 1925, and *Mantrap*, *Kid Boots*, and *Dancing Mothers*, all released in 1926. In 1927 she was a sensation in a film written especially for her by Elinor Glyn and titled, simply and provocatively, *It*. Thereafter known universally as "the It Girl," Bow was the embodiment of beauty, abandon, and sex appeal for the moviegoers of the Jazz Age. Others of the thirty-odd movies in which she starred included *Hula*, 1927, *Rough House Rosie*, 1927, *Wings*, 1927, *The Fleet's In*, 1928, *Ladies of the Mob*, 1928, *Three Week-Ends*, 1928, *Dangerous Curves*, 1929, and *The Saturday Night Kid*, 1929. Unable to make the transition from silent movies to the talkies, in part because of her strong Brooklyn accent, and further hampered by some highly publicized scandals, she retired in 1931. After unsuccessful comeback attempts in *Call Her Savage*, 1932, and *Hoopla*, 1933, she spent most of the rest of her life living quietly on a Nevada cattle ranch owned by her husband, former cowboy star (and later lieutenant governor of Nevada) Rex Bell, whom she had married in 1931. Bow died in West Los Angeles, California, on September 27, 1965.

Boyd, Belle 1844–1900 Confederate spy and lecturer

Born on May 9, 1844, in Martinsburg, Virginia (now West Virginia), Isabelle, known as Belle, Boyd attended Mount Washington Female College, Baltimore, from 1856 to 1860 and had entered society in the national capital when the Civil War broke out. Returning then to Martinsburg, she joined in fund-raising activities on behalf of the Confederacy. When the town was occupied by Union forces in July 1861, she associated freely with officers, gleaning bits of military information which she sent by messenger to Confederate authorities. The interception of one of these messages brought her only a reprimand. Within a few months she was appointed a courier for General P. G. T. Beauregard and General Thomas J. Jackson. After being arrested and briefly detained in Baltimore in early 1862, she went to live with an aunt in Front Royal, Virginia. There, she later wrote, she eavesdropped on General James Shields and his staff and then made a fifteen-mile night ride through lines to deliver the intelligence thus gained. Boyd's most noted service came in May 1862, when she learned that Jackson, who was planning to recapture the town, could by speeding his advance prevent Union forces from destroying the bridges out of town in their retreat. She ran into the field between opposing lines, her "dark blue dress and fancy white apron" making her a conspicuous target, and waved the Confederates on. Whether or not she materially aided the attack, she later claimed to have been thanked by Jackson. In July, after the Union retaking of Front Royal, she was arrested and held for a month in Old Capitol Prison in Washington, D.C. By the time she was exchanged south, she was a heroine throughout the Confederacy. In June 1863 she returned to Martinsburg and the next month was again arrested. Released in December, she was banished south. In March 1864 she sailed on a blockade runner from Wilmington, North Carolina, with dispatches for Confederate agents in England. The ship was captured, and Boyd was taken to Boston and then banished to Canada.

Boyd made her way from Canada to London, where she married the naval officer who had had charge of her captured vessel (he was subsequently disciplined for neglect of duty). After he died early in 1865, she published her two-volume memoir, *Belle Boyd in Camp and Prison*. In 1866 she turned to the stage, making her debut in *The Lady of Lyons* in Manchester and then returning to the United States to make a tour of the South. She appeared in New York in *The Honeymoon* in 1868. She retired in 1869, but in 1886, her third marriage having brought her into financial difficulties, she began a career as a lecturer on her own exploits. She died on a speaking tour in Kilbourn (now Wisconsin Dells), Wisconsin, on June 11, 1900.

Boyle, Kay 1902–1992 poet, short-story writer and novelist

Born on February 19, 1902, in St. Paul, Minnesota, Kay Boyle grew up mainly in Europe, where she received a cultured education. Financial difficulties brought the family back to the United States and to Cincinnati, where in her youth she began writing prolifically in various forms. In June 1923 she married Richard Brault, a young French student, and after a year in New York City they lived in France for several years. Soon she was publishing poems and short stories regularly in such periodicals as *Broom*, *transition*, and Harriet Monroe's *Poetry*; and in 1929 she published her first book, a collection entitled *Wedding Day and Other Stories* (American edition 1930). Her first novel, *Plagued by the Nightingale*, appeared in 1931. In that year she divorced her first husband and married Laurence Vail, an expatriate American writer with whom she lived in the French Alps until July 1941. During that period she published *Year Before Last*, 1932, *Gentlemen, I Address You Privately*, 1933, *The First Lover and Other Stories*, 1933, *My Next Bride*, 1934, *The White Horses of Vienna and Other Stories* (the title story of which won the O. Henry Prize for 1935), 1936, *Death of a Man*, 1936, *Monday Night*, 1938, *Glad Day*, a volume of poems, 1938, *The Youngest Camel*, a children's novel, 1939, and *The Crazy Hunter*, three novellas, 1940. In 1941 she won a second O. Henry Prize for her short story "Defeat."

Her writing was marked by great intelligence and sophistication, finely wrought and sometimes almost private language, and, particularly early on, a fascination for the morbid, decadent, and fastidious. Throughout her career she was a keen and scrupulous student of the interior lives of characters in desperate situations. After the fall of France she and her large family returned to the United States and settled in the Hudson River valley of New York. *Primer for Combat* appeared in 1942. She was divorced from Vail that year and in 1943 married Baron Joseph von Franckenstein. During the war she published *Avalanche*, 1943, and afterward, living in occupied Germany, where her husband was a State Department officer, she produced *Frenchmen Must Die*, 1946, *Thirty Stories*, 1946, *1939*, 1948, *His Human Majesty*, 1949, *The Smoking Mountain*, a collection of stories set in postwar Germany, 1951, and *The Seagull on the Step*, 1955. During

1946–1953 she was a regular correspondent of *The New Yorker*. Subsequent books included *Three Short Novels*, 1958, *Generation Without Farewell*, 1960, *Collected Poems*, 1942, *Nothing Ever Breaks Except the Heart*, a collection of stories, 1966, *Pinky, the Cat*, 1967, *The Autobiography of Emanuel Carnevali*, 1967, *Being Geniuses Together*, 1968, *Pinky in Persia*, 1968, *Testament for My Students*, a book of poems, 1970, *The Long Walk at San Francisco State*, 1970, and *The Underground Woman*, 1975. From 1963, the year in which her husband died, she was a member of the faculty of San Francisco State College.

She was a political activist throughout her life and protested against McCarthyism in the 1950s, the Vietnam war in the 1960s, and the U.S. bombing of Libya in the 1980s. She described herself as "a dangerous radical cleverly disguised as a perfect lady." Her later works include the collection *Fifty Stories*, 1980, *Words That Must Somehow be Said: The Selected Essays of Kay Boyle 1927–1984*, 1985, and *Collected Poems*, 1991. She died in Mill Valley, California, on December 27, 1992.

Bradley, Lydia Moss 1816–1908 philanthropist

Born in Vevay, Indiana, on July 31, 1816, Lydia Moss early demonstrated qualities of determination and ability. In May 1837 she married Tobias S. Bradley and moved with him to Peoria, Illinois, where over the next three decades he prospered in land and banking. His death in 1867 left unbegun their plan to endow an educational institution in memory of their six children who had all died young, but it left her the financial means to pursue it.

Bradley actively managed her estate and through wise investment, principally in Peoria real estate, greatly increased it. Various other philanthropies, including church gifts and a home for aged women, engaged her while she worked toward her major goal. A charter for Bradley Polytechnic Institute was obtained in 1876, but not until 1897 were the first buildings erected, Bradley Hall and Horology Hall. With a $2 million endowment and a campus of 28 acres, Bradley was from the first firmly established. It aimed at providing both academic and practical training and was a pioneer particularly in the field of domestic science. Bradley died in Peoria on January 16, 1908. The college, as it was called, later added art and music schools, and in 1920, discontinuing its academy, became a regular college and awarded its first baccalaureate degrees. In 1946 it became Bradley University.

Bradstreet, Anne 1612?–1672 poet

Born probably in 1612 in Northampton, England, Anne Dudley was the daughter of Thomas Dudley, chief steward to Theophilus Clinton, the Puritan Earl of Lincoln. In 1628 she married Simon Bradstreet, a protégé of the Earl's, and in 1630 accompanied him and her parents to America. They were members of John Winthrop's party, the first settlers on Massachusetts Bay. At first dismayed by the rude life of the settlement, she soon reconciled herself to it, and, in the midst of her husband's public duties — he was an assistant in the Massachusetts Company and was twice governor of the colony — and her private ones as mother of eight, she found time to write poetry. Her early work, largely imitative and influenced by that of the sixteenth-century French poet Du Bartas, was conventional, dull, and easily forgotten. It was first published in London (where, unknown to her, her brother-in-law, the Reverend John Woodbridge, had taken a copy of her manuscript) in 1650 as *The Tenth Muse Lately Sprung Up in America*.

Bradstreet's later work, unpublished until after her death, became her chief claim to attention. Less derivative, it was often, as in "Contemplations," graceful and pleasant, and occasionally, as in "To My Dear and Loving Husband," deeply moving in its simple beauty. Much of it concerned her personal reflections, and the warmth and frank humanity that pervaded them struck a welcome contrast to the Puritan stereotype. She died on

September 16, 1672, in North Andover, Massachusetts. In 1678 an American edition of *The Tenth Muse* appeared under the new title *Several Poems Compiled with great variety of Wit and Learning* and included some of her later work. The first satisfactory edition of her work was edited by John Harvey Ellis in 1867.

Bradwell, Myra Colby 1831–1894 publisher and lawyer

Born in Manchester, Vermont, on February 12, 1831, Myra Colby grew up in Portage, New York, and from 1843 in Schaumberg township, near Elgin, Illinois. She was educated in schools in Kenosha, Wisconsin, and Elgin. After a few years as a schoolteacher she married James B. Bradwell, a law student, in May 1852 and moved with him to Memphis, Tennessee, where they taught and then operated their own private school. In 1854 they returned to Illinois and settled in Chicago, where in 1855 James Bradwell was admitted to the bar. He enjoyed considerable success, rising to the Cook County bench in 1861 and to the state legislature in 1873. Myra Bradwell had shared in his legal studies but did not follow up on that interest for some years. During the Civil War she was active in the work of the Northwestern Sanitary Commission, and later she involved herself in other charitable activities.

In October 1868 Bradwell launched a distinguished career with the publication of the first weekly number of the *Chicago Legal News*, of which she was both editorial and business manager. A special act of the legislature made issues of the paper containing laws, ordinances, and court opinions admissible as evidence in state courts. The Chicago Legal News Company was established at the same time to publish other periodical publications and to print legal forms, stationery, and other material. Bradwell was, by special charter, enabled to serve as president of both enterprises without the usual disabilities of married women. In 1869 she helped organize Chicago's first woman suffrage convention, and later in the year she and her husband were active in the founding of the American Woman Suffrage Association in Cleveland.

In that same year Bradwell passed the qualifying examination and applied to the Illinois supreme court for admission to the state bar; the court's refusal, on the ground that she was a woman, was upheld by the U.S. Supreme Court in May 1873. Meanwhile the Illinois legislature opened all professions to women in 1872, and although she did not renew her application for the bar she was made an honorary member of the state bar association and subsequently served four terms as its vice-president.

Through the *Chicago Legal News*, which continued to publish regularly even after its plant was destroyed in the Chicago fire of 1871, she editorially supported woman suffrage, railroad regulation, improved court systems, zoning laws, and other reforms. She drafted and — with the aid of Elizabeth Cady Stanton, Mary Livermore, and others — secured passage of a bill in 1869 removing some disabilities from married women. Later she supported her husband's successful efforts to secure legislation making women eligible to serve in school offices and as notaries public and the equal guardians of their children. She was a representative of Illinois at the Centennial Exposition in Philadelphia in 1876 and played a major role in winning the World's Columbian Exposition of 1893 for Chicago. In 1890 the Illinois supreme court, on its own initiative, took up her 1869 application again and admitted her to the bar; in March 1892 she was admitted to practice before the U.S. Supreme Court. Bradwell died in Chicago on February 14, 1894. She was followed into the law and the *Chicago Legal News* by her daughter, Bessie Bradwell Helmer.

Brady, Alice 1892–1939 actor

Born in New York City on November 2, 1892, Alice Brady was the daughter of theatrical manager William Brady by his first wife, Rose Marie Rene, who died a few years later. Educated in a convent school in Madison, New Jersey, and at the New England

Conservatory of Music, she abandoned plans for an operatic career and, over her father's objections, entered the theater, making her Broadway debut in a minor role in his 1910 production of *The Mikado*. The next year she appeared under an assumed name in *The Balkan Princess*, and in 1912, as Alice Brady, she won wide acclaim in *Little Women*. After an extensive national tour with DeWolf Hopper's Gilbert and Sullivan opera company in 1914 she moved to Hollywood and made a series of motion pictures, many for her father's company, including *As Ye Sow*, 1914, *The Gilded Cage*, 1914, *La Boheme*, 1916, *Betsy Ross*, 1917, and *Woman and Wife*, 1918. In 1918 she returned to Broadway in the hit *Forever After* and subsequently enjoyed great successes in *Zander the Great*, 1923, *Old Mama*, 1925, *The Bride of the Lamb*, 1926, Eugene O'Neill's *Mourning Becomes Electra* (with Alla Nazimova), 1931, *Mademoiselle*, 1932, and many other plays. During the 1930s she returned to the screen to appear in, among other films, *The Gay Divorcee*, 1934, *My Man Godfrey*, 1936, *Three Smart Girls*, 1937, *In Old Chicago*, for her portrayal of Mrs. O'Leary in which she won an Academy Award, 1937, and *Young Mr. Lincoln*, 1939. Brady died on October 28, 1939, in New York City.

Brant, Mary 1736?–1796 Native American leader

Born about 1736, probably in the Mohawk valley of New York, Mary Brant, known usually as Molly, was of the Mohawk tribe, the daughter of a sachem and an elder sister of Joseph Brant. Sometime in the late 1750s she came to the attention of Sir William Johnson, hero of Crown Point in the French and Indian War and superintendent of Indian affairs for the northern colonies. She became his mistress following the death of his wife and bore him nine children at Fort Johnson and later Johnson Hall, his manorial estate. She also managed his household and entertained the many distinguished guests, Native American and colonial alike, who visited.

After Sir William's death in July 1774 Brant relinquished Johnson Hall to his eldest son by his wife, Sir John Johnson, and moved with her children to a farm near Canajoharie, New York. She and all her family were Loyalists during the Revolution: her brother Joseph became a feared leader of warriors, notorious for the Cherry Valley Massacre of November 11, 1778; her eldest son Peter was credited with the capture of Ethan Allen at Montreal in September 1775; and she herself conveyed intelligence on American movements and supplied ammunition to the British before the battle of Oriskany, August 6, 1777. Her influence, both as daughter of a sachem and as consort of the popular Sir William, was decisive in bringing the entire Iroquois nation into the British camp, and much of the war she spent in the Tory stronghold of Niagara. After the war she settled in Ontario, where she and other Loyalist refugees founded the town of Kingston. In the same year, 1783, she was granted a British pension for her services. Like her brother, she was in her last years a devout member of the Episcopal church. She died in Kingston, Ontario, on April 16, 1796.

Breckinridge, Madeline McDowell 1872–1920 social reformer

Born in Woodlake, near Frankfort, Kentucky, on May 20, 1872, Madeline McDowell grew up from the age of ten in "Ashland," the Lexington, Kentucky, home built by her great grandfather, Henry Clay. She was educated in Lexington and at Miss Porter's School in Farmington, Connecticut, and during 1890–1894 she studied intermittently at the State College (now University) of Kentucky. In November 1898 she married Desha Breckinridge, editor of the *Lexington Herald* and brother of Sophonisba P. Breckinridge.

In 1900 Breckinridge began her career in social reform by urging the establishment of a settlement house near Proctor, Kentucky, a poor rural town in a mountainous region she had visited on horseback the year before. In the same year she took part in a citizen movement against corruption in local politics and helped found the Women's Emergency Committee, shortly reorganized as the Lexington Civic League. The League agitated successfully for the establishment of playgrounds and kindergartens in poorer districts of the city, and after Breckinridge had observed the work of Judge Ben B. Lindsey's juvenile court in Denver in 1903–1904 (where she had gone to recuperate from a flare-up of the tuberculosis that plagued her all her life) the League undertook campaigns for legislation setting up a juvenile court system, regulating child labor, and compelling school attendance.

In 1900 Breckinridge also led in founding the Lexington Associated Charities, which organized community charity along modern casework lines and of which she was a director from 1907. In 1905 she began editing a serious and thoughtful woman's page in the *Lexington Herald*. From 1905 she was active in local, county, and state tuberculosis societies. She helped secure establishment of the state Tuberculosis Commission in 1912 and served as its vice-president until 1916, in which year her fund-raising campaign culminated in the opening of the Blue Grass (later the Julius Marks) Sanatorium in Lexington. In 1906 she was appointed to the industry and child labor division of the State Federation of Women's Clubs, and in 1908–1912 she headed the federation's legislative division, through which she campaigned successfully for legislation granting women the vote in school elections. In 1910–1912 she also served a term as a director of the General Federation of Women's Clubs. In 1912 the Civic League established the Abraham Lincoln School and Social Center, to which she thereafter gave much attention in fund-raising and innovative programming.

From 1912 to 1915 and again from 1919 to her death Breckinridge was president of the Kentucky Equal Rights Association, which worked to secure legislation recognizing the rights of married women to enjoy their own earnings, to make wills, and to be equal guardians of their children, as well as legislation limiting working hours for women, providing for women physicians in state mental hospitals, and establishing other similar reforms. In 1913–1915 she was a vice president of the National American Woman Suffrage Association, on whose behalf she traveled and spoke widely, demonstrating a remarkable gift for oratory. The ratification of the Nineteenth Amendment by the Kentucky legislature in January 1920 was largely credited to her efforts. In 1920 she attended the International Women's Suffrage Alliance convention in Geneva and later in the year undertook an extensive campaign tour on behalf of the League of Nations and the Democratic party. She died in Lexington on November 25, 1920.

Breckinridge, Sophonisba Preston 1866–1948 educator, social worker and writer

Born in Lexington, Kentucky, on April 1, 1866, Sophonisba Breckinridge was the daughter of a liberal lawyer, journalist, and later congressman who provided her ample opportunity for education. She graduated from Wellesley College in 1888. After a time as a schoolteacher in Washington, D.C., she took up the study of law in her father's office and in 1895 became the first woman to be admitted to the Kentucky bar. Legal practice failed to interest her, however, and she soon moved to Chicago, where she became secretary to Marion Talbot, dean of women at the University of Chicago, and enrolled in the graduate school. In 1901 she became the first woman anywhere to receive a Ph.D. in the field of political science, and three years later she was the first to graduate from the law school of the university. She had served as assistant dean of women since 1902, and in 1904 she also became an instructor in the department of household administration, advancing to assistant professor in 1909.

In 1907 Breckinridge became interested in the Women's Trade Union League and in Jane Addams's Hull-House, where she became a resident and remained until 1920. Also in 1907 she became an instructor and then dean of the Chicago School of Civics and Philanthropy, and the following year she succeeded Julia C. Lathrop as head of the school's research department. In 1908, with Grace Abbott and others, she organized the Immigrants' Protective League, of which she served a short time as director and then until 1942 as secretary. In 1911 she was a vice-president of the National American Woman Suffrage Association. Her championship of women's trade unions and of legislative regulation of wages and hours of employment helped make those questions national issues, particularly as part of the Progressive party's 1912 platform. Much of her work in the Chicago School of Civics and Philanthropy, where the practical training of social workers took precedence over scientific sociological research, was reflected in such books as *The Delinquent Child and the Home*, with Edith Abbott, 1912, *Truancy and Non-Attendance in the Chicago Schools*, with Abbott, 1917, and *New Homes for Old*, 1921. She also wrote *The Modern Household*, with Marion Talbot, 1912, out of her early coursework at the University of Chicago, and *Madeline McDowell Breckinridge*, a biography of her sister-in-law, 1921.

In 1915 she joined in organizing the Woman's Peace party and then accompanied Jane Addams and others to the international Congress of Women at The Hague, where she helped found the Women's International League for Peace and Freedom. In 1920 she prompted and oversaw the takeover by the University of Chicago of the Chicago School of Civics and Philanthropy, which then became the Graduate School of Social Service Administration. In that year she advanced to associate professor in that school as well as in the department of household administration (she continued also as assistant dean of women), and in 1925 she became a full professor. In 1929 she was named Samuel Deutsch Professor of Public Welfare Administration and dean of pre-professional social service students. Publications from this period included *Family Welfare Work in a Metropolitan Community*, 1924, *Public Welfare Administration*, 1927, *Women in the Twentieth Century*, 1931, *Marriage and the Civic Rights of Women*, 1931, *The Family and the State*, 1934, *Social Work and the Courts*, 1934, and *The Illinois Poor Law and its Administration*, 1939. She helped found the journal *Social Service Review* in 1927 and served thereafter on its editorial staff. She was active in international organizations, serving as a delegate to the first Child Welfare Congress in Geneva in 1925, to the First International Conference of Social Work in Paris in 1928, to the Pan-American Child Congress in Lima in 1930, and under Secretary of State Cordell Hull to the Pan-American Congress in Montevideo in 1933. In 1934 she was chosen president of the American Association of Schools of Social Work. She became professor emeritus in 1933 and continued to teach a full schedule until 1942. She died in Chicago on July 30, 1948.

Brent, Margaret 1600?–1671? colonial landowner

Born about 1600 in Gloucester, England, Margaret was the daughter of Richard Brent, Lord of Admington and Lark Stoke. In 1638, with her sister, two brothers, and a number of indentured servants, she sailed for America and in November settled in St. Marys, Maryland. Her original land grant, 70½ acres that she called "Sisters Freehold," was the first made to a woman in Maryland. It was increased by the proprietor of the colony, Lord Baltimore, and over the next few years was further augmented through family connections, business transactions, and bounties offered for the transportation of more colonists, until she became a leading landowner in the colony. She aided the governor, Leonard Calvert, in an armed dispute with William Claiborne of Virginia in 1644–1646, herself raising a troop of soldiers. Calvert, who according to some reports was her brother-in-law, appointed her executor of his estate. Upon his death in May 1647 she took charge of the estate and shortly thereafter received a court appointment as attorney for the proprietor as well. She liquidated some of Lord Baltimore's holdings in order to pay the soldiers who had fought Claiborne, averting thereby a mutiny and possibly a civil war. In January 1648 she went before the assembly to request two votes in its proceedings, one for herself as a freeholder (she was in fact one of the largest landowners in the colony) and one as attorney for the proprietor. She was refused, although the assembly subsequently defended her when Lord Baltimore condemned her having sold his property. As a result she left Maryland and settled anew in Westmoreland County, Virginia, in 1650 and remained there, living in semifeudal splendor, until her death sometime before May 1671.

Brice, Fanny 1891–1951 entertainer

Born in New York City on October 29, 1891, Fannie Borach, daughter of a barkeeper on the city's Lower East Side, took "Brice" as a stage name. She appeared first at thirteen in a talent contest at Keeney's Theatre in Brooklyn, where she sang "When You Know You're Not Forgotten by the Girl You Can't Forget" and won first prize. After that she left school to undertake a theatrical career. She was at various times a pianist, a singer, and an assistant to the projectionist in a movie theater. At fifteen she won a place in the chorus line of the George M. Cohan-Sam Harris production *Talk of New York* but was dismissed as soon as it became obvious that she could not dance.

In one of the many burlesque houses where she sang, Florenz Ziegfeld discovered and hired Brice (influenced in part by her rendition of "Sadie Salome," a song given her by Irving Berlin) for the *Ziegfeld Follies* at $75 a week. She was a *Follies* perennial after 1910, and her comic routines and parodies were highly popular. Already famous as a comedienne, she first attained real stardom in the 1921 edition of the *Follies*, in which she introduced a French torch song, "My Man," which became her trademark. Other songs identified with her were "Second Hand Rose," "I Should Worry," and "Rose of Washington Square." She appeared with such major Broadway performers as W. C. Fields, Eddie Cantor, and Will Rogers in the *Follies* and in such other shows as *The Honeymoon Express*, 1913, *Nobody Home*, 1915, *Why Worry?*, 1918, *Music Box Revue of 1924*, *Fanny*, a serious production by David Belasco in 1926, *Fioretta*, 1929, and Billy Rose's *Sweet and Low*, 1930, and *Crazy Quilt*, 1931. (She was married to Rose from 1929 to 1938.) In the last she introduced the character of Baby Snooks, a mischievous brat she had first played in vaudeville in 1912 and later often played for friends. Baby Snooks later became a *Follies* favorite, and in that character she was featured on radio from 1936 until her death. She was seen in a few motion pictures, including *My Man*, 1928, *Be Yourself!*, 1930, *The Great Ziegfeld*, 1936, and *Everybody Sing*, 1938. She died on May 29, 1951, in Hollywood. Her life was the subject of the film *Rose of Washington Square*, 1939, and of *Funny Girl*, a 1964 Broadway musical (starring Barbra Streisand) that was made into a movie in 1968.

Bridgman, Laura Dewey 1829–1889 first successfully taught blind deaf-mute

Born on December 21, 1829, in Hanover, New Hampshire, Laura Bridgman was struck by scarlet fever at the age of two and left blind and deaf. Her other senses were also affected, but she retained the sense of touch, which she developed sufficiently to learn to sew and knit. In 1837 her case came to the attention of Samuel Gridley Howe, director of the Perkins Institution for the Blind, then in Boston. He brought her to the school in October and began to attempt, against prevailing opinion and experience, to teach her by touch. By attaching words made of raised letters to common objects he was able eventually to convey to her the idea of names. Inspired by the sudden revelation of the possibility of communication, she went on to learn the letters and the manual alphabet and with these was able to study a number of advanced subjects, from arithmetic to geography. She was the first blind deaf-mute ever known to have been taught successfully, and Howe's achievement drew much attention, especially after Charles Dickens visited the school in 1842 and enthusiastically described Bridgman's accomplishments in his *American Notes*. She remained at the school for the rest of her life and gradually assumed household duties and helped teach other pupils. In 1887 a jubilee celebration was held to mark the fiftieth anniversary of her coming to the school. She died on May 24, 1889.

Briggs, Emily Pomona Edson 1830–1910 journalist

Born on September 14, 1830, in Burton, Ohio, Emily Edson grew up there and, from 1840, near Chicago. She attended local schools, taught briefly, and about 1854 married John R. Briggs, with whom she settled in Keokuk, Iowa. They remained in Keokuk, where John Briggs was part owner of the *Daily Whig* (later the *Gate City*), until 1861, when he secured appointment as assistant clerk of the U.S. House of Representatives.

In Washington, D.C., Emily Briggs soon discovered a taste for observing and commenting on the political scene. A letter to the *Washington Chronicle*, in which she defended women seeking government employment, caught the attention of the paper's owner (and her husband's immediate superior), who hired her to write a daily column. Under the pseudonym "Olivia" she wrote her column for over 20 years for the *Chronicle* and its sister paper, the *Philadelphia Press*. Her comments on public affairs were always incisive, and her column, while paying some attention to society and fashion, was quite unlike those of the general run of women journalists of the day.

During the Lincoln administration Briggs became the first woman to report directly from the White House — she became personally close to the Lincoln family — and later she was among the first to be admitted to the congressional press gallery. One of the first woman journalists to acquire a national reputation, she was elected first president of the Woman's National Press Association upon its organization in 1882. In later years she became a noted Washington hostess. In 1906 a collection of her columns was published in volume form as *The Olivia Letters*. She died in Washington, D.C., on July 3, 1910.

Britton, Elizabeth Gertrude Knight 1858–1934 botanist and writer

Born in New York City on January 9, 1858, Elizabeth Knight grew up for the most part in Cuba, where her family owned a sugar plantation. She attended schools in Cuba and New York and in 1875 graduated from Normal (now Hunter) College. For ten years she served on the staff there, the last two as an assistant in natural science, and during that time she laid the foundation of her reputation as a leading amateur botanist. By 1883 she had specialized in bryology, the study of mosses, and had published her first scientific paper in the field.

In August 1885 she married Nathaniel L. Britton, a geologist at Columbia College. He soon turned to botany, and over the next several years the two made numerous field trips together to the West Indies. She was given charge, on an unofficial basis, of the moss collection of the Columbia botany department, and gradually she built it into a major one, notably with the purchase of the collection of August Jaeger of Switzerland in 1893. In 1886–1888 she was editor of the *Bulletin* of the Torrey Botanical Club, of which she had been a member since 1879. Supported by the Torrey Botanical Club and other interested persons, the Brittons took the lead in urging the establishment of a botanical garden in New York. The New York Botanical Garden was incorporated in 1891, and in 1896 Nathaniel Britton became first director of the 250–acre (from 1915 nearly 400 acre) establishment in Bronx Park. The Columbia College herbarium was transferred there in 1899, and Britton became unofficial curator of mosses; in 1912 she received appointment as honorary curator of mosses. She was active in most other phases of the Botanical Garden's management as well.

In 1902 Elizabeth Britton was a founder and in 1902–1916 and 1918–1927 secretary and treasurer of the Wild Flower Preservation Society of America. Through the society and various publications she led movements that succeeded in saving numerous endangered wildflower species around the country. From 1916 to 1919 she was president of the Sullivant Moss Society, which she had helped found in 1898 and which in 1949 became the American Bryological Society. She published over 340 signed scientific papers during her career and had 15 species and 1 moss genus (Bryobrittonia) named for her. She died in the Bronx, New York, on February 25, 1934.

Brooks, Maria Gowen 1794?–1845 poet

Born about 1794 in Medford, Massachusetts, Abigail Gowen grew up in a prosperous and cultured family. After the death of her father in 1809 she came under the guardianship of John Brooks, a Boston merchant and the widower of her elder sister Lucretia. In August 1810 she married Brooks, who was more than 30 years her senior. Financial reverses led to their removal from Boston to Portland (then Massachusetts, now Maine), where she found life unsatisfactory. In 1819 she legally changed her given name to Mary Abigail; she later gradually adopted the name Maria.

In retreat partly from provincial Portland and partly from an infatuation with a young Canadian officer, she turned to poetry, and in 1820 she published anonymously a small volume called *Judith, Esther, and Other Poems*. After the death of her husband in 1823 she went to live with a brother on a coffee plantation near Matanzas, Cuba. A short time later she went to Canada, where she became engaged to and then estranged from her officer and twice attempted suicide. On regaining her health she returned to the Cuban plantation, to which she had fallen heir, and began work on a verse romance *Zóphiël; or, the Bride of Seven*, based on a tale in the apocryphal Book of Tobit. She published the first canto of the poem in Boston in 1825 under the name "Mrs. Brooks." In 1826 she began a correspondence with the English poet Robert Southey. The poem was complete by 1829, when she moved to Hanover, New Hampshire, where her son Horace was preparing for West Point.

In 1830 Gowen traveled to Europe with another brother and met Washington Irving and through him Lafayette, who used his influence to assist Horace's acceptance at West Point. In 1831 she was in England and spent several weeks as Southey's guest. He undertook to supervise the publication in London of *Zóphiël*, which appeared in 1833 under the name "Maria del Occidente." By that time she had returned to America, and in 1834 she published a private edition of *Zóphiël* in Boston. For several years she lived near West Point while Horace was a student and then an assistant professor there. In 1838 she published serially in the Boston *Saturday Evening Gazette* a curious fictionalized autobiography entitled *Idomen: or, the Vale of Yumuri*. No commercial publisher would issue the work as a book, so in 1843 she issued a private edition in New York.

In December 1843 she returned hurriedly to Cuba, where her eldest son and a stepson had died. She died in Matanzas on November 11, 1845, leaving unfinished a verse romance on "Beatriz, the Beloved of Columbus." Despite the championship of Southey, Griswold, and others, her works had limited public appeal even in their day.

Brown, Alice 1856–1948 novelist, short-story writer and biographer

Born in Hampton Falls, New Hampshire, on December 5, 1856, Alice Brown attended a local school and Robinson Seminary in nearby Exeter, from which she graduated in 1876. She then taught school for several years in a number of New Hampshire towns and in Boston, meanwhile contributing short stories to various magazines. Her success as a writer allowed her to give up teaching and move to Boston in 1884. She found a position on the staff of the *Christian Register* and in 1885 on that of the *Youth's Companion*, with which she was associated for some years. Her first novel, *Stratford-by-the-Sea*, was published in 1884 and was followed by *Fools of Nature*, 1887, and *Meadow Grass*, 1895.

In 1895 she collaborated with her close friend Louise I. Guiney on *Robert Louis Stevenson: A Study*, and in 1896 she published *By Oak and Thorn*, a volume of travel impressions of England, and *The Life of Mercy Otis Warren*. Thereafter novels and collections of stories appeared at a rapid rate under such titles as *The Day of His Youth*,

1897, *Tiverton Tales* (perhaps her best work), 1899, *King's End*, 1901, *Margaret Warrener*, 1901, *The Mannerings*, 1903, *The Merry Links*, 1903, *Judgment*, 1903, *High Noon*, 1904, *Paradise*, 1905, *The Country Road*, 1906, *Rose MacLeod*, 1908, *Country Neighbors*, 1910, *The Secret of the Clan*, 1912, *Robin Hood's Barn*, 1913, *Bromley Neighborhood*, 1917, *Homespun and Gold*, 1920, *Old Crow*, 1922, and *The Mysteries of Ann*, 1925. She also wrote a volume of poems, *The Road to Castalay*, 1896, and several plays, including *Children of Earth*, which in 1914 won a $10,000 competition sponsored by producer Winthrop Ames and which was a critical success but a popular failure; other plays were *The Golden Ball*, 1929, *The Marriage Feast*, 1931, and *The Kingdom in the Sky*, 1932. Her dialect tales of New Hampshire folk gradually lost their appeal as popular interest in local-color writing waned early in the century, and she never again attained the success of her work in that vein. In 1921 she published a biography of Louise Guiney. She wrote nothing after 1935, and she died in Boston on June 21, 1948.

Brown, Charlotte Emerson 1838–1895 clubwoman

Born in Andover, Massachusetts, on April 21, 1838, Charlotte Emerson was the daughter of a clergyman and a relative of Ralph Waldo Emerson. She received an excellent education, in part from her father and a brother and in part at Abbot Academy in Andover. She had a particular aptitude for languages and mastered several, ancient and modern. She taught school for a year in Montreal, traveled abroad, and in 1858 moved with her family to Rockford, Illinois. There she worked as secretary to another brother, a manufacturer, taught modern languages at Rockford Seminary (now College), and became active in club organizing. She founded Euterpe, a musical club, and others.

In July 1880 Emerson married the Reverend William B. Brown, and after a three-year sojourn abroad, during which she continued her studies in languages and music, they settled in East Orange, New Jersey. She soon became president of the local Woman's Club. In March 1889, at a meeting called by Sorosis, the New York women's club, the General Federation of Women's Clubs was organized. Brown was one of a committee of seven chosen to form the federation and was elected its first president. Under her presidency the membership grew rapidly from some 50 cultural clubs to several hundred, representing tens of thousands of members, and the formation of state federations, beginning with Maine's in 1892, went forward rapidly. She remained president until the federation's convention in Philadelphia in May 1894, when she was succeeded by Ellen Henrotin of Chicago. She was also interested in foreign missions and worked on behalf of the Woman's Board of Missions of the Congregational Church. She died in East Orange, New Jersey, on February 5, 1895.

Brown, Hallie Quinn 1850–1949 educator, lecturer and clubwoman

Born in Pittsburgh on March 10, 1850, Hallie Brown was the daughter of former slaves. From 1864 she grew up in Chatham, Ontario, and in 1870 she entered Wilberforce University in Wilberforce, Ohio. After her graduation in 1873 she taught in plantation and public schools in Mississippi and in South Carolina. In 1885–1887 she was dean of Allen University in Columbia, South Carolina, and during that period, in 1886, she graduated from the Chautauqua Lecture School. After four years of teaching public school in Dayton, Ohio, she served as lady principal of Tuskegee Institute, Alabama, under Booker T. Washington in 1892–1893.

In 1893 Brown was a principal promoter of the organization of the Colored Woman's League of Washington, D.C., which the next year joined other groups to form the National Association of Colored Women. In 1893 she was appointed professor of elocution at Wilberforce University, but her teaching duties were limited by her frequent and extensive lecture tours, notably in Europe in 1894–1899. Her lectures on African-American life in America and on temperance were especially popular in Great Britain, where she appeared twice before Queen Victoria. She was a speaker at the 1895 convention of the World's Woman's Christian Temperance Union in London and a representative of the United States at the International Congress of Women there in 1899. Her formal connection with Wilberforce lasted until 1903, although in 1910 she was highly effective in raising funds for the school during another British visit. She served as president of the Ohio State Federation of Colored Women's Clubs in 1905–1912 and of the National Association of Colored Women in 1920–1924; during the latter period she helped begin a campaign to preserve the Washington, D.C., home of Frederick Douglass. In the 1920s she was also active in Republican politics. She addressed the party's national convention in 1924 and subsequently directed campaign work among African-American women on behalf of President Calvin Coolidge. Among her published works were *Bits and Odds: A Choice Selection of Recitations*, 1880, *First Lessons in Public Speaking*, 1920, *Homespun Heroines and Other Women of Distinction*, 1926, and *Pen Pictures of Pioneers of Wilberforce*, 1937. She died in Wilberforce, Ohio, on September 16, 1949, at the age of ninety-nine.

Brown, Helen Gurley 1922– writer and editor

Born on February 18, 1922, in Green Forest, Arkansas, Helen Gurley grew up there, in Little Rock, and from 1932 in Los Angeles. After attending public schools she was a student at Texas State College for Women (now Texas Women's University) in 1939–1941 and at Woodbury Business College in 1942. For several years she held secretarial positions with Music Corporation of America, the William Morris Agency, and other firms. In 1948 she became a copywriter for the advertising firm of Foote, Cone & Belding. Her ability to write bright, arresting prose enabled her to progress rapidly in that field, and she had already won two of her three Frances Holmes Advertising Copywriters awards when she moved over to the Kenyon & Eckhardt agency as copywriter and account executive in 1958.

In September 1959 Gurley married David Brown, a motion picture producer. She left advertising in 1962 when her first book, *Sex and the Single Girl*, became an immediate and controversial best-seller. Her advice to young single women on matters of career, fashion, love, entertainment, and other topics, expressed in her singularly sprightly prose, emphasized the positive benefits of unmarried life and provoked wide comment and some criticism by recognizing that sex was a part of that life. *Sex and the Office*, 1964, continued in the same vein, and for a time she conducted a syndicated newspaper advice column, "Woman Alone," as well.

In 1965 Brown was named editor of the venerable but foundering *Cosmopolitan* magazine. Drawing on ideas she and her husband had developed earlier for an unrealized magazine project, she quickly remade *Cosmopolitan* into a splashy, upbeat magazine aimed at the young women, single or married, who had formed the audience for *Sex and the Single Girl*. *Cosmopolitan* became more daring graphically — a movement that culminated in a highly publicized nude male centerfold spread in 1972 — and a trend-setter in youthful lifestyle. Circulation and advertising revenues shot upward as the new format proved extremely popular with its intended audience.

Helen Gurley Brown also wrote *Helen Gurley Brown's Outrageous Opinions*, 1966, *Helen Gurley Brown's Single Girl's Cookbook*, 1969, *Sex and the New Single Girl*, 1970, *Having It All*, 1982, and *The Late Show: A Semiwild but Practical Survival Plan for Women over 50*, 1993. She received the New York Women in Communication Award in 1985 and established the Helen Gurley Brown Research Professorship at Northwestern University. She was inducted into the Publisher's Hall of Fame in 1988.

Brown, Martha McClellan 1838–1916 temperance leader

Born on April 16, 1838, in Baltimore, Martha McClellan grew up from 1840 in

Cambridge, Ohio. In November 1858 she married the Reverend W. Kennedy Brown, with whom she moved to a succession of Methodist pastorates in Pennsylvania and Ohio over the next several decades. Shortly after her marriage she enrolled in the Pittsburgh Female College and graduated in 1862. A member from 1861 of the Independent Order of Good Templars, a fraternal temperance society, she became a noted temperance lecturer in the years following the Civil War and in 1867 was elected to the state executive committee of the Ohio Templars as grand vice-templar. In 1868 she became editor of the *Alliance Monitor* in Alliance, Ohio, and retained that post until 1876; from 1870 the paper was owned by her husband. She played a large role in laying the groundwork for the organization of the national Prohibition party in 1869. In 1872–1874 she was grand chief templar of Ohio. She attended the 1873 international convention of Templars in London, and in 1874–1875 she was world supreme vice-templar.

At the height of a temperance prayer crusade that swept Ohio in 1873–1874 Brown seized the opportunity to create a more broadly based temperance organization than the Templars, and in February 1874 in Columbus, Ohio, she led in founding what apparently was the first women's state temperance society. That August, at Chautauqua Lake, New York, she and two others planned a national society, and she is believed to have drafted the call for the convention that met in Cleveland in November and organized the Woman's Christian Temperance Union. Failing to win the presidency of the new group, probably because of her identification with the Templars, she withdrew. In 1876 she withdrew as well from the Templars when that group declined to admit African-American members.

Brown then concentrated her efforts on the Prohibition party, becoming vice president of the convention that year and serving on the executive committee in 1876–1880. In 1877 she helped organize the National Prohibition Alliance, a speakers bureau closely associated with the Prohibition party. She served as the Alliance's secretary and principal lecturer until its dissolution in 1882. She served again on the party's executive committee in 1884–1886 and 1892–1896, but in 1896 she broke with the party when the convention dropped from its platform the woman suffrage plank that she had been instrumental in making one of the party's goals in 1869. From 1882 to 1892 she served as vice-president and professor of art, literature, and philosophy in the Cincinnati Wesleyan Woman's College, a financially shaky institution of which her husband was president. She resumed her connection with the Templars to make lecture tours of Great Britain in 1881, 1891, and 1911, but in later years she occupied herself chiefly with local philanthropies in Cincinnati. Martha Brown died in Dayton, Ohio, on August 31, 1916.

Brown, Olympia 1835–1926 clergyman and social reformer

Born in Prairie Ronde, Michigan, on January 5, 1835, Olympia Brown was refused admission to the University of Michigan because of her sex and instead attended Mount Holyoke College for a year and then Antioch College, graduating in 1860. Three years later, under the inspiration of Antoinette Blackwell, she graduated from the theological school of St. Lawrence University and in June 1863 was ordained in the ministry of the Universalist church, becoming the first American woman to be ordained by full denominational authority. (Blackwell's ordination in a Congregational church rested on the autonomous authority of a single congregation.) She served churches in Weymouth, Massachusetts, in 1864–1870 and Bridgeport, Connecticut, in 1870–1876.

At the same time Brown's long latent interest in women's rights was aroused by a meeting with Susan B. Anthony in 1866, and she became one of the cause's leading champions in the West. She campaigned vigorously but unsuccessfully for universal suffrage in Kansas in 1867. In 1868 she was a founder of the New England Woman Suffrage Association. Following her marriage to John H. Willis in April 1873 she retained her maiden name. In 1878 she moved to a pastorate in Racine, Wisconsin, but she resigned it in 1887 to devote herself to suffrage work. From 1884 to 1912 she was president of the Wisconsin Woman Suffrage Association, and she traveled and spoke widely on its aims. In 1884 she was elected a vice-president of the National Woman Suffrage Association. In 1887 she attempted to vote in a municipal election in Racine, was refused, and instituted a lengthy and ultimately unsuccessful suit against the officials responsible. In 1892 she led in founding the Federal Suffrage Association in Chicago, and she served as its vice-president until 1902, when it was reorganized as the Federal Equality Association. She was president of the Association, which later readopted its original name, from 1903 to 1920. She also later joined the Congressional Union led by Alice Paul.

Brown published *Acquaintances, Old and New, Among Reformers* in 1911 and managed her husband's newspaper (the *Racine Times*) and printing business from his death in 1893 until 1900. In 1914 she moved to Baltimore. There she continued an active and independent existence until her death on October 23, 1926.

Brown, Trisha 1936– dancer and choreographer

Born on November 25, 1936, in Aberdeen, Washington, Trisha Brown studied modern dance and graduated with a B.A. in dance from Mills College in Oakland, California. Her style began developing after she met Yvonne Rainer while studying with Anna Halprin in 1960, and together Brown and Rainer became two of the founding members of the experimental Judson Dance Theater in 1962. From 1970 through 1976, Brown was also one of the founding members of the improvisational Grand Union, and in 1970 she formed her own company, the Trisha Brown Dance Company, initially an all-female dance company.

Brown was influenced by what was then called avant-garde dance, a style developed most prominently by Merce Cunningham during the 1960s and 1970s. Although this type of dance was grounded in Martha Graham's technique (Cunningham had been a student of Graham's), avant-garde dance evolved in reaction to the more structured and formal classical ballet and classical modern dance. Some of the underlying tenets of avant-garde dance were the beliefs that dance could be divorced from music, that dance was not merely a vehicle of expression for the choreographer but could be its own subject matter, that dances could be themeless and plotless, and that dancers on stage could move in ways that were unrelated to each other. In addition, Anna Halprin taught Brown and her other students to move in ways that attended to their bodies' internal rhythms.

During this period Brown developed several experimental pieces. Her first, *Leaning Duets and Falling Duets*, choreographed from 1968 to 1971, involved dancers supporting and testing each other's strength. *Walking on the Wall*, 1970, showed dancers in an unexpected relationship with the environment: dancers moved while hanging in harnesses and while perpendicular to a wall. In *Accumulating Pieces*, 1971, the dance was built up from a series of discrete gestures, each gesture building on the previous one. Her *Roof Piece*, 1973, employed fifteen dancers, each on a different Manhattan roof, following each other's sequence of movements, while the audience watched from another roof. At this time she also did the quartet *Locus*, 1975, a piece that had no costumes or lighting effects; *Man Walking Down the Side of a Building*, outside a lower Manhattan warehouse; and *Spiral*, in a park in Minneapolis in which the dancers walked down trees and were parallel to the ground.

By the late 1970s and 1980s, she began to incorporate design and music into her pieces and to work in traditional theaters instead of outdoors. Now classified as a postmodern choreographer, she went on to choreograph *Glacial Decoy*, 1979, which featured a backdrop of black and white photos designed by Robert Rauschenberg; *Son of Gone*

Fishin', 1981, with music by Robert Ashley; *Set and Reset*, 1983, with costumes and film clips by Rauschenberg and a score by Laurie Anderson; and *Lateral Pass*, 1985, a piece designed by sculptor Nancy Graves. Brown also produced an essay in Anne Livet's *Contemporary Dance*, 1978, and two videos, *Set and Reset* and *Newark*.

Brunswick, Ruth Jane Mack 1897–1946 psychoanalyst

Born in Chicago on February 17, 1897, Ruth Mack graduated from Radcliffe College in 1918, and, having been refused admission to Harvard Medical School because of her sex, she graduated from Tufts Medical School in 1922. She then traveled to Vienna to be psychoanalyzed by Sigmund Freud. She soon became one of the inner circle of students around Freud and in 1925 began practicing psychoanalysis herself. She was a member of the Vienna Psychoanalytic Society and an instructor at the Psychoanalytic Institute. In 1932 she became an editor of the American journal *Psychoanalytic Quarterly*. One of her most notable early papers concerned her continuing treatment in 1926–1927 of one of Freud's most famous cases, the Wolf-Man. She was widely respected as a brilliant, thorough, and effective clinician.

Mack was married (for the second time) in March 1928 in Vienna to Mark Brunswick, an American composer. In 1938 the Brunswicks left Nazi-occupied Vienna and settled in New York City. There she joined the New York Psychoanalytic Society, taught courses in psychoanalytic technique and dream analysis at the New York Psychoanalytic Institute, and kept up a private practice in spite of declining health. In 1944 she resumed her connection with the *Psychoanalytic Quarterly*, which she had dropped in 1938. Her professional publications, while few, were of classic quality and contributed greatly to the full development of Freudian theory, particularly with regard to questions of childhood trauma and parental attachment. In her clinical practice she was especially interested in the treatment of psychoses often regarded as hopeless. Ruth Brunswick died in New York City on January 24, 1946.

Pearl Buck

Buck, Pearl Sydenstricker 1892–1973 novelist and short-story writer

Born on June 26, 1892, in Hillsboro, West Virginia, Pearl Comfort Sydenstricker was raised in Chenchiang in eastern China by her Presbyterian missionary parents. Initially educated by her mother and a Chinese tutor, she was sent at fifteen to a boarding school in Shanghai. Two years later she entered Randolph-Macon Woman's College in Virginia, graduating in 1914 and remaining for a semester as an instructor in psychology. In May 1917 she married missionary John L. Buck; although later divorced and remarried, she retained the name professionally. She returned to China and taught English literature in Chinese universities in 1925–1930. During that time she briefly resumed studying in the United States at Cornell University, where she took her M.A. in 1926. She began contributing articles on Chinese life to American magazines in 1922.

Buck's first published novel, *East Wind, West Wind*, 1930, was written aboard a ship headed for America. *The Good Earth*, 1931, a poignant tale of a Chinese peasant and his slave-wife and their struggle upward, was a best-seller, won a Pulitzer Prize and the Howells Medal, and established her as an interpreter of the East to the West. The book was made into a stage play and an Academy Award-winning film. With *Sons*, 1932, and *A House Divided*, 1935, it formed a trilogy, *The House of Earth*. Pearl Buck was awarded the Nobel Prize for Literature in 1938. Subsequently she wrote biographies of her parents, *The Exile* and *Fighting Angel*, both 1936 (published together as *The Spirit and the Flesh* in 1944), and a long series of novels and short story collections, including *The First Wife*, 1933, *The Mother*, 1934, *The Patriot*, 1939, *Dragon Seed*, 1942, *The Promise*, 1943, *The Dragon Fish*, 1944, *Pavilion of Women*, 1946, *Peony*, 1948, *Imperial Woman*, 1956, *Letter from Peking*, 1957, *The Living Reed*, 1963, and *The Three Daughters of Madame Liang*, 1969. She also published several novels under the pseudonym John Sedges, including a best-seller, *The Townsman*, 1945. Buck wrote a number of children's books and three volumes of autobiography, *My Several Worlds*, 1954, *A Bridge for Passing*, 1962, and *For Spacious Skies*, 1966. Her interest in cultural understanding led her to found the East-West Association in 1941. In 1949 she founded Welcome House and in 1963 the Pearl S. Buck Foundation, both dedicated to the care of unwanted children. She died in Danby, Vermont, on March 6, 1973.

Burk, Martha Jane 1852?–1903 "Calamity Jane," frontier figure

Born in Princeton, Missouri, probably in 1852 (and possibly on May 1 of that year), Martha Jane Cannary moved with her parents to Virginia City, Montana, in 1864 or 1865. There she became an expert marksman and rider. She dressed habitually as a man and acquired few of the conventional feminine refinements. By 1867 both of her parents were dead, and she roamed at large through the mining districts, reputedly drinking and cussing with the best of them. She wandered into Wyoming in the 1870s and, according to some (her not notably reliable self included), scouted for the cavalrymen commanded by Colonel George Custer and General Nelson A. Miles. She tagged along with the Newton-Jenney geological expedition into the Black Hills in 1875 and after the gold strike of 1876 became a fixture in Deadwood, South Dakota. She was a companion of "Wild Bill" Hickok, although stories that they were married are most probably untrue.

Cannary's nickname, "Calamity Jane," is variously explained: one tradition assigns it to her generosity toward the unfortunate, particularly during the smallpox epidemic of 1878, while another holds that it derived from the warning she gave men who seemed about to offend her. She is said to have been a mail carrier in Deadwood for some years. She was almost certainly not, as has also been said, a stage driver or pony express rider. She was at various times a prostitute. She left after the mining boom ended and in 1885, in El Paso, Texas, married one Clinton Burk (or Burke), who shortly thereafter deserted her. Her fame beyond the saloons and camps of the West derived from her fanciful portrayal as the beautiful companion of "Deadwood Dick" in a series of dime novels of the 1870s and 1880s. She exhibited herself briefly in a traveling show in 1896 and appeared at the Pan-American Exposition in Buffalo, New York, in 1901. Her last years were spent in poverty in Livingston, Montana, and then in Terry, South Dakota, where she died on August 1, 1903. She was buried in Deadwood beside Wild Bill.

Burlin, Natalie Curtis 1875–1921 musicologist

Born in New York City on April 26, 1875, Natalie Curtis attended the National Conservatory of Music in her native city and subsequently studied piano with outstanding teachers in Berlin, Paris, Bonn, and Bayreuth. In 1900, however, while on a visit to Arizona, she became suddenly so deeply interested in the customs and lore and especially the music of the Native Americans of the region that she gave up her planned concert career. With phonograph and later simply with pencil and paper she visited the villages and camps of the Zuñi, Hopi, and other tribes and recorded their songs, poetry, and tales. By appealing to President Theodore Roosevelt, a family friend, she won removal of a ban that had been placed on Native Americans' performing their own music, and her own warm personality earned her admission to their ceremonies. In 1905 she published *Songs of Ancient America*, consisting of three Pueblo corn-grinding songs, but her major publication in the field was *The Indians' Book*, 1907, which enjoyed two later editions and remains a vital source book for students and scholars of the subject. The lore and music in the book were drawn from 18 tribes, mainly Southwestern but also from as far away as Maine and British Columbia.

In 1911 Curtis aided David Mannes in organizing the Music School Settlement for Colored People in New York City, and she also helped arrange for the first concert of African-American music by African-American performers at Carnegie Hall in March

1914. In July 1917 she married Paul Burlin, a painter. A period of study at Hampton Institute, Virginia, enabled her to produce the four-volume *Hampton Series Negro Folk-Songs*, 1918–1919, unretouched transcriptions of great musicological value, and *Songs and Tales from the Dark Continent*, 1920, transcribed from two African students at Hampton. She also published *Songs from a Child's Garden of Verses by Robert Louis Stevenson*. While in Paris to address an art historians' congress she was killed by an automobile on October 23, 1921.

Burnett, Frances Eliza Hodgson 1849–1924 author

Born in Cheetham Hill, Manchester, England, on November 24, 1849, Frances Hodgson grew up in increasingly straitened circumstances after the death of her father in 1854. In 1865 the family emigrated to the United States and settled in New Market, near Knoxville, Tennessee, where the promise of support from a maternal uncle failed to materialize. Frances helped support the family in various ways and in 1868 managed to place a story with *Godey's Lady's Book*. Within a few years Hodgson was being published regularly in *Godey's*, *Peterson's Ladies' Magazine*, *Scribner's Monthly*, and *Harper's*. In September 1873, after a year's visit to England, she married Dr. Swan Moses Burnett of New Market. During 1875–1876 they lived in Paris, where Dr. Burnett took advanced medical training.

Shortly after their return to Tennessee Burnett published her first novel, *That Lass o' Lowrie's*, 1877, which had previously been serialized in *Scribner's*. Like her short stories, the book combined a remarkable gift for realistic detail in portraying scenes of working-class life — unusual in that day — with a plot consisting of the most romantic and improbable of turns. It had a large sale in England and America and ended the Burnetts' financial problems. They moved to Washington, D.C., where she produced the novels *Haworth's*, 1879, *Louisiana*, 1880, *A Fair Barbarian*, 1881, and *Through One Administration*, 1883, and a play, *Esmeralda*, 1881, written with William Gillette, that was a great Broadway hit with Annie Russell in the title role.

In 1886 Burnett's most famous and successful book appeared. First serialized in *St. Nicholas* magazine, *Little Lord Fauntleroy* was intended as a children's book, but it had its greatest appeal to mothers, many of whom over the next decades plagued their sons with the long curls and lace and velvet outfits favored by the book's hero. *Little Lord Fauntleroy* sold over half a million copies, and Burnett's income was increased by her dramatized version, which quickly became a repertory standard on the order of *Uncle Tom's Cabin*. In 1888 she won a lawsuit in England over the dramatic rights to *Little Lord Fauntleroy*, establishing a precedent that was incorporated into British copyright law in 1911.

Later books, all in her vein of unremittingly sentimental romanticism, included *Sara Crewe*, 1888, *The Pretty Sister of José*, 1889, *Little Saint Elizabeth*, 1890, *Two Little Pilgrims' Progress*, 1895, *A Lady of Quality*, 1896, *The Making of a Marchioness*, 1900, *A Little Princess*, 1905, *The Shuttle*, 1907, *The Secret Garden*, 1910, *The Lost Prince*, 1914, and *Head of the House of Coombe*, 1921. Her plays *A Lady of Quality*, 1896, and *The First Gentleman of Europe*, 1897, were also successful in production. In 1893 she published a memoir of her youth, *The One I Knew Best of All*. From the mid-1890s she lived mainly in England, but in 1909 she built a house in Plandome, Long Island, New York, where she died on October 29, 1924. Her son Vivian Burnett, the model for Little Lord Fauntleroy, wrote a biography of her in 1927 entitled *The Romantick Lady*.

Burton, Virginia Lee 1909–1968 author and illustrator of children's books

Born on August 30, 1909, in Newton Centre, Massachusetts, Virginia Burton was a much younger half-sister of Harold H. Burton, later justice of the Supreme Court. She grew up from the age of seven in Sonora, California. After graduating from high school she studied both dancing and drawing, for a time at the California School of Fine Arts, and later she continued taking art lessons at the Boston Museum School. In 1929 she became a sketch artist for the *Boston Transcript*. In 1937 she published her first book, a children's story written, designed, and illustrated by herself and entitled *Choo Choo*. In 1939 she published *Mike Mulligan and His Steam Shovel*, in 1941 *Calico, the Wonder Horse*, and in 1942 *The Little House*, which won the Caldecott Medal for best illustrated children's book of the year. Later books included *Katy and the Big Snow*, 1943, *Maybelle the Cable Car*, 1952, and a play, *Life Story*, 1962. The appeal of her books was such that all but a few are still in print today. In addition to her own books she also illustrated *Song of Robin Hood* by A. B. Malcolmson, 1947, and an edition of Hans Christian Andersen's *The Emperor's New Clothes*, 1949. During the 1940s she taught graphic design and organized the Folly Cove Designers, whose linoleum block prints were popular. She died on October 15, 1968, in Boston.

Butler, Mother Marie Joseph 1860–1940 religious and educator

Born in Ballynunnery, County Kilkenny, Ireland, on July 22, 1860, Johanna Butler was educated in parish and private schools and in 1876 became a novice in the Congregation of the Sacred Heart of Mary in Béziers, France. She took Marie Joseph as her name in religion. In 1879 she was sent as a teacher to the order's convent school in Oporto, Portugal, where in April 1880 her novitiate ended and she entered into full membership in the order. In 1881 she was transferred to a convent school in Braga, Portugal, where she became superior in 1893.

In 1903 Mother Marie Joseph was directed to take charge of the order's school in Sag Harbor, Long Island, New York. She also had responsibility for expanding the work of the order in the United States, and to that end in December 1907, aided by a gift of land from a cousin, she opened Marymount School in Tarrytown, New York. By 1919 the school had developed into a college for Catholic women, and under her guidance it became a leader in Catholic higher education for the modern world. Other Marymount schools were later established to spread the work of the original: in 1923 Marymount Academy of Los Angeles, now Marymount College in Palos Verdes Estates; in 1923 Mariemont in Paris; in 1930 Mariamonte in Rome; in 1936 the two-year Marymount Manhattan College in New York City. In all 14 schools, 3 of them colleges, in the United States and 23 schools, novitiates, and other institutions in other countries were opened by the order under her influence. In 1926 she was elected Mother General of the Congregation of the Sacred Heart of Mary, making her the first American head of a Catholic order based in Europe. In 1927 she was naturalized a U.S. citizen. In addition to educational institutions she founded the Mother Butler Mission Guilds for social service and instituted the retreat movement for laywomen. She died in Tarrytown, New York, on April 23, 1940. In 1948 her cause for canonization was opened.

Cabrini, Frances Xavier 1850–1917 saint of the Roman Catholic Church

Born in Sant'Angelo Lodigiano in Lombardy, Italy, on July 15, 1850, Maria Francesca Cabrini was determined from her childhood to make religious work her life's vocation. She was educated by the Daughters of the Sacred Heart in Arluno, and at eighteen she became a schoolteacher in Vidardo. Delicate health prevented her from becoming a missionary, but her remarkable efforts in an orphanage in Codogno, where she went in 1874, earned her the name Mother Cabrini and led her bishop to encourage her to take religious vows in September 1877. She did not join a formal order. In November 1880 she founded the Missionary Sisters of the Sacred Heart of Jesus, which won papal recognition in March 1888. As superior, she saw the new order grow rapidly to seven convents in as many years. Her intention was to extend the order's orphanage and missionary work to China, but instead she was directed by Pope Leo XIII to utilize her abilities among the Italian poor in the United States.

Mother Cabrini arrived in New York City in March 1889 and from then until her death lived there and in Chicago. For a quarter century she traveled extensively throughout the Americas and in Europe founding convents, schools, orphanages, and hospitals. The New York City orphanage, opened in April 1889, was moved to West Park, New York, in 1890. A school in Granada, Nicaragua, was opened in 1891, followed by institutions in Panama, Peru, Argentina, and Brazil as well as several European cities. Columbus hospitals were established in New York City in 1892, in Chicago in 1905, and in Seattle in 1916. Schools and orphanages were opened in New York City, Philadelphia, Chicago, New Orleans, Denver, Los Angeles, Seattle, and elsewhere. She became a naturalized American citizen in 1909. The order she had founded was given final papal approval in 1907, and in 1910 Mother Cabrini was named superior general for life. By 1917 the order comprised 67 houses and over 1500 daughters. After her death in Chicago on December 22, 1917, proceedings were instituted that led to her beatification in November 1938 and her canonization by Pope Pius XII on July 7, 1946. She was the first American citizen to attain sainthood.

Calderone, Mary Steichen 1904– physician and writer

Born in New York City on July 1, 1904, Mary Steichen was the daughter of photographer Edward Steichen. She was educated privately in New York and France and graduated from Vassar College in 1925. For a time she studied acting but did not make a career of it. In 1935, having ended a first marriage, she entered the medical school of the University of Rochester. She graduated in 1939, interned for a year at Bellevue Hospital in New York, and then took further training at the Columbia University School of Public Health, from which she received an M.P.H. degree in 1942. In November 1941 she married Dr. Frank A. Calderone, a noted public health official.

After four years as a school physician in Great Neck, New York, she became medical director of the Planned Parenthood Federation of America in 1953. In that post she traveled and spoke widely on the topics of birth control and family planning and directed the federation's extensive research activities. She also wrote numerous articles for popular and professional periodicals, edited *Abortion in the United States*, 1958, and wrote *Release from Sexual Tensions*, 1960, and *Manual of Contraceptive Practice*, 1964, a pioneering medical text.

In May 1964 she became executive director of a new organization, the Sex Information and Education Council of the United States, known as SIECUS, which she had led in forming. She resigned from Planned Parenthood two months later. The goal of SIECUS was to promote research, discussion, and education in the wider field of human sexuality and thereby to develop a mature and responsible public attitude toward its various aspects. SIECUS was particularly active in developing sex education materials for young people. She remained executive director until 1975 and served as president of SIECUS from 1975 to 1982.

From 1982 to 1988 she was an adjunct professor of the program in Human Sexuality at New York University. She published two books dealing with children and sexuality, *The Family Book About Sexuality*, written with Eric W. Johnson, 1981, and *Talking with Your Child About Sex: Questions and Answers for Children from Birth to Puberty*, with James W. Ramey, 1982. Calderone continued to be a frequent and popular lecturer and was the recipient of numerous professional and humanitarian awards.

Caldicott, Helen Broinowski 1938– physician and anti-nuclear activist

Born in Melbourne, Australia, on August 7, 1938, Helen Broinowski graduated in 1961 from the University of Adelaide Medical School with bachelor of medicine and bachelor of surgery degrees, together the equivalent of an American M.D. She married William Caldicott, also a physician, in 1962; they became parents of three children. She worked as a general practitioner and pediatric intern, then founded and directed a cystic fibrosis clinic at Queen Elizabeth Hospital in Adelaide.

She began her antinuclear activism in 1971 with a warning to the Australian public about the potential consequences of the French government's atmospheric testing of nuclear weapons in the South Pacific. Pointing out the extent to which radioactive fallout was already present in food and water, she eventually enlisted scientists, newspaper editors, and the general public to oppose the tests. Her efforts led to demonstrations and boycotts of French products, and contributed to the 1972 electoral victory of the Labor Party, which opposed the testing. Her efforts to ban the Australian export of uranium were resisted by government and mining interests, but they influenced the Australian Council of Trade Unions to pass a 1975 resolution against the mining, transport, and sale of uranium, a ban which held until 1982.

In 1975 Caldicott and her family moved to the U.S.; settling in Boston, she became an associate at Children's Hospital Medical Center and an instructor in pediatrics at Harvard Medical School, 1977–80. There she published *Nuclear Madness: What You Can Do!*, with Nancy Herrington and Nahum Stiskin, in 1978. In this book and in numerous public lectures and television appearances, Caldicott explained the consequences of nuclear technology in vivid, accessible language.

In 1978 Caldicott took on the challenge of reviving an organization known as Physicians for Social Responsibility. Redirecting it to focus on the health risks posed by nuclear power, she oversaw an influx of new members in the aftermath a year later of an accident at the Three Mile Island nuclear reactor near Harrisburg, Pennsylvania. She also founded a Washington lobbying group, Women's Action for Nuclear Disarmament, in 1980.

Her views on the nuclear industry were featured in the 1982 film, *If You Love This Planet*, which was produced by the National Film Board of Canada. Although it won an Academy Award, the U.S. Department of Justice declared the film political propaganda and monitored its distribution. In 1983 Caldicott resigned as president of Physicians for Social Responsibility, citing differences between her goals and those of the wider membership. She received numerous humanitarian honors and was nominated for the Nobel Peace Prize in 1985.

In 1984 Caldicott published *Missile Envy: The Arms Race and Nuclear War*. A subsequent book, *If You Love This Planet: A Plan to Heal the Earth*, 1992, addressed broader environmental issues.

Caldwell, Sarah 1928?– opera producer, director, and conductor

Born about 1928 in Maryville, Missouri, Sarah Caldwell grew up in Fayetteville, Arkansas. She was a musical prodigy and before the age of ten was giving public violin recitals. After graduating from high school at fourteen, she studied briefly at Hendrix College and at the University of Arkansas before traveling to Boston to enter the New England Conservatory of Music. On completing her studies there she passed up offers to play with orchestras in order to work as assistant to Boris Goldovsky of the New England Opera Theater. Under Goldovsky she learned stage techniques, direction, and production and also did much scholarly work on operatic scores and librettos. Her first production on her own, of Ralph Vaughan Williams's *Riders to the Sea* in 1946, attracted the notice of Serge Koussevitsky, who offered her a post at the Berkshire Music Center at Tanglewood. For six summers she taught and assisted there while continuing to study conducting and stagecraft under Koussevitsky and Goldovsky. In 1952 she was appointed to head the opera workshop at Boston University, where she remained for five years, during which her productions included the American premiere of Hindemith's *Mathis der Maler*.

In 1957 Caldwell left the university to organize the Boston Opera Group (from 1965 the Opera Company of Boston), an independent company that notwithstanding its shoestring finances soon established a remarkable reputation in staging operas. Beginning with a performance of Offenbach's *Voyage to the Moon* in June 1958, from a score that Caldwell had edited, the Opera Group mounted productions in gymnasiums, old movie theaters, or wherever accommodations could be found. Later, when contributions and grants were more readily available, the group settled in the old Orpheum Theatre, still a less than ideal setting for opera. (The company did not find a permanent home until October 1978, when it bought the elegant Savoy Theatre.)

From the beginning the group was known for daring and innovation. Caldwell's understanding of opera as equally musical and visual experiences enabled her to mount spectacularly theatrical productions, and her scholarly bent brought to the Boston stage many new works along with the traditional operatic repertoire. Her scrupulously high standards and ingenuity more than overcame lack of resources and soon attracted performers of the highest caliber, including Joan Sutherland, Renata Tebaldi, Marilyn Home, Nicolai Gedda, and Boris Christoff. (Beverly Sills sang her first *Norma* and *Lucia di Lammermoor* under Caldwell's direction.) Among the Opera Group's productions were American premieres of Nono's *Intolleranza*, Schoenberg's *Moses und Aron*, Schuller's *The Fisherman and His Wife*, Bartok's *The Miraculous Mandarin*, Mussorgsky's *Boris Godunov* in the composer's own orchestration, the full version of Berlioz's *Les Troyens*, the five-act French edition of Verdi's *Don Carlos*, Glinka's *Russian and Ludmilla*, and Michael Tippett's *The Ice Break*, along with an amazing production of the rarely attempted *War and Peace* by Prokofiev and stagings of lesser-known works such as Kurka's *The Good Soldier Schweik*, Smetana's *The Bartered Bride*, and Berg's *Lulu*. In 1967–1968 Caldwell also directed the short-lived American National Opera Company.

Her production skills sometimes overshadowed her ability as a conductor, but gradually she became recognized in that field as well. She conducted the New York Philharmonic Orchestra in November 1975 and in January 1976 became the first woman to conduct at the Metropolitan Opera in New York, leading a production of *La Traviata* with Beverly Sills. In April 1977 she produced *Ariadne auf Naxos* with the New York City Opera.

She made great efforts to use opera to help countries communicate. In 1982 she drew up an agreement between the Opera Company of Boston and Imelda Marcos, First Lady of the Philippines, to advise and assist in the creation of an opera company in the Philippines. Later, she organized Making Music Together, an American-Soviet performing arts venture, which brought 285 Soviet performers to Boston in 1988 for collaborative musical concerts, ballet and opera performances with their American counterparts. In 1991 the second leg of the venture took place with American performers traveling to the Soviet Union for four months of performances.

Acknowledged one of the great operatic producers in the world, she has often been referred to as the "first lady of American opera."

Caldwell, Taylor 1900–1985 novelist

Born on September 7, 1900, in Manchester, England, Janet Taylor Caldwell came to the United States with her family in 1907 and settled in Buffalo, New York. From an early age she was interested chiefly in writing. From 1923 to 1931 she worked in various capacities in Buffalo offices of the U.S. Labor Department and the Immigration and Naturalization Service. She worked her way through the University of Buffalo (now the State University of New York at Buffalo), taking her degree in 1931.

Caldwell's first published work, a novel entitled *Dynasty of Death*, 1938, created a minor sensation in its portrayal of a family of munitions makers. The saga was continued in *The Eagles Gather*, 1940, and *The Final Hour*, 1944. Other books, typically dramatic tales set in the past and nearly all very popular, included *The Earth Is the Lord's*, 1940, *Time No Longer* (under the pseudonym Max Reiner), 1941, *The Strong City*, 1942, *The Arm and the Darkness*, 1943, *The Turnbulls*, 1943, *The Wide House*, 1945, *This Side of Innocence*, 1946, *There Was a Time*, 1947, *Melissa*, 1948, *Let Love Come Last*, 1949, *The Balance Wheel*, 1951, *The Devil's Advocate*, 1952, *Maggie — Her Marriage*, 1953, *Never Victorious, Never Defeated*, 1954, *Tender Victory*, 1956, *Sound of Thunder*, 1957, *Dear and Glorious Physician*, 1959, *Your Sins and Mine*, 1959, *The Listener*, 1960, *A Prologue to Love*, 1961, *Grandmother and the Priests*, 1963, *The Late Clara Beame*, 1963, *To See the Glory*, 1963, *A Pillar of Iron*, 1965, *No One Hears But Him*, 1966, *Dialogues With the Devil*, 1967, *The Beautiful Is Vanished*, 1967, *Testimony of Two Men*, 1968, *Great Lion of God*, 1970, *On Growing Up Tough*, 1971, *The Captains and the Kings*, 1972, *Glory and the Lightning*, 1974, *To Look and Pass*, 1974, *The Romance of Atlantis* (with Jess Steam), 1975, *Ceremony of the Innocent*, 1976, and *Bright Flows the River*, 1978.

A founding sponsor of the New York State Conservative Party, Caldwell included antiliberal political commentary in her novels. She remained an extremely popular writer throughout her life. Her 1981 novel *Answer As A Man* made the *New York Times* bestseller list before its official publication date. A number of her books were dramatized for motion pictures or television.

Her husband from May 1931, Marcus Reback, was a frequent collaborator on her books until his death in 1970. Caldwell died at her home in Greenwich, Connecticut, on August 30, 1985.

Calkins, Mary Whiton 1863–1930 philosopher, psychologist and educator

Born in Hartford, Connecticut, on March 30, 1863, Mary Calkins grew up mainly in Buffalo, New York, and moved with her family to Newton, Massachusetts, in 1880. She graduated from Smith College in 1885, and after a European journey with her family, during which she briefly attended Leipzig University, she joined the faculty of Wellesley College as a tutor in Greek in 1887. She advanced to instructor in 1889. In 1890 she began advanced studies in psychology and philosophy at Clark University and then at Harvard, where she studied under William James, Josiah Royce, and Hugo Münsterberg. She completed all the requirements for the Ph.D. and was recommended by the department for the degree in 1896, but Harvard declined to award it to a woman.

From 1890 to 1894 she was an instructor in psychology at Wellesley, and she subsequently advanced to associate professor of psychology in 1894 and of psychology and philosophy in 1896, and to professor of philosophy and psychology in 1898. In 1891 she established at Wellesley one of the earliest laboratories for experimental psychology in the country and the first in a women's college. Her own work in the field dealt primarily with such topics as space and time consciousness, emotion, association, color theory, and dreams. Her theory of "self-psychology" held, in contrast to the behaviorist view then in the ascendant, that the conscious self is the central fact of psychology. In the field of philosophy she acknowledged Royce's idealism as the chief influence leading to her own system of "personalistic absolutism."

Calkins' writings included more than a hundred papers in professional journals of psychology and philosophy, *An Introduction to Psychology*, 1901, *The Persistent Problems of Philosophy*, which went through five editions, 1907, *A First Book of Psychology*, 1909 and three subsequent editions, and *The Good Man and the Good*, 1918. In 1905 she became the first woman to be elected president of the American Psychological Association, and in 1918 she was accorded a similar honor by the American Philosophical Association. She was the first American woman to attain distinction in either field. Outside of academic life she interested herself in the Consumers' League, the American Civil Liberties Union, pacifism, socialism, and the cause of Sacco and Vanzetti. She retired from active teaching at Wellesley with the title of research professor, and she died in Newton, Massachusetts, on February 26, 1930.

Callas, Maria 1923–1977 opera singer

Born in New York City on December 3, 1923, Maria Anna Sofia Cecilia Kalogeropoulos was the daughter of Greek immigrants. She early developed an interest in singing and at fourteen, after the family had returned to Greece, traveled with her mother to enter the Royal Conservatory in Athens. Shortly thereafter, in late 1938, she made her operatic debut in Athens in *Cavalleria Rusticana*. Her career began in earnest in August 1947, when she appeared in Verona in *La Gioconda*. Soon, under the tutoring of conductor Tullio Serafin, she made debuts in Venice, Turin, and Florence. In 1949 she first appeared in Rome, Buenos Aires, and Naples, and in 1950 in Mexico City. Her powerful soprano voice, capable of sustaining both lyric and coloratura roles, was, although not perfect in control, intensely dramatic; combined with her strong sense of theater and her scrupulously high artistic standards, it took her quickly to the forefront of contemporary opera stars. Her talents made possible the revival of nineteenth-century bel canto works, notably those of Bellini and Donizetti, that had long been dropped from standard repertoires.

Callas made her debut at the prestigious La Scala in Milan in 1950, singing in *I Vespri Siciliani*. In 1952 she appeared at Covent Garden, London. Her American debut took place in November 1954 at Chicago's Lyric Opera, and in October 1956 her debut in *Norma* at the Metropolitan Opera in New York City drew a record audience. Her recordings were enthusiastically received, and she was one of the most popular singers of the period. Her much-publicized temperament, which led to several lengthy feuds with rivals and managers, reinforced in the public mind her status as prima donna but led also to her gradual withdrawal from the operatic stage. Her series of master classes at the Juilliard School in New York in 1971 was a great success. An attempt with tenor Giuseppe di Stefino to stage a production of *I Vespri Siciliani* in Turin in 1973 was less one. She retained nonetheless her powerful presence and her legion of adulatory followers around the world. Her last operatic performance was in *Tosca* at the Met in 1965. In 1973–1974 she made a final world concert tour. She died in Paris on September 16, 1977.

Cannon, Annie Jump 1863–1941 astronomer

Born on December 11, 1863, in Dover, Delaware, Annie Cannon graduated from Wellesley College in 1884. For several years thereafter she traveled and dabbled in photography and music. In 1894 she returned to Wellesley for a year of advanced study in astronomy, and in 1895 she enrolled at Radcliffe in order to continue her studies under Professor Edward C. Pickering. In 1896 she was named an assistant in the Harvard Observatory. There, joining Williamina P. S. Fleming, she devoted her energies to the ambitious project, begun in 1885 by Pickering, the observatory's director, of recording, classifying, and cataloging the spectra of all stars down to those of the ninth magnitude. The scheme of spectral classification by surface temperature used for the project and later (1910) universally adopted was largely her work, developed out of Pickering's and Fleming's earlier systems, and she eventually obtained and classified spectra for more than 225,000 stars, publishing them in nine volumes as the *Henry Draper Catalogue*, 1918–1924.

In 1911 Cannon succeeded Fleming as curator of astronomical photographs at the observatory, and in 1938 she was named William Cranch Bond Professor of Astronomy. After 1924 she extended her work, cataloging tens of thousands of additional stars down to the eleventh magnitude for the *Henry Draper Extension*, published in two volumes in 1925 and 1949. The work was an invaluable contribution to astronomy, bearing strongly on countless other problems and areas of research and exerting major influence on the evolution of the science from one of mere observation to one of great theoretical and philosophical content. In the course of her work she also discovered some 300 variable stars and 5 novae. Among the numerous honors and awards accorded her were the first honorary doctorate from Oxford University to be awarded to a woman, 1925, and the Henry Draper Medal of the National Academy of Sciences in 1931. In 1933 she established the Annie J. Cannon Prize of the American Astronomical Society. Cannon officially retired from the observatory in 1940 but carried on research until her death in Cambridge, Massachusetts, on April 13, 1941.

Cannon, Harriet Starr 1823–1896 religious

Born on May 7, 1823, in Charleston, South Carolina, Harriet Cannon was left an orphan at the age of one and was reared by an aunt in Bridgeport, Connecticut. She attended local schools and studied music privately. In 1851 she moved to Brooklyn, New York, to be near her elder sister and supported herself by giving music lessons. The death of her sister in 1855 was a great loss, and in February 1856 she entered the Episcopal Sisterhood of the Holy Communion headed by Sister Anne Ayres. She became a full member in February 1857. In 1858 she was given charge of a ward in the newly opened St. Luke's Hospital, staffed by the order. A growing disagreement with the rule of the order, which she had hoped would be more traditionally conventual, culminated in her being asked to leave St. Luke's in early 1863; four others of like mind left with her. In September 1863 they were invited by Bishop Horatio Potter to take charge of the House of Mercy, a rescue house and reformatory for young women. A year later they also took over the Sheltering Arms orphanage and in February 1865 St. Barnabas' House for homeless women and children. After much planning the informally associated sisters became the founding members of the Community of St. Mary in February 1865, the first women's monastic order constituted by an Anglican bishop. In September Sister Harriet was elected first superior of the order. She made her life vows in February 1867. At first the order was met with widespread suspicion of their very Roman Catholic like rule; they were dismissed from St. Barnabas' in 1867 and from Sheltering Arms in 1870. They made a success, however, of St. Mary's School in New York City, opened in 1868, and followed it with St. Gabriel's School in Peekskill, New York, in 1872, St. Mary's School in Memphis, Tennessee, in 1873, and Kemper Hall in Kenosha, Wisconsin, in 1878. St. Mary's Free Hospital for Poor Children opened in New York City in 1870, and city missions serving immigrant neighborhoods were established in New York in 1880 and in Chicago in 1886. Mother Harriet died at St. Mary's convent at Peekskill, New York, on April 5, 1896.

Caraway, Hattie Ophelia Wyatt 1878–1950 public official

Born on February 1, 1878, near Bakerville, Tennessee, Hattie Wyatt grew up there and in nearby Hustburg. In 1896 she graduated from Dickson Normal School in Dickson,

Tennessee, and for a time thereafter taught school. In February 1902 she married Thaddeus H. Caraway, with whom she settled in Jonesboro, Arkansas. She devoted herself mainly to homemaking while her husband graduated from lawyer to congressman to senator.

On his death in November 1931 Caraway was appointed by the governor to fill his seat until a special election could be held; she was the second woman to be seated in the U.S. Senate, following Rebecca L. Felton nine years earlier. In January 1932, however, she became the first woman to be elected to the Senate as she was thus confirmed for the remainder of the term. She took her duties seriously and proved their equal. Nonetheless surprise was general when, while presiding over the Senate (another first for a woman) on May 9, 1932, she announced her candidacy for a full term. In the Democratic primary campaign in Arkansas she faced strong opposition, but with the aid of a barnstorming campaign whirl by Senator Huey Long of Louisiana she won the August primary, a victory tantamount to election. She was duly elected in November and began her full term in March 1933.

In her voting Caraway generally supported the New Deal and other legislation of the Roosevelt administration; she opposed isolationism, supported veterans and organized labor, and in 1943 became the first woman in Congress to co-sponsor the Equal Rights Amendment. She served as chairman of the Committee on Enrolled Bills and on October 28, 1943, served as president pro tem of the Senate, both firsts for women. Her reelection in 1938 after a primary victory over Rep. John L. McClellan firmly established her as a senator in her own right, and her dry humor and homely sayings made her a favorite national figure. In the 1944 Democratic primary in Arkansas she was defeated by Rep. J. William Fulbright, and she left the Senate in 1945. She was promptly appointed to the Federal Employees' Compensation Commission (later the Bureau of Employees' Compensation) by President Roosevelt. In July 1946 she was appointed to the Employees' Compensation Appeals Board. She resigned that post for health reasons in January 1950, and she died in Falls Church, Virginia, on December 21, 1950.

Carroll, Anna Ella 1815–1893 political theorist and pamphleteer

Born on August 29, 1815, near Pocomoke City, Maryland, Anna Carroll was a member of one of the state's most prominent families. In 1829–1830 her father served as governor. Family financial reverses obliged her to conduct a boarding school for a time in the late 1830s. After several years of obscurity she emerged in the 1850s as a spokesman for the virulently anti-Catholic and antiforeign "Know-Nothing" (American) party. She published a series of lectures on the Catholic menace in 1854 and *The Great American Battle*, a Know-Nothing apology, in 1856, and in the latter year she campaigned widely for Millard Fillmore, the Know-Nothing candidate for president. Her next book, *The Star of the West*, 1857, was in much the same vein, and she continued to publish newspaper articles on anti-Catholic topics. At the outbreak of the Civil War she settled in Washington, D.C., as an ardent Unionist and began writing letters, articles, and pamphlets in support of the federal government.

In *The War Powers of the General Government*, 1861, and *The Relation of the National Government to the Revolted Citizens Defined*, 1862, both published at her own expense, Carroll outlined a constitutional theory under which the secession of Southern states and the formation of the Confederacy were legal nullities. She held that the general rebellion was merely the sum of individual acts of rebellion, that the states would automatically resume their former relation to the central government when the rebellion had been put down, and that therefore the executive power superseded the legislative in prosecuting both war and reconstruction. This theory was precisely that under which President Abraham Lincoln exercised war-time authority and which he pressed against the competing claims of Congress. In mid-1862, in the belief that she had a firm agreement to be paid for her services — a former assistant secretary of war had made her some vague assurances — she carried a demand for $50,000 all the way to Lincoln and was rebuffed. She continued to press her claim in various ways, but in 1870 it was eclipsed by a far more spectacular one, namely, that she had originated the military strategy that had broken the Confederacy.

In 1861 she had visited St. Louis and there met Charles Scott, a riverboat pilot and amateur strategist who outlined to her his plan for a Union invasion of the South along the Tennessee River. Later that year she submitted a lengthy memorandum to the War Department on the plan, crediting Scott. General Ulysses S. Grant's successful drive up the Tennessee to Forts Henry and Donelson in February 1862 seemed to prove that the Scott plan had been adopted, and as late as 1865 Anna Carroll acknowledged Scott's authorship publicly. In 1870, however, she claimed it herself and petitioned Congress for payment. With the aid of a long-time friend, a Texas politician and railroad investor, she secured by various questionable means affidavits from a number of prominent persons, many of which she apparently altered to strengthen them. Her petitions and memorials to Congress continued to appear until her death, and while the claim was never officially accepted, she became something of a cause célèbre among feminists. She died in Washington, D.C., on February 19, 1893.

Carson, Rachel Louise 1907–1964 biologist and science writer

Born in Springdale, Pennsylvania, on May 27, 1907, Rachel Carson early developed a deep interest in the natural world. She entered Pennsylvania College for Women with the intention of becoming a writer but soon changed her major field of study from English to biology. Graduating in 1929, she went to The Johns Hopkins University for graduate work and in 1931 joined the faculty of the University of Maryland, where she taught for five years; she received her M.A. from Johns Hopkins in 1932. From 1929 to 1936 she also taught in the Johns Hopkins summer school and pursued postgraduate studies at the Marine Biological Laboratory in Woods Hole, Massachusetts.

In 1936 Carson took a position as aquatic biologist with the U.S. Bureau of Fisheries (from 1940 the Fish and Wildlife Service), where she remained until 1952, the last three years as editor-in-chief of Service publications. An article in the *Atlantic Monthly* in 1937 served as the basis for her first book, *Under the Sea Wind*, published in 1941. It was widely praised, as were all her books, for its remarkable combination of scientific accuracy and thoroughness with an elegant and lyrical prose style. *The Sea Around Us*, 1951, became a national best-seller, won a National Book Award, and was eventually translated into 30 languages. In 1951 a Guggenheim fellowship enabled her to begin work on her third book, *The Edge of the Sea*, published in 1955.

Her final book *Silent Spring*, 1962, was also a best-seller, but unlike its predecessors it raised a national controversy. In it Carson examined the widespread and rapidly growing use of chemical pesticides and herbicides and charged that indiscriminate use of such substances held great danger of permanently upsetting the natural ecological balance in the world. The book aroused public opinion and gave rise to governmental inquiries into the problem; before any substantive results were achieved, however, she died at her home in Silver Spring, Maryland, on April 14, 1964. Among her numerous awards were the 1952 John Burroughs Medal, the 1954 Gold Medal of the New York Zoological Society, and the 1963 Conservationist of the Year award of the National Wildlife Federation.

Carter, Betty 1930– jazz singer

Born in Flint, Michigan, on May 16, 1930, Lillie Mae Jones moved with her family to Detroit during World War II, taking advantage of the new factory job opportunities that the war had created for African-Americans. Her parents were both amateur musicians, and she studied piano at the Detroit Conservatory of Music. Her strongest musical influence, however, was the bebop jazz of musicians such as Charlie Parker. ("Bebop was my life," she said.) At age 16 she began singing in Detroit clubs, and after 1946 she worked in black bars and theaters in the Midwest, at first under the name Lorene Carter.

Inspired by vocalists Billie Holiday and Sarah Vaughan, Carter strove to create a style of her own; influenced by the improvisational nature of bebop, she felt each performance should be unique. One night in 1948, after singing with Lionel Hampton, Hampton asked Carter to join his band. Her insistence on improvising, however, repeatedly annoyed Hampton — he called her "Betty Be-bop" — and prompted him to fire her seven times in 2½ years. Carter left Hampton's band in 1951 for an engagement at the Apollo Bar, then performed around the country in such jazz clubs as Harlem's Apollo Theater and the Vanguard in New York, the Showboat in Philadelphia, and Blues Alley in Washington, D.C. In clubs like these she performed with such jazz artists as Charlie Parker, Dizzy Gillespie, Miles Davis, Max Roach, Muddy Waters, T-Bone Walker, Thelonious Monk, Moms Mabley, Ray Bryant, and Gigi Gryce.

After touring with Ray Charles from 1960 to 1963 and recording with him the album *The Invisible Betty Carter*, 1961, Carter took time off to get married and to raise two sons, Myles and Kagle. Her marriage did not last, however, and Carter returned to the stage in 1969 — "you got to do what you got to do," she said — backed by a small acoustic ensemble consisting of piano, drums and bass. In 1971 she released her first album on her own label, Bet-Car Records.

Beginning in the 1970s, Carter toured the college circuit, appearing or conducting jazz workshops at Harvard, Dartmouth, and Goddard College. After appearing at Carnegie Hall as part of the Newport Jazz Festival in 1977 and 1978, she developed a larger, international audience; this led to concert tours through both the U.S. and Europe. Her solo albums include *Betty Carter*, 1953, *Out There*, 1958, *The Modern Sound of Betty Carter*, 1960, *The Audience with Betty Carter*, 1980. She appeared in Howard Moore's musical, *Don't Call Me Man* at the Billie Holiday Theater in Brooklyn, 1975. Her album *Look What I Got!*, 1989, won a Grammy Award.

Cary, Alice and Phoebe 1820–1871 and 1824–1871 writers and poets

Born near Cincinnati, Alice on April 26, 1820, and Phoebe on September 4, 1824, the Cary sisters grew up on a farm and received little schooling. Nevertheless they were for their time well educated, Alice by their mother and Phoebe by Alice, and they early developed a taste for literature that could not be dampened by their unsympathetic stepmother, whom their father married in 1837.

Alice's first published poem appeared in the *Sentinel*, a Cincinnati Universalist newspaper, when she was eighteen; for ten years thereafter she continued to contribute poems and prose sketches to various periodicals with no remuneration. Phoebe began to write under Alice's guidance and had her first poem published in a Boston newspaper about the time of Alice's first. Their work attracted the favorable notice of Edgar Allan Poe, Horace Greeley, John Greenleaf Whittier, and Rufus W. Griswold, through whose recommendation in 1850 they published *Poems of Alice and Phoebe Carey* [sic], some two-thirds of which was the work of Alice. The book's modest success encouraged them to move to New York City.

In New York City, Alice and Phoebe took a house and lived frugally while establishing themselves as regular contributors to *Harper's*, the *Atlantic Monthly*, and other periodicals. Alice, much more prolific than her sister, enjoyed the higher reputation during her lifetime, although Phoebe was later held in greater critical esteem for the wit and feeling of her poems. Their salon became a popular meeting place for the leading literary lights of New York, and both women were famed for their hospitality.

Among Alice's books were two volumes of reminiscent sketches entitled *Clovernook Papers*, 1852 and 1853, *Hagar, A Story of To-day*, a novel, 1852, *Lyra and Other Poems*, 1852, *The Maiden of Tiascala*, 1855, *The Clovernook Children*, 1855, *Married, Not Mated*, a novel, 1856, *Pictures of Country Life*, 1859, *Ballads, Lyrics, and Hymns*, 1866 *Snow-Berries: A Book for Young Folks*, 1867, *The Bishop's Son*, a novel, 1867, and *The Lover's Diary*, 1868. Phoebe, much of whose time was devoted to keeping house and, in later years, to caring for Alice, published only *Poems and Parodies*, 1854, and *Poems of Faith, Hope and Love*, 1868, but one of her religious verses, "Nearer Home" (sometimes called, from the first line, "One Sweetly Solemn Thought") became widely popular as a hymn.

Both sisters were supporters of the women's rights movement of the day. Phoebe was for a short time an assistant editor of Susan B. Anthony's paper *Revolution*. In 1868 Alice reluctantly agreed to serve as first president of Sorosis, the pioneer women's club founded by Jane Croly. After a long illness Alice died in New York City on February 12, 1871; exhausted by grief and stricken with malaria, Phoebe died soon after, on July 31, 1871, in Newport, Rhode Island.

Cary, Annie Louise 1841–1921 singer

Born in Wayne, Maine, on October 22, 1841, Ann Louisa Cary, as she was originally named, grew up in Yarmouth and Gorham and graduated from Gorham Seminary in 1860. She then went to Boston to study music and singing. There she sang with church choirs and with the Handel and Haydn Society. A benefit concert at Boston Music Hall produced the necessary funds for continuing her studies in Europe, for which she set out in August 1866. After a year under Giovanni Corsi in Milan she overcame her moral misgivings about opera and accepted an operatic engagement in Copenhagen, where she made her debut in January 1868 in Verdi's *Un ballo in maschera*. For the next two seasons she continued to appear in operatic roles in Stockholm, Oslo, and Hamburg while studying in the summer with Mme. Pauline Viardot-Garcia in Baden-Baden and Giovanni Bottesini in Paris.

In April 1870 Cary made her London debut at Covent Garden in Donizetti's *Lucrezia Borgia*. That year she was engaged by a company organized by the German-American impresarios Max and Maurice Strakosch and featuring Christine Nilsson. With that company Annie Cary made her New York concert debut at Steinway Hall in September 1870 and won universal praise; Anton Rubinstein called her voice "the most beautiful I have ever heard in the whole world." Her New York operatic debut came in October 1871 in the Nilsson company's production of Flotow's *Martha*. She was thereafter established as the preeminent contralto in both concert and opera on the American stage and perhaps in the world. Her rich dramatic voice, three-octave range, and command of the grand style kept her foremost for a decade.

In November 1873 Cary sang Amneris in the American premiere of *Aïda* at the New York Academy of Music, and in an 1874 New York production of *Lohengrin* she became the first American woman to sing a Wagnerian role in America. She took part in the American premieres of Verdi's *Requiem* in New York in November 1874, Bach's *Magnificat* in Cincinnati in May 1875, Bach's *Christmas Oratorio* in Boston in May 1877, and Boito's *Mefistofele* in New York in November 1880. She also appeared in numerous major festivals. In 1876 and 1877 she sang in Moscow and St. Petersburg, and in 1879–1881 she toured in the company of British impresario Colonel James H. Mapleson. Her final operatic performance was in *Un ballo in maschera* in Philadelphia in April 1881. Her voice had been troubling her for some time, and following an appearance in New York in May 1882 she retired. In June 1882 she married Charles M. Raymond, a New York banker. She sang occasionally in later years with a church choir. She died in Norwalk, Connecticut, on April 3, 1921.

Cary, Elisabeth Luther 1867–1936 art and literary critic

Born in Brooklyn, New York, on May 18, 1867, Elisabeth Cary was educated at home by her father, a newspaper editor, and for ten years studied painting with local teachers. She became deeply interested in literature and began her career by publishing three translations from the French: *Recollections of Middle Life*, by Francisque Sarcey, 1893, *Russian Portraits* by E. Melchior de Vogüé, 1895, and *The Land of Tawny Beasts* by "Pierre Maël" (Charles Causse and Charles Vincent), 1895. In 1898 she published her first original work, a critical appreciation entitled *Tennyson: His Homes, His Friends, and His Work*. A similar *Browning, Poet and Man*, 1899, was followed by *The Rossettis: Dante Gabriel and Christina*, 1900, *William Morris, Poet, Craftsman, Socialist*, 1902, *Emerson, Poet and Thinker*, 1904, and *The Novels of Henry James*, 1905. Her critical scheme placed emphasis on moral earnestness, refinement, and beauty of expression, values that informed her own writing as well as that of her subjects. Subsequent books dealt with art and artists and included *The Art of William Blake*, 1907, *Honoré Daumier*, 1907, *The Works of James McNeill Whistler*, 1907, and *Artists Past and Present: Random Studies*, 1909. In 1905 she had begun writing and publishing a small art monthly called the *Scrip*.

In 1908 Adolph S. Ochs, publisher of the *New York Times*, was impressed by a copy of the magazine and offered Cary a job as art critic for his newspaper. There had been no such position before, and over the next 28 years she worked diligently to make it an integral part both of the newspaper and of the New York art scene. Her calm and conscientious reviews of gallery and museum shows over the years struck a consistent note of open-minded, genuine interest through the turmoil of early twentieth-century art. While devoted to standards of an earlier era, she was willing and eager to find them expressed in new modes. After 1927 she gave up much of the chore of reviewing and wrote mainly feature articles, often on her own field of particular interest, printmaking. She died in Brooklyn on July 13, 1936.

Cassatt, Mary Stevenson 1844–1926 painter

Born on May 22, 1844, in Allegheny City (now part of Pittsburgh), Pennsylvania, Mary Cassatt lived in Europe for five years as a young girl. She was tutored privately in art in Philadelphia and attended the Pennsylvania Academy of the Fine Arts in 1861–1865, but she preferred learning on her own and in 1866 traveled to Europe to study. Her first major showing was at the Paris Salon of 1872; four more annual Salon exhibitions followed.

In 1874 Cassatt chose Paris as her permanent residence and established her studio there. She shared with the Impressionists an interest in experiment and in using bright colors inspired by the out-of-doors. Edgar Degas became her friend; his style and that of Gustave Courbet inspired her own. Degas was known to admire her drawing especially, and at his request she exhibited with the Impressionists in 1879 and joined them in shows in 1880, 1881, and 1886. Although she was known to be an American artist, she was generally identified with the French group. Her depictions of mothers and children were celebrated examples of her warm, individual style, which was characterized by the combination of delicate color and strong line. The etchings she produced were compared in quality to James Whistler's. Equally fine were her color prints and pastels, many of which displayed the influence of Japanese art.

From 1876 Cassatt's works were exhibited in the United States, where they were the earliest examples seen in the Impressionist manner. She had a one woman exhibition in the Gallery of Durand-Ruel in Paris in 1891 and another and larger one in 1893. Through her influence on wealthy friends and relatives she oversaw the purchase of a great many Impressionist masterpieces for American private and public collections. Her eyesight began to fail about 1900; she ceased work by 1914 and died at Château de Beaufresne, her country home in Mesnil-Theribus, north of Paris, on June 14, 1926.

Castillo, Ana 1953– poet and novelist

Born on June 15, 1953, in Chicago, Ana Hernandez del Castillo was the daughter of Mexican-American parents who migrated from the Southwest to Chicago. She graduated from Northeastern Illinois University in 1975 with a degree in art education. There she became involved in Latino artistic, activist and intellectual circles of the 1970s, joining such organizations as the Latino Brotherhood of Artists and the Movimiento Artistico Chicano. She was part of the groundswell of Latina writers in the U.S. exploring their ethnic identities through the lens of sexual politics and their sexual politics through their ethnic origins.

During this period, her interest in writing and peforming poetry grew, and her first collection of poems, *Otro Canto*, 1977, was published as a chapbook with the help of a grant from the Illinois Arts Council. Two years later, shortly after receiving an M.A. in social sciences from the University of Chicago, she published a second chapbook, *The Invitation*, 1979, in which female speakers described the experience of the erotic in their own terms.

Her work then took a theatrical turn. From 1981 to 1982 she created and managed the Al Andalus flamenco performance troupe. She also adapted *The Invitation* to music, and the poems were performed at the 1982 Soho Art Festival in New York City. In 1983 her play, *Clark Street Counts* was performed by the Chicana Raza Group.

Castillo's work draws on the sometimes contradictory political influences of militant ethnic and economic struggles and feminist and lesbian perspectives. *Otro Canto* took a revolutionary Marxist stance on the plight of the urban poor. *Women are not Roses*, 1984, explored the difficulties of poor and working class women who must choose between devoting their energies to erotic relationships or to class struggle. Castillo characterized these arenas as feminine and masculine, respectively, and looks at how women claim their own sexuality as they negotiate between them.

The Mixquiahuala Letters, 1986, extended her exploration of Latina women's attempts to appropriate their sexuality, and of the reactions of men in the Anglo and Latino communities to these attempts. Written in an experimental form, the novel consists of letters sent over 10 years between two Latina women, arranged to be read in three different versions for three different types of reader: "The Conformist," "The Cynic," and "The Quixotic."

Castillo's other works included *Zero Makes Me Hungry*, 1975, and *My Father was a Toltec*, 1988, two collections of poetry. She was also the editor, with Cherrié Moraga, of the 1988 Spanish language edition of *This Bridge Called My Back: Writings by Radical Women of Color*, which she translated with Norma Alarcon. In 1993 she published another novel, *So Far from God*.

Cather, Willa Sibert 1873–1947 novelist

Born on December 7, 1873, near Winchester, Virginia, Willa (originally Wilella) Cather moved with her family to frontier Nebraska when she was nine and grew up in the village of Red Cloud from the age of ten. In 1895 she graduated from the University of Nebraska. She was a journalist for a few years in Pittsburgh, managing and editing the *Home Monthly* magazine in 1896–1897 and then reviewing drama and music for the *Pittsburgh Daily Leader*, and in 1901 she became a schoolteacher.

In 1903 Cather published a book of verse, *April Twilights*, and in 1905 a collection of short stories entitled *The Troll Garden*. The latter won her a position as managing editor of *McClure's Magazine*, where she remained until resigning in 1912 to devote herself

HOLLINGER

Willa Cather

entirely to writing. Her first novel, serialized in *McClure's* and then published as *Alexander's Bridge*, 1912, was a somewhat contrived work, but largely under the influence of the writer Sarah Orne Jewett she found her true literary inspiration in the frontier life of her childhood. *O Pioneers!*, 1913, and *My Antonia*, 1918, set the themes that were to infuse her best work, the heroic spirit of the Bohemian, Swedish, Russian, German, French, and other pioneers she had known and their conquest of hardships. *One of Ours*, 1922, won a Pulitzer Prize; that novel, like *A Lost Lady*, 1923, mourned the passing of the frontier and the virtues associated with it. *The Song of the Lark*, 1915, *Youth and the Bright Medusa*, 1920, and *Lucy Gayheart*, 1935, expressed the converse truth of the often stifling conventionality of small town life.

Cather's disillusionment with the values of the modern age deepened with the years and was reflected in *The Professor's House*, 1925, *My Mortal Enemy*, 1926, and in the essays collected in *Not Under Forty*, 1936. In *Death Comes for the Archbishop*, 1927, and *Shadows on the Rock*, 1931, she turned to an earlier era, that of the French missionaries in America, to recapture a heroism lost to the modern world. *Obscure Destinies*, three stories, appeared in 1932, and in 1940 she published her last novel, *Sapphira and the Slave Girl*. She died in New York City on April 24, 1947.

Carrie Chapman Catt

Catt, Carrie Clinton Lane Chapman 1859–1947 reformer

Born on January 9, 1859, in Ripon, Wisconsin, Carrie Lane grew up there and from 1866 in Charles City, Iowa. She worked her way through Iowa State College (now University), graduated in 1880, and after a short time spent reading law became a high school principal in Mason City in 1881. Two years later she was appointed superintendent of schools, one of the first women to hold such a position. In February 1885 she married Leo Chapman, publisher and editor of the *Mason City Republican*. In 1886 he died while visiting California preparatory to moving there and before Carrie Chapman could join him. Stranded on her arrival in San Francisco, she worked briefly as a newspaper reporter there and then returned to Iowa in 1887.

A short time later Chapman joined and became an organizer for the Iowa Woman Suffrage Association. In June 1890 she married George W. Catt, a Seattle, Washington, engineer who encouraged her to continue her suffrage work. As an organizer Catt was highly successful. In 1895 she was named chairman of the organization committee in charge of field work of the National American Woman Suffrage Association, and in 1900 she was elected to succeed Susan B. Anthony as president of the association. In 1904 in Berlin she was a founder of the International Woman Suffrage Alliance, of which she served as president until 1923 and thereafter as honorary chairman. In 1904 she resigned the presidency of the national organization to care for her husband, who died the next year.

At the outbreak of World War I Catt joined Jane Addams and others in forming the Woman's Peace party. In 1913–1915 she led a brilliant although unsuccessful woman suffrage campaign in New York, and in December 1915 she was again elected president of the National American Woman Suffrage Association. Buoyed by the nearly $1 million bequest of Miriam Leslie, the organization adopted Catt's "Winning Plan" and opened a massive drive for a constitutional amendment to provide national woman suffrage. The success of a second New York State referendum in 1917, followed by President Woodrow Wilson's conversion to the cause of suffrage in 1918 attested the effectiveness of Catt's flexible strategy of working at both federal and state levels to build support for woman suffrage. Tireless lobbying in Congress (directed by Maud Wood Park) and then in state legislatures finally produced a ratified Nineteenth Amendment in August 1920. The final triumph was in large part a tribute to her imaginative and tactful leadership.

The year before, she had prepared for victory by laying the groundwork for what was organized in 1920 as the League of Women Voters to undertake necessary educational work; she was honorary president of the league for the rest of her life. In 1923 she published *Woman Suffrage and Politics: The Inner Story of the Suffrage Movement* with Nettie R. Shuler. In 1925 Catt founded the National Committee on the Cause and Cure of War and served as its chairman until 1932 (thereafter as honorary chairman). She was active also in support of the League of Nations, for relief of Jewish refugees from Germany, and on behalf of a child-labor amendment. She strongly supported the United Nations after World War II. Widely honored as one of the outstanding women of her time, Catt died in New Rochelle, New York, on March 9, 1947.

Channing, Carol 1923– actor and singer

Born on January 31, 1923, in Seattle, Washington, Carol Channing grew up in San Francisco. She left Bennington College in early 1941, during her second year there, to seek a career in show business. Praise for a small part in Marc Blitzstein's short-running *No For an Answer* was an early boost, and in 1941–1942 she was for several months an understudy in Cole Porter's *Let's Face It*. After a dramatic role in the unsuccessful *Proof Through the Night* in December 1942 she turned to nightclub work, evolving an act that included impressions and satirical bits. For a number of years she made little progress in her chosen profession and was forced to take other jobs for support.

In 1948, however, Channing won a role in *Lend an Ear*, a satirical revue staged in Los Angeles by Gower Champion. In December the show moved to New York, where it lasted for a year and brought Channing considerable critical attention. In December 1949 she opened on Broadway in the leading role of Lorelei Lee in an adaptation of Anita Loos's *Gentlemen Prefer Blondes*. Her characterization of the coy, gold-digging Lorelei, highlighted by the show-stopping song "Diamonds Are a Girl's Best Friend," was a sensation; the show ran nearly two years on Broadway and another year on tour. Over the next several years she appeared in Leonard Bernstein's *Wonderful Town* in 1953, *The Vamp*, an unsuccessful 1955 musical comedy, and *The First Traveling Saleslady*, a 1956 motion picture of little distinction, and then returned to nightclub work for a time. In 1961–1962 she starred in *Show Girl*, a musical revue, and in 1962–1963 she teamed with George Burns for a while.

In January 1964 Channing returned to Broadway in *Hello, Dolly!*, a Jerry Herman adaptation of *The Matchmaker* by Thornton Wilder. Her realization of the role of the brassy, indomitable Dolly Gallagher Levi was her second unique and classic creation in American musical comedy, and it won her a Tony Award for best musical comedy actress. In 1967 she won a Golden Globe Award for her supporting role in the motion picture *Thoroughly Modern Millie*, and in 1968 she was given a special Tony award. In 1971 she appeared in *Four On a Garden*, and in January-November 1974 she revived one of her great characters in a revue titled *Lorelei*. She also revived her leading role in *Hello, Dolly!* in New York and London from 1977 to 1980, and again in 1985. A frequent guest star of many television shows, she also hosted her own TV specials. She starred briefly with Mary Martin in the comedy *Legends* in 1985–1986, and played the White Queen in *Alice in Wonderland*, 1986.

Chapman, Maria Weston 1806–1885 abolitionist

Born in Weymouth, Massachusetts, on July 25, 1806, Maria Weston spent several years of her youth living with the family of an uncle in England, where she received a good education. In 1828 she was appointed lady principal of the Young Ladies' High School in Boston, a post she held until her marriage in October 1830 to Henry G. Chapman, a merchant. Within a short time, under the influence of her husband and his family, all followers of William Lloyd Garrison, she entered into the movement for the abolition of slavery, a step that placed her outside the pale of most of Boston society. In 1832 she helped organize the Boston Female Anti-Slavery Society. She edited *Right and Wrong in Boston*, the annual report of the society, from 1836 to 1840 and braved public hostility to circulate petitions. When Garrison was mobbed while attempting to address the society in October 1835, the meeting adjourned in stately procession to Chapman's home. She quickly became a valued lieutenant to Garrison, occasionally editing his newspaper, the *Liberator*, and in 1839–1842 she edited the *Non-Resistant*, organ of the New England Non-Resistance Society. She was a leader in the Massachusetts Anti-Slavery Society and was instrumental in forwarding the work of Sarah and Angelina Grimké and others.

In 1836 she published a collection of *Songs of the Free, and Hymns of Christian Freedom*. In May 1838 she addressed the Anti-Slavery Convention of American Women in Philadelphia in defiance of a threatening mob. (The mob returned the next day and burned down the hall.) In 1839 she published *Right and Wrong in Massachusetts*, a pamphlet on the split in abolitionist ranks. From 1839 to 1846 and occasionally thereafter she edited the annual *Liberty Bell*, a gift book sold to support abolitionist work. In 1840 she was elected to the executive committee of the American Anti-Slavery Society. She assisted Garrison in establishing the *National Anti-Slavery Standard* in 1840, and after a period of public inactivity occasioned by her husband's death in 1842 she became co-editor of the journal in 1844. From 1848 to 1855 she lived in Paris; in the latter year she returned to Boston and published *How Can I Help to Abolish Slavery?* For a time during the Civil War she lived in New York City, and she later settled in her native town of Weymouth. In 1877 she published an edition of the autobiography of Harriet Martineau, an old friend, to which she appended a lengthy memoir. She died in Weymouth, Massachusetts, on July 12, 1885. The essayist and poet John Jay Chapman was her grandson.

Chase, Mary Ellen 1887–1973 literary critic and educator

Born in Blue Hill, Maine, on February 24, 1887, Mary Ellen Chase attended local public schools. She graduated from the University of Maine in 1909 and for nine years thereafter taught school. During that period she published her first novel, *His Birthday*, 1915, and two books for children, *The Girl from the Bighorn Country*, 1916, and *Virginia of Elk Creek Valley*, 1917. In 1918 she became an instructor at the University of Minnesota and undertook graduate studies in English that earned her a Ph.D. in 1922. In that year she was appointed an assistant professor. In 1926 she joined the faculty of Smith College as an associate professor; she advanced to full professor in 1929. Her academic writings included *The Art of Narration*, with W. F. K. Del Plaine, 1926, *Thomas Hardy from Serial to Novel*, 1927, *The Writing of Informal Essays*, with M. E. Macgregor, 1928, *Constructive Theme Writing*, 1929, and *The Bible and the Common Reader*, 1944. More important were her novels, *Uplands*, 1927, *Mary Peters*, 1934, *Silas Crockett*, 1935, *Dawn in Lyonesse*, 1938, *Windswept*, 1941, *The Plum Tree*, 1949, and *The Edge of Darkness*, 1957; in them she wrote evocatively of the Maine coast and its people, of whom her characterizations were subtle and penetrating portraits.

Others of her books included *Mary Christmas*, for children, 1926, *The Golden Asse and Other Essays*, 1929, *The Silver Shell*, for children, 1930, *A Goodly Heritage*, autobiography, 1932, *This England*, essays, 1936, *It's All About Me*, for children, 1937, *The Goodly Fellowship*, autobiography, 1939, *Jonathan Fisher, Maine Parson*, biography, 1948, *Abby Aldrich Rockefeller*, biography, 1950, *Recipe for a Magic Childhood*, autobiography, 1951, and *The White Gate: Adventures in the Imagination of a Child*, autobiography, 1954. She retired from Smith College in 1955 and died in Northampton, Massachusetts, on July 28, 1973.

Chesnut, Mary Boykin Miller 1823–1886 diarist

Born near Camden, South Carolina, on March 31, 1823, Mary Miller was the daughter of a prominent South Carolina politician and grew up in an atmosphere of public service and interest in affairs. When she was twelve the family moved to Mississippi, but her education was continued at a girls' school in Charleston. The family was financially pressed for a time following her father's death in 1838, but in April 1840 she married James Chesnut, Jr., a wealthy and respected young lawyer of Camden. Over the next 20 years, as his career took him eventually to Washington, D.C., as a U.S. senator, she kept up the journal she had begun in her schooldays, gradually elaborating it into a detailed daily record of persons and events, rumors and opinions.

With the coming of secession and the Civil War she consciously aimed to make her diary a record of great and small events for the use of future historians. Her husband's prominence — he served, among other capacities, as aide to General P. G. T. Beauregard and as commanding general of South Carolina reserves — placed her in close proximity to the centers of activity, and she was personally acquainted with most of the governmental, military, and social leaders of the Confederacy. The enduring value of her diary lay in its skillful and vivid writing and in its intelligence. Chesnut was an ardent Southern patriot but not a blind one; her character sketches, comments on Confederate politics, and particularly her long-held opposition to slavery revealed an independent and vigorous intellect. Her access to information and opinion at the highest levels of the Confederacy provided the best possible material for her writing.

After the Civil War Chesnut helped her husband in his attempts to rebuild their personal lives and his political career in Camden. She also revised her entire journal during the mid-1870s and devoted time to other writing as well. She died in Camden, South Carolina, on November 22, 1886. An edition of portions of her diary, under the title *A Diary from Dixie*, was published in 1905 by Isabella D. Martin, to whom it had been willed, and a larger edition was prepared by Ben Ames Williams in 1949.

Child, Julia 1912– cookery expert

Born on August 15, 1912, in Pasadena, California, Julia McWilliams graduated from Smith College in 1934 and for several years worked at various minor jobs. At the outbreak of World War II she took a job as clerk with the Office of Strategic Services, and while serving in that capacity in Ceylon she met Paul C. Child, whom she married in September 1946. By that time she had developed an interest in cooking, and when Paul Child, then a Foreign Service officer, was assigned to Paris in 1948 she found opportunity to pursue it. She attended classes at the famous Cordon Bleu cooking school and became acquainted with Simone Beck and Louisette Bertholle, both gourmets and cooks of reputation. In 1951 the three opened their own school, L'École des Trois Gourmandes. Branches of the school were later opened in other cities. After several years of collaboration the three partners produced a book on French cooking for the American market; published in 1961 as *Mastering the Art of French Cooking*, it was warmly received by critics and the public alike and came to be considered perhaps the best book in the field in English.

In 1961 the Childs settled in Cambridge, Massachusetts. In 1962, after a remarkable appearance on a book-review program on a Boston educational television station, she was invited to prepare some pilots for a possible series on cooking. The pilots were successful, and in February 1963 she began a regular series called "The French Chef." It was an immediate hit and was soon distributed to scores of other stations in the educational network (now the Public Broadcasting Service).

Besides providing clear and simple instruction and demystifying the art of fine cooking, the program attracted viewers by the thousands by its sheer entertainment value. Child's hearty, vivacious, and expert approach to her work, together with her aplomb in the face of inevitable mishaps and the program's candor in showing all, were irresistible attractions for a constantly growing audience. She won a Peabody Award in

1965 and an Emmy in 1966 for the series. In 1968 much of the content of the series was published as *The French Chef Cookbook*. In 1970, with Simone Beck, she published a second volume of *Mastering the Art of French Cooking*. In 1970 a second series of "The French Chef" was begun, while programs from the first series continued to be repeated on public television stations around the country with unabated success. She subsequently published *From Julia Child's Kitchen*, 1975, and *Julia Child and Company*, 1978. The latter title was also that of her new television series of 1978, in which she dealt with a broader and more native American gastronomic field. She also began hosting cooking segments on the American Broadcasting Company's morning show "Good Morning, America."

Child launched a new series, *Julia Child and More Company*, following a book of the same title in 1979, which won the American Book Award. She wrote a column for *McCall's* magazine from 1975–1982 and was the food editor for *Parade* from 1982–86. *The Way to Cook*, six one-hour videos with recipe booklets and a book of the same title, appeared in 1989. Her fifth series, *Dinner at Julia's*, which aired in 1983, featured a different chef each week preparing a meal under Child's ever-inquisitive gaze. Another book, *Cooking with Master Chefs*, was published in 1993.

Child, Lydia Maria Francis 1802–1880 author, editor and abolitionist

Born on February 11, 1802, in Medford, Massachusetts, into an abolitionist family, Lydia Francis spent one year in a seminary but was primarily influenced in her education by her brother, a Unitarian clergyman and later a professor at the Harvard Divinity School. Her first literary ventures, *Hobomok*, 1824, describing early Salem and Plymouth life, and *The Rebels*, 1825, describing pre-Revolutionary Boston, were received not for their artistic merit but for their interest as re-creations of real life. She also produced several practical volumes, including *The Frugal Housewife*, which went through 21 editions within a decade of its first appearance in 1829, and *The Mother's Book*, 1831. From 1825 to 1828 she conducted a private school in Watertown, Massachusetts. In 1826 she founded the nation's first monthly magazine for children, the *Juvenile Miscellany*. In October 1828 she married David L. Child, an editor, through whom she came under the influence of William Lloyd Garrison.

In 1833 Child published *An Appeal in Favor of That Class of Americans Called Africans*, which was considered an outrageous abolitionist document because it contained a proposal to educate African-Americans. Child suffered social ostracism and had her membership in the Boston Athenaeum revoked. The *Juvenile Miscellany* died in 1834, and the popularity of her books fell off sharply, although her novel *Philothea*, 1836, enjoyed some success. The *Appeal* also won support. It converted some to abolitionism and brought about a new awareness of the issue among groups that previously had ignored it. In 1840 she became a member of the executive committee of the American Anti-Slavery Society. From 1841 to 1844 she and her husband edited the *National Anti-Slavery Standard*, a weekly newspaper published in New York City. In 1843–1845 she published two very successful volumes of *Letters from New York*, originally columns contributed to the *Boston Courier*.

In 1852 the Childs settled permanently on a farm in Wayland, Massachusetts. They continued to contribute liberally, from a small income, to the abolitionist movement. Among her later books were three volumes of *Flowers for Children*, 1844–1847, *Fact and Fiction*, 1846, *The Progress of Religious Ideas, through Successive Ages*, 3 volumes, 1855, *Autumnal Leaves*, 1857, *The Freedmen's Book*, 1865, *An Appeal for the Indians*, 1868, and *Aspirations of the World*, 1878. Having persevered for many years in challenging her contemporaries with difficult questions on social injustice, she died in Wayland, Massachusetts, on October 20, 1880.

Chisholm, Shirley Anita St. Hill 1924– public official

Born on November 30, 1924, in Brooklyn, New York, Shirley St. Hill was the daughter of parents from British Guiana (now Guyana) and Barbados. She passed part of her childhood in Barbados and then returned to Brooklyn, where she attended high school and graduated from Brooklyn College in 1946. While teaching nursery school and later serving as director of the Friends Day Nursery in the Brownsville section of Brooklyn, she studied elementary education at Columbia University and received an M.A. degree in 1952. During that period, in October 1949, she married Conrad Q. Chisholm. In 1953 she became director of the Hamilton-Madison Child Care Center in Manhattan, and in 1959 she became a consultant to the division of day care of the New York City Bureau of Child Welfare. Her interest in neighborhood and city problems led her into political activity, and her work in local organizing, along with her outspoken independence and her command of Spanish, made her popular with the predominantly black and Puerto Rican people of her district.

In 1964 Chisolm ran as an independent Democrat for the state legislature and won, and in reelection campaigns in 1965 and 1966 (the district was reapportioned in that period) she increased her appeal at the polls. Her effectiveness in the state assembly prompted her to run for Congress in 1968 from the newly created Twelfth District centered on the impoverished Bedford-Stuyvesant neighborhood of Brooklyn. After a victory in the Democratic primary she handily defeated Republican-Liberal candidate James L. Farmer, former chairman of the Congress of Racial Equality, in November.

In January 1969 Chisolm became the first African-American woman to enter Congress. There she continued an effective spokesman for minority rights and urban needs. She was reelected in 1970, 1972, 1974, 1976, 1978, and 1980. In 1972 she entered several Democratic presidential primaries and at the party's national convention received 151 delegate votes for the nomination. She was the author of *Unbought and Unbossed* (a campaign slogan of hers), 1970, and *The Good Fight*, 1973, and was the recipient of numerous honors and awards.

She retired from Congress in 1982 but remained active on the lecture circuit. She held the position of Purington Professor at Mount Holyoke College, took a year as a visiting scholar at Spelman College in 1985, and retired from teaching in 1987. She continued to be involved in poltics, working on Jesse Jackson's presidential campaigns in 1984 and 1988, and founding the National Political Congress of Black Women in 1984. President Clinton nominated her as Ambassador to Jamaica in 1993, but she withdrew her name citing a progressive eye disorder.

Chopin, Kate O'Flaherty 1851–1904 novelist

Born in St. Louis on February 8, 1851, to a prominent family, Katherine O'Flaherty received her education in a convent school, supplementing it with her own wide reading. In June 1870 she married Oscar Chopin, with whom she lived in his native New Orleans and later on a plantation near Cloutiersville, Louisiana, until his death in 1882. Soon afterward Chopin returned to St. Louis. She began writing of her experiences in the South, and after an undistinguished first novel, *At Fault*, 1890, her powers developed rapidly. She became a regular contributor of stories to children's magazines and to the leading literary journals of the day and published two collections, *Bayou Folk*, 1894, and *A Night in Acadie*, 1897, which were quickly recognized as major additions to the local-color genre. Her lush descriptions of Louisiana scenes, her sympathetically realistic delineations of Creole and Cajun characters and society, and her finely wrought plots won her a lasting place in American literature.

Chopin's second full-length novel, *The Awakening*, 1899, a bold and penetrating psychological study of a young woman's sexual and artistic longings, proved too candid about its subject for many critics, however; their attacks on its portrayal of mixed marriage and other commonplaces of bayou life may have contributed to her virtually giving up writing. Chopin died in St. Louis on August 22, 1904.

Churchill, Jennie Jerome 1854–1921 society figure

Born in Brooklyn, New York, on January 9, 1854, Jeanette Jerome was the daughter of a prosperous financier and a socially ambitious mother. In 1867 she and her two sisters were taken to Paris by their mother following a scandalous escapade of their father's, and her education and introduction to society followed the manner of European upper classes. In 1873 she met and charmed young Lord Randolph Churchill, son of the Duke of Marlborough, and they were married in April 1874. Her American vivacity, her wit, and her beauty assured her of social success in London. Although she was an asset she took no active part in her husband's political career, however. His death in 1895 left her for some time at loose ends.

In 1899 Churchill founded and edited the few numbers of the lavish but short-lived *Anglo-Saxon Review*. During the Boer War she raised money for and staffed and equipped a hospital ship, the *Maine*, which did valuable work in South Africa. She also turned to writing, producing a volume of discreet *Reminiscences of Lady Randolph Churchill*, 1908, *Her Borrowed Plumes*, a play that was produced with Mrs. Patrick Campbell starring, 1909, *The Bill*, another play that was successfully staged in 1913, and *Short Talks on Big Subjects*, 1916, a collection of articles originally published in *Pearson's Magazine*. In July 1900 she married the much younger Lieutenant George F. M. Cornwallis-West, whom she divorced in 1914, and in June 1918 she married the also younger Montagu Porch. Increasingly eccentric in her late years, she died in London on June 29, 1921. Sir Winston L. S. Churchill (1874–1965), later prime minister, was her elder son.

Cisneros, Sandra 1954– poet and short story writer

Born in Chicago on December 20, 1954, Sandra Cisneros was the only daughter of a Mexican father and a Chicana mother. She grew up in poverty, and her family moved often and traveled regularly to Mexico City for visits to her paternal grandmother. The only girl among six brothers, she was a shy, introverted child who spent her time reading and observing her surroundings in the many poor neighborhoods where she lived.

She came to love books — she had a library card even before she could read — and while she spoke Spanish at home, she always read and wrote in English. At Loyola University she received a B.A. in English in 1976. In the late 1970s she enrolled in the Iowa Writers' Workshop and wrote poetry. There she began to identify herself as a Chicana writer — "a yellow weed among the city's cracks" — and her writing took on a distinctive voice. Her first work of fiction, *The House on Mango Street*, was a series of 44 interwoven tales narrated by a young girl in a Chicago ghetto; published by a small press in 1984, it won the Before Columbus American Book Award in 1985. Cisneros received her M.A. from the University of Iowa, later teaching for two years at Latino Youth Alternative High School in Chicago. During this time she received local celebrity when one of her poems was selected to be posted in Chicago buses.

In 1986 she received a Dobie-Paisano fellowship and relocated to Texas, where she finished *My Wicked, Wicked Ways*, 1987, her first book of poetry. Until she received a fellowship from the National Endowment for the Arts, she was unable to make a living from her writing; for a while she passed out fliers in supermarkets and laundromats trying to recruit students for a writing workshop. She eventually made contact with Susan Bergholtz, a literary agent who had been trying to track down Cisneros for over three years; Bergholtz got her a contract with Random House, making her the first Chicana to receive a major publishing contract. In 1991 she published *Woman Hollering Creek and Other Stories*, short stories about Chicanas on both sides of the Texan-Mexican border.

When Random House took over the publication of *The House on Mango Street*, Cisneros immediately began to receive national attention. *Loose Woman*, a collection of poems, was published in 1994; she won a MacArthur Foundation Fellowship the following year.

Clapp, Cornelia Maria 1849–1934 zoologist and college professor

Born in Montague, Massachusetts, on March 17, 1849, Cornelia Clapp graduated from Mount Holyoke Seminary in 1871, and after a year of teaching school in Andalusia, Pennsylvania, she returned to Mount Holyoke as an instructor in mathematics. Later she also taught gymnastics. A growing interest in natural history was given encouragement in 1874, when she was selected to attend the summer Anderson School of Natural History conducted by Louis Agassiz at Penikese Island in Buzzards Bay. Soon she was teaching zoology at Mount Holyoke, where she developed a vivid laboratory method of instruction that proved highly effective. She continued her own education on numerous field trips, two in groups led by David Starr Jordan of Indiana University, and in formal studies at the Massachusetts Institute of Technology, at Williams College, at Syracuse University, where she received a Ph.D. degree in 1889, and at the University of Chicago, where she took a second doctorate in 1896.

In 1896, eight years after Mount Holyoke became a college, Clapp helped organize the department of zoology, and in 1904 she was named professor of zoology. From its opening in 1888 she was involved in the work of the Marine Biological Laboratory at Woods Hole, Massachusetts. She carried on research there, primarily in the field of embryology, and served as librarian in 1893–1907 and as a trustee in 1897–1901 and again in 1910. She retired as professor emeritus from Mount Holyoke in 1916 but continued for several years to summer at Woods Hole. She published little during her career, but her influence as a teacher wa great and enduring in a period when the world of science was just opening to women. In 1923 Clapp Hall, housing the science departments and laboratories, was dedicated at Mount Holyoke. She died in Mount Dora, Florida, her winter home, on December 31, 1934.

Clare, Ada 1836?–1874 writer and actor

Born in Charleston, South Carolina, about 1836, Jane McElhenney was of a prosperous and well connected family. From about eleven she grew up under the care of her maternal grandfather, who took her on visits to Northern resorts, where she became interested in the world of actors and writers. About 1854 she struck out on her own. In New York City she began contributing love poems and sketches to periodicals — the first appeared in the *Atlas* in January 1855 — using the pseudonyms "Clare" and later "Ada Clare," and at the same time she sought a career on the stage. An amateur appearance in *The Hunchback* in August 1855 was not encouraging, but in performances in such works as *Love and Revenge*, *The Wife*, *Hamlet*, *The Marble Heart*, *Jane Eyre*, and Dion Boucicault's *The Phantom* over the next year she gradually developed her theatrical skills. A broken affair with the pianist and composer Louis M. Gottschalk led to her sailing to Paris, where she bore a son (never acknowledged by Gottschalk) in 1857. From Paris she sent comments on the theater to the *Atlas*.

By March 1859 Clare was back on the New York stage in *Antony and Cleopatra*. From 1859 to 1864 she contributed a column of sprightly commentary on subjects from theater to politics to the *Saturday Press* and later to the *Leader*. During that period she became a member of the celebrated journalistic and literary group, including Walt Whitman, Bayard Taylor, Fitz-James O'Brien, William Winter, George Arnold, Adah Menken, and others, that collected at Pfaff's Cellar on Broadway. Her charm and wit quickly earned her the nickname "Queen of Bohemia" among the group. Early in 1864 she sailed to San Francisco, where she wrote for the *Golden Era* and later for the *San Francisco Bulletin*. To the latter she sent a notable series of letters from a visit to

Hawaii. After an unsuccessful appearance in a production of *Camille* in December 1864 she returned to New York. In 1866 she published a novel, *Only a Woman's Heart*. Later she toured the South under the name "Agnes Stanfield" in *The Merry Wives of Windsor* and, after her marriage to fellow actor J. Franklin Noyes in September 1868, in various other plays. She had been appearing in *East Lynne* in Rochester, New York, when she died in New York City on March 4, 1874.

Clark, Marguerite 1883–1940 actor

Born in Avondale (now part of Cincinnati), Ohio, on February 22, 1883, Helen Marguerite Clark was educated in public schools and in a convent school in St. Martin, Ohio. Her success in a number of amateur theatricals, together with the encouragement of an elder sister, her guardian from the age of thirteen, directed her to a career on the stage. She sang in the chorus of the Strakosch Opera company in Baltimore in 1899 and made her New York debut in 1900 as a chorus girl in a production of *The Belle of Bohemia*. Parts in *The Burgomaster* and *The New Yorkers* in 1901 and *The Wild Rose* in 1902 led to her winning the ingenue role of Polly, opposite DeWolf Hopper, in *Mr. Pickwick* in 1903, a role that brought her her first popularity. Over the next decade her fame grew as she appeared in Victor Herbert's *Babes in Toyland* in 1903; *Happyland* with Hopper in 1905; *The Pied Piper* in 1908; *The King of Cadonia*, a revival of *Jim the Penman*, *Lights of London*, and the very popular *Baby Mine* in 1910; simultaneously in evening performances of *The Affairs of Anatol* with Lionel Barrymore and matinees of *Snow White* for children in 1912; and *Prunella* in 1913.

In 1914 Clark accepted a lavish offer from Adolph Zukor and signed on with his Famous Players film company (soon to become Famous Players-Lasky and eventually Paramount). Her first film, *Wildflower*, was a great success and was followed over the next five years by such films as *The Crucible*, *Goose Girl*, *Gretna Green*, *Seven Sisters*, *Still Waters*, *Molly Make Believe*, *The Prince and the Pauper* (in which she played both roles), *Topsy and Eva* (another double role, in a screenplay based on *Uncle Tom's Cabin*), *Come Out of the Kitchen*, *Rich Man Poor Man*, *Golden Bird*, *Snow White*, and others. Her tiny figure and air of sweet youthful innocence made her enormously popular and the chief competitor of Mary Pickford for the affection of the motion picture public. Her performance on stage and screen of Snow White was said to have shaped the much later Walt Disney animated version.

During World War I Clark did publicity films and tours on behalf of Liberty Loan drives. In August 1918 she married Harry P. Williams, a New Orleans businessman, and on the expiration of her contract she retired from the movies in 1919. She returned only to appear in *Scrambled Wives* in 1921. After her husband's death in 1936 she briefly managed his Wedell-Williams Air Service before selling it to Eastern Air Lines. She died in New York City on September 25, 1940.

Clarke, Helen Archibald and Porter, Charlotte Endymion 1860–1926 and 1857–1942 writers, editors and literary critics

Born in Philadelphia on November 13, 1860, Helen Clarke was of a deeply musical family, and music early became an abiding love. She attended the University of Pennsylvania (where her father, Hugh A. Clarke, had been professor of music since 1875) as a special student for two years, before women were formally admitted to the school, and received a certificate in music in 1883. Helen Charlotte Porter, who later adopted the middle name "Endymion," was born in Towanda, Pennsylvania, on January 6, 1857. She graduated from Wells College in 1875, studied for a time at the Sorbonne, and in 1883 became editor of *Shakespeariana*, a journal published in Philadelphia by the Shakespeare Society of New York. An article on Shakespeare's music by Helen Clarke that was accepted for the *Shakespeariana* by Charlotte Porter brought the two together, and a second mutual interest in Robert Browning cemented the friendship. In 1887 Porter resigned from *Shakespeariana* and a short time later became editor of the *Ethical Record*.

In January 1889, after several months of planning, the two women launched a new monthly, *Poet Lore*, "devoted to Shakespeare, Browning, and the Comparative Study of Literature." The magazine found an immediate and growing audience among the proliferating literary clubs and societies across the nation, most if not all of them sharing the Victorian literary standards and interests of the editors. In 1891 they moved *Poet Lore* to Boston when a publisher there offered them free office space in exchange for three pages of advertising per issue. In 1896 *Poet Lore* became a quarterly. Much of the critical and commentary material published in the magazine was written by the editors themselves, singly or in collaboration. Its contents faithfully followed the original dedication, leaning heavily on Shakespeare and Browning studies, but over the years it also introduced to a wide American audience works (usually translated by the editors) of Ibsen, Björnson, Strindberg, D'Annunzio, Lagerlöf, Bourget, Hauptmann, Gorki, Maeterlinck, Schnitzler, Tagore, and other moderns. Little American writing found its way into *Poet Lore*.

Clarke and Porter also published a two-volume edition of Browning's poems in 1896; a volume of *Clever Tales*, translated short stories, 1897; an edition of *The Ring and the Book*, 1898; a 12-volume complete edition of Browning's works in 1898; *Browning Study Programmes*, 1900; a six-volume edition of Elizabeth Barrett Browning's works in 1900; and the 12-volume "Pembroke" edition of Shakespeare in 1912. Clarke's dramatization of Browning's *Pippa Passes* was staged in Boston in 1899, and Porter's version of his *Return of the Druses* was done in 1902.

In 1903 they sold *Poet Lore*, and although they continued for many years as editors of the magazine they gave increasing time to other projects. Porter spent several years in preparing a 40-volume *First Folio Edition of Shakespeare*, 1903–1913, and in 1919 published *Lips of Music*, a collection of verse. Clarke, who in 1892 had published a book of songs entitled *Apparitions*, also wrote *Browning's Italy*, 1907, *Browning's England*, 1908, *A Child's Guide to Mythology*, 1908, *Longfellow's Country*, 1909, *Hawthorne's Country*, 1910, *The Poets' New England*, 1911, and *Browning and His Century*, 1912, along with a number of musical cantatas and operettas for children. As well as being both long-time members and officers of the Boston Browning Society, they were active in other organizations. They founded the American Music Society, of which Clarke was president, and the American Drama Society (later the Drama League of America), of which Porter was president. Helen Clarke died in Boston on February 8, 1926, after which Charlotte Porter lived mainly at their former summer home on Isle au Haut in Penobscot Bay, Maine. She died in Melrose, Massachusetts, on January 16, 1942.

Clarke, Martha 1944– choreographer and dancer

Born on June 3, 1944, in Baltimore, Maryland, Martha Clarke grew up in a musical family in the suburb of Pikesville and attended progressive private schools. She demonstrated a keen interest in dance in her early teens as a student at the exclusive Perry-Mansfield School of Theater and Dance in Steamboat Springs, Colorado. There she was cast as a child in *Dance for Walt Whitman* by choreographer Helen Tamiris.

Her teachers noticed her talent, and with their encouragement she attended summer sessions at the Connecticut College School of Dance, where she worked with such luminaries as José Límon and Alvin Ailey. She skipped her senior year in high school, enrolling instead at the Juilliard School in New York City. She studied the Martha Graham technique and became enamored of the work of Anthony Tudor, whose explorations of the human psyche through ballet-style movements would have a lasting effect on her. After leaving Juilliard, she joined the modern dance company of Anna Sokolow, under whose direction she discovered an emotional expressionism she later said was at the root of all her subsequent work.

Clarke's marriage to sculptor Philip Grausman, whom she later divorced, took her to Rome. After the birth of their son, the couple returned to the U.S.; Clarke took a five-year hiatus from dance, which ended when Grausman became an artist in residence at Dartmouth College. There the Pilobolus Dance Theater, an acrobatic troupe, was beginning to attract notice. She began working with the group's teacher, Alison Chase, and the two joined the previously all-male ensemble in 1973.

Although Pilobolus's process was primarily a collaborative one, Clarke created six solos that were incorporated into the group's performances. She later described her time with Pilobolus as a contentious period characterized by much competition and discord in the group. Tired of the demands of the collaboration, she left Pilobolus in 1979, eager to pursue her own vision as a choreographer.

Her next dance venture was Crowsnest, a chamber group she formed with another Pilobolus member, Robert Morgan Barnett, and French dancer and choreographer, Félix Blaska. Her work with the trio attracted critical admiration, particularly for dramatic and imaginative solos such as *Fallen Angel*, in which she danced to a Gregorian chant clad in an evening gown and bird mask, and *Nachturn*, in which she parodied Romantic ballet by hobbling and leaping across the stage bare-breasted and clad in swathes of white tulle.

Clarke's work with Crowsnest reflected her evolution from dance to performance art, a change that began in 1977 when she worked with actress Linda Hunt on a show called *Portraits*, based on Hunt's dramatic monologues and Clarke's dance solos. The two continued their collaboration in 1982 with *A Metamorphosis in Miniature*, a musical adaptation of Kafka's *Metamorphosis*.

Two years later, Clarke created a phantasmagorical series of sketches called *The Garden of Earthly Delights*, based on the work of the fifteenth century surrealist painter Hieronymus Bosch. The off-off-Broadway opening in November 1984 received rave reviews from critics, and the piece has since been performed in several cities in the U.S. and abroad.

Her next performance piece — on which she collaborated with composer Richard Peaslee — was *Vienna: Lusthaus*. Also inspired by visual art, the piece evokes the decadence of fin de siècle Europe as it slides toward world war. Later pieces included *The Hunger Artist*, about the life of Kafka, and *Miracolo d'Amore*, an exploration of erotic love that debuted in the spring of 1988 at the Spoleto Festival U.S.A. in Charleston, S.C.

Clarke was the subject of a 1981 documentary by Joyce Chopra, *Martha Clarke, Light and Dark: A Dancer's Journey*, which was broadcast on PBS. She received grants from the Guggenheim and Rockefeller Foundations and the National Endowment for the Arts, as well as a MacArthur Foundation Fellowship.

Clarke, Mary Frances 1803–1887 religious

Born in Dublin, Ireland, on March 2, 1803, Mary Clarke was drawn early to the religious life. For some years after the death of her father she successfully carried on his leather business and cared for her family. In 1831, while nursing victims of a cholera epidemic, she met four like-minded young women with whom, the next year, she opened Miss Clarke's School for poor Catholic children. In 1833 they decided to carry their work to America, and in September they began teaching in Philadelphia. Under the guidance of the Reverend Terence J. Donaghoe they formally organized themselves on All Saints Day, November 1, 1833, as the Sisters of Charity of the Blessed Virgin Mary. Sister Mary immediately became Mother Mary, superior of the fledgling order. In 1843, on invitation by Bishop Matthias Loras and Father Pierre De Smet, Mother Mary and four sisters made their way to the still primitive frontier village of Dubuque, becoming the first Roman Catholic nuns in Iowa Territory. Under her leadership the Sisters of Charity opened and staffed St. Mary's Female Academy in 1843; the school was renamed Mt. St. Joseph's Academy and moved to nearby St. Joseph's Prairie in 1844, but it returned to Dubuque in 1859. It subsequently developed into Mt. St. Joseph College and in 1928 was renamed Clarke College. Mother Mary, a reclusive figure even within her order, governed the sisters until her death in Dubuque on December 4, 1887. In March 1885 the order had received its decree of final papal approbation and confirmation from Pope Leo XIII.

Clarke, Rebecca Sophia 1833–1906 writer of children's literature

Born in Norridgewock, Maine, on February 22, 1833, Rebecca Clarke was educated at home and in the local Female Academy. In 1851 she traveled out to Evansville, Indiana, to teach school, but growing deafness forced her to give up that post. She lived thereafter in her native town. She had written for her own amusement since childhood, but in 1861, on invitation, she contributed a story to the *Memphis Daily Appeal.* Within a short time she was publishing stories for children regularly in Sara Jane Lippincott's *Little Pilgrim* magazine and in the Boston *Congregationalist* under the pseudonym "Sophie May." Her first series of Prudy Parlin stories was collected in six volumes in 1863–1865, and several such series followed, including the Dotty Dimple stories in 1867–1869, Little Prudy's Flyaway series in 1870–1873, the Quinnebasset series in 1871–1891, the Flaxie Frizzle stories in 1876–1884, and Little Prudy's Children series in 1894–1901.

The great popularity of Clarke's stories and books among children rested on her humor, her fidelity to the ways and thoughts of children, and her avoidance of the wooden didacticism of much of the literature intended for young readers of that day. The everyday details of village life were the material from which she constructed her moral yet lively tales, and her native village and its people, particularly her own nieces and nephews, were her models. A few books for adults, such as *Drone's Honey*, 1887, and *Pauline Wyman*, 1897, were not successful. She died in Norridgewock, Maine, on August 16, 1906.

Cleveland, Emeline Horton 1829–1878 physician and college professor

Born in Ashford, Connecticut, on September 22, 1829, Emeline Horton grew up from 1831 in Madison County, New York. After attending local schools she became a schoolteacher herself until she was able to afford to enroll at Oberlin College, from which she graduated in 1853. She then entered the Female (later Woman's) Medical College of Pennsylvania in Philadelphia and took her M.D. degree in 1855. During that time she married the Reverend Giles B. Cleveland in March 1854. Her husband's ill health ended their plan to undertake missionary work, and after a year of private practice in the Oneida valley of New York, Cleveland became a demonstrator of anatomy at the Female Medical College in 1856. A short time later she was named professor of anatomy and histology. In 1860–1861, with the support of Dr. Ann Preston of the college, she took advanced training in obstetrics at the school of the Maternité hospital in Paris and then returned to Philadelphia as chief resident at the rechartered Woman's Medical College, a post she held until 1868. From 1862 she was also professor of obstetrics and diseases of women and children, and she carried on an extensive private practice as well.

Cleveland's professional reputation was unsurpassed among women physicians; on several occasions she was consulted by male colleagues, and she was admitted finally to membership in several local medical societies. Her work at the college, where she had early established training courses for nurses and for nurse's aides, the latter a pioneering venture, was capped by her service as dean, succeeding Preston, in 1872–1874. In 1875 she performed the first of several ovariotomies, apparently the earliest recorded instance of major surgery performed by a woman. In 1878 she was appointed gynecologist to the department for the insane at Pennsylvania Hospital. Cleveland died in Philadelphia on December 8, 1878.

Cline, Maggie 1857–1934 singer

Born in Haverhill, Massachusetts, on January 1, 1857, Margaret Cline, daughter of Irish immigrant parents, went to work at twelve in a local shoe factory. At seventeen she decided to seek a career on the stage. Over the next several years she performed with vaudeville companies around the country. The golden era of vaudeville, roughly the 1890s and a few years on either side, was also the period of Irish songs, and Maggie Cline was the great female exponent of both. Tall, muscular, red-haired, "the daughter of Hercules and descendant of Stentor," she put over such songs as "How McNulty Carved the Duck," "Nothing's Too Good for the Irish," and "Slide, Kelly, Slide," as no one else could. Her rendition of Joseph Flynn's "Down Went McGinty to the Bottom of the Sea," a comic production enlisting the collaboration of stagehands, musicians, and audience alike, was a great hit from 1889. Her greatest success was with "Throw Him Down, McCloskey," written for her by John W. Kelly in 1890. It was the story of a pugilistic encounter, and Maggie Cline's performance — perhaps rather enactment — of it regularly aroused the audience at Tony Pastor's or any other vaudeville house to rapture. She sang it, she once estimated, 75,000 times, earning the nickname "Brunnhilde of the Bowery." After her retirement in 1917 she lived quietly in Red Bank, New Jersey. She died in Fair Haven, New Jersey, on June 11, 1934.

Cline, Patsy 1932–1963 singer

Born Virginia Patterson Hensley in Winchester, Virginia, on September 8, 1932, Patsy Cline began to sing with local country bands while a teenager, sometimes accompanying herself on guitar. She first recorded on the Four Star label in 1955, but it was with the advent of television culture in the late 1950s that she gained a wider audience. Cline began appearing on the radio and on "Town and Country Jamboree," a local television variety show; broadcast every Saturday night from Capitol Arena in Washington, D.C., it featured such future country music stars as Jimmy Dean, Roy Clark, George Hamilton IV, and Mary Klick.

Cline's big break came on January 28, 1957, when she sang "Walkin' after Midnight" as a contestant on the CBS television show "Arthur Godfrey's Talent Scouts." She took first prize, winning the opportunity to appear on Godfrey's morning show for the next two weeks, gaining national exposure both for herself and for her song. The song made both the pop and country charts, a split that would mark the remainder of Cline's singing career.

Three years later, she became a member of the "Grand Ole Opry," the Nashville country-music troupe whose radio broadcasts largely defined the genre. Cline preferred traditional country music, which included vocal tricks like yodeling and growling; however, the industry, battered by the popularity of rock-and-roll, was trying to appeal more to a pop audience. After her recording of "I Fall to Pieces" remained on the charts for thirty-nine weeks straight, Decca began to market Cline as a pop singer, backed by strings and vocals. She was never comfortable with this categorization, however: she persisted in yodeling on her records, she dressed as a cowgirl until 1962, and she disliked her three hit pop songs, "Walkin' after Midnight," "I Fall to Pieces," and "Crazy," (written by a young Willie Nelson).

Cline's life was cut short on March 5, 1963, by an airplane crash that also killed fellow entertainers Cowboy Copas and Hawkshaw Hawkins. In her short career, however, she was responsible for ushering in the modern era of American country vocalists; she figures prominently, for instance, as Loretta Lynn's mentor in Lynn's autobiography, *Coal Miner's Daughter*, 1976. Cline was elected to the Country Music Hall of Fame in 1973.

Clinton, Hillary Diane Rodham 1947– lawyer and First Lady

Born on October 26, 1947 in Chicago, Illinois, Hillary Diane Rodham was the daughter of two staunch Republicans. Her father owned a drapery manufacturing business, and her mother was a homemaker. From the age of four, she grew up in Park Ridge, Illinois, a suburb of Chicago. In high school she was active in student government and the debating team, was a National Merit Scholarship finalist, and was a member of the National Honor Society. She graduated high school in 1965 and attended Wellesley College where she was the head of the local chapter of the Young Republicans. After the assassinations of Malcolm X in 1965, and Dr. Martin Luther King Jr. and Robert F. Kennedy in 1968, along with the violence at the Democratic National Convention in Chicago in 1968, she joined the Democratic party. In 1968 she worked on Eugene McCarthy's unsuccessful presidential campaign. She was also active in a movement to admit more African-American students to Wellesley.

In 1969 she earned her B.A. in political science and was the first student at Wellesley ever asked to deliver the commencement address. She enrolled at Yale Law School where she met her future husband Bill Clinton. While at Yale, she served on the editorial board of the law review, and worked as a volunteer for the congressional lobbying and advocacy group that would later become the Children's Defense Fund. She prolonged her education a year in order to work at Yale's Child Study Center where she helped research the book *Best Interests of the Child*, 1973, by Anna Freud, Joseph Goldstein, and Albert Solnit. At that time, she also performed legal research for the Carnegie Council on Children as her interest and expertise in children's rights continued to grow.

After graduating from law school in 1973 she worked briefly for the Children's Defense Fund in Cambridge, Massachusetts. In 1974 she moved to Washington, D.C., to work on the House Judiciary Committees's inquiry into the impeachment of President Richard Nixon. When the staff was disbanded that same year she was offered a number of positions at prestigious law firms; instead of taking them she moved to Fayetteville, Arkansas, and along with Bill Clinton, taught at the University of Arkansas School of Law. In 1975 she married Clinton, though she retained her maiden name until 1982. In 1976 her husband was elected state attorney general of Arkansas and the couple moved to Little Rock. While her husband began his political career, she taught law as an adjunct professor at the University of Arkansas and directed the school's legal-aid clinic. In 1978 she worked for her husband's successful campaign for governor while working at the Rose law firm. After moving into the governor's mansion her husband appointed her chairperson of the Rural Heath Advisory Committee, which worked toward providing health care to people in isolated areas. In 1980 she was made a partner at the Rose firm and she gave birth to her daughter, Chelsea Victoria Clinton.

Bill Clinton was reelected governor of Arkansas four times between 1984 and 1990. Throughout Bill Clinton's 10 years as governor she participated in various public service programs providing either aid to children, or health care services to the disadvantaged. At the same time she also served on the boards of several high-profile corporations.

Bill Clinton was elected President in 1992 and in 1993 he appointed his wife to head the Task Force on National Health Care Reform. The plan her committee drafted proposed providing health insurance to all Americans by cutting spending through government regulation of medical services, raising taxes on alcohol and tobacco, and instituting "managed competition" into the health-care system. Although it was well-received by the public, the policy was defeated after a heated, and often nasty, partisan debate. After this loss, her problems escalated, as the so-called "Whitewater" affair gained national attention. At the core of the controversy was her dealings in Little Rock real estate while her husband was governor of Arkansas. There were serious allegations that she used her position at the Rose law firm, and as the governor's wife, in a series of unethical — and possibly criminal — business moves. While some dismiss the allegations as partisan mud-slinging, Congress began an official investigation into the charges, including appointing a special prosecutor and calling on the President and First Lady to testify under oath on the issue (an unusual occurrence in U.S. political history).

Hillary Clinton was the only First Lady to have her own successful career prior to moving to the White House. Throughout Bill Clinton's presidency, she was a controversial figure: loved by some as a role model for modern women, criticized by others for her independent — some would say, "unladylike" — nature. There is no question, however, that she forced the nation to re-examine the role of women in society and politics, as well as the national expectations of the First Lady.

Close, Glenn 1947– actor

Born on March 19, 1947, in Greenwich, Connecticut, Glenn Close was raised there, in Switzerland, and in the Belgian Congo (now Zaire), where her father ran a medical clinic. She decided as a child to become an actress. She sang with the "Up with People" touring company between high school and college, 1965–70. After graduating from William and Mary College with a B.A. in drama in 1974, she joined the New Phoenix Repertory Company in 1974 and made her Broadway debut with the company's production of William Congreve's *Love for Love*. She performed in regional and off-Broadway productions and in made-for-television movies to increasing acclaim. In 1980 she was nominated for a Tony Award as outstanding featured actress in a musical for her performance in *Barnum*.

Cast in her first movie, *The World According to Garp*, 1982, Close earned an Academy Award nomination for best supporting actress. She earned another nomination for her performance in the commercially successful *The Big Chill*, 1983, and was praised for her roles in *The Natural*, 1984, *Jagged Edge*, 1985, and *Fatal Attraction*, 1987, one of the largest grossing films of that year. She earned an Obie Award for best off-Broadway performance in 1982 for her role in *The Singular Life of Albert Nobbs*; a Tony Award for best actress for her performance in *The Real Thing*, 1984; and an Emmy nomination for her performance in the made-for-television movie *Something About Amelia*, 1984. Harvard University's Hasty Pudding Theatricals named her woman of the year in 1990. Her performance in *Death and the Maiden*, 1992, earned her both a Tony Award for best actress and a Drama League of New York Distinguished Performance award.

Coates, Florence Van Leer Earle Nicholson 1850–1927 poet

Born in Philadelphia on July 1, 1850, Florence Earle was educated in private schools in New England and at the Convent of the Sacred Heart in Paris. Subsequently she studied music in Brussels. In September 1872 she married William Nicholson, who died five years later; in January 1879 she married Edward H. Coates, a Philadelphia financier. For some two decades thereafter her life was one of social leadership, including membership in such organizations as the Society of Mayflower Descendants, the Colonial Dames of America, the Browning Society, of which she was president in 1895–1903 and 1907–1908, and the New Century Club. Her interest in literature was, in her own view, profoundly influenced by Matthew Arnold, who was a visitor at the Coates home and a correspondent. Her own poems began appearing in various leading magazines during the 1890s and soon won a distinguished following; among those who praised her work were Edmund Clarence Stedman, William Butler Yeats, and Thomas Hardy.

In their day Coates' poems were esteemed for craftsmanship and refinement of sentiment and thought rather than for feeling or originality. They were collected in several volumes, including *Poems*, 1898, *Mine and Thine*, 1904, *Lyrics of Life*, 1909, *The Unconquered Air and Other Poems*, 1912, her collected *Poems* in two volumes, 1916, and *Pro Patria*, 1917. Her "Ode on the Coronation of King George V," 1911, was forwarded to the king himself by the British consul in America. In 1915 she was elected "poet laureate of Pennsylvania" by the state Federation of Women's Clubs. She died in Philadelphia on April 6, 1927.

Cole, Johnnetta 1936– anthropologist and educator

Born on October 19, 1936, in Jacksonville, Florida, Johnnetta Betsch was expected to join the African-American life insurance firm her maternal great-grandfather had founded and for which her father worked. Instead, she followed in the footsteps of her educator mother, who taught college English before joining the company herself after her husband's death.

Besides her mother, Betsch's earliest influences were African-American women schoolteachers and librarians; she also credited Mary MacLeod Bethune, the pioneering African-American. At the age of 15, she entered Fisk University, where her contact with the writer Arna Bontemps, then the school's librarian, introduced her to an intellectual world that deeply attracted her. She left Fisk and followed an older sister to Oberlin, where she graduated with a degree in sociology in 1957. While a doctoral student in anthropology at Northwestern University, she met Robert Cole, a fellow graduate student; they were married from 1960 to 1982. Cole received her Ph.D. in 1967, after field work on traditional and wage-earning labor in Liberia.

After teaching at the University of California at Los Angeles and at Washington State at Pullman, Cole worked for 13 years at the University of Massachusetts at Amherst, where she taught in the African-American Studies and Anthropology departments. In time she was promoted to the position of provost of undergraduate education. A pivotal figure in the development of the school's African-American Studies program, she became closely associated with the academic journal *Black Scholar*. In 1983 she moved to Hunter College, where she directed the Latin American and Caribbean Studies program.

In 1987 Cole became the seventh president and the first African-American woman president of Spelman College, the oldest African-American women's college in the U.S. Describing herself as the first Spelman president with an explicitly feminist vision, she expressed a commitment to making the school a center for scholarship about African-American women. Calling herself "Sister President," she became known as a strong advocate for the liberal arts curriculum in a changing society.

Her writings focused on race, gender and class in the pan-African world. In addition to many scholarly articles and a regular column in *McCall's* magazine, she wrote *Anthropology for the Eighties: Introductory Readings*, 1982; *All American Women: Lives that Divide, Ties that Bind*, 1986; *Anthropology for the Nineties*, 1988; and *Conversations: Straight Talk with America's Sister President*, 1993. She was president of the Association of Black Anthropologists and the International Women's Anthropology Conference, and the recipient of numerous awards.

Collins, Marva 1936– educator

Born in Monroeville, Alabama, on August 31, 1936, Marva Delores Knight's most formidable early influence was her father, Henry Knight, Jr., an undertaker, merchant and cattle buyer. Even as a very young child, she spent much time following him on his daily rounds as he tended his various businesses. As a relatively prosperous African-American — his home had store-bought furniture — her father sometimes received death threats from white townspeople, many of whom remained committed to racial segregation and white supremacy. Watching him face down such threats, his daughter was inspired by his pride, self-confidence and tenaciousness, qualities that would mark her own life as well.

A relatively privileged child, she attended the Bethlehem Academy in Monroeville, a strict, old-fashioned school that was influential in the development of her later educational methods. Denied access to the public library, however, her reading was limited to tin-can labels, Bible-school books and books her father brought her from Mobile. Upon graduating from the all-black Eschambia County Training School in Atmore, Alabama, she enrolled in Clark College in Atlanta, studiying there for a degree in secretarial sciences. Since secretarial jobs were not open to African-Americans back home in Alabama, however, she turned upon graduation to teaching, a field she had never expected to enter.

From 1957 she taught bookkeeping, typing, shorthand and business law at Monroe County Training School. In 1959 following a visit to Chicago, she moved there, breaking away from her family for the first time. Within a year she was married to Clarence Collins. In 1961 she applied to work in the Chicago school system. Despite her lack of a formal teaching certificate, she was hired at first as a full-time substitute, and she later obtained regular teaching positions. Quick to take the Chicago educational establishment to task for its apathy, neglect and hostility toward the poor, largely black, inner-city students, she set high standards for her students and expected co-workers to be as prepared and enthusiastic as she was. In this setting she occasionally clashed with other teachers, some of whom seemed more interested in enforcing rules and proprieties than in educating underserved children.

Shunning the prescribed curriculum in favor of the "basics," Collins adopted unorthodox teaching methods that combined such traditional practices as memorization with more innovative teaching methods. To inspire her students to read, she assigned them classic texts that others considered too challenging. Perceived as a maverick, she inspired as much wrath as praise.

In 1975 Collins left the Chicago school system, using her $5,000 retirement money to found the private Daniel Hale Williams Westside Preparatory School. With financial assistance from the government-funded Alternative Schools Network, she began by meeting with her daughter and three neighborhood children in the basement of Daniel Hale Williams University. Soon the enrollment had increased to twenty children, prompting her husband to renovate an empty apartment in the couple's West Side home in 1976 to accommodate the growing school. Charging $80 a month in tuition, and enrolling many children considered uneducable by the standards of Chicago public schools, Collins operated Westside Preparatory according to the teaching principles she had developed during her unorthodox career.

In 1979 Westside Prep gained national prominence following a story on "60 Minutes," including an interview with Collins. Enthusiasts backed the school's claim that many children had moved from below to above grade level, and they cited standardized testing to prove the effectiveness of her methods. Highly laudatory coverage followed in *Time*, *Good Housekeeping*, *People*, *Jet*, *Newsweek*, *Ebony* and *Black Enterprise*, and in 1981 CBS aired a drama, "The Marva Collins Story," starring Cicely Tyson and Morgan Freeman.

Her popularity and achievements brought offers of several powerful and prestigious positions, including U.S. Secretary of Education, membership on the Chicago school board and superintendency of the Los Angeles school system. She refused them all, however, to remain with her school. The positive press coverage largely ended in 1982; an educational magazine charged her with inflating test scores and with accepting Federal monies, which she had said would compromise her independence. She also faced accusations of plagiarism, of harassing parents about tuition payments, and of barring students from school unless their tuition was paid.

Appearing on the "Phil Donahue Show," both with and without her attorney, Collins responded to her critics, many of whom were Chicago teachers who resented her generalizations about the local public schools. Opponents also accused her of fueling right-wing attacks on public education. Despite the controversy, she retained many supporters, including the rock star Prince, who funded a teacher training program so that Collins could impart her methods to other inner-city teachers.

Her husband retired in 1978 to devote more time to helping her run the school. She too later resigned, but remained involved at Westside Prep working with a staff committed to carrying forward her educational philosophy. A popular speaker, she traveled widely to promote her ideas in the U.S. and abroad. Her many awards include Educator of the Year from Phi Delta Kappa and the Chicago Urban League, the United Negro College Fund Award, the Fred Hampton Image Award, the Sojourner Truth Award, and the Reading Reform Foundation Award. She was active on the National Advisory Board of Private Education and the National Department of Children, Youth, and Family Services.

Comstock, Anna Botsford 1854–1930 naturalist, illustrator and college professor

Born near Otto, Cattaraugus County, New York, on September 1, 1854, Anna Botsford attended schools in her native town and the Chamberlain Institute and Female College in nearby Randolph. After a year of teaching school in Otto she entered Cornell University in 1874, but she left after two years. In October 1878 she married John Henry Comstock, a young entomologist on the Cornell faculty from whom she had taken an interest in insect illustration. Throughout their marriage she functioned as his assistant, usually informally but in 1879–1881, when he was chief entomologist in the U.S. Department of Agriculture, with a formal appointment. There she prepared the drawings for his *Report of the Entomologist* (on citrus scale insects) of 1880. After their return from Washington, D.C., to Ithaca, New York, she reentered Cornell and took her degree in natural history in 1885. She studied wood engraving at Cooper Union, New York City, in order to prepare illustrations for her husband's *Introduction to Entomology*, 1888. In 1888 she was one of the first four women admitted to Sigma Xi, national honor society for the sciences.

Anna Comstock made engravings for the more than 600 plates in Professor Comstock's *Manual for the Study of Insects*, 1895, and for *Insect Life*, 1897, and *How to Know the Butterflies*, 1904, both of which she helped write as well. Her engravings were also widely exhibited in major expositions and won several prizes. Books written and illustrated by herself included *Ways of the Six-Footed*, 1903, *How to Keep Bees*, 1905, *Confessions to a Heathen Idol*, a novel, 1906, *The Handbook of Nature Study*, which went through more than two dozen editions, 1911, *The Pet Book*, 1914, and *Trees at Leisure*, 1916. In 1895 she was appointed to the New York State Committee for the Promotion of Agriculture, under whose auspices she planned and conducted an experimental course of nature study for public schools. When the program was approved for statewide use through the extension service of Cornell she wrote and spoke in its behalf, helped train teachers, and prepared classroom materials, and in 1897 she was appointed an assistant in nature study at Cornell. In 1899 she advanced to assistant professor, the first woman to hold that rank at Cornell; in 1900 she reverted to lecturer, but in 1913 she was again appointed assistant professor and in 1920 she was promoted to professor.

Comstock lectured frequently to teachers' and farmers' institutes and at universities as far from home as Stanford. She was a contributing editor of *Nature-Study Review* in 1905–1917 and editor in 1917–1923 and was on the staff of *Country Life in America*. In 1922 she retired from Cornell as professor emeritus, but she continued to teach in the summer session. In 1923 she was chosen one of the twelve greatest living American women in a poll by the League of Women Voters. She died in Ithaca, New York, on August 24, 1930.

Comstock, Elizabeth Leslie Rous 1815–1891 minister and social reformer

Born on October 30, 1815, in Maidenhead, Berkshire, England, Elizabeth Rous was educated in Quaker schools in Islington and Croydon and subsequently taught in the

Quaker schools in Croydon and Ackworth. In April 1848 she married Leslie Wright, who died three years later. She kept a shop in Bakewell, Derbyshire, until 1854, when she emigrated to Canada and settled in Belleville, Ontario. There she again kept a shop and, inspired by the work of the English Quaker reformer Elizabeth Fry, gradually took on the role of Quaker minister.

In 1858 Rous married John T. Comstock of Rollin, Michigan, where she went to live. Her public ministry quickly came to include abolitionism and work on the Underground Railroad, on which Rollin was a highly active station. A demand grew and spread for her services as a public speaker, not only among Quaker assemblies but also among reform groups and other bodies. In 1862 she addressed the Michigan legislature, and in October 1864 she and a group of other Quaker leaders held a remarkable interview and prayer meeting with President Abraham Lincoln.

During the Civil War Comstock traveled widely ministering to those in hospitals and prison camps and to refugee slaves. Her interest in the plight of the freedmen continued unabated after the war, and she wrote and spoke frequently in their behalf. In 1879–1880 she served as secretary of the Kansas Freedmen's Relief Association after large numbers of dispossessed former slaves had migrated to that state. Prison reform, temperance, peace, women's rights, and home-mission welfare work also engaged her attention, and by her emphasis on the last, an early form of social agency work adapted to the rapidly growing cities, she was of considerable influence in reshaping the Quaker social outlook and work to the new realities of an urban-industrial age. In 1885, following her husband's death, she settled in Union Springs, New York, where she died on August 3, 1891.

Conboy, Sara Agnes McLaughlin 1870–1928 labor leader

Born in Boston on April 3, 1870, Sara McLaughlin went to work in a candy factory at eleven. Over the next several years she worked in a button factory and then in various carpet mills, becoming a skilled weaver. During that time she married Joseph P. Conboy, a Boston letter carrier, who died two years later. Her success in leading the employees of the Roxbury mill where she was then employed in a strike for higher wages and union recognition thrust her into a position of prominence in labor circles. She became an organizer for and in October 1915 secretary-treasurer of the United Textile Workers of America. She proved a highly effective fund-raiser and lobbyist on behalf of legislation protecting women and children in factories.

Conboy was the only woman at a conference on labor called by President Woodrow Wilson in 1918, and in 1920 she was given by her colleagues the unique honor of representing the American Federation of Labor at the conference of the British Trades Union Congress in Portsmouth, England. In September 1921 she was one of four women who took part in a conference on unemployment called by President Warren G. Harding. She was also an active member of the National Committee on Prisons and Prison Labor, the New York State Housing Commission, and other organizations. Conboy — "Aunt Sara" to thousands of the men and women she worked with and for — was among the very first women to achieve a position of influence in the highest levels of organized labor. She died in Brooklyn, New York, on January 7, 1928.

Cone, Claribel and Etta 1864–1929 and 1870–1949 art collectors

Born in Jonesboro, Tennessee, Claribel on November 14, 1864, and Etta on November 30, 1870, the Cone sisters, daughters of German immigrant parents, grew up in Baltimore and attended public schools there. Claribel then entered the Woman's Medical College of Baltimore, graduated in 1890, and after interning at the Blockley Hospital for the Insane in Philadelphia returned to Baltimore, where she took some advanced training at the new Johns Hopkins University Medical School. From 1894 to 1903 she carried on research under Dr. William H. Welch at Johns Hopkins and taught pathology at the Woman's Medical College.

In the 1890s Claribel and Etta together developed an informal salon where musicians, artists, intellectuals, and professional people found great delight in Claribel's unconventionality and taste in antiques and Etta's cuisine. Etta, shy and submissive, also had pronounced taste in art and, perhaps through acquaintance with Leo and Gertrude Stein, became interested in the French Impressionists. She began buying paintings in 1896, and from 1902, by which time both their parents were dead and they had a handsome income, they were both ardent collectors. They spent increasing amounts of time in Europe. Visits to the Steins' Paris apartment brought them into contact with contemporary French art and artists; they bought their first Picasso in 1905, a Matisse in 1906.

The closing of the Woman's Medical College in 1910 ended Claribel's medical career. She was in Munich when World War I broke out in August 1914 and chose to remain there for the duration rather than risk travel in wartime. On her return to Baltimore in 1921 she rented a large apartment in the same building as hers and Etta's and arranged it as a private museum for their growing collection. Set off by Renaissance textiles and furniture, the collection of paintings eventually included works by Renoir, Manet, Cézanne, Degas, and Bonnard and a large number by Matisse, with whom Etta in particular enjoyed a long friendship. Claribel Cone died suddenly in Lausanne, Switzerland, on September 20, 1929, leaving her part in the collection to the disconsolate Etta. Etta continued her quiet life, summering in Europe, especially in Italy, and wintering in Baltimore, where she cared for and occasionally opened the museum for small showings or concerts. At her death in Blowing Rock, North Carolina, on August 31, 1949, the great collection went to the Baltimore Museum of Art along with a bequest of $400,000 for the construction of a new wing to contain it.

Connelly, Cornelia Augusta 1809–1879 religious

Born in Philadelphia on January 15, 1809, Cornelia Peacock was orphaned at an early age and reared in the strongly Episcopalian household of her older half sister. In December 1831 she married Pierce Connelly, an Episcopalian clergyman, and moved with him to Natchez, Mississippi, where he was rector of Trinity Church. In 1835, following his lead, she became interested in the Catholic church, and she and her husband soon became converts to that faith. They spent two years in Rome and then moved to Grand Coteau, Louisiana, where they taught in Catholic schools.

In 1840 Connelly announced his intention to enter the priesthood; the only way for him to do so was to obtain from his wife a deed of separation and for her to enter a convent. Although she was the mother of two children (two others had died), she agreed to the conditions. The separation was granted in March 1844 and the children were placed in convent schools, whereupon she entered the Sacred Heart Convent of Trinità del Monti in Rome. Her husband was ordained the following year, and in June 1845 she took her first vow.

In 1846 Cornelia Connelly was chosen to establish an order of teaching nuns among English Catholics and Irish immigrants in England. The order was established in October 1846, and in December 1847 she took vows and was made first superior of the Society of the Holy Child Jesus. Her husband subsequently attempted to gain control of the order through her and, failing in that, left the church and instituted civil proceedings for the restitution of his conjugal rights. This action also failed, and for the rest of his life he conducted a public campaign of vilification against her. She bore all such trials with equanimity, devoting her energies to the expansion of her order, which grew apace. After the original school at Derby was moved to St. Leonards-on-Sea, Sussex, in 1848, other schools were opened in London, Liverpool, Preston, and in 1862–1867 in Towanda (for a year only), Philadelphia, Sharon Hill, and West Philadelphia, Pennsylvania. In 1870 a school was opened in Toul, France (moved to Neuilly-sur-Seine in 1876). In 1863 she published a *Book of Studies* on educational practice. Her governance of the order was firm and not without controversy. In 1874 the Bishop of Southwark removed much of her authority. She died in St. Leonards, England, on April 18, 1879, and in 1959 she was proposed for beatification.

Connolly, Maureen Catherine 1934–1969 tennis player

Born in San Diego, California, on September 17, 1934, Maureen Connolly began playing tennis at the age of ten. After a few months of training under a professional teacher she entered her first tournament and in 1947 won the girl's fifteen-and-under title in the Southern California Invitational. By the time she was fifteen she had won more than 50 championships and had failed to win only 4 tournaments. In 1949 she became the youngest girl ever to win the national junior championship, and she successfully defended the title the following year. In 1951, her second year in women's division play, she won eight major tournaments and lost three, and helped the U.S. Wightman Cup team to victory. In September of that year she won the national women's singles championship at Forest Hills and was just a few months short of being the youngest woman ever to hold that title. Dubbed "Little Mo" by an affectionate press, Connolly was deceptively slight and engaging off court, but in action she displayed awesome power in her drives and a distractingly expressionless face. In 1952 she retained her U.S. title and won the prestigious Wimbledon championship in England. The next year she became the first woman to achieve the tennis "grand slam," winning the Australian, French, English, and U.S. championships. In 1954 she won her third Wimbledon title and second French title. From 1951 through 1954 she was a regular Wightman Cup team member and did not lose a single match in four years of cup play. An Associated Press sportswriters' poll named her woman athlete of the year in 1952, 1953, and 1954. In 1954 she suffered a crushed leg in a horseback riding accident and never again entered tournament play. She was subsequently a tennis instructor. In 1968 she was elected to the National Lawn Tennis Hall of Fame. She died in Dallas, Texas, on June 21, 1969.

Cooke, Rose Terry 1827–1892 poet and short-story writer

Born on February 17, 1827, near Hartford, Connecticut, Rose Terry was of a well-to do family. While overcoming her childhood ill health, she gained from her father a love of nature and from her mother a mastery of household management and lore. She graduated from the Hartford Female Seminary in 1843 and for some years thereafter taught school and was a governess in Burlington, New Jersey. From 1848 she devoted herself principally to writing. Her first published piece was a story in *Graham's Magazine* in 1845; the first of note was a poem, characteristically titled "Trailing Arbutus," which appeared in the *New York Daily Tribune* in April 1851. By 1857 her work had brought her sufficient reputation that she was invited by James Russell Lowell to contribute the leading story to the first issue of the *Atlantic Monthly*.

Cooke's poems, which were collected in a volume in 1861 (and again in 1888), included generally facile nature lyrics and some frontier ballads of rather more originality, but it was her stories that brought her recognition. In them the scenes and characters of backcountry New England were faithfully captured in every homely detail and trick of speech. The melancholy often suggested by her subjects was frequently relieved by a humor of her own. As a forerunner of the later local colorists she provided a valuable record of the time and place, although technically her fictions suffered on comparison with later writers. Her stories were collected in *Happy Dodd; or, She Hath Done What She Could*, 1878, *Somebody's Neighbors*, 1881, *The Deacon's Week*, 1885, *Root-Bound and Other Sketches*, 1885, *The Sphinx's Children and Other People's*, 1886, and *Huckleberries Gathered from New England Hills*, 1891. In addition she published an unsuccessful novel, *Steadfast*, 1889, and some 50 stories for children in various magazines. In April 1873 she married Rollin H. Cooke, with whom she settled in Winsted, Connecticut. The financial difficulties of her years there accounted for the potboiler quality of much of her writing of the period. In 1887 the Cookes moved to Pittsfield, Massachusetts, where she died on July 18, 1892.

Coolbrith, Ina Donna 1841–1928 poet

Born on March 10, 1841, in Nauvoo, Illinois, the first major Mormon settlement, Josephine Donna Smith was a niece of Joseph Smith, founder of Mormonism. A short time later her widowed mother took the family to live in St. Louis. About 1851 the family traveled by wagon train to California, and young Josephine, on the saddle of famed scout James P. Beckwourth, became the first white child to cross Beckwourth Pass through the Sierra Nevadas. She attended school in the small town of Los Angeles and in September 1858 married Robert B. Carsley, from whom she was divorced three years later. By that time she had published a few poems in the local newspaper under the name "Ina." In 1862, adopting the name Ina Donna Coolbrith (her mother's maiden name), she moved to San Francisco, where she taught school and continued to write and publish and became a recognized member of the San Francisco literary group that included Bret Harte, Mark Twain, Ambrose Bierce, Charles W. Stoddard, and Cincinnatus H. Miller, whose nickname "Joaquin" she is said to have suggested. When Harte began editing the *Overland Monthly* in 1868 she became an editorial assistant. Her poems appeared not only in California publications but also in *Harper's*, *Scribner's*, and other national magazines, and the popularity of her verse spread to England.

While not of the first rank, Coolbrith's work avoided sentimentality, didacticism, and stilted prosody, and in that excelled much of what passed for good poetry in that day. In 1874 she became a librarian in the Oakland Public Library, where her influence over young people was later attested by such as Jack London and Isadora Duncan. In 1881 a volume of her poems entitled *A Perfect Day* was published by subscription. Ill health forced her to resign her library post in 1893, but from 1897 to 1899 she was librarian of the San Francisco Mercantile Library, and in 1899 she became librarian of the Bohemian Club, of which she was made an honorary member, the only woman ever so honored. In 1894 she published *The Singer of the Sea* and in 1895 a collection of *Songs from the Golden Gate*. The earthquake and fire of April 1906 destroyed her home and much work in manuscript. She remained nonetheless a central feature of San Francisco's cultural life, her home a popular salon for artists and writers. For the 1915 Panama Pacific Exposition she called a World Congress of Authors, and in that year she was designated poet laureate of California by act of the legislature. She died in Berkeley, California, on February 29, 1928.

Coolidge, Elizabeth Penn Sprague 1864–1953 philanthropist

Born in Chicago on October 30, 1864, Elizabeth Sprague was of a wealthy family that early encouraged her to study music. In her youth she appeared on a few occasions as a pianist with the Chicago Symphony Orchestra, of which her father was a sponsor. She married Dr. Frederic S. Coolidge of Boston in November 1891. They lived in Boston until 1901, when they moved to Pittsfield in the Berkshire hills of western Massachusetts. Coolidge's career in philanthropy began after the death of her father in 1915. She and her mother gave the memorial Sprague Hall (a music building) to Yale University, and a short time later, after her mother's death, she endowed a pension fund for the Chicago Symphony. In 1916 she organized what became the Berkshire Quartet, and from 1918 to 1924 she sponsored annual Berkshire Chamber Music festivals in Pittsfield. In 1920 she founded an annual competition for musical compositions. In 1925 she created the

Elizabeth Sprague Coolidge Foundation to build an auditorium, complete with organ, for the Library of Congress and to sponsor concerts of chamber music there. The auditorium was opened in October 1925.

Over the years Coolidge commissioned works for the Library of Congress concerts and festivals from such composers as Charles M. Loeffler, Frederick Stock, Howard Hanson, Igor Stravinsky, Serge Prokofieff, Béla Bartók, Walter Piston, Samuel Barber, Ernest Bloch, Benjamin Britten, Maurice Ravel, Ottorino Respighi, Arnold Schoenberg, William Schuman, Aaron Copland, Paul Hindemith, and Darius Milhaud. Several works were made for Martha Graham's dance troupe. In 1932 she established the Elizabeth Sprague Coolidge Medal for "eminent services to chamber music." She also sponsored concerts in many other cities in the United States and Europe and supported at various times the Pro Arte, Kolisch, Budapest, Roth, and Coolidge quartets. She died in Cambridge, Massachusetts, on November 4, 1953.

Cooney, Joan Ganz 1929– television producer

Born on November 30, 1929, in Phoenix, Arizona, Joan Ganz attended Dominican College of San Rafael, California, and the University of Arizona. After graduating from the latter in 1951 she became a reporter for the *Arizona Republic* in 1953. In 1954 she moved to New York City, where she wrote publicity copy for the National Broadcasting Company for a year and for the dramatic television series "The United States Steel Hour" from 1955 to 1962. In 1962 she joined the educational television station in New York, WNET, as a producer of documentary programs on public affairs. In February 1964 she married Timothy J. Cooney. Her study of the anti-poverty program in New York won a local Emmy award in 1966. In that year she made for the Carnegie Corporation a study of the possible use of television for preschool education. The ubiquity of television, its frequency of use by young children, and its readily demonstrable ability to teach (if only commercial jingles until then) suggested that a well designed program could provide useful and effective instruction as well as entertainment to preschoolers. Acting on her own conclusions, she began soliciting financial backing from foundations and federal agencies to develop such an approach to television.

In 1968 Cooney founded the Children's Television Workshop with $8 million in funds, and a year later, after more research on children's tastes in television, the first concrete results were shown in several pilot versions of a program called, in allusion to the Arabian Nights story of Ali Baba, "Sesame Street." The show went on the air in November 1969 over the National Educational Television network of some 190 stations and quickly drew an audience numbering in the millions, a popularity unprecedented on public television. "Sesame Street" aimed to teach the alphabet, numbers, and basic reasoning, and to raise the general level of awareness of its young and particularly its disadvantaged viewers, and to that end it employed fast pacing, animated segments, soft rock music, slapstick comedy, the irrepressible Muppets, and live actors in a set suggesting an urban tenement district street.

In 1970 "Sesame Street" won Emmy and Peabody awards, among other honors. The Children's Television Workshop continued to turn out "Sesame Street" segments, also produced in Spanish-language versions, and another program, "The Electric Company," aimed at helping older children learn to read. In 1974 it experimented with a program on health aimed at adults and called "Feeling Good." Cooney was president of the Workshop from 1970–1988, and chairwoman and chief executive officer from 1988–1990; she stepped down as CEO in 1990, but continued to chair the executive committee. In 1991 she was appointed by President Bush to the first board of the New American Schools Development. She was inducted into the Academy of Television Arts and Sciences Hall of Fame in 1989.

Cooper, Sarah Brown Ingersoll 1835–1896 educator

Born in Cazenovia, New York, on December 12, 1835, Sarah Ingersoll, a cousin of orator and agnostic Robert G. Ingersoll, was educated at Cazenovia Seminary in 1850–1853. After a year as a schoolteacher she attended Emma Willard's Troy Female Seminary in 1854. She then served as governess on the plantation of a former governor of Georgia until September 1855, when she married Halsey F. Cooper, editor of the *Chattanooga Advertiser*. At the outbreak of the Civil War they left Tennessee for New York, but a federal appointment for her husband took them to Memphis in 1863. Relief work, Bible classes, and the death of a daughter combined to strain her health, and after two years of fruitless convalescence in Minnesota she moved with her husband to San Francisco in 1869. After recovering her health she began contributing articles and reviews to various periodicals.

Cooper began a highly popular Bible class in her Presbyterian church in 1871, and ten years later she led it into the Congregational church after a heresy trial in which she was convicted of denying the doctrines of infant damnation and eternal punishment. In 1878 she was deeply impressed by the work of Kate Douglas Smith (later Wiggin) with underprivileged children at the Silver Street Kindergarten, and in 1879 she and members of her Bible class opened the Jackson Street Kindergarten. Her success there led to the opening of others and in 1884 to her organization of the Golden Gate Kindergarten Association to supervise them. As director and superintendent she guided the development of the association for the next 12 years as it grew to incorporate 40 kindergartens enrolling nearly 3600 pupils at a time. (Phoebe A. Hearst contributed an office building to house the association.) Nearly 300 kindergartens based on her model sprang up in other cities around the country and abroad. In 1891 the Golden Gate Kindergarten Free Normal Training School was opened by the association, and in 1892, at Saratoga, New York, Cooper helped found and was elected first president of the international Kindergarten Union.

Cooper was in addition a popular and frequent public speaker and was active in numerous other organizations, including the Associated Charities of San Francisco, the Pacific Coast Women's Press Association, of which she was president, the Century Club, and the General Federation of Women's Clubs. She delivered an address at the World's Columbian Exposition of 1893 in Chicago, where she was also one of five women delegates to the Pan-Republic Congress. In 1895 she helped found and was chosen first president of the Woman's Congress. In her work her constant companion and secretary was her elder daughter Harriet, especially following the suicide of Halsey Cooper in 1885. In 1896 Harriet suffered an acute attack of depression, however, and after several unsuccessful attempts on her own life and that of her mother she turned on the gas in their San Francisco apartment on the night of December 10–11, 1896, and asphyxiated them both.

Cooper, Susan Augusta Fenimore 1813–1894 writer and philanthropist

Born on April 17, 1813, at Heathcote Hill, the maternal De Lancey manor in Mamaroneck, New York, Susan Fenimore Cooper was the daughter of James Fenimore Cooper, whose devoted companion and amanuensis she was to be until his death. She was educated at home in Cooperstown, New York, until 1817, when the family moved to New York City; there, and from 1826 to 1833 in Europe, she attended private schools. In 1836 the family again settled in Cooperstown. With her father's encouragement she began to write and in 1845 published a novel, *Elinor Wyllys; or, the Young Folk of Longbridge*, under the pseudonym "Amabel Penfeather." Her volume of fresh and graceful observations of nature and country life drawn from her journal, *Rural Hours*, 1850, was very successful, enjoying several reprintings and appearing in revised editions in 1868 and

1887. In the same vein but less successful were *Rhyme and Reason of Country Life*, 1854, and *Rural Rambles*, 1854. In 1859 she published *Mount Vernon, a letter to the Children of America.* As her father's literary executor she produced *Pages and Pictures, from the Writings of James Fenimore Cooper*, 1861, and the prefatory essays in the Household Edition of his works, published in 1876–1884. She also published some magazine articles on her father and *William West Skiles, a Sketch of Missionary Life In Valle Crucis in Western North Carolina, 1842–1862*, 1890. In 1865 she founded Thanksgiving Hospital in Cooperstown and in 1873 the Orphan House of the Holy Savior, which she personally superintended as it grew to house nearly a hundred children. She died in Cooperstown, New York, on December 31, 1894.

Coppin, Fanny Marion Jackson 1837–1913 educator and missionary

Born a slave in Washington, D.C., in 1837, Fanny Jackson was bought into freedom by an aunt while still a small girl, and she grew up in New Bedford, Massachusetts, and Newport, Rhode Island. She determined to get an education and, while employed as a domestic servant, studied on her own to win admission to the Rhode Island State Normal School. In 1860 she entered Oberlin College. While there she taught in the preparatory department. On graduating in 1865 she took a job teaching Latin, Greek, and mathematics at the Institute for Colored Youth in Philadelphia, where she served also as principal of the girls' high school department. In 1869 she became head principal of the Institute; she was the first African-American woman in the country to hold such a position, and she lost little time in exerting great influence on the course of the school. In 1871 she introduced a normal-school department, and within a few years teacher training had far exceeded the classical course in enrollment. To the ordinary work of teacher training she added a practice teaching system in 1878. In 1889, after a ten-year campaign of convincing the school's managers and raising funds, she opened an industrial training department offering instruction in ten different trades. Education in both academic and vocational fields was to her equally a moral and a practical matter and a central tool in the struggle to end discrimination against her race.

After a period of ill health Jackson resigned her post with the Institute in 1902. (The Institute was moved to Cheyney, Pennsylvania, in 1904 and became a state normal school in 1920 and Cheyney State College in 1951.) In 1881 she married the Reverend Levi J. Coppin, who in 1900 became a bishop of the African Methodist Episcopal church. In 1888 Coppin served as president of the Women's Home and Foreign Missionary Society of the A.M.E. church and was a delegate to the Centenary Conference on the Protestant Missions of the World in London. In 1902 the Coppins sailed for Cape Town, South Africa, and over the next decade she worked tirelessly among native black and "colored" women in that country, organizing mission societies and promoting temperance. She also founded the Bethel Institute in Cape Town. After her return to the United States she settled again in Philadelphia, where she died on January 21, 1913. In 1926 the High and Training School of Baltimore was renamed the Fanny Jackson Coppin Normal School (now Coppin State College) in her memory.

Corbin, Margaret 1751–1800 Revolutionary heroine

Born on November 12, 1751, in what is now Franklin County, then on the western Pennsylvania frontier, Margaret Cochran, having lost both of her parents in an Indian raid when she was five, grew up with relatives. She married John Corbin in 1772, and when he enlisted in the First Company of Pennsylvania Artillery for service in the Revolution she followed him east. On November 16, 1776, Corbin was manning a gun on a ridge near Fort Washington, New York, when he was killed during a Hessian advance. Observing from nearby, Margaret immediately leaped to the gun and continued to serve in her husband's stead until she was felled by grapeshot wounds. Upon the surrender of the

American position she was not taken among the prisoners. She made her way to Philadelphia and there, completely disabled, came to the attention of the state's Executive Council, by which she was granted temporary relief in June 1779. The next month the Continental Congress approved the granting of a lifetime soldier's half-pay pension to her. She was thereafter included on military rolls and in April 1783 was formally mustered out of the Continental army. She lived in Westchester County, New York, until her death on January 16, 1800. Her story has sometimes been confused with that of Mary McCauley, "Molly Pitcher."

Cori, Gerty Theresa Radnitz 1896–1957 biochemist

Born in Prague, Austria-Hungary (now Czech Republic), on August 15, 1896, Gerty Radnitz was educated in a girls' school and at the Realgymnasium of Tetschen before entering the German University of Prague in 1914. She graduated in 1920 with a medical degree, and in August of that year she married a fellow student, Carl F. Cori. For two years she worked as an assistant in the Karolinen Children's Hospital in Vienna. In 1922 the Coris came to the United States, where both joined the staff of the New York State Institute for the Study of Malignant Diseases in Buffalo. There Gerty Cori was an assistant pathologist from 1922 to 1925 and an assistant biochemist from 1925 to 1931. In 1928 they became naturalized citizens. In 1931 the Coris moved to Washington University, St. Louis, where they joined the department of pharmacology. Gerty Cori held the post of research associate from 1931 to 1943 and that of research associate professor from 1943 to 1947. In 1946 they moved together from the department of pharmacology to that of biochemistry.

Their early work in Buffalo on metabolism in tumor cells had led them into a program of investigation of carbohydrate metabolism in general. In a series of papers in the 1920s and 1930s they published their findings on the influence of the hormones epinephrine and insulin on carbohydrate metabolism; on the mechanism whereby liver glycogen is converted to glucose; on the conversion of muscle glycogen to lactate; on their discovery in 1936 of glucose-1-phosphate (sometimes called the Cori ester), an intermediate phase in glycogen conversion; on their discovery in 1938 of the catalytic enzyme phosphorylase, which plays a central role in the process; and on other aspects of the process. Their elaboration of glycogen metabolism led to their dramatic synthesis of glycogen in the test tube in 1939. These discoveries brought them the 1947 Nobel Prize for Physiology or Medicine jointly with Bernardo A. Houssay of Argentina; Gerty Cori was the third woman, and the first American woman, to receive a Nobel Prize in the sciences. In the same year she was named professor of biochemistry at Washington University, a post she held for the rest of her life. From 1950 she sat on the board of directors of the National Science Foundation. The Coris' subsequent work led to the complete elucidation of the molecular structure of glycogen in 1952. Gerty Cori also contributed greatly to the understanding of glycogen storage diseases of children. She died in St. Louis on October 26, 1957.

Cornell, Katharine 1893–1974 actor and producer

Born on February 16, 1893, in Berlin, Germany, Katharine Cornell was the daughter of American parents with whom she returned to Buffalo, New York, later in that year. Her interest in the theater came naturally — her father was an amateur actor and an associate in theatrical management of Jessie Bonstelle. She wrote, directed, and appeared in several plays in school, and in 1916 she joined the Washington Square Players in New York City. She later worked with one of Bonstelle's touring stock companies and in October 1919 received favorable attention for her portrayal of Jo in the first London production of *Little Women*. In March 1921 she made her Broadway debut in Rachel Crothers's *Nice People* at the Klaw Theatre, and later in the year she won her first lead in

Clemence Dane's *A Bill of Divorcement*, vaulting into stardom in the role. Subsequently she appeared in *Will Shakespeare*, 1923, *The Way Things Happen* and George Bernard Shaw's *Candida*, both 1924, and Michael Arlen's *The Green Hat*, 1925, among others. The last was directed by Guthrie McClintic, her husband since September 1921 and thereafter director of nearly all her plays.

After *The Letter*, 1927, *The Age of Innocence* (an adaptation from Edith Wharton) 1928, and *Dishonored Lady*, 1930, Cornell began managing her own productions and immediately scored a triumph in *The Barretts of Wimpole Street*, 1931, in which she played Elizabeth Barrett Browning. After a long Broadway run she broke with current theatrical practice by taking the production's first-string cast on an extended and highly successful road tour. In seven months in 1933–1934 she and her company traveled 17,000 miles back and forth across the country. Celebrated for their excellence, her later productions included Thornton Wilder's *Lucrece*, 1932, *Alien Corn*, written for her by Sidney Howard, 1933, *Romeo and Juliet*, 1934, Shaw's *Saint Joan*, 1936, Maxwell Anderson's *The Wingless Victory*, 1937, *No Time for Comedy*, 1939, *The Doctor's Dilemma*, 1941, and *The Three Sisters*, 1942. During World War II she entertained troops in Europe with *The Barretts of Wimpole Street* and in 1943 appeared in a movie, *Stage Door Canteen*. She returned to Broadway in 1946 with *Antigone* and a revival of *Candida* and followed with *Antony and Cleopatra*, 1947, *That Lady*, 1949, Somerset Maugham's *The Constant Wife*, 1951, *The Dark is Light Enough*, 1955, and *Dear Liar*, 1960. During the 1950s she also appeared on television in productions of *The Barretts of Wimpole Street* in 1956 and *There Shall Be No Night* in 1957. During her thirty years of stardom she shared with Lynn Fontanne and Helen Hayes claim to the rank of first lady of the American theater. Following the death of her husband in 1961 Cornell retired from the stage. She died at her home in Vineyard Haven, Massachusetts, on June 9, 1974.

Corson, Juliet 1841–1897 cookery teacher and writer

Born on January 14, 1841, in Roxbury (now part of Boston), Massachusetts, Juliet Corson grew up from the age of six in New York City. Delicate health kept her from school, and her education was largely acquired in the extensive library of an uncle. By the age of eighteen she was supporting herself by working as librarian of the Working Women's Library. She supplemented her income by contributing verse and sketches to various periodicals, and eventually she had a regular column on topics of interest to women in the *New York Leader*. Subsequently her work as an indexer for the *National Quarterly Review* led to a staff writing job.

In 1873 Corson joined in organizing and became secretary of a Free Training School for Women, where courses were offered in sewing, bookkeeping, and proofreading. The next year she introduced a course in cooking, hiring a chef to demonstrate while she lectured out of a reading knowledge of the subject. The success of this and a similar course the next year led her to establish in November 1876 the New York Cooking School. For a textbook she wrote a *Cooking Manual*, 1877. The success of her pioneering venture in cookery education was bolstered by the wide circulation of her pamphlet *Fifteen Cent Dinners for Families of Six*, 1877, occasioned by the railroad strike of that year and published and distributed at her own expense. By 1878 she was traveling and lecturing widely; after a lecture at a public school in Montreal in December 1878, at which the chef she had engaged failed to appear, she did her own demonstration cooking while lecturing. Under the auspices of the U.S. Bureau of Education she lectured before the Washington, D.C., Training School for Nurses in 1878 and prepared an influential circular, *Training Schools of Cookery*, 1879. She also published *Twenty-five Cent Dinners for Families of Six*, 1878, *Cooking School Text-Book*, 1879, *Juliet Corson's New Family Cook Book*, 1885, *Miss Corson's Practical American Cookery*, 1886, and *Family Living* *on $500 a Year*, 1887, and a large number of articles. Her lecture tours covered the nation, and she was constantly consulted by governments and organizations. For a time in 1890–1891 she edited the *Household Monthly*. She presided over the New York State cooking school exhibit at the 1893 World's Columbian Exposition in Chicago, where she was honored for her work. She died in New York City on June 18, 1897.

Cowl, Jane 1883–1950 actor and playwright

Born in Boston on December 14, 1883, Grace Bailey grew up from the age of three in Brooklyn, New York. She attended public schools and in 1902–1904 Erasmus Hall, during which time she made her first stage appearance, under the name Jane Cowl, in David Belasco's 1903 production of *Sweet Kitty Bellairs*. Over the next several years she played many small parts while studying the craft of acting and perfecting her technique under Belasco's painstaking direction. She also took a few courses at Columbia University. Her first major role was in *Is Matrimony a Failure?* in 1909, and in it she won high critical praise. After two seasons with the Hudson Theatre stock company in Union Hill, New Jersey, she returned to Broadway in the fall of 1910. The failure of *The Upstart* was followed by the success of *The Gamblers* that year, and in September 1912 she achieved star billing in *Within the Law*, which ran for over 540 performances at the Eltinge Theatre. *Common Clay* was also a success for her in 1915.

In 1917 Cowl appeared in her first motion picture, a Samuel Goldwyn production called *The Spreading Dawn* made in Fort Lee, New Jersey. In February of that year she opened on Broadway in *Lilac Time*, which she had written in collaboration with Jane Murfin, a friend since they had played together in Belasco's *The Music Master* in 1904. *Lilac* was a moderate hit in New York and on tour, but Cowl's and Murfin's next two efforts, *Daybreak*, 1917, and *Information Please*, 1918, were failures. In 1918–1919 Jane Cowl starred in *The Crowded Hour*. Late in 1919 she opened in *Smilin' Through*, written by her and Murfin under the pseudonym "Alan Langdon Martin" (they suspected sex discrimination might have contributed to their previous failure). *Smilin' Through* was a theatrical phenomenon, running for 1170 performances on Broadway. In 1922, after the short-lived *Malvaloca*, she scored a personal triumph in *Romeo and Juliet*, in which she established a world record for Shakespearean productions of 856 consecutive performances (157 in New York, the rest on tour across the country). By this time she was acclaimed the most beautiful woman on the American stage. A dry spell followed, *Pelleas and Melisande*, 1923, *Antony and Cleopatra*, 1924, *The Depths*, 1925, and *One Trip of the Silver Star*, 1925, were unsuccessful. Success came again in Noel Coward's *Easy Virtue* in New York in 1925 and London in 1926. She was again a hit in Robert Sherwood's comedy *The Road to Rome* in 1927. *The Jealous Moon*, which she wrote with Theodore Charles, 1928, a revival of *Paolo and Francesca*, 1929, another of *Art and Mrs. Bottle*, 1930, *Twelfth Night*, a production she designed, 1930, and *Camille*, 1931, were all brief ventures. *First Lady*, by George S. Kaufman and Katherine Dayton, 1934, was a success; Thornton Wilder's *The Merchant of Yonkers*, 1938, was not; and John Van Druten's *Old Acquaintance*, opening in December 1940, was her last substantial run. For a number of years thereafter she played stock theaters and tried various revivals around the country. Her final New York stage appearance was in *The First Mrs. Fraser* in 1948. In 1943 she appeared as herself in the movie *Stage Door Canteen* (she was a co-director of the actual Stage Door Canteen operated during World War II by the American Theatre Wing), and from 1949 she had feature parts in several unmemorable films. Jane Cowl died in Santa Monica, California, on June 22, 1950.

Crabtree, Lotta 1847–1924 actor

Born in New York City on November 7, 1847, Charlotte Crabtree grew up from the age of four in California, where her father went in the Gold Rush of the early 1850s. At the

Grass Valley mining camp she met Lola Montez, who taught her a bit of dancing and stagecraft, and in 1855 she first performed before an audience of miners. Her lively, diminutive figure immediately captivated the audience, and, with her mother, she began touring the wild camps of California. In 1859 she began appearing in variety theaters in and around San Francisco, where her singing, dancing, and melodramatic roles, many written for her, kept her in the limelight.

Crabtree's first acting role was in *Loan of a Lover*, performed in Petaluma. She made her New York debut at Niblo's Garden in June 1864 with little success. After three years of touring the country, however, she returned to Wallack's Theatre in *Little Nell and the Marchioness*, adapted for her from Dickens's *The Old Curiosity Shop*, and was a sensation. From then until her retirement she enjoyed huge popularity at home and in England. Her infectious gaiety, perennially winsome, childlike appearance, and occasionally saucy and sweetly risqué manner made her a versatile performer and ranked her in the forefront of the emerging theater of burlesque extravaganza. From 1870 she toured with her own company in plays that showcased her unique talents. Among her most popular roles were those she played in *Firefly*, *Hearts Ease*, *Topsy*, *The Little Difference*, *Musette*, *Mam'zelle*, *Nitouche*, and *Zip*. Most often known simply as "Lotta," Crabtree left the stage in 1891 and lived in quiet retirement at her estate on Lake Hopatcong, New Jersey. She was honored by a special day at the Panama-Pacific Exposition in San Francisco in 1915, and during World War I she made a few appearances for soldiers and veterans. She died in Boston on September 25, 1924, leaving an estate of some $4 million.

Crandall, Ella Phillips 1871–1938 nurse

Born on September 16, 1871, in Wellsville, New York, Ella Crandall grew up in Dayton, Ohio. She graduated from the two-year course at the Philadelphia General Hospital School of Nursing in 1897 and two years later returned to Dayton as assistant superintendent of the Miami Valley Hospital and director of its newly founded school of nursing. Her outstanding work there earned her a position of influence within the Society of Superintendents of Training Schools for Nurses. In 1909 she moved to New York City, entered the New York School of Philanthropy, and for a year served as a superintendent in the visiting nurse service of Lillian Wald's Henry Street Settlement House. In 1910–1912 she was on the graduate nursing faculty of Teachers College, Columbia University.

In 1911 she served on a commission established to study the need for organized public health work and the developing and still undefined role of nurses in the field. From the commission's work emerged in 1912 the National Organization for Public Health Nursing, of which Ella Crandall became executive secretary. Until her resignation eight years later she labored indefatigably to develop public health nursing into a recognized profession with high professional standards and rigorous training. To keep in contact with the hundreds of individual nurses engaged, often as not in isolation, in public health work from city slums to mountain fastnesses required constant travel on her part. Her forceful leadership, expressed personally in her travels and frequent addresses as well as through the organization's journal *Public Health Nurse* (later *Public Health Nursing*) succeeded in giving coherence and standing to the profession.

During World War I Crandall served also on the nursing committee of the American Red Cross and as executive secretary of the National Emergency Committee on Nursing of the General Medical Board of the Council of National Defense. After her resignation as head of the Public Health Nursing organization in 1920 she continued to be active on committees involved in various aspects of public health and in 1922–1925 was associate director of the American Child Health Association. In 1927 she was named executive secretary of the newly established Payne Fund, a philanthropic foundation sponsoring research in education. She held the post until her death in New York City on October 24, 1938.

Crandall, Prudence 1803–1890 educator and social reformer
Born in Hopkinton, Rhode Island, on September 3, 1803, Prudence Crandall grew up in a Quaker household and was educated at the New England Friends' Boarding School in Providence. After a brief period of teaching school in Plainfield, Connecticut, she moved to Canterbury, Connecticut, and there in 1831 opened a private girls' academy, which was soon recognized is one of the best of its kind in the state. When early in 1833 she admitted to the school a young African-American girl, she was immediately the focus of heated protest and controversy. In March 1833, on the advice of William Lloyd Garrison and others, she announced that she would the next month open on the same premises a new school for "young ladies and little misses of color." The local citizenry were even more outraged and embarked upon a campaign of unremitting persecution and ostracism. In May the Connecticut legislature was prodded into enacting a bill forbidding the establishment of schools for nonresident African-Americans without the consent of local authorities.

In a case that received wide publicity and enlisted the aid of Arthur Tappan, Samuel J. May, and other prominent abolitionists, Crandall was indicted and convicted under the so-called "Black Law" and imprisoned until July 1834, when the court of appeals reversed her conviction on technical grounds. Local opposition increased to the point of mob violence, however, and in September 1834 she was forced to give up her school. With her husband, Calvin Philleo, a Baptist minister whom she had married in August, she moved to Illinois; after his death in 1874 she went to live with her brother in Elk Falls, Kansas. In 1886 the Connecticut legislature attempted amends with a small pension. She died in Elk Falls, Kansas, on January 28, 1890.

Crane, Caroline Julia Bartlett 1858–1935 clergyman and reformer
Born on August 17, 1858, in Hudson, Wisconsin, Caroline Bartlett grew up there and in Hamilton, Illinois. She graduated from Carthage College in nearby Carthage, Illinois (now in Kenosha, Wisconsin), in 1879, and, suppressing for a time her long-standing wish to enter the ministry, she then taught school for four years in Iowa. In 1884–1885 she was on the staff of the *Minneapolis Tribune*. After a brief stint as city editor of the *Oshkosh Daily Times* in Wisconsin she obtained appointment in 1886 as pastor of the small All Souls Unitarian society in Sioux Falls, Dakota Territory.

In October 1889, having by that time obtained some regular training in divinity at the University of Chicago, Bartlett was ordained formally in the ministry and installed as pastor of the First Unitarian Church of Kalamazoo, Michigan. Her warmth and enthusiasm soon attracted a growing congregation. In 1892 the congregation adopted a nonsectarian and essentially creedless organization, and in 1894, as the People's Church, it moved into a new building designed as a social, education, and community center. The People's Church, emphasizing practical service, included a public kindergarten, a gymnasium, manual training and domestic science departments, musical societies, and other attractions. Later the church turned to civic and sociological studies. In December 1896 Reverend Bartlett married Dr. Augustus W. Crane. In 1898 she resigned her pastorate.

Caroline Crane's second career, as an urban sanitarian, came about almost by chance. Visiting slaughterhouses in Kalamazoo in 1901 for background information for a lecture on meat preparation, she discovered that highly unsanitary conditions were the rule. Visits to other cities yielded similar results. Relevant state laws were inadequate, so she personally lobbied a bill permitting local inspection and regulation through the Michigan legislature and then pushed a model ordinance through the Kalamazoo city council. In

1903–1904 she founded the Women's Civic Improvement League, which undertook to identify and publicize unsanitary and unsightly conditions around the city and managed a demonstration project in neighborhood sanitation. She also organized the Charity Organizations Board, which coordinated all public welfare work in the city and operated visiting nurse and family counseling services and a program of public employment for beggars. Her successes led to a great demand for her services as a consultant to other cities, work she was eventually forced to place on a professional fee basis. By 1917 she had conducted consultant sanitation inspections in 62 cities in 14 states. After that time she largely retired, although she remained active in Kalamazoo affairs. She died in Kalamazoo, Michigan, on March 24, 1935.

Crapsey, Adelaide 1878–1914 poet

Born on September 9, 1878, in Brooklyn, New York, Adelaide Crapsey grew up in Rochester, New York. She was the daughter of Reverend Algernon Sidney Crapsey, an Episcopal clergyman who later, in 1906, was defrocked after a celebrated heresy trial. After attending Kemper Hall preparatory school in Kenosha, Wisconsin, she entered Vassar College, from which she graduated in 1901. She taught at Kemper Hall in 1902–1904 and then spent a year at the School of Classical Studies of the American Academy in Rome. From 1906 to 1908 she taught at Miss Lowe's School in Stamford, Connecticut, but by the latter year she was in the grip of tuberculosis; for the next three years she sought to restore her health in Italy and England.

During that time Crapsey also carried on the analytic investigations that were to be published, uncompleted, as *A Study in English Metrics*, 1918. In 1911 she returned to America and took a post as instructor in poetics at Smith College, but her health forced her to give it up in 1913 to enter a sanatorium at Saranac Lake, New York. During her last year she wrote much of the verse that was to make her famous. Her deep interest in meter and rhythm led her to devise a new verse form, the cinquain, a 5-line form of 22 syllables that was ideally suited to her own poised, concise, and delicate expression. She died in Rochester, New York, on October 8, 1914. The next year her own selection of cinquains and verses in other forms appeared as *Verses*, a volume that was immediately taken up by literati, particularly of the younger generation. Expanded editions in 1922 and 1934 contained some of her earlier and previously unpublished work.

Cratty, Mabel 1868–1928 social worker

Born in Bellaire, Ohio, on June 30, 1868, Mabel Cratty attended public schools, studied briefly at Lake Erie Seminary (now College), and graduated from Ohio Wesleyan University in 1890. She then taught school for several years at the Wheeling Female Seminary in West Virginia, in Kent, Ohio, and from 1892 in Delaware, Ohio, where from 1900 to 1904 she was principal of the high school. A growing interest in the work of the Young Women's Christian Association led to her becoming a member of the Ohio state committee of the YWCA in 1902.

In 1904 Cratty moved to Chicago to take the post of associate general secretary of the American Committee of the YWCA. With the merging of the American Committee and the rival International Board in December 1906, Mabel Cratty became executive secretary of the home department under the unified National Board of the YWCA. A short time later she moved up to general secretary of the National Board, a post she retained for the rest of her life. As chief of the professional staff she bore the principal responsibility for developing and expanding the organization, and for such work she proved to be eminently suited. She was supported in everything by the president of the National Board, Grace H. Dodge, and by a rapidly growing staff, to whom she easily delegated authority and often credit for the work of the YWCA.

Although Cratty kept herself largely from public notice, her leadership was so effective that by 1928 the number of YWCA branches in the country had increased from fewer than 300 to more than 1300 and its membership from some 143,000 to over 600,000; the national staff had grown from 14 people based in one room to 189 occupying a 12-story headquarters building in New York City. A measure of her influence was her success in keeping the YWCA in the forefront of involvement in social and internationalist issues during the disillusioned 1920s. She attended seven world YWCA conferences and visited branches in many nations. She was also active in the work of the Camp Fire Girls, the Institute of Pacific Relations (whose 1927 conference in Honolulu she attended), the National Committee on the Cause and Cure of War (which she helped Carrie Chapman Catt organize), and other groups. She died in New York City on February 27, 1928.

Crocker, Lucretia 1829–1886 educator

Born in Barnstable, Massachusetts, on December 31, 1829, Lucretia Crocker graduated from the State Normal School in West Newton in 1850 and remained there for four more years as an instructor in geography, mathematics, and natural science. During 1857–1859 she was professor of mathematics and astronomy at Antioch College, where she had been called by the president of the college, Horace Mann. In 1859 she returned to Boston to care for her parents.

Over the next 15 years Crocker remained involved in education in a variety of ways: she taught science at a private Boston school operated by a former pupil, was active in promoting the education of African-American children, was secretary and then chairman of the executive committee of the Boston School for Deaf-Mutes (founded by Sarah Fuller in 1869), helped found the Woman's Education Association of Boston in 1872, and in 1873–1876 headed the science department of the Society to Encourage Studies at Home, a correspondence school. In December 1873 she was one of four women elected to the Boston School Committee after the New England Women's Club had agitated for female representation. The legality of their election was challenged successfully, but a year later, after the state legislature had passed legislation permitting women to sit on the committee, Lucretia Crocker, Lucretia P. Hale, and four other women were elected and seated.

In 1876 Crocker was elected by the committee to the newly created and powerful six-member Board of Supervisors. During her ten years on the board she directed her efforts in particular toward the improvement of science education in the Boston public schools. She worked to secure equipment, materials, and books of the highest quality for the schools and to improve the quality of teaching, the latter most effectively through the Teachers' School of Science, which she ardently supported. She introduced the teaching of zoology and mineralogy in the schools and in 1883 published *Methods of Teaching Geography: Notes on Lessons*. Her dedication to science education led to her election to the American Association for the Advancement of Science in 1880. She died in Boston on October 9, 1886.

Croly, Jane Cunningham 1829–1901 journalist and clubwoman

Born in Market Harborough, Leicestershire, England, on December 19, 1829, Jane Cunningham came to the United States with her family in 1841. She grew up in Poughkeepsie and then Wappingers Falls, New York, and taught for a time in a district school. From an early age she was interested in writing. In 1855 she went to New York City to seek a career. In short order she had placed a regular column, "Parlor and Sidewalk Gossip," with the *Sunday Times and Noah's Weekly Messenger*. By 1857 she was sending the column to the *Baltimore American*, the *Richmond Enquirer*, the *Louisville Journal*, and the *New Orleans Delta* as well, creating what was probably the first syndicated woman's column, which she signed in the fashion of the day with a pen name, "Jennie June." In February 1856 she married David G. Croly, also a journalist. In 1859 they moved to Rockford, Illinois, where he founded the short-lived *Daily News*, and in 1860 they returned to New York City, where they both joined the staff of the new *World*. From 1862 to 1872 she managed the *World*'s woman's department. During much of that time she also contributed a woman's column, along with pieces of dramatic and literary criticism, to the *Weekly Times*. She was the chief staff writer for *Mme. Demorest's Mirror of Fashions* from its founding in 1860 by Ellen L. C. Demorest, and she retained that post, through the magazine's growth into *Demorest's Illustrated Monthly Magazine* in 1864, until 1887. She also was associated with or contributed to at various times *Godey's Lady's Book* (in 1887–1889), *Woman's Cycle*, which she founded in 1889 and which merged with the *Home-Maker* the next year and became the *New Cycle* in 1893–1896, the *Graphic Daily Times*, the *New York Times*, the *Messenger*, and other periodicals, and she continued as New York! correspondent for a number of newspapers in other cities. In 1866 she published *Jennie June's American Cookery Book*.

Croly's columns on fashion advocated moderate dress reform while gently satirizing the more radical alternatives, and her commentaries on other topics of interest to women were similarly clearheaded and sensible. Her dedication to equal rights for women was predicated on the assumption of responsibility for self-betterment and productive effort by women. She believed that suffrage and related reforms would result naturally from women's assuming their properly equal place in the economic system. Three collections of her columns were published in book form, *Jennie Juneiana: Talks on Women's Topics*, 1869, *For Better or Worse; A Book for Some Men and All Women*, 1875, and *Thrown on Her Own Resources*, 1891.

In 1868 Croly was indignant when the New York Press Club sponsored a men-only reception for Charles Dickens, and her response was to found in March 1868 Sorosis, a club for women. She prevailed upon her friend Alice Cary to serve as first president of Sorosis; she herself was president in 1870 and again from 1875 to 1886. In 1889 she called a national convention of women's clubs at which, in March of that year, the General Federation of Women's Clubs was organized with Charlotte E. Brown as president. In the same year Croly founded and became first president of the Women's Press Club of New York. In 1892 she was named professor of journalism and literature at Rutgers University. Her last major work was the writing of her *History of the Woman's Club Movement in America*, 1898. She died in New York City on December 23, 1901. The third of her five children, Herbert David Croly (1869–1930), became famous as a political thinker and founding editor of the *New Republic*.

Crosby, Fanny 1820–1915 hymn writer and poet

Born in Southeast, Putnam County, New York, on March 24, 1820, Frances Jane Crosby lost her sight to an eye infection and medical ignorance at the age of six weeks. She nonetheless grew up an active and happy child in North Salem, New York, and from 1828 in Ridgefield, Connecticut, where her widowed and remarried mother took her. From 1835 to 1843 she attended the New York Institution for the Blind in New York City. Her inclination to versify was encouraged by a visiting Scottish phrenologist, who examined her and proclaimed her a poet. Thereafter she was the school's chief ornament. She contributed a poetic eulogy on President William Henry Harrison to the *New York Herald* in 1841 and subsequently published verses in other newspapers. She was featured in a troupe of students who made public appearances in Hudson River towns in 1842 and before joint sessions of Congress in January 1844 and April 1847. In 1844 she published her first volume, *The Blind Girl and Other Poems*, and in 1851 her second, *Monterey and Other Poems*. From the latter year she began writing verses to be set to music.

With George F. Root, music instructor at the school, Crosby wrote a successful cantata, "The Flower Queen"; and she also wrote lyrics for scores of songs, some of which, such as "Hazel Dell," "There's Music in the Air," and "Rosalie, the Prairie Flower," were widely popular. After her graduation Fanny Crosby remained at the New York Institution for the Blind as a teacher of English grammar and rhetoric and of ancient history until 1858, in March of which year she married Alexander Van Alstyne, also blind, a former pupil and then also a teacher at the school. In that year she published her third volume, *A Wreath of Columbia's Flowers*.

About 1864 Crosby began writing hymns. Like her poetry, her hymns suffered generally from cliché and sentimentality, but they also displayed an occasional gleam of more than ordinary talent. Their most striking quality, however, was their number: Fanny Crosby wrote in all between 5500 and 9000 hymns, the exact count hidden by her having used a great many pseudonyms (as many as 200, according to some sources) to preserve her modesty. The best known of her hymns included "Safe in the Arms of Jesus," "Rescue the Perishing," "Jesus the Water of Life Will Give," "Blessed Assurance," "The Bright Forever," "Savior, More Than Life to Me," and "Pass Me Not, O Gentle Savior." They were especially popular in the Methodist Church, which for a time observed an annual "Fanny Crosby Day." Most prominent among her many musical collaborators was Ira D. Sankey. In 1897 she published a final volume of poetry, *Bells at Evening and Other Verses*, and she later wrote two volumes of autobiography, *Fanny Crosby's Life-Story*, 1903, and *Memories of Eighty Years*, 1906. Her last years were passed in Bridgeport, Connecticut, where she died on February 12, 1915.

Crothers, Rachel 1878–1958 playwright, producer, and director

Born on December 12, 1878, in Bloomington, Illinois, Rachel Crothers graduated from the Illinois State Normal University (now Illinois State) in 1892. She studied dramatics in Boston and New York City and for a time appeared with various theatrical companies, later giving up performing to teach. Her career as a playwright began with a few minor, one-act efforts, bearing such titles as *The Rector*, *Nora*, and *The Point of View*, which were produced in 1902–1904 at the Savoy and Madison Square theaters. Her first full-length Broadway play, *The Three of Us*, which opened in October 1906 at the Madison Square, was a highlight of the season; and for the next three decades she maintained the extraordinary average of a Broadway play a year, the majority of them popular and critical successes. Her accomplishment was made the more remarkable by the fact that she produced and directed nearly all of her plays herself. Her audiences were particularly delighted by her mastery of dialogue, her characterizations, especially of women, and her deft and often humorous advocacy of established ideals and verities in the face of contemporary social ferment. Among her greatest hits were *Myself-Bettina*, in which Maxine Elliott starred, 1908, *A Man's World*, 1909, *He and She*, 1911, *Young Wisdom*, 1914, *The Heart of Paddy Whack*, 1914, *Old Lady 31*, 1916, *A Little Journey*, 1918, *Nice People*, 1921, *Mary the Third*, 1923, *Expressing Willie*, 1924, *A Lady's Virtue*, 1925, *Venus*, 1927, *Let Us Be Gay*, 1929, *As Husbands Go*, 1931, *When Ladies Meet*, 1932, and her last play, *Susan and God*, 1937.

During World War I Crothers founded the Stage Women's Relief Fund, and in 1932 she helped found the Stage Relief Fund, of which she remained a director until 1951. In 1940 she led in organizing the American Theatre Wing, which operated the famed Stage Door Canteens, and remained its executive director until 1950, when she became president emeritus. Rachel Crothers died in Danbury, Connecticut, on July 5, 1958.

Cummins, Maria Susanna 1827–1866 novelist

Born in Salem, Massachusetts, on April 9, 1827, Maria Cummins was educated at home and at a fashionable girls' school in Lenox, Massachusetts. She thereafter lived all her life with her family in Dorchester, Massachusetts. She became interested in writing during her schooldays, and the publication of some of her early short stories encouraged her. In 1854 she published her first novel, *The Lamplighter*, which was a huge and immediate success, selling 40,000 copies in a few weeks and 70,000 in a year. *The Lamplighter* combined sentimentality, piety, and improbability in about equal portions and was perfectly suited to the rudimentary taste of a newly awakened reading public. It was the book to which Nathaniel Hawthorne was specifically referring in his famous complaint that "America is now wholly given over to a d—— d mob of scribbling women." English, French, and German editions were equally successful; the book had few peers as a literary phenomenon. Maria Cummins's later novels, *Mabel Vaughan*, 1857, *El Fureidis*, 1860, and *Haunted Hearts*, 1864, showed progress in technique but failed to achieve the popularity of her first. Maria Cummins died in Dorchester, Massachusetts, on October 1, 1866.

Cunningham, Kate Richards O'Hare 1877–1948 socialist and reformer

Born near Ada, Ottawa County, Kansas, on March 26, 1877, Kathleen Richards grew up and attended school there and, from 1888, in Kansas City, Missouri. After brief attendance at a normal school in Nebraska she taught for a short time in a rural school. She then became in apprentice machinist in the Kansas City shop where her father worked and joined the International Order of Machinists union. On her own time she devoted herself to temperance work, the local Florence Crittenton mission, and religion.

Gradually, however, Richards began to doubt the value of social work and meliorative reforms. Reading Henry George, Ignatius Donnelly, Henry Demarest Lloyd, and other radical authors and in particular hearing a speech by Mary Harris "Mother" Jones converted her to socialism. She joined the Socialist Labor party in 1899 and two years later followed the majority faction that decamped to form the more moderate Socialist Party of America. In the latter year she attended the International School of Social Economy, conducted in Girard, Kansas, under the auspices of the weekly socialist paper *Appeal to Reason*. There she met Francis P. O'Hare, whom she married in January 1902. Their honeymoon, a socialist organizing and lecture tour, inaugurated the career they shared for 15 years. Crisscrossing the Great Plains states and lecturing as far away as Great Britain, Canada, and Mexico, Kate O'Hare was one of the socialist cause's most effective proselytizers.

In 1904 O'Hare published a socialist novel, *What Happened to Dan?* (revised and enlarged in 1911 as *The Sorrows of Cupid*), which enjoyed wide circulation. About 1912 she and her husband became copublishers and coeditors of the weekly *National Rip-Saw*, published in St. Louis (it was renamed the *Social Revolution* in 1917). In 1910 Kate O'Hare ran for a Kansas congressional seat on the Socialist ballot, and in 1913 she represented the party at the Second International in London. In 1917, as chair of the party's Committee on War and Militarism, she spoke coast-to-coast against U.S. entry into World War I.

In July of that year, following an address in Bowman, North Dakota, O'Hare was indicted under the new federal Espionage Act. Convicted, she entered the Missouri State Penitentiary in April 1919; Emma Goldman was one of her fellow prisoners. From prison she published *Kate O'Hare's Prison Letters*, 1919, and *In Prison*, 1920. In May 1920 she was a leading contender for the Socialist party's vice-presidential nomination and was passed over only because, with presidential candidate Eugene V. Debs also in prison, at least one candidate free to campaign was needed. Later that month, as the culmination of a nationwide campaign by socialists and civil libertarians, her sentence was commuted; she later received a full pardon from President Calvin Coolidge. She stumped vigorously for Debs in 1920. In 1922 she organized the Children's Crusade, a march on Washington, D.C., by children of antiwar agitators still in prison to demand immediate amnesty for all. In 1923 she and her husband joined the Llano Cooperative Colony, a settlement modeled on 19th-century utopian communities, near Leesville, Louisiana. There they resumed publication of their newspaper, retitled *American Vanguard*, and helped found Commonwealth College.

By 1924 Kate O'Hare had largely abandoned socialist agitation for prison reform, and in 1924–1926 she conducted a national survey of the contract-labor practice of prisons. She continued to teach at Commonwealth College for two years after the dissolution of the Llano community and the college's move to Mena, Arkansas, in 1926. In November 1928, having divorced her first husband, she married Charles C. Cunningham, a San Francisco lawyer. In 1934 she was active in Upton Sinclair's "End Poverty in California" campaign for the governorship. In 1939 Governor Culbert L. Olson appointed her assistant director of the California Department of Penology. Under her influence a far-reaching program of reforms was instituted that in a year transformed the state prison system into a model of its kind. She left the post after a year but continued, on invitation of Governor Earl Warren, to attend sessions of the State Crime Commission. She died in Benicia, California, on January 10, 1948.

Curzon, Mary Victoria Leiter 1870–1906 vicereine of India

Born in Chicago on May 27, 1870, Mary Leiter was the daughter of Levi Z. Leiter, merchant and early partner of Marshall Field. From 1881 she grew up in Washington, D.C., where her family entertained the most distinguished native and foreign personages. In April 1895, after a two-year engagement, she married George Nathaniel Curzon, member of the British Parliament, diplomat, and Asian expert. Her wealth no less than her beauty had attracted his serious attentions, while her devotion to him was uncomplicated and unquestioning. In 1898 he was appointed viceroy of India and created Baron Curzon of Kedleston, Mary Curzon became Baroness Curzon and vicereine of India, to that time and for long afterward the highest political rank ever attained by an American woman. She proved fully up to the elegant pomp and pageantry that Curzon relished, and she was furthermore his most steadfast supporter, especially as his early successes in the post gave way to frustration and failure. Her ceremonial responsibilities, together with the climate and other difficulties, bore heavily on her health, however. Trips to England did not restore her, and by the time they returned to England after Curzon's resignation in August 1905 she was failing. She died in London on July 18, 1906.

Cushman, Charlotte Saunders 1816–1876 actor

Born on July 23, 1816, in Boston, Charlotte Cushman was obliged to leave school at thirteen to help support her family. Nonetheless, encouraged by her musically gifted mother to train for the opera, she joined a Boston company and appeared in April 1835 as Countess Almaviva in *The Marriage of Figaro*. She was engaged to perform in New Orleans, where, it was said, her instructor attempted to force her natural contralto voice into the soprano range, and her voice failed. She soon met a visiting English actor in New Orleans who offered to give her instruction in dramatics. Under his guidance she appeared in April 1836 as Lady Macbeth in a striking performance.

Cushman moved to New York City and secured engagements with several small theaters. In 1837 she appeared as Meg Merrilies in *Guy Mannering*, one of her most successful roles. In 1839 she created a striking Nancy Sykes in *Oliver Twist*. She was a serious student not only of stagecraft but of character, and she went to great lengths to perfect her characterizations. She was stage manager for the Walnut Street Theatre in Philadelphia from 1842 to 1844 and there met William Macready, a formidable English tragedian and manager, who took her as a pupil and encouraged her to perform in London. On his advice she set sail in 1844. She made her London debut in *Fazio* opposite Edwin Forrest in February 1845 and was a huge success; within weeks London was at her feet. She subsequently played Queen Katherine in Shakespeare's *Henry VIII*, Lady Macbeth,

Romeo (opposite her sister Susan as Juliet), and other standard roles. Her gift for comedy was small, and her emotional enactments of tragic figures were sometimes held to be excessive even for the day.

From 1849 through 1852 Cushman toured the United States, where she was acclaimed as the foremost actress of her time. Her success in such roles as Hamlet and Cardinal Wolsey (in *Henry VIII*) rested on her commanding presence and her mastery of the grand manner. In 1852 she retired, in a fashion, from the stage. She lived in England and Italy for the next 18 years and continued to make occasional appearances. In 1857 she returned to the United States, giving a series of farewell performances until 1858, when she settled in Rome. Two years later, back in her native land, she gave a farewell to audiences in New Haven, Connecticut. She returned to Rome and remained there until 1870. Criticized for her farewells and reappearances, she was defended on the ground that she suffered from frequent depressions resulting from her enactment of tragic roles. In 1870 she returned to America permanently and settled in Boston. A final series of farewells in 1874–1875, including a public tribute in New York City in November 1874 and her last performance, in June 1875 in Easton, Pennsylvania, ended her long career. She died at her home in Boston on February 18, 1876.

Cushman, Vera Charlotte Scott 1876–1946 social worker

Born in Ottawa, Illinois, on September 19, 1876, Vera Scott was the daughter of a Scotch-Irish immigrant merchant whose business eventually became part of the great mercantile firm of Carson Pirie Scott & Company of Chicago. She grew up in Ottawa and, during 1887–1891, in Salina, Kansas, and was educated at Ferry Hall in Lake Forest, Illinois, and at Smith College, from which she graduated in 1898. She retained through life the religious inclination of her family and in college became active in the work of the Young Women's Christian Association branch at Smith, serving as its president. She continued her interest in the YWCA after graduation and after her marriage in October 1901 to James S. Cushman, a New York City businessman. In 1905 she became a member of Grace H. Dodge's committee to unify the national YWCA movement, and from its formation in December 1906 she was a member of the unified National Board. Between then and her resignation from the board in 1936 she also served several terms as vice-president. She was also a leader of YWCA work in New York City. She helped facilitate the merger of YWCA activities in New York in 1912 and was elected first president of the unified organization. In 1913 she was vice-chairman of the "Whirlwind Campaign" that raised $4 million in 14 days for the city and national YWCAs. In May 1917 the YWCA established the War Work Council under her chairmanship to direct the contribution of the association to the war effort. Under her leadership $170 million was raised to finance the establishment and staffing of 140 Hostess Houses near army and navy camps and bases, military hospitals, and ports of embarkation and debarkation. The houses provided lodging and recreation for nurses, Signal Corps workers, and other women engaged in war work. Hostess Houses and other service centers were operated during World War I in nine countries by the YWCA. In 1919 Cushman was one of six women to receive the Distinguished Service Medal for her work. From 1924 to 1938 she was a vice-president of the World Council of the YWCA. She was also active on the Women's Board of Foreign Missions of the Presbyterian Church, a delegate to the international Suffrage Convention in Geneva in 1920, and vice-president of the League of Nations Non-Partisan Association in 1923. While on her way to a Florida vacation, she died in Savannah, Georgia, on February 1, 1946.

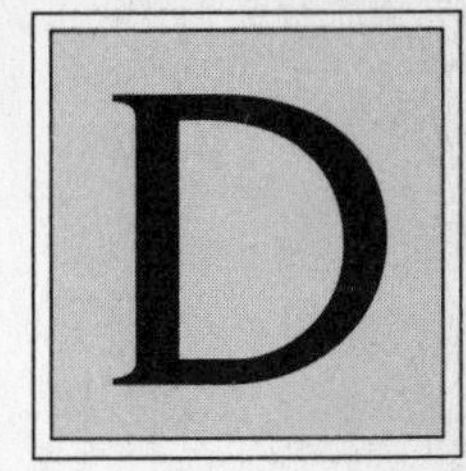

Dare, Virginia 1587–1587? colonial figure

Born on August 18, 1587, on Roanoke Island, now in North Carolina, Virginia was the first child to be born in America of English parents. Her parents, Eleanor (Ellinor, Elyonor) and Ananias Dare, had been among the 116 persons accompanying Governor John White (father of Eleanor Dare) on the second colonizing expedition to Sir Walter Raleigh's Virginia patent. They landed on Roanoke Island, the site of the earlier unsuccessful colony, in July 1587. On August 27, nine days after his granddaughter Virginia's birth, Governor White sailed back to England for supplies. War with Spain delayed his return to Roanoke until 1590, and upon landing he could find no trace of the colonists except for a cryptic inscription hinting that they had gone to seek shelter from hostile natives among the friendly Croatan tribe. It is believed that what survivors of the "Lost Colony" there may have been were absorbed into the Croatan tribe.

Darling, Flora Adams 1840–1910 writer, historian and organizer

Born in Lancaster, New Hampshire, on July 25, 1840, Flora Adams was educated at Lancaster Academy. In March 1860 she married Edward I. Darling of Louisiana. He died during the Civil War (no records confirm her later claim that he was a Confederate army officer), and after some difficulty she made her way back north. She soon instituted a claim against the federal government for recompense for valuables allegedly stolen from her luggage by Union soldiers. Prosecuting the claim became one of her chief occupations, and it was not ultimately settled until 1903, when she won a modest award. She was employed at various times in Washington, D.C., and during the 1880s she began to write for publication. *Mrs. Darling's Letters, or Memories of the Civil War*, 1883, was followed by *A Social Diplomat and A Winning, Wayward Woman*, both novels of 1889, *Senator Athens, C.S.A.*, 1889, *Was It a Just Verdict?*, 1890, and others, and she also contributed numerous romantic and sensational short stories to various magazines.

In October 1890 Darling was one of the founding members of the Daughters of the American Revolution and was elected vice president general in charge of organization. It was ever afterward her claim that she and two friends had originated the idea for such an organization some months earlier and that she had issued the call for the October meeting. The DAR's official history disputes the claim. Her talent for organization was put to good use in the early months of the society's existence, but her instinct for controversy and self-dramatization soon brought her into conflict with the national board, and in the summer of 1891 she resigned and was removed from her office almost simultaneously. In November 1891 the Darling Chapter of the DAR in New York City followed her in reorganizing as the rival Daughters of the Revolution. The DR differed from the DAR in insisting upon lineal rather than collateral descent from patriot forebears and upon strong state as opposed to national authority in the organization. In January 1892 Darling founded the Daughters of the United States of the War of 1812 (later the United States Daughters of 1812), of which she was for several years president. Later activities included efforts to establish various sorts of educational institutions, none to any effect. She published *A War Episode, or The Darling Claim vs. the U.S.*, 1900, her own version of the *Founding and Organization of the Daughters of the American Revolution and Daughters of the Revolution*, 1901, *1607–1907: Memories of Virginia*, a volume of verse, 1907, and *The Senator's Daughter*, 1907. Flora Darling died in New York City on January 6, 1910.

Darragh, Lydia Barrington 1729–1789 revolutionary heroine

Born in Dublin, Ireland, in 1729, Lydia Barrington married William Darragh, a teacher, in November 1753; shortly thereafter they emigrated to America, settling in Philadelphia. She worked as a nurse and midwife with considerable skill and success. In a story first published in 1827 and later elaborated upon, she was credited with saving General George

Washington's army: during the British occupation of Philadelphia General William Howe had his headquarters opposite the Darragh house. On the night of December 2, 1777, the adjutant general and other officers commandeered one of her rooms for a secret conference, and, listening at the keyhole, she learned of their plan to attack Washington at Whitemarsh, eight miles away, two nights later. On the morning of the day, December 4, she let it be known that she needed flour from the Frankford mill and obtained a pass to leave the city for that purpose. Once away, she made for Whitemarsh. Encountering Colonel Thomas Craig, a friend, on the road, she told him what she had learned and then, securing her flour, hurried home. The British march that night found the Continental army at arms and ready to repel, and Howe was forced to return to Philadelphia. Darragh lived in Philadelphia until her death on December 28, 1789.

Dauser, Sue Sophia 1888–1972 nurse and naval officer

Born in Anaheim, California, on September 20, 1888, Sue Dauser attended Stanford University for two years, 1907–1909, and in 1911 entered the California Hospital School of Nursing, Los Angeles, graduating in 1914. In September 1917 she joined the naval reserve, going on active duty the next month. In July 1918 she entered the regular navy. After duty at Base Hospital No. 3 in Edinburgh, Scotland, during the final months of World War I, she served tours of duty at naval hospitals in Brooklyn and San Diego and aboard ship. In 1923 she sailed on the *Henderson* on President Warren G. Harding's Alaskan visit and attended him during his last illness. She later served on Guam, in the Philippines, and at San Diego, Puget Sound, and Mare Island and Long Beach, California.

In 1939 Dauser was named superintendent of the Navy Nurse Corps. Her task in that post was twofold: to organize and administer a greatly expanded Nurse Corps in preparation for and then throughout World War II, and to secure for navy nurses equitable rank and privileges. In July 1942 Congress provided for relative rank for nurses (title and uniform, but not the commission, pay, or other benefits of regular rank), and she became a lieutenant commander. Pay was made equivalent in December 1942. In December 1943 she was promoted to (relative) captain, equivalent to Florence A. Blanchfield's army colonelcy and the highest naval rank yet attained by a woman.

In February 1944 temporary commissions were authorized for army and navy nurses. Captain Dauser retired as superintendent of nurses in November 1945 and was awarded the Distinguished Service Medal soon thereafter. Under Dauser the Navy Nurse Corps had grown from 600 members to 11,500. She lived afterward in retirement in La Mesa, California, until her death in Anaheim on March 8, 1972.

Davenport, Fanny Lily Gypsy 1850–1898 actor

Born in London on April 10, 1850, Fanny Davenport was the daughter of Edward L. Davenport, an American actor who later became one of the most popular of his day until his death in 1877. Fanny grew up in Boston from 1854 and took naturally to the theater from an early age. She essayed her first speaking part at the age of six and took a substantial role in *Faint Heart Never Won Fair Lady*, produced by her father and J. W. Wallack, Jr., at Niblo's Garden, New York City, in February 1862. At fifteen, in May 1865, she played her first adult part in *Still Waters Run Deep* in Boston. She then joined a stock company in Louisville, with which she appeared in *The Black Crook*, and shortly afterward joined the company of Louisa Lane Drew's Arch Street Theatre in Philadelphia. In 1869 she moved to Augustin Daly's Fifth Avenue Theatre company in New York City. She gained much experience under Daly and enjoyed considerable success in a wide variety of roles, particularly in W. S. Gilbert's *Charity* in 1874 and Daly's own *Pique*, in 1876.

In 1877 Davenport bought the rights to *Pique* from Daly and formed her own touring company with herself as starring attraction. She gradually expanded the repertory of her company and had several increasingly successful seasons. One of her touring hits was Anna E. Dickinson's *An American Girl* in 1880. While in England in 1882 she purchased American rights to Victorien Sardou's *Fédora*, which was at the time a great hit for Sarah Bernhardt in Paris. From its New York premiere in October 1883 through tours lasting until 1887, *Fédora* was an equally great and lucrative success for Fanny Davenport in America. Several Sardou productions followed: *La Tosca* in 1888, *Cleopatra* in 1890, and *Gismonda* in 1894. Her last undertaking, a lavish production of F. A. Mathews's *A Soldier of France* in 1897, was an expensive failure. After a final stage appearance at Chicago's Grand Opera House in March 1898 she retired exhausted to her vacation home in South Duxbury, Massachusetts, where she died on September 26, 1898.

Davis, Bette 1908–1989 actor

Born on April 5, 1908, in Lowell, Massachusetts, Ruth Elizabeth Davis was known from an early age as Bette. After graduating from Cushing Academy in Ashburnham, Massachusetts, in 1925, she decided to seek a career in the theater and for a time studied at the John Murray Anderson Dramatic School in New York City. She made her earliest appearances in small parts with stock companies in Rochester, New York, and Dennis, Massachusetts. A brief stint with the Provincetown Players led to her Broadway debut in *Broken Dishes* at the Ritz Theatre in November 1929. A subsequent Broadway role in *Solid South* won her a film contract. In Hollywood she again began in small roles in minor productions, including *Bad Sister*, 1930, *Seed*, 1930, and *Waterloo Bridge*, 1931, but in 1932 her performance opposite George Arliss in *The Man Who Played God* won her considerable attention. She failed, however, to win a part in a substantial production until 1934, when she appeared in *Of Human Bondage*, in which she was at last able to display some of her vast imaginative and emotional range. For *Dangerous*, 1935, she won an Academy Award, and after roles in *Border Town*, 1935, *Front Page Woman*, 1935, *The Petrified Forest*, 1936, *Marked Woman*, 1937, and other pictures she won a second Oscar for her forceful acting in *Jezebel*, 1938.

Often plagued by mediocre scripts, over which she fought some spectacular legal battles with Warner Brothers studio, Davis nonetheless turned in a great many performances of the highest caliber, demonstrating endless versatility in such films as *Juarez*, 1939, *The Private Lives of Elizabeth and Essex*, 1939, *Dark Victory*, 1939, *The Letter*, 1940, *The Great Lie*, 1941, *The Little Foxes*, 1941, *The Man Who Came to Dinner*, 1941, *In This Our Life*, 1942, *Now, Voyager*, 1942, *Watch on the Rhine*, 1943, *Mr. Skeffington*, 1944, *The Corn Is Green*, 1945, *A Stolen Life*, 1946, *June Bride*, 1948, *All About Eve*, 1950, *The Star*, 1953, and *The Virgin Queen*, 1955. She returned to Broadway in a revue, *Two's Company* (which also featured the dancing of Nora Kaye), in 1952 and later appeared on the stage in *The Night of the Iguana*. Among her later films, in many of which she took to its limit her ability to portray with great depth and conviction various bizarre or disturbed characters, were *A Pocketful of Miracles*, 1961, *Whatever Happened to Baby Jane?*, 1962, *Dead Ringer*, 1964, *Hush, Hush, Sweet Charlotte*, 1964, *The Nanny*, 1965, *The Anniversary*, 1967, *Bunny O'Hare*, 1970, *Madam Sin*, 1971, and *The Game*, 1972, and *The Whales of August*, 1987. In 1962 she published *The Lonely Life*, an autobiography.

Recognition of her achievements was widespread. She received ten Oscar nominations, the Cesar Award of the French Film Industry, and Best Actress for *All About Eve* in 1951 from both the Cannes Film Festival and the New York Film Critics. She was the first woman to be awarded the American Film Institute Life Achievement Award in 1977. In 1987 she received the Kennedy Center Honors for Lifetime Achievement in the Performing Arts, and in 1989 the Lincoln Center Film Society Honor. She died in Neuilly-sur-

Seine on October 6, 1989, en route home from the San Sebastian Film Festival in Spain where she had been honored for her lifetime achievement.

Davis, Katharine Bement 1860–1935 penologist, social worker and writer

Born on January 15, 1860, in Buffalo, New York, Katharine Davis grew up there, from 1863 in Dunkirk, New York, and from 1877 in Rochester. She graduated from the Rochester Free Academy in 1879 and for ten years thereafter taught high school science in Dunkirk. In 1890 she entered Vassar College as a junior, and after graduating in 1892 she pursued further studies at Columbia University. In the summer of 1893 she served as director of the New York State Exhibit of a model workingman's home at the World's Columbian Exposition in Chicago. From that year until 1897 she was head resident at the St. Mary's Street College Settlement in Philadelphia. In 1897 she undertook doctoral studies at the University of Chicago, and after work there and at the universities of Berlin and Vienna she received her Ph.D. in economics in 1900.

In January 1901 Davis began work as superintendent of the newly opened state reformatory for women at Bedford Hills, New York. Over the next 13 years the institution became famous for its actively experimental approach to penology. Davis instituted a prison farm, courses in various vocational subjects, and a cottage system. She was particularly interested in identifying various classes of reformable, habitual, and incorrigible offenders, and her work in that field induced John D. Rockefeller, Jr., to establish a Laboratory of Social Hygiene on property adjacent to the reformatory in 1912 to further such research. In 1909, during a European trip, she won international acclaim for her work in organizing self-help relief programs following a disastrous earthquake in Messina, Sicily.

In January 1914 Davis was appointed commissioner of corrections for New York City by the newly elected reform mayor, John Purroy Mitchel. She was the first woman to hold a top-level post in the government of that city. She moved quickly to improve conditions in the city's 15 penal institutions, especially to suppress drug traffic, segregate women prisoners, and upgrade dietary and medical facilities. A riot at the Blackwell's Island prison in the summer of 1914 was quelled mainly by her intelligent handling of the situation. She established the New Hampton Farm School for delinquent boys and laid plans for a separate detention home for women (ultimately opened in 1932). In 1915, principally as a result of her efforts, the New York legislature enacted a program of indeterminate sentencing and parole supervision, and in December of that year she was named first chairman of the city parole board to direct the new system. She held the post until the end of the reform administration in 1918.

From 1918 until her retirement in 1928 Davis was general secretary and member of the board of directors of the Bureau of Social Hygiene, the department of the Rockefeller Foundation that had operated the Bedford Hills laboratory. There she directed research into narcotics trade and addiction, the "white slave trade," various forms of delinquency, and other aspects of public health and social hygiene. During World War I she headed the women's section for social hygiene of the Commission on Training Camp Activities, and after the war she made a European tour of inspection for the Young Women's Christian Association and helped raise relief funds. In 1929 she published *Factors in the Sex Life of Twenty-two Hundred Women*; she was also author of a great many articles in professional and popular journals. She died in Pacific Grove, California, on December 10, 1935.

Davis, Paulina Kellogg Wright 1813–1876 feminist and social reformer

Born on August 7, 1813, in Bloomfield, New York, Paulina Kellogg grew up from 1817 on the frontier near Niagara and from 1820, when her parents died, in the home of a strict and religious aunt in LeRoy, New York. Her plan to become a missionary was abandoned when she married Francis Wright, a merchant of Utica, New York, in January 1833. The two were active and enthusiastic supporters of temperance, abolition, women's rights, and other reforms. They helped organize an antislavery convention held in Utica in October 1835 and endured mob violence for their pains. After her husband's death in 1845 Wright continued active in reform work. For a time she toured with a lecture on physiology and hygiene, using an imported female mannequin for demonstrations.

In April 1849 Wright married Thomas Davis, a jewelry maker and Democratic politician of Providence, Rhode Island. She took the lead in planning and arranging the first National Woman's Rights Convention, over which she presided in Worcester, Massachusetts, in October 1850. She accompanied her husband to Washington, D.C., when he served a term in Congress in 1853–1855 and while there, in February 1853, she established *Una*, one of the first women's-rights periodicals. *Una* continued to appear, with the editorial assistance of Caroline Dall, until late in 1855. In 1868 Davis was among the founders of the New England Woman Suffrage Association. In the 1869 split of the national suffrage movement she followed Susan B. Anthony into the National Woman Suffrage Association. She played a large part in organizing the association's convention in New York City in 1870. In 1859 and again in 1871 she traveled to Europe to study painting. She died in Providence, Rhode Island, on August 24, 1876.

Davis, Rebecca Blaine Harding 1831–1910 essayist and writer

Born on June 24, 1831, in Washington, Pennsylvania, Rebecca Harding grew up in Huntsville, Alabama, and in Wheeling, Virginia (now West Virginia). In 1848 she graduated from the Washington (Pennsylvania) Female Seminary. She was an avid reader and in her youth began dabbling in the writing of verse and stories. Some of her early pieces were published, but her reputation as an author of startlingly realistic, sometimes grim portraits of life began only with the publication of her story "Life in the Iron Mills" in the *Atlantic Monthly* in April 1861. In 1861–1862 the *Atlantic* serialized a story that appeared in book form in the latter year as *Margaret Howth*. In March 1863 she married L. Clarke Davis of Philadelphia, later an editor of the *Philadelphia Inquirer* and later still of the *Philadelphia Public Ledger*.

Over the next three decades Davis' fiction, children's stories, essays, and articles appeared regularly in most of the leading magazines of the day, and from 1869 she was for several years also a contributing editor of the *New York Tribune*. Her books included *Waiting for the Verdict*, 1868, *Dallas Galbraith*, 1868, *Pro Aris et Focis — A Plea for Our Altars and Hearths*, 1870, *Berrytown*, 1872, *John Andross*, 1874, *A Law unto Herself*, 1878, *Natasqua*, 1886, *Silhouettes of American Life*, 1892, *Kent Hampden*, 1892, *Doctor Warrick's Daughters*, 1896, *Frances Waldeaux*, 1896, and the autobiographical *Bits of Gossip*, 1904. Her later fiction failed to live up to the promise of her early work and grew instead increasingly conventional. Davis died in Mount Kisco, New York, on September 29, 1910. Of her children, the eldest, Richard Harding Davis (1864–1916) became the foremost American reporter of his day.

Day, Dorothy 1897–1980 journalist and reformer

Born in New York City on November 8, 1897, Dorothy Day grew up there, in California, and in Chicago. In 1914, aided by a scholarship, she entered the University of Illinois, where she remained for two years. While a student she read widely among socialist authors and soon joined the Socialist party. In 1916 she returned to New York City and joined the staff of the *Call*, a Socialist newspaper; she also became a member of the Industrial Workers of the World (IWW). In 1917 she moved from the *Call* to the *Masses*, where she remained until the magazine was suppressed a few months later by the government. After a brief period on the successor journal, the *Liberator*, she spent more than a year in 1918–1919 working as a nurse in Brooklyn. For several years thereafter she continued in journalism in Chicago and New Orleans. In 1927, following years of doubt and indecision, she joined the Roman Catholic church, an act that for some time estranged her from her earlier radical associates.

Then in 1932 Day met Peter Maurin, a French-born Catholic who had developed a program of social reconstruction — which he called "the green revolution" — based on communal farming and the establishment of houses of hospitality for the urban poor. The program aimed to unite workers and intellectuals in joint activities ranging from farming to educational discussions. In 1933 Day and Maurin founded the *Catholic Worker*, a monthly newspaper, to carry the idea to a wider audience. Within three years the paper's circulation had grown to 150,000, and the original St. Joseph's House of Hospitality in New York City had served as the pattern for similar houses in a number of other cities. The *Catholic Worker* took boldly radical positions on many issues and during World War II was an organ for pacifism and for the support of Catholic conscientious objectors.

In later years both Day and the newspaper agitated against nuclear weaponry and preparations for nuclear war. For several years she was jailed repeatedly for refusing to comply with New York City's compulsory civil-defense drills. She later took part in demonstrations for civil rights, against the Vietnam war, and in support of farm workers organizing in California. The number of settlement houses directly connected with the *Catholic Worker* dwindled in later years, but there remained a significant number taking their inspiration from it. The newspaper continued to appear nine times a year at a penny a copy and enjoyed a circulation of some 90,000 in the late 1970s. Day lived in the New York City house or at the *Catholic Worker's* farm in Tivoli, New York, in voluntary poverty. In 1952 she published an autobiography, *The Long Loneliness*.

A professed anarchist, Dorothy Day was widely considered in later years one of the great Catholic lay leaders of the time. She protested the Vietnam War and was arrested in 1973 while demonstrating in California in support of Cesar Chavez and the United Farm Workers. She died at the House of Hospitality on the Lower East Side of New York on November 29, 1980.

Margaret Deland

Deland, Margaret 1857–1945 novelist and short-story writer

Born on February 23, 1857, in Allegheny, Pennsylvania, Margaretta Wade Campbell grew up in the home of an aunt and uncle in nearby Maple Grove (now part of Allegheny) and later in Manchester. She attended Pelham Priory school in New Rochelle, New York, and then studied design for a year at Cooper Union in New York City. In 1876 she became a drawing instructor at the Female Normal College of New York (now Hunter College). In May 1880 she married Lorin F. Deland, with whom she lived thereafter in Boston. Under the influence of the Reverend Phillips Brooks they took up the cause of unwed mothers and over a span of 4 years took some 60 such women and their infants into their home in the belief that the love and care of the child would transform the mother. Margaret Deland also began writing verse for a greeting-card firm. A short time later a few of her poems were published in *Harper's Magazine*, and in 1886 a collection of them was published as *The Old Garden*.

In 1888 she published her first novel, *John Ward, Preacher*. The book was a sensation for its portrayal of the irreconcilable and destructive conflict between the rock-ribbed Calvinist minister and his wife who cannot accept the doctrine of eternal damnation. The conflict of ideas played little part in her subsequent novels, which, while presenting skillfully drawn characters with realistic problems and emotions, were essentially comedies or minor tragedies of middle-class domesticity, insulated from the social and economic issues of the larger world.

Deland's novels and short-story collections included *A Summer Day*, 1889, *Philip and His Wife*, 1890, *Sidney: the Story of a Child*, 1892, *The Wisdom of Fools*, 1897, *Old Chester Tales*, 1899, *Dr. Lavender's People*, 1903, *The Common Way*, 1904, *The Awaken-*

ing of Helena Richie, 1906, *The Iron Woman*, 1911, *The Voice*, 1912, *Partners*, 1913, *The Hands of Esau*, 1914, *Around Old Chester*, 1915, *The Rising Tide*, 1916, *Small Things*, 1919, *The Vehement Flame*, 1922, *New Friends in Old Chester*, 1924, *The Kays*, 1926, *Captain Archer's Daughter*, 1932, and *Old Chester Days*, 1935. The stories of "Old Chester," based loosely on the Maple Grove and Manchester of her childhood, were her most enduring work. She published two volumes of autobiography, *If This Be I*, 1935, and *Golden Yesterdays*, 1941. During World War I she did relief work in France, for which she was decorated with the Legion of Honor. In later years her fiction declined in popularity, but in November 1926 she was elected to the National Institute of Arts and Letters. She died in Boston on January 13, 1945.

Delano, Jane Arminda 1862–1919 nurse

Born in Townsend, New York, on March 12, 1862, Jane Delano attended Cook Academy in nearby Montour Falls. She taught school for two years and in 1884 entered the Bellevue Hospital Training School for Nurses in New York City. She graduated in 1886. During a yellow fever epidemic in 1887–1888 she served as superintending nurse at an emergency center near Jacksonville, Florida; even though the source of the disease was not yet known, she insisted on the use of mosquito netting in the center. In 1889 she was superintendent of nurses in a mining company hospital in Bisbee, Arizona Territory, where she faced a typhoid fever epidemic. From 1890 to 1895 she was assistant superintendent of nurses and an instructor at the University of Pennsylvania Hospital School of Nursing. Over the next five years she was engaged in a variety of activities and undertook brief courses of study at the University of Buffalo Medical School and the New York School of Civics and Philanthropy. In 1900–1902 she directed the girls' department of the New York City House of Refuge on Randall's Island, and from 1902 to 1906 she was superintendent of the nursing schools of Bellevue and its associated hospitals. From 1906 to 1908 she was largely out of professional life while she attended her mother in her last illness.

Since the Spanish-American War it had been clear that the nation lacked a proper organization of nurses that could supply the needs of war or major disaster. The Red Cross had become a potential source of such aid with the reorganization sparked by Mabel Boardman in 1905, but an institutional bridge between the Red Cross and the nursing profession was required. This was supplied by the creation of the National Committee on Red Cross Nursing Services in 1909. The members of the committee were chosen by the Red Cross and by the Nurses' Associated Alumnae, the principal professional organization, and Jane Delano was named chairman. In the same year she was elected to a two-year term as president of the Nurses' Associated Alumnae (which in 1911 became the American Nurses' Association), and she was also appointed superintendent of the Army Nurse Corps. In a stroke she was thus placed in position to direct the national organization of nursing work and of a reserve nursing capacity available for national emergency. She retained the army post until 1912 and that with the Red Cross for the rest of her life. She came into conflict with Boardman in 1912 over the issue of keeping the Red Cross Nursing Service a strictly professional service; she prevailed and then consented to Boardman's creation of an auxiliary corps of volunteer nurses' aides, for which she and Isabel McIsaac wrote *American Red Cross Textbook on Elementary Hygiene and Home Care of the Sick*, 1913.

As a result of her efficient organizing, including the appointment of Clara Noyes to head the bureau of nursing in the department of military relief, the Nursing Service was able to supply 8000 nurses to the Army Nurse Corps on the entry of the United States into World War I in April 1917, and during the course of the war Jane Delano saw to the mobilization of upwards of 20,000 nurses for duty overseas, as well as a great number of nurses' aides and other workers. Early in 1918 the Department of Nursing was created within the Red Cross under her direction. The influenza epidemic that swept Europe and America in 1918–1919 vastly increased the demand for her and the Red Cross's services. Already exhausted by her labors, she fell ill while on a European inspection tour and died in Savenay, France, on April 15, 1919.

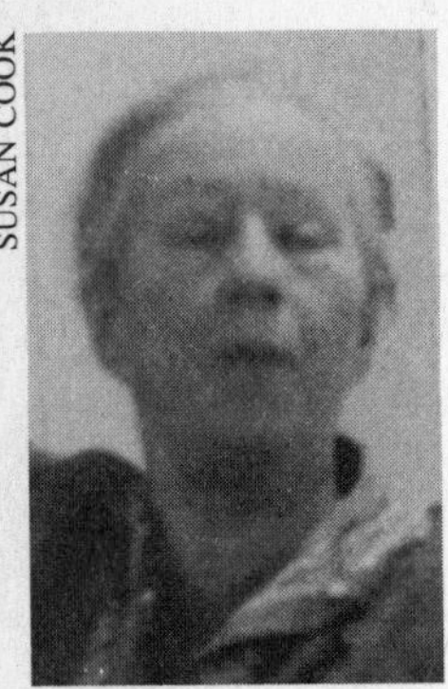
SUSAN COOK

Agnes de Mille

de Mille, Agnes George 1905–1993 choreographer

Born in New York City in 1905 (or 1908 or 1909, according to various sources), the daughter of William C. de Mille, noted American playwright, the niece of motion picture producer Cecil B. DeMille, and the granddaughter of Henry George, Agnes de Mille studied ballet and choreography under several famous teachers. She made her dancing debut in 1928 and for several years was a touring dancer and actress in the United States and England and on the Continent, during which time she danced principal roles in a number of Antony Tudor ballets and composed dance sequences for a 1936 English film version of *Romeo and Juliet*.

de Mille's first major composition was *Rodeo*, to music of Aaron Copland, which was danced by the Ballet Russe de Monte Carlo in New York City in October 1942. She was also a guest artist and choreographer with Ballet Theatre for a number of years. For that company (later the American Ballet Theatre) she created *Tally-Ho*, 1944, *Fall River Legend*, based on the story of Lizzie Borden, 1948, *The Harvest According*, 1952, *The Bitter Weird*, 1962, *The Wind in the Mountains* and *The Four Marys*, both 1965, and others. Her own company, the Agnes de Mille Dance Theatre, toured 126 cities in 1953–1954.

It was de Mille's dances for the Broadway musical *Oklahoma!* in 1943 that not only made her a leading American theatrical artist but also introduced dance to a wide American public that might never have known much about it without her. In *Oklahoma!* she was the first choreographer to integrate dance into the plot as well as the mood of a musical play. *Oklahoma!* was followed by a long series of Broadway shows, among them *One Touch of Venus*, 1943, *Bloomer Girls*, 1944, *Carousel*, 1945, *Brigadoon*, 1947, *Gentlemen Prefer Blondes*, 1949, *Paint Your Wagon*, 1951, *The Girl in Pink Tights*, 1954, and *110 in the Shade*, 1963. Most of these became spectacular movies as well, and for the film versions, too, she created innovative dance episodes.

The recipient of many prizes and awards, she was during the 1940s and 1950s the leading choreographer on Broadway, and one of the foremost in the United States. She received the Kennedy Center Career Achievement Award in 1980 and earned the National Medal of the Arts in 1986. In 1973 she established the Heritage Dance Theatre, a folk-oriented company, which toured until 1975. In addition she continued to choreograph ballets for the American Ballet Theatre including *A Rose for Miss Emily*, 1971, *Texas Fourth*, 1976, and *The Informer*, 1988. Her final ballet, *Other*, for the American Ballet Theater in 1992, dealt with a young woman and death. She wrote several books, among them *Dance to the Piper*, 1952, *And Promenade Home*, an autobiography, 1958, *To a Young Dancer*, 1962, *The Book of the Dance*, 1963, *Lizzie Borden: a Dance of Death*, 1968, *Speak to Me, Dance With Me*, 1973, and *Where the Wings Grow*, another work of autobiography, 1977. In 1981 she published a memoir, *Reprieve*, with Dr. Fred Plum, which dealt with her recovery from a cerebral hemorrhage in 1975. Her later books include *America Dances*, 1980, and her controversial commentary, *Martha: The Life and Work of Martha Graham*, 1991. She died in her home in New York City on October 7, 1993.

Demorest, Ellen Louise Curtis 1824–1898 businesswoman

Born in Schuylerville, New York, on November 15, 1824, Ellen Curtis graduated from Schuylerville Academy at eighteen and then opened a millinery shop. She later moved the business to Troy and then to New York City, where in April 1858 she married William J.

Demorest. During a brief residence in Philadelphia Ellen Demorest conceived the idea of mass-produced accurate paper patterns for home dressmaking. In 1860 she and her husband returned to New York City, where she opened "Madame Demorest's Emporium of Fashions" on Broadway and he began publishing the quarterly *Mme. Demorest's Mirror of Fashions*, which featured, in addition to the obligatory color fashion plates, a pattern stapled into each copy. The patterns were also distributed by themselves, soon through a nationwide network of agencies as they proved immensely popular; in their peak year, 1876, three million patterns were sold. The success of the magazine led to its becoming the expanded *Demorest's Illustrated Monthly Magazine* and *Mme. Demorest's Mirror of Fashions* in 1864 (*Illustrated* was dropped from the name in 1865), featuring the reporting and commentary of "Jennie June" (Jane Croly).

While her husband established a mail-order operation to deal in sewing aids and other merchandise, Demorest developed a cheap hoopskirt and a new line of corsets, cosmetics, and other products, at the same time presiding over her Emporium. In addition to her business, she supported her husband in his reform work, especially the temperance crusade, and interested herself in projects for the betterment of opportunities for women. She employed a great many women herself, including a large number of African-American women on the same terms as their white co-workers, and she was active in the management of the New York Medical College for Women and the Welcome Lodging House for Women and Children. In 1868 she joined Jane Croly in organizing Sorosis, of which she became vice-president and treasurer. In the 1880s the business declined, in large part because of their failure to patent their paper pattern idea and the consequent competition of Ebenezer Butterick and others. At the same time William Demorest became more deeply involved in the Prohibition party. In 1887 Demorest sold the pattern business. Widowed in 1895, she died in New York City on August 10, 1898.

Dempsey, Sister Mary Joseph 1856–1939 hospital administrator

Born on May 14, 1856, in Salamanca, New York, Julia Dempsey grew up there and on a farm near Rochester, Minnesota. After finishing local school she entered the Third Order Regular of St. Francis of the Congregation of Our Lady of Lourdes in August 1878, taking the name Sister Mary Joseph. She taught school in various places over the next several years and was in Ashland, Kentucky, when she was called back to Rochester in 1889 to help staff the new St. Mary's Hospital, built by her order in the wake of a disastrous tornado. The hospital medical staff consisted of Dr. William W. Mayo and his two sons, Charles H. and William J. Mayo. Sister Joseph studied nursing under a local nurse and in 1890 became Dr. William J. Mayo's first surgical assistant, a post she held until 1915. In that work she displayed rare skill and judgment. In September 1892 she was also appointed superintendent of St. Mary's Hospital, a task she was to fill for the rest of her life. During that nearly 40 years the hospital underwent six major expansions, growing from 45 to 600 beds and in time incorporating the most modern and efficient facilities, particularly for surgery. In 1906 she opened St. Mary's Hospital School for Nurses, which trained both sisters and laywomen. In 1915 she helped organize the Catholic Hospital Association of the United States and Canada and was chosen its first vice-president. In addition to her work at St. Mary's, her remarkable administrative and medical skills contributed greatly to the success of the Mayo brothers in establishing their world famous surgical practice and their Mayo Clinic. Sister Joseph died in Rochester, Minnesota, on March 29, 1939.

Dennett, Mary Coffin Ware 1872–1947 reformer

Born on April 4, 1872, in Worcester, Massachusetts, Mary Ware grew up there and from 1882 in Boston. After graduating from Miss Capen's School for Girls in Northampton, Massachusetts, she entered the school of the Boston Museum of Fine Arts. From

1894 to 1897 she taught design and decoration at the Drexel Institute in Philadelphia. In 1898, after a European visit, she and a sister opened a handcraft shop in Boston, specializing in leather and gilt leather work. After her marriage in January 1900 to William H. Dennett, a Boston architect, she worked with him as an interior decorator for a time. Gradually other interests drew her away. She served as field secretary of the Massachusetts Woman Suffrage Association in 1908–1910, and on her appointment as corresponding secretary of the National American Woman Suffrage Association in the latter year she moved to New York City. She held that post until 1914. She then became active in pacifist and socialist groups. She was field secretary of the American Union against Militarism from 1916, and on the entry of the United States into World War I she resigned her post with the women's section of the Democratic National Committee and helped found the People's Council, a radical antiwar group.

In 1915 Dennett had become involved in another issue, that of birth control. She led a group who took over and reorganized Margaret Sanger's National Birth Control League in that year. The work of the League was redirected from protest to public education and lobbying for the repeal of restrictive legislation. In 1918 the Voluntary Parenthood League was established, absorbing the older organization, and Mary Dennett was a director until 1925. During 1922–1925 she edited the *Birth Control Herald*. Throughout the period she was at odds with Sanger, who had moved to the conservative position of advocating modification of legislative restrictions on birth control information.

When the Voluntary Parenthood League voted in 1925 to support Sanger's position on restricting such information to doctors, Dennett resigned to carry on alone. In 1926 she published *Birth Control Laws*, a careful study of the legal situation and the arguments for free dissemination of information. An essay on sex as a natural and joyful part of life which had been published originally in the *Medical Review of Reviews* in 1918 and subsequently widely distributed in pamphlet form was banned from the mails as obscene in 1922. In 1928 Dennett was indicted for having continued to answer requests for the pamphlet through the mail. Her conviction in 1929 roused a national storm of protest. With the aid of the American Civil Liberties Union she won a reversal of her conviction in the federal court of appeals in March 1930. In that year she published an account of the case in *Who's Obscene?*, and in 1931 she published *The Sex Education of Children*. In 1941–1944 she was first chairman of the World Federalists. She died in Valatie, New York, on July 25, 1947.

Deren, Maya 1917–1961 filmmaker

Born Eleanora Derenkowsky in Kiev, Russia, in 1917, she emigrated to the U.S. with her parents in 1922. Encouraged by her mother to obtain a broad education, she attended L'Ecole Internationale in Geneva, Switzerland, Syracuse University, 1933–35, New York University, 1936, the New School for Social Research, 1937–39, and Smith College, 1939. She was national student secretary for the Young People's Socialist League in 1936 and a contributor to left-wing periodicals. She married Gregory Bardacke, a labor organizer, in 1935, but they were divorced in 1938.

In 1940 she proposed to Katherine Dunham that they write a book for young people about dance. Although the project was never realized, she became Dunham's personal secretary and accompanied her on the national tour of *Cabin in the Sky*, 1940–41. In 1942 she published an essay on dance in Haitian culture and married Alexander Hammid, a Czech cinematographer. With Hammid she produced *Meshes of the Afternoon*, 1943; one of the most influential works in the American experimental film canon, it was credited with establishing the independent avant-garde film movement in the U.S. Its innovative camera imagery and narrative structure depict a web of dream events that move between subjective and objective experience. In *At Land*, produced on her own in 1944, she used imaginative editing and camera techniques to express a trance state. Her films *Study in Choreography for Camera*, 1945, and *Ritual in Transfigured Time*, 1946, have been repeatedly cited as significant achievements in the representation of dance movement in space on film.

In the unfinished film *Witch's Cradle*, 1943, Deren explored Surrealist conceptions of time and space. She won a Guggenheim Fellowship in 1946 and in 1947 became the first woman and the first American to win the Grand Prix International for avant-garde film for her first four films at the Cannes film festival. She published a monograph, *An Anagram of Ideas on Art, Form and Film*, 1946. Lecturing, teaching and writing extensively on independent film, she founded the Creative Film Foundation in 1955 to provide funding and support for independent filmmakers.

Deren traveled to Haiti in 1947 to research and film voudoun culture, work which became the basis for her book *Divine Horsemen: The Living Gods of Haiti*, 1953. She produced the films *Meditation on Violence*, 1948, a study of movement in Chinese martial arts, and *The Very Eye of Night*, 1954, a major achievement in the filmic representation of dance. In 1960, thirteen years after divorcing Hammid, she married Teiji Ito, a composer with whom she had collaborated since the mid-1950s. She died on October 13, 1961, leaving several major projects, including her film on Haiti, unfinished.

de Wolfe, Elsie 1865–1950 actor and decorator

Born in New York City on December 20, 1865, Ella Anderson de Wolfe was educated privately in New York and in Edinburgh, Scotland, where she lived with maternal relatives. Through that connection she was presented at Queen Victoria's court in 1883 and introduced to London society. Soon after her return to New York in 1884 she became a devotee of amateur theatricals, then a popular form of charitable fund raising. In 1890 the death of her father left the family in somewhat straitened circumstances, and Elsie de Wolfe turned to the professional stage. She was assisted in entering the field by her close friend, Elisabeth Marbury, a theatrical agent. She made her debut in Charles Frohman's production of Sardou's *Thermidor* (for which she had prepared at the Comédie Française) in October 1891. From New York the production went on tour for two years. In 1894 she became a regular member of Frohman's company based at the Empire Theatre. A more than competent actress noted especially as one of the best dressed on the American stage, she appeared successfully over the next few years in *The Bauble Shop*, 1894, *The Marriage of Convenience*, 1897, *Catherine*, 1898, and other productions. In 1901 she formed her own company and presented Clyde Fitch's *The Way of the World* on Broadway and in a two-year tour. Her final appearance on the stage was in an unsuccessful production of Pinero's *A Wife Without a Smile*, 1905.

At the suggestion of Elisabeth Marbury de Wolfe turned to interior decoration, then an almost exclusively masculine field. Her reputation as a set designer, her success in decorating the house she and Marbury shared, and connections in society all aided her. Architect Stanford White helped her win a commission to do the Colony Club, New York's first social club for women. Her striking success there firmly established her as America's first woman professional interior decorator. Her pronounced taste helped shape that of her generation. Vivid greens and yellows, airy treatment of space, often through the clever use of mirrors, and eclecticism and economy in furniture and appointments all set a sharply anti-Victorian tone. The effect was at once classical and modern. A series of articles by her in *Good Housekeeping* and the *Delineator* was collected into the widely influential *The House in Good Taste*, 1913. Her wealthy clients brought her wealth, and she and Marbury became noted hostesses. In 1903 they bought and began restoring the Villa Trianon in Versailles, which became a second center for their entertaining.

During World War I de Wolfe remained in France and won the Croix de Guerre and the Legion of Honor for her hospital relief work, particularly among gas-burn cases. After the war she concentrated more on entertaining at Villa Trianon, which became a regular stop for the international set, and less on the decorating firm, which was left to run itself. In March 1926 she married Sir Charles Mendl, a British diplomat in France. In 1935 she published an autobiography, *After All.* On the outbreak of World War II they moved to Hollywood, California; Lady Mendl was restored to American citizenship, which had been lost by her marriage, by special act of Congress. After the war she returned to Villa Trianon, where she died on July 12, 1950.

Dewson, Mary Williams 1874–1962 economist and political organizer

Born in Quincy, Massachusetts, on February 18, 1874, Mary Dewson graduated from Wellesley College in 1897. For three years she worked as a research economist for the Woman's Educational and Industrial Union of Boston (then led by Mary M. K. Kehew), and in 1900 she was appointed superintendent of the Massachusetts Girls' Parole Department, a post she held for 12 years. In 1911 she served also as secretary of the Commission on Minimum Wage Legislation for Massachusetts. From 1912 to 1917 she engaged in dairy farming. She returned to public service in the latter year and for two years served as zone chief of the Bureau of Refugees of the American Red Cross in France. In 1919–1924 she was research secretary of the National Consumers' League, and from 1925 to 1931 she was president of the Consumers' League of New York.

In 1928 Eleanor Roosevelt prevailed upon Dewson to help organize women within the Democratic party, and thenceforth she was politically and personally close to the Roosevelt family. She took an active role in Franklin D. Roosevelt's gubernatorial campaign in New York in 1930, and in his presidential campaign in 1932 she was chairman of the Women's Division of the Democratic National Campaign Committee. In 1933 James A. Farley appointed her director of the Women's Division of the Democratic National Committee. The next year she became director of the General Advisory Committee of the Women's Division. During 1933–1935 she sat on the Consumers' Advisory Board of the National Recovery Administration (originally under the chairmanship of Mary H. Rumsey). She again headed women's campaign activities in the party in 1936, a task that involved considerable travel through the country, and in 1936–1937 she was vice-chairman of the Democratic National Committee. She served as well on the advisory council of the President's Advisory Committee on Economic Security, where much of the planning for the Social Security system was done, and in 1937 Roosevelt named her to the Social Security Board, where she sat as the only woman member until ill health forced her to resign in 1938. She emerged from retirement in 1940 to take part in Roosevelt's third presidential campaign. In later years she was a director of the Franklin D. Roosevelt Foundation and of the International Migration Service. She died in Castine, Maine, on October 22, 1962.

Diaz, Abby Morton 1821–1904 novelist and writer of children's literature

Born in Plymouth, Massachusetts, on November 22, 1821, Abigail Morton absorbed from her father at an early age a taste for reform. Among her early involvements was a juvenile antislavery society. From early 1843 until 1847 she lived and taught school at the experimental Brook Farm community, of which her father had been an original trustee. In October 1845 she married Manuel A. Diaz of Havana, from whom she was separated a few years later. For some time she taught singing and dancing and did practical nursing in Plymouth.

In May 1861 the *Atlantic Monthly* published Diaz's story "Pink and Blue," and she was launched on a career as a writer. Her stories for children appeared in numerous periodicals — *St. Nicholas*, *Wide Awake*, *Our Young Folks*, *Hearth and Home*, and others — and her long series of books began with *The Bybury Book*, 1868, and *The King's Lily and Rosebud*, 1869. In 1870 she published one of her most successful and enduring books, *The William Henry Letters*, whose sequels, *William Henry and His Friends*, 1872, and *Lucy Maria*, 1874, were also very popular. Subsequent books included six volumes of the Story Tree Series, *Story Book for Children*, 1875, *Christmas Morning*, 1880, *Jimmy-johns*, 1881, *Polly Cologne*, 1881, and *Bybury to Beacon Street*, 1887. Her books for young people emphasized her belief in the essential goodness of children, and the consequent humor and affection of her treatment of her characters accounted for her popularity. She also wrote a number of books intended for older readers, including *Neighborhood Talks*, 1876, *Domestic Problems*, 1884, *In The Strength of the Lord*, 1889, *Only a Flock of Women*, 1893, and *The Religious Training of Children*, 1896. Diaz was deeply concerned about the effects on culture and morals of the decay of the traditional village and the growth of the industrial city. The impact of these social trends on women led her to take the lead in organizing the Women's Educational and Industrial Union of Boston, of which she was a director from 1877 to 1881, president from 1881 to 1892, and vice-president from 1892 to 1902. She was also a member of the New England Women's Club and a vice-president of the Massachusetts Woman Suffrage Association. She died in Belmont, Massachusetts, on April 1, 1904.

Dickey, Sarah Ann 1838–1904 educator

Born near Dayton, Ohio, on April 25, 1838, Sarah Dickey had almost no schooling until she was sixteen, but her determined progress thereafter was rapid. At nineteen she secured a teacher's certificate. After six years of teaching in her native region she went to Vicksburg, Mississippi, in 1863 to teach in a freedmen's school operated by her church, the United Brethren in Christ. In 1865 she entered Mount Holyoke Female Seminary (now Mount Holyoke College) and worked her way through, graduating in 1869. She then returned to Mississippi. She taught for a year in a freedmen's school in Raymond, and in 1871 she moved to nearby Clinton, where she began working to fulfill her dream of opening an academy for African-American students.

Dickey secured support among the local black community despite threats from the Ku Klux Klan and enrolled a board of trustees of prominent Mississippians. In 1873 a charter was granted for the Mount Hermon Female Seminary, which opened in October 1875 in a large brick house situated on 160 acres. Patterned after Mount Holyoke in its work-study system, Mount Hermon had to deal with largely unprepared students. A primary course was instituted to prepare students for the regular work of the seminary. Dickey held standards high, as evidenced by the fact that only a single student ever received the diploma of the seminary for having finished the entire course. A number, however, completed the three- (later four-) year normal course and became teachers. Money was a constant problem, as neither her church, the American Missionary Society, nor the state of Mississippi provided any. Nonetheless Mount Hermon played an important part in the lives of Mississippi African-Americans for nearly 50 years. In addition to her teaching and money-raising activities, Dickey also reared a number of African-American children left in her care and was a constant friend to those in her community. In 1896 she was ordained a minister of the United Brethren church. She died in Clinton, Mississippi, on January 23, 1904. Mount Hermon Seminary passed into the hands of the American Missionary Association, which closed it in 1924 in favor of its own Tougaloo College.

Dickinson, Anna Elizabeth 1842–1932 lecturer

Born in Philadelphia on October 28, 1842, Anna Dickinson grew up in poverty. Her formal education took place mainly at the Friends' Select School of Philadelphia, but she was an avid reader and early developed the habit of expressing herself on public questions. At fourteen she published an article in William Lloyd Garrison's *Liberator*. In

1860 she addressed the Pennsylvania Anti-Slavery Society, and in early 1861 she spoke in Philadelphia on "Women's Rights and Wrongs" to such effect that she received invitations to speak from several platforms throughout New England. For a short time in 1861 she held a position at the U.S. mint in Philadelphia, but she was fired in December for publicly accusing General George B. McClellan of treason in the loss of the battle of Ball's Bluff. Thereafter she devoted herself to the platform. An address in Boston arranged by Garrison was followed by a tour of New England in the fall of 1862 with a lecture on "Hospital Life."

In 1863 Dickinson stumped New Hampshire and then Connecticut on behalf of Republican candidates, spoke at Cooper Union in New York City and the Academy of Music in Philadelphia, and then toured the recently draft-riot-torn mining districts of Pennsylvania for the Republicans. In January 1864 she addressed a gathering, including President Abraham Lincoln, at the U.S. Capitol in Washington, D.C. Her oratory was marked by fiery passion and remarkable vituperation, and these, with the novelty of her sex and youth, made her enormously popular. After the Civil War she went on the lyceum circuit, delivering addresses across the country on "Reconstruction," in which she advocated harsh treatment of the South, "Woman's Work and Wages," "Whited Sepulchres," her attack on Mormonism, "Demagogues and Workingmen," "Between us be Truth," on the "social evil" (venereal disease), and her favorite, "Joan of Arc." She published *What Answer?* on the topic of interracial marriage, 1868, *A Paying Investment*, on various social reforms, 1876, and *A Ragged Register (of People, Places, and Opinions)*, a memoir, 1879.

Dickinson's considerable income went as fast as it came, and when her popularity as a lecturer dwindled she turned to other fields. In May 1876 she appeared in Boston in a play of her own, *A Crown of Thorns*; both she and the play were dismissed by critics. She wrote several more plays, most of which remained unproduced and unpublished, although *An American Girl* was a success for Fanny Davenport in 1880. After a ridiculed appearance as Hamlet in 1882 she retired from the public view.

In 1888 Dickinson returned to the platform at the invitation of the Republican National Committee, but her undiminished gift for denunciation and epithet now proved an embarrassment, and she was let go. Growing signs of mental instability led to her incarceration in a state hospital in Danville, Pennsylvania, for a short time in 1891. On her release she sued those responsible and was awarded nominal damages. She lived out the rest of her life quietly in New York City and in Goshen, New York, where she died on October 22, 1932.

Dickinson, Emily Elizabeth 1830–1886 poet

Born on December 10, 1830, in Amherst, Massachusetts, Emily Dickinson was the daughter of a prominent lawyer who was later a congressman and treasurer of Amherst College. She attended Amherst Academy and spent a year at the Mount Holyoke Female Seminary, but her dislike of being away from home led her to return permanently to her father's house in 1848. Her residence there was interrupted only by a visit to Washington and Philadelphia in 1855 and a few brief trips to Boston and Concord. During her youth she was quite lively and outgoing, but she became progressively reclusive as the years passed. Although she never married she apparently experienced deep, if ambiguous, emotional involvements on a few occasions, the second during the 1850s with the Reverend Charles Wadsworth, who may have been the inspiration for the otherwise imaginary lover alluded to in some of her poems of the early 1860s. (Another possibility is Samuel Bowles, Massachusetts publisher of the *Springfield Republican*.) She seems to have written occasional verse from her school days, and she continued to write until her death, but the major portion of her work, and the best of it, was produced during the years 1858–1866.

AMHERST COLLEGE LIBRARY SPECIAL COLLECTIONS

Emily Dickinson

Typically short, condensed pieces, her poems combined spare lyricism and metaphysical speculation with highly unorthodox diction and meter and meticulous craftsmanship. The provinciality and narrowness of her outward life belied both the scope of her thought and the subtlety of her style. She showed her work to only a few persons outside her family circle. In 1862 she sent a few verses to the popular critic Thomas Wentworth Higginson, who was at once charmed and baffled by them; in a remarkable correspondence that continued for more than 20 years he gently counseled against publication. During her life none of her poems were published with her consent, although several did appear: one was published anonymously in 1878 through the agency of Helen Hunt Jackson, a schoolmate and lifelong friend and the shy poet's leading literary champion, and a few were printed in Bowles's *Republican*.

Dickinson's father died in 1874, and the next year her mother became an invalid. She kept more and more to herself until at length she rarely ventured from the house, but she maintained correspondence with a few intimates until her death in Amherst on May 15, 1886. Her sister Lavinia subsequently discovered hundreds of poems neatly bundled and tucked away. She prevailed upon Mabel Loomis Todd and the still dubious Higginson to help prepare a slender volume, *Poems by Emily Dickinson*, 1890. The book met with generally unfavorable critical response, but it was sufficiently well received by the public to warrant the publication of *Poems: Second Series*, 1891, and *Poems: Third Series*, 1896. By 1945 nearly all of Emily Dickinson's poetry — 1,775 pieces — and much of her surviving correspondence had been published, and her position as one of the world's foremost poets was secure.

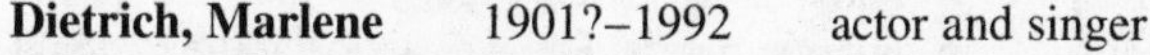

Dietrich, Marlene 1901?–1992 actor and singer

Born on December 27, probably in 1901 (she claimed 1904), in Berlin, Germany, Maria Magdalene, as she was named, was the daughter of Ludwig Dietrich, a Royal Prussian police officer, and Josephine Felsing, the daughter of a jeweler. Her father died when she was still very young, and her mother remarried Colonel Baron von Losch, who was killed fighting in World War I. She studied at a private school and learned both English and French by the time she was twelve years old. As a teenager, she studied to be a concert violinist, but a wrist injury forced her to abandon her plans for a musical career.

She turned to the arts of the stage and enrolled in Max Reinhardt's *Deutsche Theaterschule*, a school of dramatic arts, and changed her name to Marlene because her family disapproved of her decision to become an actress. Later, she joined Reinhardt's theater company. In 1923 she attracted the attention of Rudolf Sieber, a casting director at UFA film studios; he began casting her in small film roles. They married the following year and, after the birth of their daughter, Maria, she returned to theater and film. They were separated in 1929.

In the same year director Josef von Sternberg saw Dietrich in a show while he was in Germany and cast her as the haughty and amoral female lead in *The Blue Angel*, 1930, Germany's first talking film. The film's success catapulted Dietrich into stardom. Von Sternberg brought Dietrich to the U.S. and signed her with Paramount Pictures. She developed her femme fatale film persona with von Sternberg in *Morocco*, 1930, *Dishonored*, 1931, *Shanghai Express*, 1932, *Blond Venus*, 1932, *The Scarlet Empress*, 1934, and *The Devil is a Woman*, 1935. Later she worked for such directors as Lang, Lubitsch, Wilder and Hitchcock. Her visibility as a star made her a trend-setter — she wore mannish clothes and launched an entire fashion craze of American women wearing pants and other men's apparel.

By World War II, Dietrich refused to work in Germany despite personal appeals made by Adolf Hitler, and her films were temporarily banned there. She became a U.S. citizen in 1937 and worked during the war entertaining the troops by singing numbers like "Falling in Love Again." In the 1950s, while still making movies, Dietrich began a career as an international cabaret star, performing in Las Vegas and in London. She took her cabaret act to Russia in 1964 and performed at the Edinburgh Festival in 1965. She made her Broadway debut in 1967.

Some of her later films include: *Witness for the Prosecution*, 1958, *The Monte Carlo Story*, 1958, *Touch of Evil*, 1958, and *Judgment at Nuremberg*, 1961. She toured as a concert and cabaret singer until 1975; *Marlene*, her memoirs, were published in 1989. Dietrich died in Paris on May 6, 1992.

Diggs, Annie LePorte 1848–1916 reformer and politician

Born on February 22, 1848, in London, Ontario, Annie LePorte moved with her family to New Jersey in 1855. In 1873, after completing school, she went to Kansas, where in September of that year she married Alvin S. Diggs of Lawrence. In the late 1870s her interest in the temperance crusade drew her into her first acquaintance with politics. In August 1881 she helped form the nonpolitical Kansas Liberal Union among radical and free thinkers of various stripes. A few months later, during a visit to Boston, she was elected a vice-president of the Free Religious Association, succeeding Lucretia Mott.

During 1882 Diggs and her husband published the short-lived *Kansas Liberal* from their home. During the 1880s she worked for woman suffrage and was active in the developing agitation for cooperative association among farmers and workers. She wrote a column on Farmers' Alliance news for the *Lawrence Journal* for a time and then became an associate editor of the *Alliance Advocate*. She played a central role in transforming the Kansas Farmers' Alliance into a political body, the People's (later Populist) party, and became one of its most effective speakers and organizers. She was active at the national Populist conventions in Ocala, Florida, in December 1890, at Cincinnati in May 1891, and at Omaha in July 1892, and she was a principal feature of Populist election campaigns in Kansas in 1894 and 1896. In these campaigns she was associated with Mary E. Lease, whom she generally disliked and distrusted. In 1894, as vice-president of the Kansas Equal Suffrage Association, she helped manage an unsuccessful campaign for a woman suffrage amendment to the Kansas constitution. In May 1897 she was elected president of the Kansas Woman's Free Silver League, and as part of the silver movement's takeover of the Populist party she helped effect the Populist-Democrat fusion ticket for the 1898 election. From that year to 1902 she held the post of state librarian under the fusion state administration. In 1899 she became president of the Kansas Equal Suffrage Association. Her control of the fusion convention of 1900 earned her the epithet "Boss" Diggs from leaders of the regular Democrats. In 1902 she traveled to England to attend the International Cooperative Congress as the representative of the Western Cooperative Association of Kansas City. She remained abroad for two years, sending back articles and letters to newspapers on reform movements in Europe. In 1905 she was elected president of the Kansas Woman's Press Association. In 1906 she suddenly moved to New York City, and thereafter she took no part in political affairs. She published two books, *The Story of Jerry Simpson*, on her fellow Kansas Populist, 1908, and *Bedrock*, 1912. She lived in Detroit from 1912 until her death on September 7, 1916.

Dix, Dorothea Lynde 1802–1887 teacher, social reformer, and humanitarian

Born on April 4, 1802, in Hampden, Maine (then still part of Massachusetts), Dorothea Dix left her unhappy home at the age of twelve to live and study in Boston with her grandmother. By the age of fourteen she was teaching in a school for young girls in Worcester, Massachusetts, employing a curriculum of her own devising that stressed the natural sciences and the responsibilities of ethical living. In 1821 she opened her own school in Boston. In 1824 she published a science textbook entitled *Conversations on Common Things*, and in 1825 she edited *Hymns for Children*. Dix's books included *Evening Hours*, 1825, *Meditations for Private Hours*, 1828, and *The Garland of Flora*, 1829. She continued her school and its successor until 1836, when increasingly serious bouts with tuberculosis forced her to abandon teaching and leave Boston.

After nearly two years in England Dix returned to Boston, still a semi-invalid, and found to her amazement that she had inherited a sum of money sufficient to support her comfortably for life. But her Calvinist beliefs enjoined her from inactivity. Thus in March 1841, when a young clergyman asked her to begin a Sunday school class in the East Cambridge House of Correction, she accepted the challenge. In the prison she first observed the treatment of insane and disturbed persons, who were thrown in with criminals, irrespective of age or sex. They were left unclothed, in darkness, without heat or sanitary facilities; some were chained to the walls and flogged. Profoundly shocked, and supported by Samuel Gridley Howe and others of her mind, she traveled for nearly two years throughout the state, observed the same conditions in institutions everywhere, and in January 1843 submitted to the Massachusetts legislature a detailed report of her thoroughly documented findings. Her dignity, feverish compassion, and determination, as well as the issue itself, moved the legislators; and despite public apathy, disbelief, and occasional active opposition, a bill was passed for enlargement of the Worcester insane asylum. She then moved on to Rhode Island and later New York.

In the next 40 years Dix inspired legislators in 15 U.S. states and in Canada to establish state hospitals for the mentally ill. Her unflagging efforts directly prompted the building of 32 institutions in the United States. She carried on her work even while on a convalescent tour of Europe in 1854–1856, notably in Italy, where she prevailed upon Pope Pius IX to inspect personally the atrocious conditions she had discovered. Where new institutions were not required, she fostered the reorganization, enlargement, and restaffing, with well trained, intelligent personnel, of already existing hospitals.

In 1845 Dix published *Remarks on Prisons and Prison Discipline in the United States* to advocate reforms in the treatment of ordinary prisoners. In June 1861 she was appointed superintendent of army nurses for Civil War service. She was ill suited to administration, however, and had great difficulty with the post. The secretary of war, Edwin Stanton, was obliged to restrict her authority in October 1863, but she remained in the post until September 1866. After the war she returned to her work with hospitals; when she died on July 17, 1887, it was in a hospital in Trenton, New Jersey, that she had founded.

Dodge, Grace Hoadley 1856–1914 social worker

Born in New York City on May 21, 1856, Grace Dodge was of a wealthy family long active in philanthropic work. She was educated privately, for a time at Miss Porter's School in Farmington, Connecticut. From 1874 she devoted herself to social work. From Sunday School teaching she moved to teaching in the schools of the Children's Aid Society. In 1876 she joined the New York State Charities Aid Association headed by Louisa Lee Schuyler, with which she was to remain associated for many years. After a time as an instructor in one of Emily Huntington's kitchen garden classes she helped form the Kitchen Garden Association in 1880. In 1884 she led in transforming the association into the Industrial Education Association, which undertook to provide manual training classes for boys as well as domestic skills classes for girls. Dodge, as vice-president of the association, was its effective executive head. Her work there won her appointment as one of the first two women to serve on the city Board of Education, a post she held from 1886 to 1889. In 1881 she led an informal series of gatherings of working girls that soon became a regular club devoted to recreation, practical education, and self-improvement. Similar clubs sprang up around the city, and in 1885 Grace Dodge assisted them in forming the Working Girls' Association of Clubs; in 1890 a national association was established, and she was chosen director, a post she held until 1896.

In her work with working girls as with others, Dodge was remarkable for her direct, unassuming manner; although she contributed heavily to the financial support of such groups, she was never guilty of patronizing them. In the later 1880s the Industrial Education Association encountered a shortage of trained teachers of domestic and industrial skills for its own classes and for the classes it had been successful in having incorporated into the public schools. In turning its attention to teacher training, it quickly found itself working closely with Columbia University; Columbia's president, Frederick A. P. Barnard, was an honorary member of the association, while the association's head from 1887, Nicholas Murray Butler, was a Columbia professor. In 1889 the association was given a provisional charter for the New York College for the Training of Teachers, which in 1892 became Teachers College and moved to a Morningside Heights campus given by Dodge. In 1898 it was formally affiliated with Columbia University. Grace Dodge served as treasurer from 1892 to 1911 and for many of those years personally made up the budget deficit.

In 1905 Dodge took the initiative in reconciling the two rival groups that sought to control the Young Women's Christian Association movement, the largely Eastern and upper-class international Board and the Midwestern and evangelical American Committee. She planned and underwrote a meeting of representatives from both groups in New York City, and when a unified National Board was agreed upon in December 1906 she was elected president. It was a post that required much application, and in addition to her labor she contributed considerable money, including, with one of her brothers, nearly a sixth of the $4 million raised in the YWCA's "Whirlwind Campaign" of 1913.

Other activities of Dodge included the Girls' Public School Athletic League, which she founded in 1905, the New York Travelers' Aid Society, which she organized in 1907 by consolidating several smaller groups, the American College for Girls at Constantinople, of which she was president of the board of trustees from 1911, and the American Social Hygiene Association, which she formed from several other groups in 1912. She died in New York City on December 27, 1914.

Dodge, Josephine Marshall Jewell 1855–1928 philanthropist and antisuffragist

Born in Hartford, Connecticut, on February 11, 1855, Josephine Jewell was of a prominent family. She left Vassar College after three years in 1873 to accompany her father, who had just been appointed U.S. minister to Russia, to St. Petersburg. She returned with him in 1874 and in October 1875 married Arthur M. Dodge, member of a family active in New York business and philanthropy (he was an uncle of Grace H. Dodge). In New York City she became interested in the day nursery movement and in 1878 began sponsoring the Virginia Day Nursery to care for children of working mothers in the city's East Side slums. In 1888 she founded the Jewell Day Nursery, whose aim was not only day-care but also the education of immigrant children in "American" values. She demonstrated a similar model day nursery at the World's Columbian Exposition in Chicago in 1893. In 1895 she founded and became first president of the Association of Day Nurseries of New York City, which grew eventually to have 100 member nurseries, and in 1898 she became president of the National Federation (later Association) of Day Nurseries, which had 700 members. From 1899 she became increasingly active in opposition to woman suffrage, which she believed would jeopardize the nonpartisan integrity of women reformers and which recent progressive legislation on women's rights, conditions of employment, and so on had rendered unnecessary. In December 1911 she led in organizing and was chosen president of the National Association Opposed to Woman Suffrage, whose organ, *Woman's Protest*, she also edited. She continued as president of the group until June 1917, when she resigned in order that the organization might shift its headquarters from New York City to Washington, D.C., where the struggle for the Nineteenth Amendment was to take place. She continued active in local anti-suffrage agitation until the issue was finally conceded in 1919. She died on March 6, 1928, while visiting Cannes, France.

Dodge, Mary Abigail 1833–1896 essayist and editor

Born in Hamilton, Massachusetts, on March 31, 1833, Abigail Dodge attended schools in her native town and for a year each in Cambridge and Ipswich. She remained at the Ipswich Female Seminary as a teacher from her graduation in 1850 until 1854. She then taught English at the Hartford Female Seminary in Connecticut in 1854–1855 and at the Hartford High School in 1855–1858. In 1858 she moved to Washington, D.C., to become governess to the children of Gamaliel Bailey, editor of the anitslavery journal *National Era*, to whom she had earlier sent a few of her poems and prose sketches. These began to appear also in various other periodicals under the pseudonym "Gail Hamilton" and to attract considerable attention for their practical wisdom and wit.

From 1860 to 1868 Dodge was back home caring for her ailing mother. During that time she published two collections of essays, *Country Living and Country Thinking*, 1862, and *A New Atmosphere*, 1865, and a strong defense of woman's right to equal educational and occupational opportunities, *Woman's Wrongs: A Counter-Irritant*, 1868. She also edited a juvenile magazine, *Our Young Folks*, with Lucy Larcom and John T. Trowbridge in 1865–1867. Her *Battle of the Books*, 1870, was a witty fictional account of her disagreements with her first publisher, Ticknor and Fields of Boston.

From 1871 Dodge spent much time in Washington, D.C., mainly in the household of James G. Blaine, whose wife was her cousin, but she also traveled extensively in America and Europe. Her articles and essays on topics from politics to religion to current affairs remained in great demand. Subsequent books by "Gail Hamilton" included *Woman's Worth and Worthlessness*, 1872, in which she continued the argument for woman's equality in the social and economic spheres with a demand that women themselves live up to such equality by giving over the pretense of helplessness and argued against woman suffrage in favor of a more indirect influence on affairs, *Sermons to the Clergy*, 1875, *What Think You of Christ*, 1877, *Our Common School System*, 1880, *A Washington Bible Class*, 1891, *Biography of James G. Blaine*, 1895, and *X Rays*, 1896. In 1872–1873 she helped edit *Wood's Household Magazine*. She died in Hamilton, Massachusetts, on August 17, 1896.

Dodge, Mary Elizabeth Mapes 1831–1905 author and editor of children's literature

Born on January 26, 1831, in New York City, Mary Mapes was well educated at home, where her parents frequently entertained such prominent men as William Cullen Bryant and Horace Greeley. Her father, a scientist and artist, moved the family to a New Jersey farm in 1847, where he also published a magazine, *Working Farmer*, on which Mary got her first taste of editorial work. In June 1851 she married William Dodge, a lawyer whose death seven years later left her with two children to support.

Returning to New Jersey, she turned to writing, and her work quickly found acceptance in juvenile magazines. Her first book for children, *Irvington Stories*, appeared in 1864 and was followed the next year by *Hans Brinker; or The Silver Skates*, a carefully researched story of Dutch youth that came to rank as a classic of children's literature and went through more than a hundred editions during its author's lifetime. Combining a wholesome sense of adventure with a simple and cheerful outlook, Dodge's work was highly successful in a field where morbid sermonizing and stifling didacticism had often dominated. Subsequent books included *A Few Friends and How They Amused Themselves*, 1869, *Rhymes and Jingles*, 1874, *Theophilus and Others*, 1876, *Donald and Dorothy*, 1883, and *The Land of Pluck*, 1894. Her stories were printed in the leading periodicals of the day, and she was acknowledged the preeminent children's author in America.

In 1868 Dodge became associate editor of *Hearth and Home*, with Harriet Beecher Stowe and Donald Grant Mitchell ("Ik Marvel"). In 1873 she was named the first editor of the newly founded *St. Nicholas Magazine* (the name was her suggestion) for children. She held the position for the rest of her life, building the periodical into the foremost in its field. Her success was aided by the participation of her literary friends, among them Bryant, Henry Wadsworth Longfellow, and John Greenleaf Whittier, and by such other leading authors as Rudyard Kipling, Mark Twain, William Dean Howells, Louisa May Alcott, Frances Hodgson Burnett, and Alfred, Lord Tennyson, some of whom wrote their only juvenile works for her. Her editorial acumen was remarkable, and her high standards for writing and art made *St. Nicholas* an unequaled feast for its readers. Two books for young children were compiled from her own contributions to *St. Nicholas* — *Baby Days*, 1876, and *Baby World*, 1884. Dodge died on August 21, 1905, at her summer home in Onteora Park, New York.

Dole, Elizabeth Hanford 1936– lawyer and director of the American Red Cross

Born on July 29, 1936 in Salisbury, North Carolina, Elizabeth Hanford attended Duke University, graduating Phi Beta Kappa with a B.A. in political science in 1958. After doing graduate studies at Oxford University she entered Harvard University, receiving her M.A. in education in 1960 and her J.D. in 1965, where she was one of 15 women in a class of 550. Her first stint in politics was as a greeter on Lyndon B. Johnson's campaign train in 1960. While she was a Democrat early in her life, she later became an independent before eventually joining the Republican party.

After being admitted to the Bar of the District of Columbia in 1966, she became a staff assistant at the U.S. Department of Health, Education and Welfare. In 1967 she left her government position to practice law privately in Washington, D.C., and in 1968 she moved back into the public sector, working first as assistant director, then as director of the President's Committee on Consumer Interests under President Johnson. She continued to work as a public official for a number of years, holding jobs in the administrations of presidents Nixon, Ford, Carter, Reagan, and Bush. She worked on the Federal Trade Commission in 1973, and under Ronald Reagan served as secretary of the Department of Transportation. One of her most notable accomplishments in this position was writing a bill in 1983 mandating a high, center-mounted third brake light on all passenger automobiles, believed by many to have saved not only lives, but millions of dollars in repair and medical costs. While many praised her for her actions, her critics accused her of ignoring key safety issues, particularly those related to air travel.

While working in the Office of Consumer Affairs under Nixon, she had met Kansas Senator Bob Dole, whom she married in 1975. Three times in her career she resigned from her job to work for her husband's campaigns, as Gerald Ford's vice-presidential candidate in 1976, and in his own presidential bids in 1980 and 1988 (all unsuccessful). Some criticized her for this decision, in particular feminist groups who questioned her priorities.

In 1990 she resigned from her position as labor secretary under President George Bush to head the American Red Cross. She left a 25-year career in government because she "felt a calling" to join a nonprofit organization.

When Senator Bob Dole announced his intention to run for President in 1996, she once again took time off from her work to help her husband campaign — this time assuring the public that she was only taking a leave of absence, and that she fully intended to return to her post even if her husband won the election. Dole proved to be a key figure in her husband's campaign, drawing both praise and criticism for her stated intention to be a combination career woman and First Lady. While Hillary Clinton blazed a trail for the First Lady to be career-minded and powerful in the president's administration, the nation had yet to see a First Lady with her own separate career as Elizabeth Dole intended. Many in the Republican party, however, stated that they would like to see Elizabeth Dole herself make a bid for the presidential nomination. While she insisted this was not something she thought about seriously, she also never ruled out the idea.

Doolittle, Hilda 1886–1961 poet

Born on September 10, 1886, in Bethlehem, Pennsylvania, Hilda Doolittle entered Bryn Mawr College in 1904 and while a student there formed friendships with Marianne Moore, a fellow student, and with Ezra Pound and William Carlos Williams, who were at the nearby University of Pennsylvania. Ill health forced her to leave college in 1906. Five years later she traveled to Europe for what was to have been a vacation but became a permanent stay, mainly in England and Switzerland. Her first published poems, sent to *Poetry* magazine by Pound, appeared under the initials H. D., which remained thereafter her nom de plume. Other poems appeared in Pound's anthology *Des Imagistes*, 1914, and in the London journal *The Egoist*, edited by Richard Aldington, whom she married in October 1913.

H.D.'s first volume of verse, *Sea Garden*, 1916, established her as an important voice among the radical young Imagist poets. Subsequent volumes included *Hymen*, 1921, *Heliodora and Other Poems*, 1924, *Collected Poems*, 1925, *Hippolytus Temporizes*, 1927, *Red Roses for Bronze*, 1931, a translation of Euripides' *Ion*, 1937, *Collected Poems*, 1940, and a trilogy comprising *The Walls Do Not Fall*, 1944, *Tribute to the Angels*, 1945, and *Flowering of the Rod*, 1946. Over the years her sharp, spare, and rather passionless manner mellowed and took on rich religious and mystic overtones, becoming in the process less modernist and more open to the wider heritage of poetic tradition. H. D. published also a number of prose works, including four novels — *Palimpsest*, 1926, *Hedylus*, 1928, *The Hedgehog*, 1936, and *Bid Me to Live*, 1960 — and the semi-autobiographical *Tribute to Freud*, 1956. From 1916 to 1920 she edited *The Egoist*. *Helen in Egypt*, verse, was her last book, appearing shortly after her death in Zürich, Switzerland, on September 27, 1961.

Dorr, Julia Caroline Ripley 1825–1913 novelist and poet

Born on February 13, 1825, in Charleston, South Carolina, Julia Ripley accompanied her father to New England in 1830 and settled with him in Rutland, Vermont, in 1837. In 1847 she married Seneca M. Dorr, with whom she lived in Ghent, New York, until 1857, when they returned to Rutland.

Dorr had enjoyed writing verse since childhood, but none had ever been published until her husband, without her knowledge, sent one of her poems to the *Union Magazine*. In 1848 *Sartain's Magazine* published one of her short stories as winner of a prize contest. She published her first book, *Farmingdale*, a novel, in 1854 under the pseudonym "Caroline Thomas." Under the same name she published two more novels, *Lanmere*, 1856, and *Sybil Huntington*, 1869. Under her own name she published *Expiation*, a novel, 1873, *Bride and Bridegroom*, a book of advice, 1873, three books of travel: *Bermuda*, 1884, *"The Flower of England's Face"*, 1895, and *A Cathedral Pilgrimage*, 1896, *In Kings' Houses*, another novel, 1898, and at least ten volumes of verse, from *Poems*, 1872, to *Last Poems*, 1913, and including *Friar Anselmo, and Other Poems*, 1879, *Daybreak, an*

Easter Poem, 1882, *Afternoon Songs*, 1885, *Afterglow: Later Poems*, 1900, and *Beyond the Sunset: Latest Poems*, 1909, and a volume of collected poems in 1892.

Dorr's poetry was not greatly distinguished but was praised by such as Oliver Wendell Holmes and Ralph Waldo Emerson and was widely popular for its grace and easy conventionality. Dorr died in Rutland, Vermont, on January 18, 1913.

Douglas, Helen Mary Gahagan 1900–1980 actor and public official

Born on November 25, 1900, in Boonton, New Jersey, Helen Gahagan was educated privately and in 1920–1922 attended Barnard College. In the latter year she left college to seek a career on the stage. After a Broadway debut in the short-lived *Manhattan* that year she appeared in a number of plays over the next several years, including *Young Woodley* in 1925–1926, *Trelawney of the Wells* in 1926, and *Diplomacy* in 1928, and gained a reputation as a competent actress and a stunningly beautiful woman.

In 1928 Gahagan left the theater to study operatic singing and made several successful appearances on European stages. In 1930 she returned to New York and the legitimate theater. In *Tonight or Never*, David Belasco's last Broadway production, she met Melvyn Douglas, whom she married in April 1931. Notable stage appearances over the next few years included *Moor Born*, 1934, *Mary of Scotland*, 1934, *Mother Lode*, 1934, and *And Stars Remain*, 1936, and in 1935 she starred in a film version of *She*.

During the 1930s Gahagan Douglas became sharply aware of the social dislocations of the Depression, and, becoming convinced that the Republican party she had followed by family tradition had little to offer by way of solutions, she became active in Democratic and New Deal politics. She was appointed to the national advisory committee for the Works Progress Administration in 1939 and to the California state committee of the National Youth Administration in 1940, and in the latter year she was a delegate from California to the Democratic national convention and was chosen to the party's national committee. During 1941–1944 she was vice-chairman of the Democratic state central committee in California and chairman of its women's division. In 1942–1943 she was a member of the board of governors of the California Housing and Planning Association. In 1944 she won election to the House of Representatives from California's 14th District, and she held the seat through two reelections from January 1945 to January 1951. She was a staunch supporter of President Harry S. Truman's Fair Deal policies, and in 1946 Truman appointed her a delegate to the United Nations General Assembly.

In 1950 Gahagan Douglas ran for a Senate seat from California but was defeated by Richard M. Nixon after a campaign that later became proverbial for "red-baiting" and vicious politics. Thereafter she became known as a lecturer and author. In 1963 she published *The Eleanor Roosevelt We Remember*. In 1964 she was appointed by President Lyndon B. Johnson to head a delegation to the inauguration of President V. S. Tubman of Liberia. In the same year she was honorary cochair of the Women's International League for Peace and Freedom.

Douvillier, Suzanne Théodore Vaillande 1778–1826 dancer and mime

Born in Dôle, France, probably on September 28, 1778, Suzanne Vaillande was apparently an illegitimate child. Little is known of her childhood beyond the fact that she attended school in Paris and may have studied dancing in the ballet school of the Paris Opéra. By 1790 she was in Santo Domingo, French West Indies, where she formed a professional and personal alliance with Alexandre Placide, a multitalented theatrical figure. In 1791 they made their way to the United States, and in January 1792 Madame Placide, as she was billed (although they were not married), appeared at the John Street Theatre in New York City in *The Bird Catcher*, a ballet by Placide presented as an afterpiece to the regular program. *The Bird Catcher* is generally held to be the first ballet piece to have been presented in New York. They remained in New York for several months and presented a number of ballets, including *The Woodcutters*, *The Old Schoolmaster Grown Young*, and *The Philosophers, or The Merry Girl*, and several pantomimes. Later in 1792 they appeared in Philadelphia and Boston; in 1793 they were in Newport; and in 1794 they settled in Charleston, South Carolina. There, in addition to Placide's works, Madame Placide appeared in Maximilien Gardel's *La Chercheuse d'Esprit* and *Le Déserteur Français*, Jean-Georges Noverre's *Les Caprices de Galathée*, and in 1796 her own *Echo and Narcissus*.

In June 1796 Placide fought a duel with Louis Douvillier, a singer and dancer who had joined the company a year earlier, over the affections of Madame Placide. In the aftermath she married Douvillier. She and her husband performed in Norfolk, Virginia, Philadelphia, New York, and elsewhere before settling in New Orleans in 1799. She remained on the stage in ballet and pantomime until 1818. She was the first woman to work as a choreographer in America, and from about 1813 she was probably also the first to design and paint stage scenery. She died in New Orleans on August 30, 1826.

Dove, Rita Frances 1952– poet and educator

Born August 28, 1952, in Akron, Ohio, Rita Frances Dove grew up as one of four children in a middle-class, African-American family where the value of books and education were stressed continually. Her father, Ray, was the first African-American research chemist in the history of the American rubber tire industry. Shortly before her eighteenth birthday, she was ranked one of the top hundred high school students in the country and invited to the White House as a Presidential Scholar. In 1973, she received a bachelor's degree at Miami University in Oxford, Ohio. Although her parents wanted her to be a lawyer, she realized in her junior year that she was destined to be a writer. After graduating from college, she received a Fulbright Fellowship and attended the University of Tübingen, West Germany 1974–75, where she delighted in studying American foreign policy from a foreign perspective. Back in the U.S., she enrolled in the Iowa Writers' Workshop and earned an M.F.A. in 1977. In 1979 she married Fred Viebahn, a German-born novelist.

Dove's poetry began to appear in major periodicals in 1974 and touched on many different subjects. As she said once to an interviewer, "no subject is essentially boring; and no topic unfit for a poem." Among her early works were *Ten Poems*, 1977, and *The Only Dark Spot in the Sky*, 1980. *The Yellow House on the Corner*, 1980, is notable for its poems written from the perspective of slaves. *Thomas and Beulah*, 1986, a collection of narrative verse named after her maternal grandparents and loosely reminiscent of their lives, was awarded a Pulitzer Prize for poetry in 1987. *Museum*, 1983, she has said, "is a concentrated attempt to portray the underside of a museum — the politics behind the artifacts, the stories behind the legends." Other volumes of her poetry include *The Other Side of the House*, 1988 and *Grace Notes*, 1989.

Always interested in the artifice of language, Rita Dove understood poetry as dependent upon language — its sounds and its rhythms as well as its meanings. In addition to poetry, she wrote *Fifth Sunday*, 1985, a collection of short stories; *Through the Ivory Gate*, 1992, a novel; and *The Darker Face of the Earth*, 1994, a verse drama. She began teaching English Literature at the University of Virginia in 1989. She served as poetry editor of *Callaloo* and as advisory editor of *Gettysburg Review* and *TriQuarterly*. She has been awarded numerous grants and fellowships, including a Guggenheim fellowship, 1983, and a Mellon fellowship, 1988. In 1991 she served as a juror in the poetry divisions for the Pulitzer Prize, the National Book Award, and the Ruth Lilly Poetry Prize. In 1993, she was appointed Poet Laureate of the U.S. by the Library of Congress — the youngest person and first African-American to be so honored.

Downey, June Etta 1875–1932 psychologist and educator

Born on July 13, 1875, in Laramie, Wyoming, June Etta Downey graduated from the University of Wyoming in 1895. After a year of teaching school in Laramie she resumed her education at the University of Chicago, where in 1898 she took a master's degree in philosophy and psychology. In that year she joined the faculty of the University of Wyoming as an instructor of English, and the next year she became an instructor of philosophy as well. In the summer of 1901 she studied psychology under Edward Bradford Titchener at Cornell University. She was promoted to assistant professor of English and philosophy in 1902 and to professor in 1905.

In 1904 Downey published a volume of poems titled *Heavenly Dykes*. After a sabbatical year of further study at the University of Chicago, she was awarded her Ph.D. in 1908, and on her return to the University of Wyoming she became head of her department. She soon gave up the teaching of English to concentrate on philosophy and psychology, and the title of her professorship was changed formally to philosophy and psychology in 1915. A gifted and often ingenious experimenter, Downey followed her principal interest in the psychology of aesthetics into many areas of the arts and the mental processes associated with them. Work in muscle reading, handwriting, handedness, color perception, and such topics led to deeper investigations into personality and creativity. Her work resulted in more than 60 articles in professional journals and several books, including *Graphology and the Psychology of Handwriting*, 1919; *Plots and Personalities*, with Edward E. Slosson, 1922; *The Will-Temperament and Its Testing*, a report on her attempt to test clinically aspects of personality other than intelligence, 1923; and *Creative Imagination: Studies in the Psychology of Literature*, 1929. She also published *Kingdom of the Mind*, a book on experimental psychology for young readers, in 1927. Recognized as an outstanding scholar in her field by election to the Society of Experimentalists and membership on the council of the American Psychological Association in 1923–1925, she was also an inspiring teacher and a valuable asset to her university in its early years. She died in Trenton, New Jersey, on October 11, 1932.

Drake, Frances Ann Denny 1797–1875 actor

Born on November 6, 1797, in Schenectady, New York, Frances Ann Denny grew up in Albany. In 1815 she joined a theatrical troupe organized by Samuel Drake to bring entertainment to the wilds of Kentucky. On the journey to that state she made her stage debut in Cherry Valley, New York, in the comedy *The Midnight Hour*. Her debut in tragedy occurred in Cooperstown in *Adelgitha*. During the Kentucky tour she revealed great potential talent.

About 1819 Denny struck out on her own, and after appearances in Montreal and Boston she made her New York debut in April 1820 in *Man and Wife* at the Park Theatre. She remained at the Park until her marriage in 1822 or 1823 to Alexander Drake, a son of her former manager and a gifted comedian. By 1824 she had attained star status in New York and was noted especially for her portrayal of tragic heroines, although she continued to appear in comedies as well.

After that year Drake performed mainly in the West, where she gained a reputation as the "tragedy queen" of the American stage and was sometimes known as the "Star of the West." She won high praise from the visiting English critic Frances Trollope, who liked virtually nothing else about America. On her occasional returns to the New York stage she appeared opposite James William Wallack, Junius Brutus Booth, Thomas S. Hamblin, and other leading actors. Her final New York appearance was in 1835, but she continued to act until the late 1840s. She was without doubt the leading actress on the American stage in the period before the rise of Charlotte Cushman. Drake retired to a farm near Louisville, Kentucky, and died there on September 1, 1875.

Draper, Ruth 1884–1956 monologist

Born on December 2, 1884, in New York City, Ruth Draper was of a well-to-do family and was a granddaughter of Charles A. Dana, editor of the *New York Sun*. She was educated privately. Her career grew from a habit of writing sketches about persons she knew or had observed and performing them at parties. In 1911 she began performing professionally at clubs and schools. She appeared at the Neighborhood Playhouse in 1915 and in 1916 made her only appearance in a full-length play, *A Lady's Name*, at the Maxine Elliott Theatre.

In 1917 Draper made her New York debut as a monologist in a program of one-act pieces, all of which were failures except for the one she had written entitled *The Actress*. She thereafter performed only her own material. (Henry James once wrote a monologue for her that she is said never to have used.) In 1918 she spent several months in France entertaining American troops. Her London debut at Aeolian Hall in 1920 in a bill of her own works was a great success and established her as the preeminent practitioner of her art. An extensive tour of the United States in 1924–1928 was punctuated by a command performance before King George V at Windsor Castle in 1926. In 1928–1929 she played 18 consecutive weeks at the Comedy Theater in New York. She made several highly successful foreign tours in the 1930s and 1940s between engagements in the United States and Great Britain.

Draper's monologues and monodramas were delicately crafted works that revealed a deep understanding of human character, conveyed with great skill and deft suggestion. She used a minimum of stage props, no scenery, and virtually nothing in the way of costume or makeup change, yet she could people the stage at will. Her repertory eventually grew to 39 pieces with such titles as "Three Generations at a Court of Domestic Relations," "At an English House Party," "The Miner's Wife," "A French Dressmaker," "Opening a Bazaar," "In County Kerry," "The Italian Lesson," "At an Art Exhibition," and "Vive La France." In them she conjured up some 58 principal characters, endowing each with full individuality. A command of languages and dialects played a large part in her characterizations as well. Her final performance was on December 26, 1956, at the Playhouse Theatre in New York City. She died in New York on December 30, 1956.

Drew, Louisa Lane 1820–1897 actor

Born in London on January 10, 1820, Louisa Lane was the daughter of actors and at an early age began playing child parts. In June 1827 she arrived in New York with her widowed mother, and three months later she made her American debut at the Walnut Street Theatre in Philadelphia as the Duke of York in *Richard III* with Junius Brutus Booth. She later appeared with Edwin Forrest in a Baltimore production of *William Tell* and in March 1828 made her New York debut in *The Spoiled Child* at the Bowery Theatre. Her career as a highly popular child actress ended in the early 1830s, and after a brief retirement she joined the stock company of the Bowery Theatre in 1833. She learned so well from her adult apprenticeship that in 1838 she was engaged by the Walnut Street Theatre at the unprecedented salary of $20 weekly. Over the next 12 years she toured constantly and with great success. She was twice married in that time; in July 1850 she was married a third time, to John Drew, also an actor. Their three children, Louisa, John, Jr., and Georgiana (later the wife of Maurice Barrymore), were all to carry on the family theatrical tradition. For eleven years John and Louisa Drew continued to tour, together and separately.

In 1853 John Drew became part lessee of the Arch Street Theatre in Philadelphia, but his taste for management was fickle and he often absented himself for extensive tours. In August 1861 the theater's owner prevailed upon Louisa Drew to assume the management, and it was reopened as Mrs. John Drew's Arch Street Theatre. For 31 years she remained as manager. She quickly built up one of the most brilliant repertory companies in the history of the American stage. It lasted until 1878, when the company was disbanded and the theater given over to touring companies.

During the early years of the resident company Drew appeared with it regularly in the roles she was best known for — Lady Teazle, Peg Woffington, and especially Mrs. Malaprop, a role that was virtually her property. No one was more knowledgeable than she about the traditional repertory and stage business, and her exacting standards were legendary. In 1880 she played her favorite role of Mrs. Malaprop in Joseph Jefferson's touring production of *The Rivals*. In May 1892 she gave up management of her theater and moved to New York. She made a few appearances after that, including Jefferson's all-star revival of *The Rivals*, with Julia Marlowe and others, in 1896, and then settled in Larchmont, New York, where she died on August 31, 1897. Her *Autobiographical Sketch of Mrs. John Drew* was published in 1899.

Drexel, Katharine Mary 1858–1955 religious

Born in Philadelphia on November 26, 1858, Katharine Drexel was of the well known banking family. She was educated privately and early took an interest in the family philanthropies. Following the death of her stepmother in 1883 and her father in 1885 she inherited a half-share of a $14 million trust fund. She continued the work earlier undertaken by the family of founding and endowing schools and churches for African-Americans and Native Americans in the South and West.

In January 1887 Drexel had a private audience with Pope Leo XIII in which she suggested the need for nuns to staff the mission schools she had financed. Instead of recommending an order, he challenged her to devote her life as well as her fortune to the missions. In 1889 she became a novice with the Sisters of Mercy in Pittsburgh. In February 1891 she took her final vows and, with a few companions, founded the Sisters of the Blessed Sacrament for Indians and Colored People, of which she was superior general. The community moved from the Drexel summer home in Torresdale, Pennsylvania, to the new St. Elizabeth's Convent in Cornwells Heights the next year. (The community received final papal approval in May 1913.) A vigorous program of establishing schools and missions began with St. Catherine's Boarding School for Pueblo Indians in Santa Fe, New Mexico, in 1894. A school for African-American girls was opened in Rock Castle, Virginia, in 1899. Subsequently schools and houses for the order were established in Columbus, Ohio, Chicago, Boston, Arizona, and Tennessee, and in 1915 Xavier University was founded in New Orleans.

Mother Katharine's work took her to visit most of the order's establishments, and she continued to supervise its activities closely until late in her life. Her golden jubilee in 1941 was the occasion for high praise of her work, to which she had devoted her life and $12 million. At her death in Cornwells Heights, Pennsylvania, on March 3, 1955, the Sisters of the Blessed Sacrament had grown to some 500 members in 51 convents, and they had established 49 elementary schools, 12 high schools, and Xavier University.

Drinkwater, Jennie Maria 1841–1900 novelist

Born on April 12, 1841, in Yarmouth, Maine, Jennie Drinkwater was educated in the schools of her native town and at Greenleaf's Institute in Brooklyn, New York. In her youth she began contributing pieces to religious periodicals, and beginning with *Tessa Wadsworth's Discipline*, 1879, she wrote more than 30 novels that attained considerable popularity with young readers. In March 1880 she married the Reverend Nathaniel Conklin of New Vernon, New Jersey. Her other books, published under her maiden name, were *Electa*, 1881, *Bek's First Corner*, 1883, *The Fairfax Girls*, 1886, *From Flax to Linen*, 1888, *Marigold*, 1889, *Second Best*, 1891, *Looking Seaward*, 1893, and *Shar Burbank*,

1898. In 1874 she originated the Shut-in Society, whose purpose was to provide comfort and amenities to invalids. The idea spread rapidly, and in 1885 the society was incorporated in New York State. Local Shut-In societies brought fruit, flowers, reading matter, and sometimes even food and medicine to those requiring care or simply company. Organized informally, the movement persisted in many communities. Conklin died on April 28, 1900.

Duchesne, Rose Philippine 1769–1852 religious

Born in Grenoble, France, on August 29, 1769, Rose Duchesne was of a family well known and influential in affairs on both her father's and mother's sides. She was educated for a year in a convent school and otherwise by private tutors. At eighteen she became a novice of the Visitation Order at Sainte-Marie-d'en Haut, near Grenoble, and she took the habit in September 1788. On the closing of the convent in 1792 as a result of the French Revolution she returned home. For nearly ten years she carried on private devotions and charity. When changed political conditions allowed the reopening of convents, she obtained possession of Sainte-Marie-d'en-Haut and attempted to bring back the scattered Visitation nuns. Failing in that, she gathered a few companions and in 1804 joined the four-year-old Society of the Sacred Heart; Sainte-Marie became that order's second convent. A boarding school was begun a short time later. In 1815 she was elected secretary general of the order and sent to Paris to establish a convent there.

Three years later a long-standing ambition to work among Native Americans was brought closer when she and four companions were given permission by Mother General (now Saint) Madeleine Sophie Barat, founder of the order, to sail to Louisiana. They arrived in New Orleans in May 1818 and in St. Louis in August after a difficult journey. At the direction of Bishop William V. Du Bourg, on whose invitation they had come to America, they established the first free school west of the Mississippi River in St. Charles, Missouri. They encountered great hardship in the frontier village and after a year had to abandon the school. In 1819 they established a small convent in Florissant, Missouri, and opened a boarding school, a free parish school, an orphanage, a novitiate for the order, and a short-lived school for Native American girls. One of the sisters was dispatched to Louisiana to open a convent and school in Grand Coteau in 1821 and a second convent in St. Michael's in 1825. In 1827 Mother Duchesne accepted the gift of a house and land in St. Louis, where an orphanage, an academy, and a parish school were built. In 1828 the mission in St. Charles was reopened. Despite lack of resources the schools operated by Mother Duchesne's nuns were highly regarded and well attended. In 1841, at the age of seventy-one, she was at last permitted by Mother Barat to attempt work among Native Americans. In cooperation with a Jesuit mission under Father Pierre-Jean de Smet she established a school for girls of the Potawatomi tribe at Sugar Creek, Kansas. Ill and unable to speak the pupils' language, she did no teaching there; but her presence was formidable and influential, and the natives called her "Quah-kah-ka-num-ad," "Woman who prays always." A year later she was called back to the St. Charles, Missouri, convent, where she remained in seclusion until her death on November 18, 1852. In May 1940 she was declared beatified by Pope Pius XII.

Duff, Mary Ann Dyke 1794–1857 actor

Born in London in 1794, Mary Ann Dyke early took up the study of ballet under the ballet master of the King's Theatre. In 1809 she and her two sisters made their dancing debut at the Dublin Theatre, Dublin. At a subsequent performance in Kilkenny she met the poet Thomas Moore, who fell in love with her. She is said to have inspired several of his love lyrics. In 1810, however, she married Moore's friend John R. Duff, an actor — Moore then married her sister Elizabeth — and sailed with him to Boston. She made her American debut in *Romeo and Juliet* at the Federal Street Theatre on December 31, 1810.

She and her husband played in Boston until 1812, then in a Philadelphia company until 1817, when they returned to Boston.

Until that time Duff's principal theatrical asset had been extraordinary beauty; her acting was generally considered mediocre. But when her husband became ill and the support of their large family fell to her, she applied herself with a will and made astonishing progress. In February 1818 her Juliet was acclaimed a triumph. Both Edmund Kean, with whom she played in Boston in 1821, and Junius Brutus Booth the elder, who played Hamlet to her Ophelia in New York in September 1823, declared her the leading tragic actress on the English-speaking stage. By 1827 that opinion was general. Her powerful yet subtle emotional force found its greatest range in the majestic and pathetic heroines and won her the epithet of "the American Siddons." In 1827–1828 she was only a modest success in a British tour.

Personal difficulties began to contribute to a decline of Duff's career. Her husband died in 1831, and she managed her business affairs poorly. A brief marriage to actor Charles Young in 1833 added to her problems. She enjoyed some success on the New York, Baltimore, and Philadelphia stages in the middle 1830s; her last New York appearance was in November 1835. In 1836 she married Joel G. Seaver (later spelled Sevier), with whom she moved to New Orleans. She appeared on the local stage a few times for charity, the last in May 1838. Her later years were marked by the deaths of several of her children and separation from her husband. She returned to New York City, where she lived in obscurity until her death there on September 5, 1857.

ARNOLD GENTHE

Isadora Duncan

Duncan, Isadora 1878–1927 dancer

Born on May 27, 1878, in San Francisco, the daughter of a poet and a musician, Isadora Duncan was the youngest of four children, all theatrically inclined. Soon after she was born, her mother and father were divorced, and for some years the family lived in poverty. She attended school only to the age of ten and had virtually no formal discipline in her home life. She taught dancing to the children in her neighborhood and with her sister developed a spontaneous style in which they attempted to symbolize music, poetry, and the elements of nature. They won attention in San Francisco and traveled on a spare budget to Chicago and New York City, where Isadora joined the company of theatrical manager Augustin Daly in 1896. She, her mother, a sister, and a brother embarked on a cattle boat to London in 1900. While dancing in a public park, she was discovered by a woman who introduced her through a series of private performances to the elite of London. Similar introductions brought her fame in Paris in 1902. In that year she was briefly a member of Loie Fuller's troupe in Vienna. On her own she was hailed in Germany and Hungary, and after traveling briefly in Greece — she had been profoundly influenced by Greek sculptures she had seen in the British Museum — she returned to Berlin to begin a dancing school for children.

Disapproving of what she considered the restrictive bonds of matrimony, Duncan bore two children out of wedlock — a daughter by designer Edward Gordon Craig, born in 1905, and a son by Paris Singer, born in 1910. She made successful Russian tours in 1905, 1907, and 1908; on the first she made a deep impression on choreographer Michel Fokine and on Sergei Diaghilev, who was soon to become the leading ballet impresario in Europe, and on the last she brought about the fruitful alliance of Craig with Konstantin Stanislavski, producer and theorist of the stage. An American tour in 1908 managed by Charles Frohman was unsuccessful, while Paris appearances in 1909 brought her her accustomed acclaim.

At the height of her career, in 1913, Duncan's two children and their nurse were drowned in an accident. She attempted to forget the tragedy through work, but World War I intervened and she was forced to move her new dancing school first to the United States and then to South America, Athens, and Paris in turn. Finally the school disbanded. In 1921 the Soviet government offered her another school in Moscow. There she met and in May 1922 married Sergei Yesenin, a wild, dashing poet of the Revolution. On a tour through the United States at the height of the post-war "Red Scare" they were everywhere attacked as Bolshevist spies; as a result she bade a bitter farewell to the United States. Impoverished, they made their way back to the Soviet Union. Their poverty was such that they had to sell her furniture. Yesenin went berserk, deserted her, and committed suicide in 1925. The school she had created continued under other management, and she never performed again.

Duncan's influence was nonetheless permanent. Her teaching and dancing had freed ballet from its conservative restrictions and presaged the development of modern expressive dance. Her interpretations of music by Gluck, Brahms, Wagner, Chopin and Beethoven were not recorded, but her unrestrained performances in bare feet and loose Grecian-style garb helped to free women's dress and manners as well as the art of the dance. Her last years were spent in France. She died on September 14, 1927, in Nice, strangled when the long scarf she was wearing caught in a wheel of the car in which she was riding. Her autobiography, *My Life*, appeared in 1927.

Dunham, Katherine 1910– dancer, choreographer, and anthropologist

Born in Chicago on June 22, 1910, Katherine Dunham grew up there and in nearby Joliet. She early became interested in dance and while a student at the University of Chicago formed a dance group that performed in concert at the Chicago World's Fair in 1934 and with the Chicago Civic Opera company in 1935–1936. On graduating with a degree in anthropology she undertook field studies in the Caribbean area and in Brazil, first with a team from Northwestern University in 1936 and then for nearly two years on a Rosenwald fellowship. By the time she received her M.A. from the University of Chicago, she had acquired a vast knowledge of the dances and rituals of the black peoples of tropical America. In 1938 she joined the Federal Theatre Project in Chicago and composed a ballet, *L'Ag'Ya*, based on Caribbean dance.

In 1939 Dunham was involved with the cultural studies program of the Federal Writers' Project and then became dance director for productions of the New York Labor Stage, including *Emperor Jones* and *Pins and Needles*. In 1940 she choreographed and appeared in the Broadway hit *Cabin in the Sky*. In the same year she formed an all-black dance troupe and staged *Tropics and le Jazz Hot — From Haiti to Harlem*, a highly successful revue. Her Tropical Revue troupe toured regularly from 1943 and presented a number of original dance works, including *Shango*, *Bahiana*, *Rites du Passage*, *Bal Nègre*, and, in forms inspired by the dances of Northern urban blacks, *Flaming Youth* 1927, *Blues*, *Burrell House*, *Ragtime*, and *Floyd's Guitar Blues*. She appeared with such major musical organizations as the San Francisco Symphony Orchestra in 1943 and the Los Angeles Symphony in 1945 and later made numerous highly successful tours of the Americas and of Europe.

Dunham choreographed and starred in dance sequences in many motion pictures, including *Carnival of Rhythm*, 1942, *Star Spangled Rhythm*, 1942, *Stormy Weather*, 1943, and *Casbah*, 1947, and in such stage productions as *Carib Song*, 1945, and *Windy City*, 1946. From 1945 she directed the Katherine Dunham School of Cultural Arts in New York City, and in 1961 she opened a school in Port-au-Prince, Haiti, where she had a home. She was choreographer for the Metropolitan Opera's 1963 production of *Aida*. In 1966 she was an adviser to the State Department on the World Festival of Negro Arts in Dakar, Senegal, and in 1966–1967 she was artistic adviser to the president of Senegal. A frequent lecturer in colleges and universities, she was artist in residence at Southern Illinois University and a founder and director of the University's Performing Arts

Training Center in East St. Louis from 1967. She sought actively to involve local gang members in this program and to break the cycle of ghetto life through involvement in her school. She wrote numerous articles on dance, often under the pseudonym Kaye Dunn; two autobiographical books, *Katherine Dunham's Journey to Accompong*, 1946, and *Touch of Innocence*, 1959; and *Island Possessed*, 1969. In 1979 she was the recipient of the Albert Schweitzer Music Award, and she was a Kennedy Center honoree in 1983. She won the Capezio Dance Award in 1991. She made headlines in 1992 for her 47-day hunger strike protesting the U.S. government's policy of refusing entry to Haitian refugees, a fast she ended only at the request of exiled Haitian president Jean-Bertrand Aristide upon his visit to East St. Louis.

Duniway, Abigail Jane Scott 1834–1915 pioneer, suffragist and writer

Born in Groveland, Illinois, on October 22, 1834, Abigail Scott was of a large and hardworking farm family and received only scanty schooling. In 1852 the family made the arduous wagon trek to Oregon, during which her mother and a brother died. They settled in Lafayette, where Abigail taught school until she married Benjamin C. Duniway in August 1853. Over the next ten years she led just such a life of farm drudgery as she had known as a child, although she was able to find time to write *Captain Gray's Company*, 1859, a tale of crossing the Plains to Oregon and the first novel to come out of the Pacific Northwest. The Duniway farm was lost in 1862 to a poor business deal entered into by her husband without her knowledge, and shortly afterward he was accidentally disabled. To support the family she operated a boarding school in Lafayette until 1866, when she became a teacher in Albany. Later she ran a successful millinery and notions store for five years.

The resentment over women's legal disabilities that had been growing in Duniway for years, given impetus by the loss of the farm, prompted her to move to Portland in 1871 and establish the *New Northwest*, a newspaper dedicated to women's rights and to woman suffrage as the prerequisite for legal reform. Later that year she managed a Northwest speaking tour by Susan B. Anthony. In 1873 she led in organizing the Oregon Equal Suffrage Association, of which she was chosen president a short time later. In 1875 she published a volume of poems, *My Musings*, and in 1876 *David and Anna Matson*, a long poem. She traveled and spoke constantly throughout the state, forming local suffrage groups and building support for the cause. She also lobbied and addressed the state legislature on several occasions.

A number of reforms in the legal status of women passed the legislature, but Duniway's main goal, equal suffrage, eluded her. A statewide vote on an equal suffrage amendment to the state constitution in 1884 failed to support the measure. In that year she was elected a vice-president of the National Woman Suffrage Association. Her efforts nonetheless bore fruit elsewhere, as she was given much credit for the adoption of woman suffrage by Washington Territory in 1883 and, after she closed the *New Northwest* in 1887 and moved with her family to Idaho, by that state in 1896. In 1894 she had returned to Portland, Oregon, and in 1895 had become editor of the weekly *Pacific Empire*, through which she resumed the battle for woman suffrage. She was also again chosen president of the Oregon Equal Suffrage Association, which had fallen into inactivity after the defeat of 1884. A second referendum in 1900 also failed. In 1905 the National American Woman Suffrage Association mounted its own Oregon campaign, including an appearance by retired president Susan B. Anthony; Duniway resigned from the state organization and played no part in the campaign, which failed in the 1906 referendum.

In 1905 she published her second novel, *From the West to the West*. She subsequently returned to leadership of the state group and led referendum campaigns in 1908 and 1910, both of which failed. By 1912 she was confined to a wheelchair and could play little part in the campaign of that year that finally succeeded in writing woman suffrage into the

Oregon constitution. She nevertheless was accorded major credit for the victory because of her decades of groundwork, and she was given the privilege of drawing up the official proclamation and signing it with the governor. She then became the first Oregon woman to register for the vote. In 1914 she published *Path Breaking: An Autobiographical History of the Equal Suffrage Movement in Pacific Coast States*. She died in Portland, Oregon, on October 11, 1915.

Duston, Hannah 1657–1736? colonial heroine

Born in Haverhill, Massachusetts, on December 23, 1657, Hannah Emerson was married to Thomas Duston (or Dustin or Dustan) in December 1677. During King William's War (1689–1697) the French under Count Frontenac frequently incited Indians to raid English settlements, and on March 15, 1697, a band of Abnakis made such a raid on Haverhill. Twenty-seven women and children were killed in the raid. Hannah Duston, less than a week from childbed, was captured along with her infant daughter and a nurse, Mary Neff; Thomas Duston managed to escape with their seven other children. The baby was killed by an Indian, who bashed its head against a tree, and Hannah and Mary were marched northward by their captors. After a hundred miles they paused at an island (afterward known as Penacook or Dustin Island) in the confluence of the Merrimack and Contoocook rivers above the site of present-day Concord, New Hampshire. Here the two women were held and told that after a short journey to a further village they would be stripped and scourged. On the island they met Samuel Lennardson (or Leonardson), an English boy captured more than a year before. On the night of March 30 Hannah and the boy secured hatchets and attacked their captors; ten were killed, nine by Hannah. The three captives then stole a canoe and escaped, but Hannah turned back and scalped the ten corpses so as to have proof of the exploit. They reached Haverhill safely and on April 21 presented their story to the General Court in Boston, which awarded 25 pounds to Hannah Duston and half that sum to each of her companions. Hannah Duston lived out the rest of her life quietly, moving after the death of her husband in 1732 to Ipswich, Massachusetts, where she died, probably in early 1736.

Dyer, Mary ?–1660 religious martyr

Born on a date unknown, probably in Somersetshire, England, Mary Barrett left little record of her early life. In October 1633 she was married in London to William Dyer, with whom she came to America about 1635 and settled in Boston. She became a subscriber to the antinomian religious views of Anne Hutchinson and in 1638 followed her into banishment in Rhode Island. Her husband joined in the founding of Portsmouth, Rhode Island, and became a leading figure in the new colony.

In 1652 Mary Dyer returned to England with her husband and remained for five years, during which time she became a member of the Society of Friends. On returning to New England in 1657 she took up missionary work on behalf of the Quakers. Severe anti-Quaker laws passed in 1657 and 1658 made her work in Massachusetts extremely perilous. She suffered imprisonment in Boston in 1657 and expulsion from New Haven in 1658 in the course of her missionary travels. In 1659 she was again imprisoned briefly in Boston, where she had gone to visit two other imprisoned Friends, and then in September she was formally banished, a sentence that carried the threat of execution should she return. She nonetheless did return in October; arrested and condemned, she was reprieved while atop the gallows (two others were hanged that day) by the intercession of her son and the governors of Connecticut and Nova Scotia and again expelled.

In May 1660, in obedience to her conscience and in defiance of the law, she returned once more to Boston. An appeal to her to acquiesce in banishment failed, and she was hanged publicly on June 1, 1660. Her death came gradually to be considered a martyrdom even in Massachusetts, where it hastened the easing of anti-Quaker statutes.

Eagels, Jeanne 1890–1929 actor

Born in Kansas City, Missouri, on June 26, 1890, Amelia Jean Eagels was educated in public and parochial schools. From an early age she took part in amateur theatricals, and after leaving school she worked at small jobs until, at fifteen, she found a spot in a traveling tent show. The next seven years were spent touring the Midwest and playing mainly melodramatic roles. Gradually she began receiving bit parts in legitimate theatrical productions. She attracted some attention in 1911 in a New York musical called *Jumping Jupiter*. More substantial parts came in the touring production of *The Outcast* in 1915–1916, opposite George Arliss in a touring company of *Disraeli* and later in *The Professor's Love Story* in 1917, and in David Belasco's *Daddies* in 1918.

A woman of driving ambition despite frail health, Eagels achieved fame in a single role, that of Sadie Thompson in *Rain*, an adaptation of a Somerset Maugham story that opened at the Maxine Elliott Theatre in November 1922 and played for four years, nearly 1,500 performances, there and on tour. During that time, in August 1925, she married Edward H. (Ted) Coy, a former Yale football star. They were divorced three years later. Her last stage role was in *Her Cardboard Lover*, which opened in New York in March 1927 and later went on tour. For missing several performances in Milwaukee and St. Louis she was suspended by the Actors Equity Association in April 1928. She then turned to motion pictures and vaudeville. She had earlier made *Man, Woman and Sin*, a 1927 silent film with John Gilbert; later she appeared in *Jealousy* and *The Letter*, both 1929. Although hampered professionally by health and lack of training and personally by unstable temperament, she was an actress of great potential power, as *Rain* had demonstrated. Before a second role equally suited to her came along she died in New York City on October 3, 1929, of a self-administered sedative overdose following eye surgery.

Amelia Earhart

Earhart, Amelia Mary 1897–1937 aviator

Born on July 24, 1897, in Atchison, Kansas, Amelia Earhart moved often with her family and completed high school in Chicago in 1916. She was an army nurse in Canada during World War I and later attended briefly Columbia University and the University of Southern California. She learned to fly in 1920–1921 despite her family's protests and in July 1922 bought her first plane, a Kinner Canary. She lived for a time with her mother in Massachusetts, where she taught briefly in the University of Massachusetts extension program, and in 1926 was a resident of the Denison House Settlement in Boston.

In 1928 Earhart was chosen by publisher and promoter George Palmer Putnam to take part, as passenger and standby pilot, in a transatlantic flight; on June 17–18 she thus became the first woman to fly the Atlantic (Newfoundland to Wales). Widely hailed both as an aviator and as an inspiring example for the cause of feminism, she became aviation editor for *Cosmopolitan* magazine in 1928. In the same year she published *20 Hrs., 40 Min.* on the transatlantic flight. In 1929 she took part in the first Women's Air Derby, from Santa Monica, California, to Cleveland. She also helped found and was elected first president of the Ninety-Nines, a club for women pilots. Married in February 1931 to George Putnam, she continued to use her maiden name. In 1928–1931 she was vice-president of Luddington Airlines, Inc., an early passenger service in the East. With Putnam handling publicity and financing she undertook a number of acclaimed flights. On May 21–22, 1932, she became the first woman to solo across the Atlantic, piloting her Lockheed Vega from Newfoundland to Ireland in a record 14 hours 56 minutes. The flight brought her the Harmon Trophy, the Distinguished Flying Cross, and other honors. In that year she published *The Fun of It*.

In various airplanes and autogiros Earhart set a number of altitude and speed records. In January 1935 she made the first solo flight from Honolulu to the U.S. mainland (a greater distance than the Atlantic crossing) and in May of that year the first non-stop

Mexico City-New York flight. In the same year she became a career counselor to women at Purdue University. In 1937 she attempted a round-the-world flight with Frederick J. Noonan as navigator in a twin-engined Lockheed Electra bought for her by the Purdue trustees for research. After a false start that ended with a takeoff accident in Honolulu, she set out again eastward from Miami, Florida, on June 1. On July 2, flying from New Guinea to Howland Island in the central Pacific, trouble developed aboard her plane; radio contact was broken and never resumed. No trace of the plane was ever discovered. Despite the extreme unlikelihood of her having survived, speculation as to the nature of her flight and its true outcome — including the notion that hers was a clandestine intelligence mission for the U.S. Navy — continued for decades. Earhart's *Last Flight* appeared in 1937.

Earle, Alice Morse 1851–1911 writer and antiquarian

Born in Worcester, Massachusetts, on April 27, 1851, Mary Alice Morse was educated in her native city and in Boston. She married Henry Earle of New York in April 1874 and lived thereafter in Brooklyn Heights, New York. Her writing career began in 1890, when at the suggestion of her father she wrote an article on old Sabbath customs at her forebears' church in Chester, Vermont, for the *Youth's Companion*. The next year an expanded version of the article was published by the *Atlantic Monthly*, and later in 1891 she published her first book, *The Sabbath in Puritan New England*, which enjoyed considerable success.

Earle's interest in her own family's past and in antiques of the colonial period, supplemented by tireless research, provided impetus and material for a great many more articles and books over the next several years: *China Collecting in America*, 1892, *Customs and Fashions in Old New England*, 1893, *Costume of Colonial Times*, 1894, *The Life of Margaret Winthrop*, 1895, *Colonial Dames and Goodwives*, 1895, *Colonial Days in Old New York*, 1896, *Curious Punishments of Bygone Days*, 1896, *Home Life in Colonial Days*, 1898, *In Old Narragansett: Romances and Realities*, 1898, *Child Life in Colonial Days*, 1899, *Stage-Coach and Tavern Days*, 1900, *Old Time Gardens*, 1901, *Sun Dials and Roses of Yesterday*, 1902, and *Two Centuries of Costume in America, 1620–1820*, 1903. In addition she helped compile *Early Prose and Verse*, 1893, edited the *Diary of Anna Green Winslow, a Boston School Girl of 1771*, 1894, and contributed to *Historic New York*, 1897, and *Chap-Book Essays*, 1897. Her historical research and writing, as the titles of her books indicate, concentrated on the homely details of ordinary everyday life — manners, customs, handicrafts — rather than the world of politics and affairs, and her popular exposition of her findings helped spark a renewal of public interest in the American past. In January 1909 she nearly drowned when the ship on which she meant to sail to Egypt was struck by another and wrecked near the Nantucket lightship. Her health failed after that incident, and she died in Hempstead, Long Island, New York, on February 16, 1911.

Eastman, Mary Henderson 1818–1887 writer

Born in 1818 in Warrenton, Virginia, Mary Henderson was a granddaughter of Commodore Thomas Truxtun, a hero of the naval war with France. In June 1835 she married Lieutenant Seth Eastman, an army officer then on the faculty at West Point. In 1841 she accompanied him to Minnesota Territory, where Captain Eastman took command of Fort Snelling. The opportunity thus afforded Eastman of closely observing and learning to know the Mdewkanton Sioux of the region bore fruit in 1849 in her *Dahcotah; or, Life and Legends of the Sioux around Fort Snelling*, which was later said, on little real evidence, to have influenced Henry Wadsworth Longfellow's "Song of Hiawatha." In that year the Eastmans moved to Washington, D.C.

In 1852 Eastman published *Aunt Phillis's Cabin; or, Southern Life as It Is*, a hastily composed answer to *Uncle Tom's Cabin* in which she stoutly defended the South and the institution of slavery. The book brought her considerable fame. A series of tales published in the periodical press was collected in *The Romance of Indian Life*, 1853, which was followed by *The American Aboriginal Portfolio*, 1853, and *Chicora and Other Regions of the Conquerors and the Conquered*, 1854 (republished in 1855 as *The American Annual: Illustrative of the Early History of North America*), all of which were illustrated by her husband. Her writings on Native Americans, although often sentimental and to some extent shaped by commonplace prejudices, had the invaluable advantage of being drawn from first-hand knowledge; unlike many writers in the field, Eastman had taken the time to learn the language of her subjects. From 1855 to 1867 she and her husband were much apart as his duties took him from place to place while she and her children remained mainly in Washington, D.C. During that time she wrote little: *Fashionable Life*, a collection of conventional and sentimental stories, 1856, *Jennie Wade at Gettysburg*, a long verse narrative, 1864, and a few magazine articles. In 1879, four years after her husband's death, she published *Easter Angels*, a verse work. She died in Washington, D.C., on February 24, 1887.

Eckstorm, Fannie Pearson Hardy 1865–1946 writer and ornithologist

Born in Brewer, Maine, on June 18, 1865, Fannie Hardy was the daughter of a well known fur trader, outdoorsman, naturalist, and taxidermist, from whom she early absorbed a love and deep knowledge of the wilderness, wildlife, and Native Americans. She graduated from Smith College, where she had founded the college Audubon society, in 1888, and in 1889–1891 she served as superintendent of public schools in her native town. (She is said to have been the first woman to hold such a post in Maine.) In 1891, at her father's suggestion, she wrote two series of articles for *Forest and Stream* magazine in which she called for fair administration of game laws, which she felt in Maine were disadvantaging the native hunter, whose livelihood often depended on hunting, as against the sport hunter from outside. After a year as a reader for the Boston publishing firm of D. C. Heath she married the Reverend Jacob A. Eckstorm of Chicago in October 1893. They lived for a year in Oregon and then moved to Eastport, Maine. In 1898 they moved to a pastorate in Providence, Rhode Island, but Reverend Eckstorm died in 1899, and his widow and two children then settled in Brewer, Maine.

During that period Eckstorm had contributed several articles to such journals as *Bird-Lore* and the *Auk*, and in 1901 she published her first two books, *The Bird Book* for children and *The Woodpeckers*. *The Penobscot Man*, 1904, celebrated the lumbermen and river drivers she had grown up among and learned legendary tales about, and *David Libbey: Penobscot Woodsman and River Driver*, 1907, recounted the life of one such man. She wrote several articles on Native American legends and a widely noted critique on Thoreau's *Maine Woods* in 1908, contributed to Louis C. Hatch's *Maine: A History*, 1919, and published *Minstrelsy of Maine*, with Mary W. Smyth, 1927, and *British Ballads from Maine* with Smyth and Phillips Barry, 1929. In 1932 she published *The Handicrafts of the Modern Indians of Maine*, and she secured her reputation as the leading authority on the Penobscot tribe with *Indian Place-Names of the Penobscot Valley and the Maine Coast*, 1941, a work that benefited greatly from her own intimate firsthand knowledge of the region from the canoeist's point of view. Her last book was *Old John Neptune and Other Maine Indian Shamans*, 1945. She died in Brewer, Maine, on December 31, 1946.

Eddy, Mary Morse Baker 1821–1910 founder of Christian Science

Born in Bow, New Hampshire, on July 16, 1821, Mary Baker received little formal education but read at home with the aid of her brother, a Dartmouth student. She was from childhood in poor health, subject to seizures and nervous collapse. She achieved some local note as a versifier, especially after the family's move in 1836 to Sanbornton Bridge (later Tilton), New Hampshire, where in 1842 she attended the town academy. She married George W. Glover in December 1843 and moved with him to South and later North Carolina, but he died in June of the following year.

Mary Baker Eddy

Mary Glover lived then in retirement with her family until 1853, at first in a state of nervous prostration but later able to teach school from time to time and to publish odd bits of verse and fiction. Her son George, born shortly after his father's death, was reared by foster parents. In June 1853 she married Daniel Patterson, a dentist and homeopath. Her continuing ill health, exacerbated by Patterson's frequent absences and their poverty, aroused her interest in spiritual healing, and in October 1862 she sought help from the notable practitioner Phineas Parkhurst Quimby of Portland, Maine. She was, she attested, cured immediately. She became a disciple devoted to spreading Quimby's methods and fame. He died in January 1866 and the same year, having suffered a relapse. Patterson separated from her husband (she divorced him in 1873), resumed the name Glover, and again retired from the world.

Her recovery, against all odds, followed upon her taking up her Bible, and she was later to date her original discovery of Christian Science to 1866. For several years she lived in various towns while slowly clarifying her thoughts on health, religion, and reality. In 1870 she began her own career of healing and teaching. Gradually she abandoned Quimby's methods and from her reading of the New Testament evolved her own system, and in 1875, having established herself in Lynn, Massachusetts, she published the first of many versions of *Science and Health*, espousing the doctrine that Mind is the sole reality and that the infirmities of the body, like the body itself, are illusory and susceptible to cure by purely mental effort, as exemplified by her reading of Jesus's words in the New Testament. She gathered a group of followers, one of whom, Asa G. Eddy, she married in January 1877.

The "Church of Christ, Scientist" was chartered in 1879. In 1881 the Massachusetts Metaphysical College was chartered, and it continued under her leadership for eight years. Late in 1881 the church and the college were moved to Boston. In 1883 Eddy began to publish the monthly *Christian Science Journal*, which enabled her to extend her influence beyond the immediate New England area. The powerful personal influence she exerted on her students made them extraordinarily effective proselytizers for the church across the country, and the number of branch churches, societies, and members grew rapidly. *Science and Health* was regularly revised, with a *Key to the Scriptures* being added in 1883; the book was in its 382nd edition at her death.

In 1889 Eddy left Boston for Concord, New Hampshire, where she remained until 1908. Distance did not diminish her control over the church, however. In 1895 she founded what came to be called the "Mother Church" in Boston. The membership rolls continued to grow, and she created an effective and largely autocratic organization to oversee the affairs of the church. The bylaws and edicts promulgated by Eddy for the governance of the church and its rapidly multiplying branches were collected in the *Church Manual*, first issued in 1895 and much revised until 1908. In her late years her rule over the church was troubled by several instances of apostasy or simple rivalry, notably that of Augusta Stetson, who was ultimately excommunicated in 1909.

In 1906 the Mother Church edifice was joined by a great "Extension," still a Boston landmark. The *Journal* was joined by the weekly *Christian Science Sentinel* in 1898 and by the daily *Christian Science Monitor* in 1908. In 1908, maintaining her almost complete seclusion, she moved to Chestnut Hill, near Boston. She retained control of the church, despite declining health, until her death on December 3, 1910, in Chestnut Hill.

Edelman, Marian Wright 1939– lawyer, children's advocate and civil rights activist

Born June 6, 1939, in Bennettsville, South Carolina, Marian Wright was named after Marian Anderson, whom Wright heard sing at a young age. The youngest of five children, she was raised by her parents, Arthur Jerome Wright and Maggie Leola Bowen Wright, who instilled in their children a respect for community service. Her father, a Baptist minister, was himself a role model in their community; his response to segregation, for example, had been to open a playground and canteen for African-Americans behind his church.

Wright attended Marlboro Training High School and moved to Atlanta, Georgia, to attend Spelman College in 1956. A Merrill scholarship enabled her to spend her junior year abroad, studying at the Sorbonne University in Paris and at the University of Geneva; while in Europe that year, she also took part in a study tour of East Germany, Poland, Czechoslavakia, and the U.S.S.R.

Upon graduating from Spelman in 1960, she at first wanted to pursue graduate work in Russian studies. But the events of the times — particularly the state of civil rights in the U.S. — caused her instead to study law, on the theory that as a lawyer she could be a more effective agent of social change. She entered the Yale University Law School in the fall of 1960.

In 1963 Wright went to Mississippi to work on registering African-American voters. One of the first two interns at the Legal Defense and Educational Fund of the National Association for the Advancement of Colored People (NAACP), she became a staff attorney in its New York office. In 1964, she returned South and became the first African-American woman to pass the bar in the state of Mississippi. In private practice, she took on school-desegregation cases, fought for funding of one of the largest Head Start programs in the country, and helped civil-rights demonstrators get out of jail. She founded the Legal Defense and Educational Fund in Jackson, Mississippi, and served as its director until 1968. Later that year she moved to Washington, D.C., to start the Washington Research Project of the Southern Center for Public Policy, a public interest law firm that later became the parent organization of the Children's Defense Fund.

Also in 1968, she married Peter Edelman, a former legislative assistant to Robert F. Kennedy. She moved to Boston in 1971 to become the director of Harvard University's Center for Law and Education, but she visited Washington, D.C., frequently and she founded the Children's Defense Fund there in 1973, becoming its president. The CDF quickly became the nation's most effective organization advocating for children and their rights.

Edelman's lifelong commitment to social change and her skill and persistence as a lobbyist earned her the moniker of "children's crusader." In 1980, she became the first African-American and the second woman to chair the Board of Trustees of Spelman College. She has written many articles and books, including *Children Out of School in America: A Report*, 1974, *School Suspensions: Are They Helping Children?* 1975, and *Portrait of Inequality: Black and White Children in America*, 1980. In *Families in Peril: An Agenda for Social Change*, 1987, Edelman argues that the poverty-caused misery that has stricken black families in the U.S. for so long now has spread to white families and children. *The Measure of Our Success: A Letter to My Children and Yours*, 1992, is dedicated to her parents and all their grandchildren. Her many honors include a MacArthur Foundation Fellowship, 1985, and more than fifty honorary degrees.

Ederle, Gertrude Caroline 1906– swimmer

Born on October 23, 1906, in New York City, Trudy Ederle early became an avid swimmer and between 1921 and 1925 held 29 different national and world amateur records. She broke seven records in a single afternoon in a meet at Brighton Beach, New York, in 1922. In 1924 she was a member of the U.S. Olympic team and helped win a gold medal in the 400 meter freestyle relay. In 1925 she made an unsuccessful attempt to swim the English Channel. After setting records in the Battery-to-Sandy Hook swim in that year and the eight-mile swim down the Miami River the next, she returned to France in 1926 to try again. In the face of widespread doubt that a woman could swim the Channel at all, she set out from Cape Gris-Nez near Calais on August 6 and, beating through a heavy sea that forced her to swim 35 miles to cover the 21-mile distance, arrived at Dover after 14 hours 31 minutes, bettering the world record by 1 hour 59 minutes.

Ederle was greeted on her return to New York City by a ticker-tape parade and the journalistic and public adulation enjoyed by many overnight heroes during the 1920s. She toured for a time as a professional swimmer, but a series of misfortunes, culminating in a back injury in 1933 that left her in a cast for four years, took her out of the limelight. She made a brave comeback, however, and in 1939 appeared in Billy Rose's Aquacade at the New York World's Fair. Ederle later became a swimming instructor for deaf children and in 1958–1960 was a member of President Dwight D. Eisenhower's Youth Fitness Committee. She was inducted into the International Swimming Hall of Fame in 1965. A New York City park was named in her honor in 1975, and in August 1976 the 50th anniversary of her Channel swim was marked by celebrations in her native city.

Edmonds, Sarah Emma Evelyn 1841–1898 soldier

Born in December 1841 in New Brunswick (probably in York County), Sarah Edmonson, or Edmondson, received scant education as a child, and sometime in the 1850s she ran away from home. For a time she was an itinerant seller of Bibles, dressing as a man and using the name Frank Thompson. She gradually made her way west and by 1861 was living in Flint, Michigan. Shortly after the outbreak of the Civil War she enlisted, as Frank Thompson, in a volunteer infantry company in Flint that became Company F, 2nd Michigan Infantry. Her disguise was a complete success for nearly a year. She took part in the battles of Blackburn's Ford and first Bull Run and in the Peninsular campaign of May-July 1862; and at Fredericksburg, December 13, 1862, she was an aide to Colonel Orlando M. Poe. Twice or more she undertook intelligence missions behind Confederate lines "disguised" as a woman. She accompanied the 2nd Michigan to Kentucky early in 1863 and in April, for reasons that are now unclear, deserted.

Taking the name Sarah Edmonds, she worked as a nurse for the United States Christian Commission. In 1865 she published a lurid and very popular fictional account of her experiences as *Nurse and Spy in the Union Army*. She married in 1867 and thereafter moved often — to Michigan, Illinois, Ohio, Louisiana, Kansas. In 1882, living then in Fort Scott, Kansas, she began securing affidavits from old army comrades in order to apply for a veteran's pension, and in July 1884 the pension was granted by Congress to "Sarah E. E. Seelye [her married name], alias Frank Thompson." She later moved to La Porte, Texas, where she died on September 5, 1898. A short time before, she had in Houston become the only woman to be mustered into the Grand Army of the Republic as a regular member.

Edson, Katherine Philips 1870–1933 reformer and public official

Born on January 12, 1870, in Kenton, Ohio, Katherine Philips was well educated in public schools and private academies. While studying music at a Chicago conservatory she met and married Charles F. Edson in October 1890. They settled in Antelope Valley, California, where Katherine Edson soon became active in organizing support for woman suffrage. In 1900 they moved to Los Angeles, and she joined the Friday Morning Club, a pioneering women's club (founded nine years earlier by Caroline M. Severance) and the original inspiration for her work in Antelope Valley. Through the Friday Morning Club's various public reform and health campaigns she became involved in public affairs. In 1910 she was chosen a member of the board of the California Federation of Women's Clubs, a post she held for six years. Also in 1910 she campaigned for Hiram W. Johnson for governor. She played a significant part in the campaign that secured a woman suffrage amendment to the state constitution in 1911. In 1912 she was elected to the Los Angeles Charter Revision Commission and became the first woman to be named to the executive committee of the National Municipal League. She also became a member of the Progressive party's state central committee.

In the same year Governor Johnson appointed Edson a special agent of the California Bureau of Labor Statistics. In that post she carried out investigations of violations of or shortcomings in state labor law. Her investigation and lobbying resulted in closing a loophole by which student nurses had escaped the protection of the eight-hour law for women, and she drew up a comprehensive wages and hours law that, with Johnson's strong support, was enacted by the legislature in 1913. She was then appointed to the five-member Industrial Welfare Commission created under the law to set standards of hours, wages, and working conditions; she became executive commissioner in 1916. In that year she became a member of the Republican party's state central committee.

During World War I Edson served the federal government as industrial mediator for California and the navy as a mediator and inspector of labor conditions at firms working under navy contracts. In 1920 she was a delegate to the Republican national convention, and notwithstanding her support for Governor Johnson's unsuccessful bid for the presidential nomination she was named to the party's national executive committee, on which she served for four years. In 1921 she was appointed by President Warren G. Harding an adviser to the U.S. delegation to the Washington Limitation of Arms Conference. In 1927 she became chief of the California Division of Industrial Welfare. She was relieved of her post and her membership on the Industrial Welfare Commission by a new administration in 1931, but she loyally remained as an adviser to her successor, a patronage appointee. In 1932 she was elected to the board of directors of the National League of Women Voters (she had been a director of the California League since 1922). She died in Pasadena, California, on November 5, 1933.

Einstein, Hannah Bachman 1862–1929 social worker

Born in New York City on January 28, 1862, Hannah Bachman was educated at the New York Chartier Institute. She married William Einstein, a clothing manufacturer, in June 1881. She soon developed an interest in charitable work, and from its founding about 1890 she was active in the Temple Emanu-El Sisterhood, which undertook a program of direct relief and home visitation to needy families. In 1896 she became a trustee of the United Hebrew Charities of New York. In 1897 she was chosen president of the Sisterhood, a position she held until 1922, and in 1899 she became president of the New York Federation of Sisterhoods. Courses at Columbia University and at the New York School of Philanthropy sharpened her understanding of social problems and welfare methods. She was named chairman of the relief committee of the United Hebrew Charities in 1903.

Einstein's interest came to focus on the plight of working mothers and their children. She became convinced that maintaining the integrity of the family was of paramount importance to society and that therefore there was a public obligation to support widowed or abandoned mothers so that they might devote full time to the rearing of their children. No such form of public relief then existed, and private agencies either disagreed with the idea or lacked resources for it. In 1909 she organized and became president of the Widowed Mothers' Fund Association to pursue her goal. Within a year she had begun to campaign for the reform of the public welfare system to include a "mother's pension." Overcoming the objections of welfare officials, who preferred institutional to "outdoor" relief, and of private agencies, who opposed public relief generally, she won enough influential support, notably that of Sophie Loeb of the New York *Evening World*, to induce the New York legislature to establish a State Commission on Relief for Widowed Mothers in 1913. The commission appointed an investigating committee, headed by Einstein, to report on the need for new legislation. Legislation authorizing the creation of local Child Welfare Boards to administer public aid to dependent widows with children was defeated by the legislature in 1914 but passed on a second try in 1915. With the creation of the New York City Child Welfare Board, Einstein became chairman of its central families committee; she held that post for the rest of her life. She subsequently served as president of the New York State Association of Child Welfare Boards and helped found the National Union of Public Child Welfare Officers. The movement she had begun in 1909 spread by 1920 to nearly every state. She died in New York City on November 28, 1929.

Elders, Joycelyn 1933– pediatrician and government official

Born on August 13, 1933, in Schaal, Arkansas, Minnie Joycelyn Jones was the oldest of eight children born to Haller and Curtis Jones. She grew up in a three-room cabin without electricity or an indoor toilet. Medical care was virtually inaccessible, and was never sought except for life-or-death emergencies.

Her parents were sharecroppers, and the entire family worked and saved to put aside money for clothes and bus fare to send Joycelyn Jones to college. At the age of fifteen she entered Philander Smith College in Little Rock, on a scholarship from the United Methodist Church. That year, she saw a doctor for the first time in her life, and for the first time she considered the possibility of becoming a physician herself. Subsequently, she met Edith Urby Jones, the first African-American woman to attend the University of Arkansas Medical School, who encouraged her to persevere, despite the obstacles.

Working as a maid to put herself through college, Elders graduated in 1952 in just three years. She joined the U.S. army and trained to become a physical therapist. She attended the University of Arkansas Medical School on the G.I. Bill and was the only woman to graduate in 1960. That year she married Oliver Elders, a high school basketball coach. Elders later remembered that she refused to participate in the protests of the early civil rights movement, noting in an interview that, "I didn't have time for a social conscience." Still she never failed to challenge the racial stereotypes she encountered or to speak her mind about issues at hand.

She served her internship at the University of Minnesota Hospital, in Minneapolis, from 1960 to 1961, then returned to Arkansas for a residency at the University of Arkansas Medical Center in Little Rock, where she rose to chief pediatric resident in 1963 and became a pediatric research fellow in 1964. She earned an MS degree in biochemistry from the university in 1967 and joined the faculty at the medical school in 1967, rising to full professor by 1976.

She first met Governor Bill Clinton in the 1970s when he attended the funeral of her brother, a veterinarian who had been tragically murdered. He appointed her to the office of director of public health in Arkansas in 1987. Elders's extraordinary achievements during her tenure there included: a project to reduce the levels of teen pregnancy through availability of birth control, counseling, and sex education at school based clinics; a tenfold increase in early childhood screenings, from 4,000 in 1988 to 45,000 in 1992; a 24-percent rise in the immunization rate for two-year-olds; from 1990 to 1992 a 17-percent increase in the number of women participating in the state's prenatal care program; expansion of the availability of HIV testing and counseling services, breast cancer screenings, and around-the-clock care for elderly and terminally ill patients; and full development of a philosophy of preventive medicine.

On July 1, 1993, President Bill Clinton nominated Elders for the post of surgeon general, a post historically used to raise public consciousness about the nation's most pressing health care problems and concerns. Her confirmation process was lengthy and controversial, involving personal attacks on various financial dealings, as well as her outspokenness on sex, sex education, and condom distribution, matters she considers central to the national health care agenda. In a bruising public battle that included being dubbed the "condom queen" by conservative groups, Elders was finally confirmed by the full Senate on September 8, 1993. While Elders fared better than many of Clinton's other controversial appointees from that period, she found the process debilitating: "When it was all over I remember thinking, 'I came to Washington, D.C. like prime steak, and after being here a while I feel like poor-grade hamburger.' "

As surgeon general, Elders was responsible for: the Commissioned Corps, a 6000-member service that can be dispatched to trouble spots as needed; the Public Health Service's offices of population affairs, minority health, and women's health; and the President's Council on Physical Fitness and Sports. Once in office, Elders did not back down from controversial positions, saying, "Bill Clinton didn't pick me to be a rubber stamp for him . . . If that was all he wanted, he would have left me in Arkansas." Elders saw a punitive attitude behind conservative opposition to sex education and preventive measures, a deeply held belief "that fornication must be punished, and that teenage pregnancy and the bad things that happen after are the natural punishment." Such continued outspokenness further provoked conservatives, and she was removed from office by President Clinton in December 1994 after giving a similarly candid answer to a doctor's question about what sex education curricula should say about masturbation.

Among Elders's awards were the National Governors' Association Distinguished Service Award, the American Medical Association's Dr. Nathan Davis Award, the DeLee Humanitarian Award, and the National Coalition of 100 Black Women's Candace Award for Health Science. Elders wrote more than 150 articles on hormone-related illnesses and on children's growth patterns. She received honorary degrees from Morehouse College, Yale University, Philander Smith College, Hendrix College and LeMoyne Christian College.

Elion, Gertrude Belle 1918– biochemist and pharmacologist

Born on January 23, 1918, in New York City, Gertrude Belle Elion, daughter of Russian émigré, Bertha Cohen, and Lithuanian émigré, Robert Elion, attended public high school in the Bronx. After her father went bankrupt during the crash of 1929, Elion enrolled tuition-free at Hunter College in 1933, where she majored in chemistry. She graduated with the highest honors from Hunter in 1937, but was unable to obtain a graduate assistantship at any of the fifteen schools to which she applied, as they were not accepting women as graduate students.

Elion moved from one job to another, working first as assistant organic chemist at the Denver Chemical Company for a year, teaching chemistry and physics in New York City high schools for a year, and working as a research chemist at Johnson & Johnson for a year. During this time she also took classes part-time and received her M.S. degree from New York University in 1941. When she discovered that to obtain a Ph.D., she would have to quit working and attend school full-time, Elion left the Brooklyn Polytechnic Institute and never acquired her doctorate. In later years, however, Elion would receive honorary doctorate degrees from many schools, including George Washington University, Hunter College, Duke University, Columbia University, and the University of Michigan.

During World War II, jobs opened up for women in fields that were previously reserved for men. In 1944, Elion accepted a position as a senior research chemist at the Wellcome

Research Laboratories, where she would spend twenty years. Between 1966 and 1983 she served as head of experimental therapy and taught pharmacology at Duke University and at the University of North Carolina.

Elion had begun working on nucleic acids in the 1940s, initiating her life's work of synthesizing and perfecting drugs used to treat diseases such as cancer and leukemia. An early breakthrough was the drug 6-mercaptopurine, which would be widely used in the chemotherapy of children with leukemia. Elion and her team went on to develop drugs successfully used in cancer chemotherapy; to treat autoimmune disorders; to ensure successful organ transplants; to treat acute rheumatoid arthritis, malaria, herpes, gout, and hyperuricemia. Her immunosuppressant, Imuran, was used during the first heart transplant. Later Elion's work was recognized as leading the way for the development of azidothymidine (AZT), currently one of the most effective treatments for acquired immunodeficiency syndrome (AIDS).

During the 1980s, Elion served on various committees for the World Health Organization's Division of Tropical Disease Research and as the chairperson of WHO's Steering Committee on the Chemotherapy of Malaria. Elion's many awards included the Garvan Medal, 1968, the President's Medal from Hunter College, 1970, and the National Medal of Science, 1991. In 1988 she and her collaborator George Hitchings won the Nobel prize for medicine or physiology.

Ellet, Elizabeth Fries Lummis 1812?–1877 historical writer

Born in Sodus Point, New York, most probably in October 1812 (some sources give 1818), Elizabeth Lummis began writing verse as a child. She was educated at the Female Seminary in Aurora, New York. In 1834 her translation of Silvio Pellico's *Euphemio of Messina* was published anonymously, and the next year she published *Poems, Translated and Original*. Probably in 1835 she married William H. Ellet, a professor of chemistry at Columbia College, New York, with whom she moved to Columbia, South Carolina, in 1836. Her *Characters of Schiller*, 1839, was followed by *Scenes in the Life of Joanna of Sicily*, 1840, and *Rambles About the Country*, 1840, and a number of poems and articles on literature for various leading magazines. In 1848 she and her husband returned to New York City.

In that year, after considerable research among authenticated and mainly primary sources, Ellet published *Women of the American Revolution* in two volumes, to which a third was added in 1850. The work (illustrated by Lilly M. Spencer) sketched the lives of some 160 women who had played a part in or commented on or merely observed the events of the Revolution; it long remained the major work in a theretofore entirely neglected field and enjoyed several successful editions. From related materials she drew *Domestic History of the American Revolution*, 1850. Others of her books included *Evenings at Woodlawn*, a collection of German legends, 1849, *Family Pictures from the Bible*, 1849, *Watching Spirits*, 1851, *Novelettes of the Musicians*, 1852, *Pioneer Women of the West*, similar to her earlier work on the Revolution, 1852, *Summer Rambles in the West*, 1853, *The Practical Housekeeper*, 1857, *Women Artists in All Ages and Countries*, 1859, *Queens of American Society*, 1867, and *Court Circles of the Republic*, with Mrs. R. E. Mack, 1869. She was a figure of New York literary society and was the source of some mischievous gossip concerning Edgar Allan Poe and later Rufus W. Griswold. She died in New York City on June 3, 1877.

Elliott, Harriet Wiseman 1884–1947 educator and public official

Born on July 10, 1884, in Carbondale, Illinois, Harriet Elliott attended the academy of Park College in Missouri and then taught school for a few years before entering Hanover College, Indiana, from which she graduated in 1910. After a brief period as a high school principal and another spent in travel she undertook graduate studies, first in history and later in political science, at Columbia University, from which she received a master's degree in 1913. She then joined the faculty of the State Normal and Industrial College of North Carolina (from 1919 the North Carolina College for Women) in Greensboro, with which she remained associated for the rest of her life, becoming professor of history and political science in 1921. She played an active role in the unsuccessful campaign for woman suffrage in North Carolina in 1915.

During World War I, despite her earlier activity on behalf of various peace groups, Elliott headed the education department of the North Carolina division of the Woman's Committee of the Council of National Defense; later, in 1925, she took part in Carrie Chapman Catt's Conference on the Cause and Cure of War. In 1930 she participated in the White House Conference on Children called by President Herbert Hoover. An ardent New Dealer, she served on the advisory committee of the North Carolina Emergency Relief Administration in 1933–1935. In the latter year she was named dean of women of her college, which three years earlier had become the Women's College of the University of North Carolina (now the University of North Carolina at Greensboro). In the same year she took a leave of absence to direct a grass-roots educational program in government and specifically New Deal agencies instituted by the Women's Division of the Democratic National Committee. For six months she organized study groups and lectured around the country to great effect. In 1936 she was a delegate to the Democratic national convention. In April 1939 she was a participant in a White House Conference on Children in a Democracy called by President Franklin D. Roosevelt, and in May 1940 she was a member of the Washington Conference on Unemployment among Young Women called by Eleanor Roosevelt, whose friend she soon became. She served also in 1939–1940 as president of the North Carolina Social Service Conference.

In May 1940 President Roosevelt named Elliot the consumer representative among the seven members of the National Defense Advisory Commission; she was the only woman among the seven. In April 1941 she was appointed associate administrator of the Office of Price Administration and Civilian Supply and chief of its consumer division, but after several months of ceaseless labor, principally in public education on voluntary price controls, she resigned in December when the mandatory controls she then believed were necessary were not instituted. She was nonetheless appointed to an advisory committee of the Consumer Division of the OPA shortly thereafter. In June 1942 she was named to organize and head a women's division in the Treasury Department by Secretary of the Treasury Henry Morgenthau. Over the next three years her division enlisted more than a million women to sell war bonds and stamps. She represented the State Department at the London Educational Conference held in 1945. A highly effective teacher and organizer of women, Harriet Elliott died in Carbondale, Illinois, on August 6, 1947.

Elliott, Sarah Barnwell 1848–1928 novelist and suffragist

Born on August 29, 1848, in Savannah, Georgia, Sarah Elliott grew up there and in Sewanee, Tennessee, where her father, an Episcopal bishop, was chancellor of the University of the South. She was educated by tutors and by her own efforts and from an early age took an interest in writing. In 1879 she published her first novel, *The Felmeres*. In 1886 she studied briefly at The Johns Hopkins University. She published a short novel, *A Simple Heart*, in 1887 and followed it in 1891 with *Jerry*, a novel first serialized in *Scribner's Magazine*. *Jerry* told of a simple boy from the Cumberland Mountains of Tennessee who is slowly but inevitably corrupted and destroyed by the inhuman forces of postbellum America. As an early and successful example of literary naturalism the book was a sensation, widely reprinted and translated. *John Paget*, 1893, and *The Durket Sperret*, 1898, both novels, *An Incident and Other Happenings*, a collection of earlier stories set in the South and Southwest, 1899, and *The Making of Jane*, a novel, 1901, were less popular but also interesting in their interplay of moral codes and amoral realities. In 1900 she wrote a biography of Sam Houston. She also wrote three plays, at least one of which, *His Majesty's Servant*, was produced in London. Residence in New York City in 1895–1902 exposed her to new ideas, and after her return to Sewanee she helped form the Tennessee Equal Suffrage Association, of which she was president in 1912–1914. In 1912 she became the first woman to address the Tennessee legislature. After 1914 she took little part in public affairs. She died in Sewanee, Tennessee, on August 30, 1928.

Emerson, Ellen Russell 1837–1907 ethnologist

Born on January 16, 1837, in New Sharon, Maine, Ellen Russell was educated at the Mount Vernon Seminary in Boston. In February 1862 she married Edwin R. Emerson of Portland, Maine. From a childhood meeting with Henry Wadsworth Longfellow she had had a strong interest in Native American lore and legend, and with the years her studies grew more serious and systematic. John Wesley Powell of the Smithsonian Institution's Bureau of American Ethnology and other scholars provided her encouragement and assistance. In 1884 she published *Indian Myths; or Legends, Traditions, and Symbols of the Aborigines of America Compared with Those of Other Countries, including Hindostan, Egypt, Persia, Assyria and China*, a voluminous study in comparative ethnology that was long of great value to students in the field.

From 1886 to 1889 Emerson studied under Gaston Maspero in Paris and other leading ethnologists in Germany and Italy. In 1891 she published *Masks, Heads, and Faces, with Some Considerations Respecting the Rise and Development of Art*, a study of primitive design from pictographic writing to pottery decoration, with particular attention to Mexican and Native American artifacts. Her last book, a collection of essays entitled *Nature and Human Nature*, appeared in 1902. Emerson was widely honored for her work and was a member of a number of international learned societies, in which she was forced in late years to give up active participation because of ill health. She died in Cambridge, Massachusetts, on June 12, 1907.

Eustis, Dorothy Leib Harrison Wood 1886–1946 philanthropist and dog breeder

Born in Philadelphia on May 30, 1886, Dorothy Harrison was educated at the Agnes Irwin School in her native city and at the Rathgowrie School in Eastbourne, England. In October 1906 she married Walter A. Wood, a businessman and political figure of Hoosick Falls, New York. In that place her husband operated an experimental farm where selective breeding of dairy cattle was carried on. The remarkable intelligence and loyalty of her German shepherd dog, Hans, further stimulated her thinking about practical genetics. In 1917, two years after her husband's death, she moved to Radnor, Pennsylvania, and in 1921 to Vevey, Switzerland, where she soon established a kennel and began experimenting in selective breeding of dogs.

In June 1923 Dorothy Wood married George M. Eustis, who joined in her enthusiasm, as did Elliott S. Humphrey, an American horse breeder and trainer. Gradually they evolved a strain of German shepherd of great intelligence and loyalty and excellent disposition. Dogs from the Fortunate Fields kennel were soon earning great respect for work with the Swiss army and with various city police units throughout Europe.

In 1927 George Eustis learned of a school in Germany that trained dogs as guides for blind veterans. An article on the school for the *Saturday Evening Post* by Dorothy Eustis entitled "The Seeing Eye" late in that year brought an inquiry from Morris S. Frank, a blind insurance salesman of Nashville, Tennessee. Frank traveled to Switzerland early in 1928 to receive Buddy, a specially trained dog from Dorothy Eustis's kennels, and to learn how to work with it, When he returned to Nashville he and Buddy received wide publicity, prompting yet more inquiries from blind persons. In 1929 Dorothy Eustis returned to the United States, incorporated The Seeing Eye, and established a training school for dogs and owners in Nashville, whence it was moved to Morristown, New Jersey, the next year. In 1932 the school settled permanently in Whippany, New Jersey.

Dorothy Eustis remained president of The Seeing Eye until 1940; from 1929 to 1933 she was also president of L'Oeil Qui Voit, a Swiss school for training dogs and instructors. Much of her own fortune went into The Seeing Eye, and with wise management no outside fund raising was required after 1958. From the first she established a policy of restricting the sale of her guide dogs to blind persons of sufficient maturity, strength, ambition, and financial means to support and benefit fully from the freedom thus made possible. She died in New York City on September 8, 1946. By that time The Seeing Eye had already supplied more than 1300 guide dogs to blind persons.

Evans, Elizabeth Glendower 1856–1937 reformer

Born on February 28, 1856, in New Rochelle, New York, Elizabeth Gardiner grow up from the age of three in Boston. She was educated privately. In May 1882, after a five-year engagement, she married Glendower Evans, a promising young lawyer, who died suddenly in 1886. Thereafter his widow used the name Elizabeth Glendower Evans. She soon developed an interest in a variety of social reform movements. In 1886 she was appointed a trustee of the Massachusetts reformatory system, a post she held until 1914. She contributed greatly to the development of a modern and progressive penal system by the state. Later she became active in the Women's Trade Union League.

A visit to Great Britain in 1908–1909 left Evans a committed socialist, and thereafter she took an increasingly active role in labor organizing. She was deeply involved in a weavers' strike in Roxbury, Massachusetts, in 1910 and even more so in the widely publicized Lawrence textile strike of 1912, where her personal prominence and credibility helped expose police brutality to public view. In 1911–1912 she supported personally and financially the successful campaign for a minimum-wage law in Massachusetts. She was also a member of the National American Woman Suffrage Association, and in 1915 she accompanied her friend Jane Addams to the International Congress of Women at The Hague. From 1913 to 1935 she was a contributing editor of *La Follette's Magazine* and its successor, *The Progressive*.

In the 1920s Evans was a national director of the American Civil Liberties Union. Of her many and varied involvements that in the Sacco and Vanzetti case was the most publicized and probably the deepest. She was at the center of fund-raising activities for the defense of the two anarchists accused of robbery and murder, and she became personally close to them, especially to Nicola Sacco. The publicity that aroused the interest of the nation and then of the world in the case stemmed in large part from her efforts, and she was instrumental in enlisting the active support of prominent liberals and radicals, many of them friends of long standing. When all proved of no avail, Sacco addressed his last words, "Farewell, Mother," to her. Thereafter she lived for the most part in retirement. She died in Brookline, Massachusetts, on December 12, 1937.

Everleigh, Ada and Minna 1876–1960 and 1878–1948 madams

Born, according to the most credible evidence, near Louisville, Kentucky, Ada on February 15, 1876, and Minna on July 5 or 13, 1878, the sisters were probably originally named Lester. Early marriages failed for each of them, and they became actresses in a traveling company. In 1898, having come into a legacy of some $35,000, they opened a high-class brothel in Omaha, where the Trans-Mississippi Exposition supplied ready customers. It was at this time that they adopted the name Everleigh.

In less than two years the Everleigh sisters had doubled their investment, which they liquidated to buy out a flourishing brothel at 2131 South Dearborn Street in Chicago. In February 1900, after elaborate redecorating, they opened the Everleigh Club. In the eleven years they were in business theirs was, in the words of the Chicago Vice Commission, "probably the most famous and luxurious house of prostitution in the country." Furnished with tapestries, oriental rugs, statuary, gold-framed nude paintings, a library filled with expensively bound volumes, and a music parlor featuring a $15,000 gold-leaf piano, the Everleigh Club missed no chance for opulence. A dozen downstairs parlors, decorated along various themes such as the Silver Parlor, the Gold Parlor, the Rose Parlor, or the Japanese Throne Room, catered to groups, while the more private indulgences took place in equally luxurious upstairs chambers. The dining room, suggesting a private Pullman car, featured dinners and suppers for the epicure — caviar, oysters, duck, capon, lobster. Even the $650 gold cuspidors placed about the club became legendary. These sybaritic surroundings catered to a clientele that included captains of industry, political bigwigs, the occasional European noble or even royal, and others who could command the prices: $10 for admission, $12 for a bottle of wine, $50 for dinner, $25 for supper, and $50 for an evening with one of the carefully chosen and trained hostesses. The club was expanded into the adjoining property in 1902, as the sisters' contributions to the First Ward Democratic organization, headed by "Bathhouse John" Coughlin and Michael "Hinky-Dink" Kenna, kept the forces of law at bay. Popular reform was not so easily stayed, however, and public pressure gradually built, forcing the city administration to take official notice.

A vice commission appointed in 1910 reported on nearly 600 houses of prostitution in Chicago, but the Everleighs' was the most visible and the politically necessary first target. On orders of the reform mayor, Carter H. Harrison, Jr., the club was closed in October 1911. The sisters retired with an estimated million dollars in cash and $200,000 in jewelry. After an extensive European tour they returned to Chicago, but their notoriety made a quiet retirement there impossible, and they settled in New York City. In their remaining years of theatergoing and poetry reading they resumed the surname Lester. Minna died on September 16, 1948, after which Ada moved to Virginia, where she died on January 3, 1960.

Evert, Christine Marie 1954– tennis player

Born on December 21, 1954, in Fort Lauderdale, Florida, Chris Evert was the daughter of a noted tennis player. She early began taking lessons from her father and soon demonstrated natural ability of a high order. Her style evolved rapidly to feature a powerful two-hand backhand and a degree of concentration that sometimes unnerved opponents. Her rise to the top of world competition was rapid: victories over Margaret Smith Court in 1970 and in the Virginia Slims Masters tournament in St. Petersburg, Florida, in April 1971 earned her a place on the U.S. Wightman Cup team at the age of sixteen, the youngest player ever. In cup competition in August she defeated Virginia Wade soundly in the crucial match to give the United States the victory.

In September 1971 Evert became virtually an overnight favorite with three remarkable come-from-behind victories in the U.S. Open tournament at Forest Hills; she lost a semifinal match to Billie Jean King. Five months later she demolished King, 6–1, 6–0, in the Women's International Tennis Tournament in Fort Lauderdale, a tournament played on clay, her preferred surface. She was again a member of the victorious Wightman Cup team in 1972, and in June she advanced to the semifinal round of her first Wimbledon tournament before losing to Evonne Goolagong. Later in the month she defeated Goolagong in the Bonne Bell Cup tournament in Cleveland. At Forest Hills in September she again lost her semifinal match, but in October she won the Virginia Slims with a victory over Kerry Melville, who had beaten her in the U.S. Open.

In December Evert turned professional. She won her first professional tournament in her home town in March 1973. After graduating from high school that spring she went on to an indifferent year of tennis in which she lost the Italian championship in the final match with Goolagong, lost the Wimbledon final to King, and lost the U.S. Open semifinal match to Margaret Court. She was again a Wightman Cup player for the victorious U.S. team. In 1974 her victories in the French and Italian championships and especially her victory at Wimbledon over Olga Morozova highlighted a remarkable 56-match winning streak. Wimbledon was also notable in that the women's and men's singles titles were won for the first time by an engaged couple; her engagement to Jimmy Connors was later broken. In 1975 she retained her Italian and French titles, lost the Wimbledon semifinal to Billie Jean King, and won her first U.S. Open with a final victory over Evonne Goolagong Cawley. In 1976 she won her second Wimbledon title over Cawley and her second U.S. Open. In 1977 she lost a quarter-final match at Wimbledon to Virginia Wade, but won her third U.S. Open at Forest Hills. In 1978 she lost the Wimbledon final to Martina Navratilova but bounced back to win her fourth consecutive U.S. Open. She again lost the Wimbledon final to Navratilova in 1979.

During these years Evert was a dominant player on the professional circuit, and in February 1978 she signed to play for the Los Angeles Strings of the World Team Tennis tour. Despite her occasional troubles on grass courts, she compiled one of the most spectacular records in sports in clay court competition: as of April 1978 she was undefeated on clay in 118 matches in 24 tournaments. Her earnings and endorsements made her one of the most financially secure young athletes in the world.

Following her marriage to tennis player John Lloyd in April 1979 she adopted the name Evert Lloyd. She continued to be successful on the courts; among other championships she won the United States Open again in 1980 and 1982, Wimbledon in 1981, and the Virginia Slims tournament in 1987. She retired from professional tennis in 1989, becoming a commentator on tennis events for the National Broadcasting Company, a special advisor to the United States National Tennis Team, and president of the Women's Tennis Association from 1982–1991.

In 1985 the Women's Sports Foundation voted her the greatest woman athlete in the past 25 years Among her many other honors are the Women's Sports Foundation Flo Hyman Award, 1990, the Women's Tennis Association Award, 1992, for her years of service to the sport, and a Lifetime Achievement Award from the March of Dimes, 1993.

Fairchild, Mary Salome Cutler 1855–1921 librarian

Born in Dalton, Massachusetts, on June 21, 1855, Salome Cutler graduated from Mount Holyoke Seminary in 1875 and in 1876–1878 was a teacher there. A period of ill health followed. With her recovery came an interest in the relatively new field of librarianship. After cataloguing a small country library in 1884 she sought the assistance of Melvil Dewey of Columbia College in finding a position. Dewey hired her as a cataloguer in the Columbia library, and in January 1887, when he opened his pioneering School of Library Economy, she became an instructor in cataloguing. In 1889 she was named head cataloguer of the Columbia library, but shortly afterward she left the college with Dewey and the school when he transferred his work to Albany.

Fairchild became vice-director of what was reorganized as the New York State Library School, and, with Dewey deeply involved in other work, she was its chief administrator and guiding spirit for the 16 years of her association with it. Under her direction a strong curriculum was made stronger, entrance requirements were raised to include a difficult examination and, from 1902, a bachelor's degree, and the scope of library training was broadened to meet her ideal of the librarian as a professional educator in the public service. From 1889 she also served as librarian of the New York State Library for the Blind in Albany. In 1891 the University of the State of New York awarded her a bachelor's degree in library science. From 1892 to 1898 she was a member of the council of the American Library Association, and in 1893 she chaired a committee of the association that established a 5000-volume model library and compiled a catalogue for it at the World's Columbian Exposition in Chicago. In 1894–1895 and again in 1900–1901 she was vice-president of the association. In July 1897 she married Edwin M. Fairchild, a minister of Troy, New York.

In 1905, following closely upon Dewey's rancorous resignation, Fairchild fell ill and was forced to retire from her position with the library school and the library for the blind. Her professional activities were limited thereafter to a few months as director of the Drexel Institute Library School in Philadelphia in 1909–1910 and membership on the council of the American Library Association again in 1909–1914. She was a frequent contributor of articles to professional journals. Fairchild died in Takoma Park, Maryland, on December 20, 1921.

Falconer, Martha Platt 1862–1941 social worker

Born in Delaware, Ohio, on March 17, 1862, Martha Platt attended school in her native town and in Philadelphia, where she went to live with an older sister on the death of her mother in 1877. Later she moved to Kansas for her health, and there in March 1885 she married Cyrus Falconer. In 1888 they moved to Oak Park, Illinois, a suburb of Chicago. She soon became active in a number of forms of social work, including teaching at the Chicago Commons settlement and serving as one of Cook County's first probation officers when that program was begun under the new juvenile court in 1899. From 1898 she also served on the staff of the Illinois Children's Home and Aid Society, eventually becoming assistant superintendent.

In January 1906 Falconer became superintendent of the girls' division of the Philadelphia House of Refuge. She moved quickly to change what was little more than a penal institution into a leader in the still largely experimental field of rehabilitation. With the removal of the institution to a farm near Glen Mills, Pennsylvania, the Sleighton Farm institution, as it became known (formally the girls' division of the Glen Mills Schools), adopted the cottage system of residence, with young women college graduates in supervisory posts and a student government to help teach responsibility and self-reliance. The great success of her program at Sleighton Farm led to the widespread adoption of many of its features at other institutions across the country.

During World War I Falconer took leave of absence to serve the War Department's Commission on Training Camp Activities as head of a committee on the care of camp followers and other girl delinquents. She returned to Sleighton Farm after the war, but in November 1919 she moved to New York City to become director of the department of protective social measures of the American Social Hygiene Association. From 1924 until her retirement in 1927 she was executive secretary of the Federation Caring for Protestant Children in New York City (later the Federation of Protestant Welfare Agencies). In 1928 she was a delegate to the International Conference of Social Work in Paris on appointment by New York's Governor Franklin D. Roosevelt. In retirement she occasionally served as a consultant to agencies and institutions in the field of rehabilitation of delinquents. Martha Falconer died in East Aurora, New York, on November 26, 1941.

Farley, Harriet 1813?–1907 writer and editor

Born in Claremont, New Hampshire, on February 18 probably of 1813 (some sources say 1817), Harriet Farley grew up from 1819 in Atkinson, New Hampshire, where she was educated in the local academy headed by her father. In 1837, to help support her family and possibly also to seek a certain independence, she made her way to Lowell, Massachusetts, and obtained a position in a textile mill. She eagerly threw herself into the lectures and other activities that promoted culture among the girl operatives of the Lowell mills, and in December 1840 she attracted some attention when her reply to Orestes Brownson's criticisms of the working conditions in the mills was published by the *Lowell Offering*. The *Lowell Offering*, a magazine written by and for the mill girls, changed ownership in October 1842, and Harriet Farley was invited to become editor. Harriot Curtis, another mill girl, became her coeditor in 1843.

Under Harriet Farley's direction the *Offering* was a literary magazine of the most conventional sort, publishing moral and inspirational pieces that were meant to demonstrate the intelligence and refinement of the working girls and women of Lowell. The magazine attracted much attention as far away as Great Britain, where an anthology of pieces from it was published in 1844. The determined respectability of the magazine foundered in the rising tide of labor unrest of the middle 1840s, however. Explicitly refusing to discuss the issues of hours, wages, and working conditions, the *Offering* lost its appeal to its own audience. Criticism of the magazine, led by Sarah Bagley, led to its demise in December 1845.

In 1847 Farley published *Shells from the Strand of the Sea of Genius*, a collection of homilies, many of them originally published in the *Offering*. In September of that year she revived the magazine as the *New England Offering*, but after less than three years it went under again in March 1850. She then moved to New York City, where she contributed to *Godey's Lady's Book*. In 1851 she edited a collection of her father's *Discourses and Essays on Theological and Speculative Topics*, and in 1853 she published *Happy Nights at Hazel Nook*, a children's book. After her marriage in 1854 to John I. Donlevy she wrote no more, but after his death she published a Christmas book, *Fancy's Frolics*, 1880. She died in New York City on November 12, 1907.

Farmer, Fannie Merritt 1857–1915 cookery expert

Born in Boston on March 23, 1857, Fannie Farmer grew up there and in Medford, Massachusetts. She suffered a paralytic stroke during her high school years that forced her to end her formal education. She recovered sufficiently to find employment as a mother's helper, and she soon developed such an aptitude and fondness for cooking that her parents encouraged her to enter the eight-year-old Boston Cooking School. She graduated in 1889 and was asked to remain as assistant director; in 1894 she became head of the school. Although reticent, she nevertheless became much sought after as a lecturer at schools and social gatherings. She left the school in 1902 to open her own Miss

Farmer's School of Cookery, which was designed to train housewives rather than teachers, institutional cooks, or servants. For a year at Harvard she conducted a course in dietetic and invalid cooking, and with her sister, Cora Farmer Perkins, she wrote a regular column for the *Woman's Home Companion* from 1905 to 1915.

Farmer's lasting contribution was twofold: the introduction of standardized level measurements in recipes and the *Boston Cooking School Cookbook*, first published in 1896 and still a best seller in a modernized version, frequently revised, *The Fannie Farmer Cookbook*. Its 12 editions in the first 70 years had sales totaling nearly 4 million copies. Recipes for everyday and classic dishes were accompanied by sections on formal entertaining, proper management of the home and service staff, use of kitchen equipment, and etiquette. Her largely intuitive knowledge of diet planning predated the modern science of nutrition. She stressed in her cookbook the "knowledge of the principles of diet [as an] essential part of one's education. Mankind will eat to live, will be able to do better mental and physical work, and disease will be less frequent." Her recipes were all personally tested and, thanks to accurate measurements, easy to follow successfully.

Farmer's other books included *Chafing Dish Possibilities*, 1898, *Food and Cookery for the Sick and Convalescent*, which she thought her most important, 1904, *What to Have for Dinner*, 1905, *Catering for Special Occasions, with Menus and Recipes*, 1911, and *A New Book of Cookery*, 1912. She died in Boston on January 15, 1915; her cooking school continued under a successor until 1944.

Farnham, Eliza Wood Burhans 1815–1864 reformer and writer

Born on November 17, 1815, in Rensselaerville, New York, Eliza Burhans grew up from the age of four in Maple Springs, New York, in the unhappy home of foster parents. At fifteen she came into the care of an uncle, and she briefly attended the Albany Female Academy. In 1835 she went to live with a married sister in Tazewell County, Illinois, where in July 1836 she married Thomas Jefferson Farnham, a lawyer who soon won fame as a Western explorer. In 1840 they settled in Washington Hollow, near Poughkeepsie, New York. While her husband was working on his widely read *Travels in the Great Western Prairies*, 1841, she began taking an interest in reform movements. One of her earliest published essays, in *Brother Jonathan* magazine in 1843, was in opposition to political rights for women, a step she feared would actually reduce the influence of women.

In 1844 Farnham won appointment as matron of the women's division of Sing Sing prison. She instituted a highly advanced regime, eliminating the ban on speaking among inmates and setting up a system of discussions, privileges, and useful training. Her liberal approach to penology won her numerous enemies, however, and in 1848 she was forced to resign. During that period, in 1846, she had published her first book, *Life in Prairie Land*. She then worked briefly with Samuel Gridley Howe at the Perkins Institution in Boston, helping to train the deaf-mute Laura Bridgman, until she heard of the death of her husband in September 1848 in San Francisco. The following spring, after a period of ill health, she set out for San Francisco accompanied by a small number of unmarried women she had recruited to bring refinement to the disorderly city. After a difficult cruise around the Horn she arrived in California and late in 1849 bought a farm in Santa Cruz County. In March 1852 she married William Fitzpatrick, whom she divorced in 1856. In that year she returned to New York City and published *California, In-doors and Out*. Among her activities over the next several years was the organizing of several parties of destitute women to seek homes in the West; she personally conducted some of the companies to their destinations.

In 1859 Farnham published *My Early Days*, a fictionalized memoir reissued in expanded form in 1864 as *Eliza Woodson, or, The Early Days of One of the World's Workers*.

In 1859 she returned to California, where she delivered a number of public lectures and in 1861 became matron of the female department of the Stockton Insane Asylum. She returned to New York City in 1862. She joined the Women's Loyal National League in 1863 and in July of that year volunteered for service as a nurse in the aftermath of the battle of Gettysburg. In 1864 her magnum opus, several years in the preparation, was published as *Woman and Her Era*, in which she expounded the natural superiority of women over men and attributed the disabilities laid on women in the practical spheres to the unconscious recognition by men that women were not meant to labor or serve on an equal footing but were rather to occupy a higher station from which their moral influence would shape the course of events. Farnham died in New York City on December 15, 1864. Her fictional *The Ideal Attained* appeared in 1865.

Farrar, Geraldine 1882–1967 opera singer

Born in Melrose, Massachusetts, on February 28, 1882, Geraldine Farrar was the daughter of a professional baseball player. She displayed musical talent from early childhood, and although her dislike of practice led to her abandoning the piano she did continue her voice lessons, under Mrs. J. H. Long in Boston, Emma Thursby in New York City, and in 1899–1900 under Trabadelo in Paris. In 1900 she traveled to Berlin, where an audition won her a three-year contract with the Royal Opera House. Her debut occurred there in October 1901 in *Faust*. During her stay in Berlin she studied under Lilli Lehmann. During 1904–1907 she sang at the Monte Carlo Opera, making her debut there opposite Enrico Caruso in *La Bohème* in March 1904. In March 1905, with only five days of rehearsal, she sang the world premiere of Mascagni's *Amica*. In those years she was the toast of several European capitals.

Farrar made her American debut at the Metropolitan Opera House, New York City, in Gounod's *Roméo et Juliette* in November 1906. In February 1907 she sang Cio-Cio-San in the Met's first performance of *Madama Butterfly*, a performance that also featured Louise Homer and Caruso and for which Puccini himself was present. Her youth, her beauty, and her richly dramatic soprano voice made her a sensation in the role, which she repeated 95 times in her Metropolitan career. A second role that she made her own was that of the Goose Girl in Humperdinck's *Königskinder*; from the world premiere in December 1910 she sang the role some 30 times. Others among the 23 roles she sang during her Metropolitan career were Carmen, which she carried against much skepticism (the role was firmly identified with Emma Calvé) in November 1914, Thaïs in 1917, Suor Angelica in 1918, Zaza in 1920, and Louise in 1921.

After a final performance in *Zaza* in April 1922 — a performance for which the Met was more packed with her fans than usual and during which the streets outside were crowded with eager "Gerry flappers," as her teenage admirers were known — she retired from the Met, although she subsequently made a number of concert tours. She enjoyed a minor second career in silent motion pictures, beginning with *Carmen* in 1915 and including *Maria Rosa*, 1916, *Joan the Woman*, 1917, *The Woman God Forgot*, 1917, *The Turn of the Wheel*, 1918, *The Hell Cat*, 1918, *The World and Its Woman*, 1919, *Flame of the Desert*, 1920, and *The Woman and the Puppet*, 1920. Her final public appearance was at Carnegie Hall in November 1931. In 1938 she published an autobiography, *Such Sweet Compulsion*. She lived in retirement in Ridgefield, Connecticut, until her death there on March 11, 1967.

Farrar, Margaret Petherbridge 1897–1967 editor

Born in New York City on March 23, 1897, Margaret Petherbridge was educated at the Berkeley Institute in Brooklyn and at Smith College, from which she graduated in 1919. After a year as a secretary in a bank she found a position with the *New York World*, where she soon found herself in charge of the weekly crossword puzzle, a Sunday feature the

World had pioneered in December 1913. By 1922 crossword puzzles were catching on with a wide public, and within a couple of years they were a genuine national craze, inspiring considerable comment in the form of articles, jokes, and cartoons.

In 1924 Petherbridge joined F. Gregory Hartswick and Prosper Buranelli in editing the *Cross Word Puzzle Book*, the first such book ever published. It seemed such a gamble that the publisher, Simon & Schuster, issued it under another imprint. It was instead a huge success, selling nearly 400,000 copies in its first year, and successors appeared at the rate of about two a year thereafter under her editorship. She later also edited a series of similar books for Pocket Books and a *Crossword Puzzle Omnibus* series. Meanwhile, in May 1926, she married John C. Farrar, author and publisher.

Crossword puzzles became an established department of most newspapers, where they attracted their legions of loyal fans. The only major American daily to hold out against the tide was the *New York Times*, which had also never fallen for the comic strip. But in February 1942 the Sunday edition of the *Times* began printing a crossword puzzle, and in September 1950 it became a daily feature as well, in both instances under Farrar's editorship. She remained at the *Times*, for which she also edited 18 collections of puzzles, until her retirement in December 1968. Appointed to the position of director at the publishing firm Farrar, Straus and Giroux in 1974, she served in that post for the rest of her life. She died in New York City on June 11, 1984, while working on her 134th book of crossword puzzles. Her record of publishing from 1924–1984 represents the longest running continuous series in American publishing history.

Farrell, Eileen 1920– singer

Born on February 13, 1920, in Willimantic, Connecticut, Eileen Farrell was the daughter of former vaudevillians who later became music teachers. With her family she moved to Storrs, Connecticut, and then to Woonsocket, Rhode Island. After graduating from high school in 1939 she traveled to New York City to study singing, and in 1940, following a failure to win a place on "Major Bowes' Original Amateur Hour," she auditioned successfully for membership in studio choral and ensemble groups on the CBS radio network. The next year she began her own program, "Eileen Farrell Sings," on which for six years she performed vocal works ranging from operatic arias to popular songs. In 1947 she began making regular concert tours, extending her field to South America two years later, and received wide acclaim for her consistently brilliant performances.

An extended engagement with the New York Philharmonic Orchestra in 1950–1951, during which she sang in the American premiere performance of Milhaud's *Les Choëphores*, was the beginning of a long association with that organization, and in 1953 she became a regular performer with the Bach Aria Group as well. A popular guest on television variety programs, she continued to mix classical and popular music in her repertoire and in 1957 began her formal operatic career in *Il Trovatore* with the San Francisco Opera Company. Her mastery of a wide variety of soprano roles steadily raised the critical estimation of her singing, and after an appearance in Gian-Carlo Menotti's 1959 Festival of Two Worlds in Spoleto, Italy, where hers was considered by many the outstanding performance (in Verdi's *Requiem* and some song recitals), she at last made her debut with the Metropolitan Opera Company in New York in December 1960 in Gluck's *Alcestis*.

Firmly established thereafter as one of the best American dramatic sopranos, Farrell continued to win success and the highest critical and popular acclaim for her concert appearances and recordings. She is one of the few opera singers to have been successful with popular songs; she recorded *I Gotta Right to Sing the Blues*, her first crossover album, in 1960. In the mid-1970s she taught both classical and popular voice at Indiana

University. Although she no longer performs publicly, she has continued to record songs of composers such as Harold Arlen, Rodgers and Hart, Alec Wilder and Johnny Mercer.

Suzanne Farrell

Farrell, Suzanne 1945– ballet dancer

Born in Cincinnati on August 16, 1945, Roberta Sue Ficker began studying ballet at the age of eight. She continued those studies while attending Catholic parochial schools, and in 1960 she won a scholarship to the School of American Ballet, the training school of the New York City Ballet. She made her first New York appearance in a minor role in the New York City Ballet's annual Christmas production of *The Nutcracker* in 1960. She joined the company's corps de ballet in 1961, by which time she had adopted the professional name Suzanne Farrell. In 1962 she became a featured dancer and made her first appearance in a featured role in *Serenade* during the company's summer tour.

Farrell's first solo performance was in the premiere of John Taras's *Arcade* in March 1963. In April she created the lead role in George Balanchine's *Movements for Piano and Orchestra*. While mastering various roles in the company's repertoire — *La Valse*, *Concerto Barocco*, *Agon*, *Liebeslieder Walzer*, *Donizetti Variations*, *A Midsummer Night's Dream*, *Ivesiana*, *Glinkaiana*, *Stars and Stripes*, *Prodigal Son*, *Symphony in C*, and many others, mostly Balanchine works — she created roles in *Meditation* in December 1963, *Clarinade* in April 1964, and *Don Quixote*, in which she attained stardom in May 1965. A short time later she was named principal dancer in the New York City Ballet. Often thought of as the "Balanchine ballerina par excellence," she combined a light, gentle presence and a certain cool assurance with flawless technique to create her stage persona. Subsequent major roles were those in *Variations*, which premiered in April 1966, *Bugaku*, *The Four Temperaments*, *The Jewels*, which premiered in April 1967, *Ballet Imperial*, *Metastaseis & Pithoprakta*, which premiered in January 1968, and a new version of *Slaughter on Tenth Avenue* in April 1968.

In 1969 Farrell left Balanchine and the New York City Ballet, and in 1970 she became the principal dancer in Ballet of the 20th Century, a Brussels-based company whose repertory was largely the work of Maurice Béjart. She created roles in Béjart's *Sonate*, 1970, *Les Fleurs du mal*, 1971, *Nijinsky, Clown de Dieu*, 1971, *Ah, vous dirais-je Maman*, 1972, *Golestan*, 1973, *Farah*, 1973, and *I Trionfi*, 1974. In 1975 she returned to the New York City Ballet, where she created roles in Balanchine's *Tzigane*, 1975, and *Union Jack*, 1976, and Jerome Robbins's *Piano Concerto in G*, 1975, and continued a principal exponent of what appeared to be a renaissance of interest in ballet.

She retired from performing in 1989 following hip surgery, but remained with the New York City Ballet until 1993 as a teacher and coach for dancers re-creating Balanchine roles. She was named Artistic Director of the Fort Worth Ballet and also worked with the Balanchine Trust, formed after his death in 1983. She published an autobiography, *Holding On to the Air*, in 1990. She received a *Dance* magazine award in 1976, the New York City Award of Honor in 1979, an Emmy in 1985, a Golden Plate award from the American Academy of Achievement, and the New York State Governor's award in 1988.

Fassett, Cornelia Adele Strong 1831–1898 painter

Born in Owasco, New York, on November 9, 1831, Cornelia Strong was married to Samuel M. Fassett of Chicago in August 1851. Her artistic training was at the hands of teachers in New York City and in Europe, where she stayed for three years. In Chicago she won a large local reputation with her paintings, but her major career awaited her removal to Washington, D.C., in 1875. There the fame she gained as a hostess enabled her to win a great many prominent sitters for portraits, including three presidents — Ulysses S. Grant, Rutherford B. Hayes, and James A. Garfield — as well as Vice-President Henry Wilson and many more.

In February 1877 Fassett attended and painted the meeting of the Electoral Commission (appointed to settle disputed ballots in four states in the 1876 presidential election) in the Supreme Court chamber. Her finished painting, "The Florida Case before the Electoral Commission," was an astounding piece of work, depicting faithfully some 260 prominent Washington figures engaged in or attending the hearing. The painting was subsequently purchased by Congress to be hung in the Capitol. In later years Fassett took up miniature painting. She died in Washington, D.C., on January 4, 1898.

Feinstein, Dianne Goldman 1933– politician

Born on June 22, 1933 in San Francisco, California, Dianne Emiel Goldman grew up in the city's upscale Presidio Terrace district. Her father was a surgeon and medical school professor and her mother was a former nurse and model who suffered from a brain disorder and was mentally ill. Though it was difficult growing up with a mother who was prone to sudden furious outbursts, Goldman was an intelligent and happy child. She attended public school through the eighth grade, and eventually became the only Jewish student at an elite Catholic high school. She credited her father and her uncle Morris, who took her to sessions of the San Francisco Board of Supervisors, as her early influences. In 1951 she entered Stanford University, first as a pre-med student, and then as a political science and history major. After graduating in 1955 with her B.S. degree, she began interning at the Coro Foundation in San Francisco, an organization whose goal was to provide young people with political experience.

She married prosecuting attorney Jack Berman in 1956 and divorced him three years later, after the birth of their daughter Katherine. For the next few years she devoted herself to caring for her daughter, although she remained interested in politics, working as a volunteer on John F. Kennedy's presidential campaign and becoming active in civil rights demonstrations.

From 1960 to 1966 she worked on the California Women's Board of Terms and Parole. In 1962 she married Bertram Feinstein, a surgeon, and they were together until his death in 1978. She served as the chairperson of San Francisco's Advisory Committee for Adult Detention from 1966 to 1968, and in 1969 she won a seat on the San Francisco Board of Supervisors. She served for nine years, acting as the first female president for a number of those years. Some of the issues she dealt with on the board included increasing the number of police officers on foot patrol and working toward criminal-justice reform.

In 1971, and again in 1975, she ran unsuccessfully for mayor of San Francisco. In 1978 Mayor George Moscone and the first openly gay city supervisor Harvey Milk were assassinated. As president of the Board of Supervisors she succeeded to the mayoral position. Just a few days prior to the assassinations, the Reverend Jim Jones and his followers in the People's Temple cult — most of whom were former Bay Area residents — committed mass suicide at their compound in Guyana. Her strong leadership skills during this difficult time in the city's history earned her much respect and public support. She was elected mayor in her own right in 1979, serving until 1988. While in office, she received high marks for improving city services such as garbage collection and transportation, and for furthering gay rights. In 1982, however, she opposed a measure that would have granted registered domestic partners the right to some benefits, such as insurance. Her stance cost her the support of much of her constituency and even fueled an unsuccessful movement to recall her.

After serving the maximum of two terms, she ran as the Democratic candidate for governor of California in 1990, losing to Republican Senator Pete Wilson. Her platform favored the death penalty which she had previously opposed, drawing much criticism for her change of heart. When Wilson won the election and vacated his Senate position, she was elected to his seat. She was sworn into office in November of 1992 for a special two-year term and was reelected to a full six-year term in 1994.

In office Feinstein wrote legislation that included a ban on the manufacture, sale, and possession of semiautomatic military combat weapons, and drafted the California Desert Protection Act, which called for the protection of more than three million acres of desert, national parks, and nature reserves. She served on the Senate Judiciary Committee, the Foreign Relations Committee, and the Rules and Administration Committee. She married her third husband, Richard Blum in 1980.

Felton, Rebecca Ann Latimer 1835–1930 reformer and public official

Born near Decatur, Georgia, on June 10, 1835, Rebecca Latimer, grew up in a family of liberal views and received a good private education. She graduated from Madison Female College in Madison, Georgia, in 1852 and in October 1853 married Dr. William H. Felton, with whom she settled near Cartersville. The family suffered heavily during the Civil War, when Sherman's march forced them to flee their farm. In the 1870s, while rebuilding their home, both Feltons became active in public affairs. Felton soon proved an able and canny politician in assisting Dr. Felton's campaigns for Congress in 1874, 1876, and 1878, to which she contributed speeches, newspaper pieces, and campaign strategy. She served as his secretary in Washington, D.C., and in 1881, after Dr. Felton's defeat and return to Cartersville, she helped found and edit a local newspaper. In 1884–1890 Dr. Felton sat in the Georgia legislature, and during that period Rebecca Felton again managed his election campaigns, drafted bills and speeches, and advised on policies and tactics.

By that time she was as well or better known publicly, and she continued in the public eye for several decades as a leader of several reform movements, notably those for prison reform, especially for the ending of the much abused system of convict-leasing, for state liquor prohibition (both these ends were achieved in 1908), and for women's rights, including suffrage and the admission of women to the state university. Her newspaper articles and letters, together with speeches around the state and appearances before the legislature, made her the most influential woman in Georgia. She served on the board of lady managers of the World's Columbian Exposition in Chicago in 1893 and was chairman of the women's executive board of the Cotton States and International Exposition in Atlanta in 1894–1895. In 1899 she began contributing a regular column, "Mrs. Felton's Timely Talks," to the *Atlanta Journal*; she continued to write it until 1927. In 1912 she was a delegate to the Progressive Republican national convention in Chicago. She published *My Memoirs of Georgia Politics* in 1911 and *Country Life in Georgia in the Days of My Youth* in 1919.

In 1920 Felton took an active part in the political campaign that elected the former Populist but more recently racist and nativist Thomas E. Watson to the Senate. On Watson's death in September 1922 the governor of Georgia appointed Felton to the office ad interim, an act intended only as a gesture since Congress was adjourned and an actual successor would soon be elected. But Felton, eighty-seven years old, persuaded the elected successor, Walter F. George, to delay his appearance in the reconvened Senate; and on November 21, 1922, she took her seat, the first woman ever to do so. The next day she made a brief address and then yielded the seat to George. She returned to Cartersville, continued her newspaper work for some years, and in 1930 published a third autobiographical work, *The Romantic Story of Georgia Women*. She died in Atlanta on January 24, 1930.

Ferber, Edna 1887–1968 writer

Born on August 15, 1887, in Kalamazoo, Michigan, Edna Ferber grew up there and in Appleton, Wisconsin. After graduating from high school in 1905 she worked for a time as a reporter for a local newspaper, moving later to jobs with the *Milwaukee Journal* and then the *Chicago Tribune*. After the publication of her first novel, *Dawn O'Hara*, in 1911,

Edna Ferber

she devoted herself to writing. She soon became a prolific producer of magazine stories that were highly popular both at their first publication and in such collections as *Buttered Side Down*, 1912, *Roast Beef Medium*, 1913, *Emma McChesney & Co.*, 1915, *Fanny Herself*, 1917, *Cheerful — by Request*, 1918, *Half Portions*, 1919, *The Girls*, 1921, *Gigolo*, 1922, *Mother Knows Best*, 1927, and *One Basket*, 1947. Her novel *So Big*, 1924, placed her in the ranks of the best-selling authors of the day and also was sufficiently esteemed by critics to win a Pulitzer Prize.

Ferber's acute observations of American social life combined with a strong flair for characterization in a series of novels set in picturesque places and times — *Show Boat*, 1926, which Jerome Kern and Oscar Hammerstein II adapted for the great musical of the same name in 1929, *Cimarron*, 1930, *Saratoga Trunk*, 1941, *Giant*, 1952, and *Ice Palace*, 1958, all made into successful motion pictures. Ferber also collaborated with George S. Kaufman on a number of plays, including *Minick*, 1925, *The Royal Family*, 1927, *Dinner at Eight*, 1932, *Stage Door*, 1936, *The Land Is Bright*, 1941, and *Bravo!*, 1949. Several of the plays became movies as well. Although her stories and novels were occasionally dismissed by some critics as merely popular romances, there was in them a constant undercurrent of serious exploration and celebration of the American character and the American land. She published two autobiographical volumes *A Peculiar Treasure*, 1939, and *A Kind of Magic*, 1963. Ferber died in New York City on April 16, 1968.

Ferguson, Abbie Park 1837–1919 educator

Born in Whately, Massachusetts, on April 4, 1837, Abbie Ferguson was the daughter of a Congregational minister. She graduated from Mount Holyoke Seminary in 1856 and then taught school for 13 years, first in Niles, Michigan, in 1856–1858, and then in New Haven, Connecticut. During 1869–1871 she lived in France as tutor and companion to two young American girls. In 1873 she learned that the Reverend Andrew Murray, a Dutch Reformed minister of Cape Colony, South Africa, had appealed to Mount Holyoke for assistance in establishing a girls' school in South Africa on the work-study principle established by Mary Lyon. Abbie Ferguson and Anna Elvira Bliss (1843–1925), also a Mount Holyoke graduate, answered the appeal and in November 1873 arrived at Cape Town. They made their way to Wellington, Murray's home, and with funds he had already raised opened Huguenot Seminary in January 1874 with 54 girls.

The seminary was an immediate success with the Calvinist and largely rural people of Cape Colony, as it promised to train the teachers needed to staff church-oriented schools. In 1875 the seminary was divided into a lower department under Bliss and an upper under Ferguson; the upper placed ten graduates among those certified as teachers by the colony's educational authority at the end of that year. In 1884 a Collegiate Department was established, although among South Africans higher education for women was widely viewed with suspicion. Ferguson was also deeply interested in the vast opportunity for missionary work that Africa presented, and through the Women's Missionary Society (later the Vrouwen Zending Bond) that she and Bliss formed at Huguenot she worked toward the conversion of a continent. In 1890 a school for entering students was opened in Pearl, and Huguenot Seminary was thereafter limited to secondary and collegiate work. Branches of the seminary were opened in Bethlehem, Orange Free State, and in Greytown, Natal (both now part of the Republic of South Africa). In 1898 the Collegiate Department of Huguenot awarded its first two bachelor's degrees and was reorganized as Huguenot College, of which Ferguson was president from then until her retirement in 1910.

As the only women's college in South Africa, Huguenot was chronically short of money, space, and faculty, but Abbie Ferguson's dedication overcame every obstacle. On her return from convalescent leave in Europe and the United States in 1905–1906 she fought off a faculty plan to merge Huguenot with Victoria College at Stellenbosch and then undertook a strenuous fund-raising campaign that made possible the erection of Ferguson Hall. In 1907 the college was formally chartered by act of Parliament. After her retirement, at which time Bliss succeeded her as president, she devoted much time to organizing and fund-raising through a network of Past Pupils Unions that she had earlier formed and that she merged into the Huguenot General Union in 1914. In 1916 Huguenot College became a constituent of the newly chartered University of South Africa (from 1920 it was Huguenot University College). Abbie Ferguson died at Huguenot on March 25, 1919.

Ferguson, Elizabeth Graeme 1737–1801 writer

Born in Philadelphia on February 3, 1737, Elizabeth Graeme grew up in a wealthy and influential family at a country estate, Graeme Park, outside the city. About 1757 she became engaged to William Franklin, son of Benjamin Franklin, but the opposition of both families to such a marriage, along with William's absence in London with his father, ended the matter. During 1764–1765 she was in London, where she met several leading literary and scientific figures. Her mother's death in the latter year left her the mistress of Graeme Park, and she soon established something like a literary salon. Her translation of Fénelon's *Télémaque*, made while she was recovering from her broken engagement, circulated in manuscript and gave her a certain literary reputation of her own. Other writings of the period included a metrical version of the Psalms, a wide and lively correspondence, and a remarkable journal. Virtually none of her writings were published in her lifetime.

In April 1772 Graeme married Henry H. Ferguson, who, however, spent much of his time in England while she remained at Graeme Park, which she inherited later that year on the death of her father. In the Revolution her husband was a Loyalist, while she gave mild support to the Whig cause. In October 1777 he prevailed upon her to carry from the Reverend Jacob Duché, formerly chaplain of the Continental Congress but later a Loyalist, to General George Washington a letter urging Washington to surrender. Washington chided her for her part in the episode. The next year Governor George Johnstone, a British peace commissioner, persuaded her to carry to Joseph Reed, Pennsylvania delegate to the Continental Congress and an aide to Washington, an offer of 10,000 guineas for help in obtaining peace terms advantageous to Britain. Reed's reply became famous: "He was not worth purchasing, but such as he was, the King of Great Britain was not rich enough to do it." Ferguson's part, that of compliant go-between, caused her trouble nonetheless. Her husband had already been attainted and proscribed, and late in the war Graeme Park was confiscated. It was restored to her in 1781, but she lost it through financial reverses in 1791. Her last years were difficult. She died near Graeme Park on February 23, 1801.

Ferraro, Geraldine Anne 1935– politician and attorney

Born on August 26, 1935, in Newburgh, New York, Geraldine Ferraro was the daughter of Italian immigrants. Her father died when she was eight years old, leaving the family with little money. Her mother worked crocheting beads on dresses to support her two children. Geraldine attended Marymount College in Manhattan on a scholarship; she majored in English, taking a B.A. in 1956. She taught English in public schools in Queens while attending the Fordham University Law School at night. She earned her J.D. degree in 1960, passed the New York bar exam that summer; she married John Zaccaro a week later.

During the next 14 years, although she became involved in local politics, Ferraro devoted her attention to raising her three children. When her youngest child entered school in 1974, she accepted a position as an assistant district attorney in the Investigations Bureau in Queens; in 1975, she transferred to the Special Victims Bureau, which she helped to create to handle cases of domestic violence and rape. In 1978, she was elected to the U.S. House of Representatives from New York's Ninth Congressional District, running as a Democrate on a platform supporting law and order, the elderly, and neighborhood preservation. Reelected in 1980 and 1982, she represented a predominantly blue-collar, Catholic constituency while advancing a liberal and feminist political agenda.

In 1980 she was elected secretary of the Democratic caucus, and she took a seat in the House Steering and Policy Committee. In 1984 she was appointed chair of the 1984 Democratic platform committee, the first woman to hold the post. That same year, Democratic party presidential candidate, Walter Mondale, selected Ferraro to be his running mate, making her the first woman on a major party's national ticket. The presidential bid was unsuccessful, however, and Mondale lost to Ronald Reagan.

Since 1984, Ferraro has written *Ferraro: My Story*, 1985, an autobiography; she has been active campaigning and lecturing on behalf of female political candidates; she held a fellowship at the Harvard Institute of Politics, 1988; and she ran unsuccessfully for the U.S. Senate in 1992.

Fields, Dorothy 1905–1974 songwriter

Born on July 15, 1905, in Allenhurst, New Jersey, Dorothy Fields was the daughter of Lew M. Fields of the vaudeville comedy team of Weber and Fields. After graduating from high school in New York City she taught drama and published a few poems in magazines before she found her career. Her lyrics for Jimmy McHugh's song "Our American Girl" led to their successful collaboration on *Blackbirds of 1928*, a lavish Cotton Club show featuring "I Can't Give You Anything But Love, Baby" (a song first heard in the short-lived *Delmar's Revels* in 1927) and "Diga Diga Doo."

For *International Revue* in 1930 Fields and McHugh wrote "On the Sunny Side of the Street" and "Exactly Like You," and for that year's *Vanderbilt Review* they wrote "Blue Again." Also in 1930 they contributed songs to the motion pictures *Love In the Rough* ("Go Home and Tell Your Mother") and *Every Night at Eight*. They wrote songs for the movies *Singin' the Blues* and *Cuban Love Song* in 1931, *Dinner at Eight* and *Clowns in Clover* in 1933, and *Every Night at Eight* ("I'm In the Mood for Love") and *Hooray for Love* in 1935, and they contributed "Lovely to Look At" to the 1935 film version of Jerome Kern's *Roberta*. In 1934 they wrote "Lost in a Fog" for the Dorsey brothers' band. In 1935 she worked with Kern on the score of the film *I Dream Too Much*, featuring Lily Pons, and in 1936 they wrote the score for *Swingtime*, including "A Fine Romance," "Waltz in Swing Time," and the Academy Award winning "The Way You Look Tonight." Also in 1936 she collaborated with her older brother Herbert Fields (1898–1958) on the screenplay for the film *Riviera*; they followed with screenplays for *Love Before Breakfast*, 1936, and *Fools for Scandal*, 1938.

In 1939 Dorothy Fields worked on *Stars in Your Eyes*, a Broadway musical with Ethel Merman and Jimmy Durante. She worked with Kern again on the movies *Joy of Living*, 1938, and *One Night in the Tropics*, 1940. She and Herbert again collaborated on lyrics for Cole Porter's *Let's Face It* on Broadway in 1941 and on *The Father Takes a Wife*, a film of the same year. In 1943 they again joined Cole Porter to produce *Something for the Boys*, and the same team wrote *Mexican Hayride*, 1944. In 1945 Herbert and Dorothy Fields wrote the book and Dorothy wrote the lyrics to Sigmund Romberg's melodies for the very successful *Up in Central Park*. Their book, Irving Berlin's music, and Ethel Merman's performance made *Annie Get Your Gun* the great Broadway hit of 1946. Most of their Broadway shows also became motion pictures. *Arms and the Girl*, 1950, featured their book and Dorothy's lyrics to Morton Gould's tunes.

In 1951 Fields wrote lyrics to Arthur Schwartz's music for the Broadway production of

A Tree Grows in Brooklyn and collaborated with Schwartz and Harold Arlen on songs for *Excuse My Dust* and *Texas Carnival*. In 1954 she and Herbert Fields wrote the book and she wrote the lyrics for *By the Beautiful Sea* (music by Arthur Schwartz), and in 1959, with composer Albert Hague, they produced the hit *Redhead*. With composer Cy Coleman she produced the hit show *Sweet Charity*, 1965, and *Seesaw* and *PIN-UPS*, both 1973. Dorothy Fields was elected to the Songwriters Hall of Fame in 1971. She died in New York City on March 28, 1974.

Fillmore, Myrtle Page 1845–1931 religious leader

Born in Pagetown, Morrow County, Ohio, on August 6, 1845, Mary Caroline Page, who later took the name Myrtle, grew up in a strict Methodist home. After a year at Oberlin College in 1868–1869 she became a schoolteacher; she taught in Clinton, Missouri, in 1869–1875, in Denison, Texas, in 1875–1878, and again in Clinton in 1878–1881. In March 1881 she married Charles Fillmore (1854–1948), a railroad man and real estate developer whom she had met in Denison. They moved to Colorado, where land booms in Gunnison and later in Pueblo engaged Charles Fillmore's attention, but the collapse of the boom in 1884 prompted them to move to Kansas City, Missouri.

Myrtle Fillmore's incipient tuberculosis, which had benefited from the Colorado air, soon worsened. Orthodox medical treatment was of no avail, and in 1886 she turned to mental healing as described in a series of lectures by a Dr. E. B. Weeks, a student of the ex-Christian Scientist Emma Curtis Hopkins. Fillmore found her health greatly improving; her husband, skeptical at first, soon joined in her enthusiasm as he found his leg, which had been stunted and weak since a childhood accident, growing stronger. They resolved to devote themselves to evangelizing for "practical Christianity," an active faith able to effect solutions to physical, mental, financial, and other problems.

In April 1889 they began publication of a magazine called *Modern Thought*, which was subsequently renamed *Christian Science Thought*, *Thought*, and in 1895 *Unity*. In 1893 they began publishing a second magazine, *Wee Wisdom*, for children. In 1890 they organized the Society of Silent Unity, which offered the service of effective prayer on behalf of beset persons who wrote to request it. From the outset their idea was to found not a denomination but a school devoted to teaching the fundamental truth that unified all sects. Eventually, however, the organizational structure came to resemble closely that of a denomination, with a training school turning out ministers and with hundreds of separate Unity "churches" throughout the Midwest and in California. A basic text, *Lessons in Truth*, was published in 1908 by one of their most influential converts, Dr. Harriette Emilie Cady of New York City, a former homeopathist.

The Unity School of Christianity grew rapidly, and after World War I the Fillmores bought a large tract of land at Lee's Summit, Missouri, and began building a permanent home for the Unity movement called Unity Farm, which grew ultimately to 1300 acres. Until 1922 Unity was connected with the International New Thought Alliance, but thereafter it went its own way. Myrtle Fillmore's influence on the development of the Unity doctrine of the power of prayerful thought and on the practical organization of the school's activities was inseparable from that of her husband, who held the title of president. She died at Unity Farm on October 6, 1931. The Unity movement continued to prosper under her husband, who was succeeded in turn by their sons.

Finley, Martha 1828–1909 writer of children's books

Born on April 26, 1828, in Chillicothe, Ohio, Martha Finley grew up there and in South Bend, Indiana. In 1853, after the deaths of both her parents, she moved to New York City; later she moved to Philadelphia and then to Phoenixville, Pennsylvania. She taught school for a time and then turned to writing, at first for Sunday school publications under the name "Martha Farquharson." A few early attempts at children's novels were not particularly successful, but with *Elsie Dinsmore*, 1867, she found a formula that would bring her fame and fortune.

The tale of a preternaturally virtuous young girl valiantly resisting various relatively petty temptations in the name of a somewhat fundamentalist Christianity found a wide audience that grew, over the course of 27 sequel volumes that took Elsie to grandmotherhood, to some 25 million readers in America and Britain. In addition to the Elsie Dinsmore series Martha Finley also produced a seven-volume series beginning with *Mildred Keith*, 1878, a nine-volume "Do-Good Library," a twelve-volume "Pewit's Nest" series, and a "Finley" series of books for adults, a total of more than a hundred books. Single volumes for children appeared under such titles as *Willie Elton, the Little Boy Who Loved Jesus*, 1864, *The Little Helper*, 1868, *Milly; or the Little Girl who Tried to Help Others and to do them Good*, 1868, *Our Fred; or Seminary Life at Thurston*, 1874, and *Twiddletewit, a Fairy Tale*, 1898. Her books were generally ignored in their day by critics, a fact which affected not at all their enormous popularity with an uncritical audience; when the fashion for priggishness in literary children passed, they were all but forgotten. Martha Finley lived in Elkton, Maryland, from 1876 until her death there on January 29, 1909.

Fisher, Clara 1811–1898 actor

Born in England, probably in London, on July 14, 1811, Clara Fisher made her stage debut in December 1817, at the age of six, in a children's adaptation of David Garrick's *Lilliput* at the Drury Lane Theatre. Her performance in that and in an afterpiece of excerpts from *Richard III* captivated the audience. She subsequently appeared at Covent Garden and then began a ten-year period of touring up and down Great Britain, winning popular acclaim in a variety of child's and adult's roles.

Fisher came to America in 1827 and made her debut at the Park Theatre, New York City, in September in *The Will*. Despite the weakness of the play she was a sensation, and in appearances in leading theaters in virtually every major American city over the next seven years she only added to her popular success. Her characterizations of both male and female roles were imbued with a buoyant spirit and great charm. In the craze of adulation that attended her, her name was given to babies, race horses, stagecoaches, and steamboats, and she was generally esteemed the leading actress of the American stage. After her marriage in December 1834 to James G. Maeder, an Irish musician, she continued to act, but less frequently and increasingly seldom as a star. She was the Singing Witch in the performance of *Macbeth* that was the occasion of the Astor Place riot of May 10, 1849. In later years she played with various stock companies, including those of Mrs. John Drew's Arch Street Theatre and of Augustin Daly. At various times she taught dramatics and elocution. She played the Nurse in the Maurice Barrymore-Helena Modjeska production of *Romeo and Juliet* that closed Booth's Theatre, New York City, in April 1883. Her last performance was at Ford's Theatre, Baltimore, in 1889. She died in Metuchen, New Jersey, on November 12, 1898.

Fisher, Dorothy Canfield 1879–1958 writer

Born on February 17, 1879, in Lawrence, Kansas, Dorothea Frances Canfield graduated from Ohio State University, of which her father was then president, in 1899 and after further studies at the Sorbonne in Paris entered Columbia University and took her Ph.D. in 1904. She was for a time secretary of the Horace Mann School in New York City, but in May 1907, upon her marriage to John R. Fisher, she moved to a farm in Arlington, Vermont, that had been in her family for generations; the farm remained her home for the rest of her life. In 1907 her first novel, *Gunhild*, was published, and she followed it with *Squirrel Cage*, 1912, *The Bent Twig*, 1915, *Hillsboro People*, a collection of fictional Vermont sketches, 1915, and *Understood Betsy*, 1917, a novel that became a minor classic of children's literature. During World War I she and her husband traveled to France to work in a number of relief projects, and her experiences there resulted in the stories collected in *Home Fires in France*, 1918, *The Day of Glory*, 1919, and *Basque People*, 1931.

Fisher was throughout her life deeply interested in education, both of children and adults, and she published a number of works on aspects of the subject, including *The Montessori Mother*, 1913, *Mothers and Children*, 1914, *Why Stop Learning?*, 1927, and *Our Young Folks*, 1943. Her fictional writings — calm, commonsensical appraisals of American life marked by profound concern for the characters — were perennially popular and included also *The Brimming Cup*, 1921, *Rough Hewn*, 1922, *Raw Material*, 1923, *The Home-Maker*, 1924, *Made-to-Order Stories*, 1925, *Her Son's Wife*, 1926, *The Deepening Stream*, 1930, *Bonfire*, 1933, *Fables for Parents*, 1937, *Seasoned Timber*, 1939, *Nothing Ever Happens*, 1940, *American Portraits*, 1946, *Four Square*, 1949, *Something Old, Something New*, 1949, and *A Harvest of Stories*, 1956.

Fisher wrote several nonfiction works on American history and other topics, most notably *Vermont Tradition: The Biography of an Outlook on Life*, 1953. She was active in numerous educational and charitable organizations, serving as president of the American Association for Adult Education and during World War II providing the principal inspiration for the Children's Crusade for Children. She was also a member of the editorial board of judges of the Book of the Month Club from its inception in 1926 until 1951. Fisher died in Arlington, Vermont, on November 9, 1958.

JILL KREMENTZ

M.F.K. Fisher

Fisher, M.F.K. 1908–1992 author

Born on July 3, 1908, in Albion, Michigan, Mary Frances Kennedy grew up in Whittier, California, where her father owned and operated a local newspaper, *The Whittier News*. As an adolescent she became interested in food and cooking and spent hours on end watching and assisting the family cook. Along with cooking, she also spent a great deal of her free time reading and writing. She briefly attended college in Illinois and California before she married Alfred Fisher, a doctoral student in literature. Together they moved to Dijon, France, in 1929. In France, her passion for food and culinary delights blossomed. Food and eating were much more than just a means of biological sustenance to her — they were a celebration of life.

In 1932, she and her husband moved to Los Angeles, California, and she began combining her passion for food and her interest in literature by writing pieces about cooking and eating. Unlike traditional cookbooks and other food writing, her pieces were more about lifestyle than about the particulars of specific dishes or cuisines. Her first book, *Serve it Forth*, a collection of her essays, was published under the pseudonym M.F.K. Fisher in 1937, introducing a new genre to American literature: the food essay. She continued to refine this genre throughout her life. *Serve it Forth*, along with her next two books, *Consider the Oyster*, 1941, and *How to Cook a Wolf*, 1942, were well-received, but it was not until *The Gastronomical Me* was published in 1943 that she began to be recognized as a highly skilled writer, as well as a critical success. In that book, she wrote: "Our three basic needs, for food and security and love are so mixed and mingled and entwined that we cannot straightly think of one without the others."

In 1949 she published the definitive translation of French gastronomist Jean Anthelme Brillat-Savarin's *The Physiology of Taste*, and in 1954 five of her gastronomic books were published together as her most famous work, *The Art of Eating* — a mix of recipes, social commentary, travel writing, and compelling stories — which became a modern classic. In one of the many often-anthologized pieces in *The Art of Eating*, "Borderland," she writes about the intense pleasure of eating tangerine sections that have been placed on a warm radiator until they have grown "plumper, hot and full," while watching the afternoon goings-on from the windowsill of a Strasbourg pension. All told, she published 15 books, most celebrating food and life, including *A Cordiall Water*, 1961, a slim volume on folk cures that became a cult favorite. She also wrote a novel, *Not Now But Now*, 1947, a screenplay, and the children's book *The Boss Dog*, 1991. In 1971 she wrote the memoir *Among Friends*, and in 1983 she published *Sister Age*, about growing old.

In 1938 she divorced Al Fisher, and married the artist Dillwyn Parrsh. He died in 1941, and she married Donald Friede, a literary agent in 1945. Their marriage ended in divorce in 1951. Fisher had two daughters, Anna, born in 1943 and Kennedy in 1946. In 1952 she and her sister, Norah, rented separate houses on vineyards in St. Helena, in Napa Valley, California. She bought Bouverie Ranch in neighboring Glen Ellen in 1971, where she lived the rest of her days living life as she wrote about it: cooking, writing, eating, and celebrating. She died on June 22, 1992, at age 83, after a lengthy battle against Parkinson's disease.

Fiske, Fidelia 1816–1864 missionary

Born on May 1, 1816, in Shelburne, Massachusetts, Fidelia Fisk (she later restored the ancestral final "e") early exhibited a serious interest in religion. She was said to have read Cotton Mather's *Magnalia Christi Americana* and Timothy Dwight's *Theology* by the age of eight. At seventeen she began teaching in district schools. In 1839 she entered Mount Holyoke Seminary, and, after a year's absence owing to typhoid fever, she graduated in 1842 and was promptly appointed to the faculty. Influenced by Mary Lyon, she responded to a call the next year from the American Board of Commissioners for Foreign Missions for a missionary to the Nestorian Christians of Persia. She sailed from Boston in March 1843 and in June landed at Urmia (now Rezaiyeh, Iran), legendary birthplace of Zoroaster.

After mastering the Syriac language Fiske labored under severe physical and cultural difficulties to build a small day school into Urmia Seminary, a boarding school for girls that won wide repute. She was virtually a mother to her pupils, who had first to be rescued from the tradition of educational neglect and early marriage to attend the school. Her services as a nurse for the region about Urmia and her missionary work into the countryside and among mountain tribes gradually won her respect and helped set an example that contributed to the slow improvement of the lot of Persian women. The school had grown to an enrollment of some 40 pupils by 1858, when ill health forced her to return to the United States. While serving as an unofficial chaplain at Mount Holyoke and traveling and speaking widely on her missionary work she wrote *Memorial: Twenty-Fifth Anniversary of the Mt. Holyoke Female Seminary*, 1862, and contributed to Thomas Laurie's *Woman and Her Saviour in Persia*, 1863. It was her intention to return to Persia when her health was restored, and for that reason she declined the offer of the principalship of Mount Holyoke in 1863. Her health did not improve, however, and she died in Shelburne, Massachusetts on July 26, 1864. Her *Recollections of Mary Lyon* was published in 1866.

Fitzgerald, Ella 1918–1996 singer

Born on April 25, 1918, in Newport News, Virginia, Ella Fitzgerald was orphaned early in life and was reared in an orphanage in Yonkers, New York. In 1934, at an amateur show at the Apollo Theater in Harlem, she was discovered by bandleader Chick Webb, who immediately hired her and became her musical mentor. With his band she made her first recording, "Love and Kisses," in 1935. Their recorded version of "A-Tisket, A-Tasket," released in 1938, became a nationwide hit. Following Webb's death in 1939 she took over his band for a time and then became a solo performer, successfully touring nightclubs and theaters across the country and abroad.

A singer of great flexibility and imagination, Fitzgerald was able to instill life and

Ella Fitzgerald

interest into the poorest of materials, and with good songs she created classic renditions. Her repertoire ranged from blues, through Dixieland and calypso to popular ballads — among her most popular record albums were those of songs by Irving Berlin, George Gershwin, Cole Porter, and Rodgers and Hart — and she appeared and recorded with such greats as Louis Armstrong, whom she rivaled in scat singing, and Duke Ellington. From 1946 she toured regularly with Norman Granz's Jazz at the Philharmonic group and in 1956 began recording for his Verve label. In 1955 she appeared in the movie *Pete Kelly's Blues*.

Known around the world as "the First Lady of Song," Fitzgerald was the acknowledged favorite female vocalist of most top jazzmen and popular musicians and regularly won top honors in polls conducted by such trade magazines as *Metronome* and *Downbeat*. In 1968 she was voted top female singer by the International Jazz Critics' Poll. Others among her most popular single recordings were "That's My Desire," "Oh, Lady Be Good," "Manhattan," and "I'm Thrilled." Her recordings continued to be immensely popular and she won twelve Grammy awards, including Best Female Jazz Vocalist in 1981, 1984 and 1990.

Fitzgerald was the first recipient of the Society of Singers lifetime achievement award, 1989, an award that now bears the name "Ella" in her honor. Elected honorary chairman of the Martin Luther King Foundation in 1968, she was also honored at the Kennedy Center in 1979 and was awarded the National Medal of the Arts in 1987. She was named a Commander of the French Order of Arts and Letters, 1990, was honored with the Presidential Medal of Freedom, 1992, and, with Billie Holiday and the Ink Spots, was an early inductee into the Apollo Hall of Fame, 1993.

Fitzgibbon, Sister Irene 1823–1896 religious

Born in Kensington, London, on May 11, 1823, Catherine Fitzgibbon came to the United States with her parents in 1832 and grew up in Brooklyn, New York, She attended parish schools there and in January 1850 entered the novitiate of the Sisters of Charity, taking the name Sister Mary Irene. Sister Irene taught at St. Peter's Academy in New York City until 1858, when she became superior of St. Peter's convent. In the years during and after the Civil War the care of foundling infants became an increasingly serious problem in New York City. No public or private charity had yet taken up the problem, and the practice of putting the infants into the care of prisoners or the inmates of almshouses was wholly unsatisfactory. Archbishop John (later Cardinal) McCloskey proposed that the Sisters of Charity establish a home for such children and chose Sister Irene to direct it.

In October 1869 the Foundling Asylum (later the New York Foundling Hospital) opened with a staff of four sisters under Sister Irene. The next month, with Mrs. Paul Thébaud, she organized the Foundling Asylum Society, an organization of laywomen to support the work of the asylum. In 1873 the asylum moved to much larger quarters on a site donated by the city and with a large state appropriation to help erect a new building. Forced to evolve her own methods of dealing with foundlings and with unwed mothers, Sister Irene initiated a program of placing children whenever possible in foster homes, with provision for legal adoption when desired. Needy unwed mothers were given shelter and encouraged to keep and care for their own babies. To further these programs she founded three allied institutions: St. Ann's Maternity Hospital in 1880, the Hospital of St. John for Children in 1881, and Nazareth Hospital for convalescent children at Spuyten Duyvil, New York City, in 1881. She also founded the Seton Hospital for tuberculosis patients in 1894. In that year, the 25th anniversary of the opening of the Foundling Asylum, it was estimated that 26,000 children had thus far been saved. Sister Irene died in New York City on August 14, 1896.

Flanner, Janet 1892–1978 journalist

Born in Indianapolis on March 13, 1892, Janet Flanner was of a literary family. She attended the University of Chicago in 1912–1913 and then returned to Indianapolis and took a job with the *Indianapolis Star*, becoming the paper's first movie critic in 1916. She subsequently worked for a time at a girls' reformatory in Pennsylvania. A brief marriage brought her back to Indiana in 1920, and a short time later she moved to New York City to try her hand at serious writing. A European tour ended in her settling in Paris in 1922. In 1926 she published a novel, *The Cubical City*. In 1925 she had been asked to contribute a biweekly "Paris Letter" to the newly founded *New Yorker* magazine.

The letters — sketches of Parisian life, especially among the "smart set," and often reflecting through them the effects of politics and public affairs — were characterized from the first by remarkable degrees of sensibility, wit, and clarity. As analyses of the serious aspects of French society and culture they were unique, and they proved one of the most valuable of the *New Yorker*'s assets. An occasional letter dealt with a particular interest of hers, ingenious and bizarre crimes. Harold Ross, first editor of the magazine, gave Flanner the nom de plume "Genêt," which continued to appear after her pieces for some years. For 14 years, until her return to the United States, she was the sole author of the "Paris Letters"; later she also wrote a number of "London Letters" and several penetrating contributions to the *New Yorker*'s "Profile" series, notably those on Hitler, Thomas Mann, Edith Wharton, Cocteau, Gide, Picasso, Camus, Sartre, Colette, Stravinsky, Josephine Baker, Ravel, Piaf, and Elsa Maxwell, among many others. Those and other pieces comprised *An American in Paris*, published in 1940. *Pétain: The Old Man of France* appeared in 1943.

With the Allied liberation in 1944 Flanner returned to France and continued to contribute regularly to the *New Yorker*. In 1957 she published *Men and Monuments. Paris Journal, 1944–1965*, a collection of her pieces edited by William Shawn (editor of the *New Yorker*) that won a National Book Award, 1965; *Paris Journal, 1965–1971*, also edited by Shawn, 1971; *Paris Was Yesterday, 1925–1939*, edited by Irving Drutman, 1972; and *London Was Yesterday, 1934–1939*, edited by Drutman, 1975, preserved her magazine pieces. Her final Paris Letter was published in the *New Yorker* in September 1975, a month short of the 50th anniversary of her first. She also translated a number of French works, including *Chéri* and *Claudine à L'École* by Colette and *Ma Vie avec Maeterlinck* by Mme. Georgette Le Blanc. Janet Flanner died in New York City on November 7, 1978.

Fleming, Williamina Paton Stevens 1857–1911 astronomer

Born in Dundee, Scotland, on May 15, 1857, Mina (as she was called) Stevens was educated in public schools and from fourteen was a teacher as well as student. In May 1877 she married James O. Fleming, with whom she emigrated to America and settled in Boston the next year. The failure of her marriage in 1879 forced her to seek employment, and she soon became housekeeper for Edward C. Pickering, professor of astronomy and director of the Harvard College Observatory. Before the year was out Pickering had called her to work at the observatory as a temporary employee, and in 1881 she became a permanent member of the staff. From clerical and simple computation work she graduated to more difficult and responsible tasks, eventually taking over the observatory's work in the still rudimentary field of stellar classification by photographic spectra. She made numerous improvements in Pickering's original scheme of classification and used the "Pickering-Fleming system" to produce her *Draper Catalogue of Stellar Spectra*, covering 10,351 stars, in 1890. Her work provided much of the foundation for the much larger undertaking of Annie J. Cannon.

In addition to carrying on her own work with the observatory's rapidly growing collection of photographs and supervising a staff of computers, Fleming also edited all of the observatory's publications, and in 1898 she was formally appointed curator of astronomical photographs by the Harvard Corporation; she was the first woman to hold a corporation appointment at the university. A major product of her research on stellar spectra was her identification of 222 variable stars. That accomplishment stemmed directly from her discovery of emission lines in the spectra of a number of known red variables, a discovery that provided a highly useful tool in the search for others. Her posthumously published paper on "Stars Having Peculiar Spectra" listed 28 novae, of which she had discovered 10, and 107 Wolf-Rayet stars' of which she had found 94. Among her many honors she was in 1906 the first American woman elected to membership in the Royal Astronomical Society. She died in Boston on May 21, 1911.

Fletcher, Alice Cunningham 1838–1923 ethnologist

Born on March 15, 1838, to American parents visiting Havana, Cuba, Alice Fletcher grew up in New York City, where she received an excellent education. She taught school for a number of years, lectured occasionally on various topics, and was an early member and secretary of Sorosis and in 1873 a founder and secretary of the Association for the Advancement of Women. A growing interest in archaeology and ethnology led to extensive reading in those fields, guided by Frederic Ward Putnam, director of Harvard's Peabody Museum, and by 1878 to field work with Indian remains in Florida and Massachusetts.

In 1879 a meeting with Susette La Flesche ("Bright Eyes"), then making her first eastern speaking tour, turned Fletcher's interest toward the Omaha people. In 1881 La Flesche introduced her to the Omaha, in whose villages and teepees she lived for several months. While studying their ways and observing firsthand the squalid existence to which they had been reduced, she became convinced that the Omaha were threatened with further dispossession by the Indian Bureau. After written appeals had failed to accomplish anything, she traveled herself to Washington, D.C., in 1882, drafted a bill calling for the division of the common tribal land into individual holdings, and lobbied it through Congress. President Chester A. Arthur then appointed her in April 1883 to personally manage the division of land. Assisted by Francis La Flesche, a brother of Bright Eyes, she worked for a year to complete the task. In 1885 she wrote a lengthy report on *Indian Education and Civilization* for the U.S. Senate. In 1886 the Peabody Museum, to which she had sent a great many Native American artifacts and relics, granted her the title of "assistant." In the same year she traveled to Alaska at the request of Secretary of the Interior Lucius Q. C. Lamar to study the educational needs of Native Americans and Eskimos. The passage of the Dawes Act of 1887, growing out of Fletcher's work on behalf of the Omahas and pushed by the publicity and petition campaign of Mary L. Bonney and others, established the severalty principle for all tribes.

In that year Fletcher was appointed a special agent of the Interior Department to direct the allotment of tribal land among the Winnebago in Nebraska. The job took her two years to complete, and she then undertook the same task with the Nez Percés in Idaho, where she worked until 1893. She took great pains to secure, usually against heavy local opposition, the best possible tracts and to allot them fairly. During these years she continued her scholarly work, contributing several papers to publications of the Peabody Museum, where she held from 1891 a life fellowship endowed especially for her, and to reports of the Bureau of American Ethnology of the Smithsonian Institution. A paper on Omaha songs delivered to the International Congress of Anthropologists in Chicago in 1893 led to a series of articles in popular and scholarly journals on Native American music and to *Indian Story and Song from North America*, 1900, and *The Hako: A Pawnee*

Ceremony, 1904. In these works, as in her major publication *The Omaha Tribe*, 1911, she was greatly assisted by Francis La Flesche, whom she had taken into her home as her formally adopted son. In 1896 she was elected vice-president of the American Association for the Advancement of Science, and in 1902 she was a founder of the American Anthropological Association. From 1899 to 1916 she was on the editorial board of the *American Anthropologist*, to which she was also a frequent contributor, and in 1908 she led in founding the School of American Archaeology (later the School of American Research) in Santa Fe, New Mexico. She was elected president of the American Folk-Lore Society in 1905. She died in Washington, D.C., on April 6, 1923.

Flower, Lucy Louisa Coues 1837–1921 welfare worker

Born on May 10, 1837, probably in Boston, Lucy Coues grew up in Portsmouth, New Hampshire, and attended local schools. After a year at Packer Collegiate Institute in Brooklyn, New York, in 1856–1857 she worked for two years as a draftsman in the U.S. Patent Office in Washington. In 1860 she moved to Madison, Wisconsin, and became a teacher in the public schools, and in 1862–1863, when the city's public schools were closed, she operated a private school. She married James M. Flower, a Madison lawyer, in September 1862. After their move to Chicago in 1873 she devoted herself to a variety of philanthropic activities, especially those dealing with children.

Lucy Flower became a member of the board of the Half-Orphan Asylum in 1875 and later of that of the Chicago Home for the Friendless. In 1880, with Dr. Sarah Stevenson and others, she helped found the Illinois Training School for Nurses, the first such school in Chicago, of which she was president for 11 years and a director until 1908. She led in agitation for the establishment of a state industrial school for dependent boys and in 1886 drafted legislation to that end. The bill was defeated in the Illinois legislature, but the public interest in the idea she had aroused eventuated in the opening of such a school under private auspices in Glenwood, Illinois, in 1889. In 1887 she joined in organizing the Protective Agency for Women and Children, and in 1888 she helped form the Lake Geneva Fresh Air Association to provide vacations for poor urban children. In 1890–1891 she served as president of the influential Chicago Woman's Club. She was appointed to the Chicago Board of Education in 1891, a post she held for three years and in which she was effective in seeing to the introduction of kindergartens and of manual and domestic training classes for the lower grades. In 1894 she was elected by a large majority to the post of trustee of the University of Illinois; she was the first woman to hold a statewide elective office in Illinois. In the same year she took part in the organization of the Chicago Bureau of Charities and was chosen its vice-president.

In the later 1890s Flower lent her influence to the faltering campaign for the establishment of a juvenile court system in Chicago. With assistance particularly from Jane Addams and Julia Lathrop, she organized support for the plan among other welfare and social service leaders and the city's legal establishment, helped draft enabling legislation, and saw her work come to fruition in July 1899 with the creation of the Cook County Juvenile Court, the first of its kind anywhere in the world. She founded the Juvenile Court Committee to raise money for probation officers' salaries, and she served frequently as a court adviser. In 1902 Lucy Flower moved with her husband to Coronado, California, where, after several years as an invalid, she died on April 27, 1921.

Flynn, Elizabeth Gurley 1890–1964 political radical

Born on August 7, 1890, in Concord, New Hampshire, Elizabeth Gurley Flynn was the daughter of working-class socialists. She grew up in Manchester, New Hampshire, in Adams, Massachusetts, and from 1900 in the Bronx, New York City. While still in grammar school she was active in local socialist clubs, and in 1906 she joined the Industrial Workers of the World. She left high school in 1907 to devote full time to IWW organizing around the country. She took part in the IWW's "free speech" campaigns in Missoula, Montana, in Spokane, Washington, and in other western cities and was arrested several times. Back east she helped organize the Lawrence, Massachusetts, textile strike of 1912 and the Paterson, New Jersey, strike of 1913. She raised relief and legal defense funds for the Mesabi iron miners' strike in Minnesota in 1916. In 1918 she helped establish and until 1922 served as secretary of the Workers' Liberty Defense Union; in 1920 she was a founder of the American Civil Liberties Union; and in 1927–1930 she was chairman of International Labor Defense. In the post-World War I years she was mainly engaged in legal defense of labor and political agitators and aliens who were victimized by the "Palmer raids" of Attorney General A. Mitchell Palmer and threatened with deportation. She was also a key fund and support raiser in the Sacco and Vanzetti case.

After a lengthy period of ill health Flynn resumed her political activities in the 1930s, and in 1937 she joined the Communist party. Three years later she was removed from the national committee of the American Civil Liberties Union for her Communist party membership. She was a tireless organizer and writer on behalf of the party, and she gained a reputation as a rousing platform speaker. She was arrested along with 12 other Communist leaders in 1951 and in 1953 was convicted of violating the 1940 Smith Alien Registration Act. She was confined in the federal women's reformatory in Alderson, West Virginia, from January 1955 to May 1957. Her *I Speak My Own Piece: Autobiography of "The Rebel Girl"* was published in 1955. ("The Rebel Girl" was a song written by the IWW's minstrel, Joe Hill, and inspired by the young Gurley Flynn.) In March 1961 she was chosen chairman of the national committee of the Communist Party of the United States. She was the first woman to hold the post, and she retained it until her death. A suit carried to the Supreme Court (*Aptheker v. Secretary of State*), challenging the constitutionality of a provision of the 1950 Subversive Activities Control Act that denied the issuance of passports to Communists, was won in 1964, and she promptly secured a passport in order to visit the Soviet Union. While there she died in Moscow on September 5, 1964.

Follett, Mary Parker 1868–1933 writer and lecturer

Born on September 3, 1868, in Quincy, Massachusetts, Mary Follett attended Thayer Academy in nearby Braintree, from which she graduated in 1884, and in 1888 she entered the Society for the Collegiate Instruction of Women at Harvard, which a short time later became Radcliffe College. Her attendance at Radcliffe was interrupted by a year at Newnham College, Cambridge, in 1890–1891 and later by the death of her mother, and she finally graduated in 1898. By that time she had published her first book, *The Speaker of the House of Representatives*, 1896, a pioneering study that she had conducted with the aid of historian Albert Bushnell Hart. After returning to Boston from further study abroad she associated herself with the Roxbury Neighborhood House. In 1900 she organized the Roxbury Debating Club and in 1902 the Highland Union, a social and educational club for young men, and the Roxbury Industrial League for Boys. The Industrial League made pioneering after-hours use of community school buildings, and from 1908 to 1920 Follett headed a committee of the Women's Municipal League of Boston devoted to developing community centers in neighborhood schools throughout the city. She was active in the Women's Municipal League's work for minimum wage legislation and also with the Boston Placement Bureau and its successor from 1917, the Boston Department of Vocational Guidance.

In 1918 Follett published *The New State*, in which she described an organic form of democracy based on spontaneous organization along natural neighborhood lines. Her next book, *Creative Experience*, 1924, expanded on the social and psychological implications of her earlier work, setting forth an idealistic interpretation of the creative interaction of people and groups toward a constructive synthesis of views and goals. The particular application of her ideas to industrial management and labor relations led her into a career as a lecturer, beginning with a series of papers read to the Bureau of Personnel Administration in New York City in 1925. Her books, papers, and lectures were of lasting influence on the practice of business administration, combining as they did keen insights into individual and group psychology with a knowledge of scientific management and a dedication to a broad, positive social philosophy. She interested herself also in the work of the International Labor Office and the League of Nations. From 1928 she lived in London. After a series of lectures to the department of business administration of the London School of Economics in early 1933 she fell ill, and in October she returned to Boston, where she died on December 18, 1933.

Foltz, Clara Shortridge 1849–1934 lawyer and reformer

Born on July 16, 1849, in Indiana, probably in New Lisbon, Clara Shortridge grew up in Wayne County, Indiana, and from about 1858 in Mount Pleasant, Iowa. She taught school in her youth and in December 1864 married Jeremiah R. Foltz. She followed him to Portland, Oregon, in 1872, and they moved to San Jose, California, a short time later. Widowed in 1877, she undertook the reading of law in the office of a local attorney. On discovering that the California constitution limited admission to the bar to white males, she drew up an amendment striking out those limiting qualifications and, aided by Laura D. Gordon and others, pushed it through the legislature, where it passed in April 1878. Five months later she became the first woman admitted to legal practice in California. The next year she was denied admission to the state-supported Hastings College of Law in San Francisco; she brought suit and, again with Gordon's help, argued her case successfully up to the state supreme court. In December 1879 she and Gordon were the second and third women admitted to practice before the state supreme court.

Foltz served as clerk of the state assembly's judiciary committee in 1879–1880. Her private legal practice in San Francisco grew rapidly, and in 1893 she organized the Portia Law Club with other women lawyers of the city. During 1887–1890 she lived in San Diego, where she founded and edited the daily *San Diego Bee*. Later she resided and practiced briefly in New York City. A growing practice in corporate law led her into such sidelines as organizing a women's department for the United Bank and Trust Company of San Francisco in 1905 and publishing a trade magazine, *Oil Fields and Furnaces* (later merged into the *National Oil Reporter*). From 1906 she lived and worked in Los Angeles. She played a leading role in the campaign that secured the vote for women in state elections in 1911, and shortly thereafter she served for a year or two as the first woman deputy district attorney in Los Angeles.

From 1910 to 1912 Foltz was the first woman member of the State Board of Charities and Corrections, a post awarded her on the strength of her long efforts for reforms in criminal procedure and prison administration, including the appointment of public defenders for indigent defendants and the segregation of adult and juvenile prisoners. She was also responsible for legislation that allowed women to serve as executors and administrators of estates and to hold commissions as notaries public. In 1916–1918 she published the *New American Woman* magazine. Long active in state politics — she had run for the office of presidential elector as early as 1884, on the Equal Rights ballot headed by Belva A. Lockwood — she was seriously considered for several high appointments in the 1920s, but none were realized. In 1930, at eighty-one, she entered the Republican gubernatorial primary and received a respectable vote. She died in Los Angeles on September 2, 1934.

Fonda, Jane 1937– actor and businesswoman

Born in New York City on December 21, 1937, Jane Fonda was raised among actors — her father, Henry, and her brother, Peter. Her mother, Frances Seymour Brokaw, was a

Boston society woman whose family descended from Samuel Adams. She grew up in Los Angeles where she attended the Brentwood Town and Country School. Later she attended the Greenwich Academy in Connecticut and the Emma Willard School in Troy, New York. When Fonda was 13 years old, her mother, while a patient at a private sanatorium, took her own life. Eight months later her father married Susan Blanchard.

Fonda first appeared on stage with her father the summer after her graduation from the Emma Willard School and appeared with him again the following summer at the Cape Playhouse in Dennis, Massachusetts. She had no intention of making acting a career, however — she said she was "terrified of acting" — and her father neither encouraged nor discouraged her in this direction. She had enrolled at Vassar College in the fall of 1955, but left college after two years and traveled to Paris to study art. When she returned to the U.S., she settled in New York City to study both art and music. She also worked briefly for the *Paris Review*.

In 1958, Fonda became one of Lee Strasberg's students at the Actors Studio in New York City, where she was introduced to Method acting, an acting style in which actors draw on personal memories and emotions to perform. She supported herself by working as a fashion model for magazines such as *Vogue*. After a 1959 screen test given by Joshua Logan, one of her father's oldest friends, she was offered a five-year contract to perform in one movie a year. She made her Broadway debut in *There Was a Little Girl*, 1960, a controversial play about the effects of rape on a young girl and the people close to her. The play was unsuccessful, as were her follow-up Broadway outings, *Invitations to a March*, 1960, and *The Fun Couple*, 1962. In her last stage role in 1963, she starred in Eugene O'Neil's *Strange Interlude* at the Actors Studio. Her film debut was in the campus comedy *Tall Story*, 1960, and it was followed by *A Walk on the Wild Side*, 1962, *Period of Adjustment*, 1962, *The Chapman Report*, 1962, *In the Cool of the Day*, 1963, and *Sunday in New York*, 1964.

In 1963 she traveled to France again. She met and married film director Roger Vadim and accepted roles in several of his films, while also shooting *Cat Ballou*, 1965, *The Chase*, 1966, *Barefoot in the Park*, 1967, *Hurry Sundown*, 1967, and *Any Wednesday*, 1967, in the United States. In 1970, her five-year marriage to Vadim ended, primarily because their political views increasingly differed; she had been politicized by the student uprising in Paris in 1968 and by the Vietnam War. Back in the U.S. she became an antiwar activist. A trip to North Vietnam in 1972, during which she appealed to American airmen over Radio Hanoi to stop the bombing, particularly angered opponents, who called her "Hanoi Jane." Among her most determined opponents was the Nixon administration itself, which placed her and her friends under F.B.I. surveillance.

During this time Fonda starred in *They Shoot Horses, Don't They?*, 1969, a role for which she earned a Best Actress award from the New York Film Critics, and in *Klute*, 1971, for which she received another New York Film Critics' Award as well as an Oscar. In 1973, she married Tom Hayden, a founder of the Students for a Democratic Society, and spent the next few years working on his unsuccessful campaign for a seat in the U.S. Senate. After 1975 she returned to her film career, starring in *Fun With Dick and Jane*, 1977, and *Julia*, 1977. By 1977, with producer Bruce Gilbert, Fonda had formed her own production company, IPC Films. IPC — which stood for "Indochina Peace Campaign" — set out to make entertaining movies that carried a social message, and she starred in several of them. Her role in *Coming Home*, 1978, about a Vietnam veteran and his lover, earned her an Oscar; in *The China Syndrome*, 1979, a woman news reporter exposes the cover-up of a nuclear plant accident; and in *Nine to Five*, 1980, with Lily Tomlin and Dolly Parton, women office workers kidnap their male boss and run the office without him. IPC later produced *On Golden Pond*, 1981, in which she starred alongside her father, who died four months after receiving an Oscar for his role. In 1984, she won an

Emmy award for her portrayal of the title role in *The Dollmaker*, a made-for-television movie.

After battling bulimia for years, she began her own public fitness campaign in the late 1970s. She opened her first "Workout" studio in Beverly Hills, California, and began offering fitness classes that stressed aerobic exercises performed to the beat of recorded music. She was given major credit for the vast popularity that aerobics enjoyed in the 1980s. Her workout studio soon developed into a chain, and their great success led to a series of bestsellers that included: *Jane Fonda's Workout Book*, 1981, *Jane Fonda's Workout Book for Pregnancy, Birth and Recovery*, 1982, and *Women Coming of Age*, 1984. In turn the books spawned a series of bestselling records and videocassettes for at-home exercisers, and even an eponymous line of exercise clothing.

Later films included *Agnes of God*, 1985, *The Morning After*, 1986, and *Stanley and Iris*, 1990. She largely curtailed her acting career after her marriage in 1991 to communications tycoon Ted Turner, but made occasional forays back into the spotlight. In 1994 she narrated "A Century of Women," a television series that celebrated women's achievements in the 20th century.

Fontanne, Lynn 1887–1983 actor

Born in London about 1887 (probably on December 6), Lynn Fontanne was drawn to things theatrical at an early age, and in her youth she was taken as a pupil by Ellen Terry. Her first real stage role came in 1905 in *Alice-Sit-by-the-Fire*, and her first London appearance was in pantomime at the Drury Lane Theatre in 1909. Roles in *Lady Frederick* and *The Young Lady of Seventeen* followed, and in November 1910 she made her New York debut as part of a touring company. She first attracted special attention in *Milestones* in London in 1914. In 1916 she returned to New York at the invitation of Laurette Taylor, with whom she appeared in *The Harp of Life*, *Out There*, and others. While playing in *The Wooing of Eve*, 1917, she met Alfred Lunt (1893–1977); they appeared together in *A Young Man's Fancy* in summer stock in 1919. In 1920 she appeared in *Chris*, an early version of Eugene O'Neill's *Anna Christie*, and in 1921 she was a great success in the George S. Kaufman-Marc Connelly comedy *Dulcy*.

In May 1922 Fontanne and Lunt were married, and thereafter they appeared together on the stage almost invariably, becoming the most famous husband-and-wife acting team, perhaps the most famous team of any sort, in the contemporary theater. In 1923 they played *Sweet Nell of Old Drury*, but their joint career began in earnest with their appearance in the Theatre Guild production of Molnar's *The Guardsman* in 1924. Subsequently they played Shaw's *Arms and the Man*, 1925, *The Goat Song*, 1926, Shaw's *Pygmalion*, 1927, *The Brothers Karamazov*, 1927, S. N. Behrman's *The Second Man*, 1927, *Caprice* (Lunt's London debut), 1929, Behrman's *Meteor*, 1929, *Elizabeth the Queen*, 1930, *Reunion in Vienna*, 1931, Noel Coward's *Design for Living*, 1933, *Taming of the Shrew*, 1935, Robert Sherwood's *Idiot's Delight*, 1936, *The Sea Gull*, 1938, Behrman's *Amphitryon 38*, 1938, Sherwood's *There Shall Be No Night*, 1940, Behrman's *The Pirate*, 1942, Terence Rattigan's *Love in Idleness*, 1944, Behrman's *I Know My Love*, 1949, Coward's *Quadrille*, 1952, *The Great Sebastian*, 1956, and Friedrich Dürrenmatt's *The Visit*, 1958, after which they retired from the stage.

In 1958 the Broadway Theatre was renamed the Lunt-Fontanne in their honor. While their work in serious drama was respected, it was the sophisticated comedies of S. N. Behrman and Noel Coward in which they excelled. They came out of retirement in 1965 to do *Magnificent Yankee* for the "Hallmark Hall of Fame" television series, winning Emmy awards for their performances. Two years later Fontanne appeared alone in a television production of *Anastasia*; it was her first performance without Lunt since *Strange Interlude* in 1928. In 1964 Lynn Fontanne and Alfred Lunt were awarded jointly the Presidential Medal of Freedom. She received an Emmy Award in 1965 and a Gold Medal for diction from the American Academy of Arts and Letters in 1935. In retirement they lived in the farmhouse they had owned in Genesee Depot, Wisconsin, since their marriage. Fontanne survived Alfred Lunt's death in Chicago in August 1977. She died in Genesee Depot on July 30, 1983.

Foote, Mary Anna Hallock 1847–1938 novelist and illustrator

Born in Milton, New York, on November 19, 1847, Mary Hallock grew up in a literary home and early displayed artistic talent. She attended Poughkeepsie Female Collegiate Seminary and in 1864–1867 the women's art school of the Cooper Institute in New York City. For several years thereafter she was quite successful as an illustrator for books and magazines, including *Scribner's Monthly*, *Harper's Weekly*, and the *Century*. In February 1876 she married Arthur D. Foote, a civil and mining engineer with whom she lived thereafter in various mining districts in the West. The colorful scenes amidst which she lived called forth from her pen not only drawings but also written description and eventually fiction. From her years in Leadville, Colorado, came *The Led-Horse Claim*, published in book form in 1883 after it had been serialized in the *Century*, *John Bodewin's Testimony*, 1886, and *The Last Assembly Ball*, 1889. From Boise, Idaho, came *The Chosen Valley*, 1892, *Coeur d'Alene*, 1894, and *In Exile and Other Stories*, 1894. She and her family then settled in Grass Valley, California.

Subsequent books included *The Cup of Trembling and Other Stories*, 1895, *The Little Fig Tree Stories*, 1899, *The Desert and the Sown*, 1902, *A Touch of Sun and Other Stories*, 1903, *The Royal Americans*, 1910, *A Picked Company*, 1912, *The Valley Road*, 1915, *Edith Bonham*, 1917, and *The Ground Swell*, 1919. As pictures of Western life among miners, Mexicans, and others, her novels and stories, illustrated by herself, rivaled at their best the works of Bret Harte. At the insistence of her various editors, however, she frequently submitted with little resistance to the dictates of Victorian gentility and formulaic fiction and lost much of realism thereby. Her work soon passed out of circulation. Her last years were spent in Hingham, Massachusetts, where she died on June 25, 1938.

Force, Juliana Rieser 1876–1948 museum director

Born in Doylestown, Pennsylvania, on December 25, 1876, Juliana Reiser (she later changed the name to Rieser) was educated in local schools and at an early age went to work as a secretary. She later headed a secretarial school in New York City and then became secretary to Helen Hay Whitney, wife of a prominent financier. In 1912 she married Dr. Willard B. Force. In 1914 Helen Whitney's sister-in-law, Gertrude Vanderbilt Whitney, established the Whitney Studio to show the work of young modernist artists who had difficulty finding exhibition space in conservative galleries. Force was asked to assist in managing the studio. The next year they formed and Force became director of the Friends of the Young Artists, which sponsored exhibitions and made judicious purchases.

The informal association of artists and others that developed was organized in 1918 as the Whitney Studio Club with a clubhouse on West 4th Street where Force presided. Her innate taste and receptivity to ideas more than made up for her lack of formal art training, and she soon became a central figure in the art world of New York. To Gertrude Whitney's artist friends — Robert Henri, John Sloan, Arthur B. Davies, William Glackens, and others — were soon added an even younger generation, including Stuart Davis, Edward Hopper, and Reginald Marsh, all of whom had their first exhibitions at the Whitney Studio Club. Moved to larger quarters in 1923, the club was disbanded in 1928 when it appeared it had served its purpose of nurturing a native modern art. During 1928–1930 a Whitney Studio Gallery exhibited on West 8th Street. On the refusal of the Metropolitan Museum of Art to accept Gertrude Whitney's offer in 1929 to donate her personal collection of contemporary works of art, the Whitney Museum of American Art was established in 1930 with Force as director.

Opened in November 1931, the Whitney Museum reflected in its informal and warm interior the taste of its director. She inaugurated a pioneering series of monographs on living American artists in 1931; organized morning and evening lecture series by art historians, critics, and others; and staged a variety of exhibitions of contemporary and historical art, folk art, primitives, and other unusual genres. The Whitney Museum came to be a major force in American art, and Juliana Force was central to its influence. In 1933–1934 she helped organize and then served as a regional director of the federal Public Works of Art Project. In 1942 she became first chairman of the American Art Research Council. She headed the Committee for a New York State Art Program in 1945 and was a trustee and officer of the American Federation of Arts and the American Association of Museum Directors. She remained director of the Whitney Museum until her death in New York City on August 28, 1948.

Fossey, Dian 1932–1985 primatologist

Born in San Francisco, California, on January 16, 1932, Dian Fossey was permitted as a child to keep only goldfish as pets. She entered the University of California at Davis as a preveterinary student, but transferred to San Jose State University where she earned a B.A. in 1954. During her undergraduate years she became a prize-winning equestrienne, and so she naturally headed to Kentucky for her first job in 1956 after completing her clinical training. She became director of occupational therapy for the Kosair Crippled Children's Hospital in Louisville, remaing there for seven years. During that time, she became increasingly curious about gorillas and began making plans that would take her to see them in their indigenous African habitat.

In 1963 she planned a seven-week safari, paid for with a personal bank loan. Her initial stop was with Mary and Louis Leakey, in their camp at Olduvai Gorge, where they were engaged in a hunt for clues to early human life. There she dubiously distinguished herself by shattering her ankle while scurrying down a hill to examine a newly found fossil. Nonetheless, she made her way to Zaïre (then called the Congo) two weeks later for her first meeting with the reclusive mountain gorilla.

Although stunned and impressed by her meeting with the giant gorilla, she returned to her job in Kentucky. In 1966 Louis Leakey visited her there to encourage her to return to Africa and to pursue her dream of studying gorillas. On the "advice" of her new mentor, Fossey had her appendix removed as a supposedly prophylactic measure for life as a researcher on the African continent. This tip was later revealed to be Leakey's way of testing Fossey's resolve, but she never wavered. By late 1966 she was back in Africa, funded initially by the Wilkie Brothers' Foundation and the National Geographic Society. She visited Jane Goodall in Tanzania to learn methods of fieldwork and data collection, then went alone to the Congo.

She quickly learned methods of imitation that gained the curiosity and trust of the huge, usually skittish, gorillas and developed regular observations of three different groups. Political troubles ended her research after seven months and armed guards took her into custody. Escaping into Uganda by a ruse, she was warned that her return would entail certain death. Instead, she turned to tiny Rwanda to establish the Karisoke Research Centre in the Parc National des Volcans that abutted the area previously studied.

There Fossey resumed her work, employing innovative methods that allowed her to study the gorillas at close range. She imitated their sounds, pretended to eat similar food and mimicked their grooming practices. In Rwanda she studied fifty-one gorillas living in four stable groups. She found them to be vegetarian nomads, who, despite their fearsome image, were quite peaceful in their behavior. What particularly intrigued Fossey were the strong family ties that existed among members of the same group. They nursed one another and adjusted the pace of group movement to accommodate members weakened by sickness or injury.

Fossey left Africa briefly in 1970 to complete work for a doctorate at Cambridge University. In 1974 she received her degree in zoology with the completion of her dissertation, *The Behavior of the Mountain Gorilla*. After several years of living and working as a lone Westerner, Fossey decided she needed research assistance and accepted a series of student volunteers who made broader kinds of research possible. Working with Fossey and the indigenous trackers and other Africans who had helped Fossey keep her camp supplied, the new researchers began a parasitology project through examining gorilla dung. They also helped to complete a census of the gorilla groups that Fossey had already studied.

Motivated by the killing of Digit, one of her favored gorillas, whose death was announced on CBS News, Fossey generated international media coverage in 1978 in her battle against poachers. Six months later, despite the publicity and increased anti-poaching patrols, two more gorillas were killed, decimating one of the groups she had been studying. Fossey later denied reports of a nervous breakdown following those deaths, but she never denied the grief she experienced.

In 1980, needing respite from Africa to restore herself to physical and emotional health, she returned to the U.S. to accept a visiting associate professorship at Cornell University. While teaching, Fossey also completed *Gorillas in the Mist*, 1983, which received positive reviews from the mass media but was criticized by specialists for its attempt to appeal to a popular audience by sacrificing its scientific content. Her work was also published in *National Geographic* and she was featured in a number of the television specials.

Fossey completed her contract at Cornell and returned home to Africa, telling interviewers and journalists that she was more comfortable with gorillas than with people. Back in Rwanda, she resumed her campaign against poachers who were once again encroaching on the parkland. Fossey's body was discovered slain, near the Karisoke Center on December 26, 1985. Though no assailant was ever identified, it is widely suspected she was killed by the poachers against whom she had struggled for so long.

Foster, Abigail Kelley 1810–1887 reformer

Born on January 15, 1810, in Pelham, Massachusetts, Abby Kelley grew up in Worcester, Massachusetts. She was reared a Quaker, attended Quaker schools, and later taught in a Quaker school in Lynn, Massachusetts. She became a follower of William Lloyd Garrison and in 1835–1837 was secretary of the Lynn Female Anti-Slavery Society. In 1838 she joined Garrison in founding the New England Non-Resistant Society. She took part in the first and second woman's national antislavery conventions in New York City in 1837 and in Philadelphia in 1838, and at the latter made her first address to a mixed audience, a stirring speech that prompted abolitionist leaders to urge her to take to the platform regularly. She acceded to the idea, resigned her teaching job, and in May 1839 began a career as a reform lecturer. That career was a stormy one, bringing vituperation and sometimes even mob violence upon her as she was denounced regularly from the pulpit as one sort or another of fallen woman for daring to mount the public platform.

At the convention of the American Anti-Slavery Society in 1840 Foster's appointment to the business committee was the occasion for a split in the ranks of the delegates; her conservative opponents, led by Arthur and Lewis Tappan, left to form the American and Foreign Anti-Slavery Society, leaving her ally Garrison in complete control of his own organization. Her almost ceaseless lecturing took her as far west as Indiana and Michigan, and her travels were marked not only by personal abuse but also, more immediately, by frequent hardship. In December 1845 she married Stephen S. Foster, a companion on the abolitionist lecture circuit. They continued to travel and lecture together until 1861, although after 1847 Abigail Foster spent much of each year at their Worcester, Massachusetts, farm. During the 1850s she added appeals for temperance and women's rights to her addresses.

Foster's zeal and radicalism — she was outspokenly anticlerical and anti-government almost to the point of anarchism — stirred opposition even among sympathizers occasionally, and in the late 1850s she went as far as to break with Garrison. After the Civil War age and ill health limited her activities. She made a fund-raising tour of New England on behalf of the American Anti-Slavery Society in 1870. On three occasions in the 1870s she and her husband refused to pay taxes on their farm on grounds that she was politically unrepresented by being denied the vote; on each occasion the farm was bought by friends at public auction and returned to them. At a convention in 1880 marking the 30th anniversary of the first national women's rights convention in Worcester, she delivered an address that showed all her fire as of old. She died in Worcester, Massachusetts, on January 14, 1887.

Foster, Hannah Webster 1758–1840 novelist

Born in Salisbury, Massachusetts, on September 10, 1758, Hannah Webster received the genteel education prescribed for young girls of that day. In April 1785 she married the Reverend John Foster, a Unitarian minister, with whom she settled in Brighton, Massachusetts. In 1797, signing herself merely "A Lady of Massachusetts," she published *The Coquette; or The History of Eliza Wharton*, a highly sentimental novel that enjoyed much success. Advertised as "founded on fact," *The Coquette* was loosely based on an actual case of seduction, elopement, and tragic death. It both followed and in some particulars, notably characterization, transcended the imperatives of the formula for such fiction, in which to stray from the path of virtue was to invite inevitable and terrible retribution. The book exhibited also in its epistolary form the marked influence of Samuel Richardson's *Clarissa Harlowe*. Sales of the book warranted 13 editions during the author's lifetime and kept it in print for decades after her death, and in an 1866 edition her name was placed on the title page for the first time. Her second book, *The Boarding School; or, Lessons of a Preceptress to her Pupils*, 1798, was a failure. Little is known of Hannah Foster's life outside her books. She died in Montreal on April 17, 1840.

Fowler, Lydia Folger 1822–1879 physician, writer and reformer

Born in Nantucket, Massachusetts, on May 5, 1822, Lydia Folger attended local schools and in 1838–1839 the Wheaton Seminary in Norton, Massachusetts. She taught at Wheaton in 1842–1844. In September 1844 she married Lorenzo Niles Fowler, a well known phrenologist and one of a family of promoters in that field. Lydia Fowler soon took to the lecture circuit as a phrenologist herself, and she wrote *Familiar Lessons on Physiology*, 1847, *Familiar Lessons on Phrenology*, 1847, and *Familiar Lessons on Astronomy*, 1848, for the family publishing firm of Fowlers & Wells. In 1849 she entered Central Medical College, an eclectic institution in Syracuse, New York. During her second term, by which time the college had moved to Rochester, New York, she served also as principal of the female department. On graduating in June 1850 she became the second woman, after Elizabeth Blackwell, to receive a medical degree.

In 1851 Fowler was appointed professor of midwifery and diseases of women and children at the college, becoming thereby the first women professor in a medical college in America. From the closing of the school in 1852 until 1860 she lived and practiced in New York City. She also lectured frequently to women on hygiene and physiology, championed the further opening of the medical profession to women, and became active in the women's rights and temperance movements. During 1860–1861 she studied medicine in Paris and London, and in 1862 she became an instructor in clinical midwifery at the New York Hygeio-Therapeutic College. In 1863 she and her husband moved to London permanently. In that year she published a temperance novel, *Nora: The Lost and Redeemed*. *The Pet of the Household and How to Save It*, 1865, was a collection of lectures on child care, and *Heart-Melodies*, 1870, was verse. She died in London on January 26, 1879.

Fox, Della May 1870–1913 actor and singer

Born in St. Louis on October 13, 1870, Della Fox began appearing in juvenile theatricals while a schoolgirl. At thirteen she made her first professional appearance in *Editha's Burglar*, an adaptation of a Frances Hodgson Burnett story by Augustus Thomas, who was also in the troupe. The play toured in the Midwest and Canada between 1883 and 1885. For the next five years Della Fox sang with a succession of touring opera companies, her professional skills benefiting especially from her training in the company of Heinrich Conned. In February 1890 she made her New York debut at Niblo's Garden in *The King's Fool*. In May of that year she played opposite DeWolf Hopper in the operetta *Castles in the Air*, and their joint success led to their appearing together again in *Wang* in 1891 (followed by a lengthy tour), *Panjandrum* in 1893, and *The Lady or the Tiger*, 1894.

Fox's first true starring role came in *The Little Trooper* at the Casino Theatre, New York, in August 1894. That and subsequent performances in *Fleur-de-Lis*, 1895, *The Wedding Day*, with Lillian Russell, 1897, and *The Little Host*, which opened in New York in December 1898 and in which she then toured the country with her own company, brought her to the pinnacle of success. She was said to be for a time the highest paid performer on the American variety stage. Her diminutive but plump figure helped project the winning impression of a precocious child, and her "Della Fox curl" was imitated by girls across the country. From 1899 she suffered intermittent bouts of ill health, brought on in part by alcohol and drugs. In December 1900 she married Jacob D. Levy, a New York diamond broker, and thereafter she appeared on the stage but seldom. She returned to performing in the 1912 season and gave her last performance in *Rosedale* at the Lyric Theatre, New York City, in April 1913. She died in New York City on June 15, 1913.

Fox, Margaret and Catherine 1833?–1893 and 1839?–1892 spiritualists

Born near Bath, New Brunswick, Margaret possibly on October 7, 1833, and Catherine, known as Kate, possibly in 1839, the Fox sisters moved with their family to a farm near Hydesville in Wayne County, New York, in 1847. The next year there began to spread through the neighborhood stories about strange sounds — rappings or knockings — in the Fox house. The noises were ascribed to spirits by many, including Margaret and Kate, and soon the curious, the gullible, and the skeptical alike were coming in droves to observe for themselves. In an excitable place and age, sensation spread rapidly. An elder sister, Ann Leah Fish of Rochester, quickly began managing regular public demonstrations of her sisters' mediumistic gifts. She took them home with her, and soon the "Rochester rappings," in a code whereby "actual communication" could be made with the spirits, were famous throughout the region.

In 1850 the three traveled to New York City to begin holding regular, and quite lucrative, seances. Prominent intellectual and literary figures took them seriously. Horace Greeley was persuaded of the authenticity of the sessions and in the *New York Tribune* enthusiastically endorsed the Fox sisters' activities. With their subsequent tours of the country, spiritualism became a fad and the subject of major controversy as well. Dozens of imitators, including Victoria Claflin Woodhull, began performing as mediums, and a great deal of cultist and pseudo-religious crusading sprang up. No body of more or less organized spiritualist thought or technique had previously existed, and modern spiritualism and mediumism dates from the time of the Fox sisters. Margaret attracted the attention of the explorer Elisha Kent Kane, who tried to persuade her to give up spiritualism and to seek an education; after his death in 1857 she claimed to have entered into a common-law marriage with him and in 1865 published his letters to her, possibly somewhat altered, as *The Love-Life of Dr. Kane*. After her conversion to Roman Catholicism in 1858 she seldom served as a spirit medium. For Kate a Society for the Diffusion of Spiritual Knowledge was established in 1855 to sponsor free public sittings. Her seances gradually came to feature not only rappings but music, materializations, spirit writing, and other manifestations.

By the mid-1860s the stress of publicity and performing, together with the cultist aspects of spiritualism that they never really comprehended, had driven both sisters to drink. In the 1870s the sisters traveled to England, where spiritualism attracted a considerable following. Kate married one Henry D. Jencken in December 1872 and thereafter used the name Fox-Jencken. She returned to the United States in 1885. Three years later her drunkenness led to her children being taken from her. Shortly thereafter Margaret appeared at the New York Academy of Music and confessed that the entire matter of spirit rapping had been a hoax. She and Kate had begun it, she said, as a prank on their superstitious mother and had contrived the sounds by various means but principally by movements of their toes. The ranks of confirmed spiritualists, by then legion, condemned her confession as a shabby lie, told probably for money and possibly under the influence of alcohol. Soon thereafter she retracted the confession and returned to spiritualism for her livelihood. Both sisters' last years were passed in poverty. Kate died in New York City on July 2, 1892; Margaret died in Brooklyn, New York, on March 8, 1893.

Frankenthaler, Helen 1928– artist

Born in New York City on December 12, 1928, Helen Frankenthaler was educated in private schools and at Bennington College, where she studied art and from which she graduated in 1949. She then settled in New York and began painting. Further study at the Art Students' League and under Hans Hoffman, together with the particular influence of Arshile Gorky, Jackson Pollock, and others of the burgeoning abstract expressionist school, formed her work. She developed her own approach to painting, however, imitative of none of her teachers. Viewers of her exhibits, first in a Bennington show in New York City in 1950 and the next year in a "New Talent Show" and the "Ninth Street Show," quickly detected in her work a daring, unprogrammatic willingness to treat each painting as a new task with its own peculiar problems and rewards. She also conveyed to the canvas a variety of emotional states and moods keyed to colors and to lyrical or dramatic composition. Her experiments in stains and other media and in "action painting" highlighted her openness to various modes and her determination to evolve a personal style.

Annual shows at the Tibor de Nagy Gallery and later at the Emmerich Gallery spread Frankenthaler's reputation, as did special shows in various cities in America and abroad, notably Paris (1961, 1963), Milan (1962), London (1964, 1969), Berlin (1969), and Montreal (1971). She was one of four U.S. painters represented at the Venice Biennale in 1966. She was represented regularly in major shows at the Whitney Museum, where she had a solo retrospective in 1969. She taught drawing and painting at various times at New York University, Hunter College, the University of Pennsylvania, Yale and Princeton, and she was the recipient of numerous awards and prizes for her paintings. Despite the trend in New York galleries in the 1980s of showing, almost exclusively, the work of new, young artists, Frankenthaler has continued to have one-woman shows regularly at the André Emmerich Gallery in New York and the Knoedler Gallery in London. The Guggenheim Museum exhibited her work in an individual show in 1985, and the Museum of Modern Art in New York launched a retrospective in 1989.

Frankland, Lady Agnes Surriage 1726–1783 colonial figure

Born in Marblehead, Massachusetts, in the early spring of 1726, Agnes Surriage went to work as a maid in a local tavern at an early age. A pretty and charming girl, barefoot and in tattered dress, she attracted the attention of Charles Henry Frankland, collector of the port of Boston and ten years her elder, who secured her parents' permission to take her to Boston and educate her. By 1746, when Frankland succeeded to the baronetcy of Thirsk in the North Riding of Yorkshire, Agnes had become his mistress, to the distress of Boston society. Sir Harry, as he was known, bought some 480 acres in Hopkinton, Massachusetts, built a mansion, and installed Agnes and his natural son by a previous liaison. In 1754 he traveled to England to settle a lawsuit concerning the estate and attempted unsuccessfully to have Surriage accepted by his family. They then set out on a European tour.

They were in Lisbon on the occasion of the terrible earthquake of November 1, 1755, and Sir Harry was caught out of doors and was buried in rubble. Agnes searched for and found him, whereupon, according to the legend handed down later, Sir Harry married her. (There are indications, however, that a marriage may have occurred some months earlier.) They returned to Boston in 1756, and Lady Frankland was easily taken into society, where her charm and kindliness made her a favorite. In 1758–1764 they lived in Lisbon, where Sir Harry was British consul general, and from 1764 until his death in 1768 they lived in Bath, England. Lady Frankland then returned to the Hopkinton estate and lived there until the Revolution, when she removed to England. She died in Chichester, England, on April 23, 1783. Her spectacular and romantic rise to riches from the lowliest beginnings long attracted the attention of novelists and poets from Oliver Wendell Holmes to Sir Arthur Quiller-Couch, who kept her story alive in a variety of published works.

Franklin, Aretha 1942– singer

Born on March 25, 1942, in Memphis, Tennessee, Aretha Franklin was one of the five children of Reverend Clarence L. Franklin and Barbara Siggers, who died when Franklin was 10 years old. By then she was teaching herself piano and singing gospel at local churches. While attending high school in Detroit, she toured as the featured singer with her father's evangelist group. Her first solo recordings with Chess Records were hymns she sang at her father's church.

In 1960, with the help of a friend of the family, jazz bass player Major Holley, Franklin moved to New York City to try pop music. She studied dancing and voice and hired a manager. In 1961 she signed a five-year contract with Columbia Records, recorded ten albums in six years, including *The Electrifying Aretha Franklin*, *Laughing on the Outside*, *Runnin' Out of Fools*, and *Unforgettable*, a tribute to her mentor Dinah Washington.

When she signed with Atlantic Records in 1966, she reframed her popular style to include gospel and blues, and her first single for that label, "I Never Loved a Man The Way I Loved You," soon sold a million copies. Her number-one hit single "Respect," 1967, topped both the rhythm-and-blues chart and the pop chart, and it was heralded at the time as an unofficial black national anthem.

With *Lady Soul*, 1968, Franklin acquired the moniker "Queen of Soul." That year she also recorded *Aretha Now* and *Aretha in Paris*, opened the Democratic national convention in Chicago with her version of "The Star Spangled Banner," and appeared on the cover of the June 21, 1968, issue of *Time* magazine. Between 1967 and 1969, she also won four Grammy awards.

During the 1970s Franklin recorded *Spanish Harlem*, 1971, *Amazing Grace*, 1972, *Young, Gifted and Black*, 1972, *Hey Now Hey*, 1973, and *Something He Can Feel*, 1976. In 1980 she signed with Arista, releasing *Aretha* in 1981. She appeared in the Universal film *The Blues Brothers* in 1980 and collaborated with rock artists George Michael and

Annie Lennox on the album *Who's Zoomin' Who?*, 1985. The feminist overtones of her earlier hit single, "Respect," were invoked anew in her collaboration with Lennox on "Sisters Are Doin' It for Themselves," which also incorporated an interracial theme. By the mid-1990s she had won a total of 10 Grammy awards and 21 gold records.

Freeman, Mary Eleanor Wilkins 1852–1930 writer

Born on October 31, 1852, in Randolph, Massachusetts, Mary Wilkins moved with her family to Brattleboro, Vermont, in 1867. She lived at home after studying for a year in 1870–1871 at Mount Holyoke Female Seminary (now Mount Holyoke College), read widely on her own, and began writing children's stories and verse. In 1883, by which time both her parents had died, she returned to Randolph to live with friends, and in that year she published in a Boston newspaper her first story for adults. She continued to publish in newspapers and magazines, becoming a regular and favorite contributor to *Harper's Bazaar* and *New Monthly*. Early collections of her stories included *A Humble Romance*, 1887, *A New England Nun*, 1891, *The Pot of Gold*, 1892, *Young Lucretia*, 1892, *Comfort Pease and Her Gold Ring*, 1895, *The People of our Neighborhood*, 1898, *Silence*, 1898, *The Jamesons*, 1899, *The Love of Parson Lord*, 1900, and *Understudies*, 1901.

Narrated in a firm and objective manner with occasional subtle undertones of humor or irony, Freeman's stories were deft character studies of somehow exceptional people who, trapped by poverty or other handicaps in sterile, restrictive circumstances, react in various ways against their situations. Her use of New England village and countryside settings and dialects placed her stories in the "local color" school, and her work thereby enjoyed an added vogue; nevertheless, she avoided the sentimentality then current in popular literature. Her novels, including *Jane Field*, 1893, *Pembroke*, 1894, *Madelon*, 1896, *Jerome, a Poor Man*, 1897, and *The Heart's Highway*, 1900, were generally of less interest than her stories, serving mainly to emphasize her mastery of the shorter form. In January 1902 she married Dr. Charles M. Freeman of Metuchen, New Jersey, where she lived for the rest of her life.

Later collections of her stories included *Six Trees*, 1903, *The Wind in the Rose Bush*, 1903, *The Givers*, 1904, *The Fair Lavinia*, 1907, *The Winning Lady*, 1909, *The Green Door*, 1910, *The Yates Pride*, 1912, *The Copy-Cat*, 1914, and *Edgewater People*, 1918. Other novels were *The Portion of Labor*, 1901, *The Debtor*, 1905, *"Doc" Gordon*, 1906, *By the Light of the Soul*, 1906, *The Shoulders of Atlas*, 1908, *The Butterfly House*, 1912, and *An Alabaster Box* (with F. M. Kingsley), 1917. She also wrote a play, *Giles Corey, Yeoman*, 1893. In 1926 she was awarded the Howells Medal of the American Academy of Arts and Letters. She died in Metuchen, New Jersey, on March 13, 1930.

Frémont, Jessie Ann Benton 1824–1902 writer

Born near Lexington, Virginia, on May 31, 1824, Jessie Benton was the daughter of Senator Thomas Hart Benton of Missouri. She grew up in Virginia, her mother's native state, in Washington, D.C., and in St. Louis. She was well educated, mainly privately, and was notably independent and spirited. In 1840 she met Lieutenant John C. Frémont, a young officer in the Topographical Corps, and in October 1841, against her father's strong opposition, they were secretly married. Senator Benton chose to make the best of it and began using his considerable influence to further Frémont's career as an explorer. At the conclusion of his first expedition to the Wind River country, during which time Jessie Frémont continued to serve as her father's hostess and occasionally translated secret Spanish documents for the State Department, Frémont benefited greatly from his wife's help in preparing his official report. As Frémont was preparing to leave on his second expedition in 1843, she intercepted and suppressed an order from Washington that she feared threatened his command. She urged him to leave at once and then wrote to authorities in Washington explaining what she had done. She was largely responsible for the literary quality of the 1844 report on his second expedition; it was printed as a Senate document in an edition of 10,000 copies and widely sold in a commercial edition as well. In 1849, following Frémont's third expedition, his controversial role in the conquest of California, and his court-martial, she sailed to San Francisco to join him.

They lived at a huge estate at Mariposa until 1850, when they moved to Washington, D.C., following Frémont's election to the Senate. After their return to California in 1851 they grew wealthy, and in 1855 they moved to New York City for a time. She took what little part custom allowed in her husband's presidential campaign in 1856, and afterward they returned to California. She was, as ever, her husband's most loyal partisan in his troubled Civil War service, first as commander of the Western Department in St. Louis and later in field command in Virginia. *The Story of the Guard: A Chronicle of the War*, 1863, reprinted her articles in the *Atlantic Monthly* defending him. After Frémont's bankruptcy in 1873 she took up writing with a will. Articles, memoirs, travel sketches, and stories of hers appeared in leading magazines. Many of them were collected in *A Year of American Travel*, 1878, *Souvenirs of My Time*, 1887, *Far-West Sketches*, 1890, and *The Will and the Way Stories*, 1891. She was also the principal author of her husband's *Memoirs of My Life*, 1887. They moved to Los Angeles in 1887, and she remained there after her husband's death until her own on December 27, 1902.

Friedan, Betty Naomi Goldstein 1921– writer and social reformer

Born on February 4, 1921, in Peoria, Illinois, Betty Goldstein graduated from Smith College with a degree in psychology in 1942 and after a year of graduate work at the University of California at Berkeley settled in New York City. She worked at various jobs until June 1947, when she married Carl Friedan. For ten years thereafter she lived as a housewife and mother in New York suburbs while doing freelance work for a number of magazines. In 1957 a questionnaire that she circulated among her Smith classmates suggested to her that a great many of them were, like her, deeply dissatisfied with their lives. She planned and undertook an extensive series of studies on the topic, formulating more detailed questionnaires, conducting interviews, discussing her results with psychologists and other students of behavior, and finally organized her findings, illuminated by her personal experiences, in book form as *The Feminine Mystique*, 1963.

The book was an immediate and controversial best seller and was translated into a number of foreign languages. Friedan's central thesis was that women as a class suffered a variety of more or less subtle forms of discrimination, but that they were in particular the victims of a pervasive system of delusions and false values under which they were urged to find personal fulfillment, even identity, vicariously through the husbands and children to whom they were supposed cheerfully to devote their lives. This restricted role of wife-mother, whose spurious glorification by advertisers and others was suggested by the title of the book, led almost inevitably to a sense of unreality or general spiritual malaise in the absence of genuine, creative, self-defining work. The growing public discussion that followed the publication of the book was bolstered by Friedan's lectures and radio and television appearances around the country.

In October 1966 Friedan founded the National Organization for Women (NOW), a civil-rights group dedicated to equality of opportunity for women. As president of NOW she directed campaigns for the ending of sex-classified employment notices, for greater representation of women in government, for child-care centers for working mothers, for legalized abortion, and other reforms. Although it was later occasionally eclipsed by younger and more radical groups, NOW remained the largest and probably the most effective organization in the women's movement. Friedan stepped down from the presidency in March 1970 but continued to be active in the work that had sprung largely from her pioneering efforts, helping to organize the Women's Strike for Equality, held on

August 26, 1970, the fiftieth anniversary of woman suffrage, and leading in the campaign for ratification of the proposed Equal Rights Amendment to the U.S. Constitution. A founding member of the National Women's Political Caucus (1971), she said it was organized "to make policy not coffee." In 1973 she became Director of the First Women's Bank and Trust Company.

In 1976 she published *It Changed My Life: Writings on the Women's Movement*, and in 1981 *The Second Stage*, in which she argued that the women's movement was being misrepresented by some feminists whose aim was to put down men, marriage and the family. Although some viewed the latter book as a softening, even a recantation, of her earlier views, Friedan dismissed criticisms from both the left and right, saying she was merely "dealing with the reality of today's evolving family." *The Fountain of Age*, 1993, dealt with the psychology of old age and urged society to rid itself of the view that aging is about loss and depletion.

Friedan received the Eleanor Roosevelt Leadership Award in 1989.

Friedman, Esther Pauline and Pauline Esther 1918– and 1918– syndicated columnists

The Friedman sisters, Esther Pauline (Ann Landers) and Pauline Esther (Abigail Van Buren), identical twins, were born on July 4, 1918, in Sioux City, Iowa. They both attended the city's Central High School and its Morningside College and were married in a double ceremony on the same day, July 2, 1939 — Esther to Jules W. Lederer and Pauline to Morton Phillips. For the next 16 years their ways parted: Esther Lederer lived for the most part in Chicago, sister Pauline Phillips in Minneapolis, Eau Claire, Wisconsin, and San Francisco. Both were active at various times in local Democratic politics and in the Red Cross Grey Ladies. In 1956 their lives and careers resumed parallel courses. In the fall of the previous year Lederer had entered a contest to find a successor to Ruth Crowley, who wrote an advice-to-the-lovelorn column for the *Chicago Sun-Times* under the pen name "Ann Landers." Lederer, although she was the only nonprofessional to enter the competition, won it, and her first column appeared in October 1955. Its success was rapid. Her commonsensical and sometimes astringent replies to questions from readers appealed to thousands and then millions of readers in the United States and abroad.

Although Phillips insisted that her sister's decision to write a column had no effect on her own course, she did submit in the late fall of 1955 some sample columns to the editor of the *San Francisco Chronicle*. He immediately dropped the paper's regular columnist and substituted Phillips, who chose the pen name "Abigail Van Buren." Her column first saw the light in January 1956. Like her sister's, it was soon enormously successful, and by the later 1960s the two were far and away the leaders in the field. Not surprisingly, their styles were very similar, and they both based their advice on traditional mores. Each was quick to consult professionals in law, medicine, psychology, and other fields when necessary. Abigail Van Buren published *Dear Abby*, 1958, *Dear Teen-Ager*, 1959, *Dear Abby on Marriage*, 1962, *The Best of Dear Abby*, 1981, and *Dear Abby on Planning Your Wedding*, 1988. Ann Landers's books included *Since You Ask Me*, 1961, *Ann Landers Talks to Teen-Agers About Sex*, 1964, and *Truth is Stranger*, 1968, and *The Ann Landers Encyclopedia, A to Z: Improve Your Life Emotionally, Medically, Sexually, Socially, Spiritually*, 1978.

Throughout their careers, both sisters also received many awards for public service. Lederer (aka Landers) served on the board of directors of the Dialogue for the Blind, the Rehabilitation Institute of Chicago and the American Cancer Society, while Phillips (Van Buren) served on the board of directors of the Lupus Foundation, the American Foundation for AIDS Research, and the American Federation for Aging Research.

Frietschie, Barbara Hauer 1766–1862 patriot

Born on December 3, 1766, in Lancaster, Pennsylvania, Barbara Hauer, daughter of German immigrant parents, grew up there and from about the age of ten in Frederick, Maryland. In May 1806 she married John C. Frietschie (later sometimes spelled Fritchie). Little else is known of the first 96 years of her life. In early September 1862 the Army of Northern Virginia paused in Frederick during General Robert E. Lee's invasion of Maryland. On marching out of town on September 10 the troops passed Frietschie's house, and she may have waved a small Union flag from the porch or a second-floor window. There may also have been some small incident as a result. Whatever the actual case, the story soon grew up in Frederick that Frietschie, who was known to be intensely patriotic, had somehow defied the Confederate army. The story's connection with fact was broken by Frietschie's death at her home on December 18, 1862.

The tale was heard by the novelist Emma D. E. N. Southworth, who passed it on to John Greenleaf Whittier. In October 1863 he published in the *Atlantic Monthly* his verse version, "Barbara Fritchie," in which the story was much elaborated. In the poem, the flag flying from her house was riddled by Confederate bullets at the order of General Thomas J. "Stonewall" Jackson. Fritchie then caught up the flag herself and waved it, crying "Shoot, if you must, this old gray head/But spare your country's flag." Jackson, deeply touched, then ordered his men to cease firing, warning "Who touches a hair of yon gray head/Dies like a dog! March on!" Whittier's version quickly became canonical, and the enduring popularity of the poem kept Frietschie's name alive. Despite its meager factual basis — the one thing known certainly of the events of that day is that Jackson did not pass her house — the endurance of the tale led to the erection of a memorial in 1913 and the building of a replica of her house (the original having been razed a few years after her death) in 1926.

Fuller, Loie 1862–1928 dancer

Born on January 15, 1862, in Fullersburg (now part of Hinsdale), Illinois, Marie Louise Fuller grew up there and in Chicago. She made her stage debut in Chicago at the age of four, and over the next quarter-century she toured with stock companies, burlesque shows, vaudeville, and Buffalo Bill's Wild West Show, gave temperance lectures and Shakespearean readings, and appeared in various legitimate productions in Chicago and New York City. She began to achieve notice in Nat Goodwin's burlesque *Little Jack Sheppard* in New York in 1886, and in 1887 she starred in Charles Frohman's production of *She*. In 1888 she attempted a Caribbean tour with her own company, but bankruptcy ended the attempt in Havana. She appeared in several plays in London in 1889–1890.

While rehearsing *Quack, M.D.* in 1891 Fuller hit upon the idea of using a voluminous skirt of transparent china silk, in which she twirled under a pale green light. The effect on the audience was remarkable. She began experimenting with varying lengths of silk and different colored lighting and gradually evolved her "Serpentine Dance," which she first presented in the revue *Uncle Celestin* in New York in February 1892. After a week her success was such as to make possible her own show at the Madison Square Theatre. Later in the year she traveled to Europe and in October opened at the Folies Bergère in her "Fire Dance," in which she danced on glass, illuminated from below. She quickly became the toast of avant-garde Paris. Toulouse-Lautrec, Rodin, and Jules Cheret used her as a subject, writers dedicated works to her, and daring society women sought her out. She lived and worked mainly in Europe thereafter. At the Paris Exposition Universelle in 1900 she appeared in her own theater. Her later experiments in stage lighting, a field in which her influence was deeper and more lasting than in choreography, included the use of phosphorescent materials and silhouette techniques.

In 1908 Fuller published a memoir, *Quinze Ans de Ma Vie*, to which Anatole France contributed an introduction; it was published in English translation as *Fifteen Years of a Dancer's Life* in 1913. During World War I she entertained Allied troops and engaged in relief work for which she was later decorated by several nations. After the war she danced infrequently, but from her school in Paris she sent out touring dance companies to all parts of Europe; such groups continued to tour for a decade after her death. In 1923 she staged the inferno scene for a Paris Opéra production of Berlioz's *Damnation de Faust*. In 1926 she last visited the United States, in company with her friend, Queen Marie of Rumania. Her final stage appearance was her "Shadow Ballet" in London in 1927. She died in Paris on January 1, 1928.

Fuller, Margaret 1810–1850 writer, critic and social reformer

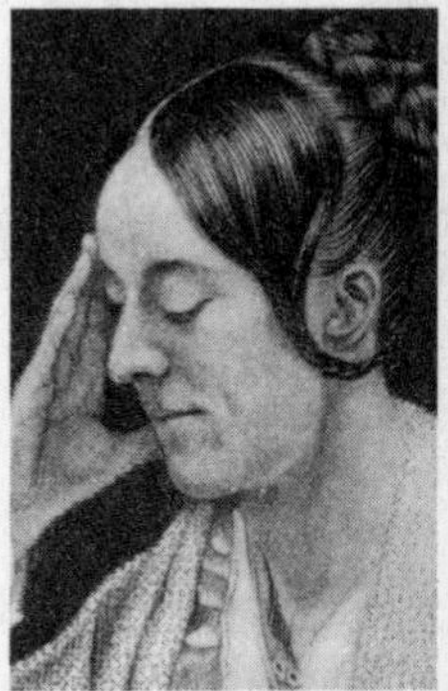

Margaret Fuller

Born in Cambridgeport (now part of Cambridge), Massachusetts, on May 23, 1810, Sarah Margaret Fuller was an extremely precocious child. Under the severe tutelage of her father she more than compensated for the inaccessibility of formal education to females of the time, but while she acquired wide learning at a very early age, the strain permanently impaired her health. She taught school for a number, of years — for one, 1836–1837, at Bronson Alcott's Temple School in Boston — and wrote occasional critical essays for the *Western Messenger*. Important friendships formed in this period included those with Ralph Waldo Emerson, William Ellery Channing, Elizabeth Peabody, Theodore Parker, and Orestes Brownson. In 1839, settling in the then-suburban Jamaica Plain, she began a series of public "conversations" in Boston intended to further the education of women. A brilliant conversationalist, she enjoyed great success, and the series was repeated yearly until 1844. In 1840, as a result of her close association with Emerson and the Concord circle, she became editor of the Transcendentalist magazine, the *Dial*, to which she contributed a considerable number of essays, reviews, and poems. She gave up the editorship in 1842.

Fuller's first book, on a western tour with James Freeman Clarke and his sister, was *Summer on the Lakes, in 1843*, 1844. In 1844 Horace Greeley invited her to become the literary critic for the *New York Tribune*, and during the next two years she established herself as the leading American critic of the time. In 1845 she published her pioneering and classic feminist work, *Woman in the Nineteenth Century*. The following year a collection of her essays was published as *Papers on Literature and Art*. Shortly thereafter she sailed for Europe, where, her reputation having preceded her, she met and mingled with the leading literary figures. Her letters to the *Tribune*, written by the first American woman to work as a foreign correspondent, were later collected in *At Home and Abroad*, 1856.

In Rome in 1847 Fuller met the Marchese Angelo Ossoli, an impoverished Italian nobleman and ardent republican. They became lovers and were married, secretly, apparently in 1849. They both became deeply involved in the revolution of 1848–1849 in Italy, led by Giuseppe Mazzini, whom she had met earlier in England. When the revolutionary Roman republic was crushed in July 1849 they fled to Rieti and thence to Florence, and there she wrote a history of the episode. In May 1850 she sailed with her husband and their child for the United States. On July 19 the ship was wrecked off Fire Island, New York, and all aboard perished. Her memoirs, edited by Emerson, Clarke, and W. H. Channing, were published in 1852, and in 1859 another collection of her essays appeared as *Life Without and Life Within*. Most of her writings have not withstood the passage of time, but she is nonetheless remembered for her sheer brilliance, her determination to win her place, and not least for her vivid if demanding personality and the friendships she worked tirelessly to make fruitful.

Fuller, Sarah 1836–1927 educator

Born on February 15, 1836, in Weston, Massachusetts, Sarah Fuller grew up in nearby Newton Lower Falls. After graduating from the Allan English and Classical School in

West Newton she became a schoolteacher. From 1855 to 1869 she taught in Newton and then in Boston. In 1869 she studied for three months under Harriet B. Rogers at the Clarke School for the Deaf in Northampton, Massachusetts, in order to prepare for her new post of principal of the Boston School for Deaf-Mutes, which opened with ten pupils in November of that year. It was the first such institution in the country to be operated on a day-school basis, and in the first five years of her principalship the enrollment increased sixfold. In 1870 she learned of Alexander Melville Bell's system of "Visible Speech" for teaching the deaf, and it was at her invitation that his son, Alexander Graham Bell, came to the United States the next year to teach the system to the school's faculty.

Fuller was an early and powerful advocate of teaching deaf children to speak rather than to sign, and she also believed in beginning such instruction at an early age. In both stands she went against the prevailing opinion of her organized colleagues. Her *An Illustrated Primer*, 1888, was aimed at teachers. In that year Mr. and Mrs. Francis Brooks, parents of a deaf daughter, endowed the Sarah Fuller Home for Little Children Who Cannot Hear to promote her methods among children of nursery school age. (The home lasted until 1925; the endowment later became the Sarah Fuller Foundation for Little Deaf Children of the Boston Children's Medical Center.) In 1890, with Alexander Graham Bell, Caroline A. Yale, and others, she helped found the progressive American Association to Promote the Teaching of Speech to the Deaf, of which she was a director from 1896. In the same year, 1890, she had briefly for a pupil the ten-year-old Helen Keller. In 1910 she retired as principal of her school, which had been known since 1877 as the Horace Mann School for the Deaf. She died in Newton Lower Falls, Massachusetts, on August 1, 1927.

Fulton, Mary Hannah 1854–1927 physician and missionary

Born on May 31, 1854, probably in Ashland, Ohio, Mary Fulton was educated at Lawrence University in Appleton, Wisconsin, and at Hillsdale College, Michigan. She graduated from the latter in 1874, took a master's degree in 1877, and for three years taught in public schools in Indianapolis. In 1880 she entered the Woman's Medical College of Pennsylvania, and on graduating in 1884 she set out for south China, where her elder brother, a minister, had preceded her. Under the auspices of the Presbyterian Board of Foreign Missions she began her medical practice in Canton. From September 1885 to the spring of 1886 she practiced in Kwai Ping, Kwangsi Province, but intense antiforeign agitation forced her and her brother to abandon that mission and return to Canton. She established two dispensaries there in 1887. While conducting her practice amid tens of thousands needing her services, she taught pediatrics at Canton Hospital, where she also directed the care of women patients. Fund-raising tours of the United States in 1891–1893 and 1903–1904 helped build in 1900 and support thereafter a church for her brother, in which she took space for a dispensary, and then in 1902 the David Gregg Hospital for Women and Children. The hospital included a training school for nurses.

Later in 1902 the Hackett Medical College for Women opened, providing a three- (shortly afterward four-) year course for Cantonese-speaking Christian women. Fulton directed these institutions and carried on her own medical practice until ill health forced her to seek less strenuous work in the more moderate climate of Shanghai in 1915. By that year the Hackett Medical College had graduated more than 60 physicians. In Shanghai she made translations into Cantonese of numerous English textbooks on medicine and nursing. She also raised funds to build the Cantonese Union Church of Shanghai to house the congregation she had organized. In 1918 she returned to the United States and settled in Pasadena, California. In her late years she wrote *"Inasmuch": Extracts from Letters, Journals, Papers, etc.*, a memoir of her work that also included a strong plea for continued support of missionary work in China. She died in Pasadena on January 7, 1927.

Furbish, Catharine 1834–1931 botanist

Born in Exeter, New Hampshire, on May 19, 1834, Kate Furbish grew up in Brunswick, Maine, and attended local schools there. From an early age she was deeply interested in the natural flora of her region. Attendance at a series of lectures on botany in Boston about 1860, together with a course in drawing in Portland, Maine, prepared her for her life's work. In 1870 she set herself the task of collecting, classifying, and making watercolor drawings of the flora of Maine. Her inheritance from her merchant and manufacturer father enabled her to devote her life to the work. With boundless energy and courage she traveled the state for 38 years, penetrating the most inaccessible wilderness areas in search of new specimens. Her paintings were extremely accurate and were widely praised by professional botanists.

In 1895 Furbish founded the Josselyn Botanical Society of Maine, of which she served as president in 1911–1912. She contributed a number of articles to botanical journals. In 1908 she gave her 16 folio volumes of watercolors, her "Illustrated Flora," to Bowdoin College. Her large collection of dried plants went to the New England Botanical Club, which placed it in the Gray Herbarium at Harvard, and her collection of ferns went to the Portland Society of Natural History. Two of her botanical discoveries were named for her: *Aster cordifolius* L., var. *furbishiae*; and *Pedicularis furbishiae*, the Furbish lousewort, an unassuming but unique species that became the center of a public controversy in 1976 when the proposed Dickey-Lincoln dam on the upper St. John River in Maine threatened the plant's only habitat. Kate Furbish continued her chosen work until her death in Brunswick, Maine, on December 6, 1931.

Gág, Wanda Hazel 1893–1946 artist and author of children's books

Born on March 11, 1893, in New Ulm, Minnesota, Wanda Gág was the daughter of a Bohemian immigrant artist. Through high school she helped support her family by contributing drawings to a juvenile supplement to the *Minneapolis Journal*. After graduating from high school in 1912 she taught a year in a one-room country school and saved money to support her family through the next year while she attended the St. Paul Art School on a scholarship. Later she attended school at night while working as a commercial artist by day. During 1915–1917 she attended the Minneapolis School of Art with aid from the *Minneapolis Journal*. In 1917 she traveled to New York City and entered the Art Students' League, where she studied under John Sloan and other noted teachers. From 1918 she made a precarious living from various forms of commercial art, but in 1923 she cut those ties and moved to an abandoned farm in Connecticut to concentrate on developing her own style and aesthetic. From 1924 to 1930 she lived in similar fashion near Glen Gardner, New Jersey.

A show of Gág's drawings, lithographs, and woodcuts at the Weyhe Gallery in New York City in 1926 brought her first recognition as a serious artist, and subsequent shows there in 1928, 1930, and 1940 increased her reputation. Her works were purchased by many leading museums in America and abroad, and she was represented in the Museum of Modern Art's 1939 exhibition of "Art in Our Time." At the suggestion of a children's book editor she wrote and illustrated *Millions of Cats*, 1928, which eventually became a classic children's book. Royalties permitted her to buy a farm in the Muscanetcong Mountains of New Jersey that she named "All Creation." Subsequent books for children included *The Funny Thing*, 1929, *Snippy and Snappy*, 1931, *A.B.C. Bunny*, 1933, *Gone Is Gone*, 1935, and *Nothing at All*, 1941. She also translated and illustrated *Tales from Grimm*, 1936, *Snow White and the Seven Dwarfs*, 1938, *Three Gay Tales from Grimm*, 1943, and *More Tales from Grimm*, 1947. *Growing Pains: Diaries and Drawings for the Years 1908–1917*, 1940, was a memoir based on her journals. Wanda Gág died in New York City on June 27, 1946.

Gage, Matilda Joslyn 1826–1898 feminist

Born in Cicero, New York, on March 25, 1826, Matilda Joslyn received an advanced education from her father and completed her formal schooling at the Clinton Liberal Institute in Clinton, New York. In January 1845 she married Henry H. Gage, a merchant, with whom she settled in Fayetteville, New York. Domestic duties largely filled the next several years, but in September 1852 she attended the National Woman's Rights Convention in Syracuse, New York, and made her first public address, a task she found exceedingly difficult. Her youth and stylish dress attracted notice, however, and helped offset the conventional notion of feminists. From its founding in 1869 she was a member of Elizabeth Cady Stanton's National Woman Suffrage Association and a contributor to its newspaper, the *Revolution*. In the same year she helped found and became vice-president and secretary of the New York State Woman Suffrage Association.

Never comfortable on the platform, Gage was an effective advocate with her pen. Her writings included the pamphlets *Woman as Inventor*, 1870, *Woman's Rights Catechism*, 1871, *Who Planned the Tennessee Campaign of 1862? Or Anna Ella Carroll vs. Ulysses S. Grant*, 1880, and *The Dangers of the Hour*, 1890. In 1875 she was elected president of both the state and national suffrage organizations, but she relinquished the national post to Stanton in 1876; she retained the state presidency until 1879. With Stanton and Susan B. Anthony she drafted a "Declaration of Rights" for women that was presented at the Fourth of July observance at the Philadelphia Centennial Exposition in 1876. During 1878–1881 she edited the monthly *National Citizen and Ballot Box* published by the National Woman Suffrage Association. She was a coauthor with Stanton and Anthony of the first three volumes of the *History of Woman Suffrage*, 1881–1886. In 1880 she lobbied the national conventions of the Republican, Democratic, and Greenback-Labor parties in an unsuccessful attempt to have them include woman suffrage in their platforms.

In 1890, after several years of growing friction within the National Woman Suffrage Association, Gage broke away to found the Woman's National Liberal Union, of which she was thereafter president. The Union was more radical than the older suffrage groups, and it reflected in particular her belief that the established churches were a major bulwark of male supremacist teaching, a view she expanded on in her book *Woman, Church, and State*, 1893. In her later years her public involvement in the suffrage movement gave way to declining health. She wrote but could not deliver an address to the fiftieth anniversary convention of the women's rights movement in Washington, D.C., in February 1898. She died in Chicago on March 18, 1898.

Gale, Zona 1874–1938 writer

Born on August 26, 1874, in Portage, Wisconsin, Zona Gale determined at an early age to be a writer. She attended public schools, graduated from the University of Wisconsin in 1895, and for six years was a newspaper reporter for the *Evening Wisconsin* and then the *Milwaukee Journal*, during which time she received her master's degree in literature from Wisconsin in 1899. In 1901 she moved to New York City and joined the staff of the *Evening World*. For years she spent her free time writing unpublishable romantic stories, poems, and even a novel.

In 1903 Gale became a freelance writer and sold her first story to *Success* magazine. In 1905 she began publishing a series of local-color stories set in "Friendship Village," based on her home town. Her first book, *Romance Island*, a novel, appeared in 1906, and it was followed by *The Loves of Pelleas and Etarre*, a collection of stories, 1907, *Friendship Village*, a collection, 1908, *Friendship Village Love Stories*, 1909, *Mothers to Men*, a novel set in Friendship Village, 1911, *Christmas*, a novel, 1912, *When I Was a Little Girl*, an autobiographical work, 1913, *Neighborhood Stories*, from Friendship Village, 1914, and *Peace in Friendship Village*, 1919. A prize from *Delineator* magazine in 1911 for an uncharacteristically realistic and unsentimental story enabled her to return to Portage to live, but it also marked the beginning of a slow growth in her writing toward maturity. *Heart's Kindred*, 1915, was a weak novel propagandizing against war. The suspicion aroused during World War I by her pacifism and her involvement in such organizations as the Women's Trade Union League and the American Civic Association forced her to reassess the meaning of small-town life in the Middle West. *A Daughter of the Morning*, 1917, dealt with working conditions of women, and *Birth*, 1918, depicted an entirely different side of Portage, here called "Burage." *Miss Lulu Bett*, 1920, a short novel, was a village comedy, and a dramatized version of it that opened on Broadway in December 1920 won the Pulitzer Prize for drama in 1921.

Subsequent books, in which Gale displayed a new, impressionistic style and later a leaning toward mysticism, included *The Secret Way*, a collection of poems, 1921, *Faint Perfume*, a novel, 1923, *Preface to a Life*, a novel, 1926, *Yellow Gentians and Blue*, stories, 1927, *Portage, Wisconsin and Other Essays*, 1928, *Borgia*, a novel, 1929, *Bridal Pond*, stories, 1930, *Old-Fashioned Tales*, 1933, *Papa La Fleur*, a novel, 1933, *Frank Miller of Mission Inn*, a biography, 1938, and *Magna*, a novel published posthumously in 1939. She also wrote several plays, including *Mister Pitt*, 1924, based on *Birth*. She was active in politics as an ardent supporter of the Progressivism of Senator Robert M. La Follette. She was an outspoken supporter of woman suffrage, prohibition, abolition of capital punishment, Sacco and Vanzetti, and other liberal causes of the day. She sat on the board of regents of the University of Wisconsin in 1923–1929. Zona Gale died in Chicago on December 27, 1938.

Galli-Curci, Amelita 1882–1963 opera singer

Born in Milan, Italy, on November 18, 1882, Amelita Galli studied piano and composition at the Royal Conservatory of Milan, from which she graduated in 1903. As a singer she was entirely self-taught. She made her operatic debut as Gilda in *Rigoletto* in the provincial city of Trani in 1909 and later in the year appeared in Rome in *Don Procopio*. Over the next several years she toured Europe and South America with various opera companies. In February 1910 she married Luigi Curci, Marchese of Simeri, and she used the name Galli-Curci thereafter. Her American debut occurred in Chicago in November 1916, when she sang *Rigoletto* at the Auditorium Theatre to great acclaim. She remained with the Chicago Opera Association until 1921, during that time making her New York debut in *Dinorah* at the Lexington Theatre in January 1918. In November 1920 she first appeared at the Metropolitan Opera of New York in *La Traviata*. Having divorced her first husband, she married her accompanist, Homer Samuels, in January 1921, becoming an American citizen thereby.

From 1921 to 1930 Galli-Curci sang regularly with the Met. Among her best roles were those in *Madama Butterfly*, *Der Rosenkavalier*, *Lakmé*, *Roméo et Juliette*, *Lucia di Lammermoor*, and *I Puritani*. Her florid coloratura soprano was of unsurpassed beauty, and she was a popular recording artist; her "Caro nome" from *Rigoletto*, recorded about 1919, was ever afterward considered one of the greatest operatic recordings ever made. Her last performance at the Met was in *Il Barbiere di Siviglia* in January 1930. For several years thereafter she maintained a heavy schedule of concert appearances. A goiter required her to undergo a throat operation in 1936, and her return to the stage in a Chicago Civic Opera production of *La Bohème* in November won a great ovation. She retired the next year. She died in La Jolla, California, on November 26, 1963.

Garbo, Greta 1905–1990 actor

Born in Stockholm, Sweden, on September 18, 1905, Greta Lovisa Gustafsson grew up in modest circumstances and on leaving school at fourteen held various jobs. While working as a department store clerk she met Erik Petschler, a motion picture director who gave her a small part in *Peter the Tramp* in 1922. From 1922 to 1924 she studied in the Royal Dramatic Theatre School in Stockholm, and in 1924 she played a major role in *The Story of Gösta Berling*. The film's director, Mauritz Stiller, gave her the name Garbo and secured for her a contract with Metro-Goldwyn-Mayer in Hollywood in 1925. She remained with MGM for 16 years and made 24 films, beginning with *The Torrent*, 1926; later silent films, including *Flesh and the Devil*, 1927, *Love*, 1927, *Wild Orchids*, 1929, and *The Kiss*, 1929, quickly established her as a star who captivated audiences with her subtle and mysterious allure. Unlike many stars of the silent movies — and unlike her favorite leading man, John Gilbert — she more than successfully made the transition to sound film with *Anna Christie*, 1930, in which her first spoken words on the screen revealed a low, husky voice to match her beauty. (The promotional campaign for the film had relied heavily on the simple declarative "Garbo talks!").

Subsequent movies, among them *Romance*, 1930, *Susan Lennox — Her Fall and Rise*, 1931, *Inspiration*, 1931, *Mata Hari*, 1932, *Grand Hotel*, 1932, *As You Desire Me*, 1932, *Queen Christina*, 1933, *The Painted Veil*, 1934, *Anna Karenina*, 1935, *Camille*, 1936, and *Conquest*, 1937, won Garbo a following that was almost a cult, and in *Ninotchka*, 1939, she displayed an unexpected gift for comedy. Her last film, *Two-Faced Woman*, 1941, was less successful. Garbo retired after its release and became a near-recluse, living mostly in New York City, traveling often under an assumed name, and refusing interviews or publicity of any kind. She became a U.S. citizen in 1951. She won the New York Film Critics' Award for Best Actress for *Anna Karenina* in 1935, and for *Camille* in 1936. In 1955 she received an Academy Award for her "series of luminous and unforgettable performances." Her insistence on complete privacy recalled a famous line from one of her films, usually quoted, not quite accurately, as "I want to be alone," and helped make her literally a legend in her own time. Her films, frequently revived, became classics, and she remained for many the epitome of unfathomable glamour. She died in New York City on April 15, 1990.

Garden, Mary 1874–1967 opera singer

Born on February 20, 1874, in Aberdeen, Scotland, Mary Garden came to the United States with her parents when she was seven and lived in Chicopee, Massachusetts, and Hartford, Connecticut, before settling in Chicago. She early began studying violin and piano and receiving voice lessons, and in 1897 she traveled to Paris to continue her voice training. A soprano, she made her public debut in April 1900 in Gustave Charpentier's *Louise* at the Opéra-Comique when, as understudy, she filled in for the stricken regular soprano. She was an immediate success and subsequently sang in *La Traviata* and other operas. In 1902 she was chosen by Claude Debussy to sing the female lead in the premiere of his *Pelléas et Mélisande* at the Opéra-Comique in April, and her interpretation of that role remained her most famous.

Others among Garden's major roles were those in *Le Jongleur de Notre-Dame*, after Jules Massenet had rewritten the tenor part for her; in Massenet's *Thaïs*, in which she made her American debut at the Manhattan Opera House in November 1907; in Richard Strauss's *Salomé*, in which she created a sensation; in Février's *Monna Vanna*; and in Montemezzi's *L'Amore dei Tre Re*. Acclaimed not only for her brilliant and highly individual singing but also for her remarkable dramatic ability in appearances throughout Europe and in London and New York City, she joined the Chicago Civic Opera in 1910 and starred with it until 1931, serving also as general director of the Chicago Opera Association in 1921–1922. She retired from the operatic stage in 1931 but remained active for 20 years more in musical circles, making numerous national lecture and recital tours and serving as an audition judge for the National Arts Foundation. Her autobiography, *Mary Garden's Story*, written with Louis Biancolli, appeared in 1951. Garden died in Aberdeen, Scotland, on January 3, 1967.

Gardener, Helen Hamilton 1853–1925 writer, reformer and public official

Born on January 21, 1853, in Winchester, Virginia, Alice Chenoweth grew up from 1855 in Greencastle, Indiana. She attended high school in Cincinnati and graduated from the Cincinnati Normal School in 1873. After two years as a schoolteacher she married Charles S. Smart in 1875 and moved with him to New York City in 1880. There she contributed to newspapers, studied biology at Columbia University, lectured on sociology at the Brooklyn Institute of Arts and Sciences, and came under the influence of the famous freethinker, Colonel Robert G. Ingersoll. She gave a series of lectures on freethinking in 1884 and published them in 1885 as *Men, Women, and Gods, and Other Lectures*, which she signed Helen Hamilton Gardener, a name she subsequently used privately as well. She came to wide attention among feminists in 1888 with her carefully researched refutation of a widely publicized claim by a leading neurologist that female brains were inherently and measurably inferior to male brains.

In 1890 Gardner published *Is This Your Son, My Lord?*, a novel whose outspoken and lurid attack on the double standard gave it a wide sale. She followed it with *A Thoughtless Yes*, a collection of stories, 1890, *Pray You, Sir, Whose Daughter?*, 1892, *Pushed By Unseen Hands*, stories, 1892, and *An Unofficial Patriot*, 1894, a fictionalized biography of her father that was later successfully dramatized by James A. Herne as *Griffith Davenport, Circuit Rider*. Many of her articles on social questions, which appeared in numerous magazines, were collected in *Facts and Fictions of Life*, 1893. In 1897 she was briefly coeditor of the *Arena* magazine. After her husband's death in 1901 and her second marriage in 1902 she spent five years in world travel before settling in Washington, D.C. There she gradually began using her wide social and political contacts to further the cause of woman suffrage.

In 1913 Gardner was appointed to reorganize the Congressional Committee of the National American Woman Suffrage Association, lately gutted by mass resignations of radical suffragists and followers of Alice Paul. In 1917 she was elected a vice-president of the association. Her contacts, notably with President Woodrow Wilson and Speaker of the House Champ Clark, along with her wit and tact, made her a central figure in the practical business of maneuvering the federal suffrage amendment through a maze of obstacles. Known as the association's "diplomatic corps," she became vice-chairman of the Congressional Committee in 1919. In April 1920 she was appointed by Wilson to the U.S. Civil Service Commission, the highest federal position occupied by a woman to that time. She served effectively until her death in Washington, D.C., on July 26, 1925.

Gardner, Helen 1878–1946 art historian and educator

Born on March 17, 1878, in Manchester, New Hampshire, Helen Gardner grew up there and, from about 1891, in Chicago. She graduated from the University of Chicago with a degree in Latin and Greek in 1901 and became a teacher at the Brooks Classical School; from 1905 to 1910 she was assistant principal of the school. In 1915 she enrolled in the graduate school of the University of Chicago to study art history. She received a master's degree in 1917, held a fellowship in the art history department in 1917–1918, and continued to take courses in the field until 1922. About 1919 she was named to head the photograph and lantern slide department of the Ryerson Library of the Art Institute of Chicago. In 1920 she began lecturing on art at the Institute, and in 1922 she resigned her library post to devote full time to teaching and to developing an art history curriculum at the Institute school.

The lack of a broad, comprehensive, single-volume textbook on art history prompted Gardner to write one herself, and the resulting *Art Through the Ages*, 1926, was very well received by other teachers and by the public. In readability, breadth of coverage, and wealth of illustration, her book far surpassed other available works, and it remained a widely used text for decades. In 1932 she published *Understanding the Arts*, aimed at a wide general audience. She had been named an assistant professor in the Art Institute school in 1929, and in 1933 she became professor and head of the department of art history. A second edition of *Art Through the Ages*, greatly expanded, appeared in 1936; between them the first two editions sold over 260,000 copies. Gardner retired from the Art Institute school in 1943. Despite declining health she managed to complete work on the manuscript of a third edition of *Art Through the Ages* (published in 1948) before her death in Chicago on June 4, 1946.

Gardner, Isabella Stewart 1840–1924 socialite and art collector

Born in New York City on April 14, 1840, Isabella Stewart was the daughter of a wealthy businessman. She was educated privately and in a Paris finishing school. In April 1860 she married John L. Gardner, a businessman who belonged to a prominent and long established Boston family, and went to live in his city, which she adopted as her own. Boston's Brahmin society failed to reciprocate. Her household was a quiet one until the 1870s, when, after a bout of illness and despondency and an exhilarating European convalescence, she began arranging social affairs that soon dazzled and occasionally titillated conservative Boston. A brilliant and unconventional woman, she attracted and was attracted by musicians, artists, actors, and interesting people of all kinds, and she came close to scandalizing Boston society by attending boxing exhibitions by John L. Sullivan and Gentleman Jim Corbett. In music she became known as a patroness of the

Boston Symphony and of countless students, for whom she once arranged a private recital by Ignace Paderewski. She also developed a deep interest in art.

Advised by her protégé and close friend Bernard Berenson, Gardner began collecting paintings and objets d'art and with her husband made numerous trips to Europe and the Orient to add to her collection. After her husband's death in 1898 she continued her interest in art, eventually assembling one of the world's finest collections of Renaissance and Dutch masterpieces, interspersed with sculpture, Oriental art, and major works by such contemporaries as John Singer Sargent and James A. M. Whistler. In 1899 she began to build on Fenway Court a gallery in the form of a 15th-century Italian villa. She took an active part in designing and even in the actual construction of the building, arranged her art collection along with personal memorabilia in it, and opened it to the public in January 1903. It was a fitting monument to one who was acknowledged to be one of the most remarkable women of her time. Gardner died in Boston on July 17, 1924. By her will the Isabella Stewart Gardner Museum was given to Boston as a public institution with the proviso that the collection be maintained precisely as she had arranged it — nothing was to be added, removed, or rearranged. As a monument to personal taste the museum and its collection remain unique.

Garland, Judy 1922–1969 actor and singer

Born on June 10, 1922, in Grand Rapids, Minnesota, Frances Gumm was the daughter of former vaudevillians with whom she later moved to Los Angeles. She began appearing on the vaudeville and variety stage at a very early age and for a few years toured with her two older sisters in a singing act, the Gumm Sisters. She had already adopted, at George Jessel's suggestion, the name Judy Garland when in 1935 she was signed for motion pictures by Metro-Goldwyn-Mayer. Her first film appearance was in a short, *Every Sunday*, 1936. She followed with such movies as *Pigskin Parade*, 1936, *Listen, Darling*, 1937, and *Broadway Melody of 1938*, 1937, in which she sang "Dear Mr. Gable" (usually known as "You Made Me Love You"), and began her climb to stardom. Her popular partnership with Mickey Rooney began in *Thoroughbreds Don't Cry*, 1937, and continued through *Love Finds Andy Hardy*, 1938, *Babes in Arms*, 1939, *Babes on Broadway*, 1941, and *Girl Crazy*, 1943, in which she sang "I Got Rhythm" and "Embraceable You."

In 1939 Garland made a classic and perennially popular film version of *The Wizard of Oz*, in which she sang what became her lifelong theme, "Somewhere Over the Rainbow;" she won a special Academy Award for her performance. Among her later movies of note were *Strike Up the Band*, 1940, *For Me and My Gal*, 1942, *Presenting Lily Mars*, 1943, *Meet Me in St. Louis*, (which featured the "Trolley Song"), 1944, *The Harvey Girls* ("The Atchison, Topeka, and Santa Fe"), 1946, *Till the Clouds Roll By* ("Look for the Silver Lining"), 1946, *The Pirate*, 1948, *Easter Parade* (with Irving Berlin's title song), 1948, *Words and Music* ("Johnny One Note"), 1948, *In the Good Old Summertime*, 1949, and *Summer Stock* ("Get Happy"), 1950.

Stardom proved a heavy burden, and Garland began experiencing personal and health problems that led to the termination of her MGM contract in 1950. She toured with great success as a singer, both in the United States and in Europe, attracting devoted fans in droves and establishing a following that occasionally assumed the dimensions of a cult. In 1954 she returned to the screen in *A Star Is Born*. She continued to make concert appearances through the late 1950s and early 1960s despite bouts with illness, overweight, and drugs. During one of her emergent periods she played a supporting dramatic role in *Judgment at Nuremberg*, 1962, that brought her an Academy Award nomination. She also appeared in *I Could Go On Singing*, 1962, and *A Child Is Waiting*, 1963. A short-lived television variety program and personal appearances in London, New York City, and elsewhere marked her last years. Judy Garland, one of the most popular entertainers of her day and the idol of millions around the world, died in London on June 22, 1969. Her daughter, Liza Minnelli (1946–), later became a film and musical-comedy star in her own right.

Garrett, Mary Elizabeth 1854–1915 philanthropist

Born in Baltimore on March 5, 1854, Mary Garrett was the daughter of a wealthy businessman. Her own education extended through secondary school, but she early acquired an interest in higher education for women. One of her closest friends from youth was Martha Carey Thomas, whom in 1885 she joined in establishing the Bryn Mawr School for Girls in Baltimore, a secondary school of remarkably high academic standards. As in most of her involvements, Mary Garrett's support was heavily financial. In 1889 she headed the Baltimore committee of Carey Thomas's campaign to raise a $100,000 gift to the Johns Hopkins University medical school to induce it to admit women students; she herself contributed nearly half that sum. When the trustees of the school delayed its opening until a much larger sum of money was on hand, she offered a further $306,977 on certain conditions, accepted after three months of negotiation, including that the medical school forever remain a graduate school.

In 1893 Garrett made a financial offer to the trustees of Bryn Mawr College to help persuade them to award the vacant presidency to Carey Thomas. After her friend's installation as president she spent some $50,000 in improvements to the presidential residence. She also made up the college's annual deficits on several occasions, and her gifts to Bryn Mawr eventually totaled nearly $350,000. She became a director of the college in 1906. She influenced the National American Woman Suffrage Association to hold its 1906 convention in Baltimore and provided lavish hospitality for the delegates, especially for the aging and unwell Susan B. Anthony. She accepted the chairmanship of a committee appointed to raise funds for a permanent endowment for the association. In that same year she made another and far from inconsequential gift to Johns Hopkins in commissioning John Singer Sargent to paint a group portrait of "The Four Doctors," William H. Welch, William Osler, William S. Halsted, and Howard A. Kelly. Sargent had earlier painted her portrait at the request of the university trustees. After several years of ill health she died in Bryn Mawr, Pennsylvania, on April 3, 1915; she left the bulk of her estate to Carey Thomas.

Garrett, Mary Smith and Emma 1839–1925 and 1846?–1893 educators

Born in Philadelphia, Mary on June 20, 1839, and Emma apparently in 1846, the Garrett sisters led obscure early lives. Emma graduated from Alexander Graham Bell's course for teachers of the deaf at the Boston University School of Oratory in 1878 and became a teacher of speech at the Pennsylvania Institution for the Deaf and Dumb in Mount Airy, Pennsylvania, that year. An advocate of the teaching of vocal speech rather than sign language to deaf students, she was given charge of the newly established Oral Branch of the institution in 1881, and in the same year she began teaching summer courses in vocal instruction for other teachers. Mary also became a teacher at the institution. In 1884, at the invitation of civic leaders in Scranton, Pennsylvania, Emma removed to that city to become principal of a day school that shortly afterward was named the Pennsylvania Oral School for Deaf-Mutes. In 1885 Mary left Mount Airy to open a private school for the teaching of speech to deaf children in Philadelphia.

Emma's school, which became a state institution in 1885, grew rapidly through her strenuous fund-raising activities. In 1889 Mary joined her in Scranton as a teacher. Their observations of children of various ages soon convinced them that deaf children could master speech far more easily if they were exposed to and trained in it from a very early age. By pamphlet and personal appeal Emma Garrett secured an appropriation from the Pennsylvania legislature and a gift of land from a Philadelphia philanthropist, and in February 1892, having left the Scranton school, the Garrett sisters opened the Pennsylvania Home for the Training in Speech of Deaf Children Before They Are of School Age, more simply known as the Bala Home for its nearness to that Philadelphia suburb. With Emma as superintendent and Mary as secretary the school opened with 15 students. Students were admitted as young as two and underwent a six-year residential course of study. The state took over support of the school in 1893. In that year they took their students to Chicago to give demonstrations of their methods and success at the World's Columbian Exposition. While there Emma Garrett's mental health broke, and on July 18, 1893, she took her own life. Mary Garrett succeeded to the post of superintendent of the Bala Home and retained it for the rest of her life.

By lectures, pamphlets, and journal articles Mary continued to promote the ideas of teaching speech to deaf children and beginning at an early age, and by persuasive lobbying she obtained passage of laws in 1899 and 1901 requiring the exclusive use of oral methods in all state institutions for the deaf. During 1899–1901 she joined Hannah Kent Schoff in campaigning for a juvenile court and probation system in Pennsylvania. She was a member from 1902 of the National Congress of Mothers (later the National Congress of Parents and Teachers) and chairman of its department of legislation (later of child welfare) from 1906 to 1920, during which time she directed the Congress's work for child labor, marriage law, and other reforms. She served also as corresponding secretary of the Pennsylvania Congress of Mothers in 1911–1915 and as its first vice-president in 1915–1925. Mary Garrett died in North Conway, New Hampshire, on July 18, 1925.

Gerould, Katharine Elizabeth Fullerton 1879–1944 writer

Born in Brockton, Massachusetts, on February 6, 1879, Katharine Fullerton was of staunchly New England lineage for many generations on either side. She was schooled privately in Boston and France, graduated from Radcliffe College in 1900, took a master's degree in 1901, and taught English and writing at Bryn Mawr College from 1901 until her marriage in June 1910 to Gordon H. Gerould, a Princeton professor. In 1900 she had won a prize from *Century* magazine for the best short story by an undergraduate with "The Poppies in the Wheat," which showed the strong influence of Henry James. Her second story, "Vain Oblations," was written while on leave from Bryn Mawr in 1908–1909; during that leave she traveled to England and met James. Later short stories, generally moral tales spun from the confrontation of well bred protagonists with exotic situations and temptations, reflected the influences of Joseph Conrad, Rudyard Kipling, and others. Published mainly in *Atlantic Monthly*, *Harper's*, and *Scribner's*, many of her stories were collected in *Vain Oblations*, 1914, *The Great Tradition*, 1915, and *Valiant Dust*, 1922.

Critically well received and frequently anthologized, Gerould's stories were marked by a refined and somewhat detached style and subtle insight. Her novels, *A Change of Air*, 1917, *Lost Valley*, 1922, *Conquistador*, 1923, and *The Light That Never Was*, 1931, were less successful both in form and manner. She achieved greater success, and stirred widespread controversy among critics and journals of opinion, with her essays. Her literary criticism tended to be narrow, and her essays on social and political topics revealed a marked distaste for democratic manifestations in art, manners, and public affairs. She stoutly defended a traditional hierarchical order of society, spiritual over material values, and the superiority of breeding to training. Collections of her essays appeared as *Modes and Morals*, 1920, and *Ringside Seats*, 1937. She also published two volumes of travel sketches, *Hawaii: Scenes and Impressions*, 1916, and *The Aristocratic West*, 1925. She died in Princeton, New Jersey, on July 27, 1944.

Gibbons, Abigail Hopper 1801–1893 reformer

Born in Philadelphia on December 7, 1801, Abigail Hopper was of a pious Quaker family with a deep tradition of good works. She attended Friends' schools and in 1821 established her own school for Quaker children. In 1830 she moved to New York City and became a teacher in a Quaker school there. In February 1833 she married James S. Gibbons, a Quaker merchant of substantial means; they lived in Philadelphia until 1835 and thereafter in New York City. They were active abolitionists and leading members of the Manhattan Anti-Slavery Society, and their home became a refuge for runaway slaves. In 1842 the Friends Meeting in New York disowned Gibbons's father and husband for abolitionist activities, whereupon she resigned from the society.

Other causes also attracted her support, including temperance, abolition of capital punishment, relief of the poor, and especially prison reform. Gibbons became a leading figure in the female department of the Prison Association of New York, founded in 1845 by her father and others, and in 1846 she was elected to a committee of women in charge of a halfway house (later the Isaac T. Hopper Home, named for her father) for discharged women prisoners. She continued active in the female department long after its reorganization as the independent Women's Prison Association and Home in 1853. In 1859 she became resident of the German Industrial School. She was also a frequent visitor to the city children's asylum on Randall's Island. For nearly four years during the Civil War she worked as a volunteer nurse in army camps and hospitals around Washington, D.C., and during that time she was noted for her outspoken criticisms of army medical management and practice. In her absence her house was sacked by a mob during the New York anti-draft riots of July 1863.

After the war Gibbons resumed her connections with the Women's Prison Association, of which she became president, and with the Hopper Home, and over the next several years she often lobbied the state legislature for financial support. She founded the Labor and Aid Society to help veterans find work and to provide relief to war widows and orphans. She helped found in 1873 the New York Diet Kitchen Association, which provided food to the ailing poor upon a physician's prescription. She also helped establish the Protestant Asylum for Infants and was president of the New York Committee for the Prevention of State Regulation of Vice. She was in large part responsible for the legislation that created a women's reformatory in New York City in 1892. She died in New York City on January 16, 1893.

Gibson, Althea 1927– tennis player

Born on August 25, 1927, in Silver, South Carolina, Althea Gibson grew up there and in New York City. She began playing tennis at an early age under the auspices of the New York Police Athletic League and in 1943 won the state Negro girls' singles championship. Five years later she won the national Negro women's title and held it for ten consecutive years. While attending Florida Agricultural and Mechanical University she continued to play in tournaments around the country and in 1950 became the first African-American tennis player to enter the national grass court championship tournament at Forest Hills, Queens, New York. The next year she entered the prestigious All-England tournament at Wimbledon, again as the first African-American ever invited. She graduated from Florida A. & M. in 1953 and was appointed an athletic instructor at Lincoln University, Jefferson City, Missouri.

Until 1956 Gibson had only fair success in match tennis play, winning several minor titles but no major ones. In that year she joined a tennis team sent on a world goodwill tour by the State Department, and on the tour her game suddenly jelled. She won a number of tournaments in Asia and Europe, including the French and Italian singles titles and the women's doubles title at Wimbledon. In 1957 she returned to Wimbledon to win the women's singles and doubles titles. She was welcomed home with a ticker-tape reception in New York City. Later in the year she took the U.S. women's singles championship at Forest Hills. She repeated all three victories in 1958 and in both years was a member of the successful U.S. Wightman Cup team. Having overcome considerable early racial prejudice and having worked her way, on the strength of her smashing serves and deft returns, to top rank in world amateur tennis, she turned professional in 1959. She won the women's professional singles title in 1960, and she later took up professional golf as well. Her autobiography, *I Always Wanted to Be Somebody*, appeared in 1958. In 1971 she was elected to the National Lawn Tennis Hall of Fame. In 1973 she became national director of and technical adviser to a program to bring tennis to inner-city children. From November 1975 to January 1977 she served as New Jersey state athletic commissioner. She ran unsuccessfully for the New Jersey legislature in 1977. She was recreation manager for the city of East Orange, New Jersey, from 1980 to 1983 and has been a special consultant on the New Jersey Governor's Council on Physical Fitness and Sports since 1988. She was inducted into the International Tennis Hall of Fame, 1971, the Black Athletes Hall of Fame, 1974, the South Carolina Hall of Fame, 1983, and the Florida Sports Hall of Fame, 1984.

Gilbert, Anne Jane Hartley 1821–1904 dancer and actor

Born on October 21, 1821, in Rochdale, Lancashire, England, Anne Hartley grew up in London. At twelve she began studying dance in the ballet school of Her Majesty's Theatre, Haymarket. She danced in the corps at Her Majesty's and Drury Lane theaters until 1846, when she married George H. Gilbert, a dancer and manager. Barnstorming tours by the two of them through England and Ireland produced enough money for them to emigrate to America. They arrived in New York in October 1849, made their way to the Wisconsin frontier, and took up farming. The venture was a failure, and by the next year they had returned to the stage in Milwaukee. Later in 1850 they joined a theatrical company in Chicago, for which they arranged and performed ballets. Gilbert soon began taking small acting roles as well, the more so after an injury suffered by her husband ended his dancing career. In 1857 she joined the company of John Ellsler in Cleveland. Character parts, especially old women, became her specialty, and she attracted considerable notice in an Ellsler production of *Pocahontas*. In 1858, as a member of Lewis Baker's company in Louisville, she played Lady Macbeth opposite Edwin Booth.

Gilbert made her New York debut in September 1864 in *Finesse*, presented by the company of Mrs. John Wood at the Olympic Theatre. Over the next several years she appeared with that company in *Martin Chuzzlewit*, *A New Way to Pay Old Debts*, *David Copperfield*, *Our Mutual Friend*, and other popular pieces. Under different management she was a hit in *Caste* at the Broadway Theatre in 1867, and later in that year she played opposite Edwin Forrest in a series of Shakespearean productions. In 1869 she joined the company of Augustin Daly, under whose management she remained for 30 years, except for a period in 1877–1880, when Daly was without a theater and Gilbert appeared in A. M. Palmer's company. With Daly she appeared in *Play*, *Dreams*, *Frou-Frou*, *The Big Bonanza*, *Man and Wife*, *Pique*, and many others. *Needles and Pins*, which opened in November 1880, first brought together in Daly's company Gilbert, Ada Rehan, John Drew, and James Lewis, who in their years together became known as "The Big Four," a team unrivaled in ensemble technique and universally acclaimed among lovers of the theater. After Daly's death in 1899 Gilbert acted under Charles Frohman's management in *The Girl and the Judge*, *Mice and Men*, and others. In October 1904, at the age of eighty-three, she had her first starring role in *Granny*, an adaptation from French by Clyde Fitch commissioned specifically for her. She was a great success from the play's opening at the Lyceum Theatre in New York, and a month later she took it to Chicago, where it opened at Powers' Theatre. A few days later, on December 2, 1904, she died in her Chicago hotel.

Gilbert, Linda 1847–1895 welfare worker

Born on May 13, 1847, probably in Rochester, New York, Zelinda Gilbert, as she was christened, grew up from the age of five in Chicago. In childhood her daily path to convent school took her past the Cook County Jail. She eventually developed an acquaintance with one of the prisoners and discovered from him that there was no reading material in the jail. Her resolve to establish a library in the jail was fulfilled in 1864, when she donated some 4000 miscellaneous volumes. She then formed a plan to place libraries in every prison in Illinois and to provide other services for prisoners. As a fund-raising device she advertised a lottery, but a bit of naive fraud regarding the prizes brought the scheme to naught.

About 1872 Gilbert moved to New York City, where in September 1873 she established the Gilbert Library and Prisoners' Aid Fund. Her Fund had to compete with such established agencies as the Prison Association and the Women's Prison Association for money, and to that end she proved somewhat adept at securing endorsements and publicity, although her penchant for the grandiose worked against her in the long run. A "Grand Testimonial Concert" at Barnum's Hippodrome in April 1875 was poorly attended, and before long a general skepticism attached to her undertakings. Her *Sketch of the Life and Work of Linda Gilbert*, 1876, published in the hope of attracting a permanent endowment for her work, made inflated claims. The Gilbert Library and Prisoners' Aid Society, incorporated in 1876, was of genuine, if limited service; prison libraries were supported, small personal items were distributed to prisoners, and support and sometimes employment were offered to released prisoners. The society lasted until 1883. Linda Gilbert died in Mount Vernon, New York, on October 24, 1895.

Gilder, Jeannette Leonard 1849–1916 editor and writer

Born on October 3, 1849, in Flushing, New York, Jeannette Gilder grew up there and in Bordentown, New Jersey. Her education was irregular. In 1864 she helped support her large family, left fatherless that year by the Civil War, with a job in the office of the New Jersey adjutant general. In 1865–1866 she attended the Bridgeton Female Seminary in southern New Jersey. In 1868, after a brief clerical employment at the Philadelphia mint, she joined the staff of the *Newark Morning Register*, which had recently been established by Richard Watson Gilder, destined to be the most famous of her five talented brothers. She later became an editor of the paper, and for a time she was Newark correspondent for the *New York Tribune*. In 1875 she moved to New York City and secured a job as literary editor of James Gordon Bennett's *New York Herald*. Before long her reviews and criticism of music and drama as well as literature made her a central figure in the cultural life of the city, and she numbered many of the leading writers, artists, and actors of the day among her friends. In January 1881 she and another brother, Joseph B. Gilder, established the *Critic*, a biweekly (later weekly) journal of criticism and review that enjoyed a long life and earned for itself an important place in New York and, indeed, American cultural affairs. She contributed a regular column, "The Lounger," and helped edit the *Critic* until 1901, when she became sole editor.

For several years up to 1906 Gilder also edited the monthly *Reader*. During this period she also contributed columns to *Harper's Bazaar*, the New York *Commercial Advertiser*, and the *London Academy*, and under the pen name "Brunswick" she was a New York correspondent for the Boston *Saturday Evening Gazette* and later the Boston *Evening Transcript*; she also corresponded at various times with newspapers in Philadelphia, Chicago, and London. In 1906 the *Critic* was absorbed by *Putnam's Monthly*, of which she was associate editor until it in turn was absorbed by the *Atlantic Monthly* in 1910. Her gift for editorial work also produced several books, including *Essays from "The Critic"* with Joseph Gilder, 1882, *Representative Poems of Living Poets*, 1886, *Pen Portraits of*

Literary Women, with Helen Gray Cone, 1887, *Authors at Home*, with Joseph Gilder, 1888, *Masterpieces of the World's Best Literature* in eight volumes, 1905, and *Heart of Youth*, young people's poetry, 1911. Her attempts at literary creation met with indifferent success.

Gilder wrote several plays, including *Quits*, produced in Philadelphia in 1877, *Sevenoaks*, based on Josiah G. Holland's novel of that name, 1878, and *A Wonderful Woman*, 1878. In 1887 she published a novel, *Taken by Siege*, about literary life in New York. Her *Autobiography of a Tomboy*, 1900, and *The Tomboy at Work*, 1904, were more successful. For many years she served in addition as New York agent for a number of authors and publishers. In later years she supplied book columns to *McClure's* magazine, *Woman's Home Companion*, and the *Chicago Tribune*. She died in New York City on January 17, 1916.

Gill, Laura Drake 1860–1926 educator

Born on August 24, 1860, in Chesterville, Maine, Laura Gill graduated from Smith College in 1881 and remained in Northampton, Massachusetts, as a faculty member of Miss Capen's School for girls, operated by her aunt. She remained there as a teacher of mathematics for 17 years, taking time off to receive a master's degree from Smith in 1885 and to pursue advanced studies at the universities of Leipzig and Geneva and at the Sorbonne during 1890–1893. On the outbreak of the Spanish-American War in 1898 she joined the Red Cross. She had charge of the first party of Red Cross nurses sent to Cuba. She later had responsibility for nurse selection and placement at army hospitals in Tennessee and on Long Island. After the war she helped organize the schools of Cuba under the governorship of General Leonard Wood, and she also undertook relief work among Cuban orphans. In 1901 she was named dean of Barnard College. During her seven years in that post she planned and saw begun in 1907 the college's first dormitory, and she established the Bachelor of Science degree.

In 1909, at the request of the Women's Educational and Industrial Union of Boston, Gill moved to that city and established the first vocational placement bureau for college women. The problems experienced by educated women in finding suitable employment had first come to her attention during her work with nurses, and her experience as dean of Barnard and as president of the Association of Collegiate Alumnae had sharpened her sense of the need for organized assistance in that field. In 1911 she joined the staff of the University of the South in Sewanee, Tennessee, where she engaged in organization work for three years. She was similarly employed at Trinity College in Durham, North Carolina, in 1914–1915. During World War I she served as a special agent in field organization for the U.S. Employment Service of the Department of Labor. In 1919 she became an educational worker at Pine Mountain Settlement in Kentucky, and in 1922 she became a house mother and teacher at Berea College. She died in Berea, Kentucky, on February 3, 1926.

Gillespie, Mother Angela 1824–1887 religious

Born near Brownsville, Pennsylvania, on February 21, 1824, Eliza Maria Gillespie was educated at a private girls' school in her native town and, in 1836–1838, at a girls' school run by the Dominican Sisters in Somerset, Ohio. In the latter year she moved with her widowed mother to Lancaster, Ohio. In 1840 she entered the Visitation Academy in Georgetown, D.C., along with her Ohio cousin, Ellen Ewing (daughter of Senator Thomas Ewing and future wife of General William T. Sherman), and she graduated in 1842. She returned to Lancaster for nine years, busied herself with charitable work, and from 1847 to 1851 taught in a parish school. During 1851–1853 she taught at Saint Mary's Seminary (a nondenominational, state-supported school) in Saint Marys City, Maryland. Her long-standing inclination toward the religious life culminated in January 1853 in her deciding to enter the Sisters of Mercy convent in Chicago. On her way there she stopped to visit her brother, a seminarian at the University of Notre Dame. There she met the Reverend Edward F. Sorin, founder of the university, who turned her instead to the Sisters of the Holy Cross, a French order whose one American convent was at Bertrand, Michigan.

Gillespie took the habit and the name Sister Mary of Saint Angela in April and was sent to the order's novitiate in Caen, France. After taking her final vows in December 1853 she returned to Bertrand, Michigan, as director of studies of Saint Mary's Academy, and in April 1854 she became superior of the convent. In 1855 St. Mary's Academy was moved to a new site near Notre Dame and became St. Mary's College. A believer in full educational opportunities for women, Mother Angela instituted courses in advanced mathematics, the sciences, modern foreign languages (taught by native speakers), philosophy and theology, art, and music. By 1856 nuns of the Holy Cross order were teaching in parochial schools in Chicago, and in 1858 the order established Saint Angela's Academy in Morris, Illinois. In 1860 she began publishing a graded series of *Metropolitan Readers* for use in elementary through college-level courses.

In October 1861 Mother Angela offered the nursing services of the order to General Ulysses S. Grant. Within a short time Holy Cross sisters (80 of them during the course of the war) were employed in army hospitals in Paducah and Louisville, Kentucky, and later in Cairo, Illinois, Memphis, Tennessee, Washington, D.C., and elsewhere, as well as aboard hospital ships on the Mississippi. The order's main efforts went into the conversion of a row of riverfront warehouses in Mound City, Illinois, into a clean and efficient 1500-bed military hospital that was regarded by such as Mary A. Livermore of the Northwestern Sanitary Commission to be the best in the country. From 1866 Mother Angela was largely responsible for editing *Ave Maria*, a Catholic periodical founded by Father Sorin.

The expansion of the order and of its educational work proceeded rapidly under Mother Angela's direction. Among the 45 institutions founded by the order between 1855 and 1882 were Saint Mary's Academy in Austin, Texas, in 1874, Saint Catherine's Normal Institute in Baltimore and Saint Mary of the Assumption in Salt Lake City in 1875, and Holy Cross Academy in Washington, D.C., in 1878. In 1869 difficulties between the American and French branches of the order led to the establishment of the American branch on an independent basis, with Mother Angela, as provincial superior, under the authority of Father Sorin as superior. Although she had been preceded by two mothers superior, Mother Angela was firmly established as the effective founder of her order in America. She died at Saint Mary's Convent, South Bend, Indiana, on March 4, 1887.

Gilman, Caroline Howard 1794–1888 writer and publisher

Born in Boston on October 8, 1794, Caroline Howard grew up in a succession of nearby towns until her widowed mother settled in Cambridge in 1804. Her schooling was similarly irregular. She wrote verse for her private amusement from an early age, but she was mortified when one of her poems was printed without her knowledge in a local newspaper about 1811. In 1817 she allowed a second to appear in the *North American Review*. In December 1819 she married Samuel Gilman, a Unitarian minister with whom she moved to Charleston, South Carolina. Her writing career was slow to develop. In 1832 she began publishing the weekly *Rose-Bud, or Youth's Gazette*, one of the earliest children's magazines in America. It became the *Southern Rose*, with a somewhat broader family audience in 1835, and Gilman continued to edit and publish it until 1839. In it she serialized her first novel, published in book form in 1834 as *Recollections of a Housekeeper* under the pseudonym "Clarissa Packard." The book was a portrait of domestic life in New England; its Southern counterpart, *Recollections of a Southern Matron*, appeared in 1838.

In these books, as in much of her writing, Gilman's aim was to explain one section of the nation to the other, to display the essential unity between them that she perceived as founded on the domestic level, and to offset thereby the growing stresses between North and South on the political level. Subsequent books included *The Poetry of Travelling in the United States*, humorous sketches, 1838, *The Lady's Annual Register and Housewife's Memorandum-Book for 1838*, a domestic almanac, 1838, *The Letters of Eliza Wilkinson during the Invasion of Charleston*, an edited collection, 1839, *Tales and Ballads*, 1839, *Love's Progress*, a romance, 1840, *Ruth Raymond*, 1840, *Oracles from the Poets*, selections intended for family reading aloud, 1844, *The Sibyl, or, New Oracles from the Poets*, 1848, *Verses of a Life Time*, her own poems, 1849, *A Gift Book of Stories and Poems for Children*, 1850, and *Oracles for Youth*, 1852. During the Civil War she lived in Greenville, South Carolina, and was active in Confederate volunteer and relief work. Her home and possessions in Charleston were destroyed, but she returned to that city in 1865 and lived there until 1882, when she joined a daughter in Washington, D.C. She died in Washington on September 15, 1888.

Gilman, Charlotte Anna Perkins Stetson 1860–1935 feminist, lecturer, writer and publisher

Charlotte Perkins Gilman

Born in Hartford, Connecticut, on July 3, 1860, Charlotte Perkins grew up in poverty, her father having essentially abandoned the family. Her education was irregular and limited as the family moved often, but she did attend the Rhode Island School of Design for a time. In May 1884 she married Charles W. Stetson, an artist. She soon proved to be radically unsuited to the domestic routine of marriage, and after a year or so she was reduced to melancholia, which eventuated in complete nervous collapse. A California trip in 1885 was helpful, however, and in 1888 she moved with her young daughter to Pasadena. She divorced her husband in 1894, and after his remarriage shortly thereafter to a close friend of hers she sent her daughter to live with them. The entire affair was the subject of scandalous public comment.

After her move to California Perkins began writing poems and stories for various periodicals. Among her stories "The Yellow Wall-Paper," published in *The New England Magazine* in January 1892, was outstanding in its starkly realistic first-person portrayal of the mental breakdown of a physically pampered but emotionally starved young wife. In 1893 she published *In This Our World*, a volume of verse. For a time in 1894, after her move to San Francisco, she edited with Helen Campbell the *Impress*, organ of the Pacific Coast Woman's Press Association. She also became a noted lecturer during the early 1890s on such social topics as labor and woman's place, and after a short period of residence at Jane Addams's Hull-House in Chicago in 1895 she spent the next five years in national lecture tours. In 1896 she was a delegate to the International Socialist and Labor Congress in London, where she met George Bernard Shaw, Beatrice and Sidney Webb, and other leading socialists.

In 1898 Perkins published *Women and Economics*, a manifesto that attracted great attention and was ultimately translated into seven other languages. The book was a radical call for economic independence for women, and in it she dissected with keen intelligence much of the romanticized convention surrounding the ideas of womanhood and motherhood. Her notions of redefining domestic and child-care chores as social responsibilities to be centralized in the hands of those particularly suited and trained for them reflected her earlier interest in the Nationalist clubs following Edward Bellamy, and she expanded on the ideas in *Concerning Children*, 1900, and *The Home*, 1903. In June 1900 she married a cousin, George H. Gilman, with whom she lived in New York City until 1922. *Human Work*, 1904, continued the arguments of *Women and Economics* but to less public response. Later books included *What Diantha Did*, 1910, *The Man-Made World*, in which she distinguished the characteristic virtues and vices of male and female and attributed the ills of the world to the dominance of the male's, 1911, *The Crux*, 1911, *Moving the Mountain*, 1911, *His Religion and Hers*, 1923, and *The Living of Charlotte Perkins Gilman: An Autobiography*, 1935.

From 1909 to 1916 Gilman edited and published the monthly *Forerunner*, a magazine of feminist articles, views, and fiction. She also contributed to other periodicals. Aside from addresses to the International Council of Women in 1899 (London) and 1904 (Berlin), the International Suffrage Convention in 1913 (Budapest), and others and joining Jane Addams in the founding of the Woman's Peace Party in 1915, she was little involved in the organized movements of the day. She lived in Norwich, Connecticut, from 1922 until her husband's death in 1934, when she moved to Pasadena, California. There, after treatments for cancer had proved ineffective, she took her own life on August 17, 1935.

Gilmer, Elizabeth Meriwether 1870–1951 journalist

Born near Woodstock, Tennessee, on November 18, 1870, Elizabeth Meriwether received little in the way of formal schooling before her marriage in November 1888 to George O. Gilmer. A short time later he fell victim to incurable mental illness and was incapacitated until his death in an asylum in 1931. Forced to seek her own support, Gilmer suffered a nervous collapse. During her convalescence she began writing stories and sketches of life in her native region. In 1896 one of them attracted the notice of a neighbor, Eliza P. Nicholson, owner of the New Orleans *Picayune*, who gave her a job as a reporter. Following the custom of women reporters in writing under an alliterative pseudonym, she chose the name "Dorothy Dix" and began writing a Sunday advice column for women under the title "Sunday Salad." The column was a remarkable success, and in a short time Gilmer became editor of the women's department and assistant to the editor of the *Picayune*. In 1901 she accepted a lucrative offer from William Randolph Hearst to move to his New York *Journal*. She continued her column, now called "Dorothy Dix Talks," on a thrice-weekly basis while working also as a reporter specializing in "sob-sister" coverage of sensational murder stories.

Among the celebrated cases and trials Gilmer covered were the Nan Patterson trials in 1904 and the Harry Thaw-Stanford White murder and trial in 1906. In 1917 she left Hearst to join the Wheeler Syndicate in order to devote full time to her column, which interested her far more than did sob-sister reporting. Publishing six times weekly, she began devoting half her columns to printing actual letters from readers seeking advice; the other three continued to be her own sermonettes. At the peak of her popularity she received upwards of 2000 letters a week from readers. Her only real challenger in the field was "Beatrice Fairfax" (Marie Manning). She moved her column to the Ledger Syndicate in 1923 and to the Bell Syndicate in 1933, and by 1940 it was appearing in 273 newspapers and being read by an estimated 60 million people in the United States and several foreign countries. She continued to write it until World War II. She also published several books: *Mirandy*, 1914, *Hearts à la Mode*, 1915, *Mirandy Exhorts*, 1922, *My Trip Around the World*, 1924, and, based on her column, *Dorothy Dix, Her Book*, 1926, and *How to Win and Hold a Husband*, 1939. She died in New Orleans on December 16, 1951.

Ginsburg, Ruth Bader 1933– attorney and U.S. Supreme Court justice

Born in Brooklyn, New York, on March 15, 1933, Ruth Bader attended public schools, where she excelled academically; the day before her high school graduation in 1950, at which she was scheduled to speak, her mother died of cervical cancer. Bader attended Cornell University on a scholarship and earned a B.A. in government. She married fellow Cornell student, Martin D. Ginsburg, in 1954, and both decided to pursue careers in law.

Two years later the Ginsburgs moved to Cambridge, Massachusetts. Martin resumed his studies, having finished a tour of duty in the navy, and Ruth entered the Harvard Law School, where she was one of only 9 women in a class of over 500 students. She nevertheless was named editor of the *Harvard Law Review* before transferring to Columbia University Law School in 1958 when her husband went to work in New York City.

Ginsburg graduated first in her class of 1959, but she was unable to find a job in a law firm; neither mothers nor Jews were being hired. She eventually found employment as a clerk with a federal district judge in New York. After working two years on a Columbia Law School project that sent her to Sweden, she received an honorary degree in 1963 from the University of Lund for her work there. She joined the faculty of Rutgers University Law School the same year. She also began taking on cases for the American Civil Liberties Union (ACLU), with a particular interest in sex discrimination cases. After becoming the first woman to receive tenure at Columbia Law School, 1972, she became general counsel to the ACLU, where she was known for exposing the gender biases of existing laws when she presented her arguments.

President Jimmy Carter nominated her to the U.S. Court of Appeals for the District of Columbia; she was sworn in on June 30, 1980. In 13 years on that court, she wrote more than 300 opinions; viewed as a centrist, she voted more often with Republican-appointed colleagues than with fellow Democrat-appointed judges. Though a strong supporter of abortion rights, she was a critic of the Supreme Court's 1973 *Roe v. Wade* decision, arguing that the right to an abortion is not an issue of privacy, as the Court had ruled, but one of equality and sex discrimination. President Bill Clinton nominated Ginsburg to the Supreme Court on June 15, 1993, and the Senate overwhelmingly (96–3) approved her nomination. She took the oath of office on August 10, 1993, becoming only the second woman to accede to the high court.

Gish, Lillian Diana and Dorothy 1893–1993 and 1898–1968 actors

Born in Ohio, Lillian in Springfield on October 14, 1893, and Dorothy in Massillon on March 11, 1898, the Gish sisters grew up from about 1900 in New York City, although they later moved often as the family's precarious fortunes dictated. In 1902, upon the suggestion of a theatrical acquaintance, both girls were given parts in road-company productions, Dorothy appearing in *East Lynne* and Lillian in *Convict's Stripes*. For the next ten years they continued to tour with various companies, often together but occasionally separately. They attended school sporadically, for the most part in Ohio, where their mother returned to live. During their years as child actresses they formed close friendships with Mary Pickford (then still known as Gladys Mary Smith), who in 1912 introduced them to D. W. Griffith. Immediately struck by their beauty and charm, he gave them small parts in a series of silent movies, beginning with *An Unseen Enemy*, 1912, and the next year placed them under contract to his studio. Almost from the start Lillian was the more popular of the two. An extra measure of winsome appeal in such two-reelers as *The Musketeers of Pig Alley*, 1912, *The Mothering Heart*, 1913, and *Judith of Bethulia*, 1914, won her a large and growing audience of admirers; and from her appearance in *Birth of a Nation*, 1915, she was established as one of Hollywood's top stars, soon becoming known as the "First Lady of the Screen." In *Intolerance*, 1916, and *Broken Blossoms*, 1919, she became almost a symbol of the idealized innocent, vulnerable heroine.

Dorothy, the more vivacious sister, attracted a following of her own in *The Mountain Rat*, 1914, *The Mysterious Shot*, 1914, and other films. They appeared together in several of Griffith's greatest films, including *Home, Sweet Home*, 1914, *The Sisters*, 1914, *Hearts of the World*, 1918, and *Orphans of the Storm*, 1922. In 1920 Lillian directed Dorothy in *Remodeling Her Husband*. They left Griffith in 1922, Dorothy going to Paramount Studios and Lillian to the Tiffany Company and in 1925 to Metro-Goldwyn-Mayer.

Subsequent films of Dorothy's included *Romola*, 1924, in which Lillian also appeared; *Clothes Make the Pirate*, 1925; and two movies made in England, *Nell Gwyn*, 1926, and *Madame Pompadour*, 1927. Lillian's later films included *The White Sister*, 1923, *La Bohème*, 1926, *The Scarlet Letter*, 1926, *The Wind*, 1928, and *One Romantic Night*, her first sound picture, 1930.

With the coming of the talkies they both left the screen for a time and returned to the stage. Dorothy enjoyed a number of Broadway and London successes in *Young Love*, 1928, *The Inspector General*, 1930, *By Your Leave*, 1934, *Missouri Legend*, 1938, *Life With Father* (on tour), 1940, *Magnificent Yankee*, 1946, *The Man*, 1950, and other plays. She continued to appear on the stage and from time to time in films, notably *Our Hearts Were Young and Gay*, 1944. Her last performances were in a 1956 Broadway revival of *Life with Father* and in the film *The Cardinal*, 1963. She died in Rapallo, Italy, on June 4, 1968.

Lillian played on the stage in *Uncle Vanya* with great success in 1930 and subsequently appeared in *Camille*, 1932, *Nine Pine Street*, 1933, *Within the Gates*, 1934, *Hamlet*, 1936, *The Old Maid*, 1936, *The Star Wagon*, 1937, *Life with Father*, 1940, in which she enjoyed a record run in Chicago while Dorothy was starring with the road company, *Mr. Sycamore*, 1942, *Magnificent Yankee*, 1946, *Crime and Punishment*, 1947, *The Curious Savage*, 1950, *The Trip to Bountiful*, 1953, *The Family Reunion*, 1958, *All the Way Home*, 1960, *I Never Sang for My Father*, 1967, and many others. Her last Broadway appearance was in *A Musical Jubilee* in 1975. She continued also to appear occasionally in movies, among them *The Commandos Strike at Dawn*, 1943, *Miss Susie Slagle's*, 1946, *Duel in the Sun*, 1947, *Night of the Hunter*, 1955, *The Unforgiven*, 1960, *The Comedians*, 1967, *A Wedding*, 1978, *Hambone and Hillie*, 1984, *Sweet Liberty*, 1986, and her final film *The Whales of August*, with Bette Davis, 1987. She also appeared on television in a number of distinguished dramatic presentations, most notably in *Arsenic and Old Lace* with Helen Hayes in 1969. Her autobiographical *The Movies, Mr. Griffith and Me* appeared in 1969, and was followed by two more volumes of memoirs, *Dorothy and Lillian Gish*, 1973, and *An Actor's Life for Me*, 1987. She was awarded a special honorary Academy Award in 1971 and was honored at the Kennedy Center in 1982. She received a lifetime achievement award from the American Film Institute in 1984 and the D. W. Griffith Award for her outstanding career in motion pictures in 1987.

Ellen Glasgow

Glasgow, Ellen Anderson Gholson 1873–1945 novelist

Born in Richmond, Virginia, on April 22, 1873, Ellen Glasgow, daughter of a wealthy and socially prominent family with Old Virginia roots on her mother's side, was educated mainly at home. Of her physically and emotionally troubled childhood little is known. In 1897 she published her first novel, *The Descendant*, anonymously. It was followed by *Phases of an Inferior Planet*, 1898. With *The Voice of the People*, 1900, she began a series of novels depicting with what she intended to be Zolaesque realism the social and political history of Virginia since 1850. The series continued in *The Battle-Ground*, 1902, *The Deliverance*, 1904, *The Romance of a Plain Man*, 1909, *The Miller of Old Church*, 1911, *Virginia*, 1913, *Life and Gabriella*, 1916, and *One Man in His Time*, 1922. Other books of that period were *The Wheel of Life*, 1906, *The Ancient Law*, 1908, *The Builders*, 1919, and *The Shadowy Third and Other Stories*, 1923.

Genuine critical success came with *Barren Ground*, 1925, which had a grimly tragic theme set in rural Virginia, as did the later *Vein of Iron*, 1935. With a brilliant and increasingly ironic treatment Glasgow examined the decay of Southern aristocracy and the traumatic encroachment of modern industrial civilization in three comedies of manners, *The Romantic Comedians*, 1926, *They Stooped to Folly*, 1929, and *The Sheltered Life*, 1932. Her last novel, *In This Our Life*, 1941, had a similar theme and although not her best work was awarded a Pulitzer Prize. In 1940 she had been awarded the Howells

Medal of the American Academy of Arts and Letters. In 1943 Glasgow published a collection of critical essays entitled *A Certain Measure*. She died in Richmond, Virginia, on November 21, 1945. Her memoirs were published in 1954 as *The Woman Within*, and in 1966 an epilogue to *In This Our Life* was at last published as *Beyond Defeat*.

Glaspell, Susan Keating 1876–1948 playwright and novelist

Born in Davenport, Iowa, on July 1, 1876, Susan Glaspell graduated from Drake University in 1899. During college she had published a few short stories in the *Youth's Companion* and worked as college correspondent for a local newspaper, and on graduating she became a reporter for the *Des Moines Daily News*. In 1901 she returned to Davenport to devote herself to writing. Her stories, mainly local-color pieces set in "Freeport" (Davenport), were soon appearing regularly in such magazines as the *Ladies' Home Journal*, the *American*, and *Harper's*. In 1903 she briefly pursued graduate studies in English at the University of Chicago. In 1909 she published her first novel, *The Glory of the Conquered*, a romance of little distinction that nonetheless enjoyed some success. After a year in Paris she produced a second novel, *The Visioning*, 1911. In that year she moved to New York City. In 1912 a collection of previously published stories appeared under the title *Lifted Masks*. In April 1913 she married George Cram Cook, a literary and radical son of a wealthy Davenport family and a friend of Susan Glaspell's for many years. They quickly became central figures in the life of Greenwich Village. In 1915 she published *Fidelity*, a novel, and together with her husband *Suppressed Desires*, a satirical one-act play on popular Freudianism.

That year at their summer home in Provincetown on Cape Cod, George Cook organized a group of local artists as an amateur theater group that staged a number of one-act plays in a converted fish warehouse. The next year Eugene O'Neill was introduced to the group, which soon became more formally organized as the Provincetown Players and began presenting a winter season of performances at the Playwright's Theatre in Greenwich Village. Susan Glaspell wrote several one-acters for the group, notably *Trifles*, 1916, and also *Close the Book*, 1917, *A Woman's Hour*, 1918, and *Tickless Time*, 1919, and four full-length plays, including *Bernice*, 1919, and especially *Inheritors*, 1921, and *The Verge*, 1921, which displayed a marked insight into character and considerable dramatic talent. In 1922 she and her husband established themselves at Delphi, Greece, where he died two years later. She then returned to New York. In 1927 she published a biography of George Cook, *The Road to the Temple*. Subsequently she published *The Comic Artist*, a play on which she collaborated with Norman H. Matson (to whom she was married for a time), 1927, *Brook Evans*, a novel, 1928, *Fugitive's Return*, a novel, 1929, *Alison's House*, a play that was awarded the Pulitzer Prize, 1930, and four more novels, *Ambrose Holt and Family*, 1931, *The Morning Is Near Us*, 1939, *Norma Ashe*, 1942, and *Judd Rankin's Daughter*, 1945. She died in Provincetown, Massachusetts, on July 27, 1948.

Gleason, Kate 1865–1933 businesswoman

Born in Rochester, New York, on November 25, 1865, Kate Gleason began helping out in her father's small toolmaking business when she was eleven. After graduating from high school in 1884 she briefly attended Cornell University; she studied there again briefly in 1888. Returning to her father's business, she became secretary and treasurer of the firm in 1890. Her position made her the firm's chief sales representative as well, and she was evidently the first woman to travel in such a line of goods. Her efficient representation of the firm in travels that took her several times across the country and to Europe helped bolster its profits and made possible an expansion of the factory. A much greater expansion followed on the rapidly growing demand in the early years of the new century for beveled gears. The elder Gleason had been perfecting a machine to cut beveled gears, formerly the product of inaccurate handwork, since 1874; and the new demand created primarily by the automobile industry, together with Kate Gleason's very effective promotion, put the Gleason firm solidly in the forefront of a vital segment of the machine-tool business. So strongly was she identified with the Gleason bevel-gear planer that she was credited by many (including Henry Ford) with having invented it, and she was awarded memberships in the Verein Deutscher Ingenieure in 1913 and the American Society of Mechanical Engineers in 1914, in both cases as the first women ever so honored.

After resigning her position with her father's company in 1913 Kate Gleason engaged in a variety of enterprises. In 1914 she was appointed receiver for another machine-tool firm in East Rochester, which she quickly restored to solvency. During 1917–1919 she acted as president of the First National Bank of East Rochester while the permanent president was absent on war-related work. Becoming interested in the depressed condition of East Rochester, she undertook a number of projects to stimulate the economy of the city, the largest of which was an innovative housing development. Using standardized plans and mainly unskilled workmen, a hundred six-room cement houses were built. This experiment in mass production in housing led to her becoming the only woman member of the American Concrete Institute. In the years immediately following World War I she also invested much time and money in the restoration of much of the French village of Septmonts, notably its twelfth-century castle tower. In the early 1920s she began developing a resort complex at Beaufort, South Carolina, and later in the decade she made plans for and a small start on a development in Sausalito, California. She died in Rochester, New York, on January 9, 1933, leaving an estate of nearly one and a half million dollars to various philanthropies.

Glueck, Eleanor Touroff 1898–1972 criminologist

Born in Brooklyn, New York, on April 12, 1898, Eleanor Touroff graduated from Barnard College in 1919 and then entered the New York School of Social Work, from which she took a diploma in 1921. At Harvard University, where she enrolled in the Graduate School of Education, she met Sheldon Glueck, whom she married in April 1922. In 1923 she received a master's degree in education and in 1925 a doctorate. During that time, in 1921–1922, she also worked at the Dorchester, Massachusetts, Welfare Center. In 1925 she became a research criminologist in the department of social ethics at Harvard, where her husband was an instructor. Her first book, *The Community Use of Schools*, appeared in 1927. In 1928 she moved to the Harvard Law School as a research assistant in the Crime Survey; the next year Sheldon Glueck joined the Law School as assistant professor, and in 1930 Eleanor Glueck was given a regular faculty appointment as research assistant. From 1925 their joint researches centered on studies of criminal character and behavior.

Encouraged by Dr. Richard C. Cabot of the Harvard Medical School and Massachusetts General Hospital, Eleanor and Sheldon Glueck undertook a detailed study of former inmates of the Massachusetts Reformatory, publishing their heavily documented findings as *500 Criminal Careers*, 1930, a pioneering work in the field. Subsequent follow-up studies of the same men were published as *Later Criminal Careers*, 1937, and *Criminal Careers in Retrospect*, 1943. The parallel *Five Hundred Delinquent Women*, 1934, conducted at the Massachusetts Reformatory for Women (then under Superintendent Jessie D. Hodder), and their *One Thousand Juvenile Delinquents: Their Treatment by Court and Clinic*, 1934, and *Juvenile Delinquents Grown Up*, 1940, the former reporting a study suggested by then-Professor (later Justice) Felix Frankfurter, rounded out a body of work that constituted virtually the whole of extant scientific literature on criminals, the efficacy of various penal and rehabilitative theories, and recidivism.

Subsequent books by the Gluecks included *Unraveling Juvenile Delinquency*, 1950, in which they published their controversial Social Prediction Tables by which they claimed potential delinquents could be identified by the age of six, *Delinquents in the Making*, 1952, *Physique and Delinquency*, 1956, *Predicting Delinquency and Crime*, 1959, *Family Environment and Delinquency*, 1962, *Ventures in Criminology*, 1964, *Delinquents and Nondelinquents in Perspective*, 1968, *Toward a Topology of Juvenile Offenders: Implications for Therapy and Prevention*, 1970, and *Identification of Predelinquents*, 1972. In 1953 Eleanor Glueck's title in the Harvard Law School became research associate in criminology. She and her husband shared numerous honors for their work. Eleanor Glueck died in Cambridge, Massachusetts, on September 25, 1972.

Goddard, Mary Katherine 1738–1816 printer and publisher

Born on June 16, 1738, in either Groton or New London, Connecticut, Mary Goddard grew up in the latter town. In 1762 she and her widowed mother moved to Providence, Rhode Island, where her elder brother William had opened a printing office. Both she and her mother assisted in the business, and from the summer of 1765, when William moved to Philadelphia, they operated it themselves, including the editing and publishing of the *Providence Gazette* from 1766 and the issuing of the annual *West's Almanack*. Late in 1768 they sold the business and rejoined William in Philadelphia. Mary Goddard assisted in the publishing of William's *Pennsylvania Chronicle* until August 1773, when he moved to Baltimore and she took over sole responsibility for the Philadelphia business. In February 1774 she sold that interest and moved to Baltimore, where she soon took over William's weekly *Maryland Journal* and the *Baltimore Advertiser*.

From May 1775 Goddard's role as editor and publisher was formally acknowledged in the paper's colophon. She maintained the newspaper and the printing business through the Revolution. In 1775 she also became postmaster of Baltimore; she was probably the first woman to hold such a position in America. In January 1777 she issued the first printed copy of the Declaration of Independence to include the signers' names. In March 1783 the *Maryland Journal* became a semiweekly. In January 1784, following a quarrel, William displaced his sister as publisher of the newspaper; she nonetheless still managed to issue an almanac in her own name late in that year. She continued as postmaster until October 1789, when she was replaced by a male appointee who could undertake the travel necessary to supervise the operations of the postal service through the South. Her removal was widely protested in Baltimore. She operated a bookstore until 1809 or 1810, and she died in Baltimore on August 12, 1816.

Goldman, Emma 1869–1940 anarchist

Emma Goldman

Born on June 27, 1869, in Kaunas (or Kovno), Lithuania (variously a part of Poland and Russia), Emma Goldman grew up there, in Königsberg, East Prussia, and in St. Petersburg. Her formal education was limited, but she read much on her own and in St. Petersburg associated with a radical student circle. In 1885 she emigrated to the United States and settled in Rochester, New York. There, and later in New Haven, Connecticut, she worked in clothing factories and came into contact with socialist and anarchist groups among fellow workers. In 1889 she moved to New York City, determined to join the anarchist cause. She formed a close association with Alexander Berkman, who was imprisoned in 1892 for an attempt to assassinate Henry Clay Frick during the Homestead steel strike. The following year she herself was sent to jail in New York City for inciting to riot by a fiery speech to a group of unemployed workers.

Upon her release Goldman embarked on lecture tours of Europe in 1895, of the United States, and again of Europe in 1899. Leon Czolgosz, the assassin of President William McKinley, claimed to have been inspired by her, although there was no direct connection netween them and by that time had relinquished her earlier tolerance of viiolance as an acceptable means of achieving her social ends. In 1906 Berkman was freed and he and Goldman resumed their joint activities. In that year she founded *Mother Earth*, a periodical that she edited until its suppression in 1917. In 1908, by a legal stratagem, her naturalization as a U.S. citizen was revoked. In 1910 she published *Anarchism and Other Essays.* She spoke often and widely, not only on anarchism and social problems but also on the current European drama of Ibsen, Strindberg, Shaw, and others, which she was instrumental in introducing to American audiences. Her lectures on that topic were published in 1914 as *The Social Significance of the Modern Drama.* She also lectured on "free love," by which she meant that uncoerced attachment between two persons to whom conventions of law and church were irrelevant, and on birth control, a topic that landed her briefly in jail in 1916.

When World War I broke out in Europe Goldman opposed U.S. involvement, and when that nevertheless came about she agitated against military conscription. In July 1917 she was sentenced to two years in prison for these activities. By the time of her: release in September 1919 the nation was in the throes of hysteria over a largely imaginary subversive network of Communist elements. Goldman — "Red Emma," as she was called — was declared a subversive alien and in December, along with Berkman and 247 others, was deported to the Soviet Union. Her stay there was brief. Two years after leaving she recounted her experiences in *My Disillusionment in Russia*, 1923. She remained active, living at various times in Sweden, Germany, England, France, and elsewhere, continuing to lecture and writing her autobiography, *Living My Life*, 1931. She joined the antifascist cause in Spain during the civil war there and while working in its behalf died in Toronto, Canada, on May 14, 1940.

Goldmark, Josephine Clara 1877–1950 social researcher

Born in Brooklyn, New York, on October 13, 1877, Josephine Goldmark was the daughter of a well-to-do and cultivated family. After her father died in 1881, she grew up under the influence of Felix Adler, founder of the Ethical Culture movement, who earlier had married one of her sisters. (A few years later another sister married Louis D. Brandeis.) She graduated from Bryn Mawr College in 1898 and studied English an additional year at Barnard College. While working as a tutor at Barnard in 1903–1905, she became a volunteer assistant to Florence Kelley of the National Consumers' League. Within a short time she became publications secretary of the League and then chairman of its committee on legal defense of labor laws. The first of the painstakingly researched, massively detailed, and dramatically argued reports on social conditions that were to be her career appeared in 1907 under the title *Child Labor Legislation Handbook.* Five years of work went into the next one, *Fatigue and Efficiency*, published by the Russell Sage Foundation in 1912, in which she was able to demonstrate that excessive working hours were not only injurious to workers but also to overall productivity. She directed the research and compilation of facts that went into many of her brother-in-law's famous "Brandeis briefs," notably the one filed in *Muller v. Oregon* in 1908, and after his appointment to the Supreme Court in 1916 she frequently served Felix Frankfurter in a similar capacity.

In 1911–1913 Goldmark served with Frances Perkins, Robert Wagner, Alfred E. Smith, and others on a committee investigating the disastrous fire at the Triangle Shirtwaist Company in New York City in which 146 workers died. She published the *Case for the Shorter Work Day* in 1916 and *The Case against Nightwork for Women* in 1918. In 1919 she was named secretary of the Rockefeller Foundation's Committee for the Study of Nursing Education headed by Dr. C.-E. A. Winslow of Yale. As principal investigator for the committee, she examined more than 70 schools of nursing over the next four years. The resulting report, *Nursing and Nursing Education in the United States*, 1923, generally known as the Winslow-Goldmark report, was of great effect in prompting the upgrading of nursing education, particularly through the establishment of university affiliations and national accreditation procedures. She also served for a time as director of the New York Visiting Nurses Service. In the 1920s she and Florence Kelley directed a campaign to secure protection for workers with radium paint in the manufacture of instrument dials. Her last book on social problems, *Democracy in Denmark*, appeared in 1936. Josephine Goldmark passed her last years in Hartsdale, New York, and died in White Plains, New York, on December 15, 1950. Her biography of Florence Kelley, *Impatient Crusader*, was published in 1953.

Goodridge, Sarah 1788–1853 painter

Born in Templeton, Massachusetts, on February 5, 1788, Sarah Goodridge attended district schools and briefly, at seventeen, a school in Milton, Massachusetts, where she had gone to live with the family of an elder brother. From an early age she had been interested in drawing. Opportunity for instruction in art did not exist, however, and as for material she was generally limited to drawing on birch bark with a pin or on a sanded floor with a stick. When her brother moved to Boston she accompanied him and there was given a few lessons by a man in his household. Until 1820 she lived alternately in Boston in winter and in summer in Templeton, where she taught school on occasion and began making and selling portraits in crayon and watercolor. She studied oil painting for a time, but a meeting with an artist from Hartford, who introduced her to miniature painting on ivory, settled her choice of medium.

From 1820 Goodridge lived in the home of her sister in Boston and worked steadily in miniature portraiture. Through a friend she met Gilbert Stuart, who criticized her work, gave her further instruction in technique, and in 1825 sat for a portrait that he declared the only true likeness ever done of him. Other famous subjects of her miniatures included Isaiah Thomas, General Henry Lee, Theophilus Parsons, Daniel Webster, and General Henry Knox, the last a copy of one made by Stuart for her instruction, the only miniature painted by him. Commissions given her over the next three decades were sufficient to support several members of her family in addition to herself. She exhibited her work on five occasions between 1827 and 1835 at the Boston Athenaeum, and in 1828–1829 and again in 1841–1842 she visited Washington, D.C., with her work. In the late 1840s her output began to decline from the two or three miniatures a week she had normally painted, and with the failure of her eyesight she gave up painting entirely in 1851 and settled in Reading, Massachusetts. She died in Boston on December 28, 1853.

Goodwin, Doris Kearns 1943– author

Doris Kearns Goodwin

Born on January 4, 1943 in Rockville Centre, New York, Doris Helen Kearns graduated magna cum laude from Colby College in 1964 and received her Ph.D. from Harvard University in 1968. While working on her doctorate degree, she was an intern at the State Department, and then at the House of Representatives. She later became a research associate at the Department of Health, Education and Welfare. She was working as special assistant to Willard Wirtz in 1968 when she co-authored an article for *New Republic* in which she was extremely critical of President Lyndon B. Johnson. When she met Johnson at a White House reception a few months later, he surprised her and asked her to dance. Trying to appear open-minded and unthreatened by his critics and the growing anti-Vietnam sentiment in the nation, he suggested that she be assigned to work with him in the White House. Soon afterward, Johnson asked her to help him write his memoirs, beginning a friendship that would last the rest of Johnson's life.

Many critics believed that Johnson enlisted her aid as a calculated political move. They felt he wanted to be remembered favorably and therefore sought out writers that would paint a positive picture of him. She spent a number of years visiting Johnson at his home in Austin, Texas, while she was a professor at Harvard, collecting information and getting to know the former President. Her book, *Lyndon Johnson and the American Dream*, published in 1976 (three years after Johnson's death), impressed critics with its skillful writing, as well as its intelligent and down-to-earth portrayal of Johnson. She neither sugar-coated nor glossed over the events in Johnson's life. She simply presented a researched critical study of the former president, his actions and policies, and what she believed to be his motivations.

After the much-hailed publication of her book, she was contracted to write a biography of John F. Kennedy — a project that took almost 10 years to complete — and the critical response was similar to her first book. In 1975 she married Richard Goodwin, a writer and political consultant who worked as a speech writer and advisor to Robert and John Kennedy. Since her husband had been a friend of the Kennedy family for over 25 years, she had access to information, both verbal and written, that no Kennedy biographers before her had. She was praised for her ability to use this information to write a detailed history of her subjects without invading their privacy. *The Fitzgeralds and the Kennedys: An American Saga*, 1987, chronicled three generations of the Fitzgerald and Kennedy families. The book provided an exploration of Irish immigrant families over several generations. Made into a television movie, the work was considered not only historically accurate and important, but a gripping, compassionate tale as well.

In 1994 she once again utilized her skill for writing fascinating accounts of the lives of American leaders in *No Ordinary Time*, a biography of Franklin and Eleanor Roosevelt. The book was a great success and she was awarded a Pulitzer Prize for it in 1995. Other of her notable accomplishments included acting as a regular panelist on a weekly television program in Boston, and appearing as a political commentator on numerous national television programs such as "Nightline," "Today," and "Good Morning America."

Gordon, Anna Adams 1853–1931 reformer

Born in Boston on July 21, 1853, Anna Gordon attended public schools in Newton, Massachusetts, and was a student at Mount Holyoke Seminary (now College) in 1871–1872 and at Lasell Seminary in Auburndale, Massachusetts, in 1873–1875. In 1877, at a Boston revival meeting held by evangelist Dwight L. Moody, she met Frances Willard, and within a short time she had become Willard's private secretary. She took up residence with Willard in Evanston, Illinois. In 1879 she followed her friend and employer into the work of the Woman's Christian Temperance Union, of which Frances Willard was that year elected president. With Willard and alone she traveled throughout the country for a number of years, lecturing and organizing local branches and children's auxiliaries of the WCTU. She was particularly interested in the organization's appeal to children through the Loyal Temperance Union, for which she wrote a number of marching songs, and in 1891 she became superintendent of juvenile work for the new World Woman's Christian Temperance Union.

On the death of Frances Willard in 1898 Gordon became vice-president of the national WCTU under Lillian M. N. Stevens. She published *The Beautiful Life of Frances E. Willard* in 1898 and *What Frances E. Willard Said* in 1905. In 1910 she founded the Young Campaigners for Prohibition. In 1914 she succeeded Stevens as president of the WCTU and promptly moved the organization into the burgeoning campaign for a federal prohibition amendment. She was instrumental in persuading President Woodrow Wilson to take various steps short of outright prohibition during World War I, such as prohibiting the use of foodstuffs for the manufacture of alcoholic beverages, and with the ratification of the Eighteenth Amendment in January 1919 she urged the WCTU to become interested in enforcement. She also turned the organization's attention to other causes, including Americanization of immigrants, child welfare, and the condition of women in industry. In 1924 she headed a highly successful membership and fund-raising drive by the WCTU.

Having been elected president of the World WCTU in 1922 after two years as vice-president, Gordon resigned the presidency of the national organization in 1925 to devote full time to the larger task. Other books by her included *Toots and Other Stories*, 1906, *White Ribbon Hymnal*, 1911, *Young People's Temperance Chorus Book*, 1911, *What Lillian M. N. Stevens Said*, 1914, *Marching Songs for Young Crusaders*, 1916, *Jubilee Songs*, 1923, and *Everybody Sing*, 1924. Anna Gordon died in Castile, New York, on June 15, 1931.

Gordon, Laura de Force 1838–1907 lawyer, editor and reformer

Born in North East, Erie County, Pennsylvania, on August 17, 1838, Laura de Force attended local schools. In 1862 she married Dr. Charles H. Gordon, with whom she lived in New Orleans during the Civil War and traveled west to Nevada in 1867. In 1870 they settled in Mokelumne, California. (Four years later the town changed its name to Lodi.) Laura Gordon had for some years been an occasional public lecturer, and the trip west by wagon shortly became one of her topics. In February 1868 she delivered in San Francisco a call for equal rights for women, one of the first such public appeals to be made in the West. She lectured on suffrage throughout the region and in 1870 contributed materially to the founding of the California Woman Suffrage Society, of which she served as president in 1877. In 1871 she was nominated for state senator by her local Independence party. In 1873 she became editor of the woman's department of the *Narrow Gauge*, a semiweekly paper published in Stockton, California. Later, in September of that year, she began publishing and editing the *Stockton Weekly Leader*. Her editorial ability, bolstered by the novelty of a woman editor, made the paper an immediate success, and in May 1874 it became a daily. In 1875 she moved the paper to Sacramento, where it appeared as the *Weekly Leader* until she sold it a year later. From that year to 1878 she edited the Oakland *Daily Democrat*. In 1877 she published *The Great Geysers of California and How to Reach Them*.

While covering the 1877–1878 session of the state legislature for her paper and also for the *Sacramento Bee*, Gordon lobbied effectively in behalf of a bill drafted by Clara S. Foltz to admit women to the practice of law in California. Later in 1878, having sometime before divorced her husband, she applied for admission to the Hastings College of Law in San Francisco. She and Foltz, who also had applied, were denied admission, whereupon they instituted a suit against the school. They argued their case jointly in district court and in the fall of 1879 before the state supreme court and won. Gordon had meanwhile been reading law privately, and in December 1879 she and Foltz were the second and third women admitted to the California bar. She practiced in San Francisco for five years and then moved to Stockton. She won a large reputation at the bar, notably — and remarkably — as a criminal lawyer; a number of her successful defenses in murder cases were widely discussed. In February 1885 she was admitted to practice before the U.S. Supreme Court. She campaigned on numerous occasions for the Democratic party and remained a forceful supporter of woman suffrage. From 1884 to 1894 she was again president of the California Woman Suffrage Society. She died in Lodi, California, on April 5, 1907.

Graham, Isabella Marshall 1742–1814 educator and philanthropist

Born in Lanarkshire, Scotland, on July 29, 1742, Isabella Marshall grew up in Elderslie, near Paisley, in a religious family and received a good education. In 1765 she married Dr. John Graham, an army surgeon whom she accompanied to Canada in 1767. They lived successively in Quebec, Montreal, and Fort Niagara and on the island of Antigua, where Dr. Graham died in 1773. She then returned with her children to Scotland and opened a small school in Paisley. Later she opened a boarding school for girls in Edinburgh, where she also was active in various charitable enterprises, notably a "penny Society," a fund for mutual relief in case of sickness to which the poor subscribers contributed a penny weekly. The society later became the Society for the Relief of the Destitute Sick. In 1789 she returned to America and settled in New York City, where she opened a girls' school that was immediately successful. She also continued her charitable work and in November 1797 led a group of women, including Elizabeth Bayley Seton (later Saint Elizabeth), in organizing the Society for the Relief of Poor Widows with Small Children, of which she became "First Directress." She gave up teaching the next year to devote full time to philanthropy.

The society was one of the earliest organizations of its kind in America, and under Graham's leadership it distributed assistance to hundreds of needy widows. The society also sought work for them and established a house for needlework. From 1802, when a state charter was granted, the society received money from the legislature to supplement that raised by public appeal. She presided over a meeting in March 1806 at which the Orphan Asylum Society was founded, largely as a result of the labors of her daughter, Joanna Graham Bethune. She taught in the asylum's Lancasterian school and from 1810 was a trustee of the managing society. She was chosen president of the board of ladies in charge of the Magdalen House of the Magdalen Society on its organization in 1811. In 1814, shortly before her death, she led in founding the Society for the Promotion of Industry Among the Poor. She died in New York City on July 27, 1814.

Graham, Katharine Meyer 1917– newspaper publisher

Born in New York City on June 16, 1917, Katharine Meyer grew up in Washington, D.C., and attended private schools. She entered Vassar College in 1935, transferred to the University of Chicago a year later, and graduated in 1938. After a year as a reporter for the *San Francisco News* she joined the editorial staff of the *Washington Post*, which her father had bought in 1933. She also worked in the editorial and circulation departments of the *Sunday Post*. In June 1940 she married Philip L. Graham, a lawyer. From 1945 she gave up her career in favor of her family. In 1946 Philip Graham became publisher of the *Post*, and in 1948 he and Mrs. Graham bought the voting stock of the corporation from her father. She remained apart from active involvement in the business as her husband built up the paper and acquired the rival *Times-Herald* in 1954, *Newsweek* magazine in 1961, and several radio and television stations.

In September 1963, following her husband's death by suicide, Katharine Graham assumed the presidency of the Washington Post Company. (Later, in January 1969, she also assumed the title of publisher.) After a period of study of the newspaper's situation she moved forcefully to make it into a journal of national importance. Greatly increasing the editorial budget and expanding the staff, she built up a corps of reporters and editors that made the *Post* a formidable competitor to such established national papers as the *New York Times* and the *Los Angeles Times*. In particular the *Post* built a reputation for aggressive investigative reporting: in 1971 it and the *New York Times* published lengthy excerpts from the classified "Pentagon Papers" after fighting judicial prior restraint orders in the Supreme Court, and in 1972–1974 it was the *Post*, and specifically reporters Carl Bernstein and Robert Woodward, working under editor Benjamin C. Bradlee, who pursued the Watergate story into the White House, uncovering obstruction of justice that involved President Nixon himself and winning their paper a Pulitzer Prize in the process. Throughout these and other controversial cases, when the *Post* was criticized not only by political leaders — Vice-President Spiro T. Agnew was particularly harsh — but frequently also by less uncompromising journalists, Graham staunchly upheld her editors' decisions. In 1973 she moved up from president to chairman of the board of directors and chief executive officer of the Washington Post Company. She handed over the position of publisher to her son in 1979, and, retaining her control of the company as chairman and CEO, she expanded *Newsweek* and increased the scope of the company by purchasing more television stations and moving into cable television and cellular telephone operations. She stepped down as CEO in 1991. She was, in addition, a leading capital hostess and the recipient of numerous honors and awards.

Graham, Martha 1893–1991 dancer and choreographer

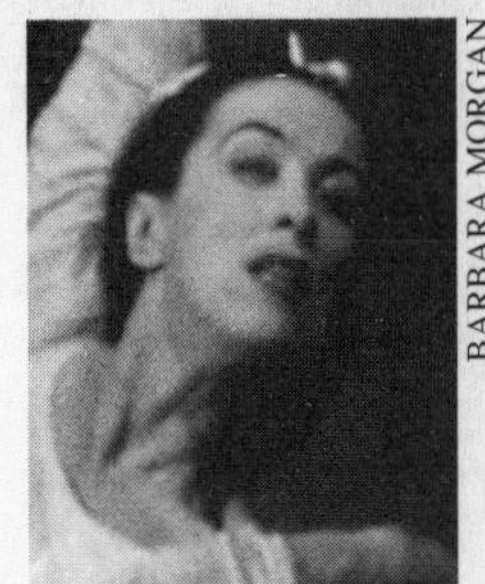

Martha Graham

Born in Pittsburgh on May 11, 1893, Martha Graham grew up in Santa Barbara, California, from the age of ten, and after completing her formal education in California schools she devoted herself to dancing. She studied with Ruth St. Denis and Ted Shawn at their influential Denishawn school in Los Angeles from 1916 and in New York City from 1920. Her first professional appearance was in 1920 as a lead dancer in Shawn's highly successful *Xochitl*, a modern ballet derived from Aztec legend. In 1923 she joined the *Greenwich Village Follies*, with which she remained for two seasons, and afterward she worked to develop her own dancing style. She taught at the Eastman School of the Theatre in Rochester, New York, in 1924–1925 and there experimented with group arrangements. In April 1926 she premiered as a solo dancer in New York City, introducing works of her own creation, and began to acquire an audience of discriminating and enthusiastic admirers. Interpretations of Ernest Bloch's *Baal Shem Suite* and of Claude Debussy's *Nuages et Fêtes*, and her own *Désir*, *Tanagar*, and *Revolt*, were among the works in her early repertoire.

In 1927 she founded the Martha Graham School of Contemporary Dance in New York. In the 1930s, with her own dance company, she introduced *Primitive Mysteries*, *Incantation*, and *Dolorosa*, dances that reflected her fascination with Mexican Indians and their religious rituals. She studied in Mexico in 1932 as the first dancer to receive a Guggenheim fellowship. With *Frontier*, 1935, she began using stage decor and inaugurated her long association with sculptor-designer Isamu Noguchi. Later she also employed designs by Alexander Calder.

Among Graham's most famous dance pieces were *El Penitente*, 1940, *Letter to the World*, based on the life and poetry of Emily Dickinson, 1940, *Punch and Judy*, 1941, *Deaths and Entrances*, on a theme suggested by the Brontës, 1943, *Hérodiade*, 1944, *Appalachian Spring* (to music of Aaron Copland), 1944, *Cave of the Heart*, inspired by the Medea legend (music of Samuel Barber), 1946, *Errand into the Maze*, on the Minotaur legend (Gian-Carlo Menotti), 1947, *Night Journey*, the tale of Jocasta (William Shuman), 1947, *Judith* (Shuman), 1950, *Seraphic Dialogue*, on Joan of Arc, (Norman Dello Joio), 1955, *Clytemnestra*, 1958, *Embattled Garden*, on the Eden myth, 1958, *Episodes: Part 1* (Anton Webern), 1959, *Alcestis*, 1960, *Phaedra*, 1962, *Circe* (Alan Hovhaness), 1963, *The Witch of Endor* (Schuman), 1965, *A Time of Snow* (Dello Joio), 1968, *The Archaic Hours*, 1969, *Mendicants of Evening*, 1973, *Myth of a Voyage*, 1973, *Holy Jungle*, 1974, *Lucifer*, 1975, *Ecuatorial* and *The Owl and the Pussycat*, 1978, *Acts of Light*, 1981, *Rite of Spring*, 1984, *Persephone*, 1987, and *Maple Leaf Rag*, 1990. Her introduction of completely new techniques based on the contraction and release of the torso was a break from classical ballet and created a completely new form of dance and theatre.

As a creator of dances Graham never allowed her work to settle into any one hackneyed set of movements or moods. Over the course of her career, in over 150 dance pieces from solos to full-scale works, she was passionately interested in the power of dance to reveal inner identity, the soul hidden by and often at odds with the outer appearance. Her many interpretations of Greek myth made particular use of this contrast in the characters of tragic heroines. In *A Dancer's World*, a 1957 film, she both explained and demonstrated her techniques and philosophy of dance. In 1964 she founded the Batsheva Dance company in Tel Aviv and in 1967 the London Contemporary Dance Theatre. Acknowledged the foremost American exponent of her art, she performed in major cities of the United States and made numerous foreign tours. Graham retired from performing in 1970, but she continued thereafter as choreographer of her troupes and as director of the Martha Graham Center of Contemporary Dance. In 1973 she published *The Notebooks of Martha Graham*. In October 1976 she was awarded the Medal of Freedom by President Gerald R. Ford (whose wife Betty had once been a student of hers). Other awards include the Aspen Award in the Humanities, 1965, the Kennedy Center Honors, 1979, Knight of the Legion of Honor from France, 1983, the Paris Medal of Honor, 1985, the National Medal for Arts, 1985, Denmark's Ingenio et Arti Medalion, 1987, and several honorary doctorates. She died in New York City on April 1, 1991.

Grant, Zilpah Polly 1794–1874 educator

Born on May 30, 1794, in Norfolk, Connecticut, Zilpah Grant attended local schools and to the extent her frail health allowed worked to help her widowed mother keep the family farm. From fifteen she taught in district schools in Paug (now East Norfolk), Winchester, and other nearby towns. In 1820 she seized an opportunity to further her own education and entered the Female Seminary of Byfield, Massachusetts, operated by the Reverend Joseph Emerson. A year later she became a teacher in the school. Later still she taught in a girls' school in Winsted, Connecticut, and in 1823–1824 she was again at Emerson's school, which had moved to Saugus, Massachusetts. In 1824 she accepted the position of preceptress of the newly endowed Adams Female Academy in what is now East Derry, New Hampshire. She was accompanied there by her younger colleague from the Reverend Emerson's school, Mary Lyon. She established a rigorous three-year course with examinations required for promotion from one grade to the next and with a diploma awarded for successful completion.

The academy flourished and gained a considerable reputation. The intrusion of the trustees, however, prompted Grant to leave in 1828, taking Lyon and a number of pupils with her, and to establish the Ipswich Female Seminary along the same lines in Ipswich, Massachusetts. In spite of her convalescent absence in 1832–1833 the school prospered, and with Lyon she began to plan a New England Female Seminary for Teachers. But in 1835 Mary Lyon left to begin the work that would lead to the founding of Mount Holyoke Seminary, and four years later the Ipswich Seminary closed. Grant moved to Dedham, Massachusetts, and in September 1841 married William B. Banister, a lawyer and politician of Newburyport. (He died in 1853). In 1852 she became a member of the board of managers of the American Woman's Educational Association, founded by Catharine Beecher, and was active in the program to recruit and train teachers for schools in the West, making a tour of colleges and seminaries for that purpose in 1855–1856. In the latter year she published a pamphlet of *Hints on Education.* Her last years she devoted increasingly to religion. She died in Newburyport, Massachusetts, on December 3, 1874.

Grasso, Ella 1919–1981 public official

Born on May 10, 1919, in Windsor Locks, Connecticut, Ella Rosa Giovanna Oliva Tambussi was educated in parochial schools and at the private Chaffee School in Windsor. She graduated from Mount Holyoke College with honors in 1940 and took an M.A. in 1942. In August 1942 she married Thomas A. Grasso. During World War II she served as assistant director of research for the Connecticut office of the War Manpower Commission. Grasso also became active in local Democratic politics, and in 1952 she was elected to the state legislature. She was reelected in 1954. During 1956–1958 she sat on the Democratic National Committee. In 1958 she was elected Connecticut's secretary of state, a post in which she served three terms, until 1970. In 1970 and again in 1972 she was elected to Congress, where she compiled a strongly liberal voting record.

In 1974 Grasso campaigned successfully for the Democratic nomination for governor and in November decisively defeated her Republican opponent. With her inauguration in January 1975 she became the first woman to serve as governor of Connecticut and the first woman to hold a state governorship solely on her own merits (all previous women governors had been wives of former governors). A major concern of her administration was restoring solvency to the state treasury, a task made more difficult by the strong popular opposition to a state income tax. An inherited budget deficit was turned into a surplus within four years as she maneuvered adroitly to retain the support of the many fragmented groups that made up her constituency. In September 1978 Grasso fought off a primary challenge by her lieutenant governor and was nominated for a second term. She was reelected by a large majority in November and began a second four-year term, but resigned on New Year's Eve in 1980 because of illness. She was described as a symbolic rather than doctrinaire feminist leader who was opposed to legalized abortion, did not actively support affirmative action, and supported the proposed Equal Rights Amendment but did not campaign for it. She was a popular politician who, in 28 years as a public figure, never lost an election. She died in Hartford on February 5, 1981.

Gratz, Rebecca 1781–1869 philanthropist

Born in Philadelphia on March 4, 1781, Rebecca Gratz was the daughter of a well known merchant and patriot. She grew up a celebrated beauty, and the Gratz home was frequently visited by Edward Malbone, Thomas Sully (both of whom made portraits of Rebecca), Washington Irving, and Fanny Kemble. In 1801 she helped organize and became first secretary of the Female Association for the Relief of Women and Children in Reduced Circumstances. In 1815 she helped found the Philadelphia Orphan Asylum, of which she served as secretary from 1819 to 1859. In 1819 she organized and became secretary of the Female Hebrew Benevolent Society.

In 1838, after some 20 years of active interest in improving religious education for Jewish children, Rebecca Gratz, through the Female Hebrew Benevolent Society, founded the Hebrew Sunday School Society of Philadelphia, of which she served as president until 1864. The society was the first such organization in the United States and served as a model for others like it. The fame she enjoyed in her own day and the enduring interest in her rest not on her philanthropies, however, but on the well attested tradition that she served as the model for the heroine Rebecca in Sir Walter Scott's *Ivanhoe*. Story has it that Washington Irving met Scott and, on learning of his intention to include Jewish characters in his next novel, told him about his Philadelphia friend. Scott later wrote Irving after the publication of *Ivanhoe*: "How do you like your Rebecca? Does the Rebecca I have pictured compare well with the pattern given?" Rebecca Gratz died in Philadelphia on August 27, 1869.

Grau, Shirley Ann 1929– writer

Born in New Orleans on July 8, 1929, Shirley Ann Grau attended the Booth School in Montgomery, Alabama, and in 1950 graduated from Newcomb College, Tulane University, in New Orleans. She remained at Tulane for an additional year of graduate study in English literature. Her first published story appeared in *New World Writing* in 1953, and in 1955 she published a collection entitled *The Black Prince, and other Stories*, which received considerable critical attention. *The Hard Blue Sky*, 1958, her first novel, challenged readers with its setting in an exotic community on a Louisiana coastal island and with its near absence of plot. The treatment of character, and the lyrical quality of the writing itself, accounted for the novel's great interest. In *The House on Coliseum Street*, 1961, *The Keepers of the House*, which won a Pulitzer Prize, 1964, *The Condor Passes*, 1971, and *Evidence of Love*, 1977, she continued to explore the inner recesses of characters cut off, whether by poverty, geography, race, or other circumstances, from their fellow men. She also continued to publish short stories in the *New Yorker*, *Saturday Evening Post*, *Atlantic Monthly*, *Mademoiselle*, and other magazines, some of which were collected in *The Wind Shifting West*, 1973. *Nine Women*, a collection of short stories, was published in 1986.

Green, Anna Katharine 1846–1935 mystery writer

Born on November 11, 1846, in Brooklyn, New York, Anna Green grew up and attended public schools there and, from the age of ten, in Buffalo. She graduated from

Ripley Female College (now Green Mountain College) in Poultney, Vermont, in 1866. Her early poetic ambitions were bolstered by a meeting while in college with Ralph Waldo Emerson. Her first book, however, was something entirely different: a detective tale entitled *The Leavenworth Case*, 1878, which sold over 150,000 copies. Edgar Allan Poe and Wilkie Collins were virtually her only predecessors in the writing of such fiction; her fictional detective, Ebenezer Gryce, anticipated in some respects the later Sherlock Holmes. *A Strange Disappearance*, 1880, and *Hand and Ring*, 1883, followed, and after publishing two largely ignored volumes of verse, *The Defense of the Bride and Other Poems*, 1882, and *Risifi's Daughter*, 1887, she returned permanently to detective novels.

Among Green's mysteries were *Behind Closed Doors*, 1888, *Forsaken Inn*, 1890, *Marked "Personal"*, 1893, *The Doctor, His Wife, and the Clock*, 1895, *The Affair Next Door*, 1897, *Lost Man's Lane*, 1898, *Agatha Webb*, 1899, *The Circular Study*, 1900, *The Filigree Ball*, 1903, *The House in the Mist*, 1905, *The Millionaire's Baby*, 1905, *The Amethyst Box*, 1905, *The Woman in the Alcove*, 1906, *The Chief Legatee*, 1906, *The Mayor's Wife*, 1907, *The House of the Whispering Pines*, 1910, *Initials Only*, 1911, *The Mystery of the Hasty Arrow*, 1917, and *The Step on the Stair*, 1923. While their literary value was not great — she never outgrew the Victorian conventions of romantic love scenes, stilted dialogue, and circumlocution — they were tightly plotted, well constructed, and engrossing. Her knowledge of criminal law, gained from her lawyer father, helped give an air of realism to the novels. She is generally credited with having established the detective novel as a genre and as one of the most popular forms of fiction, and in her books the formulas that were to characterize the field were first outlined. From November 1884 she was married to Charles Rohlfs, an actor turned designer who later achieved fame for his unique art nouveau furniture. Anna Green Rohlfs died in Buffalo, New York, on April 11, 1935.

Green, Anne Catherine Hoof 1720?–1775 printer

Born about 1720, probably in the Netherlands, Anne Hoof apparently was brought to America as a child and grew up in Philadelphia. In April 1738 she married Jonas Green, a printer employed by Benjamin Franklin and Andrew Bradford. Later in that year they moved to Annapolis, where he became printer to the province of Maryland. In January 1745 he began issuing the *Maryland Gazette*. Anne Green undoubtedly helped in the printing shop and learned the business well, for after Jonas Green's death in April 1767 the newspaper continued to appear without interruption. In that year she also issued the volumes of *Acts and Votes and Proceedings* of the provincial assembly on schedule. Assisted by her son William until his death in August 1770 and there after by her son Frederick, she maintained the private and public sides of the business with great ability. In June 1768 she was given formal appointment as provincial printer. The almanacs, pamphlets, and books, notably the *Deputy Commissary's Guide*, 1774, by Elie Vallette, that issued from her press were typographically distinguished examples of her craft. The *Maryland Gazette* was the province's principal source of news in the period leading up to the Revolution, and in its pages the issues of the day were hotly debated. John Dickinson's celebrated *Letters from a Pennsylvania Farmer* were first published in that journal. Little is known of Anne Green's personal life. She died on March 23, 1775, probably in Annapolis.

Green, Henrietta Howland 1834–1916 financier

Born in New Bedford, Massachusetts, on November 21, 1834, Henrietta Howland Robinson came of a wealthy family; she was connected on the maternal Howland side to one of the great mercantile families of New England. She was reared in a home of Quaker austerity, however, and schooled privately. In 1865 both her father and a maternal aunt died, leaving her in their wills a total of about $10 million in outright bequests and trust funds. Her suit to secure her aunt's entire estate on the basis of a deathbed will dragged on for five years until the will was adjudged a forgery in 1871. In July 1867 she married Edward H. Green, but by mutual consent their finances were kept separate, and she managed hers with single-minded dedication both before and after his death in 1902. Steeped in business and finance from childhood, Hetty Green devoted her life to increasing her fortune. She became a major and feared operator on Wall Street, where in addition to extensive holdings in railroad and other stocks and in government bonds she maintained a considerable liquid fund for lending purposes. In the aftermath of the Panic of 1907 a number of major investors found themselves in her debt. She also invested heavily in mortgages and real estate, particularly in Chicago.

As her fortune grew, Hetty Green, sometimes called the "witch of Wall Street," continued to live with her son and daughter in inexpensive lodgings, avoiding all display of wealth and virtually all society. Her eccentricities made her a favorite subject for newspaper gossip, and all manner of stories were circulated concerning her miserliness. Perhaps the most widely repeated was that of her supposed refusal to hire a doctor to treat her son's injured leg, resulting eventually in a forced amputation. She often appeared publicly in shabby dress, and she was known to seek medical treatment for herself at charity clinics. Reputed, probably correctly, to be the richest woman in America, she lived for much of her later life in a small apartment in Hoboken, New Jersey. On her death in New York City on July 3, 1916, she left an estate of more than $100 million.

Greene, Belle da Costa 1883–1950 librarian and bibliographer

Born on December 13, 1883, in Alexandria, Virginia, Belle Greene grew up there and in Princeton, New Jersey, after the separation of her parents. Unable to afford college, she went from public school into a job at the Princeton University library. She soon mastered cataloguing, served in the reference department, and became deeply interested in the library's rare book collection. This interest brought her to the attention of Junius Spencer Morgan, a collector, who recommended her to his uncle, J. Pierpont Morgan, whose large and haphazard collection of early books and manuscripts was about to be placed in its own building in New York City. From 1905 to 1908 Belle Greene worked to bring order to Morgan's great collection. Her ability and her forthright personality led Morgan to place increasing trust in her judgment, and from 1908 she was traveling regularly to Europe as his agent, seeking out and purchasing additions to the Morgan Library collection. She worked indefatigably on these trips to increase her own knowledge of books and manuscripts, a pursuit in which she profited greatly by the tutelage of Sydney Cockrell of the Fitzwilliam Museum in Cambridge and later that of Bernard Berenson in Italy. She became a well known and respected figure to the leading libraries, galleries, and dealers in Europe.

The death of Morgan in 1913 left Greene for a time in an uncertain position, for J. P. Morgan, Jr., had shown little interest in his father's collection. World War I interrupted her worries, however, and she threw herself wholeheartedly into war work. By 1920 the younger Morgan had discovered an interest in the library, and Belle da Costa Greene resumed her European researches. In 1924 Morgan transformed the library into an incorporated and endowed educational institution and named Greene director. She held the post for 24 years, during which she made it a world center for scholarly research. Photographic and information services, together with programs of lectures and publications, were soon established. She had a genius for friendship as for scholarly bibliography, and the two qualities dovetailed in her work for the library. Her European trips continued until 1936; declining health marked the years from then until her retirement in November 1948. In 1949 an exhibition was mounted at the Morgan Library in her honor, and work began by a group of scholars on a festschrift in her honor. She died in New York City on May 10, 1950. The volume of *Studies in Art and Literature for Belle da Costa Greene* appeared in 1954.

Greenfield, Elizabeth Taylor 1817?–1876 singer

Born a slave in Natchez, Mississippi, probably in 1817, Elizabeth Taylor accompanied her mistress to Philadelphia in her childhood. When her mistress joined the Society of Friends and freed her slaves, Elizabeth chose to remain with her and took her surname, Greenfield. Encouraged by Mrs. Greenfield, young Elizabeth devoted time to developing her manifest musical talent. She continued to study after Mrs. Greenfield's death in 1845, eventually concentrating on her singing, and in 1851 she gave her first public performances in Buffalo, New York. During 1851–1852 she made a concert tour of several cities from Boston to Chicago. A testimonial concert in March 1853 arranged by friends in Buffalo raised funds to finance a trip to Europe for additional training. A London manager who was to have handled a British concert tour for her defaulted, leaving her stranded. She sought help from Lord Shaftesbury and was further aided by the recently arrived Harriet Beecher Stowe and by the Duchess of Sutherland, who became her especial patroness. She gave her first London performances in May 1853 and over the next months sang in several cities in England and Ireland. Her voice — full, resonant, with remarkable range — was accented by her plain appearance and the charm of her imperfect training. She attracted an enthusiastic following, by whom she was affectionately dubbed "the Black Swan," and on May 10, 1854, she sang for Queen Victoria at Buckingham Palace. Money for her vocal studies still lacked, however, and in July 1854 she returned to America. Settling in Philadelphia, she became a vocal teacher and for some years gave occasional concerts. She died in Philadelphia on March 31, 1876.

Greenhow, Rose O'Neal 1815?–1864 Confederate spy

Born in Maryland, probably in Montgomery County, about 1815, Rose O'Neal grew up there and in Washington, D.C., in the elegance of prewar Southern society. In 1835 she married the prominent physician and historian Robert Greenhow. She became a leading hostess of Washington, a confidante of several powerful political figures, notably John C. Calhoun and James Buchanan, and a party to various intrigues, especially those of the Cuban General Narciso López. In 1850 the Greenhows moved to Mexico City and then to San Francisco. After her husband's death in 1854 Rose Greenhow returned to Washington, D.C., where after the election of Buchanan as president in 1856 she was again a major social figure. Although she had long been a staunchly pro-slavery Southerner, she remained in Washington after the outbreak of the Civil War.

Greenhow was soon recruited as a Confederate spy. In July 1861 she secured and forwarded by courier information about movements of General Irvin McDowell's army toward Manassas Junction, Virginia. In August she was arrested by Allan Pinkerton, head of the Union secret service, and confined to her home. She somehow managed to continue sending information from there and, after her incarceration in January 1862, even from Old Capitol Prison. In March she was examined by a War Department commission, and in June she was exiled south. Greeted as a heroine in the Confederacy, she was handsomely rewarded by President Jefferson Davis. In August 1863 she sailed for Europe as an unofficial agent of the Confederacy, and later that year she published her prison diary, *My Imprisonment and the First Year of Abolition Rule at Washington*. Her celebrity having preceded her, she was presented at the British and French courts and was reportedly courted by Lord Granville. On October 1, 1864, weighed down by gold sovereigns, she drowned in the sinking of a small boat in which she was attempting to run the federal blockade of Wilmington, North Carolina.

Gregory, Cynthia 1946– ballet dancer

Born in Los Angeles on July 8, 1946, Cynthia Gregory began taking ballet lessons at the age of five. She later studied with Michel Panaieff, Robert Rossellat, and Carmelita Maracci, and while still a child she appeared in productions of the Los Angeles Civic

SUSAN COOK

Cynthia Gregory

Light Opera and the Santa Monica Civic Ballet. In 1958 choreographer Gower Champion gave her a small role in his musical motion picture *The Girl Most Likely*. After advanced lessons with Jacques d'Amboise of the New York City Ballet she entered the school of the San Francisco Ballet in 1961. Later in that year she joined the company's corps de ballet, and in 1962 she became a soloist. In San Francisco she learned roles in such standards as *Swan Lake* and *The Nutcracker* and in such modern pieces as George Balanchine's *Symphony in C* and *The Seven Deadly Sins* and John Cranko's *Beauty and the Beast*.

In 1965 Gregory moved to New York City and won a place in the American Ballet Theatre, where she became a soloist in 1966 and principal dancer in 1967. She danced roles in such classic romantic works as *Giselle*, *Les Sylphides*, *The Sleeping Beauty*, and *Swan Lake*. Her Odette/Odile in David Blair's version of *Swan Lake* in 1967 was hailed by critics, and over the next few years she made the role virtually her own. At the same time she demonstrated an equal gift for dramatic roles in such modern works as Antony Tudor's *Dark Elegies*, *Undertow*, and *Lilac Garden*; Michael Smuin's *Gartenfest*, *Schubertiade*, and *The Eternal Idol*, in the last two of which she created the principal roles; José Limon's *The Moor's Pavane*; Dennis Nahat's *Brahms Quintet*, in the premiere of which she danced in 1970; Alvin Alley's *The River* (music by Duke Ellington), in its 1971 premiere; Glen Tetley's *Gemini*; and Eliot Feld's *Intermezzo* and *At Midnight*. Her performance opposite Rudolf Nureyev in his revival of Marius Petipa's *Raymonda* in 1975 was a dazzling success, calling forth in their fullest her virtuoso technique and her magnetic stage presence. At the end of 1975 she left the American Ballet Theatre suddenly, but after nearly a year of quiet retirement in California she rejoined the company in October 1976 and quickly regained her standing as, in Nureyev's phrase, "America's prima ballerina assoluta." Her performance in a revival of Agnes de Mille's *Fall River Legend* in May 1979 was greeted as a triumph. She was the recipient of a *Dance* magazine award in 1975. She became a permanent guest artist with the Cleveland San Jose Ballet in 1986. She retired from the American Ballet Theatre in 1991, having received numerous awards including the Dance Educators of America Achievement Award, in 1983 and 1987, the International Arts Club's Citation of Merit, 1991, and San Francisco's Cyril Magnin Award, 1986. She has published two books, *Ballet is the Best Exercise*, 1986, and *Cynthia Gregory Dances Swan Lake*, 1990.

Griffing, Josephine Sophia White 1814–1872 reformer

Born in Hebron, Connecticut, on December 18, 1814, Josephine White married Charles S. S. Griffing in September 1835. About 1842 they moved to Ohio and settled in Litchfield. Within a short time Josephine Griffing became active in the antislavery cause and made her home a station on the Underground Railroad. Soon she was also active in the new women's rights movement as well. From 1851 to 1855 she was a paid agent of the Western Anti-Slavery Society, and in 1853 she was elected president of the Ohio Woman's Rights Association, of which she had been a founding member. She traveled and spoke widely on behalf of both causes and was a frequent contributor to newspapers, particularly the *Anti-Slavery Bugle* of Salem, Ohio. In 1863–1865 she was a lecturer for the Women's Loyal National League, a group concerned with the full implementation of emancipation. At the end of the Civil War she moved to Washington, D.C., to help deal with the problem of the landless and jobless freedmen.

In 1865 Griffing became the general agent of the National Freedman's Relief Association of the District of Columbia, which collected and distributed funds, food, and fuel to, and established temporary settlements for, the thousands of former slaves who had converged on Washington. Through her many also found jobs and homes. She lobbied effectively for the creation of the federal Freedmen's Bureau, and, although she disapproved its military character and impersonality, she cooperated with it and for two brief periods in 1865 and 1867 was employed by it. During the latter period she was especially effective in maintaining employment offices for freedmen in several Northern cities. She continued her work with the National Freedman's Relief Association of the District of Columbia for some years after the dissolution of the Freedmen's Bureau in 1869. During that time she continued also her support of the women's rights movement. She helped found and was first vice-president of the American Equal Rights Association in 1866, was a founder and president of the Universal Franchise Association of the District of Columbia in 1867, and in 1869 followed Susan B. Anthony and Elizabeth Cady Stanton into the National Woman Suffrage Association, of which she was chosen corresponding secretary. She died in Washington, D.C., on February 18, 1872.

Sarah M. Grimké

Grimké, Sarah Moore and Angelina Emily 1792–1873 and 1805–1879 social reformers

Born in Charleston, South Carolina, Sarah on November 26, 1792, and Angelina on February 20, 1805, the Grimké sisters came of a wealthy and aristocratic family. They early developed an antipathy toward both slavery and the limitations on the rights of women. Sarah, who had early objected to the rather thin education made available to her, made a number of visits to Philadelphia, where she became acquainted with the Society of Friends; at length, in 1821, she became a member and left her Southern home permanently. Angelina followed in 1829 and also became a Quaker. In 1835 Angelina wrote a letter of approval to William Lloyd Garrison that he subsequently published in his abolitionist newspaper, the *Liberator*. From that time on, the sisters were deeply involved in the abolitionist movement, Angelina always taking the lead. In 1836 she wrote a pamphlet, *An Appeal to the Christian Women of the South*, in which she urged those addressed to use their moral force against slavery. The institution, she argued, was harmful not only to African-Americans but to women. Sarah followed with *An Epistle to the Clergy of the Southern States*. Their public identification with the abolitionist cause rendered them anathema in their native city and state and even strained their Quaker friendships.

Under the auspices of the American Anti-Slavery Society, the Grimké sisters began to address small groups of women in private homes; this practice grew naturally into appearances before large mixed audiences. The General Association of Congregational Ministers of Massachusetts issued a pastoral letter in July 1837 strongly denouncing women preachers and reformers, and the sisters thereafter found it necessary to crusade equally for women's rights. Their fellow abolitionists split over the question of whether this was an extraneous issue, but the sisters were firm in their belief that it had to be dealt with if women were to be of effect in the abolitionist or any other cause. Their lectures at Odeon Hall, Boston, in the spring of 1838 attracted thousands. There followed Angelina's *Appeal to the Women of the Nominally Free States*, 1837, and Sarah's *Letters on the Equality of the Sexes and the Condition of Woman*, 1838. In May 1838 Angelina married the abolitionist Theodore Dwight Weld. After collaborating with Angelina's husband on *Slavery As It Is: Testimony of a Thousand Witnesses*, 1839, the sisters retired from public activity. They assisted in Weld's school in Belleville and later Perth Amboy, New Jersey, in 1848–1862. In 1863 the three moved to West Newton, Massachusetts, and in 1864 to Hyde Park, now in Boston. There the sisters died, Sarah on December 23, 1873, and Angelina on October 26, 1879.

Guérin, Mother Theodore 1798–1856 religious

Born in Étables, Côtes-du-Nord, France, on October 2, 1798, Anne-Thérèse Guérin, daughter of a naval officer, was privately educated. In 1823, after caring for her invalid mother for some years, she entered the community of the Sisters of Providence at Ruillé-sur-Loir, and in September 1825 she took her final vows in the order as Sister Theodore. She was then appointed superior of the order's school in Rennes. In 1833 she was transferred to the school at Soulaines. In 1840 she and five other sisters were dispatched to answer a call from the bishop of Vincennes, Indiana, to establish the order there. In October 1840 they arrived and established the convent of St. Mary-of-the-Woods near Terre Haute with Mother Theodore as superior. Within a month the first novices were accepted into the convent, and in July 1841 the Institute of St. Mary's, the first academy for girls in Indiana, was opened; it received a state charter in 1846 and eventually (1909) became Saint Mary-of-the-Woods College. In her 16 years as superior of the American branch of the Sisters of Providence, Mother Theodore oversaw the firm establishment of the mother house and the opening of ten schools throughout Indiana in addition to the Institute of St. Mary's. She died in St. Mary-of-the-Woods on May 14, 1856.

Guinan, Mary Louise Cecilia 1884–1933 actor and hostess

Born in Waco, Texas, on January 12, 1884, Mary Guinan at a young age went on the stage. For a number of years she barnstormed with stage companies and rodeos, and she had already made and broken two marriages when she arrived in New York City in 1905. There she won parts of increasing importance in a series of musical comedies and revues, including *Miss Bob White*, *The Hoyden*, *The Gay Musician*, and *The Passing Show of 1913*. She entertained troops in France during World War I. She had a highly successful career as a film actress in perhaps as many as 200 silent two-reelers, in which typically she portrayed a blunt, aggressive, blond Western heroine in the dime-novel tradition of Calamity Jane.

In 1924 Guinan began the career that made her famous. After a spontaneous performance one night as mistress of ceremonies at a party following a show at New York's Winter Garden, she was taken up by bootlegger and racketeer Larry Fay, who installed her as hostess of his El Fay Club. Perched on a stool in the center of the club, armed with a whistle and her own booming voice, "Texas" Guinan single-handedly created an atmosphere of camaraderie unique among nightclubs of prohibition-era New York. Each newcomer was greeted with a loud "Hello, sucker!" and she maintained her rule over the convivial chaos with a stream of wisecracks. Her good-humored challenges were effective in spurring club visitors to ever greater heights of extravagance, and her particular name for the free-spending out-of-towner, a "big butter-and-egg man," entered the vernacular. After the police closed the El Fay Club, she reappeared almost immediately at the Del Fay and in succession at the Texas Guinan Club, the 300 Club, the Club Intime, and Texas Guinan's Salon Royale. In a short time she became one of the best known figures of a decade ever eager for titillation. Her diamonds were equally celebrated. Arrested several times for operating a speakeasy, she was never convicted, and her ownership of any of the clubs was never proved.

Guinan returned to the Broadway stage with her own revue, *Padlocks of 1927*, and made two talking pictures, *Queen of the Night Clubs*, 1929, and *Broadway Thru a Keyhole*, 1933. In 1931, after her road company was refused permission to perform in France, she renamed her revue *Too Hot for Paris* and took it on a western tour. She fell ill and died in Vancouver, British Columbia, on November 5, 1933.

Guiney, Louise Imogen 1861–1920 poet and essayist

Born on January 7, 1861, in Roxbury (now part of Boston), Massachusetts, Louise Guiney was educated at Elmhurst, a convent school in Providence, Rhode Island. On graduating in 1879 she rejoined her family in Auburndale, Massachusetts. The death of her father two years earlier had left them in poverty, and to help support them she began contributing to various newspapers and magazines. Her poems, collected in *Songs at the Start*, 1884, and *The White Sail and Other Poems*, 1887, and her essays, collected in *Goose Quill Papers*, 1885, soon attracted the attention of the Boston literary establishment, and the verse in *A Roadside Harp*, 1893, and the essays in *Monsieur Henri*, 1892, *A*

Little English Gallery, 1894, and *Patrins*, 1897, brought her to the center of aesthetic life in Boston. Oliver Wendell Holmes, Thomas Bailey Aldrich, Thomas W. Higginson, and Edmund Clarence Stedman were among her friends and patrons, and on visits to England in the 1890s she added Edmund Gosse, William Butler Yeats, and others. During 1894–1897 she served as postmaster of Auburndale, and later she was employed in the Boston Public Library. A walking tour of England with her friend Alice Brown in 1895 led to their collaboration on *Robert Louis Stevenson — A Study*, 1895. Her own models in literature were chiefly Tennyson and Hazlitt.

When, toward the end of the 1890s, her health and her muse both deserted her, Guiney turned to scholarship, concentrating mainly on the Cavalier poets. From 1901 she lived happily in England, where she did research at the Bodleian Library at Oxford and explored the Cotswold countryside. Later books included *England and Yesterday*, 1898, *Martyr's Idyll and Shorter Poems*, 1899, *Hurrell Froude*, 1904, *Robert Emmet — His Rebellion and His Romance*, 1904, *The Blessed Edmund Campion*, 1908, and *Happy Ending*, her collected verse, 1909 (revised 1927). She died at her home in Chipping Campden, Gloucestershire, on November 2, 1920. Her unfinished anthology of Catholic poets from Sir Thomas More to Alexander Pope, prepared in collaboration with Geoffrey Bliss, was published as *Recusant Poets* in 1939.

Guthrie, Janet 1938– automobile racer

Born on March 7, 1938, in Iowa City, Iowa, Janet Guthrie grew up there and in Miami, Florida. She was an adventurous child and at seventeen earned a pilot's license. After graduating from the University of Michigan in 1960 she worked as a research and development engineer for Republic Aviation for six years. During that time she was one of four women to qualify for the scientist-astronaut program of the National Aeronautics and Space Administration; she was subsequently disqualified when the Ph.D. degree was made a requirement. From 1962 she was an avid sports car enthusiast, and in 1963 she began racing regularly in her Jaguar XK 140. Over the next several years she enjoyed increasing success on the Sports Car Club of America circuit, winning several major races and placing well in many others, and in 1966 she gave up her full-time job and became a freelance technical editor in order to devote more time to racing. From that year to 1971 she was a member of an all-woman racing team sponsored by the Macmillan Ring-Free Oil Company.

Later, under other sponsorships, Guthrie won, among others, the 1973 "B sedan" class North American road racing championship and the 1975 Vanderbilt Cup. Early in 1976 she was offered an opportunity to try out for the Indianapolis 500, the premier American event for Formula One cars. A 15th-place finish in her first Formula One race, the Trenton 200 in May 1976, demonstrated her ability to handle the big cars. She failed to qualify for Indianapolis, however, and for the rest of 1976 and early 1977 she gained speedway experience in a series of top stock car races. She qualified in speed trials for the 1977 Indianapolis 500 and on May 29 became the first woman to participate in that race. Mechanical troubles forced her to retire from the race after 27 laps. In 1978 she again qualified and for the first time finished, placing ninth in the field despite the handicap of a broken wrist. She qualified for the Indianapolis 500 again in 1979 but was forced out of the race early by mechanical problems. Having overcome both skepticism and on occasion outright hostility, Guthrie established herself as an outstanding professional race driver. She was inducted into the Women's Sports Hall of Fame in 1980. Translating her driving experience into the business world, she became a highway safety consultant for the Metropolitan Life Insurance Company from 1980 to 1987.

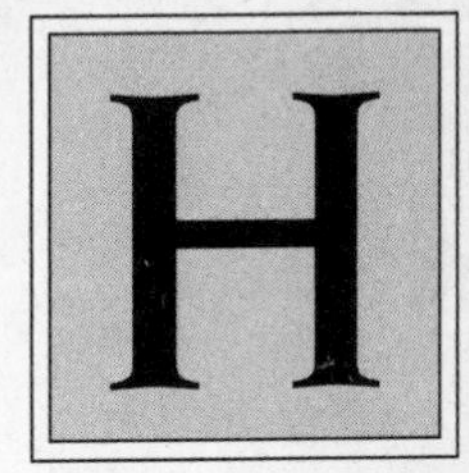

Hale, Louise Closser 1872–1933 actor and novelist

Born in Chicago on October 13, 1872, Louise Closser grew up and attended school in Indianapolis and La Porte, Indiana. After study at the American Academy of Dramatic Arts in New York City and Emerson College of Oratory in Boston she made her theatrical debut in 1894 in a Detroit production of *In Old Kentucky*. For several years she appeared in various minor roles. During that time, in August 1899, she married Walter Hale, an actor and artist. In the 1903 Broadway season she was a hit in Shaw's *Candida*. In April 1907 she made her London debut in her most popular role, that of Miss Hazy in *Mrs. Wiggs of the Cabbage Patch*. Subsequent appearances were in *Blue Bird* in 1910, *The Rainbow* in 1912–1913, *The Marriage of Columbine* in 1914, *The Clever Ones* in 1915, *His Bridal Night* in 1917, *For the Defense* in 1919, Eugene O'Neill's *Beyond the Horizon* in 1920, Zona Gale's *Miss Lulu Bett* in 1920, *Peer Gynt* in 1923, Rachel Crothers's *Expressing Willie* in 1924, *The Ivory Door* in 1927, and *Paris* in 1928. During those years of theatrical success, as she became one of the most popular and respected character actresses on the American stage, she led a second career as an author.

Hale's first novel, *A Motor Car Divorce*, appeared in 1906 and was followed by *The Actress*, 1909, *The Married Miss Worth*, 1911, *Her Soul and Her Body*, which was something of a sensation and was later made into a play, 1912, *Home Talent*, 1926, and *Canal Boat Fracas*, 1927. She also wrote several travel books illustrated by her husband: *We Discover New England*, 1915, *We Discover the Old Dominion*, 1916, and *An American's London*, 1920.

In 1929 Louise Hale left the legitimate stage for Hollywood. Among the films in which she was featured were *The Hole in the Wall*, 1929, *Paris*, 1929, *Big Boy*, 1930, *Dangerous Nan McGrew*, 1930, *Devotion*, 1931, *Shanghai Express*, 1932, *Letty Lynton*, 1932, *The White Sister*, 1933, *Another Language*, 1933, and *Dinner at Eight*, 1933. She died in Los Angeles on July 26, 1933.

Hale, Lucretia Peabody 1820–1900 writer

Born in Boston on September 2, 1820, Lucretia Hale was an elder sister of Edward Everett and Alexander Hill Hale and with them grew up in a cultivated family much involved with literature. She was educated privately at Elizabeth Peabody's school and others and through much of her life was in delicate health. In 1850 she and her brother Edward collaborated on a novel, *Margaret Percival in America*. She began publishing stories in the leading periodicals in 1858. Over the next 30 years she produced a large number of books, many of them on religious subjects or on the art of needlework. *Struggle for Life*, a novel, appeared in 1861 and was followed by *The Lord's Supper and its Observance*, 1866, and *The Service at Sorrow*, 1867. She collaborated with her brother Edward and others on *Six of One by Half a Dozen of the Other*, a novel, 1872, and in 1888 she published a book of games as *Fagots for the Fireside*, but her major reputation was gained by a series of whimsical sketches, many first published in magazines (beginning with "The Lady Who Put Salt in Her Coffee" in *Our Young Folks* for April 1868), that filled two books, *The Peterkin Papers*, 1880, and *The Last of the Peterkins*, 1886.

The Peterkins, a family of quite Bostonian and quite ingenuous folk devoted to self-improvement and lofty notions, encountered in the sketches a variety of difficulties arising from their scatterbrained naïveté and were rescued from disaster in each case by the commonsensical Lady from Philadelphia. The little tales were engagingly humorous and immensely popular, attaining over the years the status of classics of children's literature.

In addition to writing, Hale also helped her brother Edward edit his *Old and New Magazine* from 1870 to 1875. She was interested in education and in 1874 was one of the first six women, including Lucretia Crocker, elected to the Boston School Committee; she served two terms, until 1876. She also occasionally instructed students in her home or through a correspondence school. Her last years were marked by failing health. Her last book, *The New Harry and Lucy*, appeared in 1892. She died in Belmont, Massachusetts, on June 12, 1900.

Hale, Sarah Josepha Buell 1788–1879 editor and writer

Born on October 24, 1788, in Newport, New Hampshire, Sarah Josepha Buell was educated by her mother, by an older brother, a Dartmouth student, and later by her husband, David Hale, a lawyer, whom she married in October 1813. She submitted some articles to newspapers early in her married life but devoted herself principally to her home and to raising five children until her husband died in 1822. Left in financial straits, she then embarked on a literary career. Her poems were printed over the signature "Cornelia" in local journals and gathered in *The Genius of Oblivion*, 1823. A novel, *Northwood, a Tale of New England*, 1827, brought her an offer to go to Boston as editor of a new publication, the *Ladies' Magazine* (from 1834 the *American Ladies' Magazine*), which she accepted in 1828.

As editor Hale wrote most of the material for each issue herself — literary criticism, sketches of American life, essays, and poetry. Editorially and personally she supported patriotic and humanitarian organizations, notably the Boston Ladies' Peace Society and the Seaman's Aid Society, which she founded in 1833, and she staunchly advocated education for women and opportunities for women to teach, although she always remained apart from formal feminist movements and advised her readers to shun unfeminine involvement in public affairs. She also published during this period *Poems for Our Children*, 1830, containing her single most famous piece, "Mary Had a Little Lamb," and in 1834–1836 edited the *Juvenile Miscellany* magazine for children.

In 1837 Louis A. Godey took over the *American Ladies' Magazine* and established Hale as editor of his *Lady's Book*, soon known as *Godey's Lady's Book*, which he had established seven years earlier in Philadelphia. She moved to that city in 1841. With Godey she made the *Lady's Book* into the most influential and widely circulated women's magazine published in the country up to that time. (By 1860 its circulation was reputedly 150,000.) The magazine was especially noted for its colored fashion plates, and its literary pages were often filled by the likes of Nathaniel Hawthorne, Ralph Waldo Emerson, Edgar Allan Poe, Henry Wadsworth Longfellow, and Harriet Beecher Stowe. She continued to call for female education in the liberal arts and for more women teachers (her articles aided the founding of Vassar College), and she wrote of women as America's cultural and moral cornerstone whose uplifting influence should be wielded in the home and in schools and not through political power. *Godey's Lady's Book* was ever respectful of the highest decorum and of the cheerful aspects of life, and no hint of the social and political turmoils of the day crept into its pages.

In later years Hale liberalized her outlook so far as to approve women doctors, if only to treat those ailments of women that she felt were otherwise better endured than examined by male physicians. She was also active in promoting child welfare, and she published a number of books, including cookbooks, poetry, and prose. Her major achievement in book form was the *Woman's Record, or Sketches of Distinguished Women*, issued in 1853, 1869, and 1876; in the course of this ambitious project she completed some 36 volumes of profiles of women, tracing their influence through history on social organization and literature. She retired from *Godey's* in December 1877, at the age of eighty-nine. She died in Philadelphia on April 30, 1879.

Haley, Margaret Angela 1861–1939 educator and organizer

Born in Joliet, Illinois, on November 15, 1861, Margaret Haley attended public and convent schools and from 1876 taught in a succession of schools around Chicago. She took courses at the State Normal University (now Illinois State University) and at Cook County Normal School (now Chicago State University) at various times, and continued to teach in a Chicago elementary school. She was an early member of the Chicago Teachers' Federation, formed in March 1897, and rose quickly in the organization to become a district vice-president by 1900. In 1901 she left teaching to become a full-time business agent for the union. Her first successful fight for the union was against the Chicago Board of Education's refusal to honor a promised salary increase in 1899 and its rescission of an earlier one in 1900. Attacking the board's claim of poverty, Haley and the union president, Catharine Goggin, investigated the city tax revenues and discovered that five large public utility firms were seriously underassessed. A court case was fought to the Supreme Court, which in 1907 ratified a lower court's order that the utilities be reassessed. She had again to go to court to force the Board of Education to apply the increased revenue to salary increases. In 1902 she led the Chicago Teachers' Federation into the Chicago Federation of Labor.

About that time Haley also took over the moribund National Federation of Teachers, of which she became president, and used it with great skill to force the larger and more important National Education Association, until then entirely dominated by college presidents and administrators, to become more responsive to the needs of grade-school teachers. She achieved a major victory in Illinois with the enactment in 1907 of a state pension plan for teachers. She was also a vigorous supporter of a range of progressive reforms, including woman suffrage, child labor legislation, direct primaries and the referendum, and direct election of U.S. senators, and she threw the weight of her union behind them. In 1910 she was instrumental in securing the election of Ella Flagg Young, superintendent of Chicago schools, as president of the National Education Association.

During 1915–1917 Haley led a battle between the Chicago Teachers' Federation and the Board of Education over the federation's affiliation with the labor movement. The outcome was her agreement to take the union out of the Chicago Federation of Labor in exchange for the enactment of a state tenure law for teachers. She remained nonetheless active in the Women's Trade Union League, of which she was a national vice-president, and from its founding in 1916 she worked as an organizer for the American Federation of Teachers. In addition to her indefatigable efforts on the political and legal fronts she also edited and largely wrote the Chicago Teachers' Federation *Bulletin* from 1901 to 1908 and *Margaret Haley's Bulletin* in 1915–1916 and again from 1925 to 1931. She remained active into the 1930s. After a period of semiretirement she died in Chicago on January 5, 1939.

Hallaren, Mary Agnes 1907– army officer

Born in Lowell, Massachusetts, on May 4, 1907, Mary Hallaren was educated at the state teachers college in Lowell. While teaching in Lexington, Massachusetts, she traveled extensively in Europe, the Near East, and South America. In July 1942 she entered the Officer Candidate School of the newly organized Women's Army Auxiliary Corps. In July 1943, with the rank of captain, she was named commander of the first battalion to go overseas (the WAAC was redesignated the Women's Army Corps in that month and became a component of the Army of the United States). She served as director of WAC personnel attached to the Eighth and Ninth Air Forces, and in March 1945, by which time she had advanced to lieutenant colonel, she was appointed director of all WAC personnel in the European theater.

In June 1946 Hallaren became deputy director of the WAC, and in May 1947 she succeeded Colonel Westray B. Boyce as director, taking the rank of colonel. With the enactment on June 12, 1948, of the Women's Armed Services Integration Act the WAC became a component of the Regular Army; in consequence, in December of that year,

Colonel Hallaren became the first woman to receive a commission in the Regular Army (except for those in the Medical Corps, made part of the Regular Army in 1947). She continued as director until January 1953, when she was succeeded by Colonel Irene O. Galloway, and she retired from the army in 1960.

In 1965 Hallaren became director of the Women in Community Service division of the U.S. Labor Department. She retired from this position in 1978, but continued to consult to WICS and other organizations. In retirement she remained active in civic affairs, serving for many years on the board of directors of the WAC Foundation and lecturing on the history of women in the Army.

Hamer, Fannie Lou Townsend 1917–1977 civil rights activist

Born in Ruleville, Mississippi, on October 6, 1917, Fannie Lou Townsend was the youngest of 20 children. By the time she was six, she was working the fields with her sharecropper parents. Amid poverty and racial exploitation, she received only a sixth-grade education.

In 1942 she married Perry "Pap" Hamer with whom she adopted two girls, one of whom died in 1967. Her civil rights activism began with a mass meeting organized in August 1962 by the Student Nonviolent Coordinating Committee (SNCC), where she answered a call for volunteers to challenge voter registration procedures that excluded African-Americans. Her civil-rights activity cost her and her husband their jobs at the Marlow Plantation. Despite this and other harassments, she continued her civil-rights work, becoming a field secretary for SNCC and a registered voter in 1963.

In 1964 she became vice-chairperson of the Mississippi Freedom Democratic Party (MFDP), established after unsuccessful attempts by African-Americans to work with the all-white Mississippi Democratic Party. She ran as an MFDP candidate for Congress in the Second Congressional District of Mississippi. As a leader of the MFDP she gave a nationally televised address to the Credentials Committee at the 1964 Democratic National Convention describing the violence and injustices suffered by civil rights activists, including a jailhouse beating which left her crippled.

Hamer published *To Praise Our Bridges: An Autobiography*, 1967. As a member of the Democratic National Committee for Mississippi 1968–1971 and the Policy Council of the National Women's Political Caucus, 1971–1977, she actively opposed the Vietnam War and worked tirelessly on projects to improve economic conditions in Mississippi, including the Delta Ministry, the Freedom Farms Corporation, and the Young World Developers. She was awarded honorary degrees from several universities, including Tougaloo College, Howard University, and Morehouse College. She died on March 15, 1977.

Hamilton, Edith 1867–1963 educator, historian and writer

Born on August 12, 1867, in Dresden, Germany, of American parents, Edith Hamilton grew up in Fort Wayne, Indiana. From a very early age she was an eager student of Greek and Roman literature. She attended Miss Porter's School in Farmington, Connecticut, and following her graduation from Bryn Mawr College with an M.A. degree in 1894 she spent a year in 1895–1896 at the universities of Leipzig and Munich (she was the first woman to attend classes at Munich). In 1896 she returned to the United States and was appointed headmistress of the Bryn Mawr School in Baltimore, a preparatory institution founded 11 years earlier by Mary E. Garrett and others. She remained headmistress for 26 years. In 1922 she retired to devote herself to her classical studies and writing.

Hamilton published a number of articles on aspects of Greek life and art, and in 1930 her first book, *The Greek Way*, appeared. Vivid and engaging as well as thoroughly scholarly, the book was a critical and popular success. It was followed by *The Roman Way*, 1932, which was equally well received. Hamilton turned to other sources of tradition in *The Prophets of Israel*, 1936, and later in *Witness to the Truth: Christ and His Interpreters*, 1949. Others of her books included *Three Greek Plays*, translations from Aeschylus and Euripides, 1937, *Mythology*, 1942, *The Great Age of Greek Literature* (an expansion of *The Greek Way*), 1943, *Spokesmen for God* (an expansion of *The Prophets of Israel*), 1949, and *The Echo of Greece*, 1957. While visiting Greece in 1957 at the age of ninety, she was made an honorary citizen of Athens in recognition of her devotion to the ancient ideals of that city. Hamilton died in Washington, D.C., on May 31, 1963.

Hancock, Joy Bright 1898–1986 naval officer

Born in Wildwood, New Jersey, on May 4, 1898, Joy Bright graduated from the Pierce School of Business Administration in Philadelphia in 1918 and promptly enlisted in the naval reserve. From 1919 she worked as a civilian for the navy at various stations and at the Department of the Navy in Washington, D.C. In 1924 she married Lieutenant Commander Lewis Hancock, a naval aviator who died in the crash of the dirigible *Shenandoah* the following year. In 1928 she took a civil pilot's license, and after a period of study at George Washington University and elsewhere she joined the navy's Bureau of Aeronautics. Her *Airplanes in Action* appeared in 1938. She also edited the newsletter that became the *Naval Aviation News*. Shortly after the creation of the new women's naval reserve, the Women Accepted for Volunteer Emergency Service (WAVES), in July 1942 she joined, becoming a lieutenant in October, lieutenant commander in November 1943, and commander in March 1945. In February 1946 she was named assistant director of the WAVES, and in July she became director with the rank of captain.

The women's reserve passed out of existence in October 1948, but under provisions of the Women's Armed Services Integration Act of June 12, 1948, the Navy was authorized to offer regular commissions to women. In October Captain Hancock was among the first eight women so commissioned, taking rank of permanent lieutenant commander and temporary captain, which made her the navy's highest ranking woman. She was appointed assistant chief for women of the Bureau of Personnel and continued as ex officio director of WAVES (the name, though unofficial, persisted) until her retirement in June 1953. She was succeeded in that post by Captain Louise K. Wilde. In 1972 she published an autobiography, *Lady in the Navy*. Hancock received the Legion of Merit for her wartime service. She died on August 20, 1986, in Bethesda, Maryland.

Hanks, Nancy 1927–1983 public official

Born on December 31, 1927, in Miami Beach, Florida, Nancy Hanks grew up there and in Montclair, New Jersey. She graduated from Duke University in 1949 and two years later settled in Washington, D.C., where she held a succession of government jobs of increasing responsibility. In 1953 she became an assistant to Nelson A. Rockefeller, who was then serving as undersecretary of the newly created Department of Health, Education and Welfare. She remained with Rockefeller through his work with the Special Projects Office in the White House, and from 1956 to 1969 she was executive secretary of the Special Studies Project of the Rockefeller Brothers Fund. During that period she worked closely with Nelson and then with Laurance Rockefeller. Following up on a study by the Rockefeller staff on the state of the performing arts in America, she became a member of the board of directors of the Associated Councils of the Arts and in June 1968 president of the group.

In October 1969, following nomination by President Richard M. Nixon and confirmation by the Senate, Hanks became chairman of the National Endowment for the Arts and of its advisory arm, the National Council on the Arts. She proved to be a successful saleswoman for the endowment: her first annual appropriation from Congress was $16.4 million, compared to the $9 million of the year before. In distributing the money she broke new ground for the National Endowment by subsidizing national tours of dance companies, orchestras, and opera and theater groups, enabling such exponents of the arts to perform for audiences that would otherwise not have had the opportunity. Grants were also made to place working poets, musicians, dancers, and other artists in public schools, particularly those in the inner city, where schoolchildren could learn firsthand of the arts and their human meaning. By 1975 she had firmly established a reputation as a remarkably effective lobbyist in behalf of her own budget requests; in that year Congress appropriated $82 million for the National Endowment for the Arts. She resigned her post in October 1977, at the expiration of her second term, and returned to private life. She served as a Trustee and Vice Chairman of the Rockefeller Brothers Fund and was Executive Secretary of the Fund's Special Studies Project. In 1982 she received the Founders Award for Civic Leadership from the National Arts Endowment. She died in New York City on January 7, 1983.

Lorraine Hansberry

Hansberry, Lorraine 1930–1965 playwright

Born in Chicago on May 19, 1930, Lorraine Hansberry grew up in a relatively well-to-do family. She was interested in writing from an early age and while in high school was drawn especially to the theater. She attended the University of Wisconsin in 1948–1950 and then briefly the school of the Art Institute of Chicago and Roosevelt University. Moving to New York City, she held various minor jobs and studied at the New School for Social Research while concentrating mainly on her writing. In 1958 she raised funds from a number of people to produce her play *A Raisin in the Sun*. Tryouts in New Haven, Philadelphia, and Chicago were successful, and in March 1959 the play opened at the Ethel Barrymore Theatre on Broadway. It was the first play by a African-American women ever to be produced on Broadway, and it was a great hit.

A Raisin in the Sun, the story of a African-American family in Chicago and their frustrations and aspirations, won the New York Drama Critics' Circle award for best play of 1959. It ran until June 1960 and subsequently was made into a motion picture. Lorraine Hansberry's second play, *The Sign in Sidney Brustein's Window*, opened at the Longacre Theatre in October 1964 and had a short run. One of the most promising young playwrights in America, she died after two years of intermittent hospitalization for cancer, in New York City on January 11, 1965. In 1969 a selection of her writings and drawings was published as *To Be Young, Gifted, and Black*, edited by Robert Nemiroff.

Hapgood, Isabel Florence 1850–1928 translator and writer

Born in Boston on November 21, 1850, Isabel Hapgood grew up there, in Jersey City, New Jersey, and in Worcester, Massachusetts. Her formal education ended in 1868, after three years at Miss Porter's School in Farmington, Connecticut, but she continued her studies of languages on her own. By the 1880s she had mastered virtually all of the Romance and Germanic languages and several of the Slavic. Her career as a translator began in 1886 with the publication of her translations of Tolstoy's *Childhood, Boyhood, Youth*, Gogol's *Taras Bulba* and *Dead Souls*, and a selection of *Epic Songs of Russia*. During 1887–1889 she toured Russia and met Tolstoy.

Living in New York City thereafter, Hapgood produced a stream of books: translations of Tolstoy's *What to Do?*, 1887, Victor Hugo's *Les Misérables*, 1887, Edmondo de Amicis's *Cuore*, 1887, Tolstoy's *Life*, 1888, and *Sevastopol*, 1888, Hugo's *Notre Dame de Paris*, 1888, and *Toilers of the Sea*, 1888, Ernest Renan's *Recollections and Letters*, 1892, Armando P. Valdés's *Faith* and *The Origin of Thought*, 1892, Sonya Kovalevsky's *Recollections of Childhood*, 1895, Pierre de Coubertin's *The Revolution of France under the Third Republic*, 1897, Gorky's *Foma Gordyeef*, 1901, and *Orloff and His Wife*, 1901, Abbé Joseph Roux's *Méditations*, 1903, the 16-volume *Novels and Stories of Ivan Turgenev*, 1903–1904, Dostoevski's *The Brothers Karamazov*, 1905, Chekhov's *The Seagull*, 1905, Nikolai Leskov's *The Steel Flea*, 1916, Ivan Bunin's *The Village*, 1923, and Leskov's *The Cathedral Folk*, 1924.

Hapgood's pioneering work in introducing Russian literature to English-language readers was especially valuable. In addition she wrote *Russian Rambles*, 1895, a lively account of her visit to that country, *A Survey of Russian Literature*, 1902, for the Chautauqua Literary and Scientific Circle, and many magazine articles. For 22 years she was a correspondent, reviewer, and editorial writer for the New York *Evening Post* and the *Nation*. She made a second visit to Russia in 1917 and only through personal acquaintances there escaped being caught up in the turmoil of the revolution. She died in New York City on June 26, 1928.

Hardey, Mother Mary Aloysia 1809–1886 religious

Born on December 8, 1809, in Piscataway, Maryland, Mary Ann Hardey grew up there, in Baltimore, and from 1815 on a plantation in Opelousas, Louisiana. During 1822–1824 she attended the school conducted by the Society of the Sacred Heart (lately introduced into America by Mother Philippine Duchesne) at Grand Coteau, Louisiana, and in September 1825 she entered the novitiate there. Sent to the order's new convent at St. Michael's, Louisiana, Sister Aloysia took her first vows in March 1827 and her final vows in July 1833. By that time she had already had charge of the girls' school at St. Michael's for a time, and in 1836, at the age of twenty-six, she was named superior of St. Michael's. In 1841 she was directed by the secretary general of the Society of the Sacred Heart to establish the order's first convent in the East, and in the fall of that year it opened in New York City. The next year, after a trip to France during which she met Mother (later Saint) Madeleine Sophie Barat, founder of the order, she became superior of the New York convent. In 1844 she was appointed mother provincial for eastern North America, which then included schools in Pennsylvania and Quebec. (Her title was changed to superior vicar in 1851.)

In addition to the New York convent school, which in 1847 moved to Manhattanville, New York, (it later became the College of the Sacred Heart and later still Manhattanville College) and became a highly successful educational institution, she established over the course of 27 years 16 houses for the order from Halifax, Nova Scotia, to Havana, Cuba, and as far west as Detroit. (The house in Cincinnati was built in 1869 with help from Sarah Peter.) During the Civil War she had additional responsibility for houses in the West cut off from their provincial superior at Grand Coteau. In 1864 she transferred her headquarters from Manhattanville to Kenwood, near Albany. In 1871 she was named assistant general of the Society of the Sacred Heart with responsibility for the houses in the British Empire and North America. She made an arduous farewell tour of the North American houses from Canada to Cuba to Kansas and in 1872 arrived at the mother house in Paris. Her last visit to the United States was in 1882–1884. She died in Paris on June 17, 1886. In 1905 her remains were brought to the United States and reinterred in the convent in Kenwood, New York.

Harkness, Anna M. Richardson 1837–1926 philanthropist

Born on October 25, 1837, in Dalton, Ohio, Anna Richardson was married at sixteen, in February 1854, to Stephen V. Harkness, thirty-five, a businessman with whom she moved to Cleveland in 1866. In the 34 years of their marriage Stephen Harkness prospered greatly, having become an early and major investor in John D. Rockefeller's Standard Oil Company. At his death in 1888 Anna Harkness and her three children were left with over $150 million. In 1891 she moved to New York City, where her eldest son, Charles W. Harkness, established an office to manage the estate and she devoted herself to quiet philanthropy. Until 1916 she concentrated mainly on giving to churches and home and foreign missions. After Charles's death in 1916 the scope of her philanthropy broadened.

In 1917 Anna Harkness gave $3 million to Yale to build what became Harkness Quadrangle, named in memory of her son. She became particularly interested in supporting medical research and education, but the increased complexity of dealing with large numbers of applications made it impossible for her to continue her practice of personally assessing each one. In 1918, therefore, she established the Commonwealth Fund with an endowment of $20 million and a board of directors with full discretion. The Commonwealth Fund, one of the major philanthropic foundations in the country and one of the very few established by a woman, gave its particular support over the years to medical schools, to the building of hospitals and clinics in rural areas, and to a program of fellowships to allow British students to study in the United States.

Harkness's personal benefactions continued with another $3 million gift to Yale for faculty salaries in 1920, and in 1922 she gave a 22-acre site valued at $4 million to Columbia University in New York City for a new medical center for the College of Physicians and Surgeons and Presbyterian Hospital. She also gave liberally to the New York Public Library, the Museum of Natural History, the Metropolitan Museum of Art, and other cultural and educational institutions. By the time of her death in New York City on March 27, 1926, Anna Harkness had managed her original $50 million share of the estate into $85 million and had given away over $40 million of it. Her will distributed the rest mainly to philanthropic institutions, including an additional $22 million to the Commonwealth Fund.

Harlow, Jean 1911–1937 actor

Born in Kansas City, Missouri, on March 3, 1911, Harlean Carpenter grew up from the age of ten in the Los Angeles home of her maternal grandfather. She left private school in Lake Forest, Illinois, at sixteen to be married and settled in Beverly Hills, California. In 1928 she was persuaded to register with the Central Casting Bureau in Hollywood, and soon, under the name Jean Harlow (Harlow was her mother's maiden name), she was playing small parts in short films, many of them silent comedies directed by Hal Roach. Her first screen credit was in a Laurel and Hardy comedy, *Double Whoopee*, in 1928. After a small role in *The Saturday Night Kid* with Clara Bow, 1929, she was chosen by Howard Hughes to star in his *Hell's Angels*, 1930, in which she was an immediate sensation.

A rapid succession of movies followed — among them *Platinum Blonde*, 1931, *The Secret Six*, 1931, *Public Enemy*, 1931, *Iron Man*, 1931, *The Beast of the City*, 1932, and *Red Dust*, 1932 — all designed to exploit Harlow's worldly-wise manner and her striking, frankly sensual beauty. The design was enormously successful, and despite her lack of dramatic ability Harlow became, virtually overnight, one of Hollywood's top box-office attractions. Her often daring wardrobe, her enticing languor alternating with a wisecracking, sardonic humor, and her platinum blonde hair were all, with varying degrees of success, widely copied. In *Red-Headed Woman*, 1932, she displayed a knack for light comedy in a script by Anita Loos, and thereafter she concentrated on such roles, notably in *Dinner at Eight*, 1933, *Bombshell*, 1933, *Hold Your Man*, 1933, *Reckless*, 1934, *China Seas*, 1935, *Libeled Lady*, 1936, and *Personal Property*, 1936. Her last years were marked by unhappy marriages and serious bouts of illness. She died in Los Angeles on June 7, 1937, at the age of twenty-six. Her last film, *Saratoga*, was released a month later.

Harper, Ida A. Husted 1851–1931 journalist and suffragist

Born in Fairfield, Franklin County, Indiana, on February 18, 1851, Ida Husted grew up there and from the age of ten in Muncie, Indiana. She attended local schools and after a year at Indiana University became in 1869 principal of the high school in Peru, Indiana. In December 1871 she married Thomas W. Harper, a lawyer, with whom she settled in Terre Haute. While her husband became a prominent attorney and politician and an associate of Eugene V. Debs, she began writing for local newspapers, although not without his disapproval. For 12 years, at first under a male pseudonym, she contributed a column entitled "A Woman's Opinions" to the *Terre Haute Saturday Evening Mail*, and for 9 years after 1884 she wrote a woman's column for the *Firemen's Magazine* (later the *Locomotive Firemen's Magazine*), a union publication.

In 1887 Harper helped organize and became secretary of a state woman suffrage society. She was divorced in February 1890. During February-May of that year she was editor of the *Terre Haute Daily News*, and on moving to Indianapolis in the latter month she joined the staff of the *Indianapolis News*. During 1893–1895 she attended Stanford University, and in 1896 she had charge of press relations for the National American Woman Suffrage Association's campaign for a state suffrage amendment in California. As a result of her work in that campaign she was asked by Susan B. Anthony to become the suffrage leader's official biographer. In 1897 she took up residence in Anthony's home in Rochester, New York. The first two volumes of the *Life and Work of Susan B. Anthony* appeared in 1898; a third was published in 1908. She also collaborated with Anthony on the fourth volume of the latter's *History of Woman Suffrage*, 1902.

Harper served meanwhile as chairman of the press committee of the International Council of Women in 1899–1902 and was a delegate to council conventions in London in 1899 and Berlin in 1904. During 1899–1903 she edited a woman's column in the New York *Sunday Sun*, and from 1909 to 1913 she edited the woman's page in *Harper's Bazaar*. She was also a correspondent for newspapers in Chicago, Boston, Philadelphia, Washington, D.C., and New York City. In 1916, when the bequest of Miriam Florence Leslie made possible the establishment of the Leslie Bureau of Suffrage Education within the National American Woman Suffrage Association, the association's president, Carrie Chapman Catt, named Harper to head it. The steady stream of letters, articles, and pamphlets that issued from her office in Washington, D.C., played a large role in the successful campaign for passage of the Nineteenth Amendment. In 1922 she published the fifth and sixth volumes of the *History of Woman Suffrage*, bringing the story up to 1920. She died in Washington, D.C., on March 14, 1931.

Harriman, Florence Jaffray 1870–1967 diplomat

Born in New York City on July 21, 1870, Florence Jaffray Hurst grew up in a wealthy and socially well connected family and was educated privately. In November 1889 she married J. Borden Harriman, a New York banker, and for many years led the life of a young society matron interested in charitable and civic activities. She was a founder, with Elisabeth Marbury, Anne Morgan, and others, and from 1903 to 1916 first president of the Colony Club. She was also a leader in the National Civic Federation, the Consumers' League, and other organizations, and after campaigning for Charles Evans Hughes for governor in 1906 she served from then until 1918 on the board of managers of the New York reformatory for women at Bedford. As a result of her campaigning for Woodrow Wilson in 1912, during 1913–1916 she was the sole woman member of the Federal Industrial Relations Commission. Following the death of her husband in December 1914 she moved to Washington, D.C., where she became known as a political hostess of the first importance.

During World War I Harriman served with the Red Cross Motor Corps and was appointed by President Wilson chairman of the Committee on Women in Industry of the Council of National Defense. During the Republican administrations from 1921 to 1932 her Washington home was a bastion of Democratic society. In 1923 she published a lively memoir, *From Pinafores to Politics*. From 1924 she was Democratic national committeewoman for the District of Columbia, and she was regularly a delegate to the party's national conventions. With the return of a Democratic administration under President Franklin D. Roosevelt she again found herself near the center of power, and in June 1937 Roosevelt appointed her U.S. minister to Norway. She was the second American woman, after Ruth Bryan Rohde, to hold ministerial rank.

After the outbreak of World War II Harriman had added to her task of maintaining good U.S.-Norwegian relations the problems of evacuating U.S. nationals from Norway and protecting U.S. rights. In November 1939 she succeeded in obtaining the release and return to American hands of the freighter *City of Flint*, which had been captured on the high seas by the German warship *Deutschland* and had been taken into a neutral Norwegian port by its prize crew after developing engine trouble. With the German invasion of Norway in April 1940 she was forced to flee Oslo. She made her way to Sweden, where she arranged for the safety of other Americans and of members of the Norwegian royal family, returning with them to the United States in August. In 1941 she published her record of her service in Norway as *Mission to the North*. She lived mainly in retirement thereafter. In April 1963 she was the first person to receive the newly created Citation of Merit for Distinguished Service from President John F. Kennedy. She died on August 31, 1967, in Georgetown, D.C.

Harris, Patricia Roberts 1924–1985 public official

Born on May 31, 1924, in Mattoon, Illinois, Patricia Roberts grew up there and in Chicago. She graduated from Howard University in 1945, pursued graduate studies for two years at the University of Chicago, and from 1946 to 1949 was a program director for the Young Women's Christian Association in Chicago. In 1949 she returned to Washington, D.C., where she took further graduate work at American University and worked as assistant director of the American Council on Human Rights in 1949–1953. For six years thereafter she was executive director of the national headquarters of Delta Sigma Theta sorority. In September 1955 she married William B. Harris, a professor of law at Howard University. She graduated from the law school at George Washington University in 1960 and was admitted to the District of Columbia bar in the same year. After a year in the criminal division of the U.S. Department of Justice she became associate dean of students and lecturer in law at Howard University. During 1962–1965 she was vice-chairman of the National Capital Area Civil Liberties Union. She relinquished the deanship in 1963 but remained on the Howard faculty as assistant professor, advancing to associate professor two years later.

In July 1963 Harris was named by President John F. Kennedy co-chairman, with Mildred McAfee Horton, of the National Women's Committee for Civil Rights. In March 1964 she was appointed also to the Commission on the Status of Puerto Rico, and in May 1965 President Lyndon B. Johnson named her U.S. ambassador to Luxembourg. On receiving Senate confirmation in June she became the first African-American woman to hold ambassadorial rank. During her tenure in that post she served also in 1966–1967 as an alternate U.S. delegate to the United Nations General Assembly. In August 1967 she rejoined the Howard law faculty as a full professor; in 1969 she served as dean of the law school until leaving to enter private legal practice. During 1968–1969 she served on the National Commission on the Causes and Prevention of Violence, and from 1969 to 1973 she was a member of the Carnegie Commission on the Future of Higher Education. In December 1976 she was chosen by President-elect Jimmy Carter to be secretary of Housing and Urban Development. She held that post from January 1977 to August 1979, when she became secretary of Health, Education and Welfare, later renamed Health and Human Services. She was the first African-American woman member of a presidential cabinet, remaining in this position until Carter was defeated in the 1980 election.

She returned to George Washington University in 1981 as a fulltime Professor of Law. In 1982 she ran for mayor of Washington, D.C., but lost the Democratic primary to incumbent Marion S. Barry. She died in Washington, D.C., on March 23, 1985.

Harrison, Elizabeth 1849–1927 educator

Born on September 1, 1849, in Athens, Kentucky, Elizabeth Harrison grew up in Midway, Kentucky, and from the age of seven in Davenport, Iowa. After graduating from high school she remained at home until 1879, when, following the death of her mother, she visited Chicago. There she encountered the fledgling kindergarten movement and promptly enrolled in a training class for kindergarten teachers. She assisted in her teacher's kindergarten during 1880, conducted her own in Marshalltown, Iowa, in 1881, and in January 1882 sought further training in Susan E. Blow's school for kindergartners in St. Louis. Another period of teaching kindergarten in Chicago later in 1882 was followed by another of study under Maria Kraus-Boelté in New York in January-June 1883. She then settled in Chicago and became the city's most active organizer of kindergarten activities and teachers. She helped found the Chicago Kindergarten Club, a discussion association of kindergarten teachers, in that year, and she soon had attracted and was lecturing regularly to groups of interested parents.

Harrison began training teachers for kindergartens in 1885, and in 1887 she led in formally establishing a school for kindergarten teachers and mothers that four years later was incorporated as the Chicago Kindergarten College. From 1887 to 1894 the school and the club together sponsored annual lecture series, under the name Chicago Literary Schools, by noted scholars, and in 1894, 1895, and 1896 Harrison organized national conferences of mothers that helped pave the way for the National Congress of Mothers, founded in 1897. The Chicago Kindergarten College was her principal concern, and while the high standards she set for it — notably requiring a high school diploma for entrance and insisting on a three-year training course — created a permanent threat of insolvency, the college became a model for others throughout the country. (After several changes of name it became in 1930 the National College of Education.)

Among Harrison's writings were *A Study of Child Nature*, which enjoyed more than 50 editions and was translated into 8 foreign languages after its first publication in 1890, *A Vision of Dante*, for children, 1891, *In Storyland*, 1895, *Two Children of the Foot Hills*, 1900, *Some Silent Teachers*, 1903, *Misunderstood Children*, 1908, *Offero, the Giant*, 1912, *When Children Err*, 1916, and *The Unseen Side of Child Life*, 1922. She also remained a popular lecturer. She traveled several times to Europe to stay abreast of developments in the kindergarten field, and in 1913, after inspecting the work of Dr. Maria Montessori in Rome, she wrote an influential report, *Montessori and the Kindergarten*, for the U.S. Bureau of Education.

Harrison retired from teaching and from the presidency of her National Kindergarten and Elementary College in 1920. She died in San Antonio, Texas, on October 31, 1927.

Hart, Nancy 1735?–1830 Revolutionary heroine

Born about 1735, in either Pennsylvania or North Carolina, Ann Morgan, who was known throughout life as Nancy, grew up in the latter colony. She is traditionally said to have been related to both Daniel Boone and General Daniel Morgan, although with no real evidence in either case. At a date unknown she married Benjamin Hart of Virginia, with whom she moved subsequently to South Carolina and about 1771 to Wilkes County, Georgia. She was well able to handle a rifle in the fierce and bloody internecine fighting that beset Georgia during the Revolution, Nancy Hart was a stalwart supporter of the Whig cause. A number of stories of her exploits in the war grew up and circulated for years before being written down. The best known story told of a day when five or six armed Tories arrived at her cabin and demanded that she cook them a meal. As she roasted her last turkey, shot by one of the Tories, her young daughter slipped away to arouse neighboring Whigs. Nancy plied the Tories with whiskey and contrived to get near their stacked rifles. She put two rifles out through a crack between the logs before she was detected, and she quickly took up a third to hold off the aroused Tories. One rushed her and was shot dead; another she wounded. When help arrived she vetoed the notion of shooting the rest on grounds that shooting was too good for Tories. They were accordingly taken to the woods and hanged.

Other stories told of Nancy Hart acting as a spy for Georgia patriot forces, crossing the Savannah River on a raft of logs tied with grapevines to bring back information from enemy camps. After the war the Harts moved to Brunswick, Georgia, where Benjamin Hart died. Nancy Hart later moved to Clarke County, Georgia, and then to Kentucky, where she died in 1830. The story of her Revolutionary exploit was first published in a newspaper reminiscence occasioned by the visit of the Marquis de Lafayette to the United States in 1825. In 1848 it was retold by Elizabeth F. Ellet in *Women of the American Revolution.* In 1853 Hart County, Georgia, and in 1856 its seat, Hartwell, were named in her honor.

Hasbrouck, Lydia Sayer 1827–1910 editor and reformer

Born in Warwick, New York, on December 20, 1827, Lydia Sayer early demonstrated intelligence and independence. She attended high school and Central College in Elmira, New York. In 1849 she adopted a costume of kneelength skirt over pantaloons, what soon came to be called the "bloomer" costume, and when she was refused admission to the Seward Seminary in Florida, New York, on grounds of her unconventional dress, her original motives of comfort and convenience gave way to indignation and principle. She continued to wear the costume through life and was perhaps the only one of the bloomer enthusiasts to do so (although she could not entirely conceal her irritation over the costume's having been so named by happenstance for someone who had adopted it later than she). In 1853 she was a delegate to the World's Temperance Convention in New York City, and a short time later she studied for a brief time at the Hygeio-Therapeutic College, a hydropathic institution. She practiced medicine in Washington, D.C., for a year, during which she also lectured frequently and contributed to newspapers in several cities.

In 1856 Sayer traveled to Middletown, New York, to lecture on dress reform at the invitation of John W. Hasbrouck, publisher of the local *Whig Press*. He promptly established a feminist and reform newspaper, the *Sibyl*, of which the first number appeared in July, and she remained in Middletown to edit it. Later in July she and Hasbrouck were married. The *Sibyl*, calling itself "a Review of the Tastes, Errors, and Fashions of Society," was published biweekly until 1861 and monthly thereafter, and its principal concern was dress reform, with medical education for women, a commonsense system of healthy living she called "hygeopathy," and woman suffrage also receiving attention. In 1863–1864 she was president of the National Dress Reform Association. With the waning of general interest in dress reform the *Sibyl* ceased publication in June 1864. She helped edit her husband's *Whig Press* until it was sold in 1868. They both continued their shared interest in reform. In March 1880, in the first New York State election in which women were permitted to vote and run for school offices, she was elected to the Middletown school board. In 1881 she and her husband published and edited the short-lived *Liberal Sentinel*. In later years she was active in real estate development. She died in Middletown, New York, on August 24, 1910.

Hatcher, Orie Latham 1868–1946 vocational guidance worker

Born on December 10, 1868, in Petersburg, Virginia, Orie Hatcher grew up in Richmond. She graduated from Richmond Female Institute in 1884, taught there for a year, and then entered Vassar College, from which she graduated in 1888. She then taught in a private girls' school in Louisville, Kentucky, until 1893, when she returned to the Richmond Female Institute. During the next year she taught and helped prepare for the school's transformation into the Woman's College of Richmond, in which she was professor of history, English language, and literature from 1894 to 1901. In the latter year she undertook graduate studies in English at the University of Chicago. She received her Ph.D. in 1903 and in 1904 became reader in English at Bryn Mawr College. Her doctoral thesis was published in 1905 as *John Fletcher: A Study in Dramatic Method.* In 1910 she was made chairman of Bryn Mawr's newly created department of comparative literature, and from 1912 she was associate professor of comparative literature and English literature. In 1914, when her research on Renaissance poetry in Italy was interrupted by the outbreak of World War I, she returned to Richmond.

Hatcher became involved in the Virginia Association of Colleges and Schools, a group interested in securing admission of promising woman graduates of Virginia junior colleges to the major women's colleges in the Northeast. The next year, resigning from Bryn Mawr, she became president of the reorganized Virginia Bureau of Vocations for Women, which sought more generally to improve opportunities for talented women for business and academic careers. The bureau aided in the founding of the Richmond School of Social Work and Public Health in 1917 and won the admission of women to the Medical College of Virginia in 1920. In that year, reflecting the bureau's and Hatcher's broadening perspective on the needs of women, the organization changed its name to the Southern Woman's Educational Alliance. Her interest in the general question of vocational opportunities for women, highlighted by her publication of *Occupations for Women* in 1927, led her to a still broader concern for the education of girls, especially in the rural areas of the South. The alliance began directing its funds and energies to vocational training programs in rural districts and to helping young girls find appropriate opportunities for self-help.

Eventually the education of rural boys became equally a concern. Demonstration schools were established in Konnarock, Virginia, and Breathitt County, Kentucky. In 1937 the alliance again changed its name to the Alliance for Guidance of Rural Youth. Others of her books were *Guiding Rural Boys and Girls*, 1930 (later revised with Ruth Strang as *Child Development and Guidance in Rural Schools*, 1943), *Rural Girls in the City for Work*, 1930, and *A Mountain School: A Study Made by the Southern Woman's Educational Alliance and Konnarock Training School*, 1930. Orie Hatcher served also as a vice-president of the National Federation of Business and Professional Women's Clubs in 1920–1924, as chairman of the rural section of the National Vocational Guidance Association in 1928–1938, on the executive board of the National Council of Women in 1932–1935, and on the National Occupational Conference in 1933–1939. She took part in White House conferences on children in 1939–1940 and on rural education in 1944, and in the latter year she presided over the Institute on War and Post-war Problems of Rural Youth Migration. She died in Richmond, Virginia, on April 1, 1946.

Haughery, Margaret Gaffney 1813–1882 philanthropist

Born in 1813 near Killeshandra, County Cavan, Ireland, Margaret Gaffney was brought to the United States by her parents in 1818. They settled in Baltimore. She received no schooling (she never learned to read or write), and after her parents died in a yellow fever epidemic in 1822 she lived in the home of some Welsh neighbors. After several years of working as a domestic she married Charles Haughery in October 1835. They moved the next month to New Orleans, and the next year Charles Haughery died after sailing back to Ireland for his health. For a time Margaret Haughery worked as a laundress in a New Orleans hotel, and then with her savings she bought a pair of cows and started a dairy. She was soon a familiar and welcome sight in the streets of New Orleans as she peddled and often gave away milk. Despite, or because of, her marked generosity she prospered, and by 1840 she had a dairy herd of 40 cows. In that year she contributed funds to the Sisters of Charity to enable them to open the New Orleans Female Orphan Asylum.

Over the years ten more such institutions were financed by Haughery's benefactions, notably St. Vincent's Infant Asylum, and she was ever ready to help in other ways as well, particularly as a nurse during the yellow fever epidemics that regularly swept the city. In 1858 she acquired as payment of a debt a small bakery. She gave up her dairy, expanded the bakery, and soon proved herself a master of business. Hers was reputedly the first bakery in the South to use steam, and she was credited with coming up with the notion of selling packaged crackers. At its peak her bakery was the city's largest export business. During the Civil War her charitable efforts were directed especially toward soldiers' families, and she also conducted "free markets" two or three times a week. Her personal philanthropies as well as her larger institutional ones were conducted with unassuming humility, and much of her work in that sphere was unknown to the public during her lifetime. She died in New Orleans on February 9, 1882, leaving an estate of nearly half a million dollars, most of which was left to various Catholic, Protestant, and Jewish charitable institutions. In July 1884 a statue of her, bought by public subscription, was unveiled in Margaret Haughery Park in New Orleans.

Hauk, Minnie 1851?–1929 opera singer

Born in New York City, probably on November 16, 1851 (some sources say 1852 or 1853), Minnie Hauk moved with her family soon afterward to Providence, Rhode Island; they subsequently moved about 1857 to Sumner, Kansas, and about 1860 to New Orleans. In New Orleans she received her first musical training, and she had already sung in public when in 1862 she and her mother returned to New York. There she came under the patronage of financier Leonard Jerome (father of Jennie Jerome Churchill), who sponsored her further vocal training under Achille Errani. She made her operatic debut in *La Sonnambula* at Jerome's private theater and a few weeks later, on October 13, 1866, made her public debut in the same opera at the Brooklyn Academy of Music under the name "Amalia M. Hauck." (Later she resumed her own name.) In November she appeared with Clara Louise Kellogg in *L'Etoile du Nord* at the Winter Garden. During 1867 she sang in *Don Giovanni* and *Faust*, and in December 1867, at the age of sixteen, she sang Juliette in the American premiere of Gounod's *Roméo et Juliette* at the Academy of Music. Other roles and appearances in other cities followed. In 1868, with a loan from music publisher Gustav Schirmer, she traveled to Europe.

Hauk studied for a time under Maurice Strakosch and in the spring of 1869 made her Paris debut in his company in *La Sonnambula*. In October 1869 she appeared in the same opera in London. After appearances in Holland, St. Petersburg, and Moscow, she made her Vienna debut in May 1870 in *Faust* at the Imperial Opera House. She was a leading singer at the Imperial until 1874, when she joined the new Komische Oper (later the Ring Theater) as its prima donna assoluta for the first season. Late in 1874 she joined the Berlin Royal Opera, where she remained for three years. During these years she was especially popular in *Le Roi l'a dit*, *La Part du Diable*, and *Taming of the Shrew*. In May 1978 she made her long desired appearance in *Carmen* in Brussels, a role she repeated to great acclaim in the opera's British premiere at Her Majesty's Theatre, London, in June of that year. With the same company, under Colonel James H. Mapleson's management, she sang Carmen in the opera's American premiere at the Academy of Music in New York in October 1878.

Through the 1880s Hauk continued to sing regularly in England and Europe, with occasional tours of the United States; during such a tour in 1883–1884 she sang for President Chester A. Arthur at the White House. In December 1885 she sang the title role in the American premiere of *Manon* at the Academy of Music in New York. Her last New York appearance was in *Carmen* in April 1891. In September 1891, with her own company, she sang the first Chicago performance of *Cavalleria Rusticana*. Her final

American performance was in *L'Africaine* in Philadelphia in November 1893, and her last in England was in *Cavalleria Rusticana* in February 1895. A short time later she retired from the stage. Although hers was perhaps not the greatest voice of the day, her magnetic quality as a singing actress made a permanent impression on the staging of opera. From her retirement until World War I she lived at her Villa Triebschen near Lucerne, Switzerland, with her husband (from 1881), Baron Ernst von Hesse-Wartegg. The war and her husband's death shortly afterward left her in poverty, and she was supported thereafter by funds raised by Geraldine Farrar and others. She died at Villa Triebschen on February 6, 1929.

Haven, Emily Bradley Neal 1827–1863 writer of children's literature and editor

Born on September 13, 1827, in Hudson, New York, Emily Bradley grew up from the age of six in the home of an uncle, first in Boston and later in Exeter and then New Hampton, New Hampshire. She began writing poems and stories while a schoolgirl, and under the pseudonym "Alice G. Lee" she submitted a story to *Neal's Saturday Gazette and Lady's Literary Museum* of Philadelphia, which printed it. More contributions followed, all warmly received by the magazine's editor, Joseph C. Neal, and in December 1846 the two were married. At his request she went thereafter by the name Alice. After her husband's death the next year she helped edit the *Gazette* for six years. Her particular department was "The Bird's Nest," a children's column that she conducted under the name "Cousin Alice." The stories and sketches published under that name were widely read and loved. She contributed also to other periodicals, including *Godey's Lady's Book*, *Harper's*, and *Graham's Magazine*.

Alice Neal's first book, written for use by the General Protestant Episcopal Sunday School Union, was *Helen Morton's Trial*, 1849. *The Gossips of Rivertown*, 1850, was an uncharacteristically ironic novel. From 1852 to 1859 she wrote for D. Appleton & Co. a series of "Home Books" for children with such titles as *No Such Word as Fail*, 1852, *Contentment Better Than Wealth*, 1853, *Patient Waiting No Loss*, 1853, *All's Not Gold That Glitters*, 1853, and *Out of Debt, Out of Danger*, 1855. In January 1853 she married Samuel L. Haven, a New York broker with whom she lived in Mamaroneck, New York, from 1854; after 1858 they lived in James Fenimore Cooper's former home. Alice Haven died in Mamaroneck, New York, on August 23, 1863. A memoir, *The Good Report*, was published in 1867, and a collection of her stories was published as *Home Studies* in 1869.

Hawes, Harriet Ann Boyd 1871–1945 archaeologist

Born in Boston on October 11, 1871, Harriet Boyd graduated from the Prospect Hill School in Greenfield, Massachusetts, in 1888 and from Smith College in 1892. For four years she taught ancient and modern languages, first as a private tutor in Henderson, North Carolina, and then at a girls' school in Wilmington, Delaware. In 1896 she entered the American School of Classical Studies in Athens. Recent archaeological finds in Crete had inspired her to take up studies there, but she found no encouragement for her ambition to do field work. From the Agnes Hoppin fellowship awarded her in her fourth year she saved money to finance a trip to Crete. She visited the excavation at Knossos being worked by British archaeologist Arthur J. Evans, who suggested she explore the region about Kavousi. The discovery of some Iron Age tombs there provided material for her master's thesis; the degree was awarded her by Smith in 1901. She had since 1900 held an instructorship in Greek archaeology, epigraphy, and modern Greek at Smith, and she retained the appointment until 1906, although in 1903 and 1904 she was again on leave of absence to be in the field on Crete.

From May 1901 Hawes' interest centered on a rich site she discovered at Gournia, an outlying district of Kavousi. She was the first archaeologist to discover and completely excavate an Early Bronze Age Minoan town site, and her work there won her worldwide fame. In 1904 Cretan authorities permitted her to ship to the American Exploration Society a small selection of artifacts unearthed at Gournia; these eventually entered the collections of the Metropolitan Museum in New York, the Boston Museum of Fine Arts, and the University Museum in Philadelphia. Her definitive report on the Gournia excavation was published by the American Exploration Society as *Gournia, Vasiliki and Other Prehistoric Sites on the Isthmus of Hierapetra, Crete*, 1908. In March 1906 Harriet Boyd married Charles H. Hawes, a British anthropologist. They lived in Madison, Wisconsin, in 1907–1909, in Hanover, New Hampshire, in 1910–1917, and in Boston from 1919 to 1936. Her husband collaborated with her on her popular *Crete: The Forerunner of Greece*, 1909, but for several years thereafter she abandoned scholarly work.

She had earlier served as a volunteer nurse during the Greco-Turkish War in 1897 and in the Spanish-American War in 1898, and during World War I she nursed Serbian soldiers on Corfu and in 1917 organized and led a Smith College Relief Unit to France. From 1920 to 1936 she lectured on pre-Christian art at Wellesley College. In 1936 she and her husband retired to a farm in Alexandria, Virginia. She died in Washington, D.C., on March 31, 1945.

Hayden, Melissa 1923– ballet dancer

Born in Toronto on April 25, 1923, Mildred Herman began studying dance while a schoolgirl in her native city. In 1945 she went to New York City and found a position in the corps de ballet at Radio City Music Hall. Within a few months she had been accepted by the Ballet Theatre (now American Ballet Theatre) company, in which she rose rapidly to the rank of soloist. In 1949, after a South American tour with the Ballet Alicia Alonso, she joined the New York City Ballet under George Balanchine. She attracted high critical praise in her debut with that company in *The Duel* in February 1950 and established herself as a great ballerina in creating a role in the premiere of Frederick Ashton's *Illuminations* the next month. In December she danced a principal role in Jerome Robbins's *Age of Anxiety*. Other notable performances were those in Todd Bolender's *The Miraculous Mandarin* in 1951, Robbins's *The Pied Piper* in 1951, Balanchine's *Caracole* in 1952, and Robbins's *The Cage* in 1952. In 1952 she appeared in the Charlie Chaplin film *Limelight*.

From April 1953 to May 1954 Hayden was again with Ballet Theatre, and after a retirement of nearly a year she rejoined the New York City Ballet in February 1955. She remained with that company thereafter until her final retirement in 1973. During that long period of stardom she made acclaimed appearances in Balanchine's *Ivesiana* in 1955 and in Bolender's *Still Point* in 1956, and in premieres of Balanchine's *Divertimento No. 15* (a longer version of *Caracole*) in 1956, *Agon*, 1957, *Stars and Stripes*, 1958, *Episodes*, 1959, *Liebeslieder Walzer*, 1960, *A Midsummer Night's Dream*, 1962, *Brahms-Schoenberg Quartet*, 1966, *Glinkiana*, 1966, and *Cortège hongroise*, created especially for her, 1973, and in Robbins's *In the Night*, 1970. She was a frequent guest star with the National Ballet of Canada, the Royal Ballet of London, and other companies. In 1963 she published *Melissa Hayden — Off Stage and On*. Her final performance was in *Cortège hongroise* at Wolf Trap Farm, Virginia, in September 1973.

On her retirement Hayden was awarded New York City's Handel Medallion. In 1973 she became artist-in-residence at Skidmore College, and in 1974 she established a dance school in Saratoga, New York. In 1976 she was named artistic director of the Pacific Northwest Dance in Seattle. She published *Dancer to Dancer*, 1981, offering practical advice to dancers based on her own experiences, and *The Nutcracker Ballet*, 1992, retelling the classic ballet for young readers. In 1983 she joined the dance faculty at the North Carolina School of the Arts.

Hayes, Helen 1900–1993 actor

Born on October 10, 1900, in Washington, D.C., Helen Hayes Brown made her professional debut at the age of five as Prince Charles in a Columbia Players' production of *The Royal Family*. She went to New York City in 1909 and in November made her Broadway debut at the Herald Square Theatre in *Old Dutch*. She appeared in *The Summer Widowers*, 1910, and *The Never Homes*, 1911, and then returned to Washington to resume acting with the Columbia Players and to study at the school of the Sacred Heart Convent, from which she graduated in 1917. She appeared with John Drew in *The Prodigal Husband* in 1914, and after a Broadway run in *Pollyanna* in 1916 she toured in that play in 1917–1918. Thus began a long and distinguished career paralleled only by that of Ethel Barrymore.

Hayes was hailed for her performances in *Penrod*, 1918, *Dear Brutus*, 1918, *Clarence*, 1919, *Bab*, 1920, *The Wren*, 1921, *To the Ladies*, 1922, *We Moderns*, 1924, George Bernard Shaw's *Caesar and Cleopatra*, 1925, James M. Barrie's *What Every Woman Knows*, 1926, *Coquette*, 1927, *Mr. Gilhooley and Petticoat Influence*, 1930, Maxwell Anderson's *Mary of Scotland*, written for her, 1933–1934, Laurence Housman's *Victoria Regina*, generally regarded as her most brilliant role, 1935–1939, *Ladies and Gentlemen*, 1939, *Twelfth Night*, 1940, Anderson's *Candle in the Wind*, 1941, as Harriet Beecher Stowe in *Harriet*, 1943, Barlie's *Alice-Sit-by-the-Fire*, 1946, Anita Loos's *Happy Birthday*, for which she won a Tony Award, 1946, Tennessee Williams's *The Glass Menagerie* in London, 1948, again on Broadway in Joshua Logan's *The Wisteria Trees*, 1950, *Mrs. McThing*, 1952, a Paris revival of Thornton Wilder's *The Skin of Our Teeth*, 1955, *Time Remembered*, 1957, and Eugene O'Neill's *A Touch of the Poet*, 1958.

Hayes movie career included warmly received roles in *The Sin of Madelon Claudet*, for which she won an Academy Award, 1931, *Arrowsmith* and *A Farewell to Arms*, both 1932, *The White Sister*, *Another Language*, and *Night Flight*, all 1933, *What Every Woman Knows*, 1934, *Vanessa Her Love Story*, 1935, *My Son John*, 1952, and *Anastasia*, 1956. On radio she starred in 1935 in the "New Penny" series, in 1936 in the "Bambi" series, in 1940 and 1941 in the "Helen Hayes Theatre," in 1945 in "This Is Helen Hayes," in 1948–1949 in "Electric Theatre," and in 1956 in "Weekday." She also acted in television productions of *Dear Brutus*, 1956, *Springtime USA*, 1956, *One Rose for Christmas*, 1958, *Ah, Wilderness!*, 1959, *Woman: The Lonely Years*, 1960, *Four Women in Black*, 1961, and others.

In November 1955, in recognition of her 50 years on the stage, New York's Fulton Theatre was renamed the Helen Hayes Theatre in her honor. From 1928 to his death in 1956 she was married to playwright Charles MacArthur. Hayes continued to be active in the theater, on television, and in motion pictures, appearing in the films *Candleshoe*, 1978, and *Hopper's Silence*, 1981, and on television in *Murder is Easy*, 1982, *A Carribean Mystery*, 1983, and as Jane Marple in *Murder with Mirrors* in 1985. She served on the National Arts Council from 1966 to 1970 and again from 1971. Her performance in *Airport*, 1970, won her an Academy Award for supporting actress. Her autobiography, *A Gift of Joy*, with L. Funke, appeared in 1965. She also published *Twice Over Lightly: New York Then and Now*, a guidebook and memoir, with Anita Loos, 1971, *A Gathering of Hope*, 1983, *Our Best Years*, a novel, with Marion Gladney, 1984, *Where the Truth Lies*, a mystery novel, with Thomas Chastain, 1988, and *My Life in Three Acts*, another autobiography, with Katherine Hatch, 1990.

In 1979 she was awarded the Laetare Medal by the University of Notre Dame. She received the American Exemplar Medal in 1978, the Kennedy Center Honors in 1981, the Medal of Freedom in 1986, and the Medal of the Arts in 1988. In her honor the annual Helen Hayes Awards were established for artistic achievement in professional theater in Washington, D.C. She died on March 17, 1993, in Nyack, New York.

Head, Edith 1898?–1981 fashion designer

Born in Los Angeles at a date undisclosed but possibly about 1898, Edith Head, daughter of a mining engineer, grew up in various towns and camps in Arizona, Nevada, and Mexico. She attended high school in Los Angeles, graduated from the University of California, and subsequently took a master's degree from Stanford University. After a time as a schoolteacher and some additional study at the Otis Institute and the Chouinard Art School, she submitted some fashion designs to the head designer at Paramount Studios and was promptly hired. For several years she worked her way up from sketcher to designer by way of apprentice assignments and such minor but memorable accomplishments as designing Dorothy Lamour's sarong for the Bob Hope-Bing Crosby *Road* pictures.

In 1938 Head became chief designer at Paramount in charge of a costume department with a staff of hundreds. She was the first woman to head a design department at a major studio. She was thereafter directly or indirectly responsible for the costuming in all Paramount films, and she gradually became known even outside the industry as perhaps the leading practitioner of her craft. In 1967, when Paramount was bought by Gulf and Western, she became Chief Costume Designer at Universal Studios where she remained until 1981. Recognition of her talent came in the form of a remarkable number of Academy Awards: for black and white design (separate award from color design until 1969) for *The Heiress* (with Gile Steele), 1949; *All About Eve* (with several collaborators), 1950; *Samson and Delilah*, color, 1950; *A Place in the Sun*, black and white, 1951; *Roman Holiday*, black and white, 1953; *Sabrina*, black and white, 1954; *The Facts of Life*, black and white, 1960; and *The Sting*, 1973.

Head was the author of *Dress Doctor*, combining some autobiography with design sketches, written with J. K. M. Ardmore, 1959, and *How to Dress for Success*, with Joe Hyams, 1967. Noted especially for her ability to create designs suited to particular actors and actresses as well as to their roles, Edith Head was the acknowledged dean of Hollywood costume designers. She died in Hollywood on October 24, 1981.

Hearst, Phoebe Apperson 1842–1919 philanthropist

Born in Franklin County, Missouri, on December 3, 1842, Phoebe (originally Phebe) Apperson attended local schools and was herself a teacher briefly before she married George Hearst in June 1862. George Hearst, 22 years older than his wife, had already made a fair beginning on what was to become a large fortune in western mining holdings. At home in San Francisco Hearst soon became a noted hostess.

Phoebe also devoted much thought and time to self-improvement, and she made a number of lengthy trips, notably in 1873 and again in 1878–1880 across the country and to Europe. With the increase and stabilization of the family fortune she became interested in various philanthropies, particularly Sarah B. Cooper's Golden Gate Kindergarten Association, for which she erected an office building. She also built kindergartens, libraries, and other institutions in the Utah, Montana, and Dakota towns where her husband had mining interests. On his appointment to the U.S. Senate in 1886 she accompanied him to Washington, D.C. She continued there her practice of lavish entertainment and her philanthropic interests. After her husband's death in 1891 she was obliged to devote much time as well to the affairs of the estate. In that year she made a large gift to the University of California to endow several scholarships for women students.

In 1893 Hearst founded and became first president of the Columbian Kindergarten Association, and four years later the training school for kindergarten teachers she financed was opened. In 1896 she sponsored an architectural competition for a full campus plan for the University of California at Berkeley, and toward the realization of the winning plan she contributed the Hearst Memorial Mining Building and Hearst Hall. She also underwrote, with an amateur's enthusiasm, several archaeological expeditions to Florida, Mexico, Italy, Egypt, and Russia, and in 1901 she built the University Museum to house the artifacts brought back from them. She also helped support the new department of anthropology for a number of years. From July 1897 almost without interruption until her death she served as a regent of the university. In February 1897 she had helped found the National Congress of Mothers, forerunner of the National Congress of Parents and Teachers. Others of her benefactions went toward the restoration of Mount Vernon, the building of the National Cathedral, and the support of the National Cathedral School in Washington, D.C. In 1915 she was honorary president of the women's board of the Panama-Pacific Exposition. Her last years were spent at La Hacienda del Pozo de Verona, her home near Pleasanton, California. She died there on April 13, 1919. Her son was William Randolph Hearst (1863–1951).

Heinemann, Barbara 1795–1883 religious leader

Born on January 11, 1795, in Leitersweiler, Alsace, Barbara Heinemann (or Heynemann) grew up in poverty and received no schooling. From the age of eight she worked in various menial capacities. An intensely religious nature led her to the Community of True Inspiration, a Pietist sect founded in 1714 and revived about 1817 by Christian Metz and others. On Christmas Day 1818 Barbara Heinemann had a powerful religious experience and received the gift of oral prophecy, a principal element in the doctrine of the Inspirationists. She taught herself to read the Bible shortly thereafter. Overcoming the suspicion of elders in the sect, who for a time expelled her, she traveled widely with Metz to other centers of Inspirationists and helped spark the rebirth of the sect. Her marriage in 1823, however, marked her fall from grace in the eyes of her colleagues, and she lived as an ordinary member of the sect for over a quarter of a century. She and her husband, George Landmann, were among the 800 Inspirationists who followed Metz to America in 1842–1843 and established the Ebenezer Society in Erie County, New York.

In 1849 the gift of prophecy once again became manifest in Barbara Heinemann and she was accepted again as a *Werkzeug*, an instrument of God, and thereby a leader of the society. She ratified Metz's prophecy ordaining in 1854 the establishment of a new settlement far to the west, away in particular from the encroaching city of Buffalo. Land was bought in Iowa County, Iowa, and a network of seven settlements, known collectively as the Amana Society, was established. The frugal, spiritual, and communal lives of Amana's residents were directed by Metz and Heinemann together until Metz's death in July 1867 and thereafter by Barbara Heinemann alone, aided by a Great Council of the Brethren. Her pious, contentious, and sometimes willful nature made the task of holding the community together more difficult, especially as a new generation grew up to be tempted by the increasingly attractive world beyond Amana. The community did nonetheless continue to prosper as the most successful of the many communistic experiments tried in America in the 19th century. Barbara Heinemann died at Amana, Iowa, on May 21, 1883. No *Werkzeug* appeared to succeed her, but the society persisted in largely its original form until 1932, when by vote of its members it became a joint stock enterprise.

Hellman, Lillian 1905–1984 playwright

Born in New Orleans on June 20, 1905, Lillian Hellman attended New York and Columbia Universities in 1922–1924. After a year working in a New York publishing house she began reviewing books for the *New York Herald Tribune* in 1925, and from 1927 to 1930 she was employed as a play reader. At the same time she began devoting more and more time to her own writing. Her first major success came with her play *The Children's Hour*, which opened on Broadway in November 1934, ran for 691 perfor-

Lillian Hellman

mances, and was later frequently revived and several times made into motion pictures. After the unsuccessful *Days to Come*, 1936, she again scored a hit with *The Little Foxes*, which opened in February 1939 starring Tallulah Bankhead. It was also twice made into a movie. Subsequent plays, in which she continued to draw powerful and bitter pictures of intolerance and exploitation, included *Watch on the Rhine*, which won a New York Drama Critics' Circle Award and was also later adapted for the screen, 1941, *The Searching Wind*, 1944, *Another Part of the Forest*, 1946, *The Autumn Garden*, 1951, *Toys in the Attic*, which won her a second Critics' Circle Award, 1960, and others.

From 1935 Hellman wrote often for the movies, both original scenarios and adaptations of some of her own plays. Among her film scripts were those for *The Dark Angel*, 1935, *These Three* (film title of *The Children's Hour*), 1936, *Dead End*, 1937, *The Little Foxes*, 1941, *The North Star*, 1943, *The Searching Wind*, 1946, and *The Chase*, 1965. Hellman also adapted a number of works for the stage, including Jean Anouilh's *The Lark*, 1955, and *My Mother, My Father, and Me*, 1963, from Burt Blechman's novel *How Much?* She wrote the book for *Candide*, 1956, a musical based on Voltaire's story, with Richard Wilbur, who wrote the lyrics, and Leonard Bernstein, who composed the score. In 1964 she was awarded the gold medal for drama by the National Institute of Arts and Letters and the American Academy of Arts and Letters. She edited Anton Chekhov's *Selected Letters*, 1955, and *The Big Knockover*, 1966, a collection of stories and short novels by Dashiell Hammett, with whom she had had a long personal relationship. In 1969 she published *An Unfinished Woman*, an autobiographical memoir that won a National Book Award, and in 1973 she published *Pentimento: A Book of Portraits*, a further volume of autobiography. *Scoundrel Time*, 1976, was her controversial memoir of persons and politics. In 1980 she published *Maybe*, her last autobiographical work.

Both Hellman and Hammet were left wing sympathizers and were called to testify before the House Committee on Un-American Activities. Hammet was imprisoned in 1951. When Hellman was called in 1952, she became the first person to refuse to implicate others and made herself famous with her statement: "I cannot and will not cut my conscience to fit this year's fashions." She was not imprisoned but was blacklisted. She died on June 30, 1984, near her home on Martha's Vineyard, Massachusetts.

Helmer, Bessie Bradwell 1858–1927 lawyer and editor

Born in Chicago on October 20, 1858, Bessie Bradwell was the daughter of Myra Colby Bradwell. She graduated from Chicago High School first in her class in 1876. From Northwestern University she received a bachelor's degree in 1880 and a master's in 1882, and in the latter year she also graduated first in her class from Union College of Law in Chicago and was admitted to the Illinois bar. In December 1885 she married Frank A. Helmer, also a lawyer. Following her mother's death in 1894 she became assistant editor of the *Chicago Legal News*, and in 1907 she succeeded her father as editor in chief of the newspaper and president of the company that published it. She retained both posts for the rest of her life, and from 1905 to 1923 she was also editor of Hurd's *Revised Statutes of the State of Illinois*. In addition she edited nine volumes of *Reports of Cases Determined in the Appellate Court of Illinois*.

Helmer was an early and active member of the Association of Collegiate Alumnae (now the American Association of University Women) and served as president of the organization in 1890–1891. In 1890 she also became a member of a new committee established by the organization to oversee the awarding of fellowships to promising women graduate students, and the next year she succeeded Alice Freeman Palmer as chairman of the committee. For the next 15 years she devoted much of her time to raising funds for the fellowship program and to selecting recipients. Bessie Helmer died in Battle Creek, Michigan, on January 10, 1927.

Hentz, Caroline Lee Whiting 1800–1856 writer

Born in Lancaster, Massachusetts, on June 1, 1800, Caroline Whiting was a vivacious and intelligent girl who early demonstrated a flair for writing. In September 1824 she married Nicholas Marcellus Hentz, a French immigrant teacher of morbid disposition. From 1826 to 1830 they lived in Chapel Hill, North Carolina, where Nicholas Hentz taught languages and letters at the university. Shortly after their move to Covington, Kentucky, Caroline Hentz entered a verse drama, *De Lara, or the Moorish Bride*, in a competition and won. The play was produced and favorably received at the Tremont Theatre in Boston and the Arch Street Theatre in Philadelphia in 1831. The next year her *Constance of Werdenberg, or The Forest League* was produced at the Park Theatre, New York City, and her *Lamorah, or The Western Wilds* was produced in Cincinnati. She and her family moved to Cincinnati in that year. From 1834 they lived in a succession of Southern towns — Florence, Alabama, in 1834–1843, Tuscaloosa in 1843–1845, Tuskegee in 1845–1847, and Columbus, Georgia, in 1847–1854 — and until 1849 her family duties and the task of helping run the private girls' schools opened by her husband prevented her from writing more than some short stories and one highly successful book, *Aunt Patty's Scrap Bag*, 1846.

In 1849 her husband became permanently invalid, and Caroline Hertz began writing in earnest. Her novels, most serialized first and then published in book form, included *Linda, or The Young Pilot of the Belle Creole*, 1850, *Rena, or The Snow Bird*, 1851, *Marcus Wariand, or The Long Moss Spring*, 1852, *Helen and Arthur, or Miss Thusa's Spinning Wheel*, 1853, *The Planter's Northern Bride*, a two-volume rebuttal of *Uncle Tom's Cabin* that brought her widespread gratitude in the South, 1854, *Robert Graham: A Sequel to Linda*, 1855, and *Ernest Linwood, or The Inner Life of the Author*, 1856. Despite their lack of literary quality the novels achieved great popularity (they were republished as late as 1889) through the device of featuring female protagonists who were preternaturally noble and self-sacrificing and male characters of tyrannical and otherwise unpleasant habits. Her short stories were collected in such volumes as *The Victim of Excitement and Other Stories*, 1853, *Wild Jack*, 1853, *Courtship and Marriage, or The Joys and Sorrows of American Life*, 1856, and *The Banished Son, and Other Stories of the Heart*, 1856. Hentz died in Marianna, Florida, on February 11, 1856.

Hepburn, Katharine 1909– actor

Born in Hartford, Connecticut, on November 8, 1909, Katharine Hepburn graduated from Bryn Mawr College in 1928 and immediately sought a theatrical career. After a period of study and working in summer stock she made her Broadway debut in a small role in *Night Hostess* at the Martin Beck Theatre in September 1928. After other parts in *These Days*, 1929, *A Month in the Country*, 1930, and *Art and Mrs. Bottle*, 1930, she drew considerable attention with her performance in *The Warrior's Husband*, 1932, and was given a film contract by RKO Studios.

In Hollywood Hepburn appeared in a rapid succession of movies, including *Bill of Divorcement*, 1932, *Christopher Strong*, 1933, *Morning Glory*, for which she won an Academy Award, 1933, *Little Women*, 1933, *Spitfire*, 1934, *The Little Minister*, 1934, *Alice Adams*, 1935, *Mary of Scotland*, 1936, *A Woman Rebels*, 1936, *Quality Street*, 1937, *Stage Door*, 1937, *Bringing Up Baby*, 1938, and *Holiday*, 1938, the last for Columbia. She returned to the stage, touring in *Jane Eyre*, and to Broadway in *The Philadelphia Story*, 1939, which had been rewritten with her own sharp, aristocratic manner in mind. The 1940 MGM film version with Cary Grant brought her a New York Film Critics' Circle Award.

In 1942 Hepburn made *Woman of the Year*, the first of a series of highly popular movies with her long-time friend Spencer Tracy; with Tracy she also appeared in *Keeper of the*

Flame, 1942, *Without Love*, 1945, *Sea of Grass*, 1947, *State of the Union*, 1948, *Adam's Rib*, 1949, *Pat and Mike*, 1952, and *Desk Set*, 1957. Others of her films of that period included *Dragon Seed*, 1944, *The African Queen*, 1951, *Summertime*, 1955, *The Rainmaker*, 1956, and *Suddenly, Last Summer*, 1959, and she continued also to appear occasionally on the stage, for a time especially in Shakespearean roles. For *Long Day's Journey into Night*, 1962, she won a Cannes Film Festival award, and for *Guess Who's Coming to Dinner*, 1967, which was Tracy's last film, she won another Academy Award. With *The Lion in Winter*, 1968, she became the only woman ever to win three Oscars for best actress.

Subsequently Hepburn appeared in *The Mad Woman of Chaillot*, 1969, *The Trojan Women*, 1971, *A Delicate Balance*, 1973, and *Rooster Cogburn*, 1976, and in the 1969 Broadway production of *Coco*. Her later films include *On Golden Pond*, 1981, for which she won her fourth Oscar for best actress, and *The Ultimate Solution of Grace Quigley*, 1985. Her Broadway performance in *West Side*, 1981, was greeted with critical acclaim. Among her rare television performances were those in *Love Among the Ruins*, with Sir Laurence Olivier in 1975, *The Corn Is Green*, 1979, *Mrs. Delafield Wants to Marry*, 1986, and *Laura Lansing Slept Here*, 1988. A decided individualist in private life, she brought to all her roles a sinewy strength and an aura of confidence that could range from frank cheerfulness to roaring zeal to ultrafeminine hauteur. Her comic and dramatic versatility was attested to both by her four Oscars and by her eight other nominations for the award. She published *The Making of the African Queen*, 1987, and an autobiography, *Me*, 1991. In 1990 she received the Kennedy Center honors and the American Comedy Lifetime Achievement Award.

Hewins, Caroline Maria 1846–1926 librarian

Born on October 10, 1846, in Roxbury (now part of Boston), Massachusetts, Caroline Hewins grew up in nearby Jamaica Plain and West Roxbury. She graduated from Eliot High School in Jamaica Plain, attended the Girls' High and Normal School in Boston in 1862–1863, and taught school for a few years thereafter. In 1866–1867 she was an assistant at the Boston Athenaeum, where she learned bibliography and the rudiments of librarianship. She then studied for a time at Boston University and the Massachusetts Institute of Technology.

In 1875 Hewins secured the post of librarian of the Young Men's Institute, a private subscription library in Hartford, Connecticut. She oversaw the merging of the Institute with the Hartford Library Association in 1878 and its transformation by stages into a free library in 1892. (The name Hartford Public Library was adopted in 1893.) A principal interest of hers from her first days at the Young Men's Institute was to increase the library's usefulness and appeal to children. She took personal interest in children's reading, prevailed upon schools to join the Institute so that she could supply suitable books to the classroom, and in 1878 began publishing reading suggestions for children in the Institute's newly established bulletin.

In 1882, at the invitation of Frederick Leypoldt, editor of *Publishers' Weekly*, Hewins compiled *Books for the Young: A Guide for Parents and Children*, a pioneering work that greatly influenced the development of children's library collections. Her own collection at the Hartford Public Library, although not for years given its own department, was heavily patronized by young readers. Finally in 1904 funds were allocated by the trustees to establish a separate children's department with its own librarian. In 1895 she opened a branch library, also with a children's section, in the Social Settlement of Hartford, where she herself lived for 12 years. Her eminence in the field of library science was recognized in her election as secretary and in 1912 president of the Connecticut Library Association, of which she had been a founder in 1891, and as council member in 1885–1888 and

1893–1902 and vice-president in 1891 of the American Library Association. In 1923 she published *A Traveler's Letters to Boys and Girls* and in 1926 *A Mid-Century Child and Her Books*, a personal memoir. She died in Hartford, Connecticut, on November 4, 1926.

Hill, Grace Livingston 1865–1947 novelist

Born on April 16, 1865, in Wellsville, New York, Grace Livingston grew up in a succession of towns in New York, New Jersey, and Ohio as her clergyman father moved from pastorate to pastorate. She was educated in public schools and for a time at the Cincinnati Art School and at Elmira College. Encouraged by her aunt, Isabella Macdonald Alden, she early developed an interest in writing. Her first book, *A Chautauqua Idyl*, was published in 1887 after first appearing as a magazine serial. In December 1892 she married the Reverend Thomas G. F. Hill, with whom she lived in Germantown, Pennsylvania, until his death in 1899. She then settled in Swarthmore, Pennsylvania, and took up writing seriously.

Over the next 48 years she published some 78 novels with such titles as *A Little Servant*, 1890, *Katharine's Yesterday*, 1896, *In the Way*, 1897, *An Unwilling Guest*, 1901, *The Angel of His Presence*, 1902, *The Story of a Whim*, 1902, *The Girl from Montana*, 1907, *Marcia Schuyler*, her first big success, 1908, *Dawn of the Morning*, 1910, *The Best Man*, 1914, *The Obsession of Victoria Gracen*, 1915, *The Witness*, 1917, *The Enchanted Barn*, 1918, *The Red Signal*, 1919, *Cloudy Jewel*, 1920, *The Tryst*, 1921, *The City of Fire*, 1922, *Coming Through the Rye*, 1926, *The White Flower*, 1927, *The Prodigal Girl*, 1929, *Ladybird*, 1930, *Happiness Hill*, 1932, *Matched Pearls*, 1933, *Rainbow Cottage*, 1934, *Beauty for Ashes*, 1935, *April Gold*, 1936, *Daphne Dean*, 1937, *Stranger Within the Gates*, 1939, *Crimson Mountain*, 1942, *A Girl to Come Home To*, 1945, and *Where Two Ways Met*, 1947.

Hill's books were aimed generally at the adolescent girl reader of rural or small-town background, and they presented her own stern moral code in confrontation with an endless variety of challenges in the modern world, from bolshevism to jazz to motion pictures. By her death her books had sold some 4 million copies, and they continued to be reprinted for two decades. Some of them originally appeared under the name Marcia Macdonald, and after her second marriage in 1904 (which ended in separation) a few appeared under the name "Grace Livingston Hill-Lutz." In 1918 she collaborated with Evangeline Booth on the non-fictional *War Romance of the Salvation Army*. For a number of years she also wrote a syndicated newspaper column entitled "The Christian Endeavor Hour." She died in Swarthmore, Pennsylvania, on February 23, 1947.

Hill, Patty Smith 1868–1946 educator

Born in Anchorage, Kentucky, on March 27, 1868, Patty Hill was the daughter of educated and progressive parents and was early encouraged to develop her intellectual and creative nature. She graduated from the Louisville Collegiate Institute in 1887 and then enrolled in a newly opened kindergarten normal course in that city. On completing the course in 1889 she was given charge of the demonstration kindergarten, and in 1893 she became head of the Louisville Free Kindergarten Association and its Louisville Training School for Kindergarten and Primary Teachers. Her success in introducing new methods and materials into the kindergarten classroom soon attracted wide attention in the field. In 1893, with her sister Mildred J. Hill, she published *Song Stories for the Kindergarten*, which included "Good Morning to All," later better known as "Happy Birthday to You." In the summer of 1896 she studied under psychologist G. Stanley Hall at Clark University. In 1904–1905 she delivered a series of lectures at Columbia University Teachers College. An alternating series by Susan Blow, the conservative exponent of pure Froebelian methods, created a striking and useful counterpoint.

In 1906 Patty Hill joined the Teachers College faculty. She was elected president of the

International Kindergarten Union in 1908. From 1910 she was head of the newly organized kindergarten department of the college. In her work to introduce more flexible, natural methods into a field that had become in large part rigidly doctrinaire, she drew liberally upon the methods of behavioral psychology, in particular benefiting from the suggestions and criticisms of such Columbia colleagues as Edward Lee Thorndike and John Dewey. Dewey's ideas of socialization and project-directed activities were tested in the college's experimental Horace Mann Kindergarten, and with the aid of Thorndike's experimental techniques a list of specific forms of behavior to be learned by kindergarten pupils was determined. This "habit inventory" was published in 1923 as *A Conduct Curriculum for the Kindergarten and First Grade* and constituted a concrete alternative to the Froebelian system. From 1922 she also championed the nursery school as an extension down to two-year-olds of the vital task of socialization. She was made a full professor in that year. In 1924 she led in organizing the Institute of Child Welfare Research at Teachers College, and in 1925 she was a founder of the National Association for Nursery Education.

Although she wrote little, her influence spread through the country with the teachers she trained, and her reform of the kindergarten curriculum was a permanent one. She was the inventor of Patty Hill blocks, large construction blocks with which children could build structures big enough to play in. After her retirement from Columbia in 1935 she devoted much time to the Hilltop Community Center for underprivileged children in the neighborhood. She died in New York City on May 25, 1946.

Hills, Carla Anderson 1934– lawyer and public official

Born in Los Angeles on January 3, 1934, Carla Anderson attended private schools and in 1951 entered Stanford University, where she was an outstanding tennis player as well as student. After graduating in 1955 she entered Yale Law School, from which she received her law degree in 1958. In September 1958 she married Roderick M. Hills. After her admission to the California bar in 1959 she worked for two years as an assistant U.S. attorney in Los Angeles. In 1962 she and her husband and others formed the law firm of Munger, Tolles, Hills, & Rickershauser, in which she gained experience in antitrust and securities cases. She was a coauthor of *Federal Civil Practice*, 1961, and the editor of *Antitrust Advisor*, 1971.

She was president of the Los Angeles chapter of the Federal Bar Association in 1963 and of the National Association of Women Lawyers in 1965. She was admitted to the bar of the U.S. Supreme Court in the latter year. In 1972 she was adjunct professor of antitrust law at the University of California at Los Angeles for a semester.

In the autumn of 1973 Hills was offered the post of assistant U.S. attorney general, but the offer became void when the attorney general, Elliot L. Richardson, resigned in the "Saturday night massacre" episode of the Watergate affair. In February 1974, however, she was again offered the post by Richardson's successor, William B. Saxbe, and in April she took office as assistant attorney general in charge of the Justice Department's civil division. In February 1975 she was nominated by President Gerald R. Ford to be secretary of the Department of Housing and Urban Development. She was confirmed, over some questions regarding her lack of experience in the field, and sworn in in March. She retained the post until the accession of a Democratic administration in January 1977, when she was succeeded by Patricia Roberts Harris.

In 1978 she opened a Washington, D.C., branch of the Los Angeles law firm Latham & Watkins and remained there until 1986 when she became a partner with Weil, Gotshal & Manges. In 1989 she was appointed U.S. Trade Representative for the Bush administration. In this position she focused on breaking down the Japanese trade barriers affecting

US satellites, supercomputers and semiconductors, as well as successfully urging the European community to phase out farm subsidies which undercut American and other foreign farmers. In 1993 she founded her consulting firm, Hills and Company, and also teamed up with other members of the Bush administration, Brent Scowcroft, Lawrence Eagleburger, and Robert Gates, to form the Forum for International Policy.

Hinkle, Beatrice Moses 1874–1953 psychiatrist

Born in San Francisco on October 10, 1874, Beatrice Moses was educated privately. She married Walter S. Hinkle, a lawyer and assistant district attorney, in 1892, and a short time later she entered the Cooper Medical School (later taken over by Stanford University). She graduated in 1899 shortly after her husband's death. Later in the year she was appointed San Francisco's city physician; she was the first woman physician in the country to hold a public health position. In the course of her work she became interested in psychotherapy, and in 1905 she moved to New York City and became associated with Dr. Charles R. Dana. In 1908 they established at Cornell Medical College the nation's first psychotherapeutic clinic.

In 1909 Hinkle traveled to Vienna to study with Sigmund Freud. During her years there she gradually aligned herself with the psychoanalytic group that gravitated about Carl Jung. She returned to New York in 1915 and the next year joined the faculties of Cornell Medical College and the New York Post-Graduate Medical School. In the same year she published *The Psychology of the Unconscious*, a translation from Jung. She was among the earliest practitioners of Jungian analysis in America, and she made numerous contributions to the conceptual framework of the theory. Her major written work, *The Recreating of the Individual*, 1923, was noted particularly for its chapters on women and artists. She also published a number of articles in journals and a translation of Dirk Coster's *The Living and the Lifeless*, 1929. In later years she expanded her practice to include a small private sanatorium adjacent to "Roughlands," her Washington, Connecticut, retreat. She died in New York City on February 28, 1953.

Hodder, Jessie Donaldson 1867–1931 prison superintendent and reformer

Born in Cincinnati on March 30, 1867, Jessie Donaldson grew up in the home of her grandmother; little else is known of her early life. She moved to New York City in 1890 and a short time later entered into a common-law marriage with Alfred L. Hodder, a student of William James. They lived in Germany and Italy for a time and from 1893 near Bryn Mawr College, where Alfred Hodder secured an instructorship. Jessie Hodder and her two children went abroad in 1898, but Alfred failed to join them as he had promised; he subsequently denied them and married again. In 1906 Jessie Hodder returned to the United States and settled in Boston, where a letter of introduction from Mrs. William James to Elizabeth Glendower Evans won her a job as house mother at the Industrial School for Girls in Lancaster, Massachusetts.

In 1908 Hodder became a counselor for unwed expectant mothers, syphilitics, and alcoholics in the social services department of Massachusetts General Hospital. She quickly revealed a strong aptitude for such work and soon pioneered in advising that unwed mothers keep and rear their children. In December 1910 she was appointed superintendent of the Massachusetts Prison and Reformatory for Women (formerly the Reformatory Prison for Women, where Ellen Cheney Johnson had instituted a pioneer program of rehabilitation), which the next year, at her urging, changed its name to simply the Massachusetts Reformatory for Women. She quickly made substantive changes in the same vein: windows were unblocked, and a vigorous program of education and recreation was instituted. Educational opportunities offered ranged from the elementary level to university extension, and new recreational facilities included sports, music, and drama.

While not an original theorist, Hodder was quick to draw on advanced thinking in criminology, penology, and sociology. In particular she adopted the notion of classifying prisoners, pioneered by Katharine Bement Davis at the Bedford Hills Reformatory for Women in New York. The mentally ill were identified and held separate from the rest of the prison population, which constituted the reformable inmates. Careful examinations, record-keeping, and follow-up studies conducted by a research department staff from 1912 produced a scientifically valuable body of data while contributing greatly to the effectiveness of reform. Not the least of her accomplishments was securing legislative support for, or at least acquiescence in, such far-reaching institutional changes.

Independent testimony to the value of Hodder's work appeared in 1934 in Sheldon and Eleanor Glueck's *Five Hundred Delinquent Women*, a study carried out at the Massachusetts Reformatory. In 1925 she was the sole woman delegate to the International Prison Congress in London, and she was a member of the National Crime Commission appointed by President Calvin Coolidge in 1927 and of a committee of the Wickersham Commission on Law Observance and Enforcement appointed by President Herbert Hoover in 1929. Jessie Hodder died at her home in the reformatory, in Framingham, Massachusetts, on November 19, 1931.

Hoffman, Malvina 1887–1966 sculptor

Born in New York City on June 15, 1887, Malvina Hoffman, daughter of a noted English pianist, was educated privately. She leaned strongly toward an artistic career from an early age, and after several years studying painting she took up sculpture with Herbert Adams and then Gutzon Borglum. She went to Paris in 1910 and studied in the studio of Auguste Rodin. Her "Russian Dancers" won first prize in an international art exposition in that year. She opened a studio of her own in New York City in 1912, but from 1913 to 1915 she was again in Paris. In the latter year her "Pavlowa Gavotte" and "Bacchanale Russe" (the latter, figures of Anna Pavlova and Mikhail Mordkin, now in Luxembourg Gardens, Paris) won wide attention.

During World War I Hoffman was active in Red Cross work and was American representative for Appui aux Artistes, an organization for the relief of needy artists that she had helped found in France. In 1918–1919 she was deeply involved in postwar relief work, making in the latter year a tour of inspection of the Balkan countries for Herbert Hoover. Her first major postwar sculpture was "The Sacrifice," a war memorial for Harvard University. A massive group, "To the Friendship of the English Speaking People," was dedicated at Bush House, London, in July 1925. She became especially known for her portrait sculptures, and among her subjects were Ignace Paderewski (several times), Anna Pavlova (several times), John Muir, John Keats, and Ivan Mestrovic.

Hoffman's skilled, finely detailed portraits brought her in 1930 a remarkable commission from the Field Museum of Chicago to execute a series of 110 life-size figures (25 full-figure, 85 in bust) of human racial types. For five years she alternated periods in her Paris studio with journeys to every portion of the globe, often under considerable hardship, to observe and model the various types called for in the plan. (She had already spent 1926–1927 in Africa for a similar purpose.) Leading anthropologists were consulted along the way. Of the 110 figures finally completed for the Hall of Man (which was dedicated in June 1933, before completion), 97 were cast by her in bronze, the remaining 13 being done in marble or stone. In 1936 she published a memoir, *Heads and Tales*, and in 1939 *Sculpture Inside and Out*. Other notable sculptures were a series of 26 stone panels for the facade of the Joslin Clinic in Boston, the American Battle Monument (World War II) at Épinal, France, and a bronze "Mongolian Archer," which won a gold medal from the Allied Artists of America in 1962. Widely honored for her work, Malvina Hoffman died at her studio-home in New York City on July 10, 1966.

Hoge, Jane Currie Blaikie 1811–1890 welfare worker

Born in Philadelphia on July 31, 1811, Jane Blaikie was educated at the Young Ladies' College in that city. In June 1831 she married Abraham H. Hoge, a Pittsburgh merchant. Over the next several years, in addition to caring for her large family, Jane Hoge found time to serve as secretary of the Pittsburgh Orphan Asylum. In 1848 the Hoges moved to Chicago, where in 1858 Jane Hoge helped found and direct the Home for the Friendless. The enlistment of two of her sons in the Union army at the beginning of the Civil War drew her into volunteer nursing work at Camp Douglas, near Chicago.

By late 1861 Hoge and her friend Mary A. Livermore were working with the Chicago (later Northwestern) Sanitary Commission under Eliza Chappell Porter. About that time they were also appointed agents of Dorothea Dix, superintendent of army nurses, to recruit nurses for service in hospitals in the Western department. In March 1862 they made a tour of army hospitals in Cairo and Mound City, Illinois, in St. Louis, in Paducah, Kentucky, and elsewhere. In December 1862, after attending a general conference of U.S. Sanitary Commission leaders in Washington, D.C., the two women were appointed associate directors of the Chicago branch. The work demanded of them was great and ceaseless. By letters, addresses, and other means they aroused and maintained at high pitch the work of upwards of a thousand local aid societies throughout the Northwest in collecting and forwarding clothing, medical and hospital supplies, food, and other materials. During 1863 Jane Hoge made three trips to the front in the Vicksburg campaign, combining inspection of the logistics system with nursing of soldiers.

During July-October 1863 Hoge and Livermore temporarily stepped aside from their posts to organize and direct the great Sanitary Fair in Chicago, a two-week fund-raising extravaganza that raised over $70,000 for the Chicago office. Their success prompted the holding of similar events in eastern cities in 1864. At the end of the war a great many public tributes were paid to Hoge and Livermore for their work. In 1867 Hoge published an account of her wartime experiences as *The Boys in Blue*. In 1871 she organized a fund-raising campaign that financed the founding of the Evanston College for Ladies, which opened in September of that year under Frances Willard. From 1872 to 1885 she headed the Woman's Presbyterian Board of Foreign Missions in the Northwest. She died in Chicago on August 26, 1890.

Hokinson, Helen Elna 1893–1949 cartoonist

Born in Mendota, Illinois, on June 29, 1893, Helen Hokinson grew up in Moline, Illinois, in Des Moines, Iowa, and from 1905 again in Mendota. After graduating from high school in 1913 she studied for five years at the Chicago Academy of Fine Arts while supporting herself by doing fashion illustration. In 1920 she moved to New York City and studied for a time at the New York School of Fine and Applied Art. In addition to illustration she did some painting as well. She also had a keen interest in cartooning, and the acceptance of one of her early efforts by the newly founded *New Yorker* magazine in 1925 decided her career.

Over the next two dozen years Hokinson drew more than 1700 cartoons, published principally in the *New Yorker* and nearly all of them detailing the life of the middle-aged American matron. Her characters, slightly overweight, behatted, and ranging in mental state from outright addled to merely puzzled, populated garden clubs, literary societies, civic meetings, and luncheons, and they entertained numberless notions and aspirations that were at once ridiculous and engagingly innocent. Hokinson's cartoons lampooned with a gentle touch that won her great popularity, not only among the satirically inclined but also among the very ranks of those she chided. From 1931 she worked in collaboration with James Reid Parker, a *New Yorker* contributor. Her cartoons, with his captions, were collected in several volumes: *So You're Going to Buy a Book!*, 1931, *My Best Girls*,

1941, *When Were You Built?*, 1948, *The Ladies, God Bless 'Em*, 1950, *There Are Ladies Present*, 1952, and *The Hokinson Festival*, 1956. She continued to publish her cartoons regularly until her death in an airplane accident near Washington, D.C., on November 1, 1949.

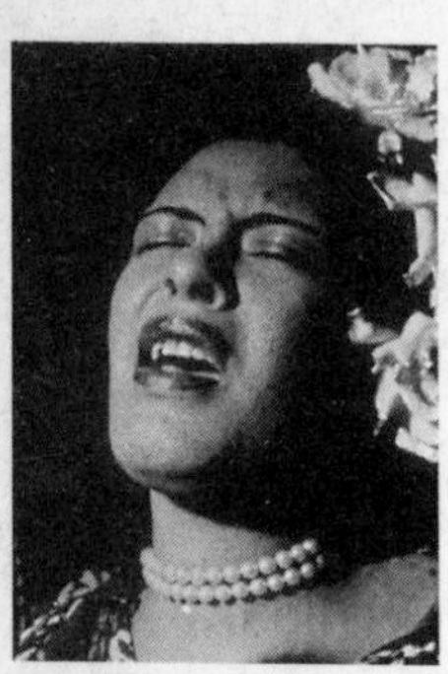

Billie Holiday

Holiday, Billie 1915–1959 singer

Born on April 7, 1915, in Baltimore, Eleanora Fagan was the daughter of a professional musician who for a time played guitar with the Fletcher Henderson band. She later adopted the name Billie from a favorite movie actress, Billie Dove; Holiday was her father's name. She grew up in poverty in a ghetto area of Baltimore. As a child, in return for running errands for a local brothel keeper, she was allowed to linger and listen to recordings by Bessie Smith and Louis Armstrong. In 1928 she moved with her mother to New York City, and after three years of subsisting by various means she found a job singing in a Harlem nightclub. She had had no formal musical training, but with an almost instinctive sense of musical structure and with a wealth of experience gathered at the root level of jazz and blues she developed a singing style that was deeply moving, individual, and inimitable.

In 1933 Holiday made her first recordings, with Benny Goodman and others. Two years later a series of recordings with Teddy Wilson and members of Count Basie's band brought her wider recognition and launched her career as the leading jazz singer of her time. She toured with Basie and with Artie Shaw in 1937 and 1938 and in the latter year opened at the plush Café Society in New York City. From about 1940 she performed exclusively in cabarets and in concert. Her recordings between 1936 and 1942 marked her peak years. During that period she was often associated with saxophonist Lester Young, who gave her the nickname "Lady Day" (it was she, in turn, who dubbed him "Pres"). In 1947 she was arrested for a narcotics violation and spent a year in a rehabilitation center.

No longer able to obtain a cabaret license to work in New York City, Holiday nonetheless packed New York's Carnegie Hall ten days after her release. She continued to perform in concert and in clubs outside of New York, and she made several tours during her later years. The constant struggle with heroin addiction more and more affected her voice, although not her style. Among the songs identified with her were "Strange Fruit," "Fine and Mellow," "The Man I Love," "Billie's Blues," "God Bless the Child," and "Driving Me Crazy." In 1956 she wrote an autobiography, *Lady Sings the Blues* (with William Dufty). She died in New York City on July 17, 1959.

Hollander, Nicole 1939– cartoonist

Born in 1939, Nicole Hollander grew up on Chicago's west side, in one of the few Jewish families in a predominantly Italian neighborhood. Her mother was a hospital employee whose strong network of female friendships taught her daughter the value of the company of women; like all the women in Hollander's family, her mother worked full time out of necessity throughout the 1940s and 1950s. Hollander's father was a union carpenter who was passionate about the labor movement and progressive politics. He often got angry at his employers and walked off the job, several times attempting to start his own businesses, including two unsuccessful delicatessens.

Out of this environment came the down-to-earth toughness, the feminist consciousness, and the quirky, ironic sense of humor that informed Hollander's work as one of less than a handful of female syndicated cartoonists. With an MFA in painting, in 1976 Hollander published her first comic strip, "The Feminist Funnies," in *The Spokeswoman*, a national feminist newsletter she designed and illustrated.

Three years later, *I'm in Training to be Tall and Blonde*, her first book of cartoons, was published by St. Martin's Press. The book introduced Sylvia, the middle-aged, working class, outspoken heroine whom Hollander said was inspired by the way her mother and her friends dressed and talked when she was growing up. In 1981, *Sylvia* became a nationally syndicated comic strip, and Hollander began a series of battles with syndicates and newspaper editors over the feminist content of her work.

In 1982, she took control and began syndicating her own work, which meant not only creating the strip but reproducing it, sending it to outlets, and billing customers. Sylvia, her menagerie of irreverent cats, and a cast of characters including bartenders, waitresses, and an alien lover appeared in more than fifty newspapers. The strip's popularity spawned a line of greeting cards and calendars, a musical revue, and thirteen books, among them *Everything Here is Mine: Sylvia's Unhelpful Guide to Cat Behavior*, 1992, published by Avon.

In 1983 Hollander received the Wonder Woman Foundation Award for Women of Achievement over 40, and in 1985 she joined the likes of Alexander Haig, Moshe Dayan, and Robert Redford as a recipient of Yale's Chubb Fellowship for Public Service.

Holley, Marietta 1836–1926 writer and humorist

Born near Pierrepont Manor, New York, on July 16, 1836, Marietta Holley attended district school until she was fourteen. She studied and then taught piano and from an early age wrote verses for her own amusement. A few were printed in local newspapers, and in April 1867 one appeared in the nationally circulated *Peterson's Magazine*. In the same magazine in July 1871 appeared the first of her humorous dialect sketches featuring the commonsensical "Samantha Allen" and the sentimental caricature "Betsy Bobbet." The sketch was signed "Josiah Allen's Wife," which soon became as familiar a pseudonym as Artemus Ward, Josh Billings, or Major Jack Downing.

In 1873 Holley's first book appeared as *My Opinions and Betsy Bobbet's*. Some 20 similar volumes followed, including *Samantha at the Centennial*, 1876, *My Wayward Pardner*, 1880, *Miss Richard's Boy*, 1882, *Sweet Cicely, or Josiah Allen as a Politician*, 1885, *Samantha at Saratoga*, 1887, *Samantha Among the Brethren*, 1890, *Samantha on the Race Problem*, 1892, *Samantha at the World's Fair*, 1893, *Josiah's Alarm*, 1893, *Samantha in Europe*, 1895, *Round the World with Josiah Allen's Wife*, 1899, *The Borrowed Automobile*, 1906, *Samantha on Children's Rights*, 1909, *Who Was to Blame*, 1910, and *Josiah Allen on the Woman Question*, 1914.

Written in the tradition of droll Yankee humor, the books were highly popular at home and abroad, not least because of their successful portrayal of Samantha, a strong advocate of women's rights, as the plainspoken voice of sanity opposed to the hysterical and conventional views of Betsy and Josiah. Despite her views and the urgings of Frances Willard and Susan B. Anthony, Marietta Holley took no part in organized action for women's rights, temperance, or other reforms. She also published a few other volumes, such as *Miss Jones' Quilting*, 1887, *Tirzah Ann's Summer Trip*, 1892, and *The Widder Doodle's Love Affair*, 1893. She died at her ancestral farm near Pierrepont Manor, New York, on March 1, 1926.

Holmes, Mary Jane Hawes 1825–1907 novelist

Born in Brookfield, Massachusetts, on April 5, 1825, Mary Jane Hawes was encouraged by her parents in gaining an education and in her early attempts at writing. She began teaching in district schools at thirteen, and two years later her first published work appeared. In August 1849 she married Daniel Holmes, a Yale graduate with whom she lived and taught school in or near Versailles, Kentucky, for three years. From 1852 they lived in Brockport, New York. In 1854, the year after Daniel Holmes's admission to the bar, Mary Holmes published her first novel, *Tempest and Sunshine; or, Life in Kentucky*.

Nearly two score novels and collections of stories followed, all cut from the same pattern of conventional domestic tales embodying the simplest of moral codes, in which only black and white were admitted, and all written in sentimental and undistinguished prose. They included *English Orphans*, 1855, *The Homestead on the Hillside, and Other Tales*, 1856, *Lena Rivers*, her best known book, 1856, *Meadow Brook*, 1857, *Dora Deane; or the East India Uncle*, 1858, *Cousin Maude*, 1860, *Marian Gray*, 1863, *Darkness and Daylight*, 1864, *Hugh Worthington*, 1865, *The Cameron Pride: or, Purified by Suffering*, 1867, *Rose Mather*, 1868, *Ethelyn's Mistake*, 1869, *Millbank*, 1971, *Edna Browning*, 1872, *West Lawn*, 1874, *Edith Lyle*, 1876, *Daisy Thornton*, 1878, *Forrest House*, 1879, *Chateau d'Or*, 1880, *Madeline*, 1881, *Queenie Hetherton*, 1883, *Bessie's Fortune*, 1885, *Gretchen*, 1887, *Marguerite*, 1890, *Paul Ralston*, 1897, *The Tracy Diamonds*, 1899, *The Merivale Banks*, 1903, *Rena's Experiment*, 1904, and *Connie's Mistake*, 1905. Her vast appeal to young girls and women enabled her publishers to sell upward of 2 million copies of her books, many in paperbound editions. She died in Brockport, New York, on October 6, 1907.

Holt, Winifred 1870–1945 welfare worker

Born in New York City on November 17, 1870, Winifred Holt was a daughter of publisher Henry Holt. She was educated in private schools and, informally, by the artists and writers who were frequent guests of her parents. While on an extended visit to Italy in the mid–1890s to convalesce from one of her many illnesses, she discovered a talent for sculpture, and after her return to New York in 1897 she studied with Augustus Saint-Gaudens and others. On another trip to Italy in 1901 she encountered at a concert a group of blind students to whom the government had provided unsold tickets. Their obvious enjoyment deeply impressed her, and after her return to New York in 1903 she established the Ticket Bureau for the Blind to provide concert and theater tickets.

During 1904–1905 Holt attended the Royal Normal College and Academy of Music for the Blind in London, and in November 1905 she and her sister Edith organized the New York Association for the Blind, of which Winifred Holt remained secretary until 1914. At a time when the blind were believed capable only of accepting charity, the new organization devoted itself to educating the public, including the blind, to the possibilities of rehabilitation and vocational training to make the blind self-supporting. (A committee within the association pursued a second objective, in cooperation with Louisa Lee Schuyler and others, and in 1915 became part of the National Committee for the Prevention of Blindness.) Winifred Holt's fervid dedication to her chosen cause and her abilities as a public speaker and fundraiser enabled the association to grow rapidly from a small group meeting at her home to a major welfare organization overseeing courses of instruction in sewing, typing and stenography, broommaking, piano tuning, and other marketable skills. From a rented loft the classrooms, workshops, and offices were moved to a permanent location, The Lighthouse, in February 1913.

The organization's success owed much to Winifred Holt's ability to enlist the active support of prominent persons: President William Howard Taft opened a fund-raising exhibit of blind workers' skills and products at the Metropolitan Opera House in 1911 and dedicated The Lighthouse in 1913; and Elihu Root, Carl Schurz, Charles Evans Hughes, Richard Watson Gilder, Mark Twain, and Helen Keller (of whom she made a fine sculpture bust) were among others involved. She worked with the New York City Board of Education to end the segregation of blind children in separate classrooms and to introduce Braille teaching materials, and she founded a magazine, *Searchlight*, for children. Lighthouses were begun in several other American cities in imitation of the New York original, and during World War I Holt was engaged by the French government to establish Lighthouses in Bordeaux and Paris for blinded soldiers. The international Lighthouse movement eventually spread to some 34 nations.

Holt's many honors for her work included the gold medal of the National Institute of Social Sciences in 1914 and membership in the French Legion of Horror in 1921. In 1922 she published *The Light Which Cannot Fail*, a record of her work. In November 1922 she married Rufus G. Mather, with whom she continued active in the Lighthouse movement. She died in Pittsfield, Massachusetts, on June 14, 1945.

Homer, Louise Dilworth Beatty 1871–1947 opera singer

Born on April 30, 1871, in Shadyside (now part of Pittsburgh), Pennsylvania, Louise Beatty grew up there and from 1882 in West Chester. After graduating from high school she helped support her family by working in Philadelphia as a secretary in a Quaker school and then as a court stenographer. Singing was an avocation until 1893, when she moved to Boston to pursue musical studies seriously. She became a member of the famous choir of the First Universalist Church there and was introduced to the world of opera by one of her teachers, the composer Sidney Homer, whom she married in January 1895. In 1896 they traveled to Paris, where she studied under Fidèle Koenig. A successful concert appearance was followed by her operatic debut in *La Favorita* at Vichy in June 1898. She sang at Angers in the 1898–1899 season, at Covent Garden, London, in the summer of 1899, in Brussels in 1899–1900, and again at Covent Garden in 1900. Maurice Grau, manager of the Metropolitan Opera of New York, was impressed by her full, wide-ranging, and dramatic contralto and signed her to a three-year contract in 1900. She remained with the Met for 19 years.

Homer's American debut occurred with the Metropolitan company in San Francisco in *Aïda* in November 1900, and a month later she made her New York debut in the same opera. Her astounding ability to learn a new role quickly was demonstrated when she replaced Ernestine Schumann-Heink in *Tristan und Isolde* on ten days' notice in San Francisco in December 1901, in her singing *Tannhäuser* in St. Louis with no orchestral rehearsal in the same month, and when she stepped into a 1903 production of *Das Rheingold* on a day's notice. Other notable performances were in *Rigoletto* on the night of Enrico Caruso's American debut in November 1903, the American premiere of *Hänsel und Gretel* in November 1905, the Metropolitan's first production of *Madame Butterfly*, with Geraldine Farrar (and with Puccini himself present) in February 1907, in *Aïda* in Arturo Toscanini's American debut in November 1908, and in *Orfeo ed Euridice* with Alma Gluck in December 1909. A perennial favorite with audiences was her performance opposite Caruso in *Samson et Dalila*.

Homer's greatest popularity came not from the stage, however, but from her second career as a recording artist. Beginning as early as 1902 she recorded for the Victor Talking Machine Company, first on cylinders and later on disks. Arias, oratorio selections, hymns, and ballads recorded by her were enormously popular: in 1919 alone, over 332,000 copies of 69 recorded selections were sold. Among her most popular recordings were duets and quartets with Alma Gluck, Geraldine Farrar, Caruso, and others. After leaving the Met in 1919 she sang four seasons, 1922–1926, with the Chicago Opera, made guest appearances with companies in San Francisco and Los Angeles, and made numerous concert and festival appearances. Her final performance at the Met was in *Il Trovatore* in March 1929. She gave up recording in the same year and devoted herself thereafter to the care of her ailing husband and her family. She died in Winter Park, Florida, on May 6, 1947.

Hooker, Isabella Beecher 1822–1907 suffragist

Born in Litchfield, Connecticut, on February 22, 1822, Isabella Beecher was a daughter of the Reverend Lyman Beecher and a half sister of Henry Ward and Catharine Beecher and Harriet Beecher Stowe. She grew up from 1826 in Boston, from 1832 in Cincinnati, and from 1835 in Hartford, Connecticut, and was educated mainly in schools founded by her sister Catharine. In August 1841 she married John Hooker, a law student and descendant of Thomas Hooker, the founder of Hartford. They lived in Farmington,

Connecticut, for ten years and then returned to Hartford, where John Hooker and a brother-in-law bought a hundred-acre wooded tract, built houses for themselves, and sold lots to Harriet Beecher Stowe, Charles Dudley Warner, Mark Twain, and other prominent and congenial figures.

Isabella Hooker's interest in the law and the legal status of women was first aroused early in her marriage by her husband's reading to her from Blackstone (whose position was that in marriage, man and wife are one person before the law, and that the woman has no separate legal existence). John Stuart Mill's essay on "The Enfranchisement of Women," which she read in 1861, ten years after its first appearance, further stimulated her, as did his later *The Subjection of Women.* Under the influence of Caroline M. Severance she overcame her earlier disdain for crusading reformers and became an associate of Susan B. Anthony, Elizabeth Cady Stanton, Paulina Wright Davis, and other women's-rights advocates. She helped organize the New England Woman Suffrage Association in 1868, and her "Mother's Letters to a Daughter on Woman's Suffrage" appeared anonymously in *Putnam's Magazine* in November and December of that year. In 1869 she called and presided over the convention that organized the Connecticut Woman Suffrage Association. From 1870 until success was achieved in 1877 she lobbied the Connecticut legislature vigorously in favor of a married women's property bill drafted by her husband.

Hooker was a prominent speaker at the 1870 convention of the National Woman Suffrage Association in Washington, D.C., and she planned and financed a special convention in January 1871 at which a federal constitutional suffrage amendment was drawn up and presented to Congress. For a number of years she was much of the time in Washington, lobbying and testifying in behalf of the amendment. Her association with Victoria Woodhull dated from that campaign and soon became quite close. She sided with Woodhull when the latter publicly accused the Reverend Henry Ward Beecher of adultery and was thereafter shunned by most of her family. She also followed Woodhull into Spiritualist circles and for a time was convinced that she would soon be chosen by spirit powers to lead a matriarchal government of the world. She published *Womanhood: Its Sanctities and Fidelities* in 1874. She remained active in suffrage work for most of her life, continuing as president of the state organization until 1905. She was involved in planning the first International Convention of Women in 1888. In 1892 she supported Olympia Brown's Federal Suffrage Association. In 1893 she was one of Connecticut's two representatives on the Board of Lady Managers of the World's Columbian Exposition in Chicago. Isabella Hooker died in Hartford, Connecticut, on January 25, 1907.

Hope, Lugenia Burns 1871–1947 activist, social reformer and clubwoman

Born on February 19, 1871, in St. Louis, Missouri, Lugenia D. Burns was the youngest of Ferdinand and Louisa Bertha Burns's seven children. She was able to attend school for a while until the family fell on hard times. As an adolescent she worked, often full-time, for several charitable and settlement organizations, including Hull-House and the King's Daughters.

Between 1890 and 1893 she attended the Chicago Art Institute, the Chicago School of Design, and the Chicago Business College. She met John Hope, a native of Georgia and a theology student at Brown University, in 1893. They were married during the Christmas holidays of 1897 and moved to Nashville, Tennessee, where John Hope had a teaching position at Roger Williams University.

While in Nashville, Lugenia Hope continued her tradition of community service and conducted classes in arts and crafts and physical education for the women students of Roger Williams. The following year John Hope accepted a position as classics instructor at Atlanta Baptist College (later Morehouse University). For more than three decades, the

Hopes lived and worked in Atlanta. In 1906 John Hope became the first black president of Morehouse College and was central in establishing the school as a nationally respected center for African-American education. Lugenia Hope supported her husband and contributed her own ideas to this mission.

Soon after arriving in Atlanta, Lugenia Hope became involved in a group trying to provide child-care centers to Atlanta's West Fair community. Under her leadership this group evolved into the Neighborhood Union, the first female-run, social welfare agency for African-Americans in Atlanta. From 1908 to 1935, as chairperson of its Board of Managers, she offered critical leadership as the organization provided medical, recreational, employment, and educational services in Atlanta's African-American communities and agitated for the rights of black Atlantans. By 1930 the structure of the Neighborhood Union had also been a model adopted by communities in Haiti and Cape Verde.

At the beginning of World War I, the Union ran the Atlanta YWCA's War Work Councils to serve African-American soldiers who were stationed in segregated units and barred from the recreational activities available to white soldiers through the base canteens and other USO-related entertainments. As a result of their success, she was approached to coordinate a nationwide network of Hostess Houses that eventually provided both African-American and Jewish soldiers, and their families, with a wide variety of services from recreation to relocation counseling. She served as director throughout the war.

Hope was also a founding member of the Atlanta Branch of the National Association of Colored Women's Clubs. Through her club work, she became involved in national reform activities and particularly in the efforts to challenge racial discrimination within various reform organizations.

In the spring of 1920, Hope called a conference of African-American women at Morehouse College to plan a challenge to the practices of segregation and white-domination within the national YWCA. Demanding that the YWCA move toward being an interracial rather than biracial institution, the women sent a memo directly to the national board for action at its South Atlantic field meeting in July. Following the inadequate response they received from that meeting, her group successfully lobbied the Tuskegee biennial meeting of the National Association of Colored Women to refuse to endorse the work of the YWCA, and began to develop, in conjunction with the NAACP and the Urban League, a parallel, but independently run, organization to replace the YWCA services within African-American communities in the South.

Believing that increased, interracial contact on a basis of equality was the only long-term solution to these institutional problems, she invited nine white Southern women to the Tuskegee meeting. It was there that the first interracial meeting of African-American and white Southern women was planned. The historic Memphis Conference on October 6–7, 1920, received a seven-point program that had been developed at Tuskegee. While the conference has been viewed as the beginning of women's organized interracial work, it was not without controversy. The white women in charge of the final meeting altered the Tuskegee program without the consent of the African-American women who wrote it. They excised the demand for "all rights and privileges granted American womanhood," for fear that the white women gathered would reject it as premature. With characteristic acidity, Hope responded to a member of the white leadership, "Ignorance is ignorance wherever found, yet the most ignorant white woman may enjoy every privilege that America offers. Now . . . the ignorant Negro woman should also enjoy them."

Several years later, in criticizing the resistance of the white women's organization, the Association of Southern Women for the Prevention of Lynching, to federal antilynching legislation, she spoke out again with characteristic honesty: "It is difficult for me to understand why my white sisters so strenuously object . . . After all, when we yield to public opinion and make ourselves say only what we think the public can stand, is there not a danger that we may find ourselves with our larger view conceding what those with the narrow view demand?"

Hope developed a style that went beyond the traditional racial politics of the period. Despite her use of traditional connections between the African-American elite and the white power structure, she never compromised her principles to maintain those alliances. She criticized sharply the widespread belief that African-Americans had to prove their readiness for citizenship. She had a life-long reputation for frank speech, in public and in private, and was extremely assertive in all her organizational work. Yet, she was tireless in her efforts to organize and uplift the African-American community through the resources of its own people.

In 1932 after her husband had assumed the presidency of Atlanta University, she became the First Vice President of the Atlanta chapter of the NAACP. As such, she organized citizenship schools that offered six-week classes, taught by Atlanta University faculty members, on voting, democracy, and the Constitution. Other chapters around the country used such strategies and later modified them for use in the early stages of the civil rights movement. That year Hope was nominated for the Spingarn Award, the NAACP's highest honor.

Her husband died in 1936, whereupon her own health began to suffer from years of constant activity. She moved away from Atlanta, first to New York City, then to Chicago, and finally to Nashville to be near relatives. She died in August of 1947; at her request, her body was cremated and her ashes released from the tower of Graves Hall over the Morehouse campus.

Hopkins, Emma Curtis 1853–1925 religious leader

Born in Killingly, Connecticut, on September 2, 1853, Emma Curtis was educated at the Woodstock Academy in Woodstock, Connecticut, where she was subsequently a teacher for a time. In July 1874 she married George Hopkins, also a teacher. Of the next few years of her life little is known. In December 1883 she was in Boston and enrolled in a course in Christian Science conducted by Mary Baker Eddy. She joined the staff of the *Christian Science Journal* shortly thereafter and in September 1884 became editor of the monthly. After about a year she left that post, and by 1886 she had broken with Eddy and settled in Chicago. In 1887 she established the Christian Science Theological Seminary in her home and began taking students. From 1887 to 1897 she published a magazine, *Christian Metaphysician*, and she was also a frequent lecturer.

Hopkins' personal magnetism was widely testified to, and the gentle persuasiveness of her unsystematic theology, which she later called "Spiritual Science," drawing on the Bible and other sacred texts, philosophers, and mystics, spread her influence abroad. At length students of hers were conducting classes in San Francisco, Kansas City, Boston, New York, and elsewhere. Among those directly influenced by her were Charles and Myrtle Fillmore, founders of Unity, Malinda E. Cramer and Nona L. Brooks, founders of Divine Science, Annie Rix Militz, founder of The Home of Truth, and Ernest Holmes, founder of Religious Science. Thus within the loose amalgamation of the many religio-metaphysical groups that were known collectively as the New Thought movement, Emma Hopkins became known as the "Teacher of Teachers." In 1920–1922 she published *High Mysticism* in 12 small volumes. She spent her later years in New York City, where her students included Ella Wheeler Wilcox, Mabel Dodge Luhan, and John Jay Chapman. She died in New York City on April 25, 1925.

Hopkins, Juliet Ann Opie 1818–1890 administrator

Born on May 7, 1818, on a plantation in Jefferson County, Virginia, Juliet Opie was educated privately. In 1837 she married A. G. Gordon, a navy lieutenant who died in

1849; in 1854 she married Arthur F. Hopkins, a justice of the Alabama supreme court. She lived thereafter in Mobile, Alabama. At the outbreak of the Civil War she volunteered her services to the state and was sent to Richmond, Virginia, where she superintended the Alabama section of the Chimborazo Hospital. In November 1861 the Alabama legislature appointed Judge Hopkins state hospital agent, apparently with the understanding from the beginning that he was to have the title while Juliet Hopkins had the actual job. Certainly it was she who proved a resourceful and effective administrator in overseeing the establishment, staffing, supply, and management of base and field hospitals. The high quality of medical care and the superior conditions in hospitals under her direction became widely known throughout the Confederacy and won public praise from such as General Joseph E. Johnston. She several times went into the field to help with the wounded and at Seven Pines (Fair Oaks), May 31, 1862, was herself wounded and left with a permanent limp.

When the state hospitals were merged into the Confederate Medical Department in 1863, Hopkins' work was largely ended. Among the honors tendered Hopkins' was the use of her likeness on the Alabama 25-cent and 50-dollar bills. After the war she moved to New York City; she died while visiting Washington, D.C., on March 9, 1890, and was buried with military honors in Arlington National Cemetery.

Hopper, Grace Brewster Murray 1906–1992 mathematician and computer scientist

Grace Murray Hopper

Born in New York City on December 9, 1906, Grace Murray, whose father believed that his daughters should have the same educational opportunities as his son, attended Vassar College and received a B.A. in mathematics in 1928. At Yale University she earned an M.A. and a Ph.D. in mathematics, and returned to Vassar to teach mathematics. In 1930 she married Vincent Foster Hopper; the couple divorced in 1945.

During World War II, she took a leave of absence from Vassar and joined WAVES (Women Accepted for Volunteer Emergency Service) as a commissioned lieutenant, junior grade. Her naval assignment took her to Harvard, where she worked on the Bureau of Ordnances Computation Project. In 1945, while working on the Mark I computer that her team at Harvard developed, she discovered a moth in the computer's circuitry and coined the term "bug" to refer to computer glitches.

In 1946 Hopper left active naval duty and resigned from Vassar in order to pursue a career that combined academic, business and military positions. She remained at Harvard as a faculty member, and then joined the Eckert-Mauchly Computer Corporation in Philadelphia, where she wrote code for the first commercial, large-scale, electronic computer (Univac I). Her work also led to the development of the first practical compiler, 1952, which translates instructions from a computer programmer into codes the computer reads. In the 1960s she helped develop COBOL (Common Business-Oriented Language), a widely-used computer language that allows commands to be written using an English-based vocabulary rather than in machine code.

In 1966 Hopper retired from the navy as a commander but was recalled to active duty the following year to oversee the standardization of the navy's computer languages. In 1982, she became the oldest officer on active duty in the armed services, and in 1983, President Ronald Reagan promoted her to the rank of commodore, which was elevated to rear admiral in 1985. Her retirement in 1986 marked forty-three years of service in the military.

During her long career she published over 50 articles on software and programming languages and was honored many times. In 1969, the Data Processing Management Association selected her as its first computer sciences "Man of the Year." President Bush awarded her the National Medal of Technology in 1991 — the first time the award was given solely to a woman. She held honorary doctorates from many universities and New Hampshire decreed November 7, 1983, as Captain Grace Murray Hopper Day in honor of the dedication of the Grace Murray Hopper Center for Computer Learning at Brewster Academy in Wolfeboro. Known for her unorthodox, blunt style, and for smoking unfiltered cigarettes, she once called the women's movement "tommyrot and nonsense." She died at her home in Arlington, Virginia on January 1, 1992.

Hopper, Hedda 1890–1966 actor and columnist

Born on June 2, 1890, in Hollidaysburg, Pennsylvania, Elda Furry early developed a love for the stage and at eighteen ran away from her sternly Quaker family to seek her fortune in the theater. After a period in the chorus of an opera company she made her Broadway debut in *The Motor Girl*, 1909. While playing a role in *A Matinee Idol* a short time later she met DeWolf Hopper, whom she married in May 1913. It was at his suggestion — reportedly to end the confusion arising from the similarity of her first name with those of his four earlier wives — that she changed her name to Hedda. After a brief retirement she returned to the stage and in 1915 made her film debut in Louis B. Mayer's *Virtuous Wives*. She subsequently appeared in scores of movies but failed to attain stardom and eventually found her career fading. (She and her husband were divorced in 1922.) For a few years she worked at other jobs, including real estate sales and fashion commentary.

In 1936 Hopper began broadcasting regularly on radio, reporting from Hollywood on the latest gossip about the stars and moguls of the movies. Two years later she began writing a Hollywood gossip column for the Esquire Syndicate, subsequently moving it to the syndicate of the *Des Moines Register and Tribune* and in 1942 to the *Chicago Tribune–New York Daily News* syndicate. Hopper's detailed knowledge of the faces and foibles of the film colony served her as a reservoir of valuable information and gave her a ready entrée into the most private affairs of the leading characters. Her large readership and the publicity outlets she commanded made her a powerful arbiter of the morals and mores of the industry. Her rivalry with the earlier-established Louella Parsons grew into a celebrated feud, to which she added others no less publicized over the years. Generally considered to be more friendly and tolerant than her archrival, she remained for the rest of her life a popular, if somewhat feared, figure in Hollywood, noted for her lively and often ungrammatical language, her numberless exotic hats, and later her markedly right-wing political views. She wrote two volumes of memoirs, *From Under My Hat*, 1952, and *The Whole Truth and Nothing But*, 1963. She died in Hollywood on February 1, 1966.

Lena Horne

Horne, Lena Calhoun 1917– singer and entertainer

Born on June 30, 1917 in Brooklyn, New York, Lena Calhoun Horne had a father who left home when she was three, and consequently she was raised by her mother, the former Edna Scottron, an actress, and her grandmother, Cora Calhoun Horne, a prominent member of the NAACP. At age 16 she left school to help support her ailing mother and took a job at the legendary Cotton Club in Harlem, thus beginning her long, successful career in entertainment. She spent two years at the Cotton Club, appearing in shows with entertainers such as Cab Calloway and working her way up from the chorus to featured spots. She was well liked by audiences and eventually she began starring in her own shows. In 1935 she left the Cotton Club and joined the Noble Sissle orchestra under the name Helena Horne.

In 1937 she married Louis J. Jones. Though they did not divorce until 1944, the couple had two children, Gail, born in 1937, and Edwin, in 1940. After the birth of her son, she was hired to sing for Charlie Barnet's orchestra, making her one of the first black performers to sing with a prominent white band. She sang with Barnet on several recordings and was discovered by the record producer John Hammond. He helped her get a show in a club in Greenwich Village, which in turn led to her first solo show at Carnegie Hall. Her career continued to flourish and she began working with other jazz greats like Artie Shaw, as well as recording several of her own albums. She also began appearing regularly on national radio shows.

In 1942 she left New York City to perform in Los Angeles, California, and once there began a successful stint in films. She appeared in a number of movies throughout her career beginning with *Cabin in the Sky* in 1943, and including *Meet Me In Las Vegas*, 1956. Her role in the film *Stormy Weather*, 1943, included her rendition of the title song; a song that would become her trademark. After her introduction to film, almost every project she was attached to was successful. The Broadway musical she starred in, *Jamaica*, ran for 555 performances; her album, *Lena Horne at the Waldorf-Astoria*, became one of the best-selling recordings by a female performer in RCA history; and her television specials, including *Lena in Concert*, 1969, and *Harry and Lena* (with singer Harry Belafonte in 1979), were both critical and popular successes. In 1974 a new generation of filmgoers was introduced to her through her role in *The Wiz*, an all-black version of *The Wizard of Oz*. A remarkably charismatic entertainer, she was one of the most respected and widely loved singers of popular music in her time. Though she was primarily known as an entertainer, she was politically and socially active as well. Beginning with her campaigning for Franklin D. Roosevelt, she was noted for her work with civil rights and political organizations such as the NAACP, and as an actress, she refused to play roles that stereotyped African-American women, such as prostitutes and maids.

In 1947 she married Lennie Hayton, a marriage that lasted until his death in 1971. Her retrospective performances *Lena Horne: The Lady and Her Music*, 1981, won a Drama Critics Circle award and a special achievement Tony Award. She was awarded an honorary degree from Howard University in 1979, and received a Kennedy Center honor for lifetime contribution to the arts in 1984.

Horne, Marilyn Bernice 1934– opera singer

Born on January 16, 1934 in Bradford, Pennsylvania, Marilyn Bernice Horne was the child of music aficionados: her father was a semi-professional tenor who sang in churches and various bands for a number of years. She sang for audiences even as a toddler and when she was two, her family moved to Southern California, settling in the suburb of Long Beach. She sang in choirs and other groups and eventually studied voice at the University of Southern California under William Vennard, participating in the master classes of Lotte Lehmann (the renowned German soprano). To pay her school tuition, she sang on various film soundtracks, most notably acting as the dubbed voice of Dorothy Dandridge in the 1954 film *Carmen Jones*. Her passion and calling however, were for opera. The same year she worked on *Carmen Jones*, she made her operatic debut as Hàta in *The Bartered Bride* with the Los Angeles Guild Opera. She then left school and headed for Europe to begin her career as a mezzo-soprano, performing the role of Giulietta at the Gelsenkirchen Opera in 1956. She continued for three seasons at the Gelsenkirchen, taking on such roles as Fuliva in *Ezio*, and Marie in *Wozzeck*.

Upon returning to the U.S. she repeated her role in *Wozzeck* at the San Francisco Opera in 1960. Later that year she married the conductor Henry Lewis (whom she divorced in 1976) and under his direction made a number of appearances. Her debut at La Scala came in 1969 in *Oedipus Rex*. She first appeared at New York's Metropolitan Opera in 1970 as Adalgisa in *Norma* and subsequently became one of the Met's principal singers. At the Met she sang with Joan Sutherland, beginning a professional association that would last many years. Sutherland's husband, the conductor Richard Bonynge, became her coach and helped shape her voice. Soon her wide range and vocal flexibility were impressing the worldwide opera community. Her biggest impact on opera however, was her ability to perform roles originally written for the *castrati* of long ago; roles that were written for voices with both power and an upper range, previously only accessible to men who had undergone castration. She repeatedly made operatic history, demonstrating her vocal power by reviving roles that hadn't been performed in over a century. Some of the difficult roles she undertook to critical success included Handel's Rinaldo, Malcolm in Rossini's *La Donna del Lago*, and Arsace in *Semiramide*.

She proved to be a popular success as well. She accompanied the conductors Igor Stravinsky and Leonard Bernstein and gave many recitals, including those at the White House for both Presidents Ronald Reagan and George Bush. She impressed and awed the entire country when she performed the national anthem and several other selections at the inauguration of President Bill Clinton in 1993. In November of 1995, Horne announced that she would be accepting a position as director of the vocal program at The Music Academy of the West, overseeing the program and teaching master classes. Her autobiography, *Marilyn Horne: My Life*, (written with Jane Scovell) was published in 1983.

Horney, Karen Danielssen 1885–1952 psychoanalyst

Born on September 16, 1885, in Hamburg, Germany, Karen Danielssen was of Dutch and Norwegian parentage. She studied medicine at the universities of Freiburg, Göttingen, and Berlin, taking her M.D. degree from the last in 1911. (In 1909 she married Oscar Horney, a lawyer, from whom she was separated in 1926 and divorced in 1937.) After a period of medical practice she became interested in psychoanalysis, and from 1913 to 1915 she studied under Karl Abraham, a close associate and disciple of Sigmund Freud. From 1915 to 1920 she engaged in clinical and out-patient work in connection with Berlin psychiatric hospitals, and in the latter year she joined the teaching staff of the newly founded Berlin Psychoanalytic Institute. Although she adhered in the main to the outlines of Freudian theory, she early began to disagree in particular with Freud's view of female psychology, which he saw as essentially derivative of male psychology. Unaffected by the worshipful awe that held many early Freudians to received dogma, she forthrightly rejected such notions as penis envy (except as a basis for neurosis) and other manifestations of male bias in psychoanalytic theory. A series of articles with such titles as "The Flight from Womanhood," 1926, "Inhibited Femininity," 1926, "Distrust Between the Sexes," 1931, and "The Dread of Woman," 1932, located the source of much female psychiatric disturbance in the very male-dominated culture that had produced Freudian theory.

In 1932 Horney became associate director of the Institute for Psychoanalysis in Chicago. She moved two years later to New York City, where she carried on her practice, did research, and taught at the New School for Social Research. Her first book, *The Neurotic Personality of Our Time*, 1937, was widely read. *New Ways in Psychoanalysis*, 1939, was a thorough critique of Freudian practice and contributed to her being disqualified as an instructor and training analyst by the New York Psychoanalytic Institute in 1941. She promptly founded the Association for the Advancement of Psychoanalysis and some time later the American Institute for Psychoanalysis, through both of which broad research into new aspects of psychoanalysis was fostered.

The aspects of Freudian doctrine Horney rejected were, in addition to its view of women, its emphasis on the rigidity of instincts and the dominating roles of libido and death instinct in the psyche, its disregard of moral values, and its consequently pessimistic view of human life in general. She continued to emphasize the role of social and cultural pressures in the genesis of neurosis, and in her clinical method analyst and analysand were collaborators in a search for self-understanding and integration. Other books by her were *Self-Analysis*, 1942, *Our Inner Conflicts*, 1945, and *Neurosis and*

Human Growth, 1950. She died in New York City on December 4, 1952. The Karen Horney Foundation was established in New York in that year and gave rise in 1955 to the Karen Homey Clinic. In 1967 a collection of her papers was published as *Feminine Psychology*.

Horton, Mildred Helen McAfee 1900–1994 educator and naval officer

Born on May 12, 1900, in Parkville, Missouri, Mildred McAfee was the daughter of a noted Presbyterian clergyman and granddaughter of the founder of Park College. She graduated from Vassar College in 1920, taught school for a year in Godfrey, Illinois, and for another year in Chicago, and in 1922–1923 was director of girls' work in a Chicago church. During 1923–1926 she was on the faculty of Tusculum College, Greeneville, Tennessee, and in 1927 she was named dean of women and professor of sociology at Centre College, Danville, Kentucky. She received an M.A. degree from the University of Chicago in 1928. From 1932 to 1934 she worked as executive secretary of the Vassar alumnae association, and in the latter year she was named dean of college women at Oberlin College. In 1936 she was chosen the seventh president of Wellesley College.

McAfee served, immediately after the entry of the United States into World War II, on a committee planning a women's naval reserve program. The committee's work led to the establishment on July 30, 1942, of the WAVES (Women Accepted for Volunteer Emergency Service), of which McAfee became director, with relative rank of lieutenant commander, on August 3. The WAVES were from the start fully a part of the naval reserve (unlike the army's women's reserve, until July 1943 an auxiliary corps) and McAfee was thus its first woman officer. By September 1945 the WAVES reached a peak strength of 86,000 officers and enlisted women, and an estimated 50,000 navy men were released to service afloat or abroad by their work. Commander McAfee's rank was raised to captain in 1944, and she resigned from service in February 1946, returning to Wellesley.

In August 1945 McAfee married the Reverend Douglas Horton, the first world leader of the Congregational Christian Churches. Thereafter she too assumed an active role in international church affairs, serving as president of the American Board of Commissioners for Foreign Missions, 1950–1953, and as vice-president of the National Council of Churches of Christ in the USA.

Mildred Horton continued as president of Wellesley until 1949. From 1950 to 1953 she was president of the National Social Welfare Assembly; in 1959–1961 she was president of the American Board of Commissioners for Foreign Missions; in 1962 she was a delegate to the United Nations Educational, Scientific, and Cultural Organization (UNESCO); and in 1963–1964 she served as cochairwoman, with Patricia Roberts Harris, of the National Women's Committee for Civil Rights. Horton, who lived in later years in New Hampshire, also served as president of the Association of American Colleges. She died in Berlin, New Hampshire, on September 2, 1994.

Horwich, Frances Rappaport 1908– educator

Born in Ottawa, Ohio, on July 16, 1908, Frances Rappaport graduated from the University of Chicago in 1929 and for three years thereafter taught school in the Chicago suburb of Evanston. In June 1931 she married Harvey L. Horwich. In 1933 she took a master's degree from Teachers College, Columbia University, and until 1935 she supervised nursery schools in Chicago for the federal Works Progress Administration. From 1935 to 1938 she was director of junior kindergartens in suburban Winnetka. During 1938–1940 she was dean of education in the Pestalozzi Froebel Teachers College in Chicago, and during 1940–1943 she was counselor to student teachers at the Chicago Teachers College (now Chicago State University), meanwhile taking a Ph.D. from Northwestern University in 1942. After two years as director of the Hessian Hills School in Croton-on-Hudson, New York, and a year as visiting professor of education at the University of North Carolina, she returned to Chicago in 1946 as professor of education at Roosevelt College (now University).

In 1952 Horwich was invited by the National Broadcasting Company to develop a nursery school program for television. "Ding Dong School," a half hour program conducted by Horwich as "Miss Frances," premiered on the Chicago NBC affiliate station in October 1952 and within a few weeks had become a regular one-hour network program five mornings weekly. The first educational television program to be aimed at the preschool audience, "Ding Dong School" became greatly popular with both children and parents, and it earned high marks from educators and child psychologists as well. In addition to being the program's creator, writer, and on-camera personality, Horwich also published a series of *Ding Dong School Books* beginning in 1954, she also wrote *Miss Frances' All-Day-Long Book*, 1954, *Miss Frances' Story Book of Manners for the Very Young*, 1955, *Miss Frances' Story Book of Pets for the Very Young*, 1956, *Safety on Wheels*, 1960, *Stories and Poems to Enjoy*, 1962, *From Miss Frances' Desk*, 1964, and *The White House*, 1964, and for parents, *Have Fun With Your Children*, 1954, and *The Magic of Bringing Up Your Child*, 1959.

"Ding Dong School" remained on the NBC network until December 1956 and was continued by a Chicago station in 1957–1959; from 1959 to 1965 it was in syndication. In 1955–1956 Horwich was also supervisor of children's television for NBC. She later served as an educational consultant to the Curtis Publishing Company in 1962–1964 and to Field Enterprises Educational Corporation in 1965–1966. She continued to appear occasionally as "Miss Frances" on local television and from 1968 to 1970 was a consultant to the Chicago Head Start preschool program. She was the recipient of numerous honors and awards for her work.

Hosmer, Harriet Goodhue 1830–1908 sculptor

Born in Watertown, Massachusetts, on October 9, 1830, Harriet Hosmer was reared by her father, a physician widowed when she was four, to be a vigorous and independent young woman. While attending a girls' school in Lenox, Massachusetts, she was encouraged by the actress Fanny Kemble to pursue her natural talents into the art of sculpture. She established a studio at home and made what progress she could on her own. She furthered her knowledge of anatomy by taking private lessons from a professor of anatomy in St. Louis. In 1852 she traveled to Rome to study under the noted English sculptor John Gibson while living under the care of another older friend, the actress Charlotte Cushman. While slowly distinguishing herself as an artist, she also became a favorite in the English and American colonies in Rome, numbering the Brownings among her friends.

In 1856 Hosmer delivered her first commissioned work, "Oenone," to the father of a former classmate in St. Louis, and in 1857 her second, "Beatrice Cenci," went to the St. Louis Mercantile Library. Her next piece, an amusing figure of "Puck," proved a great success: 50 copies were sold, including one to the Prince of Wales. In 1860 she was commissioned by the state of Missouri to produce a monumental bronze statue of Senator Thomas Hart Benton, the finished work was placed in Lafayette Park, St. Louis, in 1868. In 1862 she exhibited "Zenobia" in London with great success, and in 1865 her "Sleeping Faun" was purchased by Sir Benjamin Guinness for the city of Dublin. Other notable works of the period were "Walking Faun," "Browning Hands," "Death of the Dryads," "Siren Fountain," and "Heroine of Gaeta," a figure of the Queen of Naples unveiled in 1871.

Until the end of the century Hosmer lived mainly in England, making frequent visits to

Rome. She maintained a large studio and enjoyed a considerable income. Her originality of character, energy, and genius for friendship made her a much loved figure in European artistic and aristocratic circles. Her position as the foremost American woman sculptor of the century was unchallenged, although critical estimation of her doggedly neoclassical style never afterward placed her in the first rank of artists. Her last major work was a statue of Queen Isabella commissioned by the city of San Francisco and unveiled there in 1894. From about 1900 she lived in Watertown, Massachusetts. In her last years she devoted much time and mechanical ingenuity to the problem of perpetual motion. She died in Watertown on February 21, 1908.

Howard, Ada Lydia 1829–1907 educator

Born on December 19, 1829, in Temple, New Hampshire, Ada Howard was educated at New Ipswich Academy, Lowell High School, and Mount Holyoke Seminary (now College), graduating from the last in 1853. After a period devoted to studies under private tutors she returned to Mount Holyoke in 1858 as a teacher. During 1861–1862 she taught at Western College for Women (now Western College) in Oxford, Ohio, and from 1866 to 1869 she was principal of the women's department at Knox College in Galesburg, Illinois. In the latter year she opened her own school for girls, Ivy Hall, in Bridgeton, New Jersey.

In 1875 Howard was selected by founder and treasurer Henry F. Durant to become first president of Wellesley College, which opened in September of that year. Until Durant's death in October 1881 her task was that of executor of policies set by him. She presided over the faculty of 20 to 30 women, itself a novelty not unattended by controversy, and lent her own dignified presence to the fledgling and experimental college. Ill health forced her to resign in November 1881, and thus she never had the opportunity to run the college on her own; its administration passed to Alice E. Freeman (Palmer). Ada Howard divided her last years between Methuen, Massachusetts, and Brooklyn, New York. She died in Brooklyn on March 3, 1907.

Howard, Blanche Willis 1847–1898 novelist

Born in Bangor, Maine, on July 21, 1847, Blanche Howard attended public schools through high school and then spent a year in a private school in New York City. From girlhood she intended to be a writer, and the success of her first novel, *One Summer*, 1875, a light and fresh romantic story that sold over 50,000 copies in a short time, confirmed her in her ambition. Later that year she sailed for Europe, whence she contributed to the *Boston Evening Transcript* a series of lively weekly articles on European sights, travel, legend, art, and other matters of interest. *One Year Abroad*, 1877, her next book, was a direct outgrowth of her newspaper articles. She settled in Stuttgart, Germany, where she studied music, philosophy, science, and other subjects and tutored and chaperoned visiting American girls. Richard Wagner was among her friends, and Franz Liszt is said to have praised her piano playing.

Howard continued to write novels: *Aunt Serena*, 1881, *Guenn: a Wave on the Breton Coast*, 1884, *Aulnay Tower*, 1885, *Tony, the Maid*, 1887, *The Open Door*, 1889, *A Battle and a Boy*, 1892, *A Fellowe and His Wife*, 1892, *Seven on the Highway*, 1897, *Dionysius the Weaver's Heart's Dearest*, 1899, *The Garden of Eden*, 1900, and *The Humming Top; or, Debit and Credit in the Next World*, 1903 (the last two published posthumously). Romantic tales set in various European locales, the novels were popular on both sides of the Atlantic. In 1890 she married Dr. Julius von Teuffel, court physician to the king of Württemburg, becoming thereby the Countess von Teuffel. After a period of insanity he died in 1896. The Countess thereafter divided her time between Stuttgart and the Isle of Guernsey. She died in Munich on October 7, 1898.

Howe, Julia Ward 1819–1910 writer and social reformer

Born in New York City on May 27, 1819, Julia Ward came of a well-to-do family and was educated privately. In April 1843 she married Samuel Gridley Howe and took up residence in Boston. Always of a literary bent, she published her first volume of poetry, *Passion Flowers*, in 1854; this and subsequent works, including *Words for the Hour*, poems, 1857, *Leonora, or the World's Own*, a drama produced in New York City in 1857, and *A Trip to Cuba*, 1860, had little success. For a while she and her husband published the *Commonwealth*, an abolitionist newspaper, but for the most part he kept her out of his affairs and strongly opposed her involving herself in any sort of public life. In February 1862 the *Atlantic Monthly* published her poem "Battle Hymn of the Republic," to be set to an old folk tune also used for "John Brown's Body." The song, written during a visit to an army camp near Washington, D.C., in 1861, became the semiofficial Civil War song of the Union army, and Howe became famous.

After the war Howe involved herself in the woman suffrage movement. In 1868 she helped form and was elected the first president of the New England Woman Suffrage Association, an office she held until 1877, and from 1869 took a leading role in the American Woman Suffrage Association. She was president of the New England Women's Club, of which she had been a founder in 1868, almost continuously from 1871 (in which year she succeeded Caroline M. Severance). She was later active in the General Federation of Women's Clubs. She also took up the cause of peace and in 1870 published her "Appeal to Womanhood Throughout the World," a call for an international conference of women on the subject of peace. In 1871 she became first president of the American branch of the Woman's International Peace Association.

Howe continued to write throughout her life, publishing travel books, poetry, collections of essays, and biographies under such titles as *From the Oak to the Olive*, 1868, *Modern Society*, 1880, *Margaret Fuller*, 1883, *Is Polite Society Polite?*, 1895, *From Sunset Ridge: Poems Old and New*, 1898, *Reminiscences*, 1899, and *At Sunset*, 1910. She founded a short-lived literary journal, *Northern Lights*, in 1867 and was a founder in 1870 and an editor for 20 years thereafter of the *Woman's Journal*. She was a frequent traveler until extreme old age. She was again president of the New England Woman Suffrage Association from 1893 to 1910. In 1908 she became the first woman to be elected to the American Academy of Arts and Letters. She was an American public institution by the time of her death on October 17, 1910, in Newport, Rhode Island. Of her children the best known was Laura Elizabeth Howe Richards.

Howland, Emily 1827–1929 educator and reformer

Born on November 20, 1827, near Sherwood, New York, Emily Howland grew up much under the influence of Quaker grandparents. She attended local schools until sixteen, when she was obliged to take over care of the home from her ailing mother. Chafing at the narrow bounds of her life, she threw herself into abolitionist activity in the 1850s and in the fall of 1857 took over Myrtilla Miner's school for black children in Washington, D.C. She returned home two years later but in 1863 traveled again to Washington to teach in a series of freedmen's schools in and around the city. In 1867 she prevailed upon her father to buy a 400-acre tract of land at Heathsville, Virginia, where she settled a number of freedmen and established a school. In the summer of that year she returned to Sherwood, New York, to nurse her mother in her last illness, and she remained at home for the rest of her life. She nonetheless continued to support the Virginia school for over 50 years until the state of Virginia took it over.

In 1871 Howland helped found the Sherwood Select School, a Quaker institution, and she was its chief supporter from 1882, when she built a new schoolhouse, until it was taken over by the state of New York in 1927, whereupon it was renamed the Emily

Howland School. Her interest in the education of African-American students resulted in her support of over 30 institutions in the South, especially Booker T. Washington's Tuskegee Institute. She was also an active supporter of the women's suffrage movement. Her services to education were recognized in the award of an honorary doctorate by the University of the State of New York in 1927, when she was ninety-nine. She died at one hundred and one, on June 29, 1929, in Sherwood, New York.

Humphrey, Doris 1895–1958 dancer and choreographer

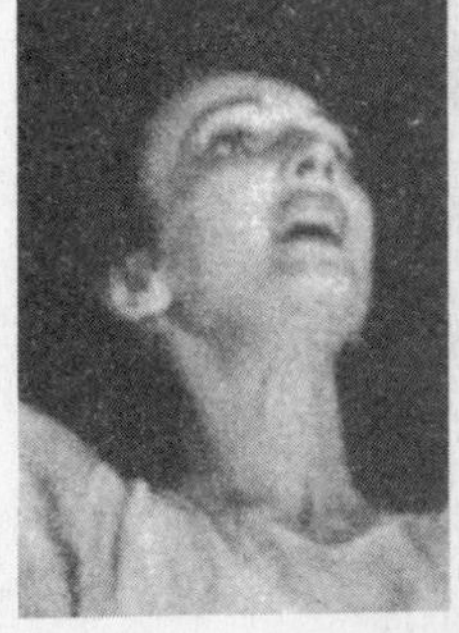
Doris Humphrey

Born on October 17, 1895, in Oak Park, Illinois, Doris Humphrey was of deep New England ancestry, including Elder Brewster and Ralph Waldo Emerson among her forebears. She was an avid and talented student of dance from an early age, and in 1917, after graduating from high school and teaching dance herself in Chicago for four years, she joined the Denishawn dance school and company in Los Angeles. She soon became a leading soloist in the company's strongly Asian repertoire, and by 1920 she was experimenting in choreography. Her first major work, to Alexander MacDowell's *Sonata Tragica*, was presented in 1925. The piece was subsequently performed without musical accompaniment, and it was credited by Humphrey's mentor, Ruth St. Denis, with being the first American modern dance piece to embody such innate rhythm. After a two-year tour of Asia she and another Denishawn dancer, Charles Weidman, directed the Denishawn House in New York City until 1928, when they left to form the Humphrey-Weidman school and company.

Humphrey's systematic and rigorous investigation of the phenomenon of human movement convinced her that it occurred always in the region between static balance and irreversible unbalance, between motionlessness and the out-of-control fall, a region she called "the arc between two deaths." Thus much of her early choreography was based on an exploration of this region by the technique of fall and recovery. Such works as *Color Harmony*, *Water Study*, both 1928, *Air on a Ground Bass*, 1929, *Drama of Motion*, 1930, and *The Dance of the Chosen*, subsequently retitled *The Shakers*, 1930, were highly individual and innovative and attracted much attention as they gradually revealed her striking talent for creating ensemble and theatrical works. She was engaged to create dances for a number of Broadway productions, including *Americana*, 1932, Moliere's *School for Husbands*, 1933, and *Life Begins at 8:40*, 1934. From 1934 she was also on the staff of the Bennington College School of Dance.

Doris Humphrey's choreographic masterpiece, a trilogy comprising *Theatre Piece*, *With My Red Fires*, and *New Dance*, was completed (but not performed as a whole) in 1936. Subsequent works included *The Race of Life*, inspired by James Thurber, 1937, *Passacaglia in C Minor*, to music of Bach, 1938, *New Dance* and *Song of the West*, 1940, *El Salon Mexico* to music of Aaron Copland, and *Inquest*, 1944, the last work in which she performed. Limited by arthritis to choreography thereafter, she was artistic director for the dance company of José Limón (who had begun his career in the Humphrey-Weidman school) from its formation. For Limón she created *Lament for Ignacio Sánchez Mejias*, 1946, *Day on Earth* to music of Copland, 1947, *Story of Mankind*, 1947, *Quartet No. 1* (also known as *Night Spell*), 1951, *Deep Rhythm*, 1953, *Ruins and Visions*, 1953, and *Theatre Piece No. 2*, 1956. Her later works displayed a deep interest in gesture as a universal language as opposed to the stylized code of classical dance. She was on the faculty of the Juilliard School of Dance from its organization in 1952 and founded the Juilliard Dance Theatre in 1955. She died in New York City on December 29, 1958; her book, *The Art of Making Dances*, appeared in 1959.

Hunt, Harriot Kezia 1805–1875 physician and reformer

Born in Boston on November 9, 1805, Harriot Hunt was reared in a family of liberal social and religious views and educated privately. She opened a school of her own in her parents' house in 1827. The lengthy illness of her sister in the early 1830s, during which a series of physicians demonstrated the futility of a variety of therapies, induced Harriot and her sister to begin studying in 1833 under an English couple named Mott who apparently cured the sister. In 1835 the two sisters opened their own practice in the face of considerable prejudice. Finding the body of medical knowledge of the day to be largely incoherent but rejecting the current enthusiasm for harsh medications, they concentrated on the study of physiology and the practice of good hygiene. Diet, bathing, rest, and exercise formed the core of their medicine, along with a sizable dose of commonsense and sympathetic insight that amounted to a sort of psychotherapy. They enjoyed considerable success, particularly in cases of hysterical or psychosomatic ailments with which orthodox physicians had failed. After her sister's marriage in 1840 Harriot Hunt continued in practice alone.

In 1843 Hunt formed the Ladies Physiological Society under whose auspices she conducted a course of lectures for women on physiology and hygiene. In 1847, on learning of Elizabeth Blackwell's admission to the Geneva Medical College, she applied for permission to attend lectures at the Harvard Medical College and was denied. She conducted a second series of lectures in 1849, this time in a working-class district of Boston. In 1850 she attended the national women's rights convention in Worcester, Massachusetts, where she met the leaders of the movement and threw in her lot with theirs. For a number of years she lectured frequently on women's rights and the abolition of slavery. A second application to Harvard late in 1850 was successful, but the vigorous protest of the male medical students prevented her from taking advantage of it. In 1853, in recognition of her pioneering work for women in medicine, the Female Medical College of Philadelphia awarded her an honorary medical degree. Her autobiography, *Glances and Glimpses*, was published in 1856. She continued to practice medicine and to support the feminist cause late in life. The 1868 meeting at which the New England Women's Club was organized with Julia Ward Howe as president was held at her home. She died in Boston on January 2, 1875.

Hunt, Mary Hannah Hanchett 1830–1906 temperance leader

Born in South Canaan, Connecticut, on June 4, 1830, Mary Hanchett attended local schools and, after a year of teaching in a country school, the Amenia Seminary, Amenia, New York, for a year and then the Patapsco Female Institute near Baltimore. After graduating from the last she remained for a time as a science teacher and collaborated with Almira Hart Lincoln Phelps, principal of the school, on a series of science textbooks. In October 1852, after a year as a governess on a Virginia plantation, she married Leander B. Hunt, with whom she settled in East Douglas, Massachusetts. They moved in 1865 to the Boston suburb of Hyde Park (now part of Boston). In the middle 1870s, while helping her son Alfred E. Hunt, later a distinguished chemist and engineer, study for a chemistry course at the Massachusetts Institute of Technology, she became interested in the existing literature on the physiological effects of alcohol.

Hunt's interest in the temperance movement had been inherited from her father, and she soon began advocating the promoting of temperance on scientific grounds, an idea that had been proposed before but never effectively applied. In 1878, having drawn up a series of graded lessons, she persuaded the Hyde Park school board to adopt them for use in physiology and hygiene classes in the local schools. Her experience in attempting the same thing in other Massachusetts towns soon showed her the necessity of a greater force than individual persuasion. At that point, in 1879, she was invited by Frances E. Willard to present her ideas to the national convention of the Woman's Christian Temperance Union. In 1880 the WCTU established a Department of Scientific Temperance Instruction, of which Hunt was named national superintendent. A year's experiment with a program of lectures and petitions at the local level convinced her that only legislation could accomplish the goal of making temperance instruction mandatory in public schools.

In 1882 a state-by-state campaign was mounted to secure such legislation, beginning in Vermont, where a law to that effect was passed in November. Hunt traveled widely to direct the state campaigns, supervised the production of suitable textbooks, and from 1892 edited the *Scientific Temperance Monthly Advices* (later the *School Physiology Journal*) for teachers. By 1901 the desired legislation had been adopted in every state, and from 1886 a federal law required temperance instruction in schools under federal control. In 1890 she was named to a position in the World's WCTU comparable to the one she held in the national organization. She published *A History of the First Decade of the Department of Scientific Temperance Instruction in Schools and Colleges*, 1891, and *An Epoch of the Nineteenth Century*, 1897. Her campaign was not without its controversial aspects, and outright opposition to it climaxed in the 1903 report of a distinguished "Committee of Fifty" educators, scientists, clergymen, and the like. She continued to direct her campaign until her death in Dorchester, Massachusetts, on April 24, 1906, after which it soon waned.

Hunter, Alberta 1895–1984 singer, songwriter, nurse

Born in Memphis, Tennessee, on April 1, 1895, Alberta Hunter's life was full of contradiction and dramatic turns. She was the second daughter of Charles Hunter, a sleeping-car porter, and Laura Peterson Hunter. Her father abandoned the family soon after Alberta's birth. Her mother, who worked as a domestic in a brothel, refused to discuss her job with the children. Laura Hunter remarried in about 1906, but Alberta did not get along with her new step-father, her step-sister or her older sister, La Tosca.

Although the reports of dates and age vary, she ran away at about the age of 11, accompanying a teacher who was eloping and had a free child pass for the train to Chicago. She borrowed a dime to make the trip and once there looked up another friend from Memphis, who got her a job cleaning and peeling potatoes in a boardinghouse for $6 a week, plus room and board. Hunter soon began to look for other work; by dressing up to look older was able to sneak into clubs where she persisted in asking for a chance as a singer. She started out at Dago Frank's, a semi-discreet brothel, and soon moved to Hugh Hoskins' club where she met many of the leading pickpockets and con men of Chicago. In 1915 she moved to the Panama Café, home to many leading blues singers of the day. The headline performers sang downstairs and Hunter was the mainstay "upstairs."

Sometime between 1913 and 1915, her mother moved to live with her. The two women shared a home for most of the rest of her mother's life. Her mother never discussed the break-up of her second marriage and Hunter never discussed with her mother her numerous romantic liaisons with women. After one such affair, threats from an angry boyfriend forced Hunter to relocate quickly to New York. Unlike other women performers such as Ethel Waters, Hunter was discreet about her lesbian relationships, including her two long term lovers, one in Chicago and one in New York.

Although Hunter bought several homes in New York and was based there for most of the rest of her life, the town always represented a constant struggle for work. Upon her initial arrival she played club dates and recorded for several labels using the name of her half-sister, Josephine Beatty, to by-pass exclusive contracts. She traveled on the Keith vaudeville circuit because it provided steady work; it was especially hard, however, on African-American performers, who were forced to perform in raggedy, country-clothes, assigned the early acts (played to half-empty houses), and pressured constantly not to upstage the white performers whom these shows featured.

Hunter's original song "Downhearted Blues" brought her recognition in 1923 when it was recorded by Bessie Smith, and in 1926 she replaced Smith in the leading role of *How*

Come? on Broadway. In 1927, Hunter began her legendary travels between New York, Europe and Chicago, performing in nightclubs and theatre productions, most successfully in Europe, including the 1928 London production of *Showboat* with Paul Robeson. She returned to the U.S. in 1929, but the depression eroded even the dubious security of vaudeville; in 1933 she headed back to Europe where work was more plentiful and racism less acute. She traveled between Paris, London and Amsterdam. In 1935 she played a role in the English film *Radio Parade* and was part of the final sequence shot in color. In 1937 she caught the attention of NBC executives while taking part in a radio show broadcast from Europe for an audience in the U.S. (That broadcast was also the first time her mother had heard her perform.) She returned briefly to New York for a job with NBC radio and permanently, in late 1938, when the State Department warned U.S. citizens that war in Europe was imminent.

War in Europe meant hard times for older black performers who had found work there. Hunter toured extensively for the USO during World War II, including the battlefields of both the Atlantic and the Pacific, and again later during the Korean War. After World War II she performed in England with Snub Mosley, toured Canada and played long residences in Chicago. During the 1954–55 season, she understudied for a Broadway role in *Mrs. Patterson* but never came on stage. She retired from active performing in 1954.

Against the advice of friends, Hunter then began a second career as a practical nurse. Lying about her age, she enrolled in a three-year YWCA training program. She was offered a job before her training ended, and she completed twenty years of service before reaching the mandatory retirement age of 70. (She was actually 82.) By all accounts she was an excellent practical nurse and had particularly good rapport with her patients.

Unbeknownst to her nursing colleagues, she was coaxed into making two recordings during that period, with Lovie Austin in 1961 and Jimmy Archey in 1962. In 1977 when completing a form requesting welfare, she indicated that she was actively looking for work and had only left nursing because she had been forced to retire. Five months after her retirement party, she returned to performing at The Cookery, a nightclub in Greenwich Village, New York. Her comeback led to greater fame than she had ever experienced during her earlier singing career. Hunter continued performing actively and recording, granting interviews and appearing in videos and on television until a few months before her death at home, on Roosevelt Island, New York, on October 17, 1984.

Huntington, Emily 1841–1909 welfare worker

Born on January 3, 1841, in Lebanon, Connecticut, Emily Huntington grew up in Norwich, Connecticut. Her education culminated in two years at the Wheaton Seminary in Norton, Massachusetts, in 1856–1858. She worked in a mission school operated by the Congregational Church in Norwich from 1859 until she moved to New York City in 1872. She soon obtained the post of matron of the Wilson Industrial School for Girls, a mission school in an East Side tenement district populated largely by poor immigrant families. Beyond their poverty, Huntington was struck especially by her charges' utter ignorance of domestic skills. She began reorganizing and revitalizing the school's so-called "housework" classes and in 1875 published a lesson plan as *Little Lessons for Little Housekeepers*. A visit to a kindergarten exhibit suggested to her other procedures and approaches to teaching domestic skills, and in a short time she had loosely adopted Froebelian kindergarten techniques to the teaching of sewing and cooking and so on, a system she called "kitchen garden." The new program of instruction was an immediate success, and to help meet the demand for it she began training volunteer teachers.

Fourteen industrial schools and missions in New York and several in other cities had adopted the kitchen garden idea by 1879.

In 1880 one of Huntington's volunteers, Grace H. Dodge, led in organizing the Kitchen Garden Association, and similar associations soon sprang up in other cities. Huntington developed a "cooking garden" course for girls during the early 1880s, and another of her teachers, Mrs. L. B. Briant, devised the "farm garden" course for boys. For her courses she wrote *Children's Kitchen-Garden Book*, 1881, *The Cooking Garden*, 1885, *How to Teach Kitchen Garden*, 1901, and *Introductory Cooking Lessons*, 1901. In 1892 she left the Wilson school to become superintendent of the New York Cooking School. Having contributed substantially to the growth of general interest in practical education, she also was an original member from 1899 of the Lake Placid Conference on Home Economics, forerunner of the American Home Economics Association. She died in Windham, Connecticut, on December 5, 1909.

Hurst, Fannie 1889–1968 writer

Born on October 18, 1889, in Hamilton, Ohio, Fannie Hurst grew up and attended schools in St. Louis. She graduated from Washington University in 1909, by which time she had already published a few articles and other short pieces in various periodicals. During 1910–1911 she studied at Columbia University, With the aim of gathering material for her pen she worked at various times as a waitress, as a nursemaid, and in a sweatshop, and she made a sea voyage to Europe in steerage. Her first book, *Just Around the Corner*, a collection of short stories, appeared in 1914. In rapid succession and with growing success she produced *Every Soul Hath Its Song*, stories, 1916, *Land of the Free*, a play, 1917, *Gaslight Sonatas*, stories, 1918, *Humoresque*, stories, 1919, *Stardust*, her first novel, 1921, *The Vertical City*, stories, 1922, *Lummox*, 1923, *Appassionata*, 1925, *Mannequin*, 1926, *Song of Life*, stories, 1927, *A President Is Born*, 1928, *Five and Ten*, 1929, *Procession*, stories, 1929, *Back Street*, 1931, *Imitation of Life*, 1933, *Anitra's Dance*, 1934, *Great Laughter*, 1936, *We Are Ten*, stories, 1937, *Lonely Parade*, 1942, *Hallelujah*, 1944, *The Hands of Veronica*, 1947, *Anywoman*, 1950, *The Man with One Head*, 1953, *Anatomy of Me*, an autobiography, 1958, *Family!*, 1960, *God Must Be Sad*, 1961, and *Fool — Be Still*, 1964.

Fannie Hurst

Hurst's novels and stories told tales of ordinary people, often women, in sentimental, florid, and occasionally overwritten prose. Despite their stylistic shortcomings they were nonetheless imbued with vitality and unmistakable touches of real life and close observation of places and characters. A number were turned into successful motion pictures, for some of which she wrote screenplays. Fannie Hurst was active in numerous organizations: she was president of the Authors' Guild in 1937, chairman of the Woman's National Housing Commission in the same year, a member of the National Advisory Committee to the Works Progress Administration in 1940–1941, a member of the Mayor's Committee on Unity in New York City in 1945–1947, and U.S. delegate to the World Health Organization assembly in Geneva in 1952. She was also a trustee of the Russell Sage Foundation and active in the Urban League. She died in New York City on February 23, 1968.

Hurston, Zora Neale 1903–1960 novelist

Born on January 7, 1903, in Eatonville, Florida, the first incorporated all-black city in the nation, Zora Hurston attended local schools until the age of thirteen. After a time as a domestic she resumed her education at the academy of Morgan College in Baltimore. She attended Howard University from 1921 to 1924 and in 1925 won a scholarship to Barnard College, where she studied anthropology under Franz Boas. She graduated from Barnard in 1928 and for two years pursued graduate studies in anthropology at Columbia University.

Zora Neale Hurston

During those years and until 1932 she also conducted field studies in folklore among African-American people in the South. For a short time she was amanuensis to Fannie Hurst. In 1934 she published her first novel, *Jonah's Gourd Vine*, which was very well received by critics for its portrayal of African-American life uncluttered by stock figures or sentimentality. *Mules and Men*, a study of folkways among the African-American population of Florida, followed in 1935. *Their Eyes Were Watching God*, a novel, 1937, *Tell My Horse*, a blend of travel writing and anthropology based on her Guggenheim fellowship-sponsored investigations in Haiti, 1938, and *Moses, Man of the Mountain*, a novel, 1939, firmly established her as a major African-American author. Some critics placed her in the first rank of American literature. For a number of years she was on the faculty of North Carolina College for Negroes (now North Carolina Central University) in Durham. She also wrote for Warner Brothers motion picture studio for a time and was on the staff of the Library of Congress. She contributed to magazines from time to time, and an article of hers on Senator Robert A. Taft for the *Saturday Evening Post* was said to have been the origin of his nickname "Mr. Republican." *Dust Tracks on a Road*, 1942, an autobiography, was highly regarded.! Her last book, *Seraph on the Suwanee*, a novel, appeared in 1948. Despite her early promise, by the time of her death in Fort Pierce, Florida, on January 28, 1960, Zora Hurston was little remembered by the general reading public. Her work proved of lasting significance, however, to folklorists and students of rural life in the South.

Husted, Marjorie Child 1892?–1986 home economist and businesswoman

Born about 1892 in Minneapolis, Marjorie Child attended public schools and graduated from the University of Minnesota in 1913. She remained at the university to take a degree in education the next year. After a period as secretary of the Infant Welfare Society of Minneapolis she joined the Red Cross during World War I and served as director of the information and publicity service and later as assistant director of field service in the northern division. After the war she was associated with the Women's Cooperative Alliance until 1923, when she secured the post of supervisor of promotional advertising and merchandising for the Creamette Company of Minneapolis. A year later she moved to the Washburn-Crosby Company, a flour milling and sales firm, as field representative in home economics. In October 1925 she married K. Wallace Husted.

In 1926 Marjorie Husted organized a home service department for Washburn-Crosby whose staff answered letters from consumers on various topics in homemaking over the standardized signature "Betty Crocker," a name first employed in that manner in 1921. Washburn-Crosby was one of several firms merged in 1928 to create General Mills, and to the new consolidated company it contributed both the "Gold Medal flour" label and its home service department with Betty Crocker. The department was renamed the Betty Crocker Homemaking Service in 1929 with Husted as director. Under her guidance Betty Crocker became the personification of the company, an epitome of the competent, friendly American homemaker. A portrait by a leading commercial artist, Neysa Mc-Mein, helped fix the image of Betty Crocker, whose likeness and signature appeared on a growing number of consumer items and became as well known to the public as any real woman. Husted was the voice of Betty Crocker on radio interview shows.

In 1946 Husted was promoted to the job of consultant to the officers and executives of General Mills, and in 1948 she was made consultant in advertising, public relations, and home service. She also served in 1948 as a consultant to the U.S. Department of Agriculture on food conservation. Honors accorded her for her achievements included the 1949 Advertising Woman of the Year Award from the Advertising Federation of America and the Outstanding Achievement Award of the Women's National Press Club, also in 1949. In April 1950 she left General Mills to form her own consulting firm,

Marjorie Child Husted and Associates. She died on December 23, 1986, in Minneapolis, Minnesota.

Hutchinson, Anne 1591–1643 religious leader

Born in Alford, Lincolnshire, England, probably in the spring of 1591, Anne Marbury was the daughter of a silenced clergyman and grew up in an atmosphere of learning. In August 1612 she married William Hutchinson, a merchant. She became a follower of John Cotton, a Puritan minister of nearby Boston, and in 1634, a year after Cotton had gone to Massachusetts Bay, she sailed for the newer Boston with her husband and family, arriving in September. Her kindliness and intellect soon won her a position of influence in the community, and when she organized regular religious meetings in her home she attracted large numbers of people, including leading merchants and many ministers. At first concerned only with discussion of recent sermons, she gradually began to use the meetings to expound her own theological views, which she attributed generally to Cotton. In opposition to the orthodox "covenant of works," with its demand for righteousness in the faithful, she set forth a "covenant of grace," holding that faith alone was necessary or sufficient for salvation and that the elect were thereby relieved of the burden of sin. Her teachings were viewed by conservatives as a veiled attack on the theocratic polity of the Puritan settlements, and factions quickly formed in what came to be known as the Antinomian Controversy.

Principal among Hutchinson's supporters were her brother-in-law, the Reverend John Wheelwright, John Cotton, and the governor, Sir Henry Vane; ranged against them were the deputy governor, John Winthrop, and the rest of the clergy of the colony, led by the Reverend John Wilson. In 1637 Winthrop won the governorship from Vane, who returned to England, and in September a synod of churches was called at which Hutchinson and her adherents were denounced. Cotton recanted and became one of her severest critics; Wheelwright was banished. After being convicted by the General Court in November of "traducing the ministers," Hutchinson was also banished from Massachusetts Bay, and a short time later, despite a confused recantation extracted from her by Cotton, she was formally excommunicated. Early in 1638 she moved with her family and others to the island of Aquidneck, now called Rhode Island. Following the death of her husband in 1642 she resettled at what is now Pelham Bay, Long Island, where in August 1643 she was killed by Indians in what was considered by many in Massachusetts Bay to be an act of divine judgment.

Hyatt, Anna Vaughn 1876–1973 sculptor

Born in Cambridge, Massachusetts, on March 10, 1876, Anna Hyatt was the daughter of noted Harvard paleontologist Alpheus Hyatt. She was educated privately and began her study of sculpture with Henry H. Kitson in Boston. She later attended the Art Students' League in New York City for a time. Gutzon Borglum was among the teachers who aided her. Her first one-woman exhibition of her work was in Boston in 1900, when she showed some 40 characteristic pieces — animal figures, delicately and accurately modeled and endowed with a spirit almost of life itself. In 1903 the Metropolitan Museum of Art made its first of many acquisitions of her sculptures. In 1907 she traveled to France. For a year she occupied a studio in Auvers-sur-Oise and executed, among other works, a large jaguar that was shown in the Paris Salon exhibition of 1907. In 1908 she was in Naples, where she modeled a large lion that was cast in bronze and later placed in Dayton, Ohio. She returned to Paris a year later and in the Salon of 1910 won honorable mention for her equestrian statue of Joan of Arc, replicas of which were erected in New York City in 1915 and subsequently in several other cities.

Other works of note included "Diana and the Chase" (which won Hyatt a second Saltus Medal from the National Academy of Design in 1922, two years after her first),

"El Cid Campeador," an equestrian figure erected in Seville in 1927 (for which she was awarded the Grand Cross of Alfonso XII by King Alfonso XIII), "Bulls Fighting" in 1928, "Don Quixote" in 1942, "Boabdil" in 1944, "Fighting Stallions," a 17-foot statue cast in aluminum and erected at Southwest Texas State Teachers College in 1951, figures of José Martí, Abraham Lincoln, and Andrew Jackson, a fox statue in Lancaster, New Hampshire, and a number of pieces for the grounds of the Hispanic Society of America in New York. Among other honors bestowed on her were the Rodin Gold Medal in Philadelphia in 1917, membership in the French Legion of Honor in 1922, and gold medals from the American Academy of Arts and Letters, the National Sculpture Society, and other groups. Her works were in the collections of more than 200 museums and galleries throughout the world. In 1965 she gave a casting of her mounted figure of José Martí to the city of New York, and it was placed on Central Park South at the Avenue of the Americas. From March 1923 she was married to poet and philanthropist Archer M. Huntington. She died in Redding, Connecticut, on October 4, 1973.

Hyman, Libbie Henrietta 1888–1969 zoologist

Born in Des Moines, Iowa, on December 6, 1888, Libbie Hyman graduated from the University of Chicago in 1910 and remained to take her Ph.D. in 1915. From 1916 to 1931 she held a research appointment there. Her work concentrated on the physiology and morphology of lower invertebrates, particularly the flatworms. She was best known for her textbooks and reference works on invertebrate and vertebrate zoology; they included *A Laboratory Manual for Elementary Zoology*, 1919, *A Laboratory Manual for Comparative Vertebrate Zoology*, 1922, *Comparative Vertebrate Anatomy*, 1942, and her monumental six-volume *The Invertebrates*, 1931–1968, left uncompleted at her death. From 1937 to her death she held an honorary research appointment to the American Museum of Natural History in New York City. She was president of the Society of Systematic Zoology in 1959 and editor of the journal *Systematic Zoology* from 1959 to 1963. Among her numerous honors were the Elliot Gold Medal in 1951, the gold medal of the Linnaean Society of London in 1960, and a gold medal for distinguished achievement in science from the American Museum of Natural History in 1969. She died in New York City on August 3, 1969.

Irwin, Agnes 1841–1914 educator

Born on December 30, 1841, in Washington, D.C., Agnes Irwin was a great-great-granddaughter of Benjamin Franklin and a daughter of a congressman from Pennsylvania. She was educated privately and early displayed remarkable intelligence and love of learning. In 1862, six years after her father's death, she moved with her family to New York City and became a teacher in a private school. In 1869 she accepted the principalship of a private school in Philadelphia that shortly afterward was renamed the Agnes Irwin School. For 25 years she maintained high standards at the school, acquiring in the process a reputation that extended beyond Philadelphia.

In 1894 Irwin's name was suggested for the post of dean of the newly chartered Radcliffe College, formerly the Society for the Collegiate Instruction of Women at Harvard. In May she stepped into the new and demanding job. She worked well with Elizabeth Cary Agassiz, president of the college, who left the administration of the school mainly to the dean. Irwin quietly worked to expand the Radcliffe curriculum, calling more and more on the resources of Harvard, and by 1902 she had created a program capable of awarding doctoral degrees. During her tenure four dormitories were built, the first opened in 1901, thus making Radcliffe more accessible to young women from other parts of the country. A gymnasium, a library, and an administration building were also built during that time. From 1899, when Agassiz became honorary president and withdrew still more from the management of the college, Irwin was the effective head of the college. The appointment of a Harvard faculty member, LeBaron R. Briggs, as president to succeed Agassiz in 1903 came as a great disappointment to Irwin, who apparently believed she had originally been assured of the succession. She remained at Radcliffe until 1909, and during 1901–1907 she served also as president of the Woman's Education Association of Boston. In 1909 she returned to Philadelphia. She was president of the Head Mistresses' Association of Private Schools from 1911 to 1914. She died in Philadelphia on December 5, 1914.

Irwin, May 1862–1938 actor and singer

Born on June 27, 1862, in Whitby, Ontario, Ada Campbell attended a convent school for several years. In 1875, after her father's death had left the family in poverty, her mother got her and her elder sister Georgia an engagement in a Rochester, New York, variety theater. In December 1875 they made their first professional appearance at the Adelphi Theatre in Buffalo, where they were billed as the "Irwin Sisters." A midwestern tour under their new names, May and Flo Irwin, was followed by a New York City debut at the London Theatre in January 1877. In October of that year they began a run at Tony Pastor's New York Music Hall. After six years of vaudeville and burlesque with Pastor's company, May left in 1883 to join Augustin Daly's stock company — then featuring Ada Rehan and John Drew — and made her first appearance on the legitimate stage in December in Pinero's *Girls and Boys*. For Daly she appeared in *The Magistrate*, *A Night Off*, *The Recruiting Officer*, and other pieces and made her London debut in August 1884 in *Dollars and Sense*.

By 1887 Mary Irwin had decided that she preferred the free-and-easy world of vaudeville to repertory work, and in that year she signed with the Howard Athenaeum of Boston. She toured with that troupe for two years, and in 1889–1890 she toured in the popular *City Directory*. She returned to the legitimate stage in 1893 in Charles Frohman's *His Wedding Day*, in the afterpiece to which, *The Poet and the Puppets*, a burlesque on *Lady Windermere's Fan*, she was a hit singing "After the Ball." Later in the year she appeared in *A Country Sport*, the first of a series of full-length farces in which she had her greatest success. In *The Widow Jones*, 1895, she sang an old St. Louis levee song, "I'm Looking for de Bully," in a style that quickly became popular as "coon-shouting" for its use of African-American dialect and a rhythm that became known as ragtime. The song was published in 1896 as "May Irwin's Bully Song." *The Widow Jones* also provided a brief scene for Thomas A. Edison's "Vitascope" cinematic camera in which May Irwin and her leading man, John Rice, shared a prolonged kiss; *The Kiss*, one of the earliest commercially distributed films, was denounced from the pulpit across the country. In *Courted into Court*, 1896, she sang "Mister Johnson, Turn Me Loose" and introduced "A Hot Time in the Old Town."

In 1897 Irwin began appearing under her own management. Her productions included *The Swell Miss Fitzwell*, 1897, *Kate Kip, Buyer*, 1898, *Sister Mary*, 1899, *Madge Smith, Attorney*, 1900, *Mrs. Black is Back*, 1904, *Mrs. Wilson, That's All*, 1906, and George Ade's *Mrs. Peckham's Carouse*, 1907. Her good humor, wit, and buxom figure made her one of the most popular performers of the day. Subsequently she appeared in *The Mollusc*, 1908, Booth Tarkington and Harry Leon Wilson's *Getting a Polish*, in which she sang Irving Berlin's "The Opera Rag," 1910, *She Knows Better Now*, 1911, *Widow by Proxy*, 1913, *No. 13 Washington Square*, 1915, and *On The Hiring Line*, 1919. She was briefly master of ceremonies for a small revue, *The '49ers*, in 1922 and then retired to her farm in Clayton, New York. She died in New York City on October 22, 1938.

Isom, Mary Frances 1865–1920 librarian

Born on February 27, 1865, in Nashville, Tennessee, Mary Isom grew up and attended public schools in Cleveland. She attended Wellesley College for a year, 1883–1884, but ill health prevented her completing her education. In 1899, following the death of her widower father, she entered the Pratt Institute Library School in Brooklyn, New York, from which she graduated in 1900. The next year she took the job of cataloger of the newly acquired John Wilson Collection at the Library Association, a private subscription library in Portland, Oregon. In January 1902 she was appointed librarian of the institution, which at that time was converted to a free public library. To the burden of organizing a greatly expanded library to serve a similarly multiplied community of users was added a year later the responsibility, mandated by state law, of making the library available to all the rural communities of Multnomah County. Within five years she had established a network of three branch libraries and eleven reading rooms around the county along with an efficient book circulation system.

In 1904 Isom organized the Oregon Library Association, and in 1905 she was principally responsible for the passage of legislation creating the Oregon State Library Commission, of which she was a member until her death. She helped found the Pacific Northwest Library Association in 1909 and served as its president in 1910–1911. In 1912–1913 she was second vice-president of the American Library Association. The rapidly growing demands on the Portland library made necessary the establishment of seven large permanent branches in 1911–1913, and in the latter year, crowning a long period of deep involvement in every phase of the project, she saw opened the new Multnomah County Public Library. During World War I she was active in organizing libraries for hospitals and army and lumber camps in Oregon and Washington. For six arduous months she organized hospital libraries in France. In declining health in her last years, she continued her work until her death in Portland, Oregon, on April 15, 1920.

Jackson, Helen Hunt 1830–1885 writer

Born in Amherst, Massachusetts, on October 15, 1830, Helen Maria Fiske was the daughter of a professor of classics at Amherst College and from an early age was a close friend of Emily Dickinson. She was educated privately. She married Edward B. Hunt, an army officer, in October 1852, and his death in 1863 and that of her younger son in 1865 (the elder had died in 1854) left her alone, in despair, and without resources. She turned to writing. After publishing some poems in the *New York Evening Post* and the *Nation* she moved in 1866 to Newport, Rhode Island, and with the encouragement of Thomas W. S. Higginson began contributing poems and prose sketches to various periodicals, principally the *New York Independent* and *Hearth and Home*.

As an author Hunt was successful from the outset, although throughout much of her career she signed little of her work, using instead of her own name such pseudonyms as "Saxe Holm" and "H. H." Her first book, a volume entitled *Verses*, appeared in 1870 and was followed by such popular but minor efforts as *Bits of Travel*, 1872, *Bits of Talk About Some Matters*, 1873, *Mercy Philbrick's Choice*, 1876, *Hetty's Strange History*, 1877, and *Nelly's Silver Mine*, 1878. From October 1875, when she married William S. Jackson, a banker, she lived in Colorado Springs, Colorado. Her life in the West generated in her a deep sympathy for Native Americans. She described the consistently shoddy and cruel treatment of Native Americans by the government in *A Century of Dishonor*, 1881, the considerable impact of which was greatly surpassed by that of her subsequent novel *Ramona*, 1884. While *Ramona* aroused something of a public outcry on behalf of the Native Americans, its great and lasting popularity was due in large part to its picturesque and romantic setting in old California. It continued to sell through more than 300 printings and was made into a motion picture at least three times. As a result of the publication of *A Century of Dishonor* she had been appointed in 1882 by the Department of the Interior to investigate the condition of the Mission Indians of California. Her report in July 1883 made no impression on the government. Jackson died in San Francisco on August 12, 1885.

Jackson, Mahalia 1911–1972 gospel singer

Born in New Orleans on October 26, 1911, Mahalia Jackson was the third of six children of a longshoreman and barber who preached on Sundays in a neighborhood church. She attended public schools in New Orleans and was brought up in a strict religious atmosphere involving, among other things, disapproval of all kinds of secular music. Her father's family included several entertainers, but she was forced to confine her own musical activities to singing in his choir and listening — surreptitiously — to recordings of Bessie Smith and Ida Cox as well as of Enrico Caruso. When she was sixteen she went to Chicago and joined the Greater Salem Baptist Church choir, where her remarkable contralto voice soon led to her selection as a soloist. She was popular in storefront and tent churches but for a long time was not accepted by the larger, more formal black congregations because of the syncopated rhythms of her songs. But her fame grew, and in 1934 her first recording, "God Gonna Separate the Wheat from the Tares," became very popular and led to a series of other recordings.

Jackson's first great hit (altogether, eight of her records sold more than a million copies each) was "Move on Up a Little Higher," which appeared in 1945. It, and indeed all of her other famous songs, including "I Believe," "He's Got the Whole World in His Hands," "I Can Put My Trust in Jesus," "Just Over the Hill," "When I Wake Up in Glory," and "Just a Little While to Stay Here," were gospel songs — songs with texts drawn from biblical themes and strongly influenced by the harmonies, rhythms, and emotional force of blues. Despite her admiration for Bessie Smith, and despite the fact that she is said to have possessed the greatest potential blues voice and style since the death of Smith, Jackson resolutely refused to sing anything but religious songs, or indeed to sing at all in surroundings that she considered inappropriate. Thus she would never sing in a nightclub or in any place where liquor was served. But she sang on the radio and on television and, starting in 1950, performed to overflow audiences in annual concerts at Carnegie Hall in New York City.

Jackson was enormously popular abroad; her version of "Silent Night," for example, was one of the all time best-selling records in Denmark. She made a notable appearance at the Newport Jazz Festival in 1957 — in a program devoted entirely, at her request, to gospel songs — and she sang at the inauguration of President John F. Kennedy in January 1961. She sang in churches and in prisons and hospitals as well as in concert halls and in command performances before heads of state. In her later years she was closely associated with the civil rights movement, but she also suffered from ill health, and although advised by her doctors to curtail her demanding schedule, she refused to do less than all she could to help heal the divisions, as she said, between black and white people in the United States and elsewhere. She died in Evergreen Park, Illinois, on January 27, 1972, after a lifetime devoted to making "a joyful noise unto the Lord."

Jackson, Mercy Ruggles Bisbe 1802–1877 physician and educator

Born in Hardwick, Massachusetts, on September 17, 1802, Mercy Ruggles received what was for the time a good education. In June 1823 she married the Reverend John Bisbe, with whom she moved to Hartford, Connecticut, the next year and later to Portland, Maine. After his death in 1829 she supported herself and her children by operating a girls' school until 1832, when she opened a drygoods store. In 1835 she married Captain Daniel Jackson of Plymouth, Massachusetts. Her long-standing interest in medicine, particularly the treatment of children (of which she had 11 herself), was given added impetus in 1848 when a regular Plymouth physician began giving her books and medicines. Soon she had a thriving practice in homeopathic medicine. After her second husband's death in 1852 she entered the New England Female Medical College, from which she graduated in 1860.

Mercy Jackson then settled and began a practice in Boston. In 1861 she applied for membership in the American Institute of Homeopathy (headquartered in Philadelphia) but was rejected on account of her sex. Her annual reapplications were similarly rejected until 1871, in June of which year the Institute admitted her and two other women. Two years later she was admitted to both the Massachusetts and the Boston Homeopathic societies. Also in 1873 she was appointed adjunct professor of the diseases of children at the newly opened Boston University School of Medicine. She continued to teach and to carry on a large practice until her death. She was also a supporter of and lecturer on the causes of temperance and woman suffrage and a frequent contributor to the Boston *Woman's Journal*. She died in Boston on December 13, 1877.

Jacobi, Mary Corinna Putnam 1842–1906 physician

Born in London on August 31, 1842, Mary Putnam was the daughter of George Palmer Putnam, founder of the publishing firm of G. P. Putnam's Sons, and an elder sister of Herbert Putnam, later librarian of Congress. The family returned from England in 1848, and Mary grew up in Staten Island, Yonkers, and Morrisania, New York. She was educated in private and public schools and early demonstrated great intellectual promise. In April 1860, before she was eighteen, she had a story published in the *Atlantic Monthly*. Her scientific bent determined her on a medical career. She graduated from the New York College of Pharmacy in 1863 and from the Female (later Woman's) Medical College of Pennsylvania in 1864. During that period she twice ventured to Union-occupied areas in the South to care for ailing family members.

After a few months at the New England Hospital for Women and Children in Boston,

Putnam decided in 1866 to seek further training in Paris. There she attended clinics, lectures, and a class at the École Pratique until she decided to seek admission to the École de Médecine. Her persistence finally secured a directive from the minister of education forcing the faculty to admit her in 1868. Her course was a distinguished one, and she graduated in July 1871 with a prize-winning thesis. (Although she had been the first woman admitted, she was the second graduated.) During her stay in Paris she contributed letters, articles, and stories to the *Medical Record*, *Putnam's Magazine*, the *New York Evening Post*, and *Scribners Monthly*.

In the fall of 1871 Putnam returned to New York City, opened a practice, and accepted the post of lecturer on materia medica in Dr. Elizabeth Blackwell's Woman's Medical College of the New York Infirmary for Women and Children. The quality of her own education had highlighted for her the meagerness of that available to most women aiming for a medical career, and in 1872 she organized the Association for the Advancement of the Medical Education of Women (later the Women's Medical Association of New York City) to begin redressing that shortcoming; she was president of the association from 1874 to 1903. At the Woman's Medical College, where she became professor of materia medica and therapeutics in 1873, she was a demanding teacher whose standards were viewed by some colleagues as unrealistically high. In July 1873 she married Dr. Abraham Jacobi, generally considered the founder of pediatrics in America. In the same year she began a children's dispensary service at Mount Sinai Hospital. From 1882 to 1885 she lectured on diseases of children at the New York Post-Graduate Medical School. She opened a small children's ward at the New York Infirmary in 1886. She resigned her professorship at the Woman's Medical College in 1889 but continued to be a force for improved education for women. From 1893 she was visiting physician at St. Mark's Hospital. In addition to clinical work and teaching she found time for writing as well.

Mary Jacob's bibliography ran to more than a hundred titles, mainly in pathology, neurology, pediatrics, and medical education, and one of her essays won the 1876 Boylston Prize from Harvard. Her books included *The Value of Life*, 1879, *Essays on Hysteria, Brain-Tumor, and Some Other Cases of Nervous Disease*, 1888, *Physiological Notes on Primary Education and the Study of Language*, 1889, and *"Common Sense" Applied to Woman Suffrage*, 1894. While she did little original research, her contribution to the status of women within the medical profession was incalculable. She also took an interest in social causes. She helped found the Working Women's Society (from 1890 the New York Consumers' League) and the League for Political Education. After several years of declining health ending in invalidism she died in New York City on June, 10, 1906.

Jacobs, Frances Wisebart 1843–1892 welfare worker

Born on March 29, 1843, in Harrodsburg, Kentucky, Frances Wisebart grew up in Cincinnati. She attended public schools and then taught school until February 1863, when she married Abraham Jacobs, a storekeeper of Central City, Colorado. In 1874 they moved to Denver. There Frances Jacobs quickly became active in charitable work, which had only lately become organized in the city. She was elected president of the Hebrew Benevolent Ladies Aid Society, and in 1874 she was an original officer of the non-sectarian Ladies' Relief Society. In 1887 she led in organizing the Charity Organization Society, a federation of existing charitable groups intended to coordinate their various efforts and to conduct joint appeals for funds. She was secretary of the Charity Organization Society until her death.

Unlike many women of position who involved themselves in such work, Jacobs took her post with the utmost seriousness and risked the occasional criticism of colleagues — and not infrequently her health — by personally investigating charity cases and distributing food and other relief. In 1890 she served as president of the Ladies' Relief Society. She was also interested in the kindergarten movement and organized a kindergarten association in Denver. On her death in Denver on November 3, 1892, she was eulogized by leading citizens from the governor of Colorado down, and in 1900 she was the only woman among the 16 Colorado pioneers chosen to be memorialized in stained-glass portraits in the state capitol.

Jamison, Cecilia Viets Dakin Hamilton 1837–1909 children's literature writer, novelist and writer

Born in 1837 in Yarmouth, Nova Scotia, Cecilia Dakin grew up there and from about 1852 in Boston. She was educated privately in Boston, New York, and Paris. Her first ambition was to be a painter, and it was while she was pursuing that goal, with a studio in Boston, that she married one George Hamilton about 1860. Some time later she traveled to Rome to continue her studies and remained there for three years. While there she met Henry Wadsworth Longfellow, to whom she showed the manuscript of a novel she had written. He praised it highly and undertook to have it published. By the time it appeared in 1872 under the title *Woven of Many Threads*, Hamilton had returned to America, established studios in both Boston and New York City, and successfully divided her time between writing and painting. Her first book to be published was *Something To Do: A Novel*, 1871, and it was followed by *A Crown from the Spear*, 1872, *Ropes of Sand and Other Stories*, 1873, *My Bonnie Lass*, 1877, and *Lilly of San Miniato*, 1878.

Among Hamilton's best known portraits of the period were one of Longfellow (now at Tulane University) and one of naturalist Louis Agassiz (now at the Boston Society of Natural History). In October 1878 she married Samuel Jamison, a lawyer with whom she lived on a plantation near Thibodeaux, Louisiana, until 1887 and thereafter in New Orleans. During the 1880s Cecilia Jamison became well known as a writer of juvenile literature as well as of adult romances. She was a frequent contributor to *St. Nicholas*, and many of her novels were serialized in *Harper's*, *Scribner's*, and *Appleton's*. Her books included *The Story of an Enthusiast*, 1888, *Lady Jane*, 1891, *Toinette's Philip*, 1894, *Seraph, the Little Violiniste*, 1896, *Thistledown*, 1903, and *The Penhallow Family*, 1905. After her husband's death in 1902 she lived in Massachusetts; she died in Roxbury (now part of Boston) on April 11, 1909.

SUSAN COOK

Judith Jamison

Jamison, Judith 1944– dancer and choreographer

Born May 10, 1944, in Philadelphia, Pennsylvania, Judith Jamison was the daughter of John Jamison, a steelworker with musical aspirations, and Tessie Jamison, a part-time teacher and former athlete. She began taking dance lessons at age six at the Judimar School of Dance, where for eleven years she studied tap, acrobatics, jazz and ballet. She also took piano and violin lessons as well as acting lessons, and she was an active member of the Mother Bethel African Methodist Episcopal Church. At seventeen she graduated from high school and enrolled as a psychology major at Fisk University. Three semesters later she transferred to the Philadelphia Dance Academy (now the University of the Arts).

In 1964, Agnes de Mille invited Jamison to dance in her new ballet, *The Four Marys*, at New York's Lincoln Center. In the fall of 1965, while auditioning unsuccessfully for a Harry Belafonte television special, she attracted the attention of Alvin Ailey. She performed her debut with the Alvin Ailey Dance Company (now the Alvin Ailey American Dance Theater) in "Conga Tango Palace" at the Harper Festival in Chicago in 1965. In time, she became Ailey's leading dancer. In 1971 Ailey choreographed *Cry* expressly for her; a fifteen-minute solo depicting the struggles of black women, it has become her signature piece. She traveled extensively with the Ailey company worldwide, and appeared as a guest artist with numerous other American and European dance companies.

In 1972, President Nixon appointed Jamison as an advisor to the National Council on the Arts. Also that year, she married Miguel Godreau, a former member of the Alvin Ailey American Dance Theater Company. In 1980, she left the company to star in the Broadway musical hit *Sophisticated Ladies*. She herself began experimenting with choreography and the Alvin Ailey American Dance Theater premiered her first work, *Divining*, in 1984. She established her own twelve-member troupe, the Jamison Project, in 1987. After Ailey's death in 1989, she took on the responsibilities of artistic director of the Ailey troupe and of its school of more than three thousand students. In doing so, she became the first African-American woman to direct a major modern dance company. Jamison's choreographies include *Just Call Me Dance*, 1984, *Time Out*, 1986, *Time In*, 1986, *Into the Life*, 1987, *Tease*, 1988, *Forgotten Time*, 1989, *Rift*, 1991, and *Hymn*, 1993, for which Anna Deveare Smith wrote the libretto. With Howard Kaplan, Jamison has written *Dancing Spirit: an Autobiography*, published in 1993.

Jarvis, Anna M. 1864–1948 founder of Mother's Day

Born in Grafton, West Virginia, on May 1, 1864, Anna Jarvis was of a prosperous family. She was educated at Mary Baldwin College. She emerged into public life in 1907, when, following a memorial service in May of that year for her late mother, she began a one-woman campaign to have one day a year set aside in honor of mothers. (Others had had similar ideas; as early as 1872 Julia Ward Howe suggested it.) On the second Sunday in May 1908, churches in Grafton and Philadelphia, where Jarvis then lived, held observances honoring mothers, and the custom of wearing carnations on that day was begun then. A tireless letter-writing campaign directed at state governors and legislatures and at congressmen resulted in Mother's Day observances being established in nearly every state by 1913, and in May 1914 President Woodrow Wilson signed a joint resolution of Congress recommending the observance of Mother's Day by government offices. The next year the President was authorized to proclaim a national Mother's Day each year on the second Sunday of May.

Incorporating herself as the Mother's Day International Association, Anna Jarvis extended her efforts to other nations. The volume of her correspondence was such that at length she was forced to buy the house next door simply for storage. At one time it was estimated that mother's days were being observed in 43 countries. The commercialization of Mother's Day by florists, confectioners, and greeting card firms outraged her, and she devoted much of the rest of her life, and her modest inheritance, to the largely unavailing attempt to maintain the purity of the holiday. Her threat of a lawsuit in 1923 did succeed in preventing a planned commercial celebration of Mother's Day in New York City. Her health broke down completely in 1943, and she spent her last years in a sanatorium in West Chester, Pennsylvania, where she died on November 24, 1948.

Jemison, Mae 1956– astronaut and doctor

Born in Decatur, Alabama, on October 17, 1956, to a maintenance supervisor and a schoolteacher, Mae Jemison moved with her family to Chicago at the age of three. There she was introduced to science by her uncle and developed interests throughout her childhood in anthropology, archaeology, extinct species, evolution, and astronomy. While a student at Morgan Park High School, a visit to a university sparked her interest in biomedical engineering, and after graduating in 1973, she entered Stanford University on a National Achievement Scholarship. There she received degrees in chemical engineering and African-American studies, becoming involved in dance and theater as well.

In 1977 Jemison entered medical school at Cornell, where she pursued an interest in international medicine. After volunteering for a summer in a Cambodian refugee camp in Thailand, she studied in Kenya in 1979 on a grant from the International Travelers Institute. She graduated from medical school in 1981 and completed her internship with the Los Angeles County-USC Medical Center in 1982. After a short time as a general practitioner with a Los Angeles medical group, Jemison became a medical officer with the Peace Corps in West Africa. There she managed health care for Peace Corps and U.S. Embassy personnel and worked in conjunction with the National Institutes of Health and the Center for Disease Control on several research projects, including development of a Hepatitis B vaccine.

After returning to work as a physician for a health maintenance organization in Los Angeles, Jemison applied to NASA to be an astronaut. Her attempt to join the space program was aborted by the explosion of the space shuttle *Challenger* in January 1986, after which NASA temporarily suspended applications. When she reapplied in October 1986, Jemison was one of 15 accepted out of two thousand applicants.

Jemison completed her training as a mission specialist with NASA in 1988. She became an astronaut office representative with the Kennedy Space Center at Cape Canaveral, working to process space shuttles for launching and to verify shuttle software. Next, she was assigned to support a cooperative mission between the U.S. and Japan designed to conduct experiments in materials processing and the life sciences. In August 1992, STS–47 Spacelab J became the first successful joint U.S.-Japan space mission.

Her maiden space flight came with the week-long September 1992 mission of the shuttle *Endeavor*. The only African-American woman astronaut (at the time there were 18 other women and 5 black men in the space program), Jemison expressed pride in her own heritage on that mission by taking into space a poster of dancer-choreographer Judith Jamison performing "Cry," a dance dedicated to the lives of African-American women.

Jemison, Mary 1743–1833 Indian captive

Born in 1743 aboard the ship bearing her immigrant parents from northern Ireland to America, Mary Jemison grew up on a farm near the site of present-day Gettysburg, Pennsylvania. On April 5, 1758, a raiding party of French soldiers and Shawnee descended on the farm. Mary's two eldest brothers escaped, but three other children and the parents were killed. Mary was carried off and soon afterward adopted by a Seneca family, who treated her well. She lived with them in the Ohio country and in 1760 was married to a Delaware warrior who died not long afterward. In 1762 she and her infant son moved to the Seneca territory in western New York, settling in a town on the Genesee River near what is now Geneseo, New York. She married a Seneca warrior in 1765 and by him bore several children, all of whom took her surname. Her husband was a leader in the Cherry Valley massacre of November 1778, and the next year she was forced to relocate to the Gardeau Flats near Castile, New York, when the retaliatory expedition under General John Sullivan destroyed her town. She lived there in her log cabin until 1831.

At the end of the Revolution, for various reasons, Jemison refused an offer of repatriation. She owned the largest herd of cattle in the region. A tribal grant in 1797 made her one of the largest landowners around, and her title was confirmed by the state in 1817, in which year also she was naturalized. In her personal life she lived largely by Native American customs. She was noted for her generosity, cheerfulness, and a vigor that remained with her into her eighties. As a result of an interview in 1823, Dr. James E. Seaver published the next year *A Narrative of the Life of Mrs. Mary Jemison*, which quickly became one of the most popular in the genre of captivity stories and eventually ran through some 30 editions. Known popularly as "the White Woman of the Genesee," Mary Jemison was a figure of great interest to her neighbors and to travelers in the region. In 1831, white settlement in the district having become oppressively thick, she sold her land and moved to the Buffalo Creek Reservation near Buffalo, New York. She died there on September 19, 1833. In 1874 her remains were removed to a spot near her old Genesee home, in what later became Letchworth State Park. A statue of her by Henry K. Bush-Brown was unveiled there in 1910.

Jewett, Sarah Orne 1849–1909 short story writer

Born on September 3, 1849, in South Berwick, Maine, Theodora Sarah Jewett, who in later life did not use her first name, was often taken by her physician father on visits to the fishermen and farmers of the area, and she developed a deep and abiding love of their way of life and of the sights and sounds of her surroundings. These experiences, and reading in her family's ample library, formed the bulk of her education. Although she also attended the Berwick Academy, graduating in 1865, she considered her schooling insignificant compared to the learning she gained on her own. During her childhood she began to write of the perishing farms and neglected, shipless harbors around her. She published her first story, "Jenny Garrow's Lovers," in the *Flag of Our Union* in 1868 and followed it with "The Shipwrecked Buttons" in the *Riverside Magazine for Young People* and "Mr. Bruce" in the *Atlantic Monthly* in 1869. Her early pieces were signed "Alice Eliot" or "A. C. Eliot." Numerous later sketches of a New England town, "Deephaven," that resembled South Berwick, were published in the *Atlantic Monthly* and were collected in *Deephaven*, 1877, her first book.

There followed many other collections of stories and vignettes, often first published in the *Century*, *Harper's*, or the *Atlantic*: *Old Friends and New*, 1879, *Country By-Ways*, 1881, *The Mate of the Daylight and Friends Ashore*, 1883, *A White Heron*, 1886, *The King of Folly Island and Other People*, 1888, *Strangers and Wayfarers*, 1890, *A Native of Winby*, 1893, *The Life of Nancy*, 1895, *The Country of the Pointed Firs*, 1896, and *The Queen's Twin*, 1899. She wrote three novels — *A Country Doctor*, 1884, *A Marsh Island*, 1885, and *The Tory Lover*, 1901 — but sustained narrative was not her forte. She also wrote a number of books for children, including *Play Days*, 1878, *Betty Leicester*, 1889, and *Betty Leicester's English Christmas*, 1897.

Jewitt's best book, *The Country of the Pointed Firs*, portrayed, like *Deephaven*, the isolation and loneliness of a declining seaport town and the unique humor of its people. The sympathetic but unsentimental portrayal of this provincial and rapidly disappearing society made her an important local-color writer, and in this she was a profound influence on Willa Cather. The best of her writing resembled nineteenth-century French fiction, especially that of Gustave Flaubert, whom she greatly admired, in its naturalism, precision, and compactness. She frequently visited Boston and other large cities but lived and wrote in the same house in which she was born. Her writing career ended after a disabling accident in 1902. She died in South Berwick on June 24, 1909. Her collected poems were published posthumously as *Verses*, 1916.

Jhabvala, Ruth Prawer 1927– novelist and screenwriter

Born in Cologne, Germany, on May 7, 1927, to Polish Jewish parents, Ruth Prawer fled Nazi Germany to England with her family in 1939. Educated near London, she attended Queen Mary College, London University, from 1945–1951, receiving an M.A. in English literature in 1951. In 1951 she married Cyrus Jhabvala, an architect, and moved with him to India, where she had three daughters and began to write.

Her early fiction was set in India; her position as an expatriate allowed her to write with the viewpoint of both an insider and an outsider. Her novel, *Heat and Dust*, which won the Booker Prize in 1975, explored Indian themes while working with new narrative techniques and experimental forms. Although she went on to write more than ten novels and several collections of short stories, she became best known for her work as a screenwriter.

In 1961, filmmakers James Ivory and Ismail Merchant approached her about creating a film of her fourth novel, *The Householder*, the story of an arranged marriage between a schoolmaster and a young woman. She agreed, beginning one of the longest creative collaborations in the history of the cinema. Three decades later she had written sixteen screenplays for Merchant and Ivory, including adaptations of two of her own novels. Her screenplays of E.M. Forster's *A Room with a View*, 1986, and *Howard's End*, 1992, both earned Academy Awards for Best Adapted Screenplay.

She was awarded a Guggenheim fellowship in 1976 and a MacArthur fellowship in 1984. She took up permanent residence in New York City in 1975 and became an American citizen in 1986. Her subsequent literary interests moved away from Indian subjects and settings in favor of American ones. *In Search of Love and Beauty*, 1983, *Three Continents*, 1987, and *Poet and Dancer*, 1993, are all set in Manhattan.

Johnson, Ellen Cheney 1829–1899 prison superintendent and reformer

Born on December 20, 1829, in Athol, Massachusetts, Ellen Cheney grew up there and in Weare, New Hampshire. After attending Weare public schools and an academy in Francestown, New Hampshire, she taught for a time in Weare. From her youth she was an ardent supporter of the cause of temperance. In her early twenties she married Jesse Crane (or Cram) Johnson, with whom she settled in Boston. During the Civil War she was a leading figure in the U.S. Sanitary Commission as a founder and member of the executive and finance committees of the New England Women's Auxiliary Association of the commission. The distribution of surplus funds to soldiers' dependents at the end of the war took her frequently to various correctional institutions, where she quickly developed an interest in the plight of female prisoners. About 1867 she called the first of several meetings of reform-minded women at her home that led in 1874 to the establishment of the Temporary Asylum for Discharged Female Prisoners in Dedham and in 1877 to the passage of legislation authorizing the establishment of the Massachusetts Reformatory Prison for Women in Sherborn, near Framingham.

Johnson was a member of the state prison commission from 1878, and in January 1884 she became superintendent of the women's reformatory. She soon introduced an innovative and strongly humanitarian regime into the institution. While a large working vegetable and livestock farm provided work, food, and supplemental income, the inmates were encouraged to develop their abilities through a graded system of earned privileges, training classes in domestic skills and child care, elementary schooling for those needing it, compulsory library patronage, and recreational activities. A system of supervised outside domestic employment with local families was also devised. It was her policy not to know the inmates' histories; each was making a new beginning under her care. While her rehabilitative methods were sometimes seen as sentimental, her insistence on the justness of punishment was a tempering quality. The Sherborn facility became a much-visited model institution under her direction. She died in London on June 28, 1899, while attending the congress of the International Council of Women.

Johnson, Helen Louise Kendrick 1844–1917 writer and editor

Born on January 4, 1844, in Hamilton, New York, Helen Kendrick grew up there and from 1850 in Rochester and Clinton, New York. Her schooling was irregular, concluding with a year, 1863–1864, at the Oread Institute in Worcester, Massachusetts, but she learned much from her father, a professor of Greek. Through a travel sketch she wrote for the *Rochester Democrat* in 1867 she met the assistant editor, Rossiter Johnson, whom she married in May 1869. They lived in Concord, New Hampshire, where he edited the *New Hampshire Statesman*, until 1873, when they moved to New York City. Her stories and sketches written for her husband's newspaper were collected in her first book, *Roddy's Romance*, for children, 1874.

Two more Roddy books followed by 1876, and Johnson went on to produce *Tears for the Little Ones: A Collection of Poems and Passages Inspired by the Loss of Children*, 1878, *Our Familiar Songs and Those Who Made Them*, which collected over 300 standards and favorites and was long in print, 1881, *Illustrated Poems and Songs for Young People*, 1884, the six-volume "Nutshell Series," a collection of epigrams, 1884,

Raleigh Westgate; or, Epimenides in Maine, a novel, 1889, *A Dictionary of Terms, Phrases, and Quotations*, with H. P. Smith, 1895, *Woman and the Republic*, a collection of articles and arguments against woman suffrage, 1897, *Great Essays*, from Montaigne and others, 1900, and *Mythology and Folk-Lore of the North American Indian*, 1908. During 1894–1896 she edited the *American Woman's Journal*, and she was a frequent contributor to newspapers, magazines, and *Appleton's Annual Cyclopaedia*, of which her husband was editor from 1883 to 1902. She was active in the Henry Street Settlement and was the founder of the Meridian Club in 1886 and of the antisuffrage Guidon Club in 1910. She died in New York City on January 3, 1917.

Johnson, Osa Helen Leighty 1894–1953 explorer, filmmaker and writer

Born in Chanute, Kansas, on March 14, 1894, Osa Leighty attended local schools. In May 1910 she married adventurer and photographer Martin E. Johnson. For two years they played the vaudeville circuit with an exhibit of photographs Martin Johnson had taken in the South Seas while accompanying Jack London on his voyage of the *Snark*. By 1912 they had accumulated the funds to return to the South Sea islands and make a motion-picture record of cannibal and head-hunting tribesmen. Thenceforward they alternated lengthy photographic trips into the field with lecture and exhibition tours at home. They were in the Solomon and New Hebrides Islands in 1914, North Borneo in 1917–1919 and again in 1935, and in 1921–1922, 1923–1927, 1928–1929, and 1933–1934 in various parts of Africa. In the field Martin Johnson was the principal photographer, while Osa was guard, hunter, and pilot. They made motion-picture records of wildlife for the American Museum of Natural History and gathered much valuable geographical and ethnological information.

Their motion pictures, which were highly successful in commercial distribution, included *Jungle Adventures*, 1921, *Head Hunters of the South Seas*, 1922, *Trailing African Wild Animals*, 1923, *Simba, The King of Beasts*, 1928, *Across the World*, 1930, *Wonders of the Congo*, 1931, *Congorilla*, 1932, *Baboons*, 1935, and *Borneo*, 1937, along with such short features as *Cannibaland*, *The Adventurous Orang*, and *Wings over Africa*. They also collaborated on several books: *Cannibal-Land*, 1922, *Camera Trails in Africa*, 1924, *Lion*, 1929, *Congorilla*, 1931, and *Over African Jungles*, 1935. On her own Osa Johnson wrote *Jungle Babies*, 1930, and *Jungle Pete*, 1932.

After Martin Johnson's death in February 1937 Osa continued in the work they had begun together. In that year she led a large expedition from Twentieth-Century Fox into the African bush to film sequences for the motion picture *Stanley and Livingstone*. She produced four more films on her own — *Jungles Calling*, 1937, *I Married Adventure*, 1940, *African Paradise*, 1941, and *Tulagi and the Solomons*, 1943 — and wrote *Osa Johnson's Jungle Friends*, 1939, *I Married Adventure*, the nonfiction best seller of 1940, *Pantaloons, the Story of a Baby Elephant*, 1941, *Four Years in Paradise*, 1941, *Snowball, the Baby Gorilla*, 1942, *Bride in the Solomons*, 1944, and *Tarnish, the True Story of a Lion Cub*, 1945. She also designed a line of accurately detailed animal toys for the National Wildlife Federation. She died in New York City on January 7, 1953.

Johnston, Annie Fellows 1863–1931 children's literature writer

Born on May 15, 1863, in Evansville, Indiana, Annie Fellows, an elder sister of Albion Fellows (Bacon), grew up there and in nearby McCutchanville. She attended district schools and at seventeen taught for a year. During 1881–1882 she attended the University of Iowa, and after three more years of teaching in Evansville she worked as a secretary until October 1888, when she married William L. Johnston, a widower with three children. Inspired by that ready-made audience, she began contributing stories to the *Youth's Companion*, which, along with *St. Nicholas*, *Little Corporal*, and other magazines, had been among her own favorite childhood reading. Although she had dabbled in writing since her youth, she did not take it up seriously until after her husband's death in 1892. In 1894 she published her first book, *Big Brother*, which was followed by *Joel: A Boy of Galilee*, 1895, and nearly 50 more.

A visit to the Pewee Valley, near Louisville, Kentucky, where her stepchildren had relatives and where she was charmed by the almost antebellum style of life and in particular by one spirited little girl, led Johnston to write *The Little Colonel*, 1896, the first in a series of twelve books that included also *Two Little Knights of Kentucky*, 1899, *The Little Colonel's House Party*, 1900, *The Little Colonel's Holidays*, 1901, *The Little Colonel's Hero*, 1902, *The Little Colonel at Boarding School*, 1903, *The Little Colonel in Arizona*, 1904, and *The Little Colonel's Knight Comes Riding*, 1907. In 1898 she settled in the Pewee Valley and lived there the rest of her life, except for the years 1901–1910, when she took her stepson to Texas for his health. Johnston's of her books included *In League with Israel*, 1896, *Songs Ysame*, with her sister Albion Bacon, 1897, *Cicely*, 1902, *Aunt 'Liza's Hero*, 1903, *The Quilt that Jack Built*, 1904, *In the Desert of Waiting*, 1905, *Mary Ware, the Little Colonel's Chum*, the first in a second series, 1908, *The Jester's Sword*, 1909, *Mary Ware in Texas*, 1910, *Travellers Five*, 1911, *Promised Land*, 1912, *Georgina of the Rainbows*, 1916, *Georgina's Service Stars*, 1918, and *The Road of the Loving Heart*, 1922. Inspirational, sentimental, and cheerful, her books were enormously popular with young girls and had sold over a million copies at the time of her death in the Pewee Valley of Kentucky on October 5, 1931.

Johnston, Henrietta ?–1729 artist

Born sometime before 1670, probably in Ireland, Henrietta Deering was married to the Reverend Gideon Johnston in Dublin in April 1705. Of her earlier life nothing is known. Two years later they emigrated to America and settled in Charles Towne (now Charleston), South Carolina. Their life there was hard: beset by poverty and illness, Henrietta Johnston cared for her husband, who was also often ill, served as his secretary, kept the house, cared for her children, and found time to supplement their meager income by doing portraits of the wealthy, the powerful, and the prominent. Apparently untrained, she employed native talent to produce portraits of frank, unadorned directness. They were small, generally 9 by 12 inches and never larger than 14 by 16, and were done in pastels, a technique only then coming into widespread use. She was almost certainly the earliest worker in that medium and quite possibly the earliest woman artist in America. Some 40 portraits by her are known, most done between 1707 and 1720. She was forced to support herself after her husband's death in 1716, and she may have done so in part by boarding in the homes of her subjects. A number of portraits done in New York as late as 1725 have been attributed to her. The place and date of her death are unknown, but she was buried in Charles Towne on March 7, 1729.

Johnston, Mary 1870–1936 novelist

Born on November 21, 1870, in Buchanan, Botetourt County, Virginia, Mary Johnston grew up there, in New York City, and in Birmingham, Alabama, as her father's varied business interests led him from place to place. She was frequently ill as a child and gained her education largely at home in her father's extensive library. After her mother's death in 1889 she took charge of the household. Her first book, *Prisoners of Hope*, a tale of 17th-century Virginia, 1898, was an immediate success in a period when the historical romance was greatly popular, but it was eclipsed by the astounding half-million-copy sale of her second, *To Have and to Hold*, a story of early Jamestown, 1900. In 1902 she moved to Richmond, Virginia.

The majority of Johnston's novels dealt with Virginia's history. They included *Audrey*, 1902, *Sir Mortimer*, 1904, *Lewis Rand*, 1908, *The Long Roll*, 1911, *Cease Firing*, 1912,

Hagar, 1913, *The Witch*, 1914, *The Fortunes of Garin*, 1915, *The Wanderers*, 1917, *Foes*, 1918, *Michael Forth*, 1919, *Sweet Rocket*, 1920, *Silver Cross*, 1922, *1492*, 1922, *Croatan*, 1923, *The Slave Ship*, 1924, *The Great Valley*, 1926, *The Exile*, 1927, *Hunting Shirt*, 1931, *Miss Delicia Allen*, 1933, and *Drury Randall*, 1934. She also wrote a play, *The Goddess of Reason*, 1907, which was produced in New York in February 1909 starring Julia Marlowe; *Pioneers of the Old South*, a volume in the Yale Chronicles of America series, 1918; and several magazine stories. Many of her later books were marked by her growing interest in mysticism, and *Silver Cross* featured some nearly baffling stylistic tricks. Mary Johnston was involved in a number of progressive organizations, including the Equal Suffrage League of Virginia, which she helped Ellen Glasgow to found in 1909, the Consumers' League, the National Municipal League, and the Women's International League for Peace and Freedom. From 1913 she lived on an estate near Warm Springs, Virginia, and she died there on May 9, 1936.

Jones, Amanda Theodosia 1835–1914 poet, editor and inventor

Born on October 19, 1835, in East Bloomfield, New York, Amanda Jones grew up and attended school there and, from 1845, in Black Rock, near Buffalo. She graduated from the normal course at the East Aurora Academy in 1850 and for four years taught school. In 1854 some verses of hers were printed in the Methodist *Ladies' Repository* of Cincinnati, and she devoted herself thereafter to writing. Her work was frequently interrupted by bouts of illness and periods of convalescence and faddist courses of therapy. Her first book, *Ulah, and Other Poems*, appeared in 1861. During the Civil War she contributed a series of patriotic poems to *Frank Leslie's Illustrated Newspaper*, and in 1867 her second book, titled simply *Poems*, was published. By that time she had become a full convert to spiritualism and was convinced that she was a medium. A spirit contact having informed her that she was destined for some great work, she moved to Chicago in 1869 and for some years was associated with various periodicals. She edited the *Universe*, was literary editor of the *Western Rural*, edited the *Bright Side*, a children's magazine, and contributed to the *Interior*, *Scribner's*, the *Century*, the *Outlook*, *Youth's Companion*, and others.

In 1872 Jones began working on an idea that had come to her for a food preserving process. In collaboration with Professor LeRoy C. Cooley of Albany, New York, she developed a process using vacuum and heated fluid, and in June and July 1873 five patents covering their work were granted, two to Cooley, one of which he assigned to her, one to them jointly, and two to her. An attempt to establish the Jones process commercially failed. In 1880 she went to the Pennsylvania oilfields to develop a liquid fuel burner for use in furnaces and boilers and in March of that year was awarded a patent. Again her attempt to commercialize her invention came to naught. For a time she operated a working women's home in Bradford, Pennsylvania. In 1882 she published a collection of poems as *A Prairie Idyl*. Back in Chicago in 1890 she organized the Woman's Canning and Preserving Company to exploit her process, and so far as possible she saw to it that the officers, employees, and stockholders of the company were women. A dispute with other officers in 1893 resulted in her abandoning the business and moving to Junction City, Kansas, where she continued to write and to experiment.

Jones' books included *Flowers and a Weed*, 1899, *Rubáiyát of Solomon and Other Poems*, 1905, *Poems 1854–1906*, 1906, *A Mother of Pioneers*, 1908, and *A Psychic Autobiography*, 1910. She contributed a series of articles on her fuel burner work to *Steam Engineering and Engineer* journals in 1903 and 1904. She was awarded four more patents in 1903–1906 for developments in her canning process and three others in 1904, 1912, and 1914 for valves and other refinements in her burner. She died in Junction City, Kansas, on March 31, 1914.

Jones, Mary Harris 1830–1930 "Mother Jones," labor leader

Born in Cork, Ireland, on May 1, 1830, Mary Harris was brought to America some time after 1835 by her father, who had preceded the rest of the family in emigrating. She grew up and attended school in Toronto, Ontario, and later worked as a schoolteacher in Monroe, Michigan, and Memphis, Tennessee, until, in 1861, she married a certain Jones, a member of the Iron Molders' Union, in Memphis. In 1867 her husband and her four children died in a yellow fever epidemic in Memphis, and four years later she lost all her possessions and her dressmaking business in the Chicago fire. She began to attend meetings of the newly formed Knights of Labor and from that time devoted her life to speaking and organizing in the cause of working people.

For more than half a century Mother Jones appeared wherever there were labor troubles: in Pittsburgh during the great railroad strike in 1877, in Chicago at the time of the Haymarket riot of 1886, in Birmingham in 1894, among the anthracite coal miners of Pennsylvania in 1900–1902, in the Colorado coalfields in 1903–1906, in Idaho in 1906, where she was involved in a copper mine strike, in Colorado again in 1913 and 1914, in New York City in 1915–1916, where she was active in the garment- and streetcar-workers' strikes, and throughout the country in 1919 in the nationwide steel strike of that year. In 1923, at the age of ninety-three, she was still working among striking coal miners in West Virginia.

A passionate organizer, Mother Jones counted among her more spectacular achievements the leading of a march of miners' wives who routed strikebreakers with brooms and mops in the Pennsylvania coalfields in 1902, and the leading of a march of striking child textile workers from Kensington, Pennsylvania, to President Theodore Roosevelt's Long Island home in 1903 to dramatize the case for abolition of child labor. In 1905 she helped found the Industrial Workers of the World. She was often at odds with the leadership of the unions she worked for or with but never lost her simple and undoctrinaire sympathy for the working people. Her several collisions with the law included a conviction by a West Virginia militia military court in 1913 for conspiracy to commit murder. A short time later, under threat of a Senate investigation, the newly elected governor set aside her 20-year sentence. A little old woman in a black bonnet, she was a compelling speaker and a fierce adversary of capitalists and industrialists everywhere. On her hundredth birthday she was honored by a reception at her home in Silver Spring, Maryland, during which she read a congratulatory telegram (one of many) from one of her old enemies, John D. Rockefeller, Jr., and made a fiery speech for the motion-picture cameras. She died in Silver Spring six months later, on November 30, 1930.

Jones, Matilda Sissieretta Joyner 1869–1933 concert opera singer

Born on January 5, 1869, in Portsmouth, Virginia, Sissieretta Joyner grew up there and from about 1876 in Providence, Rhode Island. In her childhood she began singing with a Providence church choir, and for a time she studied at the Providence Academy of Music. In September 1883 she married David R. Jones, from whom she was divorced by 1898. She may have undertaken further studies at the New England Conservatory of Music in 1886 or 1887, but that, like much of her early and late life, is obscure. In 1888 she made her singing debut in New York City, and during the last half of the year she toured the West Indies as a featured artist with the Jubilee Singers of Fisk University. Her rich, powerful soprano voice quickly inspired a newspaper critic to dub her "the Black Patti" (after Adelina Patti, the foremost operatic diva of the day), although she herself disliked the epithet.

Until 1896 Jones sang in concert, opera, and vaudeville halls in solo recitals or with such groups as the Patrick Gilmore band. She appeared at a "Grand African Jubilee" at Madison Square Garden in April 1892, sang for President Benjamin Harrison at the White House in that year, and appeared at the World's Columbian Exposition in Chicago in 1893. Her tours took her to Canada, England, and continental Europe. The demands of audiences and managers forced her to include much spiritual and ballad material in her repertoire, but whenever possible she preferred selections from grand and light opera. From 1896 to 1916 she toured continually with a troupe called, to her distaste, the Black Patti Troubadors, a motley group whose productions included blackface minstrel songs, "coon" songs, acrobats, and comedians. Madame Jones, as she preferred to be known, restricted herself to operatic selections, which over the years she was able to expand into larger excerpts with costumes and scenery. Performing almost exclusively for white audiences who saw in her an oddity, she was nonetheless widely acclaimed the premier African-American singer of her time. After the breakup of the Black Patti Troubadors in 1916 she lived in obscurity until her death in Providence, Rhode Island, on June 24, 1933.

Jones, Sybil 1808–1873 preacher and missionary

Born on February 28, 1808, in Brunswick, Maine (then still part of Massachusetts), Sybil Jones grew up in Augusta. She was reared in the Quaker religion. Her schooling ended with a year at the Friends Boarding School in Providence, Rhode Island, in 1824–1825, after which she taught school until her marriage in June 1833 to Eli Jones, a distant relative and a Quaker preacher. They settled a short time later in Dirigo, Maine. Soon Sybil, who had earlier begun hesitantly to speak in meeting, was accepted as a minister on the strength of her increasingly eloquent and earnest preaching. In 1840, accompanied by her husband, she made a preaching and visiting tour of New Brunswick and Nova Scotia. In 1842 she visited meetings throughout New England, and in 1845 she traveled to all the yearly meetings in Ohio, Indiana, Maryland, and North Carolina.

Observing the plight of the African-American in the South, Jones began to brood upon that problem and eventually became convinced of a call to preach to the former slaves and African natives in Liberia. She and her husband sailed for Monrovia in July 1851 and preached for some months, returning in December. During 1852–1854 they visited meetings in England, Ireland, Norway, Germany, France, and Switzerland. In 1860, after six years at home, Sybil Jones traveled to Indiana meetings and then again journeyed through the South. During the Civil War she visited military hospitals. In April 1867 she and her husband sailed to England, whence with two English Quakers they made their way through southern France and Greece to Syria and Palestine. Their visit was cut short by her ill health, but in 1869 they returned. She helped found the Friends Girls School in Ramallah, Palestine, and made a great impression on both the Moslems and on other missionaries working in the region, notably Theophilus Waldmeir. With her return home from that journey her evangelical missionary work, in which she had been a pioneer and moving spirit among Quakers, came to an end. She died in Dirigo, Maine, on December 4, 1873.

Jordan, Barbara 1936–1996 public official

Born on February 21, 1936, in Houston, Texas, Barbara Charline Jordan was the youngest of three daughters raised by Benjamin and Arlyne Patten Jordan in the then-segregated city of Houston. Though not affluent, her family was close-knit and, as a young person, she was particularly close to her maternal grandfather, a former minister. The only non-church-going member of the family, he encouraged her to think independently and warned against the pitfalls of mediocrity.

She attended Phyllis Wheatley High School in Houston and was an excellent student. After hearing Chicago lawyer Edith Sampson speak, she decided to become an attorney herself. In addition to her studies, she chose to sharpen her oratorical skills. In 1952 she placed first in the state Ushers Oratorical Contest and won a trip to Chicago, where she won the national contest.

After high school she attended Texas Southern University and pursued a degree in government. She became a member of the debate team that tied with Harvard University — one of her proudest college moments. Following graduation, her debate coach persuaded her to attend Boston University Law School.

She later described the transition to Boston University as one of the most difficult of her life: "I was doing sixteen years of remedial work in thinking." When she graduated three years later — one of only two women, both African-Americans from Houston — she passed the Massachusetts Bar. She moved to Tuskegee Institute in Alabama and taught there for one year before returning to Texas and gaining admittance to the bar there. Although she had job offers in Boston, she decided to practice in Texas.

Campaigning for the Kennedy/Johnson ticket in 1960, Jordan developed a block-worker program for the 40 predominantly African-American precincts of Harris County. The astoundingly successful 80% voter turnout propelled her into politics. In 1962 and again in 1964 she was defeated for the Texas House of Representatives, but she did not waver in her commitment to politics. Despite family pressure to marry, she made a permanent decision against it, preferring immersion in the world of politics, public speaking, and public life. In 1965 Harris County was reapportioned, creating the new Eleventh District, comprised entirely of precincts easily won by Jordan in previous elections. Elected in 1966, she went to Austin as the first African-American member of the Texas State Senate since 1883, as well as the first woman ever elected to that legislative body.

Friends and opponents alike attributed her success in Texas politics to her knowledge of the rules of the game. Despite her apparent differences, she went to great lengths to fit in, reasoning that it was the best strategy for effectiveness. She sought advice on committee assignments. She caught Lyndon Johnson's eye and was invited to the White House for a preview of his 1967 civil rights message. Her own legislative work focused on the environment, antidiscrimination clauses in state business contracts, and urban legislation, the last being a political hot potato in a state dominated by rural interests.

She remained in the Texas State Senate until 1972, when she was elected to U.S. House of Representatives. Jordan's assignment to the Judiciary Committee turned out to have dramatic consequences as the Watergate scandal evolved into calls for the impeachment of Richard Nixon. Her nationally televised speech calling for impeachment focused on the constitutional violations committed by the administration and went down in the public record as one of the most memorable and most meticulously reasoned speeches during the impeachment process.

Jordan's reputation in the House was one of effectiveness. In general, she advocated legislative initiatives to improve the lives of minorities, the poor and the disenfranchised. Her agenda items included passage of expanded workers' compensation and strengthening the Voting Rights Act of 1965 to cover Mexican-Americans in the Southwest.

Her oratorical abilities continued to win accolades. In 1976 she delivered a dramatic keynote address to the Democratic National Convention, generating an enthusiastic media response and speculation about Jordan as a possible choice for vice president. In 1978 Jordan decided to retire from Congress and accept a position at the Lyndon B. Johnson School of Public Affairs of the University of Texas at Austin. In 1982 she was appointed to the Johnson Centennial Chair in National Policy. She continued as a faculty member and minority recruiter. She said her decision to leave politics came from the impulse to focus more on the nation as a whole than on serving the constituents of a particular district, "to free my time in such a way that it could be structured by the country's needs as I perceived them."

Barbara Jordan received honorary degrees from many institutions, including Harvard, Princeton and the University of Cincinnati. She was the recipient of the Eleanor Roosevelt Award in 1984. Despite her absence from Washington, she retained an influence in political affairs. In 1991 Jordan was appointed advisor on ethics in government by the newly elected governor of the state of Texas, Ann Richards. In 1992 she reprised her keynote appearance at the Democratic National Convention.

Barbara Jordon died in Austin, Texas on January 17, 1996.

Jordan, Elizabeth Garver 1865–1947 journalist and novelist

Born in Milwaukee on May 9, 1865, Elizabeth Jordan graduated from high school in 1884, and after a course at a business school she was appointed editor of the woman's page of *Peck's Sun* (published by George W. Peck, author of *Peck's Bad Boy*). Later she worked as a secretary and contributed to the *St. Paul Globe* and the *Chicago Tribune*. In 1890 she went to New York City and got a job on Joseph Pulitzer's *World*. Her exclusive interview with the First Lady, Mrs. Benjamin Harrison, at the Harrisons' vacation house at Cape May, New Jersey, won her the status of full-fledged reporter. Her particular knack for interviewing led to a series of Sunday features called "True Stories of the News," human-interest stories that took her to hospitals, jails, slums, asylums, and other scenes of human tragedy or comedy. Among the sensational stories she covered were the Helen Potts murder and the Lizzie Borden trial.

In the meantime Jordan also began writing short stories, many of them based on her own unique fund of experiences, and in 1895 published a successful collection of them as *Tales of the City Room*. In 1897 she was named assistant Sunday editor of the *World*. In 1900 she succeeded Margaret Sangster as editor of *Harper's Bazaar*, a post she held for 13 years. During that time she produced a number of novels and collections of stories under such titles as *Tales of the Cloister*, 1901, *Tales of Destiny*, 1902, *May Iverson, Her Book*, the first of a series featuring that popular heroine, 1904, *Many Kingdoms*, 1908, and *May Iverson Tackles Life*, 1913. Her play *The Lady from Oklahoma* had a brief Broadway run in April 1913.

From 1913, when *Harper's Bazaar* was taken over by William Randolph Hearst, to 1918 Jordan was a literary advisor for Harper & Brothers, to whom she brought such authors as Zona Gale, Eleanor H. Porter, Dorothy Canfield Fisher, and Sinclair Lewis. In 1915 she collaborated on *The Story of a Pioneer*, Anna Howard Shaw's autobiography, and she also organized *The Whole Family*, an innovative novel to which such authors as William James, William Dean Howells, Elizabeth Stuart Phelps Ward, and Henry Van Dyke contributed a chapter each. After a brief stint in 1918 as editorial director for Goldwyn Pictures she turned to writing.

Jordan's own later books included *Lovers' Knots*, 1916, *Wings of Youth*, 1917, *The Girl in the Mirror*, 1919, *The Blue Circle*, 1920, *Red Riding Hood*, 1924, *Black Butterflies*, 1926, *Miss Nobody from Nowhere*, 1927, *The Devil and the Deep Sea*, 1928, *The Night Club Mystery*, 1929, *The Fourflusher*, 1930, *Playboy*, 1931, *Young Mr. X*, 1932, *Daddy and I*, 1934, *The Life of the Party*, 1935, *The Trap*, 1936, *First Port of Call*, 1940, *Faraway Island*, 1941, *Herself*, 1943, *Miss Warren's Son*, 1944, and *The Real Ruth Arnold*, 1945. Her autobiographical *Three Rousing Cheers* appeared in 1938. From 1922 to 1945 she was a regular drama critic for the Catholic weekly *America*. She was also an ardent supporter of the woman suffrage movement and a noted hostess. She died in New York City on February 24, 1947.

Judson, Ann Hasseltine 1789–1826 missionary

Born in Bradford, Massachusetts, on December 22, 1789, Ann (christened Nancy) Hasseltine attended the Bradford Academy and then taught school for several years. In February 1812 she married Adoniram Judson, a young and zealous Congregationalist missionary about to embark for Asia. They sailed together from Salem two weeks later, bound for Calcutta. In accompanying her husband, Ann Judson became the first American woman to enter the field of foreign missions. Shortly after their arrival in June 1812 they both converted to the Baptist doctrine and were baptized by English Baptist missionaries. The break with their Congregational sponsors, the American Board of Commissioners for Foreign Missions, left them without support for a time, and the hostility of British authorities in India, particularly after news of the outbreak of the War of 1812 reached Calcutta, placed them in actual jeopardy. They escaped Calcutta by night, and after a brief stay on the Isle of France (Mauritius) they decided to take their mission to Burma.

They arrived in Rangoon in July 1813. Ann Judson learned Burmese along with her husband, and while he labored to produce his Burmese New Testament and dictionary she assisted him in writing tracts and catechisms and from 1819 held services for Burmese women. Although from 1814 they received support from a Baptist missionary society organized in the United States for that purpose, life remained hard. Ill health compelled Ann Judson to return to America by way of England in 1821, and while recuperating in Baltimore she wrote and published *A Particular Relation of the American Baptist Mission to the Burman Empire*, 1823.

In December 1823 she arrived again in Rangoon and made the journey up the Irrawaddy River to the new capital, Ava, whence her husband had moved the mission. In June 1824, at the outbreak of the first Burmese War with Britain, Adoniram Judson was seized by Burmese authorities and imprisoned. Through his 17 months of imprisonment, first in Ava and later in Oung-pen-la (Aungbinle), during which he was starved and tortured, his wife underwent incredible hardships to stay near, caring for him when permitted to and nursing her infant daughter and an adopted Burmese girl while suffering herself. After his release in November 1825 they returned to Rangoon to recover from their ordeal. Exhausted and prey to a tropical fever, Ann Judson died in Amherst, the British headquarters near Rangoon, on October 24, 1826. Her story was long a favorite subject of poets and novelists.

Judson, Sarah Hall Boardman 1803–1845 missionary

Born on November 4, 1803, in Alstead, New Hampshire, Sarah Hall grew up in Danvers and then Salem, Massachusetts. Responsibilities in the home prevented her from completing her schooling, but she continued her studies on her own and for a while taught school. She published poems from time to time in the *Christian Watchman* and the *American Baptist Magazine*, and a meeting with Ann Hasseltine Judson in 1823 stimulated her interest in foreign missions. One of her poems attracted the notice of George D. Boardman, a seminary student, whom she married in July 1825 after his graduation from Andover. Two weeks later they sailed for Burma. The Anglo-Burmese war compelled them to wait in Calcutta for a year, but in the spring of 1827 they arrived at the British post of Amherst, near Rangoon, where the redoubtable pioneer missionary Adoniram Judson was then stationed. A short time later they moved on to Moulmein and early in 1828 to Tavoy, where they established contact with the Karen people. Sarah Boardman shared in the struggle to establish schools and a church for the Karens, a task made the more difficult by recurrent illnesses, the loss of two of her three children, and an anti-British revolt in mid–1829 that forced them to flee for their lives. George Boardman died in February 1831 and his widow resolved to carry on his work alone. With moral support from Judson she labored for three years to reestablish the schools closed in the revolt and to evangelize among the jungle villages around Tavoy. In April 1834 she and Judson were married. For the next 77 years she worked with him in Moulmein. She made a special study of the Peguan language and translated tracts, the New Testament, and Judson's *Life of Christ* into it. She also compiled a Burmese hymn book and translated the first part of *Pilgrim's Progress* into Burmese. She fell ill shortly after the birth of her eighth child by Judson (of whom five survived to maturity), and in May 1845 she sailed for America to recuperate. She died on September 1, 1845, while her ship was anchored at St. Helena.

Kaahumanu ?–1832 ruler of Hawaii

Born on the island of Maui, probably between 1768 and 1777, Kaahumanu was of distinguished parentage, her mother having been married to the late king of Maui. Early in life she was betrothed to Kamehameha, whom her father had served as counselor. Theirs was a stormy but enduring relationship. She supported him in his efforts to unite the islands of the archipelago under his central authority and shared largely in their governance. From his death in May 1819 until 1823 she occupied the position of kuhina nui, a sort of co-ruler, in the government of Kamehameha II. During that period she exerted her considerable influence to improve the position of women in Hawaiian society. She worked in particular to overcome the taboos placed on women in the islanders' traditional religion and scored a major victory in persuading Kamehameha II to eat publicly with women. She encouraged the Protestant missionaries from New England who began arriving in 1820 and learned to read and write from them.

In 1823 Kamehameha II left the islands; to visit England, and from that time Kaahumanu ruled the islands; from 1824, when Kamehameha II died in England, she ruled as regent for the boy Kamehameha III. In the latter year she anticipated Kamehameha III's later introduction of constitutional government in promulgating what amounted to a code of laws, the first in the islands' history, which included a provision requiring universal literacy. In 1825 she publicly converted to Christianity, taking the baptismal name Elizabeth. She traveled much among the islands, promoting the evangelizing and educational work of the missionaries, until her death in the Manoa Valley of Honolulu on June 5, 1832.

Kael, Pauline 1919– film critic

Born in Petaluma, California, on June 19, 1919, Pauline Kael graduated from the University of California at Berkeley in 1940. For a number of years she made a precarious living with various minor jobs while pursuing interests in playwriting, filmmaking, and literature. She had been an avid fan of the movies since childhood, and in 1953 she published her first piece of film criticism in *City Lights* magazine in San Francisco. Other articles followed in *Partisan Review*, *Moviegoer*, *Kulchur*, and other journals and then appeared regularly in *Film Quarterly*. For several years from 1955 she broadcast film reviews over the radio stations of the Pacifica network, and during that time she also managed a pair of art film cinemas in Berkeley.

Kael's reputation among film buffs and fellow critics for honest, lively, and penetrating criticism led to the publication in 1965 of a collection of her articles in book form under the characteristic title *I Lost It at the Movies*. The book was a best seller and won her assignments from such major general circulation magazines as *Life*, *Holiday*, *Mademoiselle*, and *McCall's*. She was the regular film reviewer for *McCall's* for some months in 1966 and for the *New Republic* in 1967, and in 1968 she joined the *New Yorker*, where her column appeared weekly for six months a year for the next 11 years.

The intelligence and wit that marked Kael's reviews were rendered the more effective by her cool, clearsighted dismissal of both the overblown promotions on the one hand and the pretentious intellectualizing on the other that marked the poles of the world of film. She had, moreover, remarkable insight into the sociological import of the movies — their meaning within contemporary culture, as understood by their audiences. The great success of her subsequent collections of reviews — *Kiss Kiss Bang Bang*, 1968, *Going Steady*, 1970, *Deeper Into Movies*, 1973, which won the National Book Award, and *Reeling*, 1976 — suggested that she was the preeminent American film critic of the day. In *The Citizen Kane Book*, 1971, she published the script of that classic film along with a lengthy introduction and voluminous notes. A popular speaker and television guest, she was widely honored for her work and in 1970 was chairman of the National Society of

Film Critics. In 1979 she took leave of absence from the *New Yorker* to work as the executive consultant on film projects to Paramount Pictures. She returned to the *New Yorker* in 1980 where she remained until 1991. Her later collections of reviews include *When the Lights Go Down*, 1980, *Nights at the Movies*, 1982, *Taking It All In*, 1984, *State of the Art*, 1985, *Hooked*, 1989, and *Movie Love*, 1991.

Kahn, Florence Prag 1866–1948 public official

Born on November 9, 1866, in Salt Lake City, Utah, Florence Prag grew up from 1869 in San Francisco. She graduated from the University of California at Berkeley in 1887. Her ambition to study law was frustrated by the family's finances, and for 12 years she taught high school English and history. In March 1899 she married Julius Kahn, an actor turned politician and at that time the Republican congressman from California's Fourth District. Over the next quarter-century she took a deep interest in his career and in public issues. At his death in December 1924 she decided to seek his congressional seat, and in a special election in February 1925 she won it. Although she chafed somewhat at her distinctly minor committee assignments — of her appointment to the Indian Affairs Committee she commented "The only Indians in my district are in front of cigar stores" — she served patiently.

Winning the regular nomination and election in 1926, Kahn soon laid to rest doubts as to her ability to fill the job, and in 1928 she won assignment to the Committee on Military Affairs, on which her husband had given distinguished service before and during World War I. She later also served on the Appropriations Committee. She was notably successful in securing federal money for her district in the form of numerous military installations and financing for the San Francisco Bay Bridge. Her wit in floor debate made her a gallery favorite, and she was widely accounted among the more effective members of Congress. She served through the 74th Congress, retiring to San Francisco in January 1937 after her defeat in the Democratic landslide of 1936. She died in San Francisco on November 16, 1948.

Kander, Lizzie Black 1858–1940 welfare worker and cookery expert

Born in Milwaukee on May 28, 1858, Lizzie Black graduated from Milwaukee High School in 1878 and in May 1881 married Simon Kander, a businessman and local politician. From the age of twenty she was an active member of the Ladies Relief Sewing Society of Milwaukee, a group that collected and repaired discarded clothing and distributed it among poor immigrant families. She served as president of the society in 1894–1895, and the next year she was chosen president of the newly organized Milwaukee Jewish Mission, whose purpose was to offer vocational and domestic training to children. In 1900 the Mission joined with a similar organization, the Sisterhood of Personal Service, to establish Milwaukee's first social settlement, known simply as "The Settlement," of which Kander became president also. With financial support from the Federated Jewish Charities of Milwaukee, the Settlement offered training in vocational and domestic skills as well as classes in English, American history, and music, established a gymnasium, organized boys' and girls' clubs, and otherwise served as a community center. The cooking classes, in which Kander was personally involved, were especially popular, and to facilitate the distribution of recipes a collection of them was printed in book form in 1901 as *The Settlement Cook Book: The Way to a Man's Heart*.

Advertising space was sold to finance the first edition, but the book proved to have great appeal beyond the cooking classes of the Settlement, and from the second edition it not only paid for itself but began returning profits to the Settlement. Kander continued to collect recipes from friends, teachers, and cooks around the world and to help edit subsequent editions; from 1914 she had sole editorial responsibility. By the late 1970s, when *The Settlement Cook Book*'s subtitle was "Treasured Recipes of Seven Decades," the book had sold more than a million copies. During Kander's presidency the Settlement prospered greatly, and in 1911 it moved into new and larger quarters under a new name, the Abraham Lincoln House. She remained president until 1918. (Abraham Lincoln House became the Jewish Community Center in 1931.) She served also on the Board of School Directors of Milwaukee from 1907 to 1919 and was largely responsible for the creation of a girls' vocational high school. Kander died in Milwaukee on July 24, 1940.

Kanter, Rosabeth Moss 1943– social scientist and writer

Born on March 15, 1943, in Cleveland, Ohio, Rosabeth Moss was the daughter of an attorney and a schoolteacher. In 1963 she married Stuart Alan Kanter, who died in 1969. After graduating from Bryn Mawr with honors in 1964, she went on to do graduate work in sociology at the University of Michigan, where she received her M.A. in 1965 and her Ph.D. in 1967. Her education also included postdoctoral studies at Harvard University from 1975 to 1976.

Kanter began her teaching career as an instructor in sociology at the University of Michigan in 1967. She taught in the Brandeis University sociology department from 1967 to 1977, interrupted by a year at Harvard, 1973–74. She was a professor of sociology at Yale University from 1977 to 1986. In 1986, Kanter was appointed to an endowed chair at the Harvard Business School as Professor of Business Administration.

As an undergraduate, Kanter began pursuing her fascination with "how a complex world is put together," an interest that would shape her career as an academic, business consultant, and prolific writer. While her earliest books were about the way collective life is organized in communes, her concern would eventually turn to how corporations are structured and managed in a changing society.

Men and Women of the Corporation, 1977, was a pioneering look at the ways in which work is organized and performed in large companies. She later noted that it documented the last gasp of a bureaucratic corporate model that was about to be replaced. *A Tale of "O"* continued her analysis of corporate organization, focusing on how corporate culture discriminates against those who do not fit its stereotypes and assumptions. In *The Change Masters*, 1983, she investigated the elements that make some corporations innovate and grow while others suppress initiative and stagnate. It recorded the cases of the first bold attempts to transform the old style of corporate life

When Giants Learn to Dance, 1989, was the result of a wide-ranging five-year study of top American corporations, documenting changing management strategies and practices that, in her view, represent the future of successful businesses in the U.S. She said of this work that it brought together intellectual knowledge gleaned from her academic work at Yale and Harvard and the practical knowledge emerging from her association with Goodmeasure, the Boston-based business consulting firm she co-founded in 1977.

Kanter's other books included *Commitment, Communes and Utopias in Sociological Perspective*, 1972, *Communes: Creating and Managing the Collective Life*, 1973, *Another Voice: Feminist Perspectives on Social Life and Social Science*, (edited with Marcus Millman, 1975), and *Work and Family in the USA: Critical Review and Research and Policy Agenda*, 1977. She contributed also to many texts on sociology, gender roles, and organizational development, and to sociology, education, psychology, and psychiatry journals.

Käsebier, Gertrude Stanton 1852–1934 photographer

Born on May 18, 1852, in Des Moines, Iowa, Gertrude Stanton grew up there, in Leadville, Colorado, and in New York City. In May 1874 she married Eduard Käsebier, a New York businessman. After many years of deferring her interest in art she entered the Pratt Institute in Brooklyn about 1888 and studied painting there until 1893. In that year she traveled to Paris for further study, and she spent several months of each of the next four years there. During that time her interest shifted from painting to photography, which she pursued in Paris and Germany. After a short apprenticeship to a photographer in Brooklyn in 1897, she established her own studio on Fifth Avenue in Manhattan. She quickly attained success as a portrait photographer and soon attracted the attention of other pioneers in the fledgling field of serious photography.

In 1902 Käsebier was a founding member, along with Edward Steichen, Clarence H. White, Alvin Langdon Coburn, and others, of Alfred Stieglitz's Photo-Secession group of young camera artists, and in 1903 her work was featured in the first issue of Stieglitz's influential quarterly journal, *Camera Work*. She also became a member of the somewhat older Linked Ring group in England. Her work continued to appear in *Camera Work* and was featured in other journals, such as *Photo-Era* and *Photographic Art*, in Gustav Stickley's *Craftsman* magazine, and in such general circulation magazines as *McClure's*, *Scribner's*, *Munsey's*, and *Everybody's*. Among her major efforts were series on African-Americans, on Auguste Rodin, and on mothers and children.

Käsebier's exhibition in 1906 at the Little Galleries of the Photo-Secession (later known as the 291 Gallery) firmly established her as a leading professional photographer and photographic artist. She was the first woman to be so recognized. When Stieglitz and other avant-gardists began to discard the aesthetic of the original Photo-Secession, Gertrude Käsebier, Coburn, and White formed in 1916 the Pictorial Photographers of America to continue working in what was becoming an outmoded manner. Among her subjects as a portraitist were many leading artists of the day — Stieglitz himself, John Sloan, George Luks, Gelett Burgess, Robert Henri, Jan Kubelik, Stanford White, and others. Her final exhibition was mounted at the Brooklyn Institute of Arts and Sciences in 1926. She died in New York City on October 13, 1934.

Kassebaum, Nancy Landon 1932– U.S. Senator

Born on July 29, 1932 in Topeka, Kansas, Nancy Landon was the daughter of Alfred M. Landon, the governor of Kansas and the Republican candidate for President in 1936. Through her father's career she became interested in politics at a very early age, though it would be years before she would enter the political arena herself. She grew up in Topeka, attending public schools, and graduated from the University of Kansas with a B.A. in political science in 1954. In 1956 she earned a master's degree in diplomatic history from the University of Michigan. That same year, she married Philip Kassebaum, whom she had met as an undergraduate. She eventually gave birth to four children and for the next 15 to 20 years concentrated on raising her family. While a homemaker, she was also the vice president of Kassebaum Communications, a family-owned business that operated two radio stations. She also worked in state politics, serving on the Kansas Governmental Ethics Commission and Kansas Committee on the Humanities. In 1972 she was elected to the school board in Maize, Kansas, serving until 1975.

After she and Philip Kassebaum legally separated in 1975, her life and career aspirations changed dramatically. She moved to Washington, D.C., and began working for Senator James B. Pearson of Kansas as a caseworker. While her duties in this position were primarily bureaucratic — helping constituents solve conflicts with federal agencies — her interest in the larger scope of legislative politics was piqued. In 1978, when Pearson announced he would not seek reelection, she decided to run for office. Though she was one of nine candidates seeking the Republican nomination, she won the primary and went on to defeat Bill Roy, a former Democratic congressman. When she entered office in 1979 she was the only woman in the Senate.

As a freshman senator, she sat on the Banking, Housing and Urban Affairs Committee, the Budget Committee, the Commerce, Science and Transportation Committee, and the Special Committee on Aging. She later became a member of the prestigious Foreign

Relations Committee as well as the Committee on Labor and Human Resources. While she was often labeled a "Liberal Republican," her stance on various issues, as well as her stubbornness and perseverance in her ideals, made pigeonholing her difficult. She was known for standing her ground, but not before delving deeply into issues and collecting the facts before arriving at her position. Early in her career, she supported the Equal Rights Amendment, but had refused to demand the extension of the deadline for its ratification (thereby forfeiting the support of the Kansas Women's Political Caucus at the time). She took a strong stand for farmers by opposing the grain embargo against the Soviet Union during the presidency of Jimmy Carter and engineered legislation to provide federal aid for a troubled railroad serving grain farmers in Kansas. Later, however, she refused to support farmers's demands for federally guaranteed prices. Always strongly supported by her constituency, she was a senator who tackled subjects other Republican politicians shied away from. She was known for supporting welfare reform, changes in the federal student loan and financial assistance program, and the National Endowment for the Arts. In the 1980s she worked toward ending apartheid in South Africa. In 1994, never a senator who voted simply to appease her party, she voted in support of Democratic President Bill Clinton's crime bill, much to her colleagues dismay. The fact that she was always in touch with the needs and concerns of her constituents, however, was amply attested by her reelection to office time and again.

Kaye, Nora 1920–1987 ballet dancer

Born in New York City in 1920, Nora Koreff began taking dance lessons at the Metropolitan Opera Ballet School at the age of eight. At fifteen she joined the Met's corps de ballet, and in the fall of 1935 she joined George Balanchine's American Ballet company when it became the Met's resident dance troupe. By that time she had altered her surname to Kaye. She also studied under Michel Fokine. For a time in the later 1930s she became interested in Broadway and danced in a number of musical productions, including *Virginia*, 1937, *Great Lady*, 1938, and *Stars in Your Eyes*, 1939. For nine months she was a member of the Radio City Music Hall ballet.

In 1939 Kaye returned to classical dance as an original member of the corps of the Ballet Theatre (later American Ballet Theatre) where she developed rapidly under the instruction of Antony Tudor. Her first substantial character role was in Tudor's *Gala Performance* in February 1941. Other small parts followed in various works, but in April 1942 she burst into the ranks of prima ballerinas with her performance as Hagar in the world premiere of Tudor's *Pillar of Fire*. As Ballet Theatre's leading dramatic ballerina, she subsequently danced major roles in Tudor's *Dark Elegies*, Fokine's *Bluebeard* and *Apollo*, Tudor's *Lilac Garden* and *Dim Lustre*, Massine's *Mademoiselle Angot* and *Romeo and Juliet*, Balanchine's *Waltz Academy* (premiere, October 1944), Nijinska's *Harvest Time*, Kidd's *On Stage!* (premiere, October 1945), Semenoff's *Gift of the Magi* (premiere, October 1945), Taras's *Graziana* (premiere, October 1945), Jerome Robbins's *Facsimile* (premiere, October 1946), Ashton's *Les Patineurs*, and Agnes de Mille's *Fall River Legend*, the leading role of which had been choreographed with her in mind, although illness delayed her dancing it until after the premiere in April 1948. Other productions in which she starred included Fokine's *Petrouchka*, Balanchine's *Theme and Variations*, and Tudor's *Nimbus*.

In February 1951 Kaye left Ballet Theatre for the New York City Ballet, with which she appeared in Robbins's *The Cage* (premiere, June 1951), his *Age of Anxiety*, and Tudor's *La Gloire* (premiere, February 1952). In 1952 she also appeared in Bette Davis's Broadway revue *Two's Company* in choreography by Robbins. From 1954 to 1959 she was again with Ballet Theatre, now called American Ballet Theatre, where she danced in *Winter's Eve*, *Journey*, and *Paean*. She saw herself as a very American ballet dancer, compelled to question the traditions, interpretations, and movement of ballet. She advised younger dancers "not to accept until you understand (at least to your own satisfaction), and not to dance any role, ancient or new, until you do understand." In August 1959 she married choreographer Herbert Ross, with whom the next year she formed the Ballet of Two Worlds, a company that presented Ross's *Angel Head*, *Rashomon Suite*, and *The Dybbuk*. She retired from performing in 1961. In 1964 she was named assistant to the director of the American Ballet Theatre, and she served as the Associate Artistic Director from 1977–1983. She and her husband produced the motion picture *The Turning Point* in 1977, and collaborated again in 1987 on Ross' film *Dancers*. She died at her home in Santa Monica, California, on February 28, 1987.

Keene, Laura 1820?–1873 actor and theatrical producer

Born in London about 1820, Mary Moss, as her name is believed to have been originally, grew up in obscurity. She was married about 1846 to one John Taylor, who later was banished to Australia. She turned to the stage to support herself and made her London debut in *The Lady of Lyons* in October 1851 under the name of Laura Keene. The next year she joined the theatrical company of Madame Vestris, with whom she soon gained a wide reputation in the comedies and extravaganzas produced at the Royal Lyceum Theater in London. In 1852 she traveled to the United States to appear with the New York City company of James W. Wallack. Her American debut at Wallack's Lyceum in September was a great success, but she soon left Wallack to appear under her own management at the Charles Street Theatre in Baltimore in December 1853, and then, in March 1854, in San Francisco, where she was the principal attraction at the Metropolitan Theatre. After an unsuccessful Australian tour with Edwin Booth she returned to San Francisco, where she reigned supreme in the theater and tried her hand also at management and production with the staging of a number of popular and tastefully conceived extravaganzas.

In 1855 Keene returned to New York City to play at the Metropolitan Theatre, which she renamed Laura Keene's Varieties Theatre. The next year she moved to the newly constructed Laura Keene's Theatre. For eight years she was a major theatrical producer, the first woman in the United States to achieve that status, and her company included such eminent figures as Joseph Jefferson, Dion Boucicault, and Edward A. Sothern. One of her greatest successes was the production of *Our American Cousin*, which premiered in America in October 1858 and had a record run in New York City. It was during her appearance in her revival of that play at Ford's Theatre, Washington, D.C., in April 1865 that President Abraham Lincoln was assassinated (and it was she who recognized the assassin as John Wilkes Booth). After giving up her theater in May 1863 her career gradually declined. She continued to act, touring with various companies throughout the country, to write, and to lecture, and in 1869–1870 she attempted a comeback as manager of the Chestnut Street Theatre, Philadelphia, but, lacking fresh material and caught by changing tastes in entertainment, she faded from public notice. In 1872 she helped found and edit *The Fine Arts*, a short-lived magazine. Laura Keene died in Montclair, New Jersey, on November 4, 1873.

Kehew, Mary Morton Kimball 1859–1918 reformer

Born in Boston on September 8, 1859, Mary Kimball was educated privately in her native city and in Europe. In January 1880 she married William B. Kehew, a Boston merchant. In 1886 she joined the nine-year-old Women's Educational and Industrial Union of Boston, an early and somewhat tentative association of philanthropically minded women of position working to alleviate the condition of the growing population of working women in Boston. Becoming a director of the Union in 1890 and succeeding Abby Morton Diaz as president in January 1892, she moved forcefully to make the Union a more organized and effective social tool. To the employment guidance, legal aid, and similar services of the Union were soon added full courses of instruction in dressmaking in 1895, housekeeping in 1897, and salesmanship in 1905. In 1905 a research department was organized to conduct thorough and scientific sociological studies of working and living conditions of Boston women and to help formulate legislative proposals in the areas of hours and wages regulation, factory inspection, and consumer protection. In 1910 an appointment bureau was formed to help place the rapidly growing numbers of college women in suitable employments.

Alongside and complementary to Kehew's work with the Union was her deep involvement in fostering the growth of labor unions among women. In 1892 she invited to Boston Mary Kenney (O'Sullivan) an organizer for the American Federation of Labor from Chicago, to help her form the Union for Industrial Progress, under whose auspices unions were organized among women bookbinders and laundry workers by 1896, tobacco workers in 1899, and needle-trade workers in 1901.

At the organizing convention of the National Women's Trade Union League in Boston in 1903 Kehew was elected first president, with Jane Addams as vice-president. Among her other activities were involvement in the founding in 1902 of Simmons College, which took over some of the educational work of the Educational and Industrial Union, and the founding of the Denison House settlement, of the Public School Association, of the Massachusetts Association for Promoting the Interests of the Blind in 1903 (growing out of a committee within the Union, and in 1906 taken over by the state of Massachusetts), of the Loan and Aid Society for the Blind, of Woolson House, a settlement for blind women, and of *The Outlook for the Blind*, a magazine. She was also active in the Milk and Baby Hygiene Association, the Civil Service Reform Association, the State Commission for Industrial Education, and other groups. Despite her avoidance of personal publicity, her energy and executive ability, together with a talent for working with people of all classes, placed her at the center of reform and progressive activity in Boston. She remained president of the Union until 1913 and was acting president and chairman of the board from 1914 until her death in Boston on February 13, 1918.

Kellas, Eliza 1864–1943 educator

Born in Mooers Forks, New York, on October 4, 1864, Eliza Kellas attended schools in Mooers and Malone and at sixteen became a teacher in the former town. Seven years later she entered the Potsdam Normal School (now the State University of New York College at Potsdam), where on graduating in 1889 she remained as a member of the faculty. In 1891 she was appointed principal of the school of practice at the Plattsburgh Normal School (now State University of New York College at Plattsburgh) and in 1895 she became preceptress of the Normal School. In the later 1890s she studied briefly at the University of Michigan and at the Sorbonne in Paris. She resigned her post in 1901 and from then until 1905 traveled widely as a governess and companion. In the latter year she entered Radcliffe College.

She graduated in 1910 and pursued graduate studies there for a year until, at the recommendation of Agnes Irwin, the lately retired dean of Radcliffe, she was selected for the post of principal of the Emma Willard School (before 1895 the Troy Female Seminary) in Troy, New York. When she entered upon her new duties in February 1911 at the school's brand-new campus, the gift of Margaret Olivia Sage, Kellas faced an institution whose standards had slipped seriously for several decades from its founder's original vision. With energy and determination she set about restoring those high standards of scholarship and deportment. She succeeded also in raising money among alumnae for several more new buildings. Her own character and moral example became a significant force in the lives of the students and helped make the school within a few years one of the leading institutions of its kind in the country. At her suggestion and with funds supplied by Sage, the old campus of the Emma Willard School was reactivated in September 1916 as the Russell Sage College of Practical Arts, devoted to vocational training for young women. Kellas served as president of Russell Sage College from its opening while continuing as principal of the Emma Willard School.

The college grew quickly, granted its first degrees in 1920, and in 1927, at Kellas's urging, severed its legal and financial connections with the preparatory school. A school of nursing was opened in the college in 1923. In 1928 Kellas retired from the presidency of the college, having seen it firmly established, and devoted herself thereafter entirely to the Emma Willard School, of which she retained the principalship until 1942, when she retired. She died in Troy, New York, on April 10, 1943.

Keller, Helen Adams 1880–1968 writer and lecturer

Born on June 27, 1880, near Tuscumbia, Alabama, Helen Keller was afflicted at the age of 19 months with an illness (possibly scarlet fever) that left her blind, deaf, and mute. She was examined by Alexander Graham Bell at the age of six; as a result he sent to her a twenty-year-old teacher, Anne Sullivan (Macy) from the Perkins Institution for the Blind in Boston, which Bell's son-in-law directed. Sullivan, a remarkable teacher, remained with Helen from March 1887 until her death in October 1936.

Helen Keller

Within months Helen had learned to feel objects and associate them with words spelled out by finger signals on her palm, to read sentences by feeling raised words on cardboard, and to make her own sentences by arranging words in a frame. During 1888–1890 she spent winters in Boston at the Perkins Institution learning Braille. Then she began a slow process of learning to speak — feeling the position of the tongue and lips, making sounds, and imitating the lip and tongue motions — under Sarah Fuller of the Horace Mann School for the Deaf in Boston. She also learned to lip-read by placing her fingers on the lips and throat of the speaker while the words were simultaneously spelled out for her. At fourteen she enrolled in the Wright-Humason School for the Deaf in New York City, and at sixteen she entered the Cambridge School for Young Ladies in Massachusetts. She won admission to Radcliffe College in 1900 and graduated cum laude in 1904.

Having developed skills never approached by any person so handicapped, Keller began to write of blindness, a subject then taboo in women's magazines because of the relationship of many cases to venereal disease. The pioneering editor Edward W. Bok accepted her articles for the *Ladies' Home Journal*, and other major magazines — *The Century*, *McClure's*, and the *Atlantic Monthly* — followed suit.

She wrote of her life in several books, including *The Story of My Life*, 1902, *Optimism*, 1903, *The World I Live In*, 1908, *Song of the Stone Wall*, 1910, *Out of the Dark*, 1913, *My Religion*, 1927, *Midstream*, 1929, *We Bereaved*, 1929, *Peace at Eventide*, 1932, *Helen Keller's Journal*, 1938, *Let Us Have Faith*, 1940, *Teacher: Anne Sullivan Macy*, 1955, and *The Open Door*, 1957. In 1913 she began lecturing, primarily on behalf of the American Foundation for the Blind, for which she later established a $2 million endowment fund, and her lecture tours took her several times around the world. Her efforts to improve treatment of the deaf and the blind were influential in removing the handicapped from asylums. She also prompted the organization of commissions for the blind in 30 states by 1937. Awarded the Presidential Medal of Freedom in 1963, she died in Westport, Connecticut, on June 1, 1968, universally acknowledged as one of the great women of the world.

Kelley, Florence 1859–1932 reformer

Born in Philadelphia on September 12, 1859, Florence Molthrop Kelley was frequently ill as a child and was educated mainly at home. She entered Cornell University in 1876 and, after a course of study again delayed by illness, graduated in 1882. She was refused admission to the graduate school of the University of Pennsylvania in the latter year, but after a year spent conducting evening classes for working women in Philadelphia she traveled to Europe, where an encounter with M. Carey Thomas led to her enrolling in the University of Zurich. There she came under the influence of European socialism and made a translation of Friedrich Engels's *The Conditions of the Working-class in England in 1844* that was published in New York in 1887. She returned to the United States in 1886 with her husband, Lazare Wischnewetzky, a Polish-Russian medical student she had married in June 1884. In New York City they were active in the Socialist Labor party, until they were expelled in 1887, and in various reforms. She published a pamphlet on *Our Toiling Children* in 1889.

In 1891 she and her husband separated; they were subsequently divorced and she moved to Chicago and resumed her maiden name. She became a resident at Jane Addams's Hull-House settlement and quickly took her place among the most active and effective workers there. In 1892 she conducted complementary investigations into slum conditions in Chicago (for Carroll D. Wright, federal commissioner of labor) and into sweatshops in the tenements (for the Illinois Bureau of Labor Statistics). Her reports, together with her contributions to *Hull-House Maps and Papers*, 1895, were a vivid picture of terrible working and living conditions and a forceful challenge to take action. The Illinois law of 1893 that limited working hours for women, regulated tenement sweatshops, and prohibited child labor was in large part the direct result of her published findings, and in consequence she was appointed by Governor John Peter Altgeld to the job of chief factory inspector, a post created by the same legislation. The four annual reports compiled by her and her staff of 12 investigators (one of whom was Mary Kenney O'Sullivan) were highly effective in exposing continuing violations of the laws, but the slowness of prosecution led Florence Kelley to enroll in the law school of Northwestern University. She graduated in 1894 and was subsequently admitted to the bar.

In 1897 she was relieved of her position by a new and unsympathetic governor. She remained at Hull House two more years and then in 1899 moved to New York City to become general secretary of the new National Consumers' League, which had grown out of Josephine Shaw Lowell's Consumers' League of New York. She took up residence at Lillian Wald's Henry Street Settlement and set about the work of promoting federal hours-and-wages and child labor legislation and other reforms. Through her and her able assistant Josephine Goldmark, Goldmark's brother-in-law Louis D. Brandeis was brought into the legal fight for industrial reform. She organized some 60 local and state Consumers' Leagues over the years and helped organize and attended international conferences of Consumers' Leagues in Geneva in 1908 and Antwerp in 1913. She traveled and spoke indefatigably, contributed numerous articles to magazines, published *Some Ethical Gains through Legislation*, 1905, and *Modern Industry*, 1913, and edited Edmond Kelly's volume on *Twentieth Century Socialism*, 1910. With Lillian Wald she led in organizing the New York Child Labor Committee in 1902, and two years later she was a founder of the National Child Labor Committee. Her efforts contributed greatly to the creation of a federal Children's Bureau in 1912.

Her early successes in winning passage of minimum-wage legislation in several states and passage of a federal child labor law in 1916 later give way to frustrating reverses before the Supreme Court, reverses that called forth her notable talent for invective.

In addition to her work with the Consumers' League, of which she remained general secretary until her death, Kelley was a founder of the National Association for the Advancement of Colored People in 1909, a member of the Intercollegiate Socialist Society from 1911 and president in 1918–1920, a member of Eugene V. Debs's Socialist Party of America from 1912, a longtime member of the National Conference of Charities and Corrections (later the Conference on Social Work) and for several years vice-president of the National American Woman Suffrage Association. During 1917–1918 she was secretary of the federal board of control of labor standards for army clothing. She died in Philadelphia on February 17, 1932.

Kellogg, Clara Louise 1842–1916 opera singer

Born on July 9, 1842, in Sumterville (now Sumter), South Carolina, Clara Kellogg grew up in Birmingham (now Derby) in her parents' native Connecticut and from about 1855 in New York City. From about fourteen she studied music and singing privately and at the Ashland Seminary and Musical Institute in the Catskill Mountains. In 1860 she made an undistinguished concert and opera tour that ranged as far west as Detroit. She made her New York debut in February 1861 in a production of *Rigoletto* at the New York Academy of Music, and a week later she achieved some success in a Boston production of Donizetti's *Linda di Chamounix*. Despite the dampening effect of the Civil War she managed to build a career in the next few years, singing in *La Sonnambula*, *La Fille du Regiment*, and other operas, in Boston, Chicago, and other cities.

In November 1863 Kellogg sang Marguerite in the New York premiere of Gounod's *Faust* at the Academy of Music. The role was long identified with her, and in it she made her London debut at Her Majesty's Theatre in November 1867. From 1868 to 1873 she toured the major opera houses of America, in 1872 as co-star of an opera company organized by her and the Austrian prima donna Pauline Lucca. During 1873–1876 she headed her own English Opera Company, a pioneering effort at presenting opera in English in which she closely supervised every detail. Thereafter she again toured as a solo artist in concert and opera performances, capped by a successful tour to Russia in 1880–1881. Her career faded thereafter, owing perhaps to the inadequacy of her early training and the consequent early fading of her voice, especially in the upper register. In her prime, however, hers was a soprano of some power and beauty, and she was the first native American prima donna and the first to achieve success in Europe. In November 1887 she married impresario Carl Strakosch (nephew of the better known Max and Maurice Strakosch, the former of whom had been her manager) and shortly thereafter retired. In 1913 she published *Memoirs of an American Prima Donna*. She died in New Hartford, Connecticut, on May 13, 1916.

Kellogg, Louise Phelps 1862–1942 historian

Born in Milwaukee on May 12, 1862, Eva Louise Kellogg, who dropped her first given name, grew up and attended school there and from 1870 in Evanston, Illinois. In 1882 she graduated from Milwaukee Female College (later Milwaukee-Downer College and now part of Lawrence University). After several years of teaching in private schools she entered the University of Wisconsin as a junior in 1895 and graduated in 1897. She remained to pursue graduate studies in American history under Frederick Jackson Turner, and during 1898 1899 she studied at the Sorbonne and the London School of Economics. She received her Ph.D. at Wisconsin in 1901, and her thesis, published as *The American Colonial Charter*, 1903, was awarded the Justin Winsor Prize. Until his death in 1913 she assisted Reuben G. Thwaites of the Wisconsin Historical Society in editing and publishing some 40 volumes of documents from the society's collection.

After 1913 Kellogg worked alone to produce *Frontier Advance on the Upper Ohio*, 1916, *Frontier Retreat on the Upper Ohio*, 1917, and *Early Narratives of the Northwest, 1634–1699*, 1917. In 1923 her two-volume edition of *Charlevoix's Journal of a Voyage to North America* was published by the Caxton Club. She wrote two narrative histories, *The French Régime in Wisconsin and the Northwest*, 1925, and *The British Régime in Wisconsin and the Northwest*, 1935, and edited H. E. Cole's *Stage Coach and Tavern Tales of the Old Northwest*, 1930. She also published numerous articles. In 1930 she became the first woman to be elected president of the Mississippi Valley Historical Association (later the

Organization of American Historians), and she was also a member of numerous other professional and honorary societies, including the British Royal Historical Society. She died in Madison, Wisconsin, on July 11, 1942.

PHILIPPE HALSMAN

Grace Kelly

Kelly, Grace Patricia 1929–1982 actor and princess of Monaco

Born in Philadelphia on November 12, 1929, the daughter of a wealthy contractor and former Olympic oarsman, the sister of another Olympic oarsman, and the niece of playwright George Kelly, Grace Kelly was educated in convent and private schools. She then attended the American Academy of Dramatic Arts in New York City, working as a photographer's model to pay her own tuition. After several seasons of summer stock she made her Broadway debut in November 1949 in August Strindberg's *The Father*. She appeared in a number of television dramas in the early 1950s. Her first film part, a small one, was in *Fourteen Hours*, 1951, but the next year she appeared as Gary Cooper's Quaker wife in *High Noon* and her career began to blossom.

Signed to a seven-year contract by Metro-Goldwyn-Mayer, she was featured in *Mogambo*, 1953, and starred in *Dial M for Murder* and *Rear Window*, both in 1954. In December of that year *The Country Girl*, a screen version of the play by Clifford Odets in which she starred opposite Bing Crosby, was released, and she won an Academy Award for her performance. Other pictures followed, including *To Catch a Thief*, 1955, and *High Society*, 1956, but her movie career was cut short, to the mixed distress and delight of her fans, when on April 18, 1956, she married Prince Rainier III of Monaco and retired from the screen. She remained active in charitable and cultural work and became the mother of three children. (Without an heir, the principality of Monaco would be ceded to France.) She resisted attempts to lure her back into performing, although she lent her narration to one or two documentary films and gave occasional poetry readings, and in 1976 she joined the Board of 20th Century-Fox Film Corporation. She died on September 14, 1982, in Monte Carlo after a car accident.

Kemble, Fanny 1809–1893 actor and diarist

Born in London on November 27, 1809, Frances Anne Kemble was the daughter of the actors Charles Kemble and Maria Theresa De Camp and the niece of the two most distinguished English actors of the later eighteenth century, John Philip Kemble and his sister Sarah Siddons. She was educated mainly in France and early in life showed little interest in the stage. Later, however, in order to save her father from bankruptcy, she made her debut in his company at Covent Garden in London in October 1829, playing Juliet. Her success was instantaneous, and she was able to recoup the family's and indeed the theater's fortunes, at least for a time. She was an even greater success in 1830 in *The Hunchback*, which Sheridan Knowles wrote for her.

In 1832 she came with her father to the United States and enjoyed the same immediate success from her debut in *Fazio* at New York's Park Theatre in September. She subsequently appeared also in *The Hunchback* and as Juliet to her father's Romeo, he being then fifty-seven. She toured for two years, winning acclaim everywhere; her appearance in Washington, D.C., enraptured the likes of Daniel Webster and Chief Justice John Marshall. In June 1834 she married Pierce Butler, a Philadelphian who was also a Georgia planter, and retired from the stage, a profession she had endured rather than pursued. But she was shocked and disturbed to see at first hand the plantation that was the source of her husband's wealth, and as she learned more about the institution of slavery she drew away from her husband (whose family, in turn, disdained her career, her antislavery sentiments, and especially the somewhat satirical journal she published in 1835) from the South, and finally from the United States.

The discovery of Butler's infidelity led to her return to London in 1846. After a year in Rome she reluctantly returned to the stage, playing for a time opposite William Macready.

In 1848 she happily abandoned acting for public readings from Shakespeare, a far more congenial task. In 1849, the year her husband was granted a divorce on grounds of abandonment, she returned to America and established herself in a cottage in Lenox, Massachusetts. (She is credited with having been one of the first to wear, in 1849, the costume later famous as "bloomers.") She continued to give successful readings until 1862, when she returned again to England. She wrote several plays and published a volume of poems in 1844, a volume of *Notes on Some of Shakespeare's Plays* in 1882, and several volumes of reminiscence, including *A Year of Consolation*, 1847, *Record of a Girlhood*, 1878, *Records of Later Life*, 1882, and *Further Records*, 1890, but her most lasting writing was *Journal of a Residence on a Georgian Plantation*, 1863, which was adapted from her diary of 1838–1839 and issued during the Civil War to influence British opinion against slavery. From 1867 to 1877 she lived in Pennsylvania near her daughter, mother of the novelist Owen Wister. She returned to England in 1877 and lived in London until her death there on January 15, 1893.

Kerr, Jean Collins 1923– writer and critic

Born in Scranton, Pennsylvania, in July 1923, Jean Collins graduated from Marywood College in her native city in 1943. In August 1943 she married Walter F. Kerr, then a professor of drama at Catholic University of America, where she had attended summer sessions, and later drama critic for the New York *Herald Tribune* and the *New York Times*. She received an M.F.A. degree from Catholic University in 1945.

In March 1946 their collaborative adaptation of Franz Werfel's novel *The Song of Bernadette* was produced on Broadway. It was a commercial failure but a worthy apprentice piece. Jean Kerr alone wrote *Jenny Kissed Me*, which was produced in December 1948 with only slightly greater success. *Touch and Go*, for which the Kerrs wrote sketches and lyrics, ran for 176 performances from its opening in October 1949, and Jean Kerr's sketches in John Murray Anderson's *Almanac* in 1953–1954 were highly praised. With Eleanor Brooke she wrote *King of Hearts*, a comedy directed by Walter Kerr that opened in April 1954 and ran for 279 performances. In 1957 she published a collection of comic sketches on domestic life, some of them previously printed in magazines, under the title *Please Don't Eat the Daisies*. The book was a best seller and spawned a popular motion picture and later a television series under the same title. *The Snake Has All the Lines*, 1960, was in the same vein as the earlier book. *Mary, Mary* opened on Broadway in March 1961 and enjoyed a huge success, running for 1572 performances before closing in December 1964. Her next play, *Finishing Touches*, ran from February to July 1973. Other books of hers included *Poor Richard*, a play, 1964, *Penny Candy*, 1970, *How I Got To Be Perfect*, a collection of essays, 1978, and *Lunch Hour*, a play, 1980. One of the leading producers of light comic prose, Jean Kerr was the recipient of a number of honors, including, with her husband, the 1971 Laetare Medal from the University of Notre Dame.

King, Billie Jean 1943– tennis player

Born in Long Beach, California, on November 22, 1943, Billie Jean Moffitt was athletically inclined from an early age. At eleven she gave up softball — she was an outstanding shortstop — for tennis, and she worked at it so assiduously that at fourteen she won the Southern California championship in the girls fifteen and under category and advanced to the quarter finals of the national tournament. In 1959 she advanced to the final round of the Eastern grass court championship tournament, and in 1960 she reached the final round of the national girls eighteen and under tournament.

In 1961, with Karen Hantze, she was half of the youngest pair ever to win the Wimbledon women's doubles title. With the same partner she retained the title the next year and also reached the quarter finals in singles competition, defeating top-seeded Margaret Smith along the way. In 1963 she lost the Wimbledon singles final to Smith. For a year or two her game made little progress. She spent several months of 1964 training in Australia. In September 1965, shortly after winning her third doubles title at Wimbledon, she married Larry King, a classmate at Los Angeles State College (now California State College at Los Angeles).

In 1966 King came into her own with victories in singles, doubles, and mixed doubles in the U.S. Lawn Tennis Association's indoor tournament, the South African singles, and the Wimbledon singles. In 1967 she won the U.S. indoor singles and mixed doubles, retained the South African title, retained her Wimbledon singles and won the doubles and mixed doubles titles, won the U.S. women's singles title at Forest Hills without the loss of a single set, and won the U.S. doubles and mixed doubles titles as well. She was the first woman to sweep the U.S. and British singles, doubles, and mixed doubles titles in a single year since 1938.

In 1968, playing as a professional, she won the Australian singles and mixed doubles, the U.S. indoor singles and doubles, and at Wimbledon the doubles and her third consecutive singles. She won no major national tournaments in 1969. In 1970 she won the doubles at Wimbledon and the mixed doubles in the French Open. Her successes in the confused but prospering women's professional tour were capped in 1971 when she became the first woman athlete ever to win $100,000 in a year. In that year she also won the U.S. Open singles and mixed doubles, the U.S. indoor singles, the U.S. clay court singles and doubles, and the Wimbledon doubles and mixed doubles. In 1972 she won the U.S. singles, the French singles and doubles, and the Wimbledon singles and doubles. In 1973 she won the U.S. mixed doubles and swept the singles (in a final against Chris Evert) doubles, and mixed doubles at Wimbledon again.

The highlight of the year, however, was her heavily publicized match in September against Bobby Riggs, a colorful former champion and self-styled "male chauvinist pig," before a record live audience of 30,000 and a world television audience estimated at 60 million. Her victory brought her a $100,000 purse, the largest ever for a tennis match. She was named the top woman athlete of the year for 1973. That year also saw the culmination of her long battle for equal prize money and treatment for women professionals in the major tournaments, a battle that had caused her suspension a number of times.

She won her fifth U.S. singles title in 1974, along with the U.S. doubles, the U.S. indoor singles, and the Wimbledon mixed doubles. In 1975 she won the U.S. indoor doubles and her sixth Wimbledon singles, the latter with a remarkable rally against Chris Evert, for a record-tying total of 19 Wimbledon titles. She won the U.S. mixed doubles in 1976, but from that year she concentrated on playing with the New York Apples of the World Team Tennis tour. She published *Tennis to Win*, 1970, and *Billie Jean*, with Kim Chapin, 1974. She was involved as well in the creation of *WomenSports* magazine in 1974. In July 1979, with Martina Navratilova, she won the doubles final for her record 20th Wimbledon title.

One of the most influential figures in the movement for equality for women athletes, she founded the Women's Tennis Association in 1973, serving as its president from 1973 to 1975, and again from 1980 to 1981. She retired from competitive tennis in 1984 and the same year became the first woman commissioner in professional sports in her position with the World Team Tennis League. She was inducted into the Women's Sports Hall of Fame in 1980, the International Tennis Hall of Fame in 1987, and the National Women's Hall of Fame in 1990. She published a second autobiography, *The Autobiography of Billie Jean King*, with Frank Deford, 1982, and *We Have Come A Long Way, The Story of Women's Tennis*, with Cynthia Starr, 1988.

King, Carol Weiss 1895–1952 lawyer

Born in New York City on August 24, 1895, Carol Weiss was of a wealthy family. She attended Horace Mann School, graduated from Barnard College in 1916, and then entered

New York University Law School. In 1917 she married George C. King, an author. She graduated from law school in 1920, was admitted to the bar, and began her practice from an office in the firm of Hale, Nelles, and Schorr. From the first her interest was in defending the victims of antiradical hysteria whose civil rights had in one way or another been violated. Her involvement particularly in cases turning on immigration law soon made her the preeminent expert in that field. She generally confined herself to research and writing briefs, eschewing courtroom work in favor of better known, often conservative, lawyers.

Of the great many Supreme Court cases in which King was involved, *Bilokumsky v. Tod*, 1923, *Mahler v. Eby*, 1924, *Tisi v. Tod*, 1924, *Vatjauer v. Commissioner of Immigration*, 1927, and others bore on the deportation of aliens and the due process of law therein required; *Powell v. Alabama*, 1932, the first of the "Scottsboro Boys" cases, upheld the right of trial by a fairly chosen jury; *De Jonge v. Oregon*, 1937, and *Herndon v. Lowry*, 1937, reversed convictions of Oregon and Georgia radicals under the "clear and present danger" test; *Bridges v. Wixon*, 1945, and *Bridges v. U.S.* , 1953, defended Harry Bridges, radical president of the International Longshoremen's and Warehousemen's Union, against deportation proceedings; and *Carlson v. Landon*, 1952, and *Zydok v. Butterfield*, 1952, defended against prosecutions brought under the McCarran Internal Security Act. The last case was the only one in which she appeared to argue before the Court. Carol King was active in the International Labor Defense, the National Lawyers Guild, the Joint Anti-Fascist Refugee Committee, and other civil libertarian groups.

In 1932 she founded the *International Juridical Association Bulletin*, which she edited until 1942, when it merged with the *Lawyers Guild Review*. Shortly after her court appearance in *Zydok* she died, on January 22, 1952, in New York City.

Kingston, Maxine Hong 1940– novelist and teacher

Born on October 27, 1940, in Stockton, California, Maxine Hong was the oldest of the six American-born children of Chinese immigrant parents. (Two older children born to her parents in China had died in childhood.) Hong's father, a scholar, had left China in 1924 and immigrated to New York City; unable to find work as a poet or calligrapher, he took a job in a laundry. Hong's mother had remained behind in China, using the money he sent her to attend midwifery training and to establish a successful practice in China, before joining him in the U.S. in 1939.

In Stockton her parents' new laundry became their children's second home and a center for family and community gatherings. As such, it served as a seedbed for the talk-story tradition that surfaced later in Hong Kingston's books. This oral tradition was conducted in Say Yup, the Cantonese dialect Maxine Hong spoke as a child. With no experience speaking English, she remained silent through her first several years of school. But by the time she was nine, she was writing poetry in English, transforming the communal gift for story-telling into a solitary and written activity.

Despite her family's indifference, she continued to work hard at school and eventually built a strong academic record. She attended the University of California at Berkeley as a scholarship student. At first majoring in engineering, she soon declared English literature as her official major. The turbulence and the sense of profound change that was emerging on the Berkeley campus already in the early 1960s suited her. She graduated in 1962 and, unable to make a living writing full-time, obtained a teaching certificate in 1965. While still at Berkeley, she met aspiring actor Earll Kingston. They were married in November 1962 and had a son in 1964. The couple taught at Sunset High School in 1966–67 in Hayward, California, then moved to Hawaii where she held a series of high school and ESL teaching jobs for the next ten years.

In 1976 Kingston published her first book, *Woman Warrior: Memoirs of a Girlhood among Ghosts*. A memoir, it combines myth, family history, folk tales and memories of the pleasures and pain of growing up within two conflicting cultures. The problem of expression is a central concern — the silencing of Chinese women both in China and in the U.S. and the silencing of the Chinese immigrant who must learn, often in the face of ridicule, both a new language and the culture where that language is used. The three central characters are women — Kingston, her mother, and the mythical warrior Fa Mu Lan — and the issue of self-expression is individually resolved for each of the characters.

Woman Warrior was an immediate critical success and became a best-seller. It won the 1976 National Book Critics' Circle Award for nonfiction, and *Time* magazine named it one of the top ten nonfiction books of the decade. The book's success enabled Kingston to begin writing full-time. In 1977 she became visiting professor of English at the University of Hawaii in Honolulu. In 1980 she won a writing fellowship from the National Education Association.

In her second memoir, *China Men*, 1980, Kingston told the story of Chinese immigration, this time through the experiences of the men in her family. Using the narrative techniques of *Woman Warrior*, she related their stories of virtual slave labor, loneliness and discrimination. *China Men* also vividly portrayed the rarely documented violence employed to drive Asian-Americans from their homes and communities, once their physical labor was no longer required to "open" the West coast to settlement by Anglo-Americans.

While her memoirs were of immigrant families, Kingston's work belonged firmly in the tradition of American writing. She argued that her books were an essential component than in her third mass-market book, *Tripmaster Monkey: His Fake Book*, 1989, in which the main character (Whittman Ah Sing, named after Walt Whitman) narrates a peculiarly 20th-century American odyssey; the book combines Eastern and Western literary traditions while emphasizing the Americanness of its characters. Defining "fake" as meaning fictional, Kingston explained that its presence in the title was meant to indicate a move away from her earlier autobiographical and generational accounts. After *Tripmaster Monkey* was published, Chinese critics attacked Kingston for her distortions of Chinese tradition. She responded that her work made no claims to uphold tradition, that it emerged from a "low" rather than "high" Chinese cultural form, with more roots in peasant stories than in traditional Chinese myths. Its "distortions," she said, were part of its heritage, reflecting the impact of an immigrant culture encourntering, and being transformed by, Anglo-American culture.

In addition to her memoirs and novel, Kingston published poems, short stories, and articles. Her collection of twelve prose sketches, *Hawaii One Summer*, was published in a limited edition with original woodblock prints and calligraphy in 1987. In 1980 a Buddhist sect named her a Living Treasure of Hawaii; she was the first Chinese-American to receive that honor. She won the American Book Award for nonfiction for *China Men*, the Asian/Pacific Women's Network Woman of the Year Award and a Guggenheim Fellowship in 1981. In 1983 she won the Hawaii Writer's Award. In the mid–1980s, she and her husband moved to Oakland, California.

Kinzie, Juliette Augusta Magill 1806–1870 pioneer and writer

Born on September 11, 1806, in Middletown, Connecticut, Juliette Magill was a descendant on her mother's side of Roger Wolcott, colonial governor of Connecticut. She was educated at home, in a New Haven boarding school and briefly at Emma Willard's Troy Female Seminary in Troy, New York. In August 1830 she married John H. Kinzie, son of Chicago pioneer John Kinzie and himself Indian agent at Fort Winnebago (now Wisconsin, but then still part of Michigan Territory). They lived at Fort Winnebago until

1834, when they moved to Chicago. In that newly incorporated town Juliette Kinzie quickly became a social and cultural leader.

In 1844 she published anonymously a *Narrative of the Massacre at Chicago*, an account of the 1812 Fort Dearborn massacre that she compiled from Kinzie family records and reminiscences. Her version of the event soon became the standard and accepted one. It was amplified and included in her major written work, *Wau-bun: The "Early Days" in the North-west*, 1856, a combination of travel accounts and personal experiences of her early years at Fort Winnebago, including the Black Hawk War of 1832, together with Native American legends, further early history of Chicago, and particularly the story of John Kinzie. The book, a valuable if imperfectly reliable picture of the period, was a considerable success in its day and has continued to be reprinted. It was largely responsible for fixing the reputation of John Kinzie as a founding father of Chicago. In 1869 Mrs. Kinzie published *Walter Ogilby*, a novel; *Mark Logan, the Bourgeois*, also a novel, appeared posthumously in 1887. She died in Amagansett, New York, on September 15, 1870, as the result of a pharmacist's error.

Kirchwey, Freda 1893–1976 editor and publisher

Born on September 26, 1893, in Lake Placid, New York, Freda Kirchwey was the daughter of a Columbia University Law School professor and dean and later (1915–1916) warden of Sing Sing Prison. She attended the Horace Mann School in New York City, graduated from Barnard College in 1915, and then became a reporter for the *New York Morning Telegraph*. In 1917–1918 she wrote for *Every Week* magazine, and in 1918 she joined the editorial staff of the liberal journal *The Nation*, then 53 years old and under the editorship of Oswald Garrison Villard. She advanced quickly to editor of the international relations section and in 1922 to managing editor. In 1925 she edited a collection of *Nation* articles on *Our Changing Morality*. She succeeded Villard as editor in 1933, and in 1937 she bought the journal.

Under her management and editorship *The Nation* continued to be, with the *New Republic*, a leading national forum and advocate of liberal policies as well as a source of informed comment and criticism on the arts and society. *The Nation* strongly supported the New Deal, opposed isolationism and neutrality in the years preceding World War II, and spoke out against hysteria and repression in the name of anticommunism in the 1940s and 1950s. In 1947 she transferred ownership of the magazine to The Nation Associates, of which she was thereafter president. In 1955 she retired as editor (she was succeeded by Carey McWilliams). In later years she devoted much time to such organizations as the Committee for World Disarmament, the Women's International League for the Rights of Man, and the National Association for the Advancement of Colored People. She died on January 3, 1976, in St. Petersburg, Florida.

Kirkpatrick, Jeane Jordan 1926– political scientist and U.S. ambassador to the United Nations

Born on November 19, 1926 in Duncan, Oklahoma, Jeane Duane Jordan was the daughter of an oil wildcatter who moved his family from small town to small town constantly trying to strike it rich. In 1946 she received her A.A. degree from Stephens College in Columbia, Missouri, and entered Barnard College. She earned an A.B. from Barnard and her master's degree in political science from Columbia University in 1950. After working as a research analyst with the Office of Intelligence Research at the U.S. State Department, she studied at the Institute of Political Science in Paris, France. In 1955 she married Evron M. Kirkpatrick, also a political scientist, with whom she later had three sons. Early in her career she served on a number of Democratic party committees and worked intermittently for the United States Department of Defense, in between raising her sons and traveling extensively with her family. Between 1956 and 1962 she worked as a research associate with the "Communism in Government" project of the Fund for the Republic Organization. In 1967 she joined the faculty of Georgetown University, where she became a full professor of political science in 1973. As an active Democrat, she worked on the campaigns of former Vice President and presidential candidate Hubert Humphrey, including his reelection to the Senate in 1970 and his unsuccessful bid for the presidential nomination in 1972.

During the 1970s she published a number of articles and books, many of which criticized the Democratic party. In a widely read article in *Commentary* in 1979 she sharply criticized President Jimmy Carter's foreign policy. In 1980 she, along with other neo-conservative Democrats, met with Carter and unsuccessfully tried to persuade him to adopt a tougher anti-Soviet policy. Around this time, Republican presidential candidate Ronald Reagan began to take an interest in her views, and during his 1980 campaign he hired her as his foreign policy adviser. After winning the election, Reagan nominated her for U.S. ambassador to the United Nations, a position she held for four years. She was given cabinet rank in the Reagan administration and was also a member of his national security team. During her years as U.N. ambassador she was known for her hard-line anti-communist stance — particularly directed at the Soviet Union — and for her tolerance for non-communist, authoritarian regimes, most notably in Central America.

Heavily criticized for her views and actions, she was constantly under public scrutiny. She was accused of accepting bribes, falsifying tapes that implicated Soviet forces in the shooting down of a Korean passenger jet, and advocating the dismantling of India, all of which she vehemently denied.

In 1985 she resigned from her position and officially joined the Republican party. She returned to teaching at Georgetown University but remained active in politics, serving as chief foreign policy adviser to senate Republicans. She was a frequent public speaker and also became a fellow at the American Enterprise Institute, a conservative think tank. She wrote a column syndicated by The *Los Angeles Times*, as well as both popular and scholarly articles and books. In 1990 she published *The Withering Away of the Totalitarian State*.

Kirkus, Virginia 1893–1980 critic, editor and writer

Born on December 7, 1893, in Meadville, Pennsylvania, Virginia Kirkus grew up in Wilmington, Delaware. She attended private schools and in 1916 graduated from Vassar College. After taking courses at Columbia University Teachers College she taught in a private school in Delaware in 1917–1919. She then held a series of writing and editorial jobs in New York City, and in 1922 she published *Everywoman's Guide to Health and Personal Beauty*. From 1925 to 1932 she headed the children's book department of the publishing firm of Harper Brothers.

In 1933, after a trip to Europe, she launched the Virginia Kirkus Bookshop Service, an entirely original idea in the field of publishing and selling books. Arranging with publishers — only 20 or so at first, but eventually nearly every firm of any size in the industry — to receive advance galley proofs of books, she read them and wrote out brief critical evaluations of their literary merit and probable popular appeal that were then sent out to subscribing bookshops in the form of a bimonthly bulletin. Bookshop managers were thus given an informed and unbiased opinion on which to base their orders and promotions. The scheme was a success from the beginning as Kirkus proved to be right in her evaluations some 85 percent of the time, particularly in identifying "sleepers" — books not likely otherwise to receive their due attention. In addition to her work in preparing her bulletins, including the reading of upwards of 700 books a year, she also wrote *A House for the Week Ends*, on her experiences in remodeling her Redding,

Connecticut, home, 1940, and *First Book of Gardening*, 1956. She was also a trustee and in 1952–1953 president of the Mark Twain Library in Redding.

She retired from the Kirkus Service in 1962. In 1980 the Service, then owned by the *New York Review of Books*, had 4,600 subscribers and reviewed 4,500 books a year. She died on September 10, 1980, in Danbury, Connecticut.

Knight, Margaret E. 1838–1914 inventor

Born on February 14, 1838, in York, Maine, Margaret Knight grew up there and in Manchester, New Hampshire. From an early age she demonstrated a knack for tools and invention, and she was said to have contrived a safety device for controlling shuttles in powered textile looms when she was twelve. In 1868, at which time she was living in Springfield, Massachusetts, she invented an attachment for paper-bag folding machines that allowed them to produce square-bottomed bags. After working to improve her invention in Boston she patented it in 1870. She later moved to Ashland, Massachusetts, and there received patents for a dress and skirt shield in 1883, a clasp for robes in 1884, and a spit in 1885. Later still, in Framingham, Massachusetts, she received six patents over a span of years for machines used in the manufacturing of shoes.

Other inventions of hers included a numbering machine and a window frame and sash, both patented in 1894, and several devices relating to rotary engines, patented between 1902 and 1915. While not the first woman to receive a patent, Margaret Knight was one of the most prolific of women inventors, with about 27 patents to her credit, and unusual in her interest in heavy machinery. She failed to profit much from her work, however. She died in Framingham, Massachusetts, on October 12, 1914, and was called in a local obituary a "woman Edison."

Knight, Sarah Kemble 1666–1727 diarist

Born in Boston on April 19, 1666, Sarah Kemble was the daughter of a merchant and received a good education. Sometime before 1689 she married Richard Knight, of whom little certain is known. She is said to have taken over the family business after her father's death in 1689, and it may have been in that connection that she set out on horseback in October 1704 for New Haven and then New York. Her undertaking such a journey alone, and her successful completion of it, speak volumes for her energy, self-reliance, and courage. She returned to Boston in March, having kept along the way a detailed journal account of her travels and adventures, her food and lodgings, the people she met and their speech and customs.

From about 1706 she was known as Widow Knight as well as Madam Knight. She is said to have been a scrivener in Boston and also, almost certainly without factual basis, to have been a schoolteacher and to have had young Benjamin Franklin for a pupil. About 1714 she followed her married daughter to New London, Connecticut. She prospered over the next several years as a shopkeeper and accumulated property in Norwich and New London. In 1718 she was fined for selling liquor to Native Americans. At her death in New London, Connecticut, on September 12, 1727, she left a sizable estate. Her diary passed into private hands and lay unknown until 1825, when it was published as *The Journal of Madam Knight* by Theodore Dwight, Jr. The graphic and often humorous account of her journey proved to be of enduring interest, and the *Journal* was frequently reprinted thereafter. It has remained a valuable historical source and a unique literary work.

Knox, Rose Markward 1857–1950 businesswoman

Born in Mansfield, Ohio, on November 18, 1857, Rose Markward was educated in public schools. In her early twenties she moved with her family to Gloversville, New York, where she went to work in a glove factory. In February 1883 she married Charles B.

Knox, a salesman, with whom she lived in Gloversville, in New York City, and then in Newark, New Jersey. In 1890 they decided to invest their $5000 savings in a prepared gelatine business to be located in Charles Knox's hometown, Johnstown, New York, where the presence of several tanneries would assure the supply of raw materials. From the first Rose Knox interested herself in both the details of the business and the challenge of expanding the market for gelatine. It was in large part owing to her efforts that gelatine evolved from a delicacy and invalid food into a common household staple. Her booklet of personally tested *Dainty Desserts*, 1896, helped interest women in the product.

On her husband's death in June 1908 Knox ignored the advice of friends and retained control of the business. She discarded many of Charles Knox's peripheral business ventures and his promotional devices — racehorses, balloon ascensions, and others aimed primarily at men — and concentrated on selling gelatine to the American housewife. A second booklet on *Food Economy*, 1917, a newspaper column of recipes and hints called "Mrs. Knox Says," and continued research, half a million dollars worth over the years in her own experimental kitchen and at the Mellon Institute, kept the company growing. A larger plant was opened in 1911, and in 1915 the firm was capitalized at $300,000; ten years later capitalization was increased to $1 million.

In 1916 Knox bought a half-interest in the Kind and Landesmann firm of Camden, New Jersey, from which the Knox firm had been buying gelatine, and in 1930 she became vice-president of the reorganized Kind and Knox Gelatine Company. She built a new plant in Camden to produce flavored gelatine in 1936. Her treatment of employees was notably brisk and fair, and they were remarkably loyal to the firm. The Knox company remained the leading manufacturer and distributor of gelatine, selling 60 percent of its product to home and institutional consumers and 40 percent for industrial (especially photography) and medical use.

She was the first woman member of the American Grocery Manufacturers' Association and became in 1929 its first woman director. As she became more widely known in her later years, she was recognized as one of the nation's outstanding businesswomen. Knox was active in various civic and philanthropic activities in Johnstown. She retired from the presidency of Knox in 1947 in favor of her son James and took the title of chairman of the board. She died in Johnstown, New York, on September 27, 1950.

Kraus-Boelté, Maria 1836–1918 educator

Born on November 8, 1836, in Hagenow in the German grand duchy of Mecklenburg-Schwerin, Maria Boelté was of a prominent family and was privately educated. As a young woman she became interested in the work of Friedrich Froebel in the education of children and spent two years studying his methods under his widow in Hamburg. She then went to London and taught in a kindergarten operated by one of Froebel's pupils, Bertha Rongé. She ran the kindergarten on her own after Rongé's return to Germany and initiated garden activities and nature study among her pupils. Work done by her pupils was displayed at the London International Exhibition in 1862.

In 1867, after a brief period as a student in the South Kensington School of Art, she returned to Hamburg and taught in the Froebel Union training school for kindergarten teachers. Illness prevented her from joining Froebel's training school, but she subsequently opened a kindergarten and training courses in Lübeck. In 1871 she returned to London, and in 1872, at the request of Elizabeth Peabody, she came to the United States. On her arrival in New York in September she established a kindergarten and mothers' classes in a private school.

In 1873 Boelté married John Kraus, a German-born kindergartner who had come to America in 1851 and was at the time attached to the U.S. Bureau of Education; she was known thereafter by the surname Kraus-Boelté. They had corresponded previously, and each had studied the other's work. In the autumn of 1873, John Kraus having resigned his position, they opened the New York Seminary for Kindergartners with a model kindergarten. One of the earliest and, because of Kraus-Boelté's association with Froebel, most authoritative and influential centers of kindergarten work in America, the school trained hundreds of orthodox Froebelian teachers and taught thousands of children. Some time after its opening primary classes were added, but they were discontinued in 1890.

In 1877 the two published *The Kindergarten Guide* in two volumes. After John Kraus's death in 1896 his widow continued to operate the training school. In 1899–1900 she was president of the Kindergarten Department of the National Education Association. Largely at her urging the New York University School of Education offered a summer course in kindergarten education in 1903. Kraus-Boelté taught the course, believed to be the first given under college auspices, and similar ones in 1904 and 1907. She retired in 1913 and died in Atlantic City, New Jersey, on November 1, 1918.

Kreps, Juanita Morris 1921– economist and public official

Born in Lynch, Kentucky, on January 11, 1921, Juanita Morris graduated from Berea College in 1942 and then pursued graduate studies in economics at Duke University, taking her M.A. degree in 1944 and her Ph.D. in 1948. At the same time she was on the faculty of Denison University as an instructor in economics from 1945 and as assistant professor from 1947 to 1950. In August 1944 she married Clifton H. Kreps, also an economist. During 1952–1954 she lectured at Hofstra College (now University) during 1954–1955 she lectured at Queens College, and in 1955 she returned to Duke as assistant professor. She advanced to full professor in 1968 and in 1972 was appointed James B. Duke Professor of Economics. She served also as director of undergraduate studies in economics, as dean of the women's college and assistant provost in 1969–1972, and as vice-president of the university from 1973 to 1977. From 1972 to 1977 she was the first woman to sit on the board of directors of the New York Stock Exchange.

As an economist specializing in labor demographics, she concerned herself in particular with the position of women in the labor force, a changing role whose implications, she pointed out, were often missed or ignored but which would continue to profoundly alter the overall structure of society. Her published works included *Principles of Economics*, with Charles E. Ferguson, 1962, *Automation and Employment*, 1964, *Taxation, Spending, and the National Debt*, 1964, *Lifetime Allocation of Work and Leisure: Essays in the Economy of Aging*, 1971, *Sex in the Marketplace: American Women at Work*, 1971, *Contemporary Labor Economics*, with others, 1974, and *Sex, Age, and Work: the Changing Composition of the Labor Force*, 1975. She also edited *Aid, Trade, and Tariff*, with Clifton H. Kreps, 1953, *Our Natural Resources: Their Development and Use*, 1955, *Employment, Income and Retirement Problems of the Aged*, 1963, *Technology, Manpower, and Retirement*, 1967, and *Women and the American Economy: A Look to the 1980s*, 1976.

Her prominence in her field brought her directorships of several major corporations. In 1976 she was called on by President-elect Jimmy Carter for briefings on various economic issues, and the impression she left was such that in December he nominated her for the post of secretary of commerce. Despite her lack of bureaucratic and governmental experience she was widely endorsed and in January 1977 was confirmed by the Senate and sworn in. She stated in confirmation hearings her conviction that the Department of Commerce ought properly to concern itself not only with the needs of business but with those of labor and the consuming public as well. She resigned from the cabinet in October 1979. From 1985 to 1992 she served as the chairman of the board of overseers of the Teachers Insurance and Annuity Association and the College Retirement Equities Fund.

Krim, Mathilde 1926– medical researcher and health educator

Born on July 9, 1926, in Como, Italy, Mathilde Galland was educated at the University of Geneva, where she received her doctorate in 1953. That same year she entered into a brief marriage with a Bulgarian medical student; following their divorce, she married Arthur B. Krim, chairman of United Artists, in 1958.

She worked on biomedical research projects at the Weizmann Institute of Science at Rehovot, Israel, from 1953 to 1959, and at Cornell Medical College in New York City until 1962. In that year she began working as a researcher at New York's Memorial Sloan-Kettering Cancer Center, where she eventually became head of the interferon laboratory. From 1986 to 1990 she was a research scientist in the Department of Pediatrics at St. Luke's Roosevelt Hospital Center and Columbia University. In 1990 she became adjunct professor of public health and management at Columbia University.

It was while directing Sloan Kettering's interferon laboratory in 1980 that Krim learned about AIDS; from then on she devoted her considerable talents and energies as a researcher, fund-raiser, and public health educator to fight against the disease. In 1983 she used more than $100,000 of family monies to found the AIDS Medical Foundation. She set to work raising additional money, much of it from the Hollywood celebrity circles in which she and her husband Arthur, by then chairman of Orion Pictures, traveled. After merging with a similar organization in 1985, Krim's group became known as the American Foundation for AIDS Research (AmFAR), which as of 1992 had donated more than $43 million to AIDS causes.

The bulk of AmFAR's funds went to research, often supporting short-term financing to allow scientists to pursue ideas that were too new to be able to attract federal money. AmFAR was also instrumental in the development of a network of 45 centers for community-based clinical research trials, which reached out to patients who might not otherwise have participated in research programs. In addition to research, AmFAR was active in education and lobbying efforts, and it played a key role in the passage of the so-called Ryan White Act authorizing health care services for people with AIDS. The organization was also involved in debates on a number of controversial policy issues, including condom distribution in schools and the legal entry of HIV-infected people into the U.S.

As AmFAR's founder and cochair, Krim was involved in AIDS issues on the local, national, and international level. She was an advisor to New York City Mayor David Dinkins on AIDS issues, testifying before the New York City Board of Education in favor of school condom distribution in 1991. At the United Nations's World AIDS Day Conference in 1990, she stressed the responsibility of affluent nations to work with developing countries in fighting the epidemic, sharing "knowledge as well as financial and technical resources."

In a 1992 interview, Krim stressed the need for the U.S. to heed the lessons of the AIDS crisis for our health care system, noting "long before AIDS, we needed a national health insurance system; we needed better, accelerated drug development; we needed nursing homes for people with chronic diseases and hospices for people with terminal diseases. AIDS has made these needs obvious and acute because of all the suffering it causes and the urgency and costs it entails."

Kugler, Anna Sarah 1856–1930 medical missionary

Born in Ardmore, Pennsylvania, on April 19, 1856, Anna Kugler was the daughter of a prominent Lutheran lay leader and public official. She was educated in public and private schools. In 1879 she graduated from the Woman's Medical College of Pennsylvania. After three years as an assistant physician in the State Hospital for the Insane in Norristown, she sailed for India in August 1883 under the sponsorship of the Lutheran

Women's Missionary Society. Although she was sent out as a teacher, the Missionary Society being reluctant to enter the field of medical missionary work, it was as a physician as well that she undertook her work at Guntur Mission in Madras State. As the only woman physician in the state she soon found medical work among the local women filling what time was left over from school and evangelical work.

In 1885 she was at last formally designated a medical missionary and granted a small fund for supplies. In August 1886 she opened the first dispensary among the Telegu people. Money was hard to come by, and it was not until 1893 that a separate dispensary building was erected. A residence for medical missionaries followed in 1895 (only a year after the arrival of the first assistant Kugler was given, a nurse), and a 50-bed hospital in 1898. In the meantime Kugler returned to the United States for additional training in 1889 and to take part in the Lutheran Women's Congress held in conjunction with the World's Columbian Exposition in Chicago in 1893. Later a maternity and surgical building, a children's ward, a nurses' home, and other buildings were added to the medical compound at Guntur. A nurses' training school was established and graduated its first class in 1901. Dr. Kugler also took an active role in the establishment of the Union Mission Tuberculosis Sanitarium in Arogyavarum, where she was for a time physician-in-charge, and of the Medical College for Women in Vellore, which opened in 1917. Her memoir, *Guntur Mission Hospital*, 1928, was written following a serious illness that occasioned her final trip to the United States. She died at Guntur Mission, India, on July 26, 1930.

Kuhn, Maggie 1905–1995 social activist

Born on August 3, 1905, in Buffalo, New York, Margaret E. Kuhn was raised in the North because her parents, who had lived in the South, found racial segregation intolerable. After the family moved to Cleveland, Maggie attended high school and enrolled in the Flora Stone Mather College of Case Western Reserve University in 1922. She majored in English and sociology while also organizing a college chapter of the League of Women Voters.

After graduation, Kuhn began training as a high school teacher, yet chose to take a job with Cleveland's Young Women's Christian Association where she worked for the next eleven years organizing young YWCA women. Kuhn explained how these years had confirmed her radicalism: "So many of our members at the YWCA were women working for rotten-paying clerical or commercial jobs . . . My work with these women as they started to organize and unionize cemented my radicalism."

After resigning from the YWCA in the late 1930s, she began twenty-five years of work with the United Presbyterian Church in New York City, serving as its associate secretary in the office of church and society, as coordinator of programming in the division of church and race, and as an editor of and writer for *Social Progress*, the church magazine. An activist for such social causes as women's rights, medical care, housing, and the elderly, she used her own experience in the church ministry to write *Get Out There and Do Something About Injustice*, 1972, and *Maggie Kuhn on Aging*, 1977, which argued that the church should "launch a massive attack on ageism in all its oppressive and constraining forms." She resented the church's mandatory retirement policy, and, after she was forced to retire in 1970 at the age of 65, she began meeting with other retirees about social issues that concerned them. Opposition to U.S. involvement in the Vietnam War became their first issue, and they became militant activists against the war.

This organization, committed to bridging the gap between young and old people, was at first called the Consultation of Older and Younger Adults for Social Change. "We realized that the young and the old in this society are equally discriminated against." The organization was dubbed the "Gray Panthers" by a television newsman who likened them to the militant Black Panthers, and the name held. The Gray Panthers set up an office in 1971 in a church basement in Philadelphia, from where they launched a crusade to end age discrimination and other social injustices. In 1973 Kuhn's organization merged with Ralph Nader's Retired Professional Action Group and began a study of nursing homes that resulted in *Nursing Homes: A Citizens' Action Guide*, 1977. Speaking on the problems of medical care for the aged, Kuhn charged that "doctors prey on the infirmities of the old." During the Carter Administration, she criticized the welfare reform bill, asserting that "public welfare in this country does not need re-forming; it needs radicalization." Through the group's Media Watch, Kuhn also challenged the generally negative portrayal of the elderly on television. The Gray Panthers went on to call for the elimination of the profit motive from the U.S. health care system. At meeting s of the American Medical Association the group would present position papers as well as stage protests.

The first, general convention of the Gray Panthers in 1975, was attended by delegates from over 30 states; by 1977 when Kuhn convened the second biennial convention, there were about 350 delegates representing about 70 affiliate Gray Panther groups. While recommending legislation that made health care free and available to all people, the groups also adopted a resolution calling for "the right to sexuality at all ages and the right to celebrate and express it."

Kuhn was honored with the Award for Justice and Human Development of the Witherspoon Society, 1974; the Distinguished Service Award in Consumer Advocacy of the American Speech and Hearing Association, 1975; the Freedom Award of the Women's Scholarship Association of Roosevelt University, 1976; the Annual Award of the Philadelphia Society of Clinical Psychologists, 1976; the Peaceseeker Award of the United Presbyterian Peace Fellowship, 1977; the Humanist of the Year Award of the American Humanist Association, 1978; and an honorary doctorate from Swarthmore College, 1978.

Kuhn and the Gray Panthers focused on maintaining Social Security benefits during the 1980s as they fell under attack by the Reagan Administration. In the early 1990s, a campaign for a national health care system was the top priority of the Gray Panthers. Other priorities for the 1990s included federal support for housing, reduced military spending, and a clean and safe environment. Kuhn remained the national convener of the organization that she founded. She died in her Philadelphia home on April 22, 1995.

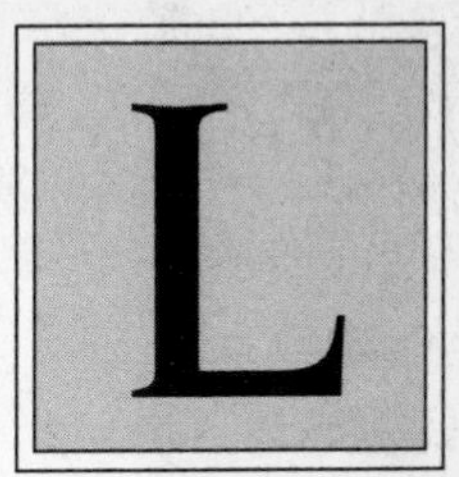

Ladd-Franklin, Christine 1847–1930 logician and psychologist

Born in Windsor, Connecticut, on December 1, 1847, Christine Ladd grew up there, in New York City, and, following the death of her mother in 1860, in Portsmouth, New Hampshire. She attended schools in those places and in 1865, after two years' attendance, graduated first in her class from the Wesleyan Academy in Wilbraham, Massachusetts. She then entered Vassar College. She left after a year, taught school for a year, and then returned for a second year and received her degree in 1869. At Vassar, Maria Mitchell had interested her in astronomy, from which she moved on to physics. For the next nine years she taught science in a succession of secondary schools while continuing on her own the study of mathematics.

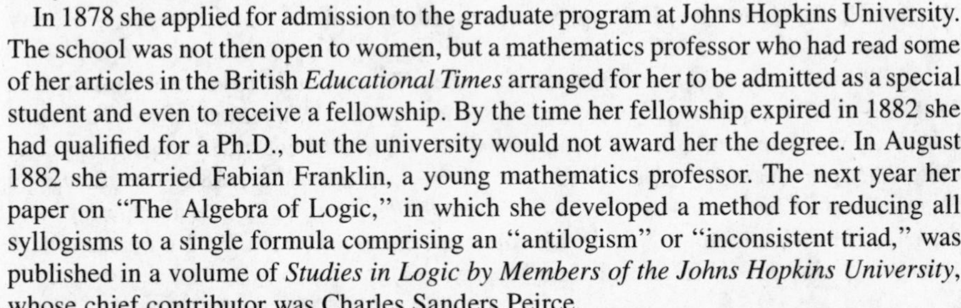

In 1878 she applied for admission to the graduate program at Johns Hopkins University. The school was not then open to women, but a mathematics professor who had read some of her articles in the British *Educational Times* arranged for her to be admitted as a special student and even to receive a fellowship. By the time her fellowship expired in 1882 she had qualified for a Ph.D., but the university would not award her the degree. In August 1882 she married Fabian Franklin, a young mathematics professor. The next year her paper on "The Algebra of Logic," in which she developed a method for reducing all syllogisms to a single formula comprising an "antilogism" or "inconsistent triad," was published in a volume of *Studies in Logic by Members of the Johns Hopkins University*, whose chief contributor was Charles Sanders Peirce.

From about 1886 Ladd-Franklin devoted much time to the study of vision, in particular the problems of binocular vision and color vision. During a year, 1891–1892, in Germany she studied with G. E. Müller at Göttingen and carried on experimental work in the Berlin laboratory of Hermann von Helmholtz. At the International Congress of Psychology in London in 1892 she presented her theory of color vision, which avoided the principal defects of those of her German mentors while introducing a plausible evolutionary mechanism to explain the rise of color perception. The Ladd-Franklin theory was for many years a leading contender in the field, and its originator, always an eager controversialist, warmly promoted it. She later served as associate editor for logic and philosophy of J. M. Baldwin's three-volume *Dictionary of Philosophy and Psychology*, 1901–1905, and from 1904 to 1909 she was a lecturer in psychology and logic at Johns Hopkins. In 1910 she and her husband, who had turned to journalism, moved to New York City. There she lectured on logic and psychology at Columbia University, and from 1914 to 1927 she held formal appointment as a lecturer in psychology at Columbia. She continued to conduct research and published her last paper in 1926, at the age of seventy-nine. In that year Johns Hopkins at last awarded her a Ph.D. Her collected papers appeared as *Colour and Colour Theories* in 1929. She was a frequent speaker at scientific congresses and an effective advocate of greater academic opportunities for women. She died in New York City on March 5, 1930.

La Flesche, Susette 1854–1903 Native American leader

Born in 1854 in a village of the Omaha tribe near present-day Bellevue, Nebraska, Susette La Flesche was the daughter of Iron Eye (Joseph La Flesche), the half-French chief of the Omahas. Her mother was the daughter of a Native American woman and a U.S. army surgeon. She attended the reservation school and the Elizabeth Institute in New Jersey, a private seminary from which she graduated in 1873. She then returned to the Omaha reservation as a teacher. In 1877 the federal government mistakenly assigned to the Sioux the traditional homeland of the Ponca Indians in the region of the Nebraska-Dakota border. The Poncas were then forcibly removed to the unfamiliar Indian Territory.

Within a couple of years a third of the Poncas sickened and died, and early in 1879 the Ponca chief, Standing Bear, led a band of 34 followers off the reservation and back to

Nebraska. Military authorities captured the group and held them at Fort Omaha pending their return south. In April a habeas corpus hearing brought about at the instigation of Thomas H. Tibbles of the *Omaha Herald* resulted in the release of the Poncas and the establishment of a legal precedent in recognizing Native Americans as persons before the law. Tibbles then arranged a lecture tour of the East with Standing Bear, Susette La Flesche as interpreter, and her younger brother Francis La Flesche (later an ethnologist and protégé of Alice C. Fletcher). Susette La Flesche used her Indian name, Inshta Theumba or Bright Eyes, on the tour, and with her natural beauty and her native costume she made a deep impression on eastern audiences. The sympathy thus aroused in influential circles, led by such as Helen Hunt Jackson, Edward Everett Hale, Alice Fletcher, Wendell Phillips, and Mary L. Bonney, eventuated in the passage of the Dawes Severalty Act in 1887.

In July 1881 Susette La Flesche married Tibbles. She continued to lecture regularly and in 1886–1887 toured England, where she attracted much attention. She also began contributing stories and articles to *St. Nicholas* and other magazines and newspapers, edited the anonymous *Ploughed Under, The Story of an Indian Chief*, 1881, and illustrated Fannie Reed Giffen's *Oo-Mah-Ha Ta-Wa-Tha (Omaha City)*, 1898. She and her husband later lived in Washington, D.C., in Lincoln, Nebraska, and from 1902 on a farm near Bancroft, Nebraska, where she died on May 26, 1903.

Lamb, Martha Joanna Reade Nash 1826–1893 writer, editor and historian

Born in Plainfield, Massachusetts, on August 13, 1826, Martha Nash attended schools in Goshen, Easthampton, and Northampton, Massachusetts. She taught school for a few years in New Jersey and Ohio, and in September 1852 she married Charles A. Lamb, with whom she moved in 1857 to Chicago. There she was associated with Jane Hoge in the founding of the Home for the Friendless and the Half-Orphan Society and with Hoge and Mary A. Livermore in the Chicago Sanitary Fair in 1863. In 1866, probably having divorced her husband, she moved to New York City.

Turning to literary work to support herself, she produced eight volumes of children's stories in 1869 and 1870, *Spicy*, a novel, in 1873, and a number of articles and stories published in periodicals. In 1877 and 1881 appeared the two volumes of her *History of the City of New York: Its Origin, Rise, and Progress*, which far surpassed Mary L. Booth's pioneering history of 1859 in its extensive and imaginative use of documentary sources. Other books of hers included *The Homes of America*, 1879, several Christmas annuals such as *The Christmas Owl* and *The Christmas Basket*, and *Historical Sketch of New York for the Tenth Census*, 1883.

In May 1883 Lamb bought the six-year-old and financially shaky *Magazine of American History*, of which she was editor for the rest of her life. Under her guidance the journal became an important and successful one. She published historical documents, reviews, and scholarly articles, and herself contributed more than 50 signed articles and uncounted unsigned ones. From her own contributions to the magazine developed such books as *Wall Street in History*, 1883, and *Unpublished Washington Portraits*, 1888.

She was a member of more than a score of historical and patriotic societies and was widely honored for her work; she was twice invited to the White House, in 1886 by President Grover Cleveland and in 1889 by President Benjamin Harrison. She died in New York City on January 2, 1893. The *Magazine of American History* was sold by her heirs and ceased publication eight months later.

Landes, Bertha Ethel Knight 1868–1943 clubwoman and public official

Born in Ware, Massachusetts, on October 19, 1868, Bertha Knight grew up from 1873 in Worcester, Massachusetts. She was a younger sister of Admiral Austin M. Knight. After attending public and private schools she entered Indiana University and graduated in 1891. She then taught high school in Worcester until her marriage in January 1894 to Harry Landes, with whom she moved that year to Rockland, Maine, and the next to Seattle, Washington. In Seattle she became active in civic and women's club activities. She was deeply involved in organizing Red Cross work during World War I and was a member of the Minute Women of Washington, a wartime speakers bureau. She served as president of the Woman's Century Club of Seattle in 1918–1920 and of the Seattle City Federation of Women's Clubs in 1920–1922. In 1922 she was elected by a large vote to the Seattle city council. In the same year she organized the Women's City Club.

In 1924 she was reelected to the city council, which subsequently chose her as its president. When Mayor Edwin J. Brown left Seattle to attend the 1924 Democratic National Convention in New York City, Landes became acting mayor. She promptly opened a vigorous campaign against the vice and gambling that had given the city its "wide open" reputation. Her campaign included relieving the police chief of his job. Mayor Brown reinstated the chief on his return, but lines were drawn for the next city election. In March 1926 Landes defeated Brown and became the first woman to serve as mayor of a major American city. Her administration was a measured success, but her higher plans for eliminating the patronage system, instituting a city manager government for a unified city and county, expanding the public park system, and ending the traditionally open vice were largely frustrated. In 1928 she was defeated for reelection. In later years she served as president of the Washington State League of Women Voters and in 1930–1932 of the American Federation of Soroptimist Clubs. She died in Ann Arbor, Michigan, on November 29, 1943.

Lane, Gertrude Battles 1874–1941 editor

Born on December 21, 1874, in Saco, Maine, Gertrude Lane attended public schools and the private Thornton Academy in her native town, graduating from the latter in 1892. She then traveled to Boston, where she worked as a private tutor for a year. After taking a stenographic course she secured an editorial position with the American Biographical Dictionary Company. During her seven years in that job she also studied English at Simmons College and contributed to the *Boston Beacon*. In 1903 she moved to New York City and joined the staff of the *Woman's Home Companion*. Her manifest editorial talents enabled her to advance rapidly: she became managing editor of the magazine in 1909 and editor in chief in 1912.

Backed by the resources of the Crowell Publishing Company, which had bought the *Woman's Home Companion* shortly before she joined it, Gertrude Lane systematically built it into a leading publication in its field. Although she was less innovative than Edward Bok of the *Ladies' Home Journal*, whose lead she followed in some respects, she had a firm notion of the sort of magazine the mothers and homemakers of America needed. Practical advice in home decorating, food preparation, fashion, family health, and related topics was presented in the most up-to-date and appealing form. The "Better Babies Bureau" was a particularly successful department of the magazine. From 1935 she relied much on a unique nationwide network of 1500 unpaid reader-editors, whose comments and answers to detailed questionnaires provided invaluable insights into the needs and preferences of the reader-consumer. She had a keen eye for the sort of fiction that would attract her readers and paid high prices for work from Kathleen Norris, Ellen Glasgow, Willa Cather, Edna Ferber, Pearl Buck, Booth Tarkington, Sinclair Lewis, and others. Other contributors included four presidents — Taft, Wilson, Coolidge, and Hoover — and during the 1930s Eleanor Roosevelt, who had a regular page. Lane was shrewd in the equally essential task of promotion and made the *Companion* page a much sought commodity among advertisers.

By 1937 the *Woman's Home Companion* was the leading woman's magazine in the country, and by 1941, after 29 years of Lane's editorship, it was the third largest of all American magazines, with a circulation of over 3.6 million and advertising revenues of over $5.9 million. From 1929 she was a vice-president of Crowell Publishing. In addition to her editorial work she served in the Food Administration under Herbert Hoover during World War I and helped plan the 1930–1931 White House Conference on Child Health and Protection. After several years of declining health she died in New York City on September 25, 1941.

Laney, Lucy Craft 1854–1933 educator

Born in Macon, Georgia, on April 13, 1854, Lucy Laney was the daughter of free black parents. She attended the private Lewis High School (later Ballard Normal School) in Macon and in 1873 graduated from Atlanta University. For twelve years she taught in public schools in Macon, Milledgeville, Augusta, and Savannah, Georgia. In January 1886, with a state charter and encouragement from the Presbyterian Board of Missions for Freedmen, she opened a private school in an Augusta church. Within two years the enrollment of the school increased from 5 to 234, and it continued to grow through providing a solid academic education to students whose other options were limited to vocational training or the few poor public schools for African-Americans. Finances were a perennial problem. The church provided no support, and Lucy Laney was obliged to spend much time seeking out individual benefactors. A large gift early in the school's history from Francina E. H. Haines led to the school's being named the Haines Normal and Industrial Institute, and other gifts over the years made possible the erection of several brick buildings on a four-acre campus.

The school was able to attract outstanding students and teachers; among the latter, in 1896–1897, was Mary McLeod Bethune.

By 1917 the school had a faculty of more than 30 and a student body of some 900. It pioneered in kindergarten education in Augusta and opened in the 1890s a nurses' training department that became eventually the school of nursing at University Hospital. In its later years the lower grades were dropped, and Haines Institute provided a four-year high school course and a year of college-level instruction. An austere, strict, and widely admired educator, Lucy Laney continued to direct the activities of the school until her death in Augusta, Georgia, on October 23, 1933. Haines Institute closed in 1949.

Lange, Dorothea 1895–1965 photographer

Born in Hoboken, New Jersey, in 1895, Dorothea Lange studied at the New York Training School for Teachers and then, pursuing an early interest in photography, with photographer Clarence White, a member of the Photo-Secession group, at Columbia University. She opened a portrait studio in San Francisco in 1916, and her reputation as an innovator grew rapidly. In the 1930s she was selected by the state of California and later by the federal Farm Security Administration to record the migration of farm people from the Dust Bowl of the Great Plains region, especially Oklahoma. She lived for some time with the migratory workers — the "Okies" — and the undertaking resulted, with the help of her husband, Paul S. Taylor, in *An American Exodus: A Record of Human Erosion*, 1939.

Lange's first exhibition was held in 1934, and thereafter her skill as a documentary photographer was firmly established. Her most famous portrait, "Migrant Mother, Nipomo, California," 1936, which hangs in the Library of Congress, was selected by a University of Missouri panel in 1960 as one of the 50 best photographs of the preceding half-century. In 1942 she gave up a Guggenheim fellowship to make a photographic record of the Japanese internment on the West Coast. Later she made a number of photo-essay contributions to *Life* magazine. She died on October 11, 1965, in San Francisco. She was honored the next year by a retrospective show at the Museum of Modern Art in New York City.

Langer, Susanne Knauth 1895–1985 philosopher

Born in New York City on December 20, 1895, Susanne Katherina Knauth graduated from Radcliffe College in 1920 and, after graduate study at Harvard and at the University of Vienna, received her M.A. from Radcliffe in 1924 and her Ph.D. in 1926. She joined the Radcliffe faculty the next year as a tutor in philosophy and remained until 1942, the year of her divorce from the historian William L. Langer, whom she had married in September 1921. She was an assistant professor of philosophy at the University of Delaware in 1943 and from 1945 to 1950 was a lecturer in philosophy at Columbia. During the next few years she was a visiting professor at a number of institutions, and she joined the faculty of Connecticut College in 1954, remaining there until 1962, when she became professor emeritus and resident research scholar.

Over the years Langer published a series of important works in philosophy that led to her being considered among the leading American philosophers of the twentieth century. The first, *The Practice of Philosophy*, 1930, was followed by *An Introduction to Symbolic Logic*, 1937, and in 1942 by *Philosophy in a New Key: A Study in the Symbolism of Reason, Rite, and Art*, which reached its third edition in 1957. In that book, soon considered a classic, she applied some of the ideas of Ernst Cassirer to various art forms, especially music, and suggested that they employ their own characteristic non-discursive symbolic languages capable of expressing and conveying non-rational meanings, such as emotional states, and as such are as communicative as conventional language. *Feeling and Form*, 1953, extended the analysis. *Problems of Art* appeared in 1957, *Philosophical Sketches* in 1962, and *Mind: An Essay on Human Feeling*, three volumes, 1967–1982. She also edited *Reflections on Art: A Source Book of Writings by Artists, Critics, and Philosophers*, 1958. She died on July 17, 1985, at her home in Old Lyme, Connecticut.

Larcom, Lucy 1824–1893 poet, educator, and editor

Born on May 5, 1824, in Beverly, Massachusetts, Lucy Larcom grew up there and from 1835, after the death of her sea captain father, in Lowell. Before long she had finished her schooling and followed her older sisters into the mills. From about 1840 she was a frequent contributor of verse to the *Operatives Magazine* and the better known *Lowell Offering*. In 1846 she made her way to Illinois, where for three years she taught school in Looking Glass Prairie (approximately the site of present-day Highland) and from 1849 to 1852 attended Monticello Seminary in Godfrey. On her graduation she returned to her native town.

In 1854 she published her first book, *Similitudes from Ocean and Prairie*, a series of prose poems. Also in 1854 her poem "Call to Kansas" won a prize offered by the New England Emigrant Aid Company. *Ships in the Mist* appeared in 1859 and *The Sunbeam and Other Stories* in 1860. From 1854 to 1862 she taught at Wheaton Seminary (later College) in Norton, Massachusetts, where she contributed several innovative ideas on courses and methods.

After 1862 she lived mainly in Beverly and Boston and devoted herself largely to literary work. She was an editor of *Our Young Folks* magazine from 1865 to 1873, and in 1869 she published a volume of *Poems*. Her verses, mainly conventional in language and marked by sentiment, piety, and effusions on nature, became widely popular. They were published in *St. Nicholas*, *Youth's Companion*, *Atlantic Monthly*, and other periodicals and collected in *Childhood Songs*, 1873, *Wild Roses of Cape Ann, and Other Poems*, 1881, and in a "Household Edition" in 1884. *An Idyl of Work*, 1875, was a blank verse narrative of mill life; other volumes included the autobiographical and still valuable *A New England Girlhood*, 1889, *Easter Gleams*, 1890, *As It Is In Heaven*, 1891, *The Unseen Friend*, 1892, and *At the Beautiful Gate and Other Songs of Faith*, 1892. She assisted John Greenleaf Whittier, a friend since her Lowell days, in editing the anthologies *Child Life*,

1871, and *Songs of Three Centuries*, 1883. Lucy Larcom died in Boston on April 17, 1893.

Lathrop, Julia Clifford 1858–1932 social worker and reformer

Born in Rockford, Illinois, on June 29, 1858, Julia Lathrop attended Rockford Seminary (later College) for a year and then entered Vassar College, from which she graduated in 1880. Over the next ten years she worked as secretary to her father (a lawyer who had just served a term in Congress), studied some law, and interested herself in various reform movements. In 1890 she moved to Chicago and joined Jane Addams at the newly established Hull-House settlement. Her first opportunity to undertake the sort of arduous, detailed, and passionately devoted work that characterized her career came in July 1893, when, at Governor John P. Altgeld's appointment, she took a place on the Illinois Board of Charities. She immediately began a personal inspection of all 102 county almshouses and farms in the state. She interrupted that work during the winter of 1893–1894 to make an inspection of the county charity institutions in Cook County. Her stark descriptions of the Cook County infirmary, asylum, and other institutions were printed as a chapter in *Hull-House Maps and Papers*, 1895.

In 1898 and again in 1900 she traveled to Europe to study modern methods of staffing and organizing charity institutions. Her statewide inspections were reflected in *Suggestions for Visitors to County Poorhouses and to Other Public Charitable Institutions*, 1905. She was particularly disturbed by the treatment of the mentally ill, who were often thrown in with the physically ill and with no provision for separating the young and the old. From that time she was a strong advocate of extramural care for mental patients, and later, in 1909, she became a charter member of Clifford W. Beers's National Committee for Mental Hygiene. In 1901 she resigned from the Illinois Board of Charities in protest against the low quality of the staffs of most of the institutions under its purview. She served again on the board from 1905 until her plan for its reorganization was adopted in 1909.

Lathrop's interest in the problem of finding trained personnel to staff public institutions led her to join Graham Taylor in organizing the Chicago Institute of Social Science in 1903–1904. She lectured regularly at the school, which shortly was renamed the Chicago School of Civics and Philanthropy, and in 1907, assisted by Sophonisba Breckinridge, she established its research department, of which she served for a year as director. She continued a trustee of the school until it became the School of Social Service Administration of the University of Chicago in 1920. She was active in other fields as well: in 1899 she joined Lucy Flower in the campaign that secured the creation of the world's first juvenile court system in Cook County, and she headed the Juvenile Court Committee organized to raise funds for the salaries of probation officers. In 1908 she joined Sophonisba Breckinridge and Grace Abbott in forming the Immigrants' Protective League.

In 1912 President William Howard Taft appointed Julia Lathrop to head the newly created federal Children's Bureau of the Department of Commerce and Labor. She was the first woman to head a statutory federal bureau at the appointment of the president with consent of the Senate. With a limited budget and staff she first undertook a study of infant mortality and developed a plan for uniform birth registration. Subsequent studies by the bureau centered on child labor, mothers' pensions, illegitimacy, juvenile delinquency, nutrition, and the mentally retarded. Following passage of the Keating-Owen Child Labor Act in 1916 a Child Labor Division was created within the bureau to enforce it, and Lathrop brought in her old associate Grace Abbott to direct the division. (The law was declared unconstitutional in 1918, as a second one of 1919 was in 1922). During World War I the bureau took on added responsibilities for children of servicemen and of working mothers and other matters. During 1918–1919 she also served as president of the National Conference of Social Work. In May 1919 a national conference on child welfare highlighted a "Children's Year" declared by the Children's Bureau.

Lathrop also campaigned hard for the Sheppard-Towner Act, offering federal funds to states for programs of maternity and infant care, which was passed shortly after her resignation for reasons of health in 1921. (She was succeeded by Grace Abbott.) From 1922 she lived in Rockford, Illinois. In that year she was elected president of the Illinois League of Women Voters, and in the same year she was appointed to a presidential commission investigating conditions at the immigration station at Ellis Island, New York. She contributed articles to various periodicals and a chapter to *The Child, the Clinic, and the Court*, 1925. From 1925 to 1931 she served as an assessor for the Child Welfare Committee of the League of Nations. She died in Rockford, Illinois, on April 15, 1932.

Lathrop, Mother Mary Alphonsa 1851–1926 writer and religious

Born in Lenox, Massachusetts, on May 20, 1851, Rose Hawthorne was the youngest child of Nathaniel Hawthorne. In her childhood the family traveled much in Europe; when in America they lived mainly in Concord, Massachusetts. Rose attended various schools and was also educated by tutors. In 1868 she accompanied her widowed mother to Dresden, Germany, and in 1870 to London, where she took some courses in art. In September 1871 she married George P. Lathrop, with whom she returned to Boston. There and from about 1881 in New York City, while her husband worked as a journalist and editor, she published a number of stories and sketches in the *Atlantic Monthly*, *St. Nicholas*, *Harper's*, *Appleton's*, and other periodicals. In 1888 she published a volume of poems, *Along the Shore*, and in 1894 she and her husband, converts to the Catholic faith three years earlier, published *A Story of Courage* on the founding of the Visitation Order in Georgetown, D.C. Her series of articles on her father for the *Atlantic Monthly* was later published in book form as *Memories of Hawthorne*, 1897.

In 1895 she and her husband were separated. The next year, after a period of retreat and in response to a variety of causes, she decided to devote her life to the care of persons suffering incurable cancer. She had had occasion to see the sort of care available in public institutions, and she resolved to provide comfort and attention to those unable to afford private hospitalization. After a three-month nursing course at the New York Cancer Hospital she established herself in rooms in the Lower East Side tenement district. She moved to larger quarters in 1897, and in 1898 she and her first associate, Alice Huber, organized themselves as the Servants of Relief for Incurable Cancer.

In September 1899 they became Sister Mary Alphonsa and Sister Mary Rose, lay sisters of the Dominican third order, and in December 1900 they took the habit and their first vows. The small community became the Dominican Congregation of St. Rose of Lima, and Sister Alphonsa became Mother Alphonsa. From 1899 the community operated the 15-bed St. Rose's Free Home in New York City, and in 1901 it acquired the 40-bed Rosary Hill Home in Sherman Park (later Hawthorne), New York. In addition to her work with patients Mother Alphonsa also devoted much time to writing, the proceeds all going to the order. She also founded a magazine, *Christ's Poor*, in 1901. She made her final vows in 1909. She continued her work without interruption until her death at Rosary Hill on July 9, 1926. She was succeeded by Sister Mary Rose as superior of the order, which continued to grow.

Latimer, Mary Elizabeth Wormeley 1822–1904 historian and translator

Born in London on July 26, 1822, Mary Wormeley was the daughter of American-born parents. Her father was a naturalized British subject and an admiral in the Royal navy. Her education was acquired haphazardly during the family's constant travels in Europe, and she early learned to mix easily with the socially prominent, making her debut at the court of Louis Philippe. In the mid–1840s the family returned to the United States and lived in Boston and Newport, Rhode Island. In 1852 she published her first book, a novel entitled *Amabel*. Her second, *Our Cousin Veronica*, appeared in 1856, in which year she married Randolph B. Latimer of Baltimore. Her writing career was suspended for 20 years in favor of home and family, but in 1876 she resumed literary work. Her stories were published in various magazines but not collected.

Latimer's books included *France in the Nineteenth Century*, 1892, *Russia in the Nineteenth Century*, 1893, *Turkey in the Nineteenth Century*, 1893, *England in the Nineteenth Century*, 1894, *Italy in the Nineteenth Century and the Making of Austro-Hungary and Germany*, 1896, *My Scrap Book of the French Revolution*, 1898, *Judea from Cyrus to Titus; 537 B.C.–70 A.D.*, 1899, and *The Last Years of the Nineteenth Century*, 1900. Lively and well researched, her histories were widely popular. She also produced a number of translations, including Ernest Renan's *History of the People of Israel*, with J. H. Allen, 1888–1896, Louis Ulbach's *The Steel Hammer* and *For Fifteen Years*, both 1888, George Sand's *Nanon*, 1890, and J. C. L. de Sismondi's *The Italian Republics*, 1901, *The Love Letters of Victor Hugo, 1820–22*, 1901, and *Talks of Napoleon at St. Helena with General Baron Gourgaud*, 1903. Mary Latimer died in Baltimore on January 4, 1904.

Lauder, Estée 1908– businesswoman and chemist

Born Josephine Esty Mentzer, probably on July 1, 1908, in New York City, Estée Lauder grew up in the European-style home of her French Catholic and Hungarian Jewish mother and her Czechoslovakian father. Determined to become "100 percent American," she learned her first marketing lessons as a child in her father's hardware store: assertive selling, perfectionism, quality products, and, above all, attention to outward appearance. Drawn to fashion and beauty at an early age, she was introduced to her true vocation by an uncle, a European skin specialist who came to stay with her family at the outbreak of World War I. She apprenticed herself to her uncle as he produced skin creams from natural ingredients, learning his trade secrets and helping him to develop new products.

After her youthful marriage to Joseph Lauder and the birth of their first son, she continued to invent new beauty products in her own kitchen. She also studied to be an actress, but soon learned that her theatrical instincts were better applied to marketing than to performance. After demonstrating her products to the owner of the beauty salon she frequented, she was invited to open a concession at the salon's newest branch. There she would perform free demonstrations for customers, and give each purchaser a free gift — innovations that Lauder claimed were prototypes for selling techniques widely in use today. Through tireless networking she built a devoted clientele, expanding her operations to other shops and hiring a sales staff.

Lauder's growing success led to a tumultuous period in her personal life, and she and Joseph Lauder were divorced in 1939. In 1942 the couple remarried, and he became a full partner in the business. A second son was born in 1944, and two years later, Lauder opened her first factory in a former restaurant. From then on, the Estée Lauder company was a family business, with Lauder in charge of marketing and sales, Joseph Lauder in charge of the factory. Both sons also became steeped in the business as they grew up.

In 1953 the company branched into perfumes. Lauder traveled widely to introduce her products personally to department stores throughout the U.S., and in the 1960s the company built an international division. In 1967 she began marketing products for men, and in 1968 she started developing an extremely successful line of hypoallergenic women's skin care products.

In her 1985 autobiography, Lauder described what she saw as some of the basic principles underlying her success — personally opening the Estée Lauder counter at each new store herself; hiring saleswomen who were walking advertisements for the products; always offering a free gift to the customer; and retaining a focus on one's personal love for and involvement with the company. She also expressed a determination that the models for her products not be dehumanized and that the focus always be on the whole woman rather than her facial or body parts.

Law, Sallie Chapman Gordon 1805–1894 Confederate nurse and patriot

Born on August 27, 1805, in Wilkes County, North Carolina, Sallie Gordon grew up under the influence of her father, a veteran of the Revolution. In June 1825 she married Dr. John S. Law, with whom she lived in Forsythe, Georgia, until 1834 and then in Columbia, Tennessee. In 1844, her husband having died, she settled in Memphis. On the outbreak of the Civil War in April 1861 she organized the Southern Mothers' Hospital in Memphis. From its original 12-bed capacity it quickly expanded, and after the battle of Pittsburg Landing (Shiloh) in April 1862 it handled hundreds of wounded Confederate soldiers. Law was highly effective in gathering supplies and often ventured into the field to distribute them personally to the soldiers.

With the Union capture of Memphis in June 1862 she converted the hospital's assets into opium, morphine, and quinine and herself carried those valuable drugs through Union lines to the South. A hospital in La Grange, Georgia, where she stopped to assist was named for her. At Columbus, Georgia, she gathered a huge stock of clothing and other supplies and distributed them among the poorly equipped men of General Joseph E. Johnston's division. Johnston honored her with a review of 30,000 soldiers. At the end of the war her hospital organization became the Southern Mothers' Association, one of the first Civil War memorial societies, and she remained its president until 1889, when it was absorbed into the newly founded Confederate Historical Association. Law died in Memphis, Tennessee, on June 28, 1894.

Lawrence, Gertrude 1898–1952 singer and actor

Born in London on July 4, 1898, Gertrud Alexandra Dagmar Lawrence Klasen (she later changed the spelling of her first name) was the daughter of music hall performers, and from an early age she was trained to follow their career. She made her stage debut in December 1908 in a pantomime *Dick Whittington* in Brixton. Subsequently she appeared in *Babes in the Wood*, 1910, *The Miracle*, 1911, *Hannele*, 1913, and other musicals and plays, and for a time she toured in minor revues. In 1916 she began appearing in André Charlot's intimate revues in London: *Some*, 1916, *Cheep*, 1917, *Tabs*, during which she stepped into the lead when Beatrice Lillie fell ill, 1918, and *Buzz-Buzz*, 1919. For two years she performed in nightclubs, but in 1921 she returned to Charlot to replace Beatrice Lillie in *A to Z*, in which she introduced "Limehouse Blues," her first hit song.

She appeared with Noel Coward, whom she had known for ten years, in his *London Calling*, 1923, and in January 1924 made her New York debut as one of the stars of *Charlot's Revue*, with Lillie and Jack Buchanan, at the Times Square Theatre. In 1926 she starred in George and Ira Gershwin's *Oh Kay!*, which moved to London the next year, and in 1928 in their *Treasure Girl*. In 1928 she played her first straight dramatic role in *Icebound* in London, and in 1929 she appeared opposite Leslie Howard in *Candle-Light*.

Lawrence's greatest role was in Noel Coward's *Private Lives*, written with her in mind, in which she opened opposite the author at the Phoenix Theatre, London, in September 1930. Both the play and the stars set the tone that would characterize comedies of manners for a decade or more: sophistication, brittle wit, and chic. *Private Lives* was a great success in New York as well from its opening in January 1931 at the Times Square.

In 1933 she appeared in Cole Porter's musical *Nymph Errant*, and in 1936 she rejoined Coward in his *Tonight at 8:30* (originally *Tonight at 7:30* in its London production). She later appeared in Rachel Crothers's *Susan and God*, 1937, *Skylark*, 1939, and the Moss Hart-Kurt Weill musical *Lady in the Dark*, which was another triumph for her, 1941. Throughout her career, her singing and dancing, both accomplished but not exceptional, merely supported her compelling stage presence, what Coward called her "star quality." On the strength of it she remained for a quarter-century one of the most popular stars on the American and British stages. During World War II she was active in the Stage Door Canteen and entertained troops in Europe and the Pacific. In 1945 she published an autobiography, *A Star Danced*. After the war she appeared in *September Tide*, 1948, a film version of *The Glass Menagerie*, 1950, and others, and in March 1951 she opened on Broadway in Rodgers and Hammerstein's *The King and I*. During the run of that musical she died in New York City on September 6, 1952.

Lazarus, Emma 1849–1887 poet and essayist

Born in New York City on July 22, 1849, Emma Lazarus came of a wealthy family and was educated privately. She early displayed a talent for poetry, and her first book, *Poems and Translations*, 1867, was praised by Ralph Waldo Emerson, to whom her next, *Admetus and Other Poems*, 1871, was dedicated. These and subsequent volumes — the prose *Alide: An Episode of Goethe's Life*, 1874, a verse tragedy, *The Spagnoletto*, 1876, and a fine translation of *Poems and Ballads of Heinrich Heine*, 1881 — were cosmopolitan in flavor, sometimes technically excellent, but lacking in real distinction.

About 1881, however, with the wave of immigration to the United States from European and Russian ghettoes, Lazarus turned from literary dilettantism and took up the defense of persecuted Jews and of Judaism and began to work for the relief of immigrants. She published numerous essays in the *Century* and the weekly *American Hebrew* on the pogroms and persecutions and the often equivocal attitude of the Christian West. She was an early advocate of a Jewish homeland in Palestine. In 1882 she produced *Songs of a Semite*, which included such powerful pieces as "The Dance to Death," "The Banner of the Jew," and "The Crowing of the Red Cock." Her sonnet on the Statue of Liberty, "The New Colossus," written in 1883, was chosen to be inscribed on the base of the monument, and it remains a most moving and eloquent expression of an American ideal: "Give me your tired, your poor," the sonnet concludes, "Your huddled masses yearning to breathe free, / The wretched refuse of your teeming shore. / Send these, the homeless, tempest-tost to me, / I lift my lamp beside the golden door!" Her last book, a series of prose poems published under the title *By the Waters of Babylon*, appeared in 1887. After four years of declining health and intermittent depression Emma Lazarus died in New York City on November 19, 1887.

Leach, Abby 1855–1918 educator

Born in Brockton, Massachusetts, on May 28, 1855, Abby Leach was a precocious student and early developed an abiding interest in Latin. She graduated from Brockton High School in 1869 and from the Oread Collegiate Institute in Worcester, Massachusetts, in 1871. She taught at Brockton High School from 1871 to 1873 and at Oread Institute from 1873 to 1878; during 1876–1878 she served also as preceptress. In 1878 she went to Cambridge, Massachusetts, and sought private instruction in Greek, Latin, and English from Harvard professors. William Watson Goodwin, professor of Greek, was sufficiently impressed by her knowledge of that language to take her on as a private student, and he persuaded colleagues to do likewise.

She was an inspiration for — and one of the first students enrolled in — the classes opened to women in September 1879 at the "Harvard Annex" under the auspices of what became the Society for the Collegiate Instruction of Women and later Radcliffe College. While studying there she also taught at the Girls' Latin School in Boston. In 1883 she became instructor in Greek and Latin at Vassar College. In recognition of her work at

Harvard, Vassar granted her a bachelor's and a master's degree in 1885. She later studied for a time at Johns Hopkins University and in 1886–1887 at the University of Leipzig. She advanced to associate professor in 1886 and to full professor and head of the Greek department at Vassar in 1889. For 29 years thereafter she was an inspiring and occasionally awesome presence at Vassar.

The determination that had marked her own quest for education carried over into her teaching, and she took the instilling of classical ideals of reason and conduct as part of her task. She contributed articles to a number of scholarly journals, one of which became a chapter, "Fate and Free Will in Greek Literature," in Lane Cooper's *The Greek Genius and Its Influence*, 1917. From 1888 she served on the committee of managers of the American School of Classical Studies in Athens. She was president of the American Philological Association in 1899–1900 and of the Association of Collegiate Alumnae (later the American Association of University Women) in 1899–1901. She died in Poughkeepsie, New York, on December 29, 1918.

Lease, Mary Elizabeth Clyens 1850–1933 lecturer and political reformer

Born on September 11, 1850, in Ridgway, Elk County, Pennsylvania, Mary Clyens grew up on a farm in McKean County and graduated from St. Elizabeth's Academy, Allegany, New York, in 1868. She became a schoolteacher and in 1870 moved to Kansas to take a job in a Catholic girls' school in Osage Mission. In January 1873 she married Charles L. Lease, a pharmacist with whom she lived in Kingman County, Kansas, later in Denison, Texas, and from 1883 in Wichita, Kansas. According to her unsubstantiated later claim, in 1885 she was admitted to the Kansas bar. She was in any case active in public affairs. Her career as a public speaker dates from that year, when she began speaking on behalf of Irish home rule and raising funds for the Irish National League.

Lease's considerable ability as a speaker fired her taste for political battle, and later in 1885 she was one of the speakers before the Union Labor party's state convention in Wichita. She edited the *Union Labor Press* during the state campaign of 1888 and the *Colorado Workman* during a visit to that state in 1889. In 1891 she was elected "master workman" of a local Knights of Labor assembly in Kansas. From that period she was prominent in the Farmers' Alliance and its offspring, the Populist (People's party) movement in Kansas. She stumped the state in 1890, delivering about 160 speeches, spoke in the West and South in 1891, and at the party's Omaha convention in July 1892 seconded the nomination of James B. Weaver for president. In 1893, after the People's party victory in Kansas elections, she received an appointment as president of the State Board of Charities. She was the orator of choice on Kansas Day at the World's Columbian Exposition in Chicago in 1893, where she also attended the World Peace Congress and was elected national vice-president. Her bid that year for the U.S. Senate, however, failed, despite a growing number of supporters.

Her forte was political agitation rather than administration, and her popularity derived mainly from her powerful and colorful oratory. She was perhaps best known for her advice to Kansas farmers to "raise less corn and more Hell" (a line that may well not have been original with her). The fact that she was occasionally known as Mary Ellen led opponents to dub her Mary Yellin. Her erratic nature made it difficult for other Populist organizers, notably Annie L. Diggs, to work with her. In 1894 she was removed from her post on the Board of Charities.

In 1896 Lease broke with the Populist mainstream in opposing the nomination of William Jennings Bryan for president.

After 1896 her influence in Kansas waned and she decided to go east, joining the *New York World* as a political writer. She remained active as a speaker in New York for numerous reform causes, including prohibition, woman suffrage, and birth control, and she later joined forces with the Theodore Roosevelt Progressives in the Bull Moose campaign. She never returned to Kansas except for a short visit in 1902 to obtain a divorce. From 1908 until her retirement from public life in 1918 she was an occasional lecturer for the New York City Board of Education. Her major written work, *The Problem of Civilization Solved*, 1895, proposed to end militarism, poverty, and business monopoly by a complex scheme of colonization of tropical regions, nationalization of certain utilities, free trade, and other reforms. She died on October 29, 1933, at Callicoon, New York.

Leavitt, Henrietta Swan 1868–1921 astronomer

Born on July 4, 1868, in Lancaster, Massachusetts, Henrietta Leavitt grew up there, in Cambridge, Massachusetts, and from 1885 in Cleveland, Ohio. She attended Oberlin College for two years, 1886–1888, and then transferred to the Society for the Collegiate Instruction of Women (later Radcliffe College), from which she graduated in 1892. Following an interest aroused in her senior year, in 1895 she became a volunteer assistant in the Harvard Observatory. In 1902 she received a permanent staff appointment. From the first she was employed in the observatory's great project, begun by Edward C. Pickering, of determining the brightnesses of all measurable stars. In this work she was associated with the older Williamina Fleming and the more nearly contemporary Annie J. Cannon.

She soon advanced from routine work in examining variable stars to a position as head of the photographic photometry department. A new phase of the work began in 1907 with Pickering's ambitious plan to ascertain photographically standardized values for stellar magnitudes. The vastly increased accuracy permitted by photographic techniques, which unlike the subjective eye were not misled by the different colors of the stars, depended upon the establishment of a basic sequence of standard magnitudes for comparison. The problem was given to Henrietta Leavitt, who began with a sequence of 46 stars in the vicinity of the north celestial pole. Devising new methods of analysis, she determined their magnitudes and then those of a much larger sample in the same region, extending the scale of standard brightnesses down to the 21st magnitude. These standards were published in 1912 and 1917.

She then established secondary standard sequences of from 15 to 22 reference stars in each of 48 selected "Harvard Standard Regions" of the sky, using photographs supplied by observatories around the world. Her North Polar Sequence was adopted for the Astrographic Map of the Sky, an international project undertaken in 1913, and by the time of her death she had completely determined magnitudes for stars in 108 sky areas. Her system remained in general use until improved technology made possible photoelectrical measurements of far greater accuracy. One result of her work on stellar magnitudes was her discovery of 4 novae and some 2400 variable stars, the latter figure comprising more than half all those known even by 1930.

Leavitt's outstanding achievement was her discovery in 1912 that in a certain class of variable stars, the Cepheid variables, the period of the cycle of fluctuation in brightness is highly regular and proportional to the actual luminosity of the star. (The subsequent calibration of the period-luminosity curve allowed Edwin Hubble, Harlow Shapley, and others to determine the distances of many Cepheid stars and consequently of the star clusters and galaxies in which they were observed.) Leavitt continued her work at the Harvard Observatory until her death in Cambridge, Massachusetts, on December 12, 1921.

Leavitt, Mary Greenleaf Clement 1830–1912 reformer and missionary

Born on September 22, 1830, in Hopkinton, New Hampshire, Mary Clement grew up and attended school there and in Thetford, Vermont, and at sixteen began teaching in country schools. Later she studied at the Massachusetts State Normal School in West Newton, and after graduating in 1851 she taught for periods in Boston and Quincy. In June 1857 she married Thomas H. Leavitt, a Boston businessman who ultimately proved an improvident husband and father. In 1867, in order to support herself and her children, she opened a private school in her home. A few years later her husband left her; they were divorced in 1878. By that time Mary Leavitt had become interested in the rapidly growing temperance movement. She helped organize the Boston Woman's Christian Temperance Union and in 1877 met Frances Willard, who urged her to employ her gifts in a wider arena.

In 1881 Leavitt closed her school and began lecturing regularly throughout New England on behalf of temperance and the New England Woman Suffrage Association. The next year she was named to head the newly organized Franchise Department of the national WCTU. In 1883–1884 she made a lecture and organizing tour of the Pacific coast states for the WCTU. In 1884 Frances Willard persuaded her to undertake a foreign missionary tour for temperance. She set out in November of that year for the Sandwich (Hawaiian) Islands, whence she proceeded to New Zealand, Australia, Japan, China, India, Africa, Europe, and Great Britain. Her unprecedented journey took her nearly seven years. In the course of it she spoke to over 1,600 meetings through some 229 interpreters in 47 languages. She organized 86 branches of the WCTU and 24 men's temperance societies. Her style of travel was extremely frugal, and her expenses were met by contributions along the way, a small amount of support from the World's WCTU after it was organized in 1885, and out of her own pocket. Along the way she sent back letters to the WCTU journal, the *Union Signal*, and collected several million signatures on the "Polyglot Petition" calling for a halt to the international traffic in opiates and other drugs.

After Leavitt's return to the United States in 1891 she reported to the Boston convention of the World's WCTU, where she was chosen honorary president. A short time later she undertook another temperance mission, this one to Latin America. Neither that trip nor those of later WCTU missionaries began to match her extraordinary seven-year mission, however. In the later 1890s she became estranged from the WCTU and in particular from Frances Willard, whom she attacked in letters and speeches. She passed her last years in Boston, where she died on February 5, 1912.

Le Clercq, Tanaquil 1929– ballet dancer

Born in Paris on October 2, 1929, Tanaquil Le Clercq was the daughter of American parents (her father by naturalization) and grew up in New York City. She began taking ballet lessons at four and at seven became a pupil of Michael Mordkin. Her regular education was obtained at the Lycée Français de New York and from private tutors. In 1940 she entered the School of American Ballet, where she studied under George Balanchine. Her first professional performance occurred at Ted Shawn's Jacob's Pillow Festival in Lee, Massachusetts, in August 1945, and in 1946 she became an original member of the Ballet Society upon the organization of that company by Balanchine and Lincoln Kirstein. She danced in the premieres of Balanchine's *Four Temperaments* in November 1946, *Divertimento* in January 1947, *Orpheus* in April 1948, and other ballets. She remained a principal dancer when the company became the New York City Ballet in 1948.

Over the next several years Le Clerq emerged as one of the company's most individual stylists and a particularly fine exponent of Balanchine's choreography. (She was married to Balanchine from 1952 to 1969.) Among the Balanchine works in which she appeared were *Bourrée Fantasque*, with Maria Tallchief, which was premiered in December 1949; *La Valse*, premiered in February 1951; *Caracole* (later revised as *Divertimento No. 15*) in 1952; *Western Symphony*, premiered in September 1954; *Ivesiana*, premiered in September 1954; and works from the repertoire such as *Apollo*, *Symphony in C*, and *Swan Lake*.

She also created roles in premieres of Frederick Ashton's *Illuminations*, with Melissa Hayden, in March 1950, and Jerome Robbins's *Age of Anxiety* in February 1950, *The Pied Piper* in December 1951, *Afternoon of a Faun* in May 1953, and *The Concert* in March 1956. During a European tour with the New York City Ballet in 1956 she was stricken with polio, which abruptly ended her dancing career. She was the author of *Mourka; the Autobiography of a Cat*, 1964, and *The Ballet Cook Book*, 1967. In later years she was a teacher at the school of the Harlem Dance Theatre.

Lee, Ann 1736–1784 religious leader

Born on February 29, 1736, in Manchester, England, Ann Lee was the unlettered daughter of a blacksmith who was probably named Lees. In her youth she went to work in a textile mill. At the age of twenty-two she joined a sect known as the Shaking Quakers, or Shakers, because of the shaking and dancing that characterized their worship. (Those practices had originated among a sect known as the Camisards, or Prophets, in France in 1688, many of whose adherents had later fled to England to avoid persecution.) She married reluctantly at twenty-five and over the next few years was deeply affected by the loss of all four of her children in infancy. In the following years she agonized over her conviction of sinfulness, suffering great remorse about her marriage. After a prolonged period of penance by mortification in 1770, during which she apparently experienced a divine illumination, she began to preach a new gospel, opposing marriage and sexual relationships and affirming the dual nature of God — the original incarnation of the masculine in Christ to be followed during the present millennium by a feminine incarnation in the person of Ann Lee. Regarded thereafter as such by her followers, she was referred to as Ann the Word or Mother Ann and was celebrated as the leader of the Shakers. She was imprisoned for periods in 1772 and 1773 for preaching in the streets.

Prompted by a vision in 1774, she came to the New World with eight disciples. They arrived in New York City in August. In the spring of 1776 a colony was established at Niskeyuna (subsequently Watervliet) near Albany, New York. From about 1780 Ann Lee began proselytizing in the neighborhood and later in other parts of New York and in New England. Her evidently magnetic personality and the appeal of her doctrine of a communal life of neatness, simplicity, economy, charity, and equality of races and sexes, won wide attention. Whole congregations of Baptists joined the Shakers, and, despite occasional persecution (owing, in part, to the group's pacifism) their numbers swelled to several thousand during the next five years.

Led by Mother Ann's visions, the Shakers at Watervliet evolved beginnings of the communal life which later became the distinctive pattern of Shaker social organization. She died at Niskeyuna on September 8, 1784. After her death her followers organized the United Society of Believers in Christ's Second Appearing, which was also known as the Millennial Church and, most commonly, as the Shakers, and which by 1826 had grown to encompass 18 Shaker villages in 8 states. The intensive communal life of the Shaker settlements was of a remarkably stable nature. Within it developed styles of work that resulted particularly in distinctive furniture-making and other crafts. The Shakers gradually disappeared as an active religious sect, but their influence on American crafts and design proved permanent.

Lee, Gypsy Rose 1914–1970 entertainer and mystery writer

Born in Seattle, Washington, on January 9, 1914, Rose Louise Hovick escaped a formal education almost completely, since she made her stage debut about the age of four with her sister June (later well known as actress June Havoc). The place was a Knights of Pythias hall in Seattle. Under the management of their ambitious mother, June and Rose toured as "Dainty June and her Newsboys" until June eloped in 1925. Rose then became the star of "Madame Rose's Dancing Daughters." About the age of fifteen Rose, now under the name Gypsy Rose Lee, took striptease lessons from a lady known as Tessie the Tassel-Twirler.

She made her burlesque debut that year in Kansas City, and by 1931 she was in New York City, where, besides practicing her specialty at Minsky's and other palaces of burlesque, she was introduced to the writers and intellectuals of the town by Damon Runyon. It was about this time that H. L. Mencken coined the word "ecdysiast" for her, in an attempt to make respectable the skill that she had perfected far beyond most of her competitors. The wit and sophistication she brought to an art that had never known them won her a spot in the *Ziegfeld Follies* in 1936.

While stripping in the *Streets of Paris* show at the New York World's Fair in 1940, she began to write a murder mystery. She completed the first draft while touring, writing in crowded dressing rooms, in planes and trains, and in the bathtub. *The G-String Murders* was published in 1941 and became a best-seller. It was followed the next year by another successful whodunit, *Mother Finds the Body*.

In 1942 she appeared in a Broadway show, *Star and Garter*, to rave reviews. She was featured in several films, including *Stage Door Canteen*, 1943, in which she performed a satire on the striptease, and was the star of her own television talk show for several years in the later 1960s. Her autobiographical *Gypsy: A Memoir*, 1957, became the basis for a hit Broadway musical and a motion picture. She died on April 26, 1970, in Los Angeles.

Lee, Mary Ann 1824?–1899 dancer

Born in Philadelphia probably about July 1824 (many sources say 1823), Mary Ann Lee was the daughter of theatrical performers. She performed frequently in children's roles in Philadelphia theaters and in December 1837 first appeared as a dancer in *The Maid of Cashmere* (English version of Daniel Auber's *La Dieu et la Bayadère*) at the Chestnut Street Theatre, a presentation that was also the dancing debut of the slightly older Augusta Maywood. The production and the two young stars were sensations. In March 1838 they appeared together in *The Dew Drop, or La Sylphide*, a version of Philippe Taglioni's classic ballet, in Philadelphia and Baltimore. Mary Ann Lee made her New York debut in an interlude selection from *The Maid of Cashmere* at the Bowery Theatre in June 1839. Subsequently she danced in *The Sisters* there. Between dancing engagements she also acted and sang in a variety of shows.

To her original instruction in Philadelphia under Paul Hazard, formerly of the Paris Opéra, was added further training by James Sylvain, partner of the famed European ballerina Fanny Elssler, and possibly by Taglioni. She was a great popular favorite by 1844, when she traveled to Paris to study under Jean Coralli, ballet master of the Paris Opéra and principal choreographer of *Giselle, ou Les Wilis*, the premier romantic ballet and a favorite display piece for ballerinas.

On her return to Philadelphia late in 1845 Lee formed with G. Washington Smith a small ballet company and on tour presented a series of European dance works, including Francois Albert's *La jolie fille de Gand*, Taglioni's *La Fille du Danube*, which she retitled *Fleur des Champs*, and in January 1846 at the Howard Athenaeum in Boston the first American production of *Giselle*. In April she took *Giselle* to New York City.

The company toured as far as Charleston and New Orleans before she disbanded it in May 1847 and retired. A few months later she married a Philadelphia businessman. She later returned to the stage on a few brief occasions, appearing in *La Muette de Portici* in 1852 and 1853. Although not a dancer of the first rank, she was the leading and favorite American ballerina of the day (her friend Augusta Maywood having left America permanently in 1838). She died in Philadelphia on January 25, 1899.

Leech, Margaret Kernochan 1893–1974 writer and historian

Born on November 7, 1893, in Newburgh, New York, Margaret Leech attended private schools and in 1915 graduated from Vassar College. For several years she worked in publishing, advertising, and public relations, and after World War I she was active in reconstruction work in France. She then turned to literary work. Her first novel, *The Back of the Book*, was published in 1924 and was followed by *Tin Wedding*, 1926, and *The Feathered Nest*, 1928. She also collaborated with Heywood Broun on the well received biography *Anthony Comstock: Roundsman of the Lord*, 1927. From August 1928 until his death in 1939 she was married to Ralph Pulitzer, publisher of the *New York World*. After the failure of *Divided by Three*, a play written with Beatrice Kaufman and produced in 1934, she turned to history.

Years of research among original documents and other materials went into *Reveille in Washington, 1860–1865*, published in 1941 after serialization in the *Atlantic Monthly*. The lively, dramatic, and panoramic story of life in the national capital during the Civil War was a best seller and was awarded the Pulitzer Prize for history in 1942. An even longer period of research and writing went into In *The Days of McKinley*, 1959, which won both the Pulitzer Prize for history and the Bancroft Prize of Columbia University in 1960. Margaret Leech died in New York City on February 24, 1974.

Le Gallienne, Eva 1899–1991 actor and director

Born in London on January 11, 1899, Eva Le Gallienne, daughter of poet Richard Le Gallienne, was brought up there and in Paris. She was educated at the Collège Sévigné, and during World War I, unable to return to Paris, she studied at Tree's Academy (later the Royal Academy of Dramatic Art) in London. She made her stage debut in *The Laughter of Fools* at London's Prince of Wales Theatre in May 1915. Although she received excellent notices, it was a number of years before she could gain any but small parts in plays, either in Britain or in the United States, where she made her debut in New York City in *Mrs. Boltay's Daughters* at the Comedy Theatre in October 1915. She subsequently appeared in *Bunny*, 1916, *Mr. Lazarus*, 1916, *Lord and Lady Algy*, 1917, *The Off Chance*, 1918, *Lusmore*, 1919, and other plays.

Le Gallienne's first big successes came in 1920, when she portrayed Elsie Dover in *Not So Long Ago* at New York's Booth Theatre and then on tour, and in 1921, when she starred in *Liliom*. But she still found it difficult to get satisfactory parts, and she spent the long periods between engagements reading such authors as Chekhov and Ibsen. In 1925 and 1926 she starred in her own productions of *The Master Builder* at Maxine Elliott's Theatre and *John Gabriel Borkman* at the Booth. The theatrical work for which she was best known began in October 1926, when her Civic Repertory Theatre presented its first production, *Saturday Night*, at the 14th Street Theatre in New York City. Over the next six years, until the project was ended because of the Depression, the Civic Repertory presented 1581 performances of 34 different plays and provided New York audiences with a kind of theatrical experience then almost unique, and always rare, in the United States. Productions included *The Three Sisters*, *The Mistress of the Inn*, and *Twelfth Night* in 1926, *The Cradle Song*, *The Inheritors*, and *The Good Hope* in 1927, *The First Stone*, *Improvisations in June*, *Hedda Gabler*, *The Would-be Gentleman*, and *The Cherry Orchard* in 1928. She starred in most and directed 32 of the Civic's productions.

From 1932 to 1946 Le Gallienne starred in many plays on Broadway and in summer stock, including *L'Aiglon*, 1934, *Rosmersholm*, 1935, *Camille*, 1935, *Love for Love*, 1936, *Prelude to Exile*, 1936, *Madame Capet*, 1938, *Ah, Wilderness!*, 1941, *Uncle Harry*, 1942, and *Therese*, 1945.

In November 1946 she was able once again to realize her dream of a repertory theater when the American Repertory Theatre, headed by her in association with Margaret

Webster and Cheryl Crawford, opened with a production of Shakespeare's *Henry VIII* at the International Theatre in New York. The experiment ended after one season. Le Gallienne herself, however, continued to be a mainstay of the American theater.

The autobiographical *At 33* appeared in 1934 and was followed in 1953 by another autobiographical work, *With a Quiet Heart*. She also wrote *Flossie and Bossie*, a children's book, 1949, and *The Mystic in the Theatre*, a biography of Eleonora Duse, 1966; she translated a number of Ibsen's plays, with prefaces written from the actor's point of view, and several of Hans Christian Andersen's stories. She also appeared occasionally in television dramas, winning an Emmy in 1978 for Best Supporting Actress in *The Royal Family*. In 1980 she played a supporting role in the film *Resurrection*.

Her last stage appearance was as the White Queen in the 1982 Broadway production of *Alice in Wonderland*, which she also directed and co-wrote. Among her many honors and awards was a special Tony award in 1964 for distinguished contributions to the theatre, and the Medal of Arts in 1986 for her lifetime acheivement as an actress. She died on June 3, 1991, in Weston, Connecticut.

Le Guin, Ursula Kroeber 1929– science fiction writer and essayist

Born in Berkeley, California, on October 21, 1929, Ursula Kroeber was the youngest child of psychologist, Theodora, and anthropologist, Alfred Kroeber. As a child, she read myths, legends, and science fiction. In college and graduate school she studied French and Italian literature. After receiving a B.A. from Radcliffe College, she attended Columbia University and earned her M.A. in 1952.

Ursula K. Le Guin

On a trip to France, she met and married Charles Le Guin and returned to the U.S. to teach at several universities. When the Le Guins settled in Portland, Oregon, in 1959, and with three children to care for, she began writing at night. Several published short stories brought her little success, until *Rocannon's World*, her first novel, was published in 1966 — the first of some thirty volumes of science fiction, fantasy, poetry, and essays, for which she would receive many distinguished awards.

The Left Hand of Darkness,1969, which told the story of an androgynous, warless people on an imaginary planet, won the prestigious Nebula and Hugo awards. Relying on both Taoist and Jungian thought, her *Earthsea* trilogy — *A Wizard of Earthsea*, 1968, *The Tombs of Atuan*, 1971, and *The Farthest Shore*, 1972 — explored the nature of mythic journeys and the power of naming. In 1989, she published the widely acclaimed *Dancing at the Edge of the World*, a collection of essays, speeches, and musings, covering a range of topics from abortion to travel literature, to overpopulation.

Lehmann, Lotte 1888–1976 singer

Born on February 27, 1888, in Perleberg, Prussia (now Germany), Lotte Lehmann grew up there and from 1902 in Berlin. After graduating from a girls' high school in 1904 she devoted herself to singing. She studied under Erna Tiedke, under Helene Jordan at the Königliche Hochschule für Musik in Berlin, under Eva Reinhold at Etelka Gerster's school in Berlin, and privately under Matilde Mallinger. In 1910 she was engaged by the Hamburg Municipal Theatre, where she made her debut in a small role in *Die Zauberflöte*. After several other minor roles she attracted some notice in *The Merry Wives of Windsor* and *Das Rheingold*. Greater successes soon followed in *Lohengrin* and *Der Rosenkavalier*.

In 1914 she went to the Vienna State Opera, where she made her debut in *Der Freischütz*. She was chosen by Richard Strauss to sing The Young Composer in the Vienna premiere of his *Ariadne auf Naxos* in November 1916, and she subsequently sang in the premiere of his *Die Frau ohne Schatten* in October 1919, in the Vienna premiere of Puccini's *Il Trittico* in 1920, in the world premiere of Strauss's *Intermezzo* in Vienna in 1925, and in the Vienna premiere of his *Arabella*, composed with her in mind, in 1933.

Her London debut occurred at Covent Garden in 1922, when she sang the Marschallin in *Der Rosenkavalier*, thereafter one of her great roles, and in 1925 she was a sensation in several leading European opera houses in *Fidelio*. Other productions in which she appeared were *Manon*, *La Bohème*, *Tosca*, *Die Tote Stadt*, *Eugen Onegin*, and *Otello*. She made her American debut at the Chicago Civic Opera in *Die Walküre* in October 1930.

In 1933 Lehmann was forbidden to sing in Germany after she refused Hermann Göring's offer to make her the nation's prima donna assoluta provided she sing only approved works and exclusively in Germany.

In January 1934 she made her debut at the Metropolitan Opera in New York in *Die Walküre* and was a sensation. She settled permanently in the United States in 1938 following the German annexation of Austria; she became a naturalized citizen in June 1945. Until 1946 she was the Met's leading lyric-dramatic soprano and one of the most popular and sought-after guest stars at opera houses around the world. After her final Met performance that year in *Der Rosenkavalier* she devoted herself to the concert stage. As a singer of lieder, especially those of Robert Schumann, she was incomparable. She retired from performing entirely after a final concert at New York's Town Hall in February 1951 and thereafter concentrated on teaching and occasionally directing. She published several books: *Orplid, mein Land*, a novel, 1937, which appeared in English as *Eternal Flight*, 1938; *Anfang und Aufsteig*, an autobiography, 1937, translated as *Midway in My Song*, 1938; *More than Singing* notes on interpretation, 1945; *My Many Lives*, notes and recollections of opera, 1948; and *Five Operas and Richard Strauss*, 1964. She died in Santa Barbara, California, on August 26, 1976.

Leibovitz, Annie 1949– photographer

Born Anna-Lou Leibovitz on October 2, 1949, in Westbury, Connecticut, Annie Leibovitz was the daughter of Sam Leibovitz, an Air Force officer, and Marilyn Leibovitz, a modern dance instructor who had performed with Martha Graham's company. Her family moved frequently from one military base to another when Annie was young. While this fostered closeness among the six Leibovitz children, Annie also developed a shyness she carried with her into her professional life.

In 1967 she enrolled in the San Francisco Art Institute, intending to become a painter. A night class in photography inspired the purchase of her first camera, bought in Japan en route to visit her father, then stationed in the Philippines. She used that camera to document her five months on an Israeli kibbutz and, upon her return, to shoot street scenes of San Francisco in the late 1960s.

On the basis of those photos, she was given her first commercial assignment by *Rolling Stone* magazine in 1970, photographing Grace Slick of Jefferson Airplane. Following that, at the age of twenty, she was placed on a retainer of $47 a week for the magazine where she worked for the next thirteen years. By 1973 she was chief photographer at *Rolling Stone*, photographing the expanding counter-cultural music scene, including John Lennon and Yoko Ono, Stevie Wonder, Les Paul, Bob Dylan, Jerzy Kosinski, John Belushi, Bruce Springsteen, Bette Midler, Pat Benatar, Woody Allen, Debbie Harry, Dolly Parton and Linda Ronstadt.

In 1975 she was hired by the Rolling Stones to document the group's six-month concert tour, during which she produced several famous and frequently published photos of lead singer Mick Jagger, and which introduced her to the high-powered, drug culture surrounding the group. (She later said, "It took me about five years to get off that tour.") Beginning in1983 she took some time off from the daily pressures of photojournalism. She produced a sixty-print show that toured Europe and the U.S. for the next two years. The accompanying book, *Annie Leibovitz: Photographs*, had sold 85,000 copies by 1990. When she returned to work, it was not to *Rolling Stone* but to high-gloss *Vanity Fair* under the editorship of Tina Brown, thereby broadening her range of possible subjects well beyond the world of rock and roll. In 1986 she moved further into advertising photography, working for such clients as Honda, American Express, and the Gap. The American Express ad campaign won particular acclaim for its artistry and a Clio Award in 1987.

In the spring of 1991, Leibovitz had her first museum exhibit at the National Portrait Gallery in Washington, D.C., one of only two such exhibits ever devoted to a living photographer by the Portrait Gallery. A companion book, *Photographs: Annie Leibovitz 1970–1990*, was published in October 1991.

Her earliest photos were in black-and-white. It was while at *Rolling Stone* that she developed her trademark vivid primary colors, which, combined with the newsprint surface of the 1970s *Rolling Stone*, gave her work its most distinctive quality. Continued use of vivid, even garish, colors marked her later work at *Vanity Fair* and her advertising photographs. In some of her 1990s work she returned to black-and-white.

Her modus operandi as a photographer was always to spend large amounts of time with the subjects she photographed, typically spending two days observing every detail of their daily lives. She claimed that she retained her childhood shyness, making her awkward in the presence of strangers. Ironically, this awkwardness, along with an absence of awe in the presence of stars, was what enabled her to form an intimate and relaxed relationship with her subjects and to enlist them in the portrait process. Leibovitz viewed her photographic sessions as "a collaboration" and insisted it was this arrangement that produced some of her best photographs: Christo swathed in wrapping in cloth, Bette Midler buried in a bed of roses, naked John Lennon wrapped fetus-like around Yoko Ono and Ella Fitzgerald in a red suit standing in front of her 1959 Mercedes convertible. A photographer of celebrities who herself became a celebrity, she asserted "I'm not the people I photograph. It's more of a service I perform."

Leitzel, Lillian 1892–1931 circus performer

Born in Breslau, Germany, in 1892 (some sources give 1893), Leopoldina Alitza Pelikan inherited the circus tradition from both her parents. In addition to languages, dancing, and piano, she early began learning the family aerobatic routines. In her youth she became a member of the aerial team known as the Leamy Ladies, consisting of her mother and two aunts, and in 1908 she came with the act to the United States. She took "Lillian Leitzel" for her professional name. For three years she appeared with the Leamy Ladies in the Barnum & Bailey Circus. She remained in the United States when the other members returned to Europe in 1911, and for a time she toured in vaudeville. In April 1915 she opened in a solo act with the Ringling Brothers Circus in Chicago. She was a center ring attraction with Ringling Brothers in 1916, with Barnum & Bailey in 1917, with Ringling again in 1918, and from 1919 on with the merged Ringling Brothers and Barnum & Bailey, the "Greatest Show on Earth."

Leitzel's aerial act, produced with all the showmanship and drama the circus could muster, consisted of a display of gymnastic skill on roman rings suspended high above the center ring, followed by the feat that made her famous throughout the circus-loving world, the one-arm plange. Holding by one hand to a swiveled rope in the very peak of the big top, she pivoted her entire body on her shoulder sockets, turning faster and faster like a pinwheel while her mesmerized audience counted the revolutions up to 100. The grace, skill, and daring of the act, together with her own petite figure and beauty, made her Ringling's major attraction for years. In July 1928 she married Alfredo Codona (1893 – 1937), considered the greatest flying trapeze artist in circus history. While performing at the Valencia Music Hall in Copenhagen, Denmark, in February 1931, Lillian Leitzel plunged to the floor when the swivel on one of her rings broke. She died two days later, on February 15, 1931.

Lennox, Charlotte Ramsay 1720–1804 writer and translator

Born in 1720 in New York City, Charlotte Ramsay was the daughter of a British army officer who was said to have been lieutenant-governor of the colony, although no evidence for the claim survives. She grew up in Albany, New York, until the age of fifteen, when she was sent to live with relatives in England. For some years she was supported by a series of aristocratic patronesses. In October 1747 she married Alexander Lennox, a printer. In that year she published her first book, *Poems on Several Occasions*. An attempt at acting in 1748 was short-lived, as Horace Walpole's opinion that she was "a deplorable actress" was widely shared.

Her career in literature was largely opened to her by her acquaintance with Samuel Johnson and in lesser part by her association with Samuel Richardson, both of whom offered encouragement and assistance. In 1750 she published her first novel, *The Life of Harriot Stuart*. Two years later her most famous book appeared, *The Female Quixote, or the Adventures of Arabella*, a satire, somewhat in the Cervantean manner, on popular French romances and their readers. Subsequent books included *Shakespear Illustrated*, a pioneering study of the playwright's sources, 1753, *The Memoirs of M. de Bethune, Duke of Sully*, a translation, 1756, *The Memoirs of the Countess of Berci*, translation, 1756, *Memoirs for the History of Madam de Maintenon, and of the Last Age*, translation, 1757, *The History of Henrietta*, a novel, 1758, *Philander* and *Angelica, or Quixote in Petticoats*, plays, both 1758, *The Greek Theatre of Father Brumoy*, translation, 1759, *Sophia* a novel, 1762, *The Sister*, a play given one performance at Covent Garden, 1769, *Meditations and Penitential Prayers Written by the Duchess de la Vallière*, translation, 1774, *Old City Manners*, a dramatic adaptation, 1775, and *Euphenia*, a novel, 1790. During 1760–1761 she also published a short-lived periodical, *The Lady's Museum*. Her literary efforts brought her little income but much renown. Johnson honored her by quoting her in his dictionary. She died in London on January 4, 1804.

Leslie, Miriam Florence Folline 1836–1914 editor and publisher

Born in New Orleans on June 5, 1836, Miriam Folline was educated privately and acquired several languages. After the family's fortunes declined they lived in Cincinnati from about 1846 and in New York City from about 1850. Her first marriage, to one David C. Peacock in March 1854, was entered into under duress and was annulled two years later. During 1857 she made a few stage appearances in Albany, Providence, and Pittsburgh as "Minnie Montez," supposedly the sister of Lola Montez, with whom she shared the stage. In October 1857 she married Ephraim G. Squier, an amateur archaeologist and promoter who in 1861 became editor of *Frank Leslie's Illustrated Newspaper*. Miriam Squier soon began contributing to the magazine, and her ability won her the editorship of Leslie's *Lady's Magazine* when it began publication in 1863.

In 1865 she became editor of the new *Frank Leslie's Chimney Corner* and in 1871 of *Frank Leslie's Lady's Journal*, both of which enjoyed great success under her guidance. During those years she formed a personal liaison with her publisher, Frank Leslie (born Henry Carter in England in 1821). She divorced Squier in 1873 and married Leslie in July 1874. Leslie's wealth enabled her to undertake a very active social life. Her lavish entertainments at their New York City home and at their upstate Saratoga estate were widely commented on. In 1877 the Leslies, attended by a large number of friends and a retinue of servants and comforted by sumptuous accommodations, made a much publicized "transcontinental excursion." Miriam Leslie's account of the trip was published as *California: A Pleasure Trip from Gotham to the Golden Gate*, 1877.

By the time of Frank Leslie's death in January 1880 his publishing business had fallen on hard times. Miriam Leslie moved quickly and forcefully to restore it to financial health, cutting away 6 of the 12 periodicals produced by the firm and taking full advantage of her own editorial acumen to build up the remaining ones. In 1882 she changed her name legally to Frank Leslie, and within a few years her astute management had earned her the title of "the empress of journalism." Her 400 employees produced periodicals with a combined circulation that peaked at a quarter-million readers. She continued also as a prominent hostess, lectured occasionally, and wrote such books as *Rents in Our Robes*, 1888, *Beautiful Women of Twelve Epochs*, 1890, *Are Men Gay Deceivers?*, 1893, and *A Social Mirage*, 1899. In October 1891 she married William C. K. Wilde, brother of Oscar Wilde; they were separated in 1892 and divorced in 1893. In 1895 she leased the publishing business to a syndicate and retired, but within three years the syndicate failed and she was compelled to resume active management.

She also resumed the editorship of *Frank Leslie's Popular Monthly* (the other major Leslie publication, the *Illustrated Newspaper*, had been sold in 1889) and restored it to its former preeminence in the field, with a circulation of 200,000. In 1900 she relinquished the editorship and a half-interest in the company. In 1901 she returned from a European trip claiming the title of Baroness de Bazus, supposed to have descended to her from her Huguenot forebears. She lived thereafter in retirement in New York City. At her death in New York on September 18, 1914, she left in her will a major portion, amounting in the end to nearly $1 million, of her estate to Carrie Chapman Catt for the furtherance of the crusade for woman suffrage.

Levertov, Denise 1923– poet

Born on October 24, 1923, in Ilford, Essex, England, Denise Levertov was the daughter of an immigrant Russian Jew who had become an Anglican clergyman. She was educated at home. During World War II she served as a civilian nurse in London. She published her first book of poems, *The Double Image*, in 1946. In 1948 she settled in New York City with her American husband; she became a naturalized citizen in 1955. During the first years of her residence in America her poetry developed rapidly, in part under the influence of that of William Carlos Williams, and with the appearance of her second book, *Here and Now*, 1957, her early neoromanticism had been entirely displaced by her mature style of intense concentration on the particulars of common experience, conveyed in spare, unclouded language.

Subsequent books included *Overland to the Islands*, 1958, *With Eyes at the Back of Our Heads*, 1960, *The Jacob's Ladder*, 1962, *O Taste and See*, 1964, *The Sorrow Dance*, 1967, *Relearning the Alphabet*, 1970, *To Stay Alive*, 1971, *Footprints*, 1972, *The Freeing of the Dust*, 1975, *Life in the Forest*, 1979, *Light Up the Cave*, 1981, *Candles in Babylon*, 1982, *Breathing the Water*, 1987, *A Door in the Hive*, 1989, and *Evening Train*, 1992. She also translated *In Praise of Krishna: Songs from the Bengali*, with Edward Dimock, Jr., 1967, edited *Out of the War Shadow*, a collection of antiwar and anti-draft writings, 1967, and published a volume of essays, criticism, and other writings, *The Poet in the World*, 1973.

When she became active in the anti-war movement of the 1960's, her poems became more political as well. Although this was not well received by some critics, she continued to write political poetry saying, "poetry is necessary to a whole man, and that poetry be not divided from the rest of life is necessary to it. Both life and poetry fade, wilt, shrink, when they are divorced." She was a frequent visiting lecturer, professor, or artist at colleges and universities, including Drew University in 1965, Vassar College in 1966–1967, the University of California at Berkeley in 1969, the Massachusetts Institute of Technology in 1969–1970, Kirkland College in 1970–1971, the University of Cincinnati in 1973, and Tufts University in 1973–1974. From 1975 to 1979 she joined the regular Tufts faculty as professor of English. She was a poet in residence at Brandeis University from 1981 to 1983, and in 1981 she became a professor at Stanford University. She was the recipient of numerous prizes and honors for her poetry.

Lewis, Edmonia 1845–? sculptor

Born on July 4, 1845, in Greenbush, near Albany, New York, Edmonia Lewis was of African descent on her father's side and Chippewa Indian on her mother's. By the age of four she was an orphan. She grew up among the Chippewas, by whom she was called Wildfire. Through an older brother she obtained admission to the preparatory department of Oberlin College in 1859, and in 1860–1862 she attended the college proper. She then made her way to Boston, where William Lloyd Garrison introduced her to a local sculptor from whom she received a few lessons in modeling. Her first work seen publicly was a medallion featuring the head of John Brown that was advertised early in 1864. Later in the year her bust of Colonel Robert Gould Shaw, a Boston favorite who had been killed leading his black troops in the assault on Fort Wagner before Charleston, was widely praised. Sales of copies of the bust allowed her to sail in 1865 for Rome, where she was taken under wing by Charlotte Cushman, Harriet Hosmer, Hiram Powers, and other members of the American artistic community.

She quickly achieved success as a sculptor. Her "Forever Free" (now at Howard University), a composition of two figures of emancipated slaves, attracted much notice in 1868, as did her "Hagar in the Wilderness" (now in Washington, D.C.) of the same year. Her bust of Henry Wadsworth Longfellow, modeled in 1869 largely from her own observations of him in Rome, ultimately went to Harvard. Other notable works included busts of Garrison, Lincoln, John Brown, and Maria Chapman, a grave statue of "Hygeia" commissioned by Dr. Harriot K. Hunt, a number of groups inspired by Longfellow's *Hiawatha*, including "The Marriage of Hiawatha" and "The Old Arrow-Maker and His Daughter," and several pieces sent to Philadelphia in 1876 for the Centennial Exposition, most notably "The Death of Cleopatra." Her early realism gave way to a more fashionable neoclassical style that continued nonetheless to exhibit, at least in her best works, striking evidence of genuine feeling. The change of fashion after the 1870s largely ended her celebrity, but she continued to work in her Rome studio. She visited the United States only occasionally. She was reported alive in Rome as late as 1909; no death record has been found.

Lewis, Ida 1842–1911 lighthouse keeper

Born on February 25, 1842, in Newport, Rhode Island, Idawalley Zoradia Lewis, known throughout life as Ida, grew up and attended public schools there until 1857, when the family moved to Lime Rock in Newport Harbor, where her father was keeper of the lighthouse. Before long her father incurred a disability that forced her to assume much of his work. Her daily rowing of her younger siblings to the mainland for school amply prepared her for trials to come. In 1858 or 1859 she rescued four young men whose pleasure boat had capsized in the harbor. On a cold winter day in 1866 she rescued a drunken sailor whose boat had foundered in the stormy waters. In 1867, during a terrific gale, she rescued three sheepherders who had gone into the water after a valuable sheep; she subsequently also saved the sheep, which belonged to August Belmont. Later that year she rescued a man marooned on a rock. In March 1869 she rushed hatless, coatless, and shoeless to the aid of two soldiers from Fort Adams whose sailboat had overturned in a squall.

This last feat came to the notice of a New York reporter, and within weeks Ida Lewis was known throughout the nation. In July a celebration was held in her honor in Newport, and she was given a skiff, named *Rescue*. The financier James Fisk later built her a boathouse. In October 1870 she married William H. Wilson, a fisherman of Black Rock, Connecticut, but they separated after a short time and she resumed her maiden name and her duties at Lime Rock. She rescued three soldiers from a reef in 1877, two more in 1881, and as late as 1906, at the age of sixty-four, saved a woman vacationer from the water. In 1879, after more than 20 years as de facto keeper of the Lime Rock lighthouse, she was finally given the job officially by the federal government. In 1906 she was given a pension by the Carnegie Hero Fund and a gold medal by the American Cross of Honor Society. Other honors had been accorded her at various times by the Rhode Island legislature and the Life Saving Benevolent Association of New York. Ida Lewis died on Lime Rock, Rhode Island, on October 24, 1911.

Lewisohn, Irene 1892–1944 social worker and theatrical patron

Born in New York City on September 5, 1892, Irene Lewisohn was of a wealthy and cultivated family. By 1902 both her parents had died and she and her elder sister Alice were left a substantial fortune. She attended the Finch School in New York and then pursued her deep interest in dance and the theater. She and her sister also became teachers at the Henry Street Settlement, a philanthropy in which their father had been interested, and they soon began organizing various forms of amateur dramatic and variety productions. The ethnic diversity of the Henry Street district was reflected in the productions of the settlement members, and the neighborhood in turn warmly adopted the new outlet for expression. A group from the settlement called the "Neighborhood Players" staged a full-length play in 1912. In 1914 the Lewisohn sisters built a theater adjacent to the settlement, naming it the Neighborhood Playhouse, and in 1915 it was presented formally to the Henry Street Settlement.

By 1920 the Neighborhood Playhouse had evolved from an amateur enterprise of local significance into a leader in the little theater movement. A resident professional company presented a highly diverse selection of avant-garde and exotic works, notably including the premiere of Eugene O'Neill's *The First Man* in 1922, Percy MacKaye's *This Fine-Pretty World* in 1923, *The Little Clay Cart* (from the Hindu *Mrcchakatikā*)in 1924, and *The Dybbuk* in 1925; the last two were especially popular, in part owing to the designs of Aline Bernstein. For several years from 1923 the playhouse also produced an annual satirical revue called the *Grand Street Follies*. Irene Lewisohn's involvement in the playhouse was intensely personal, ranging from financial support through production and direction to occasional appearances on stage in dance roles. From 1925 her sister's participation was greatly reduced. The Neighborhood Playhouse closed as a professional theater in 1927, and the physical plant was taken over again by the Henry Street Settlement. In 1935 a special production of Federico Garcia Lorca's *Bitter Oleander* (originally *Bodas de Sangre*) marked the 20th anniversary of the founding of the playhouse.

Meanwhile, in 1928, Lewisohn helped found the Neighborhood Playhouse School of the Theater, of which she remained thereafter co-director with Rita W. Morgenthau. Her abiding interest in the theater of dance led to her creating a number of "orchestral dramas" or "musical masques," one of which was presented at the Manhattan Opera House in 1928 and another, featuring Martha Graham and the Cleveland Orchestra, in 1930. In 1931 yet another was performed in Washington, D.C., under commission of the Elizabeth Sprague Coolidge Foundation. In 1937, with Aline Bernstein, she founded the Museum of Costume Art (later the Costume Institute and later still a department of the Metropolitan Museum of Art). During the Spanish Civil War she founded the Spanish Child Welfare Association, and during World War II she was active in the Stage Door Canteen. She died in New York City on April 4, 1944.

Lhevinne, Rosina 1880–1976 pianist and educator

Born in Kiev (some sources say Moscow), Russia, on March 29, 1880, Rosina Bessie was of Dutch and Russian parentage. At the age of nine she entered the Imperial

Conservatory of Music, from which she graduated in 1898. While a student she made her public debut with the Moscow Symphony in February 1895. In June 1898 she married Josef Lhevinne, the conservatory's star pupil and destined to be a piano virtuoso of worldwide reputation. On her marriage she abandoned plans for a career as a concert pianist, although over the next several years she appeared occasionally as a soloist, notably in Vienna in 1910, St. Petersburg in 1911, and Berlin in 1912. Rather more frequently she and her husband gave duet recitals. They lived at various times in Tbilisi, Berlin, and Moscow.

In 1919, after having been interned in Berlin during World War I, they emigrated to the United States, where they had first performed in 1906 and had toured in 1907–1908. By that time Rosina Lhevinne had largely withdrawn from performing, and in 1925 she joined the faculty of the Juilliard School of Music in New York City. After her husband's death in 1944 she devoted herself more fully to her students and became in time the doyenne of piano teachers in America. Among those profiting from her skilled discipline were Van Cliburn, David Bar-Illan, John Browning, Misha Dichter, and David Pollack. In addition to her Juilliard students she taught summer master classes at the Los Angeles Conservatory from 1945 to 1956, at the Aspen Music Festival School from 1956 to 1970, and at the University of Southern California from 1971. She continued to perform publicly on occasion as well and appeared with the Roth, Gordon, and Juilliard string quartets. Her appearances as soloist with the National Orchestral Association in 1961 and with the New York Philharmonic in 1961 and 1963 were highly praised. She died in Glendale, California, on November 9, 1976.

Libbey, Laura Jean 1862–1924 novelist

Born on March 22, 1862, perhaps in Brooklyn, New York, although Milwaukee, Wisconsin, and Springfield, Massachusetts, appear in some sources, Laura Libbey at least grew up in Brooklyn and was educated privately. At an early age she began submitting articles and stories to the *New York Ledger*, the *Fireside Companion*, and the *Family Story Paper*. Her serialized stories were subsequently published in book form as cheap paperbacks by various pulp publishers, and in that form they were enormously popular. They were all virtually alike in their melodramatic plots and their happy endings of true and virtuous love rewarded. Critics seldom deigned even to notice them, but her audience of young working class girls was as voracious as she was prolific. Some 60 novels appeared over her name during the 1880s and 1890s bearing such titles as *A Fatal Wooing*, *All for Love of a Fair Face*, *A Forbidden Marriage*, *When His Love Grew Cold*, *Lotta, the Cloak Model*, *The Price of a Kiss*, *Miss Middleton's Lover*, *Only a Mechanic's Daughter*, *Olive's Courtship*, and *Lovers Once But Strangers Now*. Sales of her books were estimated to run upwards of ten million.

During 1891–1894 Libbey edited the *Fashion Bazaar* magazine in New York, and in 1899–1901 she was a regular contributor of articles to the *New York Evening World*. With James R. Garey she dramatized *Miss Middleton's Lover*, and the resulting play, *Parted on Her Bridal Tour*, was successfully produced in March 1907 at Blaney's Theatre, Brooklyn. Over the next year and a half she dictated over 150 more plays, apparently none of which was ever produced or published. Her books continued to appear as late as 1923, totaling in the end about 160, and reprinted editions of many of them continued to sell for years afterward. She died in Brooklyn on October 25, 1924.

Liliuokalani 1838–1917 queen of Hawaii

Born in Honolulu on September 2, 1838, Liliuokalani was of a high-ranking family close to the throne of Kamehameha III. She was originally named Lydia Kamakaeha Paki, the surname being that of her adoptive family, and she was educated by American missionaries at the Royal School. After a time as a member of the court of Kamehameha

IV she was married in September 1862 to John Owen Dominis, son of a Boston sea captain and himself an official in the Hawaiian government. In 1874 her brother David Kalakaua was chosen king, and in 1877, on the death of a second brother, W. P. Leleiohoku, who was heir apparent, she was named heir presumptive. She was known from that time by her royal name, Liliuokalani.

Over the next 14 years she established herself firmly in that role. She served as regent during King Kalakaua's world tour in 1881, and she was active in organizing schools for Hawaiian youth. During a world tour in 1887 she was received by President Grover Cleveland and by Queen Victoria. On the death of King Kalakaua in January 1891 Liliuokalani ascended the throne, becoming the first woman ever to occupy it. She immediately undertook to restore to the throne its traditional autocracy. The U.S.-Hawaiian Reciprocity Treaty renewed in 1887 had included provisions for ministerial government, along with granting commercial privileges and ceding Pearl Harbor as a naval base, and the government had quickly become dominated by the largely American haole, representing commercial interests. Her domineering manner, together with economic setbacks for the islands' sugar industry, led to confrontation. When she attempted to promulgate a new constitution in January 1893, a Committee of Public Safety was formed under the leadership of Sanford B. Dole, and she was forced aside. She acceded to the establishment of the Provisional Government in order to avoid bloodshed.

A revolt by her followers in 1894 was easily put down by the government of the Republic of Hawaii, and for several months thereafter she was held under house arrest in the former royal palace. In January 1895, in return for the pardoning of others imprisoned after the revolt, she formally abdicated. She fought bitterly against annexation of the islands by the United States as head of the Oni pa'a (Stand Firm) movement, whose motto was "Hawaii for the Hawaiians." Annexation nonetheless occurred in July 1898. In that year she published *Hawaii's Story by Hawaii's Queen* and composed a song ever afterward beloved in the islands, "Aloha Oe." She lived quietly thereafter in Honolulu, enjoying a government pension and the homage of islanders and visitors alike. She died in Honolulu on November 11, 1917.

Lincoln, Mary Johnson Bailey 1844–1921 educator and cookery expert

Born on July 8, 1844, in South Attleboro, Massachusetts, Mary Bailey grew up there and from about 1851 in Norton, Massachusetts, where she attended Wheaton Female Seminary. She graduated in 1864, taught school in Vermont for a term, and in June 1865 married David A. Lincoln, with whom she moved to Boston. During the 1870s, with her husband in poor health, she supplemented the family's income by sewing, cooking, and other domestic work. In December 1879, after a month's training, she became a teacher in the Boston Cooking School, which had opened the previous March under the auspices of the Woman's Education Association of Boston. She remained at the school for just over five years, until January 1885.

In addition to teaching classes of nurses, cooks, homemakers, and other teachers, she also worked to compile her *Boston Cook Book*, a thorough and lucid compilation of her recipes and methods, course outlines, and information on chemistry, physiology, and hygiene that was published in 1884. The book was a great commercial success and went through many editions. From 1885 to 1889 Lincoln taught cooking classes at the Lasell Seminary in Auburndale, Massachusetts, and during that time she published *Peerless Cook Book*, 1886, *Boston School Kitchen Text-Book*, 1887, and *Carving and Serving*, 1887. Thereafter she devoted herself to writing for various periodicals, notably the *American Kitchen Magazine*, with which she was associated from 1894 to 1904 and of which she was a part owner from 1895, and to lecture courses in cookery, which she delivered in every part of the country. In 1904 she published *What to Have for*

Luncheon. After several years of declining health she died in Boston on December 2, 1921.

Lincoln, Mary Todd 1818–1882 First Lady

Born in Lexington, Kentucky, on December 13, 1818, Mary Ann Todd grew up in a prosperous Southern home attended by numbers of servants. She was educated in private academies. In 1839 she went to live with her sister, Mrs. Ninian W. Edwards, in Springfield, Illinois. As an attractive and accomplished member of a prominent household — her sister's father-in-law was a former governor of Illinois — she attracted much attention. In particular she attracted Abraham Lincoln, then a down-at-heels country lawyer with no firm prospects. Theirs was a painful courtship, interrupted by Lincoln's melancholy self-doubt and nearly scoffed by tragedy when he took responsibility for some satirical newspaper skits that Mary Todd had written and that nearly provoked a duel. In November 1842, over her sister's objections, she married Lincoln. For the next 19 years she kept the home in Springfield. Her domestic life was a fairly happy one, despite the untimely death of one of her four sons and her husband's protracted absences on the circuit or in Congress. Gradually, however, her physical ailments and periods of nervous strain or hysteria became more frequent. Her querulousness, although in later years much exaggerated by unfriendly commentators, was genuine.

In March 1861 she began an entirely new life as mistress of the White house. Her position was a difficult one, made more so by her Southern birth, and a great deal of malicious gossip circulated. Her gracious performance as hostess drew fire, as did her alleged extravagance. The death of another son in 1862 added to the strain, and soon she was the victim of frequent bouts of almost violent irrationality. The assassination of Lincoln in April 1865 was almost more than she could bear. She secluded herself in Chicago for a time. Much of the rest of her life was haunted by a powerful delusion that she was in dire poverty, linked with an obsession to buy extravagantly. The wide public credence given the claims of William H. Herndon, Lincoln's former law partner, about her husband's relations with Ann Rutledge and other matters, together with occasional bursts of unfavorable publicity about her own life, kept her in a state of perpetual agitation.

In 1868 she traveled to Europe and lived for a time in Germany and then England. The pension allowed her at last by Congress in 1870 did nothing to assuage her fears of poverty. In 1871, shortly after her return to Chicago, her youngest son died. In 1875 her eldest son, Robert Todd Lincoln, arranged for a sanity hearing, in consequence of which she was confined for some months in a sanatorium in Batavia, Illinois. Later she was placed in the care of her sister in Springfield. A second hearing in 1876 reversed the earlier finding of insanity, leaving her free but publicly humiliated. For four years she again resided in Europe. She returned late in 1880 to Springfield, Illinois, where she remained in declining health until her death on July 16, 1882.

Lindbergh, Anne Spencer Morrow 1906– writer

Born in Englewood, New Jersey, on June 22, 1906, Anne Morrow was the daughter of Dwight W. Morrow, a prominent Wall Street lawyer and in 1927–1930 U.S. ambassador to Mexico. She attended Miss Chapin's School in New York City and in 1928 graduated from Smith College, where she won prizes for early literary efforts. She met Charles Lindbergh at her father's embassy in Mexico City in December 1927 and married him in May 1929. The fame and publicity that had been showered on him since his daring Atlantic flight of May 1927 quickly engulfed her as well. She accompanied her husband on nearly all of his flights to various parts of the world and in 1931 herself qualified for a pilot's license.

She was widely honored for her part in the development of aviation and in 1934 was the first woman to receive the Hubbard Medal of the National Geographic Society. The tragic kidnap and murder of the Lindberghs' infant son in March 1932, the sensational capture and trial of Bruno Richard Hauptmann for the crime in 1934–1935, and the incessant newspaper publicity that attended every detail of the case drove the essentially retiring couple to seek refuge in England in 1935. In that year Anne Lindbergh published her first book, *North to the Orient*, an account of their pioneering flight across Canada, Alaska, and Siberia to Japan and China in 1931. *Listen! the Wind*, 1938, told of their five-month, 30,000-mile survey of transatlantic air routes in 1933. After a year in France the Lindberghs returned to the United States in 1939. In *The Wave of the Future*, 1940, she wrote in support of Charles Lindbergh's isolationist outlook on world war. Her next book, *The Steep Ascent*, 1944, was a novel.

Subsequent books included *Gift from the Sea*, a best-selling collection of poetic essays on nature and human life, 1955, *The Unicorn and Other Poems, 1935–1955*, 1956, *Dearly Beloved: A Theme and Variations*, a novel, 1962, *Earth Shine*, two long essays, 1969, and several widely admired volumes of excerpts from her diaries and letters: *Bring Me a Unicorn*, 1972, *Hour of Gold, Hour of Lead*, 1973, *Locked Rooms and Open Doors*, 1974, *The Flower and the Nettle*, 1976, and *War Within and Without*, 1980.

Lippincott, Sara Jane Clarke 1823–1904 writer and lecturer

Born in Pompey, New York, on September 23, 1823, Sara Jane Clarke was a great-granddaughter of the Reverend Jonathan Edwards. She attended schools in Rochester, New York, and in 1843 settled with her family in New Brighton, Pennsylvania. As early as 1836 she had published some verses in Rochester newspapers, and from 1844 she was a regular contributor to magazines, notably Nathaniel P. Willis's *New Mirror* and *Home Journal*, later *Sartain's*, *Graham's*, *Union Magazine*, and later still *Hearth and Home*, *Christian Union*, *Atlantic Monthly*, *Harper's New Monthly*, and others. Her early sketches in the *Home Journal*, were signed "Grace Greenwood," and she soon adopted the name for all her writing and even used it in private life.

Her first book, a collection of magazine articles and sketches, was *Greenwood Leaves*, 1850. It was followed by *History of My Pets*, 1850, *Poems*, 1851, *Greenwood Leaves: Second Series*, 1852, and *Recollections of My Childhood and Other Stories*, 1852. In 1849–1850 she was on the staff of *Godey's Lady's Book*. During a tour of Europe in 1852–1853 she sent back a series of lively travel sketches and interviews to the *National Era* and the *Saturday Evening Post* that were later collected in *Haps and Mishaps of a Tour in Europe*, 1854, whose popularity kept it in print for 40 years.

In October 1853 Greenwood married Leander K. Lippincott, with whom she founded in Philadelphia the *Little Pilgrim*, a juvenile monthly that was, typically for the day, pious and nationalistic in tone. Her own contributions to the magazine were later collected in *Merrie England: Travels, Descriptions, Tales, and Historical Sketches*, 1855, *A Forest Tragedy and Other Tales*, 1856, *Stories and Legends of Travel and History for Children*, 1857, *Stories from Famous Ballads*, 1860, *Bonnie Scotland: Tales of Her History, Heroes, and Poets*, 1861, *Stories and Sights of France and Italy*, 1867, and *Heads and Tails: Studies and Stories of Pets*, 1875. The *Little Pilgrim* ceased publication in 1875.

From the late 1850s to the early 1870s Grace Greenwood was also a popular lecturer on the lyceum circuit; her subjects ranged from inspirational and literary ones to mild calls for such reforms as pacifism and abolition of capital punishment. During the Civil War she won much esteem, including that of President Abraham Lincoln, for her patriotic lecturing, fund-raising, and personal visiting of Union troops.

Her reminiscences of that period were published as *Records of Five Years*, 1867. In the early 1870s she was the Washington, D.C., correspondent for the *New York Times* and for papers in Philadelphia, Chicago, and elsewhere. *New Life in New Lands*, 1873, collected her articles on her many visits to Colorado and the West. In 1875 she took her daughter to Europe for her education, and she remained for more than a decade, during which she contributed letters on current topics to the *Independent*. She later lived in New York City and from 1892 in Washington, D.C. She continued to write for the *Independent* until 1903. Her later books included *Queen Victoria: Her Childhood and Womanhood*, 1883, *Stories for Home Folks*, 1885, and *Stories and Sketches*, 1892. She died in New Rochelle, New York, on April 20, 1904.

Livermore, Mary Ashton Rice 1820–1905 suffragist and reformer

Born on December 19, 1820, in Boston, Mary Rice grew up and was educated in public schools there before attending the Female Seminary in Charlestown, where she remained to teach for two years after graduation in 1836. From 1839 to 1842 she was a tutor on a Virginia plantation. The experience made her an ardent foe of slavery. She then took charge of a private school in Duxbury, Massachusetts, where she remained until her marriage in May 1845 to Daniel P. Livermore, a Universalist minister and ardent temperance advocate. Daniel Livermore served several New England parishes in the next ten years, and during that time Mary Livermore wrote for various religious and reform periodicals. They decided to emigrate to Kansas in 1857, but the illness of a daughter ended their journey at Chicago, where for 12 years they edited the *New Covenant*, a Unitarian periodical.

In 1863 she published *Pen Pictures*, a collection of essays and sketches. Soon after the outbreak of the Civil War she volunteered her services to the Chicago (later Northwestern) Sanitary Commission. Early in 1862 she and her friend Jane C. Hoge made a tour of military hospitals at St. Louis, Cairo, Mound City, and elsewhere, and in December of that year they were made co-directors of the Chicago branch of the U.S. Sanitary Commission. Their joint efforts at inspiring and maintaining a flow of supplies from local aid societies all over the upper Midwest was so successful that the Chicago office was credited with two-thirds of the material collected by the Sanitary Commission. During July-October 1863 they stepped down temporarily to organize the great Sanitary Fair, which raised over $70,000 and inspired similar efforts in several other cities. Through her work with the Sanitary Commission Livermore became convinced that extending the vote to women was the key to many social reforms, including temperance, and she began to devote an increasing amount of energy to the woman suffrage movement.

Elected president of the Illinois Woman Suffrage Association in 1868, after she had called a suffrage convention in Chicago, she launched in January 1869 the *Agitator*, a suffragist paper. Later in the year she attended the founding convention of the American Woman Suffrage Convention in Cleveland and was elected a vice-president. She moved back east to Melrose, Massachusetts, in the same year to become editor of the *Woman's Journal*, a new Boston periodical, with which the *Agitator* merged. In 1870 she helped found the Massachusetts Woman Suffrage Association. After two years she resigned the editorship of the *Woman's Journal*; the years after 1872 were devoted to a vigorous schedule of lecturing. An accomplished public speaker, she never tired in her efforts to arouse public opinion on the need for educating women and for changing the liquor laws. She remained active in the suffrage movement, serving as president of the American Woman Suffrage Association from 1875 to 1878 and succeeding Lucy Stone as president of the Massachusetts association from 1893 to 1903. She was also president of the Association for the Advancement of Women in 1873 and of the Massachusetts Woman's Christian Temperance Union from 1875 to 1885. In 1895 she retired from the lecture circuit.

Her lectures and articles were published in numerous periodicals. *My Story of the War: A Woman's Narrative of Four Years Personal Experience* appeared in 1887 and was followed in 1897 by *The Story of My Life, or, The Sunshine and Shadow of Seventy Years*.

She was joint editor, with Frances E. Willard, of *A Woman of the Century*, a highly successful compilation of biographies that first appeared in 1893. She died in Melrose, Massachusetts, on May 23, 1905.

Locke, Bessie 1865–1952 educator

Born on August 7, 1865, in West Cambridge (now Arlington), Massachusetts, Bessie Locke grew up there and in Brooklyn, New York, where she attended public schools. She later took some business courses at Columbia University. In her teens she worked as a bookkeeper in her father's fabric-printing factory, and later she managed an uncle's millinery store in North Carolina. Her interest in educational reform found early expression in the organization of industrial classes for women under the aegis of the Brooklyn King's Daughters Circle, of which she was for a time president.

About 1892 Locke visited a kindergarten conducted by a friend who had studied with Maria Kraus-Boelté. The effect of the kindergarten on the immigrant children of the tenement district in which it operated astonished her, and she became convinced that the kindergarten was of a potential importance to the future health of society equal to that of the church. Among a circle of influential citizens she collected money and formed the East End Kindergarten Union of Brooklyn. From 1896 to 1923 she was financial secretary and later trustee of the Brooklyn Free Kindergarten Society, and from 1899 she was financial secretary of the New York Kindergarten Society. Her talent as a fund-raiser was remarkable. She raised $700,000 for mission kindergartens and for five permanently endowed private kindergartens and tapped John D. Archbold, vice-president of Standard Oil of New Jersey, for $250,000 for a community center and headquarters building for the New York Kindergarten Society.

In 1909, after three years of groundwork, Locke led in founding the National Association for the Promotion of Kindergarten Education, which in 1911 became the National Kindergarten Association. She was a director and the executive secretary of the association for the rest of her life. In 1912 the National Kindergarten Association was asked to assist in establishing a kindergarten division in the U.S. Bureau of Education, and from 1913 to 1919 Bessie Locke was chief of the division. In 1917 she inaugurated in the division a series of home education articles for parents. From 1919 the articles were published by the National Kindergarten Association, and by 1952 they had circulated to an estimated 38 million people. From 1913 to 1922 she chaired the kindergarten extension division of the National Congress of Parents and Teachers. During her long career her efforts led directly to the opening of 3260 kindergartens enrolling 1.6 million pupils. She also served as a director of the National Council of Women from 1921 to 1946 and as honorary vice-president thereafter. From 1920 she was on the governing board of the National College of Education of Evanston, Illinois. Locke died in New York City on April 9, 1952.

Lockwood, Belva Ann Bennett 1830–1917 lawyer and reformer

Born at Royalton, Niagara County, New York, on October 24, 1830, Belva Bennett attended country schools until she was fifteen and then taught in them until her marriage in November 1848 to Uriah H. McNall, a local farmer who died in 1853. Belva McNall then resumed teaching and continued her own education. She graduated from Genesee College (forerunner of Syracuse University) in 1857. After college she continued as a teacher in various towns in upper New York state until 1866, when she moved to Washington, D.C. There she taught for a year and then, while operating her own private school, took up the study of law. In March 1868 she married Ezekiel Lockwood, a former minister and dentist who took over her school. After Columbian College (now George Washington University), Georgetown University, and Howard University had each refused her admission, she was enrolled in the new National University Law School in

Belva Lockwood

1871. She graduated in 1873 and in the same year was admitted to the District of Columbia bar.

Offended by the legal and economic discrimination against women in American society, Lockwood became one of the most effective advocates of women's rights of her time. Her law practice dealt primarily with pension claims against the government, but her work in Washington gave her the opportunity to lobby on behalf of legislation favorable to women. She drafted a bill for equal pay for equal work by women in government employment, and the bill was enacted into law in 1872. After being denied admission to the Supreme Court in 1876 she singlehandedly lobbied through Congress enabling legislation and in March 1879 became the first woman to be admitted to practice before the Court. She gained national prominence as a lecturer on women's rights and was active in the affairs of various suffrage organizations.

In 1884 she was nominated to run for the presidency on the ticket of the National Equal Rights party, a small California group. Despite criticism and even ridicule she conducted a dignified campaign on a broad platform of reform and won 4,149 votes in 6 states. A second campaign in 1888 was less effective. She was chosen by the Department of State to be a delegate to the International Congress of Charities, Correction, and Philanthropy at Geneva in 1896, and she attended peace congresses in Europe in 1889, 1906, 1908, and 1911. She took a prominent part in the campaign headed by Ellen S. Mussey that secured for the married women of the district equal property rights and equal guardianship of children in 1896. When the statehood bills for Oklahoma, New Mexico, and Arizona came before Congress in 1903, she prepared amendments granting suffrage to women in the proposed new states. She held office in several reform organizations, including the Universal Peace Union, the International Peace Bureau, the Nobel Peace Prize nominating committee, the League of Women Voters, and the National and American Woman Suffrage associations. Lockwood died on May 19, 1917, in Washington, D.C.

Loeb, Sophie Irene Simon 1876–1929 journalist and welfare worker

Born on July 4, 1876, in Rovno, Russia, Sophie Simon came with her parents to the United States when she was six. She grew up and attended school in McKeesport, Pennsylvania. She taught school there until her marriage in March 1896 to Anselm Loeb. The marriage was not successful, and in 1910 she obtained a divorce and moved to New York City. She soon secured a position with the *New York Evening World*, to which she had contributed occasional articles from McKeesport. In 1913 she published a book of *Epigrams of Eve*.

In the course of her reportorial work Loeb became particularly interested in the plight of widowed mothers, and she used the columns of her newspaper to publicize both the problem and the work of such leaders as Hannah B. Einstein toward a solution. In 1913 she and Einstein were appointed to the newly created State Commission on Relief for Widowed Mothers. She made a tour of several European nations in 1913–1914 to study welfare practices for the commission. Her work with the commission and on the *Evening World* contributed immeasurably to the passage by the legislature in 1915 of a bill authorizing the creation of child welfare boards in every county and the use of public money for the support of widowed mothers — the "mother's pension."

In that year Loeb was appointed to New York City's Child Welfare Board, of which she became president. During the eight years she held that post she made her board a model for others. Administrative expenses were kept to a bare minimum, while the use of trained social workers as case investigators assured maximum equity in the distribution of funds. Her effectiveness was also indicated by the increase in the board's appropriation from $100,000 in its first year to more than $4.5 million at the end of her term. During that time she also served on a commission appointed by Governor Alfred E. Smith in 1920 to codify the state's laws in the child welfare field. In the same year she published *Everyman's Child*. In 1924 she helped found and became first president of the Child Welfare Committee of America. Her belief in the importance of keeping families together and children out of orphanages was endorsed by the International Congress on Child Welfare in Geneva in 1926, which she attended, and in 1927 she submitted a report on blind children in America to the League of Nations.

Other public topics that occupied Loeb at various times included corruption in the New York Public Service Commission, an investigation of which she instigated in 1916; legislation for cheap school lunches and milk; reforms in taxi fares and driver bonding; health and safety regulations for motion picture theaters; tenement regulation, play streets, and public baths; and free maternity care for the indigent. She mediated a New York City taxi strike in 1917 in seven hours. Her 1925 tour of Palestine converted her to Zionism and resulted in *Palestine Awake: The Rebirth of a Nation*, 1926. Sophie Loeb died in New York City on January 18, 1929.

Lombard, Carole 1908–1942 actor

Born on October 6, 1908, in Fort Wayne, Indiana, Jane Alice Peters grew up there and, after her parents' divorce in 1916, in Los Angeles. Her mother enrolled her in the Marian Nolks Dramatic School, and at the age of twelve she won a part in the motion picture *The Perfect Crime*. She graduated from Los Angeles High School in 1924 and was quickly put under contract by the Fox Film Corporation. After a part in *Hearts and Spurs*, a 1925 Buck Jones western, she appeared with Edmund Lowe in *Marriage in Transit* under her new name, Carol (changed in 1930 to Carole) Lombard. An automobile accident a short time later interrupted her career until plastic surgery largely erased a disfiguring facial scar.

In 1927–1928 Lombard first displayed hints of her comedic talent in a series of Mack Sennett two-reelers. She then worked briefly for Pathé and later free-lanced in such films as *Ned McCobb'sDaughter*, *Big News*, *High Voltage*, and *The Racketeer* all in 1929, and *Fast and Loose* and *The Arizona Kid* in 1930. In 1930 she signed with Paramount Pictures. After a few wasted films she began to find her métier in such comedies as *Man of the World*, 1931, *No Man of Her Own*, 1932, *Twentieth Century*, 1934, *The Gay Bride*, 1934, *Hands Across the Table*, 1935, *The Princess Comes Across*, 1936, and *My Man Godfrey*, 1936. By the time of the last film she was a star and the leading female exponent of the "screwball comedy" genre. Her film character played her own slender blond beauty against the breezy, earthy, wisecracking realism and great energy that audiences came to love. *True Confession*, 1937, *Nothing Sacred*, 1937, *Fools for Scandal*, 1938, *In Name Only*, 1939, *Made for Each Other*, 1939, and *They Knew What They Wanted*, 1940, continued her great popularity.

Lombard's marriage to William Powell in 1931 had ended in divorce in 1933, and in March 1939 she married Clark Gable. They made one of Hollywood's most popular and publicized couples. She took fewer film roles in order to learn to share Gable's taste for outdoor life. They were noted hosts to the film colony, and Lombard was widely known as a practical joker and a raconteur of considerable talent. Shortly after the completion of *To Be or Not to Be*, 1942, she undertook one of her many cross-country promotional tours on behalf of war bonds. On January 16, 1942, on the return leg from Indianapolis to Los Angeles, the airplane in which she was a passenger crashed into Table Rock southwest of Las Vegas, Nevada, killing all 21 persons aboard.

Longshore, Hannah E. Myers 1819–1901 physician

Born on May 30, 1819, in Sandy Spring, Maryland, Hannah Myers grew up there, in Washington, D.C., where she attended a Quaker school, and from 1833 in Columbiana County, Ohio. Her interest in academic subjects, particularly science, was encouraged in her liberal Quaker home and at the New Lisbon Academy, where she adopted her middle initial to distinguish herself from a classmate of the same name. Lack of funds stood in the way of her entering Oberlin College and of her studying medicine. In March 1841 she married Thomas E. Longshore, a teacher, with whom she moved to Attleboro (now Langhorne), Pennsylvania, in 1845. There she undertook the study of medicine privately under her brother-in-law, Joseph S. Longshore, an eclectic physician. Joseph Longshore, already a reformer of zeal in many fields and no doubt stimulated by the enthusiasm and ability of his apprentice, drafted the charter and secured the establishment of the Female (later Woman's) Medical College of Pennsylvania in 1850.

Hannah Longshore entered the college in the first class and graduated in December 1851. (Ann Preston was a classmate.) During her second session she was a demonstrator as well as student, making her the first woman faculty member of a medical school in the nation. She was a demonstrator of anatomy at the New England Female Medical College in Boston in 1852, again at the Female Medical College of Pennsylvania in 1852–1853, and at the Penn Medical University, also in Philadelphia, in 1853–1857.

Longshore's private practice was slow to develop in the face of ingrained prejudices against women doctors, but the great success of several series of public lectures on physiology and hygiene eventually brought under her care an estimated 300 families. Before long her reputation was such that male colleagues referred patients to her, albeit frequently in secret. Her large practice occupied her until her retirement in 1892. She died in Philadelphia on October 18, 1901.

Longworth, Alice Roosevelt 1884–1980 socialite

Born in New York City on February 12, 1884, Alice Lee Roosevelt was the daughter of Theodore Roosevelt, then a New York assemblyman. Her mother died two days after her birth, and during her father's long absence in Dakota Territory she was reared by an aunt. After her father's marriage in December 1886 to Edith Kermit Carow and the establishment of the family seat at Sagamore Hill in Oyster Bay, Long Island, she grew up in a home of wealth, tradition, and politics. The family followed Theodore Roosevelt to Washington, D.C., back to New York City, to Albany, and in 1901 again to Washington.

His accession to the presidency in September of that year thrust young Alice into the national spotlight. Headstrong and rebellious and with a pronounced taste for the society of aristocrats and the Gilded Age wealthy, she was a favorite topic for the mass circulation yellow press, which slavishly recorded the comings and goings, the defiance of conventions, and the acid comments on contemporaries of "Princess Alice." Her reported favorite color, a shade of blue-gray, became widely popular as "Alice blue" and later inspired the song "In My Sweet Little Alice Blue Gown" (Joseph McCarthy, Harry Tierney), introduced in the musical *Irene*, 1919. Asked if he could not keep her in line, the President was quoted as saying "I can do one of two things. I can be president of the United States, or I can control Alice. I cannot possibly do both."

In February 1906 she and Ohio Representative Nicholas Longworth were married in the East Room of the White House. After her marriage Alice Longworth devoted less time to the social scene and more to politics. The Longworth house became a center of Republican conviviality, especially during Nicholas Longworth's speakership of the House of Representatives from 1925 to 1931. After his death in the latter year Alice Longworth maintained her Washington home and her position near the center of national politics and capital social life. She campaigned against her fifth cousin, once removed, Franklin D. Roosevelt, and her scathing imitation of her first cousin Eleanor was a favorite entertainment in Republican social circles during the long New Deal period. In 1934 she published a volume of memoirs entitled *Crowded Hours*, and she collaborated with Theodore Roosevelt, Jr. on *The Desk Drawer Anthology: Poems for the American*

People, published in 1937. After a period of relative eclipse her celebrity reappeared again during the Eisenhower years, when her acerbic wit and gossip were frequently the best newspaper copy in Washington. She remained thereafter a fixture of the Washington scene, earning the nickname, "Washington's other monument." She served on the America First Committee in 1940 and was the Ohio delegate to the Republican National Convention in 1936, 1940 and 1944. She died at her home in Washington, D.C., on February 20, 1980.

Loos, Anita 1888?–1981 screenwriter and novelist

Born on April 26, probably in 1888 (some sources say 1893), Anita Loos grew up in Sissons (now Mount Shasta), California, and in San Francisco, Los Angeles, and San Diego. In San Francisco her father published the *Dramatic Review*, and in this role he helped her win child's parts in several theatrical productions. At an early age she also began contributing sketches and articles to various periodicals. In 1912 she submitted a scenario to the Biograph Company that was made by D. W. Griffith into the motion picture *The New York Hat* starring Mary Pickford and Lionel Barrymore. Several more scenarios followed, and eventually she was hired by Griffith to write on a salary basis. Lillian and Dorothy Gish, Norma and Constance Talmadge, and others acted her stories on film.

His Picture in the Paper, 1916, a Douglas Fairbanks film, signaled a new departure in its use of discursive and witty titles, and its success convinced Griffith to let Anita Loos write titles for his epic *Intolerance*, 1916, and many others. Her lightly satiric touch contributed to Fairbanks's continuing popularity in several films. By 1919 she had written scenarios or titles for some 200 films and was credited with bringing a whole new dimension to films; in some circles she was known as the "O. Henrietta" of the movies.

In that year Loos married writer-director John Emerson, a frequent collaborator, and in New York City they began writing and producing their own films, notably a series of starring vehicles for Constance Talmadge including *A Virtuous Vamp*, 1919, *The Perfect Woman*, 1920, *Dangerous Business*, 1921, *Polly of the Follies*, 1922, and *Learning to Love*, 1925. They also wrote two books, *Breaking Into the Movies*, 1919, and *How to Write Photoplays*, 1921, and on her own Loos wrote two plays for Broadway, *The Whole Town's Talking*, which opened at the Bijou Theatre, New York, in August 1923, and *The Fall of Eve*, at the Booth in August 1925.

In 1926, the year after its serialization in *Harper's Bazaar*, Loos's first fictional volume appeared: *Gentlemen Prefer Blondes*, a small book whose success was immediate and astonishing. The tale of the disarmingly mindless but ineluctably blonde gold digger from Arkansas, Lorelei Lee, made Loos an international celebrity. Her stage version of the story opened at the Times Square Theatre in New York in September 1926 and later toured successfully. Over two decades later she wrote with Joseph Fields the book for a musical version that was a smash hit with Carol Channing in the lead, and in 1953 Marilyn Monroe starred in a movie version. Her next book, *But Gentlemen Marry Brunettes*, 1928, was also successful although overshadowed by its predecessor.

In 1931 Loos and her husband collaborated in writing and directing *The Social Register* for Broadway. She then moved to Hollywood and began writing scripts for MGM. Among her scripts were those for *Red-Headed Woman*, which starred Jean Harlow in 1932, *The Girl from Missouri*, 1934, *Biography of a Bachelor Girl*, 1935, *Riffraff*, 1935, *San Francisco*, 1936, *The Women*, adapted from Clare Boothe Luce's play in 1939, *Susan and God*, 1940, and *I Married an Angel*, 1942. In October 1946 *Happy Birthday*, a play she wrote especially for her close friend Helen Hayes, opened at the Broadhurst Theatre for a long run. Her dramatization of Colette's *Gigi* was produced in 1951, and she subsequently produced a number of other adaptations from French sources. *A Mouse Is*

Born, 1951, and *No Mother to Guide Her*, 1961, were novels, and *This Brunette Prefers Work*, 1956, was an autobiography. She wrote *Twice Over Lightly: New York Then and Now*, 1972, in collaboration with Helen Hayes. *A Girl Like I*, 1966, and *Kiss Hollywood Good-By*, 1974, were volumes of reminiscences. Her last work for the stage was *Lorelei* in 1974, another adaptation of *Gentlemen Prefer Blondes*. In 1977 she published *Cast of Thousands*, her memoirs and commentary on her Hollywood friends. *The Talmadge Girls: A Memoir*, 1978, drew on her early experiences writing for silent movies. She died August 18, 1981, in New York City.

Lord, Pauline 1890–1950 actor

Born on August 13, 1890, in Hanford, California, Pauline Lord grew up in San Francisco. She attended a convent school for a time, but her early attraction to the theater led her to the school of the Alcazar Theatre in San Francisco. There, at thirteen, she made her stage debut in a small role with the Belasco Stock Company in *Are You a Mason?* An invitation from Nat Goodwin, who saw her in San Francisco, brought her to New York City to join his troupe in 1905. Later she acted with stock companies in Springfield, Massachusetts, and Milwaukee for a number of years.

In January 1912 she made her New York debut on the legitimate stage in *The Talker* and attracted some attention. Vaudeville and touring engagements over the next five years were punctuated by appearances in such pieces as Elmer Rice's *On Trial*, 1915. In August 1917 she drew high critical praise for her performance in the otherwise unsuccessful *The Deluge*.

For four years Lord made do with mediocre scripts — *Under Pressure*, 1917, *Out There*, a production also featuring Minnie Maddern Fiske, Laurette Taylor, and George M. Cohan, 1917, *April*, 1918, *Our Pleasant Sins*, 1919, and *Big Game*, 1920, among others — before her first great role came along in Eugene O'Neill's *Anna Christie*. From its opening at the Vanderbilt Theatre in November 1921 the play was a sensation, largely on the strength of Pauline Lord's realization of the title role. After a national tour in 1922–1923 a similar success was scored in London, where the play opened in April 1923. In 1924 she enjoyed another, if less spectacular, success in Sidney Howard's *They Knew What They Wanted*. For several years thereafter she was again at the mercy of indifferent material: *Sandalwood*, 1926, *Mariners*, 1927, *Spellbound*, 1927, *Salvation*, 1928, *Distant Drums*, 1932, *The Truth About Blayds*, 1932, and others. *The Late Christopher Bean*, another Howard play, was a success for her in 1932. In 1934 she appeared in the motion picture version of *Mrs. Wiggs of the Cabbage Patch*.

Lord's last great Broadway role was in the dramatized version of Edith Wharton's *Ethan Frome*, with Ruth Gordon and Raymond Massey, which opened at the National Theatre in January 1936. Subsequent roles were again largely disappointing: *Suspect*, 1940, *Eight O'Clock Tuesday*, 1941, *The Walrus and the Carpenter*, 1941, and *Sleep My Pretty One* (her last Broadway role) 1944; a touring production of *The Glass Menagerie*, 1946, was well received. In the creation of wistful, beaten, vulnerable characters she was without peer, but her career was hampered by her often unwise choice of scripts. She died in Alamogordo, New Mexico, on October 11, 1950, of injuries and complications following an automobile accident.

Lorde, Audre Geraldin 1934–1992 poet and essayist

Born in New York City on February 18, 1934, Audre Lorde was the daughter of Grenadan parents trapped by the Great Depression in a land quite unlike their island home. Their daughter rebelled under their sullen and strict rule, channeling some of her alienation into political protest around such issues as civil rights. Seeing herself as a misfit, she sought out other rebels and found a community of sorts — albeit a mostly white one — in Manhattan's gay scene. She also began using poetry to record the many conflicts she found in being, in one person, a black radical and a gay feminist.

Involved for a while with the Harlem Writer's Guild, she attended Hunter College and received a B.A. in 1959; a master's degree in library science followed in 1961. For reasons never explained publicly, she married in 1962 and bore two children, Elizabeth and Jonathan. She continued writing poetry while working as a librarian at Town School in New York; she also taught English at Hunter College. In 1968 her first volume of poetry, *The First Cities*, was published, and Lorde briefly left New York to become poet-in-residence at Toogaloo College in Mississippi. There she met another woman, Frances Clayton, who would become her partner for life. Lorde returned to New York and continued to publish poetry. Three years later she first read a lesbian love poem; although it later appeared in *Ms.*, her editor did not allow her to include it in the next volume of her own poetry. That book, *From a Land Where Other People Live*, 1974, won nomination for a National Book Award; Lorde took advantage of the resulting burst of publicity to change publishers.

Fellow poet Adrienne Rich subsequently helped publicize Lorde's work, and by 1978, with the publication of *The Black Unicorn*, her reputation as a serious poet was widely acknowledged. She continued to teach and lecture widely, prodding her readers into dialogues on feminism, lesbianism, racism, and prejudice; she urged that women themselves work for change, arguing that "the master's tools will never dismantle the master's house." Her essays sounded similar themes. A collection published under the title *Sister Outsider*, 1984, became required reading in many women's studies programs and raised Lorde's profile in the women's movement generally. *Zami: Another Spelling of My Name*, a 1983 "biomythography," explored and embellished Lorde's memories as a child victim of racism and, later, as a lesbian coming of age in New York in the 1950s.

In 1980 Lorde — sometimes also known by the African name "Gamba Adisa" — teamed with African-American writer and activist Barbara Smith to create a new publishing house, Kitchen Table: Women of Color Press; its goal was ensuring that women of color have an outlet for their writings. Lorde was named poet laureate of New York State in 1991, and over the years she received honorary doctorates from Hunter, Oberlin, and Haverford Colleges.

Lorde documented a 14-year struggle with breast cancer in *The Cancer Journals*, 1980, and again in *A Burst of Light*, 1988. The latter title, which won the 1989 American Book Award, explained her decision to forego surgery and to seek alternative treatments. Those treatments did not produce a cure, and Lorde died November 17, 1992, in St. Croix, in the U.S. Virgin Islands. Her last book, *The Marvelous Arithmetics of Distance*, appeared posthumously in 1993.

Lothrop, Alice Louise Higgins 1870–1920 social worker

Born in Boston on March 28, 1870, Alice Higgins was educated in private schools. After periods as a Sunday school superintendent and as a volunteer worker with the Boston Children's Aid Society she became an agent for the Associated Charities of Boston in 1898. In 1900 she became a district secretary, and in 1903 she succeeded Zilpha Smith as general secretary of the Associated Charities. Her character, energy, and intellectual gifts fitted her perfectly to the work of organized charity, as her rapid rise in the Associated Charities attested, and in her ten years as general secretary she made a profound and lasting impression on the methods and outlook of social workers. She worked hard to broaden the impact of social work, making the field caseworker also a link to other public agencies and an informed worker for reform through social legislation.

In addition to her contributions to the passage of mothers' aid laws and her work on the

Massachusetts Child Labor Committee, the Massachusetts Commission to Investigate Employment Agencies, and the Massachusetts Civic League, Higgins concerned herself deeply with the problems of public health. She was particularly active in the battle against tuberculosis, and after an initial period of skepticism she threw the support of the Associated Charities behind the innovative program of hospital social service begun in 1905 by Dr. Richard C. Cabot at Massachusetts General Hospital. In 1904 she helped establish the Boston School for Social Workers, operated jointly by Harvard and Simmons College, and she lectured there regularly until 1920.

In 1910–1911 she helped found the National Association of Societies for Organizing Charity (later the Family Service Association of America). Farther afield, she played a large role in organizing relief services in the wake of the San Francisco earthquake and fire of 1906, the Chelsea, Massachusetts, fire of 1908, the Salem, Massachusetts, fire of 1914, and the Halifax explosion of 1917, in the last instance working closely with the Emergency Relief Unit of the Boston chapter of the Red Cross, which she had planned only the year before. She resigned as general secretary of the Associated Charities upon her marriage in May 1913 to William H. Lothrop, a Boston businessman. She was a director of the Associated Charities for the rest of her life and during World War I served also as director of civilian relief of the New England division of the Red Cross and in other capacities. She died in Newton, Massachusetts, on September 2, 1920.

Lothrop, Harriett Mulford Stone 1844–1924 writer of children's books

Born in New Haven, Connecticut, on June 22, 1844, Harriett Stone was educated at Grove Hall Seminary in New Haven. Her inclination to literature was encouraged in her cultured home. During the 1870s she began contributing stories and verses to various periodicals under the name "Margaret Sidney." In 1877 the children's magazine *Wide Awake* published her "Polly Pepper's Chicken Pie," the first of her stories about the Pepper family. A series of Pepper stories published in *Wide Awake* during 1880 was published in book form the next year as *Five Little Peppers and How they Grew*. The book proved enormously popular — it was still in print 100 years later — and it was followed by more tales of the family's adventures: *Five Little Peppers Midway*, 1890, *Five Little Peppers Grown Up*, 1892, *Phronsie Pepper*, 1897, *Stories Polly Pepper Told to the Five Little Peppers in the Little Brown House*, 1899, *Five Little Peppers Abroad*, 1902, *Five Little Peppers at School*, 1903, *Five Little Peppers and Their Friends*, 1904, *Ben Pepper*, 1905, *Five Little Peppers in the Little Brown House*, 1907, and *Our Davie Pepper*, 1916.

The sequels were less popular than the original, but by 1914 they had collectively sold over 2 million copies. Other books included *So As By Fire*, 1881, *The Pettibone Name, a New England Story*, 1882, *Hester and Other New England Stories*, 1886, *A New Departure for Girls*, 1886, *Dilly and the Captain*, 1887, *How Tom and Dorothy Made and Kept a Christian Home*, 1888, *Old Concord: Her Highways and Byways*, 1888, *Adirondack Cabin*, 1890, *Rob, a Story for Boys*, 1891, *Whittier with the Children*, 1893, *Gingham Bag*, 1896, *Little Maid of Concord Town*, 1898, *The Judges' Cave*, 1900, *Sally, Mrs. Tubbs*, 1903, *Two Little Friends in Norway*, 1906, and *Little Maid of Boston Town*, 1910. In October 1881 she married Daniel Lothrop, founder of the publishing firm of D. Lothrop & Company, which published *Wide Awake*. In 1883 they bought "Wayside," Nathaniel Hawthorne's house in Concord, Massachusetts. After her husband's death in 1892 she lived in a smaller cottage in Concord. Lothrop was active in the Daughters of the American Revolution, the Old Concord chapter of which she founded, and she was the founder of the auxiliary Children of the American Revolution, of which she was president from 1895 to 1901. She was also instrumental in the preservation and restoration of several historical homes in Concord. She died in San Francisco on August 2, 1924.

Low, Juliette Magill Kinzie Gordon 1860–1927 founder of the Girl Scouts

Born on October 31, 1860, into a prominent Savannah, Georgia, family, Juliette Gordon was named for her maternal grandmother, Juliette Magill Kinzie. She was educated at private schools in Virginia and New York City and for some years thereafter traveled widely. She married a fellow Savannahian residing in England, William M. Low, in December 1886. She divided her time between Savannah and England both before and after her husband's death in 1905. Her interest in the Scout movement stemmed from her friendship with Robert and Agnes Baden-Powell, who in 1908–1910 organized the Boy Scouts and their sister organization, the Girl Guides, in England. She formed a small troop of Girl Guides in Scotland on a visit there and two in London. She then returned to the United States and formed the first troop of Girl Guides in the nation with 16 girls in Savannah in March 1912. In 1913 she established a headquarters in Washington, D.C. (later moved to New York City), and during 1914 she traveled through New England and to Chicago organizing troops.

In 1915, by which time the name had been changed to the Girl Scouts of America (a name first suggested for a proposed but never accomplished merger of the Girl Guides with the Campfire Girls), the movement was formally organized on a national basis and Low was elected president, a post she retained until 1920. She traveled throughout the country spreading the new organization. Her charm and conviction were in large measure responsible for the rapid spread of the movement. At her retirement in 1920 she was honored with the title of founder, and her birthday was set aside as Scouts Founder's Day. Her devotion to the movement continued unabated after her retirement. Low died in Savannah on January 18, 1927. By that time Girl Scout troops were thriving in every state of the Union, and by midcentury the organization had grown to include more than 2 million members.

Lowell, Amy 1874–1925 poet and critic

Born on February 9, 1874, in Brookline, Massachusetts, Amy Lowell came from a long-prominent Massachusetts family. She was the sister of Abbott Lawrence Lowell, later president of Harvard, and of astronomer Percival Lowell. She was educated in private schools and by her mother, and until she was twenty-eight she did little but alternately live at home, where she enjoyed the life of a Boston socialite of means and breeding, and travel abroad. About 1902 — in consequence, she later wrote, of seeing Eleonora Duse during the latter's Boston season — she decided to devote her energies to poetry. It was eight years before her first piece, a conventional but not undistinguished sonnet, was published in the *Atlantic Monthly*, and two more before her first volume, *A Dome of Many-Coloured Glass*, appeared.

In 1912 she discovered Harriet Monroe's *Poetry* magazine, and on a visit to England in 1913 she met Ezra Pound and discovered his circle, the Imagists. He included a poem of hers in his anthology *Des Imagistes*, 1914, and in that year she published her second book, *Sword Blades and Poppy Seed*, which included her first experimental work with free verse and "polyphonic prose." She edited the three numbers of *Some Imagist Poets*, 1915–1917, and subsequent volumes of her own work included *Men, Women, and Ghosts*, which contained her well known "Patterns," 1916, *Can Grande's Castle*, with "The Bronze Horses," 1918, *Pictures of the Floating World*, 1919, *Fir-Flower Tablets*, a collection of translations from the Chinese, with Florence Ayscough, 1921, *Legends*, 1921, and posthumously, *What's o'Clock*, including "Lilacs," 1925, *East Wind*, 1926, and *Ballads for Sale*, 1927. Her critical work included *Six French Poets*, 1915, *Tendencies in Modern American Poetry*, 1917, and a two-volume biography of John Keats, undertaken after delivering at Yale an address commemorating the centennial of his death and published in 1925.

Amy Lowell became the leading exponent of the modernist movement in poetry in the United States and succeeded Ezra Pound as the guiding spirit of Imagism. She was a brilliant and popular conversationalist and lecturer. Unconventional in her life as in her poetry, she enjoyed a fame that edged into notoriety. Her eminence among the modern poets of the day derived perhaps less from the quality of her own verse than from her courageous and highly pragmatic leadership. Her bluff, witty, cigar-smoking, and corpulent presence went far to disarm the opposition before it could mount an offense. In 1922 she published *A Critical Fable*, a playful verse treatment of several contemporary poets patterned on the *Fable for Critics* of her collateral ancestor, James Russell Lowell. She died suddenly on May 12, 1925, in Brookline, Massachusetts.

Lowell, Josephine Shaw 1843–1905 charity worker and reformer

Born on December 16, 1843, in West Roxbury (now part of Boston), Massachusetts, Josephine Shaw was of a wealthy and publicly active family. She grew up from 1847 on Staten Island, New York, and between 1851 and 1856 in Europe, where she attended schools in Paris and Rome. Her primary education came at home, however, where affairs of the day were discussed frequently with distinguished guests. The Civil War thrust her into public service. Her brother, Robert Gould Shaw, was killed in July 1863 while leading the first regiment of African-American troops sent into combat, and in October 1864 her husband of just one year, Colonel Charles Russell Lowell, died of wounds.

She joined the Woman's Central Association of Relief, an auxiliary of the U.S. Sanitary Commission, in 1863 and later began working for the relief and education of freedmen, work her father had pioneered in. She soon became the chief fund raiser for the National Freedmen's Relief Association of New York. In 1866 she assisted in an inspection of Negro schools in Virginia for the association.

From its founding by Louisa L. Schuyler in 1872 Lowell was active in the New York Charities Aid Association. After preparing a report on the conditions of the jail and almshouse in the borough of Richmond (Staten Island) she was selected in 1875 to conduct a statewide study of the problem of able-bodied beggars. Her competent handling of that task prompted Governor Samuel J. Tilden to appoint her the first woman member of the New York State Board of Charities in 1876. During her 13 years in that post she was tireless in inspecting and reporting on the conditions in and administration of jails, almshouses, hospitals, orphanages, and other public institutions. Her agitation for reforms led directly to the establishment of the nation's first custodial asylum for mentally retarded women in Newark, New York, in 1885 and to the establishment of the House of Refuge for Women (later the State Training School for Girls) in Hudson, New York, in 1886.

In 1882, after studying the problems of waste and redundancy among the many charity groups in New York City, she led in founding the New York Charity Organization Society, an umbrella group whose aim was to coordinate and rationalize private charitable efforts in the city. She long remained the society's leader. In *Public Relief and Private Charity*, 1884, she attempted to describe a rigorous and unsentimental philosophy of public charity, holding up the rehabilitation and rendering useful to society of each subject as the sole legitimate aim of charity.

The apparent contradiction between Lowell's rather stern views and the presence in society of able-bodied and willing men unable to find work or of those whose jobs failed to pay enough to support families led her to resign from the Board of Charities in 1889 to devote herself to industrial reform. She led in organizing the Consumers' League of New York in 1890 to mobilize consumer pressure in the cause of improving wages and working conditions (she was president of the league until 1896) and she became a strong supporter of organized labor and a frequent organizer of striker relief. In 1893 she published *Industrial*

Arbitration and Conciliation. In 1894 she founded the Woman's Municipal League to mobilize politically conscious women behind reform legislation. She was also active in the movement for civil service reform. She died in New York City on October 12, 1905.

Lozier, Clemence Sophia Harned 1813–1888 physician and reformer

Born in Plainfield, New Jersey, on December 11, 1813, Clemence Harned was educated in the local academy. In 1829 or 1830 she married Abraham W. Lozier, a New York City builder. When his health failed a short time later, she opened a girls' school in their home; from 1832 to 1843 she taught some 60 girls each year. Her teaching of anatomy, physiology, and hygiene reflected a long-standing interest of her own, and during that period she also studied medicine with an elder brother who was a physician. In 1844 she moved to Albany, New York, whence she later moved to Webster, New York.

During the later 1830s and the 1840s she was active in various reform groups concerned with prostitution and its related social problems. In 1849 she entered the Central Medical College of Rochester, and in 1853 she graduated from its successor, the Syracuse Medical College. She established a highly successful and lucrative practice in New York City, specializing in obstetrics and surgery. Beginning in 1860 she lectured regularly on physiology, anatomy, and hygiene, and the success of that venture led her to obtain, not without a struggle, a charter for the New York Medical College and Hospital for Women, a homeopathic institution that opened in November 1863. It was the first women's medical school in the state. She served as president and clinical professor of diseases of women and children until 1867, when in a reorganization she became dean and professor of gynecology and obstetrics. By 1888 the college had graduated more than 200 physicians.

Dr. Lozier had an abiding interest in the suffrage movement. She contributed to the support of Susan B. Anthony's weekly *Revolution* and served as president of the New York City Woman Suffrage Society from 1873 to 1886 and of the National Woman Suffrage Association in 1877–1878. She was also active in movements for prison reform, sanitary reform, international arbitration, civil rights for African-Americans and Native Americans, temperance, and other causes. Notable among her few writings was the pamphlet *Child-Birth Made Easy*, 1870. She died in New York City on April 26, 1888.

Luce, Clare Boothe 1903–1987 writer, editor and public official

Born in New York City on April 10, 1903, Ann Clare Boothe grew up there and in Memphis and Chicago. She was educated privately, and after graduating from The Castle in Tarrytown, New York, in 1919 she studied drama for a time. She married George T. Brokaw in 1923 and was divorced from him in 1929. She was employed by the Condé Nast publications from 1930 to 1934, as an editorial assistant on *Vogue* in 1930–1931, an associate editor of *Vanity Fair* in 1931–1933, and the managing editor of the latter magazine in 1933–1934. In 1931 she published a volume entitled *Stuffed Shirts*. In November 1935 she married Henry R. Luce, publisher of *Time* and *Fortune* magazines. In the same month her first play, *Abide With Me* opened on Broadway. Her second, *The Women*, a biting satire, opened in December 1936 and enjoyed a two-year run. She subsequently contributed to Broadway and later the motion pictures *Kiss the Boys Goodbye*, 1938, and *Margin for Error*, 1940. After a lengthy European tour for *Life* magazine in 1940 she published *Europe in the Spring*, 1940.

In 1942 Luce was elected as a Republican to Congress from the 4th District of Connecticut. During her two terms in Congress she served on the Military Affairs Committee and was an outspoken critic of the Democratic administration. She delivered the keynote address at the 1944 Republican National Convention. After leaving Congress in 1947 she returned to journalism for a time. In 1952 she edited *Saints for Now*, an anthology of essays. In that year she campaigned strenuously for Dwight D. Eisenhower, and after his election as president he nominated her for the post of U.S. ambassador to

Italy. The nomination was confirmed in March 1953. She held the post until ill health forced her to resign in November 1956.

In April 1959 President Eisenhower named her ambassador to Brazil. She was confirmed over vigorous opposition led by Senator Wayne Morse. Her subsequent comments on Morse reopened the controversy, and in May she resigned. She continued thereafter to contribute articles and stories to magazines. In 1964 she made a seconding speech for Senator Barry Goldwater at the Republican National Convention.

In 1971 Luce returned to the theatrical world with a feminist play, *Slam the Door Softly*, which was produced in Los Angeles. *The Women* was revived successfully on Broadway in 1973. In 1973 she was named by Nelson A. Rockefeller to the blue-ribbon National Commission on Critical Choices for America. She sat also on the President's Foreign Intelligence Advisory Board under Presidents Nixon and Ford from 1973 to 1977, and again under President Reagan from 1982 to 1987. In 1983 she received the Presidential Medal of Freedom. She died on October 9, 1987, at her home in Washington, D.C.

Ludington, Sybil 1761–1839 Revolutionary heroine

Born on April 5, 1761, in Fredericksburg (now Ludingtonville), New York, Sybil Ludington was the daughter of Henry Ludington, a noted New York militia officer and later an aide to General George Washington. On April 26, 1777, a messenger reached the Ludington house with news of Governor William Tryon's attack on Danbury, Connecticut, some 15 miles to the southeast, where the munitions and stores for the militia of the entire region were stored. Colonel Ludington began immediately to organize the local militia. The messenger and his horse being exhausted, Sybil volunteered to bear the order for muster and to rouse the countryside. Through the night the sixteen-year-old girl rode her horse nearly 40 miles on unfamiliar roads around Putnam County, spreading the alarm. She ranged south to Mahopac and north to Stormville before returning home. In October 1784 Sybil married Edward Ogden, a lawyer, and she lived in Unadilla, New York, until her death on February 26, 1839.

Luhan, Mabel Ganson Dodge 1879–1962 writer and hostess

Born in Buffalo, New York, on February 26, 1879, Mabel Ganson was educated in private schools. From 1900 until his accidental death two years later she was married to Carl Evans, also of Buffalo. In 1903, while visiting Europe, she married Edwin Dodge, a Boston architect with whom she lived in the Villa Curonia, near Florence, until 1912. There she created in her home a remarkable salon frequented by such members of the international set as Eleonora Duse, Isadora Duncan, and other artists.

After her return to the United States and her divorce from Dodge she settled in New York City, where again her home became a principal meeting place for liberal intellectuals and radical artists and agitators. Frequent guests included John Reed, Lincoln Steffens, Amy Lowell, Walter Lippmann, Margaret Sanger, and Max Eastman. She was a major force behind the organization of the epochal Armory Show of Post-impressionist artists in 1913. In 1916 she married Maurice Sterne, an artist.

In 1918 Dodge moved to Taos, New Mexico, where a colony of artists had grown up in recent years. There again she became a hostess of note. In 1923, having divorced Sterne, she married Tony Luhan, a Pueblo Indian. Doubtless the most famous of her international guests in Taos was D. H. Lawrence, who was there for long visits in 1922–1923 and 1924–1925. In 1932 she described in intimate and sometimes painful detail her relations with Lawrence and his wife in *Lorenzo in Taos*. There followed four volumes of autobiography, collectively entitled *Intimate Memories: Background*, 1933, *European Experiences*, 1935, *Movers and Shakers*, 1936, and *Edge of Taos Desert*, 1937. She also wrote *Winter in Taos*, 1935, and *Taos and Its Artists*, 1947. She died in Taos, New Mexico, on August 13, 1962.

Lukens, Rebecca Webb Pennock 1794–1854 businesswoman

Born in West Marlboro Township, Chester County, Pennsylvania, on January 6, 1794, Rebecca Pennock was reared in a liberal and hardworking Quaker family. She attended school at home and in Wilmington, Delaware, and in 1813 she married Dr. Charles Lukens, who became a partner in her father's iron business. A few years later Charles Lukens leased the Brandywine Mill in Coatesville, Pennsylvania, from the elder Pennock and set about converting it to the production of high quality charcoal iron for use in steam boilers. At his death in 1825 he left the mill functioning but in a financially precarious state. Rebecca Lukens quickly assumed charge. She brought in her brother-in-law, Solomon Lukens, to superintend the operation of the mill, while she took over the commercial and financial duties, securing raw materials, making contracts, selling, and stabilizing the firm. Her work was complicated by expensive and protracted probate litigation of her father's and her husband's wills, which was not settled until 1853, but by the 1840s she had built a strong and widely respected business. Lukens boiler plate was used as far away as Boston and New Orleans, and George Stephenson was said to have used it in the construction of his early locomotives.

In 1847 and 1849 sons-in-law were brought into the business as partners. Lukens, the first woman in America to engage in the iron business and perhaps the first in any heavy industry, died near Coatesville, Pennsylvania, on December 10, 1854, leaving an estate of over $100,000. The Brandywine Iron Works was renamed the Lukens Iron Works in 1859 and incorporated as the Lukens Steel Company in 1890. Still in business in 1996, it was the oldest steel manufacturing firm in the nation.

Lupino, Ida 1918–1995 filmmaker and actor

Born on February 4, 1918, in London to actress Connie Emerald and stage comedian Stanley Lupino, Ida Lupino was a member, on her father's side, of one of England's oldest theatrical families. The first woman of that family to achieve professional recognition, she started acting while still in her early teens, playing a flapper in director Allan Dwan's *Her First Affair*, 1932.

In 1934 she moved to the U.S. and began acting in Hollywood, where she attained stardom with her portrayal in 1939 of Bessie in William Wellman's *The Light That Failed*. Her film career blossomed throughout the 1940s, when she starred in eight films and won a 1942 New York Critics' Best Actress Award for her work in Vincent Sherman's *The Hard Way*.

But Lupino was dissatisfied as an actress; she needed a bigger playing field for her enormous energy and talent. In 1949 she co-founded a production company originally called Emerald Productions, later known as Filmmakers. By the 1950s she had fast become the only female director of major films. Her low-budget, no-glamour projects were aimed at showing "how America lives," using off-beat scripts and little-known performers to tell stories that were down-to earth, provocative, and suggestive of the human spirit's ability to survive adversity. Her pioneering work as an independent filmmaker helped gain her a reputation as one of the most talented and gutsy women in Hollywood.

She took over the direction of her first feature in 1949 from Elmer Clifton, who had suffered a heart attack during filming. Called *Not Wanted*, it told the melodramatic story of a young woman who became pregnant out of wedlock, gave up her baby for adoption, and was sent to jail when she tried to kidnap the child. Her second film, *Never Fear*, 1950, celebrated the determination of a young woman who, struck with polio, had to give up dancing.

Outrage, 1950, recounted a woman's attempt to cope with rape and its aftermath, and *Hard, Fast and Beautiful*, 1951, tells the story of the relationship between a young woman tennis player and her ambitious mother. Lupino's two final films of the 1950s were *The Bigamist*, 1953, about a man married to two women, one of whom was played by Lupino herself, and *The Hitchhiker*, 1953, a critically acclaimed thriller about two men victimized by a psychopathic killer — Lupino's favorite of the films she directed.

Lupino returned to directing in 1966 to make *The Trouble with Angels*, a Walt Disney film about the relationship between a mischievous student at a convent school and the school's mother superior. She produced, but did not direct, two more films during the fifties, *On the Loose* and *Beware My Lovely*, both in 1951. Although best known for her work in film, both as an actress and as a director, she directed many television films, and also at times worked as a dancer, artist, singer, designer, composer and musician. She died in her California home on August 3, 1995.

Lyon, Mary Mason 1797–1849 educator

Born on February 28, 1797, in Buckland, Massachusetts, Mary Lyon began teaching in country schools in 1814 in order to finance her own further education. Between 1817 and 1821 she attended Sanderson Academy at Ashfield, Amherst Academy, and the Reverend Joseph Emerson's seminary at Byfield. At Byfield she formed a close friendship with Zilpah Grant, one of her teachers. After three years of teaching at Sanderson Academy she opened a school of her own in Buckland in 1824. During her four years there she spent summers teaching with Zilpah Grant at the Adams Female Seminary in New Hampshire and then at the Ipswich Female Seminary. She also attended lectures at Amherst College and the Rensselaer School (now Polytechnic Institute).

In 1828 she joined the Ipswich school full time. Through these years of teaching she nursed a growing conviction that the education of women, which in the early years of the nineteenth century depended upon the luck and skill of entrepreneurial teachers or on the whims of occasional male benefactors, should be placed on a firm and permanent basis. She and Grant failed to secure an endowment for the Ipswich school or to win support for a projected New England Female Seminary for Teachers. Nonetheless, her conviction led her in 1834 to undertake the raising of funds for a school devoted to the liberal education of women. Her aim was to make such an education available to students of moderate means by having the students share in the domestic work of the school and to make it of such a caliber that even the wealthy should not find better. With enthusiasm and an indomitable spirit as well as considerable tact and diplomacy she secured the necessary financial support for her plan.

A charter was obtained in 1836, and Mount Holyoke Female Seminary opened for classes at South Hadley, Massachusetts, on November 8, 1837, with about 80 students. It was an immediate success, and some 400 applicants were turned away in 1838 for lack of space. The cause of female education had entered a new era. Mary Lyon served as the principal of Mount Holyoke for 12 years, during which time the curriculum was expanded and new buildings were added. Her energy and clear vision of her goal were the key ingredients in the school's early success. In 1843 she published *A Missionary Offering*. She died in South Hadley, Massachusetts, on March 5, 1849. The school became Mount Holyoke Seminary and College in 1888 and Mount Holyoke College in 1895, and it remained one of the leading institutions of higher learning for women in the United States.

Maass, Clara 1876–1901 nurse

Born on June 28, 1876, in East Orange, New Jersey, Clara Maass graduated from the Newark German Hospital School of Nursing in 1895 and shortly afterward was named head nurse of the school. At the outbreak of the Spanish-American War in April 1898 she volunteered to serve as a contract nurse with the U.S. Army Medical Department. During her first term of service she worked at army camps in Florida, Georgia, and Cuba. She volunteered again in 1900 and was sent first to the Philippines and then back to Cuba.

Her long experience in nursing victims of yellow fever drew her into the work of the Yellow Fever Commission headed by Major Walter Reed. While at Las Animas Hospital in Havana she volunteered to take part in an experiment conducted by Major William C. Gorgas and Dr. John Guitéras on immunization against yellow fever. On August 14, 1901, she allowed herself to be bitten by an infected *Stegomyia* mosquito. The theory of the experiment was that, given prompt hospital care under controlled conditions, she should contract a mild case and recover, immune thereafter. Such had been Reed's experience during his classic demonstration of the fact that yellow fever is spread exclusively by the mosquito. Nurse Maass, however, came down with a severe case and died on August 24, 1901. She was the only woman and the only American to die during the yellow fever experiments of 1900–1901. (Dr. Jesse W. Lazear, who died in September 1900, had done so in consequence of an uncontrolled experiment undertaken before Reed began his work.) In 1952 the Newark German Hospital, which had meanwhile changed its name to Lutheran Memorial, was renamed the Clara Maass Memorial Hospital.

McAuliffe, Christa Corrigan 1948–1986 teacher and first private citizen in space

Born on September 2, 1948 in Boston, Massachusetts, Sharon Christa Corrigan was the first of five children and was raised in nearby Framingham. There she attended Marion High School, graduating in 1966. In 1970 she earned her B.A. from Framingham State College and married her high school sweetheart, Steve McAuliffe. She received her M.A. in education from Bowie State College in Maryland in 1978. In 1976 she gave birth to a son, Scott, and three years later a daughter, Caroline.

In 1970 she began her teaching career at Benjamin Foulois Junior High School in Morningside, Maryland. She taught American history, civics, and English for a number of years in the Northeast, and in 1982 she began teaching at Concord Senior High School in New Hampshire. There she taught social studies courses, including American culture, economics, law, and a course she developed herself: The American Woman. Throughout her teaching career she was considered by both her peers and students to be a dynamic and dedicated educator who was always willing to spend extra time with her class. She tutored students after school, worked to develop elaborate and original lesson plans, and was known for taking students on field trips.

In 1984 President Ronald Reagan announced his intention to pick the first private citizen in history to journey into space. After an thorough screening process the candidate chosen would accompany astronauts on the U.S. space shuttle *Challenger*. Having always had an interest in history and space, she was eager to apply and was ultimately chosen out of a field of over 10,000 applicants. In her application she proposed keeping a three-part journal of her experiences: the first part describing the training she would go through, the second chronicling the details of the actual flight, and the third related to her feelings and experiences back on earth. She also planned on keeping a video record of her activities. She was to conduct at least two lessons while onboard the space shuttle to be simulcasted to students around the world and spend the nine months following her return home lecturing to students across the U.S. The primary task of the *Challenger* mission was to launch satellites, including one that was to be released and picked up two days after observing Halley's Comet during its closest approach to the sun. Another goal of the mission, however, was directly related to McAuliffe's presence onboard the shuttle: to highlight the importance of teachers in our society and to inspire young people to look toward careers in science and technology.

There were problems with the ill-fated mission from the start. First, the launch was postponed for several days due to delays in getting the previous shuttle orbiter back on the ground. Next, the night before the launch, central Florida was hit by a severe cold front that left ice on the launchpad. The shuttle finally launched on 11:38 a.m. on January 28, 1986. Just 73 seconds after liftoff the craft exploded, sending debris cascading far out into the Atlantic Ocean for more than an hour afterward. There were no survivors. The accident — witnessed live on TV by millions of viewers worldwide — stunned the nation and immediately put a halt to future shuttle missions which did not resume until September of 1988 with the flight of the shuttle *Discovery*. While the *Challenger* accident generated speculation on problems NASA had been experiencing for a number of years, many believed that it was Christa McAuliffe's presence onboard that was most damaging to the space program's credibility, reputation, and level of public support. Never before had a civilian been directly injured as a result of U.S. space exploration. The public's trust in the safety, and by extension, necessity of shuttle launches markedly diminished in the wake of the *Challenger* disaster, and many believed it would never be completely restored.

McBride, Mary Margaret 1899–1976 journalist and broadcaster

Born on November 16, 1899, in Paris, Missouri, Mary Margaret McBride moved frequently from farm to farm with her family. Her schooling was similarly episodic until 1906, when she entered William Woods College (then actually a preparatory school). In 1916 she entered the University of Missouri, from which she graduated with a journalism degree in 1919. After a year as a reporter for the *Cleveland Press* she was publicity director for the Interchurch World Movement for several months and then a reporter for the *New York Evening Mail* until 1924. She then turned to freelance magazine writing. Her work appeared in *Saturday Evening Post*, *Cosmopolitan*, *Good Housekeeping*, and other magazines, and she also published several books, including *Jazz*, with Paul Whiteman, 1926, *Charm*, with Alexander Williams, 1927, *Paris Is a Woman's Town*, with Helen Josephy, 1929, *London Is a Man's Town*, with Josephy, 1930, *The Story of Dwight Morrow*, 1930, *New York Is Everybody's Town*, with Josephy, 1931, and *Beer and Skittles — A Friendly Modern Guide to Germany*, with Josephy, 1932.

In 1934 McBride auditioned successfully for a daily program of advice for women on radio station WOR in New York City. Using the name "Martha Deane" and exploiting her homey Missouri drawl, she projected a grandmotherly kindness and wit that proved highly popular. She continued with the program until 1940. Meanwhile she also edited the woman's page of the Newspaper Enterprise Association syndicate in 1934–1935 and in 1937 began a weekly radio program under her own name on the CBS network. In 1941 she moved from CBS to NBC, where her weekly 45-minute program of ad lib commentary and interviews drew an audience in the millions. From 1950 to 1954 she broadcast daily over the ABC network, and in the latter year she returned to NBC, where she remained until 1960. From 1960 she was heard in a syndicated program of the New York Herald Tribune Radio operation. Celebrities from politics, entertainment, and the arts appeared on her program, while her own brand of frank, folksy, down-to-earth comment made her a peerless saleswoman. While advertisers clamored for her services, she stoutly refused to push any product that she had not personally tried and liked. "Mary Margaret," as she was known to her listeners, also refused to advertise tobacco or alcohol.

During 1953–1956 McBride conducted a syndicated newspaper column for the Associated Press. Among her other books were *Here's Martha Deane*, 1936, *How Dear to My Heart*, an autobiography, 1940, *America for Me*, 1941, *Tune in for Elizabeth*, a book for girls, 1945, *Harvest of American Cooking*, 1957, *A Long Way from Missouri*, 1959, *Out of the Air*, autobiography, 1960, and *The Growing Up of Mary Elizabeth*, for girls, 1966. In her last years she conducted a thrice weekly show from her own living room for a radio station in Kingston, New York. She died in West Shokan, New York, on April 7, 1976.

McCarthy, Mary Therese 1912–1989 writer and critic

Mary McCarthy

Born on June 21, 1912, in Seattle, Washington, Mary McCarthy was left an orphan at the age of six. Reared in Minneapolis until the age of eleven by paternal grandparents, about whose harsh treatment she later recalled nothing sympathetic, she then joined her maternal grandparents in Seattle. She was educated at private schools and at Vassar College, from which she graduated in 1933. She then began a career as a critic for the *New Republic* and the *Nation*. From 1937 to 1948 she was a drama critic for the *Partisan Review*. She was encouraged to undertake fiction by her second husband, Edmund Wilson, whom she married in 1938 and divorced in 1946.

McCarthy's first story, "Cruel and Barbarous Treatment," was published in the *Southern Review* for Spring 1939. It later became the opening chapter of *The Company She Keeps*, 1942, a loosely connected series of stories. She dealt with politics, utopia, and ineffectual intellectualism in The *Oasis*, 1949. *Cast a Cold Eye*, 1950, was another series of stories. *The Groves of Academe*, 1952, which displayed her talent for biting satire, was followed by *A Charmed Life*, 1955. In 1956 and 1959 she experimented with lavishly photographed travelogues of Venice in *Venice, Observed* and of Florence in *The Stones of Florence*. *Memories of a Catholic Girlhood*, 1957, which was autobiographical — or simply more explicitly so than her fiction — was praised by many critics over her fiction, which at its best seemed to be straining to meet her own critical standards. Her theatrical criticism was collected from time to time, and her diverse interests were represented in *On the Contrary; Articles of Belief: 1946–1961*, a collection of 21 essays originally published in various periodicals. *The Group*, 1963, a novel that followed eight Vassar girls of the class (McCarthy's own) of 1933 through their subsequent careers and the intellectual fads of the 1930s and 1940s, became the most popular of all her works and was made into a film.

The most controversial of McCarthy's writings was a series of essays on the Vietnam War that first appeared in the *New York Review of Books* and were later collected in *Vietnam*, 1967, and *Hanoi*, 1968. Her confession that she went to Southeast Asia "looking for material damaging to American interests" infuriated some critics, but others emphasized the sensitivity with which she treated the suffering of the Vietnamese and the ironies of the war. Others of her books included The *Writing on the Wall*, essays, 1970, *Birds of America*, a novel, 1971, *Medina*, 1972, *The Seventeenth Degree*, which collected some earlier short works, 1974, *The Mask of State*, on the Watergate affair, 1974, *Cannibals and Missionaries*, a novel, 1979, *Ideas and the Novel*, essays, 1980, *The Hounds of Summer*, short stories, 1981, *Occasional Prose*, essays, 1985, and *How I Grew*, an autobiography, 1987. An unfinished autobiography, *Intellectual Memoirs, New York, 1936–38*, was published posthumously in 1992. She was named an officer in the French Order of Arts and Letters in 1983, and in 1984 she received both the National Medal for Literature and the MacDowell Medal. She died on October 25, 1989, in New York City.

McCauley, Mary Ludwig Hays 1754–1832 "Molly Pitcher," Revolutionary heroine

Born in Trenton, New Jersey, on October 13, 1754, Molly Ludwig lived on a small dairy farm until 1769, when her father arranged for her employment as a servant to William Irvine, a doctor in Carlisle, Pennsylvania. She was married shortly thereafter to

John Hays who, during the Revolution, served in the 7th Pennsylvania Regiment, commanded by Irvine. Molly Hays, with many other soldiers' wives, was with the regiment at the battle of Monmouth, on June 28, 1778. The day was a hot one, and Molly assisted the artillerymen in the battle by bringing drinking water in a pitcher, earning thereby the nickname "Molly Pitcher." After her husband collapsed from the heat, she took his place at his gun and served heroically for the remainder of the battle.

After the war she led an uneventful life at Carlisle. Hays died in 1789 and Molly's second marriage, to John (or George) McCauley, brought her no respite from her work as a servant. During the last ten years of her life she received a pension of $40 a year that was authorized by an act of the Pennsylvania assembly in February 1822 in commemoration of her heroism at Monmouth. She died in Carlisle on January 22, 1832. Her story, sometimes confused with that of Margaret Corbin, was revived and her grave marked in 1876. In 1916 a state monument was raised to her memory.

Barbara McClintock

McClintock, Barbara 1902–1992 geneticist

Born on June 16, 1902, in Hartford, Connecticut, Barbara McClintock liked reading, playing baseball and, as she said, "thinking about things." She took great pleasure in science. Her mother, however, worried that her child was not becoming feminine enough — that she might become "a strange person, a person that didn't belong to society" — and she opposed any further education beyond high school for her daughter. McClintock responded by spending all her free time for the next year in the library, reading and studying on her own. Her parents eventually acquiesced, and she enrolled at Cornell University in 1919 as a biology major.

Throughout college, McClintock concentrated on her studies, never distracted, she said, by close personal relationships with other persons. She received her B.S. in 1923, her M.A. two years later, and, having specialized in cytology, genetics and zoology, finished her Ph.D. in 1927. While in graduate school she began the work that would occupy her entire life, the chromosomal analysis of maize. Studying the genetics of corn, she used a microscope and a staining technique that allowed her to examine, identify and describe individual corn chromosomes.

In 1931 she and a colleague, Harriet Creighton, published "A Correlation of Cytological and Genetical Crossing-over in Zea mays," a paper that established that chromosomes formed the basis of genetics. Based on her experiments and publications during the 1930s, she was elected vice president of the Genetics Society of America in 1939 and president of the Genetics Society in 1944. She received a Guggenheim Fellowship in 1933 to study in Germany, but left early due to the rise of Nazism. When she returned to Cornell, she found that the university would not hire a female professor. Instead, the Rockefeller Foundation funded her research at Cornell for two years, until finally, in 1936, she was invited to become an assistant professor at the University of Missouri.

In 1941, McClintock moved to Long Island to work at the Cold Spring Harbor Laboratory, where she spent the rest of her professional life. In 1944, the same year that McClintock was elected a member of the National Academy of Sciences, she began research on transposition — the notion that there exist shifting and movable elements she called transposable elements (later called "jumping genes") on a chromosome that control the supposedly random movement of some genes on the chromosome. Ahead of its time, however, McClintock's work was for many years considered too radical — or was simply not considered at all — by her fellow scientists. Deeply disappointed with her colleagues, McClintock stopped publishing the results of her work and she ceased giving lectures, though she continued doing research. "They called me crazy, absolutely mad at times," she said later. Not until the late 1960s and 1970s, after biologists had determined that the genetic material was DNA, did members of the scientific community begin to verify her findings from 1951.

When recognition finally came, McClintock was inundated with awards and honors — the Kimber Genetics Award from the National Academy of Sciences, 1967; the National Medal of Science, 1970; Brandeis University's Rosenstiel Award 1978; the Albert Lasker Basic Medical Research Award 1981; Israel's Wolf Foundation Prize, 1981; and a lifetime MacArthur Laureate Award of $60,000 annually, beginning 1981, among others. In 1983, at the age of 81, McClintock became the first woman to win an unshared Nobel prize for medicine or physiology. When asked at the time about her years of neglect by the scientific community, she said only that "if you know you're right, you don't care. You know that sooner or later, it will come out in the wash." McClintock died in Huntington, New York, on September 2, 1992.

McCormick, Anne Elizabeth O'Hare 1882–1954 journalist

Born on May 16, 1882, in Wakefield, Yorkshire, England, Anne O'Hare was brought by her parents to America in early childhood. She grew up in Columbus, Ohio, and attended the academy and college of St. Mary of the Springs. Sometime before 1916 she married Francis J. McCormick, a businessman. After a time as associate editor of the *Catholic Universe Weekly* in Cleveland she became a freelance writer, contributing poems and articles to *Smart Set*, *Atlantic Monthly*, and other magazines. In 1920 she traveled to Europe and began submitting dispatches to the *New York Times*. The *Times* accepted several, and in 1922 she became a regular correspondent.

Her reports on political crises and developments, especially the rise of Fascism in Italy and the emergence of Benito Mussolini, established her as one of the most perspicacious observers on the Continent. She traveled widely and frequently and seemed to many colleagues to have an uncanny knack for arriving at the scene of major stories as they were breaking. Leading European figures whom she interviewed, with a keen perception of personality, included Adolf Hitler, Mussolini, Sir Neville Chamberlain, Joseph Stalin, Sir Winston Churchill, Léon Blum, Gustav Stresemann, Eamon de Valera, Eduard Benes, and Kurt von Schuschnigg. Her book *The Hammer and the Scythe: Communist Russia Enters the Second Decade*, 1928, was widely praised.

McCormick's dispatches to the *Times* at length earned her a regular bylined column called "In Europe" and later "Abroad." In 1936 she became the first woman to sit on the editorial board of the *Times*, a post that required her to write two unsigned pieces weekly for the paper's editorial page. In 1937 she became the first woman to win a Pulitzer Prize for journalism when she was chosen for the award for foreign correspondence. In 1939, when her reporting took her to 13 countries in 5 months, she was honored by the National Federation of Press Women, the American Women's Association, and the New York Career Tours for Women, which named her "Woman of the Year." In 1944 she was awarded the Laetare Medal by the University of Notre Dame. In 1946 and 1948 she served as a U.S. delegate to the United Nations Educational, Scientific, and Cultural Organization, and in 1947 she was elected to the National Institute of Arts and Letters. Anne McCormick died in New York City on May 29, 1954. Two volumes of her *New York Times* pieces were later edited by Marion T. Sheehan: *The World at Home*, 1956, and *Vatican Journal, 1921–1954*, 1957.

McCrea, Jane 1752?–1777 Revolutionary heroine

Born about 1752 in Bedminster (now Lamington), New Jersey, Jane McCrea went to live with a brother's family in Northumberland, New York, in 1769. A tall, attractive woman with very long blonde hair, she was courted by one David Jones, whom she had known in New Jersey. In 1776 Jones was one of several Tories from the area to join the

British army. In the summer of 1777 the approach of a large British force under General John Burgoyne down Lake Champlain and the Hudson River valley and the consequent abandonment of Fort Ticonderoga and then Fort Edward by American defenders caused a panic among the remaining settlers, who quickly began to evacuate southward. Jane McCrea declined to leave, however, for she had received a letter from David Jones, by then a lieutenant with Burgoyne, saying that he hoped soon to see her at Fort Edward. In later legend it was said they were to be married at that time.

On the morning of July 27, 1777, Jane McCrea visited a friend, Sarah McNeil, who was preparing to leave Fort Edward for safety. About noon the two women were captured by some Native American scouts whom Burgoyne had employed as an advance force. McNeil was delivered safely to British hands, but Jane McCrea was later discovered dead, several bullet wounds in her body, and scalped. Her captors claimed she had been killed by a stray bullet from an American detachment, but it was generally accepted that one of the scouts had killed her, perhaps in a quarrel over whose captive she was. The murder and scalping sent a shock of horror through the colonies; it was even felt in England, where in the House of Commons Edmund Burke denounced the use of Indian allies. In America the deed galvanized patriotic sentiment, swung waverers against the British, and encouraged a tide of enlistments that helped end Burgoyne's invasion three months later. The tale of Jane McCrea became a favorite and was much romanticized in popular versions. Among the authors who used it were Philip Freneau, Joel Barlow, and Delia S. Bacon.

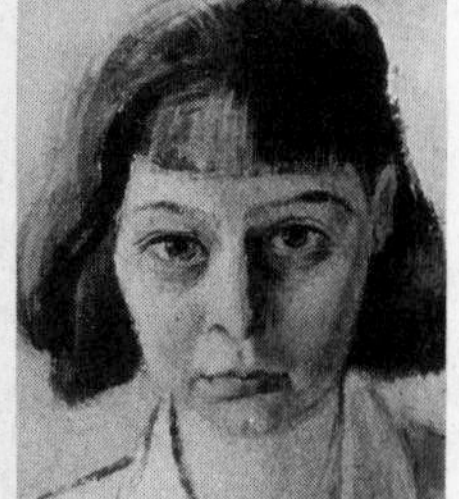

Carson McCullers

McCullers, Carson Smith 1917–1967 writer

Born on February 19, 1917, in Columbus, Georgia, Carson Smith grew up in a region that provided the setting for all of her later fiction. At seventeen she went to New York City to study at Columbia and New York universities, and in September 1937 she married Reeves McCullers. Her life after that was clouded by illness and tragedy. Repeated strokes incapacitated her for long periods, and partial paralysis confined her to a wheelchair in her later years. Her achievement as a writer, a career that was successfully launched by her first novel, *The Heart Is a Lonely Hunter*, 1940, was the outgrowth of her own character and lonely suffering.

Her fictional characters endured various physical and psychological handicaps that complicated their natural but often bizarre searches for compassion. *Reflections in a Golden Eye*, 1941, a shorter work set in a Southern army post that chronicled the unhappy life of a captain (a latent homosexual) and his wife (a nymphomaniac), confirmed her earlier success; it was made into a film released in 1967. (In 1968 *The Heart Is a Lonely Hunter* was made into a motion picture.) *The Member of the Wedding*, 1946, proved her most popular work. The sensitive portrayal of Frankie, a lonely adolescent whose attachment to her brother precipitates a crisis at his wedding, was equally successful in her dramatic version, which ran on Broadway from January 1950 to March 1951 (featuring Ethel Waters) and for which she won a New York Drama Critics' Circle award; it too was made into a movie. Her other works included *The Ballad of the Sad Café*, 1951, a collection from which the title novelette was dramatized by Edward Albee in 1963; *The Square Root of Wonderful*, 1958, another play; and *Clock Without Hands*, a novel, 1961. Carson McCullers died in Nyack, New York, on September 29, 1967.

McGinley, Phyllis 1905–1978 poet, essayist and writer of children's books

Born on March 21, 1905, in Ontario, Oregon, Phyllis McGinley grew up there, in Colorado, and in Ogden, Utah. After graduating from a parochial high school she attended the University of Southern California and the University of Utah. She taught school for a year in Ogden and then moved to New York and taught for four years in a high school in New Rochelle. A writer of verses since childhood, she began submitting them to newspapers and magazines. Franklin P. Adams printed a few in his column, "The Conning Tower," in the *New York Herald Tribune*, and gradually they began to appear also in *The New Yorker* and other periodicals.

After a stint as an advertising copywriter and another as poetry editor for *Town and Country* magazine McGinley devoted herself to writing. Her first book of poems, *On the Contrary*, 1934, was well received. It was followed by *One More Manhattan*, 1937, *Pocketful of Wry*, 1940, *Husbands Are Difficult*, 1941, *Stones from Glass Houses*, 1946, *A Short Walk from the Station*, 1951, *Love Letters*, 1954, and *Merry Christmas, Happy New Year*, 1958. In 1961 her *Times Three: Selected Verse from Three Decades*, 1960, was awarded the Pulitzer Prize for poetry. Hers was the first award of that prize to a writer of light verse. As the titles of several of her volumes suggested, her poetic world was the otherwise mundane workaday world of urban and particularly suburban life. Her trenchant but warm comments on that life charmed, amused, and fortified millions of readers for decades.

McGinley also wrote a number of books for children, including *The Horse That Lived Upstairs*, 1944, *The Plain Princess*, 1945, *All Around the Town*, 1948, *The Most Wonderful Doll in the World*, 1950, *Blunderbus*, 1951, *The Horse Who Had His Picture in the Paper*, 1951, *Make-Believe Twins*, 1953, *The Year Without a Santa Claus*, 1957, *Lucy McLockett*, 1959, *Boys are Awful*, 1962, *A Girl and Her Room*, 1963, and *How Mrs. Santa Claus Saved Christmas*, 1963.

Her essays, first published in such magazines as *Ladies' Home Journal*, *McCall's*, *Vogue*, and *Reader's Digest*, were collected in *Province of the Heart*, 1959, *Sixpence in Her Shoe*, 1964; *Wonderful Time*, 1966, and *Saint Watching*, 1969. Later collections of poems included *Sugar and Spice*, 1960, *Mince Pie and Mistletoe*, 1961 and *A Wreath of Christmas Legends*, 1967. She died in New York City on February 22, 1978.

McGroarty, Sister Julia 1827–1901 religious and educator

Born in Inver, County Donegal, Ireland, on February 13, 1827, Susan McGroarty emigrated with her family to the United States in 1831 and settled in Brown County, Ohio. Later they moved to Cincinnati, where she was educated in the convent school of the Sisters of Notre Dame de Namur. In January 1846 she entered the order. She took the habit as Sister Julia in April of that year and made her final vows in August 1848. She conducted the convent's day school for six years, and in 1854 she was sent to the new Academy of Notre Dame in Roxbury (now part of Boston), Massachusetts, as mistress of boarders. In 1860 she became the first American superior in the Belgian-based order when she took charge of the academy in Philadelphia. In addition to the regular school, attended largely by the daughters of the well-to-do, she also conducted a night school for the children of the poor and from 1877 to 1882 a school for African-American children.

In 1885 she was called back to Cincinnati to serve as assistant to Sister Superior Louise Van der Schrieck, and on the latter's death in December 1886 she succeeded as superior of the order's 26 American houses east of the Rockies. From 1892 to 1901 her jurisdiction also included the order's California province. In her 15 years as superior she founded 14 new convents, a large novitiate in Waltham, Massachusetts, and an orphanage in San Jose, California. She was deeply concerned with the quality of instruction offered in the order's 30-odd academies. She wrote a standardized course of instruction and devised a system of common general examinations prepared and graded at the Provincial House.

The lack of facilities for higher education for Catholic women prompted a number of lay and ecclesiastical leaders to prevail upon Sister Julia to establish a new institution to that end. In 1897, with the support of James Cardinal Gibbons, Apostolic Delegate

Martinelli, and the rector of Catholic University (limited to men students since its founding in 1889), she established Trinity College in Washington, D.C. The college was formally incorporated in August 1897 and opened its doors in November 1900. While overcoming the objections of Catholic conservatives, many of whom objected that the college's proximity to Catholic University amounted to co-education, Sister Julia planned a college of the highest academic standards and saw it successfully through its first year. She died at the Notre Dame convent in Peabody, Massachusetts, on November 12, 1901.

MacInnes, Helen Clark 1907–1984 novelist

Born in Glasgow, Scotland, on October 7, 1907, Helen MacInnes grew up from the age of five in Helensburgh, Dumbartonshire. She graduated from Glasgow University with an M.A. degree in 1928 and remained at the university for a year afterward as a special cataloger in the library. After a year of library work with the Education Authority of Dumbartonshire she entered the School of Librarianship of University College, London, in 1930. She graduated in 1931. In September 1932 she married Gilbert Highet, who was just beginning his academic career at Oxford. Over the next several years they collaborated on a number of translations from German. In 1938, after Highet had taught for a year as guest professor at Columbia University, he accepted a permanent post there and the family settled in New York City.

A short time later Helen MacInnes began her first book, *Above Suspicion*, which appeared in 1941. A tale of espionage in Nazi Europe, it was an immediate success, widely praised for its suspense and humor, and it was made into a motion picture in 1943. *Assignment in Brittany* followed in 1942 and was also made into a movie. *While We Still Live*, 1944, and *Horizon*, 1946, were both suspenseful tales of World War II. *Friends and Lovers*, a love story, 1947, was followed by a series of thriller novels of international intrigue and Cold War tension: *Rest and Be Thankful*, 1949, *Neither Five Nor Three*, 1951, *I and My True Love*, 1953, *Pray for a Brave Heart*, 1955, *North from Rome*, 1958, *Decision at Delphi*, 1960, *The Venetian Affair*, 1963, *The Double Image*, 1966, *The Salzburg Connection*, 1968, *Message from Málaga*, 1971, *The Snare of the Hunter*, 1974, *Agent in Place*, 1976, and *Prelude to Terror*, 1978, *The Hidden Target*, 1980, *Cloak of Darkness*, 1982, and her final book, *Ride a Pale Horse*, 1984.

Her books were nearly all best sellers and were frequently translated and reissued; several more were made into motion pictures. Critics and readers alike noted her skillful and credible portrayal of espionage and the human characters involved in it. She credited her success to thorough research and "underlying everything is the fact that I'm interested in international politics, in analyzing news, to read newspapers both on and between the lines, to deduct and add, to utilize memory."

Helen MacInnes and her husband were naturalized American citizens in 1951 (he died in 1978). She died on September 30, 1984, in New York City.

McLean, Alice Throckmorton 1886–1968 social service organizer

Born in New York City on March 8, 1886, Alice McLean was the daughter of the chairman of the board of the Phelps Dodge Corporation. As a child she traveled widely, mastered several languages, and was educated privately. An early marriage to Edward L. Tinker, a lawyer and later author and critic, ended in divorce, and she resumed her maiden name. Until 1938 Alice McLean led the life of a wealthy socialite. In that year, however, while visiting England she learned of the work of the Women's Voluntary Services, a volunteer organization doing war-related work on the home front. After studying similar groups in other European nations she returned to America in 1939 and began enlisting friends in what was at first an entirely informal series of activities aimed at promoting the idea of volunteer social service.

In 1940 she organized the American Women's Voluntary Services. Despite the prevailing mood of isolationism in the nation at that time, she succeeded in rapidly building a sizable organization interested in preparing the home front for war. By the time of Pearl Harbor AWVS numbered over 18,000 members who were training in ambulance driving, evacuation procedures, mobile kitchen operation, first aid, household conservation, fire prevention, and other techniques. The entry of the United States into the war greatly increased the number of volunteers. Training in automobile mechanics, cryptography, switchboard operation, map reading, rehabilitation, and other skills was added to AWVS's program. Volunteers provided relief and food services to armed forces posts, disaster workers, and wounded servicemen and at other times served as fire watchers, crop pickers, motor vehicle drivers, and photographers. AWVS workshops turned out more than a million new or reconditioned articles of clothing for servicemen, their families, hospitals, and other users, while publishing booklets and conducting public classes for housewives in preserving and repairing their families' own clothing.

AWVS members sold more than a billion dollars worth of war bonds and stamps during the war. By 1945 AWVS members totaled some 325,000, and the more than 200 junior auxiliary groups had enrolled over 32,000 young people. Partisanship, racial discrimination, and rivaly with other social service agencies were successfully avoided. McLean continued as president of AWVS, which was still in existence at the time of her death in Baltimore on October 25, 1968.

McMein, Neysa 1888–1949 artist

Born in Quincy, Illinois, on January 24, 1888, Margery Edna McMein was educated in local schools. After graduating from high school she entered the school of the Art Institute of Chicago, supporting herself by playing piano in nickelodeons, selling hats, and other jobs. In 1913 she went to New York City to seek a career. After a brief stint as an actress she turned to commercial art. On the advice of a numerologist she adopted the name Neysa, and she thereafter credited the change with her rapid success.

McMein studied at the Art Students' League for a few months and in 1914 sold her first drawing to the *Boston Star*. The next year she sold a cover to the *Saturday Evening Post*. Her warm pastel drawings proved highly popular, as did the chic, healthy American girls she drew, and commissions came ever more quickly. During World War I she drew posters for the U.S. and French governments and spent six months in France as a YMCA lecturer and entertainer. From 1923 through 1937 she supplied all of *McCall's* covers at a rate that peaked at $30,000 per year. She also supplied work to *McClure's*, *Liberty*, *Woman's Home Companion*, *Collier's*, *Photoplay*, and other magazines, as well as creating advertising graphics for such accounts as Palmolive and Lucky Strike. General Mills's Marjorie C. Husted commissioned her to create the image of "Betty Crocker."

Alongside a highly successful career Neysa McMein managed a brilliant social life. A gay and unselfconsciously beautiful woman, she became a regular member of the Algonquin Hotel set, with her closest friends including Alexander Woollcott, Alice Duer Miller, and Jascha Heifetz. Franklin P. Adams, Robert Benchley, Edna Ferber, Irving Berlin, and Bernard Baruch were also among her companions. Her West 57th Street studio was a popular gathering place for her circle. In May 1923 she made an unconventionally unrestrictive marriage with John C. Baragwanath, a mining engineer and author.

McMein's more private artistic ambitions lay in the field of portraiture, at first in pastels and later in oil. Among her subjects were Presidents Harding and Hoover, Edna St. Vincent Millay, Anne Morrow Lindbergh, Dorothy Parker, Janet Flanner, Katharine Cornell, Helen Hayes, Dorothy Thompson, Anatole France, Charlie Chaplin, Charles Evans Hughes, and Count Zeppelin (she had been one of the first women to fly in

Zeppelin's dirigible). Portraiture occupied more of her time with the decline in popularity of her brand of commercial art in the later 1930s. She died in New York City on May 12, 1949.

Macomber, Mary Lizzie 1861–1916 artist

Born in Fall River, Massachusetts, on August 21, 1861, Mary Macomber early demonstrated an artistic bent. She studied drawing with a local artist for some years and then at the school of the Boston Museum of Fine Arts for a year, until ill health cut short her studies. After her recovery she studied again briefly under Frank Duveneck and then opened a studio in Boston. In 1889 her "Ruth" was exhibited in the National Academy of Design show. Over the next 13 years she exhibited 25 more paintings at the National Academy and was a frequent exhibitor at other major museums and galleries.

Macomber's symbolic, allegorical, and decorative panels, revealing the influence of the Pre-Raphaelites, were widely admired. Among her more celebrated works were "Love Awakening Memory," 1892; "Love's Lament," 1893; "St. Catherine," which won the Dodge prize for best work by a woman at the National Academy show in 1897; "The Hour Glass," the first of her works in the broader, more confident style she adopted after 1898, 1900; "The Lace Jabot," a self-portrait, 1900; "Night and Her Daughter Sleep," 1903; and "Memory Comforting Sorrow," 1905. In later years she also devoted much time to portraiture. She died in Boston on February 4, 1916.

McPherson, Aimee Semple 1890–1944 evangelist

Born on October 9, 1890, near Ingersoll, Ontario, Aimee Elizabeth Kennedy was reared by her mother in the work of the Salvation Army. She was educated in public schools. In August 1908 she was married to a Pentecostal evangelist, Robert J. Semple, under whose influence she had converted to that sect (she was ordained in it in 1909) and with whom she did missionary work in China. After his death in Hong Kong in 1910 she returned to the United States. In February 1912, while working with her mother and the Salvation Army in New York City, she married Harold S. McPherson, with whom she settled in Providence, Rhode Island.

In 1915 McPherson decided to devote her life to preaching and healing. Her first preaching occurred at Mount Forest, Ontario, in August 1915, and the next summer she began a career as an itinerant evangelist. From the beginning she worked in spiritual healing and encouraged speaking in tongues and other common attributes of fundamentalist and Pentecostal Christianity. In 1917 she began writing and publishing *Bridal Call*. Under her mother's management (her husband left her in 1918 and obtained a divorce in 1921) she traveled through the United States and to England, Canada, Australia, and other countries. From 1918 she made her headquarters in Los Angeles. Her personal appeal was such that her revivals attracted thousands, from the well known to the unlettered. In April 1921 she began building her Angelus Temple in Los Angeles.

In January 1923 it was dedicated as the "Church of the Foursquare Gospel," a name deriving from her vision of a four-faced creature she equated with Ezekiel's similar vision and interpreted as typifying Christ's fourfold role as Savior, Baptizer, Healer, and Coming King. Based on tenets of hope and salvation for the needy, her Foursquare Gospel appealed especially to migrant Southerners and Midwesterners who found themselves frustrated by the complexities of life in urban Southern California. In 1927 she incorporated the International Church of the Foursquare Gospel.

A born showman, McPherson dazzled her audiences with robed choirs, costumed pageantry, an orchestra, and her own white-robed, blue-caped figure. She preached every night at the temple, and Sunday services at the temple were attended by thousands of worshipers, who sat spellbound throughout extravaganzas that included patriotic and quasi-religious music played by a 50-piece band, the breathtaking entrance of Sister

Aimee, prayers, and singing, all climaxed by a dramatic sermon. She based much of the appeal of her movement on faith healing, adult baptism by immersion, and a pervading aura of optimism and spectacle. The temple radio station broadcast her services, and she published weekly and monthly magazines and operated numerous other enterprises. She compiled a book of sermons, *This Is That*, 1923, and wrote *In the Service of the King*, 1927, and *Give Me My Own God*, 1936. She frequently made newspaper headlines, most notably in 1926, when she disappeared for several weeks (she claimed to have been kidnapped) and she was accused of a number of financial improprieties, but none was proved and none detracted from her appeal to her loyal following. During the 1930s she was dogged by numerous lawsuits — at one time 45 assorted legal actions were pending — and by disagreements with her family.

By 1944 McPherson's Foursquare Gospel movement had grown to include over 400 branches in the United States and Canada and nearly 200 missions abroad, with membership numbering some 22,000. Her Bible College, founded in 1923 and from 1926 housed in the Lighthouse of International Foursquare Evangelism next to the Angelus Temple, had graduated over 3000 evangelists and missionaries. She died on September 27, 1944, in Oakland, California, from an overdose of sleeping pills that was declared accidental. Her son Rolf McPherson continued the movement.

Macy, Anne Sullivan 1866–1936 educator

Born in Feeding Hills, Massachusetts, on April 14, 1866, Joanna Sullivan was known throughout her life as Anne or Annie. When she was eight her mother died, and two years later her father deserted the three children. Anne, whom an earlier illness had left nearly blind, and her lame brother were placed in the state almshouse in Tewksbury, where the brother died a short time later. In October 1880 Anne entered the Perkins Institution for the Blind. Surgery the next year restored some sight. She graduated from Perkins at the head of her class in 1886.

In March 1887, after several months of studying the records of Samuel Gridley Howe's work with Laura Bridgman, Sullivan arrived in Tuscumbia, Alabama, to become governess to six-year-old Helen Keller, who had been left blind, deaf, and mute by an illness contracted at the age of nineteen months. Since that time she had grown into an undisciplined, willful, and ill tempered child with no means of contact with the outer world but touch. Anne Sullivan's first task was to tame the child. She then began attempting to convey to her the idea of communication by finger spelling in her palm the names of objects. Great patience and unshakable determination were required for the job. One day in April Helen suddenly made the connection between water being pumped over her hand and the name w-a-t-e-r being spelled out simultaneously. Her progress was rapid thereafter. In 1888 the two began spending periods at the Perkins Institution, and Anne Sullivan subsequently accompanied Helen to the Wright-Humason School in New York City, the Cambridge School for Young Ladies, and finally Radcliffe College, where she painstakingly spelled out the lectures to Helen and read to her for hours each day. After Helen's graduation in 1904 they settled on a farm given by a benefactor in Wrentham, Massachusetts.

In May 1905 Anne Sullivan married John A. Macy, a younger Harvard instructor who had worked with Helen Keller on a book. The marriage ultimately proved unhappy, and from 1913 they were separated. Anne Macy continued as Helen Keller's constant companion at home and on national and later worldwide lecture tours on the Chautauqua and vaudeville circuits and later for the American Foundation for the Blind. Her frequent overexertions taxed her strength, however, and as her health declined so did her always delicate spirits. By 1935 she was completely blind. She died in Forest Hills, Queens, New York, on October 20, 1936. Her achievement in teaching Helen Keller, often minimized by uninformed commentators who celebrated only Keller's miraculous abilities, was given its full due in the pupil's book *Teacher: Anne Sullivan Macy*, 1955, and was the subject of a highly successful Broadway play, *The Miracle Worker*, by William Gibson, 1959, which was also made into a motion picture.

Madison, Dolley Payne Todd 1768–1849 socialite and First Lady

Born on May 20, 1768, in Guilford County, North Carolina, Dolley (or Dolly) Payne grew up on a plantation in Hanover County, Virginia, until 1783, when her father, under Quaker influence, sold the plantation, freed his slaves, and settled the family in Philadelphia. Dolley, an attractive and vivacious young woman, married John Todd, Jr., a Quaker lawyer, in January 1790. Todd died in a yellow fever epidemic in October 1793, leaving his widow with two young children, one of whom died weeks later. In September 1794 she married James Madison, then a member of Congress from Virginia. Her warm, cheerful, sociable manner contrasted as sharply with Madison's quietly introspective way; they proved nonetheless, or perhaps therefore, an exceedingly successful match, perfectly complementary in nearly every respect.

From 1797 to 1801 they lived at Montpellier (now spelled Montpelier), Madison's estate in Orange County, Virginia, but on his becoming secretary of state in the administration of Thomas Jefferson in 1801 Dolley Madison became the leader of Washington society and the acting hostess for the President, a widower. Her graces went far to offset the often drab social scene of the first Democratic-Republican administration. When James Madison entered the presidency in March 1809, Dolley Madison blossomed forth in finery and more formal entertainments. Her open hospitality and genuine friendliness did much to ease the strains of partisanship in Washington and to strengthen Madison's hold upon his own party.

When British troops occupied and burned Washington in August 1814, she acted quickly in salvaging a Gilbert Stuart portrait of George Washington and a great many important state documents from the President's House (as the White House was then known) before fleeing. On their return to the city the Madisons lived in the Octagon House and later in a house on Pennsylvania Avenue while the official residence was repaired. In 1817 they returned to Montpelier, where they lived quietly, save for a continuous stream of guests, until Madison's death in 1836. Dolley Madison then settled again in Washington, D.C., where she continued to be a favorite figure in society until her death on July 12, 1849.

Mallon, Mary 1870?–1938 "Typhoid Mary," typhoid carrier

Believed to have been born in the United States about 1870, Mary Mallon allegedly gave rise to the most famous outbreaks of carrier-borne disease in medical history. She was first recognized as a carrier of the typhoid bacteria during an epidemic of typhoid fever in 1904 that spread through Oyster Bay, New York, where she worked as a cook. By the time the disease had been traced to its source in a household where she had recently been employed, she had already left. She continued to work as a cook, moving from household to household, until 1907, when she was found working in a Park Avenue home.

Between 1907 and 1910 she was institutionalized at Riverside Hospital on North Brother Island (in the East River), New York City, the authorities of which finally released her on the promise that she would seek employment other than a cook. Four years later, after another outbreak of typhoid fever, she was found to be working as a cook in a sanatorium in New Jersey, and after that she remained in detention on North Brother Island until her death in New York City on November 11, 1938. Her history as a carrier implicated her in 3 deaths from typhoid and more than 50 other cases, while, as is not uncommon, she herself remained immune.

Mankiller, Wilma Pearl 1945– principal Chief of the Cherokee Nation

Born in Tahlequah, Oklahoma, on November 18, 1945, Wilma Mankiller was the daughter of Charlie Mankiller, a full-blooded Cherokee, and Irene Mankiller, who was of Dutch and Irish origin. Her early life was spent on Mankiller Flats, the farm granted to her grandfather as part of a government settlement after the forced relocation of his tribe. (The name Mankiller derives from the high military rank achieved by a Cherokee ancestor.)

Farming provided only subsistence income on Mankiller Flats; like most homes in the community, the Mankillers' had neither electricity nor running water. When the farm failed in 1957, after two years of drought, the family was again relocated, this time through a government program designed to move Native Americans from rural to urban areas, thus breaking their ties with tribal life and culture. The relocation was largely involuntary and the abrupt change in Mankiller's surroundings was as difficult for her as for the entire family. Her father eventually got a job as a warehouse worker and became a union activist.

During the 1960s, she studied sociology and got a job as a social worker. She married Hugo Olaya, an Ecuadorian businessman, with whom she had two daughters. In 1969, she became an activist in the American Native Rights movement, crediting her politicization to the occupation of Alcatraz Prison by a group protesting the atrocious treatment of all Native Americans. (The women's movement was another formative influence.) She began attending college at night, then got a job as Native American programs coordinator for the Oakland public schools.

In the mid–1970s, she divorced her husband, moved back to Oklahoma with her daughters, reclaimed her land and built a small house on Mankiller Flats. In 1977 she took a job as economic stimulus coordinator for the Cherokee Nation. Completing her degree in social science and taking courses in community planning, she initiated a number of projects aimed at greater development of the Cherokee communities in Oklahoma. Her programs emphasized a self-help philosophy and her grant-writing skills and experience at urban social work insured excellent financial and organizational support. Projects included housing renovation, improvement of rural water systems, development of commercial horticultural facilities and implementation of expanded social services.

A 1979 automobile collision severely injured her, but she emerged with renewed determination to overcome the obstacles she faced. Due to her reputation in economic and community development, she was approached in 1983 by principal Cherokee chief, Ross Swimmer, and urged to run for deputy principal chief on his ticket. Although Swimmer was a conservative, business-oriented Republican and Mankiller was more supportive of Democrats, she accepted. They won the election and pursued his agenda of attaining autonomy as a nation through the promotion of small business enterprises. They also worked together to reduce tensions in the tribe between full- and mixed-blooded Cherokees.

In 1985, Swimmer was chosen by the Reagan administration to head the Bureau of Indian Affairs in Washington D.C. Mankiller succeeded him as principal chief, thereby becoming the first woman ever to serve as chief of a major Native American tribe. Although the ascendancy of a woman caused some consternation, Mankiller was quick to point out that was not entirely without historical precedent — like many other tribes, the Cherokees were originally matrilineal. Moreover, prior to the influence of Europeans, women in some tribes helped select the chiefs.

In 1986, Mankiller married Charlie Soap, a tribal member and community activist involved in rural development work. With his fluent Cherokee he helped lay the groundwork for Mankiller's own 1987 election to chief in her own right. Her victory ushered in an administration that focused on the high unemployment rate and low levels of education, on improvement of community health care and on economic development of northeastern Oklahoma. She emphasized the necessity of retaining certain Cherokee traditions by creating the Institute for Cherokee Literacy, where summer students learn to read and write Cherokee and pass on their knowledge to other members of the community.

In 1991 Mankiller was re-elected to a second, full term. Despite the fact that the Cherokee nation had a stronger economic base than many other native tribes, she emphasized the work that remained ahead. She used media exposure ably, largely to focus greater attention on the problems and concerns of Cherokee life. Reinvestment in health care, Head Start and job training proved to be major helps but not panaceas. She cited infant mortality and the continued low-level of educational achievement as priorities for her second administration. She did not hesitate to criticize political leaders: of Ronald Reagan she had said that he "was not good on Indian issues at all. I met with him, along with some other people, and he didn't have the tiniest bit of interest in Indian issues."

Mankiller was given a Citation for Outstanding Contributions to American Leadership and Native American Culture by the Harvard Foundation, 1986. Named Woman of the Year by *Ms.* magazine in 1987, she was also inducted into the National Women's Hall of Fame in Seneca Falls, N.Y. She served on the board of the Cherokee Nation Industries, Inc., the Cherokee National Historical Society, the Indian Law Resource Center and the Oklahoma Academy of State Goals. Her autobiography, *Mankiller: A Chief and Her People*, was published in 1993.

Mannes, Clara Damrosch 1869–1948 musician and educator

Born on December 12, 1869, in Breslau, Prussia (now Wroclaw, Poland), Clara Damrosch was the daughter of Leopold Damrosch. The family came to the United States and settled in New York City in 1871, and until his death in 1885 Leopold Damrosch played a major role in fostering the growth of music as an organized public amenity in the city. Clara began studying piano at six and attended private schools. During 1888–1889 she continued her musical studies in Dresden, and on her return to New York in the latter year she began giving lessons herself. She also sang occasionally with the Oratorio Society, which her father had founded. There she met David Mannes (1866–1959), a violinist in the New York Symphony Orchestra (also founded by her father and subsequently conducted by her brother Walter). They became engaged while both were studying in Germany in 1897, and they were married in June 1898.

For a time they continued their careers separately, but in 1901 they began playing together, and in 1903, after a period of study with Eugene Ysaÿe in Belgium, they gave a series of sonata recitals that were highly acclaimed. Clara Mannes also joined her husband in teaching at the Music School Settlement on New York's Lower East Side. Their joint concert career took them on tours throughout the United States and in 1913 to London. Clara Mannes also appeared from time to time as accompanist to the Kneisel Quartet, Pablo Casals, and other artists. In 1916 they founded the David Mannes Music School, open to students of all ages and dedicated to the training not only of virtuoso talent but also of the educated amateur and lover of music. Their career as joint recitalists ended in 1917, and thereafter Clara Mannes devoted herself entirely to her duties as co-director of the school. They were both decorated by the French government in 1926 for their contributions to music education. In 1928, with Louis Untermeyer, they edited *New Songs for New Voices*, a collection of songs, many especially commissioned for the book, for children. Clara Mannes died in New York City on March 16, 1948. The Mannes School, incorporated in 1934, became Mannes College of Music in 1953.

Mannes, Marya 1904–1990 writer and critic

Born in New York City on November 14, 1904, Maria von Heimburg Mannes, known always as Marya, was the daughter of Clara Damrosch Mannes and David Mannes, both distinguished musicians. She was educated privately and benefited also from the cultural atmosphere of her home and from European travel. During the 1920s and early 1930s she contributed a number of stories and reviews to *Theatre Arts*, *Creative Art*, *International Studio*, and *Harper's* magazines and wrote a play, *Café*, that was produced, albeit unsuccessfully, on Broadway.

During that period, from 1926 to 1930, she was married to theatrical designer Jo Mielziner. From 1933 to 1936 she was a feature editor for *Vogue* magazine. For some time thereafter she lived abroad in Florence with her second husband, Richard Blow, an artist. From 1941 to 1945 she was involved in government work, first for the Office of War Information and later as an analyst for the Office of Strategic Services.

After the war Mannes resumed writing for magazines, notably the *New Yorker*, and in 1946–1947 she was a feature editor for *Glamour*. Her first book, *Message from a Stranger*, a novel, was published in 1948. In 1952 she joined the staff of *Reporter* magazine, to which she contributed essays, reviews, opinions, and verse until 1963. A collection of essays criticizing and satirizing American mores, foibles, and preoccupations appeared in 1958 as *More In Anger*, a book that occasioned widespread comment. *Subverse*, 1959, was a collection of satirical poems, many reprinted from *Reporter*.

In 1961 she published *The New York I Know*, and in 1964 *But Will It Sell*. From 1965 to 1967 she wrote a monthly column and in 1968 movie reviews for *McCall's*. She also contributed a monthly column to the *New York Times* in 1967 and in 1967–1968 was a regular commentator on a New York public television station. Later books included *They*, 1968; *Out of My Time*, an autobiography, 1971; *Uncoupling*, an account of her three divorces, written with Norman Sheresky, 1972; and *Last Rites*, a plea for laws supporting euthanasia, 1974. Marya Mannes was accounted one of the most perceptive observers of, and acerbic commentators on, the American way of life. She died on September 13, 1990, in San Francisco, California.

Manning, Marie 1873?–1945 journalist

Born in Washington, D.C., probably on January 22, 1873 (the year is not certain), Marie Manning was educated in schools in her native city, in New York City, and in London. Her long-held ambition to become a newspaperwoman came to fruition after a chance meeting at a Washington dinner party with Arthur Brisbane, an editor on the *New York World*. At his invitation she went to New York and took a job at space rates (on which basis she was paid only for the quantity of submitted material that was actually printed) on the *World*. An exclusive interview with President Grover Cleveland shortly afterward won her a regular staff position.

In 1897 she joined Brisbane and much of the rest of the *World*'s staff in going over to William Randolph Hearst's *New York Evening Journal*. There, after a year or so of turning out standard women's-page fare and sensational crime stories she was asked by Brisbane to deal with some letters sent to the paper by women requesting advice on difficult personal problems. He suggested a regular column might be made of such stuff.

On July 20, 1898, the column made its first appearance under the byline of "Beatrice Fairfax," a name Marie Manning had compounded from Dante's Beatrice and Fairfax County, Virginia, where her family owned a home. Beatrice Fairfax was an immediate success, and within a short time letters were arriving from the lovelorn and the merely puzzled at the rate of over a thousand a day. Questions of etiquette — how to win a man, how to hold a woman, what little intimacies were allowable in various circumstances —

apparently troubled or at least interested thousands of readers. Beatrice Fairfax's replies relied generally on a firm code of etiquette and the motto "Dry your eyes, roll up your sleeves, and dig for a practical solution." In the newspaper advice field she was rivaled only by "Dorothy Dix" (Elizabeth M. Gilmer).

While conducting the column Manning continued as a reporter, contributed short stories to *Harper's Magazine*, and wrote two novels, *Lord Allingham, Bankrupt*, 1902, and *Judith of the Plains*, 1903. After her marriage in July 1905 to Herman E. Gasch, a real estate dealer in Washington, D.C., she retired to devote herself to her family. The stock market crash of 1929, in which she lost heavily, brought her out of retirement. She resumed the column, now syndicated through Hearst's King Features to 200 newspapers across the country, and dealt as she had before with a new generation of problems. She also wrote *Personal Reply*, 1943, a book of advice for servicemen and their families, and *Ladies Now and Then*, 1944, an autobiography. In late years she also covered women's news from Washington for the International News Service. Marie Manning died in Washington, D.C., on November 28, 1945.

Mansfield, Arabella 1846–1911 lawyer and educator

Born on May 23, 1846, on the family farm near Sperry Station, Iowa, Belle Aurelia Babb grew up and attended school there and, from 1860, in Mount Pleasant, Iowa. She graduated from Iowa Wesleyan University in 1866. (By that time she was known as Arabella.) She then taught at Simpson College in Indianola until her marriage in June 1868 to John M. Mansfield, a professor at Iowa Wesleyan. She joined the Iowa Wesleyan faculty in that year as a teacher of English and history. With her husband she studied law as well, and together they applied for admission to the Iowa bar in June 1869. The judge who passed on their application proved sympathetic to the idea of equal rights and protection for women, and, on learning from the equally sympathetic examiners that Mansfield had passed her examination with high honors, he construed the words "man" and "male" in the state law regulating bar admissions as extending to women as well and approved her application.

Mansfield thus became the first woman to be admitted to the bar in the United States. She did not practice law, however, but continued to., teach at Iowa Wesleyan, from which she also received M.A. and LL.B. degrees in 1870 and 1872. During that time she helped organize the Iowa Woman Suffrage Society. In 1879 she and her husband joined the faculty of Indiana Asbury University, which five years later became DePauw University. After a two-year period devoted to caring for her husband, who had suffered a nervous breakdown and whom she ultimately was obliged to place in an asylum, she resumed her career at DePauw in 1886. She remained there until her death, teaching at various times history, aesthetics, and music history and serving as dean of the school of art from 1893, also as dean of the school of music from 1894, and from time to time in other administrative capacities. She died in Aurora, Illinois, on August 2, 1911.

Marble, Alice 1913–1990 tennis player and spy

Born on September 28, 1913, in California and raised in San Francisco, Alice Marble was exposed to loss early in life. At the age of seven, her father died of pneumonia, and within the same year she saw her best friend killed in an accident. Later Marble was introduced to baseball by her uncle and was captivated by the sport; in turn she impressed the local minor league baseball team and became the San Francisco Seals's mascot. She resolved then to become a professional baseball player.

Marble's older brother, Dan, put a tennis racket in her hand in the hopes of interesting her in a less masculine sport. She played aggressive tennis and pioneered the women's serve and volley style of play. Her training pitching baseballs lent itself to a powerful tennis serve, while her quick hand-to-eye coordination and speed gave her an exceptional game at the net.

Marble practiced over the next few years by emulating other players and by spending every free moment at the public courts at Golden Gate Park. At age fifteen, Marble was raped at the park by a man whose identity she never learned. Physically she recovered quite quickly, but she suffered continued anger and humiliation throughout high school; it was ten years before she was able to have an intimate, physical relationship with another person. Marble came to believe that the attack contributed to her toughness and made her focus even more intently on tennis as a source of self-esteem.

Only three years after her introduction to tennis and still without a coach, Marble traveled to Forest Hills as northern California's junior champion. Then, in 1932, she started working with the woman who would be her career-long coach, manager, mentor and principal supporter, Eleanor Tennant. Working with Tennant and Harwood "Beese" White, Marble learned the game from scratch: she changed her grip from a Western grip to Eastern one — a vital factor for success on a grass court. Marble's aggressive serve and volley game and her preference for shorts instead of a skirt shocked the tennis world; one headline read, "Marble's Playing a Man's Game!" Tennant, who was a popular tennis coach among the stars of southern California, introduced her to the likes of W. Randolph Hearst, Cary Grant, Clark Gable, Marlene Dietrich and Carole Lombard, many of whom became close lifelong friends.

On her first trip abroad in 1934, Marble collapsed during a match in Paris and was diagnosed with tuberculosis and pleurisy — she was told she would never play tennis again. With Lombard's and Tennant's support, she recovered fully and returned to competition. From 1936 to 1940, she was the top-ranked woman in the U.S.; she played at Wimbledon, where she won the mixed doubles championship with Don Budge in 1937, and again in 1938 along with the women's doubles championship with Sarah Palfrey.

Marble became the first woman of the century to win the Triple Crown at Wimbledon in 1939 — the mixed doubles with Bobby Riggs, the women's doubles with Sarah Palfrey and the women's singles titles, all in the same tournament. With increasing fame and glamour, Marble's activities began to include speaking engagements. She did a brief stint as a professional singer at the Waldorf Astoria in New York and some radio sportscasting. She also designed a line of women's tennis apparel.

Marble turned professional in 1940 just as the nation prepared for World War II. She gave exhibition tours and clinics around the country and at many military bases. Despite intense pressure from her coach to abstain from romantic involvement, Marble had a couple of brief affairs (first with a man and then a woman); in 1942 she married a soldier she met on one of her tours. Two years later, after losing her friend Lombard in a plane crash, her painful string of tragedies resumed. Days after a car accident in which she lost the child with whom she was pregnant, she learned that her husband's plane had been shot down by the Germans; he had not survived.

Despondent, she tried to kill herself. Upon recovering from her attempt at suicide, however, Marble agreed to participate in an espionage plot for the U.S. Army Intelligence. In 1945 she traveled to Switzerland to investigate financial ledgers of an ex-lover who was a Swiss investment banker harboring Nazi wealth during the war. Marble was nearly killed on the mission and lost the physical evidence she had acquired, but she used her photographic memory to recall much of the needed information.

Her tournament play was cut short by World War II. Marble continued to play in exhibition matches, hold clinics and give lectures. She also coach promising new players (including another serve and volley newcomer, Billie Jean King). She was inducted into the Tennis Hall of Fame in 1964, the winner of twelve U.S. Open and five Wimbledon titles. Marble spent her last years in Palm Desert, California; she died in 1990.

Marbury, Elisabeth 1856–1933 theatrical and literary agent

Born in New York City on June 19, 1856, Elisabeth Marbury grew up in a well-to-do and cultured home. She was privately educated, to a large extent by her father. Until 1885 she occupied herself with social activities, Sunday school teaching, and a brief but quite successful foray into poultry raising on the family's Oyster Bay farm. In that year her success in organizing a benefit theatrical performance prompted producer Daniel Frohman to advise her to devote herself to the management side of the theater. In 1888 she persuaded Frances Hodgson Burnett, who had written a dramatic version of her best-selling *Little Lord Fauntleroy* but who had little knowledge of the theater or of business generally, to take her on as business manager and agent. The association quickly proved highly profitable to both.

In 1891 she traveled to France and convinced playwright Victorien Sardou to allow her to be his representative in the English-speaking market and that of the other members of the Société des Gens de Lettres. For over 15 years she represented Sardou, Georges Feydeau, Edmond Rostand, Ludovic Halévy, Henri Meilhac, Jean Richepin, Francis de Croisset, and others. Her work on their behalf included securing suitable translations, sound productions with leading actors, and full royalties. She also represented George Bernard Shaw, James M. Barrie (whom she prevailed upon to rewrite *The Little Minister* for Maude Adams), Hall Caine, and Jerome K. Jerome, among British authors, and Rachel Crothers and Clyde Fitch among Americans. Her office was thus a center of the New York theatrical business, and for many years she worked closely with Charles Frohman and his Theatrical Syndicate in bringing order to a rapidly expanding field of enterprise. She later also worked with the rival Shubert brothers' organization.

From early in her career Marbury found time for an occasional piece of writing. *Manners: A Handbook of Social Customs*, appeared in 1888; she was coauthor of *A Wild Idea*, a play produced in 1889, and she adapted *Merry Gotham*, produced in 1892, from a French play. In 1914 she joined several other agents in forming the American Play Company, and in 1915 she turned as well to producing and helped stage *Nobody Home*, 1915, *Very Good, Eddie*, 1915, and *Love o' Mike*, 1916, all with music by Jerome Kern, and *See America First*, 1916, by Cole Porter. These works contributed significantly to the development of the characteristically American form of musical comedy. In 1913 she brought Vernon and Irene Castle, whom she had seen on one of her innumerable trips to Paris, back to New York and set them up in a fashionable dancing school that was the springboard for their brief but spectacularly popular career. From 1887 she was a close friend and companion of Elsie de Wolfe, whom she assisted in creating a career in interior decoration, and in 1903 she bought and set about restoring the Villa Trianon near Versailles, where they became noted hostesses. Also in 1903 she joined Anne Morgan, Florence J. Harriman, and others in organizing the Colony Club, the first women's social club in New York.

During World War I Marbury devoted much time to relief work for French and later American soldiers and spent several months in France working in military hospitals and giving talks to the troops. She translated Maurice Barrès's *The Faith of France*, 1918, and was decorated by the French and Belgian governments. She became active in politics in Alfred E. Smith's 1918 gubernatorial campaign in New York, and in 1920 she was a delegate to the Democratic National Convention. From that year she served on the party's National Committee. In 1923 she published an autobiography, *My Crystal Ball*. After several years of declining health Elisabeth Marbury died in New York City on January 22, 1933.

Marlatt, Abby Lillian 1869–1943 home economist and educator

Born in Manhattan, Kansas, on March 7, 1869, Abby Marlatt graduated from the

Kansas State Agricultural College (now Kansas State University of Agriculture and Applied Science) in her hometown in 1888. She remained there as a teacher while studying for her M.S. in chemistry, which she received in 1890, and she then was invited to organize a department of domestic economy in the Utah State Agricultural College (now Utah State University) in Logan, where she served as professor until 1894. In that year she joined the faculty of the Manual Training (later the Technical) High School in Providence, Rhode Island, where she organized a department of home economics. During her years in Providence she continued her own studies at Brown University and in summer sessions at Clark University. She also took part in the work of the Lake Placid Conference on Home Economics, serving as chairman in 1903 and vice-president in 1907 under Ellen H. Richards.

In 1909 Marlatt was asked by the University of Wisconsin to organize its courses in home economics, lately transferred to the college of agriculture, into a regular department. Under her leadership the department rapidly outgrew its basement quarters, and after a statewide campaign aided by women's clubs and by her own students' serving pancakes to the appropriate legislative committee, the department moved into its own building in 1914. In her 30 years as director of home economics the staff of the department grew from 2 to 25, the enrollment from 47 to 512, and the course offerings from 12 to 67. More important, Marlatt established high academic standards for her students. Basic courses in English, foreign language, and science were required, and technical courses from bacteriology to physiology to journalism greatly broadened the training available to home economics majors beyond the domestic skills courses that had once been their only education. Her department at Wisconsin set standards that were emulated by institutions across the country.

From 1912 to 1918 Marlatt served as vice-president of the American Home Economics Association, which had grown out of the Lake Placid conferences. During World War I she served at the request of Herbert Hoover as chairman of a committee on state participation in the Division of Food Conservation of the Food Administration. She was subsequently secretary of the Women's Division of the Wisconsin Council of National Defense. She retired in 1939 and died in Madison, Wisconsin, on June 23, 1943.

Marot, Helen 1865–1940 reformer, writer, librarian, labor organizer and public official

Born in Philadelphia on June 9, 1865, Helen Marot grew up in a well-to-do and cultured family and was educated in Quaker schools. In 1893 she took a job with the University Extension Society of Philadelphia. In 1896 she worked as a librarian in Wilmington, Delaware, and the next year she returned to Philadelphia and with a friend opened a private library specializing in works on social and economic topics. In 1899 she published a *Handbook of Labor Literature*. In that year she also conducted for the U.S. Industrial Commission an investigation of working conditions in the custom tailoring trades in Philadelphia, an experience that added force to her natural sympathy for the exploited. In 1902 she investigated child labor in New York City for the Association of Neighborhood Workers. Later in the year she helped form the New York Child Labor Committee, and with Florence Kelley and Josephine Goldmark she drew up a report on child labor in the city that was the principal impetus to the passage of the Compulsory Education Act by the state legislature the next year. After serving as secretary of the newly organized Pennsylvania Child Labor Committee for over a year, she returned to New York in late 1905 to become chairman of the school visiting committee of the Public Education Association of New York.

In mid–1906 Marot resigned that post to become executive secretary of the two-year-old New York branch of the National Women's Trade Union League. Her executive ability, organizing talent, and sheer drive built the group into a formidable force in labor organization. She was largely responsible for creating the Bookkeepers, Stenographers and Accountants Union of New York, a pioneering effort in organizing white-collar women. During that time she also assisted Goldmark and Kelley in assembling the data for Louis Brandeis's famous brief in the case of *Muller v. Oregon*, concerning the regulation of women's working hours. In 1909–1910 she was the principal leader and organizer of the first great strike of shirtwaist makers and dressmakers under the banner of the new International Ladies' Garment Workers' Union.

Marot resigned as executive secretary of the league in 1913 and turned to writing. After publishing *American Labor Unions*, 1914, a tract on the syndicalist Industrial Workers of the World written from her standpoint as a Fabian socialist, she served on the editorial board of the radical journal *Masses* in 1916–1917 and on the staff of *The Dial* in 1918–1920. She was also a member of the U.S. Industrial Relations Commission in 1914–1916. Her *Creative Impulse in Industry* appeared in 1918. From 1920 she lived in quiet retirement. She died in New York City on June 3, 1940.

Marshall, Clara 1847–1931 physician and educator

Born in West Chester, Pennsylvania, on May 8, 1847, Clara Marshall was of a prominent Quaker family. At the age of twenty-four, after having taught school for a time, she enrolled in the Woman's Medical College of Pennsylvania. On graduating in 1875 she was appointed a demonstrator in materia medica and practical pharmacy in the college, and in the same year she became the first woman to be admitted to the Philadelphia College of Pharmacy (of which a Marshall ancestor had been first president). After a year of study there, during which her academic standing earned her the honor of arranging the pharmaceutical display at the Centennial Exposition of 1876, she returned to the Woman's Medical College as professor of materia medica and therapeutics. She retained that post until 1905. In 1882 she served also as demonstrator in obstetrics at the Philadelphia Hospital; she was the first woman on the staff of that institution. From 1886 she was attending physician to the girls' department of the Philadelphia House of Refuge.

In 1888 Marshall was named dean of the Woman's Medical College. Under her leadership the course and facilities of the school were greatly expanded and improved. The course was lengthened from three to four years in 1893, and from 1896 instruction and laboratory work in the new field of bacteriology and related subjects were added. To supply critical clinical experience, for which the Woman's Hospital (founded in 1861 by Dr. Ann Preston) had by the 1890s begun to prove insufficient, Marshall determined to open a hospital directly associated with the college.

The small Pavilion Hospital opened in 1904. A larger hospital in permanent quarters was begun in 1907 and finally completed in 1913, representing a huge undertaking for so small an institution. The success of Marshall's work to keep the school's standards up to the demands of modern scientific training was reflected in the A rating awarded by the American Medical Association's Council on Medical Education in 1906 and in the laudatory comments of Abraham Flexner on the school in his influential and often scathingly critical report, *Medical Education*, in 1910. After 1905 Marshall gave up teaching in order to devote more time to private practice. She retired as dean in 1917 and resigned her emeritus professorship in 1923. In 1897 she had published *The Woman's Medical College of Pennsylvania: An Historical Outline*. She died in Bryn Mawr, Pennsylvania, on March 13, 1931.

Marshall, Penny 1942– actor, comedienne and director

Born on October 15, 1942, in New York City, Carole Penny Marshall was the daughter of a dance teacher and an industrial filmmaker. She attended Walton High School in the Bronx and studied dance at her mother's studio, beginning at the age of three. She first performed with her mother's dance group, the Marshallettes, and was making television appearances by the time she was in her teens. When she was fourteen, the Marshallettes won on Ted Mack's television show, *The Original Amateur Hour*, and appeared on *The Jackie Gleason Show*.

Marshall started college at the University of New Mexico in Albuquerque but left after two years to marry Michael Henry, a football player. They had a daughter, Tracy, and divorced soon thereafter. In Albuquerque she taught dance and performed before moving to Hollywood in 1967. Her brother, Garry, was already living in Hollywood and working as a comedy writer and producer, and he convinced Marshall to take acting classes there and to try a career in film. Garry also gave Marshall her first bit part in the movie *How Sweet It Is!*, 1968, which he cowrote and coproduced. In 1970 Marshall met actor Rob Reiner, who played Archie Bunker's son-in-law in ABC's hit comedy *All in the Family*. They were married one year later, a marriage that lasted until 1979.

Marshall's big television break came when her brother gave her a small part as the secretary to Oscar Madison in *The Odd Couple* in 1971. The following two years she played Miss Larson on *The Bob Newhart Show*. Between 1970 and 1975 she acted several dramatic roles on television, until one day in 1975, Marshall and Cindy Williams played in *Happy Days* as the dates of Richie Cunningham and Arthur Fonzarelli. After this episode, Garry Marshall suggested a spin-off show to ABC, which became *Laverne and Shirley*. This show featured two blue collar women working in a Milwaukee brewery during the 1950s. Marshall's father became the producer of *Laverne and Shirley*, while brother Garry became its executive producer and her sister Ronny its associate producer.

She made her directorial debut with *Jumpin' Jack Flash*, 1986, starring her friend Whoopi Goldberg. She followed with *Big*, 1988; a hit with both critics and moviegoers, it was the first film directed by a woman to gross more than $100 million at the box office. Her next film, *Awakenings*, was nominated for several Oscars, including one for best picture, but Marshall was denied a best-director nomination. Later films included *A League of Their Own*, 1992, and *Renaissance Man*, 1994. She was regarded as being in the forefront of Hollywood directors.

Martin, Anne Henrietta 1875–1951 reformer

Born in Empire City, Nevada, on September 30, 1875, Anne Martin attended Whitaker's School for Girls in Reno and graduated from the University of Nevada in 1894. She then enrolled in Stanford University, taking a second B.A. in 1896 and an M.A. in history in 1897. During 1897–1899 she headed the new history department at the University of Nevada. After two years of additional study at Columbia University, Chase's Art School in New York, and London and Leipzig universities, she returned to the University of Nevada as an instructor of art history. She resigned in 1903, and following a period devoted to family business she spent several years in travel and study in the Orient and Europe. In November 1910 she was arrested in a pro-suffrage demonstration in England. In 1911 she returned to Nevada, and the next year she became president of the state Equal Franchise Society. The campaign she headed succeeded in November 1914 with the legislature's approval of woman suffrage. The Equal Franchise Society thereupon transformed itself into the Nevada Woman's Civic League, of which she continued as president. She served also on the Nevada Educational Survey Commission.

On the national stage Martin sat on the executive committee of the National American Woman Suffrage Association, and in 1917 she became the first national chairwoman of Alice Paul's militant National Woman's party. In 1918 and 1920 she ran on an independent ticket for a U.S. Senate seat from Nevada, but her pacifism — she had joined the Woman's Peace party organized by Jane Addams and Carrie Chapman Catt in 1915 — was one of several unpopular stands that led to her defeat. Nonetheless in both elections she attracted some 20 percent of the popular vote. She remained an active member of the National Woman's party until the later 1920s and was one of its most vehement spokesmen against women's joining the established, male-dominated political parties.

In 1926 Martin became active in the Women's International League for Peace and Freedom; she was a national board member from 1926 to 1936, director of the U.S. section's western region from 1926 to 1931, and a delegate to congresses in Dublin in 1926 and Prague in 1929. She left the organization in 1936 in protest of its lack of commitment to feminist goals. Before the Second World War, as before the First, she was a stout opponent of U.S. involvement. Throughout her career as a reformer she was a frequent contributor of articles and poems to leading magazines and journals. She died in Carmel, California, on April 15, 1951.

Martin, Lillien Jane 1851–1943 psychologist

Born on July 7, 1851, in Olean, New York, Lillie (she later changed the name to Lillien) Jane Martin was a precocious child and entered Olean Academy at the age of four. At sixteen she began teaching in a girls' school in Wisconsin, and she later taught in a school in Omaha, Nebraska. By 1876 she had saved enough money to enter Vassar College, from which she graduated in 1880. From that year to 1889 she taught high school physics and chemistry in Indianapolis, and from 1889 to 1894 she was vice-principal and head of the science department of the Girls' High School in San Francisco.

In 1894 Martin traveled to Germany to enter the University of Göttingen, where she studied psychology under G. E. Müller and was awarded a Ph.D. in 1898. In 1899 she was named assistant professor of psychology at Stanford University. She continued her studies in Germany in summers, working in the universities of Würzburg in 1907, Bonn in 1908 and 1912, and Munich in 1914. Her scholarly publications of that period, nearly all in German, dealt with problems in hypnotism, aesthetics, personality, abnormal psychology, and the nature of thought and included *Zur Analyse der Unterschiedsempfindlichkeit*, 1899, *Über Asthetische Synästhesie*, 1909, *Zur Lehre von der Bewegungsvorstellungen*, 1910, *Die Projections Methode*, 1912, and *Ein Experimenteller Beitrag zur Erforschung des Unterbewussten*, 1915. At Stanford she advanced to associate professor in 1909 and to full professor in 1911, and in 1915 she became the first woman to head a department there. She retired at the mandatory age of sixty-five in 1916. She then moved to San Francisco and established herself as a consulting psychologist. She established mental hygiene clinics in the Polyclinic and Mount Zion hospitals and carried on private practice as well. In 1920 she opened at Mount Zion the first clinic for normal preschool children.

In 1929, as a result of having to deal with a problem child whose problem was actually an overbearing grandmother, Martin established the Old Age Counseling Center, the first such clinic in the world. The rest of her career was devoted to gerontological research and clinical counseling and rehabilitation. Her success in that field derived in large part from the example she herself set: an indefatigable traveler, she journeyed alone to Russia at seventy-eight, made a coast-to-coast automobile tour at eighty-one (just three years after she had learned to drive), and traveled through the jungles and mountains of South America for six months at eighty-seven.

Martin's later publications included *Personality as Revealed by the Content of Images*, 1917, *Mental Hygiene; Two Years' Experience of a Clinical Psychologist*, 1920, *Mental Training for the Pre-School Age Child*, with Clare De Gruchy, 1923, *Round the World with a Psychologist*, 1927, *Salvaging Old Age*, with De Gruchy, 1930, *Sweeping the Cobwebs*, with De Gruchy, 1933, *The Home in a Democracy*, with De Gruchy, 1938, and *Handbook for Old Age Counsellors*, 1944. In 1917–1920 she was president of the California Society for Mental Hygiene. She died in San Francisco on March 26, 1943.

Martin, Mary 1913–1990 actor

Born in Weatherford, Texas, on December 1, 1913, Mary Martin attended private schools and for a year the University of Texas. After a brief first marriage (1930–1935) she opened a dance school in Weatherford that proved a remarkable success. At various times she took voice lessons, and at length she decided to seek a career in show business. A long and frustrating period followed as any number of auditions and screen tests in Hollywood came to nothing. Finally, however, on the strength of her singing in an amateur show at the Trocadero Club, she was advised to go to New York City.

Martin was given a small part in *Leave It to Me*, a Cole Porter musical that opened at the Imperial Theatre in November 1938, and wowed the audience with her steamy rendition of "My Heart Belongs to Daddy." A hit engagement at the Rainbow Room followed, and she then returned to Hollywood to appear in a series of movies: *The Great Victor Herbert*, 1939, *Rhythm on the River*, 1940, *Love Thy Neighbor*, 1940, *New York Town*, 1941, *Birth of the Blues*, 1941, *Star-Spangled Rhythm*, 1942, and others. In October 1943 she returned to Broadway in *One Touch of Venus*, a musical with book by S. J. Perelman and Ogden Nash, music by Kurt Weill, and choreography by Agnes de Mille. According to many critics, the show was a huge success largely owing to Mary Martin's performance, and the Broadway run and subsequent tour kept her busy into 1945. Her performance won her a New York Drama Critics' award. In 1946 she appeared in *Night and Day*, a film biography of Cole Porter. In the same year she appeared on Broadway in *Lute Song* and made her London debut in Noel Coward's *Pacific 1860*. During 1947–1948 she toured in *Annie Get Your Gun*; her work in bringing that hit show to the country while Ethel Merman and the original cast were still on Broadway won her a special Tony award.

In April 1949 Martin opened at the Majestic Theatre, New York, in the Rodgers and Hammerstein musical *South Pacific*. After some 900 performances as Nellie Forbush she left the Broadway cast in 1951 and in November opened in the London production of the show. *South Pacific* brought her another New York Drama Critics' award. Later shows in which she appeared included *Kind Sir* in 1953; *Peter Pan*, for which she won a Tony award, on tour in 1954; *The Skin of Our Teeth* in Paris and then on U.S. tour in 1955; *Music with Mary Martin*, a one-woman show in 1957; *The Sound of Music*, which opened at the Lunt-Fontanne Theatre in New York in November 1959, ran for nearly two years, and brought her another Tony; *Jennie* in 1963; *Hello, Dolly* on world tour in 1965; *I Do, I Do* on Broadway and on tour in 1966–1970, and *Do You Turn Somersaults?*, 1978.

Martin also became a popular television star in such special programs as "America Applauds — An Evening for Richard Rodgers," 1951, the Ford Motor Company's 50th anniversary show (in which she sang a memorable duet with Ethel Merman), 1953, the "Rodgers and Hammerstein Cavalcade," 1954, and especially her much admired *Peter Pan*, which was first broadcast in 1955, in which year it won her an Emmy award, and frequently repeated in later years. Mary Martin also recorded albums of Broadway show tunes and other music. She published an autobiography, *My Heart Belongs*, in 1976, and in 1987 toured briefly with Carol Channing in the comedy *Legends*. She was a Kennedy Center honoree in 1989. She died on November 3, 1990, in Rancho Mirage, California.

Marwedel, Emma Jacobina Christiana 1818–1893 educator

Born on February 27, 1818, in Münden, near Göttingen, Germany, Emma Marwedel was of a family of some social standing. The deaths of her mother and then of her father during her childhood left her without means, however, and she early had to earn her own support. Nothing is known of the education that prepared her to be a teacher, but her ambition and energy are attested by her election to a directorship in an association for the promotion of public education in Leipzig in 1864 and her membership in Germany's first association for the advancement of women in 1865.

In 1867–1868 Marwedel was chosen to be the first director of the newly established Girls' Industrial School in Hamburg. During that time she also conducted a kindergarten according to Froebelian principles. It is not known whether she had studied under Friedrich Froebel or his widow. Her work in Hamburg made a deep impression on the visiting Elizabeth Palmer Peabody, as did her *Warum bedürfen wir weibliche Gewerbeschulen? und wie sollen sie angelegt sein?*, 1868, a book on industrial schools for girls drawn from her earlier observations in England, France, and Belgium. At Peabody's suggestion, Marwedel came to the United States shortly afterward and in 1870 established a women's cooperative industrial school near Brentwood, Long Island. That effort failed along with the housing development with which it was associated, and she then moved to Washington, D.C., where in 1871 she opened a private school that included a kindergarten and Froebelian training classes for teachers.

In 1876, at the invitation of Caroline Severance, Marwedel moved to Los Angeles and established the California Model Kindergarten and the Pacific Model Training School for Kindergartners, the first such school in California, whose first students included Kate Smith (Wiggin). The enterprise failed to attract sufficient support, however, and she moved to Oakland in 1877, to Berkeley in 1879, and to San Francisco in 1880. In the last city she operated her Pacific Kindergarten Normal School, along with a model kindergarten and primary classes, until her retirement in 1885 or 1886. In San Francisco she helped organize the San Francisco Kindergarten Society and the Silver Street Kindergarten, for which she recommended Kate Smith as head. She led in founding the California Kindergarten Union in 1879 and served as its first president.

Her writings, including *Conscious Motherhood; or the Earliest Unfolding of the Child in the Cradle, Nursery and Kindergarten*, 1887, *The Connecting Link, to Continue the Three-Fold Development of the Child from the Cradle to the Manual-Labor School*, 1891, and such undated pamphlets as *An Appeal for Justice to Childhood and Games and Studies in Life Forms and Colors of Nature for Home and School*, together with lecturing on Froebelian theory and practice, occupied her last years. She died in San Francisco on November 17, 1893.

Mathews, Ann Teresa 1732–1800 religious

Born in Charles County, Maryland, in 1732, Ann Mathews grew up in a deeply religious home in a time when Roman Catholics labored under legal disabilities and other discriminations in Maryland. In 1754 she traveled to Hoogstraeten, Belgium, to enter an English contemplative order of Discalced Carmelites. She took the habit as Sister Bernardina Teresa Xavier of St. Joseph in September 1754 and made her profession in November 1755. She later became mistress of novices in the monastery, and in 1774 she was elected prioress.

She had doubtless long considered the idea of establishing the order in America when, in rapid succession, the American Revolution swept away the legal disabilities of Catholics there, and Joseph II, Holy Roman Emperor, dissolved the monasteries in the Netherlands in 1782. The complex task of raising money and securing permissions took until 1790. In April of that year Mother Bernardina sailed with four companions, Sister Eleanora and Sister Aloysia, both nieces of hers, Sister Clare Joseph Dickinson, and Father Charles Neale. In July they settled at Chandler's Hope on the Port Tobacco River in Charles County, Maryland, where Father Neale had grown up. The monastery established there was the first of any religious order in the United States. (The Ursuline convent in New Orleans, dating from 1727, was in what was still French territory.) Three months later the monastery was moved a short distance upriver. Novices were attracted from the surrounding region, and by 1800 the monastery housed 14 nuns. Mother Bernardina served as prioress until her death on June 12, 1800. She was succeeded by Mother Clare Joseph.

Maxwell, Elsa 1883–1963 columnist, songwriter, and professional party-giver

Born in Keokuk, Iowa, on May 24, 1883, Elsa Maxwell grew up in California and attended Miss West's School in San Francisco. She left school at the age of fourteen but later claimed to have continued her education at the University of California and the Sorbonne. Although she never had a music lesson, she began to earn a living as a theater pianist and accompanist in her early teens. She left San Francisco in 1905 as an odd-jobs girl in a Shakespearean troupe and subsequently appeared in vaudeville and for a time in South African music halls. In 1907 she began a song-writing career that resulted in some 80 published compositions.

About the same time Maxwell started meeting socially important people, showing up at soirées in the United States and in Europe and working her way up the social ladder into the international set. By the end of World War I she was giving parties for royalty and high society throughout Europe. During 1925–1926 she organized the International Motor Boat Races at the Lido in Venice, and in 1926, under the auspices of the Prince of Monaco, she planned the Monte Carlo Beach Club, the Casino Hotel, and the Piscine Restaurants of Monte Carlo. Her renowned parties were noted not only for the guests she was able to attract but also for the novelties she devised to keep them amused. She was credited with inventing the "scavenger hunt" that became a popular party game in the 1930s. Maxwell returned to New York City in the early 1930s, but New York during the Depression was not her cup of tea, and she went to Hollywood in 1938, where she appeared in several not very successful movie shorts, including *Elsa Maxwell's Hotel for Women*, 1939, and *The Lady and the Lug*, 1940. She later appeared in *Stage Door Canteen* in 1943.

Her radio program, "Elsa Maxwell's Party Line," began in 1942; she also wrote a syndicated gossip column. All the while she continued to organize parties for prominent social figures. In 1936 her "I Live by My Wits" was published serially in *Harper's Bazaar*. In 1938 her "Life of Barbara Hutton" was serialized in *Cosmopolitan*. Her autobiography, *R.S.V.P.*, appeared in 1954. In 1957 she published *How to Do It; the Lively Art of Entertaining* and began making weekly television appearances on Jack Paar's "Tonight" show. Maxwell died in New York City on November 1, 1963.

May, Geraldine Pratt 1895– air force officer

Born on April 21, 1895, in Albany, New York, Geraldine Pratt grew up there and in Tacoma, Washington. She graduated from the University of California, Berkeley, in 1920 and for a number of years was a social worker and then an officer of the Camp Fire Girls organization in San Francisco and Sacramento. In 1928 she married Albert E. May and for several years thereafter lived in Tulsa, Oklahoma. In July 1942, having returned to California, May enlisted in the Women's Army Auxiliary Corps. She was in the first class to graduate from WAAC officers training school in Des Moines, Iowa, and was commissioned a second lieutenant. After several months of recruiting duty she was transferred to work with the Army Air Corps and in March 1943 became WAAC staff director for the Air Transport Command, receiving promotions to captain in April and to major in November. Personnel under her command were assigned to 41 different bases from Hawaii to India and North Africa.

In May 1945 she was promoted to lieutenant colonel, and in October 1946 she was assigned to duty with the General Staff. In January 1947 she was named WAC (the name was changed in July 1943) staff director with Army Ground Forces. The signing into law of the Women's Armed Services Integration Act on June 12, 1948, established the

Women in the Air Force (WAF) as a regular component of the air force, and two days later May was appointed first director of the WAF with the rank of colonel. She remained in that post until resigning in June 1951. She was succeeded as WAF director by Colonel Mary J. Shelley.

Mayer, Maria Goeppert 1906–1972 physicist

Born on June 28, 1906, at Kattowitz, Germany (now Katowice, Poland), Maria Goeppert earned a doctorate in physics at the University of Göttingen under a committee of three Nobel Prize winners, including Max Born, in 1930. In January of that year she married the American physical chemist Joseph E. Mayer, and a short time later she accompanied him to Johns Hopkins University in Baltimore. Over the next nine years she was associated with Johns Hopkins as a volunteer associate. During that time she collaborated with Karl Herzfeld and her husband in the study of organic molecules. She became a citizen in 1933. In 1939 she and her husband both received appointments in chemistry at Columbia University. Their *Statistical Mechanics* appeared in 1940. Although they remained at Columbia throughout World War II, Maria Mayer also lectured at Sarah Lawrence College in 1942–1945 and conducted research on isotopes for the atomic bomb project.

After the war Mayer's interests centered increasingly in nuclear physics, and in 1946 she became a senior physicist at the Argonne National Laboratory and volunteer professor of physics in the Enrico Fermi Institute for Nuclear Studies at the University of Chicago. She received a regular appointment as full professor in 1959. In 1948–1949 she published several papers concerning the stability and configuration of protons and neutrons that comprise the atomic nucleus. She developed a theory that the nucleus consists of several shells or orbital levels, and that the distribution of protons and neutrons among these shells produces the characteristic degree of stability of each species of nucleus. A similar theory was developed at the same time in Germany by Johannes H. D. Jensen, with whom she subsequently collaborated on *Elementary Theory of Nuclear Shell Structure*, 1955. The work established her as a leading authority in the field, and in 1963 she and Jensen and Eugene P. Wigner of Princeton shared the Nobel Prize for Physics for their theoretical contributions. Also noted for her work in quantum electrodynamics and spectroscopy, Mayer accepted an appointment at the University of California at San Diego in 1960, as did her husband. She died in San Diego on February 20, 1972.

Mayo, Mary Anne Bryant 1845–1903 farm organizer

Born near Battle Creek, Michigan, on May 24, 1845, Mary Anne Bryant became a district school teacher after her graduation from Battle Creek High School. In April 1865 she married Perry Mayo, with whom she settled on a farm in Marshall Township, Calhoun County. She and her husband were much interested in self-improvement and in community self-help and betterment organizations. In the early 1870s they became active in the Patrons of Husbandry (known as the Grange) and in the organization of Farmers' Institutes, and both were elected to offices in their county Grange. Mary Mayo in particular became a highly active and effective organizer for the Grange. She served as lecturer, as chairman of the woman's work committee, and from 1891 as chaplain of the state Grange, and she traveled constantly throughout Michigan, visiting township Granges and local gatherings of every sort to forward the work of the Grange.

Mayo was especially concerned with bringing women and children into full participation in Grange organizations and Farmers' Institute meetings. Under the aegis of the Grange she developed the "Fresh Air" plan whereby children of the urban poor were taken into Granger homes for country vacations. She labored long to establish separate women's meetings and courses within the Farmers' Institute framework, and she also succeeded, after more than ten years of effort, in securing the creation of a women's department (1897) in its own building (1900) at the Michigan State Agricultural College (now Michigan State University). She served also on the board of the Michigan State Industrial Home for Girls in Adrian. Mary Mayo died on April 21, 1903. In September 1931 a new dormitory for women at Michigan State College was named in her honor.

Maywood, Augusta 1825–1876 dancer

Born in 1825, probably in New York City, Augusta Williams was the daughter of itinerant English actors. Her mother divorced her father and in 1828 married another English actor, Robert C. Maywood, whose name young Augusta took. The family settled at length in Philadelphia. Augusta began studying ballet under Paul H. Hazard in 1836, and in December 1837 she made her public debut at the Chestnut Street Theatre in *The Maid of Cashmere* (Taglioni's ballet from Daniel Auber's opera *Le Dieu et la Bayadère*). She and her co-star, fellow student Mary Ann Lee, were a great success. Enthusiastic audiences encouraged a rivalry between the two dancers. In March 1838 the two appeared together in *The Dew Drop, or La Sylphide*, a version of Taglioni's *La Sylphide*, in New York City. In May of that year Maywood took Augusta to Paris, where she studied under Jean Coralli and Joseph Mazilier, respectively ballet master and principal dancer at the Paris Opéra. In November 1839 she made her Paris debut at the Opéra in Coralli's *Le Diable boîteux* and was a great popular and critical success. In November 1840 she eloped with Charles Mabille, also a dancer. They returned to Paris in time and were married, but, their Opéra contracts broken, they were consigned to dancing engagements in Marseille, Lyon, Lisbon, and other smaller cities over the next five years. In 1845 she left Mabille and went to Vienna, where she danced with great success at the Kärntnertor Theatre until late in 1847. After a short engagement in Budapest she went to Milan in 1848 and made her La Scala debut.

In 1849 Maywood was prima donna assoluta at La Scala, and for the next nine years she was the unchallenged darling of the Italian dance public. Among the ballets in which she appeared were *Giselle*, *Le Diable amoureux*, *La Gypsy*, *Faust*, *La Silfide*, and, after she began touring with her own company — she was the first ballerina to do so — her own ballet versions of *Uncle Tom's Cabin* and of Termanini's *Rita Gauthier*, the latter based on Dumas's *La Dame aux Camélias*. In 1848 and again in 1854 she returned triumphantly to Vienna. Her marriage in 1858 to Carlo Gardini, an Italian physician, journalist, and impresario, occasioned her retirement. They settled in Vienna, where she opened a school of ballet. She taught until 1873 and in later years lived on Lake Como. The first American dancer to win international acclaim, she died in obscurity in Lemberg, Austrian Galicia (now Lvov, Ukraine), on November 3, 1876.

Mead, Margaret 1901–1978 anthropologist

Margaret Mead

Born on December 16, 1901, in Philadelphia, Margaret Mead was the daughter of an economics professor and a sociologist. She entered DePauw University in 1919 and transferred to Barnard College a year later. Courses under Franz Boas and Ruth Benedict of Columbia University led her to choose anthropology as her field. She graduated from Barnard in 1923, took her M.A. from Columbia in 1924, and, after several years as one of Boas's own graduate students, received her Ph.D. in 1929. In 1926 she was appointed assistant curator of ethnology at the American Museum of Natural History in New York City.

In 1925–1926 Mead made the first of many field trips to the South Seas, to the island of Tau in Samoa, where she observed the development of native children through adolescence. The tangible result of her field work was *Coming of Age in Samoa*, 1928, a book that enjoyed enormous popularity (it was still in print 50 years later) and that not only established Mead's reputation virtually overnight but also made cultural anthropology a topic accessible to a wide lay audience. On a second trip, during 1928–1929, she investigated the development of social behavior in children of the Manus in the Admiralty Islands in the western Pacific, from which sprang *Growing Up in New Guinea*, 1930. Her expedition of 1931–1933 was also to the New Guinea area, where she studied three tribes, the Arapesh, Mundugumor, and Tchambuli, for *Sex and Temperament in Three Primitive Societies*, 1935. The three books appeared together as *From the South Seas* in 1939.

Using a method that came to characterize much of her work — contrasting the values of two or more cultures — Mead prompted significant questioning of rigid social standards. Like Ruth Benedict, she stressed the impermanence and relativity of human values and their dependence on time and environment. In 1932 she published the results of her study of an unnamed Native American tribe ("the Antlers") in *The Changing Culture of an Indian Tribe*. She edited and published 13 papers by Columbia graduate students as *Cooperation and Competition Among Primitive Peoples*, 1937, to refute the notion of primitive society as a Darwinian jungle. During 1936–1939 she did field work in Bali and New Guinea, producing *Balinese Character: A Photographic Analysis*, 1942, with Gregory Bateson (her husband from 1936 to 1951) and *Growth and Culture: A Photographic Study of Balinese Childhood*, 1951, with Frances MacGregor.

Using essentially the same techniques she applied to primitive cultures, Mead explored American cultural standards in *And Keep Your Powder Dry*, 1942. During World War II she wrote pamphlets for the Office of War Information to aid communication between British and American troops. One of her most important books appeared in 1949: *Male and Female: A Study of the Sexes in a Changing World*. It examined traditional male-female relationships, using observations from the Pacific and the East Indies for reference in discussing such topics as the mother's influence in perpetuating male and female roles and the different concepts of marriage held by various cultures.

Mead also published *Soviet Attitudes Toward Authority*, 1951, *New Lives for Old*, 1956, *People and Places*, 1959, *Continuities in Cultural Evolution*, 1964, *Anthropology: A Human Science*, 1964, *Family*, with K. Heyman, 1965, *Anthropologists and What They Do*, 1965, *Culture and Commitment*, 1970, *A Way of Seeing*, with R. Metraux, 1970, *A Rap on Race*, with James Baldwin, 1971, *Twentieth Century Faith*, 1972, and *Ruth Benedict*, 1974, and numerous papers. She edited *Childhood in Contemporary Cultures*, with M. Wolfenstein, 1955, and Ruth Benedict's *Anthropologist at Work*, 1959. At the American Museum of Natural History she advanced to associate curator in 1942 and to curator in 1964, remaining in that post until 1969, when she became curator emeritus. From 1954 she was an adjunct professor of anthropology at Columbia University, and from 1968 to 1970 she was also chairman of the social sciences division at Fordham University. She served on national public health and mental health councils and was a frequent visiting lecturer at universities as well as being a popular and frequent public lecturer. *Blackberry Winter*, a volume of autobiography, appeared in 1972.

Mead was president of the World Federation for Mental Health in 1956–1957, of the World Society for Ekistics in 1969–1971, of the Scientists' Institute for Public Information in 1970–1973, of the Society for Research in General Systems in 1972–1973, and of the American Association for the Advancement of Science in 1975. As late as 1973 she was still making field trips to New Guinea. In late years she was something of a national oracle as a social critic of unsurpassed influence and celebrity. She died in New York City on November 15, 1978.

Mears, Helen Farnsworth 1872–1916 sculptor

Born in Oshkosh, Wisconsin, on December 21, 1872, Helen Mears was, according to the little information and few anecdotes of her childhood that survive, destined from earliest age for sculpture. She attended public schools and Oshkosh State Normal School (now a branch of the University of Wisconsin). In 1892 she won a commission for a sculpture of a woman and winged eagle design entitled "Genius of Wisconsin" for the Wisconsin Building at the World's Columbian Exposition in Chicago. While executing the work at the Art Institute of Chicago, she received some encouragement from Lorado Taft. The success of the piece, which was later installed in the Wisconsin State Capitol, enabled her to travel to New York City and enroll in the Art Students' League. Shortly afterward she became an assistant to and student of Augustus Saint-Gaudens. In 1897–1899 she studied in France and Italy.

On her return to New York City in 1899 Mears established a studio on Washington Square and embarked on a brief but highly successful career as a professional sculptor. Her craftsmanship, artistic sensibility, and energy won her a place among her colleagues. Among her commissions were bronze busts of George Rogers Clark (for the Milwaukee Public Library) and Dr. William T. G. Morton (Smithsonian Institution), bas-relief portraits of Saint-Gaudens (Peabody Institute, Baltimore) and Edward MacDowell (Metropolitan Museum), a three-panel bas-relief work entitled "The Fountain of Life," which was exhibited successfully at the Louisiana Purchase Exposition in St. Louis in 1904 and elsewhere, and a full-length statue of Frances E. Willard, commissioned by the State of Illinois and placed in Statuary Hall of the U.S. Capitol in 1905. A number of pieces were left in various degrees of incompleteness at her death in New York City on February 17, 1916.

Meloney, Marie Mattingly 1878–1943 journalist and editor

Born on December 8, 1878, in Bardstown, Kentucky, Marie Mattingly grew up there and in Washington, D.C. She was educated privately and by her mother, who at various times edited the *Kentucky Magazine* and taught at Washington College for Girls. Marie Mattingly's early ambition for a career as a pianist was ended by a disabling accident, and in 1895 she took a job as a reporter for the *Washington Post*. A series of sketches of various political personages won her the job of chief of the Washington bureau of the *Denver Post* in 1897, when she was eighteen. In November 1899 she scored a journalistic coup when she discovered, quite by chance, the unannounced wedding of Admiral George Dewey. Another brief stint on the *Washington Post* staff was followed by a period of convalescence in Arizona.

In 1900 Mattingly moved to New York City, where she worked briefly for the *World*, for the *Herald*, and in 1901–1904 for the *Sun*, to which she contributed a column called "Men About Town." After her marriage in June 1904 to William B. Meloney, an editor on the *Sun*, she retired to domestic life for a decade. In 1914 she became editor of the *Woman's Magazine*, a post she held until the magazine died in 1920. During 1917–1920 she was also associate editor of *Everybody's*. From 1921 to 1926 she edited the *Delineator*.

As a woman's magazine editor Meloney promoted various campaigns, including relief for postwar Europe, for which she was decorated by the governments of France and Belgium; cancer research, toward which she raised $100,000 to purchase a gram of radium for Madame Curie in 1921; and the Better Homes in America movement, of which she became vice-president under Herbert Hoover upon its incorporation in 1924. In 1926 she became editor of the Sunday magazine of the *New York Herald Tribune*. In 1930 she organized the first of what became an annual Herald Tribune Forum on Current Problems, a prestigious event that soon drew statesmen from around the world to its platform. In 1935 she became editor of *This Week*, an experimental Sunday magazine published by the *Herald Tribune* and distributed with it and a number of other newspapers around the country; it eventually reached a circulation of 6 million. She resigned as editor in 1942 and thereafter held the title of editorial director. Maloney died in Pawling, New York, on June 23, 1943.

Menken, Adah Isaacs 1835?–1868 actor and poet

Born into a Jewish family, probably in Chartrain, a suburb of New Orleans, and probably on June 15, 1835, the later Miss Menken apparently was given the names Adah Bertha, and her surname was apparently originally Theodore, but other facts concerning her early life are obscured by later and confused publicity stories. Her father died when she was two or three, and her mother was left without means until she married a man named Josephs. Adah became fluent in several languages, including Hebrew, German, Spanish, and French, and displayed a talent for singing and dancing as well. She was later to claim that in her youth she rode horses in a circus, modeled for a sculptor, and danced in the New Orleans French Opera House. She married Alexander Isaac Menken in Livingston, Texas, in April 1856 and thereafter retained his name on the stage through several marriages, all of them short-lived. She appeared on the stage at Shreveport, Louisiana, in *The Lady of Lyons* as early as 1857 and made her debut in New Orleans the same year in *Fazio*. She began to publish verse about that time; several poems appeared in the *Cincinnati Israelite* during 1857–1859 and in the *New York Sunday Mercury* in 1860–1861.

Menken first appeared on the stage in New York City in March 1859, when she played in *The Soldier's Daughter* at Purdy's National Theatre, but it was not until she opened in Albany, New York, in a dramatic adaptation of Lord Byron's *Mazeppa*, in June 1861, that she achieved lasting recognition. Appearing in the play's climactic scene almost nude and strapped to a running horse, she created a sensation in several cities, including Albany, Baltimore, and in 1863 San Francisco. Strikingly beautiful, the central figure in a scandalous divorce case (in September 1859, in the belief that Alexander Menken had divorced her, she married pugilist John C. Heenan; Menken then announced they were still married and proceeded to obtain a divorce, while Heenan denied their marriage) as well as in various rumored infidelities, and a talented poet who received encouragement from Walt Whitman, she numbered Mark Twain, Joaquin Miller, Bret Harte, and others of California's literary circle and in the East even Henry Wadsworth Longfellow among her friends and admirers.

Her fame preceded her to London, where she opened in *Mazeppa* at Astley's Theatre in October 1864. Her literary entourage there soon included Charles Dickens, A. C. Swinburne, and D. G. Rossetti. In 1865 she had a run in New York City and the following year another, and she made a successful U.S. tour before returning to Europe in August 1866. Everywhere she played before record audiences. Her performances in such pieces as *Dick Turpin*, *The French Spy*, *Three Fast Women*, and *The Child of the Sun* were generally respectfully received, but always the demand was for *Mazeppa*. About six weeks after the birth of her second son in Paris (George Sand was the godmother) she opened in late December 1866 in *Les Pirates de la Savane* (which also included a sensational horse-and-nudity scene) at the Théâtre de la Gaité. She received acclaim unprecedented for an American actress, and added Théophile Gautier and Dumas père to her train. The Paris engagement was interrupted by performances in Vienna, and in the fall of 1867 she returned to Astley's Theatre in London. She gave what proved to be her last performance at the Sadler's Wells Theatre in May 1868. She died in Paris at the age of thirty-three, on August 10, 1868, a month after she had collapsed during a rehearsal for a revised version of *Les Pirates*. Eight days later her *Infelicia*, a collection of poems that was dedicated to Dickens, appeared in London.

Merman, Ethel 1909–1984 singer and actor

Born on January 16, 1909, in Astoria, New York, Ethel Agnes Zimmerman attended public school in Long Island City. She worked as a secretary and sang in nightclubs and vaudeville — including an engagement with the song and dance team of Clayton, Jackson, and (Jimmy) Durante at the Palace Theatre in 1929 — before opening in George Gershwin's musical *Girl Crazy* at the Alvin Theatre in October 1930, billed as "Ethel Merman." Without any formal musical training she became an immediate sensation and launched a new hit song, "I've Got Rhythm." *Girl Crazy* ran for 272 performances. Virtually everything she appeared in after that was a success, and she soon was recognized as the large-voiced, bouncy queen of a new era of musical comedy.

Merman's triumphant debut was followed by an appearance in *George White's Scandals* of 1931, in which her rendition of "Life is Just a Bowl of Cherries" became another hit. "Eadie Was a Lady," from *Take a Chance*, 1932, was so popular that the lyrics appeared in the *New York Times* after the Broadway opening. The success of Cole Porter's *Anything Goes*, 1934, was repeated in the movie version, 1936, in which she starred with Bing Crosby. Other memorable shows included *Red, Hot and Blue!*, 1936, *Stars in Your Eyes*, 1939, *Du Barry Was a Lady*, 1939, *Panama Hattie*, 1940, *Something for the Boys*, 1943, and *Annie Get Your Gun*, 1946, which was her biggest success, running for 1147 performances. She appeared also in several motion pictures, including *The Big Broadcast*, 1932, *We're Not Dressing*, 1934, *Kid Millions*, 1934, *Strike Me Pink*, 1936, *Alexander's Ragtime Band*, 1938, and *Stage Door Canteen*, 1943.

After a two-year run in *Call Me Madam*, for which she won a Tony award in 1951, she announced it would be her last Broadway show, but she returned to do *Happy Hunting*, 1956, and enjoyed another huge success in *Gypsy*, 1959. In 1970 she stepped into the title role of *Hello, Dolly!* and won the Drama Desk award. Other movies included *Call Me Madam*, 1953, *There's No Business Like Show Business*, 1954, and *It's a Mad, Mad, Mad, Mad World*, 1963. The apparently ageless first lady of the American musical comedy stage, Merman was noted for her unflagging humor only slightly less than for her "wake 'em up in the last row" voice. In 1955 she published an autobiography, *Who Could Ask for Anything More?*

During the 1950s and 1960s she made numerous appearances on television as well as in nightclubs (one of her most notable television appearances was a duet with Mary Martin on the Ford Motor Company's 50th anniversary show in June 1953), and into the 1970s she continued to be a popular television guest star. She won a special Tony in 1952 for career achievement and a Pied Piper award in 1982 from the American Society of Composers, Authors and Publishers for her contribution to American music. In 1978 she published *Merman*, a second autobiography. She died on February 15, 1984, at her home in New York City.

Merritt, Anna Lea 1844–1930 artist

Born in Philadelphia on September 13, 1844, Anna Lea was educated privately. From an early age she displayed artistic talent, and after studying with William H. Furness in Philadelphia for several years she went to Europe. There she studied mainly in Dresden and from 1871 in London. By the middle 1870s she was exhibiting paintings regularly at the Royal Academy, and in 1876 her submission won a medal at the Centennial Exposition in Philadelphia. In April 1877 she married her British teacher, Henry Merritt. With marriage she gave up her career, but after her husband's death just three months later she resumed it. She wrote a memoir of her husband and supplied 23 small etchings for *Henry Merritt: Art Criticism and Romance*, 1879.

Major works of Merritt's brush over the next decades included "Taming the Bird," exhibited at the National Academy of Design in New York in 1883; "Camilla," shown at the Paris Exposition of 1889; "Love Locked Out," which in 1890 became the first work of a woman artist to be purchased for the National Gallery of British Art (known as the Tate Gallery); "Eve Overcome by Remorse" and a mural decoration for the Women's Building at the World's Columbian Exposition in Chicago in 1893, both of which won medals; a series of eight murals for St. Martin's Church, Chilworth, Surrey, done in 1893–1894; "Piping Shepherd," bought by the Pennsylvania Academy of Fine Arts in 1896; and such other paintings as "Eve Repentant," "Merry Maids," and "I Will Give You Rest" and portraits of James Russell Lowell, Mrs. Arnold Toynbee, and General John A. Dix. She also won medals for paintings shown at the Atlanta Exposition in 1895 and at the Pan-American Exposition in Buffalo, New York, in 1901. She continued to exhibit at the Royal Academy until 1906. In 1902 she published *A Hamlet in Old Hampshire*, a portrait of Hurstbourne Tarrant, her home from 1890. After several years of failing eyesight she died in London on April 7, 1930.

Merry, Ann Brunton 1769–1808 actor

Born in London on May 30, 1769, Ann Brunton grew up there and in Norwich, where her father, a former grocer and tea dealer who had turned to the stage in 1774, later managed the Theatre Royal. Under his management she made her stage debut in Bath in *The Grecian Daughter* in February 1785. Subsequent highly successful performances there and in Bristol led to her London debut in *The Roman Father* at Covent Garden in October 1785. Over the next seven years she delighted Covent Garden audiences in such plays as *Romeo and Juliet*, *The Orphan*, *The Distressed Mother*, *Jane Shore*, *Much Ado About Nothing*, *The Conscious Lovers*, *Lorenzo*, and *Road to Ruin*. In August 1791 she married Robert Merry, the high-living leader of the Delia Cruscan group of extremely minor poets. The next year she retired from the stage, but by 1796 Robert Merry's extravagance made it necessary for her to accept an offer from a Philadelphia theater manager.

They arrived in the United States in October 1796, and in December Ann Merry made her American debut in *Romeo and Juliet* at Philadelphia's Chestnut Street Theatre. She made her New York debut in August 1797, when she appeared in *Venice Preserved* at the Greenwich Street Theatre. She continued to appear with the Chestnut Street company, which traveled on occasion to New York, Baltimore, Washington, D.C., and Annapolis, for the rest of her life. The simple grace, gentleness, and lovely voice that had won much attention in London made her the unchallenged reigning tragic actress on the American stage. Her husband died in 1798, and in January 1803 she married the manager of the company, Thomas Wignell. On his death a few weeks later she took up management of the company with his partner, Alexander Reinagle. She was married a third time in August 1806 to a fellow actor, William Warren. She died during a Southern tour, in Alexandria, Virginia, on June 28, 1808.

Messick, Dale 1906– cartoonist

Born in 1906 in South Bend, Indiana, Dalia Messick grew up in Hobart. She was interested in drawing from an early age, but her difficulties with school delayed her graduation from high school until she was twenty. She studied briefly at the Art Institute of Chicago and then held a series of jobs as engraver, sign painter, and commercial artist. After a time as a designer of greeting cards in Chicago and later in New York City she began experimenting with various ideas for newspaper comic strips. The prevailing prejudice against women in that profession led her to change her name to Dale, but nonetheless for a number of years she made no headway. After some samples of her work were ignored by Joseph Medill Patterson of the *New York Daily News* in 1939 they were taken up by one of his assistants, Mollie Slott, who had had a hand in developing such successful strips as "Little Orphan Annie," "Terry and the Pirates," and "Winnie Winkle." Together they worked out a strip featuring a beautiful red-haired heroine. Originally a bandit, the heroine was ultimately made a newspaper reporter and given the name Brenda Starr.

"Brenda Starr, Reporter" first appeared in June 1940 as a Sunday strip in several papers of the Chicago Tribune-New York News Syndicate. Its success enabled it to become a daily strip in October 1945, and in that year a motion picture serial featuring the intrepid Brenda was produced. Despite the often profound improbability of the story line and the sometimes uncertain artwork, "Brenda Starr" remained thereafter a highly popular comic strip. The romantic aura pervading Brenda's adventures in exotic settings and her perennial pursuit of her mystery-man lover, Basil St. John, along with her impossibly glamorous appearance and the apparent ease with which she held down the post of top reporter for the *Flash*, made her a favorite especially among young girl readers. Dale Messick, who later supervised a staff of assistants in turning out the strip, was virtually the only woman to create and maintain a major newspaper comic strip. The comic strip received a Reuben award nomination for best comic strip in 1975 and again in 1982. In 1989 a second movie version of Brenda Starr was released starring Brooke Shields.

Mesta, Perle 1889–1975 socialite and diplomat

Born on October 12, 1889, in Sturgis, Michigan, Perle Skirvin was the daughter of a former salesman who struck it rich in oil and real estate in Oklahoma and Texas. She grew up in Oklahoma City and was educated privately. In 1917 she married George Mesta, a wealthy Pittsburgh manufacturer. While he was serving in Washington, D.C., during World War I, she had her first introduction to politics and Washington society. After the war they traveled extensively in Europe. By the time of his death in 1925 Mesta had acquired a large acquaintanceship in the worlds of business and politics.

In 1929 Mesta settled in Newport, Rhode Island, where she soon became a leading hostess. About 1935 she began to devote much time to active political work. She joined the National Woman's party and became an effective lobbyist on behalf of the Equal Rights Amendment; she was also chairman of the party's public relations committee for a time. In electoral politics she supported the Republican party until 1940 and the Democratic party thereafter. About that time she moved her residence to Washington, D.C., and soon became one of the capital's leading hostesses. She was an early patroness of Senator Harry S. Truman and was greatly helpful to him in the elections of 1944 and especially 1948, when she served on the finance committee of the Democratic campaign. (She had earlier been hostess to Margaret Truman's coming-out party in 1946.) She was co-chairman of Truman's inaugural ball in January 1949. In June of that year Truman nominated her for the post of U.S. minister to Luxembourg, and she was confirmed and sworn in in July. She was the first to hold the post, diplomatic relations with the duchy having previously been handled by the ambassador to Belgium. She served in the post until replaced by the Republican administration of President Dwight D. Eisenhower in September 1953.

Her appointment had served to inspire Irving Bering to write a hit musical, *Call Me Madam*, in which Ethel Merman starred in 1950–1952. During the 1950s Mesta continued to reign as Washington's premier hostess, as the informal charm and gaiety of her entertaining attracted the cream of international society. The advent of a new social atmosphere with the Kennedy administration began a decline in her influence. In 1960 she published *Perle: My Story*. She died in Oklahoma City on March 16, 1975.

Meyer, Annie Florance Nathan 1867–1951 writer, educator and antisuffragist

Born in New York City on February 19, 1867, Annie Nathan grew up in an unsettled home and early found her greatest pleasure in books. She was privately schooled, and in

1885 she enrolled in an extension reading course for women begun two years earlier by Columbia College as an alternative to regular admission to the college. She left after a year to marry Dr. Alfred Meyer in February 1887. Immediately afterward she began working for the creation of a fully accredited women's college to be affiliated with Columbia. She published a widely read article on the idea in the *Nation*, secured the signatures of a number of prominent men on a petition, and solicited financial support. In a stroke that broadened support for her idea, she proposed to name the college after Columbia's late president, Frederick A. P. Barnard, who had laid much groundwork for such an institution.

Modeled on Harvard's "Annex" (later Radcliffe College) in quarters Meyer had leased in anticipation of success, Barnard College opened in September 1889. From its chartering to her death more than 60 years later, Meyer remained a trustee of the college and continued to recruit students and faculty and to raise funds for the school. She was a prolific contributor of articles and short stories to such magazines as *The Bookman*, *World's Work*, *Century*, *Harper's*, *Smart Set*, and *North American Review*. For several years she was a leading opponent in print of woman suffrage. Among her books were *Woman's Work in America*, 1891, *Helen Brent, M.D.*, 1892, *My Park Book*, 1898, *Robert Annys: Poor Priest*, 1901, and *Barnard Beginnings*, 1935. She also wrote some 20 plays, of which several were published, including *The District Attorney*, 1920, *The Advertising of Kate*, 1921, *The New Way*, 1925, and *Black Souls*, 1932, and a few produced without conspicuous success. Her autobiography, *It's Been Fun*, appeared in 1951. She died in New York City on September 23, 1951.

Meyer, Lucy Jane Rider 1849–1922 social worker and educator

Born in New Haven, Vermont, on September 9, 1849, Lucy Rider attended public schools and the New Hampton Literary Institution in Fairfax, Vermont. After three years as a teacher, one in Canada and two in a Quaker school for freedmen's children in North Carolina, she entered Oberlin College, from which she graduated after two years in 1872. During 1873–1875 she attended the Woman's Medical College of Pennsylvania to prepare herself to share the life of the medical missionary to whom she had become engaged, but after his death in 1875 she returned to Vermont. She was lady principal of the Troy Conference Academy in Poultney in 1876–1877, a student of chemistry at the Massachusetts Institute of Technology in 1877–1878, and professor of chemistry at McKendree College in Illinois in 1879–1881. From 1881 to 1884 she was field secretary for the Illinois State Sunday School Association.

In May 1885 Rider married Josiah S. Meyer, a Chicago businessman who shared her deep interest in the Methodist Church and its work. In October of that year they opened the Chicago Training School for City, Home, and Foreign Missions with four students. The time and place were opportune for such a school, and theirs grew rapidly and quickly gained the support of official Methodist bodies. Wesley Memorial Hospital, the Chicago Old People's Home, and the Lake Bluff Orphanage soon evolved from their work and that of their students, and over the years some 40 philanthropic institutions grew up in a like manner.

In 1887 Meyer completed her interrupted medical studies and received her M.D. from the Woman's Medical College of Chicago. In that year she organized a number of her women students into a program of visitation and social service among the urban poor, and within a few months a core group of these social workers had banded together into what was in effect the first house of deaconesses in America. (The deaconess idea of groups of lay women serving without pay or vows had originated in Germany and had been brought to America originally by Lutherans.) The group was headed for its first year by Isabella

Thoburn, home on furlough from her missionary work in India. Meyer devoted most of her time to the deaconess movement and converted her periodical, the *Message*, founded in 1886, into the *Deaconess Advocate*, which she edited until 1914. In 1889 she published *Deaconesses: Biblical, Early Church, European, American*, a history of the movement. For a number of years there was friction between the Meyers' work and that of the Methodist Woman's Home Missionary Society, which sought to gain control of the various deaconess experiments around the country, and in 1908 she formed the Methodist Deaconess Association, of which she became secretary, to maintain the independent integrity of the Chicago deaconesses.

In 1903 she published *Mary North*, a novel. In 1917 she and her husband resigned as superintendent and principal of the Chicago Training School, whose enrollment had grown at one time to over 200 and had graduated by then over 5000 trained workers. Meyer died in Chicago on March 16, 1922.

Millay, Edna St. Vincent 1892–1950 poet

Edna St. Vincent Millay

Born on February 22, 1892, in Rockland, Maine, Vincent Millay, as she was known to her family, was reared in nearby Camden by her divorced mother, who recognized and encouraged her talent in writing poetry. Her first published poem appeared in the *St. Nicholas Magazine* for children in October 1906. She remained at home after her graduation from high school in 1909, and in four years she published five more poems in *St. Nicholas*. At nineteen she entered "Renascence," a poem of about 200 lines, in an anthology contest, and although she did not win a prize the poem was published in *The Lyric Year*, 1912, and attracted critical recognition and a patron who sent her to Vassar. She graduated in 1917.

In that year she published her first book, *Renascence and Other Poems*, and moved to Greenwich Village in New York City. There she became a lively and admired figure among the avant garde and radical literary set. To eke out a living she submitted hackwork verse and short stories under the pseudonym "Nancy Boyd" to magazines, and while her ambition to go on the stage was short-lived, she worked with the Provincetown Players for a time and wrote the one-act *Aria da Capo*, 1919, for them. In 1920 she published *A Few Figs from Thistles*, her second book of verse, and in 1921 *Second April* and two more plays, *Two Slatterns and a King* and *The Lamp and the Bell*. In the latter year she began a two-year European sojourn, during which she was a correspondent for *Vanity Fair*. She won a Pulitzer Prize in 1923 for *Ballad of the Harp-Weaver*. In July 1923 she married Eugen Jan Boissevain, a Dutch businessman with whom from 1925 she lived in a large, isolated house in the Berkshire foothills near Austerlitz, New York. In 1925 the Metropolitan Opera Company commissioned her to write an opera with Deems Taylor. The resulting work, *The King's Henchman*, first produced in 1927, became the most popular American opera up to its time and, published in book form, sold out four printings in 20 days.

Millay's youthful appearance, the independent, almost petulant tone of her poetry, and her political and social ideals made her a symbol of the youth of her time. In 1927 she donated the proceeds from her poem "Justice Denied in Massachusetts" to the defense of Sacco and Vanzetti and personally appealed to the governor of the state for their lives. The night of their execution she was arrested in the death watch outside the Boston Court House. Three later books, *There Are No Islands Any More*, 1940, *Make Bright the Arrows*, 1940, and *The Murder of Lidice*, 1942, expressed her continuing concern with contemporary affairs. She also published *The Buck in the Snow and Other Poems*, 1928, *Fatal Interview*, 1931, *Wine from These Grapes*, 1934, *Conversation at Midnight*, 1937, and *Huntsman, What Quarry?*, 1939.

The bravado and stylish cynicism of much of Millay's early work gave way in later years to more personal and mature writing, and she produced, particularly in her sonnets and other short poems, a considerable body of intensely lyrical verse. She died in Austerlitz, New York, on October 19, 1950. A final collection of her verse appeared as *Mine the Harvest* in 1954.

Miller, Alice Duer 1874–1942 writer

Born on Staten Island, New York, on July 28, 1874, Alice Maude Duer was of a wealthy and distinguished family and grew up on an estate in Weehawken, New Jersey. The family fortune was lost in a banking failure, however, and she made her way through Barnard College by selling essays, poems, and stories to *Harper's* and *Scribner's* magazines. In 1896 her first book, entitled simply *Poems*, was published. In October 1899, shortly after her graduation, she married Henry W. Miller, a businessman with whom she lived in Costa Rica until 1903. During that time she continued to publish magazine pieces. After their return to New York she taught composition at a girls' school and tutored in mathematics at Barnard until 1907, while publishing *The Modern Obstacle*, 1903, and *Caldron's Prisoner*, 1904, the first of her many romantic novels. Thereafter she devoted herself to writing. *The Blue Arch*, 1910, *Things*, 1914, and *Are Women People?*, 1915, followed. The last, a collection of satirical verses, took its title from the column she wrote for the *New York Tribune* in 1914–1917.

Miller's first great success, *Come Out of the Kitchen*, set the pattern for several subsequent novels by being serialized in *Harper's*, published in book form in 1916, and then adapted for Broadway and a motion picture. *The Charm School*, 1919, *The Beauty and the Bolshevist*, 1920, *Manslaughter*, 1921, *Priceless Pearl*, 1924, *Are Parents People?*, short stories, 1924, *The Reluctant Duchess*, 1925, *Instruments of Darkness and Other Stories*, 1926, *Forsaking All Others*, a love story in verse, 1931, *Gowns by Roberta*, which became the Jerome Kern-Otto Harbach musical hit *Roberta*, 1933, *Come Out of the Pantry*, stories, 1933, *Death Sentence*, 1934, *The Rising Star*, 1935, *Four Little Heiresses*, 1935, *Not for Love*, 1937, and *And One Was Beautiful*, 1937, followed in rapid succession. During the 1920s and 1930s she was a member of the Algonquin group of writers and wits, among whom her charming combination of the highest inherited social standing and carefree love of fun made her a much loved figure. She spent much time in Hollywood writing scenarios and advising on matters of social custom, and in 1935 she played a small role (spoiled daughter of a millionaire) in the Ben Hecht-Charles MacArthur film *Soak the Rich*.

Her greatest success came in 1940 with the publication of *The White Cliffs*, a verse tale of love and fortitude in World War II Britain. Over 700,000 copies had sold by the end of the war, while Lynn Fontanne's reading of it had been broadcast on radio twice and recorded. The motion picture *The White Cliffs of Dover*, 1944, was adapted from the story. Alice Duer Miller died in New York City on August 22, 1942.

Miller, Harriet Mann 1831–1918 writer of children's books

Born on June 25, 1831, in Auburn, New York, Harriet Mann grew up in various towns in Ohio, Wisconsin, Illinois, and elsewhere as her itinerant father drifted from place to place. Her schooling was consequently irregular. In August 1854 she married Watts T. Miller, with whom she settled in Chicago. In 1875 they moved to Brooklyn, New York. After several years devoted to domestic cares, her childhood predilection for story-writing reasserted itself. From her first in 1870 she published over the next several years hundreds of stories and articles for children. Her stories, typically sentimental tales that over the years showed an increasingly Dickensian interest in the forlorn, were generally signed "Olive Thorne." Under the name "Harriet M. Miller" she published a number of nature sketches that were distinguished by their factuality and sprightly manner. A number of these sketches were collected in *Little Folks in Feathers and Fur, and Others in*

Neither, 1875. Several of her stories were collected in *Nimpo's Troubles*, 1879, in which year she began using the name "Olive Thorne Miller" for all her work, and *Queer Pets at Marcy's*, 1880, and *Little People of Asia*, 1882, followed.

In 1885 Miller published *Bird-Ways*, the first of a series of books on birds for adults and children that became widely popular. Others included *In Nesting Time*, 1888, *Little Brothers of the Air*, 1892, *A Bird-Lover in the West*, 1894, *The First Book of Birds*, 1899, *The Second Book of Birds: Bird Families*, 1901, *True Bird Stories from My Notebook*, 1903, *With the Birds in Maine*, 1904, *The Bird Our Brother*, 1908, and *The Children's Book of Birds*, 1915. In the course of the series her reliance on firsthand field observation and her ability to convey a sense of nature's wonder both grew apace. Birds also served as a frequent lecture topic. Others of her books were *Four Handed Folk*, 1890, *The Woman's Club*, 1891, a series of "Kristy" books including *Kristy's Queer Christmas*, 1904, *Kristy's Surprise Party*, 1905, and *Kristy's Rainyday Picnic*, 1906, and *What Happened to Barbara*, 1907. She died in Los Angeles on December 25, 1918.

Miller, Marilyn 1898–1936 actor

Born on September 1, 1898, in Evansville, Indiana, Marilyn Reynolds grew up with her stepfather's name, Miller. Her parents and oldest sister formed a vaudeville act called "The Columbian Trio," which Marilyn joined as "Mlle. Sugarplum" when she was four, making her stage debut in August 1903 in Dayton, Ohio. For ten years she toured the Middle West and even abroad in the family act, which ultimately became "The Five Columbians." Her dancing attracted the attention of Lee Shubert, who spotted her at the Lotus Club in London in 1913, and for four years she appeared in Shubert revues: *The Passing Show of 1914*, *The Passing Show of 1915*, *The Show of Wonders* in 1916, and *The Passing Show of 1917*.

In 1918 she came under the management of Florenz Ziegfeld, for whom she appeared in *Fancy Free* and the *Ziegfeld Follies*. In 1920 she opened at the Amsterdam Theatre in *Sally*, which ran for three years and in which she was a sensation, especially singing Jerome Kern's "Look for the Silver Lining" and "Whip-poor-will." Her appearance in *Peter Pan* in 1924 was her only non-musical role. She became the reigning queen of musical comedy in a series of bright, splashy productions: *Sunny*, (Jerome Kern, Oscar Hammerstein, Otto Harbach) in which she sang "Who," 1925; *Rosalie* (Sigmund Romberg, George Gershwin, and others), 1928; *Smiles* (Vincent Youmans and others), in which she sang "Time on My Hands," 1930; and *As Thousands Cheer* (Irving Berlin, Moss Hart) which also starred Ethel Waters, and in which Miller and Clifton Webb sang "Easter Parade" and "Not for All the Rice in China," 1936.

Her youthful grace, small figure, dazzling smile, and blonde beauty made her seem the very embodiment of youth, and modern youth at that. The titles of her shows suggested the image she projected. She went to Hollywood to make film versions of *Sally* in 1929 and *Sunny* in 1930 and also starred in *Her Majesty, Love*, 1931. She died suddenly in New York City on April 7, 1936, of an acute infection. A film biography of her, released in 1949, was aptly titled *Look for the Silver Lining*.

Mills, Susan Lincoln Tolman 1825–1912 missionary and educator

Born on November 18, 1825, in Enosburg, Vermont, Susan Tolman grew up there and from about the age of ten in Ware, Massachusetts. She graduated from Mount Holyoke Seminary (now College) in 1845 and remained there as a teacher until her marriage in September 1848 to Cyrus T. Mills, a Presbyterian missionary with whom she sailed immediately afterward to Ceylon. For six years she assisted her husband in his work as principal of Batticotta College, taught classes in domestic skills to local girls, and helped supervise several day schools. In 1854, both in very poor health, they left Ceylon to return to Massachusetts. In 1860, fully recovered, they traveled to the Hawaiian Islands, where

Cyrus Mills became president of Oahu College for children of missionaries and Susan Mills became a teacher in the school. She introduced calisthenics for girls and brought her Mount Holyoke experience to bear in emphasizing the sciences. Cyrus Mills's ill health forced them to leave Hawaii in 1864 and settle in California.

In 1865 they bought the Ladies Seminary in Benicia and set about remaking it into a girls' school of high standing. Again Mount Holyoke provided impetus, this time in the form of several teachers whom they persuaded to come to California. In 1871 they moved the school to a more attractive and accessible site on a 60-acre tract a few miles from Oakland. Mills Seminary, as the school was renamed, soon featured the imposing Seminary Hall (later Mills Hall) as its principal building. The school was incorporated in 1877. Susan Mills served as lady principal of the seminary until her husband's death in April 1884, when she added the duties of board member and acting president. From 1885, when the school became Mills College, to 1890 she continued as lady principal under two presidents. In 1890 she was elected president of Mills College, the first women's college on the Pacific Coast, and during her 19 years in that post she worked constantly to raise standards and secure recognition for the school. Beginning in 1906 the seminary classes were progressively eliminated. She retired in 1909 and died in Oakland, California, on December 12, 1912.

Miner, Myrtilla 1815–1864 educator

Born near Brookfield, New York, on March 4, 1815, Myrtilla Miner was educated at home, at the Female Domestic Seminary in Clinton, New York, in 1839, and at the Clover Street Seminary in Rochester in 1840–1844. Her school and teaching careers were frequently interrupted by ill health. She taught at the Rochester seminary for a year and then at the Richmond Street School in Providence, Rhode Island, in 1845–1846. She then taught for a year at the Newton Female Institute in Whitesville, Mississippi, where she was refused permission to conduct classes also for African-American girls, and in 1849 in Friendship, New York. Her Mississippi experience made her receptive to an idea broached by abolitionist friends that she open a school for African-Americans, and encouragement from the Reverend Henry Ward Beecher and a contribution from a Quaker philanthropist settled the matter.

In December 1851 Miner opened the Colored Girls School in Washington, D.C. Within two months the enrollment grew from 6 to 40, and despite hostility from a portion of the community it prospered. Contributions from Quakers continued to appear, and Harriet Beecher Stowe gave $1000 of her *Uncle Tom's Cabin* royalties. The school was forced to move three times in its first two years, but in 1854 it settled on a three-acre lot with house and barn on the edge of the city. In 1856 the school came under the care of a board of trustees, among whom were Henry Ward Beecher and Johns Hopkins. While the school offered primary schooling and classes in domestic skills, its emphasis from the outset was on training teachers. Miner stressed hygiene and nature study in addition to academic subjects, which were rigorously presented. By 1858 six former students were teaching in schools of their own. By that time her connection with the school had been loosened by her worsening health, and from 1857 Emily Howland was in charge. In 1860 the school had to be closed, and the next year Miner went to California in an attempt to regain her health. A carriage accident in 1864 ended that hope, and she died on December 17, 1864, shortly after her return to Washington, D.C.

Her school had been granted a Congressional charter as the Institution for the Education of Colored Youth in 1863, but it did not reopen until after the Civil War. From 1871 to 1876 it was associated with Howard University, and in 1879, as Miner Normal School, it became part of the District of Columbia public school system. In 1929 it became Miner

Teachers College, and in 1955 it merged with Wilson Teachers College to form the District of Columbia Teachers College.

Minnigerode, Lucy 1871–1935 nurse

Born on February 8, 1871, near Leesburg, Virginia, Lucy Minnigerode was educated in private schools. She entered the Training School for Nurses of Bellevue Hospital in New York City in 1899 and in 1905 completed her studies and became a registered nurse. She was in private practice until 1910, when she became superintendent of nurses at the Episcopal Eye, Ear and Throat Hospital in Washington, D.C. Later she held a similar post at the Savannah Hospital, Georgia.

In 1914 she headed one of the first Red Cross hospital units (a unit comprised 3 surgeons, 12 nurses, and supplies) sent to Europe for war-relief work, and during 1914–1915 she served at a hospital at the Polytechnic Institute in Kiev, Russia. Her work there earned her the Cross of St. Anne, awarded her by the czar in 1915. In 1915–1917 she was director of nurses at Columbia Hospital for Women in Washington, D.C., and in 1917–1919 she was again associated with the Red Cross. In 1919 she was asked to make a tour of inspection of the hospitals of the U.S. Public Health Service. Her report led to the creation of a department of nurses within the service, and she was immediately appointed superintendent. She held that post for the rest of her life. She recruited and organized a large corps of nurses to serve in hospitals established to care for World War I veterans. Her pioneering work in that field was later taken over by the Veterans' Bureau following its establishment in August 1921. In 1925 she was awarded the Florence Nightingale Medal of the International Red Cross. By 1935 her job entailed the supervision of 650 nurses in 26 hospitals of the Public Health service. Lucy Minnigerode died in Alexandria, Virginia, on March 24, 1935.

Minor, Virginia Louisa 1824–1894 suffragist

Born on March 27, 1824, in Caroline County, Virginia, Virginia Minor grew up from the age of two in Charlottesville. Little is known of her early life. In August 1843 she married Francis Minor, a distant cousin and a lawyer with whom she settled in St. Louis in 1844. At the outbreak of the Civil War she became an active member of the St. Louis Ladies Union Aid Society, which shortly became the largest branch of the Western Sanitary Commission. The successful management by women of the complex activities of the society — collecting and distributing clothing and supplies, staffing army hospitals, helping in the field and even at the front — served to confirm the belief that she had doubtless long entertained, that women deserved political equality.

As early as 1865, when enfranchisement of former slaves was a topic of public debate, Minor was the first woman in Missouri to suggest publicly that women be granted the vote. Early in 1867 she petitioned the Missouri legislature to that end but without success. In May of that year she organized in St. Louis the Woman Suffrage Association of Missouri, said to have been the first organization anywhere devoted to the single aim of woman suffrage. She remained president of the group until 1871, when she resigned because the state group had voted to affiliate with the American Woman Suffrage Association rather than with the older National Woman Suffrage Association, of which she was a member.

Minor made a notable impact on the National Association in 1869 in proposing a legal stratagem for quickly attaining suffrage. She argued, simply, that the 14th Amendment to the Constitution implicitly guaranteed the franchise to women. The association adopted the argument and used it widely. In October 1872 she attempted to register to vote in St. Louis, and when refused she brought suit against the registrar. The test case was appealed all the way to the Supreme Court, Minor's husband serving as one of her attorneys throughout the procedure. Chief Justice Morrison R. Waite ruled in *Minor v. Happersett*, 1874, that suffrage was not conferred on anyone by the Constitution and that the question was entirely one of state discretion. Although lost, the case generated much publicity for the cause of woman suffrage.

In 1879 the National Woman Suffrage Association organized a Missouri branch, and Minor was elected president. In 1890 she became president of the state branch of the merged National American Woman Suffrage Association. She resigned for health reasons in 1892 and died in St. Louis on August 14, 1894.

Mitchell, Lucy Myers Wright 1845–1888 archaeologist

Born on March 20, 1845, in Urmia, Persia (now Rezā'īyeh, Iran), Lucy Wright was the daughter of a missionary to the Nestorian Christians. In 1860 she was brought to America, and a short time later she entered Mount Holyoke Seminary, but she left in 1864 to rejoin her father in Persia. On his death the next year she came back to the United States. She married Samuel S. Mitchell of Morristown, New Jersey, in 1867, and they traveled together to Syria as missionaries. Her husband's health failed soon afterward, however, and they left Syria; the rest of her life was spent mainly in Europe. By that time she had acquired a vernacular knowledge of Syriac and Arabic, as well as French, German, and Italian, and for a time she devoted herself to philological studies. Her dictionary of modern Syriac was never published, and the manuscript was ultimately obtained by Cambridge University.

In 1873 Mitchell turned her attention to ancient art. While living in Rome in 1876–1878 she gave parlor lectures on Greek and Roman sculpture. A number of museums and libraries granted her scholar's privileges, and many leading archaeologists of Europe assisted her in her studies. In 1883 she published *A History of Ancient Sculpture*, and a companion volume of plates, *Selections from Ancient Sculpture*. These works were well received by critics and fellow scholars, and in 1884 she became only the second woman to be elected to the Imperial German Archaeological Institute. During 1884–1886 she began studying in Berlin for a major work on Greek pottery and vase-painting. Her studies included ancient and modern Greek and photography. She fell ill, however, and died in Lausanne, Switzerland, on March 10, 1888.

Mitchell, Maggie 1832–1918 actor

Born in New York City on June 14, 1832, Margaret Julia Mitchell left school at twelve to follow her older half sisters onto the stage. While filling a variety of child's walk-on and silent roles she was coached by her parents and by an English actor friend of theirs. She made her debut in a speaking role in June 1851 in a benefit performance of *The Soldier's Daughter* at Burton's Chambers Street Theatre. In 1852 she was with the stock company at the Bowery Theatre, where she played mainly boys' parts, notably in *Oliver Twist*, and danced between acts. She then began touring, and under various managements over the next several years she appeared in Boston, Philadelphia, and other Eastern cities and gradually began traveling into the Midwest and South.

She performed in a variety of ephemeral pieces with such titles as *A Rough Diamond*, *The Loan of a Lover*, *A Middy Ashore*, *The Pet of the Petticoats*, *The Wild Irish Girl*, and *Our Maggie*, a play written for her. A specialty of hers was a bill consisting of acts from *The Lady of Lyons*, *Richard III*, and *Douglas*, in each of which she played a young hero's role. That particular bill set off a "Maggie Mitchell craze" among the young men of Cleveland in 1853.

In January 1861, at De Bar's St. Charles Theatre in New Orleans, Mitchell first appeared in a new piece, *Fanchon, the Cricket*, a secondhand adaptation by August Waldauer from George Sand's story "La Petite Fadette." Her characterization of the sprite of a heroine, which included a graceful and entrancing shadow dance, was an immediate sensation. Her Southern tour was cut short by the Civil War, and after taking *Fanchon* to Boston, where it was equally successful, she opened in it at Laura Keene's Theatre in New York in June 1862 for a six-week run. *Fanchon* remained her mainstay for 30 years. Audiences never tired of it — her admirers included the likes of Abraham Lincoln and Ralph Waldo Emerson — and even in her fifties she retained the winsome, elfin appeal that made it go. She also early obtained the rights to it, enabling her to amass a considerable estate. She occasionally played other roles, as in *Jane Eyre*, which Henry Wadsworth Longfellow greatly admired, *The Lady of Lyons*, *Ingomar*, and *The Pearl of Savoy*. After a final performance in *The Little Maverick* in Chicago in 1892 she retired from the stage. She died in New York City on March 22, 1918.

Mitchell, Margaret Munnerlyn 1900–1949 novelist

Born in Atlanta, Georgia, on November 8, 1900, Margaret Mitchell attended public schools, Woodberry's School, and Washington Seminary in Atlanta before enrolling at Smith College in 1918. When her mother died the next year, she left college and returned home. Between 1922 and 1926 she was a writer and reporter for the *Atlanta Journal*. After an ankle injury in 1926 she left the paper and, for the next ten years, worked slowly on a romantic novel about the Civil War and Reconstruction. From her family she had absorbed since earliest childhood the history of the South, the tragedy of the war, and the romance of the Lost Cause. She worked at her novel sporadically, composing episodes out of sequence and later fitting them together. She apparently had little thought of publication at first, and for six years after it was substantially finished it lay unread. But in 1935 she was persuaded by a Macmillan Company editor who had heard of it from a mutual friend to submit it.

It appeared in 1936 as *Gone With the Wind* (a line from the poem "Cynara" by Ernest Dowson). The book was an utter sensation. Within six months a million copies had been sold; 50,000 copies were sold in one day. It went on to become the largest-selling novel in U.S. publishing history, with sales passing 12 million by 1965. It was eventually translated into 25 languages and sold in 40 foreign countries. The following year the book was awarded the Pulitzer Prize. The motion-picture rights were sold to Selznick-International Pictures for $50,000. The film, which starred Vivien Leigh as Scarlett O'Hara and Clark Gable as Rhett Butler, premiered in Atlanta in December 1939 after an unprecedented period of advance promotion, including the highly publicized search for an actress to play Scarlett. It won ten Academy Awards and for decades reigned as the top money-making film of all time. Margaret Mitchell, who never adjusted to the celebrity that had befallen her and who never attempted another book, died following an automobile accident in Atlanta on August 16, 1949.

Mitchell, Maria 1818–1889 astronomer

Born on August 1, 1818, on the island of Nantucket, Massachusetts, Maria Mitchell was educated in the island schools, including the one conducted by her father. Her interest in astronomy was stimulated by her father, who let her assist in his own work of rating chronometers for the Nantucket whaling fleet and who encouraged her independent use of his telescope. From 1836 she worked as a librarian in the Nantucket Atheneum during the day (often acting as an informal teacher) and became a regular observer of the skies at night.

In October 1847 Mitchell succeeded in establishing the orbit of a new comet. The discovery gained her immediate recognition in scientific circles; the following year brought her a gold medal from King Christian VIII of Denmark and election to the American Academy of Arts and Sciences, the first woman to achieve this honor. In 1849 she was appointed a computer for the *American Ephemeris and Nautical Almanac*, and the next year she was elected to the American Association for the Advancement of

Science. A gift of a large equatorial telescope manufactured by Alvan Clark was arranged by a group of prominent American women led by Elizabeth Peabody in 1858, and her accomplishments were subsequently kept in the public eye by feminists. She traveled to Europe in 1857–1858, meeting many leading scientists, and in 1861 moved with her widowed father to Lynn, Massachusetts.

Reluctantly, but encouraged by her father, Mitchell accepted in 1865 an appointment to Vassar Female College, which opened that year in Poughkeepsie, New York. As director of the observatory and professor of astronomy there she was, in those early days, the most prominent member of the faculty. Several of her students later testified to the great influence she had as a teacher and as an example. Her own research, in which many of her students assisted, focused on the observation of the sun, Jupiter, and Saturn. Elected to the American Philosophical Society in 1869, she helped found the Association for the Advancement of Women in 1873 and served as its president in 1875–1876. She retired from Vassar in failing health in 1888 and died in Lynn, Massachusetts, on June 28, 1889.

Monk, Maria 1816–1849 writer

Born on June 1, 1816, probably in St. John's, Quebec, Maria Monk grew up in Montreal. Little is known for certain of her early life, but she was reportedly the victim of some sort of intermittent mental derangement from the time of a childhood head injury. She worked as a servant girl until her promiscuity brought her to a Catholic asylum for prostitutes, from which she was subsequently discharged in 1834 when she was discovered to be pregnant. She then formed a liaison with the Reverend William K. Hoyt (or Hoyte), head of the nativist Canadian Benevolent Association and a fanatical anti-Catholic. He took her to New York City, where he and a group of nativist agitators drew upon and embroidered Maria Monk's experiences in the asylum. Helped along by her own fevered imagination, the tale ultimately took the shape of lurid fiction: Maria had converted to Catholicism and entered the Hotel Dieu Convent (nearby the asylum in which she had lived) as a nun. There she discovered that nuns and priests engaged regularly in sexual intercourse and that the babies born of these unholy unions were killed and buried in cellar graves. This tale was published serially in the *American Protestant Vindicator* in 1835 and in book form early in 1836 as *Awful Disclosures of Maria Monk, As Exhibited in a Narrative of Her Sufferings during a Residence of Five Years as a Novice, and Two Years as a Black Nun, in the Hotel Dieu Nunnery at Montreal.*

Benefiting from the rising tide of anti-Catholic bigotry in the country, from the appetite whetted by such works as Rebecca Reed's *Six Months in a Convent*, published a short time earlier, and from a latent taste for pornography in a reading audience otherwise deprived of it, *Awful Disclosures* became a sensational best seller. A flood of denunciations and repudiations from respectable sources, Catholic and Protestant alike, was met by a greater flood of anti-Catholic replies, and sales mounted. Over 300,000 copies were sold by the time of the Civil War, and the book continued to be reprinted into the 20th century. In 1837 Maria Monk left Hoyt for the Reverend John J. L. Slocum, another of her collaborators, and he produced *Further Disclosures by Maria Monk*, 1837. She later lived in Philadelphia, where in 1838 she gave birth to another illegitimate child. In 1849 she was living in a bordello in New York City. Arrested for picking the pocket of a customer, she was sent to the almshouse on Blackwell's Island, where she died on September 4, 1849.

Monk, Meredith 1942– performance artist

Born on November 20, 1942, in Lima, Peru, where her mother was giving concerts, Meredith Jane Monk grew up in New York City and Connecticut. As a child, Monk studied piano and eurhythmics, which combines music and movement. She earned a Bachelor of Arts degree in 1964 from Sarah Lawrence College, where she studied dance with Bessie Schoenberg, Judith Dunn, and Beverly Schmidt, as well as music, acting, writing and literature. She credits that time as an important period of creative growth: "I was encouraged to work with a feeling, an idea [. . .] and let the medium and the form find itself. It seemed that finally I was able to combine movement with music and words, all coming from a single source." Among her other teachers were Vicki Starr, John Devers, and Jeanette Lovetri for voice; Ruth Lloyd, Richard Averre, and Glenn Mack for composition; and Gershon Konikow for piano.

From the beginning of her career, her interests included singing, filmmaking, choreography, and acting; she incorporated all of these elements, singly and in combination, into her vast body of work and came to refer to her work as composite theater. Monk made her performance debut in the Washington Square Galleries in 1964 and her film debut in 1966. In 1968, she organized The House, a group devoted to interdisciplinary approaches to the arts. A program from a 1971 performance describes The House as "a group of artists, actors, dancers, and a scientist who are committed to performance as a means of expression and as a means of personal and hopefully social evolution . . . Our work is full of remembered things and dreamed things and felt things." For Monk the total experience of a performance was more important than any particular message in the work.

Monk's artwork defied traditional genres. Her 1965 piece, *Duet with Cat's Scream and Locomotive*, contained sound waves perceived by the brain, but inaudible to the human ear. In *Juice*, a theater piece premiered at the Guggenheim Museum in 1969, Monk experimented with moving the audience about the room instead of changing the stage set.

A great deal of Monk's music is for voices, but it rarely contains recognizable text. "People can respond more directly, without having to go through language," she explained. "I'm trying to approach a vocal music that's both primordial and futuristic." To this end Monk used extended vocal techniques — from conventionally sung notes over a four-octave range to a wide variety of non-traditional sounds reminiscent of whining, hiccuping, laughing, and animal-like noises. As a commentator once suggested, it sounded at times as if Monk might be singing ethnic music from a culture she invented herself.

Monk received an Obie Award for her work in 1972 and was a Guggenheim Fellow that same year. The following year, in both New York and Paris, Monk performed *Education of the Girlchild*, a work without dialogue that explored movement and stillness; she revived it in 1979 and again in 1991. In 1976, she was awarded a second Obie for *Quarry*, a powerful theater piece that incorporated film with music, dance, and occasional lines of text.

In 1978, Monk founded the vocal ensemble bearing her name and with which she toured worldwide. The group performed throughout the U.S. and in festivals in London, Rome, Paris, Tokyo, Jerusalem, Stockholm, Munich, and Cologne. In addition to live performances, Monk and her performing forces made numerous recordings including *Our Lady of Late*, 1974, *Dolmen Music*, 1981, which received the German Critics Award for Best Record, and *Turtle Dreams*, 1983. In 1988, Monk wrote *Fayum Music*, a film score for voice, hammer dulcimer, and double ocarina. The following year, *Book of Days*, a feature-length film, played at the New York Film Festival; a shorter version of it aired on the PBS series *Alive from Off-Center*. In 1991, the Houston Grand Opera company premiered *Atlas*, Monk's multi-media opera. By that time her singular style, prolific body of work and long-standing success continued to make her at once a pioneer and an institution in the relatively new world of performance art. She was recognized with a MacArthur Foundation Fellowship in 1995.

Monroe, Harriet 1860–1936 editor and poet

Born in Chicago on December 23, 1860, Harriet Monroe was educated at the Dearborn Seminary in Chicago and the Convent of the Visitation in Georgetown, D.C., graduating from the latter in 1879. During the next decade her ambition to become a dramatist and a poet was encouraged by such literary figures as Robert Louis Stevenson, with whom she corresponded, William Dean Howells, Eugene Field, Edmund Clarence Stedman, and Richard Watson Gilder.

In 1888 Gilder accepted her sonnet "With Shelley's Poems" for his *Century* magazine, and in the same year she was commissioned to write a cantata for the dedication of Louis Sullivan's Auditorium Theatre in Chicago. In 1891 she published *Valeria and Other Poems*. That same year she received a $1000 commission to write a "Columbian Ode" for the opening of the World's Columbian Exposition in Chicago in October 1892. Thereafter a recognized poet, she continued to publish verse in national magazines while also serving as art and drama critic for Chicago newspapers. In 1896 she wrote *John Wellborn Root, Architect*, a memoir of her late brother-in-law, and in 1900 another volume of verse, *After All. The Passing Show: Five Modern Plays in Verse* was published in 1903, but none of the plays was performed. *The Dance of the Seasons* appeared in 1911.

Monroe would likely have remained only a minor figure but for her ambitious project to establish a forum for contemporary poets. With the confidence born of a sure critical eye she found backers and solicited work from more than 50 poets, and after a year and a half of planning and fund-raising *Poetry: A Magazine of Verse* was launched in October 1912. Young new writers were drawn to the magazine, and it quickly became the leading poetry journal in the English-speaking world. A list of its contributors, beginning with Ezra Pound (who served as London editor for the magazine's first six years) and including Marianne Moore, W. B. Yeats, Robert Frost, T. S. Eliot, Amy Lowell, Wallace Stevens, James Joyce, Edwin Arlington Robinson, William Carlos Williams, Hilda Doolittle, Vachel Lindsay, Edgar Lee Masters, and Carl Sandburg, became an index of major contemporary poets, many of whom were first brought to public attention through its pages.

Although Monroe, under whose aegis the magazine thrived for 24 years, championed the Imagists, the magazine did not confine itself to any school. Her passion for open-mindedness and innovation remained its ruling credo. The magazine survived the passing of the Chicago Renaissance, in the midst of which it had been born, as well as world war and world depression, to remain a journal of major importance. Her own writing over this period included two volumes of verse, *You and I*, 1914, and *The Difference and Other Poems*, 1924. *Poets and Their Art*, 1926, contained essays and a selection of her editorials, and in 1935 she issued a volume of her *Chosen Poems*. In 1917 she edited with Alice Henderson (the magazine's assistant editor) the influential *The New Poetry: An Anthology of Twentieth-Century Verse in English*. It was revised and reissued in 1923 and 1932. She died in Arequipa, Peru, on September 26, 1936. Her autobiography, *A Poet's Life: Seventy Years in a Changing World*, appeared in 1938.

Monroe, Marilyn 1926–1962 actor

Born in Los Angeles on June 1, 1926, Norma Jean Mortenson later took her mother's name, Baker. Her mother was frequently confined in an asylum, and she was reared by 12 successive sets of foster parents and for a time in an orphanage. In 1942 she married a fellow worker in an aircraft factory. She was divorced soon after World War II. She became a popular photographer's model and in 1946 signed a short-term contract with Twentieth Century-Fox, taking as her screen name Marilyn Monroe. After a few brief appearances in movies made by the Fox and Columbia studios she found herself jobless and returned to modeling for photographers. A nude photograph taken of her at that time for use as a calendar illustration later became a national sensation as a feature in the first issue of Hugh Hefner's *Playboy* magazine in December 1953.

In 1950 Monroe played a small uncredited role in *The Asphalt Jungle* that reaped a

GEORGE S. ZIMBEL

Marilyn Monroe

mountain of fan mail. An appearance in *All About Eve*, 1950, won her another contract from Fox and an intense publicity campaign that soon made her name a household word. In a succession of movies, including *Let's Make It Legal*, 1951, *Love Nest*, 1951, *Don't Bother to Knock*, 1952, *Clash by Night*, 1952, *We're Not Married*, 1952, *Monkey Business*, 1952, and *Niagara*, 1953, she advanced to star billing on the strength of her studio-fostered image as a "love goddess." In 1953 she starred in *Gentlemen Prefer Blondes* and *How to Marry a Millionaire* and in 1954 in *The River of No Return* and *There's No Business like Show Business*. Her fame grew steadily and became international, and she became the object of unprecedented popular adulation. In January 1954 she married baseball hero Joe DiMaggio, and the attendant publicity was enormous. With the end of their marriage less than a year later she began to grow discontented with her career.

Monroe studied for a time with Lee Strasberg at the Actors' Studio in New York City, and in *The Seven-Year Itch*, 1955, and *Bus Stop*, 1956, she began to emerge as a talented comedienne. In July 1956 she married playwright Arthur Miller and retired for a time from moviemaking, although she co-starred with Sir Laurence Oliver in *The Prince and the Showgirl*, 1957. In 1959 she won critical acclaim for the first time as a serious actress for *Some Like It Hot*. In 1960 she appeared in *Let's Make Love* and in 1961 she was seen in her last role in *The Misfits* written by Arthur Miller, whom she had divorced the year before (the movie also featured Clark Gable's final performance). Her 23 movies grossed for their first runs a total of more than $200 million, and her fame surpassed that of any other entertainer of her time.

After several months as a virtual recluse, Monroe died in her Hollywood, California, home on August 5, 1962, having taken an overdose of sleeping pills. Her early image as a dumb and seductive blonde gave way in later years to the somewhat tragic figure of a beautiful and fragile girl unable to escape the pressures and false images created for her by Hollywood publicity.

Montez, Lola 1818–1861 adventuress and dancer

Born in Limerick, Ireland, in 1818, Marie Dolores Eliza Rosanna Gilbert, the daughter of a British army officer, spent much of her girlhood in India but was educated in Scotland and England. At nineteen she eloped with Lieutenant Thomas James, whom she married in Ireland in July 1837 and with whom she returned to India. The marriage ended in separation in 1842, and the following year she launched a career as a dancer. Her debut as "Lola Montez, the Spanish dancer" in London in June 1843 was ruined when she was recognized as Mrs. James. The fiasco would probably have ended the career of anyone less beautiful and determined, but she went to the Continent and danced in Berlin, Dresden, Warsaw, St. Petersburg, and at the Paris Opéra. During her travels she reputedly formed liaisons with Franz Liszt and Alexandre Dumas, among many others.

Late in 1846 Montez danced in Munich, and Ludwig I of Bavaria was so struck by her beauty that he offered to provide her with a castle. She accepted, became Baroness Rosenthal and Countess of Lansfeld, and remained as his mistress. Under her influence (the cabinet became known as the "Lolaministerium"), he inaugurated liberal governmental policies, but his infatuation with her helped to bring about the collapse of his regime in the revolution of 1848. In March of that year Ludwig abdicated in favor of his son. Lola fled back to London, where in July 1849 she married Lieutenant George Heald, another British officer, although she had never been divorced from James. Heald later left her.

The years 1851–1853 found Montez in the United States. After a New York debut in *Betley, The Tyrolean* at the Broadway Theatre in December 1851, she appeared in 1852 in *Lola Montes in Bavaria* (the spelling of her stage name was frequently unstable), which subsequently toured Boston, Philadelphia, St. Louis, and New Orleans. In May 1853 she stunned a San Francisco audience with her "Spider Dance." Her third marriage, to Patrick P. Hull of San Francisco in July 1853, terminated in divorce soon after she settled in Grass Valley. There, among other amusements, she coached young Lotta Crabtree in singing and dancing. She settled in New York City after an unsuccessful tour of Australia in 1855–1856 and gathered a following as a lecturer on such topics as fashion, gallantry, and beautiful women. An apparently genuine religious conversion led her to take up various personal philanthropies.

Montez published *Anecdotes of Love; Being a True Account of the Most Remarkable Events Connected with the History of Love; in All Ages and among All Nations*, 1858, *The Arts of Beauty, or, Secrets of a Lady's Toilet with Hints to Gentlemen on the Art of Fascination*, 1858, and *Lectures of Lola Montez, Including Her Autobiography*, 1858. She died in New York City on January 17, 1861. The international notoriety of her heyday persisted long after her death and inspired numerous literary and balletic allusions.

Moore, Grace 1898–1947 singer and actor

Born on December 5, 1898, in Slabtown (now Nough), Tennessee, Mary Willie Grace Moore grew up in Knoxville and Jellico, Tennessee. She was educated in public schools and briefly at Ward-Belmont College in Nashville. She then went to the Wilson-Greens School of Music in Chevy Chase, Maryland. She made her public singing debut in a recital program at the National Theatre, Washington, D.C., in 1919. She then left school and went to New York City, where she sang in a nightclub to pay for vocal lessons. Unfortunately she had chosen a teacher who allowed her to injure her voice. After a period of recuperation she began studying with Dr. Mario Marafioti, who also opened his home to her and helped her find work in some minor musical comedies.

After appearing in *Suite Sixteen*, *Just a Minute*, and *Up in the Clouds*, she made her Broadway debut at the Amsterdam Theatre in the 1920 edition of the revue *Hitchy-Koo*, which featured Jerome Kern's music. After singing in *Town Gossip* she went to Paris to continue training for her hoped-for career on the operatic stage. While studying with Roger Thiral she circulated easily in café society. When she had exhausted her funds she returned to Broadway to star in Irving Berlin's *Music Box Revue of 1923*. While making a great success in that show and in the 1924 edition, in which she sang "What'll I Do" and "All Alone," she continued her studies with Dr. Marafioti. In 1925 she went back to France, where Mary Garden, long her idol and now her friend, recommended her to operatic coach Richard Barthelemy. With an audition before Giulio Catti-Casazza in June 1927 she finally won a contract with the Metropolitan Opera.

Moore's Met and operatic debut occurred in February 1928, when she sang Mimi in *La Bohème* to a warm reception. Later she sang in *Roméo et Juliette* and then made a European tour. After singing Juliette at Deauville she made a highly successful Paris debut as Mimi at the Opéra-Comique in September 1928. In the next few seasons at the Met she sang in *Carmen*, *Tosca*, *Manon*, *Faust*, *Pagliacci*, *Gianni Schicchi* and others.

In 1930 she tried her hand at movie making, going to Hollywood to appear in *A Lady's Morals*, a biography of Jenny Lind, 1930, and in *New Moon* with Lawrence Tibbett, 1931. In 1932 she returned to Broadway in the operetta *The Dubarry*. Back in Hollywood she won the starring role in *One Night of Love*, 1934, a film that featured a pioneering attempt to record operatic works with full orchestra. The film was a great popular success and brought her a medal from the Society of Arts and Sciences for her contribution to "raising the standard of cinema entertainment." She subsequently appeared in *Love Me Forever*, 1935, *The King Steps Out*, 1936, *When You're in Love*, 1937, and *I'll Take Romance*, 1937.

Meanwhile Moore continued in opera. She made her London debut at Covent Garden in *La Bohème*, in June 1935 to tremendous ovations. In France in 1938 she starred in a film version of *Louise*, and after coaching from Mary Garden and Gustave Charpentier she sang it at the Met in January 1939. In February 1941 she sang *L'amore dei Tre Re* under the conducting of the composer, Italo Montemezzi. Radio broadcasts and public appearances such as those at the Roxy Theatre, New York, in 1943 and at Lewisohn Stadium in 1944 further increased her popularity. During World War II she made numerous appearances at bond rallies, benefits, and army camp shows, for which she was decorated by several governments, and in 1946 she toured Europe to entertain occupation forces. Her autobiography, *You're Only Human Once*, appeared in 1944. She died on January 26, 1947, in an airplane crash in Copenhagen, Denmark, following a command performance there.

Moore, Marianne Craig 1887–1972 poet

Marianne Moore

Born on November 15, 1887, in St. Louis, Marianne Moore grew up there and from about the age of seven in Carlisle, Pennsylvania. She graduated from Bryn Mawr College in 1909 and then returned to Carlisle, where she attended Carlisle Commercial College for a year and then for four years taught in the Carlisle Indian School. Her first published poems appeared in 1915, when T. S. Eliot printed some in *The Egoist* in London and then Harriet Monroe printed more in *Poetry*. In 1916 she moved with her mother to Chatham, New Jersey, and two years later they settled in Greenwich Village in New York City.

While teaching in a private school and then working as an assistant librarian in the New York Public Library in 1921–1925, she established a place for herself in the literary life of Greenwich Village. A collection of her poems was edited by Hilda Doolittle and Winifred Ellerman and published without her knowledge in London in 1921 as *Poems*. In 1924 a revised version of the book was published in the United States as *Observations*, which was given a Dial award. From 1925 to its demise in 1929 Marianne Moore was acting editor of the *Dial*. In the latter year she moved to Brooklyn.

Moore's verse and literary criticism appeared in many journals and periodicals in England and the United States. Over the next decades she produced *Selected Poems*, 1935, *The Pangolin and Other Verse*, 1936, *What Are Years*, 1941, *Nevertheless*, 1944, and her *Collected Poems*, 1951, which won a Pulitzer Prize, the Bollingen Prize, and a National Book Award. Her verse was characterized by highly individual metrical forms, by wit and irony, deep moral concern, and carefully considered feeling. She often employed imagery from the natural world, but her concerns never strayed far from the human. The personal interests that formed her subjects ranged from baseball to art glass; titles of some of her best known pieces included "To a Steam Roller," "Hometown Piece for Messrs. Alston and Reese" (on the Brooklyn Dodgers), "The Labors of Hercules," "When I Buy Pictures," "The Monkeys," "Carnegie Hall: Rescued," "In Distrust of Merits," and "Tom Fool at Jamaica." Her prosody showed high craftsmanship, discipline, and precision. Among her other writings were a translation, *The Fables of La Fontaine*, 1954, *Predilections*, a collection of essays on her favorite authors, 1955, and *Idiosyncrasy and Technique*, 1958. Other books of verse included *Like a Bulwark*, 1956, *O To Be A Dragon*, 1959, *The Arctic Ox*, 1964, and *Tell Me, Tell Me: Granite Steel and Other Topics*, 1966. Her *Complete Poems*, appeared in 1967. Moore died at her New York City home on February 5, 1972.

Moran, Mary Nimmo 1842–1899 artist

Born in Strathaven, Lanarkshire, Scotland, on May 16, 1842, Mary Nimmo was brought to America in 1847 by her father, a widower. She grew up and attended school in Crescentville, then a suburb of Philadelphia, and in mid–1862 she married Thomas Moran, an artist. She began studying painting under him and before long was exhibiting at the Pennsylvania Academy of Fine Arts and at the National Academy of Design. In 1867 they made an extended visit to Europe and studied together in France and Italy. During the 1870s Thomas Moran made a reputation as a painter of Western scenes — his panoramic "Grand Canyon of the Yellowstone" was bought by Congress for the U.S. Capitol — and until her health declined Mary Moran accompanied him on journeys to the West, the South, and elsewhere.

In 1879, while her husband was visiting the Grand Tetons, Moran took up copperplate etching. Working directly from nature, she produced prints of such quality that she was promptly elected to the New York Etching Club. An exhibit of some of the club members' work in London in 1881 won her election to the Royal Society of Painter-Etchers. Over the next decade she firmly established herself as the preeminent woman worker in the field. Her etchings of landscape views around her East Hampton, Long Island, home, in the New Jersey meadows, in Georgia and Florida, and in Great Britain were widely popular. She exhibited at the World's Columbian Exposition in Chicago in 1893 and was awarded a diploma and a medal. In all her etchings numbered about 70, bearing such titles as "Evening, East Hampton," "Bridge over the Delaware," "The Goose Pond," "An Old Homestead," "Florida Forest," "Between the Gloaming and the Murk," and "Conway Castle, Wales." She died in East Hampton, New York, on September 25, 1899.

Morgan, Anne Tracy 1873–1932 philanthropist

Born in Highland Falls, New York, on July 25, 1873, Anne Morgan was the daughter of J. Pierpont Morgan and grew up amid the wealth and cultural amenities he had amassed. She was educated privately and traveled frequently. Until her late twenties she passed her time in the social world to which she had been born and in church work. Under the tutelage of Elisabeth Marbury she began to broaden her horizons about 1900. In 1903 she joined Marbury, Florence J. Harriman, and others in organizing the Colony Club, New York's first social club for women. She became active in various organizations devoted to assisting young working women, and in 1909 she established a restaurant and clubroom for workers at the Brooklyn Navy Yard. She gave her support to the strike of women shirtwaist workers in 1909 and in 1910 joined Mrs. August Belmont in founding the Working Girls Vacation Association, which became the American Women's Association in 1922. In 1915 she published *The American Girl: her Education, her Responsibility, her Recreation, her Future*.

Early in World War I Morgan established in France the American Fund for French Wounded, and early in 1917 she organized the American Friends for Devastated France, which by the end of World War I had collected and distributed an estimated $5 million in food, medicine, and other war relief, had relocated over 50,000 French villagers left homeless by war, had built orphanages, kindergartens, and clinics, and had helped restock and reequip farms. As chairman of the executive committee of the organization Anne Morgan carried the burden of its work, and in 1918 she was awarded the Croix de Guerre. (In 1932 she became the first American woman to be appointed a commander of the Legion of Honor.)

In 1924 she resumed her connection with the American Women's Association, of which she was president from 1928 to 1943. In 1939 she organized the American Friends of France in anticipation of a new war. She directed the relief work of the group, which had three relief centers ready when war broke out, until forced to leave the country in 1940. She returned to supervise postwar relief. After four years of declining health Anne Morgan died in Mount Kisco, New York, on January 29, 1952.

Morgan, Helen 1900–1941 singer

Born in Danville, Illinois, on August 2, 1900, Helen Riggins took the name Morgan in her childhood when her divorced mother remarried. She grew up in Danville and later in Chicago, and after leaving high school about 1918 she held a series of jobs in factories and stores. Various conflicting accounts of her entry into show business survive, but she apparently obtained some voice training, sang in speakeasies, and in 1920 got a job in the chorus of Florenz Ziegfeld's *Sally*. More nightclub singing in Chicago and perhaps a beauty contest in Montreal led to a small role in *George White's Scandals* in 1925. In that year she had an engagement at Billy Rose's Backstage Club, where the crowded conditions obliged her to perch on her accompanist's piano, an informal touch that soon became a trademark.

On Broadway Morgan appeared in *Americana*, in which she sat on a piano and stopped the show with "Nobody Wants Me," 1926, *Grand Guignol*, 1927, and Jerome Kern's and Oscar Hammerstein's *Show Boat* which opened at the Ziegfeld Theatre in December 1927 and in which she was a sensation singing "Bill" and "Can't Help Lovin' Dat Man." In the Kern-Hammerstein *Sweet Adeline*, 1929, she starred and sang "Don't Ever Leave Me" and "Why Was I Born?" Later shows, less successful, included *The Ziegfeld Follies* of 1931, *Memory*, 1934, *George White's Scandals* of 1936, and *A Night at the Moulin Rouge*, 1939. She also appeared in a number of motion pictures, including *Applause*, 1929, *Glorifying the American Girl*, 1930, *Roadhouse Nights*, 1930 *Marie Galante*, 1934, *Street Music*, 1935, *Go into Your Dance*, 1935, *Frankie and Johnnie*, 1935, and *Show Boat*, 1936.

Morgan's main fame, however, was as a club singer. Her small, pale appearance and her sweet, artless, somewhat thin, and blues-tinged voice made her the ideal performer of the new sort of popular song that was being written in the 1920s and 1930s: ironic, sometimes bitter, distinctly urban, and full of the disappointment, loneliness, and joyless hedonism that filled the smoky, boozy clubs that were seemingly her natural habitat. In her personal life she was unlucky in love, alcoholic, and generous to a fault. She died in Chicago on October 8, 1941.

Morley, Margaret Warner 1858–1923 biologist, educator and writer of children's books

Born on February 17, 1858, in Montrose, Iowa, Margaret Morley grew up and attended public schools in Brooklyn, New York. She studied at the Oswego Normal School (now State University of New York College at Oswego) and at New York City Normal College (now Hunter College), graduating from the latter in 1878. She conducted postgraduate studies in biology at Armour Institute (now the Illinois Institute of Technology) in Chicago and at the Woods Hole, Massachusetts, marine laboratory. She then embarked on a career of teaching, which took her to Oswego Normal, to the State Normal School (now part of the University of Wisconsin-Milwaukee) in Milwaukee, to a high school in Leavenworth, Kansas, to Armour Institute, and to the Free Kindergarten Association Training Class of Chicago. Her work in that field was eclipsed, however, by her career as an author of books on nature study and biology for children.

Morley's pioneering writings, many used as school texts at a time when nature study was beginning to be incorporated into many schools' curricula, included *A Song of Life*, 1891, *Life and Love*, 1895, *Seed Babies*, 1896, *A Few Familiar Flowers*, 1897, *Flowers and their Friends*, 1897, *The Honey Makers*, 1899, *Bee People*, 1899, *Little Wanderers*, 1899, *Down North and Up Along*, 1900, *Wasps and their Ways*, 1900, *The Insect Folk*, 1903, *Little Mitchell, the Story of a Mountain Squirrel*, 1904, *Butterflies and Bees: the Insect Folk, Vol. II*, 1905, *The Renewal of Life; How and When to Tell the Story to the Young*, for parents, 1906, *Grasshopper Land*, 1907, *Donkey John of the Toy Valley*, 1909, *The Spark of Life; How Living Things Come into the World, as Told for Girls and Boys*, 1913, *The Carolina Mountains*, 1913, *Will-o'-the Wasps*, 1913, and *The Apple-Tree Sprite*, 1915. She died in Washington, D.C., on December 12, 1923.

Morris, Clara 1847?–1925 actor and writer

Born in Toronto on March 17, probably in 1847 (some sources give 1846 or 1848), Clara Morris was the eldest child of a bigamous marriage. When she was three her father, whose name was La Montagne, was exposed, and her mother fled with her to Cleveland, where they adopted her grandmother's name, Morrison. Young Clara received only scanty schooling. About 1860 she became a ballet girl in the resident company of the Cleveland Academy of Music, shortening her name to Morris at that time. After nine years of training with that company she played a season as leading lady at Wood's Theatre, Cincinnati, in 1869. She then appeared in Halifax, Nova Scotia, for a summer and with Joseph Jefferson in Louisville before going to New York City in 1870.

Morris made her New York debut in September in *Man and Wife*, directed by Augustin Daly at his Fifth Avenue Theatre. The role had come to her by chance, but she made such an impression in it that Daly starred her in a series of highly emotional roles over the next three years in such plays as *No Name*, *Delmonico's*, *L'Article 47*, *Alixe*, *Jezebel*, and *Madeleine Morel*. She left Daly in 1873 and in November of that year starred under A. M. Palmer's management in *The Wicked World* at the Union Square Theatre. Over the next few years she had great successes in *Camille* in 1874, *The New Leah* in 1875, *Miss Multon* (an American version of a French version of *East Lynne*), her most popular role, in 1876, *Jane Eyre* in 1877, and *The New Magdalen* in 1882. She also toured extensively, especially in the 1880s, and everywhere mesmerized audiences with her emotional power. Although neither a great beauty nor a great artist, nor trained in elocution or stagecraft, she had an instinctive genius for portraying the impassioned and often suffering heroines of French melodrama. The passing of the vogue for that sort of theater, together with her uncertain health, brought her career to a close in the 1890s.

In retirement in Riverdale, New York, Morris contributed articles on acting to various magazines, wrote a daily newspaper column for ten years, and published several books, including *A Silent Singer*, stories, 1899, *Little Jim Crow, and Other Stories for Children*, 1900, *Life on the Stage: My Personal Experiences and Recollections*, 1901, *Stage Confidences*, reminiscences, 1902, *A Pasteboard Crown*, 1902, *The Trouble Woman*, 1904, *The Life of a Star*, more reminiscences, 1906, *Left in Charge*, 1907, *New East Lynne*, 1908, *A Strange Surprise*, 1910, and *Dressing-Room Receptions*, 1911. In 1904 she returned to the stage in a revival of *The Two Orphans*, and she later appeared in vaudeville. She died in New Canaan, Connecticut, on November 20, 1925.

Morris, Elizabeth 1753?–1826 actor

Born about 1753, probably in England, Elizabeth Morris left no record of her life before her marriage, at a date also unknown, to Owen Morris, an actor in Lewis Hallam's traveling American Company. Her first recorded stage appearance in America was at the Southwark Theatre, Philadelphia, in the autumn of 1772. She subsequently performed in Charleston, New York, and other American cities until the outbreak of the Revolution forced the troupe to retire to the West Indies. They returned in 1785 and resumed their touring. In 1791 she and her husband left Hallam to join a new company organized by Thomas Wignell. In 1792 the two of them were arrested in Boston some weeks into a run of *The School for Scandal*; it was reputedly Boston's first theatrical season, albeit an illegal one. In February 1794 Wignell's company opened the new Chestnut Street Theatre in Philadelphia, where Morris remained until 1810.

In the period of the 1790s and early 1800s Morris was accounted by the all but unanimous verdict of audiences and critics the leading actress on the American stage. Her elegant figure and command of the grand manner earned her that position, while the aura of mystery she cultivated helped preserve it. She may have acted as late as 1815, but in her last years she was in private life notoriously reclusive. The few appearances she made in public revealed the quaint costume of nearly a half-century before. She died in Philadelphia on April 17, 1826.

Morris, Esther Hobart McQuigg Slack 1814–1902 suffragist and public official

Born near Spencer, New York, on August 8, 1814, Esther McQuigg was apprenticed to a seamstress after being orphaned when she was eleven. In August 1841 she married Artemus Slack, and after his death three years later she moved with her young son to Peru, Illinois, where Slack had left her property. A short time later she married John Morris, a local merchant. Early in 1869 they moved to Wyoming Territory and settled in South Pass City. There she apparently exerted her considerable personality on behalf of the notion of woman suffrage. It may well have been largely owing to her that the legislator elected from her district in the first territorial election in 1869, William H. Bright, promptly introduced a bill providing for woman suffrage that was passed in December of that year.

In February 1870 Morris was appointed justice of the peace for South Pass City, a job for which, despite the rough character of the gold-mining town of saloons and fewer than 500 people, her robust frame and blunt fearlessness well suited her. In her 8½ months in the post she tried over 70 cases expeditiously and without reversal. She was the first woman ever to hold such a position. She contributed occasionally to Susan B. Anthony's *Revolution*. In 1871 she left her husband and moved to Laramie, where in 1873 she was briefly on the ballot for state representative. She later left Wyoming for New York, but she returned by 1890 and settled in Cheyenne.

In her later years Morris was increasingly honored for her role in the attainment of suffrage in Wyoming, the first success of the movement for national woman suffrage. She died in Cheyenne, Wyoming, on April 2, 1902. Her reputation continued to grow in succeeding years, and in 1960 statues of her were placed in Statuary Hall of the U.S. Capitol and before the Wyoming state house in Cheyenne.

Morrison, Toni 1931– teacher, editor, novelist and critic

Born on February 18, 1931, the second child of George and Ramah Wofford, Cloe Anthony Wofford grew up in a racially mixed, working-class neighborhood during the depression in Lorain, Ohio. Both her parents claimed Southern roots. Her maternal grandparents had lost their land in the 1890s and had never been able to recover it. They sharecropped in Alabama until heading north in search of greater opportunity. Her father's family had been Georgia sharecroppers; although the intense racial violence that he had lived through embittered him and made him strive to live independently of white people, it also gave him a deep pride and commitment to African-American culture and community.

HELEN MARCUS

Toni Morrison

Growing up in an ethnically diverse community, where African-Americans were not social outcasts, Morrison learned about the strengths and the divisions within the black community from the lively debates and dissensus within her family. Her maternal grandparents argued about whether African-Americans in the U.S. would ever improve their lot; her paternal grandfather, based on his early experiences of exploitation by white people, believed they would not; her grandmother resorted to prayer.

Her father and mother argued about whether there was any hope for the improvement of white people, her father taking the pessimistic position and preferring to live as separately as possible from the whites, while her mother was open to each new encounter. All members of her family, however, shared a deep love of and appreciation for traditional black culture. Story-telling, songs and folktales were a deeply formative part of her childhood.

Morrison could read before she entered school, continuing to read avidly as an adolescent. She graduated from Lorain High School with honors in 1949, then surprised her family by entering Howard University in Washington, D.C., in pursuit of a college degree.

While majoring in English, Morrison joined the Howard University Players, a campus theater group. During her college years she also changed her name from Cloe to Toni. She graduated from Howard in 1953 and went on to Cornell University for graduate work in English. Her M.A. thesis was on the theme of suicide in William Faulkner and Virginia Woolf. After two years teaching at Texas Southern University she returned to Howard for a teaching job that she held until 1964. Her students included Claude Brown and Stokley Carmichael. She married Harold Morrison in 1957 and bore two sons; the couple divorced in 1964.

In 1965 Toni Morrison accepted a job as textbook editor for Random House and moved to Syracuse, New York, with her two young children. In 1968 she became a senior editor for Random House in New York City. There she edited works by Angela Davis and the biography of Muhammed Ali, while promoting and encouraging the literary careers of Toni Cade Bambara and Gayl Jones.

In an autobiographical sketch, Morrison described the isolation and unhappiness she suffered in her marriage. Writing became a partial ameliorative. While still in D.C., she joined a writer's group and produced several stories, including one about a young black girl who desperately wanted to have blue eyes. The story of Pecola Breedlove was published in 1970 as *The Bluest Eye*. Told from the point of view of a nine-year-old narrator, the novel chronicled the lives of three young girls and their struggle for self-esteem in the face of Anglo-Saxon standards for beauty. The belief of Pecola Breedlove, that blue eyes were essential to finding love and happiness, her failure to move beyond that obsession, and the complicity of the African-American community in her eventual madness formed the central tragedy of the novel.

Sula, her second novel, appeared in 1973 and focused on the lives and friendship of two women growing up in the 1920s and 30s, in a Midwestern African-American community called the Bottoms. Nel Wright and Sula Peace are an unlikely pair. Their friendship ends prior to Sula's early death and is not reclaimed until Nel is on her deathbed at the end of the novel. Once again, Morrison wrestles with the issues of community and marginality. Sula, while ostracized for her outrageous behavior, is never expelled from the community. Despite her rejection of Sula, Nel is moved in the end to recognize the similarity of their circumstances despite the vast differences in how they chose to respond.

Her first two novels, *The Bluest Eye* and *Sula*, were well received by critics but sold modestly and were allowed to go out of print. In contrast, her third novel, *Song of Solomon*, was published in 1977 to great acclaim. A paperback best-seller and Book-of-the-Month Club selection, *Song of Solomon* was also the winner of the National Book Critics' Circle award. It was the first book by an African-American author to achieve such critical acclaim since Richard Wright's *Native Son* was published in 1940. It tells the story of young Milkman Dead and his struggle to find an identity for himself. Ultimately it becomes the history of his family and their struggle to survive and escape from slavery.

The novel was preceded and informed by the publication of *The Black Book*, a pictorial history of African-American life in the U.S., edited by Morrison. As editor, she oversaw the collection of a vast, diverse amount of material that reflected the common experience of African-Americans: newspaper clippings, bills of sale, sheet music, dream books, photographs and other artifacts documenting the lives and loves of everyday people. Published in 1974, the book contained materials that informed Morrison's subsequent fiction.

Song of Solomon's commercial success allowed Morrison to pursue writing full-time. *Tar Baby*, published in 1981, was also quite successful, making the *New York Times* best-seller list a month after its publication and remaining there for four months. Quite different from her earlier novels, *Tar Baby* was a blend of fantasy and realism, metaphorically rooted in the folktale about the rabbit who, trapped by a white farmer, tricks the farmer into releasing him unharmed. It was also her first novel to be set outside the geographical boundaries of the U.S.

Following the publication of *Tar Baby*, Morrison became the first African-American woman to be featured on the cover of *Newsweek* magazine. The Pulitzer Prize winning novel, *Beloved*, was published in 1987. The novel was based on an 1851 newspaper clipping about Margaret Garner, a woman who had escaped from slavery with her four children. Facing capture in Ohio and a return to slavery, Garner attempted to kill all four of her children, succeeding in killing one and injuring two others. The case became a cause celebre in abolitionist circles, and money was raised to free Garner and her remaining children.

Morrison, however, grappled with the permanent damage, the marks left indelibly on the memory of an entire people by the legacy of enslavement and survival. Through the post-slavery struggles of the Garner-inspired character, whom she called Sethe, Morrison examined the necessary conditions for true freedom and identified the African-American community as the redeemer through which release from the history of bondage must be attained. *Beloved* was the first novel in a proposed trilogy that would commemorate and celebrate little-documented episodes in African-American history.

Jazz, her sixth novel, published in 1992, is the second volume. *Jazz* moved from the era of slavery and reconstruction to the period of black migration to the urban North, and the shift in location of the African-American community from the countryside to the city.

Morrison's central concerns remained the problems of memory, community and culture for African-Americans. Beginning in the 1980s, Morrison embarked on another career, that of critic. She began in an effort to correct some of the misrepresentation and ignorance surrounding her work and that of other African-American writers. Despite the efforts of many critics to find universal (nonracial) themes in Morrison's later work, her own critical contributions denied the validity of that approach, pointing to the failure of white, Western critics to recognize and affirm the centrality of African-American culture in her fiction.

Her philosophy — that the best literature is necessarily political — recurred as a theme in her essays, especially her 1989 essay for the *Michigan Quarterly*, and in a 1992 collection titled *Playing in the Dark: Whiteness and the Literary Imagination*, which pointed to the way in which whiteness, as a racial category, masquerades behind the traditional notions of universality. According to Morrison, her fiction exposed the speciousness of identifying whiteness with universality. She affirmed that her particular representation of African-American memory and community is crucial to understanding her work.

After leaving Random House she lectured and taught at many colleges and universities, including Yale University, Bard College, SUNY-Purchase, SUNY-Albany, and Harvard University. She began teaching at Princeton University in 1989. Winner of numerous awards since the late 1970s, Morrison made history again in 1993 by becoming the first African-American woman to win the Nobel prize for literature.

Morton, Sarah Wentworth Apthorp 1759–1846 poet

Born in Boston in August 1759, Sarah Apthorp was the daughter of a well-to-do merchant and evidently acquired an unusually thorough education. From the age of ten the family lived in Braintree (now Quincy). In February 1781 she married Perez Morton, a Boston lawyer. She had formed the habit of writing verse in childhood, and in 1789 she began contributing to the "Seat of the Muses" department of the newly established *Massachusetts Magazine*. Her early poems, ranging in manner from eulogy to pastoral, were published under the name "Constantia" and later that of "Philenia." The work of "Philenia" soon attracted the notice of domestic and even British critics, who warmly praised her first volume, a long verse narrative entitled *Ouâbi: or The Virtues of Nature*, 1790, a tale of Native Americans cast in the literary "noble savage" mold.

Verses that continued to appear in the *Columbian Centinel*, the *New York Magazine*, the *Tablet* and later in the *Port Folio*, the *Monthly Anthology*, and other periodicals established Philenia as the foremost woman poet of her period in America. *Beacon Hill. A Local Poem, Historic and Descriptive*, 1797, and its sequel *The Virtues of Society. A Tale Founded on Fact*, 1799, were consciously American works of the early national period. From 1797 she lived in Dorchester (now part of Boston), Massachusetts. On a visit to Washington, D.C., in 1802 she sat for Gilbert Stuart. Her last published work, *My Mind and Its Thoughts*, appeared in 1823. In 1837, on her husband's death, she returned to Quincy, Massachusetts, where she died on May 14, 1846.

For over a century she was falsely believed to have written *The Power of Sympathy*, 1789, the first American novel, because of the similarity of the book's plot to a scandalous tragedy that had occurred in her own life — her husband's affair with her sister, followed by the sister's suicide. In 1894 authorship of the book was fixed upon William Hill Brown, a neighbor of the Mortons.

Moses, Anna Mary Robertson 1860–1961 "Grandma Moses," painter

Born on September 7, 1860, on a farm in Greenwich, New York, Anna Robertson grew up there and from the age of eleven near Easton, New York. She had only a few months' schooling during the summers of her childhood. About the age of thirteen she left home to earn her living as a hired girl. After her marriage to Thomas Moses in September 1887 the couple lived near Staunton, Virginia, until 1905. In that year they settled on a farm near Eagle Bridge, Rensselaer County, New York, where she lived the rest of her life. Thomas Moses died in 1927, and his widow continued to farm until 1936.

Anna Moses had enjoyed drawing pictures as a child, and in 1918 she tried painting a scene on the fireboard of her fireplace, but it was not until her late seventies, when arthritis forced her to give up making worsted embroidery pictures, that she turned to oil paints to occupy her time. At first she copied illustrated postcards and Currier & Ives prints, but gradually she began to recreate scenes from her childhood, as in "Apple Pickers" and "Sugaring-Off." Her early paintings were given away or sold for small sums. In 1939 several of her paintings that were hanging in a drugstore window in Hoosick Falls, New York, impressed Louis Caldor, an engineer and art collector, who then drove to her farm and bought her remaining stock of 15 paintings. In October of that year three of those paintings were exhibited at the Museum of Modern Art in New York City in a show entitled "Contemporary, Unknown Painters." From the beginning her work received favorable criticism. In October 1940 a one-woman show of 35 paintings was held at Galerie St. Etienne in New York City. In November of that year Gimbel's department store brought "Grandma" Moses to New York City on the opening day of a Thanksgiving exhibition of her works. Thereafter, her paintings were shown throughout the United States and in Europe in some 150 solo shows and 100 more group exhibits.

Grandma Moses produced some 2,000 paintings in all, mainly on masonite board. Her naive style (labeled American primitive) was acclaimed for its purity of color, its attention to detail, and its vigor. Other notable paintings included "Out for the Christmas Trees," "Catching the Thanksgiving Turkey," "The Old Oaken Bucket," "The Old Checkered House," "Black Horses," and "From My Window." From 1946 her paintings were often reproduced in prints and on Christmas cards. Her autobiography, *My Life's History*, was published in 1952. She died on December 13, 1961, at the age of a hundred and one, in Hoosick Falls, New York.

Mosher, Eliza Maria 1846–1928 physician and educator

Born in Cayuga County, New York, on October 2, 1846, Eliza Mosher was educated in local schools and at the Friends' Academy in Union Springs, New York. In 1869, over the objections of friends and family, she entered the New England Hospital for Women and Children as an intern apprentice. After a year she was forced to suspend her education to nurse her mother in her last illness, and during that year she also assisted a woman doctor in Boston. In October 1871 she entered the University of Michigan, where she completed the medical course and received her M.D. in 1875. During 1875–1877 she was in private practice with a classmate in Poughkeepsie, New York. In 1877 she was appointed resident physician at the Massachusetts Reformatory Prison for Women, newly opened at the instigation of Ellen C. Johnson. After establishing hospital facilities in the prison she was responsible for virtually all medical, surgical, and even dental care. In 1880 she was made superintendent of the prison, but an accidental injury in 1883 forced her to resign. She then returned to private practice in Brooklyn, New York, in partnership with Dr. Lucy M. Hall, a Michigan classmate and colleague at the reformatory. During 1883–1887 they also alternated semesters as resident physician and associate professor of physiology and hygiene at Vassar College.

In 1888 Mosher organized a medical training course at the Union Missionary Training Institute in Brooklyn, and the next year she became lecturer on anatomy and hygiene at the Chautauqua, New York, summer school; her association with both institutions was measured in decades. In 1896 President James B. Angell called her to the University of Michigan as dean of women and professor of hygiene. She was the first woman on the university's faculty, and she retained her posts, as well as those of director of physical education and resident physician to women students, until ill health forced her resignation in 1902. For the rest of her life she practiced medicine privately in Brooklyn. At various times she lectured at Mount Holyoke College, Adelphi College, Pratt Institute, and the Brooklyn YWCA.

In her work in educational institutions Mosher had always been interested in the fields of health maintenance and physical education and fitness, and in private research she investigated medical aspects of posture. She devised an orthopedically sound school desk and chair for children. She was a founder of the American Posture League. She was also president of the Women's Medical Society of New York, honorary president of the Medical Women's National Association, a founder of the American Women's Hospitals Committee, and from 1905 to her death senior editor of the *Medical Women's Journal*. In 1912 she published *Health and Happiness: A Message to Girls*. She died in New York City on October 16, 1928.

Mott, Lucretia Coffin 1793–1880 reformer

Born on January 3, 1793, in Nantucket, Massachusetts, Lucretia Coffin was the daughter of a Quaker sea captain. From 1804 she grew up in Boston, where she attended public school for two years in accordance with her father's wish that she become familiar with the workings of democratic principles. Later she was enrolled in a Friends' boarding school at Nine Partners, near Poughkeepsie, New York. After two years as a student she became a teacher, and she was quickly impressed by the fact that experienced women teachers were paid less than half as much as their male counterparts. In April 1811, having rejoined her family in Philadelphia, she married James Mott, a fellow teacher from the school. About 1818 she began to speak at religious meetings, and three years later she was accepted as a minister of the Friends. She joined the Hicksite (Liberal) branch of the Society when a rift occurred in the 1820s, and in that decade she began to travel about the country lecturing on religion and questions of social reform, including temperance, the abolition of slavery, and peace.

Lucretia Mott

In 1833 Mott attended the founding convention of the American Anti-Slavery Society, and immediately thereafter she led in organizing its women's auxiliary, the Philadelphia

Female Anti-Slavery Society, of which she was chosen president. She met opposition within the Society of Friends when she spoke of abolition, and attempts were made to strip her of her ministry and membership. In 1837 she helped organize the Anti-Slavery Convention of American Women, and in May 1838 mob violence against her home was narrowly averted after the burning of Pennsylvania Hall, Philadelphia, where the convention had been meeting. Rebuffed as a delegate to the World's Anti-Slavery Convention in London in 1840 because of her sex, she still managed to make her views known.

With Elizabeth Cady Stanton, Mott called a convention of women in Seneca Falls, New York, in July 1848, from which was issued a "Declaration of Sentiments" phrased in language recalling the Declaration of Independence and calling for equality before the law for women. The women's-rights and suffrage movements as organized political campaigns grew directly from that convention. Mott discussed the disabilities of women in her *Discourse on Woman*, 1850. In 1852 she presided over a women's-rights convention in Syracuse, New York. She and her husband opened their home to runaway slaves escaping via the Underground Railroad after the Fugitive Slave Law was adopted in 1850. At the organizing meeting of the American Equal Rights Association in 1866 she was chosen president. In May 1867 she joined Robert Dale Owen, Rabbi Isaac M. Wise, and others in the organization of the Free Religious Association.

A fluent, moving speaker, Mott retained her poise and femininity before the most hostile audiences. After the Civil War she worked to secure the franchise and educational opportunities for freedmen. She continued active in the causes of women's rights, peace, and liberal religion until her death. Her last address was given to the Friends' annual meeting in May 1880. She died on November 11, 1880, in her home outside Philadelphia.

Moulton, Ellen Louise Chandler 1835–1908 writer, critic and hostess

Born in Pomfret, Connecticut, on April 10, 1835, Louise Chandler was educated in a local school, where her classmates included James A M. Whistler and Edmund Clarence Stedman, and for a year, 1854–1855, in Emma Willard's Troy Female Seminary. In 1854 she published *This, That, and the Other*, a collection of verses and sketches earlier contributed to various periodicals. The book enjoyed a large sale. In August 1855 she married William U. Moulton, publisher of *True Flag*, in which some of her poems had appeared. She soon established herself as a literary and social force in Boston. Her verses, stories, and sketches became regular features of *Godey's Lady's Book*, *Atlantic Monthly*, *Scribner's*, *Youth's Companion*, *Harper's Bazaar*, and other popular magazines. They were collected in several volumes, the children's stories in several books of *Bed-Time Stories*, 1874–1880, and other pieces in *Some Women's Hearts*, 1874, *Poems*, 1877, *Swallow-Flights and Other Poems*, 1878, *Random Rambles*, 1881, *Firelight Stories*, 1883, and *Ourselves and Our Neighbors: Short Chats on Social Topics*, 1887.

Moulton's Friday salon was frequented by such figures as Ralph Waldo Emerson, James Russell Lowell, Henry Wadsworth Longfellow, John Greenleaf Whittier, Oliver Wendell Holmes, Thomas W. S. Higginson, John Singer Sargent, and others. She served as Boston literary correspondent for the *New York Tribune* in 1870–1876 and as book critic for the *Boston Sunday Herald* in 1887–1891. From a first trip to London in 1876, on which she made the acquaintance of many literary figures, she spent increasing amounts of time there until she had virtually divided her year between London and Boston. In London as in Boston her salon became a major one in the social-literary life of the city, and her personal friendships with numerous late Romantic and Pre-Raphaelite poets eased their introduction to an American readership.

Moulton's other books included *Lazy Tours in Spain and Elsewhere*, 1896, and the posthumous *Poems and Sonnets of Louise Chandler Moulton*, 1909, which collected many of the poems that were highly praised by contemporaries for their elegance, sensitivity, and lyrical beauty. She also edited several volumes, including *The Collected Poems of Philip Bourke Marston*, 1893, and *Arthur O'Shaughnessy, His Life and His Work, with Selections from His Poems*, 1894. She died in Boston on August 10, 1908.

Mowatt, Anna Cora Ogden 1819–1870 writer and actor

Born on March 5, 1819, to American parents in Bordeaux, France, Anna Ogden came to New York City with her family when she was seven. As a child she exhibited a talent for acting and a precocious interest in Shakespeare, whose plays she devoured before she was ten. In October 1834, at the age of fifteen, she married James Mowatt, a lawyer several years her senior. Under the pseudonym "Isabel" she published her first book, a verse romance titled *Pelayo, or, The Cavern of Covadonga*, in 1836. She defended it against critical attacks in *Reviewers Reviewed* the next year.

During 1837–1840 she was abroad for her health, and from Europe she contributed articles to *Godey's Lady's Book* and other magazines. Shortly afterward her husband suffered financial reverses, and in 1841 she determined to pursue a career as an author and actress. She gave a successful series of poetry readings in Boston, New York, and other cities and, under the pseudonym "Helen Berkley," wrote for the fashionable magazines. She also produced biographies, several volumes on cooking, needlework, and other domestic topics, and two novels, *The Fortune Hunter*, 1844, and *Evelyn*, 1845. Her first successful play, *Fashion; or, Life in New York*, a social satire written at the suggestion of Epes Sargent and for which she is chiefly remembered, opened in March 1845 at New York's Park Theatre.

Mowatt made her acting debut in June of that year in *The Lady of Lyons* at the Park. Her second play, *Armand, the Child of the People*, was also well received in New York City in 1847, and she later took both plays to England. Her success on the stage, the more remarkable for her complete lack of training or experience, extended to several Shakespearean roles. After four years in Britain and the death of her husband in 1851 she returned for an American tour, but recurring illness forced her from the stage in 1854. Her *Autobiography of an Actress* was published in the same year. She married William F. Ritchie in June of that year and settled in Richmond, Virginia. She became active in Ann Pamela Cunningham's Mount Vernon Ladies' Association and became vice-regent for Virginia in 1858. On the outbreak of the Civil War in 1861 she went to Europe.

Her later books included *Mimic Life; or, Before and Behind the Curtain*, 1856, *Twin Roses* 1857, *Fairy Fingers*, 1865, *The Mute Singer*, 1866, and *The Clergyman's Wife and Other Sketches*, 1867. She lived mostly in Florence during her last years but died in Twickenham, England, on July 21, 1870. *Italian Life and Legends*, 1870, appeared posthumously.

Murfree, Mary Noailles 1850–1922 writer

Born on January 24, 1850, on a plantation near Murfreesboro (named in 1811 for her great-grandfather), Tennessee, Mary Murfree grew up and attended school in Nashville. The Civil War forced a suspension of her education, but in 1867–1869 she was at Chegaray Institute, a French school in Philadelphia. With the failure of her father's business in 1869 the family returned to Murfreesboro, where Mary began writing stories for her own and her family's entertainment. In 1874 one of her stories appeared in *Lippincott's Magazine* under the name "R. Emmet Dembry," and her writing career was begun. A story in the *Atlantic Monthly* in 1878 appeared under the name "Charles Egbert Craddock," which she used thereafter. In 1881 she moved with her family to St. Louis.

Her first book, *In the Tennessee Mountains*, 1884, collected several of her stories from the *Atlantic* and was well received critically. *Where the Battle Was Fought*, her first novel, 1884, was followed by *The Prophet of the Great Smoky Mountains* (first serialized in the

Atlantic), 1885, *Down the Ravine*, a boys' story serialized in *Wide Awake*, 1885, *In the Clouds*, 1886, *The Story of Keedon Bluffs*, 1888, *The Despot of Broomsedge Cove*, 1889, *In the "Stranger People's" Country*, 1891, *His Vanished Star*, 1894, *Phantoms of the Footbridge and Other Stories*, 1895, *The Mystery of Witch-Face Mountain and Other Stories*, 1895, *The Juggler*, 1897, and *The Young Mountaineers*, 1897. The revelation in 1885 of Charles Craddock's true identity to Thomas Bailey Aldrich, editor of the *Atlantic*, and subsequently to her reading public, added greatly to her celebrity and to interest in her writing. Her knowledge of mountaineer ways and dialect enabled her to make a large contribution to the local color movement in American fiction, but her work was frequently marred by formal shortcomings in diction and development.

Murfree's later works were historical fictions for the most part, and while they showed progress in the craft of writing they lacked the spontaneity and life of her earlier work. They included *The Story of Old Fort Loudon*, 1899, *The Bushwhackers and Other Stories*, 1899, *The Champion*, 1902, *A Spectre of Power*, 1903, *The Frontiersman*, 1904, *The Storm Centre*, 1905, *The Amulet*, 1906, *The Windfall*, 1907, *The Fair Mississippian*, 1908, *The Raid of the Guerilla and Other Stories*, 1912, *The Ordeal*, 1912, and *The Story of Duciehurst*, 1914. From 1889 she lived again in Murfreesboro, Tennessee, where she died on July 31, 1922.

Murray, Judith Sargent Stevens 1751–1820 writer

Born in Gloucester, Massachusetts, on May 1, 1751, Judith Sargent was the daughter of a wealthy shipowner and merchant and received an unusually good education for a girl of her time. In October 1769 she married John Stevens, a sea captain. She began writing in the 1770s, at first in verse but soon afterward in essay form, as the intellectual ferment of the Revolutionary period awakened thoughts on woman's place and rights. In 1784, under the pseudonym "Constantia," she published a few essays in a Boston magazine, the *Gentleman and Lady's Town and Country Magazine*, beginning with one called "Desultory Thoughts upon the Utility of Encouraging a Degree of Self-Complacency, Especially in Female Bosoms." Her husband died in 1786, and in October 1788 she married John Murray, pastor of the first Universalist meetinghouse in America, of whom the Sargent family had been among the earliest supporters.

In 1790 her poems began appearing in the *Massachusetts Magazine*, and from February 1792 to August 1794 she contributed a monthly column entitled "The Gleaner," in which she commented on affairs and public questions of the day and especially on her particular interest, equal education for women. In March 1795 her play *The Medium, or A Happy Tea Party* was produced at the Federal Street Theatre in Boston, probably the first at that theater by an American author. That play and her next, *The Traveller Returned*, produced in March 1796, were unsuccessful. In 1798 Murray's "Gleaner" columns were collected and published in three volumes under that title. In 1802–1805 she published a few more poems in Boston magazines. She edited her husband's *Letters and Sketches of Sermons*, 1812–1813, and, after his death in 1815, his *Records of the Life of the Rev. John Murray, Written by Himself, with a Continuation by Mrs. Judith Sargent Murray*, 1816. In the latter year she left Boston to live with her daughter in Natchez, Mississippi. She died there on July 6, 1820.

Mussey, Ellen Spencer 1850–1936 lawyer, educator and reformer

Born in Geneva, Ohio, on May 13, 1850, Ellen Spencer was the daughter of Platt Rogers Spencer, reformer and promoter of the widely used form of handwriting called Spencerian script. At twelve she began assisting in his penmanship school, and after his death two years later and a period of nervous ill health she lived with various relatives and attended Rice's Young Ladies' Seminary in Poughkeepsie, New York, take Erie Seminary (now College) in Painesville, Ohio, and Rockford Seminary (now College) in

Rockford, Illinois. In 1869 she moved to Washington, D.C., and took charge of the ladies' department of the Spencerian Business College operated by her brother Henry.

In June 1871 she married Reuben D. Mussey, a former Union army general and a successful lawyer. She began working in his law office in 1876, after he suffered a serious illness, and she continued helping him in legal matters until his death in 1892. Although she had had no formal training in the law — only the reading she had done under her husband's supervision — and despite being refused admission to the law schools of National University and Columbian College (now George Washington University), she obtained special consideration and was allowed to qualify for the bar by oral examination, which she passed in March 1893. In 1896 she was admitted to practice before the Supreme Court.

In that year Mussey began holding informal classes for three young women who wished to read law with her. After two years of these classes, in which she was assisted by Emma M. Gillett, another lawyer, and after the denial of admission to Columbian College of her students on grounds of sex, she and Gillett established and incorporated the Washington College of Law in April 1898. From then until 1913 Mussey served as dean of the college, which proved a success in training large numbers of women, as well as men, for the bar, and she also taught classes in constitutional law, contracts, wills, equity, and other topics.

Outside the college Mussey was active in numerous reforms. In 1894 she joined the campaign for improved married women's property rights legislation, and in 1895 she successfully urged the creation of a legislative committee by the District of Columbia Federation of Women's Clubs. As chairman of the committee she led the campaign that resulted in the Married Woman's Act, passed by Congress in June 1896, which equalized the status of married women with respect to property and guardianship of children. She was instrumental in securing a congressional appropriation in 1898 for the establishment of public kindergartens in the District, and she played a major role in the establishment of a juvenile court system.

She served on the District of Columbia board of education in 1906–1912, as vice-president general of the Daughters of the American Revolution in 1907–1909, and as editor of the DAR's *American Monthly Magazine* in 1911–1912. Her legal practice included serving as counsel to the American Red Cross and for 25 years to the legations of Sweden and Norway.

The stress of a suffrage march in Washington in March 1913 brought on a stroke, and later in the year she retired as dean of the Washington College of Law. She later resumed limited activity and in 1917 became chairman of the committee on the legal status of women of the National Council of Women. She drafted and with Maud Wood Park helped secure passage in 1922 of the Cable Act, which ended the automatic loss of citizenship for women who married foreign nationals. Mussey died in Washington, D.C., on April 21, 1936.

Nathan, Maud 1862–1946 reformer

Born in New York City on October 20, 1862, Maud Nathan was an elder sister of Annie Nathan (Meyer). She attended private schools in New York and a public high school in Green Bay, Wisconsin, graduating from the last in 1876. In April 1880 she married her cousin Frederick Nathan, a New York broker. Early in her married life she involved herself in such community service organizations as the New York Exchange for Women's Work and the Women's Auxiliary of the Civil Service Reform Association, and she served also as a director of the nursing school of Mount Sinai Hospital.

In 1890 Nathan joined Josephine Shaw Lowell and others in forming the New York City Consumers' League, a group devoted to organizing the marketplace power of consumers in order to induce reforms in the industrial system. Nathan's first project for the League was an investigation of the working conditions of women sales clerks. In 1897 she became president of the New York Consumers' League, and on the organization of the National Consumers' League the next year she was elected to the executive board. The New York League under her leadership provided unofficial factory and shop inspectors, published "white lists" of employers who met standards for wages and working conditions, and lobbied for legislative protections for workers. Lobbying the New York legislature from her position as a non-voter drew Nathan into the campaign for woman suffrage.

Nathan served as first vice-president of the New York Equal Suffrage League and in 1912 was chairman of the suffrage committee of the Progressive (Bull Moose) party. She spoke throughout the state on behalf of suffrage and on several occasions addressed international suffrage conferences. She was also active at various times in the Woman's Municipal League of New York, the New York and General Federations of Women's Clubs, the League for Political Education, the League of Women Voters, and the National Council of Jewish Women. She resigned as president of the New York Consumers' League in 1917 and was named honorary president for life.

Nathan wrote *The Story of an Epoch-Making Movement*, on the work of the League, 1926, and an autobiography, *Once Upon a Time and To-day*, 1933. She died in New York City on December 15, 1946.

Carry Nation

Nation, Carry Amelia Moore 1846–1911 reformer

Born on November 25, 1846, in Garrard County, Kentucky, Carry Moore attended school sporadically as her family moved back and forth between Kentucky, Missouri, and Texas. Her childhood was marked by the family's poverty, her mother's mental instability, and her own religious enthusiasm and frequent bouts of ill health. In November 1867 she married Charles Gloyd, an alcoholic who resisted her efforts to reform him. She left him after a few months, and a short time later he died, leaving her with a child and a hatred for liquor and saloons. Despite her limited schooling she secured a teaching certificate from the Missouri State Normal School (now Missouri State University, Warrensburg) and taught school in Holden, Missouri, for four years. In 1877 she married David Nation, a Warrensburg journalist and sometimes lawyer and minister, with whom she moved to Texas in 1879. About 1889 they moved to Medicine Lodge, Kansas, where in 1892 she organized the Barber County chapter of the Woman's Christian Temperance Union. Since 1880 Kansas had been a "dry" state, but prohibition had been openly flouted, and in 1890 antiprohibitionists had begun to agitate for repeal of the law.

Carry Nation conceived the theory that since establishments selling liquor were in violation of the law, they were outside the law's protection as well. Thus she began in 1899 a series of hatchet-swinging "missions" through saloons in towns and cities in Kansas. Alone or with a few hymn-singing supporters, she invaded "joints," castigated the "rummies" present, and concluded with a highly destructive "hatchetation" of the property. Her victims included the barroom of the Hotel Carey in Wichita and in 1901 the saloon of the Kansas state senate. (In that year her husband divorced her for desertion.)

Later Nation was ejected from the gallery of the U.S. Senate. Frequently arrested for disturbing the peace, she paid her fines from lecture fees and contributions and by selling souvenir hatchets. She published a few short-lived newsletters, called variously the *Smasher's Mail*, the *Hatchet*, and the *Home Defender*, and an autobiography, *The Use and Need of the Life of Carry A. Nation*, in 1904. Her hatchetation period was brief but brought her national notoriety. She was for a time much in demand as a temperance lecturer; she customarily appeared in her deaconess's garb, holding a hatchet. Later she appeared in vaudeville, at Coney Island, and briefly in 1903 in *Hatchetation*, an adaptation of *Ten Nights in a Bar-room*. She settled in Guthrie, Oklahoma Territory, in 1905, and in Boone County, Arkansas, in 1909. Her lecture tours were shortened by declining health, to which the numerous physical assaults she had endured may have contributed. She died after a period of hospitalization in Leavenworth, Kansas, on June 9, 1911. Despite her spectacular campaign, the later enactment of national prohibition was largely the result of the efforts of more conventional reformers, who had been reluctant to support her.

Navratilova, Martina 1956– tennis player

Martina Navratilova

Born on October 18, 1956, near Prague, Czechoslovakia, Martina Navratilova grew up in a tennis-playing family — her grandmother had ranked #2 in the country before World War II, and both her stepfather and her mother served as tennis administrators for the government. At eight years of age, she played in her first tournament and, despite comments that she was too small to compete, she reached the semi-finals in the 12-and-under category. By age 14, she had won her first national title in the 14-and-under age division. Within two years, she had won three national championships and the national junior title to become the number one women's player in the country.

In 1973 she participated in an eight-week winter tournament sponsored by the United States Tennis Association. She played against Chris Evert for the first time (and lost), in Akron, Ohio, but did well enough in the tournament to qualify for the draws of major events. In 1974 she won her first Virginia Slims tournament as well as Rookie of the Year honors from *Tennis Magazine*. In 1975 she led the Czechoslovakian team to its first Federation Cup.

Facing increasing interference on the part of Czechoslovakian tennis officials who wished to control her activities and playing decisions, she defected from Czechoslovakia on September 7, 1975. She won her first Wimbledon singles title in 1978. Afterwards she was recognized as one of the best serve and volley grass court players ever: she won Wimbledon a record nine times (Helen Wills Moody's eight Wimbledon victories had stood as a record since 1938).

She was at the top of her game in the 1980s. She earned 15 Grand Slam singles titles and 25 Grand Slam doubles titles. In 1983 she posted 86 match wins and a single loss and took 16 titles. She completed a singles, non-calendar year Grand Slam sweep at the 1984 French Open during a run of six consecutive Grand Slam victories. Between 1983 and 1985 she set a record 109-match doubles win-streak with partner Pam Shriver, including eight Grand Slam titles in a row. In 1984 she had the longest consecutive streak of singles victories (74 matches). She won a rare Triple Crown in 1987 at the U.S. Open, taking the mixed doubles (with Emilio Sanchez) and the women's doubles (with Pam Shriver), as well as the women's singles titles.

In a professional career spanning more than twenty years, she exhibited extraordinary endurance at the highest level of performance: she played more than 1,600 career matches, including more singles matches than any other player, male or female. She held records for most matches won, most tournament titles, and most doubles titles. She finished the year as the #1 woman seven times between 1978 and 1992. She was ranked in the top five for nineteen years in a row. In her last appearance at Wimbledon in 1994, she reached the finals again but lost to rising star Conchita Martinez.

The sports community recognized her contributions with honors such as Female Athlete of the Decade (the 1980s) by the National Sports Review, United Press International, and the Associated Press. She also was awarded the Women's Tennis Association Player of the Year a record seven times.

In her personal life, she was one of the first sports superstars to live a publicly gay lifestyle. In the early 1990s she became increasingly vocal in the gay-rights movement, speaking at the April 1993 gay rights rally in Washington, D.C., joining the ACLU in a lawsuit against antigay legislation in Colorado, and endorsing fund-raising efforts by the National Gay and Lesbian Task Force.

Nestor, Agnes 1880–1948 labor leader

Born in Grand Rapids, Michigan, on June 24, 1880, Agnes Nestor attended public and parochial schools. In 1897 she moved with her family to Chicago, where she went to work in a glove factory. In the spring of 1898 the women glove-makers in her factory, encouraged by their unionized male colleagues, went out on strike. Agnes Nestor, articulate and stalwart in spite of her frail appearance, quickly emerged as the spokesman of the group, and in ten days of picketing all demands were met, including an end to "machine rent," which operators had been forced to pay back to the company from wages, and the establishment of a union shop.

In 1902 Nestor led her fellow women workers out of the men's union, becoming president of the newly organized women's local, and later in the year she took part in forming the International Glove Workers Union. She was elected a national vice-president of the union in 1903, a post she held until 1906; she served as secretary-treasurer from 1906 to 1913, general president in 1913–1915, vice-president again from 1915 to 1938, and director of research and education from 1938 to her death. From 1904 she was active also in the Chicago Women's Trade Union League, of which she was president from 1913 to 1948, and from 1907 she sat on the executive board of the National Women's Trade Union League. In addition to her duties to her own union, for which she gained a reputation as a highly informed and skilled negotiator, she helped organize unions in other industries, notably the needle trades, and took part in the garment workers' strikes of 1909 and 1910–1911.

Nestor was also a very effective lobbyist on behalf of social legislation. The passage of the Illinois ten-hour-day law of 1909 was largely her work, although it represented for her only a compromise on the road to the eight-hour day, which was finally achieved in 1937. She worked for child-labor, minimum wage, maternity health, and woman-suffrage legislation as well. She served on the National Commission on Vocational Education in 1914 and on the Woman's Committee, of the U.S. Council of National Defense during World War I. She died in Chicago on December 28, 1948.

Nevada, Emma 1859–1940 singer

Born on February 7, 1859, in Alpha, near Nevada City, California, Emma Wixom grew up in Nevada City and in Austin, Nevada. From an early age singing was her greatest joy, and in childhood she sang for miners and in church. She graduated from Mills Seminary (now College) in 1876. In Vienna on a European study tour in 1877 she met and was taken as a pupil by Mathilde Marchesi, with whom she remained for three years.

She made her operatic debut under the name Emma Nevada in *La Sonnambula* at Her Majesty's Theatre in London in May 1880. She was quickly recognized as one of the great coloratura sopranos of the day. Her voice, while small, was remarkably flute-like, and her art concealed what defects it suffered. For two years she sang in Trieste, Florence, and

Genoa, where Verdi is said to have heard her and arranged for her appearance at La Scala in Milan. In May 1883 she opened at the Opéra Comique in Paris in *La Perle du Brésil.* At the Opéra Comique she vied with fellow American Marie van Zandt for popular honors. Sir Alexander Mackenzie's oratorio *The Rose of Sharon*, 1884, contained a part written especially for her; she sang it at Covent Garden, London, that year.

Late in 1884 Nevada returned to America in the opera company of Colonel James H. Mapleson as alternate coloratura to Adelina Patti. She sang *La Sonnambula* at the New York Academy of Music in November 1884 and then toured the country with Mapleson's company. She received a particularly enthusiastic welcome in California, In 1885 she returned to Europe. In October of that year she married Dr. Raymond S. Palmer, who was thereafter her manager. She continued to tour Europe for several years. She gave command performances for Queen Victoria and later Edward VII and was a particular favorite of Queen Christina of Spain. Her performances in Madrid and Seville were usually the occasion of outbursts of adulation.

Nevada's favorite roles were in *Lakmé*, *Faust*, *Les Contes d'Hoffmann*, *Mireille*, *Il Barbiere di Siviglia*, *Mignon* and *Lucia di Lammermoor*. She made tours of the United States in 1899, 1901–1902, and 1907. After a final *Lakmé* in Berlin in 1910 she retired from the stage. For some years thereafter she taught voice in England. She died in Liverpool, England, on June 20, 1940.

Nevelson, Louise 1900–1988 sculptor

Born in Kiev, Russia, on September 23, 1900 (or perhaps 1899), Louise Berliawsky came to the United States with her parents in 1905 and grew up in Rockland, Maine. She graduated from high school in 1918, and in 1920 she married Charles S. Nevelson, with whom she settled in New York City. (They were later divorced.) In New York she began taking lessons in voice, dramatics, and painting, gradually concentrating on the last. In 1928–1930 she was a student at the Art Students' League, and in 1931 she studied under Hans Hofmann in Munich. In 1932–1933 she was an assistant to Diego Rivera, who was then engaged in painting a mural for the New Workers' School. In the latter year her own works of sculpture were first exhibited in New York. She was represented in a group show at the Brooklyn Museum in 1935 and had her first one-woman show at the Nierendorf Gallery in 1940. Her early works in stone, plaster, terra cotta, metals, and wood displayed striking originality in design and handling of materials, and her larger abstract pieces often revealed in architectural affinity for Aztec or Mayan forms.

By the middle 1950s Nevelson's characteristic sculptures had evolved: "assemblages," multilayered, complex, and frequently large, built up of wood and sometimes other materials (typically in the form of found objects) and painted white, black, or gold. On her use of boxes and square shapes she said, "I was born with that objective form in me and I never wanted to try to improve it." Her several shows at the Nierendorf were followed by exhibits at the Norlyst and Grand Central Moderns galleries, from which leading museums began to acquire her works for their permanent collections. She was represented in the "Nature in Abstraction" show at the Whitney Museum, New York City, in 1958, in the "Sixteen Americans" show at the Museum of Modern Art in 1959, at the Venice Biennale in 1962, at Documenta III in Kassel, Germany, in 1964, and in numerous other shows. In 1967 a major retrospective of her work was mounted at the Whitney.

Among Nevelson's major commissions were those for sculptures for the South Mall, Albany, New York, 1968; for the World Trade Center, New York City, 1978; and for St. Peter's Lutheran Church, New York, where she created the Erol Beker Chapel of the Good Shepherd in 1977. Titles of her more celebrated pieces included "Black Majesty," "Sky Cathedral," "Royal Game," "Homage to 6,000,000," "America — New York Blue," "Night Zag I," "Homage to the World," "Tropical Rain Forest," and "Mrs. N's

Palace," the last a room-size sculptural environment exhibited in 1977 after 13 years of work on it. In 1979 she created an environment of her black sculpture in Louise Nevelson Plaza in Manhattan. She worked continually until her death, completing a 35-foot black steel sculpture in 1988 for the National Institutes of Health in Bethesda, Maryland. Louise Nevelson was widely known for her unique costumes and personal adornments as well as for her other artistic achievements. Acknowledged as a major innovator in the field of sculpture, she was the recipient of numerous awards and honors for her work. She died on April 17, 1988, at her home in New York City.

Newcomb, Josephine Louise Le Monnier 1816–1901 philanthropist

Born in Baltimore on October 31, 1816, Josephine Le Monnier was the daughter of a wealthy businessman and was educated largely in Europe. After the death of her mother in 1831 and the decline of the family's fortune shortly thereafter, she lived with her father and sister in New Orleans. In December 1845 she married Warren Newcomb, a prosperous wholesale grocer of Louisville, Kentucky. For some years they lived by turns in New Orleans, Louisville, and New York City. Newcomb retired from active business in 1863 so that they might devote themselves to the rearing and education of their daughter, Harriott Sophie Newcomb. He died in 1866, leaving a fortune and Sophie to Josephine Newcomb. Sophie died at fifteen, in 1870, and after a period of despondency Newcomb set about finding a suitable memorial for her. Astute business sense enabled her to increase her wealth, and she made sizable donations to Washington and Lee University, to the Confederate Orphan Home in Charleston, South Carolina, and to other institutions. In October 1886, at the suggestion of an old friend, she gave $100,000 to the newly established Tulane University in New Orleans for the creation of the H. Sophie Newcomb Memorial College for women. Newcomb College opened in September 1887 and proved a success as the nation's first self-sufficient women's college connected with a men's college. Over the next several years Newcomb's gifts to the college totaled about $1 million. She died in New York City on April 7, 1901. Her will named Newcomb College residuary legatee, a bequest that amounted to about $2.5 million.

Ney, Elisabet 1833–1907 sculptor

Born in Münster, Westphalia (now Germany), on January 26, 1833, Franzisca Bernadina Wilhelmina Elisabeth Ney was the daughter of a stonecutter from whom she absorbed artistic ambitions. After attending Catholic schools and studying drawing privately in her home city, she entered, over her parents' misgivings, the Royal Bavarian Academy of Fine Arts in Munich. In 1855 she went to Berlin to study with Christian Daniel Rauch, through whom she was introduced to the literati and cultural leaders of that city. She exhibited her work successfully at the Berlin Exposition of 1856, and on the death of Rauch in 1857 she took over some of his unfinished commissions. Busts of Arthur Schopenhauer, a personal friend, and of King George V of Hanover established her fame. After three years in Münster working on a number of busts and statues she was married in November 1863 to Edmund Duncan Montgomery, whom she had met as a student in Munich. She retained her own name (she had by then dropped the *h* from Elisabeth) and for some years often denied she was married out of a sense that marriage somehow contradicted her stoutly feminist beliefs. They lived for a time in Madeira and then in Rome, where she prevailed upon Garibaldi to sit for a bust. In Rome she also did a bust of Bismarck on commission from Wilhelm I of Prussia, and she executed a colossal "Prometheus Bound." Her popularity grew rapidly. In late 1867 she returned to Munich as court sculptor to Ludwig 11 of Bavaria, by whom she and Montgomery were installed in a villa. The apparent irregularity of their living together, along with some possible involvement in intrigue with Bismarck, forced them to leave Bavaria in 1870. They chose to emigrate to the United States. They settled first in Thomasville, Georgia, where they hoped to establish a colony of like-minded "enlightened" émigrés, but in 1873 they settled on Liendo Plantation near Hempstead, some 40 miles from Houston, Texas. Elisabet Ney virtually abandoned sculpture for nearly 20 years to devote herself to the task of rearing their son to be a genius in her own mold; her efforts proved self-defeating.

In 1890 Ney again turned to her art with commissions for statues of Stephen F. Austin and Samuel Houston to be exhibited at the World's Columbian Exposition in Chicago three years later. In 1891 she opened a studio in Austin, Texas, where she was able to bring her forceful personality and attractive unconventionality to bear on prominent Texans to win further commissions. She made several statues of prominent Texans: two more of Houston, for the state capitol and for Statuary Hall of the U.S. Capitol; two of Austin for similar placement; of Albert Sidney Johnston for the Texas State Cemetery; and several of former governors and senators. Her last major private work was a statue of Lady Macbeth. It is generally conceded that the brilliant career she early seemed destined for was thwarted largely by her own unbending will. She died in Austin, Texas, on June 29, 1907.

Nicholls, Rhoda Holmes 1854–1930 artist and art instructor

Born in Coventry, England, on March 28, 1854, Rhoda Carleton Marion Holmes was the daughter of a vicar. She early displayed a talent for art and was sent to London to study at the Bloomsbury School of Art and then at the Kensington Museum. She sacrificed a Queen's scholarship to travel instead to Rome, where she became a member of the Circello Artistico, a group of artists of various nationalities who shared mutual criticisms. Her paintings soon won wide recognition and were exhibited in Rome and Turin, at the Royal Academy in London, and elsewhere. After three years on her brother's ostrich farm in South Africa she returned to England, where in 1884 she married Burr H. Nicholls, an American painter she had met in Italy.

In the United States Rhoda Nicholls quickly established a reputation, winning medals at the New York Prize Fund Exhibition in 1886, the World's Columbian Exposition in Chicago in 1893, the Atlanta Exposition in 1895, and other major shows. Several of her watercolors were widely reproduced, notably "Those Evening Bells." Other well known paintings included "Cherries," "A Rose," "The Scarlet Letter," "Searching the Scriptures," "Prima Vera, Venezia," and "Water Lilies." In addition to her own work, she taught art classes for many years at the William Chase School in Shinnecock, Long Island, and later it the Art Students' League in New York City, and she conducted summer classes in Gloucester and Provincetown, Massachusetts, and Kennebunkport, Maine. She also served on the staffs of the *Art Interchange* and the *Art Amateur* and was coeditor of *Palette and Brush*. In 1924 a major show of her watercolors was mounted at the Corcoran Gallery in Washington, D.C. She died in Stamford, Connecticut, on September 7, 1930.

Nichols, Clarina Irene Howard 1810–1885 journalist and reformer

Born on January 25, 1810, in West Townshend, Vermont, Clarina Howard was educated in local public schools and for a year at an academy. From April 1830 until her divorce in February 1843 she was married to Justin Carpenter, a Baptist preacher with whom she lived in Herkimer, New York. There about 1835 she apparently opened a girls' seminary. She returned to her Vermont home in 1839 and the next year began writing for the *Windham County Democrat* of Brattleboro. She married the newspaper's publisher, George W. Nichols, in March 1843. From that year she was editor of the *Democrat*, and over the next few years she gradually broadened the paper's range to include literary pieces and editorials in support of various reform movements. In 1847 a series of her editorials on the subject of married women's property rights led directly to the passage of legislation by the Vermont legislature providing for such rights. Subsequent clarifications and broadenings of the law were passed with her support in 1849 and 1850. In 1852 her campaign to secure the vote for women in district school elections, which she carried personally to the legislature, failed to win the requisite legislation.

From about 1850 Nichols was in increasing demand as a lecturer and debater, mainly on questions of women's rights. She traveled as far afield as Wisconsin, where she campaigned in 1853 for a state prohibition law. The *Democrat* ceased publication late in 1853, and in 1854 Nichols and her two older sons accompanied a New England Emigrant Aid Company party bound for Kansas Territory. She returned shortly to Vermont and the next year brought her husband out to Kansas. He died in the summer of 1855, and after yet another trip to Vermont to arrange the estate, during which time she also lectured on the problems of slavery and statehood in Kansas, Nichols settled in Wyandotte County, Kansas. She contributed articles on women's rights to the Lawrence *Herald of Freedom* and the Topeka *Kansas Tribune* and traveled and spoke throughout the territory, from early 1859 on behalf of the newly founded Kansas Woman's Rights Association. She lobbied the Wyandotte constitutional convention ceaselessly, and it was largely owing to her efforts that the final document granted to women equal rights to education, to custody of their children, and to the vote in local school matters. She campaigned for ratification of the constitution and in 1860, as the representative of the Kansas Woman's Rights Association, addressed a joint session of the first state legislature on the need for a married women's property law. (Such a law was enacted in 1867.)

In December 1863 Nichols moved to Washington, D.C., where she worked as a clerk in the Quartermaster's Department until February 1865 and then became matron of a home operated in Georgetown by the National Association for the Relief of Destitute Colored Women and Children. In 1866 she returned to Kansas, and in 1867 she joined Susan B. Anthony in the unsuccessful campaign to achieve full woman suffrage in the state. Late in 1871 she moved to Mendocino County, California, where she contributed articles to the local *Rural Press*. She died in Potter Valley, California, on January 11, 1885.

Nicholson, Eliza Jane Poitevent Holbrook 1849–1896 poet and journalist

Born in Hancock County, Mississippi, on March 11, 1849, Eliza Jane Poitevent completed her schooling with three years at the Female Seminary of Amite, Louisiana. From her graduation in 1867 she began contributing poems to various periodicals under the name "Pearl Rivers." Her verses appeared in *The South*, the New York *Home Journal and Ledger*, the *New Orleans Times*, and the *New Orleans Picayune*. In 1870 she accepted the post of literary editor of the *Picayune*,over family objections. In May 1872 she married Alva M. Holbrook, who until the preceding January had been owner and editor of the paper. She published in 1873 a volume of her collected *Lyrics*. Late in 1874 the syndicate to whom Holbrook had sold the *Picayune* failed, and the paper reverted to him. Little more than a year later, in January 1876, he died, leaving the paper and its heavy burden of debt to his widow. After due consideration Holbrook rejected the conventional advice that she liquidate and instead decided to take over active management of the *Picayune*. She thus became the first woman publisher of a daily newspaper in the Deep South. With a firm commitment to sound, principled journalism, she set about restoring the paper to solvency. Aided by her business manager, George Nicholson, whom she married in June 1878, she cleared the debt and increased the *Picayune*'s circulation manyfold. Eliza Nicholson retained editorial control and introduced a number of circulation-building innovations, including departments of interest to women and children and a Sunday society column that at first dismayed conservative New Orleans. Advice columns, comics, and quality literary features were added later. The *Picayune* became, under the guidance of Nicholson and her husband, a prosperous enterprise. In 1884 she was elected president of the Women's National Press Association. In later years she resumed writing poetry. "Hagar" and "Leah," long dramatic monologues, were published in *Cosmopolitan* in 1893 and 1894. She died in New Orleans on February 15, 1896.

Nielsen, Alice 1870?–1943 singer

Born in Nashville, Tennessee, on June 7 probably in 1870 (some sources give 1868 or 1876), Alice Nielsen grew up in Warrensburg and then Kansas City, Missouri. She was educated in parochial schools and from an early age sang in the streets for pennies. She later sang in a church choir and received some voice instruction from a local teacher. About 1886 she had the opportunity to sing in a touring juvenile production of *The Mikado*. Her marriage to Benjamin Nentwig, a church organist, in 1889 was short-lived. In 1892 she and three other singers formed the "Chicago Church Choir Company," and after an unsuccessful tour through Missouri and a stint at the Eden Musée in St. Joseph, Missouri, with that group, she joined the Burton Stanley traveling opera company. In Oakland, California, she appeared as Yum-Yum in the Stanley production of *The Mikado* in 1893. In 1894, after a period at the Wigwam, a San Francisco music hall, she joined the Tivoli Opera Company, with whom she made her grand operatic debut in *Lucia di Lammermoor*.

In 1896 Nielsen obtained an audition with the manager of the Bostonians, the nation's leading light opera company, which was then touring California. She won a position with the company and gradually worked her way up from understudy and ingenue roles to the female lead in Reginald De Koven's *Robin Hood*. She was chosen by Victor Herbert's wife to sing the lead in his *The Serenade*, which premiered in Cleveland in February 1897 and opened in New York City the next month. Her success in that operetta induced her to leave the Bostonians and to form the Alice Nielsen Comic Opera Company. Her greatest successes with her own company were Herbert's *The Fortune Teller*, in which she opened in Toronto in September 1898 and in New York later in the month, and his *The Singing Girl*, which she took from Montreal to New York in October 1899.

In 1901 Nielsen took *The Fortune Teller* to London, and during its successful run there she was encouraged by the impresario Henry Russell to study for grand opera. Financed by an English patroness, she studied in Rome for two years and made her debut in December 1903 at the Bellini Theatre, Naples, in *Faust* (according to most sources, although she herself later remembered it as *La Traviata*). After an engagement at the San Carlo Theatre, Naples, she made her London debut in the spring of 1904 in a Covent Garden presentation of *Don Giovanni*. Subsequently she sang in *Le Nozze di Figaro*, *La Bohème*, and *Rigoletto* there, and in 1905, under Russell's management, she sang *Il Barbiere di Siviglia* and *Don Pasquale*, at the New Waldorf Theatre. Under Sam and Lee Shubert she toured the United States in *Don Pasquale*, beginning with a New York debut in November 1905. A second American tour, with the San Carlo Opera Company, occupied 1907–1908.

In 1909 Nielsen joined the Boston Opera Company, with which she remained for five years, during which she sang in the American premiere of Debussy's *L'Enfant Prodigue*, in November 1910 and the world premiere of Frederick S. Converse's *The Sacrifice* in March 1911. During that period she also sang occasionally with the Metropolitan Opera Company. She returned to light opera in the autumn of 1917 in Rudolf Friml's *Kitty Darlin'* at the Casino, New York City. Her last appearances were a series of concert recitals with the Boston Symphony Orchestra between 1921 and 1923. She then lived in retirement in New York City until her death there on March 8, 1943.

Nordica, Lillian 1857–1914 opera singer

Born in Farmington, Maine, on December 12, 1857, Lillian Norton grew up from the age of six in Boston. At fourteen she began studying voice at the New England Conservatory of Music, and after her graduation in 1876 she continued her studies for a time in

New York City. She made her formal debut in concert with Patrick S. Gilmore's band at Madison Square Garden in September 1876, and she toured with the band in America and Europe until 1878. She then resumed her studies in Paris with François Delsarte and Emilio Belari and then in Milan with Antonio Sangiovanni, who secured for her an operatic debut in *Don Giovanni* at the Manzoni Theatre, Milan, in March 1879 and who gave her her stage name. She sang for two seasons in St. Petersburg, appeared in Danzig, Berlin, and other cities, and made her debut at the Paris Opéra in July 1882, when she sang the part of Marguerite in Gounod's *Faust* to great acclaim.

Having become the first American operatic singer to win renown in the demanding houses of Europe, Nordica returned home under the management of English impresario Colonel James H. Mapleson. She sang Marguerite in her American operatic debut at the New York Academy of Music in November 1883. Thereafter she was one of the most sought-after sopranos in America, in England, and on the Continent. Her London debut occurred at Covent Garden in March 1887 in *La Traviata*. Between operatic engagements she sang frequently in concerts and oratorios. In 1893 she became a regular singer at the Metropolitan Opera. Not content with her command of much of the French and Italian repertoires, a short time later she left the stage for several months to study Wagnerian opera. Her appearance in *Lohengrin* under Cosima Wagner's direction at Bayreuth in 1894 was a success, and her Isolde to Jean de Reszke's Tristan at the Metropolitan in November 1895 was a triumph.

Despite Nordica somewhat undeveloped dramatic bent and her clear, lyric soprano, her great successes in subsequent years were usually in Wagnerian roles, notably those of Elsa, Isolde, and the three Brunnhildes. The great success she enjoyed was largely the product of tireless effort. In November 1909 she appeared in the *Gioconda* that inaugurated the Boston Opera House. Her final appearance at the Met was in *Tristan und Isolde*, with Toscanini conducting, in December 1909. She continued to appear elsewhere in the United States and abroad in opera and in concert. Her final full operatic performance was a Boston production of *Tristan* in March 1913, and her last American appearance was in concert in Reno, Nevada, in June of that year. She then set out on a concert tour that was to take her around the world. She appeared in Australia in November, but shortly afterward her ship grounded in the Gulf of Papua in December. She contracted pneumonia and died of complications of the disease in Batavia, Java, on May 10, 1914. *Lillian Nordica's Hints to Singers*, which included many of her letters, was published in 1923.

Norman, Jessye 1945– opera singer

Born on September 15, 1945, in Augusta, Georgia, Jessye Norman was one of five children in a prosperous upper-middle class family. Both her mother and grandmother were pianists and her father sang in Augusta's Mt. Calvary Baptist Church, the site of Norman's earliest singing experiences. At age 16, she traveled to Philadelphia for her first important vocal competition. Though she won only words of encouragement, she stopped on her way home to sing for Carolyn Grant, the head of the voice department at Howard University. Grant offered her a full scholarship, and, two years later, Norman received her first formal voice training there and earned a bachelor's degree with honors. She continued her studies at the Peabody Conservatory in Baltimore with Alice Duschak and then at the University of Michigan with Elizabeth Mannion and Pierre Bernac.

While still a graduate student, she won the 1968 International Music Competition in Munich, making such an impression that the Berlin Deutsche Oper immediately offered her a three-year contract. She made her operatic debut with that company in 1969 as Elisabeth in *Tannhäuser*.

Norman eventually resigned when she saw that she was expected to sing roles without regard for her particular talents, experience or temperament. Such a bold decision by a young singer was characteristic of the artistic self-determination Norman exhibited throughout her career. In a world where the opera diva is revered, she has concentrated much of her energy on performing recitals and concerts. Norman was noted for her thorough scholarship and her ability to project drama through her voice — qualities that contributed to her enormous success as a recitalist. Her varied repertoire in these settings included Schubert, Mahler, Wagner, Brahms, Satie, Messaien and contemporary American composers.

Norman's extraordinary artistry and vocal gifts combined to make her one of the most versatile and internationally acclaimed singers of her time. During 1976 and 1977, several years after her major recital debuts in New York and London, Norman performed extensively throughout North America. She also toured in South America, the Middle East, Australia, Israel, and Europe.

She chose her operatic roles with great care, not only for the music, but because "to portray a character of . . . depth is more interesting to me than simply singing a pretty tune." Her commanding stage presence and rich, powerful soprano lent themselves to the larger-than-life heroines she favored in opera. Her operatic debuts included: the title role in Meyerbeer's *L'Africaine* in Florence in 1971; in *Aïda* at La Scala; and Cassandra in Berlioz's *Les Troyens* at Covent Garden in 1972.

That Norman's career choices and her huge talent have served her well in the opera world was exemplified by the auspiciousness of her 1983 debut at the Metropolitan Opera. She appeared on opening night of the Metropolitan's centennial season in a monumental production of Berloz's *Les Troyens*. She also opened the 1989 opera season in Chicago as Gluck's Alcestis, and that same year returned to the Met stage for an historic performance of that company's first single character production, *Erwartung* by Schoenberg.

Many recordings and television broadcasts bear her name; they span the breadth of her operatic and concert repertory, including some explorations of American spirituals and popular music. Known for insisting upon times of complete solitude, she greatly valued her privacy, often limiting discussions of personal matters in her interviews with the media.

Normand, Mabel Ethelreid 1893?–1930 actor

Born probably in either Rhode Island or Massachusetts, probably on November 10, 1893, Mabel Normand grew up after 1900 on Staten Island, New York. Much of her early life is obscure, including whatever scant schooling she may have received. About the age of fifteen she became an artist's model for, among others, James Montgomery Flagg. In 1909, despite her entire lack of dramatic experience, she succeeded in getting a job at the fledgling Biograph motion picture studio in New York City. There she formed a liaison with director Mack Sennett that lasted several years. In 1912 she left Biograph with Sennett and joined his new Keystone Film Company in California. While working on a Sennett film about 1913 she is said to have succumbed to impulse and thrown a custard pie at Ben Turpin, thus creating what soon became a classic film comedy bit.

Petite, impish, and gifted, Normand was the female star of the Keystone company, and when Charlie Chaplin joined it late in 1913 he learned much basic filmcraft from her. She was his leading lady in 11 films, mostly one- and two-reelers, and it was in *Mabel's Strange Predicament*, 1914, that Chaplin first appeared in his "little tramp" persona. There followed *Mabel's Busy Day*, *Mabel's Married Life*, and the great *Tillie's Punctured Romance*, 1914, in which they were joined by Marie Dressler. After Chaplin left Keystone for Essanay, Roscoe "Fatty" Arbuckle became her partner in a successful series of comedies. In 1916 Sennett organized the Mabel Normand Feature Film Company for her. The firm produced *Mickey*, which after long delays, was released in 1918 and was enormously successful. In 1917 Mabel Normand left Keystone to join the new Goldwyn Film Company, where she made such movies as *The Venus Model*, 1918, *Back to the Woods*, 1918, *Sis Hopkins*, 1919, and *Upstairs*, 1919. In 1920 Goldwyn released her from her contract — she had become increasingly difficult to work with as she explored the prerogatives of stardom — and she rejoined Sennett to make *Molly O'*, 1921.

The murder in February 1922 of William Desmond Taylor, a Hollywood director and a friend of Normand's, was the beginning of the end of her career. She was admittedly the last to see him alive, only moments before the murder, and while the case remained unsolved, the publicity, together with rumors of drug addiction and blackmail, roused a public outcry for censorship of her films. She made *Head Over Heels*, 1922, *Oh, Mabel Behave*, 1922, *Suzanne*, 1922, and *The Extra Girl*, 1923, for Sennett, but a second scandal ended her career. Her chauffeur shot a wealthy young suitor in her apartment in January 1924, reportedly in a jealous argument over her. She made one unsuccessful attempt at legitimate theater in 1925, and in 1926 she appeared in a few Hal Roach comedy shorts, but the public would no longer accept her. She died of tuberculosis on February 23, 1930, in Monrovia, California.

Norton, Eleanor Holmes 1938– lawyer, politician and educator

Born on April 8, 1938, in Washington, D.C., Eleanor Holmes was the daughter of a schoolteacher, Vela, and a civil servant, Coleman Holmes. Of her childhood, Norton said that "my sisters and I had a sense that a little girl can grow up to be somebody." After attending high school in Washington, D.C., Holmes went on to Antioch College in Yellow Springs, Ohio. She received an M.A. in American Studies and a doctor of jurisprudence from Yale University in 1963 and 1964, respectively.

In late 1964 Holmes began clerking for a federal judge in Philadelphia, where she met her future husband, Edward Norton; they married a year later. (She later said of her marriage "nobody would have married me who didn't want a woman with a career.") The Nortons moved to New York City, where she became the assistant legal director of the American Civil Liberties Union (ACLU). She worked there 5 years, specializing in freedom of speech cases. She gained national exposure in 1968 when she represented former Alabama Governor George Wallace, who was denied permission to hold a political rally at Shea Stadium. According to her, "if people like George Wallace are denied free expression, then the same thing can happen to black people. Black people understand this."

The first woman to head the New York City Commission on Human Rights, she was first appointed in 1970 by Mayor John Lindsay and again in 1974 by Mayor Abraham Beame. In 1973 she helped to found the National Black Feminist Organization, and in 1975 she coauthored *Sex Discrimination and the Law: Causes and Remedies*. In 1977, President Carter appointed her to chair of the Equal Employment Opportunity Center (EEOC), a position she held until 1981.

In 1988, while a tenured professor at the Georgetown University Law Center, she was asked by the Reverend Jesse Jackson to handle the platform discussions for his presidential campaign. Two years later she campaigned successfully for the congressional seat representing the District of Columbia, becoming one of only three black women in Congress. She has been awarded dozens of honorary doctorate degrees.

Noyes, Clara Dutton 1869–1936 nurse and educator

Born in Port Deposit, Maryland, on October 3, 1869, Clara Noyes was educated in private schools. She graduated from the Johns Hopkins Hospital School of Nursing in 1896 and remained there for a year as head nurse. In 1897 she was appointed superintendent of the nurses training school of the New England Hospital for Women and Children in Boston. Four years later she became superintendent of St. Luke's Hospital in New

Bedford, Massachusetts, where she oversaw a major expansion of the hospital and a thorough revision of nurses training. From 1910 to 1916 she was general superintendent of training schools for the Bellevue and Allied Hospitals in New York City. During her tenure there she established the nation's first hospital school for midwives. From 1912 to 1915 she was president of the National League of Nursing Education. In 1916, on the recommendation of Jane A. Delano, she took charge of the bureau of nursing of the American Red Cross's department of military relief. In that post she was in immediate command of the vast mobilization and deployment of nurses for field service in the 54 base hospitals and numerous relief expeditions organized for World War I. In 1918 she became director of field nursing in the newly organized department of nursing, and in August 1919 she succeeded Delano as director of the Red Cross department of nursing, a post she held for the rest of her life. She also served from 1919 as chairman of the National Committee of the Red Cross Nursing Service, in 1918–1922 as president of the American Nurses Association, and as first vice-president of the International Council of Nurses. Among the many honors accorded her for her work in nurses education and in World War I were the Patriotic Service Medal of the National Institute of Social Sciences in 1918, the Florence Nightingale Medal of the International Red Cross in 1923, and the French Medal of Honor in 1929. She died in Washington, D.C., on June 3, 1936.

Nuttall, Zelia Maria Magdalena 1857–1933 archaeologist

Born in San Francisco on September 6, 1857, Zelia Nuttall was the daughter of a physician. From the age of eight she lived with her family in various parts of Europe, and she was educated largely by tutors and for a year and a half at Bedford College for Women in London. In 1876 the family returned to San Francisco. In 1880 Zelia married Alphonse L. Pinart, a French ethnologist from whom she was soon separated and in 1888 divorced. Through her mother's Mexican ancestry she had early developed an interest in that country, and on a visit there in 1884 she studied some archaeological artifacts. Her paper on the small terra-cotta heads found at Teotihuacan was published in 1886 in the *American Journal of Archaeology*. The paper attracted attention in scholarly circles and won her appointment as honorary special assistant in Mexican archaeology at Harvard's Peabody Museum and, the next year, a fellowship in the American Association for the Advancement of Science. From 1886 to 1899 she lived in Europe, headquartered in Dresden but traveling widely for study and to attend scholarly congresses.

The results of Nuttall's wide-ranging investigations were published in *The Fundamental Principles of Old and New World Civilizations*, 1901, in which she traced cultural parallels between ancient Middle Eastern and American civilizations and hypothesized that culture may have been carried to the Western Hemisphere by Phoenician explorers; in *Codex Nuttall*, 1902, a facsimile of a pictographic historical record of ancient Mexico that she had discovered in a private library in England; and in *The Book of the Life of the Ancient Mexicans*, 1903, which printed in facsimile the Codex Magliabecchiano, a similar pictographic work that she had found in Florence. After a brief stay in the United States in 1899–1902 she settled in the Casa Alvarado in Coyoacán, a suburb of Mexico City. There she continued her investigations. In 1904 she was field director of the Reid-Crocker archaeological mission from the University of California, where she had already served as an adviser to the department of anthropology. In 1908 she was made honorary professor in the Museo Nacional of Mexico. From 1911 to 1917 she was abroad during Mexico's revolutionary disturbances, and during that time she published *New Light on Drake: Documents Relating to His Voyage of Circumnavigation, 1577–1580*, 1914. Much of her published work was in the form of monographs published by the Peabody Museum and the Smithsonian Institution. In her later years she became widely known as a hostess at Casa Alvarado. She died there on April 12, 1933.

Nutting, Mary Adelaide 1858–1948 nurse and educator

Born on November 1, 1858, in Frost Village, Quebec, Mary Nutting grew up in nearby Waterloo. She was educated in local schools and in convent schools in St. Johns, Newfoundland, and in Montreal. In 1881 she moved with her family to Ottawa, where she studied piano for a time. Later she gave lessons herself, and in 1882–1883 she taught music at the Cathedral School for Girls in St. Johns. In 1889 she entered the new Johns Hopkins Hospital School for Nurses with its first class. After graduating in 1891 she was a head nurse in the hospital for two years and then assistant superintendent of nurses for a year. In 1894 she became superintendent of nurses and principal of the school. At that time nursing schools, even that at Johns Hopkins, were more important as sources of cheap staffing for hospitals — at a rate of from 60 to 105 hours a week from each student — than as centers of professional training. Adelaide Nutting moved quickly to change the priorities in her school.

In 1895 Nutting presented to the trustees a detailed analysis of current student nurse employment and secured approval for a new three-year curriculum, the abolition of stipends, and the institution of scholarships to needy students. In 1901 she established a six-month preparation course in hygiene, elementary practical nursing, anatomy, physiology, and materia medica for entering students to prepare them for ward work. She also began a professional nursing library at Johns Hopkins, from which developed her later four-volume *History of Nursing*, with Lavinia L. Dock, 1907–1912. She was an early member of the American Society of Superintendents of Training Schools for Nurses of the United States and Canada (later the National League of Nursing Education), of which she was president in 1896, vice-president in 1897, secretary in 1903–1904, and president again in 1909. In 1900 she helped found the *American Journal of Nursing*, and in 1903 she was a founder and first president of the Maryland State Association of Graduate Nurses. In 1898 she served on a committee of the Society of Superintendents appointed to investigate means of improving the quality of nursing instruction. The committee's work led to the establishment the next year of an experimental program in hospital economics at Teachers College, Columbia University. Adelaide Nutting taught part-time in the program from 1899 to 1907 and then left Johns Hopkins to become a full-time professor of institutional management at Teachers College; in 1910 she became head of the new department of nursing and health. She was the first nurse to hold either such position, and she remained at Columbia until her retirement in 1925. By that time the programs she had created in hospital administration, nursing education, public health, and other fields had brought her department international recognition.

During that time Nutting was also active in other projects: she was a founder of the American Home Economics Association in 1908; she wrote *The Educational Status of Nursing*, 1912, for the U.S. Bureau of Education; she served as chairman of the committee on nursing of the General Medical Board of the Council of National Defense during World War I; she led the National League of Nursing Education's committee on education, of which she was chairman from 1903 to 1921, in producing the *Standard Curriculum for Schools of Nursing*, 1917; and she served with Josephine Goldmark and others on the Rockefeller Foundation committee that produced the landmark Winslow-Goldmark report, *Nursing and Nursing Education in the United States*, 1923. In 1926 she published *A Sound Economic Basis for Schools of Nursing*. In 1934 she was named honorary president of the Florence Nightingale International Foundation, and in 1944 the National League of Nursing Education created the Mary Adelaide Nutting Medal (modeled by Malvina Hoffman) in her honor and awarded it to her that year. She died in White Plains, New York, on October 3, 1948.

Oakley, Annie 1860–1926 marksworman

Born on August 13, 1860, on a farm in Darke County, Ohio, Phoebe Ann Moses (she later gave the family name as "Mozee") early developed an amazing proficiency with firearms. As a child she hunted game with such success that, according to legend, by selling it in Cincinnati she was able to pay off the mortgage on the family farm. When she was fifteen she won a shooting match in Cincinnati with Frank E. Butler, a vaudeville marksman. They were married in June 1876, and until 1885 they played vaudeville circuits and circuses as "Butler and Oakley" (she apparently took her professional name from a Cincinnati suburb). In April 1885 Annie Oakley, now under her husband's management, joined "Buffalo Bill" Cody's Wild West Show. Billed as "Miss Annie Oakley, the Peerless Lady Wing-Shot," she was one of the show's star attractions for 16 years, except for a brief period in 1887, when she was with the rival Pawnee Bill's Frontier Exhibition.

Oakley never failed to delight her audiences, and her feats of marksmanship were truly incredible. At 30 paces she could split a playing card held edge-on; she hit dimes tossed into the air; she shot cigarettes from her husband's lips; and, a playing card being thrown into the air, she riddled it before it touched the ground (thus giving rise to the custom of referring to punched complimentary tickets as "Annie Oakleys"). She was a great success on the Wild West Show's European trips. In 1887 she was presented to Queen Victoria, and later in Berlin she performed her cigarette trick with, at his insistence, Crown Prince Wilhelm (later Kaiser Wilhelm II) holding the cigarette. A train wreck in 1901 left her partially paralyzed for a time, but she recovered and returned to the stage to amaze audiences for many more years. She died on November 3, 1926, in Greenville, Ohio.

Oates, Joyce Carol 1938– writer

JILL KREMENTZ

Joyce Carol Oates

Born in Lockport, New York, on June 16, 1938, Joyce Carol Oates attended local schools and in 1960 graduated from Syracuse University. The next year she took an M.A. degree in English from the University of Wisconsin. She abandoned Ph.D. studies at Rice University to devote herself full time to writing, an occupation that had been hers since childhood. She contributed short stories to a number of magazines and reviews, including the *Prairie Schooner*, *Literary Review*, *Southwest Review*, *Epoch*, and others and in 1963 published a collection as *By the North Gate*, which received warm critical approval. Her first novel, *With Shuddering Fall*, appeared in 1964, and was followed by a second story collection, *Upon the Sweeping Flood*, 1965. The novels *A Garden of Earthly Delights*, 1967, *Expensive People*, 1968, and *Them*, 1969, formed a trilogy on the intertwined themes of money, morality, and violence in American life. *Them* was named for a National Book Award. *Anonymous Sins and Other Poems*, 1969, and *Love and Its Derangements*, 1970, marked her entry into another genre, as did *The Edge of Impossibility: Tragic Forms in Literature*, a collection of critical essays, 1972.

A remarkably prolific writer, Oates subsequently produced *The Wheel of Love and Other Stories*, 1970, *Wonderland*, a novel, 1971, *Marriages and Infidelities*, stories, 1972, *Do With Me What Yon Will*, a novel, 1973, *Angel Fire*, poems, 1973, *The Hungry Ghosts*, stories, 1974, *Where Are You Going, Where Have You Been?*, stories, 1974, *The Goddess and Other Women*, stories, 1974, *New Heaven, New Earth: The Visionary Experience in Literature*, essays, 1974, *The Poisoned Kiss and Other Stories from the Portuguese*, 1975, *The Seduction and Other Stories*, 1975, *The Fabulous Beasts*, poems, 1975, *The Assassins: A Book of Hours*, a novel, 1975, *Childwold*, a novel, 1976, *Crossing the Border*, stories, 1976, *The Triumph of the Spider Monkey*, 1976, *Night-Side*, stories, 1977, *Son of the Morning*, a novel, 1978, *Women Whose Lives are Food, Men Whose Lives are Money*, poems, 1978, *Unholy Loves*, a novel, 1979, *Bellefleur*, a novel, 1980, *A Bloodsmoor Romance*, a novel, 1982, *The Profane Art*, essays, 1984, *Raven's Wing*, short stories, 1986,

On Boxing, essays, 1987, *(Woman) Writer*, essays, 1988, *American Apetites*, a novel, 1989, *Because It Is Bitter and Because It Is My Heart*, a novel, 1990, *In Darkest America* and *I Stand Before You Naked*, plays, 1990, *Black Water*, a novel, 1992, *Foxfire: Confessions of a Girl Gang*, a novel, 1993, and *Haunted: Tales of the Grotesque*, a novel, 1994.

Oates also edited *Scenes from American Life: Contemporary Short Fiction*, 1973, and *The Hostile Sun: The Poetry of D.H. Lawrence*, 1973. Her play *The Sweet Enemy* was produced Off-Broadway in 1965, and *Sunday Dinner* was produced by the American Place Theatre in 1970. From 1961 to 1967 she was on the English faculty of the University of Detroit, and from 1967 to 1987 she was on that of the University of Windsor, Ontario. In 1987 she became a professor at Princeton University. Her dark, gothic tales of violent and dismal lives invited comparisons to both romantic and naturalistic writers. Among her many awards, she received an O. Henry award for continuing achievement in both 1970 and 1986, and in 1990 she won both the Rea award for the short story and the Alan Swallow award for fiction.

JOE MCTYRE

Flannery O'Connor

O'Connor, Flannery 1925–1964 short story writer

Born on March 25, 1925, in Savannah, Georgia, Mary Flannery O'Connor grew up and attended schools there and in Milledgeville, Georgia. She graduated from Georgia State College for Women (now Georgia College) in 1945 and for two years studied creative writing at Iowa State University, taking an M.F.A. degree in 1947. Her first published piece was a story in *Accent* in 1946, and in subsequent years her stories appeared in *Sewanee Review, Parisian Review, Kenyon Review, Mademoiselle*, and other periodicals. In 1952 she published *Wise Blood*, a novel that, together with her collection *A Good Man Is Hard to Find, and Other Stories*, 1955, attracted considerable critical attention. Her stark tales of variously alienated and deformed characters, recalling in some ways and yet transcending the hackneyed conventions of Southern gothic writing, were in fact moral fables informed by the author's Catholic viewpoint. *The Violent Bear It Away*, a novel, appeared in 1960, and a second collection of stories, *Everything That Rises Must Converge*, was published posthumously in 1965. She died in Milledgeville, Georgia, on August 3, 1964, of a chronic disease. Her Christian and often almost mystical concerns, expressed in stories propelled by violent incident, gave rise to comparisons of her writing with that of Dostoevsky, although some critics saw it rather is merely narrow. The power of her fictions, however, outlived their shock, and *Flannery O'Connor: The Complete Stories*, edited by Robert Giroux, 1971, won a National Book Award. Her collected lectures and essays were published as *Mystery and Manners* in 1969.

O'Connor, Sandra Day 1930– attorney and Supreme Court justice

Born on March 26, 1930, in El Paso, Texas, Sandra Day grew up on her parents isolated Lazy B Ranch, in southeastern Arizona. At age five, she was sent to El Paso to live with her maternal grandmother and to attend a private school there. She graduated from high school at sixteen and enrolled in Stanford University, where she majored in economics and obtained a B.A. degree in 1950. Two years later she completed a law degree at Stanford, finishing third in her class. Serving on the board of editors of the *Stanford Law Review*, she met John Jay O'Connor, whom she married soon after graduation in 1952.

After earning her law degree, she found that no California firms were willing to hire a woman. Entering public service instead, she worked in the San Mateo County district attorney's office. After her husband's military service in Germany, the O'Connors settled in Phoenix, where she opened her own small practice. In 1960, after the birth of the second of three sons, O'Connor gave up her practice and became a full-time homemaker.

In 1965 she returned to work outside of her home, as an Arizona assistant attorney general, a position she held until 1969. She was then chosen to replace a retiring state senator; the next year she campaigned for the same seat and won handily. In 1972

O'Connor was elected majority leader thereby becoming the first woman majority leader in any state senate. By 1974, after a hard-fought election, she won a judgeship in the Maricopa County superior court. After declining to run for governor of Arizona against incumbent Bruce Babbitt, she was nominated by Governor Babbitt as his first appointee to the Arizona Court of Appeals in 1979.

President Ronald Reagan, who during his campaign had promised to appoint a woman to the Supreme Court, nominated O'Connor for the post on July 7, 1981. Her nomination was approved by the Senate and she took the oath of office on September 26, 1981. As a member of the court, she generally supported her conservative colleagues, although she often wrote separate, concurring decisions in order to clarify the majority opinion or to show a different reasoning.

O'Keeffe, Georgia 1887–1986 painter

CARL VAN VECHTEN

Georgia O'Keeffe

Born in Sun Prairie, Wisconsin, on November 15, 1887, Georgia O'Keeffe grew up and attended schools there and, from 1902, in Williamsburg, Virginia. Determined from an early age to be a painter, she studied at the Art Institute of Chicago in 1904–1905, at the Art Students' League in New York City in 1907–1908, and subsequently under other painters, notably Arthur Dove. Beginning as an advertising illustrator, she supported herself until 1918 by teaching art at various schools and colleges around the country, including West Texas State Normal College (now West Texas State University) in 1915–1918, but after that date she devoted herself entirely to painting. In 1916 she had sent some drawings to a friend in New York City who showed them to Alfred Stieglitz, the photographer and founder of the famous 291 Gallery. Unknown to her, Stieglitz exhibited the drawings, and, when O'Keeffe moved to New York in 1918, he introduced her to such painters as John Marin, Marsden Hartley, and Charles Demuth, all of whom showed at "291." A major one-man show was mounted at the Anderson Galleries in January 1923. Stieglitz and O'Keeffe were married in December 1924.

O'Keeffe's early paintings were abstractions; in the 1920s she produced a series of lyrical and greatly magnified depictions of flowers, along with a number of careful, precise paintings of scenes of New York City and the East River. She found what became her characteristic style during a visit to New Mexico in 1929, when she became enchanted by the bleak landscape under the broad desert skies, and thereafter she often painted desert scenes, sometimes with the bleached skull of a longhorn in the foreground. She settled permanently in New Mexico after Stieglitz's death in 1946. She exhibited her work annually at the Intimate Gallery, An American Place, until 1946 and thereafter was honored in a number of retrospectives in various museums and galleries around the country. Represented in the permanent collections of most of the nation's major museums, she was generally recognized in later years as one of the most original and productive of American artists. Her stark, semi-abstract landscapes or still lifes defied categorization as to school and were instantly recognizable as hers. *Georgia O'Keeffe*, a sumptuously illustrated and produced autobiography, was published in 1976. She received a Gold Medal for painting in 1970 from the National Institute of Arts and Letters and was awarded the Medal of Freedom by President Gerald R. Ford in 1977. In 1983 she received the Radcliffe award for lifetime achievements for women and in 1985 she won a National Medal of Arts. About her need to paint until late in her life she said, "the painting is like a thread that runs through all the reasons for all other things that make one's life." She died on March 6, 1986, in Santa Fe, New Mexico.

Onassis, Jacqueline Lee Bouvier Kennedy 1929–1994 socialite, First Lady and editor

Born in Southampton, Long Island, New York, on July 28, 1929, Jacqueline Bouvier was of a wealthy and socially prominent family. She was educated in private schools.

Jacqueline Kennedy Onassis

From Vassar College, which she entered in 1947, she later transferred to George Washington University, from which she graduated in 1951, having spent a year at the Sorbonne in Paris. For two years she worked as a photographer and columnist for the *Washington Times-Herald*, until her marriage in September 1953 to Senator John F. Kennedy of Massachusetts. On Kennedy's election as president in 1960 she became the focus of national and even international popular interest. As the cultured and sophisticated First Lady, she helped set the social tone for the Kennedy administration; her quiet dignity went far to offset its otherwise often boyish air. Her personal taste in clothes was widely copied. She particularly interested herself in the White House itself and secured a number of important antique pieces for it as part of a plan to restore several of its public rooms to period authenticity. She set up a fine arts commission for the White House and hired a White House curator. In February 1962 she conducted a televised tour of the White House that was widely praised and was named for a Peabody award. On trips abroad with her husband she was warmly received and did much informally to maintain good relations with various nations. The assassination of President Kennedy as they rode together in a Dallas motorcade in November 1963 thrust her even more into the foreground of the national consciousness. After the immediate period of ceremony and mourning she withdrew slowly into the world of international society, becoming a frequent subject of society gossip and the victim of publicity seekers and paparazzi. She was linked romantically with various eligible men, but her marriage in October 1968 to Greek shipping tycoon Aristotle Onassis was a shock to her partisans and critics alike. She lived the secluded life of the extremely wealthy before and for a time after Onassis's death in 1975. From 1975 to 1977 she was a consulting editor at Viking Press. She moved to Doubleday in 1978 as an associate editor, later becoming a senior editor. She died on May 19, 1994, at her home in New York City.

O'Neill, Rose Cecil 1874–1944 illustrator, writer and businesswoman

Born in Wilkes-Barre, Pennsylvania, on June 25, 1874, Rose O'Neill grew up in Battle Creek and Omaha, Nebraska, and was educated in convent schools. Although steered by her father toward a theatrical career, she preferred art. A prize drawing for the *Omaha World-Herald* when she was fourteen led to sales of other drawings to the newspaper and to the *Great Divide* magazine of Denver. In 1893 she made her way to New York City, where she was soon selling drawings to *Truth*, *Puck*, *Cosmopolitan*, and other magazines. In 1896 she married Gray Latham, a Virginia aristocrat whom she divorced in 1901. During the marriage she signed her work "O'Neill Latham." In June 1902 she married the editor of *Puck*, Harry Leon Wilson. She illustrated several of his books, including *The Spenders*, 1902, and *The Lions of the Lord*, 1903. They were divorced in 1907. In addition to her illustrations for *Good Housekeeping*, *Life*, *Collier's*, and other leading magazines, which brought her a substantial income, she wrote *The Loves of Edwy*, 1904, and *The Lady in the White Veil*, 1909.

Wealth came with O'Neill's famous "Kewpies," sentimental little Cupid figures to which the *Ladies' Home Journal*, under Edward Bok, devoted a full page in December 1909. The Kewpies and their adventures quickly became a national rage, and from drawing them she moved on to marketing a line of Kewpie dolls, patented in 1913. These modernized American Cupids swept the country, and royalties from their sales and from *Kewpies and Dottie Darling*, 1913, *Kewpies: Their Book, Verse, and Poetry*, 1913, *Kewpie Kutouts*, 1914, and *Kewpies and the Runaway Baby*, 1928, allowed O'Neill all the leisure she required to paint in her Washington Square studio or at her villa on Capri, to entertain flamboyantly at Carabas Castle, her home in Westport, Connecticut, and to write poetry published as *The Master-Mistress*, 1922, and such extremely Gothic romances as *Garda*, 1929, and *The Goblin Woman*, 1930. Her serious drawings, exhibited at the Galerie Devambez in Paris in 1921, secured her election to the Société des Beaux Arts. She also dabbled in monumental sculpture. Late in life, her money squandered, she retired to "Bonnie Brook," her family's homestead in the Ozark hills of Missouri. She died on April 6, 1944, in Springfield, Missouri.

O'Sullivan, Mary Kenney 1864–1943 labor leader and reformer

Born in Hannibal, Missouri, on January 8, 1864, Mary Kenney received only a few years of schooling. At an early age she went to work as an apprentice dressmaker. Later she worked in a printing and binding factory, becoming a forewoman before the plant closed down. She then made her way to Chicago about 1889, where, while working in a succession of binderies, she was appalled by the squalid conditions of the city and particularly of working-class life. She took the lead in organizing the Chicago Women's Bindery Workers' Union within the Ladies' Federal Labor Union No. 2703 (A.F. of L.). She was elected a delegate to the Chicago Trades and Labor Assembly, and soon she formed a close friendship with Jane Addams, who opened Hull-House to the women bindery workers. She also assisted Florence Kelley in her sweatshop and tenement investigation in 1892. In April of that year Samuel Gompers, president of the American Federation of Labor, appointed her the Federation's first woman general organizer. During the year she held the post she organized among garment workers in New York City and Troy, New York, and printers, binders, shoe workers, and carpet weavers in Massachusetts. She then returned to Chicago, where, after lobbying for the state factory inspection law inspired by the 1892 investigation, she was appointed one of the 12 inspectors in the new Factory Inspection Department under Florence Kelley. In October 1894 she married John F. O'Sullivan, a former seaman and labor editor of the *Boston Globe*.

In Boston Mary O'Sullivan organized the Union for Industrial Progress to study factory and workshop conditions. Through the Women's Educational and Industrial Union and its president, Mary Morton Kehew, she organized rubber makers and garment and laundry workers. For a time she and her husband lived in the Denison House settlement, and they were in contact with all the leading reform and progressive figures in Boston. After her husband's accidental death in 1902 she worked as manager of a model tenement in South Boston, where she also conducted classes in English and domestic skills for her tenants. In November 1903 she attended the annual convention of the A.F. of L. and with William E. Walling, a New York settlement worker, organized the National Women's Trade Union League, of which she became secretary and later first vice-president. In 1912, after personal investigation, she broke with the Boston Women's Trade Union League and the A.F. of L. to support the strike of textile workers in Lawrence, Massachusetts. She met with leaders of the Industrial Workers of the World, who had organized the strike, and with the president of the American Woolen Company, and in doing so she contributed greatly to the settlement of the strike. In November 1914 she was appointed a factory inspector for the Division of Industrial Safety (from 1919 a part of the state Department of Labor and Industries) and she held that post until January 1934, when she retired. She died in West Medford, Massachusetts, on January 18, 1943.

Ottendorfer, Anna Sartorius Uhl 1815–1884 publisher and philanthropist

Born on February 13, 1815, in Würzburg, Bavaria (now Germany), Anna Sartorius (some sources give her surname as Behr) received a scanty education. About 1836 she emigrated to the United States and settled in New York City. Sources are divided over whether her marriage to Jacob Uhl, a printer, took place before or after she came to America. In either case, by 1844 they had bought a print shop and along with it the contract for printing the weekly *New-Yorker Staats-Zeitung*. They bought the newspaper outright the following year. Together — Anna Uhl shared in the editorial, business, and even composing room and press work involved — they built the paper into a successful institution that was distributed to other cities with sizable German communities as well. It soon became a tri-weekly and then in 1849 a daily. From the death of her husband in 1852 Anna Uhl managed the entire enterprise. In July 1859 she married Oswald Ottendorfer, a Moravian immigrant who had joined the *Staats-Zeitung* in 1851 and had become editor in 1858. She served thereafter as general manager of the paper. In later years Anna Ottendorfer took up philanthropy.

In 1875 she contributed $100,000 to build the Isabella Home for elderly women of German ancestry in Astoria, Long Island. A similar gift in 1881 established the Hermann Uhl Memorial Fund, named for a deceased son, to support the study of German in American schools, principally through the German-American Teachers' College of Milwaukee. To the New York German Hospital she gave a women's pavilion in 1882 and a German dispensary and reading room in 1884, gifts totaling $225,000. She gave lesser amounts to other institutions in Brooklyn, Newark, and elsewhere, and in her will left another $250,000 to various German-American institutions. She died in New York City on April 1, 1884.

Packard, Sophia B. 1824–1891 educator

Born in New Salem, Massachusetts, on January 3, 1824, Sophia Packard attended local district school and from the age of fourteen alternated periods of study with periods of teaching in rural schools. In 1850 she graduated from the Female Seminary of Charlestown, Massachusetts, and after teaching there for a year and in schools on Cape Cod for four years she became preceptress and a teacher in the New Salem Academy in 1855. A year later she moved to Orange, Massachusetts, where she taught for three years, and after a short-lived attempt to operate her own school in Fitchburg, Massachusetts, in partnership with her long-time companion, Harriet E. Giles, she taught at the Connecticut Literary Institution in Suffield, Connecticut, from 1859 to 1864. From 1864 to 1867 she was co-principal of the Oread Collegiate Institute in Worcester, Massachusetts. She then moved to Boston, where, after a time employed in an insurance company, she secured in 1870 the unusual position of pastor's assistant under the Reverend George C. Lorimer of the Shawmut Avenue Baptist Church and later of the Tremont Temple. In 1877 she presided over the organizing meeting of the Woman's American Baptist Home Mission Society, of which she was chosen treasurer that year and corresponding secretary the next.

In 1880 Packard toured the South to determine what form of assistance to the African-American population would be most useful. She concluded to open a school for African-American women and girls in Georgia. After persuading the Woman's American Baptist Home Mission Society to provide support, she moved to Atlanta in April 1881 and, with Giles, opened a school in a church basement. Within a few months enrollment at the Atlanta Baptist Female Seminary increased from 11 to 80, and by the next February it reached 150. In addition to teaching in the school the two women also held prayer meetings, conducted Sunday schools, and taught sewing classes. The American Baptist Home Mission Society (parent of the women's society) made a down payment on a permanent site for the school in 1882, and early in 1883 the school moved to its new home. The balance owing was paid in 1884 by John D. Rockefeller, who was impressed by an address of Packard's in Cleveland, and the school was named Spelman Seminary in honor of his wife and her parents. Rockefeller Hall, with offices, a chapel, and dormitory rooms, was built in 1886, and Packard Hall was erected in 1888. With the granting of a state charter in the latter year Packard became treasurer of the board of trustees. She continued in that post and as president of the school until her death on June 21, 1891, in Washington, D.C. At that time Spelman Seminary numbered 464 students and a faculty of 34. Giles succeeded her as president. Spelman Seminary became Spelman College in 1924, and in 1929 it affiliated, along with Morehouse College, with Atlanta University.

Page, Geraldine 1924–1987 actress

Born on November 22, 1924 in Kirksville, Missouri, Geraldine Sue Page was the daugther of a doctor and a homemaker. As a child she had aspirations of becoming a pianist or visual artist, but at 17 she appeared in her first amateur theater production, and from that point on, she never wavered from her desire to be a professional actress. Supported by her father, whom she always cited as one of her major influences, she entered the Goodman Theater Dramatic School in Chicago, where the family was then living, in 1941. Upon graduation from acting school, she and a number of her classmates and contemporaries organized their own acting company at Lake Zurich, 35 miles outside of Chicago. For the next four years she spent her summers as a stock actress at Lake Zurich, and her winters scraping by at various odd jobs in New York City, trying to find acting roles in major productions. She worked wrapping thread cones for a thread company, clerked and modeled lingerie at a dress shop, and plodded as a hat-check girl, all while acting in a number of off-Broadway productions.

In the early 1950s Jose Quintero, the director of the Loft Players at the Circle-in-the-

Square theater in Greenwich Village, "discovered" her — giving her a small but challenging role in a production of Lorca's *Yerma*. He went on to give her the lead in Tennessee Williams's play *Summer and Smoke* in 1952. While the production was a modest one, and the theater small, word of her performance as the vulnerable but eccentric Alma Winemiller spread, and theater-goers and critics flocked to the theater. This transformed her from an unknown "starving" actress to a critical and popular success. She was offered a number of roles in film at this time, but she declined, preferring Broadway theater. In 1953 she realized her dream of becoming a Broadway leading lady when she was called upon to play Lily, the idealistic, naive heroine in Vina Delmar's play, *Mid-Summer*. After completing 109 extremely well-received performances, she was a bonafide star. Although she appeared briefly in the films *Out of the Night* in 1947 and *Taxi* in 1953, she found her first starring film role in *Hondo*, 1953, opposite John Wayne. She was nominated for an Oscar for her performance.

She returned to the stage for a number of years, coming back to Hollywood in 1961 when she reprised her now legendary performance in *Summer and Smoke* in the film version of the play. For this she was once again nominated for an Academy Award, as she would be a total of eight times over the course of her career. Other films for which she was nominated — but did not receive an Oscar for — include *You're a BigBoy Now*, 1967, *Pete n' Tillie*, 1972, and *The Pope of Greenwich Village*, 1984.

She was married to actor Rip Torn and together, they founded the repertory company Stock Theater. She also worked in television, winning two Emmy awards for her performances in *A Christmas Memory* and *The Thanksgiving Visitor*. In 1985 she starred in the film *A Trip To Bountiful* and was awarded what many considered to be a long-overdue Oscar for her portrayal of an aging Southern woman who is determined to see her hometown once more before she dies.

As an actress, she was respected for her intuitiveness and creativity in capturing her often vulnerable, eccentric characters. When she died on June 13, 1987, at the age of 6s, she was still acting on Broadway in *Blithe Spirit*, for which she was nominated for yet another Tony Award. At the time of her death, her last film, *My Little Girl*, had not been released.

Paley, Grace Goodside 1922– writer

Born in the Bronx, New York City, on December 11, 1922, Grace Goodside was the youngest child of Jewish socialist immigrants. She attended Hunter College and New York University from 1938 to 1939. She married Jess Paley in 1942 and, while raising two children, wrote poetry. In her mid-thirties she began to write short stories as well.

With *The Little Disturbances of Man*, 1959, her first collection of short stories, she introduced her alter-ego, Faith Darwin, whose first person narratives would return now and again throughout her stories, to delight of faithful readers. Another collection of short stories, *Enormous Changes at the Last Minute*, was published in 1974: later three of these stories were made into a film of the same title. *Later the Same Day* was published in 1985. Her collected stories appeared in 1994, in a volume published by Farrar, Straus & Giroux. Paley's stories characteristically take place in a single setting — typically somewhere unremarkable, like a park bench or a hospital room — and are marked by wit and starkness.

Paley also published collections of poetry. In the 1960s, she was a familiar figure in Greenwich Village and was actively engaged in the antiwar movement. In 1988, she wrote the text for *Three Hundred Sixty-Five Reasons Not to Have Another War*, a calendar. She has taught at several universities, most recently at Sarah Lawrence College. She was elected to the American Academy and Institute of Arts and Letters in 1980 and was the recipient of a Guggenheim fellowship. In 1972 she married writer Robert Nichols, whose home in Vermont was a favorite retreat.

Palmer, Bertha Honoré 1849–1918 socialite
Born on May 22, 1849, in Louisville, Kentucky, Bertha Honoré grew up from the age of six in Chicago. She was educated at St. Xavier's Academy and Dearborn Seminary in Chicago and the Visitation Convent School in Georgetown, D.C. In July 1871 she married Potter Palmer, a wealthy merchant who shortly afterward became identified with the Palmer House, one of the nation's premier hotels. Her husband's position automatically qualified her for membership in Chicago's social elite. Her own abilities, tact, charm, and high goals won her undisputed leadership. In 1891 she was named chairman of the Board of Lady Managers for the World's Columbian Exposition to be held in Chicago two years later. Under her firm guidance the board created a highly effective female presence in the exposition. The Woman's Building, featuring exhibits from 47 nations, many of them obtained through Palmer's personal acquaintance with political leaders and royalty, was a highlight of the exposition and went far to demonstrate both the achievements of women around the world and the disabilities under which they yet labored. She served also as president of the Woman's Branch of the Congress Auxiliary of the exposition but delegated that work largely to her friend, Ellen M. Henrotin. Palmer was a mainstay of Jane Addams's Hull-House settlement, to which she gave liberally of both financial and personal support. During 1892–1896 she was a trustee of Northwestern University. She became first vice-president of the Chicago Civic Federation (forerunner of the National Civic Federation) on its organization in December 1893. In 1900 she was appointed by President William McKinley the only woman among the U.S. commissioners to the Paris Exposition. She was an art collector of note, and she was guided by Mary Cassatt to an early appreciation of the Impressionists. Her social sphere was extended to Newport, Rhode Island, in 1896, and the same qualities that had brought her to the fore in Chicago conquered Eastern prejudices against Midwestern and newer money. After her husband's death in 1902 she took over active management of the $8 million estate and more than doubled it in her remaining years. From 1910 she devoted much of her time to ranching and farming on her large estate in Florida. She died in Osprey, Florida, on May 5, 1918.

Palmer, Phoebe Worrall 1807–1874 evangelist and religious writer
Born in New York City on December 18, 1807, Phoebe Worrall was reared in a strict Methodist home. In September 1827 she married Walter C. Palmer, a homeopathic physician and also a Methodist. From the beginning of their married life they shared a deep interest in their religion and in the task of carrying it to others. They became active in the revivalist movement in the 1830s, and from 1835 Phoebe Palmer conducted, at first jointly with a sister and later alone, regular women's home prayer meetings. Gradually the meetings became known as the Tuesday Meeting for the Promotion of Holiness, and they became Centers of theGrowing "Holiness" movement that sought the goal of Christian perfection. By the early 1840s the hundreds who had come under her direct influence included two bishops of the Methodist Church. As the meetings grew, they were moved from her home to larger accommodations. During the 1840s Palmer also became active in charitable work among the poor and the imprisoned, and for 11 years from 1847 she was corresponding secretary of the New York Female Assistance Society for the Relief and Religious Instruction of the Sick Poor. In 1850 she led the Methodist Ladies' Home Missionary Society in founding the Five Points Mission in a notorious slum district of New York. She was also a regular contributor to the *Guide to Holiness*, the chief periodical of the perfectionist movement, and she wrote a number of books, including *The Way of Holiness*, 1845, *Entire Devotion*, 1845, *Faith and Its Effects*, 1846, *Incidental*

Illustrations of the Economy of Salvation, 1852, *Promises of the Father*, 1859, and *Pioneer Experiences*, 1868.

From 1850 Palmer evangelical activities began to branch out, as she and her husband began making annual tours of the eastern part of the country and Canada, during which they visited Methodist camp meetings and conducted their own holiness revivals. From 1859 to 1863 they lived in England, where they conducted revivals that stirred thousands. During that period, in 1862, Dr. Palmer bought the *Guide to Holiness* and named Phoebe Palmer the editor, a task she fulfilled for the rest of her life. In 1865 she published a record of her British experiences as *Four Years in the Old World*. From its organization in 1867 the National Association for the Promotion of Holiness provided the institutional framework for much of their evangelical work, which gradually extended over the entire country. Palmer continued in that work and in her Tuesday Meetings until her death in New York City on November 2, 1874.

Park, Maud Wood 1871–1955 suffragist

Born in Boston on January 25, 1871, Maud Wood attended St. Agnes School in Albany, New York, and after graduating in 1887 she taught school for eight years. She then entered Radcliffe College and graduated in three years, in 1898. In September 1897, while still a student, she married Charles E. Park, a Boston architect. At Radcliffe she found that she was one of only two students who favored woman suffrage, and in her last year she invited Alice Stone Blackwell to speak on campus. At the 1900 convention of the National American Woman Suffrage Association in Washington, D.C., the last convention to be presided over by Susan B. Anthony, she found herself virtually the only representative of the younger generation of women. That discovery prompted her to organize the College Equal Suffrage League to stir up interest and support among a seemingly apathetic generation. Her tours of colleges across the country resulted in the formation of chapters in 30 states, and in 1908 they organized as the National College Equal Suffrage Association. She was a co-founder of the Boston Equal Suffrage Association for Good Government in 1901 and was its executive secretary for 12 years. In 1916 Park went to Washington, D.C., at the invitation of Carrie Chapman Catt to become head of the congressional committee of the National American Woman Suffrage Association. Her task was to direct congressional lobbying and liaison in the implementation of Catt's "winning strategy." Her acute understanding of legislative process and the techniques of lobbying contributed immeasurably to the success of the campaign for a suffrage amendment to the Constitution. On the creation of the National League of Women Voters in 1920 to follow up on the success of the suffrage campaign, Park was chosen president of the new group and chairman of its legislative committee. In her four years in those posts she built the League into a large and broadly based organization devoted to education, good government, and social and economic reform. She resigned in 1924 for reasons of health but served again in 1925–1928 as the League's legislative counselor.

In 1924 Park organized the Women's Joint Congressional Committee, a lobbying front representing originally 10 constituent women's organizations and later 21. As permanent chairman of the committee she directed lobbying efforts that contributed to the passage of the Sheppard-Towner Act of 1921, which authorized federal aid to states for programs of maternity and child health and welfare, the Cable Act of 1922, which granted married women U.S. citizenship independent of their husbands' status, and the child-labor amendment submitted to the states in 1924. With the failure of her health in the later 1920s she retired to Cape Elizabeth, Maine, and devoted herself to writing. Her play *Lucy Stone* was produced by the Federal Theater Players at the Copley Theatre, Boston, in May 1939. She died in Melrose, Massachusetts, on May 8, 1955.

Parker, Dorothy 1893–1967 writer and critic

Dorothy Parker

Born in West End, near Long Branch, New Jersey, on August 22, 1893, Dorothy Rothschild was educated at Miss Dana's School, Morristown, New Jersey, and the Blessed Sacrament Convent School, New York City. She joined the editorial staff of *Vogue* in 1916 and the next year moved to *Vanity Fair*. In 1917 she married Edwin Pond Parker II, whom she divorced in 1928 but whose surname she retained in her professional career. She left *Vanity Fair* in 1920 in a dispute over a particularly acerbic theatrical review she had submitted and decided to try her hand at freelance writing. She collaborated with playwright Elmer Rice on *Close Harmony*, which had a short run in 1924. Her first book of light, witty, and sometimes cynical verse, *Enough Rope*, was published in 1926 and became a best seller.

In 1927 Parker became book reviewer for the *New Yorker*, and she was associated with that magazine as a staff writer or contributor for much of the rest of her career. Early in the 1920s she was one of the founders of the famous "Algonquin Round Table" at the Algonquin Hotel in Manhattan and was by no means the least of a group of dazzling wits that included Robert Benchley, Robert E. Sherwood, James Thurber, George S. Kaufman, Franklin P. Adams, and others. It was there, in conversations that frequently spilled over from the offices of the *New Yorker*, that she established her reputation as one of the most brilliant conversationalists in New York. Her rapier wit became so widely renowned that quips and mots were frequently attributed to her on the strength of her reputation alone. She came to epitomize the liberated woman of the Twenties.

The theme of the bright but heartbroken girl-about-New York was important in many of Parker's later poems, which were published in *Sunset Gun*, 1928, and *Death and Taxes*, 1931, and later collected in *Collected Poems: Not So Deep as a Well*, 1936, and in her often bittersweet short stories, collected in *Laments for the Living*, 1930, *After Such Pleasures*, 1933, and *Here Lies*, 1939. In 1933 she married Alan Campbell and thereafter collaborated with him on a number of film scenarios, including *A Star Is Born*, 1937. In the later 1940s her liberal sympathies lost her employment in the film industry, and she returned to magazine writing, contributing book reviews to *Esquire* for a time. She collaborated with Arnaud d'Usseau on a play, *Ladies of the Corridor*, that was produced on Broadway in 1953. She lived in Hollywood, California, until Campbell's death in 1963 and then returned to New York City. She died in New York City on June 7, 1967.

Parks, Rosa 1913– reformer

Rosa Parks

Born in Tuskegee, Alabama, on February 4, 1913, Rosa Lee Parks attended Alabama State Teachers College (now Alabama State University) for a time. She later moved to Montgomery, Alabama. She lived in quiet obscurity for the first 42 years of her life. In 1943 she became a member of the Montgomery chapter of the National Association for the Advancement of Colored People and served as its secretary until 1956. On December 1, 1955, while returning home from her job as a seamstress, she was ordered by the driver of the city bus on which she was riding to give up her seat to a white man. She refused. She was then arrested and fined ten dollars for her failure to comply with the city's racial segregation ordinances. The episode galvanized African-American community leaders in Montgomery into action. Under the aegis of the Montgomery Improvement Association, and led by the young pastor of the Dexter Avenue Baptist Church, Dr. Martin Luther King, Jr., a boycott of the municipal bus company was begun on December 5. The boycott lasted for 382 days before the city government bowed to public opinion aroused throughout the nation in support of the protest. City buses were thereafter run on an unsegregated basis. For her role in sparking the successful campaign, which thrust Dr. King into the leadership of a still-fledgling movement, Parks became known as the "mother of the civil rights movement." In 1957 she and her family moved to Detroit, where she was employed on the staff of U.S. Rep. John Conyers from 1965 until her retirement in 1988. In her honor the Southern Christian Leadership Council established the annual Rosa Parks Freedom Award. She was awarded the Spingarn Medal in 1979, was the first woman to receive the Martin Luther King, Jr. Nonviolent Peace Prize in 1980, and in 1990 received the Adam Clayton Powell Jr. Legislative Achievement Award. In 1987 she established the Parks Institute for Self-Development in Detroit to provide career training for young people. She published her autobiography, *Rosa Parks: My Story*, with Jim Haskins, in 1992.

Parrish, Anne 1760–1800 philanthropist

Born in Philadelphia on October 17, 1760, Anne Parrish grew up in a Quaker home where charitable works were greatly valued. Not much is known of her early life. When her parents fell victim to the yellow fever epidemic of 1793, she vowed that if they should recover she would devote the rest of her life to philanthropy. They did recover, and she was true to her vow. In 1796 she founded a school for needy girls that was later called the Aimwell School. The school quickly proved a success, and within three years she had taken on several teachers to assist her with some 50 pupils. Courses in regular school subjects were supplemented by training in domestic skills. Over the years the school moved several times to larger quarters, and it remained in operation until 1923. In 1795 Anne Parrish established the House of Industry to supply employment to poor women in Philadelphia. It was the first charitable organization for women in America, and it remained in operation for even longer than the school. Anne Parrish died in Philadelphia on December 26, 1800.

Parrish, Celestia Susannah 1853–1918 educator

Born on a plantation near Swansonville, Pittsylvania County, Virginia, on September 12, 1853, Celestia Parrish was orphaned during the Civil War and thereafter was reared by relatives. She received an irregular education, but her own desire for learning went far to supply the deficiency, and in 1869 she became a teacher in rural schools of her native county. In 1874 she moved to Danville, Virginia, where she taught school and also attended the Roanoke Female Institute (now Averett College), from which she graduated in 1876. In 1884, after a year of teaching at the Roanoke Female Institute, she entered the Virginia State Normal School (now Longwood College). On her graduation in 1886 she was given an appointment as instructor in mathematics. During 1891–1892 she studied mathematics and astronomy at the University of Michigan, and in the latter year she joined the faculty of the newly opened Randolph-Macon Woman's College in Lynchburg, Virginia. Her post required her to teach mathematics, philosophy, pedagogy, and psychology, and in order to gain competence in the last field she attended summer sessions at Cornell University in 1893, 1894, and 1895. In 1896 she received her long sought college degree from Cornell. In 1893 she had established a psychology laboratory at Randolph-Macon — probably the first in the South — and in 1895 she published a paper in the *American Journal of Psychology*.

Having come as far as she had only by dint of extraordinary persistence, Parrish began to work to make education more easily accessible to Southern women. Through articles, through her own teaching, and through the Association of Collegiate Alumnae (later the American Association of University Women), of which she was state president and national vice-president, and the Southern Association of College Women, of which she was founder in 1903 and first president, she worked to improve the quality of education available to women and to interest women in availing themselves of newly opened opportunities. In 1897, 1898, and 1899 she attended summer sessions at the University of Chicago, where she worked under John Dewey and became imbued with his ideas of progressive education. In 1902 she left Randolph-Macon to become professor of pedagogic psychology and head of the department of pedagogy at the Georgia State Normal School (now George Peabody College of Education of the University of Georgia). She persuaded philanthropist George Foster Peabody to underwrite the building of Muscogee Elementary School, which opened in 1903 as the college's laboratory school. There over the next eight years Celestia Parrish trained hundreds of teachers in progressive methods in what was the only such program in the South and one of the few in the nation.

In 1911 Parrish was appointed state supervisor of rural schools for the North Georgia District, a task that required her to oversee the work and in-service training of over 3800 teachers scattered among more than 2400 schools in 48 counties where education was given low priority. She remained in that post, traveling almost constantly to visit schools, organize teachers' institutes, and exhort public officials, until her death in Clayton, Georgia, on September 7, 1918.

Parsons, Elsie Worthington Clews 1875–1941 anthropologist

Born in New York City on November 27, 1875, into a socially prominent family, Elsie Clews attended private schools and graduated from Barnard College in 1896. She then studied history and sociology at Columbia, receiving her M.A. in 1897 and her Ph.D. in 1899. In the latter year she was appointed Hartley House fellow at Barnard. In September 1900 she married Herbert Parsons, a New York attorney and politician. From 1902 to 1905 she was a lecturer in sociology at Barnard, but with her husband's election to Congress she resigned in 1905 and accompanied him to Washington, D.C. Her first book, *The Family*, was published in 1906; a textbook and a feminist tract founded on sociological research and analysis, it contained a lengthy discussion of trial marriage, which generated some notoriety and helped it to enjoy a large sale. To avoid embarrassing her husband in his political career, she used the pseudonym "John Main" for her next two books, *Religious Chastity*, 1913, and *The Old Fashioned Woman*, 1913, the latter of which was a sharp and witty analysis of the genesis of traditional sex roles and behavior and the cultural codes that sustain them in the face of changing social, economic, and political circumstances. *Fear and Conventionality*, 1914, *Social Freedom*, 1915, and *Social Rule*, 1916, appeared under her own name.

On a trip to the Southwest in 1915 Parsons met the anthropologists Franz Boas and Pliny E. Goddard, who interested her in their work among Native Americans of the region. She spent the rest of her life studying these and other tribes herself. After further studies under Boas at Columbia, she embarked on a 25-year career of field research and writing that established her as perhaps the leading authority on the Pueblo and on other tribes in North America, Mexico, and South America. Her papers appeared in leading scientific journals, and her books included *The Social Organization of the Tewa of New Mexico*, 1929, *Hopi and Zuñi Ceremonialism*, 1933, and *Mitla: Town of the Souls*, 1936, a highly regarded product of her study of a Zapotec community in the state of Oaxaca, Mexico. Her most important book, the two-volume *Pueblo Indian Religion*, appeared in 1939.

Parsons also published a number of works on West Indian and African-American folklore, including *Folk-Tales of Andros Island, Bahamas*, 1918, *Folk-Lore from the Cape Verde Islands* (on black Cape Verdeans in Massachusetts), 1923, *Folk-Lore of the Sea Islands, South Carolina* (on the Gullah-speaking people), 1923, and *Folk-Lore of the Antilles, French and English*, three volumes, 1933–1943. Her last book, *Peguche, Canton of Otavalo*, a study of Andean culture, appeared posthumously in 1945. During the last 25 years of her life she undertook at least one field trip a year, and her voluminous notes of careful field observations shaped her professional writings, in which she avoided speculation and extrapolation.

From 1918 to her death Parsons was associate editor of the *Journal of American Folklore*. Her only teaching post in later years was a lectureship in 1919 at the newly opened New School for Social Research, where one of her students was Ruth F. Benedict. She was president of the American Folklore Society in 1918–1920, of the American Ethnological Society from 1923 to 1925, and of the American Anthropological Association in 1940–1941. She died in New York City on December 19, 1941.

Parsons, Louella 1881?–1972 newspaper columnist

Born in Freeport, Illinois, probably on August 6, 1881 (although she frequently gave 1893), Louella Oettinger obtained her first newspaper job while she was still in high school, as dramatic editor for the *Dixon (Illinois) Morning Star*. Her starting salary was $5 a week, a sum that was multiplied several hundred times before she was through. She married John Parsons in 1910. When he died four years later, she went to Chicago and became a reporter on the *Chicago Tribune*. In 1912 she had had her first contact with the movie industry, selling a script to the Essanay company for $25, and she soon began the first movie column in the country, in the *Chicago Record-Herald* in 1914. When the paper was bought by William Randolph Hearst in 1918 she was out of a job, for Hearst had not yet discovered that movies were news, but she moved to New York City and started a similar column in the *New York Morning Telegraph* that caught Hearst's attention. After some shrewd bargaining on both sides he obtained her services for his *New York American* in 1922. She was associated with various Hearst enterprises for the rest of her career. She underwent a crisis in 1925, when she contracted tuberculosis and was told she had only six months to live. She decided to spend her last days in California, but the disease went into remission and she emerged as the Hearst syndicate's Hollywood columnist.

Parsons made several attempts to start a radio program in the late 1920s and early 1930s, but it was not until 1934 that she found a successful formula: an interview program, "Hollywood Hotel," on which stars appeared gratis to publicize their films. The Radio Guild put a stop to all such free appearances in 1938, but by that time she had established herself as the social and moral arbiter of the Hollywood colony, her judgments being considered as final in most cases and her disfavor being feared more than that of any film critic. Her daily gossip column eventually appeared in 407 newspapers in the United States and other countries and was read by upwards of 20 million people. Although its items were often inaccurate and sometimes simply spiteful, it was followed religiously and thus afforded her a kind and degree of power held by no one else in Hollywood. Her nearest rival was the somewhat friendlier and more tolerant Hedda Hopper, who began her column in 1938. Volumes of memoirs appeared as *The Gay Illiterate*, 1944, and *Tell It to Louella*, 1961. With the decline of Hollywood as the center of the motion picture industry after World War II her influence also waned, but she continued to turn out her column until December 1965, when it was taken over by her assistant, Dorothy Manners, who had in fact been writing it for more than a year. Parsons died in Santa Monica, California, on December 9, 1972.

Parton, Sara Payson Willis 1811–1872 columnist and writer

Born in Portland, Maine, on July 9, 1811, Grata Payson Willis early changed her first name to Sara. She was of a family of strong literary and journalistic traditions: her father, Nathaniel Willis, founded the *Youth's Companion* in 1827, and her elder brother, Nathaniel Parker Willis, was later a poet and editor of the *New York Mirror*. She was educated in Boston and at Catharine Beecher's seminary in Hartford, Connecticut, and she then worked for the *Youth's Companion* until her marriage in 1837 to Charles H. Eldredge. He died nine years later, and in 1849 she married Samuel P. Farrington, from whom she was divorced in 1852. By that time she had begun contributing paragraphs and articles, under the name "Fanny Fern," to various periodicals, including *True Flag*, *Olive Branch*, and *Mother's Assistant*, and in 1853 a collection of her witty and chatty pieces was published in volume form as *Fern Leaves from Fanny's Port-Folio*. The book promptly sold some 80,000 copies and was quickly followed by a second series of *Fern Leaves* in 1854 and by *Little Ferns for Fanny's Little Friends* for children in 1854.

In 1855 Willis published her first novel, *Ruth Hall*, a roman à clef that satirized her brother Nathaniel and his set. In that year she was engaged by the *New York Ledger* to write a weekly column for the unprecedented sum of $100 each. She maintained that association for the rest of her life; she was not only one of the first woman columnists in the world of journalism, she was also one of the first whose columns employed satire and even downright impudence to comment on affairs of the day, particularly upon the position of women and the poor in society. Her columns were collected in *Fresh Leaves*, 1857, *Folly as It Flies*, 1868, *Ginger Snaps*, 1870, and *Caper-Sauce*, 1872. Shortly after beginning her *Ledger* connection she moved to New York City, where in January 1856 she married James Parton, the eminent biographer. Other books by Fanny Fern were *Rose Clark*, a novel, 1856, and two children's books, *The Play Day Book*, 1857, and *A New Story Book for Children*, 1864. In 1868 she joined Jane Croly, Alice Cary, and others in founding the pioneer women's club Sorosis. She died in New York City on October 10, 1872.

Patrick, Mary Mills 1850–1940 missionary and educator

Born on March 10, 1850, in Canterbury, New Hampshire, Mary Patrick grew up there, in North Boscawen, and from 1865 in Lyons (now part of Clinton), Iowa. Learning was encouraged in her home, and in 1869 she graduated from the Lyons Collegiate Institute. In 1871 she accepted appointment by the American Board of Commissioners for Foreign Missions as a teacher in a mission school in Erzurum in what is now eastern Turkey. In her four years there she learned ancient and modern Armenian and traveled some 3,000 miles on horseback through the region. In 1875 she was transferred to the American High School for Girls (also known as the Home School) in Scutari (Üsküdar), an Asiatic suburb of Constantinople. She became co-principal of the school in 1883 and sole principal in 1889. During her summers she lived in Greek villages, adding that language and Turkish to her others. After a study furlough in the United States she received a master's degree from the University of Iowa in 1890.

In that year, after much planning and the securing of a charter from the Commonwealth of Massachusetts, the American High School became the American College for Girls at Constantinople, later known as Constantinople Woman's College. Patrick served as president of the college from its opening. Summer study at the universities of Heidelberg, Zurich, Berlin, Leipzig, Paris, and Oxford led to her receiving a Ph.D. from the University of Bern in 1897. Her dissertation was published in 1899 as *Sextus Empiricus and Greek Scepticism*. Prompted by a destructive fire in 1905, the college acquired a new site in Arnavutköyü on the European side of the Bosporus. A new charter in 1908 ended the college's ties to the mission board, and in 1914 the new campus was occupied. Dr. Patrick kept the school open through the Balkan Wars, the Turkish revolution, and World War I, and through those changes it evolved from a school primarily for minority Greek, Armenian, and Bulgarian Christian women into a leading center of higher education for Turkish women. She remained president until her retirement in 1924, after which she lived in New York City and from 1932 in Palo Alto, California. Others of her books were *Sappho and the Island of Lesbos*, 1912, and, in retirement, *The Greek Skeptics*, 1929, *Under Five Sultans*, an autobiography, 1929, and *A Bosporus Adventure*, a history of the college, 1934. She died in Palo Alto, California, on February 25, 1940. The American College for Girls later affiliated with nearby Robert College for men.

Patterson, Alicia 1906–1963 newspaper publisher and editor

Born in Chicago on October 15, 1906, Alicia Patterson was of the city's journalistic dynasty. She was the daughter of Joseph Medill Patterson and the great-granddaughter of Joseph Medill of the *Chicago Tribune*; Eleanor Medill Patterson was her aunt. She was educated privately in the United States and Europe. In 1927–1928 she served an apprenticeship by working in the promotion department and then as a cub reporter for her father's *New York Daily News*. She then wrote articles for *Liberty* magazine, at that time also owned by the family. After *Liberty* was sold to Bernarr Macfadden in 1931 she freelanced a bit and attained distinction as a pilot (she set a women's New York-to-Philadelphia record) before returning in 1932 to the *Daily News*, for which she wrote book reviews for 11 years.

In 1939 Patterson and her husband, Harry F. Guggenheim (her third, married that year) bought the plant and equipment of the short-lived *Nassau County Journal*, and on September 9, 1940, they launched a new daily tabloid, *Newsday*. Alicia Patterson, in addition to holding 49 percent of the stock, was from the start publisher and editor of the paper. Innovative in format, politically independent, sensitive to local issues while providing full national and international coverage, *Newsday* quickly surpassed in circulation its chief competitor, the *Nassau Review-Star*, which went out of business in 1953. By 1954 circulation was in excess of 213,000, and by 1963 it exceeded 375,000. It was the leading competitor of the New York City dailies and over the years won numerous awards for excellence in typography and reporting. Alicia Patterson served as a trustee of the Harry F. Guggenheim Foundation and of the Fund for the Republic and in various other public service capacities. She remained publisher and editor of *Newsday* until her death in New York City on July 2, 1963; she was the last surviving member of her family still active in newspaper publishing.

Patterson, Eleanor Medill 1881–1948 newspaper publisher and editor

Born in Chicago on November 7, 1881, "Cissy" Patterson, as she was called from girlhood (she later changed her given names from Elinor Josephine to Eleanor Medill), came of one of the great American newspaper families: her grandfather, Joseph Medill, had been editor in chief of the *Chicago Tribune*, her father, Robert W. Patterson, and her cousin, Robert R. McCormick, were in turn editors and publishers of it, and her brother, Joseph Medill Patterson, was publisher of the *New York Daily News*. Patterson, however, was slated for a career in society by her ambitious mother. After a private education at Miss Hersey's in Boston and Miss Porter's in Farmington, Connecticut, she became a most eligible debutante. She spent much time with her uncle, Robert S. McCormick, U.S. envoy in Vienna and then St. Petersburg, and in April 1904 she married an impecunious Polish nobleman, Count Josef Gizycki. But the count had other interests besides his wife, and she left him after less than four years. The count followed her, abducted their baby daughter, and initiated an international episode of the greatest interest to readers of society pages on both sides of the Atlantic. It took a year to get the baby back, with the help of the enormous Patterson and McCormick fortune, and another eight years to get a divorce, which cost, it was rumored, some half a million dollars. For some years thereafter she gave herself to travel, to rearing her daughter, who in 1925 married columnist Drew Pearson, and to writing occasional newspaper pieces. As Eleanor M. Gizycka she published two novels, *Glass Houses*, 1923 (French edition; English in 1926), and *Fall Flight*, 1928. Another marriage left her a widow in 1929, and Cissy, at forty-five, was left with her social career a disaster.

Patterson decided to try her hand at the newspaper business — she had inherited an interest in the *Tribune*, but beyond membership on its board of directors had played no part in it — and in 1930 she was engaged by her old friend William Randolph Hearst to edit the *Washington Herald.* (The same year she changed her name legally to Eleanor Patterson.) She was an eccentric editor in chief, often arriving at the office in riding costume or in evening clothes. She feuded with a series of city editors in the course of proving her seriousness and determination to shape her own paper. Her involvement in the *Herald* extended to going out on many important stories herself, usually in disguise. Her editorial style tended strongly to the personal, even idiosyncratic, and included sharp wit and vituperation among its weapons. Yet she was an early crusader for home rule for the District of Columbia and for a hot lunch program for District schoolchildren (a program she underwrote herself for a time), among other reforms. In addition, she had the family genius for circulation-building publicity. Within a few years the paper's circulation had more than doubled. In August 1937 she leased the *Herald* from Hearst, together with his evening paper, the *Washington Times*, and in January 1939 she bought them outright. Against her brother's advice she combined them into a single all-day paper with six editions, the *Washington Times-Herald*. By 1943 the paper had the highest circulation in Washington and was out of the red. Her paper thrived during World War II, but it became less prosperous afterward as she appeared to lose interest in it. She died at her estate near Marlboro, Maryland, on July 24, 1948. The *Times-Herald* was sold to Colonel Robert R. McCormick's *Chicago Tribune*, in 1949 and to the *Washington Post* in 1954.

Patti, Adelina 1843–1919 opera singer

Born on February 10, 1843, in Madrid, Spain, Adela Juana Maria Patti was the daughter of Italian opera performers. When she was quite young, her parents emigrated to the United States, and she grew up in New York City. She sang from an early age and made her debut at eight, in November 1851, in concert at Tripler Hall. For three years thereafter she toured successfully in the United States, Canada, Mexico, and Cuba with Norwegian violinist Ole Bull under the management of impresario Maurice Strakosch, who had married her older sister Amalia. A period of study under her half-brother, Ettore Barili, and a brief West Indian tour with pianist Louis N4. M. Gottschalk followed, and in November 1859 she made her operatic debut in *Lucia di Lammermoor* at the New York Academy of Music. She subsequently sang *La Sonnambula*, *Il Barbiere di Siviglia*, *Martha*, and *I Puritani* in New York and on tour before traveling to London, where her debut in *La Sonnambula* at Covent Garden in May 1861 was a sensation. For the next 23 years she was a Covent Garden regular. Her Paris debut, again in *La Sonnambula*, in November 1862 was another great success, and in Vienna, St. Petersburg, Monte Carlo, Madrid, Moscow, Brussels, and elsewhere her pure, sweet soprano and dazzling technique conquered all. She made her La Scala debut in *La Traviata* in November 1877. Verdi declared her the greatest singer he had ever heard, and others, from musicians to royalty to a unanimously adulatory opera public, eagerly concurred. She was without doubt the supreme exponent of bel canto and coloratura in her day — a day that lasted well over half a century. Other works in her repertoire of 42 operas included *Linda di Chaumounix*, *Don Pasquale*, *L'Elisir d'Amore*, *Faust*, *Roméo et Juliette*, *Lakmé* and *Don Giovanni*. From 1881 she made a series of annual tours of the United States, in the course of which she received a record $5000 per concert (she occasionally got $6000). Her concert performances combined arias and ballads and usually ended with "Home, Sweet Home," a song closely identified with her and one with which she moved Queen Victoria to tears. Her final U.S. tour was in 1903–1904. Her official farewell appearance occurred at the Royal Albert Hall, London, in December 1906, but she continued to sing in concert from time to time until a last appearance at the Royal Albert Hall in October 1914 in a benefit for the Red Cross War Fund; George V and Queen Mary were among those present on the latter date. Adelina Patti lived in retirement at Craig-y-Nos, her estate in Brecknock, Wales, until her death there on September 27, 1919.

Alice Paul

Paul, Alice 1885–1977 lawyer and social reformer

Born in Moorestown, New Jersey, on January 11, 1885, Alice Paul was reared in a Quaker home and attended private schools. She graduated from Swarthmore College in 1905 and during the following year did graduate work at the New York School of Social Work and lived in the New York College Settlement. In 1906 she went to England for three years to do settlement work. During her stay there she was jailed three times for suffragist agitation. She also continued to do graduate work at the universities of Birmingham and London, and she received an M.A. degree in absentia from the University of Pennsylvania in 1907 and her Ph.D. from the same institution in 1912. In 1912 she became chairman of the congressional committee of the National American Woman Suffrage Association, but she soon differed with what she considered its timid policies, and in 1913 she and a group of like-minded militants withdrew to found the Congressional Union for Woman Suffrage, which in 1917 merged with the Woman's party to form the National Woman's party, in which she was a dominant figure during the next three decades. Her militancy in the fight for woman suffrage led to prison terms on three more occasions before the passage of the Nineteenth Amendment in 1919. Paul devoted herself after the successful conclusion of the campaign for ratification of the Nineteenth Amendment in 1920 to the study of law, taking a law degree from the Washington College of Law in 1922 and master's and doctor's degrees from American University in 1927 and 1928, but she also found time to continue her activities on behalf of equal rights for the women of the United States and of the world. She drafted and managed to have introduced into Congress in 1923 the first equal rights amendment in behalf of women. When it failed of passage, she turned her attention to the international field, concentrating with considerable success during the 1920s and 1930s on obtaining support for her crusade from the League of Nations. From 1927 to 1937 she was chairman of the Woman's Research Foundation, and she subsequently founded and represented at League headquarters in Geneva the World Party for Equal Rights for Women, known as the World Women's party. She always insisted that many of the troubles of the world had their basis in the fact that women were not allowed to exert their potential political power, and she reiterated this view when World War II broke out: it need not have occurred, she declared, and probably would not have if women had been able to have their say at the Paris Peace Conference at the end of World War I.

Elected chairman of the National Woman's party in 1942, Paul continued thereafter to work for women's rights in general and for an equal rights amendment to the Constitution in particular, a dream that was partly realized in 1970, when such an amendment passed the Congress and was referred to the states for ratification. In the interim she was able to have included in the preamble to the charter of the United Nations an affirmation of the equal rights of women and men. Long considered the elder stateswoman of the feminist movement, Alice Paul died in Moorestown, New Jersey, on July 9, 1977.

Peabody, Elizabeth Palmer 1804–1894 educator, publisher and writer

Born on May 16, 1804, in Billerica, Massachusetts, Elizabeth Peabody grew up in Salem. She was educated by her mother, who for a time operated an innovative girls' school in the home, and from an early age she exhibited an interest in philosophical and theological questions. In 1820 she opened a school of her own in Lancaster and two years later another in Boston, where she also studied Greek with the young Ralph Waldo Emerson. From 1823 to 1825 she was a teacher and governess in Maine. On her return to Massachusetts she opened another school in Brookline. Through his daughter, a student in the school, she made the acquaintance of William Ellery Channing, with whom over the next two decades she shared a remarkable intellectual intimacy. As her Socratic tutor he introduced her to the Romantic poets and philosophers of the day, and together they examined the emerging liberal theology of Unitarianism as it evolved. She also served informally as his secretary, copying down his sermons and seeing them into print. After her school closed in 1832 she supported herself mainly through writing, principally her *First Steps to the Study of History*, 1832, and through private tutoring until 1834, when she helped Bronson Alcott establish his radical Temple School in Boston and became his assistant. Her *Record of a School*, based on her journal of Alcott's methods and daily interactions with the children, was published anonymously in 1835 and did much to establish him as a leading and controversial thinker. In 1836 she returned to her family in Salem, where she remained for four years.

In 1837 Peabody became a charter member of the Transcendentalist Club, along with Margaret Fuller, Emerson, Channing, Alcott, and others. On visits to Emerson and the others in Concord she introduced to them the Salem poet-mystic Jones Very and the writer Nathaniel Hawthorne, whose family she had known from childhood and who she discovered in 1837 was the author of some stories she had admired in the *New England Magazine*. Hawthorne married her sister Sophia in 1842 (another sister, Mary, married Horace Mann in 1843).

In 1840 Elizabeth Peabody moved back to Boston and opened a bookshop in which she sold or loaned the foreign and native books and periodicals of the Romantic-Unitarian-Transcendentalist movements in thought and letters. She also published some works, including three of Hawthorne's books for children, some of Margaret Fuller's translations, and in 1842–1843 the Transcendentalist journal *Dial*. She was probably the first woman book publisher in America. Margaret Fuller held her famous conversations in the shop, which naturally became a meeting place for all the Transcendentalists. The Brook Farm experiment was largely planned there. In 1849 she published a single number of a Transcendentalist journal, *Aesthetic Papers*, which contained, among other essays, Henry David Thoreau's "Civil Disobedience." She closed the shop in 1850 and for the next ten years taught school, wrote, and worked to promote public education. Peabody's particular brand of Transcendentalism, anchored firmly in an idea of a just society informed by liberal Christianity, led her to place great emphasis on the education of the young.

In 1859 she learned of Friedrich Froebel's kindergarten work in Germany from Mrs. Carl Schurz, and the next year she opened in Boston the nation's first formal kindergarten. She continued it until 1867, when she undertook a tour of European kindergartens in order to learn more of Froebel's thought. Much of her later writing concerned kindergarten education; her books included *Moral Culture of Infancy, and Kindergarten Guide*, 1863, *Kindergarten Culture*, 1870, *The Kindergarten in Italy*, 1872, and *Letters to Kindergartners*, 1886. In 1873 she founded the *Kindergarten Messenger*, of which she was editor during its two years of life, and in 1877 she organized the American Froebel Union, of which she was first president. From 1879 to 1884 she was a lecturer at the Concord School of Philosophy of her old friend Alcott. She published *Reminiscences of Rev. Wm. Ellery Channing, D.D.*, 1880, and *Last Evening with Allston*, 1886. In her last years she was known for her eccentricity while still widely admired for her contributions to public education. She died in Jamaica Plain (now part of Boston), Massachusetts, on January 3, 1894.

Peabody, Josephine Preston 1874–1922 poet and dramatist

Born on May 30, 1874, in Brooklyn, New York, Josephine Peabody grew up there until 1884, when the death of her father and the consequent poverty of the family forced them to move to the Dorchester, Massachusetts, home of her maternal grandmother. She had early absorbed her parents' love of literature and the theater, and she read and wrote constantly. Her first published work was a poem in *The Woman's Journal* in 1888, when she was fourteen. Her formal schooling nearly ended with three years at the Girls' Latin

School in Boston in 1889–1892, but after poems of hers had been accepted by the *Atlantic Monthly* and *Scribner's Magazine* in 1894 she was enabled by a patron to attend Radcliffe College as a special student in 1894–1896. Her first volume of verse, *The Wayfarers*, appeared in 1898 and was followed by *Fortune and Men's Eyes*, a one-act play built on Shakespeare's sonnets, 1900, and *Marlowe*, a verse play on Christopher Marlowe, 1901. From 1901 to 1903 she lectured on poetry and literature at Wellesley College. After a European tour in 1902 she produced *The Singing Leaves*, a collection of poems, 1903, and *Pan*, a choric idyll produced for a state occasion in Ottawa in 1904. Peabody's early verse showed the influences of Shakespeare, Browning, and the Pre-Raphaelites, especially Christina Rossetti, and throughout her career her work was marked by delicacy, clarity, and a certain otherworldliness. In June 1906 she married Lionel S. Marks, a Harvard engineering professor with whom she toured Europe for a year before settling in Cambridge, Massachusetts. In 1908 she published *The Book of the Little Past*, a collection of poems for children, and in 1909 *The Piper*, a verse drama on the Pied Piper legend. *The Piper* won the Stratford Prize Competition over 314 other entries and in July 1910 was produced at the Memorial Theatre, Stratford-upon-Avon. It was warmly praised by critics in England and America and subsequently enjoyed successful productions in London and in January 1911 at the New Theatre, New York. *The Singing Man*, a collection of poems exhibiting her growing concern with social justice, appeared in 1911. *The Wings*, a verse drama written in 1907, was produced in Boston in 1912. *The Wolf of Gubbio*, a drama on St. Francis of Assisi, 1913, was followed by *Harvest Moon*, poems, 1916, *The Chameleon*, a comedy, 1917, *Song for the Pilgrim Women*, the Plymouth, Massachusetts, pageant piece for 1921, and *Portrait of Mrs. W.*, a play about Mary Wollstonecraft, 1922. She died in Cambridge, Massachusetts, on December 4, 1922.

Peabody, Lucy Whitehead McGill Waterbury 1861–1949 missionary

Born on March 2, 1861, in Belmont, Kansas, Lucy McGill grew up in Pittsford, New York, and from 1873 in nearby Rochester. After graduating from Rochester Academy in 1878 she taught for three years in the Rochester State School for the Deaf. In August 1881 she married Reverend Norman W. Waterbury, a Baptist minister with whom she sailed two months later to India. They worked among the minority Telugu people of Madras under the aegis of the American Baptist Missionary Union until Waterbury's death in 1886. After her return to Rochester and a brief period of teaching she became an assistant secretary of the Woman's Baptist Foreign Missionary Society. She moved to the society's Boston headquarters in 1889 and the next year became corresponding secretary of the society. In 1890 she founded the Farther Lights Society, a girls' auxiliary to the mission society, and helped promote the establishment of an annual day of prayer for missions, an idea that became known as the World Day of Prayer. In 1902 she became chairman of the Central Committee on the United Study of Foreign Missions, which had grown out of the New York Ecumenical Missionary Conference of 1900. She held the post until 1929, and in it she developed a series of textbooks for use by women's study groups and by a network of some 30 summer schools of missionary studies. In 1908 she founded and until 1920 she edited *Everyland*, a missionary magazine for children. She resigned as secretary of the Woman's Baptist Foreign Missionary Society on her marriage to Henry W. Peabody in June 1906; he died in 1908.

In 1912, largely at Lucy Peabody's instigation, the Interdenominational Conference of Woman's Boards of Foreign Missions in the United States and Canada created the Committee on Christian Literature for Women and Children, of which she became an influential member. The committee collected, translated, and published magazines for distribution around the world. In 1913 she became vice-president for the foreign department of the newly unified Woman's American Baptist Foreign Mission Society, and she was instrumental in transforming the Interdenominational Conference into the more effective Federation of Women's Boards of Foreign Missions in 1916. In 1913–1914 and 1919–1920 she made world tours of inspection of missions, the latter as chairman of a commission studying mission schools. She led a fund-raising drive in 1920–1923 to raise $2 million, upon which a $1 million pledge by John D. Rockefeller was contingent, to finance the establishment of seven women's colleges in the Orient. Traveling and lecturing indefatigably, she raised the required amount and subsequently sat on the boards of directors of three of the seven: Women's Christian College, Madras, and Women's Christian Medical College, Vellore, in India, and Shanghai Medical College. She resigned as vice-president of the WABFMS in 1921 in a dispute over ecumenism, which she supported, and in 1927 she resigned all her other denominational offices in a disagreement over missionary qualifications and modernist theology, which she opposed. She then formed the Association of Baptists for World Evangelism, which undertook new missions in the Philippines. She remained president of the group until 1934, and from 1928 she published its periodical *Message*. During the 1920s she was also a leader of opposition to the growing movement to repeal Prohibition, serving for more than ten years as president of the Woman's National Committee for Law Enforcement. She died in Danvers, Massachusetts, on February 26, 1949.

Peale, Anna Claypoole and Sarah Miriam 1791–1878 and 1800–1885
painters

Born in Philadelphia, Anna on March 6, 1791, and Sarah on May 19, 1800, the Peale sisters were daughters of James Peale, a painter, and nieces of Charles Willson Peale, a well known portraitist. Painting was a Peale family enterprise, and as James had entered his brother's studio and gradually taken over work on backgrounds and in miniatures, so Anna took over miniature work from her father. She exhibited a "Fruit Piece" at the first exhibition of the Pennsylvania Academy of Fine Arts in 1811 and three years later showed a "Frame containing three miniatures." She then traveled to Washington, D.C., to enter the studio of her uncle Charles and won his highest praise for her miniature portraits on ivory. Her sympathetic portraits, heightened by contrasting backgrounds, brought her more commissions than she could comfortably handle; among her subjects were James Monroe, Andrew Jackson, Henry Clay, and William Bainbridge. She worked at various times in Boston and Baltimore as well. In 1824 she was elected to the Pennsylvania Academy of Fine Arts, where she exhibited regularly until 1842. Following her marriage (her second) to General William Duncan in 1841 she retired. She died in Philadelphia on December 25, 1878.

Her younger sister Sarah first exhibited at the Pennsylvania Academy in 1818 with "Portrait of a Lady (second attempt)." The next year she exhibited two portraits and four still lifes. After a brief time in her uncle Charles's studio in Washington she launched an independent career as a portraitist, working in Philadelphia and Baltimore. In 1824 she was elected to the Pennsylvania Academy along with her sister, and she continued to exhibit there annually until 1831. She often shared studio and patronage with her sister. Her portraits were distinctive in their lovingly detailed furs, laces, and fabrics. Her subjects included Thomas Hart Benton, Caleb Cushing, William R. D. King, Daniel Webster, and in 1825 the Marquis de Lafayette. In 1846 she left Baltimore for St. Louis where she was the leading portraitist for 32 years. She later turned to still life painting as well. In 1878 she returned to Philadelphia to live with Anna, now widowed again. She died in Philadelphia on February 4, 1885. The Peale sisters were among the very first women to achieve professional recognition and success as artists in America.

Peck, Annie Smith 1850–1935 mountain climber

Born in Providence, Rhode Island, on October 19, 1850, Annie Peck early developed remarkable physical strength, endurance, and courage through her determined competition with her three older brothers. She attended Dr. Stockbridge's School for Young Ladies, Providence High School, and in 1870–1872 the Rhode Island State Normal School (now Rhode Island College). After teaching school in Providence and then in Saginaw, Michigan, she entered the University of Michigan in 1874 and graduated with honors four years later. She taught for short periods in schools in Cincinnati and in Montclair, New Jersey, and from 1881, when she received her master's degree from Michigan, to 1883 she taught Latin at Purdue University. In 1883–1885 she pursued advanced studies in Germany, and in the latter year she became the first woman admitted to the American School of Classical Studies in Athens. In 1886–1887 she taught Latin at Smith College.

On Peck's journey from Germany to Greece in 1885 the sight of the Matterhorn had aroused in her an interest in climbing. After a few practice climbs she tackled Mount Shasta, California, in 1888. Her ascent of the Matterhorn in 1895 brought her wide celebrity and, in Victorian society, a touch of notoriety. In 1897 she climbed the volcano Popocatepetl and Mount Orizaba in Mexico, the latter, at 18,314 feet, the highest point in the Western Hemisphere reached by a woman up to that time. She supported herself by giving parlor lectures and subsequently by lecturing on the Chautauqua and other circuits, but little money was left over for proper equipment and preparation for her more ambitious and demanding climbs; she drove herself and her hired help nonetheless. In 1900 she represented the United States at the Paris Congrès Internationale de l'Alpinisme, and while in Europe she climbed the Fünffingerspitze in the Austrian Tyrol, Monte Cristallo in the Dolomites, and the Jungfrau in Switzerland. In 1902 she helped found the American Alpine Club. She then began exploring South America for a peak on which she could make a first ascent. In 1904 she climbed the 20,867-foot Illampu peak of Mount Sorata, Bolivia. Several lesser climbs followed, and in September 1908 she conquered the north peak of Huascarán in the Peruvian Andes. Estimating the summit to be about 24,000 feet, she could claim to have reached higher than any other woman. A subsequent triangulation by French engineers sent by Fanny Bullock Workman showed the peak to be 21,812 feet, leaving her still with the American record in the Western Hemisphere. In 1911, at the age of sixty one, she climbed Mount Coropuna (21,250 feet), Peru, raising a "Votes for Women" pennant at the top.

In addition to lecturing Peck wrote occasional articles for magazines and published *A Search for the Apex of South America*, 1911, *The South American Tour*, 1913, *Industrial and Commercial South America*, 1922, and *Flying over South America — 20,000 Miles by Air*, on the feasibility of commercial aviation on that continent, 1932. In 1927 the Lima Geographical Society named the north peak of Huascarán in her honor — Cumbre Aña Peck. Her last climb was of Mount Madison, New Hampshire, when she was eighty-two. She died in New York City on July 18, 1935.

Pendleton, Ellen Fitz 1864–1936 educator

Born in Westerly, Rhode Island, on August 7, 1864, Ellen Pendleton attended local public schools and in 1886 graduated from Wellesley College. She remained at Wellesley as a tutor in mathematics, Latin, and Greek until 1888, when she received an appointment as instructor in mathematics. In 1889–1890 she pursued graduate studies at Newnham College, Cambridge, and in 1891 she was awarded an M.A. by Wellesley. In 1897 she became secretary of the college and in 1901 associate professor of mathematics, dean, and head of College Hall. She became acting president in 1910 and the next year was the first alumna to be elected president of Wellesley. She came to the post at the close of a decade of expansion and innovation, and she quickly proved to be ideally suited to administer a period of consolidation.

In her 25 years as president Pendleton saw a small growth in the student body but a remarkable eightfold increase in endowment, to nearly $10 million, and a virtual rebuilding of the physical plant. The destruction by fire of College Hall, which contained most of the classrooms and offices, the library, dormitory quarters, and other facilities, in March 1914 brought out her highest leadership and organizational talents. After an early spring vacation Wellesley students were back in class in makeshift quarters in three weeks. A $3 million fund-raising campaign financed the construction of seven new brick buildings over the next decade; eight more followed before her retirement, in all comprising six dormitories, four apartment buildings for faculty and staff, three academic buildings, an alumnae-student building, and an administration building.

On the academic side Pendleton instituted an honors program and resisted the introduction of either vocational or narrowly specialized courses of study. She was a strong supporter of academic freedom and opposed the dismissal by the trustees of Emily Greene Balch in 1918. She served at various times as president of the College Entrance Examination Board, president of the New England Association of Colleges and Secondary Schools, and vice-president of Phi Beta Kappa, and from 1923 she was the only woman juror for the American Peace Prize established by Edward Bok. She retired from Wellesley in 1936 and died a month later, on July 26, 1936, in Newton, Massachusetts.

Perkins, Frances 1882–1965 public official

Frances Perkins

Born in Boston on April 10, 1882, Frances Perkins grew up and attended public schools in Worcester, Massachusetts. She graduated from Mount Holyoke College in 1902 and for some years taught school and served as a social worker for the Episcopal church. She worked briefly with Jane Addams at Hull-House in Chicago and then resumed her studies, first at the Wharton School of Finance and Commerce of the University of Pennsylvania and then at Columbia University, where she took an M.A. in social economics in 1910. From that year until 1912 she was executive secretary of the Consumers' League of New York, for which, under its president, Maud Nathan, she directed studies of working conditions and hours and of female and child labor. She led the lobbying efforts that resulted in state legislation on factory safety standards in 1911 and on hours and wages in 1913. From 1912 to 1917 she was executive secretary of the New York Committee on Safety and from 1917 to 1919 executive director of the New York Council of Organization for War Service. She was appointed in 1919 to New York's State Industrial Commission by Governor Alfred E. Smith, and in 1923 she was named to the State Industrial Board, of which she became chairman in 1926. Smith's successor, Franklin D. Roosevelt, appointed her state industrial commissioner in 1929. She was, both before and after the onset of the Great Depression of the 1930s, a strong advocate of unemployment insurance and close government supervision of fiscal policy.

When Roosevelt entered the presidency in 1933 he named Perkins secretary of labor, making her the first woman to serve in a cabinet position. After the initial controversy of her appointment died away she settled into a 12-year term of effective administration of her department. During that time the department's activities in social service and research and fair labor standards enforcement were greatly expanded. It was, on the other hand, pointed out that most of the New Deal's innovative and controversial programs bearing on labor were established either outside the Department of Labor or upon a semi-autonomous footing within. She thus had little to do with shaping or administering the National Recovery Administration, the National Labor Relations Board, the Wages and Hours Board, or the Walsh-Healy Act. She was also of limited influence in settling the major labor disputes in the steel and auto industries that occurred in the 1930s and 1940s. Nonetheless much of the bitter criticism heaped upon the New Deal devolved upon her, allowing her at the least to establish a reputation as one of the most unflappable members of the Roosevelt administration. In 1934 she published *People at Work*. She left the cabinet in June 1945. From 1946 to 1953 she was a member of the U.S. Civil Service Commission, and in subsequent years she was a much sought-after lecturer on labor and industrial problems. *The Roosevelt I Knew*, a record of her association with the late president, was published in 1946. She died in New York City on May 14, 1965.

Perkins, Lucy Fitch 1865–1937 writer of children's books

Born on July 12, 1865, in Maples, Indiana, Lucy Fitch grew up there, in Hopkinton, Massachusetts, and in Kalamazoo, Michigan. After her graduation from Kalamazoo High School in 1883 she attended the Museum of Fine Arts School in Boston for three years. She worked as an illustrator for the Prang Educational Company in Boston for a year and then taught for four years in the School of Fine Arts of the newly opened Pratt Institute in Brooklyn, New York. In August 1891 she married Dwight H. Perkins, with whom she settled in Chicago. She abandoned her career for a time, but in 1893 she resumed it. She worked as an illustrator for the Chicago office of the Prang firm, painted mural decoration in schoolrooms, taught art, and lectured. In 1906, two years after she and her husband moved to Evanston, Illinois, she published her first book, *The Goose Girl*, a collection of rhymes for children. *A Book of Joys: A Story of a New England Summer* appeared in 1907.

With *The Dutch Twins*, 1911, Perkins began a series of geographical and historical story books that proved enormously popular. Humorous, unpedantic, and illustrated in her own whimsical style, the "Twins" series extended to 26 volumes, including *Japanese Twins*, 1912, *Irish Twins*, 1913, *Mexican Twins*, 1915, *Cave Twins*, 1916, *Belgian Twins*, 1917, *French Twins*, 1918, *Scotch Twins*, 1919, *Spartan Twins*, 1920, *Italian Twins*, 1920, *Puritan Twins*, 1921, *Swiss Twins*, 1922, *Filipino Twins*, 1923, *Colonial Twins of Virginia*, 1924, *American Twins of 1812*, 1925, *American Twins of the*, 1926, *Pioneer Twins*, 1927, *Farm Twins*, 1928, *Indian Twins*, 1930, *Pickaniny Twins*, 1931, *Norwegian Twins*, 1933, *Spanish Twins*, 1934, and *Chinese Twins*, 1935. In all, the books of the series sold more than 2 million copies and were translated into several foreign languages. Others of her books included *Cornelia*, 1919, *Robin Hood*, 1923, and *Mr. Chick*, 1926. *Dutch Twins and Little Brother*, on which she was at work at her death, was completed by her son and daughter and published in 1938. She died in Pasadena, California, on March 18, 1937.

Perry, Antoinette 1888–1946 actor and director

Born in Denver on June 27, 1888, Mary Antoinette Perry was educated at Wolcott's School in her native city. In her youth she frequently traveled in summer with an aunt and uncle who were touring actors. She made her theatrical debut in *Mrs. Temple's Telegram* at Powers' Theatre, Chicago, in June 1905; later that year she made her New York debut in the same play at the Madison Square Theatre. Over the next four years she appeared in *Lady Jim*, 1906, David Belasco's *The Music Master*, 1906, *A Grand Army Man*, 1907, and again in *The Music Master*, 1908. In November 1909 she married Frank W. Frueauff, a Denver businessman with whom she settled in New York City. During the marriage her connection with the theater was limited to aiding talented young people, notably composer Deems Taylor. Her husband died in 1922, and in 1924 she returned to the stage in Zona Gale's *Mr. Pitt*, with Walter Huston. Subsequently she appeared in *Minick*, 1924, *The Dunce Boy*, 1925, *Engaged*, 1925, *Caught*, 1925, *The Masque of Venice*, 1926, *The Ladder*, 1926, and *Electra*, 1927.

In 1928 Perry turned to directing, making her debut in that field with *Goin' Home*, at the Hudson Theatre in August of that year. Preston Sturges's *Strictly Dishonorable*, which opened on Broadway in September 1929 and ran for 557 performances, was her first great directorial success. Working with producer Brock Pemberton, with whom she shared a professional and personal alliance for two decades, she subsequently directed such plays as *Divorce Me Dear*, 1931, *Christopher Comes Across*, *Personal Appearance*, 1934,

Ceiling Zero, 1935, *Red Harvest*, 1937, Clare Boothe Luce's *Kiss the Boys Goodbye*, 1938, *Lady in Waiting*, 1940, *Cuckoos on the Hearth*, 1941, *Janie*, 1942, *Pillar to Post*, 1943, and the Pulitzer Prize-winning *Harvey*, 1944. She also staged an American Theatre Wing production of *The Barretts of Wimpole Street*, with Katharine Cornell, for Allied military audiences in Europe in 1944–1945. She served as chairman of the committee of the Apprentice Theatre of the American Theatre Council in 1937–1939, and in 1941 she was president of the Experimental Theatre of the Actors Equity Association. She was a founder of the American Theatre Wing, which operated the well known Stage Door Canteens in several cities and otherwise provided hospitality and entertainment for servicemen, and was its chairman from 1941 to 1944. She died in New York City on June 28, 1946. In 1947 the American Theatre Wing established the annual Antoinette Perry Awards — known as Tony Awards — for distinguished theatrical performance, direction, production, design, composition, and other accomplishments on the New York stage.

Perry, Nora 1831–1896 journalist and writer of children's books

Born in 1831 in Dudley, Massachusetts, Nora Perry grew up there and in Providence, Rhode Island. From childhood she composed stories and poems, and at eighteen she had her first story published in *Harper's Magazine*. She served as Boston correspondent for the *Chicago Tribune* and the *Providence Journal* for a time while continuing to contribute stories, serials, and poems to various other periodicals. Among her best known poems were "Tying Her Bonnet Under Her Chin," published in the *National Era*, and "After the Ball" (sometimes called "Maud and Madge"), in the *Atlantic Monthly*. Her later writings were principally stories for girls. Her books included *After the Ball, and Other Poems*, 1875, *Her Lover's Friend, and Other Poems*, 1880, *The Tragedy of the Unexpected and Other Stories*, 1880, *A Book of Love Stories*, 1881, *For a Woman, a Novel*, 1885, *New Songs and Ballads*, 1887, *A Flock of Girls and Their Friends*, 1887, *The Youngest Miss Lorton and Other Stories*, 1889, *Brave Girls*, 1889, *Lyrics and Legends*, 1891, *Hope Benham, a Story for Girls*, 1894, *Three Little, Daughters of the Revolution*, 1896, and posthumously *Cottage Neighbors*, 1899, *That Little Smith Girl*, 1899, *May Bartlett's Stepmother*, 1900, *Ju Ju's Christmas Party*, 1901, and *A New Year's Call*, 1903. Sentimental and simple, her stories nonetheless possessed humor and gaiety and were widely popular. Nora Perry died in Dudley, Massachusetts, on May 13, 1896.

Pettit, Katherine 1868–1936 settlement worker

Born on February 23, 1868, near Lexington, Kentucky, Katherine Rhoda Pettit was educated privately in Lexington and Louisville. In the 1890s, while working with the Woman's Christian Temperance Union and the State Federation of Women's Clubs, she first discovered the isolation, poverty, and hopelessness of the lives of Kentucky mountain people. From informally distributing flower seeds and decorative pictures to mountain women, her involvement developed into a full commitment to improve their lives. In the summer of 1899, under the aegis of the State Federation of Women's Clubs, she and a coworker established a camp on the outskirts of remote Hazard, Perry County, Kentucky, and for several weeks offered housewives instructions in healthful food preparation, gardening, and housekeeping and entertained children with songs, games, and Bible readings. They were invited to hold a similar camp, called an "Industrial," at Hindman, Knott County, in the summer of 1900, and in 1901 they set up near Sassafras, also in Knott. In 1901 they began raising funds for a permanent institution.

A fund-raising tour of eastern cities, along with contributions from organizations and local people, enabled them to open the Hindman School in August 1902. Academic subjects were taught as well as crafts and domestic and industrial skills. Through the efforts of another co-worker, treatment was made available for the endemic trachoma that left many mountain people blind. In 1913 Katherine Pettit left Hindman to establish the Pine Mountain Settlement School near Dillon, Harlan County, a task that she carried through from the clearing of a parcel of donated timberland to the erection of buildings from the lumber. While organizing classes and extension work and clinics for trachoma, hookworm, and dental care, she also encouraged the practice of traditional arts and crafts. In 1907 she published some mountain ballads from Harlan County in *Journal of American Folk-Lore*, one of the very few occasions she ventured into public print. She resigned as co-director of Pine Mountain Settlement School in 1930 and for the next five years traveled alone through Harlan County offering instruction and advice in farming and acting as agent for craftsmen. She died in Lexington, Kentucky, on September 3, 1936.

Phelps, Almira Hart Lincoln 1793–1884 educator and writer

Born in Berlin, Connecticut, on July 15, 1793, Almira Hart was a younger sister of Emma Hart (Willard). She was educated at home, in district schools, for a time by Emma, and in 1812 at an academy in Pittsfield, Massachusetts. After a year of teaching at the Berlin Academy she conducted a school of her own briefly in her family's home and then in 1816 became principal of an academy in Sandy Hill, New York. In October 1817 she married Simeon Lincoln, editor of the *Connecticut Mirror* of Hartford. After his death in 1823 she became a teacher in her sister's Troy Female Seminary, where she remained for eight years, the last as acting principal in Emma's absence.

In 1829 Lincoln published a textbook, *Familiar Lectures on Botany*, which enjoyed wide use and went through nine editions in ten years. It was followed by *Dictionary of Chemistry*, translated from a French work, 1830. Following her marriage in August 1831 to John Phelps, a lawyer, she settled with him in Guilford, Vermont. Over the next several years she published *Lectures to Young Ladies*, 1833, *Botany for Beginners*, 1833, *Geology for Beginners*, 1834, *Chemistry for Beginners*, 1834, *Natural Philosophy for Beginners*, 1836, *Lectures on Natural Philosophy*, 1836, and *Lectures on Chemistry*, 1837. She also wrote a novel, *Caroline Westerly*, 1833. In 1838 she accepted the offer of the principalship of the Young Ladies' Seminary in West Chester, Pennsylvania. When the school closed the next year, she became head of the Female Institute of Rahway, New Jersey.

In 1841 Phelps became principal and her husband business manager of the Patapsco Female Institute in Ellicott's Mills, Maryland. In her 15 years at that school she created an institution of high academic standards, with a curriculum rich in the sciences, mathematics, and natural history and designed in particular to train highly qualified teachers. The polite attainments that passed for education in most girls' schools of the time were not entirely ignored but were relegated to secondary importance. In 1856 she retired and settled in Baltimore. In her remaining years she wrote frequently for national periodicals.

Others of her books included *Ida Norman*, a novel, 1848, *Christian Households*, 1858, and *Hours with My Pupils*, 1859, and she edited *Our Country in its Relation to the Past, Present and Future*, 1864. In 1859 she became the second woman to be elected to the American Association for the Advancement of Science, following Maria Mitchell. She died in Baltimore on July 15, 1884.

Phillips, Lena Madesin 1881–1955 lawyer and clubwoman

Born in Nicholasville, Kentucky, on October 15, 1881, Anna Lena Phillips adopted the names Lena Madesin when she was eleven. She was educated at the local Jessamine Female Institute and in 1899–1901 at the Woman's College of Baltimore (now Goucher College). She attended the Peabody Institute of Music in Baltimore for a time, but an injury to her arm ended her dreams of a career as a concert pianist. Over the next decade she held various jobs: she worked in a store, sold books door-to-door, sold music, taught music at Jessamine Institute, and conducted her own music school. In 1915, after suffering a nervous breakdown, she resolved to become a lawyer. Two years later she graduated from the University of Kentucky Law School. She soon became an attorney for the Young Women's Christian Association and secretary of its National War Work Council. In 1918 she was sent to New York City to organize the National Business Women's Committee for war work. Although the war had ended before the committee was able to begin its work, the members decided to form a permanent peacetime organization for women in business and the professions.

Lena Phillips organized a convention in St. Louis in July 1919 at which was formed the National Federation of Business and Professional Women's Clubs, and from then until 1923 she was executive secretary of the federation. While traveling widely to foster the establishment of local clubs, she helped found the federation's journal, *Independent Woman*, in 1920. In 1923, after receiving a master's degree in law from New York University, she entered private practice in New York City. In 1926–1929 she served as president of the National Federation of Business and Professional Women's Clubs, and during that period she initiated the movement that culminated in a conference in Geneva in August 1930 at which the International Federation of Business and Professional Women was formed. She served as president of the International Federation from then until 1947. In 1931–1935 she was also president of the National Council of Women, and in 1933 she was president of the International Conference of Women held in conjunction with the Chicago World's Fair. She abandoned her legal practice in 1935 and for four years thereafter was associate editor of and a columnist for the *Pictorial Review*. Her work as president of the International Federation required her to travel frequently to Europe, and during and after World War II she worked to sustain and rebuild clubs and national federations there. She was also active in war relief work and the United Nations and later was chairman of the First International Conference on Public Information. She died in Marseilles, France, on May 22, 1955.

Piatt, Sarah Morgan Bryan 1836–1919 poet

Born on August 11, 1836, in Lexington, Kentucky, Sarah Bryan grew up in Versailles and, after her mother's death, in New Castle, Kentucky. She was educated at the Henry Female College in New Castle. From an early age she was a lover of English poetry, and in her youth she began to write verses herself under the influence of those of Scott, Byron, Coleridge, and Shelley. Her first published poem appeared in the *Galveston News* of Texas, whose editor had been shown it by chance. A short time later poems of hers began appearing regularly in the *Louisville Journal* and then in the *New York Ledger*. She was widely known as a poet by the time of her marriage in June 1861 to John L. Piatt, journalist, poet, and coauthor with William Dean Howells of *Poems of Two Friends*, 1860. They lived in Washington, D.C., until 1867 and then in North Bend, Ohio, until 1882. During those years Piatt produced several volumes of poetry, including *The Nests at Washington and Other Poems* with her husband, 1864, *A Woman's Poems*, 1871, *A Voyage to the Fortunate Isles and Other Poems*, 1874, *That New World and Other Poems*, 1876, and *Dramatic Persons and Moods*, 1880.

In 1882 they moved to Cork, Ireland, where John Piatt was U.S. consul until 1893. There their friends eventually included Edmund Gosse, Alice Meynell, Katharine Tynan, and Austin Dobson. Ireland proved fertile ground for her poetry, which was typically characterized by a light lyrical expression of domestic scenes and emotions with a recurrent lindertone of melancholy. In form it was frequently unconventional. Books published in that period included *An Irish Garland*, 1884, *Primrose Time*, 1886, *Child's World Ballads*, 1887, *The Little Emigrants*, 1887, *The Witch in the Glass*, 1888, *An Irish Wild Flower*, 1891, *An Enchanted Castle*, 1893, and *Pictures, Portraits, and People in Ireland*, 1893. She also collaborated with her husband on *The Children Out-of-Doors*, 1885. Her *Collected Poems* appeared in 1894. Her verse was much admired in England, where it was compared to that of Christina Rossetti and Elizabeth Barrett Browning. After their return to the United States in 1893 the Piatts lived in North Bend, Ohio, and after her husband's death in 1917 Sarah Piatt lived in Caldwell, New Jersey, until her death there on December 22, 1919.

Pickford, Mary 1893–1979 actor

Born in Toronto on April 8, 1893, Gladys Mary Smith was the daughter of actors. Soon after the death of her father she began taking child's roles in productions in which her mother was playing. From the age of five she appeared in such plays as *The Silver King*, *Bootle's Baby*, *Little Ted*, *Uncle Tom's Cabin*, *The Little Red Schoolhouse*, *East Lynne*, and *The Fatal Wedding*. The Smith family toured together, from 1906 under the name Pickford, which her mother adopted from a relative. Young Gladys made her New York debut (under her original name) in David Belasco's *The Warrens of Virginia* at the Belasco Theatre in December 1907. At fourteen she had already learned more of stagecraft than veterans much older than she, and her winsome face, topped by a mass of golden curls, made her appeal virtually irresistible. Other Belasco productions followed on Broadway and on tour.

In 1908 Pickford met David W. Griffith of the Biograph Studio and began appearing as an extra in some of his films, beginning with *Her First Biscuit* with Florence Lawrence. In two years she had roles in 74 Biograph films. Her first starring role was in *The Violin Maker at Cremona*, 1909. Over the next several years she worked in turn for Carl Laemmle's Independent Motion Picture Company; for Majestic Films; again for Biograph, for Belasco in 1913, when she was a Broadway sensation in *A Good Little Devil*, in 1913–1915 for Adolph Zukor's Famous Players Company (during that time her salary rose from $500 to $2000 per week); for American Film Company; and in 1916 again for Famous Players, which created the Mary Pickford Studios to produce her films and the Artcraft Company to distribute them.

Pickford's meteoric rise from an anonymous player to a star with her own production company was attributable not only to the phenomenal popularity of her films but also to her dedication to her craft and her meticulous care in creating quality entertainments. The ringleted ingenue with an expression of sweet sincerity and invincible innocence that she played in such silent films as *Hearts Adrift*, 1914, *Madame Butterfly*, 1915, *Poor Little Peppina*, 1916, *The Eternal Grind*, 1916, *Hulda from Holland*, 1916, *Less Than the Dust*, 1916, *The Pride of the Clan*, 1917, *Poor Little Rich Girl*, 1917, *Rebecca of Sunnybrook Farm*, 1917, *A Romance of the Redwoods*, 1917, *The Little Princess*, 1917, *M'liss*, 1918, and *Johanna Enlists*, 1918, enthralled audiences everywhere. She was known at first as "the Biograph Girl with the Curls" and then as "Our Mary" when that much of her name was revealed; with the release of *Tess of the Storm Country* in 1914 she was firmly established as "America's Sweetheart." In 1917 First National Films paid her $350,000 each for three films, including the very successful *Daddy Long Legs*, 1919.

In 1919 Pickford took the lead in organizing the United Artists Corporation with Griffith, Charlie Chaplin, and Douglas Fairbanks. In March 1920, after the dissolution of her first marriage (1911–1919) to actor Owen Moore, she married Fairbanks, America's favorite swashbuckler. As Hollywood's leading, and perhaps America's best loved, couple they reigned happily from "Pickfair," their lavish estate. Pickford's popularity continued unabated in *Heart o' the Hills*, 1919, *Pollyanna*, 1920, *Suds*, 1920, *Little Lord Fauntleroy*, 1921, *The Love Light*, 1921, *Rosita*, 1923, *Dorothy Vernon of Haddon Hall*, 1924, *Little Annie Rooney*, 1925, *Sparrows*, 1926, *My Best Girl*, 1927, *Coquette*, her first talking picture, in which she won an Academy Award for best actress, 1929, *The Taming of the Shrew*, her only film with Fairbanks, 1929, and *Kiki*, 1931.

With *Secrets*, 1933, her 194th film, Pickford retired from the screen. Thereafter she devoted herself to United Artists' of which she was first vice-president from 1935 and for which she produced several films. She also wrote *Why Not Try God*, 1934, *The Demi-Widow*, a novel, 1935, and *My Rendezvous with Life*, 1935, and in the 1930s appeared on radio. She and Fairbanks were divorced in 1935, and in 1937 she married actor Charles "Buddy" Rogers. Her later years were given over to business and civic and charitable activities. *Sunshine and Shadow*, her autobiography, was published in 1955. She eventually became a recluse at Pickfair. She died in Santa Monica, California, on May 29, 1979.

Pierce, Sarah 1767–1852 educator

Born in Litchfield, Connecticut, on June 26, 1767, Sarah Pierce attended schools in her native town and for a time in New York City. In 1792 she opened a school in her home in Litchfield. The success of the school was such that in 1798 a group of Litchfield citizens presented her with a building to house the rapidly growing institution. Alongside Tapping Reeve's already famous Litchfield Law School, Pierce's helped make Litchfield a leading center of education in the young United States. In addition to basic subjects she taught composition, geography, history, needlework, painting, and dance. She also saw to it that her charges received an amount of physical exercise. In 1814 she brought her nephew, John P. Brace, a Williams College graduate, into the school, and he instituted classes in logic, philosophy, and the sciences. In 1825 she relinquished the principalship to him, but she continued to teach the course that was her particular love, universal history. Between 1811 and 1818 she had published four volumes of *Sketches of Universal History Compiled from Several Authors, For the Use of Schools* for that course. At its peak the school enrolled some 130 students, some of them boys. Among them were Catharine Beecher, Harriet Beecher (Stowe), and Henry Ward Beecher, children of Reverend Lyman Beecher, who provided religious instruction at the school in return for his children's tuition. In 1827 the school was incorporated as the Litchfield Female Academy. Pierce retired from teaching in 1833; the school closed about a decade later. She died in Litchfield, Connecticut, on January 19, 1852.

Pike, Mary Hayden Green 1824–1908 novelist

Born on November 30, 1824, in Eastport, Maine, Mary Green grew up and attended school in nearby Calais. From 1840 to 1843 she studied at the Female Seminary in Charlestown, Massachusetts. In September 1845 she married Frederick A. Pike, a lawyer of Calais. In 1854 she published a novel, *Ida May*, under the pseudonym "Mary Langdon." The melodramatic tale of a child of wealthy white parents who is kidnapped and sold into slavery, the book was an immediate success. Riding to some extent on the coattails of *Uncle Tom's Cabin*, published two years before, *Ida May* sold some 60,000 copies in less than two years and appeared in several British editions and in German translation. In 1856 she published *Caste: A Story of Republican Equality* under the name "Sydney A. Story, Jr." *Caste* told of a quadroon girl forbidden to marry a white man, and while it was less successful than *Ida May* it received much favorable critical comment. *Agnes*, 1858, her last book, concerned a North American protagonist in the time of the Revolution. Pike also contributed to the *Atlantic Monthly*, *Harper's*, *Graham's*, and other magazines. She later abandoned writing for landscape painting. From 1861 to 1869, while her husband sat in Congress, she lived in Washington, D.C. They then passed several years in Europe before returning to Calais. After her husband's death in 1886 she lived in Plainfield, New Jersey. She died in Baltimore on January 15, 1908.

Pinkham, Lydia Estes 1819–1883 businesswoman

Born on February 9, 1819, in Lynn, Massachusetts, Lydia Estes grew up in a Quaker family and attended Lynn Academy. For several years she taught school, and she was an ardent member of many reform groups for abolition, Swedenborgianism, phrenology, temperance, women's rights, and other causes. In September 1843 she married a young widower, Isaac Pinkham, to whom, together with her children, she devoted herself for the next 30 years. The Panic of 1873 left the family in financial straits, and it was at the suggestion of one of her sons that she thought to exploit her local reputation for an herbal medicine she had been concocting for years. Mainly an infusion of unicorn root (*Aletris farinosa*) and pleurisy root (*Asclepius tuberosa*), it was held by her and her neighbors to be a sovereign remedy for "women's weakness" and similar ills. Pinkham had ordinarily given the medicine away to anyone who wanted it, but in the 1870s she decided to sell it.

Bottled with about 18 percent alcohol as a "solvent and preservative," Lydia E. Pinkham's Vegetable Compound made its commercial appearance in Lynn in 1875. Her contribution to the astounding success of the preparation was twofold: for years she prepared the brew herself on her own kitchen stove; more important, she quickly realized the value of advertising. She wrote most of the early advertisements herself in a quaint, homely style drawn largely from that of the reform movements of her youth. She also personally answered letters from the thousands of women who, unable to bring themselves to consult male physicians, sought her advice on medical problems. She generally prescribed exercise, cleanliness, good diet, and her compound, in which she had complete confidence. Her advertised claims for it gradually grew bolder, and it was eventually recommended for men as well as women. Her sons distributed handbills, placed advertising, and sold their mother's compound in an ever-widening market. Profits were turned back into the business, and from 1879 advertising and labels featured Pinkham's own benign likeness. By 1898 the compound was the most widely advertised product in the United States. The medicine's therapeutic value, if any, was never ascertained, and at one time it was attacked by the American Medical Association as a fraud, but it appears to have soothed the psyches, if not the bodies, of its millions of purchasers for two generations. The legions of satisfied users who volunteered testimonials included many prominent temperance leaders. The business eventually became enormously profitable, but Pinkham lived to see only the promise of such results, for she died in Lynn on May 17, 1883.

ROLLIE MC KENNA

Sylvia Plath

Plath, Sylvia 1932–1963 poet and novelist

Born in Boston on October 27, 1932, Sylvia Plath grew up in Winthrop and Wellesley, Massachusetts. While attending public schools she began writing verse; she won some newspaper poetry competitions and while still in high school sold her first poem, to *Seventeen* magazine. She entered Smith College in 1951. She was a co-winner of the *Mademoiselle* magazine fiction contest in 1952. Despite her remarkable artistic, academic, and social success at Smith, she suffered from severe depression and underwent a period of psychiatric hospitalization. She graduated from Smith with highest honors in 1955 and went on to Newnham College, Cambridge, on a Fulbright fellowship. In June 1956 she married the English poet Ted Hughes. During 1957–1958 she was an instructor in English at Smith College, and the next year she attended classes at Boston University while devoting much time to her poetry.

In 1960, shortly after Plath and her husband returned to England, her first collection of poems appeared as *The Colossus*. Her second book, a strongly autobiographical novel titled *The Bell Jar*, was published in 1963 under the pseudonym "Victoria Lucas." During her last three years she wrote poetry with increasing speed, abandoning the restraints and conventions that had bound much of her early work to produce poems of almost terrifyingly stark self-revelation and confession. All the anxiety, confusion, and doubt that had haunted her were transmuted into verses of great power and pathos borne along on flashes of incisive wit. Suddenly, after a burst of productivity, she took her own life in London on February 11, 1963. *Ariel*, 1965, a collection of her later poems, helped spark the growth of something of a cult devoted to her. The reissue of *The Bell Jar* under her own name in the United States in 1966 and the appearance of small collections of previously unpublished poems, including *Crossing the Water*, 1971, and *Winter Trees*, 1971, were welcomed by critical and cultish admirers alike.

Pocahontas 1595–1617 colonial heroine

Born about 1595 or 1596, probably in the vicinity of the later English settlement of Jamestown, Virginia, Matoaka, whose pet name was Pocahontas (translated variously as "frolicsome" and "my favorite daughter"), was the daughter of Powhatan (as he was known to the English; more properly Wahunsonacock), chief of a confederation of some 30 tribes of the tidewater region. She first appeared in history in December 1607, when she interceded to save the life of Captain John Smith, military leader of the months-old Jamestown settlement, who had been taken prisoner by Native Americans. In later, perhaps fanciful versions of Smith's story, she flung herself over him as his captors prepared to club his head on a stone. At her urging Smith was released to return to Jamestown. She subsequently became a frequent visitor in the settlement, sometimes bearing gifts of food to relieve the hard-pressed settlers. Her playful nature made her a favorite, and her friendship proved valuable to the settlers in helping to preserve peace. After Captain Smith's return to England in 1609 relations between natives and settlers gradually deteriorated. Pocahontas seems to have abandoned or been abandoned by her English friends for a time. In the spring of 1613, however, Captain Samuel Argall took her prisoner with the idea of holding her hostage for a number of English prisoners held by Indians and of forcing a permanent peace. She was held in Jamestown in the most comfortable manner and treated with great courtesy. She was converted to Christianity and christened Rebecca, and in April 1614, with the approval of both Governor Sir Thomas Dale and Powhatan, she married John Rolfe, a settler who had experimentally introduced tobacco culture to Virginia. In the spring of 1616 they sailed with Governor Dale to England, where she was lionized by society and presented at the court of James I. While preparing to return to America, she fell ill and died in Gravesend, Kent, in March 1617. The tale of Pocahontas was to prove over the centuries an enduring inspiration to playwrights, novelists, and poets.

Pons, Lily 1904–1976 opera singer

Born on April 12, 1904, in Draguignan, near Cannes, France, Alice Josephine Pons was of French and Italian parentage. As a child she took up the piano, and at thirteen she entered the Paris Conservatory. Ill health and World War I interrupted her studies for several years. After the war she began playing ingenue roles at the Paris Théâtre des Variétés under the name Lily Pons. She left the theater on her marriage in 1923 to August Mesritz, a lawyer and newspaper publisher. She was encouraged to study singing by her husband, however, and in 1925 she began taking lessons from Alberti di Gorostiaga. In 1928 she made her operatic debut in *Lakmé* in Mulhouse, Alsace. After a year or so of singing in opera houses in the French provinces she came to the United States and auditioned at the Metropolitan Opera House, New York City. Pons made her debut there in January 1931 in *Lucia di Lammermoor*, and her brilliant coloratura soprano was an immediate critical and popular success. Her beauty, diminutive figure, and marked dramatic ability made her a favorite with audiences for a quarter of a century. She was long considered the most glamorous star on the operatic stage. Among her best roles were those in such bel canto works as *Rigoletto*, *Il Barbiere di Siviglia*, *Linda di Chamounix*, *Mignon*, *La Fille du Régiment*, *Le Coq d'Or* and *La Sonnambula*. She sang regularly at the Met and at the opera house of Colon, Buenos Aires, and toured widely in Europe, Great Britain, Australia, and the United States.

Pons appeared in several motion pictures, including *I Dream Too Much*, 1935, *That*

Girl from Paris, 1936, and *Hitting a New High*, 1937, and was also a popular radio performer. In June 1938, having divorced her first husband, she married conductor André Kostelanetz. In the same year she was awarded the Legion of Honor by France. She became a naturalized American citizen in 1940. During World War II she sang for troops in North Africa, Europe, and India, and she was also honored for her work on behalf of the blind. She and Kostelanetz made numerous highly successful joint concert tours until their divorce in 1958. She effectively retired as the Met's reigning diva in 1956, after a gala celebration of her 25th anniversary there, although her formal retirement did not occur until 1964. Her last public performance was at a Promenade concert of the New York Philharmonic, André Kostelanetz conducting, in May 1972. She died in Dallas, Texas, on February 13, 1976.

Pool, Maria Louise 1841–1898 writer

Born in Rockland, Massachusetts, on August 20, 1841, Maria Pool attended public schools in her hometown and for a time was herself a schoolteacher. By the age of twenty she had begun to publish stories in various magazines. She also wrote for a Philadelphia newspaper and, during her residence in Brooklyn, New York, in 1870–1877, for the *New York Tribune* and the *Evening Post*. Her sketches of New England life were well received in the period when the local color movement in American literature was just beginning, and her travels in Florida and the Carolinas also provided material for her pen. While often clumsily plotted, her tales exhibited a deep and affectionate understanding of character and a humorous sense of life. Her books included *A Vacation in a Buggy*, 1887, *Tenting at Stony Beach*, 1888, *Dally*, 1891, *Roweny in Boston*, 1892, *Mrs. Keats Bradford*, 1892, *Katharine North*, 1893, *The Two Salomes*, 1893, *Out of Step*, 1894, *Against Human Nature*, 1895, *Mrs. Gerald*, 1896, *In Buncombe County*, 1896, *In a Dike Shanty*, 1896, *In the First Person*, 1898, *Boss and Other Dogs*, 1898, and *A Golden Sorrow*, 1898, *A Widower & Some Spinsters*, 1899, and *The Meloon Farm*, 1900, were published posthumously. Maria Pool died in Rockland, Massachusetts, on May 19, 1898.

Porter, Eleanor Hodgman 1868–1920 novelist

Born in Littleton, New Hampshire, on December 19, 1868, Eleanor Emily Hodgman attended public schools until ill health forced her to leave high school; she then studied with tutors. She later studied singing at the New England Conservatory of Music in Boston. She gained local reputation as a singer in concerts and church choirs and continued her career after her marriage in May 1892 to John L. Porter, a businessman with whom she lived during the next decade in Chattanooga, Tennessee, in New York City, and in Springfield, Vermont. By the time they settled in Cambridge, Massachusetts, about 1901, however, she had abandoned music in favor of writing. Her stories began appearing in numerous popular magazines and newspapers, and in 1907 she published her first novel, *Cross Currents*. There followed *The Turn of the Tide*, 1908, *The Story of Marco*, 1911, *Miss Billy*, her first really successful book, 1911, and *Miss Billy's Decision*, 1912.

In 1913 Porter published *Pollyanna*, a sentimental tale of a most improbable heroine, a young girl whose "glad game" of always looking for and finding the bright side of things somehow reforms her eantagonists, restores hope to the hopeless, and generally rights the world. The book's immediate and enormous popularity — in countless reprinted editions it eventually sold over a million copies — must be attributed to the American reading public's eagerness for reassurance that rural virtues and cheerful optimism still existed, as well as to Porter's skill in blending dashes of social conscience and ironic distance into the sentimentalism of her message. *Pollyanna*, second on the fiction best-seller list for

1914, was followed by *Pollyanna Grows Up*, 1915. *Pollyanna* was made into a Broadway play starring Helen Hayes in 1916 and then into a motion picture starring Mary Pickford in 1920, and it inspired a veritable industry for related books and products. "Glad" clubs sprang up around the country and then abroad as *Pollyanna* was translated into several foreign languages. The name itself soon entered the American lexicon, albeit in a largely pejorative sense.

Porter's other books included *Miss Billy Married*, 1914, *Just David*, best-seller in 1916, *Six Star Ranch*, 1916, *The Road to Understanding*, a best-seller in 1917, *Oh, Money! Money!*, a best-seller in 1918, *Dawn*, a best seller in 1919, *Mary-Marie*, a best seller in 1920, *Sister Sue*, 1921, and *Hustler Joe*, 1924. Many of her more than 200 stories were collected in *Across the Years*, 1919, *Tangled Threads*, 1919, *The Tie that Binds*, 1919, and, posthumously, *Money, Love and Kate*, 1925, *Little Pardner*, 1926, and *Just Mother*, 1927. Porter died in Cambridge, Massachusetts, on May 21, 1920. A series of juvenile Pollyanna books was subsequently written by Harriet L. Smith and Elizabeth Borton.

Porter, Eliza Emily Chappell 1807–1888 educator and welfare worker

Born on November 5, 1807, in Geneseo, New York, Eliza Chappell grew up there and in Franklin, New York. After a rudimentary education she began teaching school at sixteen, and after moving with her mother to Rochester, New York, in 1828 she opened a school for small children. In 1831 she traveled to the frontier settlement on Mackinac Island (now part of Michigan) as a private tutor, and within a short time she had opened a school for mixed-race Indian children. After a trip east to recover from an illness and to secure support for the founding of more schools in the Northwest, she returned in 1833 and established a school at St. Ignace. She then moved to the small settlement of Chicago and opened a school there. In June 1835 she married the Reverend Jeremiah Porter, with whom she lived in Peoria, Illinois, for two years, in Farmington, Illinois, for three, and in Green Bay, Wisconsin, from 1840 to 1858, when they returned to Chicago. In October 1861 she became directress of the Chicago Sanitary Commission (later the Northwestern Sanitary Commission), organized to solicit, collect, and distribute food, medical, and other supplies for use by the Union army and in military hospitals.

In the spring of 1862 Porter abandoned office work for field service (by the end of the year Mary A. Livermore and Jane C. Hoge had become joint directors of the commission). She escorted a group of women volunteers to Cairo, Illinois, and there and in nearby Mound City she helped organize hospitals and direct the work of caring for the large number of casualties from the battle of Shiloh (Pittsburg Landing) in April. After recruiting more volunteer nurses she assisted in hospitals in Savannah and Memphis, Tennessee, and in the latter city she also established a school for African-American children. During July-October 1863 she was again in charge of the Northwestern Sanitary Commission while Hoge and Livermore were organizing the great Chicago Sanitary Fair. She then visited and distributed supplies to hospitals in Corinth, Vicksburg, Cairo, and Chattanooga, at the last joining "Mother" Mary Ann Bickerdyke in caring for the wounded of General William T. Sherman's army in the march to Atlanta. She and the rough-hewn Mother Bickerdyke made an effective team. In the fall of 1864 she returned to Chicago and then made a tour of inspection of military hospitals in Arkansas and elsewhere. She rejoined Sherman's army for the Carolinas campaign early in 1865. In the months following the end of the Civil War she visited hospitals in Kentucky, Alabama, and Texas. During 1866–1868 she and her husband lived in Prairie du Chien, Wisconsin. They then moved to Brownsville, Texas, where Porter reopened the coeducational Rio Grande Seminary that she had founded on her earlier visit. Over the next 15 years she conducted schools there, at Fort Sill, Oklahoma, and at Fort D.A. Russell, Wyoming, as her husband, now an army chaplain, was transferred. From his retirement in 1882 they traveled much. Eliza Porter died in Santa Barbara, California, on January 1, 1888.

Porter, Gene Stratton 1863–1924 novelist

Born in Wabash County, Indiana, on August 17, 1863, Geneva Stratton attended school in the town of Wabash, to which her family moved in 1874. Her early life in a rural area gave her a deep appreciation for and insight into nature that was to stay with her through life. In April 1886 she married Charles D. Porter of Geneva, Indiana. She and her husband made their home in Geneva, and she continued her nature studies from their luxurious home, which she called Limberlost Cabin after a nearby wild swamp area. About 1895 she began contributing a column on nature photography, a new hobby of hers, to *Recreation* magazine. Later she conducted a similar column in *Outing*. After a few years she attempted a new field, and with the success of a short story published in *Metropolitan* magazine in 1901 she decided on a career in fiction.

Porter's first novel, *The Song of the Cardinal*, appeared in 1903. *Freckles*, 1904, a sentimental tale of a poor and apparently orphaned boy who is the self-appointed guardian of the Limberlost Swamp, was a huge success, with eventual sales of nearly two million copies. Her next books, *What I Have Done with Birds*, 1907, *At the Foot of the Rainbow*, 1907, and *Birds of the Bible*, 1909, met disappointing response, but *A Girl of the Limberlost*, 1909, returned to the style and milieu of *Freckles* and was another great popular success. *The Harvester*, 1911, reached the best-seller list (it eventually sold some 1.5 million copies). *Moths of the Limberlost*, 1912, was another book of nature studies. Other novels included *Laddie*, 1913, *Michael O'Halloran*, 1915, *A Daughter of the Land*, 1918, her *Father's Daughter*, 1919, *The White Flag*, 1923, and *The Keeper of the Bees*, 1925.

Porter's sentimental romances, in which she repeatedly expressed her belief that virtue stemmed from contact with wild nature and was not to be found in urban life, stood in sharp contrast to those of the naturalistic authors of the period — Stephen Crane, Frank Norris, Theodore Dreiser, and Edith Wharton — whose works she disliked intensely. She was deeply frustrated by the low critical esteem in which her own work was held; *The Fire Bird*, 1922, a long narrative poem on Native American themes, was an unsuccessful attempt to please her critics. In 1920 she and her family moved to California. She organized a film company in 1922 to produce movie versions of her stories that she hoped would be widely used in schools and churches. She died on December 6, 1924, as the result of an automobile accident in Los Angeles.

Porter, Katherine Anne 1890–1980 writer

Born in Indian Creek in Brown County, Texas, on May 15, 1890, Katherine Anne Porter was a distant cousin of William Sydney Porter (O. Henry). Educated at private and convent schools in the South, she began to write early in life but did not publish any serious work until 1922, when her first story, "Maria Concepcion," appeared. In the meantime she supported herself with newspaper and literary hackwork in Chicago, Denver, and elsewhere. Her first collection of stories, *Flowering Judas*, appeared in 1930 and immediately established her as one of the leading American short-story writers. The purity and textured richness of her style were hailed by critics. Slow to produce the small body of work by which she was known (although she wrote quickly when finally ready to set words to paper), she produced during the 1930s only three books — *Hacienda, a Story of Mexico*, 1934, based on the Mexican experiences of Soviet film-maker Sergei Eisenstein, *Noon Wine*, 1937, and *Pale Horse, Pale Rider*, 1939, a collection that reprinted *Noon Wine* along with the title story and a story called "Old Mortality."

Although her reputation was firmly established, none of her books sold widely, and Porter supported herself primarily through fellowships, by working occasionally as an uncredited screenwriter in Hollywood, and by serving as writer-in-residence at a succession of colleges and universities. Although she had published in 1944 *The Leaning Tower*, stories, and in 1952 *The Days Before*, essays, reviews, and prefaces, and had won an O. Henry award for her 1962 story, *Holiday*, the literary world awaited with great anticipation the appearance of her only full-length novel, on which she had been working since 1941.

When *Ship of Fools* finally was published in 1962 it pleased most critics and gained Porter her first large readership. A best-seller made into a major film in 1965, it told of the ocean voyage of a group of Germans back to their homeland from Mexico in 1931, on the eve of Hitler's takeover of Germany. Her carefully crafted, ironic style was perfectly suited to the allegorical exploration of the collusion of good and evil that was her theme, and the penetrating psychological insight that had always marked her work was evident in the book. Her *Collected Short Stories* appeared in 1964 and was another popular and critical success, winning a Pulitzer Prize and a National Book Award. In 1967 she was awarded a Gold Medal from the National Institute of Arts and Letters. Later books included *A Christmas Story*, with drawings by Ben Shahn, 1967, her *Collected Essays and Occasional Writings*, 1970, and *The Never-Ending Wrong*, on the Sacco and Vanzetti case, 1977. She died on September 18, 1980, in Silver Spring, Maryland.

Porter, Sarah 1813–1900 educator

Born in Farmington, Connecticut, on August 16, 1813, Sarah Porter was a younger sister of Noah Porter, later president of Yale College. She was educated at the Farmington Academy, where she was the only girl student, and at sixteen she became an assistant teacher in the school. In 1832 she studied privately for a year under a Yale Latin professor. She continued to study on her own while teaching in schools in Springfield, Massachusetts, in Philadelphia, and in Buffalo, New York, over the next several years. An attempt to open her own school in Farmington in 1841 failed, but two years later she tried again and this time succeeded. For many years she was the only teacher at Miss Porter's School, but her ingrained intellectual curiosity had fitted her to teach Latin, French, German, chemistry, natural science, mathematics, history, geography, and music in addition to the basic subjects, and thus almost from the first her school had a reputation for academic excellence almost unique among girls' schools of the day. She also encouraged healthful exercise, and she was deeply concerned with the character development of all her charges.

As the school grew rapidly Porter acquired new facilities to keep pace, although she took care not to let it grow beyond a manageable size of about a hundred students. Her continued vigor was evident in her taking up the study of Greek and then Hebrew in her later years. She also played a leading role as a citizen of Farmington, taking the initiative in preventing the disfiguring of her lovely and picturesque native town by railroad and trolley lines. In later years she took on additional teachers, but she continued to teach her chosen subjects until just a few years before her death in Farmington, Connecticut, on February 17, 1900. Miss Porter's remains one of the outstanding girls' schools in the nation.

Porter, Sylvia Field 1913–1991 economist and journalist

Born on June 18, 1913, in Patchogue, Long Island, New York, Sylvia Field Feldman graduated from Hunter College in 1932. The previous year she had married Reed Porter, a banker. She found a job as an assistant in a Wall Street investment house, and while learning firsthand the intricacies of the market in government bonds she took supplementary courses at the School of Business Administration of New York University. During 1934–1935 she published *Reporting on Governments*, a pioneer weekly newsletter on the government bond market. In 1935 she began contributing a thrice-weekly financial column to the *New York Post*, and within a short time she was the paper's regular financial reporter as well.

Porter's column became a daily feature in 1938 under the title "Financial Post Marks" and was later syndicated to over 400 newspapers across the country. To avoid the possibility of prejudice against a woman in the traditionally male field of finance, she signed the column "S. F. Porter" for many years; later it was titled "S. F. Porter Says," and later still simply "Sylvia Porter." Her column went far beyond the printing of financial news items or investment tips; her investigations of various illicit or shady practices in commodities and securities markets prompted reforms on several occasions. In 1942 she received the National Headlines Club award for business reporting, and she was several times the Newspaper Women's Club choice for best woman columnist writing in any field. In 1978 she moved her column to the *New York Daily News* and it remained there until 1991. She contributed to magazines, notably the *Ladies' Home, Journal*, of which she was a contributing editor, and she published several books, including *How to Make Money in Government Bonds*, 1939, *If War Comes to the American Home*, 1941, *How to Live Within Your Income*, with J. K. Lasser, 1948, *Managing Your Money*, with J. K. Lasser, 1953, *How to Get More for Your Money*, 1961, *Sylvia Porter's Money Book*, 1975, *Sylvia Porter's New Money Book for the 80's*, 1979, *Sylvia Porter's Your Finances in the 1990's*, 1990, *Planning Your Retirement*, 1991, and from 1961 the annual *Sylvia Porter's Income Tax Guide*. In 1984 she launched *Sylvia Porter's Personal Finance Magazine*, which quickly grew to be the third largest periodical in its field; she sold it in 1989, however, after being hit by the stock market plunge in 1987. She died on June 5, 1991, at her home in Pound Ridge, New York.

Post, Emily Price 1872–1960 writer

Born in Baltimore on October 27, 1872 (some sources give October 3, 1873), Emily Price was educated in private schools in New York City, among them Miss Graham's Finishing School for Young Ladies. A popular debutante, she was feted by Ward McAllister, the social arbiter who coined the term "the Four Hundred." In June 1892 she married Edwin M. Post, a banker, from whom she was divorced in 1906. At the turn of the century financial circumstances compelled her to begin to write, and she produced newspaper articles on architecture and interior decoration, stories and serials for such magazines as *Harper's*, *Scribner's*, and the *Century*, and light novels, including *Flight of the Moth*, 1904, *Purple and Fine Linen*, 1906, *Woven in the Tapestry*, 1908, *The Title Market*, 1909, and *The Eagle's Feather*, 1910.

At the request of her publisher Post brought out *Etiquette in Society, in Business, in Politics, and at Home* in 1922. Immediately popular, her charming and lively presentation differed from other guides to manners in being directed to popular audiences rather than merely to the upper classes. It laid down fundamental rules that remained unchanged through the book's many printings, although she took care to remain abreast of the times in dealing with broad changes in society. Proper behavior, she believed, was a manifestation of common sense and consideration of other people. Sections of the first edition reflected the period of her own upbringing ("Chaperons and Other Conventions") and were later modified to reflect changing customs ("The Vanishing Chaperon and Other New Conventions"). She added to later editions guides to television, telephone, and airplane etiquette. Later retitled *Etiquette — the Blue Book of Social Usage*, her guide went through 10 editions and 90 printings before her death.

After 1931 Post spoke on radio programs and wrote a column on good taste for the Bell Syndicate; it appeared daily in some 200 newspapers after 1932. Her other books included *Parade*, a novel, 1925, *How to Behave Though a Debutante*, 1928, *The Personality of a House*, 1930, *Children are People*, 1940, *The Emily Post Cook Book*, with Edwin M. Post, Jr., 1949, and *Motor Manners*, 1950. She died in New York City on September 25, 1960.

Powell, Maud 1868–1920 violinist

Born on August 22, 1868, in Peru, Illinois, Maud Powell, a niece of the explorer John Wesley Powell, grew up in Aurora, Illinois. She early displayed musical talent and took up the violin. Encouraged especially by her mother, an amateur musician and composer, she studied under teachers in Aurora and Chicago. At nine she made a six-week tour in Illinois, Wisconsin, and Michigan with the Chicago Ladies' Quartet. In 1880 she was sent to Europe, where she continued her studies under Henry Schradieck in Leipzig, with Charles Dancla at the Paris Conservatory, and, after a year-long British tour in 1883, during which she played for Queen Victoria, with Joseph Joachim of the Royal High School of Music in Berlin. In 1885 she made her formal concert debut with the Berlin Philharmonic, and her American debut occurred in November of that year with the New York Philharmonic Society under Theodore Thomas. For the next seven years she toured annually with that orchestra. During that time, in January 1889, she gave one of the earliest American performances of the difficult Tchaikovsky Violin Concerto. Her repertoire was broad and included much modern work by such composers as Bruch, Sibelius, Dvorák, Lalo, and Saint-Saëns that she helped introduce to American audiences. In 1892 she was soloist with the New York Arion Society in its tour of Germany and Austria. In 1893 she played at the World's Columbian Exposition in Chicago and also delivered a paper on "Women and Music" before the Women's Musical Congress. In 1894 she organized the Maud Powell String Quartet, with which she toured for four years.

Powell's place in the first rank of contemporary violinists was ratified by her popularity with critical audiences in Europe. British and European tours in 1898 and 1900–1901, the latter including a performance for Edward VII, were highly successful. A tour in 1903 with John Philip Sousa's band included a command performance for Czar Nicholas II. She made extensive American tours in 1901–1902 and 1903–1904 and a South African tour in 1905–1906. She alternated American and European tours until 1910 and thereafter played largely in America.

Powell's technical accomplishments on the violin rested on a firm base of sensitive musicianship and understanding. From 1903 to 1907 she played a Guarnerius and thereafter a large Giovanni Battista Guadagnini. In later years she sought to extend her touring to schools, smaller towns and cities, and during World War I to army camps. She was the first violinist recorded by the Victor Talking Machine Company. She died on tour, in Uniontown, Pennsylvania, on January 8, 1920.

Prentiss, Elizabeth Payson 1818–1878 writer of children's books

Born on October 26, 1818, in Portland, Maine, Elizabeth Payson was the daughter of a well known minister and revivalist. She attended local schools and at nineteen opened a short-lived school of her own. In 1840–1841 and 1842–1843 she taught in a private girls' school in Richmond, Virginia. Ill health, which recurred throughout her life, made it difficult for her to establish herself. In April 1845 she married the Reverend George L. Prentiss, with whom she lived in New Bedford, Massachusetts, for several years, briefly in Newark, New Jersey, and from 1851 mainly in New York City. From an early age she had had an interest in writing, and as early as 1834 she had published a piece in the *Youth's Companion*.

In the early 1850s Prentiss took up writing seriously, contributing stories and articles to *Youth's Companion*, the *New York Observer*, and other periodicals. *Little Susy's Six Birthdays*, 1853, a book for children, was a considerable success and was followed by *Little Susy's Six Teachers*, 1856, and *Little Susy's Little Servants*, 1856. *The Flower of the Family*, 1853, was her first novel, and *Only a Dandelion, and Other Stories*, 1854, collected some of her earlier work. Subsequent books included *Henry and Bessie; or, What They Did in the Country*, 1855, *Peterchen and Gretchen, Tales of Early Childhood*, translated from German, 1860, *The Little Preacher*, 1867, *Fred, and Maria, and Me*, 1867, *The Old Brown Pitcher*, 1868, *Stepping Heavenward*, her greatest success, selling 100,000 copies in America and more abroad in English and in translations, 1869, *Nidworth*, 1869, *The Percys*, 1870, *The Story Lizzie Told*, 1870, *Six Little Princesses*, 1871, *Aunt Jane's Hero*, 1871, *Golden Hours*, religious verses and hymns, 1874, *Urbane and His Friends*, 1874, *Griselda*, translated from German, 1876, *The Home at Greylock*, 1876, *Pemaquid*, 1877, *Gentleman Jim*, 1878, and the posthumous *Avis Benson*, 1879. The evangelical piety of her books, many of which were thinly veiled autobiography, and their familiar reliance on scenes of everyday life found a ready audience. During 1858–1860 she and her family lived in Europe, principally in Switzerland. She died on August 13, 1878, at their summer home in Dorset, Vermont.

Preston, Ann 1813–1872 physician and educator

Born in West Grove, Pennsylvania, on December 1, 1813, Ann Preston was educated in Quaker schools there and in Chester, Pennsylvania. While caring for her younger brothers and sisters, she became active in the abolitionist and temperance movements. Later, relieved of home responsibilities, she taught school. In 1849 she published a volume of *Cousin Ann's Stories* in rhyme. Her temperance work had helped arouse an interest in physiology and hygiene. She studied those subjects as well as Latin on her own for a time, eventually began to teach classes in them to other interested women, and in 1847 became a medical apprentice in the office of a physician friend in Philadelphia. Two years later, having completed her apprenticeship, she was refused admission to all four Philadelphia medical colleges on grounds of sex. In October 1850, however, she entered the newly established Female (later Woman's) Medical College of Pennsylvania with the first class, which also included Hannah Longshore, and she graduated in December 1851. After a year of further study she was appointed professor of physiology and hygiene at the college in 1853.

A crisis was precipitated in 1858 by the action of the Board of Censors of the Philadelphia Medical Society, which effectively banned women physicians from the public teaching clinics of the city. In order to provide vital clinical experience to the college's students Dr. Preston began raising funds for a women's hospital to be affiliated with the college. A board of women managers, of which she was a member, was appointed to direct the planning and operation of the hospital. The college closed on the outbreak of the Civil War in 1861, but the Woman's Hospital opened later that year. The Woman's Medical College, operating under a new charter, opened in 1862. In 1863 Preston worked with Dr. Emeline H. Cleveland, chief resident of Woman's Hospital, to establish a training school for nurses. In 1866 she was chosen first woman dean of the Woman's Medical College. She continued in that post as well as in her professorship for the rest of her life. In 1867 she was elected to the college's Board of Corporators. She served also as consulting physician at Woman's Hospital, while her uncertain health forced her to restrict her private practice to office consultation. Under her leadership the students of the Woman's Medical College were at last admitted to the leading general clinics in Philadelphia in 1868 and 1869. In the latter year, in response to a remonstrance by the other local medical colleges and hospitals and numerous individual doctors, she published in the Philadelphia newspapers a classic argument in support of women physicians. She died in Philadelphia on April 18, 1872.

Preston, May Wilson 1873–1949 illustrator
Born in New York City on August 11, 1873, May Wilson early displayed marked artistic ability. In 1889, barely out of high school, she helped found the Women's Art Club (later the National Association of Women Artists). During 1889–1892 she attended Oberlin College. She left before graduating in order to enroll in the Art Students' League in New York City, where she remained for over four years. Under the tutelage of such artists as Robert Henri, John H. Twachtman, and William M. Chase, she developed rapidly. In 1899 she traveled to Paris to study under James A. M. Whistler, and in 1901 she studied under Chase again at the New York School of Art. Her career as a professional illustrator began in 1900, and by 1901 she was selling illustrations to the likes of *Harper's Bazaar*. The quarters she shared with two other artists at the Sherwood Studios became a popular gathering place for artists and writers. In December 1903 she married James M. Preston, a painter and associate of Henri, John Sloan, George Luks, Everett Shinn, and others in the so-called "Ashcan School" of urban realism. May Preston exhibited frequently with them and with the more formally organized Society of Illustrators, of which she was the first and for many years only woman member. She was represented at the famous Armory Show of 1913 and in 1915 was awarded a medal at the Panama-Pacific Exposition in San Francisco. Her commercial illustration found its way into the *Saturday Evening Post*, the *Woman's Home Companion*, the *Delineator*, *McClure's*, and other leading magazines, where it accompanied stories by Mary Roberts Rinehart, F. Scott Fitzgerald, Ring Lardner, P. G. Wodehouse, Alice Duer Miller, Joseph Hergesheimer, Vincent Sheean, and others. The failing market for her work in the Depression, together with a skin infection that made work difficult, largely ended her career. She died in East Hampton, Long Island, New York, on May 18, 1949.

Price, Leontyne 1927– opera singer
Born in Laurel, Mississippi, on February 10, 1927, Mary Violet Leontyne Price attended local schools there. She sang in her church choir as a girl, but it was not until she graduated from the College of Education and Industrial Arts (now Central State College) in Wilberforce, Ohio, in 1948 that she finally determined to seek a career as a singer. A scholarship, together with financial aid provided by a friend in Laurel, enabled her to study for four years at the Juilliard School of Music in New York City, where she worked under the former concert singer Florence Page Kimball, who remained her coach in later years. Her debut took place in April 1952 in a Broadway revival of Virgil Thomson's and Gertrude Stein's *Four Saints in Three Acts*. Her performance in that production, which subsequently traveled to Paris, led to Ira Gershwin's choosing her to sing Bess in his revival of *Porgy and Bess*, which played in New York City from 1952 to 1954 and then toured the United States and Europe. In October 1953 she was Samuel Barber's choice to sing the premiere performance of his *Hermit Songs* at a Library of Congress concert. The year 1955 saw her triumphant performance of the title role in the National Broadcasting Company's television production of *Tosca*,and she sang leading roles in other operas on television in the next few years.

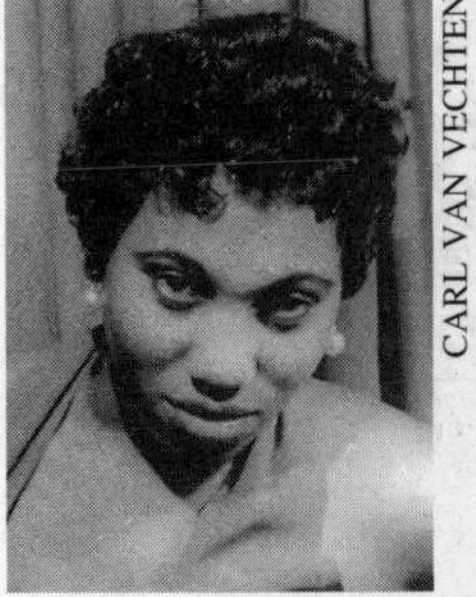
CARL VAN VECHTEN

Leontyne Price

Price's operatic stage debut, however, did not take place until September 1957, when she appeared in the American premiere of Poulenc's *Dialogues of the Carmelites* at the San Francisco Opera. She continued in San Francisco until 1960, appearing in such works as *Aïda*, *Thaïs*, and *The Wise Maidens*. By that time she was one of the most popular lyric sopranos in the country and had also made successful appearances in Vienna in 1959 and at Milan's La Scala in May 1960, where her performance in *Aïda* was warmly received.

Despite this great success — she was the first African-American singer to achieve an international reputation in opera — her debut at the Metropolitan Opera in New York was deferred until January 1961, when she appeared there in the difficult role of Leonora in *Il Trovatore*. After a brilliant performance she became one of the Met's leading regular sopranos. Later roles there included those in *Madama Butterfly*, *Don Giovanni*, *Turandot*, *Un Ballo in Maschera*, and *Ernani*. In September 1966 she sang in the world premiere of Barber's *Antony and Cleopatra*, a performance that inaugurated the Met's new house in Lincoln Center. Her performance in *La Forza del Destino* in 1967 was greeted as a triumph. She also sang frequently in Chicago, San Francisco, Milan, London, Salzburg, Rome, Vienna, and elsewhere.

In the 1970s Price reduced her operatic work somewhat to devote more time to recitals, but she scored another great success in her first performance of *Ariadne auf Naxos* in San Francisco in October 1977. She was one of the most frequently recorded opera singers, and she was the recipient of over 20 Grammy awards from the American Society of Recording Arts and Sciences. She was awarded the Presidential Medal of Freedom by President Lyndon B. Johnson in 1964, and she received the Spingam Medal of the National Association for the Advancement of Colored People in 1965, the Kennedy Center Honors in 1980, the National Medal of the Arts in 1985, and a lifetime achievement award from the National Academy of Recorded Arts and Sciences in 1989. She gave her farewell performance of *Aida* at the Metropolitan Opera in New York in 1985, but continued to give recitals, which she described as her first love. She published a book, *Aida*, based on Verdi's opera, in 1990.

Putnam, Emily James Smith 1865–1944 educator and historian

Born in Canandaigua, New York, on April 15, 1865, Emily Smith got her early education in local schools, from tutors, and by following her own curiosity. She graduated from Bryn Mawr College with the first class, that of 1889, and then attended Girton College, Cambridge, for two years. In 1891–1893 she taught at the Packer Collegiate Institute in Brooklyn, New York, and in 1893–1894 she was a fellow in Greek at the University of Chicago.

In 1894 Smith was appointed first dean of the five-year-old Barnard College, which had been headed since its opening by Ella Weed, chairman of the academic committee. Over the next six years she succeeded in greatly strengthening Barnard's academic standing by establishing a more equitable relationship with Columbia University. Columbia professors were made more accessible, other scholars of similar qualifications were added to the Barnard faculty, and Columbia's graduate courses, libraries, and other facilities were opened to Barnard women. During that period she also taught courses in Greek literature and philosophy. In April 1899 she married publisher George H. Putnam, and the next year she resigned as dean. During 1901–1904 she served as president of the League for Political Education, and in 1901–1905 she was a trustee of Barnard. In 1910 she published *The Lady: Studies of Certain Significant Phases of Her History*, a major historical study of women in society. In 1914 she resumed teaching at Barnard, first in the history department and from 1920 in the department of Greek. In 1926 she published *Candaules' Wife and Other Old Stories*, a study of Herodotus. (She also published translations of *Selections from Lucian*, 1892, Émile Fauget's *Dread of Responsibility*, 1914, Marcel Berger's *The Secret of the Marne*, 1918, and Raymond Escholier's *The Illusion*, 1921.) She helped establish the New School for Social Research in 1919 and from 1920 to 1932 was a regular lecturer there. She retired from Barnard in 1930 and a short time later went to live in Spain. The outbreak of civil war in that country forced her to leave, and she lived thereafter in Jamaica. She died in Kingston, Jamaica, on September 7, 1944.

Queler, Eve 1936– conductor

Born in New York City on January 1, 1936, Eve Rabin early displayed remarkable musical ability. She began formal piano lessons at five, and only financial problems prevented her from accepting a full scholarship to the Curtis Institute of Music in Philadelphia when she was twelve. She graduated from the High School of Music and Art in 1954 and then took courses at City College of New York, the Mannes College of Music, and Hebrew Union School of Education and Sacred Music until her marriage in December 1956 to Stanley N. Queler, a law student. For several years she worked as a church and temple organist, a rehearsal pianist, an opera coach, and in other capacities while her husband completed law school. She then returned to Mannes College, where she began the study of conducting under Carl Bamberger. She continued under Joseph Rosenstock of the Metropolitan Opera, whose original strong misgivings about her prospects in the virtually all-male field of conducting were allayed at least in part by her manifest talent. Her work with the New York City Opera, with which she was associated from 1958 as rehearsal and audition pianist and later as performing pianist and finally assistant conductor, gave her practical experience, albeit slowly. An outdoor performance in Fairlawn, New Jersey, of a truncated version of *Cavalleria Rusticana* in 1966 was her first public appearance as a conductor.

In order to provide herself with opportunities to conduct more than rehearsals Queler organized in 1967 the Opera Orchestra of New York, which also provided experience to instrumentalists and young singers. As the group developed it began attracting a public and critical following. In December 1969 the Opera Orchestra presented a concert performance of *Tosca* at Alice Tully Hall, New York City, and a year later they did *Fedora*, a seldom heard opera of the verismo school. Performances of *L'Incoronazione de Poppea* and *Belfagor* in 1971, *William Tell* and *L'Africana* in 1972, and other works established the orchestra and Eve Queler as fixtures of the New York musical scene, and they were gradually able to call on the services of major guest artists from the Metropolitan Opera.

Queler also served as associate conductor of the Fort Wayne Philharmonic in Indiana in 1970–1971, and as conductor of the Lake George Opera Festival, New York, in 1971–1972, of the Mostly Mozart Festival at Lincoln Center, New York City, in 1972, of the New Philharmonia, London, in 1973, and of the San Antonio and Montreal symphonies in 1975, among others. She was also a frequent guest conductor with such groups as the Paris Radio, the Boston, and the Puerto Rico symphony orchestras.

Quimby, Harriet 1875–1912 aviator

Born possibly on May 1, 1875, in Coldwater, Michigan (or perhaps, as she later claimed, in 1884 in Arroyo Grande, California — neither alternative is well attested), Harriet Quimby was educated in public schools. By 1902 she and her family were in any case living in California, and in that year she became a writer for the San Francisco journal *Dramatic Review* (published by the father of Anita Loos). Later she wrote also for the *San Francisco Call* and the *Chronicle* and for magazines. In 1903 she moved to New York City to become drama critic for *Leslie's Weekly*. She became interested in aviation about 1910, and following a visit to an air show at Belmont Park in October of that year she determined to learn to fly herself. She took lessons at the Moisant School of Aviation at Hempstead, Long Island, in the spring of 1911, and on August 1 she became the first woman to qualify for a license (number 37) from the Aero Club of America, the U.S. branch of the Fédération Aéronautique Internationale; she was only the second licensed woman pilot in the world, following the Baroness de la Roche of France. For a time she flew with the Moisant International Aviators, a demonstration team from the school. In October 1911 she flew as part of the inauguration ceremonies for President Francisco Madero of Mexico. She continued to contribute articles to various periodicals as well. On April 16, 1912, after nearly a month of preparation, she became the first woman to pilot an aircraft across the English Channel, guiding her French Blériot monoplane from Dover through heavy overcast to Hardelot, France. She was widely celebrated for her feat. In the summer, after participating in several other air meets, she flew to Boston to take part in the Harvard-Boston Aviation Meet. On July 1, 1912, while piloting her Blériot over Dorchester Bay, she lost control; she and a passenger both fell from the rolling craft and were killed.

Rainer, Yvonne 1934– choreographer and filmmaker

Born in 1934 in San Francisco, Yvonne Rainer moved to New York City in 1957 to study theater. She found herself more strongly drawn to modern dance than acting, however, and began studying with Edith Stephens, Syvilla Fort, and the staff of the Martha Graham School. In 1960 she returned briefly to her native city to become a part of Ann Halprin's workshop program. Back in New York later that year, she danced for Simone Forti and James Waring and studied with Merce Cunningham. She was one of the organizers of the Judson Dance Theater, a focal point for vanguard activity in the dance world throughout the 1960s, and formed her own company for a brief time after the Judson performances ended.

Rainier, who began choreographing her own works in 1961 and continued through the early 1970s, was known as a rebel in the world of modern dance. She rejected "spectacle, virtuosity, the star image, and any type of theatrical 'magic' " in favor of an approach that saw the body more as the source of an infinite variety of movements than as the purveyor of emotion or drama. Many of the elements she employed, such as repetition, patterning, tasks and games, later became standard practice in postmodern choreography.

Her best-known work, "Trio A," a section of a larger work called "The Mind is a Muscle," consisted of a simultaneous performance by three dancers that included a difficult series of circular and spiral movements. It was widely adapted and interpreted, and was often referred to in the work of other choreographers. In all, she has choreographed forty-one concert works. Her best known works included "Terrain" and "This is a Woman Who. . . ."

Rainer sometimes included filmed sequences in her dances, and in the 1970s she began to detach herself from dance to concentrate on film directing. Her films did not follow narrative conventions, instead combining reality and fiction, sound and visuals, to address major social and political issues. She directed several experimental films about dance and performance, including *Lives of Performers*, 1972, *Film About a Woman Who*, 1974, and *Kristina Taking Pictures*, 1976. Later films include *Journeys from Berlin/1971*, 1980, *The Man Who Envied Women*, 1985 and *Privilege*, 1990. She was a 1990 recipient of a MacArthur Foundation award.

Rainey, Gertrude Pridgett 1886–1939 singer

Born on April 26, 1886, in Columbus, Georgia, Gertrude Pridgett made her first public appearance about the age of fourteen in a local talent show called "Bunch of Blackberries" at the Springer Opera House in Columbus. Little else is known of her early years. In February 1904 she married Will Rainey, a vaudeville performer known as "Pa" Rainey, and for several years they toured with Negro minstrel groups as a song-and-dance team. In 1902, in a small Missouri town, as she later recalled, she first heard the sort of music that was to become known as the blues. Derived from the parallel traditions of Negro spiritual and gospel music and of field songs and hollers, both still carrying the distinctive patterns and harmonies of their African roots, the blues was evolving as a music of lament, nostalgia, and yearning.

Ma Rainey, as she was known, began singing blues songs and contributed greatly to the evolution of the form and to the growth of its popularity. In her travels she appeared with jazz and jug bands throughout the South. While with the Tolliver's Circus and Musical Extravaganza troupe she exerted a direct influence on young Bessie Smith. Her deep contralto voice, sometimes verging on harshness, was a powerful instrument by which to convey the pathos of her simple songs of everyday life and emotion. The popularization of the blues in the second decade of the century, in large part owing to the work of W. C. Handy, whose "Memphis Blues," 1912, "St. Louis Blues," 1914, and other songs became classics of the genre, opened new fields to African-American performers.

In 1923 Ma Rainey made her first phonograph recordings for the Paramount company. Over a five-year span she recorded some 92 songs for Paramount — such titles as "See See Rider," "Prove It On Me," "Blues Oh Blues," "Sleep Talking," "Oh Papa Blues," "Trust No Man," "Slave to the Blues," "New Boweavil Blues," and "Slow Driving Moan" — that later became the only permanent record of one of the most influential popular musical artists of her time. She continued to sing in public into the 1930s. She retired to her home in Columbus, Georgia, where she died on December 22, 1939.

Rand, Ayn 1905–1982 writer, lecturer and editor

Born on February 2, 1905, in St. Petersburg, Russia, Ayn Rand graduated from the University of Petrograd in 1924 and two years later emigrated to the United States. Determined from an early age to be a writer, she worked assiduously at perfecting her craft while supporting herself with a variety of jobs. In 1932 she sold her first motion picture scenario under the title *Red Pawn*. In September 1935 her first play, *The Night of January 16th*, opened at the Ambassador Theatre, New York, for a substantial run. It was revived in 1973 under the title *Penthouse Legend*. Her first novel, *We, the Living*, was published in 1936. Three more novels followed: *Anthem*, 1938, *The Fountain-head*, 1943, which became a best-seller and was later made into a motion picture, and *Atlas Shrugged*, also a best-seller, 1957. In February 1940 a second play, *The Unconquered*, had a short run on Broadway.

The political philosophy that shaped Rand's fictional work — a deeply conservative philosophy that posited individual effort and ability as the sole source of all genuine achievement, that thereby elevated the pursuit of self-interest to the role of first principle, and that scorned such notions as altruism and sacrifice for the common good as liberal delusions and even vices — found more direct expression in *For the New Intellectual*, 1961, *The Virtue of Selfishness*, 1965, *Capitalism: The Unknown Ideal*, 1966, *Introduction to Objectivist Epistemology*, 1967, *The Romantic Manifests: A Philosophy of Literature*, 1970, *The New Left: The Anti-industrial Revolution*, 1971, and *Philosophy: Who Needs It?*, 1982. She also promoted her philosophy of Objectivism as editor of *The Objectivist Newsletter* from 1962 to 1971 and of *The Ayn Rand Letter* from 1971 to 1976, and she was a frequent lecturer. Her controversial views attracted a faithful audience of admirers and followers. She was working on an adaptation of *Atlas Shrugged* for a television miniseries when she died on March 6, 1982, in New York City.

Rand, Sally 1904–1979 entertainer

Born in Elkton, Missouri, on January 2, 1904, Helen Gould Beck entered show business at an early age. Eventually adopting the name Sally Rand (suggested to her, she said, by Cecil B. DeMille), she played in vaudeville and performed as an acrobatic dancer at carnivals and for a while in the Ringling Brothers and Barnum & Bailey Circus while still in her teens. By the time she was twenty she was in Hollywood, where she appeared in a number of films, among them *The Dressmaker from Paris*, 1924, *Manbait*, 1926, *Getting Gertie's Garter*, 1927, and *King of Kings*, 1927, but never became a star.

With the onset of the Depression of the 1930s she found herself stranded in Chicago. She improvised a dance routine employing ostrich-feather fans that she performed in a speakeasy for $75 a week. Her great opportunity came with the opening in Chicago of the Century of Progress Exposition of 1933–1934. After riding a white horse to the fair, attired more or less as Lady Godiva, she received star billing at the "Streets of Paris" concession on the Midway and was credited with having made the whole fair a financial success. Her act consisted of a slow dance, with ostrich plumes as her only costume, to the music of Debussy's *Clair de Lune*. Nudity, she conceded, was not new, but she insisted that she had made it both artistic and financially successful with a new sales method. The difference between a mere performer and a star, she maintained, was merchandising. She continued to merchandise her act for more than 30 years, starring at the California Pacific International Exposition at San Diego in 1935–1936, San Francisco's Golden Gate International Exposition of 1939–1940, and on many other occasions. In 1965 she was mistress of ceremonies of the hit Broadway revue *This Was Burlesque*, and she was still occasionally presenting her dance in the 1970s. She died in Glendora, California, on August 31, 1979.

Rankin, Jeannette 1880–1973 suffragist and public official

Jeannette Rankin

Born near Missoula, Montana, on June 11, 1880, Jeannette Rankin graduated from the University of Montana in 1902. She subsequently attended the New York School of Philanthropy (later the New York, then the Columbia, School of Social Work) before embarking on a career of social work in Seattle in 1909. Caught up in the rising tide of sentiment for woman suffrage, she campaigned effectively in Washington, California, and Montana on behalf of the cause. In 1914 she became legislative secretary of the National American Woman Suffrage Association, and in that same year she led a successful campaign for woman suffrage in her native state. Two years later Montana voters elected her, as a Republican, to the United States House of Representatives. She was the first woman elected to that body. She continued the suffrage fight in Congress and introduced the first bill that would have granted women citizenship independent of the citizenship of their husbands.

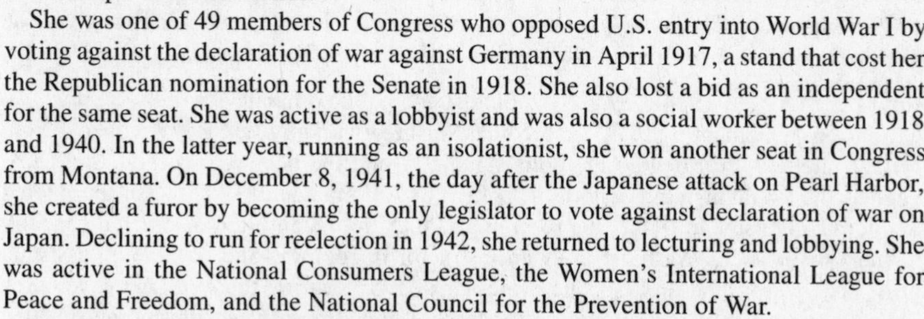

She was one of 49 members of Congress who opposed U.S. entry into World War I by voting against the declaration of war against Germany in April 1917, a stand that cost her the Republican nomination for the Senate in 1918. She also lost a bid as an independent for the same seat. She was active as a lobbyist and was also a social worker between 1918 and 1940. In the latter year, running as an isolationist, she won another seat in Congress from Montana. On December 8, 1941, the day after the Japanese attack on Pearl Harbor, she created a furor by becoming the only legislator to vote against declaration of war on Japan. Declining to run for reelection in 1942, she returned to lecturing and lobbying. She was active in the National Consumers League, the Women's International League for Peace and Freedom, and the National Council for the Prevention of War.

She remained an ardent feminist and was still lecturing on that and other modes of social reform when public opinion began to catch up to her with the beginning of the women's liberation movement of the early 1970s. In the 1960s she founded a cooperative homestead for women in Georgia. On January 15, 1968, at the age of eighty-seven, she led the "Jeannette Rankin Brigade" of 5,000 women in a march on Capitol Hill to protest U.S. involvement in the Vietnam war. She died in Carmel, California, on May 18, 1973.

Rawlings, Marjorie Kinnan 1896–1953 writer

Born in Washington, D.C., on August 8, 1896, Marjorie Kinnan attended public schools and graduated from the University of Wisconsin in 1918. The next year she married Charles A. Rawlings, a newspaperman with whom she lived in various places over the next nine years. In that time she worked for periods as a reporter and feature writer for the *Louisville Courier-Journal* and the *Rochester (New York) Journal* while attempting to establish a career as a writer of fiction. She managed to sell a few stories, but it was not until her sudden decision in 1928 to buy and settle on a 40-acre tract of orange grove near the hamlet of Cross Creek in northern Florida that she began to find her literary voice. From her first visit to the region she had felt herself attuned to the half-wild nature of the place and to the native "Crackers" who lived there. Two stories sold to *Scribner's* magazine brought her to the attention of Maxwell Perkins, editor of the works of F. Scott Fitzgerald, Ernest Hemingway, Thomas Wolfe, and others. Her "Gal Young Un" won the O. Henry Memorial Award for short stories in 1933.

Her first book, *South Moon Under*, also appeared in 1933 (the year of her divorce from

Charles Rawlings) and was followed by *Golden Apples*, 1935, and *The Yearling*, 1938, which won a Pulitzer Prize, was made into a motion picture, and over subsequent years gradually assumed the status of a classic. Many of her stories were collected in *When the Whippoorwill*, 1940. *Cross Creek*, 1942, described her life in the Florida country and displayed her striking ability to convey in poetic prose her deep feelings of kinship to nature as well as her sharp ear for dialect and the characteristic Cracker humor. *Cross Creek Cookery*, 1942, combined recipes and anecdotes of the region. *The Sojourner*, 1953, her last book, was set instead in Michigan. She was at work on a biography of Ellen Glasgow when she died near St. Augustine, Florida, on December 14, 1953. *Secret River*, a children's book, appeared posthumously in 1955.

Ray, Charlotte E. 1850–1911 lawyer

Born in New York City on January 13, 1850, Charlotte Ray was of African, Native American, and European ancestry. She was educated at Myrtilla Miner's Institution for the Education of Colored Youth in Washington, D.C., and she later taught in the preparatory and normal departments of Howard University while studying in the law school. She received a law degree in 1872 and shortly afterward was admitted to the bar of the District of Columbia.

She was the first African-American woman lawyer to practice in the United States. Her private practice was unsuccessful, however, apparently owing to racial prejudice, and by 1879 she had moved back to New York City. She taught school for a time in Brooklyn. She died in Woodside, Long Island, New York, on January 4, 1911.

Ray, Dixy Lee 1914–1994 zoologist and public official

Born on September 3, 1914, in Tacoma, Washington, Dixy Lee Ray graduated from Mills College with a degree in zoology in 1937 and the next year received an M.A. degree. She taught in public schools in Oakland, California, until 1942, when she entered Stanford University. In 1945, after receiving a Ph.D. from Stanford, she joined the faculty of the University of Washington as an instructor in zoology. She became an assistant professor in 1947 and an associate professor in 1957. During those years her research centered on studies of certain marine crustaceans and also of the various organisms that attack submerged wood. In addition to publishing a number of papers in various journals she edited *Marine Boring and Fouling Organisms*, 1959.

Ray was a leading advocate of ecological research as a prerequisite to understanding the dangers inherent in the unregulated growth of such technologies as chemical manufacture, energy production, and waste disposal. During 1960–62 she was a special consultant in biological oceanography to the National Science Foundation. In 1963 she was appointed director of the newly established Pacific Science Center in Seattle. Under her direction the center quickly developed into an important institution for encouraging public interest in and understanding of science. She served also as special assistant to the director of the National Science Foundation in 1963. In 1969 she was a member of the President's Task Force on Oceanography.

In July 1972 Ray was nominated by President Richard M. Nixon to a seat on the Atomic Energy Commission. She left the University of Washington and the Science Center upon Senate confirmation of the nomination the next month and became the first woman to undertake a full term on the commission. In February 1973 she was named to succeed James R. Schlesinger as chairman of the commission, a post that made her perhaps the most powerful woman in the federal government.

Among her priority concerns were the improvement of employment opportunities for minority group applicants and an expanded program of research on the safety of nuclear reactors. Her blunt, outspoken manner, together with her somewhat nonconformist air, made her a figure of national interest.

Following a reorganization of the Atomic Energy Commission in 1974 she moved to the Department of State as assistant secretary for oceans and international environmental scientific affairs. She resigned that post in June 1975. In 1976 she ran as a Democrat for the governorship of Washington and in winning election in November became the second woman, after Ella Grasso of Connecticut, to win a state governorship without being preceded in office by a husband.

Ray served out her term as governor to 1980. Among her awards are the United Nations Peace Medal, 1973, the American Exemplar Medal, 1978, the Outstanding Women in Energy Award, 1981 and the Susan B. Anthony Award from the Washington State Legislature, 1987. She has been a consultant to the Argonne National Laboratory and the Lawrence Livermore National Laboratory since 1987. In 1990 Ray published *Trashing the Planet: How Science Can Help Us Deal with Acid Rain, Depletion of the Ozone and Nuclear Waste*, with Lou Guzzo.

Reagon, Bernice Johnson 1942– musician, curator, historian, writer and civil rights activist

Born in Albany, Georgia, on October 4, 1942, the third of eight children, Bernice Johnson was nurtured on African-American sacred music in her father's Baptist church. She was influenced early on by her father's singing style and his connection to their community. After enrolling at Albany State College in 1959 as a music major, where she studied classical art song and arranged spirituals, she became the highest-ranking student at the school and changed her major to biology.

Johnson's first political activities were in student government and at the local NAACP Youth Chapter. When members of the Student Nonviolent Coordinating Committee (SNCC) came to Albany, she was drawn to their tactics and marched in a 1961 protest which caused her to be suspended from school and to be arrested. Still, she remembered being moved "by the hundreds and thousands of people in the streets. I was moved by hearing songs, and after hearing them all my life, for the first time, I understood what they meant."

In 1962, Johnson returned to her music studies at Spelman College in Atlanta, but left the same year to join the SNCC Freedom Singers. The group sang at political meetings and jails, drew attention to voter registration, raised money for the movement and also appeared at the 1963 March on Washington. She married Cordell Reagon, an SNCC field worker and Freedom Singer. In 1964 she left the Freedom Singers to have her first child, her daughter Toshi, who would become an accomplished musician in her own right. She later separated from her husband while pregnant with her son, Kwan; they were divorced in 1967. Reagon's first of several solo albums was released in 1966; her second was recorded in 1967: while she raised her children, she researched traditional African-American songs and stories, and organized folk festival tours that featured both African-American and white musicians.

Following this period, Reagon moved away from integrationist politics toward a more separatist stance; she wrote some of her most militant songs as a member of the Harambee Singers. After completing a degree in non-Western history at Spelman, she moved to Washington, D.C. and became the vocal director of the D.C. Black Repertory Theater. She formed the singing group Sweet Honey in the Rock from members of this company in 1972.

Sweet Honey in the Rock consisted variously of four to six women, including Reagon, performing a cappella music, ranging from traditional folk, African chant, field hollers, and Baptist hymns to the blues, jazz, and rap music. With its unique sound, the group continued to address political and personal issues, recorded many albums and performed at churches, concerts, and festivals all over the U.S. and around the world. In 1985, they coordinated the closing cultural festivities for the United Nations Decade for Women Conference in Nairobi, Kenya, and, in May of 1989, they performed to a sold-out audience at Carnegie Hall.

During the first years with Sweet Honey in the Rock, Reagon also earned a Ph.D. in history at Howard University and began working at the Smithsonian Institution as a cultural historian in the Division of Performing Arts/African Diaspora Project. Her research resulted in her article entitled "African Diaspora Women: The Making of Cultural Workers". Later she was promoted to curator of the National Museum of American History where she served as the director of the Smithsonian's program in black American culture. Her projects there included a three-record collection called *Voices of the Civil Rights Movement: Black American Freedom Songs 1960–66* and the "Wade in the Water" Series, a long-term project focusing on the history of African-American sacred song and worship traditions. The series was inaugurated in 1992 with a book on pioneers of gospel music called *We'll Understand It Better By and By* and, a series of 26 programs, which aired on National Public Radio in January of 1994. To help fund the project, she used some of the funds from her 1989 MacArthur Foundation Fellowship.

Her life and work embody her vision of herself as stated in a 1980 interview: "My identity is Black, woman, singer, historian, mother — all of these things. And I feel it is most important to demand that this society give me the space to be all of those things . . . A major part of my struggle is that human beings ought to be invited to try out their complexities and not be forced to give these narrow concepts of themselves."

Ream, Vinnie 1847–1914 sculptor

Born on September 25, 1847, in Madison, Wisconsin, Vinnie Ream grew up there, in Missouri and Arkansas, and from 1861 in Washington, D.C. At fifteen she obtained a clerkship in the Post Office Department. She took up sculpture in 1863 under the tutelage of Clark Mills, who was then finishing up work on the bronze "Liberty" for the Capitol dome. Her busts of several congressmen and other prominent persons led in 1864 to an opportunity to sculpt a bust of President Abraham Lincoln from life. That work led in turn to a $10,000 commission from Congress in August 1866 to create a full-size marble statue of Lincoln for the Capitol rotunda. It was widely suggested that the legislators had not been uninfluenced by the personal charm of the untrained eighteen-year-old artist. She was in any case the first woman to win such a commission from the federal government. She completed a plaster model for the statue in her capital studio and then, accompanied by her parents, took it to Rome in 1869 to translate it into marble.

During a brief pause in Paris she studied under Léon J. F. Bonnat and did busts of Gustave Doré and Père Hyacinthe. In Rome she studied under Luigi Majoli. She became a favorite of the artists' colonies there, became especially close to Georg Brandes, and did busts of Franz Liszt and Cardinal Antonelli.

Ream's Lincoln, done in white Carrara marble, was unveiled at the Capitol in January 1871. Although later much criticized for its lack of vigor and its manifest amateurishness, it was possessed of a naive expressiveness and was warmly received at the time. In January 1875, in competition with such men as William Wetmore Story and J. Q. A. Ward, she won a $20,000 commission from the government for a bronze statue of Admiral David G. Farragut. While at work on that statue she married Lieutenant (later Brigadier General) Richard L. Hoxie in May 1878. Her "Farragut," cast from the propeller of the *Hartford*, the naval hero's flagship, was unveiled in Farragut Square, Washington, D.C., in April 1881. The Hoxie home was on Farragut Square and was one of the most popular sources of hospitality in the city.

Ream abandoned sculpture for many years in deference to her husband's wish, but in 1906 she executed a statue of Samuel Kirkwood, Civil War governor of Iowa, for Statuary

Hall, and she completed the model for a statue of Sequoya, one of Oklahoma's contributions to Statuary Hall, shortly before her death. (It was completed by George Zolnay.) Other subjects of her earlier portrait work had included General Ulysses S. Grant, General George B. McClellan, General John C. Frémont, General George A. Custer, Senator John Sherman, Peter Cooper, Thaddeus Stevens, Horace Greeley, Francis P. Blair, Ezra Cornell, Chief Justice Morrison R. Waite, and Albert Pike. Her ideal figures included "Miriam," "The West" "America," "The Indian Girl," "Sappho," and "The Spirit of Carnival." She died in Washington, D.C., on November 20, 1914.

Reed, Mary 1854–1943 missionary

Born on December 4, 1854, in Lowell, Ohio, Mary Reed grew up mainly in nearby Crooked Tree. She graduated from high school in Malta, Ohio, and then attended Ohio Central Normal School in Worthington, from which she graduated in 1878. For the next five years she taught school. In 1884 she offered her services to the Cincinnati branch of the Women's Foreign Missionary Society of the Methodist Episcopal Church, and in November of that year she sailed for India. She was assigned to work among the Hindu women in zenanas at Cawnpore, but ill health forced her to spend a period of convalescence at Pithoragarh in the Himalayan foothills. There she studied Hindustani and visited a leper colony administered by the London-based interdenominational Mission to Lepers. Her work at Cawnpore was followed by an assignment as headmistress of a girls' school in Gonda.

Her health failed again in 1890, and Reed returned to the United States on furlough. Physicians there confirmed her premonition that she had contracted leprosy. She took the diagnosis as a call to minister to the lepers she had met in Pithoragarh. She returned there in 1891 and was appointed superintendent of the leper asylum at nearby Chandag; thereafter she was on the staffs of the Methodist Mission and of the Mission to Lepers. Her appeals for funds to improve the asylum were effective, and in a few years she had replaced the huts and stables in which the lepers had lived with substantial cottages. A grant of additional land from the Indian government enabled her to establish individual garden plots and communal grazing land. A chapel, a water supply system, a hospital, and a school were among the facilities added to the asylum, and in addition to administering the entire complex Mary Reed cared for her charges personally and taught classes in reading and religion.

Her leprosy went into remission in 1896, but she remained at Chandag for the rest of her life and sharply restricted her contact with well persons. In 52 years she left Chandag only 5 times: in 1897 she traveled 50 miles to a Woman's Foreign Missionary Society meeting near Almora; in 1899 she attended the Methodist Annual Conference in Lucknow; in 1904–1905 she took an 18-month furlough, during which she visited Palestine; in 1906 she visited the United States for the last time; and in 1924 she traveled 50 miles to obtain dental care. In 1932 her disease became active again, but by then treatment was available to control it. Widely honored for her work, Mary Reed retired as superintendent of the asylum in 1938, by which time she was virtually blind. She died at Chandag on April 8, 1943. Six years later the Mary Reed Memorial Hospital was built there by the American Mission to Lepers (now the American Leprosy Missions, Inc.).

Reed, Myrtle 1874–1911 writer

Born in Norwood Park (now part of Chicago), Illinois, on September 27, 1874, Myrtle Reed was of a religious and literary family. Her parents' ambition that she be a writer began to bear fruit when she was ten and the *Acorn*, a juvenile periodical, published a story of hers. After graduating from high school in 1893 she became a free-lance journalist. Her poems, sketches, and stories began appearing regularly in such periodicals as the *Bookman*, *Munsey's Magazine*, and the *National Magazine*, and in 1899 she published her first novel, *Love Letters of a Musician*. The popularity of that book led to *Later Love Letters of a Musician*, 1900, which was followed by *The Spinster Book*, 1901, a collection of essays on romantic love and courtship. *Lavender and Old Lace*, 1902, essentially a daydream translated into a romantic novel, was a huge success; it ran through 40 printings in the next 9 years. In that time she turned out *Pickaback Songs*, 1903, *The Shadow of Victory: A Romance of Fort Dearborn*, 1903, *The Master's Violin*, 1904, *The Book of Clever Beasts*, 1904, *At the Sign of the Jack o'Lantern*, 1905, *A Spinner in the Sun*, 1906, *Love Affairs of Literary Men*, 1907, *Flower of the Dusk*, 1908, *Old Rose and Silver*, 1909, *Sonnets of a Lover*, 1910, and *Master of the Vineyard*, 1910, books that typically appeared in lavender casings decorated with elaborate and delicate art nouveau designs.

Reed's books of what in the taste of the day was received as sweet and tender sentiment were all greatly popular. The success of *What to Have for Breakfast*, a cookbook issued in 1905 under the pseudonym Olive Green, led to nine more such books, and she also published numerous articles on domestic matters under the name Katherine LaFarge Norton. In October 1906 she married James S. McCullough, an Irish-Canadian businessman whom she had corresponded with since high school. Her romantic notions of perfection in husband, wife, and home became more and more real to her as reality fell short of them in detail after detail. The somber note that began to creep into her later books became more pronounced as it reflected her own increasing depression. She became habituated to a sedative, and on August 17, 1911, she ended her life with an overdose. Several books were then in press and appeared posthumously: *Weaver of Dreams*, 1911, *The Myrtle Reed Year Book*, 1911, *White Shield*, 1912, and *Happy Women*, 1913.

Reese, Lizette Woodworth 1856–1935 poet

Born on January 9, 1856, in Huntingdon (later Waverly, now part of Baltimore), Maryland, Lizette Reese attended the local St. John's Parish School and the public schools of Baltimore. After graduating from high school she taught at St. John's for two years, and from 1873 to 1921 she taught in various public schools in Baltimore. Her spare time was devoted almost entirely to poetry. Her first published poem, "The Deserted House," appeared in the *Southern Magazine* in June 1874. Thirteen years passed before her first volume appeared under the title *A Branch of May* in 1887. It was reissued with some added poems as *A Handful of Lavender* in 1891. Over the years her painstakingly crafted poems appeared in various periodicals, and they were later collected in such volumes as *A Quiet Road*, 1896, *A Wayside Lute*, 1909, *Spicewood*, 1920, *Wild Cherry*, 1923, *Selected Poems*, 1926, *Little Henrietta*, 1927, *White April and Other Poems*, 1930, and *Pastures and Other Poems*, 1933.

Reese's poems were at once personal and universal: universal in their concern with nature, home, and the common lot of humankind, personal in their rootedness in her own particular experience, especially her abiding delight in her rural home. In form her work remained in the traditional Victorian modes, although it often exhibited a condensed intensity that suggested some kinship with more modern poetics. Her best known piece, a sonnet entitled "Tears," appeared in *Scribner's Magazine* in November 1899. She published two volumes of prose reminiscences, *A Victorian Village*, 1929, and *The York Road*, 1931. She died in Baltimore on December 17, 1935. Some of her later poems were collected and published posthumously in *The Old House in the Country*, 1936, and an unfinished novel, *Worleys*, appeared in the same year.

Rehan, Ada 1857–1916 actor

Born on April 22, 1857, in Limerick, Ireland, Ada Crehan grew up in Brooklyn, New York, where her family settled shortly after the Civil War. She followed her older sisters onto the stage, making her debut in *Across the Continent* at the age of fourteen in Newark, New Jersey. Mistakenly billed as Rehan for her first appearance at Louisa Lane Drew's Arch Street Theatre in Philadelphia, she thereafter retained the misspelling as her stage name. She continued her apprenticeship in stock companies, playing in Louisville, Albany, and Baltimore, and she made her New York debut in *Thoroughbred* at Wood's Museum in April 1875. Four more years of supporting roles followed.

In 1879 she was invited to join the company of Augustin Daly, under whose management she first appeared in a production of Zola's *L'Assommoir* at the Olympic Theatre, New York City, in April 1879. Later that year Daly opened his Daly's Theatre in New York, and Rehan shortly became the company's leading lady. Her association with the Daly company lasted 20 years, until Daly's death in 1899, and her more than 200 roles included many from plays by Shakespeare as well as from several European comedies adapted by Daly for the American stage. She was first among equals in the "Big Four" — Ada Rehan, John Drew, Anne H. Gilbert, and James Lewis — the core of Daly's company and the secret of his success in creating an ongoing tradition of superb ensemble acting. She was already a star when she first appeared to general acclaim in London in 1884; her reception in Paris and other European capitals was equally enthusiastic.

Rehan's greatest role, first played in New York City in January 1887, was Katherine in *The Taming of the Shrew*. Other well received roles were those of Rosalind, Beatrice, Viola, and Portia. In 1893 she became a partner in Daly's London theater. She created the role of Maid Marian in Alfred, Lord Tennyson's *The Foresters*, which premiered in New York in June 1892. In 1894 she starred in a phenomenally successful London production of *Twelfth Night*. She appeared in San Francisco in 1896 as part of an American tour of that year, but she frequently returned to London during her last years on the stage.

Rehan's career effectively came to a close at the death of Daly in Paris. Her revivals of her old repertory after 1900 seemed dated and unglamorous, and she herself confessed that she was indifferent. She gave her final performance in New York City in 1905. She had prospered as an actress, however, and she subsequently lived in comfortable circumstances in England and the United States until her death in New York City on January 8, 1916.

Reinhardt, Aurelia Isabel Henry 1877–1948 educator

Born in San Francisco on April 1, 1877, Aurelia Henry grew up and attended schools there and briefly in San Jacinto, California. In 1898 she graduated from the University of California at Berkeley. After three years as an instructor in physical culture and elocution at the University of Idaho, during which time she also directed student dramatics and gave public readings, she entered graduate studies at Yale. In 1903 she was appointed to the chair in English at the Idaho State Normal School in Lewiston. Her translation of Dante's *De Monarchia* was published in 1904. In 1905 she received her Ph.D. from Yale for a dissertation on Ben Jonson's *Epicoene*, and in 1905–1906 she studied abroad, mainly at Oxford and in Italy. In 1908 she returned to her family's home in Berkeley, California, and in December 1909 she married Dr. George F. Reinhardt. On his death in 1914 she returned to work as a teacher of English in the extension service of the University of California.

Reinhardt's vivid lectures at extension centers throughout the state made a considerable impression, and in 1916 she was offered the presidency of Mills College in Oakland. In her 27 years in that post she built the college up from a small local school in precarious financial condition into a strong liberal arts institution with an international reputation. The faculty was more than doubled in size, the student body more than tripled, and the physical plant was greatly expanded. Scholars of distinction were recruited for the faculty, and academic standards were raised. Reinhardt's style of administration was intensely personal and sometimes nearly capricious, but she retained the loyalty of virtually all her associates. She had a particular flair for public relations and did much in lectures around the country to spread the reputation of Mills College and to encourage gifts to the school.

Reinhardt also served as president of the Oakland City Planning Commission in 1919, as president of the American Association of University Women in 1923–1927, as chairman of the education department of the General Federation of Women's Clubs in 1928–1930, and as moderator of the American Unitarian Association in 1940–1942. She was also active in Republican politics in California. She retired as president of Mills College in 1943 and spent much time thereafter in travel. She died in Palo Alto, California, on January 28, 1948.

Reno, Janet 1938– U.S. Attorney General

Born on July 21, 1938 in Miami, Florida, Janet Reno settled with her family on 20 acres of wilderness at the edge of the Everglades, outside of Miami when she was eight years old. There, her parents built the house she would live in for many years to come. Her father, a Danish immigrant, was a police reporter for the *Miami Herald* and her mother was an investigative reporter for the *Miami News*. While Reno's mother was considered somewhat eccentric — reportedly her pastimes included wrestling alligators and reciting poetry, and she was named honorary princess of the Miccosukee Indian tribe — Reno credits both her parents as being major influences on her life and work. She graduated from Coral Gables High School where she excelled on the debating team, and went on to Cornell University. She earned her degree in chemistry in 1960 and entered Harvard Law School. Upon graduation from Harvard in 1963, she went to work for the law firm, Brigham and Brigham. In 1967 she became the junior partner in the firm of Lewis and Reno.

She began her career in politics in 1971 when she was named staff director of the Judiciary Committee of the Florida House of Representatives. In 1973 she was named assistant to the state's attorney general in Miami and became state attorney in 1978. She was reelected to the post five times, even though she was a Democrat in a largely Republican area. She was in this position during the riots in the Liberty City section of Miami, as well as during the marked increase in crime due to burgeoning drug trafficking in the area. Reno was both applauded and criticized for her work during this time. Some believed her to be too lenient toward criminals and disagreed with her policy of frequent plea bargaining. At the same time her reformation of the juvenile justice system and her tough stance prosecuting child-abuse cases earned her a reputation as a strong children's advocate.

In 1993, after two unsuccessful nominations of other candidates, President Bill Clinton nominated her for the position of U.S. Attorney General and Congress quickly approved her nomination. Her early days in office were marked by her efforts to secure greater protection for women seeking abortions who were often victims of physical harassment from anti-abortion activists. Her most controversial decision, however, was her ordering FBI agents to conduct the final raid on the Branch Davidian cult compound near Waco, Texas. Unfortunately 86 cult members, including 17 children, were killed as a result of this police action, and she was heavily criticized for her decision. Her response was to take full responsibility for the tragedy, however, and her candor and obvious regret over the incident helped to earn her the respect of many Americans.

Over the next few years in her position as Attorney General, she drafted new legislation broadening the scope of child pornography laws. She also clashed with the White House in her efforts to regulate violence on network television, as well as over her refusal to endorse Vice President Al Gore's plan to merge the FBI and the DEA. She was respected, however, for continuing to do what she felt was right, despite the political implications.

Repplier, Agnes 1855–1950 essayist

Born in Philadelphia on April 1, 1855, Agnes Repplier was educated at home by her mother and for brief periods at Eden Hall, a Sacred Heart convent school in Torresdale, Pennsylvania, and at Agnes Irwin's private school in Philadelphia. She was a willful, self-directed student who frequently rebelled against discipline and prescribed studies. In 1871, in order to supplement her family's income, she began contributing sketches and stories to various minor and local periodicals. A short story published in *Catholic World* magazine in 1881 first brought her to national attention. After a few more stories had appeared, Father Isaac Hecker, editor of *Catholic World*, advised her to turn from fiction to the essay, and thereafter most of her writing was in that form.

From 1886 Repplier's essays appeared frequently in the *Atlantic Monthly*. Ranging in subject from literature to historical incidents to aspects of everyday life, her essays consistently displayed careful thought, discreetly marshaled erudition, fine feeling, refined taste, lightly ironic wit, and a high order of craftsmanship. They were collected in several volumes: *Books and Men*, 1888, *Points of View*, 1891, *Essays in Miniature*, 1892, *Essays in Idleness*, 1893, *In the Dozy Hours and Other Papers*, 1894, *Varia*, 1897, *Philadelphia: The Place and the People*, 1898, *The Fireside Sphinx*, 1901, *Compromises*, 1904, *A Happy Half-Century and Other Essays*, 1908, *The Cat*, 1912, *Americans and Others*, 1912, *Counter-Currents*, 1916, *Points of Friction*, 1920, *Under Dispute*, 1924, *Times and Tendencies*, 1931, *To Think of Tea!*, 1932, *The Pursuit of Laughter*, 1936, and *Eight Decades: Essays and Episodes*, 1937.

She also wrote several biographies: *J. William White, M.D.*, 1919, *Père Marquette*, 1929, *Mère Marie of the Ursulines*, 1931, *Junípero Sera*, 1933, and *Agnes Irwin*, 1934. *Our Convent Days*, 1905, was autobiographical. She was also a successful lecturer. Among the many honors accorded her were the Laetare Medal of the University of Notre Dame in 1911, membership in the American Philosophical Association in 1928, and the gold medal of the National Institute of Arts and Letters in 1935. She died in Philadelphia on December 15, 1950.

Rice, Alice Caldwell Hegan 1870–1942 writer

Born in Shelbyville, Kentucky, on January 11, 1870, Alice Hegan was educated at home and at Miss Hampton's School in Louisville. She was interested in writing from an early age and at fifteen saw her first published work in the *Louisville Courier-Journal*. She became active in church work in her youth and taught in a mission Sunday school in a slum district of Louisville known as the "Cabbage Patch." She also became a member of the Authors Club of Louisville, a group of aspiring young women writers that included Annie Fellows Johnston and Ellen Churchill Semple. With their encouragement she distilled some of her experiences in Cabbage Patch, particularly her acquaintance with a warm, humorous old woman who lived there, into a short novel, *Mrs. Wiggs of the Cabbage Patch*, 1901. The great success of that sentimental story of courage in the face of poverty and the triumph of social conscience established her career; over the next 40 years it sold more than half a million copies, was translated into several foreign languages, and was made into a play and a motion picture. In December 1902 Hegan married Cale Young Rice, a poet, with whom she lived thereafter in Louisville and traveled widely.

Subsequent books by Alice Rice included *Lovey Mary*, 1903, *Sandy*, 1905, *Captain June*, 1907, *Mr. Opp*, her most critically esteemed work, 1909, *A Romance of Billy Goat Hill*, 1912, *The Honorable Percival*, 1914, *Calvary Alley*, 1917, *Miss Mink's Soldier and*

Other Stories, 1918, *Turn About Tales*, with her husband, 1920, *Quin*, 1921, *Winners and Losers*, with her husband, 1925, *The Buffer*, 1929, *Mr. Pete & Co.*, 1933, *The Lark Legacy*, 1935, *Passionate Follies*, with her husband, 1936, *My Pillow Book*, 1937, and *Our Ernie*, 1939. From 1910 she was a devoted supporter of the Cabbage Patch Settlement, and charitable work was an avocation throughout her life. Her autobiography, *The Inky Way*, appeared in 1940. Rice died in Louisville on February 10, 1942.

Adrienne Rich

Rich, Adrienne Cecile 1929– poet, essayist and activist

Born on May 16, 1929, in Baltimore, Maryland, Adrienne Rich was brought up in a household she describes as "white and middle-class . . . full of books, with a father who encouraged me to write." She was schooled at home by her mother, a composer and pianist, until the fourth grade. In 1951, she graduated Phi Beta Kappa from Radcliffe College. That same year, she published *A Change of World*, her first book of poetry, which the poet W. H. Auden selected for the Yale Younger Poets Award. Although she married in 1953 and had three sons in six years, she continued to write.

Her early poetry is characterized by stylistic control and elegance, qualities she perfected in *The Diamond Cutters and Other Poems*, 1955. *Snapshots of a Daughter-in-Law: Poems 1954–1962*, 1963, marks a shift toward a more feminist and political poetry. In 1966, she separated from her husband (who committed suicide in 1970). She taught in the SEEK (Seek Education, Elevation and Knowledge) English program at the City College of New York from 1968 to 1970, later becoming an instructor of creative writing and assistant professor of English. The poetry of *Necessities of Life: Poems 1962–1965*, 1966, *Selected Poems*, 1967, *Leaflets: Poems 1965–1968*, 1969, and *The Will to Change: Poems 1969–1970*, 1971, reflects her involvement in the antiwar movement and the black civil rights struggle.

In the early 1970s, her poetry took on the urgent tone of militant feminism with the publication of *Diving into the Wreck: Poems 1971–1972*, 1973, which won a National Book Award. Although Rich declined the award as an individual, she accepted it on behalf of all women and donated the cash to a charitable institution. Her activism led to the publication of *Of Woman Born: Motherhood as Experience and Institution*, 1976, a prose unmasking of motherhood as mired in patriarchal assumptions.

In her monograph *Compulsory Heterosexuality and Lesbian Existence*, 1980, Rich challenges the premises of the institution of heterosexuality. Her lesbianism figures prominently in her poetry of the late 1970s and 1980s. *Twenty-One Love Poems*, 1976, became a section of *The Dream of a Common Language: Poems 1974–1977*, 1978; other collections include *A Wild Patience Has Taken Me This Far: Poems 1978–1981*, 1981, *Sources*, 1984, and *The Fact of a Doorframe: Poems Selected and New 1950–1984*, 1984, and *Your Native Land, Your Life*, 1986. With poet Michelle Cliff, she edited *Sinister Wisdom*, a lesbian-feminist journal, from 1980–1984. During this period she wrote copious essays about literature and lesbian feminism among many other issues, which are collected in *On Lies, Secrets and Silence: Selected Prose 1966–1978*, 1979, and *Blood, Bread and Poetry: Selected Prose 1979–1986*, 1986. These titles offer a perspective on the history of white feminism in the U.S.

More recently Rich has explored oppression, violence, injustice, and anti-Semitism in *Time's Power: Poems 1985–88*, 1989, and *An Atlas of a Difficult World: Poems 1988–1991*, 1991. Her voice of courage informs *What is Found There: Notebooks on Poetry and Politics*, 1993, a combination of social and cultural commentary, reflections on language and poetry, and the poets' creed — composed in passionate, lyrical prose. She has won numerous awards, fellowships and prizes, including two Guggenheim Fellowships, the Fellowship of the Academy of American Poets, the Ruth Lilly Poetry Prize, the Fund for

Human Dignity Award of the National Gay Task Force, the Lambda Book Award, and the Poets' Prize.

Richards, Ellen Henrietta Swallow 1842–1911 chemist

Born on December 3, 1842, in Dunstable, Massachusetts, Ellen Swallow was educated mainly at home. She helped her father with farm work and her mother with domestic tasks, becoming accomplished in both spheres, and after the family's move to Westford in 1859 she assisted in the village store, which her father had taken over. She attended Westford Academy for a short time. In 1863 the family moved again to Littleton, where she again helped in the store and also taught school for a time. After several disappointments she was at last able to continue her education at Vassar College, from which she graduated after two years, in 1870. Abandoning a plan, inspired by Maria Mitchell, to become a teacher of astronomy, she turned to her other great interest, chemistry, and late in 1870 became the first woman to be admitted to the Massachusetts Institute of Technology. She received a B.S. degree in 1873 and remained for two more years of graduate study, although the school declined to award her a Ph.D. In June 1875 she married Professor Robert H. Richards, head of the department of mining engineering at MIT and a brother-in-law of Laura E. H. Richards. Helping her husband in the chemistry of ore analysis and concentration led to her election as the first woman member of the American Institute of Mining and Metallurgical Engineers in 1879.

In November 1876, at her urging, the Woman's Education Association of Boston contributed funds for the opening of a Woman's Laboratory at MIT. There, as assistant director under Professor John M. Ordway, she began her work of encouraging women to enter the sciences and of providing opportunities for scientific training to capable and interested women. Courses in basic and industrial chemistry, biology, and mineralogy were taught, and through Ordway a certain amount of industrial and government consulting work was obtained. Richards published several books and pamphlet as a result of her work with the Woman's Laboratory, including *The Chemistry of Cooking and Cleaning*, 1882, and *Food Materials and Their Adulterations*, 1885.

From 1876 Richards was also head of the science section of the Society to Encourage Studies at Home. In 1882, with Alice Freeman Palmer and others, she was a founder of the Association of Collegiate Alumnae (later the American Association of University Women). The Woman's Laboratory closed in 1883, by which time its students had been regularly admitted to MIT. In 1884 Richards became assistant to Professor William R. Nichols in the institute's new laboratory of sanitation chemistry, and she held the post of instructor on the MIT faculty for the rest of her life. During 1887–1889 she had charge of laboratory work for the Massachusetts State Board of Health's survey of inland waters.

In 1890, under Richards's guidance, the New England Kitchen was opened in Boston to offer to working class families nutritious food, scientifically prepared at low cost, and at the same time to demonstrate the methods employed. In 1893 Mrs. Richards created the Rumford Kitchen at the World's Columbian Exposition in Chicago to serve cheap nutritious meals and to disseminate scientific knowledge of nutrition and food preparation. From 1894 the Boston School Committee obtained school lunches from the New England Kitchen. Richards lobbied for the introduction of courses in domestic science into the public schools of Boston, and in 1897 she helped President Mary M. K. Kehew organize a school of housekeeping in the Woman's Educational and Industrial Union that was later taken over by Simmons College.

In 1899 Richards called a summer conference of workers in the fledgling field of domestic science at Lake Placid, New York. Under her chairmanship the series of such conferences held over the next several years established standards, course outlines, bibliographies, and women's club study guides for the field, for which the name "home economics" was adopted. In December 1908 the Lake Placid conferees formed the American Home Economics Association, of which Richards was elected first president. She held the post until her retirement in 1910, and in that time she established the association's *Journal of Home Economics*. In 1910 she was named to the council of the National Education Association with primary responsibility for overseeing the teaching of home economics in public schools.

Among her other published works were *Home Sanitation: A Manual for Housekeepers*, 1887, *Domestic Economy as a Factor in Public Education*, 1889, *The Cost of Living*, 1899, *Air, Water, and Food for Colleges*, 1900, *The Cost of Food*, 1901, *The Cost of Shelter*, 1905, *Sanitation in Daily Life*, 1907, *The Cost of Cleanness*, 1908, *Laboratory Notes on Industrial Water Analysis: A Survey Course for Engineers*, 1908, *Conservation by Sanitation*, 1911, and *Euthenics: The Science of Controllable Environment*, 1912. She died in Boston on March 30, 1911.

Richards, Laura Elizabeth Howe 1850–1943 writer of children's books

Born in Boston on February 27, 1850, Laura Howe was the daughter of Julia Ward Howe and Samuel Gridley Howe. She was named for Laura Bridgman, her father's most celebrated pupil. She grew up in a cultivated home where authors, philosophers, and distinguished persons of every sort were frequent guests; her more formal education occurred in Boston private schools. In June 1871 she married Henry Richards, an architect with whom she lived in Boston until 1876 and thereafter in Gardiner, Maine. Although she had enjoyed writing for her own pleasure since childhood, it was not until 1873 that she published anything. In that year several of her nonsense rhymes and nursery songs appeared in *St. Nicholas* magazine for children. A collection of such pieces appeared in book form in 1881 as *Sketches & Scraps*, which enjoyed wide popularity, and in the same year she published a collection of stories under the title *Five Mice in a Mouse-Trap*.

Subsequent books included *The Joyous Story of Toto*, 1885, *Toto's Merry Winter*, 1887, *Queen Hildegarde*, first of a series of novels for young girls, 1889, *In My Nursery*, verses, 1890, *Captain January*, her most popular book with sales of some 300,000 copies (it was twice made into a movie), 1890, *Hildegarde's Holiday*, 1891, *Hildegarde's Home*, 1892, *Melody*, 1893, *When I Was Your Age*, a volume of childhood reminiscences, 1894, *Glimpses of the French Court*, 1893, *Marie*, 1894, *Nautilus*, 1895, *Jim of Hellas*, 1895, *Five Minute Stories*, 1895, *Narcissa*, 1896, *Isla Heron*, 1896, *Some Say*, 1896, *Hildegarde's Harvest*, 1897, *Three Margarets*, which began another series for girls, 1897, *Margaret Montfort*, 1898, *Love and Rocks*, 1898, *Rosin the Beau*, 1898, *Peggy*, 1899, *Rita*, 1900, *For Tommy*, 1900, *Quicksilver Sue*, 1901, *Mrs. Tree*, 1902, *The Hurdy Gurdy*, more verses, 1902, *The Green Satin Gown*, 1903, *The Golden Windows*, 1903, *The Merryweathers*, 1904, *Mrs. Tree's Will*, 1905, *The Piccolo*, verses, 1906, *The Silver Crown*, 1906, *Grandmother*, 1907, *The Life of Florence Nightingale For Young People*, 1909, *Up to Calvin's*, 1910, *Two Noble Lives*, about her parents, 1911, *Miss Jimmy*, 1912, *The Little Master*, 1913, *Three Minute Stories*, 1914, *The Life of Julia Ward Howe*, with her sister Maud Howe Elliott, which won the first Pulitzer Prize for biography, 1915, *The Life of Elizabeth Fry*, 1916, *The Life of Abigail Adams*, 1917, *The Life of Joan of Arc*, 1919, *Honor Bright*, 1920, *The Squire*, 1923,! *Oriental Operettas*, 1924, *Star Bright*, 1927, *Laura Bridgman*, a biography, 1928, *Stepping Westward*, an autobiography, 1931, *Tirra Lirra*, verses, 1932, *Samuel Gridley Howe*, biography, 1935, *E.A.R.*, on her young friend, the poet Edwin Arlington Robinson, 1936, and *I Have a Song to Sing You*, 1938. She also edited her father's *Letters and Journals* in two volumes, 1906–1909.

Richards was active in many civic and philanthropic organizations. She founded the local Woman's Philanthropic Union in 1895 and was its president for 26 years, and she was president of the Maine Consumers' League from 1905 to 1911. From 1900 to 1932 she assisted her husband in running Camp Merryweather, a pioneering summer camp for boys. She died in Gardiner, Maine, on January 14, 1943.

Richards, Linda 1841–1930 nurse and educator

Born on July 27, 1841, in Potsdam, New York, Melinda Ann Judson Richards grew up from the age of four in Derby and Lyndon, Vermont. She attended schools in Lyndon and an academy in nearby Barton. She worked in the Union Straw Works in Foxboro, Massachusetts, for seven years until, in 1870, she attempted to fulfill a long-standing ambition by becoming an assistant nurse at the Boston City Hospital. Instead of the training she had hoped for, however, she found only menial work among equally ill trained colleagues, and she soon left. In 1872 she enrolled in the newly opened nurses' training school at the New England Hospital for Women and Children, and in 1873 she received the first diploma awarded by the nation's first school of nursing. After a year as night superintendent at the Bellevue Hospital Training School in New York City she returned to Boston to become superintendent of the Boston Training School (later the School of Nursing of Massachusetts General Hospital), which was then a year old and still insecurely established. In three years she developed a curriculum of classroom work for trainees, succeeded in winning admission of students to all wards of the hospital, and won recognition of the superintendent of the school as superintendent of nurses for the hospital as well.

In 1877 Richards visited nurses' training schools at St. Thomas's Hospital, London, where Florence Nightingale had pioneered in the field, and at the Edinburgh Royal Infirmary, and she discussed the subject with Nightingale personally. She then returned to Boston and helped establish a training school at Boston City Hospital that was fully integrated with the organization and ward work of the hospital; she became matron of the hospital and superintendent of the school on its opening in 1878. She remained there until 1885, taking a lengthy leave of absence during that time owing to illness. In 1885 she volunteered her services to the American Board of Commissioners for Foreign Missions, under whose auspices she arrived in Japan early in 1886. Later that year she opened Japan's first training school for nurses at Doshisha Hospital in Kyoto. She supervised the school for five years.

Ill health forced Richards to return to the United States early in 1891. Over the next 20 years, as her health permitted, she served as head of the Philadelphia Visiting Nurses Society in 1891; founded a training school at the Methodist Episcopal Hospital in Philadelphia in 1892; and headed the training schools at the New England Hospital for Women and Children in 1893–1894, the Brooklyn Homeopathic Hospital in 1894–1895, the Hartford Hospital in 1895–1897, and the University of Pennsylvania Hospital in Philadelphia in 1897–1899. In 1894 she was elected first president of the American Society of Superintendents of Training Schools. During 1899–1904 she directed the training school at the Taunton Insane Hospital in Massachusetts, and in 1904 she established a school at the Worcester Hospital for the Insane, where she remained until 1905. In 1906–1909 she headed the school of the Michigan Insane Asylum in Kalamazoo, and after another year in Taunton she retired in 1911. In that year she published *Reminiscences of Linda Richards*. She died in Boston on April 16, 1930.

Richmond, Mary Ellen 1861–1928 social worker

Born on August 5, 1861, in Belleville, Illinois, Mary Richmond grew up in Baltimore largely under the care of her maternal grandmother and two aunts. After graduating from high school in 1878 she worked for two years in a New York publishing house and then returned to Baltimore, where she worked as a bookkeeper in a stationery store and later in a hotel. In 1889 she secured a job as assistant treasurer of the Baltimore Charity Organization Society. Social work quickly proved to be her destined field. To the training she received in visiting Zilpha Smith of the Boston Associated Charities she added her own reading and the practical experience of field work as a volunteer "friendly visitor." In 1891 she was named general secretary of the society, a post that had until then always been held by a man with advanced academic training.

Over the next nine years she gradually developed a coherent philosophy of social work involving professional training in case work for field workers and broad research into social conditions and problems. In 1899 she published her ideas in *Friendly Visiting Among the Poor*. From 1900 to 1909 she was general secretary of the Philadelphia Society for Organizing Charity, which she succeeded in thoroughly reorganizing and revitalizing. In *The Good Neighbor in the Modern City*, 1907, in numerous articles and speeches, and in a department she edited for the *Charities and the Commons* journal in 1905–1909, she continued to advocate the development of professional social work through scientific research, careful testing of methods, exchange of data and experience among agencies, and rational organization. In 1909 she was named director of the Charity Organization Department of the new Russell Sage Foundation in New York City, a post she held for the rest of her life. There she directed a broad program of social research and worked to develop further the methodology of professional social work.

Richmond's championship and elaboration of the case work approach were the subject of her major written work, *Social Diagnosis*, 1917. *What Is Social Case Work?* appeared in 1922. For a number of years before and after her move to New York she taught summer courses at the New York School of Philanthropy (later the New York School of Social Work). From 1910 to 1922 she conducted an annual Charity Organization Institute for advanced case work training and from 1915 an annual supervisors' conference. As a schism slowly developed between those in social work who favored tax-based governmental programs of relief for various classes of the needy and those who favored more traditional private efforts aimed at families, Richmond emerged as a leading spokesman for the latter view. In her late years she was deeply interested in the reform of marriage laws, a topic that she discussed in *Child Marriages*, 1925, and the posthumous *Marriage and the State*, 1929, both written with F. S. Hall. She died in New York City on September 12, 1928.

Rickert, Edith 1871–1938 writer, educator and literary critic

Born on July 11, 1871, in Dover, Ohio, Martha Edith Rickert grew up in La Grange, Illinois, and then in Chicago. She attended public schools and in 1891 graduated from Vassar College. While supporting herself by teaching in high schools in and around Chicago she undertook graduate studies in English and philology at the University of Chicago. She studied in Europe for a year and in 1897 returned to Vassar as an instructor of English. She received her Ph.D. from the University of Chicago in 1899. In 1900 she left Vassar and traveled to England, where over the next nine years she did research among medieval texts and produced five novels — *Out of the Cypress Swamp*, 1902, *The Reaper*, 1904, *Folly*, 1906, *The Golden Hawk*, 1907, and *The Beggar in the Heart*, 1909 — and numerous short stories.

After her return to the United States in 1909 she did editorial work for the *Ladies' Home Journal*, wrote or collaborated on several textbooks, and with Jessie Paton edited a volume of *American Lyrics*, 1912. During 1918–1919 she worked in the codes and ciphers division of the War Department with John M. Manly, with whom she subsequently collaborated on *The Writing of English*, 1919, *Contemporary British Literature*, 1921, *Contemporary American Literature*, 1922, and other handbooks and textbooks. In 1924 she became associate professor of English at the University of Chicago; she remained on the faculty there for the rest of her life, from 1930 as full professor. Her teaching fields were Chaucer and contemporary literature, the latter of which her earlier work with Manly had been instrumental in bringing into the realm of college studies.

She wrote an influential book on criticism, *New Methods for the Study of Literature*, 1927, three volumes of children's stories, *The Bojabi Tree*, 1923, *The Blacksmith and the Blackbirds*, 1928, and *The Greedy Goroo*, 1929, and a final novel, *Severn Woods*, 1930. Her last years were devoted to collaborating with Manly (who was also on the Chicago faculty) on the definitive *Text of the Canterbury Tales, Studied on the Basis of All Known Manuscripts*, which appeared in eight volumes in 1940. Before the completion of that major work she died in Chicago on May 23, 1938.

Ride, Sally 1951– physicist and astronaut

Born on May 26, 1951 in Los Angeles, California, Sally Kristen Ride grew up there and attended Westlake High School, where she became a nationally ranked tennis player. She graduated in 1968 and went on to Stanford University where she earned a B.A. in English iand a B.S. in physics in 197e. In 1978, as a Ph.D. student and teaching assistant in laser physics at Stanford, she was selected by NASA as one of six women astronaut candidates. She began her training and evaluation courses that same year. In August of 1979 she completed her NASA training, obtained her pilot's license, and earned the title Shuttle Mission Specialist. After a number of years in this position, on June 18, 1983, she became the first American woman in space. (In 1963 Soviet cosmonaut, Valentina Tereshkova was the first woman in space.) The flight of the shuttle *Challenger* lasted six days, during which time she served as flight engineer, and along with the four other astronauts onboard, deployed several satellites.

She completed a second space mission on October 13, 1984. The goal of this 13th shuttle mission was to deploy the Earth Radiation Budget Satellite as well as make scientific observations of the Earth with a large format camera. On this mission, her childhood friend Kathryn Sullivan became the first American woman to walk in space.

Had it not been for the *Challenger* disaster in 1986 and the subsequent suspension of all shuttle launches, she would have traveled in space a third time in 1986. Instead, she was appointed the astronaut office representative to the presidential commission's *Challenger* disaster investigation, responsible for questioning her NASA colleagues as well as aerospace engineers about the cause of the crash. When the investigation was completed, she continued to work for NASA as the special assistant to the administrator for strategic planning. In this post she directed a study of how NASA should proceed after completing its space station project. In the project's report, possible NASA goals outlined included a manned mission to Mars and the creation of a manned base on the moon. In August of 1987, she left NASA and returned to her alma mater Stanford University as an arms control fellow. Two years later she became the head of the Space Science Institute and a physics professor at the University of California at San Diego. All told, she logged a total of 337 hours in space.

Ride was married to fellow astronaut Steven Hawley from 1982 to 1987. She wrote the book *To Space and Back* in 1986 with Susan Okie, as well as *Voyager: An Adventure to the Edge of the Solar System* in 1992 with T. O'Shaughnessy, both children's books. She also wrote *The Third Planet: Exploring the Earth from Space* in 1994.

Riepp, Mother Benedicta 1825–1862 religious

Born on June 28, 1825, in Waal in the Bavarian province of Swabia, Maria Sybilla Riepp entered the Benedictine Convent of Saint Walburga in Eichstätt when she was nineteen. She took the habit as Sister Benedicta in August 1844. From 1849, when she made her final vows, to 1852 she was a teacher and mistress of novices in the convent. In 1852, with two companions, she sailed for America to establish the first Benedictine convent. In July of that year they settled in St. Marys, Elk County, Pennsylvania, where there was already a Benedictine monastery, and established St. Joseph's Convent and School, of which Mother Benedicta was superior.

The small community endured severe hardships for a number of years, but with the admission of 12 novices in 1853 it began a sustained growth. Sisters were sent out to establish new convents in Erie, Pennsylvania, in Newark, New Jersey, in St. Cloud, Minnesota, in Bristow, Virginia, in Pittsburgh, Pennsylvania, and elsewhere over the next several years. Jurisdictional disputes with the motherhouse in Eichstätt and with Abbot Boniface Wimmer led to her trip back to Europe in 1859 to obtain independence for the American Benedictine convents. Although she succeeded in securing independence from the motherhouse, the American convents were placed under the authority of their respective diocesan bishops. On her return to St. Joseph's she found that Abbot Wimmer had removed her as superior. She passed her last years in the convents in Erie and St. Cloud; she died in St. Cloud, Minnesota, on March 15, 1862.

Rinehart, Mary Roberts 1876–1958 mystery writer, reporter and playwright

Born in Pittsburgh on August 12, 1876, Mary Roberts attended public schools and in 1896 graduated from the Pittsburgh Training School for Nurses. In April 1896 she married Stanley M. Rinehart, a physician. She immediately began to raise a family and took up writing only as a result of difficulties created by financial losses in 1903. Her first story appeared in *Munsey's Magazine* that year, *The Circular Staircase*, 1908 her first book and first mystery, was an immediate success, and the following year *The Man in Lower Ten*, serialized earlier, reinforced her popular success. Thereafter she wrote steadily, averaging about a book a year. A long series of comic tales about the redoubtable "Tish," Letitia Carberry, appeared as serials in the *Saturday Evening Post* over a number of years and as novels beginning with *The Amazing Adventures of Letitia Carberry*, 1911.

Rinehart served as a war correspondent during World War I and later described her experiences in several books, notably *Kings, Queens and Pawns*, 1915. She produced as well a number of romances and some nine plays. Most of the plays were written in collaboration with Avery Hopwood; her greatest successes were *Seven Days*, produced at the Astor Theatre, New York, in 1909, and *The Bat*, derived from *The Circular Staircase* and produced at the Morosco Theatre, New York, in 1920. She remained best known, however, as a writer of mysteries, and the growing popularity of that genre after World War II led to frequent republication of her works. Her most memorable tales combined murder, love, ingenuity, and humor in a style that was distinctly her own.

Among her books were *When a Man Marries*, 1909, *The Window at the White Cat*, 1910, *The Case of Jennie Brice*, 1911, *Where There's a Will*, 1911, *The Street of Seven Stars*, 1914, *"K"*, 1915, *Tish*, 1916, *Bab-A Sub-Deb*, 1917, *Long Live the King*, 1917, *Twenty-Three and One-Half Hours Leave*, 1918, *The Amazing Interlude*, 1918, *Dangerous Days*, 1919, *A Poor Wise Man*, 1920, *More Tish*, 1921, *The Breaking Point*, 1922, *The Red Lamp*, 1925, *Tish Plays the Game*, 1926, *Two Flights Up*, 1928, *The Door*, 1930, *Miss Pinkerton*, 1932, *The Album*, 1933, *The State Versus Elinor Norton*, 1934, *The Doctor*, 1936, *Tish Marches On*, 1937, *The Wall*, 1938, *Familiar Faces*, 1941, *Haunted Lady*, 1942, *The Yellow Room*, 1945, *A Light in the Window*, 1948, *The Swimming Pool*, 1952, *The Frightened Wife*, 1953, and *The Best of Tish*, 1955. She wrote her autobiography, *My Story*, in 1931 and revised it in 1948. At her death in New York City on September 22, 1958, her books had sold more than ten million copies.

Ringgold, Faith 1934– artist

Born in New York City on October 8, 1934, Faith Ringgold grew up in Harlem and decided to be an artist while still in high school. She attended City College of New York, but as a woman she could not be admitted to the liberal arts program. Instead she enrolled in the School of Education, from which she graduated in 1955 with a major in art and a minor in education; she received a master's degree in 1959. After graduation, she taught art in New York City public schools before studying painting for a year in Europe. As an African-American woman Ringgold was discouraged by biases in her artistic training, which seemed to teach that the only good art is that which has evolved through European culture.

After returning to New York in 1960, Ringgold attempted to show her impressionist-style paintings, only to be told by a gallery owner that as a black artist she could not possibly produce good European-style art. After three years she left the New York art scene and worked to develop a style based on her own African-American heritage. She read black writers and studied African art, and she was deeply influenced by the Black Power movement. During this period she produced a series of paintings whose flat, matte style and interlocking shapes were reminiscent of some African art. The titles reflected her engagement in the struggle for black liberation: "The Flag is Bleeding," "US Postage Stamp Commemorating the Advent of Black Power," and "Die."

In the early 1970s she began integrating feminist concerns into her work. She painted a mural at the New York City Women's House of Detention at Riker's Island showing African-American, Latina, Asian and white women in a variety of nontraditional occupations, such as bus drivers, doctors, priests, basketball players, and even president of the United States. She also started reclaiming women's traditional art forms such as quiltmaking, and started creating fabric portrait masks of women from Harlem, many of which depict open mouths to reflect African-American women's need to find their voices.

In 1976 she branched out to performance art about African-American women's experience, using masks and soft sculptures. Her mother, dress designer Willi Posey, created the costumes, and her children were the performers. Throughout the 1970s Ringgold was active in the movement against racism and sexism in the art world. She helped to organize protests against the Whitney Museum of American Art and the Venice Biennale, and, with Kay Brown and Dinga McGannon, organized the 1971 pioneering show of African-American women artists entitled "Where We At."

Her work met with much resistance from critics and other artists. Whites saw it as too politicized and too African-American; black men saw it as too identified with Africa and objected to her use of "soft" media, calling her work more craft than art. Ringgold's response was forthright — she accused African-American men of needing to identify with white artistic standards. Decrying the lack of a place in the art world for African and female forms, she continued to work in ways that affirmed her gender and racial heritage.

Using fabric squares and narrative text to depict the lives of black women, Ringgold created a remarkable series of quilts, some of which she entitled "Who's Afraid of Aunt Jemima," "Slave Rape Story Quilt," and the autobiographical "Change: Faith Ringgold's Over 100 Pounds Weight Loss Story Quilt." In 1984 she accepted a position as professor of art at the University of California, San Diego.

Ritchie, Jean 1922– singer and folklorist

Born on December 8, 1922, in Viper, Kentucky, Jean Ritchie was the youngest of 14 children who grew up in a poor but happy family for whom the singing of traditional songs was the principal entertainment. After attending local schools and studying for brief periods at Cumberland College and the University of Kentucky, she became a schoolteacher in 1942. She later returned to the University of Kentucky, and after her graduation in 1946 she was appointed supervisor of elementary schools in her native Perry County. The next year she moved to New York City to become a social worker with the Henry Street Settlement.

In New York her ballad singing, accompanied usually by her dulcimer, attracted considerable attention among friends and coworkers, and in 1948 she sang publicly at a folk music festival at Columbia University. In 1949 she gave up social work to devote herself to her music. In 1950 she gave a concert at the Greenwich Mews Playhouse and appeared regularly on a local radio program, and she soon became a favorite artist at folk festivals and music camps and in college concerts.

Ritchie performed at the Royal Albert Hall and on the BBC radio network during a visit to Great Britain on a Fulbright scholarship in 1952. Her researches there into the roots of Appalachian folk music found their way into several of her books, which included *The Swapping Song Book*, 1952, *A Garland of Mountain Song*, 1953, *Singing Family of the Cumberlands*, about her family, 1955, *The Dulcimer Book*, 1963, *Apple Seeds & Soda Straws*, 1965, *From Fair to Fair: Folk Songs of the British Isles*, 1966, *Jean Ritchie's Dulcimer People*, 1975, and *None But One*, 1977. She remained, in concert and on records, one of the most popular exponents of the traditional ballads of her heritage.

Rittenhouse, Jessie Belle 1869–1948 poet and critic

Born on December 8, 1869, in Mount Morris, New York, Jessie Rittenhouse attended schools in nearby Conesus and Nunda and in 1890 graduated from Genesee Wesleyan Seminary in Lima. While teaching in private schools in Cairo, Illinois, and then in Grand Haven, Michigan, she began writing articles for newspapers. Some book reviews published in papers in Buffalo and Rochester attracted attention, and in 1894–1895 she was a reporter for the *Rochester Democrat and Chronicle*. In 1895 she moved to Chicago and resumed free-lance writing. Four years later, deciding to specialize in writing about literature, she moved to Boston, where she soon became a member of Ellen Louise Moulton's literary salon and an accepted member of the city's literary set. In 1900 she published a variorum edition of Omar Khayyám's *Rubáiyát* and in 1904 a volume of selections from that poem under the title *The Lover's Rubáiyát*. In the latter year she also published her first book of criticism, *The Younger American Poets*, which was well received. In 1905 she moved to New York and became poetry reviewer for the *New York Times Review of Books*, a post she held for ten years. She also reviewed for *The Bookman* until 1920. She helped found the Poetry Society of America in 1914 and served as its secretary for ten years. From 1914 to 1924 she made frequent lecture tours on which she spoke mainly on contemporary poets.

Rittenhouse edited *The Little Book of Modern Verse*, 1913, *The Little Book of American Poets*, 1915, *The Second Book of Modern Verse*, 1919, *The Little Book of Modern British Verse*, 1924, and *The Third Book of Modern Verse*, 1927, which were widely popular and effectively shaped popular acceptance of contemporary poetry. She also published several volumes of her own verse, including *The Door of Dreams*, 1918, *The Lifted Cup*, 1921, *The Secret Bird*, 1930, and *Moving Tide: New and Selected Lyrics*, 1939, the last of which was awarded the gold medal of the National Poetry Center. With Clinton Scollard, whom she married in 1924, she edited *The Bird-Lover's Anthology*, 1930, and *Patrician Rhymes*, 1932. In 1934, two years after Scollard's death, she edited his selected verses as *The Singing Heart*. Her own autobiography, *My House of Life*, appeared in the same year. In 1930 the Poetry Society of America awarded her a medal for distinguished service to poetry. Jessie Rittenhouse died in Detroit on September 28, 1948.

Rivé-King, Julie 1854–1937 pianist and composer

Born in Cincinnati on October 30, 1854, Julie Rivé was the daughter of French immigrant parents. At five she began studying piano under her mother, who had attended the Paris Conservatory, and she gave her first public performance at eight. Her mother took her in 1866 to New York, where she studied under William Mason and Sebastian Bach Mills, and during 1872–1874 she studied in Europe under Karl Reinecke, Franz Liszt, and others.

She made her European debut with the Euterpe Musical Association of Leipzig in 1874, playing Beethoven's C Minor Concerto and Liszt's Second Rhapsody. In April 1875 she played Liszt's Concerto in E Flat and Schumann's "Faschingsschwank aus Wien" with the New York Philharmonic Society in her American debut. In 1876 she married Frank H. King, an executive of the Decker Company, manufacturers of pianos. Under his management (until his death in 1900) she continued her concert career under the name Rivé-King, and by 1936, when she finally gave up performing, she had given some 4000 concerts and recitals. Her superb technique, which she could adapt to the demands of both classical and romantic works, her large repertoire, and her willingness to introduce works of American composers made her one of the most popular and influential musicians in America. Her own compositions included *Polonaise héroïque*, *Bubbling Spring*, *On Blooming Meadow*, and *Impromptu in A Flat*. From 1905 to 1936 she taught at the Bush Conservatory of Music and its successor, the Chicago Conservatory. She died in Indianapolis on July 24, 1937.

Roberts, Elizabeth Madox 1881–1941 writer

Born on October 30, 1881, in Perryville, Kentucky, Elizabeth Roberts grew up in nearby Springfield. She graduated from high school in Covington in 1900 and was admitted to the State College (now University) of Kentucky, but either ill health or lack of funds prevented her from beginning her college education at that time. For ten years she taught school in Springfield and nearby villages. In 1910 she traveled to Colorado for her health. There she wrote the verses that were published to accompany photographs of mountain flowers in *In the Great Steep's Garden*, 1915. A professor at the University of Kentucky brought her poems to the attention of Robert Morss Lovett, who encouraged her to enter the University of Chicago. She graduated with honors in 1921 and the next year published the poems that had won the university's Fiske Prize as *Under the Tree*.

Returning to her Kentucky home, she began work on her first novel, which appeared in 1926 under the title *The Time of Man*. In that and subsequent novels she created a unique body of work, in which the vivid backgrounds and authentic details, drawn from her intimate knowledge of the land and people of Kentucky, were merely the anchors of her concern with her characters' subjective lives, conveyed in her subtle, precise style and a complex but finely controlled symbolism. Other novels included *My Heart and My Flesh*, 1927, *Jingling in the Wind*, 1928, *The Great Meadow*, perhaps her finest, 1930, *A Buried Treasure*, 1931, *He Sent Forth a Raven*, 1935, and *Black Is My Truelove's Hair*, 1938. *The Haunted Mirror*, 1932, collected short stories, as did *Not by Strange Gods*, 1941; *Song in the Meadow*, 1940, collected verses. She died in Orlando, Florida, on March 13, 1941.

Robertson, Alice Mary 1854–1931 educator and public official

Born on January 2, 1854, at Tullahassee Mission in the Creek Nation, Indian Territory (now Tullahassee, Oklahoma), Alice Robertson was the daughter of missionary teachers among the Creek. She attended Elmira College in New York in 1871–1873 and then worked for six years as a clerk in the federal Office of Indian Affairs in Washington, D.C. After a brief period of teaching in the mission school at Tullahassee she became secretary to Captain Richard H. Pratt, superintendent of the Carlisle Indian School in Pennsylvania, in 1880. During 1882–1883 she made a fund-raising lecture tour to finance the building of a new mission school at Nuyaka to replace the burned one at Tullahassee. In 1885 she was given charge of a Presbyterian mission boarding school for girls in Muskogee. Under her guidance the school grew and obtained a charter as Henry Kendall College in 1894. (The school moved to Tulsa in 1907 and became the University of Tulsa in 1920.) She taught English, history, and civics at the college until 1899. In 1900 she was appointed the first federal supervisor of Creek education, and from 1905 to 1913, on appointment by her friend, President Theodore Roosevelt, she was postmistress of Muskogee. She then retired for some years to her farm. During World War I she became famous as "Miss Alice," who met every troop train passing through Muskogee and distributed coffee and refreshments to the soldiers. The canteen service that grew from her single efforts became the nucleus of the Muskogee Red Cross.

In 1920 Robertson was elected as a Republican to Congress from Oklahoma's Second District. During her term she was the only woman member of Congress. She was a regular Republican in voting, except for her opposition to the Sheppard-Towner Act of 1921 (providing for federal grants to states for programs of maternal and child health care), and she served on the Committee on Indian Affairs. After her defeat for reelection she was a welfare worker at the Veterans Hospital in Muskogee in 1923–1925. She was Washington correspondent for the *Muskogee News* for a time and later worked for the Oklahoma Historical Society. She died in Muskogee, Oklahoma, on July 1, 1931.

Robins, Margaret Dreier 1868–1945 labor leader and reformer

Born in Brooklyn, New York, on September 6, 1868, Margaret Dreier was the daughter of German immigrant parents. She attended private schools and pursued studies in history and philosophy on her own. At nineteen she volunteered for the women's auxiliary of Brooklyn Hospital, becoming secretary-treasurer of the group. In 1902 she became a member of the State Charities Aid Association's city visiting committee for insane asylums, and in 1903–1904 she was chairman of the legislative committee of the Women's Municipal League, a post in which she led a campaign for legislation regulating private employment agencies. In 1904 she joined the new Women's Trade Union League and became president of the New York branch. In June 1905 she married Raymond Robins, head of the Northwestern University Settlement in Chicago. In that city she soon met the leaders of reform and social work movements, including Jane Addams of Hull-House and Mary McDowell of the University of Chicago Settlement.

From 1907 to 1913 she was president of the Chicago branch of the Women's Trade Union League (she was succeeded in that post by her colleague Agnes Nestor), and from 1907 to 1922 she was president of the National Women's Trade Union League. She played a major role in organizing support for the strikes of 1909–1911 against the garment industry. She was the principal force behind the League's establishment of a training program for women union leaders in 1914, a program that continued until 1926, and she was for many years an editor of the League's journal, *Life and Labor*. She also served in 1908–1917 on the executive board of the Chicago Federation of Labor, and in 1915 she was appointed to the Illinois Unemployment Commission.

Robins was chairman of the League of Women Voters committee on women in industry and in 1919–1920 was a member of the women's division of the Republican National Committee. In 1919 she called an International Congress of Working Women, which met in Washington, D.C., and she was elected president of the International Federation of Working Women formed at a second such congress held in Geneva in 1921. She resigned that post in 1923. In 1924 she and her husband retired to Chinsegut Hill, an estate near Brooksville, Florida, but she continued active in public affairs. She was a member of the Republican National Committee in 1928 and headed the women in industry section of the women's division. In 1929 President Herbert Hoover named her to the planning committee of the White House Conference on Child Health and Protection. In the 1930s she became an ardent supporter of the New Deal. She was reelected to the executive board of the Women's Trade Union League in 1934. She died at her estate near Brooksville, Florida, on February 21, 1945.

Robson, May 1858–1942 actor

Born on April 19, 1858, in Wagga Wagga, New South Wales, Australia, Mary Jeanette Robison was the daughter of English immigrant parents. She grew up in a suburb of

Melbourne and, from the age of seven, in London, where her widowed mother returned. She was educated in convent and private schools in London, Brussels, and Paris. At sixteen she ran away to marry Charles L. Gore, with whom she settled in Fort Worth, Texas. They later moved to New York City, where Charles Gore's death a few years later left his widow penniless and with three children to support. She made a meager living by painting china and menu cards for Tiffany's and by teaching painting to children. An impulse moved her to obtain a small part in a stock company production of *Hoop of Gold* at the Grand Opera House in September 1883. Her portrayal of a Cockney slavey attracted considerable attention and started her on a career as a character actress of great versatility. A printer's error listed her on the program as May Robson, and she retained that name thereafter.

From 1884 to 1901 Robson played more than a hundred roles, nearly all of them comic, in the stock companies of A. M. Palmer at the Madison Square Theatre, Daniel Frohman at the Lyceum, and Charles Frohman at the Empire. She then worked under her own management, picking roles that particularly appealed to her. Among the plays she appeared in over the next several years were *Dorothy Vernon of Haddon Hall*, 1904, Clyde Fitch's *Cousin Billy*, 1905, *The Mountain Climber*, 1906, and *The Rejuvenation of Aunt Mary*, in which she attained stardom and with which she toured for a decade after its October 1907 opening in Scranton, Pennsylvania. *The Three Lights* (later called *A Night Out*), which she wrote with Charles T. Dazey, was a failure in 1911.

From 1911 Robson appeared occasionally in motion pictures for Vitagraph and other companies, but not until her 1927 film of *The Rejuvenation of Aunt Mary*, produced by Cecil B. DeMille, did she begin to make an impression on that medium. She moved to California in that year and became both a regular in movie character roles and a much loved member of the film colony. She appeared in, among others, *Strange Interlude*, 1932, *Reunion in Vienna*, 1933, *Dinner at Eight*, 1933, *Lady for a Day*, 1933, in which her portrayal of Apple Annie was a great success, and *Bringing Up Baby*, 1938, with Katharine Hepburn. She continued to work almost until her death. Shortly after completing *Joan of Paris*, 1942, she died in Beverly Hills, California, on October 20, 1942.

Rockefeller, Abby Greene Aldrich 1874–1948 philanthropist and art patron

Born on October 26, 1874, in Providence, Rhode Island, Abby Aldrich was the daughter of Nelson W. Aldrich, a businessman and at that time Providence councilman who was elected to Congress in 1878 and to the Senate in 1880. She attended Miss Abbott's School in Providence and for many years afterward led the life of a debutante in New York, Washington, D.C., and Europe. In October 1901 she married John D. Rockefeller, Jr. For a time the management of the several Rockefeller homes and the care of a large family occupied her (her children included John D. III, Nelson, Laurance, Winthrop, and David Rockefeller), but she gradually assumed a share of responsibility for the employment of the vast Rockefeller fortune. She assisted and advised her husband on the establishment of the various philanthropic foundations that were his principal work and was particularly interested in his project to restore colonial Williamsburg, Virginia. On her own she nurtured interests in the work of the YWCA, of whose national board she was a member from 1918 to 1936, the Red Cross, and the Girl Scouts. In 1919 she oversaw the building of a model home and a community center in Bayway, New Jersey, where many Standard Oil employees lived. At Columbia University in 1924 she established International House for foreign students, and in Washington, D.C., she helped furnish and equip the YWCA's Grace Dodge Hotel for women.

Rockefeller's best known achievement was her leadership in the establishment of the Museum of Modern Art in New York City in 1929; she subsequently served the museum as board member, treasurer, first vice-president, and vice-chairman of the board. Her personal art collection of over 2000 items — many the product of her knowledgeable purchases from such contemporary American artists as John Marin, Ben Shahn, Charles Sheeler, Charles Burchfield, George Bellows, John Sloan, and Georgia O'Keeffe — went to the museum during its first 17 years, and with her son Nelson she established an unrestricted purchase fund for the Modern. Her important collection of American folk art later became the Abby Aldrich Rockefeller Collection at Williamsburg, where a museum to house it was dedicated in 1957. She died in New York City on April 5, 1948.

Rogers, Edith Nourse 1881–1960 public official

Born in Saco, Maine, on March 19, 1881, Edith Nourse was educated at Rogers Hall School in Lowell, Massachusetts, and at Madame Julien's School in Paris. In October 1907 she married John J. Rogers of Lowell. After his election to Congress in 1912 they lived in Washington, D.C. During World War I she was active in volunteer work for the YMCA and the Red Cross, and in 1917 she served abroad for a time with the Women's Overseas League. Her work in military hospitals, notably Walter Reed Hospital in 1918–1922, and her inspections with her husband of field and base hospitals, led to her appointment by President Warren G. Harding as his personal representative to visit veterans' and military hospitals throughout the country in 1922.

She served President Calvin Coolidge in a similar capacity in 1923 and President Herbert Hoover in 1929. In 1924 she was a Republican presidential elector. Following her husband's death in 1925 she was elected to fill his unexpired term in Congress. In 1926 she was elected to a full term, and she was reelected regularly thereafter, serving in all 35 years as the representative of the Fifth District of Massachusetts. She was the first congresswoman from New England. Her earlier work led naturally to her appointment to the Committee on Veterans' Affairs, of which she was chairman in the 80th and 83rd congresses. She introduced the legislation, passed in March 1942 and in force two months later, that created the Women's Army Auxiliary Corps (later the Women's Army Corps). In 1944 she helped draft the "G.I. Bill of Rights" for veterans. She served also on the post office, civil service, and foreign affairs committees. She died in Boston on September 10, 1960, at which time she had served in Congress longer than any other woman.

Rogers, Harriet Burbank 1834–1919 educator

Born in North Billerica, Massachusetts, on April 12, 1834, Harriet Rogers attended local schools and in 1851 graduated from the Massachusetts State Normal School in West Newton. She taught school in various towns for several years thereafter. In 1863, through an elder sister, who had taught at the Perkins Institution for the Blind, she was asked to undertake the instruction of a young deaf girl. With little to guide her but a newspaper report of some German experiments in teaching the deaf to speak by reproducing the muscular and breath movements of a teacher, she achieved remarkable success with her little charge.

In 1865 she met Gardiner Greene Hubbard of Boston, whose daughter (later Mrs. Alexander Graham Bell) had become deaf and whom he himself had taught to speak because no one else would try. With his encouragement she opened in June 1866 a school for deaf children in Chelmsford, Massachusetts. On the chartering of the Clarke Institution for Deaf Mutes (later the Clarke School for the Deaf) in Northampton — a result of Hubbard's campaigning and a benefaction from John Clarke of that town — Harriet Rogers was appointed director. Her own pupils entered the Clarke school, which was the first chartered institution to teach deaf pupils entirely in speech, without sign language or manual alphabet. In 1871–1872 she was able to study German methods at first hand. (During that same period the inexperienced teachers at Clarke benefited from personal instruction by Alexander Graham Bell in his "visible speech" method of notation.) From 1873 she was assisted by Caroline A. Yale. Ill health forced her to take leave of absence in

1884, and in 1886 she resigned. By that time the earlier sharp breach between the older teachers of the deaf, committed to manual methods, and those they had called "visionary enthusiasts," the younger teachers of speech and lipreading, had begun to heal. She died in North Billerica, Massachusetts, on December 12, 1919.

Rogers, Mother Mary Joseph 1882–1955 religious

Born on October 27, 1882, in Roxbury (now part of Boston), Massachusetts, Mary Josephine Rogers grew up there and in nearby Jamaica Plain (also now in Boston). She attended local public schools. While a student at Smith College she organized a mission study club among other Catholic girls. After graduating in 1905 she remained at Smith for two years of advanced study in zoology. In 1908–1909 she attended Boston Normal School, and for three years thereafter she taught in Boston public schools. At the same time she helped edit *Field Afar*, a mission magazine. Shortly after the organization of the Catholic Foreign Mission Society of America (later known as the Maryknoll Missioners) in 1911, Mary Rogers volunteered her services as a secretary. She and the four other volunteers were given a house in Hawthorne, New York, in 1912. In 1914 the Maryknoll secretaries were constituted the Pious Society of Women for the Foreign Missions, and in February 1920 they were designated by the Pope a diocesan religious community, the Foreign Mission Sisters of St. Dominic (Third Order Dominicans).

In 1925, at the first general chapter of the congregation, Mary Rogers, now Mother Mary Joseph, was elected mother general, a post to which she was regularly reelected until her retirement 22 years later. The sisters numbered 22 when the first final vows were made in February 1921, and later that year the first group was sent abroad, to South China. Mother Mary Joseph established Maryknoll (later Mary Rogers) College and a motherhouse at Maryknoll, New York. She continued to work indefatigably to prepare women for missionary work around the world until her retirement in 1947. In December 1954 the congregation was placed under the direct jurisdiction of the Sacred Congregation for the Propagation of the Faith and designated the Maryknoll Sisters of St. Dominic. At the time of Mother Mary Joseph's death in New York City on October 9, 1955, there were over 1100 Maryknoll sisters working in 84 missions in 17 nations around the world.

Rohde, Ruth Bryan Owen 1885–1954 writer, public official, and diplomat

Born in Jacksonville, Illinois, on October 2, 1885, Ruth Bryan was the daughter of William Jennings Bryan, from whom she learned at an early age of public speaking, campaigning, and politics. She grew up from 1887 in Lincoln, Nebraska, and then, during her father's public service, in Washington, D.C. She attended the University of Nebraska from 1901 until her marriage in 1903 to William H. Leavitt, an artist; they were divorced in 1909. In May 1910 she married Major Reginald A. Owen, a British army officer (he died in 1927). During the first year of World War I she served as secretary-treasurer of the American Woman's War Relief Fund in London. From 1915 to 1918 she was a volunteer nurse with British forces in the Middle East. In 1918 she and her husband settled in Florida, and in 1919 she began lecturing on the Lyceum and Chautauqua circuits. She was active in numerous civic and patriotic groups as well. In 1925 she became vice-president of the board of regents and in 1926 an instructor in public speaking at the new University of Miami.

After an initial defeat in 1926 Ruth Owen ran successfully as a Democrat for the congressional seat of Florida's Fourth District in 1928. She was the first woman ever elected to Congress from the Deep South. She was reelected in 1930 but defeated in the Democratic primary in 1932. In 1931 she published *Elements of Public Speaking*. In April 1933 President Franklin D. Roosevelt appointed her U.S. minister to Denmark. On her confirmation by the Senate she became the first woman to represent the United States to a foreign country. (Sixteen years later Eugenie Moore Anderson would become the first

U.S. ambassador.) She retained the post until August 1936, when she was obliged to resign because of her marriage the previous month to Captain Borge Rohde, a Danish national and army officer. After a national campaign tour in 1936 on behalf of President Roosevelt she resumed lecturing and writing.

Rohde's others books included *Leaves From a Greenland Diary*, 1935, *Denmark Caravan*, 1936, *The Castle in the Silver Wood and Other Danish Fairy Tales Retold*, 1939, *Picture Tales From Scandinavia*, 1939, *Look Forward, Warrior*, 1943, and *Caribbean Caravel*, 1949. She continued to travel widely and to work for various peace organizations. In 1949 she served as an alternate U.S. representative to the United Nations General Assembly. She died on July 26, 1954, in Copenhagen, shortly after receiving the Distinguished Service Medal from King Frederick IX.

Rombauer, Irma von Starkloff 1877–1962 cookery expert

Born in St. Louis on October 30, 1877, Irma von Starkloff was educated in private schools in Switzerland. In October 1899 she married Edgar R. Rombauer, a lawyer. In the course of her early married life she developed an interest in cooking, an unusual leaning in that day for one of her social standing, and the Rombauer home soon became known for its fine table. In 1931, after her husband had died and her children had left home, she compiled and had privately printed a small volume of favorite recipes called *The Joy of Cooking*. The brisk sales of the book induced her to rewrite and expand it, and in 1936 a trade edition was published. The popularity of the book warranted revised editions in 1943, 1951, and 1953, the last with the aid of her daughter, Marion Rombauer Becker. By that time *The Joy of Cooking* had sold over 1.3 million copies. Subsequent editions continued to appear and to include up-to-date information on new foods and new kitchen processes.

The book's enormous success in the highly competitive field of cookbooks was traceable to its wealth of basic information on foods, measurements, menu planning, and the like, to its explicitly written, step-by-step instructions, and to the variety and time-tested reliability of its recipes. Numbers of professional chefs and authors of rival cookbooks attested to its virtual indispensability. Rombauer also wrote a *Cookbook for Girls and Boys*, 1946, and contributed to newspapers and magazines. She died in St. Louis on October 14, 1962. By 1975 *The Joy of Cooking* had sold more than 8.9 million copies.

Eleanor Roosevelt

Roosevelt, Eleanor 1884–1962 writer, diplomat, humanitarian and First Lady

Born in New York City on October 11, 1884, Anna Eleanor Roosevelt came of a prominent, well established family. Her parents died during her childhood, and she grew up in the home of her grandmother, who sent her to be schooled in England. In March 1905 she married a distant cousin, Franklin Delano Roosevelt; she was given away by her uncle, President Theodore Roosevelt. She provided constant support and aid to her husband in his career, particularly after his crippling attack of polio in 1921 and during his long convalescence. While rearing six children, she cultivated an interest in social causes, politics, and public affairs. She was in particular an active member of the Women's Trade Union League and the Democratic party. From 1927 she was a part owner and acting vice-principal of and teacher of sociology, economics, and government at the Todhunter School in New York City.

Roosevelt gradually won recognition for her political acumen, and by the time of her husband's election as governor of New York in 1928 they were acknowledged a political team. With his election to the presidency in 1932 she began 12 years as First Lady, during which she shattered many precedents, set many more, and made her position one of great, if unofficial, influence. She held the first press conference by a First Lady in 1933 and continued to hold them on a regular basis. For a time she broadcast regular 15-minute radio programs of political commentary. Her syndicated newspaper column, "My Day," which she wrote for many years beginning in 1936, changed in emphasis from women's affairs to public affairs about 1939. In that year she used it to announce her resignation from the Daughters of the American Revolution in consequence of that organization's refusal to allow Marian Anderson the use of its Constitution Hall for a concert because of her race. In 1941 her column "If You Ask Me" began appearing in the *Ladies' Home Journal*.

Because of her husband's disability much of the ceremonial and public relations work of the presidency, particularly the inspection of government works projects and the political fence-mending trips, devolved upon her, and in these travels she was able to serve as his "eyes and ears." She actively promoted liberal causes, youth movements, and social betterment, and she worked effectively for civilian defense early in World War II. In all she succeeded in becoming nearly as controversial a figure as her husband. During the war she traveled to virtually every front to visit troops.

Soon after President Roosevelt's death in 1945 Eleanor Roosevelt was named a delegate to the United Nations by President Harry S. Truman. As chairman of the UN Commission on Human Rights from 1946, she took a central role in drafting and securing the adoption of the Universal Declaration of Human Rights in 1948. She resigned her post in 1952 and for the next ten years traveled constantly, promoting her chosen causes, particularly the work of the UN. She was welcomed by heads of state around the world and was widely acknowledged to be the world's most admired woman. She remained active in Democratic politics, speaking at party conventions and campaigning in the party's behalf; she wielded considerable influence in the party's liberal and reform wings, particularly in New York State.

Roosevelt wrote prolifically, both books and articles; among her books were *This Is My Story*, 1937, *My Days*, a collection of her newspaper columns, 1938, *The Moral Basis of Democracy*, 1940, *This I Remember*, 1949, *On My Own*, 1958, *You Learn by Living*, 1960, and *The Autobiography of Eleanor Roosevelt*, 1961. In 1961 she was reappointed to the U.S. delegation to the United Nations by President John F. Kennedy. She died in New York City on November 7, 1962.

Rose, Mary Davies Swartz 1874–1941 nutritionist

Born on October 31, 1974, in Newark, Ohio, Mary Swartz grew up in Wooster, Ohio. She attended public schools and in 1894 entered Shepardson College (later part of Denison University). Her career at Shepardson was interrupted by a year of teaching school in Wooster and a year of study at Wooster College, and she graduated finally in 1901. After a year studying domestic science at the Mechanics Institute in Rochester, New York, she taught high school home economics in Fond du Lac, Wisconsin, from 1902 to 1905. In the latter year she entered Teachers College, Columbia University, from which she received a bachelor's degree in 1906. She remained another year as an assistant in the department of household arts and then began graduate work in physiological chemistry at Yale. On receiving her Ph.D. in 1909 she returned to Teachers College as its first full-time instructor in nutrition and dietetics. In September 1910 she married Anton R. Rose, a chemist. In the new department of nutrition, of which she was the founder and guiding spirit, she became assistant professor in 1910, associate professor in 1918, and full professor in 1921.

Under her direction, and with the assistance of Professor Henry C. Sherman, a pioneer nutritional chemist, the Teachers College nutrition department became a recognized national center for the training of nutrition teachers. Rose's own research ranged across such topics as the vitamin content of food, protein comparisons, effects of nutrients on anemia, metabolism, and trace elements in the diet, and she published numerous articles in professional journals as well as several books, including *A Laboratory Hand-Book for Dietetics*, a widely used textbook, 1912, *Feeding the Family*, in which food nutritive values were presented in a form useful to homemakers, 1916, *Everyday Foods in War Time*, 1918, *The Foundations of Nutrition*, another widely used text and reference book, 1927, and *Teaching Nutrition to Boys and Girls*, 1932. She was associate editor of the *Journal of Nutrition* from 1928 to 1936.

During World War I she was deputy director for New York City of the Bureau of Conservation of the U.S. Food Administration, and in 1940 she was an adviser on nutrition to the Council of National Defense. From 1933 she was a member of the Council on Foods of the American Medical Association, and from 1935 she was a member of the nutrition committee of the Health Organization of the League of Nations. She served as president of the American Institute of Nutrition, of which she had been a founder, in 1937–1938. She retired from Teachers College in 1940 and died in Edgewater, New Jersey, on February 1, 1941.

Rosenberg, Ethel 1915–1953 convicted spy

Born in New York City on September 28, 1915, Ethel Greenglass worked as a clerk for some years after her graduation from high school in 1931. She was already a member of the Communist party when she married Julius Rosenberg in June 1939. The next year Julius obtained a job as a civilian engineer with the U.S. Army Signal Corps, and the two worked together to supply secret information to agents of the U.S.S.R. In 1943 Ethel Rosenberg's brother, David Greenglass, was inducted into the army and assigned to the atomic bomb project at Los Alamos, New Mexico, as a machinist. Secret information stolen by Greenglass was passed to the Rosenbergs and by them to Harry Gold, a courier, who at length gave it to Anatoly A. Yakovlev, the Soviet vice-consul in New York City. Julius Rosenberg was fired by the army in 1945 for having lied about his party membership. In May 1950 Gold was arrested in connection with the case of confessed British spy Dr. Klaus Fuchs. The arrests of Greenglass and Julius Rosenberg followed quickly in June and July and that of Ethel Rosenberg in August. Another conspirator, Morton Sobell, a classmate of Julius Rosenberg at the College of the City of New York, fled to Mexico but was extradited.

The Rosenbergs were charged with espionage and brought to trial in March 1951; David Greenglass was the chief witness for the prosecution. They were found guilty and in April sentenced to death. (Sobell and Gold received 30-year prison terms, and Greenglass, who was tried separately, was given 15 years.) For two years the Rosenberg case was appealed through the courts and before world opinion. At issue were the constitutionality and applicability of the 1917 Espionage Act under which they were tried and the impartiality of the trial judge, Irving R. Kaufman, who in pronouncing sentence had accused them of a crime "worse than murder." Seven different appeals reached the Supreme Court and were denied, and pleas for executive clemency were turned down by President Harry S. Truman in 1952 and by President Dwight D. Eisenhower in 1953.

The case became a cause célèbre around the world, with civil libertarians, opponents of capital punishment, political sympathizers, and those who felt the trial had been unfair and the evidence perhaps falsified all organizing support for the Rosenbergs. The highly emotional so-called "death house letters" exchanged by Ethel and Julius Rosenberg during that period were widely published. In spite of all legal appeals and public protest, they were executed at Sing Sing Prison in Ossining, New York, on June 19, 1953. They were the first U.S. civilians ever executed for espionage and the first Americans to suffer that penalty in peacetime. Their case remained a subject of controversy in the ensuing years.

Ross, Betsy 1752–1836 patriot

Born in Philadelphia on January 1, 1752, Elizabeth Griscom was brought up a Quaker and educated in Quaker schools. On her marriage to John Ross, an Episcopalian, in

November 1773, she was disowned by the Society of Friends. After his death in January 1776 she took over the upholstering business he had founded. Her late husband's uncle, George Ross, was a noted patriot and a friend of George Washington, and according to the traditional account, Washington, George Ross, and Robert Morris came to Mrs. Ross's house in June 1776 and asked her to make a flag for the new country that was on the verge of declaring its independence. She suggested a design to Washington, he made a rough pencil sketch on the basis of it, and she thereupon made the famous flag in her back parlor. She is supposed also to have suggested the use of the five- rather than the six-pointed star chosen by Washington. (Whatever the source of the design, the stars-and-stripes flag was adopted by the Continental Congress in June 1777.)

There is no written contemporary record of the story, which was first publicly told in a paper before the Historical Society of Pennsylvania in 1870 and published in *Harper's Monthly* in 1873, but there is no conflicting testimony or evidence, either, and the story is now indelibly a part of American legend. Betsy Ross married Joseph Ashburn in 1777, and, after his death in a British prison in 1782, she was married for a third time in 1783 to John Claypoole. She continued the upholstering business, which became very profitable, until 1827, when she turned it over to her daughter. She died in Philadelphia on January 30, 1836. The house where she is supposed to have made the flag was marked in 1887.

Ross, Nellie Tayloe 1876–1977 public official

Born in St. Joseph, Missouri, on November 29, 1876, Nellie Tayloe married William Bradford Ross in September 1902 and went with him to Cheyenne, Wyoming, where he established a law practice. He was elected governor of Wyoming in 1922, but when he died in the middle of his term his wife was elected to serve out its remaining two years, from January 1925 to January 1927. Miriam W. "Ma" Ferguson was elected to succeed her late husband as governor of Texas on the same day in 1924, but because Ross was inaugurated two weeks before Ferguson, she is credited with having been the first woman ever to be elected governor of a U.S. state. Failing of reelection in 1926, Ross devoted herself thereafter to Democratic politics, serving in the state legislature and as the leader of Democratic women in the presidential campaigns of 1928 and 1932.

From 1928 to 1934 Ross was vice-chairman of the Democratic National Committee. She was rewarded for her valiant campaign efforts in behalf of President Franklin D. Roosevelt by being appointed director of the U.S. Bureau of the Mint in 1933, thereby becoming the first woman ever to hold the office. At the Mint she inherited an organization that had been cut to the bone because of Depression economies, but she administered it with skill until her retirement in 1953, upon the advent of Republican administration under President Dwight D. Eisenhower. From 1940 she headed the Treasury Assay Committee and was the first woman to have her likeness on a mint medal; her name also appears on the cornerstone of the U.S. gold depository at Fort Knox, Kentucky. She died in Washington, D.C., on December 19, 1977.

Rourke, Constance Mayfield 1885–1941 historian

Born on November 14, 1885, in Cleveland, Constance Rourke grew up there and from about 1892 in Grand Rapids, Michigan. She attended local public schools, graduated from Vassar College in 1907, studied at the Sorbonne for a year, worked as a research reader at the Bibliothèque Nationale and at the British Museum for two years, and in 1910 returned to Vassar as an instructor in English. In 1915 she left Vassar and moved back to Grand Rapids to devote herself to studying and writing about American cultural history. Her deep personal sense of rootedness in the culture of ordinary people, together with her ability to win the confidence of "old timers" — lumberjacks, actors, mountaineers, Native Americans, frontiersmen, miners — enabled her to track down and collect a mass of information on folk tales, songs, sayings, and history. These she worked up into articles for such magazines as the *Saturday Review of Literature*, *New Republic*, *Nation*, *Freeman*, and *Art*.

Her first book, *Trumpets of Jubilee*, 1927, attempted to define the American character and mark out the influence of popular taste through an examination of five major figures of the 19th century, Lyman Beecher, Henry Ward Beecher, Harriet Beecher Stowe, Horace Greeley, and P. T. Barnum. *Troupers of the Gold Coast, or The Rise of Lotta Crabtree*, 1928, was followed by her major work, *American Humor: A Study of the National Character*, 1931, in which she laid out her pioneering research into the various forms and characters of humor in American culture. The book's wealth of scholarship and keen analysis made it a classic study in American cultural history. Subsequent books, generally of lesser stature, included *Davy Crockett*, 1934, *Audubon*, 1936, and *Charles Sheeler: Artist in the American Tradition*, 1938. She died in Grand Rapids, Michigan, on March 23, 1941. Fragments from her projected general history of American culture were collected in *The Roots of American Culture*, edited by Van Wyck Brooks, 1942.

Rowlandson, Mary White 1635?–? Indian captive

Born about 1635 in England, Mary White was brought to America by her parents when she was still a child. They lived in Salem, Massachusetts, until 1653, when they moved to the new frontier village of Lancaster. In 1656 she married the Reverend Joseph Rowlandson, Lancaster's first regular minister. For 20 years her life proceeded in obscurity.

In February 1676, during King Philip's War, a party of Indians attacked Lancaster and laid siege to the Rowlandson house, where many townspeople had sought refuge. They overwhelmed the defenders and took 24 captives, including Rowlandson and her three children, one of whom died of wounds and starvation a week later. Rowlandson was kept a prisoner for three months, during which time she was treated for the most part as a slave. With her captors she traveled as far as the Connecticut River to the west, and north into what is now New Hampshire. Her own wounds slowly healed, and she became accustomed to her captors' meager diet. Her skill in sewing and knitting earned her rather better treatment than less fortunate captives. At one point in her ordeal she met Philip. A captured Bible given her by one of the Indians was her only solace.

In May 1676 Rowlandson was at last ransomed back to her husband for £20. Her two surviving children were returned to her some time later. In early 1677 the family moved to Wethersfield, Connecticut, where the Reverend Rowlandson died in 1678. In 1682 Mrs. Rowlandson wrote an account of her captivity for her children. It was published in Boston that year and republished in Cambridge and London. Titled (in the second edition, no copy of the first having survived) *The Sovereignty & Goodness of God, Together, with the Faithfulness of His Promises Displayed; Being a Narrative of the Captivity and Restauration of Mrs. Mary Rowlandson*, the vividly written tale quickly became a classic example not only of the captivity genre but of colonial literature generally. It ran through more than 30 editions over the years, and selections from it have been included in countless anthologies of American writing. The date and place of Rowlandson's death are not known.

Rowson, Susanna Haswell 1762?–1824 writer, actor, and educator

Born about 1762 in Portsmouth, England, Susanna Haswell was the daughter of an officer in the Royal Navy. She grew up from 1768 in Nantasket Beach, Massachusetts, where her widowed father was stationed and had remarried. The family were interned as loyalists during the first three years of the Revolution. In 1778 they returned to England. Susanna's education had consisted of wide reading in Shakespeare, the poetry of Edmund Spenser, and the Pope and Dryden translations of Homer and Virgil, and on the strength of it she obtained the post of governess to the children of the Duchess of Devonshire.

Haswell published her first novel, *Victoria*, in 1786, and the next year left the Duchess to marry William Rowson. Several other works, including *The Inquisitor or Invisible Rambler*, 1788, *Poems on Various Subjects*, 1788, *A Trip to Parnassus*, 1788, and *Mary, or the Test of Honour*, 1789, appeared before her greatest success: *Charlotte, a Tale of Truth*, 1791, entitled *Charlotte Temple* in later editions. Reprinted in Philadelphia in 1794, this sentimental story was the first best-seller in the United States. Later in 1791 appeared her essays on education, *Mentoria, or the Young Lady's Friend*, and in 1792 a semi-autobiographical work, *Rebecca, or the Fille de Chambre*.

The failure of William Rowson's business led the couple to seek theatrical careers. During 1792–1793 they played in Edinburgh and other cities, and in 1793 they came to the United States. They appeared in Baltimore, Annapolis, and Philadelphia, where she wrote a comic opera, *Slaves in Algiers*, 1794, and a light musical, *The Volunteers*, 1795. Her preoccupation with American patriotism in these and other works led to a much publicized exchange in which William Cobbett intimated that she was guilty of betrayal of England, and she responded by calling him "a kind of loathsome reptile." In 1796 she and her husband settled in Boston. She retired from the theater in 1797 after a final appearance in her own *Americans in England; or Lessons for Daughters*, a comedy.

From that year until 1822 Susanna Rowson operated a successful school for young ladies. Opened first in Boston, it moved later to Medford, to Newton, and in 1811 again to Boston. She wrote texts, songs, and poetry for her pupils, edited the *Boston Weekly Magazine* during 1802–1805, and wrote for its successor, the *Boston Magazine*, and other publications. Others of her novels were *Trials of the Human Heart*, 1795, *Reuben and Rachel*, 1798, *Sarah, the Exemplary Wife*, 1813, and a sequel to the story of Charlotte Temple, *Charlotte's Daughter, or The Three Orphans*, published posthumously in 1828. *Charlotte Temple* remained her best known work, going through more than 200 editions over the next 180 years. She died in Boston on March 2, 1824.

Royall, Anne Newport 1769–1854 writer, lobbyist and publisher

Born near Baltimore on June 11, 1769, Anne Newport endured an unsettled childhood in Pennsylvania and Virginia and while still a girl entered with her twice-widowed mother the domestic employ of Captain William Royall, a somewhat eccentric Virginia gentleman farmer, scholar, deist, Freemason, and Revolutionary War veteran. Royall became interested in her, saw to it that she was educated in his extensive library, and married her in 1797. He died 16 years later and left her most of his property, but after ten difficult years of litigation his other heirs succeeded in breaking the will, leaving her penniless at the age of fifty-four. Ill as well, Anne Royall spent several months struggling to gain a pension as the widow of a Revolutionary veteran, but although she had the assistance of John Quincy Adams her quest was not successful until 1848; even then, the pension turned out to be a mere pittance. But she was a woman of great courage, and in 1824 she began to travel and write to earn her living.

Between 1826 and 1831 Royall published ten volumes of travel accounts, of which the first, *Sketches of History, Life and Manners in the United States, by a Traveler*, 1826, was afterward the best known. The others — *The Black Book; or, A Continuation of Travels in the United States*, three volumes, 1828–1829, *Mrs. Royall's Pennsylvania*, two volumes, 1829, *Mrs. Royall's Southern Tour*, three volumes, 1830–1831, and *Letters from Alabama*, 1830 — remained valuable sources of information about the life of the period. She also published a novel, *The Tennessean*, 1827. She espoused many causes and attacked many others, and her anti-Presbyterianism resulted in 1829 in a conviction on the charge of being a common scold.

In 1830 Royall settled in Washington, D.C., and in December 1831 she began publication of a newspaper called *Paul Pry*, a weekly compilation of gossip and acerbic comment that she peddled herself, often in the corridors of the Capitol. In December 1836 *Paul Pry* was succeeded by the *Huntress*, which ran more or less continuously until July 1854, shortly before her death. A vigorous and effective lobbyist for measures of which she approved and an equally effective opponent of measures of which she did not, she became in time the conscience of Washington. She was a dangerous enemy of any corrupt politician, no matter how highly placed, although the accusations she hurled about her were not always well aimed. She was, in her friend Adams's words, "a virago errant." During her last years she suffered greatly from illness and poverty, and she died in Washington on October 1, 1854.

Rubinstein, Helena 1871–1965 businesswoman

Born in 1871 in Krakow, Poland (then part of Austria), Helena Rubinstein studied medicine briefly in Switzerland before journeying in the late 1890s to visit relatives in Australia. There the lack of cosmetics, particularly skin care products, prompted her to open a small shop in Melbourne to sell creams and the like, which at first she imported from Europe and later began manufacturing herself. In 1902 she returned to Europe and studied dermatology with several leading authorities before resuming her business. In 1908 she opened an elaborate beauty salon in London, and in 1912 another in Paris. Her clientele consisted from the beginning of wealthy and aristocratic women, many of whom broke social custom in patronizing her salons. In 1914 she opened a salon in New York, and over the next several years salons appeared as well in Chicago, Boston, Los Angeles, and other American cities. From that date she spent an increasing portion of her time in the United States.

During these years her line of trademarked beauty products grew apace and was distributed through a network of thousands of retail shops and department stores. The salons themselves existed largely for the social cachet they provided and frequently showed net losses. Overall, however, the business was extremely lucrative, and Rubinstein became one of the richest women in the world. She wrote several books on beauty and health, including *The Art of Feminine Beauty*, 1930, *This Way to Beauty*, 1936, and *Food for Beauty*, 1938, and was widely acknowledged one of the world's foremost authorities on the topic. In 1953 she established the Helena Rubinstein Foundation to support research in the areas of health, medicine, and the rehabilitation of disabled children. She continued to direct her multimillion dollar business until her death in New York City on April 1, 1965.

Wilma Rudolph

Rudolph, Wilma Glodean 1940–1994 athlete

Born in St. Bethlehem, Tennessee, on June 23, 1940, Wilma Rudolph grew up in Clarksville, Tennessee. A series of illnesses in infancy left her without the use of one leg, and only constant exercise and care, including her mother's therapeutic massages, enabled her finally to learn to walk when she was eight. Three years later she had progressed far enough to discard her specially reinforced shoe, and by the time she was in high school she had made herself into an outstanding athlete. In her sophomore year she set a state record for points scored in a season in girls' basketball. She soon came under the tutelage of the track coach at Tennessee State University in Nashville, who helped her compile a remarkable high school track record and took over her coaching full time when she entered the university in 1957. Ill health in 1958, an injury in 1959, and surgery with postoperative complications early in 1960 seriously interfered with her training, but later in 1960 she qualified for the U.S. Olympic team.

At the games in Rome Rudolph won the 100-meter dash in 11 seconds, a time disallowed for a world record because of excessive following wind; won the 200-meter dash in the Olympic record time of 23.2 seconds; and anchored the victorious U.S. 400-meter relay team, which had set a world record of 44.4 seconds in a trial heat. She was the first American woman runner to win three gold medals at a single Olympics, and her strikingly fluid style made her a particular favorite with spectators and journalists. At the New York Athletic Club meet at Madison Square Garden in February 1961 she broke her own world indoor record for the 60-yard dash, setting a new mark of 6.8 seconds, and she followed with a world record 7.8 seconds in the 70-yard dash. At the women's AAU indoor championship meet in Columbus, Ohio, in March she won the 100-yard dash in 10.8 seconds, a U.S. record, and set a world record of 25.0 seconds in a trial heat of the 220-yard dash. At a meet in Louisville, Kentucky, a short time later she lopped 0.6 second off the 26-year-old outdoor record of 8.2 seconds for the 70-yard dash. In July she ran a winning 10.8 seconds in the 100-yard at the U.S. women's outdoor championship meet in Gary, Indiana; set a new world record of 11.2 seconds in the 100-meter at a meet in West Germany; and won the 100-meter (in 11.3 seconds) in the U.S.-U.S.S.R. meet in Moscow.

She won the Amateur Athletic Union's 1961 Sullivan Award as the year's outstanding amateur athlete. In Los Angeles in July 1962 she repeated her winning time in the 100-yard in the U.S. women's outdoor meet. She retired from competition a short time later.

After graduating from Tennessee State University in 1963 she coached the university's women's track team. In 1967 she worked on Operation Champion with Vice President Hubert Humphrey to provide children and teenagers in the nation's largest ghettos with sports training from star athletes. She founded the Wilma Rudolph Foundation in Indianapolis in 1982 to encourage community-based track and field programs.

Rudolph published an autobiography, *Wilma*, in 1977. She was named to the National Track and Field Hall of Fame in 1974, the International Sports Hall of Fame in 1980, and the U.S. Olympic Hall of Fame in 1983. In 1993 she received the National Sports Award. She died of cancer in Nashville on November 12, 1994.

Rukeyser, Muriel 1913–1980 poet

Born in New York City on December 15, 1913, Muriel Rukeyser attended private schools and in 1930–1932 was a student at Vassar College. Her poems began appearing in *Poetry* magazine and other periodicals in that period. She worked on the staff of the *Student Review* in 1932–1933 and in the latter year drove to Alabama to report on the case of the Scottsboro Boys. Later she edited the *Housatonic*, a literary journal, was associate editor of the *New Theatre* magazine, took courses at Columbia University, and learned to fly at the Roosevelt Aviation School. In 1935 her first volume of poems appeared as *Theory of Flight* in the Yale Younger Poets series.

Her travels over the next few years provided material for the poems in *Mediterranean*, 1938, *U.S. 1*, 1938, and *A Turning Wind*, 1939. Her romantic and often heavily symbolic lyrics attracted considerable, if sometimes bemused, critical attention. *The Soul and Body of John Brown*, 1940, combined Old Testament themes with contemporary social problems. In 1942 she published *Willard Gibbs: American Genius*, a biography of the 19th-century mathematical physicist.

She supported herself by lecturing and working in film, but an award from the American Academy of Arts and Letters and the National Institute of Arts and Letters in 1942 and a Guggenheim fellowship in 1943 enabled her to concentrate on poetry. *Beast in View*, 1944, *The Green Wave*, 1948, *Elegies*, 1949, *Orpheus*, 1949, and *Selected Poems*, 1951, appeared in rapid succession, along with the prose *The Life of Poetry*, 1949. Later volumes included *One Life*, 1957, *Body of Waking*, 1958, *Waterlily Fire*, 1962, *The Orgy*, 1965, *The Speed of Darkness*, 1968, *20 Poems*, 1972, *Breaking Open*, 1973, *The Gates*, 1976, and her *Collected Poems*, 1978. Rukeyser also wrote several books for children, including *Come Back, Paul*, 1955, *I Go Out*, 1961, *Bubbles*, 1967, and *Mazes*, 1970, and a biography, *The Traces of Thomas Hariot*, 1971, and she published translations of the *Selected Poems of Octavio Paz*, 1963, the *Selected Poems of Gunnar Ekelöf*, with Leif

Sjöber, 1967, (which won an award for translation from the Swedish Academy), and Brecht's *Uncle Eddie's Moustache*, 1974. Her last volume of poetry, *The Collected Poems*, was published in 1978.

From 1956 to 1967 she taught at Sarah Lawrence College, and from 1967 she served on the board of directors of the Teachers-Writers Collaborative. She continued also as a lecturer. She was president of PEN American Center from 1975 to 1976.

Having taken up the cause of Spanish loyalists during the Spanish Civil War, Rukeyser remained politically active in her later years. In the 1970s she traveled to Hanoi to protest the US involvement in Vietnam and to South Korea to protest the harassment of the radical Catholic poet, Kim Chi-Ha, and she protested the execution of Kurdish socialists in Iran in 1979.

Among her honors and awards are the Copernicus Award from the Academy of American Poets, 1977, and the Shelley Memorial Award from the Poetry Society, 1977. She died in New York City on February 12, 1980.

Rumsey, Mary Harriman 1881–1934 welfare worker

Born in New York City on November 17, 1881, Mary Harriman was the daughter of financier Edward H. Harriman. She was educated in Episcopal schools and at the Brearley School in New York. In 1901 she organized among that season's debutantes the Junior League for the Promotion of Settlement Movements, dedicated to "work for a better city." (The group, later known simply as the Junior League, was soon imitated in other cities, and in 1921 it became a national organization.) She graduated from Barnard College in 1905 and for a time thereafter managed the family estate and dairy farm in Arden, New York, and gave some attention to philanthropy. In May 1910 she married Charles Cary Rumsey, a sculptor. At their farm near Middleburg, Virginia, she experimented in horse and cattle breeding and took an interest in farming cooperatives, particularly the Eastern Livestock Cooperative Marketing Association, which she helped organize. During World War I she worked with the Committee of Community Councils for National Defense.

After her husband's death in 1922 Rumsey gave herself more fully to social movements. She was named a trustee of the United Hospital Fund of New York in 1925 and elected chairman of its Women's Auxiliary. In 1929 she gave her support to the Emergency Exchange Association, which attempted to apply cooperative principles to the growing unemployment problem, and she was later active in a statewide share-the-work movement. Having switched her political allegiance to the Democratic party in 1928 along with her brother, W. Averell Harriman, she was in June 1933 appointed by President Franklin D. Roosevelt chairman of the Consumers' Advisory Board of the National Recovery Administration (among whose other members was Mary W. Dewson). Over considerable opposition by business, labor, and other segments of the bureaucracy she made the board an integral part of the code-making process of the NRA.

She worked also to encourage the formation of a network of county consumer councils across the country. She served at the same time as head of the Consumers' Division of the National Emergency Council. Her work was cut short by her death in Washington, D.C., on December 18, 1934, of complications arising from injuries sustained in a fall from her horse during a fox hunt.

Runcie, Constance Faunt Le Roy 1836–1911 composer

Born in Indianapolis on January 15, 1836, Constance Faunt Le Roy was a granddaughter of Robert Owen, the Welsh industrial reformer. She grew up in New Harmony, Indiana. She early displayed musical talent, and from 1852 to 1857 she studied piano and composition in Germany. Back in New Harmony, she organized in 1859 the Minerva Society, one of the first women's clubs in America. In April 1861 she married the

Reverend James Runcie, with whom she lived in Madison, Indiana, for a decade and then in St. Joseph, Missouri.

While continuing her interest in the women's club movement, she devoted much time to composing hymns and songs. Her earliest hymn, written in 1863, was "There Is a Land of Pure Delight." Later works included "I've Wandered Far Away," "Invocation to Love," "Das Vöglein Singt," "Take My Soul, O Lord," "Around the Lord in Glory," "Hear, O Hear Us," "I Hold My Heart So Still," "We Have Sinned Unto Death," a cantata, a "Te Deum," and *The Prince of Asturia*, an opera. Her compositions were generally well received by critics, and many became widely known. It was said that no piece of hers was ever rejected by a publisher. She also wrote numerous stories and in 1888 published a volume of *Poems, Dramatic and Lyric*. She died in Winnetka, Illinois, on May 17, 1911.

Russell, Lillian 1861–1922 singer and actor

Born on December 4, 1861, in Clinton, Iowa, Helen Louise Leonard grew up and attended convent and private schools in Chicago. About 1877 or 1878 she was taken by her mother to New York City, where her early training in voice and violin was supplemented by a year of opera study under Leopold Damrosch. Her first stage role was in the chorus of a Brooklyn company performing *H.M.S. Pinafore* in 1879. In November 1880 she made her New York City debut under the name Lillian Russell at Tony Pastor's variety theater. During subsequent appearances for Pastor she continued her studies in voice and acting, and she then toured California as the lead in *Babes in the Wood.*

Returning to New York City, she attained stardom as D'Jemma in *The Snake Charmer*, a version of Edmond Audran's comic opera *Le Grand Mogul*, in October 1881, and she then played in Gilbert and Sullivan's *Patience* and *The Sorcerer* and Offenbach's *The Princess of Trebizonde*. By 1883 she was the prima donna of the McCaull Opera Company. She made her London debut at the Gaiety Theatre in July 1883 in Edward Solomon's *Virginia and Paul* and was a great success there in his *Polly, or, the Pet of the Regiment* the next year.

Returning to the United States in 1884, Russell was in the news frequently because of her flamboyant personal life — her marriage to Edward Solomon in 1884 was annulled nine years later after his arrest for bigamy, two of her other three marriages ended in divorce, and she was for 40 years a frequent companion of Diamond Jim Brady. She also became known for her frequent contract disputes; at one time she sought an injunction to prevent any theater manager from requiring her to appear in silk tights. Celebrated for her beauty and her clear, pleasant soprano voice, she was dubbed "airy, fairy Lillian." For a generation she was the feminine ideal incarnate.

Her most difficult roles were in two Offenbach operas, as Fiorella in *The Brigands* in 1889, and in the title role in *The Grand Duchess* in 1890. During 1891–1893 she headed the Lillian Russell Opera Company. Later, under other management, she appeared in such pieces as *The Princess Nicotine*, *The Goddess of Truth*, *An American Beauty*, and *The Wedding Day*, but the vogue of the sort of buxom beauty she had epitomized was passing. She joined Weber and Fields's burlesque company in 1899 and sang in their productions — *Whirligig*, *Fiddle-dee-dee*, *Hoity-Toity*, *Twirly-Whirly*, and *Whoop-dee-doo* — until they broke up in 1904.

Her singing voice fading, Russell essayed straight comedy with *Barbara's Millions* in 1906 and was successful thereafter in other works in that genre, including *The Butterfly*, 1907, and *Wildfire*, 1908. After 1912 she appeared only rarely on the stage. She wrote articles on beauty for the women's pages of the *Chicago Herald* and the *Chicago Tribune* and in 1913 toured the country with a lecture on "How to Live a Hundred Years." During World War I she was active in the Red Cross and in Liberty Loan campaigns, and in 1922 she toured Europe as a special investigator on immigration at the appointment of President Warren G. Harding. She died in Pittsburgh on June 6, 1922, 40 years short of her goal.

Russell, Mother Mary Baptist 1829–1898 religious

Born on April 18, 1829, in Newry, County Down, Ireland, Katherine Russell was educated privately and reared in an atmosphere of religion and service. In 1848 she entered the Sisters of Mercy convent in Kinsale; she took the habit and the name Sister Mary Baptist in July 1849 and made her final vows in August 1851. She served in schools and cared for the poor and sick of Kinsale until 1854, when she was named superior of a group of eight sisters and novices sent to establish the order in San Francisco. They arrived in December 1854. A convent and a school were soon established, and after the sisters' heroic work in a cholera epidemic in 1855 they were asked by the city to take over care of the dependent sick. For that purpose the building of the former State Marine Hospital was purchased and converted into the city and county hospital. Controversy over the question of separation of church and state led Mother Mary Baptist to terminate the convent's contract with the city in 1857, and she immediately bought the building and reopened it as St. Mary's Hospital, the first Catholic hospital on the Pacific coast.

The convent also opened a House of Mercy as a shelter for unemployed women in 1855, a Magdalen Asylum for prostitutes in 1861, a home for the aged and infirm in 1872, and other charitable institutions. Mother Mary established branch houses in Sacramento in 1857 and in Grass Valley in 1863, and in addition to schools in those places the order operated St. Peter's, St. Brendan's, Our Lady of Mercy, and St. Joseph's schools in San Francisco and St. Anthony's in Oakland. The sisters again provided heroic service to the city during a smallpox epidemic in 1868, and in the Spanish-American War many served as nurses at the Presidio. Long a much loved and admired figure in the city, Mother Mary Baptist died in San Francisco on August 6, 1898.

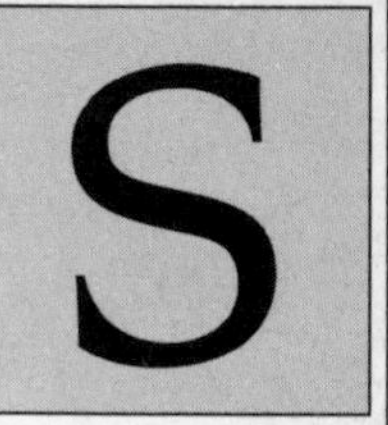

Sabin, Florence Rena 1871–1953 anatomist

Born on November 9, 1871, in Central City, Colorado, Florence Sabin grew up there and, from the age of twelve, in the Vermont home of grandparents. She attended Vermont Academy in Saxtons River and graduated from Smith College in 1893. After two years of schoolteaching in Denver she returned to Smith as an assistant in biology in 1895–1896, and in the latter year she entered the Johns Hopkins University Medical School. While a student she demonstrated particular gifts for laboratory work; her model of the brain stem of a newborn infant was widely reproduced for use as a teaching model in medical schools. After graduation in 1900 she interned in Johns Hopkins Hospital for a year and then returned to the medical school to conduct research under a fellowship awarded by the Baltimore Association for the Advancement of University Education of Women. In 1901 she published *An Atlas of Medulla and Midbrain.* In 1902, when Johns Hopkins finally abandoned its policy of not appointing women to its medical faculty, Sabin was named an assistant in anatomy. She advanced to associate professor in 1905 and to professor of histology in 1917.

For a number of years Sabin's research centered on the lymphatic system, and her demonstration that lymphatic vessels develop from a special layer of cells in certain fetal veins, rather than, as prevailing theory held, from intercellular spaces, established her as a researcher of the first rank. She then turned to the study of blood, blood vessels, and blood cells and made numerous discoveries regarding their origin and development. In 1924 she was elected president of the American Association of Anatomists, and in 1925 she was elected to the National Academy of Sciences; in both cases she was the first woman to be so honored.

In 1925 she accepted an invitation to join the Rockefeller Institute for Medical Research (now Rockefeller University), where she was also the first woman member. There she conducted research on tuberculosis, particularly the role of monocytes in forming tubercles. In 1934 she published a biography of her early mentor at Johns Hopkins, *Franklin Paine Mall: The Story of a Mind.*

Sabin retired from the Rockefeller Institute in 1938, by which time her many honors included her designation as one of the 12 greatest living American women by the League of Women Voters in 1924 and the M. Carey Thomas Award from Bryn Mawr College in 1935.

She retired to Denver, Colorado, where in 1944 she was named by the governor to a planning committee on postwar public health problems. She drew up and lobbied vigorously for a plan of complete reorganization of the state health department, securing passage by the legislature of six out of eight proposed pieces of reform legislation, and in 1948 she was appointed head of the Denver health department. She served in that post until resigning in 1953. She died in Denver a short time later, on October 3, 1953. The state of Colorado subsequently chose her as one of its two representatives in Statuary Hall of the U.S. Capitol.

Sacagawea 1786?–1812 guide and interpreter

Born about 1786, either in western Montana or eastern Idaho, Sacagawea (or Sacajawea) was a member of the Lemhi band of Shoshone Indians. Late in the year 1800 she was captured by a party of Hidatsas, or Minnetaree, Indians and taken to their village in the upper Missouri region in present-day North Dakota. There she was sold to a French-Canadian trapper, Toussaint Charbonneau, who had been living among the Indians. In 1804, when Sacagawea was eighteen, Charbonneau married her.

In the fall of 1804 the Lewis and Clark expedition arrived among the Mandan Indians near present-day Bismarck, North Dakota, to spend the winter. Lewis and Clark engaged Charbonneau as an interpreter and guide to travel with them for the rest of their journey of exploration to the Pacific Coast, and Sacagawea was allowed to accompany the party. On

February 11, 1805, Sacagawea gave birth to a baby boy who was taken along when the expedition set out again on April 7.

On August 17 they made their first contact with the Shoshones. Through the goodwill of Sacagawea's brother, who had become chief of the Lemhi, Lewis and Clark were able to obtain horses with which to continue their trek. Charbonneau and Sacagawea stayed with the expedition to the coast and between them enabled the explorers to communicate with the various tribes of the Plains and the Northwest. Except for having pointed the way through Big Hole and to what would later become known as the Bozeman Pass, however, Sacagawea did not, as later legend told, guide the expedition.

There is evidence that she and Charbonneau traveled to St. Louis in 1809 to leave their son with Clark to be educated. Sacagawea died, according to contemporary sources, on December 20, 1812, probably at Fort Manuel, near present-day Omaha. The date of her death was later brought into some doubt, however, for in 1875 an old Native American woman claiming to be Sacagawea was found among the Wind River Shoshones in Wyoming. That woman, almost certainly not the famous Sacagawea, died in 1884.

Safford, Mary Jane 1834–1891 physician

Born on December 31, 1834, in Hyde Park, Vermont, Mary Safford grew up from the age of three in Crete, Illinois. She attended schools in Illinois, Vermont, and Montreal, and during the 1850s, while living with an older brother successively in Joliet, Shawneetown, and Cairo, Illinois, she taught school. At the outbreak of the Civil War in the spring of 1861 Cairo became a town of some strategic importance because of its situation at the confluence of the Ohio and Mississippi rivers. The town was quickly occupied by volunteer troops from Chicago, and almost as quickly a variety of epidemic diseases broke out in the hastily constructed camps behind the levee.

Mary Safford began visiting the camps to tend the sick and to distribute food she had prepared herself. She gradually won the respect of officers and surgeons who had initially opposed her, and she was soon permitted to draw upon supplies collected and forwarded by the U.S. Sanitary Commission. By summer she was working closely with "Mother" Mary Ann Bickerdyke, who gave her some training in nursing and with whose bluff, robust manner her own frail appearance contrasted sharply. In November 1861 she ventured onto the battlefield at Belmont, Missouri, waving a handkerchief tied to a stick while nursing the wounded. With Mother Bickerdyke she helped transport wounded from Fort Donelson to Cairo in February 1862, and in April, following the battle of Shiloh (Pittsburg Landing), she worked aboard the hospital ship *Hazel Dell*. By that time her almost ceaseless labors had left her utterly exhausted, and she saw no more service during the war.

After an extended convalescent tour of Europe Safford returned to the United States determined to become a physician. She graduated from the New York Medical College for Women in 1869 and then pursued advanced training in Europe for three years. She studied at the General Hospital of Vienna and at several German medical centers; at the University of Breslau she became the first woman to perform an ovariotomy. In 1872 she opened a private practice in Chicago, and the next year, after her marriage to a Boston man, she moved her practice to that city and in addition became professor of women's diseases at the Boston University School of Medicine and a staff physician at the Massachusetts Homeopathic Hospital. She also interested herself in dress reform and public education in health and hygiene. In 1875 she was elected to the Boston School Committee. She retired from medical practice in 1886 and a short time later moved to Tarpon Springs, Florida, where she died on December 8, 1891.

Sage, Margaret Olivia Slocum 1828–1918 philanthropist

Born in Syracuse, New York, on September 8, 1828, Margaret Slocum attended local schools and for a year Emma Willard's Troy Female Seminary, from which she graduated in 1847. Over the next 22 years she taught school occasionally as her health permitted. In November 1869 she married the widower Russell B. Sage, a businessman who had built a fortune from wholesale groceries, banking, and railroad finance. In the 37 years of their marriage she kept their comfortable but not lavish homes in New York and elsewhere and interested herself in such movements as woman suffrage, vocational education, temperance, home and foreign missions, humane treatment for animals, and milk inspection. Russell Sage's underwriting the education of 40 Native American children, his gift of a dormitory to the Troy Female Seminary, and his gift of $50,000 to the Woman's Hospital of New York were generally attributed to her influence, as he was not otherwise known for philanthropy. At his death in July 1906 his wife was left with an estate valued in excess of $63 million.

She quickly set about becoming one of the foremost philanthropists of the day, demonstrating her long-held belief that women, the moral superiors of men, were primarily responsible for the moral progress of civilization. In April 1907 she established the Russell Sage Foundation with an endowment of $10 million. The foundation's broadly stated purpose was to foster improved social and living conditions in the United States, and the trustees were given virtually unrestricted authority in the use of its money. At the time her gift was the largest single act of philanthropy in history. In 1910 she built a new campus for the Emma Willard School (formerly the Troy Female Seminary), and in 1916, acting with the help of Eliza Kellas, she converted the old campus into Russell Sage College, devoted to the vocational education of women; the college was eventually the recipient of $1 million in gifts from her. Other gifts went to Harvard and Yale, the YMCA and the YWCA, the American Seaman's Friend Society, various museums, and the Russell Sage Institute of Pathology of the New York City Hospital. She died in New York City on November 4, 1918, and in her will she made many major bequests: The Russell Sage Foundation received an additional $5.6 million; Syracuse University, the Children's Aid Society, the Charity Organization Society of New York, and the Woman's Hospital of New York each received $1.6 million; 15 colleges, including Hampton and Tuskegee institutes, received $800,000 each; and the New York Public Library, the Metropolitan Museum of Art, the American Museum of Natural History, the New York Zoological Society, the New York Botanical Gardens, a number of missionary and tract societies, and other beneficiaries divided several millions more. Her total philanthropy in life and death was estimated at $75 million to $80 million.

Sager, Ruth 1918– geneticist

Born in Chicago on February 7, 1918, Ruth Sager graduated from the University of Chicago in 1938. After a brief hiatus she resumed her studies at Rutgers University, where she received an M.S. degree in plant physiology in 1944, and from there she went on to Columbia University, where she took her Ph.D. in genetics in 1948. During 1949–1951 she was a Merck Fellow on the staff of the National Research Council, and in the latter year she became an assistant in biochemistry at the Rockefeller Institute for Medical Research (now Rockefeller University). There, with support from the U.S. Public Health Service and the National Science Foundation, she began investigating an audacious theory that questioned a basic tenet of modern genetics, that all the genes governing heredity were to be found arranged linearly on the chromosomes of cell nuclei. A scattering of reports of anomalies in heredity experiments over decades of research lent some credence to the idea of a second genetic system outside the chromosomes. In 1953 Sager discovered a gene governing sensitivity to streptomycin that existed outside the chromosomal apparatus in the cells of the free-living green alga *Chlamydomonas*.

Her experiments showed that the many non-chromosomal genes in *Chlamydomonas* could be passed on by either partner in sexual reproduction, that they controlled a variety of hereditary characteristics, and that they replicated and remained active through successive generations. From 1955 to 1961 Dr. Sager was a research associate in zoology and from 1961 to 1965 a senior research associate at Columbia University. From 1966 to 1975 she was a professor of biology at Hunter College of the City University of New York. In the 1960s research inspired by her pioneering studies showed that chloroplasts and mitochondria in cells of organisms throughout the evolutionary chain contain genetic materials that apparently synthesize proteins and other substances and largely regulate their own development. In 1972–1973 Sager held a Guggenheim research fellowship. In 1975 Sager became a professor of cellular genetics at Harvard Medical School and chief of the Division of Genetics at the Dana Farber Cancer Institute. She was elected to the National Academy of Sciences in 1977, and in 1988 she received the Academy's Gilbert Smith Medal.

St. Denis, Ruth 1878?–1968 dancer and choreographer

Born in Newark, New Jersey, probably on January 20, 1878, Ruth Dennis grew up in Somerville. From an early age she displayed a marked interest in the theater and especially in dance. Her formal schooling ended with a brief attendance at Dwight L. Moody's Seminary in Northfield, Massachusetts, and a short time thereafter she began dancing and acting in vaudeville and musical comedy. David Belasco reputedly gave her the stage name St. Denis; she appeared in his productions of *Zaza*, *The Auctioneer*, and *Du Barry*. While touring in the last play she was inspired by a cigarette poster that featured an Egyptian scene and the goddess Isis to begin investigating Oriental art and dance.

In March 1906 at the Hudson Theatre, New York City, after a few private showings, she offered a public performance of her first dance work, *Radha*, a piece based on Hindu forms, together with such shorter pieces as "The Cobra" and "The Incense." A London performance under Charles Frohman's management later that year began a three-year European tour. She was particularly successful in Vienna, where she added "The Nautch" and "The Yogi" to her program, and in Germany. In 1910 she presented her long-planned *Egypta* and in 1913 her Japanese-inspired *O-mika*.

In August 1914 St. Denis married Ted Shawn (1891–1972), her dance partner, and the next year they opened the Denishawn School in Los Angeles. From the school soon sprang the Denishawn Company, in which both St. Denis's choreography and talented young dancers were showcased. The company's national tours were highly successful and continued until early 1932, shortly after St. Denis and Shawn separated. During a period of semiretirement from public performance she founded the Society of Spiritual Arts to promote liturgical dance. In 1940, with La Meri (Russell M. Hughes), she founded the School of Natya to continue the teaching of Oriental dance. Her performing career resumed in 1941 with an appearance at Shawn's Jacob's Pillow Festival in Massachusetts, where she continued to appear annually until 1955. In 1949 she and Shawn presented a series titled "Around the World in Dance and Song" for the Museum of Natural History in New York City. She toured in "American Dances" in 1963 and in the same year revived "Incense" in New York City. Many of her dances were recorded on film.

Known often as the "First Lady of American Dance," she profoundly influenced the course of modern dance in America. From Denishawn, the first major organized center of dance experiment and instruction in the country, students (such as Martha Graham and Doris Humphrey) went on to create new centers.

Her own theory of dance revolved around her notion of dance as spiritual expression within a religio-philosophical system, and her innovative contributions included her technique of "music visualization," an elaboration of the Dalcrozian eurhythmics she had studied as a child. Among her best known dances were "The Garden of Kama," "Ishtar of the Seven Gates," "The Feather of the Dawn," "White Jade," "The Peacock," "Japanese Flower Arrangement," "Salomé," "Black and Gold Sari," "Kwannon," and "Chrysanthemum." She published *Lotus Lights*, a volume of verse, in 1932 and *Ruth St. Denis: An Unfinished Life* in 1939. She died in Los Angeles on July 21, 1968.

St. Johns, Adela Rogers 1894–1988 journalist and writer

Born in Los Angeles on May 20, 1894, Adela Nora Rogers was the daughter of a well known criminal lawyer. Her schooling ended with her leaving Hollywood High School without a diploma. An avid reader and writer from childhood, she became a reporter for William Randolph Hearst's *San Francisco Examiner* in 1913. She moved to the *Los Angeles Herald* the next year and in December 1914 married William I. St. Johns, a *Herald* colleague. After leaving the paper in 1918 she began writing feature stories and interviews for *Photoplay* magazine and then stories based on her newspaper and Hollywood experiences for *Cosmopolitan*, *Saturday Evening Post*, and other magazines.

Three *Cosmopolitan* serials were published as books: *A Free Soul*, 1924, *The Skyrocket*, 1925, and *The Single Standard*, 1928. She also wrote a few screenplays. In the late 1920s she returned to newspaper work and covered sports for various papers of the Hearst chain and for the international News Service; among the stories she covered was the controversial Jack Dempsey-Gene Tunney "long-count" fight in 1927. She later moved on to exposé and crime stories, including the 1935 trial of Bruno Richard Hauptmann, accused kidnapper and murderer of the Lindbergh baby, and then to political reporting from Washington, D.C. Her coverage of the assassination of Senator Huey Long in 1935, of the abdication of Edward VIII in 1936, of the Democratic National Convention of 1940, and other major stories made her one of the best known reporters of the day. She said in her autobiography *The Honeycomb* that what she did not learn at school she had "learned from pimps, professional prostitutes, gamblers, bank robbers, poets, newspapermen, jury bribers, millionaire dipsomaniacs, and murderers."

She continued during that time to publish short stories, some later collected in *Never Again*, 1949, and novels, including *Field of Honor*, 1938, and *Root of All Evil*, 1940, and for a time she conducted a daily radio program, "Woman's Viewpoint of the News."

St. Johns retired from newspaper work in 1948. During 1950–1952 she taught at the Graduate School of Journalism of the University of California at Los Angeles. Her *How to Write a Short Story and Sell It* appeared in 1956 and was followed by *Affirmative Prayer in Action*, 1957, *First Step Up Toward Heaven: Hubert Eaton and Forest Lawn*, 1959, *Final Verdict*, a biography of her father, 1962, *Tell No Man*, a best-selling novel, 1966, *The Honeycomb*, an autobiography, 1969, and *Some Are Born Great*, a volume of reminiscence and anecdote, 1974. In 1970 she was awarded the Medal of Freedom by President Richard M. Nixon. She emerged from retirement in 1976 to cover the trial of Patricia Hearst for the *San Francisco Examiner*. She published another autobiography, *Love, Laughter, and Tears: My Hollywood Story* in 1978, and *No Goodbyes: My Search into Life Beyond Death* in 1981. A minister in the Church of Religious Science, she was working at the time of her death on *Missing Years*, a study of the years in Jesus Christ's life between his Bar Mitzvah and the time he turned thirty. She died on August 10, 1988, in Arroyo Grande, California.

Salmon, Lucy Maynard 1853–1927 historian

Born in Fulton, New York, on July 27, 1853, Lucy Salmon was educated at a school in Oswego, New York, at the Falley Seminary in her native town, and for a year at the high school in Ann Arbor, Michigan, where she prepared for the University of Michigan. She graduated from the university in 1876, and for five years thereafter she was assistant principal and then principal of the high school in McGregor, Iowa. She returned to the

University of Michigan to take an M.A. in history in 1883 with a thesis on "The History of the Appointing Power of the President" that was published in the *Papers of the American Historical Association* in 1886. After three years of teaching at the Indiana State Normal School (now Indiana State University) in Terre Haute, she was awarded a fellowship for a year's graduate study in American history at Bryn Mawr College. From there she went to Vassar in 1887 as that college's first history teacher; she advanced from associate professor to full professor in 1889.

Except for a leave of absence for European study and travel in 1898–1900 Salmon remained at Vassar for the rest of her life. She was a strikingly effective teacher and a pioneer in the use of the project method of individual special topic research. The number of history courses offered by the college multiplied under her influence, and she was a leader in the long drive to create a major scholarly library for Vassar. In the study of history she was similarly innovative in her use of materials reflecting the realities of daily life rather than official documents and formal pronouncements. Her pioneering use of statistical studies, in which she was assisted by Carroll D. Wright of the federal Bureau of Labor, helped make her history of *Domestic Service*, 1897, a major contribution to both history and historiography.

Other published works included *Progress in the Household*, 1906, *The Newspaper and the Historian*, 1923, *The Newspaper and Authority*, 1923, and the posthumous *Why Is History Rewritten?*, 1929, and *Historical Material*, 1933. She served on the committee of the American Historical Association that reported on *The Study of History in Schools*, 1899. She was a founder and first president of the Association of History Teachers of the Middle States and Maryland in 1903 and in 1915–1919 was the first woman to sit on the executive committee of the American Historical Association. She died in Poughkeepsie, New York, on February 14, 1927.

Samaroff, Olga 1882–1948 pianist and educator

Born on August 8, 1882, in San Antonio, Texas, Lucy Mary Olga Agnes Hickenlooper grew up there and in Galveston. While attending the school of the Ursuline convent in Galveston, she took piano lessons from her mother and then from her grandmother, who had been a concert pianist of some note. At fourteen, having received encouragement from Edward MacDowell, she was taken to Paris to continue her studies, and a year later she became the first American girl to win a scholarship to the Paris Conservatoire. She studied there under Élie Delaborde and later in Berlin under Ernst Jedliczka and Ernest Hutcheson.

During the course of an unsuccessful marriage to a Russian engineer in 1900–1904 she abandoned music, but she resumed it in the latter year and in January 1905 made her professional debut under the name Olga Samaroff with the New York Symphony, Walter Damrosch conducting, at Carnegie Hall in New York City. Good reviews led to several private engagements, and in May she made her London debut at Steinway Hall. She subsequently was invited to play with the Boston Symphony Quartet and the Boston Symphony Orchestra, and from 1906 her concert career flourished under the management of the prominent impresario Charles A. Ellis. She again gave up performing for a time after her marriage in April 1911 to Leopold Stokowski, but she resumed gradually from 1913 and toured full time again after her divorce in 1923.

A serious arm injury in 1925 prompted Samaroff to give up her performing career entirely in favor of teaching. In that year she joined the faculty of the Juilliard Graduate School of Music in New York City, with which she was associated for the rest of her life. She served also in 1926–1927 as music critic for the *New York Evening Post*. In 1928 she founded the Shubert Memorial to sponsor concerts with full orchestra for deserving young artists identified through competitions conducted by the National Federation of

Music Clubs. In 1929 she began teaching piano classes at the Philadelphia Conservatory of Music as well. From about 1930 she enjoyed considerable success with her layman's music courses, which she offered at the David Mannes Music School, at Town Hall, New York, and in Philadelphia and Washington, D.C., and she published *The Layman's Music Book*, 1935, *The Magic World of Music*, 1936, and *A Music Manual*, 1937, for use in them. The first was later reissued as *The Listener's Music Book*, 1947, after the course was presented on radio and television. Her autobiography, *An American Musician's Story*, appeared in 1939. She was a frequent guest lecturer at universities and colleges, a delegate to the International Music Education Congress in Prague in 1936, and a judge at the Concours Eugène Ysaÿe piano competition in Belgium in 1938. She died in New York City on May 17, 1948.

Sampson, Deborah 1760–1827 Revolutionary soldier

Born on December 17, 1760, in Plympton, Massachusetts, Deborah Sampson was put into service at the age of ten by her widowed mother, and she lived thereafter in Middleborough. About 1779 she left service and became a school teacher. In 1782 she decided to join the fight for independence. After one attempt was discovered, she succeeded in disguising herself as a man — she was tall, strong, and well coordinated — and enlisted in May at Uxbridge, Massachusetts, as a private in Captain George Webb's company of the 4th Massachusetts Regiment under the name Robert Shurtleff.

For over a year she served capably and without detection. Soon after the regiment was ordered to West Point she received a saber wound in a skirmish near Tarrytown, New York, and a few weeks later she took a musket ball in a fight near East Chester. This second, fairly serious wound she dressed herself rather than risk exposure. She later served in western New York and then in Philadelphia. There she fell desperately ill and was hospitalized, whereupon her secret was revealed. In October 1783 she received her formal discharge and a sum of money from General Henry Knox. She later published an account of her war experience as *The Female Review*, 1797. In April 1785 she married Benjamin Gannett and settled in Sharon, Massachusetts. In 1792 she was granted a sum of money by the Massachusetts General Court for her services in the Revolution. In 1805 she was granted a veteran's disability pension by Congress, and from September 1818 she received a full pension; she stands unique among women as a genuine Revolutionary veteran and pensioner. She died in Sharon, Massachusetts, on April 29, 1827; in July 1838 her widower, Gannett, was granted a survivor's pension.

Sanderson, Sibyl Swift 1865–1903 opera singer

Born in Sacramento, California, on December 7, 1865, Sibyl Sanderson was educated privately. She early showed remarkable vocal talent, and in 1881, at the age of fifteen, she was taken to Paris to study singing. After two years she returned home, but in 1885 she went again to Paris and early the next year entered the Paris Conservatoire, where she studied under Jean-Baptiste Sbriglia, Mathilde Marchest, and Jean and Édouard de Reszke. She made her operatic debut under the name "Ada Palmer" in 1888 at The Hague, singing the title role of Jules Massenet's *Manon*. She had by that time captivated Massenet utterly with her beauty and her voice. For her he wrote *Esclarmonde* to exploit her remarkable three-octave range, and in that opera she made her Paris debut at the Opéra Comique in May 1889. She repeated the performance a hundred times in Paris before taking it on to Brussels and then St. Petersburg. Wherever she appeared, she attracted the favor of royalty. In March 1891 she introduced Massenet's *Le Mage*, which he had written for her, at the Paris Opéra; at the Opéra Comique in 1893 she created the title role in Phryné, which Camille Saint-Saëns had written for her; and in March 1894 she sang in the premiere of Massenet's highly successful *Thaïs*, also written for her, at the Paris Opéra.

Although Sanderson had become a leading prima donna on the Continent in an amazingly short time, similar success eluded her elsewhere. Her London debut in *Manon* at Covent Garden in 1891 earned a mixed reception. Maurice Grau engaged her for the Metropolitan Opera of New York, where her debut in *Manon* in January 1895 was not successful. American audiences found her voice small and her acting cold. She repeated her earlier European triumphs in Milan in 1896, singing *Manon* and *Phryné*. In December 1897 she married Antonio Terry, a wealthy Cuban residing in France, and retired from the stage. After his death a year later and a lengthy legal wrangle over his will, she resumed singing. In 1900 she was successful in Berlin, Vienna, Budapest, St. Petersburg, and Moscow. A second American tour in 1901 repeated the failures of her first. After a final performance in *Roméo et Juliette* at the Philadelphia Academy of Music in January 1902 she returned to Paris. Later that year she scored another great success in the premiere of Reynaldo Hahn's *La Carmélite* at the Opéra Comique. Before her planned marriage to Count Paul Tolstoi, a cousin of the Russian novelist, she fell ill and died in Paris on May 15, 1903.

Sanford, Maria Louise 1836–1920 educator

Born on December 19, 1836, in Saybrook (now Old Saybrook), Connecticut, Maria Sanford grew up there and in Meriden. She attended Meriden Academy and the New Britain Normal School, and after her graduation from the latter in 1855 she taught school in various Connecticut towns for 12 years. In 1867 she moved to Parkersville, Pennsylvania, and the next year to Unionville, where in 1869, after narrowly failing of election as superintendent of schools for Chester County, she was appointed principal of the local academy. She was an innovator in pedagogy and was soon conducting regular meetings of teachers to demonstrate new methods. Later in 1869 she was appointed a teacher of English and history at the five-year-old Swarthmore College. The next year she was given professorial rank. She was an inspiring teacher who believed in using the classroom to inculcate moral and, after her late discovery of art in the 1870s, aesthetic values. She began offering public lectures on these topics as well.

Sanford resigned from Swarthmore in 1879, and after a year devoted to public lecturing she was named assistant professor of rhetoric and elocution at the University of Minnesota. She later advanced to full professor. She remained there for 29 years and in that time introduced hundreds of farm boys and girls to the worlds of poetry and art. The failure of some ill-advised real estate investments in the late 1880s left her heavily in debt, and her determination to make full restitution rather than escape through bankruptcy added various extreme economies to her other eccentricities. At times university trustees and state officials expressed displeasure with her methods or her petty money-making sidelines (such as renting art books to students), but students and alumni rallied to her support every time and she held her position until her retirement in 1909. She continued until her death to travel and lecture, particularly during World War I, when she gave patriotic addresses throughout the country. She died in Washington, D.C., on April 21, 1920. In 1958 her statue took its place as one of two outstanding Minnesotans represented in Statuary Hall of the U.S. Capitol.

Sanger, Margaret Higgins 1883–1966 social reformer

Born on September 14, 1883, in Corning, New York, Margaret Higgins was one of eleven children. She attended school in Claverack and then taught school herself until her mother's death turned her attention to medicine. She completed nurse's training at the White Plains Hospital in New York and at the Manhattan Eye and Ear Clinic. In 1900 she married William Sanger. (She retained that surname, by which she was well known, after they were divorced; she remarried in 1922.) In New York City the Sanger home became a popular meeting place for socialists and radical intellectuals and writers. She contributed articles on health to the Socialist party's organ, the *Call*; these were later collected in *What Every Girl Should Know*, 1916, and *What Every Mother Should Know*, 1917. In her nursing career she ministered primarily to maternity cases from the city's crowded Lower East Side, coming directly into contact with her patients' desperate financial circumstances and seeing those circumstances exacerbated by the birth of unplanned, unwanted children. She saw also the staggering toll of infant mortality and of deaths from self-induced abortions.

Margaret Sanger

Sanger gave up nursing in 1912 to devote herself to the cause of birth control (a term she is credited with originating). Gathering and disseminating information legally, however, was nearly impossible because of the federal Comstock Act of 1873, which classified contraceptive data with obscene matter and forbade its passage in the mails. Late in 1913 she traveled in Scotland and France as an observer of conditions there. In 1914 she returned to the United States and began publishing the *Woman Rebel*, a magazine addressed to her cause, and was indicted for sending an obscene publication through the mails. She fled to Europe on the eve of her trial and for a year continued her study of the question of birth control there. Soon after her return to New York in 1915 her indictment was quashed largely as a result of widespread sympathy aroused by the case. Also in 1914 she had founded the National Birth Control League, of which she lost control (to Mary Ware Dennett and others) during her absence in Europe. In 1917, soon after setting up the nation's first birth control clinic in the Brownsville district of Brooklyn, she was sent to the workhouse for 30 days on the charge of creating a public nuisance. But her appeal, bolstered by mounting public sympathy, led to a favorable decision from the New York Court of Appeals granting doctors the right to give advice about birth control to their patients. (In 1936 a further interpretation of the law granted doctors the right to import and prescribe contraceptive devices.)

Sanger organized numerous conventions in the United States and abroad, beginning with the Birth Control Conference in New York City in 1921 and continuing through the International Birth Control Conference in New York in 1925, the World Population Conference in Geneva in 1927, the International Contraceptive Conference in Zurich in 1930, and others. In 1921 she established the American Birth Control League, of which she served as president until 1928, to educate and mobilize public opinion behind efforts to alter restrictive legislation. In 1931 she founded the National Committee on Federal Legislation for Birth Control. In 1939 the American Birth Control League combined with the education department of the Birth Control Research Bureau and became the Birth Control Federation of America, renamed in 1942 the Planned Parenthood Federation, of which she was named honorary chairman. She was elected first president of the International Planned Parenthood Federation on its organization in Bombay, India, in 1953. She worked throughout her active career to further the cause of family planning in the Far East, notably in India and Japan. In 1935 she began the *Journal of Contraception* (later called *Human Fertility*). Her many books included *The Case for Birth Control*, 1917, *The Pivot of Civilization*, 1922, *Women, Morality, and Birth Control*, 1922, *Woman and the New Race*, 1923, *Happiness in Marriage*, 1926, *Motherhood in Bondage*, 1928, *My Fight for Birth Control*, 1931, and *Margaret Sanger: An Autobiography*, 1938. She died in Tucson, Arizona, on September 6, 1966.

Sangster, Margaret Elizabeth Munson 1838–1912 writer and editor

Born in New Rochelle, New York, on February 22, 1838, Margaret Munson grew up there, in New York City, and from 1846 in Paterson, New Jersey. She was an avid reader from an early age, and after attending Passaic Seminary and a private school in New York City she turned easily to writing. Her first story, "Little Janey," was accepted by the Presbyterian Board of Publication in Philadelphia in 1855 and won her a commission to write a hundred juvenile stories to accompany a series of illustrations. In October 1858 she married George Sangster. After his death in 1871 she resumed her writing career. She contributed several pieces to *Hearth and Home* and in 1873 succeeded Mary Mapes Dodge as editor of that magazine's children's page. A short time later she became assistant editor of the magazine, a post she held until it ceased publication in 1875. In that time she also contributed letters and essays to other periodicals, most of them reflecting her belief that she had a "mission to girlhood" to be a Christian leader. In 1876 she became editor of the family page of the *Christian Intelligencer*, to which she had been contributing for years. Subsequently she became a literary adviser to the publishing firm of Harper & Brothers, and from 1882 to 1889 she edited the "Little Postmistress" department of *Harper's Young People*. In 1889 she succeeded Mary Louise Booth as editor of *Harper's Bazaar*, which she made into a magazine of service to women. She remained with the *Bazaar* until its failure in 1899. She also contributed frequently to the *Ladies' Home Journal*, *Christian Herald*, *Youth's Companion*, and *Woman's Home Companion*.

Among Sangster's books were *Hours with Girls*, 1881, *Poems of the Household*, 1882, *On the Road Home*, verse, 1892, *Little Knights and Ladies*, 1895, *Easter Bells*, verse, 1897, *Home Life Made Beautiful in Story, Song, Sketch and Picture*, 1897, *Cheerful Todays and Trustful To-morrows*, 1899, *Winsome Womanhood*, 1900, *Lyrics of Love, of Hearth and Home, of Field and Garden*, 1901, *Janet Ward, a Daughter of the Manse*, 1902, *Eleanor Lee*, 1903, *Good Manners for All Occasions*, 1904, *What Shall a Young Girl Read?*, 1905, *Radiant Motherhood*, 1905, *Fairest Girlhood*, 1906, *The Joyful Life*, 1907, *An Autobiography: From My Youth Up; Personal Reminiscences*, 1909, *Ideal Home Life*, 1910, *A Little Book of Homespun Verse*, 1911, *Eastover Parish*, 1912, and the posthumous *My Garden of Hearts*, 1913. Pious and cheerful, sentimental and yet full of practical common sense, her writings were much loved in their day. Margaret Sangster died in South Orange, New Jersey, on June 3, 1912.

Sarandon, Susan Tomalin 1946– actor

Born on October 4, 1946 in New York City, Susan Tomalin was the first of nine children. She was raised in Edison, New Jersey, by her father, a former nightclub singer and television producer, and mother. Although a somewhat introverted child, she took an early interest in acting, constantly rehearsing plays with neighborhood children. After graduating from high school, she entered Catholic University in Washington, D.C. While in school, she worked various odd jobs and majored in drama, though she wasn't planning a career in theater. In her senior year she married a graduate student and actor, Chris Sarandon (whom she divorced in 1979). After accompanying him to an audition with an agent in New York City, she lived an all-too-familiar cliche as she was the one who gained the agent's interest. The experience spawned her desire to act professionally and she and her husband moved to New York City to pursue their acting careers in 1969. She made her screen debut in the film *Joe* in 1970.

She spent the next two years working on the television soap operas *World Apart* and *Search for Tomorrow*, and from 1972 to 1975 found a number of jobs in film, television, and very briefly, on Broadway. In 1975 she worked opposite Robert Redford in the film *The Great Waldo Pepper*. Later that year, she took on the role of Janet in the low-budget, counterculture musical *The Rocky Horror Picture Show* which quickly became a cult classic. Her next film roles were virtually ignored, however, until 1978 when she appeared in the controversial Louis Malle film *Pretty Baby*. She received favorable reviews for her portrayal of the mother of a child prostitute (played by Brooke Shields), and in 1980 she appeared in an off-Broadway production of John Ford Noonan's play *A Coupla White Chicks Sitting Around Talking*. This performance earned her critical, but not yet public, acclaim. In 1981 she and a group of other actors (including Richard Dreyfuss and Peter Boyle) formed an improvisational theater group in New York City. Later in 1981, she was nominated for an Academy Award for her portrayal of Sally, a struggling waitress aspiring to be a blackjack dealer in another Louis Malle film, *Atlantic City*.

While she continued to work in film, often to critical and popular success, she did not become a nationally recognized figure until she appeared in *Bull Durham*, 1988, playing an eccentric community college English teacher and minor league baseball groupie. While making this film she met fellow actor Tim Robbins with whom she later lived, worked, and raised children. Her role in the highly successful film *Thelma and Louise*, 1991, earned her an Academy Award nomination for Best Actress, and in 1996 she took her first Oscar for her performance in *Dead Man Walking* (directed by Robbins), based on Sister Helen Prejean's nonfiction account of her work with death row inmates. She played the role of Sister Prejean opposite Sean Penn, who played a convicted murderer awaiting execution. The role had special meaning to Sarandon, who was strongly and openly opposed to capital punishment. Throughout her career she did not hesitate to use her celebrity status to voice her opinions on social issues such as AIDS and the plight of the homeless, as well as the adverse conditions for women and children in Central America.

Schiff, Dorothy 1903–1989 newspaper publisher

Born in New York City on March 11, 1903, Dorothy Schiff was educated at the Brearley School in Manhattan and attended Bryn Mawr College for a year in 1920–1921. For some years she led the life of a wealthy debutante and socialite. During the 1930s she became interested in social service and reform. She served on the boards of the Henry Street Settlement, Mount Sinai Hospital, and the Women's Trade Union League of New York, and on the Social Service Committee of Bellevue Hospital, and she was a member of various child welfare groups. She also abandoned her inherited affiliation with the Republican party and became an active Democrat and New Dealer.

In 1939 Schiff bought majority control of the *New York Post*, the nation's oldest continuously published newspaper (founded in 1801 by Alexander Hamilton). She took the titles of director, vice-president, and treasurer and installed her second husband, George Backer, as publisher and president. With his resignation owing to illness in 1942 she became president and publisher — the first woman newspaper publisher in New York — and in 1943, divorcing Backer, she assumed the title of owner and publisher. From 1943 to 1949 she was married to Theodore O. Thackrey, who served as editor of the *Post* in that period. Under her direction the *Post* was a crusading paper devoted to liberal causes, staunchly supporting unions and social welfare legislation. It also published an array of the most popular newspaper columnists, particularly during the 1940s, when its pages featured the commentary of Franklin P. Adams, Drew Pearson, Eleanor Roosevelt, Sylvia Porter, Elsa Maxwell, Leonard Lyons, Eric Sevareid, Joseph Kraft, and others. From 1951 to 1958 Dorothy Schiff also wrote a regular Post column, "Publisher's Notebook," later called "Dear Reader." In 1961 she assumed charge of the news department and the next year took the newly created title of editor in chief. In 1976 she sold the *Post*, New York's only remaining afternoon newspaper, to Australian publisher Rupert Murdoch, who later sold it to Peter Kalikow. She remained a consultant to the *New York Post* from 1976–1981. She died on August 30, 1989, at her home in New York City.

Schlossberg, Caroline Kennedy 1957– lawyer and author

Born on November 27, 1957, in New York, New York, Caroline Kennedy was the daughter of President John Fitzgerald Kennedy and Jacqueline Bouvier Kennedy. As the daughter of the 35th President of the United States, her childhood, and that of her younger brother John, was anything but typical. From age three to six, she lived in the White House in Washington, D.C. and was educated in a special school set up by her mother.

Caroline Kennedy Schlossberg

Although a "normal" upbringing was next to impossible, Jackie Kennedy took great pains to keep her children out of the media spotlight. When John F. Kennedy was assassinated on November 22, 1963, in Dallas, Texas, the country mourned the sudden loss of a great leader, and her family's grief was witnessed by the entire nation.

Like her mother, throughout her life she constantly tried to avoid the media, presenting a very calculated image when she found herself forced to confront camera crews, reporters, and journalists. Perhaps fittingly, her early career interest was in media studies. As a teenager, she interned at NBC in London for several months and in 1979 she entered Radcliffe University earning her degree in fine arts in 1983. As a student she spent a summer working as a copy girl for the *New York Daily News* and in 1976 returned to London for a year, participating in a special course in art given by Sotheby's auction house. After graduating from Radcliffe, she began working at the film and television department at the Museum of Modern Art in New York City. She began as a researcher, eventually moving up to manager, coordinating her own productions. In 1985 she entered Columbia Law School, earning her J.D. in 1988 and passing the Bar on her first attempt. On July 19, 1986 she married Edwin Arthur Schlossberg (whom she had met at a friend's dinner party) in a wedding ceremony in Centerville, Massachusetts. While there were only a few hundred guests at the ceremony, there were over a thousand spectators outside the chapel (including numerous members of the press), cheering and waving for her on her wedding day. She and Edwin Schlossberg, the son of a wealthy Jewish textile manufacturer and the president of his own design firm, had three children together and made their home in New York City.

In 1991 she coauthored the book *In Our Defense: The Bill of Rights in Action* with Ellen Alderman. In 1995 the team also published *The Right to Privacy*, an examination of privacy from a legal and constitutional standpoint — a subject she obviously knew a great deal about. She served on the board of the John F. Kennedy Library and was active in the Kennedy Foundation. After the death of her mother in 1994, she took over her mother's position as honorary chairwoman of the American Ballet Theater and, along with her brother John, presented the annual John F. Kennedy Profile in Courage Award in memory of their father. The award honors elected officials who like John F. Kennedy, "act in accord with their conscience, even at the risk of their careers."

Schoff, Hannah Kent 1853–1940 welfare worker and reformer

Born on June 3, 1853, in Upper Darby, Pennsylvania, Hannah Kent grew up there and in nearby Clifton Heights. She attended private schools in Philadelphia and Waltham, Massachusetts. In October 1873 she married Frederic Schoff, an engineer with whom she lived in Newtonville, Massachusetts, for several years and thereafter in Philadelphia. In 1897, as representative of the New Century Club, she attended the first National Congress of Mothers in Washington, D.C., and the next year she was elected vice-president of the permanent National Congress of Mothers. In 1899 she organized the Pennsylvania Congress of Mothers, the second state branch of the national group to come into being. She served as president of the Pennsylvania Congress until 1902, when she was elected president of the National Congress of Mothers. She held that post until 1920, and in that time she established an endowment fund and a national headquarters in Washington, D.C., oversaw the multiplication of member state branches from 8 to 37 with 190,000 individual members, edited the organization's journal *Child Welfare* (later *National Parent-Teacher*) from 1906 to 1920, and approved the renaming of the organization in 1908 as the National Congress of Mothers and Parent-Teacher Associations (later the National Congress of Parents and Teachers). The national group became a major force behind proposed legislation in the areas of child labor, marriage, and education.

A Philadelphia police case in 1899, in which an eight-year-old girl, a boarding house slavey, was arrested and imprisoned for arson, moved Schoff to initiate a campaign for reform in the treatment of juvenile offenders. After securing the release and placement in a foster home of that child, she made a survey that revealed that nearly 500 children were imprisoned along with older and habitual criminals in Philadelphia. She prompted the formation of a committee of the New Century Club that compiled a summary of laws in various states affecting delinquent and dependent juveniles, and she then drew up a series of bills for the legislature. As passed in May 1901, after vigorous lobbying by Schoff and others, the legislation established a distinct juvenile court system (the nation's second, after Chicago's), separate detention homes for children, and a system of probation officers. From 1901 to 1923 she was president of the Philadelphia Juvenile Court and Probation Association, which recommended and assisted probation officers and raised funds for their salaries. In its first eight years of operation she personally observed virtually every session of the Philadelphia juvenile court. She also assisted in the establishment of such courts in several other states and in Canada, where she was the first woman ever invited to address Parliament.

In 1908 Schoff organized an international Conference on Child Welfare, sponsored by the U.S. State Department and the Congress of Mothers and held in Washington, D.C., and she subsequently organized similar conferences in 1911 and 1914. In 1909 she became chairman of the American Committee on the Causes of Crime in Normal Children, established under the aegis of the U.S. Bureau of Education. Her detailed survey of juvenile crime led to the publication of *The Wayward Child*, 1915. She was the U.S. delegate to the Third International Congress for Home Education held in Brussels in 1910. She was in large part responsible for the establishment within the U.S. Bureau of Education of the Home Education Division, of which she was a special collaborator from 1913 to 1919. She contributed to various magazines and in 1933 published *Wisdom of the Ages in Bringing Up Children*. Schoff died in Philadelphia on December 10, 1940.

Schrieck, Sister Louise Van der 1813–1886 religious

Born on November 14, 1813, in Bergen-op-Zoom, Netherlands, Josephine Van der Schrieck grew up there and from 1817 in Antwerp. She was educated in a private school and in the school of the Sisters of Notre Dame de Namur in Belgium. In 1837 she became a novice of the order, and in May 1839 she became Sister Louise.

She was one of eight sisters who volunteered to emigrate to the United States to establish the order there. They set out in September 1840 and settled in Cincinnati in October, establishing the order's first permanent home outside Belgium. A boarding school, a school for the children of the poor, and a Sunday school were soon in operation. In 1845 Sister Louise became superior of the convent, and in 1848 she became superior-provincial for all establishments east of the Rocky Mountains. During her 38 years as superior-provincial the number of foundations under her authority grew from 2 to 27, and some 800 sisters staffed the order's own academies and nearly 50 parochial elementary schools in Boston, Philadelphia, Washington, D.C., and other cities. In 1867 she sent sisters to staff a school for African-American children in Cincinnati. Night classes for adults were also operated in several cities. Under her firm, traditionalist administration the Sisters of Notre Dame de Namur flourished and provided invaluable service to the rapidly growing Catholic populations of eastern and midwestern cities. Sister Louise died in Cincinnati on December 3, 1886.

Schumann-Heink, Ernestine 1861–1936 singer

Born at Liben (or Lieben), Austria (now part of Prague, Czech Republic), on June 15, 1861, Ernestine Rössler (or Roessler) was the daughter of an Austrian army officer and grew up in poverty. Educated sporadically in convent schools, she had little opportunity for formal musical training. About 1874, however, she was able to take singing lessons from Marietta von Leclair in Graz, and in 1876 she made her first public appearance. Her opera debut, in Dresden in October 1878, was in *Il Trovatore*. She remained with the Dresden Royal Opera for four seasons, singing mostly minor roles. She was dismissed in 1882 for marrying, without permission, Ernst Heink, secretary of the company. In 1887, after he had left her, she sang in Berlin and Hamburg.

Her singing of the lead in *Carmen* on short notice in Hamburg in 1888 won her a ten-year contract and began her climb to success. She made her London debut with the Hamburg company in June 1892, singing Erda in *Siegfried* at Covent Garden. That year she divorced Heink, and the next year she married Paul Schumann, thus arriving at the hyphenated name she used for most of her professional career; she later married a third time. She sang regularly at the Bayreuth Festivals from 1896 to 1903 and occasionally thereafter. From 1897 to 1900 she was a summer regular at Covent Garden, again usually in Wagnerian roles.

In November 1898 Schumann-Heink made her American debut with the Metropolitan Opera company in a Chicago performance of *Lohengrin*. She made her New York debut in January 1899 and remained with the Met until 1903. During her years in grand opera she was more famous for Wagnerian roles than for any others she sang. After a light-opera tour in *Love's Lottery* in 1904–1905, she devoted most of her time to concert performance, with occasional returns to the grand opera stage. She became a U.S. citizen in 1905. In January 1909 she created the role of Klytemnestra in Richard Strauss's *Elektra* in Dresden, Germany.

During World War I she remained in the United States (she had sons on both sides) and made several concert tours for the Red Cross and among army camps. Her stage appearances after the war were infrequent, but when radio became popular she often sang on the air. A Carnegie Hall concert in December 1926 marked the 50th anniversary of her debut in Graz. A 20,000-mile farewell tour followed. Her farewell appearance for the Metropolitan Opera in New York City in March 1932 was in *Siegfried*. In that year she made a vaudeville tour with "Roxy and His Gang." She made a movie entitled *Here's to Romance*, 1935, but her plan to continue as a film actress was cut short by her death in Hollywood, California, on November 17, 1936, after a remarkably long career. In her prime she was considered the greatest contralto in the world, and in addition to her operatic work she had been a notable interpreter of German lieder. Her powerful, rich voice of remarkable range, her command of the grand manner, and her personal warmth and manifest kindliness made her a favorite with audiences for nearly a half-century.

Schuyler, Louisa Lee 1837–1926 welfare worker

Born in New York City on October 26, 1837, Louisa Lee Schuyler was a great-granddaughter of General Philip J. Schuyler and of Alexander Hamilton. She grew up mainly on the family's estate in Dobbs Ferry on the Hudson, and she was educated privately. As a young woman she became interested in the work of the Children's Aid Society of New York, of which her parents were supporters as well. Shortly after the outbreak of the Civil War in 1861, and after her mother had helped organize the Woman's Central Association of Relief, she was named chairman of its committee of correspondence. That position was a well placed one from which to exert forceful leadership, and under her guidance the Woman's Central Association quickly developed into the largest and most effective auxiliary of the U.S. Sanitary Commission. Her ability to organize, to inspire, and to manage efficiently and imaginatively was a mainstay of the massive effort made by the association to establish a network of local groups through which food, clothing, medical supplies, and other items were collected and forwarded to army camps and hospitals. Her exertions left her at the end of the war utterly exhausted, and for six years she convalesced mainly in Europe and Egypt.

In 1871 Schuyler turned her mind to the problem of public charity. A visit to the poorhouse in Westchester County revealed conditions in dire need of improvement. With a group of like-minded associates she formed in May 1872 the State Charities Aid Association (S.C.A.A.), which she envisioned as an umbrella organization for local groups of volunteer visitors interested in the inspection and improvement of prisons, poorhouses, workhouses, public hospitals, and schools. While working to establish and extend the work of the S.C.A.A. and to gain formal recognition of it by the state, Schuyler also devoted much time to her particular local interest, Bellevue Hospital. The most tangible result of that interest was the establishment of the Bellevue Training School for Nurses, which opened in May 1873.

From 1884 until the sought-for state legislation was obtained in 1890 she led a campaign through the S.C.A.A. to have the mentally ill removed from understaffed, ill equipped county almshouses to state hospitals. She further secured passage in 1892 of a law that provided separate accommodation and treatment for epileptics. In 1907 she was named an original trustee of the Russell Sage Foundation. From 1908 to 1915 she worked with Winifred Holt's New York Association for the Blind, the American Medical Association, the Russell Sage Foundation, and the S.C.A.A. to develop the National Committee (later Society) for the Prevention of Blindness. Among the many honors accorded her for her lifetime of service were an honorary LL.D. from Columbia in 1915 (only the second ever given by Columbia to a woman) and the Theodore Roosevelt Memorial Association medal in 1923. She died in Highland Falls, New York, on October 10, 1926.

Schwimmer, Rosika 1877–1948 feminist, pacifist, and writer

Born in Budapest, Hungary (then part of Austria-Hungary), on September 11, 1877, Rosika Schwimmer grew up and attended public and convent schools in Temesar (now Timisoara, Romania) and Szabadka (now Subotica, Yugoslavia). She also received private tutoring in languages and music. Family financial reverses obliged her to go to work as a bookkeeper in 1896, and shortly after moving back to Budapest in 1897 she organized the National Association of Women Office Workers, of which she was president until 1912. In 1903 she formed the Hungarian Association of Working Women and in 1904 the Hungarian Council of Women and, following her attendance at the International Council of Women conference in Berlin, the Hungarian Feminist Association. From 1907 she edited the monthly journal *A Nö És a Társadalom* ("Woman and Society"; later *A Nö*).

She also wrote a number of short stories, a novel, newspaper features, and articles, and in 1906 she published a translation of Charlotte Perkins Gilman's *Women and Economics*. She became known throughout Europe as a highly effective lecturer on feminist topics. In 1913 she organized and was elected corresponding secretary of the Seventh Congress of the International Woman Suffrage Alliance in Budapest.

The next year Schwimmer moved to London to serve as press secretary for the alliance, and she was stranded there by the outbreak of the European war. She immediately began organizing feminist and pacifist leaders, and in August 1914 she sailed for the United States, where she conferred with Carrie Chapman Catt, Secretary of State William Jennings Bryan, and President Woodrow Wilson. Wilson was reluctant to follow her suggestion that he become the active spokesman for neutral nations urging mediation of the war, and in 1914–1915 Rosika Schwimmer conducted a national tour to rouse popular opinion, especially among suffragists, to push him in that direction. She spoke in some 60 cities in 22 states in that tour.

She assisted Catt and Jane Addams in forming the Woman's Peace party early in 1915 and played a major role in organizing and conducting the International Congress of Women at The Hague (chaired by Jane Addams) in April-May 1915. She presented to the

Congress a plan for neutral-nation mediation and was given charge of a delegation sent to sound out opinion in 14 neutral capitals. The report of the Congress and of the surveys by her and other delegates was ignored by Wilson, but in November 1915 Henry Ford expressed interest in promoting the idea of mediation. In less than three weeks he had bought the Scandinavian-American liner *Oscar II* and installed an unofficial American mediation delegation, including himself. Rosika Schwimmer accompanied the delegation as unpaid expert adviser as *Oscar II* called at various neutral nations in Europe and gathered similarly unofficial delegations. The journey of Ford's "peace ship," widely ridiculed in the press from the beginning and further burdened with an unwisely chosen American delegation, accomplished next to nothing, and Ford himself left long before it ended. In June 1916 Schwimmer led in organizing the International Committee for Immediate Mediation, and throughout 1916 and 1917 she continued to work for an end to the war.

In October 1918 Schwimmer was named to newly independent Hungary's governing National Council of Fifteen, and the next month Prime Minister Michael Karolyi appointed her Hungarian minister to Switzerland. In 1919 she was deprived of her civil rights by the Communist government of Béla Kun that had ousted Karolyi, and in January 1920 she fled to Vienna to escape the succeeding anti-Semitic Horthy regime.

In September 1921 she came to the United States and settled in Chicago. Her hopes of establishing herself permanently were hindered by a campaign of public vilification and private blacklisting aimed at her by various patrioteering groups. She was charged variously with being a German spy, a Bolshevik agent, and a member of a Jewish conspiracy. Her application for citizenship stirred up new attacks in 1924. The federal district court in Chicago denied her application because she refused to affirm that she would bear arms in defense of the United States. An appeal won a reversal, but in May 1929 the Supreme Court ruled 6–3 against her, Justice Oliver Wendell Holmes filing a memorable dissenting opinion in her favor. Although she remained in the United States for the rest of her life, she was formally stateless.

World government was the concern that occupied Schwimmer's last years. In 1937 she formed the Campaign for World Government. She was put forward by several nations for the 1948 Nobel Peace Prize, but her death occurred before the award was to be made; none was made in that year. Her writings other than periodical pieces, lectures, and petitions, included *Tisza Tales*, a collection of Hungarian tales for children, 1928, *Chaos, War or a New World Order?*, with Lola Maverick Lloyd, 1937, and *Union Now for Peace or War?*, 1939. She died in New York City on August 3, 1948.

Scidmore, Eliza Ruhamah 1856–1928 travel writer and photographer

Born in Madison, Wisconsin, on October 14, 1856, Eliza Scidmore attended private schools and for a year, 1873–1874, attended Oberlin College. She then moved to Washington, D.C., whence she contributed letters on capital society to newspapers in New York and St. Louis. A short time later she set out on a journey to Alaska. Her magazine articles on that distant territory were collected in *Alaska, Its Southern Coast and the Sitkan Archipelago*, 1885.

Her appetite for travel whetted, she scarcely stopped after that. She spent long periods in Asia, particularly in Japan. Her articles on travel, manners, and politics appeared in such magazines as *Outlook*, *Century*, *Harper's Weekly*, and *World Today*. She was a member of the National Geographic Society from 1890, serving at various times as corresponding secretary, associate editor, foreign secretary, and member of the board of managers of the society. Her articles for the *National Geographic* magazine were generally illustrated with her own photographs. She was secretary of the Oriental Congress held in Rome in 1897 and a delegate to that in Hamburg in 1902. Her books included

Jinrikisha Days in Japan, 1891, *Appleton's Guide-Book to Alaska and the Northwest Coast*, 1893, *Java, the Garden of the East*, 1897, *China, the Long-Lived Empire*, 1900, *Winter India*, 1903, and *As the Hague Ordains*, 1907. She died on November 3, 1928, in Geneva, Switzerland; at the request of the Japanese government, her ashes were interred in Yokohama.

Scripps, Ellen Browning 1836–1932 journalist, publisher, and philanthropist

Born in London on October 18, 1836, Ellen Scripps came to the United States in 1844 with six brothers and sisters and her father, a widower. She grew up in Rushville, Illinois, attended and then taught in district schools, and in 1859 graduated from the two-year Female Department of Knox College. She then taught school again for some years. During the Civil War she worked with the U.S. Sanitary Commission and the Freedmen's Association. In 1867 she moved to Detroit to assist her elder brother, James E. Scripps, on his recently acquired and newly merged newspapers, the *Daily Advertiser* and the *Tribune*. She later returned home to Rushville to care for her ailing father, but in 1873, after his death, she again joined James, who had just launched the new *Detroit Evening News*. She read proof, contributed copy, and worked indefatigably in a variety of ways to make the venture a successful one.

In 1878 she helped her younger half-brother, Edward W. Scripps, begin his *Penny Press* in Cleveland. She gave financial support and contributed articles and columns to the *Penny Press* while continuing her work for the *Detroit Evening News*. She finally abandoned journalistic work in 1883, but she continued to invest in Edward's enterprises as he acquired several more newspapers and laid the foundation of the Scripps-McRae League (later the Scripps-Howard chain). She eventually held large interests in 16 daily newspapers around the country, and the returns on her investments multiplied. In 1891 she settled at Edward's new villa near San Diego, California, and six years later she built her own villa in La Jolla. She profited further from investments in California real estate.

From about 1900 the distribution of Scripps's large fortune through carefully planned philanthropy became one of her major concerns. The family farm in Rushville, Illinois, was converted into Scripps Memorial Park. In 1903 she and Edward established the Marine Biological Association of San Diego, which in 1912 moved to La Jolla and became a department of the University of California and which from 1925 was known as the Scripps Institution of Oceanography. She made large gifts to Knox College and to the Bishops School in La Jolla. With Edward she founded the Scripps Memorial Hospital (later the Scripps Clinic and Research Foundation) in La Jolla. She established Scripps College for Women, which opened in 1927 in Claremont, California, as one of several associated but autonomous colleges; Scripps College was the recipient of over $1.5 million from her during her lifetime. She also contributed funds for the establishment of the San Diego Zoo and the development of Torrey Pines Park. Principal among her few personal involvements in public affairs was her service from 1917 as a director of the National Recreation Association. She died in La Jolla, California, on August 3, 1932.

Scudder, Janet 1869–1940 sculptor

Born in Terre Haute, Indiana, on October 27, 1869, Netta Deweze Frazee Scudder attended public schools and at eighteen entered the Cincinnati Academy of Art, where she remained for three years. While a student in Cincinnati she adopted the first name Janet. She studied drawing, anatomy, and modeling and settled upon woodcarving as her principal interest. In 1891 she moved to Chicago, and after brief employment as a woodcarver she became a studio assistant to Lorado Taft. She helped Taft produce sculpture for the World's Columbian Exposition and, in part through him, received commissions to create statues herself for the Illinois and Indiana buildings. Late in 1893 she journeyed to Paris and entered the studio of Frederick MacMonnies as a student.

Before she left Paris in mid–1894, she had become an assistant in the studio. Settling in New York City, she shortly received her first important commission, for a seal for the New York Bar Association. Other commissions for architectural decoration and portrait medallions followed. She returned to Paris in 1896 and through MacMonnies sold several of her medallions to the Luxembourg Museum.

A trip to Florence, where she first saw works of Donatello and Verrocchio, turned Scudder to the work that was to make her famous. She immediately began work on her "Frog Fountain." In 1899 she returned to New York City, where versions of "Frog Fountain" were bought by Stanford White and by the Metropolitan Museum of Art. Her graceful, amusing garden sculptures and fountains, with their characteristic figures of chubby, joyous cherubs, became highly popular. Commissions flowed in from John D. Rockefeller and others, making her one of the most successful American sculptors of the day. She won medals at the Louisiana Purchase Exposition in St. Louis in 1904 and at the Panama-Pacific Exposition in San Francisco in 1915. A major exhibit of her works was mounted in New York in 1913. She lived again in France from 1909 until World War I, when she returned to the United States and became active in relief work with the Lafayette Fund, which she organized, the Red Cross, and the YMCA. After the war she returned to her home in Ville d'Avray, near Paris. In 1920 she was elected an associate of the National Academy of Design. In 1933 an exhibit of her paintings, an interest of her later years, was shown in New York. She left France in 1939 and died in Rockport, Massachusetts, on June 9, 1940.

Scudder, Vida Dutton 1861–1954 writer, educator, and reformer

Born on December 15, 1861, in Madura, India, Julia Vida Scudder was the daughter of a Congregationalist missionary. In 1862 she was brought to the United States by her widowed mother. She grew up in Boston, attended Miss Sanger's School and the Boston Girl's Latin School, and in 1884 graduated from Smith College. She then studied Elizabethan literature for a year at Oxford, and about that time she came under the influence of John Ruskin and various socialist authors. In 1887 she was appointed an instructor of English at Wellesley College; Smith College awarded her an M.A. degree in 1889, and at Wellesley she advanced to assistant professor in 1892 and to full professor in 1910.

In 1888 she joined the Companions of the Holy Cross, a semimonastic group of about 50 Episcopalian women devoted to prayer and the accomplishment of social harmony. She was also a member of the activist Church of the Carpenter in Boston. She was a founder of the College Settlements Association in May 1890 and of the Denison House Settlement in Boston later that year. She became a lecturer for the Society of Christian Socialists as well. In 1903 she helped organize the Women's Trade Union League, and in 1912 her support of the striking textile workers in Lawrence, Massachusetts, led to widespread newspaper criticism of her and of Wellesley; the college remained nonetheless steadfast in defense of her right to speak and act freely. She retired from teaching in 1928.

Among Scudder's written works were *The Life of the Spirit in the Modern English Poets*, 1895, *The Witness of Denial*, 1896, *Social Ideals in English Letters*, 1898, *Introduction to the Study of English Literature*, 1901, *A Listener in Babel; Being a Series of Imaginary Conversations Held at the Close of the Last Century and Reported by Vida D. Scudder*, based on her experiences at Denison House, 1903, *Saint Catherine of Siena as Seen in Her Letters*, which she edited and translated, 1905, *The Disciple of a Saint*, 1907, *Socialism and Character*, 1912, *Le Morte D'Arthur of Mallory and Its Sources*, 1917, *Brother John*, 1927, *The Franciscan Adventure; a Study in the First Hundred Years of The Order of St. Francis of Assisi*, 1931, *On Journey*, an autobiography, 1937, *The Privilege of*

Age, 1939, and *Father Huntington, Founder of the Order of the Holy Cross*, 1940. She also edited editions of works of Ruskin, Macaulay, Shelley, John Woolman, and the Venerable Bede. She died in Wellesley, Massachusetts, on October 9, 1954.

Seaman, Elizabeth Cochrane (*Nellie Bly*) 1867?–1922 journalist

Born in Cochran Mills, Armstrong County, Pennsylvania, on May 5, 1867 (or perhaps 1865), Elizabeth Cochran (she later added the final "e") received scant formal schooling. She began her career in journalism in 1885 as a reporter for the *Pittsburgh Dispatch*. It was on this paper that she began using the pen name "Nellie Bly," from a popular Stephen Foster song. Her first articles, on conditions among working girls in Pittsburgh, on slum life, and on other similar topics, marked her as a reporter of ingenuity and concern. In 1886–1887 she traveled for several months through Mexico, sending back reports on official corruption and the lives of the poor that caused her expulsion from the country; her articles were subsequently collected in *Six Months in Mexico*, 1888.

Nellie Bly

In 1887 she left Pittsburgh for New York City and went to work for Joseph Pulitzer's *New York World*. One of her first undertakings for that paper was to get herself committed to the asylum on Blackwells (now Roosevelt) Island by pretending insanity, in order to write an exposé of conditions among the patients. Her account, published in the *World* and later collected in *Ten Days in a Mad House*, 1887, precipitated a grand-jury investigation of the asylum and brought about some improvements in patient care. Similar reportorial exploits took her into sweatshops, jails (after pretending to shoplift), and the legislature (where she exposed bribery in the lobbyist system). She was far and away the best known woman journalist of her day.

The high point of her career in Pulitzer's sensational style of journalism began in November 1889 and ended in January 1890. During that period she traveled alone around the world by steamer, train, ricksha, and other commercial conveyances in the record time of 72 days, 6 hours, and 11 minutes, in a highly publicized attempt to beat the time of Phileas Fogg, the hero of Jules Verne's novel *Around the World in Eighty Days*. The resulting work, *Nellie Bly's Book: Around the World in Seventy-two Days*, 1890, was her greatest success. In April 1895 she married Robert L. Seaman, a New York businessman 45 years her senior, and retired to private life. After his death in 1910 she attended to his business interests in Brooklyn for some years with slight success. In 1919 she returned to journalism with the *New York Journal*. She died in New York City on January 27, 1922.

Sedgwick, Anne Douglas 1873–1935 writer

Born on March 28, 1873, in Englewood, New Jersey, Anne Sedgwick grew up in Irvington-on-Hudson, New York, and from the age of nine in London, where her father had business connections. In her youth she also spent two years with grandparents in Chillicothe, Ohio. She was educated privately and at eighteen took up the study of painting in Paris. In 1898 a novel she had written for private amusement was, through her father's efforts, published in London as *The Dull Miss Archinard*. The success of that book led her to turn out *The Confounding of Camelia*, 1899, *The Rescue*, 1902, *Paths of Judgment*, 1904, *The Shadow of Life*, 1907, *A Fountain Sealed*, 1907, *Anabel Channice*, 1908, and *Franklin Winslow Kane*, 1910, in rapid order.

Writing in much the same vein as Edith Wharton and, before her, Henry James, Anne Sedgwick used the contrast of the mores and morals of different cultures — American, English, French — to propel her characters through studies in social conflict. *Tante*, 1911, her first major success, was a best-seller in the United States. *The Nest*, a collection of stories, 1912, and *The Encounter*, 1914, followed. During World War I she and her husband, essayist Basil de Sélincourt (whom she had married in December 1908) left their comfortable home in Oxfordshire to work in hospitals and orphanages in France. She resumed her writing after the war, producing *A Childhood in Brittany Eighty Years*

Ago, nonfiction, 1919, *Autumn Crocuses* (in the United States *Christmas Roses*), stories, 1920, *The Third Window*, 1920, *Adrienne Toner*, 1922, *The Little French Girl*, another best-seller, 1924, *The Old Countess*, 1927, *Dark Hester*, 1929, and *Philippa*, 1930. In 1931, during her last visit to the United States, she was elected to the National Institute of Arts and Letters. After a lengthy illness she died in Hampstead, England, on July 19, 1935.

Sedgwick, Catharine Maria 1789–1867 writer

Born in Stockbridge, Massachusetts, on December 28, 1789, Catharine Sedgwick was a daughter of Theodore Sedgwick, lawyer, congressman, and later senator and judge of the state supreme court. She attended district schools and boarding schools in Albany and Boston, all for brief periods, and read widely in her father's library. From the time of her mother's death in 1807 and her father's remarriage the next year she spent much time with brothers and sisters in Albany and New York City. At the urging of her brother Theodore she undertook to write a tract on the bigotry of orthodox Calvinism — she had herself become a Unitarian and a devoted follower of William Ellery Channing — and by the time of its anonymous publication in 1822 the tract had evolved into a novel, *A New-England Tale*, which enjoyed considerable success. It was remarkable in its lively and accurate portrayal of the scenes and characters of her native Berkshire Hills. She followed with *Redwood*, 1824, *Hope Leslie*, 1827, *Clarence*, 1830, and *The Linwoods*, 1835, establishing a firm reputation as a novelist and contributing significantly to the development of a native literature.

For two decades thereafter Sedgwick's literary work consisted of stories and tracts on various moral topics that were published in periodicals and gift books and such volumes as *Home*, 1835, *The Poor Rich Man, and the Rich Poor Man*, 1836, *Live and Let Live; or Domestic Service Illustrated*, 1837, *Means and Ends; or Self-Training*, 1839, *Letters from Abroad to Kindred at Home*, 1841, *Wilton Harvey*, a collection of stories, 1845, *Morals of Manners*, 1846, *Facts and Fancies for School-Day Reading*, 1848, *Married or Single?*, her last novel, 1857, and *Memoir of John Curtis, a Model Man*, 1858. For decades she divided her time between Stockbridge and later Lenox, Massachusetts, where her summer home was a gathering place for visiting American and foreign notables, and New York City. Virtually her only venture into public affairs was her participation in the work of the Women's Prison Association of New York, of which she was "first director" from its incorporation in 1854 until her death (when she was succeeded by Sarah Platt Doremus). She died in West Roxbury (now part of Boston), Massachusetts, on July 31, 1867.

Sembrich, Marcella 1858–1935 singer

Born on February 15, 1858, in Wisnieczyk, Galicia (then part of Austrian Poland, now of Ukraine), Praxede Marcelline Kochanska was the daughter of an itinerant musician and teacher. After taking lessons from him she entered the conservatory in Lemberg (now Lvov) in 1869 and studied piano under Wilhelm Stengel. She also studied violin and harmony. In 1873 she left Lemberg for Vienna, where both Franz Liszt and the singer Mathilde Marchesi advised her to concentrate on her singing. While continuing to study piano under Julius Epstein she began vocal lessons with Victor Rokitansky of the Vienna Conservatory. In 1875 she went to Milan to study with Giovanni and Francesco Lamperti. In May 1877 she married her old teacher, Wilhelm Stengel. The next month she made her operatic debut in *I Puritani* in Athens. In 1878 she began a two-year engagement with the Saxon Royal Opera in Dresden. At that time she adopted her mother's maiden name, Sembrich, as her professional name.

In 1880 Sembrich won a five-year contract from the Royal Italian Opera company of London and made her debut there in June in *Lucia di Lammermoor* at Covent Garden. During that period she sang a command performance (with Adelina Patti) for Queen

Victoria at Buckingham Palace in 1881, sang for Czar Alexander II at the Winter Palace, St. Petersburg, in 1882, and made her American debut at the Metropolitan Opera, New York City, in *Lucia di Lammermoor* in October 1883. She sang some 55 performances of 11 different operas that season, and in April 1884, at a benefit concert for the Met's manager, Henry E. Abbey, she amazed the audience by singing a selection from *Il Barbiere di Siviglia*, playing solo violin in a De Beriot concerto, and as an encore playing a Chopin mazurka on the piano. For the next several years she sang in Austria, Germany, Russia, Scandinavia, France, and Spain. In 1895 she returned to Covent Garden, and in 1897 she gave a series of concert recitals in New York. In 1898, after a new management under Maurice Grau had reintroduced Italian opera, she returned to the Met, where she sang each season until 1909. In that period several highly publicized incidents earned her a reputation as a tempestuous prima donna. At the height of her career, the 1905–1906 season, she was paid $1000 each for 45 performances.

Among Sembrich's favorite roles were those in *La Traviata*, *Rigoletto*, *Pagliacci*, *Le Nozze di Figaro*, *Don Giovanni*, and *La Bohème*. Her voice, a brilliant and flute-like soprano of marked sweetness and remarkable range, was accounted one of the greatest of the time. She and Enrico Caruso were a favorite team; they were on tour together in San Francisco at the time of the earthquake of April 1906. She retired after a final performance of *La Traviata* in January 1909 and a farewell performance in a mixed bill the next month. She continued active on the concert stage until 1917, the year of her husband's death. Thereafter she devoted herself to teaching, both privately and from 1924 at the Juilliard School in New York City and the Curtis Institute in Philadelphia. Among her pupils was Alma Gluck. She died in New York City on January 11, 1935.

Semple, Ellen Churchill 1863–1932 geographer

Born in Louisville, Kentucky, on January 8, 1863, Ellen Semple was privately educated. She graduated from Vassar College in 1882. She taught school in Louisville while continuing informally to read history, economics, and related topics. She received an M.A. degree from Vassar in 1891 on the basis of a written examination and then traveled to Germany to study under the anthropogeographer Friedrich Ratzel at the University of Leipzig. Although not allowed to matriculate, she attended Ratzel's lectures — sitting apart from the male students — and was permanently influenced by his methods and ideas. After a year she returned to Louisville, and in 1893 she and a sister founded the Semple Collegiate School for girls, where she taught for two years. In 1895 she returned to Leipzig for further study, after which she again settled in Louisville.

Semple's first published work, an article titled "The Influence of the Appalachian Barrier upon Colonial History," appeared in the *Journal of School Geography* in 1897 and was followed by other similar writings. In 1903 she published *American History and Its Geographic Conditions*, which attracted considerable attention among professional colleagues and was adopted as a textbook by several colleges. In 1906 she was invited to lecture on anthropogeography at the University of Chicago, and she continued to lecture there for a term every other year until 1924.

Her second book, *Influences of Geographic Environment, on the Basis of Ratzel's System of Anthropo-Geography*, 1911, had been undertaken originally, at Ratzel's urging, to present his ideas to the English-speaking world. In its final form, however, the book's ideas were more Semple's than Ratzel's, and she was widely hailed by colleagues for having made a monumental contribution to the field. In 1914 the American Geographical Society awarded her its Cullum Medal. After an 18-month world tour, during which she studied methods of Japanese agriculture, Mongolian desert trade, and other geographic questions, and after a summer teaching at Oxford, she returned to work on a major study of Mediterranean geography.

She taught courses at Wellesley College in 1914–1915, at the University of Colorado in 1916, and at Columbia University in 1918. During World War I she contributed several geographical studies to the groundwork being done under Colonel Edward M. House for President Wilson's eventual role in the Paris Peace Conference. In 1921 she was named lecturer in the new Graduate School of Geography at Clark University, and two years later she advanced to professor of anthropogeography. She held that post for the rest of her life. Also in 1921 she was elected president of the Association of American Geographers, becoming the first woman to hold that office.

Semple's last book appeared in 1931 as *The Geography of the Mediterranean Region: Its Relation to Ancient History*. In 1932 she was awarded the gold medal of the Geographic Society of Chicago. She died in West Palm Beach, Florida, on May 8, 1932.

Seton, Elizabeth Ann Bayley 1774–1821 saint of the Roman Catholic Church

Born in New York City on August 28, 1774, Elizabeth Bayley was the daughter of a distinguished physician. She grew up in New York City and in nearby New Rochelle and evidently was educated privately. She married William M. Seton, a New York City merchant, in January 1794. She was much preoccupied with the problems of the poor. and devoted a good deal of time to working among them. In November 1797 she joined Isabella M. Graham and others in founding the first charitable institution in New York City, the Society for the Relief of Poor Widows with Small Children, of which she was treasurer for seven years. In 1803 she and her husband and the eldest of their five children traveled to Italy for her husband's health, but, in part perhaps as an aftereffect of his bankruptcy three years earlier, he died there in December. She returned to New York City and, as a result of her experiences and acquaintances in Italy, joined the Roman Catholic church in March 1805. She found it difficult to earn a living, in part because many friends and relatives shunned her after her conversion. For a time she operated a small school for boys.

In June 1808 Seton accepted an invitation from the Reverend William Dubourg, president of St. Mary's College in Baltimore, to open a school for Catholic girls in that city. Several young women joined in her work, and in March 1809 her long-held hope to found a religious community was realized when she and her companions took vows before Archbishop John Carroll and became the Sisters of St. Joseph, the first American-based Catholic sisterhood. In June 1809 Mother Seton and the sisters moved their home and school to Emmitsburg, Maryland. Her taking poor girls of the parish into the school was later to be seen by many as the beginning of Catholic parochial education in the United States. In January 1812 the order became the Sisters of Charity of St. Joseph under a modification of the rule of the Sisters of Charity of St. Vincent de Paul. Houses of the order were opened in Philadelphia in 1814 and in New York City in 1817. Mother Seton continued to teach and work for the community until her death in Emmitsburg, Maryland, on January 4, 1821, by which time the order had 20 communities. In 1856 Seton Hall College (now University) was named for her. Her cause was proposed in 1907. She was declared venerable in December 1959 and beatified in March 1963, and in September 1975 she became the first native-born American to be canonized.

Severance, Caroline Maria Seymour 1820–1914 reformer and clubwoman

Born on January 12, 1820, in Canandaigua, New York, Caroline Seymour grew up there and from 1824 in nearby Auburn. She attended a series of private girls' schools and graduated from the Female Seminary of Geneva, New York, in 1835. She taught in similar schools until her marriage in August 1840 to Theodoric C. Severance, a banker with whom she settled in Cleveland. From her husband's family she quickly absorbed an interest in the various reform movements of the day — temperance, abolition, women's rights, and others — and together they helped form the liberal Independent Christian

Church. She attended women's-rights conventions in Akron in 1851 and in Syracuse, New York, in 1852, and in May 1853 she presided over the first convention of the Ohio Woman's Rights Association. Also in 1853 she read a paper on "Humanity; a Definition and a Plea" before the Mercantile Library Association of Cleveland; she was subsequently invited to repeat the address in the Theodore Parker Fraternity Lecture Course in Boston. In May 1854 she presented the Ohio legislature with a memorial asking for property rights for women.

In 1855 Severance and her husband moved to Boston, whose intellectual atmosphere she found much to her liking. She became a frequent lecturer on abolitionism. In 1862 she was named to the board of directors of the New England Hospital for Women and Children, newly founded by her friend, Dr. Marie Zakrzewska. In 1866 she joined Susan B. Anthony in organizing the American Equal Rights Association, and in 1867 she joined Lucretia Mott and others in forming the Free Religious Association. In February 1868, after some months of discussion with friends, she led in founding the New England Women's Club, which preceded New York's Sorosis by a month as a pioneer organization for women. She served as president until 1871 (when she was succeeded by Julia Ward Howe). Through the club she helped establish the Girls' Latin School of Boston and worked to secure the election of women to the city school board. In 1869 Severance joined Lucy Stone in organizing the American Woman Suffrage Association.

In 1875 she and her husband moved again, this time to Los Angeles where they founded the first Unitarian congregation in that city. In 1876 she invited Emma Marwedel to establish the California Model Kindergarten and the Pacific Model Training School for Kindergartners in Los Angeles. In 1878 she organized a women's club in the Unity Church, but it lapsed in 1880 when she was absent for a time. It was again active as the Los Angeles Woman's Club in 1885–1888. In 1885 she founded the Los Angeles Free Kindergarten Association. In 1891 she formed a third women's club, the Friday Morning Club, of which she was president for three years. The Friday Morning Club became an active force behind numerous movements for reform. In 1900–1904 she served as president of the reactivated Los Angeles County Woman Suffrage League. In 1911, at the age of ninety-one, she was the first woman to register to vote under California's new woman suffrage law. She died in Los Angeles on November 10, 1914.

Sewall, May Eliza Wright 1844–1920 educator and reformer

Born in Greenfield, Wisconsin, on May 27, 1844, May Wright attended schools in Wauwautosa and Bloomington. She taught school in Waukesha for a time and then entered Northwestern Female College (later absorbed by Northwestern University), from which she graduated in 1866. (She received an M.A. degree in 1871.) Over the next several years she taught school in Corinth, Mississippi, was principal of the high school in Plainwell, Michigan, and from 1872 to 1880 was a teacher at a high school in Indianapolis. Widowed in 1875, she was married a second time in October 1880 to Theodore L. Sewall, also a teacher.

In 1882 they founded the Girls' Classical School of Indianapolis, with which Sewall was associated for a quarter-century. After her husband's death in 1895 she served as principal until 1907. During that period she also became widely known for her efforts in the women's-rights movement. She had helped found the Indianapolis Equal Suffrage Society in 1878, and in 1881–1883 she led a campaign that narrowly failed to secure woman suffrage in Indiana. From 1882 to 1890 she was chairman of the executive committee of the National Woman Suffrage Association. She was an early member of the Association of Collegiate Alumnae, founded in 1882, and the next year she helped organize the Western Association of Collegiate Alumnae, of which she was president in

1886 and 1888–1889 (both groups later were absorbed into the American Association of University Women).

In 1888 she and Frances Willard took charge of a convention of women held in Washington, D.C., to mark the 40th anniversary of the Seneca Falls women's-rights convention. From the Washington meeting emerged the National Council of Women, of which Sewall was first recording secretary and later, in 1897–1899, president. The International Council of Women, formally organized in 1889 also grew out of the Washington meeting, and she served as its president from 1899 to 1904. In 1889 she joined in organizing and was elected first vice-president of the General Federation of Women's Clubs. During 1891–1892 she traveled extensively in Europe to build support for the World's Congress of Representative Women, of which she was chairman, to be held in conjunction with the World's Columbian Exposition in Chicago in 1893. In 1900 President William McKinley appointed her U.S. representative at the Paris Exposition Universelle.

Sewall's last years were devoted principally to the cause of peace. In 1915 she called and presided over the International Conference of Women Workers to Promote Permanent Peace, held in San Francisco in conjunction with the Panama-Pacific Exposition. In December 1915 she was a member of the delegation aboard Henry Ford's peace ship *Oscar II*, managed by Rosika Schwimmer. At home in Indianapolis she had been a member of the Indianapolis Woman's Club since its founding in 1875 and had planned its clubhouse, the Propylaeum, opened in 1891. She had also been a founder in 1883 of the Indianapolis Art Association and its school (from 1902 the John Herron Art Institute) and in 1890 of the Contemporary Club.

Among Sewall's written works were *Women, World War, and Permanent Peace*, 1915, and *Neither Dead Nor Sleeping*, an account of her experiences in spiritualism, 1920; she edited *The World's Congress of Representative Women*, 1894, and other reports. She died in Indianapolis on July 23, 1920.

ROLLIE MC KENNA

Anne Sexton

Sexton, Anne 1928–1974 poet

Born on November 9, 1928, in Newton, Massachusetts, Anne Harvey attended Garland Junior College for a year before her marriage in August 1948 to Alfred M. Sexton II. They lived in New York and Massachusetts for some years and in Baltimore and San Francisco while Alfred Sexton served in the navy during the Korean War. She worked at various times as a fashion model and as a librarian. In 1954 they settled in Newton. Although she had written some poetry in childhood, it was not until the later 1950s that she began to write seriously. Her poems, showing the influence of Robert Lowell, appeared in *Harper's*, the *New Yorker*, *Partisan Review*, and other periodicals, and her first book, *To Bedlam and Part Way Back*, was published in 1960. The book won immediate attention because of the intensely personal and relentlessly honest self-revelatory nature of the poems recording her nervous breakdown and recovery. Their imagery was frequently brilliant, and their tone was both mocking and vulnerable.

In 1961–1963 Anne Sexton was a scholar at the Radcliffe Institute for Independent Study. Her second book of poems, *All My Pretty Ones*, appeared in 1962 and continued in the vein of uncompromising self-exploration. In 1964–1965 she held a traveling fellowship from the American Academy of Arts and Letters. Her *Selected Poems* was published in 1964. *Live or Die*, 1966, won a Pulitzer Prize and was followed by *Poems by Thomas Kinsella, Douglas Livingstone and Anne Sexton*, 1968, *Love Poems*, 1969, *Transformations*, 1971, *The Book of Folly*, 1972, *The Death Notebooks*, 1974, *The Awful Rowing Toward God*, 1975, and *45 Mercy Street*, edited by her daughter, Linda Gray Sexton, and published posthumously in 1976. She taught at Boston University in 1970–1971 and at Colgate University in 1971–1972. In 1969 her play *Mercy Street* was produced at the

American Place Theatre in New York City. She also wrote a number of children's books with Maxine W. Kumin, including *Eggs of Things*, 1963, *More Eggs of Things*, 1964, *Joey and the Birthday Present*, 1971, and *The Wizard's Tears*, 1975. She took her own life on October 4, 1974, in Weston, Massachusetts.

Shafer, Helen Almira 1839–1894 educator

Born on September 23, 1839, in Newark, New Jersey, Helen Shafer grew up there and later in Oberlin, Ohio. She graduated from Oberlin College in 1863. After two years of teaching in New Jersey she joined the faculty of St. Louis High School, where her work as a teacher of mathematics attracted the favorable notice of the superintendent of St. Louis schools, William Torrey Harris, later U.S. commissioner of education. In 1877 she was given the chair of mathematics at the two-year-old Wellesley College.

Her work in establishing high standards in mathematics at Wellesley was widely noted, and the quality of work done by her students was generally held to be higher than that of students at Harvard. In 1888 she succeeded Alice E. F. Palmer as president of Wellesley. Under her administration the college's curriculum was reorganized and considerably broadened, and the elective system that was long to remain in effect with few modifications was introduced. She also oversaw a liberalization of the social life of the college. Her work at Wellesley was cut short by tuberculosis; she died in Wellesley, Massachusetts, on January 20, 1894.

Shalala, Donna Edna 1941– U.S. Secretary of Health and Human Services

Born on February 14, 1941 in Cleveland, Ohio, Donna Shalala was raised by her father, a real estate salesman who was a leader in the Syrian-Lebanese community, and her mother, a physical-education teacher. Her mother, one of the people she most admired, was a former athlete who earned a law degree while working two jobs and raising twin daughters. In high school Shalala was both a dedicated student and an excellent athlete herself, winning championships in softball and tennis. She attended Western College in Oxford, Ohio, earning a B.A. in 1962. After graduation she spent two years in the Peace Corps in Iran. Upon her return, she entered Syracuse University where she earned a master's degree in social science in 1968 and a Ph.D. in 1970. She spent the next nine years teaching political science and education at the university level at the City University of New York's Bernard Baruch College and at Columbia University's Teachers College.

In 1975, while still teaching, she served as the director and treasurer of the Municipal Assistance Corporation, credited with helping rescue New York City from near bankruptcy. From 1977 to 1980 Shalala worked as the assistant secretary for policy research and development at the Department of Housing and Urban Development (HUD) in Washington, D.C. In this position, she worked primarily on women's issues — setting up shelters, establishing mortgage credits, and pressing for anti-discrimination measures.

In 1980 she returned to the university setting once again, this time as president of Hunter College in New York City, a position she held for eight years. In large part due to her success at Hunter, she was named chancellor of the University of Wisconsin at Madison in 1988, making her the first woman to preside over a Big Ten school. At Madison, among other achievements, she set out to soothe racial tensions, instituting the "Madison Plan" to create a more ethnically diverse university in both curriculum and population. In her position at the University of Wisconsin, she earned both praise for her liberal politics, self-assurance, and ability to get things done, and criticism for what some called her tendency to play both sides of the fence. All agreed, however, that fund-raising was one of her strong points; she brought in more than 400 million dollars from private sources while serving as chancellor.

In 1993 she was selected by President Bill Clinton to be Secretary of Health and Human

Services. Her main objectives in her new position included revising the financial structure of the nation's health-care system, implementing a nationwide immunization plan, and continuing and expanding AIDS research. When President Clinton's health-care plan became a hotly contested congressional issue in 1994, Shalala was a key player as both a dynamic leader with a proven track record and a strong advocate. While she didn't always act in lockstep with the Clinton administration, like the president, she believed strongly in strengthening government programs while at the same time asking more from their recipients.

Shaw, Anna Howard 1847–1919 clergyman, physician, and suffragist

Born in Newcastle-on-Tyne, England, on February 14, 1847, Anna Shaw was brought to the United States in 1851. She grew up in New Bedford and Lawrence, Massachusetts, and from 1859 on an isolated frontier farm near Big Rapids, Michigan. The absence of her father, the nervous breakdown of her mother, and the illness of an elder brother forced twelve-year-old Anna to undertake clearing the land, planting crops, finishing the poor cabin, and caring for the family. She received a year or two of schooling, which she supplemented with omnivorous reading on her own, and at fifteen she became a teacher in a frontier schoolhouse. At the end of the Civil War she moved to the home of a married sister in Big Rapids and enrolled in the local high school.

Shaw became active in the Methodist church, preached her first sermon in 1870, and was licensed to preach in 1871. In 1873 she entered Albion College, where she worked her way through two years of studies. In 1876 she entered the divinity school of Boston University, from which she graduated in 1878 after two years of nearly desperate poverty. In October 1878 she took charge of a church in East Dennis, Massachusetts. Her application for ordination (her license did not permit her to administer sacraments) was refused by the New England Conference of the Methodist Episcopal Church and then by the General Conference, which took the further step of revoking her license. Finally, in October 1880, she was granted ordination by the Methodist Protestant Church. While ministering to her East Dennis Methodist congregation and also to a nearby Congregational one, she undertook medical studies in 1883 at Boston University. She resigned her pastorates in 1885 and became a lecturer for the Massachusetts Woman Suffrage Association.

In 1886 Shaw received her M.D. degree from Boston University. She did not practice medicine, however, but instead turned to the professional lecture platform in 1887. Temperance and woman suffrage were her principal themes, and she was inevitably drawn into the organized movements for those reforms. From 1888 to 1892, at the request of Frances Willard, she headed the Franchise Department of the Woman's Christian Temperance Union. A meeting with Susan B. Anthony in 1888 led her into the work of the National Woman Suffrage Association. In 1891 she became national lecturer for the merged National American Woman Suffrage Association, and from 1892 to 1904 she was vice-president of the organization. During those years she traveled and lectured indefatigably, and she was accounted the most eloquent and moving orator in the suffrage cause. Disappointed in not succeeding Susan Anthony as president of the National American Woman Suffrage Association 1900, she did succeed Carrie Chapman Catt in 1904 and held the post until 1915. Her shortcomings as an administrator and as a political strategist contributed to the schism of militant suffragists led by Alice Paul in 1914 and the formation of the rival Congressional Union.

In April 1917, on the entry of the United States into World War I, Shaw was named chairman of the Woman's Committee of the United States Council of National Defense. Her work in that post busied her until March 1919 and earned her the Distinguished Service Medal in May. She then intended to return to the lecture circuit on behalf of the pending suffrage amendment, but former President William Howard Taft and President

A. Lawrence Lowell of Harvard prevailed upon her to exercise her oratorical skills instead in the cause of President Woodrow Wilson's League of Nations plan. In the midst of a highly successful speaking tour she fell ill, and she died at her home in Moylan, Pennsylvania, on July 2, 1919.

Sigourney, Lydia Howard Huntley 1791–1865 poet

Born in Norwich, Connecticut, on September 1, 1791, Lydia Huntley attended local schools and academies in Hartford. In 1811 she opened a school for girls in Norwich, and in 1814 she moved to Hartford and opened a similar school. In 1815 she published *Moral Pieces in Prose and Verse*, in part for the use of her pupils. Giving up her school, in June 1819 she married Charles Sigourney, a Hartford businessman. Her verse *Traits of the Aborigines of America* was published anonymously in 1822. With the decline of her husband's business about 1830 she began to turn out poetry and essays for various newspapers and magazines, as well as a great many books. The latter included *Biography of Pious Persons*, 1832, *How to Be Happy*, 1833, *Letters to Young Ladies*, her most popular work, 1833, *Poems*, 1834, *Sketches*, 1834, *History of Marcus Aurelius, Emperor of Rome*, 1836, *Select Poems*, 1838, *Pocahontas, and Other Poems*, 1841, *Poems, Religious and Elegiac*, 1841, *Pleasant Memories of Pleasant Lands*, 1842, *The Voice of Flowers*, 1846, *The Weeping Willow*, 1847, *Illustrated Poems* (a magnificently produced book that matched similar volumes devoted to Bryant and Longfellow), 1849, *Whisper to a Bride*, 1850, *Olive Leaves*, 1852, *The Faded Hope*, 1853, *Past Meridian*, 1854, *The Western Home*, 1854, *The Daily Counsellor*, 1859, *Gleanings*, 1860, and *The Man of Uz*, 1862.

Many of her 67 books reprinted topical selections from earlier ones. Her poems were especially popular features of annuals and gift books, and she herself edited one, *The Religious Souvenir*, for 1839 and 1840. She was probably the nation's most widely read poet during her lifetime. Such editors as Louis Godey of the *Lady's Book* and Edgar Allan Poe of *Graham's Magazine* vied for contributions from "the sweet singer of Hartford." Sentimental, affectedly elegant, frequently concerned with death, her writings had little literary merit; their vogue was passing already by the end of her life. She died in Hartford, Connecticut, on June 10, 1865. Her autobiography, *Letters of Life*, appeared in 1866.

Silko, Leslie Marmon 1948– poet and novelist

Born in Albuquerque, New Mexico, on March 5, 1948, of mixed Laguna Pueblo, white and Mexican ancestry, Leslie Marmon Silko commuted 100 miles a day to go to high school in Albuquerque. After graduating with honors from the University of New Mexico in 1969, she entered law school but left to do graduate work in English and pursue a writing career.

Storytelling had been a large part of Silko's life since childhood, when she listened to her great-grandmother and great aunts tell tales based in Laguna folklore and history. The stories she heard about the trickster Coyote's adventures and raids of neighboring tribes on the Laguna pueblo shaped Silko profoundly, giving her a strong sense of identity and heritage. The tales, she said, "incorporate you into them. There have to be stories. It's stories that make this a community."

Often referred to as the premier Native American writer of her generation, Silko drew on the stories of her community of origin, illuminating both ancient and contemporary themes. She combined concerns of Laguna spirituality, such as the relationship between human beings and the natural elements, with complex portrayals of contemporary struggles to retain Native American culture in an Anglo world.

Silko published *Ceremony*, 1977, to great critical acclaim. The novel tells the story of the relationship between a returning World War II veteran of mixed Laguna and Anglo heritage and a tribal wise man who attempts to help him heal the psychic wounds of war.

The title alludes not to a specific ritual or form, but to a mode of conduct and attitude toward changes in the cosmos that are inherent in tribal philosophy.

Silko's second novel, *Almanac of the Dead*, 1991, explored similar themes, this time through the lives of two Native American women. One, a survivor of the drug culture, returns to the Southwest to search for her missing child; the other, a celebrated psychic, turns her gifts to the task of transcribing the history of her people as preserved in a set of ancient texts.

After the publication of *Ceremony*, Silko began to receive recognition for her earlier collections of poetry and short stories, including *Storyteller*, 1971, and *Laguna Woman*, 1974. In 1985 she published a book of correspondence between nature poet James Wright and herself, *With the Delicacy and Strength of Lace: Letters Between Leslie Marmon Silko and James Wright*.

She taught English at Navajo Community College in Many Farms, Arizona, and the University of New Mexico. In 1978 she accepted a position to teach in the English department at the University of Arizona. She was awarded a MacArthur Foundation Fellowship.

Sill, Anna Peck 1816–1889 educator

Born in Burlington, New York, on August 9, 1816, Anna Sill attended a local rural school. At twenty she began teaching in a school in Barre, New York. In 1837 she entered Miss Phipps' Union Seminary in Albion, New York, and the next year she became a teacher there. In 1843 she opened a seminary in Warsaw, New York, and from 1846 to 1849 she headed the female department of the Cary Collegiate Institute in Oakfield, New York. For some years she had wavered between teaching and foreign missionary work; deciding at length in favor of teaching, she accepted in July 1849 an invitation to open a girls' school in Rockford, Illinois. It was the hope of Rockford's citizens that such a school would grow into the female seminary for which the Society for the Promotion of Collegiate and Theological Education in the West (founder of Beloit College) had already obtained a charter. The school opened with 60 pupils. In September 1850 it was indeed chosen as the foundation for the seminary, and in June 1852, with the seminary already crowded and a second building under construction, Anna Sill was confirmed as principal of Rockford Female Seminary. In 1854 a three-year course was instituted, and it was lengthened to four in 1865.

Anna Sill exercised a firm discipline over her students, only gradually evolved a pedagogy more advanced than rote learning of religious and classical matter, and was always primarily concerned with education as a tool of religion. Nonetheless she maintained high standards and made the school a leader in women's education in the Midwest. During the 1870s she began urging that the school be raised to collegiate status. It became a degree-granting institution in 1882, although not until ten years later was the name changed to Rockford College. Anna Sill retired in 1884 and continued to live on the campus until her death there on June 18, 1889.

Sills, Beverly 1929– opera singer

Born in Brooklyn, New York, on May 25, 1929, Belle Silverman was early destined by her mother for a career in the performing arts. At three, as Bubbles Silverman, she began a four-year stint as a regular singer on "Uncle Bob's Rainbow House," a Saturday morning radio program. She won a prize on "Major Bowes' Amateur Hour" at six, made a couple of motion-picture shorts, and became a regular on "Major Bowes Capitol Family Hour" and later on the soap opera "Our Gal Sunday," on which she played a "nightingirl of the mountains." At twelve she retired to complete her education in public schools and the Professional Children's School in New York, from which she graduated in 1945. She studied singing with Estelle Liebling for many years. For ten years she toured almost constantly with the Gilbert and Sullivan Opera Company, with the Charles Wagner Opera Company, and under other auspices, gradually developing a repertoire in grand opera.

In 1955 Sills joined the New York City Opera, making her debut in October in *Die Fledermaus*. Over the next several years she broadened her repertoire remarkably and built a reputation as a truly outstanding coloratura soprano. Her impeccable vocal precision, her musicality, her dramatic flair, and her vivid personality all combined to make her a favorite of audiences and of other musicians. Among the works in which she performed were *La Traviata*, *The Siege of Corinth*, *Faust*, *Julius Caesar*, *Lucia di Lammermoor*, *Don Giovanni*, *The Magic Flute*, and *The Tales of Hoffmann*, in which in October 1965 she dazzled critics by singing all three female roles. In July 1956 she sang in the premiere of Douglas Moore's *The Ballad of Baby Doe* and in October 1961 she sang in the premiere of his *Wings of the Dove*. In 1966 she sang Rameau's *Hippolyte et Aricie* with Sarah Caldwell's Opera Company of Boston. Her *Manon* with the New York City Opera in February 1969 was a great success, but it was eclipsed by the thunderous reception of her performance in *The Siege of Corinth* in her La Scala debut in April 1969. She made her London debut at Covent Garden in 1971 and her long-awaited Metropolitan Opera debut, again in *The Siege of Corinth*, in April 1975.

From 1971 Sills appeared also on the concert stage. Her personal charm and warmth made her popular even among non-musical audiences, and she was a frequent guest on television talk shows. In 1976 she had her own local television show in New York City, "Lifestyles with Beverly Sills," for which she won an Emmy award. She published an autobiography, *Bubbles: a Self-Portrait*, in 1978, and a second, *Beverly*, in 1987.

Among her many awards and honors are New York City's Handel Medallion in 1973, the Pearl S. Buck Women's Award in 1979, the Presidential Medal of Freedom in 1980, and the Kennedy Center honors. She retired from the opera and concert stage in 1980, having turned her skills toward management as general director of the New York City Opera in 1979. She remained in that post until 1989, also serving as president of the Board from 1980 to 1990. In 1991 she moved to the Metropolitan Opera as managing director. In 1994 Sills was the first woman elected chair of Lincoln Center.

Simms, Ruth Hanna McCormick 1880–1944 public official

Born in Cleveland on March 27, 1880, Ruth Hanna was a daughter of Mark Hanna and a niece of James Ford Rhodes. She attended the Hathaway-Brown School in Cleveland, the Masters School in Dobbs Ferry, New York, and Miss Porter's in Farmington, Connecticut. She received an education in practical spheres by accompanying her father as he attended to business and labor problems and to the organization and campaigns of the Republican party.

In June 1903 she married Joseph Medill McCormick of the Chicago newspaper family. President Theodore Roosevelt attended the wedding. She and her husband shared an interest in progressive social ideas and reform and for a time lived at the University of Chicago Settlement of Mary E. McDowell. She was active in the National Civic Federation the Women's Trade Union League, the National Child Welfare Association, and the Illinois Consumers' League. In 1913 she lobbied the Illinois legislature to great effect on behalf of the bill to grant women the franchise, and in 1913–1915 she headed the Congressional Committee of the National American Woman Suffrage Association. She also lobbied the legislature on behalf of child-labor and minimum wage legislation.

With her husband McCormick supported Roosevelt's breakaway Progressive party in 1912, but she later returned to Republican regularity. She supported military preparedness before World War I and opposed the Versailles treaty and the League of Nations afterward. In December 1918 she was named first chairman of the newly established women's executive committee of the Republican National Committee, and in 1920 she became a member of the executive committee of the national committee. In 1924 she was chosen national committeewoman from Illinois. Following her husband's defeat for reelection to his Senate seat in 1924 and his death in 1925 she became yet more active. After organizing scores of local Republican women's clubs throughout the state she ran successfully for an at-large congressional seat in 1928; her 1.7 million votes (a 400,000 plurality) led the ticket in Illinois.

In 1930 McCormick entered and won the Republican primary for a Senate seat but was defeated by Senator J. Hamilton Lewis in November after a campaign marked by charges against her of political expediency and excessive campaign expenditures. She then turned to her business interests: a group of three newspapers in Rockford, Illinois, that she had bought in the late 1920s and combined in 1930, and a radio station. In March 1932 she married Albert G. Simms, a former congressman from New Mexico. In 1934 she founded the Sandia School for Girls in Albuquerque, New Mexico. Much of her time was spent at her Illinois dairy farm and at ranches in Wyoming and later in New Mexico and then near Fort Garland, Colorado. She reentered active politics in 1939 as co-chairman of the preconvention Dewey for President Committee. In 1944 she again served on the Republican National Committee and again supported Thomas E. Dewey for the presidential nomination. She died in Chicago on December 31, 1944.

Skinner, Constance Lindsay 1877–1939 writer, critic, editor, and historian

Born on December 7, 1877, in Quesnel, British Columbia, Constance Annie Skinner (she later adopted "Lindsay," her mother's maiden name) was the daughter of an agent for the Hudson's Bay Company and grew up at a trading post on the Peace River. She was educated at home and, after the family moved to Vancouver when she was fourteen, in private schools. At sixteen she moved for her health to the home of an aunt in California. Her literary proclivities had already found outlet in the publication of stories in various newspapers, and in California she began contributing music and theatrical criticism to the *San Francisco Examiner* and the *Los Angeles Times*.

In 1910 her first play, *David*, was produced at the Forest Theatre in Carmel. She later moved to Chicago and wrote for the *Chicago American* for three years. She eventually settled in New York City, where she contributed book reviews to the *Herald Tribune* and published articles and poems regularly in the *Bookman*, the *North American Review*, *Poetry*, and other magazines. *Good Morning, Rosamund!*, her second play, was produced in New York in 1917.

Invited to contribute two volumes to the Yale University Chronicles of America series, Skinner produced *Pioneers of the Old Southwest*, 1919, and *Adventurers of Oregon*, 1920. *Adventures in the Wilderness*, with Clark Wissler and William C. H. Wood, 1925, was published in the Yale Pageant of America series. Turning to fiction, she wrote a series of adventure tales for children, all based on frontier life; they included *Silent Scot, Frontier Scout*, 1925, *Becky Landers, Frontier Warrior*, 1926, *White Leader*, 1926, *Roselle of the North*, 1927, *Tiger Who Walks Alone*, 1927, *Andy Breaks Trail*, 1928, *Ranch of the Golden Flowers*, 1928, *The Search Relentless*, 1928, *Red Man's Luck*, 1930, *Debby Barnes, Trader*, 1932, and *Rob Roy, the Frontier Twins*, 1934. She also wrote a novel for adults, *Red Willows*, 1929; *Songs of the Coast Dwellers*, a highly praised collection of poems inspired by the legends of the Squamish Indians of British Columbia, 1930; and another work of history, *Beaver, Kings and Cabins*, on the fur trade, 1933.

Skinner's histories, while vivid and highly readable, occasionally sacrificed scholarship, but they successfully evoked the landscapes that were among their principal actors. In 1935 the publishing firm of Farrar & Rinehart accepted her proposal that she edit a historical series based on the major rivers of America. The first volume in the series, Robert P. Tristram Coffin's *Kennebec: Cradle of Americans*, appeared in 1937. The series eventually extended to more than 40 volumes. Constance Skinner died in New York City on March 27, 1939, before completing her work as general editor of the series or as author of the Missouri River volume.

Smedley, Agnes 1894–1950 journalist and writer

Born in 1894 (or perhaps 1892), probably in northwest Missouri (and possibly in the town of Osgood), Agnes Smedley grew up from the age of ten in the mining town of Trinidad, Colorado. She went to work at an early age to help support the family and received little formal schooling. She left home at sixteen. Over the next several years she taught school in New Mexico, worked as a secretary and as a traveling book agent, attended the Normal School in Tempe, Arizona, in 1911–1912, attended a summer session at the University of California at Berkeley, and went through a brief unhappy marriage. About 1916 or 1917 she moved to New York City, where she worked for a magazine and attended classes at New York University. She gradually involved herself in political affairs.

Smedley became interested in the cause of Indian nationalism as represented by Lala Laipat Rai, and in March 1918 she was arrested under the Espionage Act and charged with failure to register as an agent for the Indian Nationalists, who, unbeknownst to her, had accepted funds from Germany. She was held in the Tombs in New York for some time before the charges were dismissed, and she became thoroughly disenchanted with the United States. From 1919 to 1928 she lived in Berlin with the Indian nationalist leader Virendranath Chattopadhyaya. She taught English at the University of Berlin, did graduate work in Asian studies there, and helped establish Germany's first public birth-control clinic. In part as an aid to her psychoanalysis she wrote the autobiographical novel *Daughter of Earth*, 1929.

In 1928 Smedley went to China as special correspondent for the *Frankfurter Zeitung*. From her base in Shanghai she traveled widely and reported enthusiastically on the growing Communist movement. She worked with the writers Lu Hsün and Mao Tun in preparing propaganda pieces. She lost her connection with the *Frankfurter Zeitung* in 1930 and began writing for the *Manchester Guardian*. In 1933 she published *Chinese Destinies: Sketches of Present-Day China* and in 1934, during a brief visit to New York, *China's Red Army Marches*, a glowing endorsement of the movement. She returned to China in 1935 and in 1936 began a journey to reach Communist-controlled northern China. She was in Sian in December 1936 and made English-language broadcasts on the brief capture of Chiang Kai-shek by rebellious Manchurian troops. Early in 1937 she reached Mao Tse-tung's headquarters in Yenan. She underwent great hardships to travel with the Eighth Route Army (the Red Army) during the Sino-Japanese War and in 1938 published *China Fights Back: An American Woman with the Eighth Route Army* on her experiences in Shansi Province. In January 1938 she went to Hankow, where she worked with the Chinese Red Cross Medical Corps, collected supplies for the Red Army, and served as a publicist for the Communists. On the fall of Hankow in October 1938 she made her way to join the New Fourth Army, a Communist guerrilla force in Japanese-controlled areas, with which she traveled through central China until 1940, filing reports from time to time with the *Manchester Guardian*.

After a period of illness Smedley returned to the United States in 1941. She published *Battle Hymn of China* in 1943. She wrote and spoke widely on behalf of the Chinese Communists, although to an increasingly hostile America. While she was an avid partisan, she was not a blind one, and she never joined the Communist party, her own political position being closer to anarchism than to disciplined socialism. In February 1949 General Douglas MacArthur released an army intelligence report that charged her with being a Soviet spy. She responded with outrage and threatened legal action, whereupon the secretary of the army admitted that the charge rested on no evidence. Her reputation was irreparably damaged, however, and she could find no journalistic employment. In November 1949 she sought refuge in England, where she worked to complete *The Great Road: The Life and Times of Chu Teh*, her biography of the Chinese Communist military leader that was published finally in 1956. She died in Oxford, England, on May 6, 1950. Her ashes were interred in the National Revolutionary Martyrs Memorial Park in Peking.

Smith, Abby Hadassah and Julia Evelina 1797–1878 and 1792–1886
suffragists

Born in Glastonbury, Connecticut, Abby on June 1, 1797, and Julia on May 27, 1792, the Smith sisters, youngest of five, were educated largely at home. The farm homestead where they were born was their home all their lives, except for Julia's few years as a teacher at Emma Willard's Troy Female Seminary. They were active in temperance work and local charities; reflecting the influences of both parents, they were notably independent in judgment and action. By 1869 Abby and Julia, seventy-two and seventy-seven respectively, were the only surviving members of the family. In that year, aroused by inequities in local tax rates, they attended a woman suffrage meeting in Hartford, and in October 1873 Abby traveled to New York to attend the first meeting of the Association for the Advancement of Women.

In November 1873 they attended the Glastonbury town meeting, where Abby read a spirited protest against the taxation of unenfranchised women. She and Julia thereafter refused to pay taxes unless they were granted the right to vote in town meetings. In January 1874 seven of their valued Alderney cows were seized and sold for taxes. At a second town meeting in April Abby was refused permission to speak, whereupon she mounted a wagon outside and delivered her protest to the crowd. In June authorities seized 15 acres of their pastureland, valued at $2,000, for delinquent taxes amounting to about $50. The sale of the land was conducted irregularly, however, and after a protracted suit, during the course of which the sisters were nearly driven to study law themselves, they succeeded in having it set aside. Their cows, which they had been able to buy back, were twice more taken for taxes and soon became a cause célèbre throughout the country and even abroad as newspapers spread the story. Published versions of Abby's speeches, along with witty and effective letters by both of them to various newspapers, brought them considerable prominence.

In 1877 Julia edited and published *Abby Smith and her Cows, with a Report of the Law Case Decided Contrary to Law*. (The year before she had published a translation of the Bible she had made 20 years earlier.) They spoke at numerous suffrage meetings. In January 1878 Julia testified before the Senate Committee on Privileges and Elections, then considering a suffrage amendment, and in March Abby testified before a committee of the Connecticut legislature. Abby Smith died in Glastonbury, Connecticut, on July 23, 1878. The next year Julia married and moved to Hartford, where she died on March 6, 1886.

Smith, Amanda Berry 1837–1915 evangelist and missionary

Born a slave in Long Green, Maryland, on January 23, 1837, Amanda Berry grew up in York County, Pennsylvania, after her father had bought his own freedom and that of most of the family. She was educated mainly at home and at an early age began working as a domestic. An unhappy first marriage ended with the disappearance of her husband in the Civil War and left her with a daughter. In Philadelphia in 1863 she married James Smith, a coachman and a deacon in a local Methodist church. They later moved to New York City, where in her husband's long absences she began attending the Tuesday Meetings of Phoebe W. Palmer. An experience of sanctification in September 1868 led to her first hesitant attempts at preaching. By 1869 her husband and her children had died, and she was preaching regularly in African-American churches in New York and New Jersey.

Smith's success in preaching before a white audience at a holiness camp meeting in the summer of 1870 led her to commit herself entirely to evangelism. Her travels over the next eight years took her as far afield as Tennessee and Maine, and in 1878 she sailed for England, where she spent a year evangelizing at holiness meetings. From 1879 to 1881 she was in India, where her success as an evangelist was a marvel to colleagues. After another brief stay in England she sailed late in 1881 for West Africa. For eight years she did missionary work in Liberia and Sierra Leone. Following another sojourn in Great Britain in 1889–1890 she returned to the United States. She preached in eastern cities until 1892, when she moved to Chicago.

In 1893 she published *An Autobiography*. The proceeds of the book, together with her savings, the income from the a small newspaper she published, and gifts from others enabled her to open a home for African-American orphans in Harvey, Illinois, in 1899. Eventually she resumed preaching and singing in order to support the home. In 1912, when she retired to Sebring, Florida (a retirement made possible through the beneficence of real estate developer George Sebring), the home was taken over by the state of Illinois and chartered as the Amanda Smith Industrial School for Girls. She died in Sebring, Florida, on February 24, 1915. The school continued until destroyed by fire in 1918.

Smith, Bessie 1898?–1937 singer

Born in Chattanooga, Tennessee, probably on April 15, 1898 (but perhaps 1894), Elizabeth Smith grew up in poverty and obscurity. She may have made a first public appearance at the age of eight or nine at the Ivory Theatre in her hometown. About 1919 she was discovered by Gertrude "Ma" Rainey, one of the first of the great blues singers, from whom she received some training. For several years she traveled through the South singing in tent shows and bars and theaters in small towns and in such cities as Birmingham, Atlanta, Selma, Memphis, and Savannah.

Bessie Smith

After 1920 she made her home in Philadelphia, and it was there that she was first heard by the recording director of Columbia Records. In February 1923 she made her first recordings, including the classic "Down Hearted Blues," which became an enormous success, selling more than two million copies. She continued her stage appearances in the cities of the North and her successful recording career. She made 160 recordings in all, in many of which she was accompanied by some of the great jazz musicians of the time, including Fletcher Henderson, Benny Goodman, and Louis Armstrong. Her idiom was the classic material of blues singers — poverty, oppression, stoic perseverance, and love. As the self-styled "Empress of the Blues" she played to large and predominantly black audiences in New York, Chicago, Boston, and other major cities. In 1929 she made a short motion picture, *St. Louis Blues*, that was generally banned from circulation for its realism.

In the late 1920s, when the kind of music she sang began to diminish in popularity and at the same time the advent of radio cut into the record market, her career began to wane. Excessive drinking and the breakup of her marriage nearly destroyed her and her career. When a birth of interest in jazz and blues among white audiences during the Depression of the 1930s gave hope of a renewed career, she made plans to cut more records. But she was injured in an automobile accident near Clarksdale, Mississippi, and died on September 26, 1937. The legend soon grew up that she had bled to death after being refused admittance to a white hospital. It was only decades after her death that, through the recordings she left, she was generally recognized as one of the greatest of blues singers.

Smith, Eliza Roxey Snow 1804–1887 Mormon leader and poet

Born on January 21, 1804, in Becket, Massachusetts, Eliza Snow grew up from the age of two in Mantua, Ohio. She attended a local "Grammatical Institution" and in her youth won a local reputation as a poet with verses published in various newspapers. Her family was deeply religious and in the 1820s joined the Campbellite sect of "reformed Baptists."

Mormon proselytizers came to their region of Ohio about 1830, and in 1831 Joseph Smith himself called at the Snow home. In 1835 Eliza Snow and her mother joined the Mormons, and in April she was baptized by Smith at the Mormon settlement in Kirtland.

In December 1836 Snow moved to Kirtland and became a boarding governess to Joseph Smith's children. She also conducted a school for girls. She accompanied the Mormon migration to Jackson County, Missouri, and thence back to Nauvoo, Illinois. In June 1841, after Smith's revelation concerning polygamy, she became one of Joseph Smith's plural wives. In Nauvoo she played a leading part in creating the role of women in the Mormon church. She became secretary of the Female (later Women's) Relief Society on its formation in March 1842 and pioneered in "temple work," the ritual, genealogical and administrative tasks that were to become permanent tradition.

Eliza Smith emigrated to "Deseret" — Utah — in 1847 in one of the first companies of Mormon pioneers. In 1849 she was sealed to Brigham Young as one of his plural wives. In May 1855 she was given charge of the Endowment House, where religious work was conducted before any temples were built, and in 1866 she became general president of the Women's Relief Society. In that post she oversaw the development of cooperative stores, women's classes, various charitable works, and the opening of a women's hospital in 1882. In 1869 Brigham Young gave her responsibility for the newly organized Young Ladies' Retrenchment Association, a group formed to combat a decline in public decorum.

Under her guidance the association evolved in 1878 into the Young Ladies' Mutual Improvement Association, which remained an important lay organization in the church. In 1880 she was named president of Mormon women's organizations throughout the world. In the midst of these activities she had found time to accompany her brother, Lorenzo Snow (president of the church in 1898–1901), on a missionary tour of Palestine in 1872–1873. She also continued to write throughout her life; of her several hymns, "O My Father, Thou That Dwellest" remained the best known. She published two volumes of *Poems, Religious, Historical and Political* in 1856 and 1877 and a *Biography and Family Record of Lorenzo Snow*, 1884. She died in Salt Lake City on December 5, 1887.

Smith, Hannah Whitall 1832–1911 writer, evangelist, and reformer

Born in Philadelphia on February 7, 1832, Hannah Whitall grew up in a strict Quaker home and was educated in the Friends' School. She had from childhood a deep concern with religion and a habit of introspection, In June 1851 she married Robert P. Smith, also a Quaker. During the years of their residence in Germantown, Pennsylvania, she continued to brood on religion and, in her later recollections, passed through several stages of faith and understanding. In 1865 the family moved to Millville, New Jersey, where she and her husband came under the influence of the Wesleyan-based "holiness" movement, a revivalistic creed based on sanctification by faith and the direct experience of salvation. Robert Smith soon began preaching at holiness camp meetings, and in 1889 he began publishing in Philadelphia the periodical *Christian's Pathway to Power*, to which Hannah Smith contributed frequently. She began preaching as well.

In 1874 Smith traveled to England to join her husband, who had gone over a year before, and the two became the most prominent figures in the interdenominational "Higher Life" movement that swept up masses of followers in 1873–1875. By eloquence and appearance Hannah Smith won the title of "angel of the churches" in her evangelistic addresses to huge gatherings throughout Britain. Their work there came to a sudden end in 1875 when Robert Smith was implicated in a scandal, and they returned to Philadelphia.

Hannah Smith then turned to writing. Her *Record of a Happy Life; Being Memorials of Franklin Whitall Smith*, a memoir of her late son, had appeared in 1873. In 1875 she published *The Christian's Secret of a Happy Life*, a guide to sanctification and complete surrender to divine will that was translated into several foreign languages and sold some 2 million copies around the world. Subsequent books included *John M. Whitall: The Story of His Life*, 1879, *Every-day Religion; or, the Common-sense Teaching of the Bible*, 1893, *The Unselfishness of God and How I Discovered It: A Spiritual Autobiography*, 1903, and *Walking in the Sunshine*, 1906, and she also wrote numerous pamphlets, tracts, and articles. She became a prominent advocate of providing opportunities for women to obtain college educations and in that regard was a strong influence on her niece, M. Carey Thomas. She helped found the Woman's Christian Temperance Union in 1874 and in 1883 became superintendent of its new Evangelistic Department.

In 1888 Smith and her husband moved to London, where their home was frequented by such persons as Bernard Berenson (who married their daughter Mary), Bertrand Russell (who married their daughter Alys), George Bernard Shaw, Henry and William James, Israel Zangwill, Sidney and Beatrice Webb, and George Santayana. Hannah Smith continued to work with the British Women's Temperance Association, to preach occasionally, and to write. She died in Iffley, near Oxford, on May 1, 1911. Her son, Logan Pearsall Smith (1865–1946), became a noted British essayist and critic. A collection of her essays was edited by Ray Strachey and published in 1928 as *Religious Fanaticism: Extracts from the Papers of Hannah Whitall Smith*.

Smith, Jessie Willcox 1863–1935 painter and illustrator

Born in Philadelphia on September 8, 1863, Jessie Smith was educated in private schools. At sixteen she entered the School of Design for Women in Philadelphia. During 1885–1888 she studied under Thomas Eakins at the Pennsylvania Academy of Fine Arts, and in 1886–1887 she also studied portraiture under William Sartain at the School of Design for Women. She had already sold a few drawings to *St. Nicholas* magazine when in 1894 she enrolled in a class in illustration conducted by Howard Pyle at the Drexel Institute of Arts and Sciences (now Drexel University). She also attended his informal classes at a studio on the Brandywine and in 1900 his private school in Wilmington, Delaware. Through Pyle she received her first commissions, to illustrate two books about Native Americans, and in 1897, with her friend and fellow student Violet Oakley, she illustrated an edition of Longfellow's *Evangeline*.

A bronze medal-winning exhibit at the Charleston Exposition in 1902 brought her to national attention, and in 1903 she won the Mary Smith Prize for best entry by a woman in the annual show of the Pennsylvania Academy of Fine Arts. She won a silver medal at the Louisiana Purchase Exposition in St. Louis in 1904 and a silver medal at the Panama-Pacific Exposition in San Francisco in 1915. In 1903 she and another friend, Elizabeth Shippen Green, who shared home and studio with Smith and Oakley, produced an illustrated calendar entitled "The Child" that was a large commercial success. From that time onward she received a steady flow of commissions.

Smith's illustrations, particularly of children, appeared regularly in *Ladies' Home Journal*, *Scribner's*, *Collier's*, *Harper's*, *Century*, and *Good Housekeeping*, for the last of which she painted cover illustrations regularly for many years. Advertising illustration was another lucrative field in which she became much sought-after. She illustrated a number of children's books as well, including Betty Sage's *Rhymes of Real Children*, 1903, *The Child's Book of Old Verses*, compiled by herself, 1910, P. W. Coussens's *Child's Book of Stories*, 1911, Robert Louis Stevenson's *A Child's Garden of Verses*, 1914, Louisa May Alcott's *Little Women*, 1915, Priscilla Underwood's *When Christmas Comes Around*, 1915, Charles Kingsley's *Water Babies*, 1916, Mary Stewart's *Way to Wonderland*, 1917, George MacDonald's *At the Back of the North Wind*, 1919, Ada M. and Eleanor L. Skinner's *Child's Book of Modern Stories*, 1920, Johanna Spyri's *Heidi*, 1922, the

Skinners' *Little Child's Book of Stories*, 1922, *Very Little Child's Book of Stories*, 1923, and *Child's Book of Country Stories*, 1925, and *The Children of Dickens*, 1925. She died in Philadelphia on May 3, 1935.

Smith, Kate 1909–1986 singer and TV host

Born in Greenville, Virginia, on May 1, 1909, Kathryn Elizabeth Smith started singing before audiences as a child, and by the time she was seventeen she had decided on a career in show business. She went to New York City in 1926 and landed a role in a Broadway musical, *Honeymoon Lane*, the same year. In a succession of Broadway shows she had little chance to sing, however; she was wanted mainly for comic "fat girl" roles that she despised. Her chance as a full-time singer came when she met Ted Collins, an executive with Columbia Records, in 1930. He became her manager and guided her career until his death in 1964. She appeared at the Palace Theatre in New York City for a record long-running engagement, and in May 1931 she made her radio debut.

It was on her first broadcast that she adopted her theme song, "When the Moon Comes over the Mountain." Within a short time she had become the most popular singer on radio. In 1936 she moved to a weekly half hour evening show hosted by Collins, and in 1938 she added "Kate Smith Speaks," a daytime talk program broadcast three times a week. During the 1930s her evening show became one of the most popular on the air, and in the 1940s she was known as the "First Lady of Radio." In 1933 she made a motion picture, *Hello, Everybody*. In 1938 she acquired the exclusive right to sing Irving Berlin's "God Bless America" over the air, and it was that song more than any other, with which her name was thereafter associated. In 1939 President Franklin Roosevelt introduced her to King George VI by saying, "This is Kate Smith. Miss Smith is America."

Of her more than 2000 recordings, 19 sold over a million copies each. In 1943 she appeared in the movie version of *This Is the Army*, an Irving Berlin musical. During World War II she performed notable service by selling more war bonds than anyone else — $600 million worth — and she entertained troops throughout the country with her traveling show. Smith remained on daytime radio until 1954, and in September 1950 went on television with "The Kate Smith Hour," also a daytime show. In the 1952–1953 season she added an hour-long evening show.

After 1956 she retired from television, although she returned for a season in 1960. She made a concert debut in Carnegie Hall in November 1963, and in 1964 she resumed a limited schedule of nightclub performances. Thereafter she was an occasional guest star on television. She wrote two volumes of autobiography, *Living in a Great Big Way*, 1938, and *Upon My Lips a Song*, 1960, and in 1958 published her *Company's Coming Cookbook*. In 1982 she was awarded the Presidential Medal of Freedom. She died on June 17, 1986, in Raleigh, North Carolina.

Smith, Margaret Chase 1897–1995 public official

Born in Skowhegan, Maine, on December 14, 1897, Margaret Madeline Chase attended local public schools and after graduating from high school in 1916 taught school briefly and held a series of other jobs. During 1926–1928 she served as president of the Maine Federation of Business and Professional Women's Clubs. In May 1930 she married Clyde H. Smith, a local political figure and co-owner of the Skowhegan *Independent Reporter*, for which she had earlier worked. From 1930 to 1936 she was a member of the state Republican committee, and after her husband's election to Congress in 1936 she worked as his secretary. He died in April 1940, and two months later she was chosen in a special election to complete his term. Almost immediately she displayed the independent judgment that became characteristic of her political career by breaking with her Republican colleagues to vote in favor of the Selective Service Act in September. In that month she was elected to a full term in Congress, and she was returned to her seat three more times.

During her eight years in the House of Representatives Smith served on the Naval Affairs Committee and later on the Armed Services Committee and concerned herself particularly with the status of women in the armed forces. She played a major role in the passage of the Women's Armed Services Integration Act of June 1948 that gave women equal pay, rank, and privileges. In 1948 she ran successfully for a seat in the Senate, winning it by a record plurality in Maine. In service on the Armed Forces, Appropriations, Government Operations, and Rules committees, among others, she quickly established herself as an outspoken legislator of high integrity and considerable influence. She was generally liberal on domestic issues and a strong supporter of national defense and security. She was an early opponent of Senator Joseph R. McCarthy, at a time when the majority of her Republican colleagues still considered him a great asset to the party. Reelected by large majorities in 1954, 1960, and 1966, she served in the Senate longer than any other woman. She received several votes for the presidential nomination at the 1964 Republican National Convention. Her defeat for reelection in 1972 by Rep. William V. Hathaway turned mainly on the question of her age and health; she had campaigned little.

Among her many honors were several citations as woman of the year and the *Newsweek* magazine press poll rating as Most Valuable Senator for 1960. In 1968 she published *Gallant Women*, biographies of twelve Americans for young readers, with H. Paul Jeffers, and in 1972 she published *Declaration of Conscience*, on the United States government. From 1973 she served as visiting professor at many universities, as chair of the board of Freedom House, New York City, from 1970 to 1977, and as a director of the Lilly Endowment. She died at her Skowhegan home on May 29, 1995.

Smith, Sophia 1796–1870 philanthropist

Born in Hatfield, Massachusetts, on August 27, 1796, Sophia Smith was the daughter of a prosperous farmer. She attended a local school and for one term a school in Hartford, Connecticut. In youth and young womanhood she showed little ambition, and although she enjoyed the rural social life of Hatfield she did not marry. She became deaf at forty and thereafter stayed at home much of the time. Her father died in 1836, leaving a substantial estate to his four children, three of whom continued to live on the family farm. Sophia's energetic younger sister Harriet died in 1859, and her brothers Joseph and Austin, the latter of whom had greatly multiplied his inheritance through shrewd stock speculation, followed in 1861.

At sixty-five the retiring Sophia Smith was left with a fortune. The responsibility of using it wisely caused her to seek the advice of the pastor of the Hatfield Congregational church, the Reverend John Morton Greene. She declined to contribute money to Amherst College (his alma mater) or to Mount Holyoke Female Seminary (his wife's), whereupon he suggested the foundation of a women's college. She inclined rather to the endowment of an institution for deaf-mutes and drew up her will accordingly, but the opening of the Clarke School for the Deaf in Northampton in 1868 turned her thoughts back to a women's college. Greene and two Amherst professors drew up a "Plan for a Woman's College," which Sophia Smith accepted and incorporated into a new will. A last revision of her will in 1870 provided that the college should be located in Northampton rather than in Hatfield. She died in Hatfield, Massachusetts, on June 12, 1870, and her bequest for the college amounted to over $393,000. Smith College was accordingly chartered in 1871 and opened in 1875 with 14 students; it went on to become one of the leading women's colleges in the nation.

Smith, Zilpha Drew 1852?–1926 social worker

Born probably on January 25, 1852 (although town records say 1851), in Pembroke, Massachusetts, Zilpha Smith grew up in East Boston (now part of Boston). She graduated from the Girls' High and Normal School of Boston in 1868. After working as a telegrapher for a time, she took on the demanding job of revising the index of the Suffolk County probate court. In 1879 she became registrar of the newly organized Associated Charities of Boston, in which the city's principal social welfare agencies had been consolidated. It was her task to realize in practical terms the theory that was the foundation of the Associated Charities and of the similar charity organization groups that soon sprang up in other cities: the confidential investigation and registration of all charity cases, the cooperation of agencies in handling them, and an emphasis on "friendly visiting" to attack the causes of poverty believed to lie in the family.

Under Smith's administration the Boston Associated Charities processed cases with an efficiency unmatched by similar groups. Both paid and unpaid agents were used in a system in which responsibilities were allotted by district, and she pioneered in establishing training classes for district administrators and later for agents and for volunteer friendly visitors. She also set a precedent in setting up discussion groups for agents. Representatives of charity organizations elsewhere (such as Mary Richmond of Baltimore) visited Boston frequently to study Smith's methods. From 1886 she held the title of general secretary, and she remained in that post until 1903, when she was succeeded by Alice Louise Lothrop.

From 1904 to 1918 Smith was associate director of the new Boston School for Social Workers. She also lectured occasionally at the New York School of Philanthropy and elsewhere, and she published several articles on organized charity work and the evolving technique of casework, to which she contributed both practically and theoretically. She died in Boston on October 12, 1926.

Solomon, Hannah Greenebaum 1858–1942 clubwoman and welfare worker

Born in Chicago on January 14, 1858, Hannah Greenebaum was of a well-to-do family deeply involved in local Jewish affairs. She attended public schools and for a time studied piano seriously. In 1877 she and a sister became the first Jewish members of the recently formed Chicago Woman's Club. In May 1879 she married Henry Solomon, a businessman. Family cares kept her from involvement in public affairs for several years, but in 1890 she was named to a committee of women charged with organizing a World's Parliament of Religions to be held in conjunction with the World's Columbian Exposition.

As an adjunct to the parliament she planned a Jewish Women's Congress, which on assembling in 1893 became the first such general convention of American Jewish women ever to be held. The congress established the permanent National Council of Jewish Women, of which Solomon was elected first president, a post she held until 1905. (She served thereafter as honorary president for life.) In 1896 she helped organize the Illinois Federation of Women's Clubs. In the same year she conducted a statistical survey of the schools and other public agencies available in the rapidly growing Jewish immigrant district of Chicago, and the next year she founded the Bureau of Personal Service to provide guidance to new immigrants. She headed the Bureau until it was absorbed by the Associated Jewish Charities of Chicago in 1910. In 1899 she was elected treasurer of the National Council of Women, and with Susan B. Anthony and May Wright Sewall she represented the council at the International Council of Women meeting in Berlin in 1904. She worked closely with Jane Addams and other Chicago welfare workers on matters relating to child welfare.

In 1905 she became interested in the Illinois Industrial School for Girls. Under her leadership the school was rehabilitated and in 1907 moved from Evanston to Park Ridge. She served on the school's board for many years and in 1906–1909 was president. In 1910 she helped found the Women's City Club of Chicago, for which she headed a committee of inspection of the city waste disposal system. During World War I she directed the

Chicago work of the Illinois Council of Defense. She largely retired from public service in the early 1920s. A collection of her articles and speeches was published as *A Sheaf of Leaves* in 1911, and in 1946 *Fabric of My Life*, her autobiography, appeared posthumously. She died in Chicago on December 7, 1942.

Sontag, Susan 1933– writer and critic

Born in New York City on January 28, 1933, Susan Sontag grew up in Tucson, Arizona, and later in Los Angeles and nearby Canoga Park. She attended public schools and the University of California at Berkeley for a year and in 1951 graduated from the University of Chicago. She then pursued graduate studies in English and philosophy at Harvard. While there she collaborated on *Freud: the Mind of the Moralist*, 1959, with Philip Rieff, to whom she was married in 1950–1959. She attended the University of Paris in 1957–1958, and after a short period on the editorial staff of *Commentary* she taught philosophy at the City College of New York for a year, at Sarah Lawrence College for a year, and at Columbia University for four years.

In 1962 Sontag began contributing essays and reviews to such journals as the *Partisan Review*, *Second Coming*, *New York Review of Books*, *Evergreen Review*, *Film Quarterly*, and the *Nation*. In her examinations of various facets of contemporary art, literature, and behavior, she attempted to elucidate a consistent modern aesthetic in which the immediate sensations of the observer were the paramount fact of an aesthetic transaction. Her discussions of the anti-novel, pornography, aleatory music, camp, and similar phenomena made her a principal theoretician and champion of the avant-garde.

In 1963 she published a novel, *The Benefactor*, that was well received critically and in 1966 a collection of essays under the title *Against Interpretation*, which provoked several controversies among literary and cultural critics. *Death Kit*, a novel, appeared in 1967 and was followed by *Trip to Hanoi*, originally a magazine piece that was issued in paperback in 1969, *Styles of Radical Will*, essays, 1969, an edition of Antonin Artaud's *Selected Writings*, 1976, *On Photography*, an investigation of the philosophical implications of that medium, 1977, *Illness as Metaphor*, an extended philosophical meditation based on her experiences as a cancer patient, 1978, and *I, Etcetera*, a collection of short stories, 1978. She also wrote the screenplays for and directed the motion pictures *Duet for Cannibals*, 1969, *Brother Carl*, 1971, and *Promised Lands*, 1974. In 1980 she published a collection of essays, *Under the Sign of Saturn* followed by *AIDS and its Metaphors*, 1989, and *The Volcano Lover: A Romance*, 1992.

From 1987 to 1989 she served as President of the PEN American Center. She continued to work in theatre and was one of the few Americans to travel to Sarajevo to protest the lack of American involvement in the Bosnia-Herzegovina conflict in 1993. In 1994 she produced Samuel Beckett's *Waiting for Godot* in Sarajevo. Among her many awards are the National Institute and American Academy Award for Literature, 1976, and the 1994 Montblanc Cultural Award for her humanitarian efforts in Sarajevo. She was named an officer in the French Order of Arts and Letters in 1984.

Spalding, Catherine 1793–1858 religious

Born in Charles County, Maryland, on December 23, 1793, Catherine Spalding was taken to frontier Kentucky by her widowed mother about 1799. She was later orphaned and reared by relatives. In December 1812 the Reverend (later Bishop) John David announced his plan to establish a Catholic teaching sisterhood to serve the frontier region, and the next month Catherine Spalding was one of the first three young women to answer his call. In March 1813 she was elected superior of the Sisters of Charity of Nazareth, which was established at St. Thomas's, near Bardstown. The sisters performed their own domestic and farm work, made clothing for the students of nearby St. Thomas's Seminary, visited the sick, and did other religious work. In August 1814 they opened Nazareth

Academy. The sisters took their first vows in February 1816, following which Mother Catherine was reelected superior.

She stepped down in 1819 but remained the guiding force of the group, and she served again as superior from 1824 to 1831, from 1838 to 1844, and from 1850 to 1856. During that time she saw established a school in Bardstown in 1819, St. Vincent's Academy in Union County, Kentucky, in 1820, a school in Scott County (later St. Catherine's Academy, Lexington) in 1823, a school (now Presentation Academy) in Louisville in 1831, St. Vincent's Orphan Asylum in Louisville in 1832, a hospital (now St. Joseph's) in Louisville in 1836, and the School of St. Frances at Owensboro in 1850. In addition, other sisters had been sent out to establish a school in Vincennes, Indiana, in 1824 and a school and a hospital in Nashville, Tennessee, in 1842. In 1824 the original convent moved to a new site in what is now Nazareth, Kentucky, and in 1829 the order's original Nazareth Academy received a state charter as the Nazareth Literary and Benevolent Institution. Between terms as superior Mother Catherine devoted herself to her institutions in Louisville, especially St. Vincent's Orphan Asylum. By the time of her death in Nazareth, Kentucky, on March 20, 1858, the order had grown to 145 sisters in 16 convents in Kentucky, Tennessee, and Indiana.

Spencer, Lilly Martin 1822–1902 painter

Born on November 26, 1822, in Exeter, England, Angelique Marie Martin was the daughter of French parents who emigrated to the United States in 1830. She grew up in Marietta, Ohio, and received a thorough education at home. She exhibited artistic talent from an early age and began studying drawing and oil painting with local artists. A showing of a group of paintings — portraits, genre pieces, and literary scenes — held in Marietta in 1841 was a success, and in the fall of that year she settled in Cincinnati, where in a few years she firmly established herself as a leading local artist. In August 1844 she married Benjamin R. Spencer.

In 1848 she moved to New York City, where her work had already been exhibited successfully at the National Academy of Design and the American Art-Union. The latter institution, one of a number of similar ones that flourished for a time by holding exhibitions, distributing reproductions of artworks to members, and holding annual lotteries for originals, launched Spencer as a nationally known artist. Through it and the Western Art Union, which in 1849 commissioned her "One of Life's Happy Hours," reproductions of her genre and anecdotal paintings reached thousands of homes. At an exhibit staged by the American Art-Union in 1852 her works brought higher prices than those of John J. Audubon, George Caleb Bingham, Eastman Johnson, and William S. Mount. She also received commissions for illustrations from *Godey's Lady's Book* and other magazines, illustrated such books as Elizabeth F. Ellet's *Women of the American Revolution*, 1850, and executed portraits on private commission. Among her portrait subjects were Mrs. Benjamin Harrison, Elizabeth Cady Stanton, and Robert G. Ingersoll.

In 1858 Spencer and her large family moved to Newark, New Jersey, but a few years later she took a studio in New York City, where for some years she worked on her monumental "Truth Unveiling Falsehood," which was acclaimed a masterwork on its completion in 1869. She refused as much as $20,000 for the painting; it was later lost. Her popularity declined in later years, although she continued to work. She died in New York City on May 22, 1902.

Spofford, Harriet Elizabeth Prescott 1835–1921 writer

Born on April 3, 1835, in Calais, Maine, Harriet Prescott grew up there and from 1849 in Newburyport, Massachusetts. She attended a Newburyport school and in 1853–1855 the Pinkerton Academy in Derry, New Hampshire. In part to aid the family's precarious finances, and with the encouragement of Thomas W. S. Higginson, she turned to writing.

Several of her stories were published in Boston newspapers, and in February 1859 James Russell Lowell published her tale "In a Cellar" in the *Atlantic Monthly*. Higginson soon introduced her to Boston literary society. In 1860 her first novel appeared anonymously as *Sir Rohan's Ghost*. She published *The Amber Gods*, a collection of stories, in 1863 and *Azarian: An Episode*, a novel, in 1864, before her marriage in December 1865 to Richard S. Spofford, a Newburyport lawyer. In Newburyport, for a time in Washington, D.C., where her husband's practice took them, and from 1874 in Amesbury, Massachusetts, where they built a large home, she continued to write prolifically.

Spofford's stories, essays, travel sketches, and poems appeared in the *Atlantic*, *Scribner's*, *Century*, *Harper's Bazaar*, and other leading magazines. Her published volumes included *New-England Legends*, stories, 1871, *Art Decoration Applied to Furniture*, 1878, *The Servant Girl Question*, 1881, *Poem*, 1882, *Hester Stanley at Saint Marks*, a novel, 1883, *Ballads about Authors*, 1887, *A Scarlet Poppy, and Other Stories*, 1894, *In Titian's Garden*, poems, 1897, *Old Madame, and Other Tragedies*, 1900, *The Children of the Valley*, 1901, *The Great Procession*, 1902, *Old Washington*, 1906, *The Fairy Changeling*, 1910, *The Making of a Fortune*, 1911, *A Little Book of Friends*, essays, 1916, and *The Elder's People*, stories, 1920. Her home was frequented by literary personages, especially the many women writers who were her friends. She died at her home on Deer Island in Amesbury, Massachusetts, on August 14, 1921.

Stanton, Elizabeth Cady 1815–1902 suffragist and reformer

Born on November 12, 1815, in Johnstown, New York, Elizabeth Cady was the daughter of an eminent lawyer. She received a superior education at home, at the Johnstown Academy, and at Emma Willard's Troy Female Seminary, from which she graduated in 1832. From an early age she observed her father's law practice, and many times she heard him explain to married women the details of laws that deprived them of their property and even of their children. She became interested in the abolitionist movement through her cousin, Gerrit Smith, and his daughter, Elizabeth Smith (Miller), and in May 1840 she married Henry Brewster Stanton, a prominent abolitionist. (She insisted that the word "obey" be dropped from the wedding ceremony.) Later that year they attended the World's Anti-Slavery Convention in London, and she was outraged at the denial of official recognition to several women delegates, notably Lucretia C. Mott, because of their sex. For some years thereafter the Stantons lived in Johnstown and then in Boston, where Mrs. Stanton associated with the leading liberals of the day. In 1847 they moved to Seneca Falls, New York. She spoke frequently on the subject of women's rights and circulated petitions that helped secure passage by the New York legislature in March 1848 of a bill granting property rights to married women.

Elizabeth Cady Stanton

In July 1848 she and Mott, who was visiting nearby, issued a call for a women's-rights convention to meet in Seneca Falls on July 19–20. At the meeting James Mott presided as Stanton introduced her Declaration of Sentiments, modeled on the Declaration of Independence, that detailed the inferior status of women and that, in calling for extensive reforms, effectively launched the women's-rights movement. She also introduced a resolution calling for woman suffrage that was adopted after considerable debate. From 1851 she worked closely with Susan B. Anthony; together they remained active for 50 years after the first convention, planning campaigns, speaking before legislative bodies, and addressing gatherings in conventions, lyceums, and in the streets. Stanton, the better orator and writer, was perfectly complemented by Anthony, the organizer and tactician. She wrote her own and many of Anthony's addresses, wrote countless letters and pamphlets, and contributed articles and essays to numerous periodicals, including Amelia Bloomer's *Lily*, Paulina Wright Davis's *Una*, and Horace Greeley's *New York Tribune*.

In 1854 Stanton received an unprecedented invitation to address the New York legislature; her speech bore fruit finally in new legislation in 1860 granting married women the rights to their wages and to equal guardianship of their children. During her presidency in 1852–1853 of the short-lived Woman's State Temperance Society, which she and Anthony had founded, she scandalized many of her most ardent supporters in suggesting that drunkenness be made sufficient cause for divorce. Liberalized divorce laws continued to be one of her principal issues.

The Civil War turned her back to abolitionism for a time. In May 1863 she and Anthony organized the Women's Loyal National League, which gathered more than 300,000 signatures on petitions calling for immediate emancipation. The movement to extend the franchise to African-American men after the war reemphasized the disenfranchisement of women and led her and her colleagues to redouble their efforts. In 1867 she and Anthony made an exhausting speaking and organizing tour on behalf of a proposed woman suffrage amendment in Kansas. In January 1868 she became coeditor (with Parker Pillsbury) of the newly established weekly *Revolution*, a newspaper devoted to women's rights. She continued to write fiery editorials until the paper's demise in 1870.

In May 1869 Stanton helped organize the National Woman Suffrage Association; she was named president, a post she retained throughout the organization's 21-year existence. In 1871 she and Anthony made a speaking and organizing tour of the Far West. She was the principal author of the Woman's Declaration of Rights presented at the Centennial Exposition in Philadelphia in 1876.

In 1878 Stanton drafted a federal suffrage amendment that was introduced in every Congress thereafter until substantially the same language was adopted in 1919. In addition to her labors on behalf of suffrage she became a popular lecturer on the lyceum circuit as well. With Susan Anthony and Matilda Joslyn Gage she compiled the first three volumes (1881–1886) of the six-volume *History of Woman Suffrage*, 1881–1922. She continued to contribute articles to newspapers and periodicals and published *The Woman's Bible* in two volumes, 1895–1898, and an autobiography, *Eighty Years and More*, 1898. On the merger of the National Woman Suffrage Association with the rival American Woman Suffrage Association in 1890, she was elected president of the new National American Woman Suffrage Association; she held the post until 1892. She died in New York City on October 26, 1902.

Starr, Belle 1848–1889 outlaw

Born in or near Carthage, Missouri, on February 5, 1848, Myra Belle Shirley grew up in obscurity. After the death of an elder brother, who early in the Civil War had become a bushwhacker and had perhaps ridden with William C. Quantrill's raiders, and following also the burning of Carthage in October 1863, the family moved to a farm at Scyene, near Dallas, Texas. At the end of the war the remnants of Quantrill's gang turned to undisguised outlawry, becoming notorious as the gangs led by the Younger brothers and the James brothers. They occasionally sought refuge at the Shirley farm, and Belle apparently bore a child by Thomas C. "Cole" Younger. Soon afterward she eloped with Jim Reed, a Missouri outlaw, and became his common-law wife. They lived in Los Angeles for a time and then returned to Texas. Reed was killed not long after his sensational holdup of the Austin-San Antonio stage in April 1874, and Belle Shirley was named an accessory, although not a participant, in the indictment for that crime. She operated a livery stable in Dallas for a time and continued to have sundry unsavory associations, both personal and professional.

Later she moved to Oklahoma Territory, where in 1880 she married Sam Starr, a Cherokee and long a friend of the Youngers and Jameses. Their cabin at what Belle Starr named Younger's Bend on the Canadian River (near present-day Eufaula) became a favorite hideout for outlaws of every sort. Jesse James holed up there for several months. Gradually she acquired the reputation, not certainly warranted, of a criminal mastermind whose gang preyed on travelers, ranchers, and cowboys throughout the region. In 1883 she and Sam Starr were indicted for horse stealing, and in March they were convicted by Judge Isaac C. Parker, the "hanging judge" of Fort Smith, Arkansas. They served nine months in the federal penitentiary in Detroit. She was indicted three more times in the next few years, once on a charge of taking part in a post office robbery disguised as a man, but she was never again convicted. After Sam Starr was shot and killed in December 1887, a young Cherokee named Jim July moved into her cabin. Belle Starr was shot in the back and killed at the cabin on February 3, 1889; there were several possible suspects, but no indictment was ever issued. Her gravestone, erected at Younger's Bend by her daughter, featured a carved bell and star.

A few months after her death, Richard K. Fox, publisher of the *National Police Gazette*, issued a purported biography of *Belle Starr, the Bandit Queen; or, The Female Jesse James*. Fox's picture of the beautiful Belle of Old Southern heritage who turns to crime to avenge the death of her brother, a dashing Confederate officer, long remained the popular image of her.

Stein, Gertrude 1874–1946 writer and critic

Gertrude Stein

Born on February 3, 1874, in Allegheny, Pennsylvania, Gertrude Stein was of a somewhat unsettled family. After periods in Austria and Paris, she grew up in Oakland, California. On the deaths of her parents in 1888 and 1891 she was left with a modest income. She attended the Society for the Collegiate Instruction of Women (from 1894 Radcliffe College), where she studied psychology under William James, in 1893–1897 (she received a degree in 1898) and the Johns Hopkins Medical School from 1897 to 1902. With her older brother Leo she moved in 1902 to London and in 1903 to Paris. There she and Leo quickly began collecting the works of such modern painters as Matisse, Picasso, Cézanne, Gauguin, Rousseau, Braque, Gris, and Manet. Their remarkable perspicacity and determination enabled them to amass a considerable collection, and that in turn served as the germ of what soon became the most famous salon in Paris.

Her home later became famous also as the center of the American literary expatriate movement of the 1920s; she dubbed its members the "lost generation" and was quoted to that effect in the epigraph to Ernest Hemingway's *The Sun Also Rises*. Those who frequented her home included Hemingway, F. Scott Fitzgerald, Sherwood Anderson, Wyndham Lewis, André Gide, Carl Van Vechten, Ezra Pound, Ford Madox Ford, Paul Robeson, Clive Bell, John Reed, Elliot Paul, and Jo Davidson.

Stein's writing, for which she seemed to wish to be most remembered, was as often as not baffling but to many readers fascinating nevertheless. Concerned with sound and the rhythm of words rather than with their conventional meanings, her prose style was, she claimed, a literary counterpart of abstraction or cubism in painting. A famous phrase, "Pigeons in the grass alas," was from her libretto for the opera *Four Saints in Three Acts* (which neither concerned four saints nor was presented in three acts), with music by Virgil Thomson, first produced in the United States in 1934 and many times revived.

Her books included *Three Lives*, 1909, *Tender Buttons*, 1914, *The Making of Americans*, completed in 1911 but published, with Hemingway's help, in 1925, *Lucy Church Amiably*, 1930, *Before the Flowers of Friendship Faded Friendship Faded*, 1931, *The Autobiography of Alice B. Toklas*, 1933, which was in reality her own autobiography rather than that of Toklas (her secretary and companion from 1912, when she and Leo parted), *Everybody's Autobiography*, 1937, and *Ida, a Novel*, 1941.

Among her critical and other nonfiction works were *Composition as Explanation*, 1926, *How to Write*, 1931, *Narration*, 1935, *The Geographical History of America*, 1936,

Picasso, 1938, *Paris France*, 1940, *Wars I Have Seen*, 1945, and *Brewsie and Willie*, concerning her friendships with young American servicemen in World War II, 1946. A second collaboration with Virgil Thompson produced the opera *Mother of Us All*, 1947, based on the life of Susan B. Anthony. During World War I Gertrude Stein imported a Ford motor van and enrolled herself and Toklas as an ambulance unit of the American Fund for French Wounded. In later years she and Toklas divided their time between Paris and Bilignin. Her only visit to America came in 1934, when she made a lecture tour in the wake of the success of *Four Saints*. She was not modest in her self-estimation: "Einstein was the creative philosophic mind of the century, and I have been the creative literary mind of the century." She died in Paris on July 27, 1946.

Steinem, Gloria 1934– writer, editor and feminist activist

Born in Toledo, Ohio, on March 25, 1934, Gloria Steinem spent her early years traveling around in a house trailer with her parents, until they were divorced in 1946. Gloria settled with her mother in Toledo, and for the first time she began attending school on a regular basis. Her lonely childhood was marked by the added responsibility of taking care of her mother, who was chronically depressed. She dreamed of escaping from Toledo, and planned to do so as a tap dancer. Finally, during her senior year of high school, she left, moving to Washington, D.C. to live with her older sister, Susanne.

In September 1952 she entered Smith College and earned a degree in government in 1956. She then planned to go to India to study on a Chester Bowles Asian fellowship. While waiting in England for her visa, she discovered she was pregnant. Alone, she searched for someone to perform an illegal abortion, telling no one of her situation.

In India she participated in non-violent protests against government policy there. Back in the U.S., she moved to New York City in 1960, where she undertook work as a journalist. Her first published article, a piece on the sexual revolution entitled "The Moral Disarmament of Betty Coed," appeared in a 1962 issue of *Esquire* magazine. In 1963 "I was a Playboy Bunny," an exposé recounting her experience as a waitress at Hugh Hefner's Playboy Club, became the talk of the town.

By 1968 Steinem's writing was becoming more political; she had begun writing a column, "The City Politic," for *New York* magazine. Her involvement in feminism intensified in 1968 when she attended a meeting of a radical feminist group, the Redstockings. Proud of her feminist roots — her paternal grandmother had served as president of the Ohio Women's Suffrage Association from 1908 to 1911 — Steinem founded the National Women's Political Caucus in July 1971 with Betty Friedan, Bella Abzug and Shirley Chisholm. That same year she began exploring the possibility of a new magazine for women, one that would present feminist issues and be run by and for women. The result was a sample magazine, *Ms.*, which appeared as an insert in the December 1971 issue of *New York*. The first independent issue of *Ms.* appeared in January of 1972. It included a full-page petition for safe and legal abortion, including the signatures of over fifty prominent women who had had abortions.

Her publications included *Outrageous Acts and Everyday Rebellions*, a collection of essays published in 1983, and a biography of Marilyn Monroe in 1986. *Revolution from Within*, a work on self-esteem for women was published in 1992, and *Moving Beyond Words* in 1994.

Throughout the late 1970s and 1980s, Steinem gave much of her time to political organizations. She wrote and spoke out in favor of the Equal Rights Amendment. In 1977 President Carter appointed her as one of the commissioners to the national committee on the Observance of International Women's Year. She was awarded a Woodrow Wilson Scholarship to study feminist theory, and she participated in the founding of the Coalition of Labor Union Women, Voters for Choice, and Women Against Pornography. Despite her high-profile political life, Steinem remains quiet about her private life. She never married, explaining in her own words that she "cannot mate in captivity."

Stephens, Alice Barber 1858–1932 illustrator

Born on July 1, 1858, near Salem, New Jersey, Alice Barber grew up there and in Philadelphia. She began drawing at an early age, and in 1870, while still attending public school in Philadelphia, she began taking classes at the School of Design for Women. At fifteen she began supporting herself by wood engraving, and she soon was supplying engravings to *Scribner's Monthly*, *Harper's Weekly*, *Harper's Young People*, the local *Woman's Words*, and other periodicals. In 1876 she began studying in life and portrait classes conducted by Thomas Eakins at the Pennsylvania Academy of Fine Arts.

Within a short time Barber had abandoned engraving for illustration, and her works in charcoal, color and black-and-white oil, watercolor, and other media became regular features in the *Century*, *Cosmopolitan*, *Frank Leslie's Weekly*, and the Harper publications. During 1886–1887 she studied at the Académie Julian and the school of Filippo Colarossi in Paris and visited and sketched in Italy. On her return to the United States she became a regular contributor to the *Ladies' Home Journal*. She also received numerous commissions to illustrate books, among them works of Louisa May Alcott, Margaret Deland, Bret Harte, Arthur Conan Doyle, and special editions of Longfellow's *The Courtship of Miles Standish* and Hawthorne's *The Marble Faun*. She had exhibited a pastel and an engraving at the Paris Salon in 1887; in 1890 she won the Mary Smith Prize at the Pennsylvania Academy of Fine Arts with her "Portrait of a Boy," and in 1895 she was awarded a medal at the Cotton States and international Exposition in Atlanta. The originals of her illustrations for George Eliot's *Middlemarch* and her paintings for Maria Mulock Craik's *John Halifax, Gentleman*, won a gold medal at an exhibition of women's art in London in 1899, and in 1900 she received a medal at the Exposition Universelle in Paris. From June 1890 she was married to Charles H. Stephens, an instructor at the Pennsylvania Academy.

In later years Alice Stephens taught at the School of Design for Women. In 1904 she sat on the fine arts jury of the Louisiana Purchase Exposition in St. Louis. Her later works were generally in charcoal and wash. She ceased work in 1926, and in 1929 a retrospective showing of her work was mounted by the Plastic Club of Philadelphia, of which she had been a founder. She died in Rose Valley, Pennsylvania, on July 13, 1932.

Stephens, Ann Sophia 1810–1886 editor and writer

Born in Humphreysville (later Seymour), Connecticut, on March 30, 1810, Ann Winterbotham was educated in a local school and in a school in South Britain, Connecticut. In 1831 she married Edward Stephens, a merchant with whom she settled in Portland, Maine. In 1834 her husband established and she became editor of the *Portland Magazine*, a literary monthly that continued to appear for two years. In 1836 she edited *The Portland Sketch Book*, an anthology of works by local authors.

In 1837 they moved to New York City, and Ann Stephens became associate editor of the *Ladies' Companion* magazine. In 1841–1842 she was on the staff of *Graham's Magazine*, then edited by Edgar Allan Poe, and from 1842 to 1853 she was coeditor of *Peterson's Magazine*. During those years she was also a frequent contributor to the *Lady's Wreath*, *Frank Leslie's Ladies Gazette of Fashion*, *Columbian Lady's and Gentleman's Magazine*, *Brother Jonathan*, published by her husband, and other periodicals. Her husband published her *High Life in New York*, sketches in Down East humor signed by "Jonathan Slick," in 1843. In 1854 she published *Fashion and Famine*, a novel first serialized in *Peterson's*; she followed with *Heiress of Clare Hall*, 1854, *The Old Homestead*, 1855, *Sibyl Chase*, 1860, *The Rejected Wife*, 1863, *Married in Haste*, 1870, *The Reigning Belle*, 1872, *Bertha's Engagement*, 1875, *Norston's Rest*, 1877, and many other novels. During 1856–1858 she edited her own *Mrs. Stephens' Illustrated New Monthly*; in the latter year it was merged with *Peterson's*, which continued to serialize her novels.

In 1860 she was commissioned by the Beadle & Adams Company to write the first of its new series of "Dime Novels." *Malaeska: The Indian Wife of the White Hunter* became a best-seller, and over the next four years she supplied *Myra, the Child of Adoption*, *Ahmo's Plot*, *The Indian Queen*, and three other Dime Novels to Beadle. In 1863 she edited a *Pictorial History of the War for the Union*.

Stephens was a noted literary hostess in New York City. Her popularity as an author was attested by the fact that at the time of her death a 23-volume edition of her works was in the press. She died at the home of her publisher, Charles J. Peterson, in Newport, Rhode Island, on August 20, 1886.

Stetson, Augusta Emma Simmons 1842–1928 religious leader

Born on October 12, 1842, in Waldoboro, Maine, Augusta Simmons grew up in nearby Damariscotta. She attended public schools and the Lincoln Academy in New Castle, Maine. In 1864 she married Captain Frederick J. Stetson, a member of a shipbuilding firm with whom she lived in London, in India, and in British Burma before his retirement for reasons of health. They settled in Boston, where in 1882 she enrolled in the Blish School of Oratory with the idea of becoming a professional lecturer and elocutionist.

In 1884 she attended a lecture by Mary Baker Eddy and was persuaded by Eddy herself to attend her Massachusetts Metaphysical College. On completing the three-week course in November she went to Maine to practice Christian Science. She reported a number of remarkable cures in her practice, and in 1885 she was called back to Boston as one of five preachers in Eddy's own church. In November 1886 she was sent to organize the church in New York City.

In February 1888 a Christian Science church was incorporated in New York with Stetson as preacher. Her formal ordination as pastor (a title later changed to First Reader) of the First Church of Christ, Scientist, New York City, occurred in October 1890. In 1891 she established the New York City Christian Science Institute to train practitioners. Her tall, stately figure, her elegant appearance, her rich speaking voice, and her magnetic personality attracted a large and rapidly growing following, a considerable portion of which was personally devoted to her. As the congregation grew it moved several times to larger quarters; in 1894 they met in the Scottish Rite Hall, in 1896 they bought the old Rutgers Presbyterian Church, and in 1899 work was begun on a new building, a huge granite edifice at 96th Street and Central Park West that cost more than a million dollars (it was completed without a mortgage) and that was larger than Eddy's Mother Church in Boston. It was dedicated in November 1903, and the next year Stetson moved into an adjoining home, an opulently furnished mansion built for her by her congregation.

These and other evidences of Stetson's success created anxieties in the Mother Church, where she was soon suspected of the ambition to supplant Eddy. In 1902 an edict limiting the terms of all Christian Science readers to three years was issued. Stetson duly resigned as First Reader in New York, but her influence was undiminished.

In 1909 an investigation of her was undertaken. In September her license as a Christian Science teacher and practitioner was revoked on grounds that she had taught various heresies, including that sex and procreation were evil, and had attempted to use mental means to cause harm to others. In November she was excommunicated, along with an inner circle of her followers. She continued to live in her home, however, and retained her post as principal of the New York Christian Science Institute. She continued also to proclaim her entire loyalty to Eddy. Gradually she came to interpret her trials as a call to lead the way to a higher form of Christian Science, the "Church Triumphant." After Eddy's death in 1910 Stetson predicted her resurrection. (She later also announced her own immortality.) Supported by wealthy followers, she continued to preach her version of Christian Science until her death.

Between 1918 and 1926 she directed a choral society that gave highly successful annual concerts of "spiritual music." She spent heavily on newspaper advertising and published *Reminiscences, Sermons, and Correspondence*, 1913, *Vital Issues in Christian Science*, 1915, *My Spiritual Aeroplane*, 1919, *Poems, Written on the Journey from Sense to Soul*, 1921, and *Sermons Which Spiritually Interpret the Scriptures and Other Writings on Christian Science*, 1924. In 1925 one of her students bought her a radio station, over which she spoke and read five times weekly. She died in Rochester, New York, on October 12, 1928.

Stevens, Nettie Maria 1861–1912 biologist

Born in Cavendish, Vermont, on July 7, 1861, Nettie Stevens led an entirely obscure life for her first thirty years. In 1892 she entered the State Normal School (now Westfield State College) in Westfield, Massachusetts, where she remained for four years before transferring to Stanford University. She graduated from Stanford in 1899 and received an M.A. degree in 1900. In that year she undertook graduate studies in biology at Bryn Mawr College; during 1901 she studied at the Zoological Station in Naples, Italy, and at the Zoological Institute of the University of Würzburg. She took her Ph.D. from Bryn Mawr in 1903 and remained at the college as a research fellow in biology for a year, as reader in experimental morphology for another year, and as associate in experimental morphology from 1905 to her death. In 1908–1909 she was again in Würzburg.

Her earliest field of research was the morphology and taxonomy of the ciliate protozoa; her first published paper, in 1901, had dealt with such a protozoan. Later she turned to cytology and the regenerative process. One of her major papers in that field was written in 1904 with Thomas Hunt Morgan, who would later win the Nobel Prize for work in genetics. Her investigations into regeneration led her to a study of differentiation in embryos and then to a study of chromosomes. In 1905, after experiments with the *Tenebrio molitor* beetle, she published "Studies in Spermatogenesis with Especial Reference to the 'Accessory Chromosome' " in the *Publications* of the Carnegie Institution. In that paper she announced her finding that the chromosomes known as X and Y were responsible for the determination of the sex of the individual.

This discovery, also announced independently that year by Edmund Beecher Wilson of Columbia University, not only ended the long-standing debate over whether sex was a matter of heredity or embryonic environmental influence but also was the first firm link between a heritable characteristic and a particular chromosome. Stevens continued her research on the chromosome makeup of various insects until her death in Baltimore on May 4, 1912.

Stevenson, Matilda Coxe Evans 1849–1915 ethnologist

Born on May 12, 1849, in San Augustine, Texas, Matilda Evans grew up in Washington, D.C. She was educated at Miss Anable's Academy in Philadelphia. In April 1872 she married James Stevenson, a geologist and from 1879 executive officer of the U.S. Geological Survey. She took an interest in her husband's work and in 1879 accompanied him on an expedition to New Mexico to study the Zuñi for the Bureau of American Ethnology.

For some years her assistance to her husband was largely unacknowledged, but in 1884 the British anthropologist Edwin B. Tylor visited the Stevensons, discovered the extent of her original contributions, and publicly commented on her work. On several visits to the Zuñi she studied their domestic life and in particular the roles, duties, and rituals of Zuñi women. Her first major published paper, "Religious Life of the Zuñi Child," appeared in the 1883–1884 annual report of the Bureau of American Ethnology and opened an entirely new area of anthropology in the study of children. In 1885 she helped found and became first president of the Women's Anthropological Society of America. In March 1888 her important paper on "Zuñi Religions" appeared in *Science*. On the death of her husband in July of that year she was appointed to the staff of the Bureau of American Ethnology.

In 1889 she undertook a study of the people of the Sia pueblo in New Mexico, her report on which appeared in the 1889–1890 volume of the Bureau's annual reports. The Zuñi remained her principal interest, however. She was held in great esteem by them, and in consequence she was able to learn much that had been concealed from earlier investigators. She was able, moreover, to observe changes in Zuñi culture brought about over a span of many years by contact with outsiders such as herself. The *Twenty-third Annual Report* of the Bureau in 1901–1902 published her 600-page *The Zuñi Indians: Their Mythology, Esoteric Fraternities, and Ceremonies*, her most important written work. The *Thirtieth Annual Report* of 1908–1909 printed her "Ethnobotany of the Zuñi Indians." She also contributed to *American Anthropologist* and other journals, and her subjects later included the Taos and Tewa Indians as well. She prepared an exhibit of Zuñi artifacts for the Louisiana Purchase Exposition in St. Louis in 1904. From 1904 to 1915 she lived near the San Ildefonso pueblo; when her health failed in the latter year she returned east to Oxon Hill, Maryland, where she died on June 24, 1915.

Stevenson, Sarah Ann Hackett 1841–1909 physician

Born in Buffalo Grove (now Polo), Illinois, on February 2, 1841, Sarah Stevenson was educated at the Mount Carroll Seminary and at the State Normal University (now Illinois State University) in Normal, graduating from the latter in 1863. She taught school for several years in Bloomington, Mount Morris, and Sterling, Illinois, and in the last town was also principal. She then went to Chicago and began studying anatomy and physiology at the Woman's Hospital Medical College.

After a year at the South Kensington Science School in London, where she studied under Thomas Huxley, she returned to the Woman's Hospital Medical College in Chicago and received her M.D. degree in 1874. She began her practice in Chicago in 1875 and in that year published *Boys and Girls in Biology*, a high school textbook. In 1876 she was chosen one of the Illinois State Medical Society's delegates to the American Medical Association convention in Philadelphia. Five years earlier the AMA had refused even to discuss the question of women members, but at Philadelphia the matter was dealt with quietly, and Stevenson became the association's first woman member. In 1875 she became professor of physiology and histology at the Woman's Hospital Medical College, which four years later became the Woman's Medical College and in 1891 became the Northwestern University Woman's Medical School; from 1880 to 1894 she was professor of obstetrics. She was also on the staffs of the Woman's, Provident, Mary Thompson, and, from 1881, Cook County hospitals; at the last she was the first woman staff physician.

In 1880 she joined Lucy Flower and others in founding the Illinois Training School for Nurses. She was active also in the work of the Woman's Christian Temperance Union, serving as the first superintendent of its Department of Hygiene in 1881–1882 and as president of the staff of its National Temperance (later the Frances Willard) Hospital from its founding in 1886. In 1880 she published *The Physiology of Woman*. In 1893 she was appointed to the Illinois State Board of Health (where again she was the first woman) by Governor John P. Altgeld. She retired from her large private practice in 1903 and died in Chicago on August 14, 1909.

Stewart, Eliza Daniel 1816–1908 reformer

Born in Piketon, Ohio, on April 25, 1816, Eliza Daniel was educated in local schools and in seminaries in Granville and Marietta, Ohio. In 1833 her older brother, who was

Piketon's postmaster, appointed her assistant postmaster; she was said to be the first woman ever to hold such a position officially. Soon, however, she turned to teaching school. In 1848 she married Hiram Stewart, with whom she moved to Athens, Ohio, a short time later.

About 1858 she organized an Athens lodge of Good Templars, a temperance order. During the Civil War her work in gathering supplies for the Union army and visiting sick and wounded soldiers earned her the name "Mother" Stewart, by which she continued to be known. In 1866 she and her family moved to Springfield, Ohio. There, in January 1872, she gave a temperance lecture in which she urged her listeners to seek out the wives of drunkards and to persuade them to bring suit against liquor dealers under the Adair Act, an Ohio statute that allowed such suits for damages to be brought by the wives or mothers of drunkards. A short time later she made an address to the jury in such a case, and in October 1873 she took part in a second. She organized local women in a petition drive to force the Springfield city council to adopt a local-option ordinance against liquor. In December, in response to but one of many invitations that began to come to her from other towns, she organized in Osborn, Ohio, the first Woman's Temperance League. In January 1874 she was elected president of the new Springfield Temperance Union; she became head of the county union in April and in June led in forming a statewide Temperance Union.

Throughout 1874 a largely unorganized but effective wave of temperance fervor, which came to be known as the "Woman's Crusade," swept over regions of western New York, Ohio, and parts of the Midwest. In November a general convention was called (by Martha M. Brown and others) in Cleveland to organize the movement, and Stewart played a prominent part in the founding there of the Woman's Christian Temperance Union. In 1876 she made a lecture and organizing tour of Great Britain, during which she contributed to the formation of the British Women's Temperance Association and the Scottish Christian Union. In 1879 she toured the South as chairman of the WCTU's committee on Southern work. She was a WCTU delegate to the World's Convention of Good Templars in Edinburgh in 1891, and in 1895 she delivered the opening address to the World's WCTU convention in London.

Stewart published *Memories of the Crusade: A Thrilling Account of the Great Uprising of the Women of Ohio in 1873, against the Liquor Crime*, 1888, and *The Crusader in Great Britain; or, The History of the Origin and Organization of the British Women's Temperance Association*, 1893. She died in Hicksville, Ohio, on August 6, 1908.

Stimson, Julia Catherine 1881–1948 nurse

Born on May 26, 1881, in Worcester, Massachusetts, Julia Stimson was a cousin of Henry L. Stimson, later secretary of war and of state. She grew up in Worcester and later in St. Louis and New York City. She graduated from Vassar College in 1901. After three years of further study at Columbia University she entered the New York Hospital Nurses Training School in 1904 and graduated in 1908. She was superintendent of nursing at Harlem Hospital in 1908–1911 and then joined the hospital staff at Washington University in St. Louis, where she served as administrator of hospital social service in 1911–1912. From 1913 to 1917 she was superintendent of nurses training at Barnes Hospital and at St. Louis Children's Hospital. In 1917 she received a master's degree from Washington University.

In May 1917 she sailed for France as chief nurse of American Red Cross Hospital Unit No. 21, which became Base Hospital 21, attached to British forces at Rouen. In April 1918 she was named chief nurse of the American Red Cross in France, and in November she became director of nursing for the American Expeditionary Force with responsibility for some 10,000 nurses serving in Europe. Her experiences in the war were recorded in *Finding Themselves*, 1918. In July 1919 she was appointed acting superintendent of the Army Nurse Corps and dean of the Army School of Nursing (the latter post she held until the closing of the school in 1933). Her superintendency was made permanent in December, and pursuant to the National Defense Act of June 1920 she was given the (relative) rank of major, the first nurse to hold that rank. She held that post until retiring in May 1937. She was president of the American Nurses Association from 1938 to 1944 and chairman of the Nursing Council on National Defense in 1940–1942. She was recalled briefly to active duty for recruiting work in 1942–1943. Promoted to colonel on the retired list in August 1948, she died in Poughkeepsie, New York, on September 30, 1948.

Stokes, Olivia Egleston Phelps and Caroline Phelps 1847–1927 and 1854–1909 philanthropists

Born in New York City, Olivia on January 11, 1847, and Caroline on December 4, 1854, the Stokes sisters were of a prominent banking family that viewed seriously the responsibility to use wealth for Christian ends. They grew up amid active work on behalf of temperance, abolitionism, education of African-Americans, foreign missions, bible and tract societies, the YMCA, children's hospitals, and other philanthropies. They were educated entirely at home except for Caroline's attendance at Miss Porter's School with her cousin Grace Dodge. In young adulthood they moved easily into the work their parents, especially their mother, had outlined for them. Neither married, and as their other brothers and sisters died they were left together with their remarkably similar tastes and interests. They read, attended to church work and other such activities, and, after the deaths of their parents, traveled extensively, making a world tour in 1896–1897.

Their earlier benefactions included St. Paul's Chapel at Columbia University, Woodbridge Hall at Yale, a chapel for Berea College in Kentucky, Dorothy Hall at Tuskegee Institute, a gymnasium at the Constantinople Woman's College, the open-air pulpit at the Cathedral of St. John the Divine in New York City, and money gifts to the New York Zoological Society, the New York Botanical Garden, and other institutions. Caroline Stokes passed her last years in California for her health. In 1908 she published a novel, *Travels of a Lady's Maid*. She died in Redlands, California, on April 26, 1909, leaving the bulk of her estate to establish the Phelps-Stokes Fund for the support of improved tenement housing in New York and the education of Native Americans, Africans, and American white and black students. Olivia became a major contributor to the fund and in particular a leader in the movement for model tenements. She wrote several books, including *Pine and Cedar: Bible Verses*, 1885, *Forward in the Better Life*, 1915, *Saturday Nights in Lent*, 1922, and *Letters and Memories of Susan and Anna Bartlett Warner*, on two of her closest friends, 1925. She died in Washington, D.C., on December 14, 1927.

Stokes, Rose Harriet Pastor 1879–1933 political radical

Born in Augustów, in then-Russian Poland, on July 18, 1879, Rose Wieslander took the name Pastor from her stepfather. She grew up in London, where the family moved when she was three, and from the age of eleven in Cleveland. She received only two years of schooling; the rest of her childhood from the age of four was devoted to working to help support the family. In Cleveland she worked in a cigar factory and spent her free time educating herself. She submitted several poems to the *Jewish Daily News* in New York City and in 1900 became a regular contributor. The family moved to the Bronx in 1903, and Rose Pastor joined the staff of the paper. As a result of an interview for the paper she married James G. Phelps Stokes, member of a wealthy banking family and a nephew of Olivia and Caroline Stokes, in July 1905.

James Stokes already harbored socialist inclinations, and together they undertook organizing work for the Intercollegiate Socialist Society and the Socialist party. Rose Stokes was an effective lecturer and labor organizer, and she contributed articles, reviews, and poems to such periodicals as the *Century*, *Everybody's*, and the *Independent*. In 1914, with Helen Frank, she published an English translation of Morris Rosenfeld's *Yiddish Songs of Labor and Other Poems*. In July 1917 she and her husband withdrew from the Socialist party because of its resolution condemning the entry of the United States into World War I. After the Russian Revolution later that year, however, she changed her mind, and in February 1918 she rejoined the party. In March she was indicted under the Espionage Act. Her offense was a letter to the *Kansas City Star* containing the sentence "I am for the people, while the Government is for the profiteers." She was found guilty of interfering with military recruitment and sentenced to ten years in prison. Her conviction was overturned in the Circuit Court of Appeals in 1920, but her case remained a cause célèbre and a symbol of antiradical hysteria.

In 1919 Rose Stokes joined the Communist party. She was a delegate to the Fourth Congress of the Communist International in Moscow in 1922 and contributed frequently to *Pravda* and the *Worker* (later the *Daily Worker*). She was arrested several times while picketing or demonstrating. James Stokes could not reconcile himself to her increasing radicalism and in October 1925 obtained a divorce; she refused alimony. In 1930 she was found to have cancer. Communist friends, publicly attributing her illness to a police clubbing during a demonstration the year before, raised funds for medical treatment in Europe. She died in Frankfurt-am-Main, Germany, on June 20, 1933.

Stone, Lucy 1818–1893 reformer, suffragist and publisher

Lucy Stone

Born in West Brookfield, Massachusetts, on August 13, 1818, Lucy Stone began to chafe at the restrictions placed on the female sex while she was still a girl. She took on various home chores in order to help relieve her mother's hard lot. At sixteen she began teaching — her low salary was another irritant — and supplemented her own education in short periods of study at Quaboag Seminary in Warren, Wesleyan Academy in Wilbraham, and in 1839 Mount Holyoke Female Seminary in South Hadley. Her determination to attend college derived in part from her general desire to better herself and in part from a specific resolve, made as a child, to learn Hebrew and Greek in order to determine if those passages in the Bible that seemed to give man dominion over woman had been properly translated. She entered Oberlin College in 1843 and graduated four years later.

Already an ardent abolitionist, Stone soon became a lecturer for William Lloyd Garrison's American Anti-Slavery Society. She proved an effective speaker, but before long friction developed between her and the society over her insistence on speaking for women's rights as well. Eventually a compromise was reached, and she subsequently conducted her feminist lectures on a professional basis. On several occasions she confronted hostile and even violent reactions.

In 1850 Stone led in issuing a call for a national convention on the subject of women's rights. That first such national convention (the 1848 meeting in Seneca Falls, New York, conducted by Elizabeth Cady Stanton and Lucretia Mott, had attracted largely local people) took place in Worcester, Massachusetts, and was presided over by Paulina Wright Davis. Stone's address to the convention was widely reported and drew many to the cause. She continued her lecture tours for several years, appearing frequently in "Bloomer" costume. In May 1855, despite an earlier resolution never to marry, she married Henry B. Blackwell, a Cincinnati merchant whose sisters were Elizabeth and Emily Blackwell and whose brother Samuel later married Antoinette Brown, who had been Lucy Stone's classmate at Oberlin. The marriage was performed by Thomas W. S. Higginson and included the reading by bride and groom of a protest against the marriage laws; afterward Lucy Stone retained her maiden name, becoming Mrs. Stone. After presiding over the seventh National Woman's Rights Convention in 1856 she retired for a time from public affairs to care for her daughter, Alice Stone Blackwell.

During the Civil War Stone supported the Women's Loyal National League founded by Stanton and Susan B. Anthony. In 1866 she helped found the American Equal Rights Association. In 1867 she helped organize and was elected president of the New Jersey Woman Suffrage Association. In the same year she joined in the campaigns for woman suffrage amendments in Kansas and New York. She helped organize the New England Woman Suffrage Association in 1868 and the next year moved from Orange, New Jersey, to Boston.

In 1869 a major schism occurred in the ranks of feminists. Anthony and Stanton headed one faction that favored pushing for a broad front of reforms, including labor organization and divorce law reform, and that favored defeating the proposed Fifteenth Amendment if it were not broadened to include woman suffrage; they formed the National Woman Suffrage Association in May. Lucy Stone, Julia Ward Howe, and other more conservative reformers, put off by the other faction's eclectic approach and by its acceptance of such supporters as the notorious Victoria Woodhull, formed in November the American Woman Suffrage Association. While serving on the association's executive board, Stone raised money to launch the weekly *Woman's Journal* in 1870, and in 1872 she and her husband succeeded Mary A. Livermore as editors. The journal remained over the years the staunchest and most respected journalistic voice of the suffrage movement; it continued to appear until 1917, in later years under the editorship of Alice Blackwell.

The schism in the movement was finally healed in 1890, in large part through Alice Blackwell's initiative, and Lucy Stone was thereafter chairman of the executive board of the merged National American Woman Suffrage Association. Her last lectures were delivered at the World's Columbian Exposition in Chicago in 1893. She died in Dorchester (part of Boston), Massachusetts, on October 18, 1893.

Storer, Maria Longworth Nichols 1849–1932 art patron and ceramist

Born in Cincinnati on March 20, 1849, Maria Longworth was of one of the city's leading families. She was educated privately. In May 1868 she married George W. Nichols, a writer 18 years her senior. Over the next several years they became leading patrons of the arts in Cincinnati. Her particular contribution was the May Music Festival, which she organized in 1873 and which became an annual event. In that year she also took up the new hobby of china painting. She enjoyed some success at it and gradually developed a deeper interest in ceramics, particularly after seeing an exhibit of Japanese pottery at the Centennial Exposition in Philadelphia in 1876.

By 1879 she was having ceramic pieces made to her specifications and was experimenting with glazes at a Cincinnati pottery, and in September 1880 she opened her own, which she named Rookwood, in an old converted schoolhouse. Gradually she assembled a staff — an experienced Staffordshire potter, Joseph Bailey, a chemist, and several talented men and women designers and artists — and began producing a variety of wares. The Rookwood workers developed a number of innovations in glaze, coloring, and design over the years and made theirs the foremost center of art pottery in America. The enterprise was not financially profitable for several years, but its reputation grew rapidly, and in 1889 Rookwood won a gold medal for ceramics at the Paris Exposition. By that time the founder was spending less time in ceramic work. George Nichols had died in September 1885, and in March 1886 she had married Bellamy Storer, a lawyer.

In 1889 she turned her interest in Rookwood over to William W. Taylor, and in May 1890 the Rookwood pottery was incorporated. She had little more to do with it. She continued to work in various art media, however, and in 1900 won a gold medal for bronze decoration at the Exposition Universelle in Paris.

Her husband served in Congress in 1891–1895 and in 1897–1898 was minister to Belgium. They both converted to the Roman Catholic church in 1896 under the influence of Archbishop John Ireland. Their experiences in Catholic Spain, where Bellamy Storer was U.S. minister in 1899–1902, emboldened them to dabble in church politics on behalf of Ireland. In 1899, through Theodore Roosevelt, then governor of New York, they prevailed upon President McKinley to address a letter to Pope Leo XIII urging a cardinalate for Ireland. The next year McKinley authorized them to repeat the suggestion in a papal audience.

In September 1902 President Roosevelt named Bellamy Storer ambassador to Austria-Hungary. While the new president was reluctant to press openly for Ireland, Maria Storer felt no compunction in using every tactic available to her. She conferred with Vatican officials, wrote letters, and quoted Roosevelt's earlier endorsement. In December 1905 Roosevelt wrote her demanding a written promise that she would cease her meddling; on receiving no reply he removed Storer from his post in March 1906. The affair made sensational press for some weeks, especially when the Storers took their side of the story to the public. Her pique was such that she refused to attend the wedding of her nephew Nicholas Longworth to Roosevelt's daughter Alice.

In later years she devoted time to travel and philanthropy and wrote several books: *Probation*, 1910, *Sir Christopher Leighton*, 1915, *The Borodino Mystery*, 1916 (all fiction), and *In Memoriam Bellamy Storer*, 1923. She died in Paris on April 30, 1932.

Stowe, Harriet Elizabeth Beecher 1811–1896 writer and reformer

Harriet Beecher Stowe

Born on June 14, 1811, in Litchfield, Connecticut, Harriet Beecher was a member of one of the nineteenth century's most remarkable families. The daughter of Lyman Beecher and the sister of Catharine, Henry Ward, and Edward, she grew up in an atmosphere of learning and moral earnestness. She attended Sarah Pierce's school in Litchfield in 1819–1824 and for three years thereafter her sister Catharine's school in Hartford. From 1827 to 1832 she taught at Catharine's school. In 1832 she accompanied Catharine and their father to Cincinnati, where he became president of Lane Theological Seminary and she taught in the Western Female Institute, founded by Catharine. In January 1836 she married Calvin E. Stowe, a professor at Lane. She supplemented their meager income by writing stories and sketches for periodicals, and she published a collection, *The Mayflower*, in 1843. In 1850 the Stowes moved to Brunswick, Maine, where Calvin Stowe joined the faculty of Bowdoin College.

There Harriet Stowe began to write a long tale of slavery, based on her reading of abolitionist literature and on her personal observations in Ohio and Kentucky. Her tale was published serially in the *National Era* in 1851–1852; in 1852 it appeared in book form as *Uncle Tom's Cabin, or, Life Among the Lowly*. It was an immediate sensation and was taken up eagerly by abolitionists while, along with its author, it was vehemently denounced in the South, where reading or possessing the book became an extremely dangerous undertaking. With sales of 300,000 in the first year, the book exerted an influence equaled by few other novels in history. It helped solidify both pro- and antislavery sentiment and fanned the flames that were to erupt in the Civil War. The book was translated widely and several times dramatized, the first time without Stowe's permission by George Aiken in 1852. Stowe was enthusiastically received on a visit to England in 1853, and there she formed friendships with many leading literary figures. In the same year she published *A Key to Uncle Tom's Cabin*, a compilation of documentary evidence in support of disputed details of her indictment of slavery.

In 1854 an account of Stowe's travels appeared as *Sunny Memories of Foreign Lands*. In 1856 appeared *Dred: A Tale of the Great Dismal Swamp*, another antislavery novel. From 1852 to 1864 she lived in Andover, Massachusetts, and from 1864 in Hartford. She traveled widely in the United States and to Europe and continued to produce articles, stories, and serialized novels, many of which appeared in the *Atlantic Monthly*. Her books included *The Minister's Wooing*, 1859, *The Pearl of Orr's Island*, 1862, *Agnes of Sorrento*, 1862, *The Ravages of a Carpet*, 1864, *Religious Poems*, 1867, *Oldtown Folks*, 1869, *Pink and White Tyranny*, 1871, *Sam Lawson's Oldtown Fireside Stories*, 1872, *Palmetto Leaves*, 1873, *We and Our Neighbors*, 1875, *Poganuc People*, 1878, and *A Dog's Mission*, 1881. She assisted her son Charles E. Stowe on his *Life of Harriet Beecher Stowe*, 1889. An article she published in the *Atlantic* in 1869 in which she alleged that Lord Byron had had an incestuous affair with his half-sister created an uproar and cost her much of her popularity in England, but she remained a leading author and lyceum lecturer in the United States. (The charge concerning Byron later came to be widely accepted.) After the death of her husband in 1866 she remained in Hartford until her own death on July 1, 1896.

Stratton, Dorothy Constance 1899– educator, naval officer, and public official

Born on March 24, 1899, in Brookfield, Missouri, Dorothy Stratton grew up in various towns in Kansas and Missouri. She graduated from Ottawa University in 1920, and while teaching and holding administrative posts in public schools in Renton, Washington, and from 1923 in San Bernardino, California, she took a master's degree from the University of Chicago in 1924 and a doctorate from Columbia University in 1932. In 1933 she was appointed dean of women and associate professor of psychology at Purdue University; she advanced to full professor in 1940. In June 1942 she served on the Women's Army Auxiliary Corps selection board for the V corps area, and later in the year she enlisted in the Women Accepted for Volunteer Emergency Service (WAVES) of the navy and was given a lieutenant's commission.

In November 1942 she was ordered to duty in the office of the commandant of the Coast Guard, where she developed plans and guidelines for a proposed women's reserve corps. By the end of the month she had devised a name for the corps, SPARS, derived from the Coast Guard motto Semper Paratus (Always Ready), and, with the rank of lieutenant commander, had been appointed director of the corps, which was authorized by Congress on November 23. She continued in that post, rising to the rank of captain, until 1946, and the SPARS grew during that period to some 10,000 officers and enlisted. From 1947 to 1950 she was director of personnel for the International Monetary Fund in Washington, D.C., and from 1950 to 1960 national executive director of the Girl Scouts of America. From 1962 she was a member of the President's Commission on the Employment of the Handicapped and a consultant on vocational rehabilitation to the Department of Health, Education and Welfare.

Streep, Meryl 1949– actor

Born on June 22, 1949, in Madison, New Jersey, Mary Louise was the only child in an upper-middle class family. At a very young age she acquired the nickname Meryl from her mother. She started voice training at age twelve, took up drama in high school, and pursued it in college, graduating from Vassar College in 1971 with a degree in drama and costume design. After working in summer stock theater, Streep studied drama at Yale University, where she earned her MFA in 1975. She then moved to New York City to begin her professional career as an actress.

Streep made her Broadway debut at the Lincoln Center Beaumont Theater in 1975 with *Trelawny of the Wells*, an intimate portrait of a group of thespians. What followed was an unusually successful first season in professional theater: she took leading roles in seven plays. Her early film credits included *Julia*, 1977, based on Lillian Hellman's memoir *Pentimento*, and *The Deer Hunter*, 1978, a controversial depiction of the war in Vietnam. That year she also starred in a television miniseries, *Holocaust*, about the suffering and near extermination of European Jews under the Nazi regime. In 1979 she appeared in *Kramer vs. Kramer*, the story of a painful divorce and custody battle, and in Woody Allen's *Manhattan*. The following year she starred in *The French Lieutenant's Woman*, a many-layered, dramatic love story. In *Sophie's Choice*, 1982, she played the role of a woman who endures life in a Nazi concentration camp and retreats to America after World War II. She won Oscars for her performances in *Kramer vs. Kramer* and *Sophie's Choice*.

Streep's career included many roles of political, social and historical import. She appeared in *Silkwood*, 1983, as a plant worker contaminated by radioactivity, who becomes a union activist in her efforts to expose the risks of working with plutonium. The film was based on the real-life story of Karen Silkwood who died in a mysterious car accident. In 1985 she starred in *Plenty*, about a woman's involvement in the French Resistance during World War II, and in *Out of Africa*, a film interpretation of Isak Dinesen's novel of turn-of-the-century Africa. She was nominated for Academy Awards for her roles in *Ironweed*, 1987, and *A Cry in the Dark*, 1988. In *Postcards from the Edge*, 1990, she played the role of a drug dependent actress coming to terms with her outrageous mother.

Over the years the versatility and quality of Streep's work was rewarded with many honors and awards, from the Academy of Motion Pictures, the Cannes Festival and numerous other professional circles. She was the recipient several honorary degrees.

Streeter, Ruth Cheney 1895–1990 marine officer

Born on October 2, 1895, in Brookline, Massachusetts, Ruth Cheney attended Bryn Mawr College in 1914–1916 and in 1917 married Thomas W. Streeter. They settled in Morristown, New Jersey, where she became involved in a broad range of civic activities. She had also a long standing interest in aviation and the armed forces; in memory of her brother, a World War I pilot, she and her mother sponsored an annual Cheney Award for an outstanding member of the Army Air Corps, and in 1940 she began taking flying lessons herself. She earned a commercial license in 1942. She was active in the Civil Air Patrol and various national defense committees.

On February 13, 1943, a Women's Reserve of the marine corps was formally established, and Ruth Streeter was named director with the rank of major. The women's reserve corps successfully resisted being nicknamed, an improvement over the World War I term marinettes; the corps was generally abbreviated WR. As with other women's reserve corps, the WR marines and officers were used in clerical and office work, communications, aviation support, cryptography, machine assembly and repair, and scores of other jobs that released thousands of male marines for duty overseas and combat. Trained at first in WAVES (navy) or SPARS (coast guard) camps and later in specifically marine camps, the WR reached a peak strength of 1000 officers and 18,000 enlisted by June 1944. Streeter was promoted to lieutenant colonel in November 1943 and in 1945 to colonel, and she retired in December 1945. Upon her retirement Commandant A. A. Vandergrift of the Marine Corps said her performance, "set a standard of excellence which, in my opinion, could not have been excelled and would be difficult to equal."

After the war she returned to Morristown, where she continued active in civic affairs. She was national president of the Society of Colonial Dames during 1948–1952, a delegate to the New Jersey Constitutional Convention in 1947, a Republican Presidential elector in 1960, and a member of the New Jersey Historical Sites Council in 1968–1970. Decorated with the Legion of Merit for her wartime service, she died on September 30, 1990, at her home in Morristown, New Jersey.

Streisand, Barbra 1942– singer, actor, and film producer

Born on April 24, 1942, in Brooklyn, New York, Barbara Joan Streisand (she later changed the spelling of her first name) graduated from Erasmus Hall High School there in 1959. Having determined at an early age to become an actress, she disdained less glamorous employment and immediately set out to achieve her goal. She interviewed

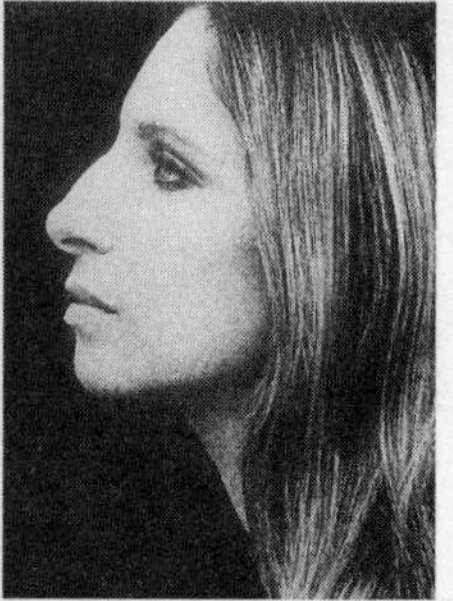

Barbra Streisand

producers, went to tryouts, and studied acting for a short time. Her first break was as a singer in a Greenwich Village nightclub. An 11-week engagement at another club led to several local television appearances, a one-night stand in an Off-Broadway play, and an engagement at the Blue Angel nightclub.

It was at the Blue Angel that Broadway producer David Merrick saw Streisand and signed her for a supporting role in the musical comedy *I Can Get It for You Wholesale*, which opened in March 1962. Her outstanding performance in that show brought her to the verge of stardom. She went on to national television guest appearances, recordings, and more nightclub appearances. In May 1963 she sang at the White House Correspondents' Dinner at the request of President John F. Kennedy. She opened on Broadway in March 1964 in *Funny Girl*, a musical comedy based on the life of Fanny Brice. Playing the lead role, Streisand won great acclaim for her singing and acting. In 1968 she starred in the film version of *Funny Girl*, for which she won an Academy Award in 1969 (the first year in which two actresses were selected for best performance, the other being Katharine Hepburn).

Streisand had by then established herself as one of the biggest names in show business and enjoyed a nationwide following through records, personal appearances, and television specials. In 1967 she was signed to play the lead in the film version of *Hello Dolly!*, which was released in 1969. In that year she received the Antoinette Perry (Tony) award as "star of the decade" for her stage work. Her later films included *On a Clear Day You Can See Forever*, 1970, *The Owl and the Pussycat*, 1970, *What's Up, Doc?*, 1972, *The Way We Were*, 1973, *For Pete's Sake*, 1974, *Funny Lady*, 1975, *A Star Is Born*, 1976, *The Main Event*, 1979, *All Night Long*, 1981, *Yentl*, which she also directed and produced, 1983, *Nuts*, which she also produced, 1987, and *The Prince of Tides*, which she also directed and co-produced, 1991. Streisand's many recordings have won her seven Grammy awards.

Stuart, Ruth McEnery 1849–1917 writer

Born on May 21, 1849, in Marksville, Louisiana, Mary Routh McEnery (she later adopted the name Ruth) grew up from the age of seven in New Orleans. She apparently attended public and private schools, and she may have taught school for a time. In August 1879 she married Alfred O. Stuart, a merchant and planter with whom she settled in Washington, Arkansas. On her husband's death in 1883 she returned to New Orleans, where she taught school for a time before turning to writing. In January 1888 she published "Uncle Mingo's 'Speculations'," a tale in authentic Negro dialect, in the *New Princeton Review*.

More stories in the local-color vein, reflecting her intimate knowledge of the many cultures of cosmopolitan New Orleans, appeared in rapid succession in various periodicals, and with *A Golden Wedding and Other Tales*, 1893, she began a series of books that included *Carlotta's Intended and Other Tales*, 1894, *The Story of Babette*, 1894, *Solomon Crow's Christmas Pockets and Other Tales*, 1896, *Sonny, a Christmas Guest*, 1896, *In Simpkinsville; Character Tales*, 1897, *Moriah's Mourning*, 1898, *Holly and Pizen*, 1899, *The Woman's Exchange*, 1899, *Napoleon Jackson; the Gentleman of the Plush Rocker*, 1902, *George Washington Jones*, 1903, *The River's Children*, 1904, *The Second Wooing of Salina Sue, and Other Stories*, 1905, *Aunt Amity's Silver Wedding, and Other Stories*, 1909, *Sonny's Father*, 1910, *The Unlived Life of Little Mary Ellen*, 1910, *The Haunted Photograph*, 1911, *Daddy Do-Funny's Wisdom Jingles*, 1913, *The Cocoon*, 1915, and *Plantation Songs*, 1916. From 1891 Stuart lived in New York City. She was a success on the lecture platform from 1893. Her reputation as a humorist and writer of dialect stories faded soon after her death in White Plains, New York, on May 6, 1917.

Surratt, Mary Eugenia Jenkins 1820?–1865 alleged conspirator

Born in Waterloo, Maryland, probably in May 1820, Mary Jenkins married John H. Surratt in 1835. In 1840 they settled on a farm in Prince Georges County, Maryland, and a short time later they opened a tavern and store at Surrattsville (now Clinton). Financial problems beset the family, and in 1862 John Surratt died. After running the tavern herself for two years, in 1864 Surratt moved to Washington, D.C., where she operated a boardinghouse. Her son, John H. Surratt, a Confederate secret agent, gathered a group of Southern sympathizers, including the actor John Wilkes Booth, and began plotting the kidnapping of President Abraham Lincoln, who was to be held hostage in Richmond, Virginia, for the release of Confederate prisoners. One kidnap attempt on March 20, 1865, failed. The fall of the Confederacy in April 1865 ended that plot, whereupon Booth announced his intention to assassinate Lincoln. Most of the conspirators, including John Surratt, abandoned Booth. Mary Surratt had apparently known nothing of all this.

After the assassination on April 14, 1865, Booth himself was killed and his three actual co-conspirators were arrested, along with Mary Surratt and four others. Amidst inflamed public opinion, the conspirators were tried by a military commission, headed by General David Hunter, that sat from May 10 until June 30, 1865. As a trial it was irregular and replete with illegal procedures, including suppression of evidence by the prosecution, all designed to implicate Jefferson Davis and the Confederate government in the plot. All eight of those arrested were convicted (a foregone conclusion), and Mary Surratt, whose boardinghouse had occasionally been used as a meeting place by the conspirators, was sentenced to be hanged along with the three actually involved in Booth's plot.

The evidence against her was weak, indeed, virtually nonexistent, and her conviction may have reflected a certain anti-Catholic bias as well as public hysteria. She was executed in Washington on July 7, 1865, along with the three others. Her son John, arrested the next year and tried in 1867 by a civil court, was released in 1868 after the majority of the jury had voted for acquittal and the government had dropped further prosecution. In his trial much of the testimony that had convicted his mother was seriously impeached.

Swain, Clara A. 1834–1910 medical missionary

Born on July 18, 1834, in Elmira, New York, Clara Swain grew up from the age of two in Castile, New York. She attended local schools and for some years from the age of fifteen alternated periods of study and teaching. In 1856–1857 she attended a seminary in Canandaigua, New York, and for seven years thereafter she taught in a public school there. In 1865 she began studying medicine under a woman physician at the Castile Sanitarium, and in 1866–1867 and 1868–1869 she attended the Woman's Medical College of Pennsylvania, receiving her M.D. degree in 1869. A short time later she responded to a call for a woman physician to work with women and orphans at the Methodist mission in Bareilly, India.

Under the auspices of the New England branch of the Woman's Foreign Missionary Society of the Methodist Episcopal Church she sailed from New York in November 1869 (in company with Isabella Thoburn) and arrived at Bareilly in January 1870. She was the first woman physician from the United States to work as a missionary in Asia. She quickly established a set of courses in anatomy, physiology, and materia medica for a class of 17 young Indian women, 13 of whom qualified in 1873 to practice routine medicine; at the same time she attended the girls of the Methodist orphanage and the residents of a village of Indian Christians and opened her general practice to all. She had great success in gaining admission to zenanas and in winning the confidence of the women in them.

In October 1871 the Nawab of Rampore gave Swain a 40-acre estate adjoining the mission, and there she opened a dispensary in May 1873 and what was apparently the first hospital for women in India in January 1874. The hospital was so planned as to allow due regard for caste and class taboos and to accommodate families and servants, with the result that patients came from as far away as Burma. Swain's case load numbered in the thousands. From early 1876 to late 1879 she took furlough and rested in Castile, New York. Her health and strength largely restored, she again worked at Bareilly from January 1880 to March 1885.

In the latter year she was invited to become palace physician to the Rajah of Rajputana and his wife, the Rani of Khetri. She accepted on condition that she be allowed to evangelize as well in the region, which had long been hostile to Christianity. The Rajah allowed her a room in the palace for a dispensary open to women of all classes, and she carried her practice into the surrounding area, frequently riding her own elephant. Except for a furlough to the United States in 1888–1889, she remained at Khetri until 1896, when she retired to Castile. She revisited India in 1906–1908 and in 1909 she published extracts from her letters over a span of a quarter-century as *A Glimpse of India*. She died in Castile, New York, on December 26, 1910. The hospital in Bareilly was later named in her honor.

Szold, Henrietta 1860–1945 Zionist leader

Born in Baltimore on December 21, 1860, Henrietta Szold was of a German-speaking Hungarian immigrant family; her father was a rabbi. After graduating from public high school in 1877 she taught French, German, Latin, science, mathematics, and history at the Misses Adams' School, a girls' academy in Baltimore, for 15 years. Having studied Hebrew and the Talmud with her father, she also taught children's and adults' classes in her father's synagogue. In 1889 she organized a night class in American history and customs for newly arrived Jewish immigrants from Eastern Europe, and the experiment was so successful that several more classes were formed to handle the demand. She also served for a time as Baltimore correspondent for the *Jewish Messenger* of New York. In 1893 she helped a Baltimore immigrant group organize Hebras Zion, perhaps the first Zionist society in America. In the same year Cyrus Adler, a family friend, named her editorial secretary of the five-year-old Jewish Publication Society. During her 23 years in that post she was largely responsible for the publication of English versions of Moritz Lazarus's *The Ethics of Judaism*, Nahum Slouschz's *Renascence of Hebrew Literature*, and other works and for a revised edition of Heinrich Graetz's five-volume *History of the Jews*. She worked on the American Jewish Year Book from its first issue in 1899 and from 1904 to 1908 was its sole editor. She also contributed articles to the *Jewish Encyclopaedia*. She was an early member of the Federation of American Zionists, organized in 1897, a member of the federation's executive council from 1899, and a contributor to its monthly *Maccabaean*. After the death of her father in 1902 she and her mother moved to New York City, where she took courses at the Jewish Theological Seminary.

A trip abroad in 1909, including a visit to Palestine, confirmed Szold in the belief that the establishment of a Jewish homeland in Palestine was of overriding importance. On her return to New York she involved herself more deeply in Zionist activities, becoming secretary of the Federation of American Zionists in 1910. On Purim (February 24) in 1912 she led the women of her Hadassah Study Circle, to which she had belonged since 1907, in forming the Hadassah Chapter of Daughters of Zion, known from its first national convention simply as Hadassah. As president Szold immediately began planning various sorts of aid programs for Palestine. Largely through a gift from Nathan Straus (of Macy's department store) Hadassah sent a team of two public health nurses to Palestine in 1913.

Szold traveled widely to organize chapters of Hadassah. Through the efforts of Justice Louis D. Brandeis and Judge Julian W. Mack she was provided a modest income in 1916 that allowed her to resign from the Jewish Publication Society and to devote full time to Zionist work. At the founding convention of the Zionist Organization of America in Pittsburgh in 1918 she was named director of the department of education. In that year she led in organizing the American Zionist Medical Unit — sponsored jointly by Hadassah, the Zionist Organization of America, and the American Jewish Joint Distribution Committee — and in forwarding its 44 doctors, nurses, and other health personnel and some 400 tons of equipment and supplies to Palestine.

In 1920 Szold went to Palestine as a member of the executive committee of the unit. She worked indefatigably to supervise and to raise funds for the unit, which in 1922 was reorganized as the Hadassah Medical Organization. In Palestine she also organized and became first president of the Histadrut Nashim Ivriot (Jewish Women's Organization). She returned to the United States in 1923. In 1926 she resigned as president of Hadassah (becoming honorary president), and in 1927 she was named by the World Zionist Organization, meeting in Basel, one of three members of the Palestine Zionist Executive Committee and supervisor of its department of health and education. She was again in Palestine in 1927–1930 and from 1931 to her death. In 1931–1933 she served in the Vaad Leumi, the executive committee of the Knesset Israel (Palestinian Jewish National Assembly). From its creation in 1933 she was director of the Youth Aliyah, an agency created to rescue Jewish children from Nazi Germany and bring them to Palestine. Late in life she founded Lemaan ha-Yeled, an institution dedicated to child welfare and research; after her death it was renamed Mosad Szold (the Szold Foundation). She died in Jerusalem, in the Hadassah-Hebrew University Hospital she had helped make possible, on February 13, 1945.

Taggard, Genevieve 1894–1948 poet

Born on November 28, 1894, in Waitsburg, Washington, Genevieve Taggard grew up from 1896 in Hawaii, where her parents were missionaries. Her life there was a happy one, in sharp contrast with the unhappiness she felt on brief returns to Waitsburg in 1905–1906 and 1910–1912. She attended the Punahou School in Honolulu and in 1914 edited its magazine, the *Oahuan*, in which her first published poem had appeared four years earlier. She left school before graduating in order to take over her father's mission school during his illness. In the fall of 1914 she entered the University of California at Berkeley. She worked her way through college, edited the literary magazine, the *Occident*, in her last year, and graduated in 1920. In December 1919 *Harper's* published the first of her poems to reach a national audience.

In 1920 Taggard moved to New York City and found a job with the publishing firm of B. W. Huebsch. In 1921 she joined Maxwell Anderson, Padraic Colum, and others in founding *The Measure: A Journal of Verse*, a monthly "little magazine" on whose editorial board she served until its demise in 1926. She was a member of the radical literary circle in New York and a frequent contributor to the *Freeman*, the *Masses*, the *Liberator*, and similar magazines. Her first volume of verse, *For Eager Lovers*, 1922, was concerned largely with marriage and motherhood and was widely praised. It was followed by *Hawaiian Hilltop*, 1923, *Words for the Chisel*, 1926, and *Travelling Standing Still*, 1928. In 1925 she edited *May Days*, an anthology of verse from the *Masses* and the *Liberator*.

After a year in California in 1922–1923, Taggard and her husband, Robert L. Wolf, settled in New Preston, Connecticut. She was an instructor in English at Mount Holyoke College in 1929–1930, and in that brief period she published *Circumference: Varieties of Metaphysical Verse, 1456–1928*, 1929, and *The Life and Mind of Emily Dickinson*, 1930, as well as a further volume of her own poems, *Monologue for Mothers*, 1929.

After a year on Majorca and Capri on a Guggenheim fellowship Taggard taught at Bennington College in 1932–1935, during which time she divorced Wolf and married Kenneth Durant, American director of the Soviet news agency Tass. From 1935 to 1946 she taught at Sarah Lawrence College and spent her free time at Gilfeather, her farm near East Jamaica, Vermont. Later volumes of verse included *Remembering Vaughan in New England*, 1933, *Calling Western Union*, her attempt to put her poetry at the service of proletarian ends, 1936, *Collected Poems: 1918–1938*, 1938, *Falcon*, 1942, *Long View*, 1942, *A Part of Vermont*, 1945, *Slow Music*, 1946, and *Origin: Hawaii*, 1947. Several of her lyrics were set to music by Aaron Copland, Roy Harris, William Schuman, and other composers. She died in New York City on November 8, 1948.

Tallchief, Maria 1925– dancer

Born on January 24, 1925, in Fairfax, a town on an Osage reservation in Oklahoma, Maria Tallchief was of Osage and Scotch-Irish descent. She began studying piano and dance as a child and continued to do so after the family's move to Los Angeles when she was seven. Gradually dance displaced piano, and while attending Beverly Hills High School she studied under Bronislava Nijinska, David Lichine, and others. Following her graduation from high school in 1942 she joined the Ballet Russe de Monte Carlo. Over the next five years she attracted much attention with roles in *Chopin Concerto*, *Scheherezade*, *Etude*, *Le Baiser de la Fée*, and other works, and she created roles in George Balanchine's *Danses concertantes* in September 1944 and *Night Shadow* in February 1946. She married Balanchine in August 1946. They left the Ballet Russe early in 1947, and after a few months as guest artists with the Paris Opéra Ballet, where she danced in his *Serenade*, *Apollon musagète*, and other works, they joined the new Ballet Society, which the next year became the New York City Ballet.

In her 18 years with that company Tallchief was the foremost exponent of Balanchine's choreography, and she was generally accounted the most technically accomplished ballerina ever produced in America. She was the company's prima ballerina in 1954–1955. Among her most important roles were those in *Symphonie concertante*, premiered in November 1947 with Tanaquil Le Clercq, *Orpheus*, premiered in April 1948, *The Firebird*, premiered in November 1949, *Bourrée fantasque*, with Le Clercq, premiered in December 1949, *Scotch Symphony*, premiered in November 1952, *Pas de dix*, premiered in November 1955, *Allegro brillante*, premiered in March 1956, and *Gounod Symphony*, premiered in January 1958, all by Balanchine, along with *The Four Temperaments*, *Caracole*, and his versions of *Swan Lake*, 1952, and *The Nutcracker*, 1954. (She and Balanchine were divorced in 1952.) She also danced in Todd Bolender's *Capricorn Concerte*, in Jerome Robbins's *The Guests*, premiered in January 1949, in Antony Tudor's *Jardin aux Lilas*, and many other works.

Tallchief's association with the New York City Ballet was interrupted by a season with the American Ballet Theatre in 1960; she retired from the New York City Ballet in 1965. Later that year she danced in the premiere of Peter Van Dyk's *Cinderella* at the Hamburg State Opera. She subsequently lived in Chicago, where she served as artistic director of the Lyric Opera Ballet from 1975 and taught occasionally. In 1981 Tallchief founded the Chicago City Ballet and was artistic director until the company folded in 1987. She was the recipient of a *Dance* magazine award in 1960.

Tamiris, Helen 1905–1966 dancer and choreographer

Born in New York City on April 24, 1905, Helen Becker began taking dance lessons at eight. She later studied with Michel Fokine and Rosina Galli, and under the latter she danced for three seasons with the Metropolitan Opera. By that time she had adopted the stage name Tamiris. She later toured South America as a ballerina with the Bracale Opera Company and appeared as a specialty dancer with the Music Box Revue in New York. After a brief period at Isadora Duncan's school in New York she made her concert debut in *Dance Moods* in 1927. During a European tour in 1928 she introduced American folk music and Negro spirituals at the Salzburg Festival; she appeared also in Berlin and Paris. In 1930 she organized her own dance company in New York, with which she appeared annually, and a school of dance that she directed until 1945.

During 1930–1932 Tamiris headed the Dance Repertory Theatre, which produced concerts jointly with Martha Graham, Doris Humphrey, and other choreographers. Her dance works of the period were deeply concerned with social issues and protest and bore such titles as *Cycle of Unrest*, *Salut au monde*, *How Long Brethren?*, and *Porterhouse Lucy Ballet*. Largely through her efforts as first president of the American Dance Association, dance was included in the program of the Federal Theater Project of the Works Progress Administration. During 1937–1939 she was the principal choreographer for the Federal Theater Project of New York. She and her company appeared at the Rainbow Room of Radio City in 1942–1943.

In 1943 Tamiris began choreographing for Broadway; shows to which she contributed included It's *Up to You*, 1943, *Up in Central Park*, 1944, *Show Boat*, 1945, *Annie Get Your Gun*, 1946, *Park Avenue*, 1946, *Inside U.S.A.*, 1948, *Touch and Go*, for which she won a Tony Award, 1949, and *Plain and Fancy*, 1955. Later she returned to concert work and continued to create dances in her characteristically vigorous manner on American themes. Others of her dance pieces included *Bayou Ballads*, *Liberty Song*, and *Dance for Walt Whitman*. In 1960 she formed the Tamiris-Nagrin Dance Company with her partner and husband, Daniel Nagrin. She died in New York City on August 4, 1966.

Tan, Amy 1952– novelist

Born in Oakland, California, on February 19, 1952, Amy Ruth Tan was the daughter of John and Daisy Tan, who had both emigrated from China in the 1940s. John Tan was a

Baptist minister and electrical engineer, her mother a vocational nurse. While still an adolescent, Tan suffered the loss of her oldest brother and her father, who both died of brain tumors within eight months of each other. Her mother then took Tan and her only other brother to Switzerland, where Amy rebelled by hanging around with a German boyfriend; when he turned out ot be a drug dealer, her mother, according to Tan, "engineered the biggest drug bust in the history of Montreux and got me hauled before a local magistrate."

After moving back to California, Tan enrolled, to please her mother, in Linfield College, a small Baptist school in Oregon. Soon she struck out on her own again, however, this time with her Italian-American boyfriend Louis DeMattei, to San Jose City College in California. She also changed her double major to English and linguistics. (Her mother, she said, "could see nothing in that as a future.") In 1974 she and DeMattei were married; he became a tax lawyer, and, after transferring again to finish her B.A. at San Jose State University, she went on to obtain an M.A. in linguistics, beginning but never completing a doctorate at the University of California at Santa Cruz and at Berkeley.

Instead she got work as a technical writer, freelancing for large companies such as IBM. Soon working an average of ninety hours a week, she found herself never turning down a job. She started writing fiction as a kind of therapy for what she considered her workaholism; her first short story, "Endgame," enabled her to join a writing group called the Squaw Valley Community of Writers in 1985. After penning another short story, "Waiting Between the Trees," she approached literary agent Sandra Dijkstra with her work.

While Tan took her first trip to China with her mother in 1987, Dijkstra sent her work off to New York publishers. Upon her return, Tan joined a new writers' group; headed by Molly Giles, it helped her refine her writing style. Meanwhile a publisher, G. P. Putnam and Sons, offered her a $50,000 advance for what would become her first novel, *The Joy Luck Club*. Hardly believing this turn of events, Tan quit her job and wrote this novel in just over four months: "I wrote it very quickly because I was afraid this chance would just slip out of my hands."

Published in 1989, *The Joy Luck Club* tells the story of generational and cultural differences between several Chinese mothers, who in 1949 had formed a social group in San Francisco called a Joy Luck Club, and their Chinese-American daughters living in the 1980s. A *New York Times* best-seller in 1989, it won the Bay Area Book Reviewers Award and the Commonwealth Club Gold Award.

Though nervous about writing her second book after the unexpected success of the first one, Tan returned to the mother/daughter theme in *The Kitchen God's Wife*, 1991. Based on her mother's life, it recounts the story of a woman who grows up in China, marries an abusive man, lives through the deaths of her first three children, and eventually emigrates to the U.S. to start a new life there. Tan's first children's book, *The Moon Lady*, was published in 1992.

Tandy, Jessica 1909–1994 actor

Born in London, England, on June 7, 1909, Jessica lost her father to cancer when she was twelve years old. Her mother maintained several jobs to support her three children. As a teenager, Jessica set her sights on acting, an art her mother encouraged. She studied at Dame Alice Owen's Girls' School from 1919 to 1924, after which she began a three-year training program at London's Ben Greet Academy of Acting. Her professional debut — for which she had to make her own elaborate costumes — took place at age 18 in a small London theater presentation of *The Manderson Girls*.

Though she went on to appear in several contemporary works, she prized classical theater above all. She focused on Shakespeare early, portraying Olivia in a 1930 Oxford

University presentation of *Twelfth Night* and later appeared in the same work again as Viola. She married and bore a child before returning to the stage as Ophelia in John Gielgud's *Hamlet*, 1934.

After emigrating to the U.S. in 1940 and ending her first marriage, she and actor-director Hume Cronyn were married in 1942 and had two children. In Hollywood her career languished, as she was too often typecast as an English maid. In 1946, however, Cronyn directed Tandy in Tennessee Williams's one-act play, *Portrait of a Madonna*, and she caught the playwright's attention. Williams cast her a year later as Blanche DuBois opposite Marlon Brando in his Broadway production of *A Streetcar Named Desire*. She won a Tony award for that performance, and the play, which ran on Broadway for two years, won both a Pulitzer Prize and the Drama Critics' Circle Award.

She returned to Elizabethan drama in 1961 in the role of Lady Macbeth at the American Shakespeare Festival in Stratford, Connecticut. Before playing Queen Gertrude in *Hamlet*, 1963, she appeared on the screen in Hitchcock's *The Birds*, 1963. She played both Hippolyta and Titania in *A Midsummer Night's Dream* at the 1976 Stratford Festival in Ontario, Canada, and Mary Tyrone in O'Neill's *Long Day's Journey into Night* at the Theatre London in Ontario, in 1977. In 1978 she earned her second Tony award, this time for her performance in *The Gin Game*, playing opposite her husband. Both she and Cronyn were admitted to the Theater Hall of Fame in 1979.

In 1983 Tandy performed in *Foxfire*, for which she received a third Tony award; she later received an Emmy award for a television adaptation. Tandy earned further critical acclaim for her role in a 1983 revival of Williams's *The Glass Menagerie*. On screen she triumphed as the feminist Miss Birdseye in the film adaptation of Henry James's *The Bostonians*, 1984.

She earned both an Academy Award and a Golden Globe award for her performance in *Driving Miss Daisy*, 1989; at age 80, she was the oldest person to win an Oscar. She continued to appear to great acclaim in films such as *Fried Green Tomatoes*, 1991, and *Used People*, 1992; two more films, *Camilla* and *Nobody's Fool*, had not yet been released when she died. Nevertheless she always claimed the stage as her first love.

Remarkable as her acting career on her own was, some of her best work was the fruit of her collaboration with Hume Cronyn in such films as *Cocoon*, 1985, and in stage productions such as *The Gin Game* and *Foxfire*. Reviewing *Foxfire*, *New York Times* critic Frank Rich captured the essence of Tandy's appeal: "Everything this actress does is so pure and right that only poets, not theater critics, should be allowed to write about her."

She received many honors, including honorary degrees from the University of Western Ontario, 1974, and Fordham University, 1985. In 1986 she received the Kennedy Center Honors for her contributions to the arts. She continued to work for years after being diagnosed with ovarian cancer in 1990. She died September 11, 1994, at her home in Easton, Connecticut.

Tarbell, Ida Minerva 1857–1944 journalist

Born on November 5, 1857, in Erie County, Pennsylvania, Ida Tarbell grew up in Rouseville and Titusville and attended public schools. In 1880 she graduated from Allegheny College in Meadville, Pennsylvania. After teaching for two years in the Union Seminary in Poland, Ohio, she became an associate editor of the *Chautauquan* in 1883. She resumed her studies at the Sorbonne and the College de France in Paris in 1891–1894 and during that time helped support herself by contributing articles to *Scribner's*, *McClure's*, and other magazines. On her return to the United States in 1894 she was personally persuaded by S. S. McClure to join the staff of his magazine. Her highly successful series of articles on the life of Napoleon was issued in volume form as *A Short Life of Napoleon Bonaparte* in 1895 and sold 100,000 copies. Her *Life of Madame Roland*

Ida Tarbell

followed in 1896 and *The Life of Abraham Lincoln*, based on another *McClure's* series, in 1900. She also collaborated with Charles A. Dana on his *Recollections of the Civil War*, 1898.

Tarbell's exhaustively researched series of 19 articles on the Rockefeller oil interests and the growth of the Standard Oil trust was collected in *The History of the Standard Oil Company*, two volumes, 1904. The articles and the book aroused public opinion and led to federal investigations into the activities of the Standard Oil Company of New Jersey, which was ultimately dissolved in 1911 under the Sherman Anti-Trust Act. The articles also helped to define a growing trend to investigation, exposé, and crusading in liberal journals of the day, a technique that came to be known as muckraking (Theodore Roosevelt's characterization, intended disparagingly but happily adopted by the muckrakers). In 1906 she left *McClure's* and with Lincoln Steffens, Ray Stannard Baker, Finley Peter Dunne, William Allen White, and others purchased the *American Magazine*, of which she was associate editor until 1915. From 1915 to 1932 she made regular lecture tours on the Chautauqua circuit.

Tarbell's later books included *The Tariff in Our Times*, from a series for the *American Magazine*, 1911, *The Business of Being a Woman*, 1912, *New Ideals in Business*, 1916, *The Rising of the Tide*, a novel, 1919, *Peacemakers — Blessed and Otherwise*, 1922, *The Life of Elbert H. Gary*, 1925, *Owen D. Young*, 1932, *The Nationalizing of Business, 1878–1898*, 1936, and *All in the Day's Work*, her autobiography, 1939. She also wrote several more books on Lincoln, including *In Lincoln's Chair*, 1920, *Boy Scouts' Life of Lincoln*, 1921, *In the Footsteps of the Lincolns*, 1924, and *Reporter for Lincoln*, 1927. She attended White House conferences on industry in 1919 and unemployment in 1921. She took no part in the woman suffrage movement and in 1915 declined to join the U.S. delegation aboard Henry Ford's "Peace Ship." She died in Bridgeport, Connecticut, on January 6, 1944.

Taylor, Elizabeth 1932– actor

Born in London on February 27, 1932, Elizabeth Rosemond Taylor was the child of transplanted American parents. She was brought to the United States shortly before the outbreak of World War II, and she grew up in Pasadena, California. Through a connection with Universal Studios, and in large part because of her English accent, she was given a small role in the motion picture *Lassie Come Home* in 1943. After appearances in *The White Cliffs of Dover* and *Jane Eyre* in 1944 she was a great success in *National Velvet* in the same year.

Over the next several years she moved from child roles to adolescent roles in such films as *The Courage of Lassie*, 1946, *Life with Father*, 1947, *Cynthia*, 1947, *A Date with Judy*, 1948, *Julia Misbehaves*, 1948, *Little Women*, 1949, *The Conspirator*, 1950, *Father of the Bride*, 1950, and *Father's Little Dividend*, 1951. She achieved recognition as an actress of talent in *A Place in the Sun*, 1951, and she secured her position as one of Hollywood's top stars in *Ivanhoe*, 1952, *Rhapsody*, 1954, *Elephant Walk*, 1954, *Beau Brummell*, 1954, *The Last Time I Saw Paris*, 1954, *Giant*, 1956, *Raintree County*, 1957, *Cat on a Hot Tin Roof*, 1958, *Suddenly, Last Summer*, 1959, and *Butterfield 8*, for which she won an Academy Award for best actress, 1960.

The usual Hollywood publicity attended Taylor's offscreen life and particularly her marriages to hotel-chain heir Conrad "Nicky" Hilton (1950–1951), actor Michael Wilding (1952–1956), producer Mike Todd (1957–1958), and singer Eddie Fisher (1959–1964). After filming the lavish and spectacular *Cleopatra*, 1963, she married her co-star, Richard Burton. She also appeared with him in *The VIP's*, 1963, *The Sandpiper*, 1965, *Who's Afraid of Virginia Woolf?*, for which she won a second Academy Award, 1966, *The Taming of the Shrew*, 1967, *The Comedians*, 1967, *Doctor Faustus*, 1968, *Boom!*, 1968, *Under Milk Wood*, 1971, and *Hammersmith Is Out*, 1972. Others among her films were

Reflections in a Golden Eye, 1967, *Secret Ceremony*, 1968, *The Only Game in Town*, 1970, *X Y & Zee*, 1972, *Night Watch*, 1972, *Ash Wednesday*, 1973, and *A Little Night Music*, 1978. She and Burton were divorced in 1974 but were again married in 1975–1976; their domestic trials, highlighted by his gifts of spectacular gems, were a virtual serial in the world tabloid press. From 1976–1982 Taylor was married to John Warner, who in 1978 was elected a Republican senator from Virginia; in 1991 she married again to contractor Larry Fortensky.

Taylor continued to star in films including *The Mirror Crack'd*, 1980, *Between Friends*, 1983, and *The Young Toscanini*, 1988. She made her Broadway debut in the 1981 production of *The Little Foxes* and appeared on stage again in *Private Lives* in 1983. She has been an active philanthropist; she initiated the Ben Gurion University-Elizabeth Taylor Fund for the Children of the Negev in 1982, and in 1985 she was founding Chair of the American Foundation for AIDS Research. She was named a Commander of Arts and Letters of France in 1985 and was awarded the French Legion of Honor in 1987. In 1993 she received the American Film Institute's Life Achievement Award and the Jean Hersholt Humanitarian Award.

Taylor, Lucy Beaman Hobbs 1833–1910 dentist

Born on March 14, 1833, probably in Franklin County, New York, Lucy Hobbs graduated from the Franklin Academy in Malone, New York, in 1849 and became a schoolteacher. While teaching in Brooklyn, Michigan, she began the study of medicine, and in 1859 she moved to Cincinnati, where, after being refused admission to the Eclectic College of Medicine because of her sex, she studied privately under one of the school's professors. At his suggestion she turned to dentistry.

She studied privately under the dean of the Ohio College of Dental Surgery and subsequently apprenticed herself to a practicing graduate of the school. Refused admission to the dental college because she was a woman, she opened a practice in Cincinnati in the spring of 1861. She practiced in Bellevue, Iowa, in 1862 and in McGregor, Iowa, in 1862–1865. In July 1865 she was elected to membership in the Iowa State Dental Society and sent as a delegate to the American Dental Association convention in Chicago. In November 1865 she was admitted to the senior class of the Ohio College of Dental Surgery, and on her graduation in February 1866 she became the first American woman to receive a dental degree. While practicing in Chicago she married James M. Taylor in April 1867; under his wife's instruction he too became a dentist. Late in 1867 they moved to Lawrence, Kansas, where they enjoyed a large practice. She largely retired after her husband's death in 1886. She died in Lawrence, Kansas, on October 3, 1910.

Teasdale, Sara 1884–1933 poet

Sara Teasdale

Born in St. Louis on August 8, 1884, Sarah Trevor Teasdale was educated privately; she graduated from Hosmer Hall in 1903. By that time she already had a reputation as a poet among her teachers and friends. With a few of the latter she helped produce the *Wheel*, a privately printed and distributed literary monthly to which she contributed some sonnets in 1904–1907. A tour of Europe and the Middle East in 1905 greatly expanded her imagination.

Her first published poem appeared in the St. Louis weekly *Reedy's Mirror* in May 1907, and later that year she published her first volume of verse, *Sonnets to Duse, and Other Poems*. Her second, *Helen of Troy, and Other Poems*, followed in 1911. *Rivers to the Sea* appeared in 1915. In 1914 she married a St. Louis businessman (rejecting a second suitor, Vachel Lindsay), and in 1916 they moved to New York City. In 1918 she won the Columbia University Poetry Society prize (forerunner of the Pulitzer Prize for poetry) and the annual prize of the Poetry Society of America for *Love Songs*, 1917. She also edited two anthologies, *The Answering Voice: One Hundred Love Lyrics by Women*, 1917, and *Rainbow Gold* for children, 1922.

Teasdale's poems were consistently classical in style: pure, openhearted lyrics usually in such conventional verse forms as quatrains or sonnets and technically excellent. But from her earlier poems to her later work in *Flame and Shadow*, 1920, *Dark of the Moon*, 1926, and *Stars To-night*, 1930, a maturing process apparently took place, with her poems evidencing an increasing subtlety and economy of expression. Her personal life was unhappy. Her marriage ended in divorce in 1929, and she lived thereafter the life of a semi-invalid. In 1932, while in London for research on a projected biography of Christina Rossetti, she was overtaken by an attack of pneumonia. Back in New York City and still in frail health, she took an overdose of barbiturates and died on the night of January 29, 1933. Her last and perhaps finest collection of verse, *Strange Victory*, was published later that year; her *Collected Poems* appeared in 1937.

Tekakwitha, Kateri 1656–1680 religious

Born in 1656, probably in Ossernenon, a Mohawk village near present-day Auriesville in upper New York State, Tekakwitha (Tegakwitha, Tegakouita) was the child of a Mohawk father and a mother who was a Christianized Algonquian. When she was four her parents and brother died in a smallpox epidemic, and she was reared thereafter by her uncle, an anti-Christian Mohawk chief. From about 1666 she lived in the village of Caughnawaga, near present-day Fonda, New York.

In 1667 Jesuit missionaries came among the tribe, and she apparently was strongly influenced by them, although she must have had contacts with Christianized Indians from time to time as well. In 1675 she asked Father Jacques de Lamberville for baptism, and after instruction she was baptized on Easter, April 18, of the following year, being given then the name Catherine (rendered Kateri in Mohawk speech). Her conversion brought her a great deal of hostility, even persecution, from fellow Native Americans, who were already suspicious of her pious ways and her refusal to marry. In 1677 she fled 200 miles to the mission of St. Francis Xavier at Sault St. Louis near Montreal. There she took her first communion on Christmas Day of 1677. She lived a life of great spirituality and asceticism that impressed all who knew her at the mission, and she became known as the "Lily of the Mohawks." In 1678 she was enrolled in the Confraternity of the Holy Family. In 1679 she took a private vow of chastity.

In 1680 Tekakwitha fell seriously ill and died on April 17 at the mission. After her death devotion to her spread among the French and the Indians of the region, and many miracles were credited to her intervention. In 1884 the third plenary council of the Roman Catholic church, meeting in Baltimore, petitioned Rome to initiate steps toward the canonization of Kateri Tekakwitha. With the formal presentation of her cause for beatification in 1932 she became the first North American Indian ever to be proposed for sainthood; in 1943 she was recognized as possessed of heroic virtue.

Temple, Shirley 1928– actor and diplomat

Born in Santa Monica, California, on April 23, 1928, Shirley Jane Temple was picked from her dancing class when she was three to appear in *Baby Burlesks*, a series of one-reel comedies mimicking serious feature films. In 1934 she appeared in her first feature-length film, the musical *Stand Up and Cheer*, in which her song-and-dance routine "Baby, Take a Bow" won the hearts of audiences everywhere. In quick succession she appeared in *Little Miss Marker*, *Change of Heart*, *Now I'll Tell*, *Now and Forever*, *Baby, Take a Bow*, and *Bright Eyes* (in which she sang "On the Good Ship Lollypop"), all in 1934, and by the end of the year she was one of Hollywood's top stars. In 1935 she was given a special Oscar by the Academy of Motion Picture Arts and Sciences for being "the outstanding personality of 1934." Her dimples and blond ringlets inspired thousands of mothers to make over their daughters for Shirley Temple lookalike contests and were copied on dolls and other toys.

Subsequent films included *The Little Colonel*, 1935, *Our Little Girl*, 1935, *Curly Top*, 1935, *The Littlest Rebel*, 1935, *Captain January*, 1936, *Dimples*, 1936, *Poor Little Rich Girl*, 1936, *Wee Willie Winkie*, 1937, *Heidi*, 1937, *Little Miss Broadway*, 1938, *Rebecca of Sunnybrook Farm*, 1938, *The Little Princess*, 1939, and *Susannah of the Mounties*, 1939. Her spirited singing and dancing, her expressiveness, and the simple optimistic sentiments of the films in which she appeared proved enominously appealing, perhaps in part by contrast with the era of the Great Depression that was her heyday. She was Hollywood's top box office attraction in 1935, 1936, 1937, and 1938.

Temple's star began to dim with *The Blue Bird*, 1940, and she was unceremoniously dropped by her studio. None of her films in the next decade were particularly successful: *Young People*, 1940, *Kathleen*, 1941, *Miss Annie Rooney*, 1942, *Since You Went Away*, 1944, *I'll Be Seeing You*, 1945, *Kiss and Tell*, 1945, *The Bachelor and the Bobby Soxer*, 1947, *That Hagan Girl*, 1947, *Fort Apache*, 1948, *Mr. Belvedere Goes to College*, 1949, *Adventure in Baltimore*, with her first husband, John Agar, 1949, and *The Story of Seabiscuit*, 1950. In 1945 she published an autobiography, *My Young Life*.

In 1950 she retired from the movies, and in December of that year she married Charles A. Black, a San Francisco businessman. She later made a brief return to entertainment with a popular television show, "Shirley Temple's Storybook," in 1957–1959 and the less successful "Shirley Temple Show" in 1960. She also became active in civic affairs and Republican politics. In November 1967 she lost a special election to fill a vacated seat in Congress. In August 1969 President Richard M. Nixon named her to the U.S. delegation to the United Nations General Assembly. In 1974 she was appointed U.S. ambassador to Ghana, and in 1976–1977 she served at the appointment of President Gerald R. Ford as chief of protocol in the State Department. Since 1973 she has been a member of the U.S. Commission for UNESCO. In 1981 she was a member of the U.S. delegation in Geneva on African Refugee Problems. Among her awards are the American Exemplar Medal in 1979 and the Gandhi Memorial International Foundation Award in 1988. Black returned to the screen for one film in 1988, *Child Star*. From 1989 to 1992 she served as ambassador to Czechoslovakia.

Templeton, Fay 1865–1939 actor

Born in Little Rock, Arkansas, on December 25, 1865, Fay Templeton was the daughter of theatrical parents — principals in the touring John Templeton Opera Company — and grew up entirely in that milieu. She was carried on stage in infancy and had her first speaking part at five. While a child she appeared in several plays, including Augustin Daly's productions of *A Midsummer Night's Dream* and *Romeo and Juliet*. She also evinced a flair for mimicry.

By the early 1880s Templeton was touring the country with her own light opera company. Her ascent to fame began with her appearance in *Evangeline* at the Fourteenth Street Theatre in New York City in October 1885. She made her London debut in *Monte Cristo, Junior* at the Gaiety Theatre in December 1886. In a succession of extravaganzas over the next decade she became celebrated equally for her singing, her acting, and her dark seductive beauty. In 1898 she appeared with the team of Joe Weber and Lew Fields in their burlesque *Hurly Burly*, in which her talents for comedy and parody found their home. She starred in Weber and Fields's *Fiddle-dee-dee* in 1900, *Hoity Toity* in 1901, and *Twirly Whirly* in 1902, all of which also featured Lillian Russell. In 1903 she appeared in *The Run-aways*, a musical, and in 1906 she starred in George M. Cohan's *Forty-five Minutes from Broadway*, in which she introduced "Mary's a Grand Old Name" and "So Long, Mary."

For a quarter-century thereafter she lived in semiretirement with her husband in Pittsburgh. She emerged to appear in such productions as Weber and Fields's *Hokey Pokey* in 1912 and several versions of *H.M.S. Pinafore*, in which, with her increasing tendency to corpulence, she made the role of Buttercup virtually her own. She appeared in a film, *Broadway to Hollywood*, in 1933, and late in that year returned to Broadway in Jerome Kern's *Roberta*, with which she then toured in 1934–1935. She retired to the Actors Fund Home in Englewood, New Jersey, in 1936 and moved the next year to San Francisco, where she died on October 3, 1939.

Teresa, Mother 1766?–1846 religious

Born about 1766 in Ireland, Alice Lalor grew up in Kilkenny. She was deeply religious from early childhood. Only the intervention of her parents, who persuaded her instead to accompany an older sister to America, prevented her from joining in the establishment of a community of Presentation nuns in Kilkenny.

By the time of her arrival in Philadelphia in January 1795 she had formed close friendships with two fellow passengers, both widows, with whom she established an informal religious community under the guidance of Father Leonard Neale. They engaged in various types of charitable work and greatly assisted Father Neale during the yellow fever epidemic of 1797–1798. In 1798 Father Neale became president of Georgetown College (now University), and the next year Lalor and her companions followed him to Georgetown, D.C. A short time later they opened a school, and in 1804 they bought a convent abandoned by a group of Poor Clares. Neale, from 1800 bishop coadjutor of the diocese, resisted suggestions that the small community become Sisters of Charity or Ursulines or Carmelites and instead recommended the Visitation order. Accordingly, in December 1816, they were recognized by Pope Pius VII as the first American foundation of the Visitation nuns, and Alice Lalor became first superior as Mother Teresa. She resigned as superior in 1819 and lived out her life in the Georgetown, D.C., convent, where she died on September 9, 1846. From the original Visitation convent 13 others eventually sprang, all with schools.

Terhune, Mary Virginia Hawes 1830–1922 writer

Born on December 21, 1830, in Dennisville, Amelia County, Virginia, Mary Hawes grew up there and from 1844 in nearby Richmond. She was well educated by private tutors and in her father's library. She also briefly attended schools in Hampden-Sydney and in Richmond. She began contributing anonymous sketches and articles to local newspapers when she was fourteen. In 1853 she won a contest for a temperance serial with "Kate Harper," which was published in the weekly *Southern Era* under the pseudonym "Marion Harland." In 1854 her first novel, *Alone*, was published privately in Richmond; two years later it appeared in a commercial edition that eventually sold more than 100,000 copies. Also in 1856 her second novel was published as *The Hidden Path*. In September 1856 she married the Reverend Edward Payson Terhune, with whom she settled in Newark, New Jersey, in 1859.

While caring for the home and several children and taking part in parish activities, she continued to write. Subsequent novels, mostly antebellum plantation romances, included *Moss-Side*, 1857, *Nemesis*, 1860, *At Last*, 1863, *Helen Gardner*, 1864, *Sunnybank*, 1867, *Husbands and Homes*, 1868, *Phemie's Temptation*, 1868, *The Empty Heart*, 1869, *Ruby's Husband*, 1870, *True as Steel*, 1872, *Jessamine*, 1873, and *My Little Love*, 1876. During 1876–1878 she and her husband traveled in Europe for her health. They lived in Springfield, Massachusetts, in 1878–1884 and in Brooklyn, New York, from 1884.

From the publication of the best-selling *Common Sense in the Household*, 1871, Terhune enjoyed virtually a second career as a writer of books on homemaking and related topics. Her books in that field included *Breakfast, Luncheon, and Tea*, 1874, *The*

Dinner Year-Book, 1878, *Eve's Daughters*, 1882, *Common Sense in the Nursery*, 1885, *The National Cook Book*, with her daughter Christine Terhune Herrick, 1896, and *Every Day Etiquette*, with another daughter, Virginia Terhune Van de Water, 1905. She edited at various times the *Home-Maker* and *Housekeeper's Weekly* magazines and contributed articles on homemaking to many others. She wrote syndicated columns on women's affairs for the Philadelphia *North American* in 1900–1910 and the *Chicago Tribune* in 1911–1917.

Terhune's later novels included *Handicapped*, 1882, *Judith*, 1883, *A Gallant Fight*, 1888, *His Great Self*, 1892, *Dr. Dale*, with her son, Albert Payson Terhune (later a well known author, especially of dog stories), 1900, and *The Carringtons of High Hill*, 1919. She also wrote several volumes of travel sketches, biography, and colonial history, including *Loitering in Pleasant Paths*, 1880, *The Story of Mary Washington*, 1892, *Home of the Bible*, 1896, *Some Colonial Homesteads and Their Stories*, 1897, *Where Ghosts Walk*, 1898, *Charlotte Brontë at Home*, 1899, *William Cowper*, 1899, *John Knox*, 1900, *Hannah More*, 1900, and *Looking Westward*, 1914. Her autobiography, *Marion Harland's Autobiography*, appeared in 1910. She died in New York City on June 3, 1922.

Terrell, Mary Eliza Church 1863–1954 writer, lecturer, educator, activist and clubwoman

Born in Memphis, Tennessee, on September 23, 1863, Mary Church was the daughter of Robert Reed Church and Louisa Ayers Church, both former slaves prominent in Memphis's growing black community. Both parents owned small, successful businesses, and they provided "Mollie" and her brother with advantages that few other African-American children of her time enjoyed. After they divorced, she was sent away at age six to attend the Antioch College Model School in Yellow Springs, Ohio; although she boarded with a black family, she was often the only African-American child in her classes there. After two years she transferred to the Antioch public schools. Meanwhile her mother and brother moved North, and she divided her summers between Memphis and New York City.

Determined to excel academically in order to disprove then-widespread theories of racial inferiority, she graduated from public high school in 1879 and entered Oberlin College, where she opted for a rigorous four-year "gentlemen's course" which stressed training in the classics. She often recounted with delight her flawless reading and translation of a Greek text during a visit to the college by Matthew Arnold; informed by her professor that Church was African-American, Arnold expressed surprise, since popular wisdom of the time held that people of African descent were incapable of such learning.

Church graduated in 1884 and returned to Memphis, in deference to her father who insisted it was not proper for a woman to enter a profession. Obedient but restless for a year, she began secretly sending out inquiries for teaching positions. Finally she accepted a job as college secretary and faculty member at Wilberforce College; a year later she moved to the M Street High School (later Dunbar High), the African-American high school in Washington, D.C., where she taught Latin.

In 1888 she received an M.A. from Oberlin and travelled to Europe, where for two years she toured France, Germany, Switzerland, Italy and England and kept journals in both French and German. Upon her return in 1891 she married Robert Terrell, a young Harvard graduate who had worked with her at Dunbar High and who had since earned a law degree in her absence. They settled in Washington. Terrell had three miscarriages there, which she attributed to the poor medical facilities available to African-Americans. During her fourth pregnancy, in 1898, she visited her mother in New York and gave birth there to a healthy baby girl she named Phyllis, after writer Phillis Wheatley.

Reacting to the same event that propelled Ida B. Wells's anti-lynching campaign — the 1892 lynching of lifelong friend Tom Moss, another successful Memphis businessman — Terrell and Frederick Douglass requested an appointment with President Benjamin Harrison and urged him, unsuccessfully, to speak out against racial violence. That same year she helped form the Colored Women's League in Washington D.C. In 1896–97 the League merged with the Federation of Afro-American Women under Josephine St. Pierre Ruffin of Boston. The newly formed group, the National Association of Colored Women (NACW), elected Terrell its first president. Dedicated to improving the lives of African-Americans, especially women, the NACW set out to challenge discrimination, poverty and injustice nationwide.

In her new position Terrell had to deal with many rivalries both in and outside her organization. In 1909 Terrell was one of two African-American women to sign the public call for the formation of the NAACP. Despite her friendship with Booker T. Washington — she supported the work of Tuskegee Institute, and Washington, its founder, repeatedly helped her husband win reappointment as a federal judge — Terrell disagreed with Washington's accomodationist strategy and became a charter member of the NAACP, a group founded by Washington's main critic, W. E. B. DuBois. As NACW president she lectured extensively on racial injustice, lynching, women's suffrage, economics, crime and various aspects of African-American history and culture. Serving as a liaison to white women's club and suffrage movements, she actively campaigned for women's suffrage until the passage of the 19th Amendment. Through the NACW she also represented African-American women in international forums; at the Berlin Congress of Women in 1904, she impressed her audience by delivering her speech in German, French and English. In 1919 she addressed the meeting of the International League for Peace and Freedom in Zurich, and in 1937 she represented African-American Women at the World Fellowship of Faiths in London.

First appointed to the District of Columbia School Board in 1895, she served until 1901 and again from 1906 to 1911. During World War I, Terrell worked for the War Risk Insurance Bureau and became involved in a protest about the treatment of African-American women. After the armistice, she worked with the War Camp Community Service as director of work among African-American girls and women. In these jobs Terrell encountered continued resistance by white people to equal treatment for African-Americans; this infuriated her, since so many black soldiers had died fighting for "democracy" abroad. In 1920 the Republican National Committee hired her to supervise women's work in the East, educating women about the right to vote and encouraging their participation in the Republican Party. In 1929 she campaigned for Ruth Hannah McCormick in her unsuccessful bid to be elected to the U.S. Senate from Illinois.

Toward the end of her life, particularly after her husband's death in 1925, Terrell became increasingly militant in both her politics and her political strategy; she joined picket lines and advocated direct action to challenge discriminatory laws and practices. In 1949, she sued after being refused readmission to the Washington branch of the American Association of University Women; although most members of the local chapter resigned in protest, Terrell was admitted by the national body. In 1949 she was elected chair of the Coordinating Committee for the Enforcement of District of Columbia Anti-Discrimination Laws, a small interracial group targeting restaurants that refused to serve African-Americans. In 1950 they brought suit against Thompson Restaurant, which had refused them service; the U.S. Supreme Court ruled in their favor in 1953, holding that segregated eating facilities in Washington were unconstitutional. Terrell also joined the campaign to free Rosa Ingram, a sharecropper sentenced to death after killing a white man in self-defense. (Ingram was finally freed in 1959.)

A 1940 autobiography, *A Colored Woman in a White World*, followed a lifetime in which she published articles and stories on topics ranging from lynching to sharecropping, from disfranchisement to racial passing. Terrell lived to celebrate the 1954 decision of the U.S. Supreme Court in *Brown vs. Board of Education*, but died two months later on July 29, 1954. She received honorary doctorates from Howard, Wilberforce and Oberlin Colleges, plus many awards from the groups and associations with which she was involved. Many women's clubs were named in her memory, as was a school in Washington, D.C.

Tharp, Twyla 1941– dancer and choreographer

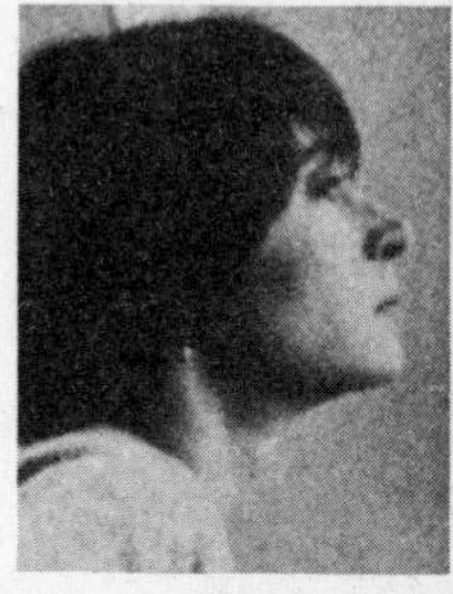

Twyla Tharp

Born on July 1, 1941, in Portland, Indiana, Twyla Tharp grew up there and in Los Angeles. From an early age she studied music: piano at first, followed by violin, viola, and music theory and composition. She also studied various forms of dance, from tap to ballet, and while a student at Barnard College she studied at the American Ballet Theatre School. She also studied privately under Richard Thomas, Martha Graham, Merce Cunningham, and others. In 1963, shortly before her graduation from Barnard, she joined the Paul Taylor Dance Company, where she soon established herself as a dancer of considerable talent and imagination. In 1965 she left the Taylor company to form her own troupe.

Tharp's first publicly performed piece of choreography, *Tank Dive*, was presented in April 1965 at Hunter College in New York City. In performances later in the year she presented *Stage Show*, a piece for the Alaska pavilion at the New York World's Fair, *Stride*, *Cede Blue Lake*, and *Unprocessed*. Through subsequent works, including *Re-Moves* and *Yancey Dance* in 1966, *Forevermore*, *Three Page Sonata for Four*, and *Generation* in 1967, *Excess*, *Idle*, *Surplus*, followed by *Disperse*, *After Suite*, *Group Activities*, *Medley*, and *Dancing in the Streets of Paris and London, Continued in Stockholm and Sometimes Madrid*, in 1969, she built a small but devoted coterie of admirers with her offbeat, technically precise explorations of various kinds and combinations of movements. Her early works generally employed no costumes, sets, properties, or music, and were frequently designed for such spaces as basketball courts, gymnasiums, outdoor areas, or bare stages.

With *Eight Jelly Rolls*, first shown at Oberlin College in January 1971 and brought to New York in September, and *The Bix Pieces*, performed in Paris in November 1971, Tharp adopted jazz music (that of Jelly Roll Morton and Bix Beiderbecke, respectively) and began creating fuller, more engaging works that appealed to larger audiences. Her choreography retained its technical brilliance, often overlaid with an air of nonchalance, while its touches of flippant humor became more marked. *Deuce Coupe*, to music of the Beach Boys, was created for the City Center Joffrey Ballet and premiered to a highly enthusiastic reception in Chicago in February 1973. *As Time Goes By*, also for the Joffrey, followed later in 1973; *In the Beginning* appeared in 1974; and in 1975 she showed *Sue's Leg*, a jazz ballet to Fats Waller's music, and *Ocean's Motion*, a dance piece to Chuck Berry's music.

She was by that time established as one of the most innovative and nonetheless popular of modern choreographers at work anywhere in the world. Subsequent works included *Give and Take*, 1976, *Push Comes to Shove* for the American Ballet Theatre, 1976, *Deuce Coupe II* for the Joffrey, 1976, and *Mud* for her own company, 1977. She also was choreographer for the motion pictures *Hair*, 1979, *Ragtime*, 1981, *Amadeus*, 1984, and *White Nights*, 1985. In 1988 she disbanded her company and moved with some of her members to the American Ballet Theatre where she was an artistic associate until 1990.

Among her other pieces are *Baker's Dozen*, 1979, *When We Were Very Young*, 1980, *The Catherine Wheel*, 1981, *Nine Sinatra Songs*, 1982, *In the Upper Room*, 1986, *Brief Fling*, 1990, and *Demeter and Persephone*, for the Martha Graham Dance Company, 1993. She received a *Dance* magazine award in 1981 and the Samuel H. Scripps American Dance Festival Award in 1990. Tharp published an autobiography, *Push Comes to Shove*, in 1992.

Thaxter, Celia Laighton 1835–1894 poet

Born on June 29, 1835, in Portsmouth, New Hampshire, Celia Laighton grew up on nearby White Island, then on Smutty-nose Island, and from 1848 on Appledore Island (all among the Isles of Shoals off the New Hampshire coast). On the last her father operated a successful resort hotel that included among its guests Ralph Waldo Emerson, James Russell Lowell, John Greenleaf Whittier, Henry David Thoreau, William Morris Hunt, Childe Hassam, Lucy Larcom, and Sarah Orne Jewett. In September 1851 she married Levi L. Thaxter, formerly her father's partner in the hotel. They lived briefly in Watertown, Massachusetts, on Star Island, in Newburyport, Massachusetts, and on Appledore before settling in Newtonville, Massachusetts, in 1856.

Celia Thaxter's homesickness for the sea and the Isles of Shoals found expression in verse, and one of her poems was printed without her knowledge in the *Atlantic Monthly* in March 1861; editor James Russell Lowell supplied the title, "Land-Locked." Thereafter her poems appeared frequently in the *Atlantic*, *Scribner's*, *Harper's*, *Century*, *St. Nicholas*, *Our Young Folks*, *New England Magazine*, and other periodicals. Her first book, *Poems*, was published in 1872 and in an expanded edition in 1874. In 1873 she published *Among the Isles of Shoals*, a collection of prose sketches. Her Newtonville home became something of a literary salon, and she was an accepted member of Boston literary society. From the late 1860s she and her husband were much apart, as he developed a distaste for the islands she loved.

Later books of hers included *Drift Weed*, 1879, *Poems for Children*, 1884, *Idylls and Pastorals*, 1886, *The Cruise of the Mystery*, 1886, and *An Island Garden*, illustrated by Childe Hassam, 1894. Her formally and morally conventional poems were distinguished mainly by the genuine emotion of their descriptions of their author's beloved picturesque Isles of Shoals. Celia Thaxter died on Appledore Island on August 26, 1894.

Thoburn, Isabella 1840–1901 missionary

Born near St. Clairsville, Ohio, on March 29, 1840, Isabella Thoburn attended local schools and the Wheeling Female Seminary in Wheeling, Virginia (now West Virginia). After a period of teaching school in Ohio she studied at the Wheeling school (which had become a college) for another year and then at the Cincinnati Academy of Design for a year. She taught in a public school in Wheeling, in a private school in New Castle, Pennsylvania, and for two years in the Western Reserve Seminary, a Methodist school in West Farmington, Ohio. She was active in relief work during the Civil War.

In 1866 Thoburn was invited by her brother James, a Methodist missionary in India, to join him in his work there. She delayed until 1869, when the formation of the Woman's Foreign Missionary Society of the Methodist Church enabled her to undertake missionary work under denominational auspices. Sailing from New York in company with Clara A. Swain, she arrived in Bombay in January 1870 and made her way thence to Lucknow. She immediately began evangelizing among the women of the zenanas, and in April she opened a girls' school in the bazaar. In 1871 the Woman's Foreign Missionary Society bought for her the seven-acre Lal Bagh estate, formerly the palace of a nobleman of the kingdom of Oudh, and she was able to begin operating a boarding school. In addition to administering and teaching in the school at Lal Bagh, which became the headquarters for women's missionary work in Lucknow. Thoburn also continued active in evangelism and conducted Sunday school classes for Eurasian and Hindu children. During 1874 she served also as principal of a girls' school in Cawnpore.

In 1880–1882 Thoburn took a furlough in the United States, and although she was recuperating from a bout of ill health she traveled throughout the country lecturing on behalf of missionary work in India. After four more years as principal at Lal Bagh she was forced by illness to take another furlough from 1886 to 1890. During that period, in 1887–1888, she served as informal head of the deaconess house organized in Chicago by Lucy Rider Meyer and taught in the Chicago Training School for City, Home and Foreign Missions. She then helped organize the Elizabeth Gamble Deaconess Home and Training School in Cincinnati and helped direct its associated Christ Hospital. Late in 1890 she returned to Lucknow. The Lal Bagh school had become the Girls' High School in 1887 and, following her suggestion, had added a collegiate department. In 1893 a teachers' course and a kindergarten were added. While serving as principal, Thoburn also edited the semimonthly Hindi-language *Rafiq-i-Niswan (Woman's Friend)* newspaper, and in 1891 she helped establish the Wellesley School for girls in Naini Tal.

A charter for a full woman's college was granted by the Indian government in 1895, and her efforts thereafter were devoted to its establishment and support. A fund-raising tour of the United States in 1899–1900 with Lilavati Singh, one of her former pupils, was a considerable success. She fell ill and died in Lucknow on September 1, 1901. The Lucknow Woman's College was renamed Isabella Thoburn College in 1903 and was later made the woman's college of Lucknow University.

Thomas, Helen 1920– journalist

Born in Winchester, Kentucky, on August 4, 1920, to Lebanese immigrants who arrived in the U.S. with $17 between them, Helen Thomas was the seventh of nine children. She moved from Winchester to Detroit with her family when she was four years old. In both localities, her father owned a grocery store, for which he kept the accounts in his head because neither he nor his wife could read or write. Despite their parents' lack of education, however, the Thomas children were raised in an atmosphere of great respect for learning, and encouragement to "be somebody" that extended to daughters as well as sons.

While attending Detroit's Eastern High School, Thomas decided to become a journalist. She joined the staff of the student newspaper, and found the work to be a perfect outlet for her boundless curiosity. After graduating in 1938 she worked for the campus newspaper at Wayne University in Detroit, where she received her B.A. in English in 1942 and moved to Washington, D.C.

She worked as a waitress until she got a job as a copy girl at the now defunct *Washington Daily News*. She was later promoted to cub reporter but soon lost her job to personnel cutbacks. Then, in 1943, she was hired by UPI (then called United Press) to write local news for radio. Although she was originally assigned stereotypically "female" subjects, Thomas's responsibilities at UPI expanded throughout the late 1940s and early 1950s. She was given a regular beat at the U.S. Department of Justice in 1955, a job that would come to include coverage of the FBI, the Department of Health, Education and Welfare, and Capitol Hill as well.

In November 1960 Thomas was given her first assignment related to the Presidency — covering the vacation of president-elect John F. Kennedy and his family in Palm Beach, Florida. Along with Associated Press reporter Frances Lewine, who became a close friend, she indefatigably trailed members of the presidential family around Palm Beach, going so far as to interview Jacqueline Kennedy's hairdresser and employees of the company that supplied diapers for John F. Kennedy, Jr. That experience whetted Thomas's taste for presidential coverage. From then on, she began showing up at presidential press conferences and briefings, where she gained a reputation for asking blunt questions with an irreverent and populist flavor.

In 1970, after UPI's chief White House correspondent Merriman Smith committed suicide, Thomas was promoted to his position. Not long afterward, the Watergate scandal gripped the country, and she distinguished herself through a number of journalistic exclusives. Much of her information was supplied by Martha Mitchell, the wife of John N. Mitchell, who served as Richard Nixon's attorney general and was later jailed for his role in the Watergate break-in and cover-up. Martha Mitchell trusted Thomas and would often confess her fears and suspicions surrounding her husband's activities in late-night phone calls. Thomas later called Mitchell "perhaps the only heroine of the Watergate tidal wave." Earlier, Thomas had been the only print journalist to accompany President Nixon on his historic trip to China in 1972.

In 1974 Thomas became UPI's White House bureau chief, the first woman to hold such a position for a wire service. This was one of a number of firsts for Thomas as a woman reporter, starting in 1959 when she and some female colleagues forced the then all-male National Press Club to allow them to attend an address to the group by Soviet premier Nikita Khrushchev. After the National Press Club finally opened its membership to women in 1971, Thomas became its first female officer. In 1975 the Gridiron Club, Washington's most exclusive press organization, invited her to become its first female member, and she became its president in 1993. She also became the first woman president of the White House Correspondents' Association in 1975.

Thomas's bold, populist style and insistence on holding presidents accountable for their actions gained her great respect among fellow journalists and the public. However, she was not without her critics. She was accused by some reporters and White House officials of being too much of an advocate for her own point of view, and by others of expressing a pro-Arab bias in regard to the Middle East, a charge she emphatically denied.

Thomas published a memoir *Dateline: White House* in 1975. She received many honorary doctorates and journalism awards, and in 1992 UPI established an annual internship in her name to be awarded to a female journalism student. In 1993 she completed fifty years as a reporter for UPI, thirty-two of which were spent covering the presidency. As the senior wire-service correspondent at the White House, she was known to television viewers as the reporter whose dignified "Thank you, Mr. President" signaled the end of White House press conferences.

Thomas, Martha Carey 1857–1935 educator and feminist

Born in Baltimore on January 2, 1857, Carey Thomas, as she preferred from her college days to be known, was the daughter of a modestly prosperous Quaker family. She early developed a taste for reading, a dedication to women's rights, and an imperious will. She attended Quaker schools in Baltimore and in Ithaca, New York, then overrode her father's objections and sought a college education. Two years after entering as a junior, she graduated from Cornell University in 1877. She spent a year at The Johns Hopkins University, where she studied privately under Professor Basil L. Gildersleeve because she was not allowed to attend classes, and then traveled to Europe to work on a doctorate in linguistics.

After three years at the University of Leipzig she was refused a degree because she was a woman; she then applied to Zurich, was accepted for examination, and received her Ph.D. summa cum laude in 1882. After a year of further work at the Sorbonne in Paris she returned to the United States and in 1884 was appointed professor of English at and dean of the newly established Bryn Mawr College for women, which opened in 1885. She was the first woman college faculty member in the country to hold the title "dean."

At Bryn Mawr Thomas quickly established herself as a leading and soon the dominant influence. She largely organized the undergraduate studies program and started the first graduate program at any women's school. In 1885 she joined her long-time friend Mary Garrett and others in founding the Bryn Mawr School for Girls in Baltimore, and in 1889 the same group organized a major fund-raising campaign that helped persuade the Johns

Hopkins faculty to open its new medical school to women. She also established scholarships for European students to study at Bryn Mawr, the first such graduate scholarships in the United States. She progressively reduced her teaching work at Bryn Mawr in favor of administration, and by 1892 she had virtually supplanted President James E. Rhoads. In 1894, with the trustees swayed in part by Mary Garrett's promise of financial support, Carey Thomas was chosen to succeed the retiring Rhoads. She continued as dean until 1908 and as president until 1922.

During that time Thomas stoutly maintained the high academic standards she had originally established for Bryn Mawr, standards unsurpassed by any men's college in America. Intellectual rigor and her own lifelong distaste for dilettantism shaped the curriculum of the college. She championed the cause of woman suffrage and worked for the passage of the Nineteenth Amendment to the Constitution, serving as president of the National College Women's Equal Suffrage League from 1908 to 1913. She was a founder in 1900 of the Association to Promote Scientific Research by Women and of the International Federation of University Women, and in 1921 she established the Summer School for Women Workers in Industry. After her retirement from Bryn Mawr in 1922 she traveled widely and luxuriously on her large inheritance from Mary Garrett. She died at her home in Philadelphia on December 2, 1935.

Thompson, Dorothy 1894–1961 journalist

Born in Lancaster, New York, on July 9, 1894, Dorothy Thompson grew up there and in Chicago, where she attended the Lewis Institute. She graduated from Syracuse University in 1914, and after a period of graduate study at the University of Vienna she spent several years in New York City doing social work and campaigning for woman suffrage. In 1920 she sailed for Europe and, while still on board ship, decided on a career in journalism.

Dorothy Thompson

She spent the next nine years in Europe. Her exclusive interview with Empress Zita of Austria after Emperor Karl's unsuccessful attempt to regain the throne in 1921 established her reputation as a reporter. She worked as a foreign correspondent for the *Philadelphia Ledger* and from 1923 for the *New York Post*, and from 1924 to 1928 she was Berlin bureau chief for the *Post*. After divorcing her first husband she married novelist Sinclair Lewis in 1928. On returning to the United States after their marriage, they divided their time between Woodstock, Vermont, and New York City. (They were divorced in 1942.) In the early 1930s she again reported from Europe. From 1936 to 1941 she wrote the thrice-weekly column "On the Record" for the *New York Herald Tribune*; the subsequent syndication of the column by the Bell Syndicate to some 170 other papers made her one of the most widely read and influential journalists in the country. From 1937 she was also a regular columnist for the *Ladies' Home Journal*, and in 1938–1939 she conducted a radio news program that attracted an estimated 5 million listeners.

During the 1930s Thompson took a vehemently anti-Fascist position in foreign affairs, and after her expulsion from Germany she lectured widely and effectively against the Hitler regime. Events in Germany drew her attention to the refugee problem, and she wrote many articles urging the United States to admit refugees who were being driven out of Europe by Fascism.

Her books included *Depths of Prosperity*, with Phyllis Bottome, 1925, *The New Russia*, 1928, *I Saw Hitler!*, 1932, *Refugees, Anarchy or Organization?*, 1938, *Political Guide*, 1938, *Let the Record Speak*, 1939, *Listen, Hans*, 1942, and *The Courage To Be Happy*, 1957. After the death in 1957 of her third husband, Maxim Kopf, she retired. She died in Lisbon, Portugal, on January 30, 1961.

Thompson, Kay 1911– entertainer and writer

Born in St. Louis in 1911, Kay Thompson early displayed a considerable talent for the piano. At sixteen she appeared as a soloist with the St. Louis Symphony. At seventeen she made her way to California, where she worked as a vocalist with the Mills Brothers. Later she was a singer and arranger for Fred Waring's band and then produced and hosted a CBS radio program, "Kay Thompson and Company." From 1942 to 1946 she was a composer and arranger for Metro-Goldwyn-Mayer studios in Hollywood, contributing to the scores of such films as *The Harvey Girls*, *The Ziegfeld Follies*, and *The Kid from Brooklyn*. In 1947 she went on the road with her own nightclub act and enjoyed success in clubs in Hollywood, Chicago, Miami, and New York City.

In 1954 Thompson staged a short-lived one-woman show at the Hotel Plaza in New York. Out of various experiences grew the idea for her first book, *Eloise*, published in 1955. *Eloise* illustrated by Hilary Knight, told of the adventures of an ill mannered, unattractive, but appealingly precocious six-year-old who was the terror of the Hotel Plaza. The book reached the best-seller list in 1956, as did its sequels *Eloise in Paris*, 1957, and *Eloise at Christmastime*, 1958. *Eloise in Moscow* followed in 1959 and *Eloise Takes a Bawth*, 1964.

The books spawned a variety of related products, including postcards, dolls, and a phonograph record. Thompson appeared in the motion pictures *Funny Face*, 1956, and *Tell Me That You Love Me Junie Moon*, 1970; she appeared also on various television programs and composed a hit song, "Promise Me Love." She published *Kay Thompson's Miss Pooky Peckinpaugh and Her Secret Private Boyfriends Complete with Telephone Numbers*, 1970.

Thorpe, Rose Alnora Hartwick 1850–1939 poet

Born on July 18, 1850, in Mishawaka, Indiana, Rose Hartwick grew up there, in Kansas, and in Litchfield, Michigan, where she graduated from public high school in 1868. From an early age she wrote poetry, much of it patterned on the sentimental verses of Lydia H. Sigourney and Felicia Hemans. In the September 1865 issue of *Peterson's Magazine* she read a short story that told how Bessie, the beautiful daughter of a forester in the England of Cromwell's time, saved her Cavalier lover Basil. Basil, convicted as a spy, was to be shot when the curfew bell rang. Bessie raced up the church steps and by clinging bodily to the clapper prevented the great bell from ringing; in the time thus gained she pleaded successfully with Cromwell for Basil's life.

Rose Hartwick turned the story into long lines of Longfellowesque trochaic heptameters and gave the poem the title "Curfew Must Not Ring Tonight." In 1870 she submitted it to the *Commercial Advertiser* of Detroit, which had published some of her earlier pieces, and from there it spread rapidly to other newspapers throughout the country. It was taken up as a favorite declamation piece and was widely anthologized and translated, but, not having taken the precaution of obtaining a copyright, Rose Hartwick profited little from the poem's great popularity. In September 1871 she married Edmund C. Thorpe. She continued to contribute verses to *Youth's Companion*, *St. Nicholas*, *Wide Awake*, and other periodicals. Her husband's carriage-making business failed in 1881, and in that year she became editor of and principal contributor to a series of moralistic monthlies published by Fleming H. Revell, including *Temperance Tales*, *Words of Life*, and *Well-Spring*.

In the same year Thorpe published *Fred's Dark Days*, a book of fiction for children; there followed *The Yule Log*, 1881, *The Fenton Family*, 1884, *Nina Bruce*, 1886, *The Chester Girls*, 1887, and *The Year's Best Days*, 1888. She also published *Temperance Poems*, 1886, *Ringing Ballads*, 1887, *Sweet Song Stories*, 1898, *The White Lady of La Jolla*, 1904, and her collected *Poetical Works of Rose Hartwick Thorpe*, 1912. Others of her best known poems included "Remember the Alamo," "The Station Agent's Story," "Mother of Mine," "God's Way is Best," and "Life's Peaceful Twilight." She and her husband later lived in San Antonio, Texas, and from 1886 in San Diego, California, where she died on July 19, 1939.

Thurber, Jeannette Meyer 1850–1946 music patron

Born in New York City on January 29, 1850, Jeannette Meyer was privately educated in New York and Paris. In September 1869 she married Francis B. Thurber, a wholesale grocer and later a lawyer and in 1881 principal organizer of the National Anti-Monopoly League. Influenced by her observations of the French system of government-sponsored music education, she soon began working toward such a system for the United States. She began by providing funds for music study abroad for American students.

In 1883 Thurber supported the free young peoples' concerts led by Theodore Thomas, and in 1884 she sponsored Thomas's first American Wagner festival. In 1885 she secured a New York state charter for a National Conservatory of Music, under the aegis of which the American School of Opera opened in December 1885. With support from such philanthropists as Andrew Carnegie and August Belmont and with Theodore Thomas as musical director, the school's resident company, a large and ambitious undertaking, mounted its first production at the New York Academy of Music in January 1886. The season, which featured the first American production of *Lakmé*, was an artistic success and a financial disaster. Reorganized as the National Opera, the company managed a second season before dissolving in June 1887.

Thurber thereafter concentrated her energies on the National Conservatory of Music, which was incorporated by act of Congress in March 1891. In 1892 she persuaded Antonin Dvorák to serve a three-year term as director of the school. It was Harry T. Burleigh, one of the African-American students who had benefited by the school's nondiscriminatory admissions policy, who brought American folk music, particularly plantation songs, to the attention of Dvorák, and at Thurber's suggestion the composer used them in several compositions, including his Symphony No. 9, *From the New World.* Despite the school's international reputation private and public support were not forthcoming, and gradually it withered. By 1920 it existed largely on paper, although Thurber continued to seek a permanent foundation for it. She died in Bronxville, New York, on January 2, 1946.

Thursby, Emma Cecilia 1845–1931 singer and educator

Born in Williamsburg (now part of Brooklyn), New York, on February 21, 1845, Emma Thursby began singing in church at the age of five. Her musical training began at the Bethlehem Female Seminary in Pennsylvania in 1857, and in 1859 her schooling ended with a few months at a convent school in Brooklyn. In that year, her father having died and the family having fallen into financial difficulty, she began giving private music lessons. She continued her own vocal studies under Julius Meyer in 1867 and Achille Errani in 1871. She was a soloist in the choir of a local Dutch Reformed church in 1865–1868 and in that of Henry Ward Beecher's Plymouth Church in 1868–1871. At the same time she began appearing on local concert stages, and in April 1868 she took part in the Brooklyn Musical Association's performance of Haydn's *Creation* oratorio. She sang also with the Brooklyn and the Boston Handel and Haydn societies. In 1872–1873 she studied under Francesco Lamperti and Antonio Sangiovanni in Milan, and in 1875 she became a pupil of Erminia Mansfield-Rudersdorff in New York.

A concert performance with Patrick S. Gilmore's 22nd Regiment Band at the Philadelphia Academy of Music in November 1874 began Thursby's rise to national and international acclaim. She made a tour of several cities with Gilmore. A year later she appeared in a joint concert with Hans von Bülow at New York's Chickering Hall, and she toured California and appeared on the Redpath Lyceum circuit with Mark Twain in 1876. She was engaged by the Church of the Divine Paternity and then by the Broadway Tabernacle, but in 1877 she gave up church singing in favor of the concert stage; she never overcame her scruples against grand opera, however. Under the management of Maurice

Strakosch she made a concert tour of the United States and Canada in 1877–1878, and in May 1878 she made her London debut at St. James's Hall. She remained in Great Britain for nearly a year. She appeared at the Théâtre de Châtelet in Paris in March 1879.

After an American tour in 1879–1880, during which she appeared with violinist Ole Bull, Thursby made a tour of Germany. In 1881 she was awarded the medal of the Société des Concerts of the Paris Conservatoire. Her European following was large and enthusiastic, attracted by a voice of bell-like clarity, flexibility, and remarkable range. After 1884 she appeared infrequently, and her last major performance occurred in Chicago in December 1895. She devoted herself thereafter to teaching, from 1905 to 1911 as professor of music at the Institute of Musical Art in New York City. Among her pupils was Geraldine Farrar. An invalid from 1924, she died in New York City on July 4, 1931.

Tingley, Katherine Augusta Westcott 1847–1929 theosophist

Born in Newbury, Massachusetts, on July 6, 1847, Katherine Westcott was educated in public schools and briefly in a convent school in Montreal. Much of her early life is obscure. An early marriage ended within months, and she may have acted with a traveling theatrical troupe. In April 1888 in New York City she married her third husband, Philo B. Tingley, an engineer. She was interested in various charitable activities as well as in spiritualism, and in her mission work on the Lower East Side she often attempted to combine the two. In the winter of 1892–1893 she met William Quan Judge, who in 1875 had helped Helena Blavatsky form the Theosophical Society.

In 1895 Judge led the American branch of the society out of the international movement based in Adyar, India, and reorganized it as the Theosophical Society in America. On his death in 1896 a secret diary, supposed to be Judge's, was found, and in it were numerous references to an unidentified person whom he had secretly appointed to succeed him as "Outer Head" of the society's Esoteric Section. The mysteriously described "Promise," "Veiled Mahatma," "Light of the Lodge," and "Purple Mother," it soon became clear, was Tingley. She moved confidently to assume power, installed her own nominee as president of the society (a position of less influence than her own), and began to reshape the organization according to her own notions. She raised funds to establish the School for the Revival of the Lost Mysteries of Antiquity. In 1896–1897 she and a few followers made a world tour, during which, she later claimed, she met with a Tibetan mahatma.

In 1897 she founded the International Brotherhood League to work for the benefit of convicts, "fallen women," and ordinary workingmen and to promote racial harmony. In April 1898 she promulgated a new constitution under which the league and the Theosophical Society were merged into the Universal Brotherhood and Theosophical Society, of which she had absolute control as "Leader and Official Head."

In February 1897 Tingley had dedicated a new headquarters for the society at Point Loma, a picturesque promontory north of San Diego, and in 1900 she established herself there. A remarkable "white city" of eclectic Asian architecture grew up at Point Loma and became a center for artists, poets, and sightseers. An active and experimental horticultural program greatly added to the beauty of the site. The School for the Revival of the Lost Mysteries of Antiquity was transferred there and evolved into the Theosophical University, which was chartered by the state of California in 1919. The Raja Yoga school and college educated about 300 children, some as a charity, with a program combining shared labor, calisthenics, music and drama, and live-in teachers. Katherine Tingley edited the weekly *Century Path* from 1907 to 1911, its successor the *Theosophical Path* from 1911 to 1929, and the bi-monthly *Râja Yoga Messenger* from 1912 to 1929.

She established theosophical schools in Cuba, Sweden, Germany, England, Massachusetts, and Minnesota, but nearly all were short-lived. Her single-minded devotion to Point Loma left the society at large open to schism; some local lodges rejoined the Adyar group, while others formed the United Lodge of Theosophists. She was sued successfully for alienation of affections in 1925 by the wife of one of her followers and lived thereafter mainly in Europe. She was severely injured in an automobile accident in Germany in 1929, and she died two months later, on July 11, 1929, at the theosophist community at Visingsö, Sweden.

Todd, Mabel Loomis 1856–1932 writer and editor

Born on November 10, 1856, in Cambridge, Massachusetts, Mabel Loomis grew up and attended private schools there and in the District of Columbia. After leaving Georgetown Seminary she studied at the New England Conservatory of Music in Boston for a time. In March 1879 she married David P. Todd, an astronomer who in 1881 joined the faculty of Amherst College. In Amherst she became a close friend of the Dickinson family; she corresponded with and frequently played the piano for the reclusive Emily Dickinson but never met her in person. She was deeply impressed by a few of Emily's poems, and when the poet died in May 1886 and several hundred poems were found neatly bundled away, the family asked her to prepare them for publication.

After nearly two years of painstaking work she was joined by Thomas W. S. Higginson, who had had a long correspondence with Emily Dickinson and had long felt that her poems were unpublishable. He undertook to polish and "correct" several of the poems chosen for publication. A volume of *Poems by Emily Dickinson* appeared in 1890 and was followed by a second volume in 1891. By herself Todd prepared a third volume, which appeared in 1896. She also published two volumes of *Letters of Emily Dickinson* in 1894. Others of her books included *Footprints*, a novel, 1883, *Total Eclipses of the Sun*, long a popular treatment, 1894, *Corona and Coronet*, based on a trip to Japan (one of many trips with her husband to observe eclipses), 1898, *A Cycle of Sunsets*, 1910, and *Tripoli the Mysterious*, 1912.

She wrote numerous articles on nature and conservation and was active in the Audubon Society. She helped organize the Boston Authors' Club and the Amherst Historical Society. She died at her summer home on Hog Island, Maine, on October 14, 1932.

Tomlin, Lily 1939– comedian and actor

Born in 1939 in Detroit, Michigan, Lily Tomlin began her career performing at Wayne State University and inventing characters for comedy routines at a local coffeehouse. She moved briefly to New York City to study mime with Paul Curtin, then returned to Detroit. By 1965 she was back in New York at work in comedy clubs and television variety shows, including *The Garry Moore Show* and *The Merv Griffin Show*.

Tomlin credited Elaine May and especially Ruth Draper for influencing her development of humorous characters. In 1969 her roles as Ernestine and Edith Ann on the weekly television comedy show *Laugh-In* catapulted her into the national limelight. She earned a Grammy award for best comedy recording for *This is a Recording*, 1971, and she collaborated with her partner, Jane Wagner, to produce the album *And That's the Truth*, 1972. She earned Emmy Awards for writing in 1974 for her television special "Lily," in 1976 for "Lily Tomlin," and in 1978 for "The Paul Simon Special." She earned an Emmy Award in 1981 as executive producer of "Lily — Sold Out" and an Emmy nomination in 1984 for her performance in "Live . . . and in Person."

Tomlin regularly performed at fundraisers to benefit the campaign for the Equal Rights Amendment, and she frequently worked for other women's causes. She made her film debut in *Nashville*, 1975, winning an Academy Award nomination for best supporting actress and a New York Film Critics Award for her performance. Her film roles included

Moment by Moment, 1978, *Nine to Five*, 1980, *All of Me*, 1984, and *Shadows and Fog*, 1992. Her one-woman shows, *Appearing Nitely* and *The Search for Signs of Intelligent Life in the Universe*, earned several awards; the latter toured nationally and was released as a film.

Tompkins, Sally Louisa 1833–1916 humanitarian and philanthropist

Born in Poplar Grove, Mathews County, Virginia, on November 9, 1833, Sally Tompkins grew up there and in Richmond. Coming from a wealthy family, she devoted most of her time to philanthropic undertakings. When the Civil War began, she turned a large house in Richmond into a hospital at her own expense and operated it as the Robertson Hospital throughout the war, until June 1865. In September 1861, following the building of several military hospitals around Richmond, President Jefferson Davis of the Confederate States issued an order discontinuing all private hospitals, but to circumvent his order in her case he commissioned Tompkins a captain in the Confederate cavalry, making her the only woman to hold a Confederate commission.

As "Captain Sally" (a title she carried the rest of her life) she was thereafter able to operate her hospital more efficiently than before and with the cooperation of the military. In the nearly four years her hospital was in operation, it cared for more than a thousand patients, of whom only 73 died, an amazing record unapproached by any other hospital in the war. After the war she continued her various philanthropies until financial reverses destroyed the family fortune. She died in Richmond on July 25, 1916, and was buried with military honors.

Towle, Katherine Amelia 1898–1986 educator and marine officer

Born on April 30, 1898, in Towle, California, Katherine Towle graduated from the University of California at Berkeley in 1920, and after a year as assistant admissions officer at the school she spent a year, 1922–1923, in advanced study at Columbia University. She then rejoined the administrative staff at Berkeley. In 1927 she was named resident dean of a private girls' school in Piedmont, California, and she became headmistress in 1929. In 1933 she resumed studies in political science at Berkeley, receiving a master's degree in 1935. From that year to 1942 she was assistant to the manager and a senior editor of the University of California Press.

In February 1943 Towle took a commission as captain in the newly established Women's Reserve (WR) of the marine corps. Until September 1944 her duties were divided between corps headquarters in Washington, D.C., and the women's training centers at Hunter College, New York City, and, from June 1943, at Camp Lejeune, North Carolina. Promoted to major in February 1944, she became in September assistant director of the WR, advancing to lieutenant colonel in March 1945, and in December 1945 she was promoted to colonel and named director to succeed Colonel Ruth C. Streeter. Towle remained in that post until June 1946, when the WR was inactivated.

During 1946–1947 she served as administrative assistant to the vice-president and provost of the University of California, and in July 1947 she was appointed assistant dean of women. With the passage of the Women's Armed Forces Integration Act of June 12, 1948, the women's reserve of the marine corps, like those of the other arms, was integrated into the active line. Colonel Towle was recalled to active duty as director in October. She retired from that post in May 1953. She then served as dean of women and associate dean of students at the University of California at Berkeley from 1953 to 1962 and as dean of students from 1962 until her retirement. During her tenure as dean of students, she ordered that political activity on the campus be limited. The students reacted with sit-ins and demonstrations and formed a protest group, the Free Speech Movement, which kept the student involvement and activism high for months. She died on March 1, 1986, in Pacific Grove, California.

Towne, Laura Matilda 1825–1901 educator

Born in Pittsburgh on May 3, 1825, Laura Towne grew up from 1833 in Boston and from 1840 in Philadelphia. She studied homeopathic medicine privately and probably attended the short-lived Penn Medical University for a time; she was also interested in abolitionism. She taught in charity schools in various northern towns and cities in the 1850s and 1860s.

Early in 1862 she responded to a call for volunteers to teach, nurse, and otherwise attend to the large population of former slaves who had been liberated in the Union capture of Port Royal and others of the Sea Islands of South Carolina. In April she arrived at St. Helena Island and became secretary and housekeeper in the headquarters of the Port Royal Relief Committee. Within a short time she was teaching school, practicing medicine, and helping to direct the distribution of clothing and other goods.

In September 1862 Towne established the Penn School, one of the earliest freedmen's schools, and laid down a rigorous curriculum patterned on the tradition of New England schools. By 1867 she had given up the practice of medicine to devote herself entirely to the school, which remained for decades the only second school available to the African-American population of the Sea Islands. From 1870 a normal department also offered teacher training courses. The school was supported for a time, and only in part, by the Pennsylvania Freedmen's Relief Association, later by the Benezet Society of Germantown, Pennsylvania, and later still by various members of Towne's family.

She herself lived on her modest inheritance and drew no salary for her work. She served the Sea Islanders also as an informal adviser in legal and other matters, as a public health officer, and as a temperance advocate. She conducted the school until her death at Frogmore, her restored plantation on St. Helena Island, on February 22, 1901. The school was renamed the Penn Normal, Industrial, and Agricultural School a short time later and was redirected toward the vocational training Towne had always resisted. In 1948 it became part of the South Carolina public school system.

Trask, Kate Nichols 1853–1922 writer and philanthropist

Born in Brooklyn, New York, on May 30, 1853, Kate Nichols was of a wealthy family and was privately educated. In November 1874 she married Spencer Trask, a banker and financier. Although she had had literary leanings from childhood, it was not until the late 1880s, in the wake of a period of illness and despondency that followed the deaths of her children, that she began to write. *Under King Constantine*, a set of three lengthy love poems, was published anonymously in 1892.

Its success warranted four more editions, and from the second the book was signed "Katrina Trask." Subsequent books, similarly signed, included *Sonnets and Lyrics*, 1894, *White Satin and Homespun*, 1896, *John Leighton, Jr.*, 1898, *Christalan*, 1903, *Free, Not Bound*, 1903, *Night & Morning*, 1907, *King Alfred's Jewel*, 1908, and *The Mighty and the Lowly*, 1915. *In the Vanguard*, 1914, was an antiwar play that was widely performed for women's clubs and church groups. With her husband she was active in various philanthropies, but her major concern came to center on Yaddo, their 300-acre estate near Saratoga Springs, New York. She entertained a mystical reverence for the spot, believing it to be a source of creative inspiration, and about 1899 she began planning for its eventual opening to other artists. That planning occupied her much of the rest of her life.

In 1913 she made public her plans for Yaddo. She died at Yaddo, after several years of semi-invalidism, on January 8, 1922. In June 1926 Yaddo was opened as an artists' colony, and it continued to serve thereafter as a summer retreat for serious artists.

Traubel, Helen 1903–1972 opera singer

Born in St. Louis on June 16, 1903 (some sources say 1899), Helen Traubel was of a musical family and at thirteen began taking vocal lessons from Vetta Karst. She left high school a short time later to devote full time to singing, and in 1925 she made her concert debut with the St. Louis Symphony. She toured midwestern and southern cities with the orchestra, sang at Lewisohn Stadium in New York City and with the New York Philharmonic in 1926, and later sang a concert series with the Philadelphia Orchestra.

Her singing was confined largely to church choirs until 1937, when Walter Damrosch invited her to create the role of Mary Rutledge in his opera *The Man Without a Country*, which was premiered by the Metropolitan Opera in May of that year. For the next two years she continued her training in New York while singing frequently on the radio. She made her New York concert debut at Town Hall in October 1939, and after a warmup performance in Chicago she made her debut in the Met's regular season as Sieglinde in *Die Walküre* in December 1939.

With the departure of Kirsten Flagstad in 1941, Traubel became the Met's leading Wagnerian soprano, a distinction she held for a dozen years. To a magnificent voice, controlled throughout its range and capable of fine emotional shading, she added a dignified and strong dramatic presence. She made several national and European concert tours, appeared in operatic productions in Buenos Aires, Mexico City, San Francisco, and other cities, and was a popular recording artist.

In 1949–1950 she served as musical supervisor for Margaret Truman, the daughter of President Harry S. Truman. She also sang frequently on radio and television. In 1950 she became part owner of the St. Louis Browns baseball team, and later in the year she published privately her first book, a mystery entitled *The Ptomaine Canary*. Her second, *The Metropolitan Opera Murders*, appeared in 1951. In 1953 the Met's general manager, Rudolf Bing, objected strenuously to her appearances in New York nightclubs, whereupon she resigned her contract. She subsequently appeared on Broadway in the Rodgers and Hammerstein musical *Pipe Dream*, 1955, and in several motion pictures. Her autobiography, *St. Louis Woman*, written with R. G. Hubler, appeared in 1959. She died in Santa Monica, California, on July 28, 1972.

Trigère, Pauline 1912– couturiere

Born in Paris on November 4, 1912, Pauline Trigère was the daughter of a tailor. She early learned to sew and helped her mother custom-tailor women's clothes. After graduating from the Collage Victor Hugo she went to work in the salon of Martial et Armand in the Place Vendôme and began learning the secrets of design and construction of women's clothing. In 1937 she moved to the United States with her mother, her brother, and two children from her dissolved marriage. She worked for New York fashion houses for five years and then in 1942 established Trigère, Inc. to produce her own designs.

With her brother Robert as salesman she achieved rapid success. Her mastery of French styling attracted major buyers across the country, and as her originality developed she assumed a position at the forefront of American couture. She was naturalized in 1944. In 1949 she was the recipient of the Coty American Fashion Critics' Award, an honor she repeated in 1951 and in 1959, on the latter occasion being inducted into the Coty Fashion Hall of Fame. While her designs were generally conservative, she made innovative use of such textiles as cotton (winning the 1959 Cotton Award thereby) and wool (in evening dresses) and devised such novelties as the reversible coat, the mobile collar, the spiral jacket, and the sleeveless coat. By 1958 Trigère, Inc. enjoyed annual sales in excess of $2 million, and the firm continued thereafter to prosper. By 1992 Trigère was the only designer to have remained in business for fifty years. She received the Silver Medal of the City of Paris in 1972 and the Lifetime Achievement Award from the Council of Fashion Designers of America in 1993.

Truth, Sojourner 1797?–1883 abolitionist

Born a slave in Ulster County, New York, in the late 1790s, Sojourner Truth, the daughter of slaves, was given at birth the name Isabella. In 1827 she took the surname Van Wagener from a family that had taken her in after she had fled from the last of a series of masters who owned her prior to the passage of the New York Emancipation Act of 1827. Little is known of her early life other than her claim that, from childhood, she had conversed with God.

One of her first acts as a free woman was to sue successfully for the return of a son who had been sold illegally to an Alabama slaveholder. She subsequently lived and worked as a servant in New York City, where she became active as an evangelist in association with Elijah Pierson, an evangelical zealot. Following the dissolution, amid a welter of court trials and popular scandal, of "Zion Hill," a utopian community established in 1833 by Pierson and one Robert Matthews at Sing Sing, New York, Isabella lived quietly for some years.

In 1843, however, the voices that followed her throughout life instructed her to adopt the new name Sojourner Truth and to take to the road as an itinerant preacher. She walked and preached through Long Island and Connecticut and by the end of the year had settled in Northampton, Massachusetts, where she first encountered and enthusiastically adopted the abolitionist cause. She became known throughout the state as a moving speaker on that topic and on that of women's rights, a movement she adopted at the Worcester, Massachusetts, convention in 1850. In that year she set out on a western tour; from headquarters in Ohio she made forays into Indiana, Missouri, and Kansas.

With her deep voice and simple message of God's mystical love, Truth was an effective preacher in spite of her illiteracy. Her usual opening, "Children, I talk to God and God talks to me!," had an electric effect on her audiences. She rivaled in eloquence the famed Frederick Douglass, with whom she frequently shared the platform. In their most famous encounter, when he urged a pre-Civil War black audience to seek justice in revolt, Truth broke the spell by asking, "Frederick, is God dead?" A large measure of her support came from widespread sales of *The Narrative of Sojourner Truth*, 1850, written by Olive Gilbert and with a preface by William Lloyd Garrison. Another edition after the Civil War was prefaced by Harriet Beecher Stowe. At the outbreak of the Civil War she solicited supplies for black volunteer regiments. Her fame preceded her to Washington, where President Abraham Lincoln received her in the White House in October 1864. She then served about a year as a counselor for the National Freedmen's Relief Association.

After the Civil War Truth continued to travel and lecture on women's rights and her idea for a western settlement for freedmen. In 1875 she retired to Battle Creek, Michigan, where she had settled her family 20 years before. She died on November 26, 1883, in Battle Creek, Michigan.

Tubman, Harriet 1820?–1913 abolitionist

Born a slave about 1820 on a plantation in Dorchester County, Maryland, Araminta Greene later adopted her mother's first name, Harriet. From early childhood she worked variously as a maid, a nurse, a field hand, a cook, and a woodcutter. About the age of thirteen an overseer struck her a heavy blow to the head, resulting in periodic spells of somnolence that came over her without warning for the rest of her life. About 1844 she married John Tubman, a free Negro.

In 1849, on the strength of rumors that she was about to be sold, she fled to Philadelphia. In December 1850 she made her way to Baltimore, whence she led her sister and two children to freedom. That journey was the first of some 19 increasingly dangerous forays into Maryland in which, over the next decade, she conducted upwards of 300

Harriet Tubman

fugitive slaves along the "Underground Railroad" to Canada. By dint of extraordinary courage, ingenuity, persistence, and iron discipline, which she enforced upon her charges, she became the railroad's most famous conductor and was known as the "Moses of her people." Rewards offered by slaveholders for her capture eventually totaled $40,000. She was celebrated among abolitionists; John Brown, who consulted her about his own plans, referred to her as "General" Tubman. About 1858 she bought from William H. Seward a small farm near Auburn, New York, where she placed her aged parents (she had brought them out of Maryland in June 1857) and herself lived thereafter. From 1862 to 1865 she served as a scout and spy, as well as nurse and laundress, for Union forces in South Carolina.

After the Civil War she settled in Auburn and began taking in orphans and old people, a practice that eventuated in the Harriet Tubman Home for Indigent Aged Negroes. The home later attracted the support of former abolitionist comrades and of the citizens of Auburn, and it continued in existence for some years after her death. In the late 1860s and again in the late 1890s she applied for a federal pension for her Civil War services. A private bill providing for $20 monthly was at length passed by Congress. She died in Auburn, New York, on March 10, 1913.

Tuchman, Barbara Wertheim 1912–1989 writer and historian

Born in New York City on January 30, 1912, Barbara Wertheim was a granddaughter of banker and diplomat Henry Morgenthau, Sr. She was educated at the Walden School in New York and early developed an interest in history, in part from her reading of Lucy Fitch Perkins's "Twins" series. She graduated from Radcliffe College in 1933 and the next year joined the staff of the Institute of Pacific Relations. After a year in Tokyo with that organization she returned to New York City in 1935 and joined the editorial staff of the *Nation*. She reported for the *Nation* from Spain during the civil war there and then wrote for the London periodical *The War in Spain*.

In 1938 she published *The Lost British Policy: Britain and Spain Since 1700*. In that year she returned to the United States. After a period as a freelance contributor to the *Nation* she became U.S. correspondent for the British *New Statesman and Nation*. In June 1940 she married Dr. Lester R. Tuchman. During 1943–1945 she was a news editor for the Office of War Information. She contributed frequently to such periodicals as the *New Republic*, *Harper's*, *Atlantic Monthly*, and *Foreign Affairs*. Her second book, *Bible and Sword: England and Palestine from the Bronze Age to Balfour*, appeared in 1956 and was followed by *The Zimmermann Telegram*, a study of a diplomatic incident in World War I, 1958.

The Guns of August, 1962, was a history of the prelude to and first weeks of World War I that became a best-seller and was awarded a Pulitzer Prize. In 1966 she published *The Proud Tower: A Portrait of the World Before the War, 1890–1914*; in 1971 *Stilwell and the American Experience in China, 1911–1945*, which won her a second Pulitzer Prize; in 1972 *Notes from China*; and in 1978 *A Distant Mirror: The Calamitous 14th Century*, also a best-seller. Her histories were strongly shaped by her method of immersing herself deeply in all facets of her subject matter, from archival records to battlefields. In 1978 she won a Gold Medal for history from the American Academy of Arts and Sciences, and in 1979 she was elected president of the American Academy and Institute of Arts and Letters, the first woman to hold the post. She published a collection of shorter writings, *Practicing History*, 1981; a discussion of historical mistakes, *The March of Folly: From Troy to Vietnam*, 1984; and an international perspective on the American revolution, *The First Salute — A View of the American Revolution*, 1988. She died on February 6, 1989, in Greenwich, Connecticut.

Tucker, Sophie 1884–1966 entertainer

Born on January 13, 1884, somewhere in Russia as her mother was on her way to join her father in the United States, Sophie Kalish grew up in Boston and then in Hartford,

Connecticut, where her mother ran a restaurant. Her father had changed the family name to Abuza after his arrival in America. From her childhood she wanted to be an entertainer, and she began by singing in the family restaurant, in part to escape table-waiting and dishwashing. After an unsuccessful early marriage that had ended in divorce by the time she was twenty, she saved enough money to leave home for New York City.

In 1906 she changed her name to Sophie Tucker and landed a few singing jobs. Her actual professional career began in December 1906, when, after a successful amateur appearance, she opened in a blackface routine at the old Music Hall in New York City. That day she launched a show business career that would span 60 years.

While on tour in 1909 Tucker was spotted by a talent scout and signed for that year's *Ziegfeld Follies*, where she appeared with Nora Bayes and was at length replaced by Eva Tanguay. She traveled the vaudeville circuits from coast to coast for more than 20 years and also made occasional appearances in England, where she gained a substantial following. In her early years on the circuit she was sometimes billed as the "Mary Garden of Ragtime." In a later act she billed herself as "Queen of Jazz" and toured with her own band. Her brassy, flamboyant style, set off by her warm and ample presence, was perfectly suited to both sentimental ballads and risqué songs, and she became a great favorite of audiences. In 1911 she first sang "Some of These Days," which became her trademark.

Tucker's first appearance at the Palace Theater in New York City, considered the summit of success in vaudeville, came in August 1914. It was in 1928, at the Palace, that she was first billed as "The Last of the Red-hot Mamas." She also appeared in numerous editions of Earl Carroll's *Vanities* and the Shuberts' *Gaieties* and in such shows as *Louisiana Lou*, 1911, *Town Topics*, 1916, *Hello Alexander*, 1919, *Round in Fifty* in London, 1922, *Charlot's Revue*, with Gertrude Lawrence, 1925, *Socrates*, 1928, *Follow a Star*, 1930, and Cole Porter's hit *Leave It to Me*, 1938.

For a time in the 1920s she operated her own New York club, Sophie Tucker's Playground. In the early 1930s, when it became apparent that vaudeville was on the way out, Tucker turned to nightclubs, while many of the other old vaudevillians either attempted the movies or slid into oblivion. She did make several films, including *Honky Tonk*, 1929, *Broadway Melody of 1937*, 1937, and *Follow the Boys*, 1944; but she preferred the live audiences a cabaret offered, and she played to them with great success for more than 30 years. She also made occasional television appearances, mainly on "The Ed Sullivan Show," during the 1950s and early 1960s.

She was eighty-one years old when illness curtailed her performing late in 1965, but until then age had little diminished her ability to belt out a rousing blues or jazz rendition of one of her standards and to regale an audience with her racy patter. She died on February 9, 1966, in New York City.

Tutwiler, Julia Strudwick 1841–1916 educator and reformer

Born on August 15, 1841, in Tuscaloosa, Alabama, Julia Tutwiler grew up there and in nearby Havana. She attended a school operated by her father, a member of the first graduating class at the University of Virginia and an educator of strongly liberal views. Later she attended Madame Maroteau's boarding school in Philadelphia for two years. During the Civil War she taught in her father's school. After a semester at Vassar College in 1866 she resumed teaching in Alabama. In 1872–1873 she studied Greek and Latin privately with professors at Washington and Lee University, and in the latter year she began a three-year period of study in Germany and France. Her studies at the Deaconesses' Institute in Kaiserswerth, Germany, contributed to her decision to devote herself to teaching. On her return to the United States in 1876 she joined the faculty of the Tuscaloosa Female College, where she taught modern languages and English literature for five years.

In 1881 she was named co-principal of the Livingston Female Academy in Livingston, Alabama. In 1882, largely at her urging, the Alabama legislature voted an appropriation that made possible the establishment in February 1883 of the Alabama Normal College for Girls as a department of the Livingston Academy, which shortly became known as Livingston Normal College (now Livingston University). In 1890 Tutwiler became sole principal; her title was later changed to president. In 1891 she was elected president of the elementary education department of the National Education Association.

After a long campaign of public education and legislative lobbying, dating from her observation of vocational education techniques in France while visiting the Paris Exposition of 1878 as representative of the *National Journal of Education*, Tutwiler finally won state support for an Alabama Girls Industrial School (later Alabama College), which opened in Montevallo in October 1896. She declined the presidency of that school. She was also responsible for securing the admission of women to the University of Alabama. Another abiding interest of hers was prison reform.

In 1880 she formed the Tuscaloosa Benevolent Association to work toward that end. A statewide examination of county jails by questionnaire induced the legislature to make improvements. Some years later she became state chairman of prison and jail work for the Woman's Christian Temperance Union. She worked for the adoption of such penal practices as classification of offenders and state inspection of jails and prisons, and she succeeded in having a pioneering prison school established, but she failed in her campaign to abolish the convict lease system. She retired as president of Livingston Normal College in 1910. She died in Birmingham, Alabama, on March 24, 1916. Her poem "Alabama," written in 1873 in Germany, was later adopted as the state song.

Tweed, Blanche Oelrichs Thomas Barrymore 1890–1950 writer and actor

Born in New York City on October 1, 1890, Blanche Marie Louise Oelrichs was of a well-to-do and socially prominent family. A mischievous child, she was expelled from the Brearley School in New York and from the Convent of the Sacred Heart in Manhattanville before completing her education under tutors. She was the reigning debutante of Newport society until her marriage in January 1910 to Leonard M. Thomas, a rising young diplomat. She soon became a fervent suffragist and occasioned much comment by bobbing her hair.

In 1914, apparently in a sudden and unprecedented inspiration, Blanche Thomas began writing poems, many of them showing the influence of Walt Whitman. One of her poems appeared in the *New York Sun*, which led to the publication of a collection of them as *Miscellaneous Poems*, 1916, which she signed "Michael Strange." (She used that name for all her published and stage work thereafter.) A volume titled simply *Poems* followed in 1919. In 1918 she adapted Toistoi's *The Living Corpse as Redemption*, which was produced successfully on Broadway with John Barrymore in the lead. On her divorce from Thomas in 1919 she began an affair with Barrymore that eventuated in their marriage in August 1920. In 1920 she wrote *Claire de Lune*, which was presented in April 1921 to mixed reviews at the Empire Theatre, New York, with John and Ethel Barrymore starring.

In 1925 Blanche Barrymore joined a summer stock company in Salem, Massachusetts, and performed in Clyde Fitch's *Barbara Frietchie*. She turned down several offers from Broadway producers eager to exploit her social stature and over the next few years chose roles in such productions as Strindberg's *Easter*, 1926, Wilde's *The Importance of Being Earnest*, 1926, Sophocles's *Electra*, 1927, Rostand's *L'Aiglon*, 1927, and *Richard III*, 1930. She also wrote another play, *Lord and Lady Byron*, about 1927, but it failed in summer tryout.

In 1928, under the management of Elisabeth Marbury, she made the first of several successful lecture tours. She divorced Barrymore in that year (Diana Blythe Barrymore was their daughter), and in May 1929 she married Harrison Tweed, a lawyer and yachtsman. In November 1935 she gave a poetry recital at Town Hall in New York City in which she read selections from her own works and those of Dorothy Parker and others, all to harp accompaniment. The next year she had a poetry and music program on a New York radio station, and it soon became a regular feature on WOR, with eventually a full orchestra accompanying her readings. Her other books included *Resurrecting Life*, 1921, *Selected Poems*, 1928, and *Who Tells Me True*, an autobiography, 1940. She died in Boston on November 5, 1950.

Tyler, Anne 1941– author

Born on October 25, 1941, in Minneapolis, Minnesota, Anne Tyler spent her early years in North Carolina and in various Quaker communities in the Midwest and South, as her parents, dedicated Quakers, searched for the ideal community to raise their family. When Tyler was 11, her family finally settled in a middle-class suburban neighborhood in Raleigh, North Carolina, where she attended Broughton High School and began to take an interest in writing and literature. In 1958 she received an Angier Duke Scholarship to Duke University. While her major at Duke was Russian, she also worked on the school's literary magazine, acted in various campus theatrical productions, and twice received the school's Anne Flexner Award for Creative Writing. Her freshman composition class was taught by the writer Reynolds Price, who was one of her early influences, as were the works of Eudora Welty and those of the major Russian writers, especially Tolstoy and Chekhov. After graduating in 1961, she did postgraduate work in Russian at Columbia University. She left school before earning her M.A., however, and worked a few odd jobs before returning to Duke University as a bibliographer. In 1963 she had a short story published in a national magazine, married Taghi Modarressi (an Iranian psychiatry student), and moved to Montreal, Canada.

HELEN MARCUS

Anne Tyler

She and her husband lived in Canada for four years, during which time she worked as a librarian at McGill University and wrote and published her first novel, *If Morning Ever Comes*, 1964, which was largely ignored by critics. Her second novel, *The Tin Can Tree*, was published in 1965. In 1967 Tyler, her husband, and their daughter Tezh (born in 1965), moved to Baltimore, Maryland. A second child, Mitra, was born in 1967. From 1970 to 1974 she published three novels (*A Slipping-Down Life*, 1970; *The Clock Winder*, 1972; and *Celestial Navigation*, 1974), but it wasn't until *Searching for Caleb* was published in 1976 that she became a nationally recognized novelist. Critics and readers alike enjoyed her smooth, witty style, her detailed descriptions of modern Southern life, and her compassionate examination of personal isolation and the breakdown of communication within the family structure. In 1982 she published *Dinner at the Homesick Restaurant*, her first book to enter the national bestseller list.

Her highly successful 1985 novel, *The Accidental Tourist*, focuses on the recently divorced Macon Leary, who writes travelguides for businessmen, who, like himself, would prefer to stay at home. Macon, like many of her characters is an idiosyncratic middle-class hero, living within a chaotic and lonely, but always hopeful, Southern family. The book was made into a film in 1988. In 1989 she was awarded the Pulitzer Prize for fiction for *Breathing Lessons*, a masterfully written novel illustrating the complications of marriage, exposing both the overwhelming happiness family can bring and the darker side of relationships.

Her later works include *Saint Maybe*, 1991, and *Ladder of Years*, 1995. She also published numerous short stories in national magazines and anthologies, and wrote a number of book reviews and articles for major newspapers and magazines.

Urso, Camilla 1842–1902 musician

Born on June 13, 1842, in Nantes, France, Camilla Urso was the daughter of an Italian flutist and a Portuguese singer. At six, despite general skepticism over her ability to master a "masculine" instrument, she began taking violin lessons. The success of her first public recital a year later convinced her parents, who took her to Paris. Persistence finally won her admission to the Paris Conservatoire, where she studied under Lambert Massart. A provincial concert tour helped finance her studies, and at ten she placed first in her final examinations.

She arrived in New York City in September 1852 to begin an American concert tour. The tour arrangements collapsed, but she gave concerts in New York City, Boston, and Philadelphia. With the Germania Society she made tours of New England and, in 1853, of other northern and western states. She subsequently toured with the company of Henrietta Sontag as far as New Orleans, and she continued to appear in New York until 1855, when she retired with her parents to Nashville, Tennessee.

Over the next seven years Urso practiced diligently. She emerged from retirement in 1863 to play with the Philharmonic Society in Boston, and later in the year she appeared with the New York Philharmonic. She toured New England with Patrick S. Gilmore's band in 1863–1864. In 1864–1865 she had her own concert company, with which she made a Canadian tour. She returned to Paris in June 1865 and scored a great success in a Pasdeloup Concert. For the next 30 years she toured regularly in the United States and abroad. In addition to regular European tours she traveled to Australia in 1879 and 1894 and to South Africa in 1895. She was acknowledged one of the preeminent violinists of the day, and her repertoire included both classic and contemporary works. She retired from performing in 1895 and settled in New York City. For some years she taught privately and at the National Conservatory of Music. She died in virtual obscurity in New York City on January 20, 1902.

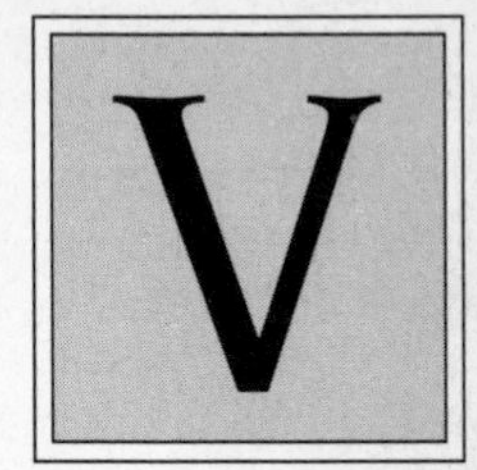

Van Deman, Esther Boise 1862–1937 archaeologist

Born on October 1, 1862, in South Salem, Ohio, Esther Van Deman grew up and attended schools there and from the early 1870s in Sterling, Kansas. She graduated from the University of Michigan in 1891 and received a master's degree the next year. Over the next 14 years she alternated periods of advanced study and of teaching: She pursued graduate work at Bryn Mawr College in 1892–1893; taught Latin at Wellesley College in 1893–1895 and at the Bryn Mawr School in 1895–1896; studied at the University of Chicago in 1896–1898, taking her Ph.D. in the latter year; taught Latin at Mount Holyoke College in 1898–1901; studied at the American School of Classical Studies in Rome in 1901–1903; and served as associate professor of Latin and archaeology at Gaucher College in 1903–1906. In 1906 she returned to the American School of Classical Studies on a fellowship from the Carnegie Institution of Washington.

In 1907, while attending a lecture in the Atrium Vestae, she noticed that the bricks blocking up a doorway differed from those of the structure itself and speculated that such differences in building materials might provide a key to the chronology of ancient structures. Further research confirmed her guess, and in 1909 the Carnegie Institution published her preliminary findings in *The Atrium Vestae*. In 1910 she was appointed to the staff of the American School. In "Methods of Determining the Date of Roman Concrete Monuments" published in the *The American Journal of Archaeology* in 1912, she outlined a basic methodology that, with few modifications, became standard procedure in Roman archaeology. The next two decades were devoted to an exhaustive study of Roman aqueducts; her studies were interrupted by World War I, when she returned briefly to the United States, by a serious nervous collapse in 1917, and by her service as Charles Eliot Norton lecturer at the Archaeological Institute of America in 1924–1925 and as Carnegie research professor of Roman archaeology at the University of Michigan in 1925–1930.

Her work on aqueducts appeared as *The Building of Roman Aquaducts* in 1934. Realizing that she had put off for too long a planned definitive work on the dating of Roman brick and concrete work, she devoted the remaining years of her life to arranging her notes. She died in Rome on May 3, 1937.

Van Lew, Elizabeth L. 1818–1900 Union agent

Born on October 17, 1818, in Richmond, Virginia, Elizabeth Van Lew was the daughter of a prosperous family of Northern antecedents. She was educated in Philadelphia. She grew up to hold strong antislavery views, and during the 1850s, under her influence, the family's domestic servants were freed. At the outbreak of the Civil War she remained firmly and publicly loyal to the United States. She made numerous visits to Union prisoners in Libby Prison, carrying in food, clothing, and other items and often carrying away military information that she was able to transmit to federal authorities. On occasion escaped prisoners were hidden in her house.

In March 1864, following General Hugh J. Kilpatrick's unsuccessful attempt to open Libby Prison during a cavalry raid on Richmond (a raid apparently planned in response to information gathered by Elizabeth Van Lew that the prisoners were soon to be moved farther south), she and her agents daringly spirited out of the city the body of Colonel Ulric Dahlgren, Kilpatrick's second-in-command and the son of Admiral John A. B. Dahlgren, who had been killed in the raid and whose remains had suffered indignities at the hands of an outraged Richmond citizenry.

During the year-long siege of Richmond and Petersburg in 1864–1865 Van Lew performed invaluable services in intelligence gathering. Her contacts reached even into Jefferson Davis's home, where she had placed one of her former servants; and her assumed manner of mental aberration, which gained her the indulgent nickname of

"Crazy Bet" around Richmond, enabled her to carry on unsuspected. Agents carried coded messages by way of various relay stations, to the Union headquarters beyond the city.

After the fall of Richmond in April 1865 she was personally thanked and given protection by General Ulysses S. Grant. Under President Grant she held the post of postmistress of Richmond from 1869 to 1877. She worked subsequently as a clerk in the Post Office Department in Washington, D.C., until the late 1880s. Van Lew then returned in poverty to Richmond, where she was still a social outcast because of her wartime activities. In later years she protested her taxes because she was denied the vote. She lived in the family mansion in Richmond, Virginia, until her death on September 25, 1900.

Van Rensselaer, Mariana Alley Griswold 1851–1934 writer and art critic

Born in New York City on February 21, 1851, Mariana Griswold was of a prosperous mercantile family and was educated privately at home and in Europe. In April 1873 she married Schuyler Van Rensselaer, an engineer and son of one of New York's old Dutch families, with whom she lived in New Brunswick, New Jersey, until his death in 1884. Her writing career began with the publication of a poem in *Harper's Magazine* and an article on art in *American Architect and Building*, both in 1876.

Other articles and reviews of contemporary artists followed, and in 1886, two years after she moved back to New York City, she published her *Book of American Figure Painters*. Her *American Etchers* appeared in the same year. Her series on "Recent American Architecture" in the *Century Magazine* gave rise to her full-length study *Henry Hobson Richardson and His Works*, 1888, long the standard work on that major figure. Her clear and incisive writings on architecture won her election as an honorary member of the American Institute of Architects in 1890. In 1889 she published *Six Portraits*, a set of studies of Renaissance and modern artists. Another *Century* series of 1887–1892 was collected in *English Cathedrals*, 1892. A series for *Garden and Forest* magazine entitled "The Art of Gardening: A Historical Sketch" was a pioneering work and led to her *Art Out of Doors*, 1893. The Society of Landscape Artists also elected her to honorary membership.

From 1894 Van Rensselaer's interests turned to social questions. She taught a class in literature at the University Settlement from 1894 to 1898 and served as president of the settlement's women's auxiliary in 1896–1898. She was a public school inspector for two years and president of the Public Education Association of New York City from 4899 to 1906, and she led a campaign to have reproductions of great works of art hung in schoolrooms. Her later writings included *Shall We Ask for Suffrage?*, a pamphlet in which she answered in the negative, 1894; *One Man Who Was Content*, a collection of stories, 1897; a two-volume *History of the City of New York in the Seventeenth Century*, a monumental work that won her an honorary degree from Columbia University, 1909; a volume of *Poems*, 1910; and *Many Children*, a collection of poems for children, 1921. In 1923 she was awarded a gold medal by the American Academy of Arts and Letters. She died in New York City on January 20, 1934.

Van Zandt, Marie 1858–1919 opera singer

Born in New York, probably in Brooklyn, on October 8, 1858, Marie Van Zandt was apparently taken to Europe as a small child by her mother, who pursued a successful career as a concert and operatic singer under the name Madame Vanzini. Marie evidently attended a convent school in Europe for a time. She soon displayed vocal abilities of her own, and her mother abandoned her own career in order to promote the daughter's. She received encouragement from Adelina Patti, studied under Francesco Lamperti in Milan, and made her singing debut in a production of *Don Giovanni* in Turin early in 1879. In May of that year she made her London debut at Her Majesty's Theatre in *La Sonnambula*.

Her Paris debut followed in March 1880 in an Opéra-Comique production of *Mignon*. Her performance there won her a five-year contract, and she attained popular stardom with dizzying speed. The height of her Paris career came in April 1883, when she created the title role in *Lakmé*, which Leo Delibes reportedly had written for her.

In November 1884 her voice failed during a performance of *Il Barbiere di Siviglia*; immediately the many cabals that had formed against her — some founded on anti-Americanism, some perhaps inspired by the rival Emma Nevada, and some perhaps arising from entirely irrelevant matters — sprang forth to destroy her reputation. She was accused, falsely, of having attempted to sing while inebriated. Her return to the Opéra-Comique stage three months later sparked riots, whereupon she secured a release from her contract. She sang successfully in St. Petersburg, Moscow, and London and in November 1891 made her American debut in *La Sonnambula* at the Auditorium Theatre in Chicago.

She spent the rest of the 1891–1892 season at the Metropolitan Opera in New York City, where she made her debut in December in *La Sonnambula*. After that single American season she returned permanently to Europe. She made a successful return to the Opéra-Comique in 1896. She retired from the stage following her marriage in April 1898 to Mikhail Petrovitch de Tscherinoff, a Russian professor and state councilor. She died in Cannes, France, on December 31, 1919.

Vaughan, Sarah Lois 1924–1990 singer

Born in Newark, New Jersey, on March 27, 1924, Sarah Vaughan was the daughter of Asbury Vaughan, a carpenter, and Ada Baylor, a laundress. Both parents were also amateur musicians. Vaughan began studying piano and organ at age 7 and began her singing career in the choir of Mt. Zion Baptist Church in Newark. After winning an amateur contest at Harlem's famed Apollo Theater in 1942, she was hired to sing with the Earl Hines Orchestra. A year later she went on to sing with the Billy Eckstine Band, where she met Dizzy Gillespie and Charlie Parker. Vaughan's singing style was influenced by their instruments — "I always wanted to imitate the horns." Gillespie, Parker and Vaughan recorded "Lover Man" together in 1945.

While she was with the Eckstine Band, Vaughan sang in New York clubs like Copacabana, Café Society Downtown, and the Onyx Club. She also toured the country, in the big cities and in the South, where being a woman apparently posed problems; audiences wanted to hear Eckstine, not her. By the mid–1940s, she began singing with John Kirby and appearing on television variety shows, including the Ed Sullivan Show.

During the 1950s her audience grew as she toured both the U.S. and Europe, giving concerts at the Paramount Theater in New York, Birdland in New York, Storyville in Boston, and Molcambo in San Francisco. She signed with Mercury Record Corporation and EmArcy, Mercury's jazz label, in 1953 to sing both pop and jazz. She also appeared in three movies in this period, *Jazz Festival*, 1956, *Disc Jockey*, 1951, and *Basin Street Revue,* 1956, and in 1956 she participated in both the Newport and New York Jazz Festivals.

A contralto with a range of three octaves, she was dubbed "the Divine One" and "Sassy" by her fans. She died on April 3, 1990, the same year in which she was inducted into the Jazz Hall of Fame.

Victor, Frances Auretta Fuller 1826–1902 writer and historian

Born on May 23, 1826, in Rome, New York, Frances Fuller grew up in Erie, Pennsylvania, and in Wooster, Ohio. She and her younger sister Metta Fuller (Victor) were educated in a female seminary in Wooster. They both contributed poems and stories to local periodicals and to the *Home Journal* of New York, and in 1848 they moved to New York City. In that year Frances Fuller published her first book, *Anizetta, the Guajira: or the*

Creole of Cuba. In 1851 the sisters together published *Poems of Sentiment and Imagination, with Dramatic and Descriptive Pieces*.

Frances left New York to help care for her now-widowed mother and younger sisters in St. Clair, Michigan, that year. In 1853 she married and homesteaded near Omaha, Nebraska Territory, but she eventually left her husband and rejoined Metta in New York. She wrote *East and West; or, The Beauty of Willard's Mill* and *The Card Claim: A Tale of the Upper Missouri*, both 1862, for Beadle and Adams's Dime Novel series edited by Metta's husband, Orville J. Victor.

In May 1862 Frances Fuller married Victor's brother, Henry C. Victor, a navy engineer, and a year later they moved to San Francisco. There she contributed to the *Golden Era*, the *Overland Monthly*, and the *San Francisco Bulletin* under the name "Florence Fane." In 1864 she and her husband settled in Oregon. She became deeply interested in local history, and over the next 13 years she produced *The River of the West*, 1870, *All Over Oregon and Washington*, a travel book, 1872, and *The New Penelope*, a collection of stories, 1877. From 1878 through 1890 she worked with Hubert H. Bancroft on his monumental 28-volume *History of the Pacific States*. Although Bancroft claimed authorship of the entire series, Victor was in fact the author of *The History of Oregon*, two volumes, 1886–1888; *The History of Washington, Idaho, and Montana*, 1890; *The History of Nevada Colorado, and Wyoming*, 1890; a large part of *The History of the Northwest Coast*, two volumes, 1884; and portions of the volumes on California and British Columbia. In 1890 she retired to Oregon, where she wrote *Atlantis Arisen*, a revision of her earlier travel book on Washington and Oregon, 1891, *The Early Indian Wars of Oregon*, 1894, and *Poems*, 1900. She died in Portland, Oregon, on November 14, 1902.

Victor, Metta Victoria Fuller 1831–1885 writer

Born on March 2, 1831, in Erie, Pennsylvania, Metta Fuller grew up there and from 1839 in Wooster, Ohio. With her elder sister Frances she attended a Wooster female seminary and began contributing stories to local newspapers and then to the *Home Journal* of New York. In 1848 she and Frances moved to New York City, where they entered into literary society. In 1851 they published *Poems of Sentiment and Imagination, with Dramatic and Descriptive Pieces*. In the same year Metta published a temperance novel, *The Senator's Son, or, The Maine Law: A Last Refuge*, which enjoyed some success in American and English editions.

She followed with *Fashionable Dissipations*, 1854, and *Mormon Wives* (or *Lives of the Female Mormons*), 1856. In July 1856 she married Orville J. Victor, an editor. For four years she assisted her husband in editing the *Cosmopolitan Art Journal*, first in Sandusky, Ohio, and then in New York City. She was editor of *Home*, a monthly magazine published by the firm of Beadle and Adams, in 1859–1860, and in 1860 she took over the editorship of the *Cosmopolitan Art Journal* when her husband turned his attention to developing a new series of cheap sensational books — the Dime Novels — for Beadle and Adams. To the series and its successors Metta Victor contributed *Alice Wilde, The Raftsman's Daughter*, 1860, *The Backwoods Bride*, 1860, and nearly a hundred more, all published anonymously. The most successful of her Dime Novels was *Maum Guinea, and Her Plantation "Children"*, 1862, which enjoyed a large sale and was praised by antislavery activists and even by President Abraham Lincoln. For Beadle and Adams she also wrote a *Dime Cook-Book*, 1859.

Others of her books, issued anonymously or under various pseudonyms, were *Miss Slimmens' Window*, 1859, *The Dead Letter*, 1886, *Too True: A Story of To-Day*, 1868, *The Blunders of a Bashful Man*, 1875, *Passing the Portal*, 1876, *A Bad Boy's Diary*, 1880, and *A Naughty Girl's Diary*, 1884. She continued through the years to contribute to numerous periodicals and commanded high prices for her stories and serials. Victor died in Hohokus, New Jersey, on June 26, 1885.

Vreeland, Diana Dalziel 1903?–1989 editor and fashion expert

Born in Paris about 1903, Diana Dalziel was the daughter of a Scottish father and an American mother in whose home the leading artists of the day were frequent guests. In 1914 the family came to the United States to escape World War I and settled in New York City. Diana attended the Brearley School, studied ballet, and grew into the life of a debutante. In March 1924 she married Thomas R. Vreeland, a banker, with whom she lived in Albany, New York, until 1928, in London until 1936, and thereafter in New York City. She became a naturalized citizen in 1925.

In 1936 she began contributing to *Harper's Bazaar* a gaily frivolous column called "Why don't you . . . ?," which became a highly popular department. In 1939 she joined the *Harper's Bazaar* staff full time and shortly thereafter was appointed fashion editor. She held that post for 23 years, becoming one of the dominant personalities on the magazine and winning acknowledgment as one of the most perspicacious and influential observers of the fashion scene.

In 1962 Vreeland left *Harper's Bazaar* and joined the staff of *Vogue*, of which she became editor in chief in January 1963. Under her strong guidance *Vogue* soon began to reflect her own taste for the novel, the bizarre, and the outrageous. The youthful and the eccentric were featured, and the photography and design were calculated to reflect the age of youth culture, rock music, and the overthrow of traditional standards. Editorial matter in the magazine often followed her own idiosyncratic way with fashion dicta: "Pink is the navy blue of India." In particular she created the notion of the Beautiful People (abbreviated BP's), a subclass of youthful, wealthy, and foot-loose members of the less exclusive international set who were supposed to set the tone of fashion, art, and society.

Diana Vreeland was removed as editor in chief of *Vogue* in May 1971, when the heady fashion excesses of the 1960s had passed. Later that year she was named special consultant to the Costume Institute of the Metropolitan Museum of Art (founded in 1937 by Irene Lewisohn). There she mounted a series of exhibitions that attracted visitors by the hundred thousand: a show of the designs of Balenciaga in 1972, a show of Paris originals from 1909 to 1939 in 1973–1974, a show of Hollywood costumes in 1974–1975, a show of Russian costumes in 1976–1977, a show of costumes from the Ballets Russes in 1978–1979, and others.

A woman of striking individuality, Diana Vreeland remained the doyenne of American high fashion. Among her numerous honors are the New York Fashion Designers award in 1963, the Council of Fashion Designers award in 1984, and the Fellow for Life award from the Metropolitan Museum of Art in 1986. She was also decorated by France's Legion of Honor, and in 1984 by France's Ministry of Culture. She published a book on fashion, *Allure*, in 1980, and her autobiography, *D.V.*, in 1984. She died on August 22, 1989, in New York City.

Walcott, Mary Morris Vaux 1860–1940 artist and naturalist

Born in Philadelphia on July 31, 1860, Mary Vaux was of a wealthy Quaker family. For several years after her graduation in 1879 from the Friends Select School in her native city she devoted herself to the care of the home and the family dairy farm. On a series of family summer vacations in the Canadian Rockies she developed into an amateur naturalist, and she soon combined that interest with her lifelong love of painting by devoting much of her vacation time to making watercolors of wildflowers. In June 1914 she married Charles D. Walcott, a geologist and paleontologist and secretary of the Smithsonian Institution. She was thereafter an active hostess in Washington, D.C., and assisted her husband in various projects.

She continued her painting, and in 1925 the Smithsonian Institution published in limited and library editions a five-volume *North American Wild Flowers*, containing 400 of her watercolors of native flowers and brief descriptions of each. The work was received with great acclaim both for the beauty and accuracy of the paintings and for the high quality of the book-making. In 1927 President Calvin Coolidge appointed her to a seat on the federal Board of Indian Commissioners formerly occupied by her brother, George Vaux; she held the post until 1932. In 1933 she was elected president of the Society of Woman Geographers. In 1935 she contributed 15 paintings to the Smithsonian's *Illustrations of North American Pitcher-plants*. She died in St. Andrews, New Brunswick, on August 22, 1940.

Wald, Lillian D. 1867–1940 nurse and reformer

Born on March 10, 1867, in Cincinnati, Lillian Wald grew up there and in Rochester, New York. She was educated in a private school, and after abandoning a plan to attend Vassar College she passed a few years enjoying an active social life. In 1889 she broke sharply with that life and entered the New York Hospital Training School for Nurses, from which she graduated in 1891. For a year she worked as a nurse in the New York Juvenile Asylum. She supplemented her training in 1892–1893 with courses at the Woman's Medical College. She was asked to organize a class in home nursing for the poor immigrant families of New York's Lower East Side, and in the course of that work she observed at first hand the wretched conditions prevailing in the tenement districts.

In the autumn of 1893, with a companion, Wald left medical school, moved to the neighborhood, and offered her services as a visiting nurse. Two years later, with aid from banker-philanthropist Jacob H. Schiff and others, she took larger accommodations and opened the Nurse's Settlement. As the number of nurses attached to the settlement grew (from the original 2 in 1893 to 92 in 1913 and to over 250 by 1929), services were expanded to include nurses' training, educational programs for the community, and youth clubs. Within a few years the Henry Street establishment had become a neighborhood center, the Henry Street Settlement. Over the years the settlement was a powerful source of innovation in the settlement-house movement and in the broader field of social work generally. The Neighborhood Playhouse was opened in connection with the settlement in 1915 through the benefaction of Irene Lewisohn. Residents at Henry Street included at various times Florence Kelley, Adolf A. Berle, Jr., Sidney Hillman, and Henry Morgenthau, Jr.

Lillian Wald exerted considerable influence beyond Henry Street as well. In 1902, at her initiative, nursing service was experimentally extended to a local public school; the project was so successful that the Board of Health soon instituted a city-wide public school nursing program, the first such program in the world. The organization of nursing programs by insurance companies for their industrial policyholders (pioneered by the Metropolitan Life Insurance Company in 1909) and of the district nursing service of the

Red Cross (begun in 1912 and later called Town and Country Nursing Service) were both at her suggestion.

In 1912 Wald's role as founder of an entirely new profession was formally acknowledged when she helped found and became first president of the National Organization for Public Health Nursing. She also worked to establish educational, recreational, and social programs in underprivileged neighborhoods. In 1912 Congress established the U.S. Children's Bureau (headed by Julia Lathrop), also in no small part owing to her suggestion, and in that year she was awarded the gold medal of the National Institute of Social Sciences.

Wald was active in other areas of reform, particularly with the National Child Labor Committee, which she and Florence Kelley helped found in 1904, the National Women's Trade Union League, and the American Union Against Militarism, which she, Kelley, and Jane Addams helped organize in 1914 and of which she was elected president. During World War I she headed the committee on home nursing of the Council of National Defense. She led the Nurses' Emergency Council in the influenza epidemic of 1918–1919. Later she founded the League of Free Nations, a forerunner of the Foreign Policy Association. She wrote *The House on Henry Street*, 1915, and *Windows on Henry Street*, 1934, both autobiographical. In 1933 ill health forced her to resign as head worker of Henry Street. She settled in Westport, Connecticut, and died there on September 1, 1940.

Walker, Alice 1944– novelist and poet

Born on February 9, 1944, in Eatonton, Georgia, Alice Walker was the eighth child of African-American sharecroppers. She spent most of her time with her five brothers. While still a child, she was accidentally blinded in one eye by one of them. Her mother gave her a typewriter and allowed her to write instead of doing chores. She excelled in school in her small, Southern town and graduated as class valedictorian.

BERNARD GOTFRYD

Alice Walker

She received a scholarship to attend Spelman College, where she became an activist. In 1963 she transferred to Sarah Lawrence College where she acquired a different perspective on the South and on the African-American community. She graduated with a B.A. in 1965 and later received an honorary Ph.D. from Russell Sage College in 1972. In the 1960s she campaigned in Georgia to register voters and to protest on behalf of those removed from the welfare rolls. During that period she also worked with Head Start in Mississippi and took a job with the Welfare Department in New York City.

Walker's first book of poetry, *Once*, 1968, comprised poems publicly acknowledging the pain and isolation of an early pregnancy and abortion, which she considered a social experience shared by others that transcended her personal experience. She was married in 1967 (and later divorced in 1976); she gave birth to Rebecca three days after finishing her first novel, *The Third Life of Grange Copeland*, 1970, a narrative that spans sixty years and three generations.

A second volume of poetry, *Revolutionary Petunias and Other Poems* and *In Love and Trouble: Stories of Black Woman*, both appeared in 1973. The latter, her first collection of short stories, bears witness to sexist violence and abuse in the African-American community. *Meridian*, 1976, about the coming of age of several civil rights workers in the 1960s was followed by *Good Night Willie Lee, I'll See You in the Morning*, 1979, a third collection of poems. *You Can't Keep a Good Woman Down*, 1981, Walker's second book of short stories, addressed violence, rape, pornography and difficult relationships.

The Color Purple, 1982, an epistolary novel loosely based on the story of Walker's great-grandmother, depicts the growing up and self-realization of an African-American woman between 1909 and 1947 in a town in Georgia. It won a Pulitzer Prize and its already broad appeal increased with the release of Steven Spielberg's popular film adaptation of it. Besides fiction and poetry, Walker published *Langston Hughes, Ameri-*

can Poet, 1974, a biography of Langston Hughes. She also recovered and championed the work of Zora Neale Hurston. In 1983 Walker published a collection of essays entitled *In Search of Our Mothers' Gardens: Womanist Prose* praising the beauty and love she found in her own heritage and introducing the term "womanist" to designate African-American feminists. *The Temple of My Familiar*, 1989, and *Possessing the Secret of Joy*, 1992, condemned the African practice of female circumcision.

Throughout her works, Walker confronted the struggle, pain, and spirituality of African-American society and history. She held several university-level teaching positions and won many literary awards, including the American Book Award, 1983, and a Guggenheim fellowship, 1979. She moved to the San Francisco area in 1979.

Walker, Maggie Lena 1867–1934 businesswoman

Born in Richmond, Virginia, on July 15, 1867, Maggie Draper was the daughter of a former slave who was then a cook in the household of Elizabeth Van Lew. She attended the Lancaster School, graduated from the Armstrong Normal School in 1883, and then taught at the Lancaster School until her marriage in September 1886 to Armstead Walker, Jr., a building contractor. Thereafter she devoted her time outside the home to the Grand United Order of St. Luke, an African-American fraternal and cooperative insurance society founded in Baltimore in 1867. Working her way up through various local and general offices, Maggie Walker became executive secretary-treasurer of the renamed Independent Order of St. Luke in 1899. At that time the order had only 3408 members in 57 local chapters and was in debt.

Walker went to work with remarkable energy and business acumen. In 1902 she founded the *St. Luke Herald* to carry news of the order to local chapters and to help in the educational work of the order, especially the training of children in habits of thrift, industry, and hygiene. In 1903 she opened the St. Luke Penny Savings Bank, of which she was president. By 1924 the Independent Order of St. Luke boasted a headquarters staff of 50 who, working from a new 4-story building in Richmond, served a membership of over 50,000 in 1500 local chapters. The order's assets approached $400,000. In 1929–1930 the Penny Savings Bank absorbed all other black-owned banks in Richmond to become the Consolidated Bank and Trust Company, of which Walker served thereafter as chairman of the board. In addition to her work with the order, Walker helped found in 1912 and served as president of the Richmond Council of Colored Women, through which she helped raise large sums for the support of Janie Porter Barrett's Virginia Industrial School for Colored Girls and for other philanthropies. Walker died in Richmond, Virginia, on December 15, 1934.

Mary Edwards Walker

Walker, Mary Edwards 1832–1919 physician and reformer

Born on a farm near Oswego, New York, on November 26, 1832, Mary Walker was of a family of singular individuals. She overcame numerous obstacles in graduating from the Syracuse Medical College in 1855, and after a few months in Columbus, Ohio, she established a practice in Rome, New York. In the same year she married one Albert Miller, also a physician, with whom she practiced but whose name she did not take; the marriage was not a happy one and they separated in 1859 and were finally divorced ten years later.

She had from an early age been interested in dress reform and was an ardent follower of Amelia Bloomer in the cause, and that interest led her also to related reforms. At the outbreak of the Civil War she traveled to Washington, D.C., to offer her services. She worked as a volunteer nurse in the Patent Office Hospital there while attempting to gain a regular appointment to the army medical service.

In 1862 Walker took time away from Washington to earn a degree from the New York Hygeio-Therapeutic College. In that year she began working in the field, and in September 1863 she finally was appointed assistant surgeon in the Army of the Cumberland by General George H. Thomas. She was apparently the only woman so engaged in the Civil War. She was assigned to the 52nd Ohio Regiment in Tennessee, and she quickly adopted standard officers' uniform, suitably modified. During April-August 1864 she was a prisoner in Richmond, Virginia. In October she was given a contract as "acting assistant surgeon," but she saw no more field service, being instead assigned to a women's prison hospital and then to an orphanage. She left government service in June 1865 and a short time later was awarded a Medal of Honor.

Walker was elected president of the National Dress Reform Association in 1866 and for some years thereafter was closely associated with Belva A. Lockwood in various reform movements. Feminist organizations widely publicized her Civil War service, but she became estranged from them over the years because of her growing eccentricity. She wore full male attire, complete to wing collar, bow tie, and top hat. Often arrested for masquerading as a man, she claimed — and the claim was given currency — that she had been granted permission to dress so by Congress; no record of any such action exists. Her view of the suffrage question was that the Constitution had already given the vote to women and that the legislation sought by organized suffragists was therefore pointless. She is said to have invented at some time in her Washington years the idea of attaching a postcard receipt to registered mail.

She published two books, the partly autobiographical *Hit*, 1871, and *Unmasked, or the Science of Immortality*, 1878. From 1887 she exhibited herself in dime museum sideshows on several occasions. She lived in Oswego from 1890. Increasingly eccentric, she wore her Medal of Honor constantly, even after it was revoked by an army board in 1917 (as were hundreds of others) because there was no record of the occasion of its award. A fall on the steps of the Capitol in Washington left her infirm, and she died in Oswego, New York, on February 21, 1919.

Walker, Sarah Breedlove 1867–1919 businesswoman

Born near Delta, Louisiana, on December 23, 1867, Sarah Breedlove was the daughter of poor farmers. She was left an orphan at six. Little is known of her early life beyond the fact that she married at fourteen in Vicksburg, Mississippi, and at twenty, then a widow, she moved to St. Louis. She worked as a washerwoman for some years and in that time began experimenting at home with various hair dressings. In 1905 she hit upon a formula for creating a smooth, shining coiffure for the ordinarily stubborn hair of African-American women, a formula combining a shampoo with a pomade preparation that she called a "hair grower" and the use of heated iron combs and vigorous brushing. She quickly achieved local success with what later became known as the "Walker Method" or "Walker System." In 1906 she moved to Denver. There she married Charles J. Walker, and thenceforward she was known as Madame C. J. Walker.

She soon gave up door-to-door selling and demonstrating to devote herself to manufacturing her products and to training a rapidly growing corps of "Walker Agents," whom she referred to professionally as hair and beauty "culturists." A second office was opened in Pittsburgh in 1908, and in 1910 the Pittsburgh and Denver offices were both transferred to Indianapolis.

The Madame C. J. Walker Manufacturing Company became one of that city's major enterprises. It employed at its peak some 3,000 persons and was by far the largest black-owned business in the nation. Walker was president and sole proprietor, and through her lectures and demonstrations before women's clubs, church groups, and lecture audiences, as well as through her likeness reproduced on the labels of her various cosmetic products, she became one of the best known figures in America. The legion of Walker agents spread her name and products throughout the United States and the Caribbean, and through the example of Josephine Baker the Walker System coiffure became popular in Europe as well.

Madame Walker interested herself in several philanthropies; recipients of substantial gifts from her included the National Association for the Advancement of Colored People, Tuskegee Institute, the Palmer Memorial Institute in Sedalia, North Carolina, and various Indianapolis institutions. She also encouraged philanthropy and community work, along with cleanliness and other personal virtues, among her employees. In 1914 she built a sumptuous townhouse in New York City, where she became hostess to leading African-American artists and intellectuals, and in 1917 she built Villa Lewaro in Irvington, New York. She died at Villa Lewaro on May 25, 1919, leaving an estate valued at more than a million dollars.

Walters, Barbara 1931– journalist

Born in Boston on September 25, 1931, Barbara Walters was the daughter of a well known nightclub proprietor. She grew up in Boston, Miami, and New York City, attended public and private schools, and in 1953 graduated from Sarah Lawrence College. After brief employment in an advertising agency she became assistant to the publicity director for New York City's NBC-affiliated television station. There she gained experience in writing and producing for television. After a short stint at another local station she was hired as a news and public affairs producer and writer by the CBS television network. She later left CBS to work for a theatrical public relations firm, but in 1961 she returned to television as a writer for the popular NBC morning show "Today." In addition to writing she did occasional feature stories herself on the air.

In 1964, when the current "Today Girl" left, Barbara Walters was given a tryout in the job, one that had traditionally involved little more than looking pretty, making small talk, and reading commercials. She soon began expanding that narrow role and gradually made herself into a regular member of the "Today" show's panel of commentators and news readers. Her intelligence and camera presence, together with the solid journalistic work that she put into her feature stories, made her one of the most popular personalities on the program, and in 1974 she was named co-host of "Today" with Hugh Downs.

Walters was particularly known for her interviews with world notables. A tenacious pursuer of elusive figures in the news, she scored numerous coups in the form of exclusive interviews with such people as Robert Kennedy, Coretta Scott King, Golda Meir, Truman Capote, Dean Rusk, Prince Philip, Mamie Eisenhower, Fred Astaire, Princess Grace of Monaco, and Henry Kissinger. Her disarmingly direct questioning drew many subjects into frequently interesting and occasionally provocative moments of self-revelation.

In 1970 Walters published *How to Talk With Practically Anybody About Practically Anything*. In 1975 she won an Emmy award for her work on "Today." She also hosted her own syndicated talk show, "Not for Women Only," and was a commentator on NBC's "Monitor" radio program. In 1976 she made headlines herself by signing a five-year contract with the ABC network that made her the first woman to co-anchor a network evening news program and, at a million dollars a year, the highest paid journalist in history. Owing in part to personal frictions the evening news spot failed to produce the increased ratings ABC had hoped for, and Barbara Walters was assigned to produce her own special shows. She continued to host "The Barbara Walters Specials," and in 1982 and 1983 she won an Emmy Award for best interviewer. From 1979 she was co-host with Hugh Downs of the ABC news show "20/20." In 1990 she was named to the Hall of Fame of the Academy of Television Arts and Sciences.

Wambaugh, Sarah 1882–1955 political scientist

Born in Cincinnati on March 6, 1882, Sarah Wambaugh was the daughter of a lawyer who later taught at Harvard. She graduated from Radcliffe College in 1902 and remained as an assistant in history and government while pursuing advanced studies in those fields until 1906. For a decade thereafter she worked with the Women's Educational and Industrial Union of Boston and took part in the woman suffrage movement. In 1916 she resumed her studies at Radcliffe, and in 1917 she was awarded an M.A. degree in international law and political science. In that year she secured a grant from the Carnegie Endowment for International Peace to finance a study of the theory, practice, and history of plebiscites, a field then new to systematic study.

Wambaugh's *Monograph on Plebiscites, With a Collection of Official Documents*, first prepared for use at the Versailles peace conference of 1919, was published in 1920 and established its author as the leading authority in the field. In 1920–1921, while studying at the London University School of Economics and at Oxford, she worked in the administrative commissions and minorities section of the League of Nations secretariat. She taught history at Wellesley College for a semester in 1921–1922. Over the next several years she observed a plebiscite in Upper Silesia, advised the League of Nations on the problems of the Saar Basin and Danzig, and advised the Peruvian government on the Tacna-Arica plebiscite. In 1927 she lectured at the Academy of International Law at The Hague.

During 1934–1935 Wambaugh helped plan and administer the Saar plebiscite, and in the latter year she lectured at the Institute for Advanced International Studies in Geneva. She served as an adviser to the United Nations mission observing Greek elections in 1945–1946 and helped plan the Jammu and Kashmir plebiscites in India in 1949. She published *La pratique des plébiscites internationaux*, 1928, *Plebiscites Since the World War*, 1933, and *The Saar Plebiscite*, 1940, along with numerous articles, many of them promoting the cause of U.S. membership in the League of Nations and the dream of a "family of nations." She died in Cambridge, Massachusetts, on November 12, 1955.

Ward, Elizabeth Stuart Phelps 1844–1911 writer

Born in Boston on August 31, 1844, Mary Gray Phelps was the daughter of a clergyman and of a popular woman writer. She grew up from 1848 in Andover, Massachusetts, and after the death of her mother in 1852 she adopted her name. She was educated at Abbott Academy and Mrs. Edwards' School in Andover and by her father, who in 1860 became president of Andover Theological Seminary. For several years she kept house for her father as he became a nervous invalid, and she devoted what free time she could find to writing. Her first published work had appeared in the *Youth's Companion* when she was thirteen; her first mature piece was a story that was published in *Harper's Magazine* in 1864.

In 1868 Phelps published her first book, *The Gates Ajar*, a sentimental and didactic novel that propounded her optimistic personal theology, in which heaven, open to all who truly repent, is a place of light, love, and the restoration of all good things known on earth. This joyous message, although clumsy as literature and suspected of unorthodoxy as theology, struck a responsive chord in the reading public. The book enjoyed a huge sale in America and in Great Britain and was translated into several foreign languages.

None of Phelps's subsequent books was so successful, although all were widely read. They included *The Trotty Book*, 1870, *Hedged In*, 1870, *The Silent Partner*, 1871, *Trotty's Wedding Tour and Story Book*, 1873, *Poetic Studies*, 1875, *The Story of Avis*, 1877, *An Old Maid's Paradise*, 1879, *Doctor Zay*, 1882, *Beyond the Gates*, 1883, *Songs of the Silent World*, 1884, *The Madonna of the Tubs*, 1887, *The Gates Between*, 1887, *Jack, the Fisherman*, 1887, *Austin Phelps*, a biography of her father, 1891, *A Singular Life*, 1895, *Within the Gates*, 1901, *Walled In*, 1907, and *Comrades*, 1911.

In October 1888 Phelps married Herbert D. Ward, several years her junior. They collaborated on three Biblical romances, *The Master of the Magicians*, 1890, *Come Forth*,

1890, and *A Lost Hero*, 1891. In 1896 she published *Chapters from a Life*, an autobiography. Elizabeth Ward died in Newton, Massachusetts, on January 28, 1911.

Ward, Hortense Sparks Malsch 1872–1944 lawyer and reformer

Born near Simpsonville, Texas, on July 20, 1872, Hortense Sparks grew up from 1883 in Edna, Texas. She was educated in public schools and at Nazareth Academy, operated by the Sisters of the Incarnate Word and Blessed Sacrament in Victoria, Texas. After a year of teaching school in Edna she married Albert Malsch, a tinner, in January 1891. She moved to Houston in 1903 and worked as a stenographer and notary. She and her husband were divorced in 1906. She began studying law by correspondence and for two years worked as a county court reporter. In August 1909 she married William H. Ward, a lawyer with whom she completed her legal studies. In August 1910 she was admitted to the Texas bar, and a short time later she and her husband formed the firm of Ward & Ward.

A letter Hortense Ward wrote to a Houston newspaper in 1912 on the need for a married women's property law in Texas attracted the notice of the *Delineator* magazine, which gave it national publicity and also distributed her pamphlet on *Property Rights of Married Women in Texas*. She lobbied vigorously and successfully on behalf of legislation to that end in 1913, and the law enacted was widely known as the Hortense Ward Law. She also worked for legislation enacting a workmen's compensation system and a 54-hour week for employed women, both of which were passed in 1913; a bill enabling women to vote in party primaries, which was passed in 1918; and other reforms.

In February 1915 Ward was admitted to practice before the U.S. Supreme Court. She ran unsuccessfully for the Democratic nomination for judge of the county court in 1920 and in 1924 campaigned on behalf of Miriam Ferguson for governor. In 1925, when all the justices of the Texas supreme court disqualified themselves in the case of *Johnson v. Darr* because it involved the Woodmen of the World, a fraternal order to which they all belonged, Ward and two other women were constituted a special supreme court to hear the case; Ward was chief justice. In the same year she was briefly acting judge of the corporation court of the city of Houston. She retired from her legal practice in 1939 and died in Houston on December 5, 1944.

Ward, Nancy 1738?–1822 Native American leader

Born about 1738, probably at Chota, a Cherokee village on the Little Tennessee River in what is now Monroe County, Tennessee, Nanye'hi was the daughter of a Cherokee mother of the Wolf clan and a Delaware father. In 1775 she distinguished herself at a battle between Cherokee and Creek bands at Taliwa (near present-day Canton, Georgia) by taking her fatally wounded husband's place in battle. She was thereafter known as "Agi-ga-u-e," or "Beloved Woman," a title that carried with it leadership of the woman's council of clan representatives and membership on the tribal council of chiefs. Her second husband was Bryant (or Brian) Ward, a white trader. Although he left the Cherokee Nation in the late 1750s and later married a white woman in South Carolina, Nancy Ward (her anglicized name) retained a strong friendship for whites.

She is credited with having secretly warned John Sevier and the Watauga Association of settlers of an impending attack by Cherokees in July 1776, and she subsequently used her prerogative as Beloved Woman to save a white woman captive from being burned at the stake. In return, her village of Chota was spared destruction by frontier militia that swept through Cherokee territory in October. She again gave warning of a Cherokee uprising in 1780 and attempted to prevent retaliation by militia forces. She made a notable plea for Indian-white friendship at the negotiation of the Treaty of Hopewell in 1785. She was a strong voice within the tribe for the adoption of farming and dairying and herself became the first Cherokee cattle-owner. Late in life she urged the tribe to stand against the rising pressure by white settlers to sell their remaining lands, but with little success. The sale of tribal lands north of the Hiwassee River in 1819 obliged her to move.

She opened an inn on the Ocoee River in southeastern Tennessee (near present-day Benton) and died there in 1822. Over ensuing years and decades, Nancy Ward, known sometimes as the "Pocahontas of the West," was the subject of numerous tales and legends in her native region, and they were given national currency by various writers, including Theodore Roosevelt in his *Winning of the West*, 1905.

Warner, Susan Bogert and Anna Bartlett 1819–1885 and 1827–1915 writers

Born in New York City, Susan on July 11, 1819, and Anna on August 31, 1827, the Warner sisters were of a prosperous family and were educated privately. From 1837, when their father suffered financial reverses, the family lived on Constitution Island in the Hudson River opposite West Point. The sisters were markedly different in temperament but worked and played together well and together developed talents for storytelling.

In 1851 Susan published a novel titled *The Wide, Wide World* under the pseudonym "Elizabeth Wetherell." Sentimental and moralistic, the book proved highly and enduringly popular; it was widely sold in several translations and was reputedly the first book by an American author to sell a million copies. She followed with *Queechy* (under her own name) in 1852, and in that year Anna published *Dollars and Cents*. Anna had earlier invented an educational game called "Robinson Crusoe's Farmyard," played with colored cards painted by both sisters; for many years the game was sold through the firm of George P. Putnam, Susan's publisher.

Over the ensuing decades they continued to write prolifically. Susan turned out *The Hills of the Shatemuc*, which sold 10,000 copies on its day of publication, 1856, *The Golden Ladder*, 1862, *The Old Helmet*, 1863, *Melbourne House*, 1864, *Daisy*, 1868, *A Story of Small Beginnings*, 1872, *Diana*, 1877, *Bread and Oranges*, 1877, *Pine Needles*, 1877, *My Desire*, 1879, *The End of a Coil*, 1880, *Nobody*, 1882, *The Letter of Credit*, 1882, *Stephen, M.D.*, 1883, and *A Red Wallflower*, 1884, among other novels. She also wrote several books for children, including *The House in Town*, 1872, *Trading: Finishing the Story of the House in Town*, 1873, *Willow Brook*, 1874, the "Say and Do Series" in 1875, and *The Flag of Truce*, 1878, and a number of works on Biblical topics, including *The Law and the Testimony*, 1853, *Walks from Eden*, 1870, *The Broken Walls of Jerusalem and the Rebuilding of Them*, 1878, and *The Kingdom of Judah*, 1878.

Anna Warner published *My Brother's Keeper*, 1855, *Hymns of the Church Militant*, 1858, *The Star Out of Jacob*, 1868, *The Fourth Watch*, 1872, *Gardening by Myself*, (the first American book to urge women to do their own gardening), 1872, *Stories of Vinegar Hill*, six volumes, 1872, *Cross Corners*, 1887, *Some Memories of James Stokes and Caroline Phelps Stokes*, 1892, and *Susan Warner*, 1909. Among her many hymns were the popular "Jesus Loves Me, This I Know" and "Jesus Bids Us Shine."

Together the sisters wrote *Mr. Rutherford's Children*, two volumes, 1853–1855, *Ellen Montgomery's Bookshelf*, 1853–1859, *Carl Krinken*, 1854, *Say and Seal*, 1860, *Books of Blessing*, 1868, *Wych Hazel*, 1876, and *The Gold of Chickaree*, 1876. For many years they conducted regular weekly Bible classes for West Point cadets.

Susan Warner died in Highland Falls, New York, on March 17, 1885. Anna continued to live alone on Constitution Island. She refused several offers to sell the island to developers because she hoped it would one day become part of the West Point reservation. Several bills authorizing the purchase of the island by the federal government failed to pass Congress, but in 1908 Margaret Olivia Slocum Sage purchased Constitution Island and presented it to the government. Anna Warner died in Highland Falls, New York, on January 22, 1915.

Warren, Mercy Otis 1728–1814 poet, dramatist, and historian

Born in Barnstable, Massachusetts, on September 14 (old style), 1728, Mercy Otis was the sister of James Otis, who was early active in the anti-British agitation over the Stamp Act of 1765. She received no formal schooling but managed to absorb something of an education from her brothers' tutors. In November 1754 she married James Warren, a Massachusetts political leader. Knowing most of the leaders of the Revolution personally, she was continually at or near the center of events during the exciting years from 1765 to 1789. Her vantage point combined with a talent for writing to make her both a poet and historian of the Revolutionary era. She wrote several plays, including *The Adulateur*, printed in the *Massachusetts Spy*, a Boston newspaper, in 1772 and published separately in 1773. It was a satire directed against Governor Thomas Hutchinson of Massachusetts, in which the war of revolution was foretold.

The Defeat, also featuring the character based on Hutchinson, followed, and in 1775 she published *The Group*, a satire conjecturing what would happen if the British king abrogated the Massachusetts charter of rights. The anonymously published *The Blockheads*, 1776, and *The Motley Assembly*, 1779, are also attributed to her. In 1788 she published *Observations on the New Constitution*, whose ratification she opposed.

She was something of a feminist, and she corresponded with her friend Abigail Adams on her belief that the relegation of women to minor concerns reflected not their inferior intellect but the inferior opportunities offered them to develop their capacities. In 1790 she published *Poems, Dramatic and Miscellaneous*, a collection of her works. In 1805 she completed a three-volume history entitled *A History of the Rise, Progress, and Termination of the American Revolution*, which remained especially useful for its knowledgeable comments on the important personages of the day. Some sharp comments in the history on John Adams led to a heated correspondence and a breach that lasted until Elbridge Gerry effected a reconciliation in 1812. Warren died on October 19, 1814, in Plymouth, Massachusetts.

Washburn, Margaret Floy 1871–1939 psychologist

Born in New York City on July 25, 1871, Margaret Washburn grew up there and in Walden and Kingston, New York. She attended public schools and the Ulster Academy in Kingston and in 1891 graduated from Vassar College. She then studied briefly at Columbia University, where she was allowed to audit courses and work in James M. Cattell's new laboratory of experimental psychology but was not admitted as a regular student. In 1892 she entered Cornell, where her studies under Edward Bradford Titchener led to her receiving a Ph.D. in psychology in 1894. For six years she was professor of psychology, philosophy, and ethics at Wells College. In 1900–1902 she returned to Cornell as warden of Sage College, a women's residence, and during that time she also taught courses in animal and social psychology.

After a year as assistant professor of psychology at the University of Cincinnati Washburn accepted the post of associate professor of psychology at Vassar. She remained at Vassar until her retirement in 1937, from 1908 as full professor. A remarkably effective teacher, she made Vassar a leading center of undergraduate training and research in psychology. The results of her fruitful joint researches with advanced students were reported in a series of *Studies from the Psychological Laboratory of Vassar College*. Her own publications included scores of articles, reviews, and notes in professional journals and two books, *The Animal Mind*, 1908, and *Movement and Mental Imagery*, 1916. The former was a summary of studies in the field that was of lasting importance, and the latter was devoted to developing her dualistic motor theory of mental activity, an attempt to find a third way between the opposed and equally one-sided schools of behaviorism and introspectionism.

Washburn served also as a cooperating editor of the *American Journal of Psychology* from 1903 to 1925 and as one of its four coeditors from 1925; she was also connected editorially with the *Psychological Bulletin*, the *Psychological Review*, the *Journal of Comparative Psychology*, and the *Journal of American Behavior*. She was president of the American Psychological Association in 1921 and vice-president of the American Association for the Advancement of Science in 1927.

In the latter year a special number of the *American Journal of Psychology* honored her. She was a member of the National Research Council in 1919–1920 and 1925–1928. In 1931 she became the second woman (after Florence R. Sabin) to be elected to the National Academy of Sciences. She died in Poughkeepsie, New York, on October 29, 1939.

Waters, Ethel 1896–1977 singer and actor

Born in Chester, Pennsylvania, on October 31, 1896, Ethel Waters grew up there and in Philadelphia in extreme poverty. Married for the first time before she was thirteen and while she was still attending convent school, she later worked as a chambermaid and scrubwoman, At the urging of friends she tried singing in a nightclub. At seventeen, billing herself as "Sweet Mama Stringbean," she was singing at the Lincoln Theater in Baltimore. It was during her engagement there that she received permission from W. C. Handy to sing his "St. Louis Blues," thus becoming the first woman to perform the song on the stage. For years she worked in vaudeville and small clubs. In 1925 she sang at the Plantation Club in New York City's Harlem, and her performance there led to offers to appear on Broadway.

In 1927 she appeared in the all-black revue *Africana*, and thereafter she divided her time between the stage, nightclubs, and eventually movies. In 1930 she was on the Broadway stage in *Blackbirds*, a revival of the popular 1924 musical, and the following year she starred in *Rhapsody in Black*. In 1933 she appeared with Marilyn Miller in Irving Berlin's musical *As Thousands Cheer*, her first departure from shows with all-black casts. Her rendition of "Heat Wave" in that show linked the song permanently to her. Accounted one of the great blues singers, she performed and recorded with such jazz greats as Duke Ellington and Benny Goodman. Several composers wrote songs especially for her, and she was particularly identified with "Dinah" and "Stormy Weather."

Waters's first straight dramatic role was in the 1938 production of DuBose and Dorothy Heyward's *Mamba's Daughters*. Two years later she spent a season on Broadway in the hit musical *Cabin in the Sky*, and she also appeared in the 1943 film version. Probably her greatest dramatic success was in the stage version of Carson McCullers's *The Member of the Wedding* in 1950, a performance for which she won the New York Drama Critics' Circle Award. She also starred in the movie version in 1953.

Among Waters's other films were *Cairo*, 1942, *Pinky*, for which she was nominated for an Academy Award, 1949, and *The Sound and the Fury*, 1959. Her autobiography, *His Eye Is on the Sparrow*, 1951, was a best-seller. In 1951 she appeared in the television series "Beulah." After the mid–1950s Waters continued in show business but at a more relaxed pace, appearing on television and occasionally in nightclubs. In the 1960s she appeared frequently with Billy Graham in his evangelistic crusades, She died in Chatsworth, California, on September 1, 1977.

Weber, Lois 1881–1939 actor, producer, and director

Born on June 13, 1881, in Allegheny (now part of Pittsburgh), Pennsylvania, Florence Lois Weber displayed musical ability at an early age. After a brief tour as a concert pianist at sixteen, she devoted some time to singing with the missionary Church Army before making her way to New York City. She took a few voice lessons there and then toured for a time with the Zig Zag stage company. She appeared in a road company of *Why Girls Leave Home* in 1904. A few months later she married W. Phillips Smalley, with whom she played stock and repertory for five years. In 1910 they decided to seek careers in the infant motion picture industry.

For a succession of small production companies — Gaumont, Reliance, Rex, and Bosworth — she and her husband turned out dozens of short and feature films. Lois Weber wrote scenarios and subtitles, acted, directed, designed sets and costumes, edited, and even developed negatives. They also worked in an experimental form of sound films, with dialogue recorded on synchronized phonograph records. In 1915 they joined Universal Pictures, and in 1917 she established Lois Weber Productions, whose films were released through Universal. She remained with Universal for her entire Hollywood career except for a brief association with DeMille Pictures in 1927.

One of the most energetic, aesthetically ambitious, and technically well grounded film makers in the industry, Weber wrote, produced, and directed such films, many of them "problem" films as suggested by their titles, as *Hypocrites*, 1914, *Scandal*, 1915, *Jewel*, 1915, *Idle Wives*, 1916, *The Dumb Girl of Portici*, 1916, *Where Are My Children?*, 1916, *Shoes*, 1916, *The People Vs. John Doe*, 1916, *The Price of a Good Time*, 1917, *The Man Who Dared God*, 1917, *The Doctor and the Woman*, 1918, *For Husbands Only*, 1918, *Borrowed Clothes*, 1919, *When a Girl Loves*, 1919, *Forbidden*, 1920, *The Blot*, 1921, *Too Wise Wives*, 1921, *What Do Men Want?*, 1921, and *A Chapter in Her Life*, 1923.

For a time following her divorce from Smalley in 1922 she was unable to work, but soon after her marriage in 1926 to Captain Harry Gantz she returned to direct *The Marriage Clause*, 1926, *Sensation Seekers*, 1927, *The Angel of Broadway*, 1927, and *Topsy and Eva*, 1927. After a seven-year absence from motion-picture work she returned to direct her last film, *White Heat*, 1934. After several years of illness Lois Weber died in Los Angeles on November 13, 1939.

Webster, Jean 1876–1916 writer

Born in Fredonia, New York, on July 24, 1876, Alice Jane Chandler Webster adopted the name Jean while attending the Lady Jane Grey School in Binghamton, New York. She graduated from Vassar College, where she was a classmate and close friend of Adelaide Crapsey, in 1901. Her interest in writing dated from an early age and doubtless profited from the fact that her father, Charles L. Webster, was Mark Twain's publisher and her maternal grandmother was his sister. She contributed a weekly column to the *Poughkeepsie Sunday Courier* while in college and at the same time started writing the stories that were collected in her first book, *When Patty Went to College*, 1903.

She soon followed with *The Wheat Princess*, 1905, and *Jerry, Junior*, 1907, both inspired by her extended visit to Italy, *The Four Pools Mystery*, published anonymously, 1908, *Much Ado About Peter*, 1909, *Just Patty*, more stories about the character perhaps modeled on Adelaide Crapsey, 1911, and *Daddy-Long-Legs*, 1912, her most popular work. *Daddy-Long-Legs*, first a serial in the *Ladies' Home Journal*, a best-seller in book form, a successful stage play in 1914 in Jean Webster's own adaptation, and in 1919 a popular Mary Pickford silent film, was not only a successful piece of fiction but also a stimulus to reform in the institutional treatment of orphans. In 1914 she published *Dear Enemy*, a sequel and also a best-seller. She died in New York City on June 11, 1916.

Wells, Carolyn 1862–1942 writer

Born in Rahway, New Jersey, on June 18, 1862, Carolyn Wells supplemented her formal education in public and private schools with an early-formed habit of voracious reading. After completing her schooling she worked as a librarian for the Rahway Library Association for some years. Her love of puzzles led to her first book, *At the Sign of the Sphinx*, a collection of charades, 1896. She followed with *The Jingle Book*, 1899, *The Story of Betty*, first of a series of novels for girls, 1899, and *Idle Idyls*, a book of verse for adults, 1900.

From 1900 Wells gave herself entirely to literary work, and over the next four decades she produced a flood of books, some 170 titles that fell into several genres: children's stories, mystery and detective stories, anthologies, and humorous and nonsense writings. Among her books were *Folly in Fairyland*, 1901, *Patty Fairfield*, beginning a second popular series for girls, 1901, *The Merry Go-Round*, 1901, *A Nonsense Anthology*, one of her best known books, 1902, *Abenaki Caldwell*, 1902, *A Phenomenal Fauna*, 1902, *Eight Girls and a Dog*, 1902, *The Pete and Polly Stories*, 1902, *The Gordon Elopement*, 1904, *Patty at Home*, 1904, *A Parody Anthology*, 1904, *The Reign of Queen Dick*, 1904, *The Staying Guest*, 1904, *A Matrimonial Bureau*, 1905, *A Satire Anthology*, 1905, *The Rubaiyat of a Motor Car*, 1906, *A Whimsey Anthology*, 1906, *Rainy Day Diversions*, 1907, *Marjorie's Vacation*, beginning another series, 1907, *The Emily Emmins Papers*, 1907, *Fluffy Ruffles*, 1907, *The Happy Chaps*, 1908, *The Clue*, 1909, *The Gold Bag*, 1911, *A Chain of Evidence*, 1912, *The Lovers' Baedecker*, 1912, *The Maxwell Mystery*, 1913, *Anybody But Anne*, 1914, *Jolly Plays for Holidays*, 1914, *The White Alley*, 1915, *Curved Blades*, 1916, *Baubles*, 1917, *Doris of Dobbs Ferry*, 1917, *The Mark of Cain*, 1917, *Faulkner's Folly*, 1917, *Vicky Vail*, 1918, *The Diamond Pin*, 1919, *The Man Who Fell Through the Earth*, 1919, *The Book of Humorous Verse*, 1920, *Raspberry Jam*, 1920, *Ptomaine Street*, 1921, *More Lives than One*, 1923, *The Fourteenth Key*, 1924, *The Book of Limericks*, 1925, *The Book of Charades*, 1927, *All at Sea*, 1927, *Anything But the Truth*, 1928, *Horror House*, 1931, *Fuller's Earth*, 1932, *The Cat in Verse*, 1935, *The Wooden Indian*, 1935, *Murder in the Bookshop*, 1936, *The Radio Studio Murder*, 1937, *The Importance of Being Murdered*, 1939, *Murder on Parade*, 1940, *The Black Night Murders*, 1941, and *Murder Will In*, 1942. Her autobiography, *The Rest of My Life*, appeared in 1937.

Carolyn Wells was especially noted for her humor, and she was a frequent contributor of nonsense verse and whimsical pieces to such little magazines as Gelett Burgess's *The Lark*, the *Chap Book*, the *Yellow Book*, and the *Philistine*. She died in New York City on March 26, 1942.

Wells, Emmeline Blanche Woodward 1828–1921 religious leader and feminist

Born in Petersham, Massachusetts, on February 29, 1828, Emmeline Woodward attended schools in her native town and in nearby New Salem. In 1842 she followed her widowed mother in converting to Mormonism. She began teaching school in 1843, but in 1844 she moved with her first husband to the Mormon settlement of Nauvoo, Illinois. Her husband deserted her the next year, and in February 1845 she became a plural wife of Newel K. Whitney, presiding bishop of the Mormon group, in a ceremony performed by Brigham Young. She accompanied the main Mormon group west to "Deseret" (Utah) in 1846–1848. In October 1852, two years after Bishop Whitney's death, she married Daniel H. Wells, a high Mormon officer; she was his seventh wife.

After a decade devoted to home cares she began involving herself in community and church affairs. She became active in the work of the influential Relief Society and in 1873 began contributing to the society's bimonthly *Woman's Exponent*, of which she became associate editor in 1875 and editor in 1877.

In 1874 Wells was elected a vice-president of the National Woman Suffrage Association. In 1878 she was proposed for the office of treasurer of Salt Lake City but was barred by territorial law from running for the office. In the mid–1880s, when Congress threatened to repeal the Utah woman suffrage law that had been enacted by the territorial legislature in 1870, she turned the *Woman's Exponent* into a powerful voice in defense of women. She spent several months in 1885 and 1886 personally lobbying in Washington, D.C. Her campaign failed, however, for in 1887 woman suffrage was repealed.

In January 1889 she led in founding the Woman Suffrage Association of Utah and through it launched a campaign that succeeded in restoring the vote to Utah women in the new state constitution that went into effect in 1896. In 1892 she became general secretary and in 1910 president of the Relief Society. She was a member of the National American Woman Suffrage Association, of the National Council of Women, and of the International Council of Women; she was secretary of the Deseret Hospital Association and the founder in 1891 of the Utah Women's Press Club.

In 1893 Wells edited *Charities and Philanthropies: Woman's Work in Utah* as part of Utah's contribution to the World's Columbian Exposition in Chicago, and in 1896 she published *Musings and Memories*, a collection of her verses. She was the author of the words of the popular Mormon hymn "Our Mountain Home So Dear." She continued to edit the *Woman's Exponent* until 1914, when it was superseded by the *Relief Society Magazine*. In her later years she was a revered figure among Mormons and widely respected nationally. She was chosen for the honor of unveiling the famous seagull monument in Salt Lake City in 1912. She died in Salt Lake City on April 25, 1921.

Wells, Mary Georgene 1928– businesswoman

Born in Youngstown, Ohio, on May 25, 1928, Mary Berg attended local schools and supplemented her education with dancing, music, and drama lessons. At seventeen she went to New York City and enrolled in the Neighborhood Playhouse School of the Theater. A year later she entered the Carnegie Institute of Technology, where she remained for two years. In December 1949 she married Burt Wells, with whom she moved back to New York in 1950. (They were divorced in 1965.)

After a stint as fashion advertising manager for Macy's department store she joined the advertising agency of McCann-Erickson, Inc., where she was a copy group head from 1953 to 1956. In the latter year she moved to Doyle Dane Bernbach, where she became copy chief and vice-president in 1963. In 1964 she accepted the offer of a senior partnership in Jack Tinker & Partners, a prestigious agency noted for its creativity. There her own imagination and drive flourished. Working especially with copywriter Richard Rich and artist Stewart Greene, she directed the development of a series of memorably amusing and award-winning television commercials for Alka-Seltzer. With the same colleagues she developed a full campaign to revamp entirely the image of Braniff International Airlines, a campaign involving painting all the firm's airplanes in bright colors and dressing the stewardesses in designer uniforms.

Early in 1966, rather than sign a long-term contract with Tinker, Wells left the agency and with her two coworkers established her own, Wells, Rich, Greene, Inc. They immediately captured the Braniff account; Philip Morris, Utica Club beer, La Rosa spaghetti, and others quickly followed, and within six months the new agency boasted over $30 million in billings. As chairman of the board and chief executive officer of one of Madison Avenue's hottest agencies, a leader in the wave of humor and wit in advertising, Mary Wells became something of a celebrity in her own right. In November 1967 she married Harding L. Lawrence, president of Braniff. In 1971 she was named advertising woman of the year by the American Advertising Federation. In 1972 she was the highest paid executive in the advertising industry, with a gross income of over $414,000.

Wells-Barnett, Ida Bell 1862–1931 journalist and reformer

Born in Holly Springs, Mississippi, on July 16, 1862, Ida Wells was the daughter of slaves. She was educated at Rust University, a freedmen's school in Holly Springs, and at fourteen began teaching in a country school. She continued as a teacher after moving to Memphis, Tennessee, in 1884 and attended Fisk University during several summer sessions. In 1887 the Tennessee supreme court, reversing a circuit court decision, ruled against her in a suit she had brought against the Chesapeake & Ohio Railroad for having been forcibly removed from her seat after she had refused to give it up for one in a "colored only" car. In 1891, in consequence of some newspaper articles she had written critical of the education offered African-American children, her teaching contract was not renewed. She thereupon turned to journalism, buying an interest in the *Memphis Free Speech*.

Ida Wells-Barnett

In 1892, after three friends of hers had been killed by a mob, Wells began an editorial campaign against lynching that quickly led to the sacking of the newspaper's office during her absence. She moved to New York City, where she continued her anti-lynching crusade, first as a staff writer for the *New York Age* and then as a lecturer and organizer of anti-lynching societies. She traveled to speak in a number of major cities and twice visited Great Britain for the cause. In June 1895 she married Ferdinand L. Barnett, a Chicago lawyer, editor, and public official. She then adopted the name Wells-Barnett. From that time she restricted her travels, but she was very active in Chicago affairs. She contributed to the *Conservator*, her husband's newspaper, and to other local journals, published a detailed look at lynching in *A Red Record*, 1895, and was active in organizing local African-American women in various causes from the anti-lynching campaign to the suffrage movement.

From 1898 to 1902 she served as secretary of the National Afro-American Council, and in 1910 she founded and became first president of the Negro Fellowship League. From 1913 to 1916 she served as a probation officer of the Chicago municipal court. She was militant in her demand for justice for African-Americans and in her insistence that it was to be won by their own efforts. While she took part in the 1909 meeting of the Niagara Movement, she would have nothing to do with the less radical National Association for the Advancement of Colored People that sprang from it. She died in Chicago on March 25, 1931.

Welty, Eudora 1909– writer

Born in Jackson, Mississippi, on April 13, 1909, Eudora Welty attended Mississippi State College for Women for a time before transferring to the University of Wisconsin, from which she graduated in 1929. She spent a year at Columbia University preparing for a career in advertising, but she evidently found the work uncongenial and soon returned to Mississippi. For a time she wrote for a radio station and for the *Commercial Appeal* of Memphis, and later she was a publicity agent for the Mississippi office of the Works Progress Administration. During that time she worked at the craft of writing.

JILL KREMENTZ

Eudora Welty

Welty's first short story was published in *Manuscript* magazine in 1936, and thereafter her work began to appear regularly, first in little magazines such as the *Southern Review* and later in such general circulation magazines as the *Atlantic Monthly* and *New Yorker*. A collection of her stories, *A Curtain of Green*, was published in 1941. The next year her short novel *The Robber Bridegroom*, was issued; a second collection of stories, *The Wide Net*, followed in 1943, and in 1946 she published her first full-length novel, *Delta Wedding*. Her 1953 story "The Ponder Heart," published in book form in 1954, won her the quinquennial William Dean Howells Medal of the American Academy of Arts and Letters; she was also six times the winner of the O. Henry Award for short stories and in 1972 the recipient of the gold medal of the National Institute of Arts and Letters. "The Ponder Heart" was made into a Broadway play in 1956.

Other books included *The Golden Apples*, 1949, *The Bride of Innisfallen*, a 1955 collection of short stones, *The Shoe Bird*, a children's book, 1964, *Losing Battles*, 1970, and *The Optimist's Daughter*, which won a Pulitzer Prize, 1972. In 1971 she published *One Time, One Place: Mississippi in the Depression*, a collection of photographs she had taken while touring the state as a publicity agent for the WPA, and in 1978 *The Eye of the Story*, a collection of essays and reviews.

The settings and characters of Welty's novels and tales were usually rural or small-town Southern, and she used to great advantage her ear for dialect and her photographic eye for telling detail. She avoided, however, the Gothic strain to which Southern regional writing is liable and in her portrayal of character achieved a universality that attracted readers around the world. She was also popular as a reader of her own stories.

In 1975 a musical version of *The Robber Bridegroom* opened on Broadway. Welty's later works include *The Collected Stories of Eudora Welty*, 1980, *One Writer's Beginnings*, a best-selling collection of lectures given at Harvard University, 1984, *Morgana: Two Stories from "The Golden Apples,"* 1988, and *Photographs*, another collection from her work with the WPA, 1989. Among her many awards are the National Medal for Literature and the Presidential Medal of Freedom, 1980, the American Book Award, 1981 and 1984, the Modern Language Association's Commonwealth Medal, 1984, the National Book Critics Circle Award, 1984, the National Medal of Arts, 1987, and the Rea Award, 1992. She was named a Knight of the French Order of Arts and Letters in 1987.

Wentworth, Cecile de ?–1933 painter

Born in New York City, apparently between 1853 and 1870, Cecilia Smith was educated in convent schools. In 1886 she went to Paris, where she studied painting with Alexandre Cabanel and Edouard Detaille. Within the next three years she married Josiah W. Wentworth, and it was as Mme. C. E. Wentworth that she first exhibited at the Paris Salon in 1889. She continued to exhibit there for 30 years. She became widely noted as a portraitist, and over the years her sitters included President Theodore Roosevelt, President William Howard Taft, Queen Alexandra of England (a portrait commissioned by the king of Spain), and General John J. Pershing. Her portrait of Pope Leo XIII won a bronze medal at the Exposition Universelle in Paris in 1900 and prompted the Pope to decorate her with the title of grand commander of the Order of the Holy Sepulchre and create her a papal marchesa. (The portrait later hung in the Vatican Museum.)

She was an *officer d'académie* from 1894 and a chevalier of the Legion of Honor from 1901. Her paintings won prizes in numerous exhibitions throughout Europe, and she was one of the very few woman artists to have works purchased for the Luxembourg Museum. Works by her were later acquired also by the Metropolitan Museum of Art in New York, the Corcoran Gallery in Washington, D.C., and other leading museums. She died in Nice, France, on August 28, 1933.

West, Jessamyn 1902–1984 writer

Born on July 18, 1902, in Jennings County, Indiana, Mary Jessamyn West grew up there and from 1909 near Yorba Linda, California. She grew up much under her mother's Quaker influence, and in 1923 she graduated from Whittier College, a Quaker institution. She taught in a rural school in Hemet, California, from 1924 to 1928 and then resumed her education with a summer at Oxford University in 1929, after which she enrolled in the University of California at Berkeley.

Before completing her work for a Ph.D. degree she fell ill and was diagnosed as having terminal tuberculosis. She spent two dispiriting years in a Los Angeles sanatorium and was then sent home to die. Instead, under her mother's constant loving care, she recovered. During her long convalescence her mother told her tales of her own Indiana farm childhood and of her more distant pioneer forebears. Jessamyn West soon began writing stories and sketches inspired by her mother's tales.

West's stories about two Quaker characters, Jess and Eliza Birdwell, began appearing in such magazines as the *Atlantic Monthly*, *Harper's*, and the *Ladies' Home Journal* and in 1945 were collected in her first book, *The Friendly Persuasion*. The book was well received by critics for its warmth, delicate artistry, and beguiling simplicity. Invited to help create a screenplay for a motion picture based on the stories (a film released in 1956), she subsequently recounted her Hollywood experience in *To See the Dream*, 1957.

Her first novel, *The Witch Diggers*, 1951, was also set in southern Indiana and featured some rather Gothic details. Later books included *Cress Delahanty*, a collection of stories, 1953, *Love, Death, and the Ladies' Drill Team*, stories, 1955, *Love Is Not What You Think*, nonfiction, 1959, *South of the Angels*, a novel, 1960, *A Matter of Time*, a novel, 1966, *Leafy Rivers*, a novel, 1967, *Except for Me and Thee*, a continuation of the story of the Birdwells, 1969, *Crimson Ramblers of the Western World, Farewell* stories, 1970, *Hide and Seek*, a volume of memoirs and reflections, 1973, *The Secret Look*, poetry, 1974, *The Massacre at Fall Creek*, a novel based on a historical incident, 1975, *The Woman Said Yes; Encounters with Life and Death*, autobiography, 1976, *Double Discovery: A Journey*, a travel diary, 1980, and *Collected Stories*, 1986. She died on February 23, 1984, in Napa, California.

West, Mae 1892?–1980 entertainer

Born in Brooklyn, New York, on August 17, 1892 (or perhaps 1893), Mae West was already acting and dancing in amateur theatricals by the time she was seven. At eight she became a member of a stock company and began playing juvenile roles. In 1906 she went into vaudeville as a partner in a song-and-dance team, and five years later, in September 1911, she opened in the Broadway musical revue *A la Broadway and Hello Paris* at the Fulton Theatre. For the next 15 years she alternated between vaudeville and Broadway shows, the latter including *Sometime*, 1918, *Demi-Tasse*, 1919, and *The Mimic World*, 1921, and she did an occasional nightclub act.

West's first great success came in April 1926 with the production of *Sex*, which she wrote, produced, and starred in, at Daly's Theatre.

The play ran for 375 performances before it was closed under pressure from the Society for the Suppression of Vice. West was convicted of "corrupting the morals of youth" and emerged from an eight-day jail sentence a national celebrity. From that time she appeared almost exclusively in vehicles that she herself wrote. For all the variety of the scripts, the constant factor was her own personality and her ability to burlesque social attitudes, especially toward sex. In 1928 she starred in the title role in the play *Diamond Lil*, a characterization that virtually became her alter ego. Her public persona became a fixture: a wisecracking, ironic, languorous, and somewhat regal woman, sure of her fatal attraction and not at all embarrassed by the practical use she makes of it. The frank sensuality of her stage presence, her opulent attire set off by her flippant double-entendres, marked her as a prime target for moralizers and censors.

In 1931–1932 she appeared in the stage version of her book *The Constant Sinner* (first published as *Babe Gordon*, 1930). She then moved to Hollywood. After starring with George Raft in *Night After Night* in 1932, she did a film version of *Diamond Lil* entitled *She Done Him Wrong*. It was in this film that she spoke to Cary Grant her most famous line: "Come up and see me sometime." For the next decade she worked almost solely in movies, making such comedies as *I'm No Angel* (in which she casually ordered her maid "Beulah, peel me a grape"), 1933, *Klondike Annie*, 1936, *Go West Young Man*, 1936, and the classic *My Little Chickadee*, which she and W. C. Fields wrote and starred in together, 1940.

During the 1930s West became one of Hollywood's highest salaried stars and invested heavily in real estate and business. In 1944 she returned to the stage with *Catherine Was Great*, and she did revivals of *Diamond Lil* from 1948 to 1951. During the mid–1950s she toured with a nightclub act consisting of herself and a "chorus" of muscle men. Subsequently she performed less frequently. She appeared occasionally on television and also made records of some of her songs. After 1943 she did not make any movies until the 1970 filming of Gore Vidal's novel *Myra Breckenridge*. The movie itself was a failure, but West wrote her own part for it, received star billing, and proved its main attraction. She emerged from retirement again to appear in the unsuccessful film *Sextette*, 1979.

West's provocative drawl and her variety of languid drapes and swivels were uniquely hers, as was the hourglass shape that inspired World War II fliers to dub their pneumatic life-vests "Mae Wests." Her autobiography, *Goodness Had Nothing to Do with It*, was published in 1959, and in 1975 she published *On Sex, Health and ESP*. She died on November 22, 1980, in Los Angeles, California.

Edith Wharton

Wharton, Edith 1862–1937 writer

Born in New York City on January 24, 1862, Edith Newbold Jones came of a distinguished and long-established New York family. She was educated by private tutors and governesses at home and in Europe, where the family resided for six years after the Civil War, and she read voraciously. She made her debut in society in 1879 and married Edward Wharton, a wealthy Boston banker, in April 1885. Although she had had a book of her own poems privately printed when she was sixteen, it was not until after several years of married life that she began to write in earnest. She contributed a few poems and stories to *Harper's*, *Scribner's*, and other magazines in the 1890s, and in 1897, after overseeing the remodeling of a house in Newport, Rhode Island, she collaborated with architect Ogden Codman, Jr., on *The Decoration of Houses*. Her next books were collections of stories, *The Greater Inclination*, 1899, and *Crucial Instances*, 1901.

Her first novel, *The Valley of Decision*, appeared in 1902. *The House of Mirth*, 1905, was a novel of manners that analyzed the stratified society she knew and its reaction to social change. The book won her critical acclaim and a wide audience. Her preoccupation with aristocratic values and, increasingly, with the importance of taste were also reflected in such works as *The Custom of the Country*, 1913, *The Glimpses of the Moon*, 1922, *Hudson River Bracketed*, 1929, and *The Gods Arrive*, 1932, but she put them aside in her most famous work *Ethan Frome*, 1911, a novelette of simple New England people that eloquently expressed the anguish of individuals doomed to live within the bleak walls of convention. *The Age of Innocence*, 1920, which won a Pulitzer Prize and was considered her best novel, explored social hypocrisy and convention with sharp irony.

Other books included *Madame de Treymes*, 1907, *The Fruit of the Tree*, 1907, *The Reef*, 1912, *Summer*, 1917, *A Son at the Front*, 1923, *Old New York*, 1924, *The Mother's Recompense*, 1925, *Twilight Sleep*, a best-seller, 1927, *The Children*, 1928, and the posthumous *The Buccaneers*, 1938, and collections of stories including *The Hermit and the Wild Woman* 1908, *Tales of Men and Ghosts*, 1910, *Xingu*, 1916, *Here and Beyond*, 1926, *Certain People*, 1930, and *Human Nature*, 1933. In 1925 she published *The Writing of Fiction* and in 1934 an autobiography, *A Backward Glance*. In all she published more than 50 books, including fiction, short stories, travel books, historical novels, and criticism.

Edith Wharton lived in France from 1907, visiting the United States only occasionally. She was divorced from Edward Wharton in 1913. In 1923, during her last visit to America, she became the first woman to receive an honorary doctorate from Yale University. She was a close friend in his last years of Henry James, with whose art her own had much in common. She died on August 11, 1937, at St. Brice-sous-forêt, near Paris.

Wheatley, Phillis 1753?–1784 poet

Born about 1753, probably in Senegal, Africa, the young girl who was to become Phillis Wheatley was kidnapped and brought to Boston on a slaveship in 1761 and purchased by a tailor, John Wheatley, as a personal servant for his wife. She was treated kindly in the Wheatley household, almost as a third daughter. In less than two years, under the tutelage of Mrs. Wheatley and her daughters, she had mastered English; she went on to learn Greek and Latin and caused a stir among Boston scholars by translating a tale from Ovid. From the age of thirteen she wrote exceptionally mature, if conventional, poetry.

Her better known pieces included "To the University of Cambridge in New England," "To the King's Most Excellent Majesty," "On the Death of Rev. Dr. Sewall," and "An Elegiac Poem, on the Death of the Celebrated Divine . . . George Whitefield," which was the first of her poems to be published, in 1770. She was escorted by Mr. Wheatley's son to London in 1773 and there her first book, *Poems on Various Subjects, Religious and Moral*, was published. Her personal qualities even more than her literary talent contributed to her great social success in London. She returned to Boston shortly thereafter because of the illness of her mistress. Both Mr. and Mrs. Wheatley died soon thereafter, and Phillis was freed.

Phillis Wheatley

In 1778 she married John Peters, an intelligent but irresponsible free Negro who eventually abandoned her. She died in Boston on December 5, 1784. Two books issued posthumously were *Memoir and Poems of Phillis Wheatley*, 1834, and *Letters of Phillis Wheatley, the Negro Slave-Poet of Boston*, 1864, Her work was frequently cited by abolitionists to combat the charge of innate intellectual inferiority among Negroes and to promote educational opportunities for people of her race.

Wheelock, Lucy 1857–1946 educator

Born in Cambridge, Vermont, on February 1, 1857, Lucy Wheelock attended schools in Underhill, Vermont, and in Reading, Massachusetts. After graduating from high school in 1874 she taught school for two years in her native village. In 1876 she enrolled in the Chauncy Hall School in Boston to prepare for college, but her discovery of the school's kindergarten opened a new field to her. On advice of Elizabeth Peabody she entered the Kindergarten Training School in Boston in 1878, and on receiving her diploma in 1879 she became a kindergarten teacher at Chauncy Hall.

In 1888, following the opening of kindergartens as part of the Boston public school system, Lucy Wheelock instituted a one-year training course for teachers at Chauncy Hall. The course proved a remarkable success, growing rapidly from its original six students as it attracted would-be kindergartners from all over the country. In 1893 the course was lengthened to two years. In 1896 the training course left the Chauncy Hall School to become the independent Wheelock Kindergarten Training School. The training of teachers for primary grades was begun in 1899 and of nursery school teachers in 1926; in 1929 the kindergarten course was lengthened to three years. Students were given training in fundamental Froebelian methods and in various innovative additions to kindergarten pedagogy and were also taught to consider the kindergarten classroom as only one element in a larger process of socialization for which they were also responsible.

Wheelock served on a committee of the National Education Association appointed in 1892 to plan a national organization of kindergartners. She helped found the resulting International Kindergarten Union in 1893 and was its second president in 1895–1899. In the kindergarten movement she occupied a mediating position between the conservative orthodox Froebelians led by Susan Blow and the progressive innovators led by Patty Smith Hill. In 1905–1909 she chaired the Committee of Nineteen appointed to study the areas of disagreement in kindergarten methodology, and she edited the committee's report, *The Kindergarten*, 1913.

She served on the committee on education of the National Congress of Mothers (later the National Congress of Parents and Teachers) from 1899 and was its chairman from 1908. She was also vice-president of the department of superintendence of the National Education Association. In addition she was active in community work in Boston, establishing free kindergartens in various poor neighborhoods and contributing to the work of settlement houses and other organizations.

Among Wheelock's published works were *Red-Letter Stories*, 1884, and *Swiss Stories for Children*, 1887, both translated from the writings of Johanna Spyri, and *Talks to Mothers*, with Elizabeth Colson, 1920; she edited *Pioneers of the Kindergarten in America*, 1923, *Kindergarten Children's Hour*, five volumes, 1924, and *The Kindergarten in New England*, 1935.

In 1929 she was appointed to the education committee of the League of Nations. She retired as director of the Wheelock School in 1939. The school, which then had 325 students and 23 faculty members, was incorporated in that year, and in 1941 it became Wheelock College. She died in Boston on October 2, 1946.

Whitcher, Frances Miriam Berry 1811–1852 writer

Born in Whitesboro, New York, on November 1, 1811, Miriam Berry early displayed marked talents for writing, usually satirical verses and humorous sketches, and for drawing caricatures. Her gifts were little appreciated in her childhood, however. She was educated in the village academy. Her first published story, "The Widow Spriggins," appeared in a Rome, New York, newspaper after she had read it to a local literary society. It was a broad burlesque of the fashionable sentimental novel and employed the dialect and rustic humor popularized by Seba Smith, Thomas C. Haliburton, and others. In 1846 *Neal's Saturday Gazette and Lady's Literary Museum* of Philadelphia published a series of her rambling monologues under the title "The Widow Bedott's Table-Talk," signed simply "Frank." In 1847–1849 *Godey's Lady's Book* published a similar series called "Aunt Magwire's Experience."

In January 1847 Miriam Berry married the Reverend Benjamin W. Whitcher, with whom she settled in Elmira, New York. She continued to write Widow Bedott and Aunt Magwire sketches and in them to satirize the pretensions, prejudices, and minor vices of village female society. Real-life townspeople who fancied themselves models for her pen were frequently outraged. Her own drawings illustrated many of her published sketches. She was the first woman to write such popular humorous works in America. She also wrote a less colloquial series of "Letters from Timberville" and a number of hymns and religious poems for *Neal's Saturday Gazette* and the *Gospel Messenger* of Utica, New York. Whitcher died in Whitesboro, New York, on January 4, 1852, leaving an unfinished novel. A collection of *Widow Bedott Papers* was published in 1856 and reportedly sold 100,000 copies within a decade. A second collection, *Widow Spriggins, Mary Elmer, and Other Sketches*, appeared in 1867, and as late as 1879 "Petroleum V. Nasby" (David Ross Locke) published a comedy, *The Widow Bedott, or a Hunt for a Husband.*

White, Alma Bridwell 1862–1946 religious leader

Born in Kinniconick, Lewis County, Kentucky, on June 16, 1862, Mollie Alma Bridwell grew up in a dour family of little means. She attended local schools and after a short time at the nearby Vanceburg Seminary became a schoolteacher. She studied for another year at the Millersburg Female College and then in 1882 moved to Bannack, Montana Territory, where she taught school for a time. In December 1887 she married Kent White, a Methodist seminarian. The marriage allowed her abiding attraction to evangelical religion to flourish. In a succession of small, out-of-the-way pastorates in Colorado, she led hymns and prayers and occasionally preached. Her tall, homely appearance and commanding voice proved of great effect, and she soon discovered the ability to move congregations to tears or to shouts of joy.

An intense experience of personal sanctification in March 1893 induced White to take the lead from her husband in organizing a series of revival meetings at which she attempted to recover the fervor and piety of primitive Methodism. Her zealous emotionalism, together with her outspoken criticisms of the decorous accommodations of the Methodist hierarchy, brought down the wrath of conservative churchmen on her and her husband, who was transferred to a still less desirable pastorate. She eventually persuaded him to resign altogether.

For a time they traveled and evangelized together in Colorado, Montana, and Wyoming, and in December 1901 Alma White founded the Methodist Pentecostal Union Church in Denver. She was ordained an elder of the new sect in March 1902. In 1902 she published *Looking Back from Beulah* on the course of her life leading to the founding of her church, and a short time later she founded the *Pentecostal Union Herald*, which in 1904 was renamed the *Pillar of Fire*. In 1907 the headquarters of the church was moved to Zarephath, New Jersey, where a tract of land had been donated by a follower. The sect grew rapidly. In 1904–1905 she made the first of 29 evangelizing missions to Great Britain. Evangelists and missionaries of the sect adopted military uniforms similar to those of the Salvation Army. In 1917 the church changed its name to the Pillar of Fire, a change reflecting Alma White's firm opposition to the rise of more primitive and undisciplined forms of pentecostalism. In 1918 she was consecrated senior bishop of the Pillar of Fire, becoming the first woman bishop of any Christian church.

In addition to a constant round of revivals, the church grew to operate two radio stations (in Denver and in New Jersey), established seven schools and, in 1921, Alma White College in Zarephath, and carried on a large program of publishing books, pamphlets, and magazines for the faithful.

Among Alma White's own books were *Golden Sunbeams*, 1909, *Demons and Tongues*, 1910, *The New Testament Church*, two volumes, 1911–1912, *Truth Stranger than Fiction*, 1913, *Why I Do Not Eat Meat*, 1914, *Restoration of Israel, the Hope of the World*, 1917, *The Story of My Life* in five volumes, 1919–1930, *My Heart and My Husband*, 1923, *The Ku Klux Klan in Prophecy*, in which she outlined Biblical sanctions for the Klan, 1925, *Klansmen: Guardians of Liberty*, 1926, *The Voice of Nature*, 1927, *Hymns and Poems*, 1931, *Radio Sermons and Lectures*, 1936, and *The Sword of the Spirit*, 1937. By 1936 the Pillar of Fire church owned property worth an estimated $4 million and had over 4,000 members in 46 congregations. Alma White died in Zarephath, New Jersey, on June 26, 1946. Her husband had left the church in 1909; she was succeeded as senior bishop by her son, Ray Bridwell White, who died five months later.

White, Ellen Gould Harmon 1827–1915 religious leader

Born on November 26, 1827, in Gorham, Maine, Ellen Harmon grew up there and, from about 1836, in Portland. A serious injury sustained at the age of nine left her facially disfigured and for some time unable to attend school. Her education ended with a brief period at the Westbrook Seminary and Female College of Portland in 1839. In 1840 she underwent a religious experience at a Methodist camp meeting, and she was baptized in that church in June 1842. A short time later she followed her family in becoming a follower of William Miller, the Adventist prophet who was preaching the return of Christ within a year or so. Undismayed by the failure of Miller's prophecy (finally fixed for October 22, 1844), Ellen Harmon retained the Adventist view.

In December 1844 Harmon experienced the first of what she would later claim were some 2,000 visions. She began an itinerant ministry to discouraged Millerites, bringing news of the future and messages of encouragement gained from her visions. In August 1846 she married the Reverend James S. White, an Adventist minister. They traveled together through New England and gradually moved farther afield, spreading the Adventist faith. In 1849, in Rocky Hill, Connecticut, Reverend White began publishing an Adventist organ, *Present Truth*, which he moved to Rochester, New York, in 1852 and then to Battle Creek, Michigan, in 1855, renaming it the *Advent Review and Sabbath*

Herald along the way. In 1851 Ellen White published *A Sketch of the Christian Experience and Views of Ellen G. White*, and in 1854 a *Supplement to the Experience and Views of Ellen C. White* followed.

After their move to Battle Creek that city became the center of Adventist activity. A meeting of representatives of scattered Adventist congregations met there in 1860 and adopted the name Seventh-Day Adventists. A formal denominational structure was adopted by a General Conference held in that city in 1863. Throughout the work of organization and the establishment of an Adventist orthodoxy, the visions of Ellen White were the major contributing factor. The scriptural interpretations that came to her were promptly accepted. Much of the church program thus revealed was published in her *Testimonies for the Church*, which grew from 16 pages in its 1855 edition to an eventual 9 volumes. Her views on health, especially her opposition to the use of coffee, tea, meat, and drugs, were incorporated into Seventh-Day Adventist practice.

In 1866 she helped establish the Western Health Reform Institute in Battle Creek; later, as the Battle Creek Sanitarium, headed by Dr. John H. Kellogg, it became famous for its work in the field of diet and health food and the model for many other sanatoriums. (It was also to become the birthplace of Kellogg's Corn Flakes, invented by Dr. Kellogg's brother Will K. Kellogg in the 1890s.) In 1874 she helped found Battle Creek College, an Adventist institution of which her husband was named president.

Under her influence the Adventist movement was actively abolitionist before the Civil War, and during the 1860s and 1870s she was a prominent temperance advocate. In 1880 she and her husband published *Life Sketches . . . of Elder James White and His Wife, Mrs. Ellen G. White*.

After her husband's death in 1881 White lived for four years in Healdsburg, California. During 1885–1888 she traveled and lectured in Europe, and from 1891 to 1900 she was an Adventist missionary in Australia. There she established a school that later became Avondale College. After her return to the United States she led a movement to remove Adventist institutions from Battle Creek. The college moved to Berrien Springs, Michigan, as Emmanuel Missionary College (from 1960 Andrews University), and in 1903 the church headquarters and newspaper relocated to Takoma Park, Maryland. From that year she lived mainly in St. Helena, California, where she died on July 16, 1915.

White, Helen Magill 1853–1944 educator

Born on November 28, 1853, in Providence, Rhode Island, Helen Magill grew up in a Quaker family that valued education for women as well as men. In 1859 the family moved to Boston, where Helen was enrolled as the only female student in the Boston Public Latin School, of which her father was a sub-master. In 1873 she was a member of the first class to graduate from Swarthmore College, of which her father was then president. She continued studies in the classics at Swarthmore and then at Boston University, where her dissertation on Greek drama won her a Ph.D. in 1877, the first to be awarded to a woman in the United States. From 1877 to 1881 she studied at Cambridge University, placing third in her tripos (honors examinations) at Newnham College in the latter year.

After a year as principal of a private school in Johnstown, Pennsylvania, she was selected in 1883 to organize Howard Collegiate Institute in West Bridgewater, Massachusetts. She remained director of Howard until 1887, when she resigned in a dispute with the trustees. She then taught briefly at Evelyn College, a short-lived women's annex to Princeton University. Illness clouded the next few years, during which she taught for a time in the high school in Brooklyn, New York. In September 1890 she married Andrew D. White, the retired president of Cornell University and a college classmate of her father's, whom she had first met at a meeting of the American Social Science Association in 1887. She accompanied him to his diplomatic posts in St. Petersburg in 1892–1894 and Berlin in 1897–1903. She took no part in public or educational affairs thereafter except, in 1913, to publicly oppose woman suffrage. She died in Kittery Point, Maine, on October 28, 1944.

White, Pearl 1889–1938 actor

Born on March 4, 1889, in Green Ridge, Missouri, Pearl Fay White grew up there and in Springfield, Missouri. She left high school in her second year to join a local theatrical stock company, and at eighteen she joined a traveling theatrical troupe. In 1910, her voice having begun to fail, she decided to seek a career in films and joined the Powers Film Company in the Bronx, New York City. She subsequently worked for the Lubin Company in Philadelphia in 1911, with the American branch of Pathé Frères in Jersey City in 1911–1912, and for Crystal Films in the Bronx in 1912 1914. For Crystal she appeared in a series of slapstick comedies.

The task of turning out a half- or full-reel comedy a week left her exhausted after a year and a half. Following an extended vacation in Europe she joined the Eclectic Film Company, a subsidiary of Pathé, in 1914 and starred in a 20-episode serial, *The Perils of Pauline*. The fifth example of an exciting and popular new film genre, *The Perils of Pauline* was one of the first to exploit the device of a cliff-hanging ending to each episode. It was a great success, in part through the sponsorship and promotion of the Hearst newspapers, and it made Pearl White a star. Over the next six years she made several more serials: *The Exploits of Elaine*, 1914–1915, *The New Exploits of Elaine*, 1915, *The Romance of Elaine*, 1915, *The Iron Claw*, 1916, *Pearl of the Army*, 1916–1917, *The Fatal Ring*, 1917, *The House of Hate*, 1918, *The Lightning Raider*, 1919, and *The Black Secret*, 1919–1920. The serials featured the heroine performing a variety of acrobatic stunts by way of escaping sundry perils; she actually did perform many of them, for she was an agile and energetic woman, but studio publicity claimed she performed them all herself, while in fact stuntmen were used frequently for the dangerous ones.

During 1919–1921 she made ten unmemorable dramatic feature films for the Fox Film Corporation. She made one more serial for Pathé, *Plunder*, 1923, and then moved to France. She had earned an estimated $2 million in her short career, and she invested it wisely. In Paris she made one film, *Terror* (*Perils of Paris* in the United States), before retiring to a life of luxury. She died in Paris on August 4, 1938. It was thought that a spinal injury suffered in a fall during the filming of *The Perils of Pauline* may have hastened her early death.

Whitman, Sarah Helen Power 1803–1878 poet and essayist

Born in Providence, Rhode Island, on January 19, 1803, Sarah Power attended schools there and a Quaker school in Jamaica, Long Island, New York. From an early age she was an avid reader of novels and of poetry, especially that of Byron. In July 1828, after a four-year engagement, she married John W. Whitman, a Boston writer and editor. Through his influence her first published poems appeared in the *Boston Spectator and Ladies' Album* under the signature "Helen." In Boston she became acquainted with literary society and was exposed to the intellectual ferment of Unitarianism and Transcendentalism. She was particularly interested in metaphysical notions and mesmerism.

Her poems appeared in Sarah J. Hale's *Ladies' Magazine* and other periodicals, and under the name "Egeria" she began publishing critical essays and articles on various topics of interest. After her husband's death in 1833 she returned to Providence. She continued to write and publish both prose and poetry and became Rhode Island's leading litterateur. In 1848 she published in the *Home Journal* of New York a playful (and anonymous) valentine poem to Edgar Allan Poe. After he learned the source of the compliment, he returned it in the second of his poems entitled "To Helen." A feverishly romantic literary courtship ensued, and in November they became engaged. Partly owing to Poe's instability and partly through the intervention of Whitman's mother the engagement was broken a month later. She published a series of articles on spiritualism in the *New York Tribune* in 1851 and a volume of verse titled *Hours of Life, and Other Poems* in 1853.

Spiritualism engaged Whitman's interest to the point that she held séances of her own and was convinced of her ability to communicate with spirits. In 1860 she published *Edgar Poe and His Critics*, a scholarly reply to the scurrilous attacks of Rufus W. Griswold and other critics. She also interested herself in the cause of woman suffrage, serving as vice-president of the Rhode Island suffrage association from its organization in 1868. She died in Providence on June 27, 1878. A volume of her collected verse was published as *Poems* in 1879.

Whitney, Adeline Dutton Train 1824–1906 writer

Born in Boston on September 15, 1824, Adeline Train was the daughter of a prosperous merchant. She attended schools in Boston and Northampton, Massachusetts. In November 1843 she married Seth D. Whitney, a merchant more than 20 years her senior, with whom she settled in Milton, Massachusetts. She began writing for publication in the late 1850s. Her poems and articles became regular features in local newspapers, and in 1859 she published her first book, *Mother Goose for Grown Folks*, a collection of characteristically humorous and didactic verses. *Boys at Chequasset*, 1862, and *Faith Gartney's Girlhood*, 1863, both juvenile novels, won her the audience that was to remain faithfully hers for four decades.

Over that span of time Whitney's message remained unchanged: the utter goodness of hearth and home. Her books included *The Gayworthys*, 1865; a series of four novels comprising the enormously popular Real Folks Series — *A Summer in Leslie Goldthwaite's Life*, 1866, *We Girls*, 1870, *Real Folks*, 1871, and *The Other Girls*, 1873; *Patience Strong's Outings*, 1868; *Hitherto*, 1869; *Pansies*, poems, 1872; *Sights and Insights*, 1876; *Odd or Even*, 1880; *Bonnyborough*, 1885; *Holy Tides*, verse, 1886; *Daffodils*, verse, 1887; *A Golden Gossip*, 1890; *White Memories*, verse, 1893; *Friendly Letters to Girl Friends*, 1897; *Square Pegs*, 1899; and *Biddy's Episodes*, 1904. True to her message, Whitney took no part in public affairs and disapproved of the woman suffrage movement. She died in Milton, Massachusetts, on March 21, 1906.

Whitney, Anne 1821–1915 sculptor

Born on September 2, 1821, in Watertown, Massachusetts, Anne Whitney grew up there and from about 1833 in East Cambridge, Massachusetts. She was educated by tutors and for a year at a private girls' school in Bucksport, Maine. In 1850 she returned with her family to Watertown (a section that later became Belmont). During the 1850s she began to write poetry and to experiment in sculpture. She had advanced to making portrait busts by 1855, and in 1859, the year she published a volume titled *Poems*, she began to study sculpture in earnest.

Whitney entered a bust of a child in the 1860 exhibit of the National Academy of Design and in 1864 and 1865 exhibited a life-size "Lady Godiva" and a colossal "Africa" in Boston and New York. She studied privately with William Rimmer in Boston for a time and in 1867 journeyed to Rome, where she remained for four years. During that time she also visited Munich. Her "Roma," inspired by the poverty of Roman peasants, was shown in London, Boston, and Philadelphia after its completion in 1869, and after her return to the United States she exhibited her statue of Toussaint L'Ouverture.

While in Rome she became acquainted with fellow sculptors Harriet Hosmer and Edmonia Lewis. A commission to execute a statue of Samuel Adams (one of Massachusetts's contributions to Statuary Hall in the U.S. Capitol) prompted her to return to

Europe in 1875 to supervise the cutting of the stone and to study in Paris. In 1876 she established a home and studio in Boston. Over the next three decades she executed portrait busts of Alice Freeman Palmer, Lucy Stone, Harriet Beecher Stowe, Mary A. Livermore, Frances Willard, Harriet Martineau, George H. Palmer, William Lloyd Garrison, and others.

She also carved a statue of Leif Ericson that was placed on the Commonwealth Avenue mall in 1887 and a statue of the seated Charles Sumner that was placed in Harvard Square in 1902. At the World's Columbian Exposition in Chicago in 1893 she exhibited a larger version of "Roma." Anne Whitney died in Boston on January 23, 1915.

Whitney, Charlotte Anita 1867–1955 suffragist and political radical

Born in San Francisco on July 7, 1867, Charlotte Whitney was the daughter of a lawyer and a niece of Supreme Court justice Stephen J. Field and of Cyrus W. Field. She was educated in public and private school, and in 1889 graduated from Wellesley College. A visit to the College Settlement House in New York City in 1893 turned her to social work, and she soon returned to California to work in the slums of Oakland.

From 1901 to 1906 Whitney was secretary of the Council of Associated Charities of Alameda County. In 1911 she became president of the California College Equal Suffrage League and second vice-president of the National American Woman Suffrage Association. She led a campaign for a woman suffrage amendment to the California constitution and subsequently joined in similar campaigns in Oregon, Nevada, and Connecticut. At the same time she became involved in the free-speech fights of the International Workers of the World.

Whitney joined the Socialist party in 1914 and in 1919 helped lead the defection of the party's radical wing and the founding of the Communist Labor party (later the Communist party). In November 1919, during the height of the postwar "Red Scare," she was arrested after a public address at the Oakland Center of the California Civic League (of which she was president from its founding that year) on five counts of criminal syndicalism. Convicted on one count, she was sentenced to 1 to 14 years. Because of ill health she served only 11 days in jail, but her appeals of the conviction dragged on for nearly 8 years before she was pardoned by the governor in June 1927.

In 1924 she ran for state treasurer on the Communist ballot and polled more than 100,000 votes. In 1935 she was convicted of distributing radical literature, lecturing without a permit, and falsely attesting Communist election petitions. She was named national chairman of the Communist party in 1936 and ran for a seat in the U.S. Senate from California in 1950. She died on February 4, 1955, in San Francisco.

Whitney, Gertrude Vanderbilt 1875–1942 sculptor and art patron

Born in New York City on January 9, 1875, Gertrude Vanderbilt was a great-granddaughter of Commodore Cornelius Vanderbilt, founder of one of America's great fortunes. She was educated by tutors and at the Brearley School in New York City. In August 1896 she married Harry Payne Whitney, a financier and internationally known sportsman. She had from childhood displayed an interest in and talent for art, and soon after her marriage she began studying sculpture under Hendrik Christian Andersen and James E. Farceur and then at the Art Students' League. Later she studied under Andrew O'Connor in Paris, where she also received some help from Auguste Rodin.

At the Pan-American Exposition in Buffalo, New York, in 1901 she exhibited a life-size ideal figure, "Aspiration." She exhibited work at the Louisiana Purchase Exposition in St. Louis in 1904, and she won awards in the New York Architectural League's competition in 1908 for her "Pan" and at the National Academy of Design in 1910 for "Paganism Immortal." Following the latter success she abandoned the use of pseudonyms and worked under her own name, her social position notwithstanding.

From 1907 Whitney maintained a studio in Greenwich Village, where she came to know such progressive young artists as Robert Henri, William Glackens, John Sloan, George Luks, and Arthur B. Davies. She bought many of their works and, to relieve their difficulty in finding exhibition space, opened the Whitney Studio in a building adjoining her work studio in 1914 and prevailed upon her sister-in-law's secretary, Juliana R. Force, to help manage it.

From that beginning evolved the Whitney Studio Club in 1918 and the Whitney Studio Galleries in 1928. While her encouragement and tangible assistance helped a great many young artists — including, in addition to those mentioned, Joseph Stella, Charles Sheeler, Reginald Marsh, Edward Hopper, John Steuart Curry, and Stuart Davis — her own collection of contemporary American art grew apace. In 1929 she offered the entire collection of nearly 500 pieces to the Metropolitan Museum of Art along with an endowment to build a new wing to house it; the Metropolitan rejected the offer out of hand. She then established the Whitney Museum of American Art, which opened in November 1931 under Force's direction. Her patronage of the arts included also the support of the Society of Independent Artists for 15 years after its founding in 1917 and of the journal *The Arts* in the 1920s.

In the meantime her own work in sculpture enjoyed continuing success. Major works of hers included the terra cotta "Aztec Fountain" for the Pan American Union Building in Washington, D.C., in 1912; the "El Dorado Fountain," which won a medal at the Panama-Pacific International Exposition in San Francisco in 1915; two panels for the Victory Arch in New York City (conveying the deep impression made on her by her relief work in World War I, when she established and worked in a field hospital in Juilly, France), 1920; the Washington Heights War Memorial, New York City, 1921, which won a medal from the New York Society of Architects; a statue of "Buffalo Bill" Cody for Cody, Wyoming, 1922; a monument for St. Nazaire, France, commemorating the first landing of American troops, 1926; the Titanic Memorial for Potomac Park, Washington, D.C., 1931; the Columbus Monument for the harbor of Palos, Spain, 1933; the Peter Stuyvesant Monument in Stuyvesant Square, New York, 1939; and "The Spirit of Flight" for the New York World's Fair of 1939–1940.

She was elected an associate of the National Academy of Design in 1940. During 1934–1935 she fought a widely publicized court battle for custody of her niece, Gloria Vanderbilt. She died in New York City on April 18, 1942.

Whitney, Mary Watson 1847–1921 astronomer

Born in Waltham, Massachusetts, on September 11, 1847, Mary Whitney graduated from public high school in 1863 and entered Vassar College with advanced standing in 1865. She immediately came under the influence of Maria Mitchell. After graduating in 1868 she returned to Waltham for a time to care for her widowed mother. She then taught school in Auburndale, Massachusetts. In August 1869 she traveled to Burlington, Iowa, to observe a solar eclipse with her own 3-inch Alvan Clark telescope. During 1869–1870 she attended, on invitation, Benjamin Peirce's class in quaternions at Harvard and his private class in celestial mechanics. In 1872 Vassar granted her a master's degree. During 1873–1876 she studied mathematics and celestial mechanics at the University of Zürich, where her younger sister was enrolled in the school of medicine.

Whitney taught at Waltham High School from 1876 to 1881 and then returned to Vassar as Maria Mitchell's assistant. In 1888 she succeeded Mitchell as professor of astronomy and director of the college observatory. She proved a popular and effective teacher. Her determination to demonstrate the capacity of women to work in the sciences on equal terms with men led to her development of an ambitious program of research at Vassar, concentrating in particular on double stars, variable stars, asteroids, comets, and the precise measurement of photographic plates. With such training her students were able to find professional positions in observatories across the country. In 1899 she was a founding member of the American Astronomical Society. She retired from Vassar for health reasons in 1910 and died in Waltham, Massachusetts, on January 20, 1921.

Whitney, Phyllis Ayame 1903– writer of children's books

Born on September 9, 1903, in Yokohama, Japan, where her American father was in business, Phyllis Whitney grew up there, in the Philippines, and in Hankow, China. Later, from the age of fifteen, she lived with her widowed mother in California and in San Antonio, Texas. She graduated from high school in Chicago in 1924. She worked in a bookstore while getting her start as a writer. The *Chicago Daily News* bought a story of hers in 1928, and over the next several years she contributed to pulp magazines, juvenile magazines, and church publications.

Her first book, *A Place for Ann*, appeared in 1941 and was followed by *A Star for Ginny*, 1942, *A Window for Julie*, 1943, *Red is for Murder*, 1943, *A Silver Inkwell*, 1945, *Willow Hill*, 1947, and *Writing Juvenile Fiction*, 1947. From 1942 to 1946 she edited the children's book page of the *Chicago Sun*, and in 1947–1948 she worked in a similar capacity for the *Philadelphia Inquirer*. She taught a course in writing juvenile fiction at Northwestern University in 1945 and was an instructor in that field at New York University from 1947 to 1958.

A prolific and perennially popular writer whose books were frequently reprinted, Phyllis Whitney subsequently produced *Ever After*, 1948, *The Mystery of the Gulls*, 1949, *Linda's Homecoming*, 1950, *The Island of Dark Woods*, 1951, *Love Me, Love Me Not*, 1952, *Step to the Music*, 1953, *A Long Time Coming*, 1954, *The Mystery of the Black Diamonds*, 1954, *The Quicksilver Pool*, 1955, *Mystery on the Isle of Skye*, 1955, *The Fire and the Gold*, 1956, *The Highest Dream* 1956, *The Trembling Hills*, 1956, *Skye Cameron*, 1957, *The Mystery of the Green Cat*, 1957, *The Secret of the Samurai Sword*, 1958, *The Moonflower*, 1958, *Creole Holiday*, 1959, *Thunder Heights*, 1960, *The Mystery of the Haunted Pool*, which won an Edgar Award from the Mystery Writers of America, 1960, *Blue Fire*, 1961, *The Secret of the Tiger's Eye*, 1961, *Window on the Square*, 1962, *The Mystery of the Golden Horn*, 1962, *Seven Tears for Apollo*, 1963, *The Mystery of the Hidden Hand*, which won an Edgar, 1963, *Black Amber*, 1964, *The Secret of the Emerald Star*, 1964, *Sea Jade*, 1965, *The Mystery of the Angry Idol*, 1965, *Columbella*, 1966, *The Secret of the Spotted Shell*, 1967, *The Mystery of the Strange Traveler*, 1967, *Silverhill*, 1967, *Hunter's Green*, 1968, *The Secret of Goblin Glen*, 1968, *The Mystery of the Crimson Ghost*, 1969, *The Secret of the Missing Footprint*, 1969, *The Winter People*, 1969, *Lost Island*, 1970, *The Vanishing Scarecrow*, 1971, *Listen for the Whisperer*, 1972, *Nobody Likes Trina*, 1972, *Snowfire*, 1973, *The Mystery of the Scowling Boy*, 1973, *The Turquoise Mask*, 1974, *Spindrift*, 1975, *The Secret of Haunted Mesa*, 1975,! *The Golden Unicorn*, 1976, *The Secret of the Stone Face*, 1977, *The Stone Bull*, 1977, *The Glass Flame*, 1978, and *Domino*, 1979. She also wrote a second guide to would-be authors, *Writing Juvenile Stories and Novels*, 1976.

Later books include *Poinciana*, 1980, *Vermilion*, 1981, *Emerald*, 1983, *Rainsong*, 1984, *Dream of Orchids*, 1985, *Flaming Tree*, 1986, *Silversword*, 1987, *Feather on the Moon*, 1988, *Rainbow in the Mist*, 1989, *The Singing Stones*, 1990, *Woman without a Past*, 1991 and *The Ebony Swan*, 1992. She published another writing guide, *Guide to Writing Fiction*, in 1982. Whitney was president of the Mystery Writers of America in 1975 and in 1988 she received their Grandmaster Award for Lifetime Achievement. In 1990 she received the Agatha Award from Malice Domestic, and the Rita Award from the Romance Writers of America.

Whittelsey, Abigail Goodrich 1788–1858 editor

Born in Ridgefield, Connecticut, on November 29, 1788, Abigail Goodrich was the daughter of a clergyman and an elder sister of Samuel Griswold Goodrich, later famous as "Peter Parley," author of scores of books for children. She received some formal education in local schools. In November 1808 she married the Reverend Samuel Whittelsey, with whom she lived in New Preston, Connecticut, until 1818; in Hartford from 1818 to 1824; in Canandaigua, New York where she served as matron of the Ontario Female Seminary, of which her husband was head, from 1824 to 1828; and in Utica, New York, where they established their own girls' seminary, from 1828. She became active in the Maternal Association of Utica and was chosen to edit its new periodical, the *Mother's Magazine*, which first appeared in January 1833. Aimed at educating mothers to their responsibilities and potentialities, the magazine quickly proved a success. It was transferred to New York City in 1834 when the Whittelseys moved there, and she continued to edit it, with one absence in 1847–1848, until 1849.

After her husband's death in 1842 she had the assistance of a brother-in-law, the Reverend Darius Mead, editor of the *Christian Parlor Magazine*. The circulation of the *Mother's Magazine* reached 10,000 in 1837. Soon after a new proprietor merged it with the rival *Mother's Journal and Family Visitant* in 1848, she resigned. In 1850 she launched *Mrs. Whittelsey's Magazine for Mothers*, which she kept up, with the aid of her son Henry, for two years and in which she continued to dispense practical advice and instruction highly colored by religious sentiment. Whittelsey died in Colchester, Connecticut, on July 16, 1858.

Whitworth, Kathryne Ann 1939– golfer

Born on September 27, 1939, in Monohans, Texas, Kathy Whitworth grew up in Jal, New Mexico. She first tried the game of golf at fifteen and took to it immediately. After graduating from high school in 1957 she attended Odessa Junior College in Texas for a semester. By 1959 her golf game had progressed to the point where she could join the professional tour. It was two years before her winnings exceeded her expenses, and in 1962 she won her first two professional tournaments and came in second in money winnings to Mickey Wright. She won eight tournaments in 1963.

She was the leading money winner on the Ladies' Professional Golf Association tour in 1965, 1966, 1967, 1968, 1970, 1971, 1972, and 1973; the LPGA player of the year seven times, in 1966, 1967, 1968, 1969, 1971, 1972, and 1973; and the Associated Press woman athlete of the year in 1965 and 1966. In 1969 she passed Mickey Wright to become the leading all-time money winner on the tour; in 1974 her career earnings totaled over $500,000 and by 1981 she was the first woman golfer to pass the million-dollar mark. She won the Vare Trophy, for best average in the LPGA tour, in 1965, 1966, 1967, 1969, 1970, 1971, and 1972. She was the winner of the LPGA championship tournament in 1967 and 1971. She won every major tournament on the tour at one time or another except for the U.S. Open, which eluded her year after year. In 1970 she was elected president of the LPGA, and she worked to considerable effect to increase the commercial appeal of the tour and consequently the size of purses offered. Kathy Whitworth was known for her strong drives but especially for her precise, unflappable short game. She was inducted into the LPGA Hall of Fame in 1975, the World Golf Hall of Fame and the Texas Sports Hall of Fame in 1982, and the International Women's Sports Hall of Fame in 1984.

Wiggin, Kate Douglas Smith 1856–1923 educator and writer

Born in Philadelphia on September 28, 1856, Kate Smith grew up there and in Portland and then Hollis, Maine. She attended a district school and for short periods the Gorham (Maine) Female Seminary, the Morison Academy in Baltimore, and the Abbott Academy in Andover, Massachusetts. In 1873 she moved with her family to Santa Barbara,

California. The death of her stepfather in 1877 left the family in perilous financial condition. At the suggestion of Caroline M. Severance, who also provided her room and board, Kate Smith entered the Pacific Model Training School for Kindergartners headed by Emma Marwedel.

For a time after completing the course she directed a private kindergarten in Santa Barbara. Through Emma Marwedel she was chosen in 1878 to become head of the first free kindergarten in the Far West, organized that summer in San Francisco. In 1880, after further training under Susan Blow and Elizabeth Peabody, she and her sister, Nora A. Smith, established the California Kindergarten Training School. She remained head of the Silver Street Kindergarten until her marriage in December 1881 to Samuel B. Wiggin, a lawyer. She continued to lecture at the training school, and even after her move to New York City in 1884 she returned each spring for the commencement exercises.

In 1883 Kate Wiggin published privately *The Story of Patsy* as a means to raise money for the school. In 1887 she published *The Birds' Christmas Carol*, also privately. Commercial editions of both books issued in 1889 were great successes. After her husband's death in 1889 she retired for a time to Hollis, Maine, and there wrote *Timothy's Quest*, 1890, a children's book. Thereafter she traveled frequently to Europe, especially after her marriage in March 1895 to George C. Riggs, a New York businessman. Subsequent books included *Polly Oliver's Problem*, for children, 1893, *A Cathedral Courtship*, 1893, *Marm Lisa*, 1896, *Penelope's Progress*, 1898, *Penelope's English Experiences*, 1900, *Penelope's Irish Experiences*, 1901, *The Diary of a Goose Girl*, 1902, *Rebecca of Sunnybrook Farm*, probably her most popular work (dramatized by Wiggin in 1910 and later made into a motion picture), 1903, *The Affair at the Inn*, 1904, *Rose o' the River*, 1905, *New Chronicles of Rebecca*, 1907, *The Old Peabody Pew*, 1907, *Susanna and Sue*, 1909, *Mother Carey's Chickens*, 1911, *Penelope's Postscripts*, 1915, *Ladies in Waiting*, 1918, *The Romance of a Christmas Card*, 1919, and *Homespun Tales*, 1920.

With her sister she also wrote and edited a number of books, including *The Story Hour*, 1890, and *The Republic of Childhood*, on Froebelian kindergarten practice, three volumes, 1895–1896. She died in Harrow, England, on August 24, 1923; later in that year her autobiography, *My Garden of Memory*, was published.

Wightman, Hazel Hotchkiss 1886–1974 tennis player

Born on December 20, 1886, in Healdsburg, California, Hazel Hotchkiss early developed a passionate love of tennis. She became one of the dominant players in the country and won the national amateur women's singles championship in 1909, 1910, 1911, and 1919. In 1923, by which time she had married George W. Wightman, she gave the Wightman Cup as the prize for an annual tournament between teams from the United States and Great Britain. She herself played for the United States in the first tournament that year and won her doubles match (the U.S. team won the tournament 7–0). In 1924 she teamed with Helen Wills to win the doubles title at Wimbledon. She was six times the U.S. doubles co-champion.

She enjoyed a remarkably long career as a tennis player: in 1950 she won the U.S. women's veterans doubles championship, which proved on research (she had not kept track) to be her 42nd national title; she won three more before she finished, the last at age sixty-eight. Along the way she also won a national women's singles championship in squash and a Massachusetts state title in table tennis, and she once made the national finals on a mixed doubles badminton team. Known as the "queen mother of American tennis," Wightman died in Chestnut Hill, Massachusetts, on December 5, 1974.

Wilcox, Ella Wheeler 1850–1919 poet and journalist

Born on November 5, 1850, in Johnstown Center, Rock County, Wisconsin, Ella Wheeler grew up there and in Windsor, Wisconsin. She attended local public schools and from an early age was an avid reader of popular literature, especially the novels of E. D. E. N. Southworth, Mary Jane Holmes, and Ouida. Her first published work, some sketches submitted to the *New York Mercury*, appeared when she was fourteen. Soon her poems were appearing in the *Waverly Magazine* and *Leslie's Weekly*. Except for a year, 1867–1868, at the University of Wisconsin, she devoted herself thereafter to writing and soon was making a substantial contribution to the family's support.

Wheeler's first book, a collection of temperance verses, appeared in 1872 as *Drops of Water*. *Shells*, religious and moral poems, followed in 1873 and *Maurine*, a highly sentimental verse narrative, in 1876. The rejection of her next book, a collection of love poems, by a Chicago publisher on grounds that it was immoral helped insure the success of the book when it was issued by another publisher in 1883 as *Poems of Passion*, a titillating title that was as racy as any of the contents. The sale of 60,000 copies in two years firmly established her reputation.

In May 1884 she married Robert M. Wilcox, a businessman with whom she lived in Meriden, Connecticut, until 1887 and in New York City until 1906. While making herself the center of a literary coterie she continued to pour out verses laced with platitudes and easy profundities; they were collected in such volumes as *Men, Women, and Emotions*, 1893, *Custer and Other Poems*, 1895, *Poems of Pleasure*, 1888, *Poems of Power*, 1901, *Poems of Sentiment*, 1906, *Poems of Progress*, 1909, *Pastels*, 1909, *Sailing Sunny Seas*, 1910, *Gems*, 1912, *Cameos*, 1914, and *World Voices*, 1918.

She also wrote much fiction, including *Mal Moulée*, 1885, *Perdita and Other Stories*, 1886, *An Ambitious Man*, 1887, *A Double Life*, 1890, *Was It Suicide?*, 1891, *Sweet Danger*, 1892, *An Erring Woman's Love*, 1892, and *A Woman of the World*, 1904. She published two works of autobiography, *The Story of a Literary Career*, 1905, and *The Worlds and I*, 1918. She contributed columns of prose and poetry to various newspapers and articles and essays to *Cosmopolitan* and other magazines.

After her husband's death in 1916 Wilcox made her long-standing interest in spiritualism the subject of a series of columns as she sought — successfully, she claimed — to contact his spirit. (Her interest in such topics had earlier found outlet in such books as *The Heart of the New Thought*, 1902, and *New Thought Common Sense*, 1908.) At his direction (she said) she undertook a lecture and poetry-reading tour of Allied army camps in France in 1918. She fell ill early in 1919, spent some time in a nursing home in Bath, England, and died at her home in Short Beach, Connecticut, on October 30, 1919.

Wilder, Laura Ingalls 1867–1957 writer

Born on February 7, 1867, in Pepin, Wisconsin, Laura Ingalls grew up in a family that moved frequently from one part of the frontier to another. Her restless father took the family by covered wagon to Minnesota, Iowa, Missouri, Kansas, Indian Territory, back to Minnesota, and to Dakota Territory. Theirs was a physically hard life but one filled with love and courage. At fifteen she began teaching in rural schools. In August 1885 she married Almanzo J. Wilder, with whom she lived in De Smet, South Dakota, in Florida, and from 1894 on a farm near Mansfield, Missouri. Some years later she began writing for various periodicals. She contributed to *McCall's Magazine* and *Country Gentleman*, served as poultry editor for the *St. Louis Star*, and for 12 years was home editor of the *Missouri Ruralist*.

Prompted by her daughter, Rose Wilder Lane, a writer, Wilder began writing down her childhood experiences in a pioneer family on a long-lost frontier. In 1932 she published *Little House in the Big Woods*, which was set in Wisconsin. *Farmer Boy*, a book about her husband's childhood, followed in 1933, and she then published *Little House on the Prairie*, a reminiscence of her family's stay in Indian Territory, 1935. The "Little House" books were warmly received by the reading public and critics alike; their warm, truthful portrayal of a life made picturesque by its very simplicity continued to charm generations of readers.

Wilder continued the story of her life in *On the Banks of Plum Creek* (Minnesota), 1937, *By the Shores of Silver Lake* (Dakota Territory), 1939, *The Long Winter* (Dakota Territory), 1940, *Little Town on the Prairie* (De Smet, South Dakota), 1941, and *These Happy Golden Years*, (De Smet), 1943. Wilder died in Mansfield, Missouri, on February 10, 1957. Her books remained in print, and their popularity was given a great boost by the success of a television series based on them that began in 1974.

Wilkinson, Jemima 1732–1819 religious leader

Born in Cumberland, Rhode Island, on November 29, 1752, Jemima Wilkinson grew up in a Quaker family and early displayed a strong interest in religion. Little detail is known of her childhood. Her attendance at meetings of a New Light Baptist congregation in the aftermath of George Whitefield's final revival tour of New England led to her dismissal from her Friends meeting in August 1776. Two months later she fell ill of a fever from which she emerged with the conviction, conveyed to her in a vision, that she had died and had been sent back to preach to a "lost and guilty, gossiping, dying World." She took the name Publick Universal Friend and thereafter answered to no other.

She began to travel and preach throughout southern New England, and by the power of her personality and of her commanding figure even more than through her rather conventional message of repentance, she soon attracted a following. Her followers included a number of influential persons, one of whom, Judge William Potter of South Kingstown, Rhode Island, freed his slaves, abandoned his political career, and built a large addition to his mansion for her use. Meetinghouses were built by her followers, known collectively as Universal Friends, in East Greenwich, Rhode Island, and New Milford, Connecticut. By 1782 she had extended her preaching as far as Philadelphia, where in 1784 she published *The Universal Friend's Advice to Those of the Same Religious Society*, largely a compilation of Biblical quotations for use in meetings.

While Wilkinson was discreetly vague about the exact nature of her mission and her relation to divinity, many of her followers openly proclaimed her a messiah, a practice that roused considerable animosity among orthodox churches against the Universal Friends and their leader. In 1788 some members of the sect, having scouted out reports of the Genesee country of western New York, began a settlement near Seneca Lake. In 1790 the Friend herself arrived at the "Friend's Settlement," which then had a population of 260. In 1794 she moved a few miles west to the vicinity of Crooked (now Keuka) Lake, where, with a small band of her most devoted followers, she established Jerusalem township. In later years the Friend's Settlement was disturbed by conflicts over ownership of the land, while outside the settlement numerous tales of dictatorial rule, harsh punishments, sexual misconduct, and other strange practices circulated widely among hostile observers.

The Universal Friend died at her home, near present-day Penn Yan, New York, on July 1, 1819. The sect she had inspired disintegrated within a few years.

Willard, Emma Hart 1787–1870 educator

Born in Berlin, Connecticut, on February 23, 1787, Emma Hart was the next-to-last of 17 children; her younger sister was Almira Hart (Lincoln Phelps). Encouraged by her father, she early began to acquire an education beyond that ordinarily thought proper for a girl, especially a farm girl. In 1802 she enrolled in the Berlin Academy, her first school, where her progress was so rapid that by 1804 she was teaching in it and in 1806 she had charge of it for a term. She also attended classes in Hartford during that time. In 1807 she taught briefly in an academy in Westfield, Massachusetts, and then became preceptress of a girls' academy in Middlebury, Vermont, where in August 1809 she married Dr. John

Willard, a physician 28 years her senior. From her husband's nephew and namesake, a student at Middlebury College who lived in their home, she first inferred the vast difference in the educational opportunities open to men and to women. She studied his textbooks and mastered such nonornamental subjects as geometry and philosophy.

In 1814 Emma Willard opened the Middlebury Female Seminary in her home and over the next few years demonstrated that women could teach and girls learn classical and scientific subjects commonly thought suited only to men. Her success prompted her to write *An Address to the Public; Particularly to the Members of the Legislature of New-York, Proposing a Plan for Improving Female Education* in 1819. The pamphlet was warmly received by such readers as Thomas Jefferson and John Adams. The legislature addressed failed to respond — several members ridiculed her outline of a course of academic studies for girls as contrary to God's will — but Governor DeWitt Clinton encouraged her to open a school in New York state.

In 1819 she moved to Waterford, New York, and opened a school. In 1821 she moved on to Troy, where the town council had raised $4000 in tax money to build a girls' school. The Troy Female Seminary opened in September 1821 and began its long history as one of the most influential schools in America. It was a pioneer in the teaching of science, mathematics, and social studies to girls, antedating Mary Lyon's Mount Holyoke Seminary by 16 years and the first public high schools for girls (in Boston and New York City) by 5. The school attracted students from families of wealth and position and by 1831 had an enrollment of over 300, more than 100 of whom were boarding students. Willard published several textbooks for use in her and other schools, including *History of the United States, or Republic of America*, 1828, and *A System of Universal History in Perspective*, 1835. She also published a volume of verse, *The Fulfilment of a Promise*, 1831; of her poems only "Rocked in the Cradle of the Deep" is remembered.

She remained head of the Troy Female Seminary until 1838, by which time hundreds of graduates, many of them teachers and all of them shaped by her philosophy, had fanned out across the country. In that same year, John Willard having died in 1825, she married Christopher Yates, who soon proved a poor husband; she left him within the year and was granted a divorce in 1843. From 1838 to 1844 she lived in Connecticut, where she worked closely with Henry Barnard to improve the public school system. In 1844 she returned to Troy, New York. Her later years were filled with travel, lecturing, and writing; among her books were *A Treatise on the Motive Powers which Produce the Circulation of the Blood*, 1846, *Guide to the Temple of Time; and Universal History for Schools*, 1849, *Last Leaves of American History*, 1849, *Astronography; or Astronomical Geography*, 1854, and *Morals for the Young*, 1857. She died in Troy, New York, on April 15, 1870. The Troy Female Seminary was renamed the Emma Willard School in 1895.

Willard, Frances Elizabeth Caroline 1839–1898 educator and reformer

Born on September 28, 1839, in Churchville, New York, Frances Willard grew up from the age of two in Oberlin, Ohio, and from six in Janesville, Wisconsin Territory. She grew up a sturdy, independent, and strong-willed child of the frontier. She was educated at home, in a district school, and briefly in a private girls' school in Janesville. In 1857 she enrolled in the Milwaukee Female College, where she remained for one term. She then transferred to the North Western Female College in Evanston, Illinois, from which she graduated in 1859. She taught school for several years: in Harlem and then Kankakee, Illinois, in 1860–1861; at the North Western Female College in 1862; at the Pittsburgh Female College in Pennsylvania in 1863–1864; at a private girls' school in Evanston in 1865–1866; and at the Genesee Wesleyan Seminary in Lima, New York, in 1866–1867.

During that time she also served as secretary of the American Methodist Ladies Centenary Association in 1865–1866 and published her first book, *Nineteen Beautiful*

Years, a biography of her deceased sister, in 1864. During 1868–1870 she made an extended world tour with a friend, and on her return she settled in Evanston. In 1871 she was named president of the new Evanston College for Ladies, a Methodist institution closely associated with Northwestern University. Financial difficulties led to the school's being absorbed by Northwestern in 1873, whereupon Frances Willard became dean of women and professor of English and art. She remained there until her constant conflicts of authority with the university's president, Charles H. Fowler (to whom she had been engaged in 1861), led her to resign in June 1874.

Just at that time the so-called "Woman's Crusade," a wave of anti-liquor agitation among women in western New York, Ohio, and other localities, was peaking, and a group of Chicago women invited Willard to become president of their temperance organization. In October 1874 she was elected secretary of the newly organized state temperance society, and in November, at the Cleveland organizing convention, she was chosen corresponding secretary of the national Woman's Christian Temperance Union. The latter post placed her in position to become acquainted with local and state WCTU leaders and led also to considerable demand for her services as a lecturer. In 1876 she also became head of the national WCTU's publications committee. In that year the national adopted the motto she had composed for the Chicago branch: "For God and Home and Native Land."

She resigned as president of the Chicago WCTU in 1877 and worked briefly as director of women's meetings for the evangelist Dwight L. Moody. Later in the year she resigned her post with the national WCTU, in large past because of the resistance of President Annie Wittenmyer to her wish to link the goals of liquor prohibition and woman suffrage. She lectured widely on suffrage for a year before being elected president of the Illinois WCTU in 1878. Assisted by her secretary and companion Anna A. Gordon, she secured more than 100,000 signatures on a "Home Protection" petition requesting the Illinois legislature to grant women the vote in matters pertaining to the liquor trade. Presented in March 1879, the petition ultimately died in committee, but Willard's lobbying efforts inspired similar campaigns in other states.

At the national WCTU's 1879 convention in Indianapolis Willard was elected president to succeed Wittenmyer; she held the post for the rest of her life. Under her leadership the WCTU quickly evolved into a well organized group able to mount campaigns of public education and political pressure on many fronts. Her linkage of suffrage and temperance was endorsed by the 1880 national convention. Among the many separate departments she established within the WCTU (eventually numbering 39) to pursue specific goals, the Franchise Department (from 1888 to 1892 under Dr. Anna Howard Shaw) was one of the most active. At Willard's invitation, Susan B. Anthony attended the 1881 convention, sparking a walkout by some conservative delegates.

Through other departments the WCTU also worked for labor legislation, programs of social health and hygiene, prison reform, international peace, and other liberal ends. Willard traveled constantly and spoke frequently — in 1883 she spoke in every state of the Union — and was a regular lecturer at the summer Lake Chautauqua meetings in New York. Lecture fees were her principal support until the WCTU voted her a salary in 1886.

Work on an international scale began in 1883 with the mission of Mary C. Leavitt and others and the circulation of the "Polyglot Petition" against the international drug trade. A convention of delegates from 21 nations met in Boston in 1891 to form the World's WCTU, of which Willard was elected president. In 1888 she joined May Wright Sewall at the International Council of Women meeting in Washington, D.C., and laid the groundwork for a permanent National Council of Women, of which she was first president in 1888–1890, and an International Council of Women. She also served as a vice-president of the Universal Peace Union and in 1889 helped organize the General Federation of Women's Clubs.

Willard's attempt to induce the WCTU to take an active role in politics ultimately failed. A "Home Protection party" organized in 1881 effected a short-lived merger with the National Prohibition party in 1882–1884, but the rank and file of prohibitionists objected as much to a woman suffrage plank as did WCTU members to party politics. Her plan to strike a coalition with the new People's party in 1892 similarly failed. Over the years she wrote frequently for periodicals and for WCTU publications, and her books included *Woman and Temperance*, 1883, *How to Win*, 1886, *Woman in the Pulpit*, 1889, *Glimpses of Fifty Years*, her autobiography, 1889, *A Great Mother*, 1894, and *A Wheel Within a Wheel; How I Learned to Ride the Bicycle*, 1895.

With Mary A. Livermore she edited *A Woman of the Century*, 1893. In her later years she spent much time in England, where she came under the influence of the Fabian socialists, a fact that caused more than usual unrest among conservatives in the WCTU. After a year of failing health she died in New York City on February 17, 1898. In 1905 a statue of her by Helen Farnsworth Mears became one of Illinois's two submissions to Statuary Hall in the U.S. Capitol.

Williams, Fannie Barrier 1855–1944 lecturer and clubwoman

Born in Brockport, New York, on February 12, 1855, Fannie Barrier attended public schools and in 1870 graduated from the local State Normal School (now the State University of New York College at Brockport). During her succeeding years as a teacher in freedmen's schools at various places in the South and in Washington, D.C., she first encountered overt racial prejudice. Later she studied for periods at the New England Conservatory of Music in Boston and at the School of Fine Arts in Washington, D.C. In 1887 she married S. Laing Williams, a lawyer with whom she settled in Chicago. While helping her husband establish his practice (at one time he was a partner of Ferdinand Barnett, husband of Ida Wells-Barnett) she became active in civic affairs as well.

She helped organize Provident Hospital and its Training School for Nurses, both interracial institutions, in 1891. In May 1893 she gave an address on "The Intellectual Progress of the Colored Women of the United States since the Emancipation Proclamation" to the World's Congress of Representative Women (held in conjunction with the World's Columbian Exposition). In September she addressed the World's Parliament of Religions. Between them the two public appearances brought her national recognition, and for a decade or more afterward she was widely in demand as a lecturer. Also in 1893 she helped found the National League of Colored Women, and she remained a leader in its successor, the National Association of Colored Women.

In 1894 Williams was proposed for membership in the prestigious Chicago Woman's Club. Debate within the club over the question verged on acrimony and lasted more than a year; one of her stoutest supporters was Dr. Sarah Stevenson. In 1895 she became the club's first African-American member. She wrote regularly for the *Chicago Record-Herald* and the *New York Age* and worked quietly in many ways to open new opportunities to black women. From 1900 she became an outspoken supporter of Booker T. Washington's program of accommodation and self-improvement. Perhaps not coincidentally, Washington used his considerable influence to secure an appointment for Laing Williams as an assistant U.S. district attorney in 1908. In 1924 the widowed Williams became the first woman and the first African-American to be named to the Chicago Library Board. In 1926 she returned to her native Brockport, New York, where she died on March 4, 1944.

Williams, Mary Lou 1910–1981 pianist, composer, arranger and educator

Born Mary Elfreida Scruggs in Atlanta, Georgia, on May 8, 1910, pianist Mary Lou Williams played a major role in the development of jazz. Characterized by Duke Ellington as "perpetually contemporary," she played vital roles in creating both the

Kansas City Big Band sound and later bebop. Known as the "First Lady of Jazz" and the "Queen of Jazz," she was versatile enough to incorporate any musical style, while her arrangements set standards for many forms of jazz and blues.

Williams's mother was a classically-trained pianist; left by her husband, she supported the family by doing housework. Even at age two Williams was picking out simple tunes. Her mother taught her to play by ear, stressing the sound and feel of the music. With perfect pitch and a highly developed musical memory, Williams stood out as a prodigy by the time she was four years old. Her new step-father bought ragtime rolls for the family's player piano and paid the young Williams to perform ragtime, blues and boogie woogie for his friends. Her uncle taught her Irish tunes, and her grandfather encouraged her in the classical European piano tradition. By age ten, Williams had a reputation as, "The Little Piano Girl" and was performing for small audiences all over Pittsburgh, including wealthy families such as the Mellons. She sometimes earned as much as twenty or thirty dollars a day from these small jobs.

Her professional debut with big bands came in 1922, at age 12, when she substituted for a pianist with the Buzz and Harris Revue, a traveling show that was visiting in Pittsburgh. Persuaded by the booking agency, her parents allowed her to accompany the band on tour for two additional weeks. Billed as Mary Lou Burley, her traveling music career had begun. She continued to tour occasionally for the next several years, even while attending high school. She performed with the Seymour and Jeanette Show, one of two African-American shows on the B.F. Keith circuit. While on tour she passed through New York City several times and played for artists such as Jelly Roll Morton, Willie the Lion Smith, Fats Waller and Duke Ellington. All these musicians were impressed by her strength as a piano player, her ability to play "like a man."

In 1926, she married John Williams, an alto and baritone saxophone player and leader of the band for Seymour and Jeanette. In 1927, the show settled in Memphis, and Mary Lou Williams became band leader when John Williams moved to Oklahoma to join the popular Andy Kirk and the Twelve Clouds of Joy.

In 1929 Williams began a successful arranging career, when she moved to Oklahoma to join John Williams with Andy Kirk. From her childhood, she had aspired to follow in the footsteps of the pianist-arranger Lovie Austin, a multitalented woman who was able to play piano with her left hand and write new arrangements with her right. During her time with Kirk, the band became well-known for her stunning solo piano and highly original arrangements, including "Froggy Bottom," "Walkin' and Swingin'," "Little Joe from Chicago," "Roll' Em," and "Mary's Idea." Williams is widely credited as a major influence for the Kansas City-Southwest Big Band sound that Twelve Clouds of Joy helped to popularize.

By the late 1930s, Williams had a reputation as one of the best arrangers in the business, writing for Earl Hines, Louis Armstrong, Duke Ellington, Tommy Dorsey, Benny Goodman, Jimmie Lunceford, Cab Calloway and many others. She remained with Kirk until 1942 when she moved to New York City and established another band with her second husband, trumpeter Harold "Shorty" Baker. Soon the couple joined Duke Ellington and Williams began arranging for the band. One of her most notable works was the popular "Trumpet No End," that Ellington began performing in 1943 and recorded in 1946. Williams's marriage to Baker ended in divorce after a year. By 1943, she was devoting herself to organizing bands and becoming a well-known solo performer at clubs all over town.

During this period, she also became very involved with a group of younger musicians in New York: Bud Powell, Thelonious Monk, Charlie Parker and Dizzy Gillespie. Already an established musician in the Swing style, she easily made the transition to bebop and began promoting the new music and the young musicians. Her apartment became a meeting place, and she was a regular performer in many of the bebop jam sessions. Important compositions in the bebop style include, "In the Land of Oo-Blah-Dee," "Tisherone," "Knowledge," "Lonely Moments," and "Waltz Boogie." The latter was recorded with one of her several women's bands known as the Girl-Stars, in 1946.

In 1945 she premiered the first of many large compositions, the twelve-movement work, *Zodiac Suite*. Performed on her new radio show as solo piano pieces, she introduced one new movement each week. Organized as tributes to various musicians and friends, and based on the phases of the zodiac, she later scored the piece for instrumental performance. In 1946, an orchestral version of three movements "Aquarius," "Scorpio," and "Pisces" was performed by the New York Philharmonic. The Carnegie Hall performance was notable for the role it played in smashing the last vestiges of the whites-only barrier to that stage, and for the Philharmonic's performance of a jazz composition, written by an African-American woman. The movement "Capricorn," was created for dancer Pearl Primus, who, like her, performed at Cafe Society. African-American dancer/anthropologist Katherine Dunham later choreographed "Scorpio" for performance as a dance piece.

She moved to Europe in 1952,and performed in Paris and London. In 1954 she walked off the stage in the middle of a lucrative Paris performance, frustrated with nightclub life and the rigors of travel and experienced an emotional crisis. She lived in the French countryside for six months before returning to the U.S. She did religious and charitable work, including work with children in Harlem; she converted to Catholicism in 1956. In 1957 she founded the Bel Canto Foundation, a group dedicated to assisting artists and musicians with medical, drug and alcohol problems. The foundation was supported with proceeds from her compositions and recordings and by a Thrift Shop.

She began performing again in 1957, first with Dizzy Gillespie at the Newport Jazz Festival and then with her own trio. She founded Mary Records, the first such company established by a woman. In the 1960s and 1970s, she composed liturgical pieces for jazz ensembles including, *Black Christ of the Andes*, a cantata, 1962, *Mass for the Lenten Season*, 1968 and *Music for Peace*, popularly known as "Mary Lou's Mass," 1970. The latter was adapted for dance and performed by Alvin Ailey's Dance Theater in 1971.

In the 1960s, Williams began teaching in Pittsburgh, at a Catholic High School. In 1975, she was appointed to the faculty of the University of Massachusetts, Amherst, and in 1977 to the faculty at Duke University. In 1970 she recorded *The History of Jazz*, a performance-lecture that spanned the entire history of jazz. In 1976, she accepted the invitation of avant-garde pianist Cecil Taylor to collaborate in a Carnegie Hall performance. The recording, *Embraced*, that was produced is noteworthy for the layering of historical blues and jazz rhythms, produced by Williams, with Taylor's contemporary contributions.

She was awarded many honors including Guggenheim Fellowships, 1972 and 1977. She received honorary doctorates from Boston, Fordham and Loyola universities. In 1978 President Jimmy Carter invited her to perform at the White House. She died at home in Durham, North Carolina, on May 28, 1981.

Wills, Helen Newington 1905– tennis player

Born in Berkeley, California, on October 6, 1905, Helen Wills was educated in private schools. She began playing tennis when she was thirteen and won her first major title, the U.S. girls' championship, in 1921, when she was fifteen. She repeated as national girls' champion in 1922 and won her first women's singles title in 1923, when she was seventeen. All together she won the U.S. championship seven times, repeating in 1924, 1925, 1927, 1928, 1929, and 1931. She won her first Wimbledon championship — the unofficial world championship — in 1927, upon the retirement of the great French star

Suzanne Lenglen, and repeated her victory seven times, in 1928, 1929, 1930, 1932, 1933, 1935, and in 1938, when she was thirty-two. To her seven U.S. and eight Wimbledon singles championships (both standing records) she added four U.S. and three Wimbledon doubles titles (she won the 1924 doubles with Hazel Hotchkiss Wightman), two U.S. and one Wimbledon mixed doubles titles, and four French singles and two doubles championships. In 1924 at Paris she won two gold medals in the only Olympic Games in which the United States entered a tennis team.

Probably the most powerful woman player up to her time, and possessing extraordinary control as well, Wills long dominated women's tennis; from 1926, when she was beaten in the U.S. finals at Forest Hills by Molla Mallory, until 1932, when she had to default in the finals against Helen Hull Jacobs because of a painful back injury, she did not lose a single set in the United States. In 10 Wightman Cup tournaments during her career she won 18 of 20 singles matches. Wills graduated from the University of California in 1927 and in December 1929 married Frederick S. Moody; she competed throughout the next decade as Helen Wills Moody. Divorced in 1937, she married Aidan Roark in October 1939 and continued for a time to compete in senior tournaments as Mrs. Roark. A second interest in art led to the mounting of several exhibitions of her drawings and paintings in New York galleries.

She wrote two books on tennis — *Tennis*, 1928, and *Fifteen Thirty*, 1937 — and a mystery, *Death Serves an Ace*, with R. W. Murphy, 1939. In 1959 she was named to the International Tennis Hall of Fame. She lived in later years in retirement in California.

Wilson, Augusta Jane Evans 1835–1909 writer

Born on May 8, 1835, in Wynnton (now part of Columbus), Georgia, Augusta Jane Evans grew up there, from 1845 in Houston, Galveston, and San Antonio, Texas, and from 1849 in Mobile, Alabama. She received little formal schooling but early became an avid reader. At fifteen she began writing a novel that was published anonymously in 1855 as *Inez: A Tale of the Alamo*, a sentimental, moralistic story laced with anti-Catholic prejudice. In 1859 she published *Beulah*, a somewhat pedantic tale concerned with religious doubt that was fairly successful, selling some 22,000 copies in less than a year.

During the Civil War she was a fervent supporter of the Confederate cause, whose rightness was a moral principle to her, and she devoted much time and energy to nursing and relief work. Her *Macaria; or, Altars of Sacrifice*, published in Richmond in 1864, was an effective morale-builder in the South, and even a northern edition, reprinted from a contraband copy, sold well. One Union general was said to have ordered his men not to read it and to have burned all available copies. *St. Elmo*, 1866, was a huge success with its Byronic hero saved to righteousness by a virtuous maiden. It was later dramatized and later still adapted for a silent film. (Its sentimentality and turgidity inspired a popular parody, *St. Twel'mo*, by William Webb.) In December 1868 Augusta Evans married Lorenzo M. Wilson, a Mobile businessman 27 years her senior. While managing his estate and later traveling with him for his health, she found time to write *Vashti*, 1869, *Infelice*, 1875, and *At the Mercy of Tiberius*, 1887. After her husband's death in 1891 she lived with relatives in Mobile and completed *A Speckled Bird*, 1902, and *Devota*, 1907. She died in Mobile, Alabama, on May 9, 1909.

Windsor, Wallis Warfield, Duchess of 1896–1986 socialite

Born in Blue Ridge Summit, Pennsylvania, on June 19, 1896, Bessie Wallis Warfield, known as Wallis, grew up there and in Maryland. She attended the Oldfields School in Cockeysville, Maryland. During World War I she married Earl W. Spencer, a navy pilot; they were divorced in the early 1920s. After living for a time in Warrenton, Virginia, she traveled to England, where she met Ernest A. Simpson, a U.S.-born British subject. They were married in 1928 and lived near London, where she became acquainted with many of the leading personalities of the day. In June 1931 she was introduced to the Prince of Wales; over the next few years they were frequently seen together at social gatherings. After his accession to the throne as Edward VIII in January 1936, the possibility of romance between them became more than an occasion of social comment. In October 1936 Wallis Simpson filed for divorce, and it soon became apparent that the King intended to marry her.

This situation initiated an unprecedented constitutional crisis, for the Church of England and other conservative factions adamantly opposed such a union, even a morganatic marriage or one that denied her the dignity of queen consort. On December 11, 1936, Edward VIII renounced his throne, and the next day he made the famous radio address to the nation which included his simple explanation: "I have found it impossible to carry on the heavy burden of responsibility and to discharge the duties of king as I would wish to do without the help and support of the woman I love." Immediately after his abdication, upon which he was created the Duke of Windsor by his brother, now George VI, he left England to live on the Continent. Simpson's divorce became final in May 1937, and she had her name changed legally to Mrs. Wallis Warfield. Mrs. Warfield and the Duke were married in France on June 3, 1937. They lived in France and traveled frequently until World War II broke out. In July 1940 King George VI named the Duke governor of the Bahama Islands, where the Duke and Duchess remained through most of World War II; he resigned his post in early 1945 and moved back to France. The couple were among the most prominent, exclusive, and newsworthy members of the "international set" of socialites and celebrities. For decades their lives consisted largely of traveling, entertaining, and being entertained a great deal. In 1956 the Duchess of Windsor published her autobiography, *The Heart Has Its Reasons*. The Duke of Windsor died in Paris on May 28, 1972, and the Duchess continued to live at her Paris home in declining health and increasing isolation. She died on April 24, 1986, in Paris and, at her husband's request, was buried beside him in the royal cemetery at Frogmore, England, near Windsor Castle.

Winfrey, Oprah 1954– talk-show host, actor and producer

Born on January 29, 1954, in Kosciusko, Mississippi, Oprah Winfrey spent her earliest years on her grandmother's farm. At six she moved to Milwaukee to live with her mother, but within a few years she began to be abused by male family members and acquaintances there. Sent at age twelve to live with her father in Nashville, Tennessee, she began to excel in school and more than once was promoted a grade level ahead of her schoolmates.

In high school, after becoming involved in extracurricular activities including drama and speech programs, she was hired to broadcast news at a local radio station. She then earned a scholarship to study speech and drama at Tennessee State University in Nashville, where, in her sophomore year, she joined WTVF-TV, a CBS affiliate, as the first African-American woman in Nashville to coanchor the local evening news.

After graduation she left WTVF for a position as reporter and coanchor for the six o'clock news with WJZ-TV, an ABC affiliate in Baltimore. In 1977 Winfrey began hosting the station's morning talk show, *People are Talking*. In 1984, she moved to WLS-TV in Chicago to host *A.M. Chicago*, a talk show which was losing its viewers to competing talk-show host Phil Donahue. Within three months, *A.M. Chicago* topped its competitor's ratings, and by 1985 Winfrey's program had been expanded to an hour and renamed *The Oprah Winfrey Show*. In 1986, her show was syndicated nationally, and Winfrey formed her own TV production company, Harpo Productions.

By 1994 *The Oprah Winfrey Show* boasted several Emmy awards and 17 million viewers, and Winfrey had become one of the most recognizable personalities in the United States. Unconstrained by journalism's demands of objectivity, Winfrey used her program to draw people out with her warmth and directness, often eliciting moving and personal tales from both guests and audience members.

Her success as a talk-show host also led to an acting career. In 1985, Winfrey appeared in Steven Spielberg's adaptation of Alice Walker's novel, *The Color Purple*. Playing the role of Sofia, she earned nominations for both an Academy award and a Golden Globe award. She later appeared in the film adaptation of Richard Wright's *Native Son* and an acclaimed TV mini-series, *The Women of Brewster Place*, 1989. A respected business-woman, she also began buying film rights to literary works, including *Beloved*, Toni Morrison's tale of slavery, and *Kaffir Boy*, Mark Mathabane's South African autobiography.

An outspoken crusader against child abuse, Winfrey established a "little sisters" program in Chicago's Cabrini-Green housing project; she also created a training program to help people of color gain production skills and access to jobs in the film and television industry. In 1986 she received the Woman of Achievement award from the National Organization for Women. The National Association for the Advancement Colored People also recognized Winfrey four times with its Image award, 1989–1992, and in 1989 it named her Entertainer of the Year.

Winnemucca, Sarah 1844?–1891 Native American leader

Born about 1844 at Humboldt Sink in what is now Nevada, Thoc-me-tony was a daughter of Winnemucca II, chief of the Paiute tribe. She lived during part of her childhood in the San Joaquin valley of California, where she learned both Spanish and English. After her return to Nevada she lived for a time with the white family of a stage company agent near Genoa; at that time she adopted the name Sarah. In 1860 she briefly attended a convent school in San Jose, California, until objections from the parents of white students forced her to leave. During the Paiute War of 1860 and the subsequent increasingly frequent clashes between Native Americans and whites, she suffered the loss of several family members, including a baby brother. She attempted the role of peace-maker on a few occasions and during 1868–1871 served as an interpreter at Camp McDermitt in northeastern Nevada. In 1872 she accompanied her tribe to a new reservation, the Malheur, in southeastern Oregon.

In 1875–1876 she was an interpreter for the reservation agent, but the appointment of a new and unsympathetic agent in the latter year ended that service as well as a period of relative quiet on the reservation. On the outbreak of the Bannock War in 1878 she offered her services to the army. After several Paiute scouts had refused to enter Bannock territory to reconnoiter for the army, and on learning that her father and several other tribesmen were being held by hostile Bannocks, she volunteered for the dangerous task. Covering more than a hundred miles of trail through Idaho and Oregon, she located the Bannock camp, spirited her father and many of his companions away, and returned with valuable intelligence for General O. O. Howard. She was scout, aide, and interpreter to Howard during the resulting campaign against the Bannocks.

In 1879 she lectured in San Francisco on the plight of her tribe — many of whose members had been exiled along with belligerent Bannocks to a reservation in Washington Territory — and on the wrongs perpetrated by dishonest civilian Indian agents. Despite slanderous responses by agents and their friends, she attracted considerable attention and was invited to Washington, D.C., where in January 1880 she spoke with President Rutherford B. Hayes and Secretary of the Interior Carl Schurz. She was promised the return of her people to the Malheur reservation and a severalty allotment of land there, but for various reasons the order to that effect issued by Schurz was not carried out.

After a year of teaching in a school for Native American children at Vancouver

Barracks, Washington Territory, and her marriage late in 1881 to L. H. Hopkins, an army officer, Sarah Winnemucca, often known among whites as "the Princess," made an eastern lecture tour to arouse public opinion. Aided by General Howard, Elizabeth Peabody, and others, the tour was a success, and sales of her *Life Among the Piutes: Their Wrongs and Claims* raised money for her expenses. She secured thousands of signatures on a petition calling for the promised allotment of reservation lands to individual Paiutes; Congress passed a bill to that end in 1884, but a new secretary of the interior, Henry M. Teller, refused to carry it out. From 1883 to 1886 she taught at a Paiute school near Lovelock, Nevada. In the latter year, following her husband's death and in ill health herself, she moved to a sister's home in Monida, Montana, where she died on October 16, 1891.

Wittenmyer, Annie Turner 1827–1900 relief worker and reformer

Born on August 26, 1827, in Sandy Springs, Ohio, Annie Turner grew up there and for part of her childhood in Kentucky. In 1847 she married William Wittenmyer, a merchant with whom she settled in Keokuk, Iowa, in 1850. At the outbreak of the Civil War, having shortly before been left a widow with a considerable estate, she soon threw herself energetically into relief work. As secretary of the Keokuk Soldiers' Aid Society she began visiting troop encampments and organizing a statewide system of local aid societies to promote the collection of hospital supplies. Her own Keokuk society became the de facto distributing agency for the state.

Under a state law of September 1862 she was appointed a paid state sanitary agent to carry on the work she had begun. In October 1863 she was elected president of the Iowa State Sanitary Commission, a group organized to resist an attempt by the all-male Iowa Army Sanitary Commission to take over the work of Iowa women. The rivalry continued into 1864, when opponents falsely accused her of mismanagement and corruption; after refuting the charges and fighting off the threat to her position she resigned as state agent in May 1864.

On her own Wittenmyer proceeded with a plan she had evolved to open special diet kitchens at army hospitals. Supported by the United States Christian Commission, she began with a kitchen in Nashville. Women recruited by her soon established similar kitchens at other hospitals, and by the end of the war her idea had been generally adopted by the army medical department. During and after the war she was also concerned with the plight of war orphans and worked on behalf of the Iowa Orphans' Home Association.

In 1868 she led in organizing the Ladies' and Pastors' Christian Union, an organization of Methodists interested in aiding the sick and needy. She was chosen corresponding secretary of the successor General Conference Society in 1871. About that time she moved to Philadelphia and founded the periodical *Christian Woman*, of which she remained editor for 11 years.

Wittenmyer joined in the "Woman's Crusade," the largely unorganized wave of temperance fervor that swept over parts of western New York, Ohio, and other midwestern states in 1873–1874. In November 1874, informally representing Methodist churchwomen, she attended the Cleveland convention at which the national Woman's Christian Temperance Union was organized and was elected the union's first president. For the next year she and Frances Willard, the WCTU's corresponding secretary, traveled widely to lecture on temperance and to organize local and state branches.

Wittenmyer also saw to the founding of *Our Union*, the WCTU's journal. She was reelected president regularly until 1879, when she lost to Willard, with whom she had split over the question of taking up the cause of woman suffrage in addition to temperance. She continued to oppose the politicization of the WCTU and supported the formation in 1890 of the splinter Non-Partisan Woman's Christian Temperance Union, of which she was president in 1896–1898.

In 1889–1890 she was president of the Woman's Relief Corps, an auxiliary of the Grand Army of the Republic. She led a campaign to establish a National Woman's Relief Corps Home for Civil War nurses and the widows and mothers of veterans, and she served as a director for such homes established in Ohio and Pennsylvania. In 1892 she lobbied Congress on behalf of a bill to provide Civil War nurses with pensions, and in 1898 she herself received a special pension. Among her written works were *Woman's Work for Jesus*, 1871, *History of the Woman's Temperance Crusade*, 1878, *Women of the Reformation*, 1884, and *Under the Guns*, 1895. She died in Sanatoga (now part of Pottstown), Pennsylvania, on February 2, 1900.

Wood, Mary Elizabeth 1861–1931 librarian and missionary

Born in Elba, New York, on August 22, 1861, Mary Wood grew up and attended public schools in nearby Batavia. In 1889 she became librarian of the newly opened Richmond Library in Batavia. In 1899 she traveled to Wu-ch'ang, China, to visit a brother who was a missionary there. At his suggestion she prolonged her visit in order to take charge of an elementary English class in the small, missionary-run Boone School. By 1904, when she received formal appointment by the (Episcopal) American Church Mission as a lay missionary, the school had grown to include a collegiate department and was in need of a library. She began slowly to build one from donations from friends and church groups. On a furlough to the United States in 1906 she raised money for a library building (Olivia Phelps Stokes was a contributor), which ultimately opened in 1910.

On subsequent furloughs she studied library science at the Pratt Institute and Simmons College. In order to extend the library's usefulness she established branches at several locations in Wu-ch'ang and in Hankow, and eventually she organized a system of traveling libraries that brought books in both Chinese and English to a wide area; one traveled as far as Peking. Beginning in 1915 she sent promising Chinese students to the United States for training in librarianship, and in 1920 she opened a library school in Boone College. Before the college was closed by the Communist regime in 1949, the library school had graduated nearly 500 librarians, many of whom went on to advanced training in the United States.

In 1923 Wood circulated a petition among Chinese leaders asking that a portion of the $6 million still unassigned from the U.S. indemnity imposed after the Boxer Rebellion be allocated to the development of public libraries in China. In 1924 she traveled to Washington, D.C., to lobby personally for the idea. Congress passed a bill remitting funds (eventually nearly $12 million) for the development of "educational and other cultural activities" under the guidance of the China Foundation for the Promotion of Education and Culture. The foundation allotted sums for the establishment of the National Library in Peking and for scholarships and expenses at the Boone Library School. From 1924 to 1930 the school, a part of Boone College, was a constituent of the Anglo-American union Huachung University, but administrative friction led to the withdrawal of the library school in the latter year. Wood devoted her remaining time to building up a permanent endowment for the school under control of a U.S.-based board (later known as the Mary Elizabeth Wood Foundation). She died in Wu-ch'ang on May 1, 1931. In 1950 the Boone Library School was absorbed by the National Wu-han University.

Woodbury, Helen Laura Sumner 1876–1933 historian and public official

Born on March 12, 1876, in Sheboygan, Wisconsin, Helen Sumner grew up there, in Durango, Colorado, from the age of five, and in Denver from thirteen. After graduating from East Denver High School she entered Wellesley College, from which she graduated in 1898. In college she became interested in social settlement work and published a free-silver campaign novel, *The White Slave or, "The Cross of Gold,"* 1896. In 1902 she began graduate studies in economics at the University of Wisconsin, where she worked as secretary to Professor Richard T. Ely and studied with Professor John R. Commons. She held an honorary fellowship in political economy in 1904–1906. She contributed to Commons's *Trade Unionism and Labor Problems*, 1905, and with Thomas S. Adams wrote *Labor Problems, a* widely used college textbook, 1905. In 1906–1907 she conducted a field investigation of woman suffrage in Colorado for the Collegiate Equal Suffrage League of New York State. Her report, *Equal Suffrage*, was published in 1909.

Resuming her studies, Sumner helped compile and edit several volumes of the *Documentary History of American Industrial Society* published by Commons's American Bureau of Industrial Research. In 1908 she received her Ph.D. for a dissertation on "The Labor Movement in America, 1827–1837," which became a major portion of the first two volumes of *History of Labour in the United States*, by Commons and several students, 1918. Her pioneering study of the "History of Women in Industry in the United States" was published by the U.S. Bureau of Labor Statistics as Volume IX of its *Report on the Condition of Woman and Child Wage-Earners in the United States* in 1910. From 1909 to 1913 she undertook various contract studies for the federal government. A European research tour led to her *Industrial Courts in France, Germany, and Switzerland*, published in 1910 as a bulletin of the Bureau of Labor Statistics.

In 1913 she joined the year-old Children's Bureau as an industrial expert, and two years later she advanced to assistant chief under Julia Lathrop. She later gave up the administrative post to serve as the bureau's chief investigator. Following her marriage in November 1918 to Robert M. Woodbury, an economist, she worked for the bureau on a contract basis. Her published work for the bureau included *Child Labor Legislation in the United States*, with Ella A. Merritt, 1915, *The Working Children of Boston: A Study of Child Labor under a Modern System of Legal Regulation*, 1922, and *Standards Applicable to tile Administration of Employment-Certificate Systems*, 1924. From 1924 to 1926 she and her husband were both on the staff of the Institute of Economics. She also contributed to the *Encyclopedia of the Social Sciences*. She died in New York City on March 10, 1933.

Woodhull, Victoria Claflin 1838–1927 spiritualist, reformer and publisher

Born on September 23, 1838, in Homer, Licking County, Ohio, into a poor and eccentric family, Victoria Claflin grew up rootless and prone to trances. That circumstance, combined with the flair for showmanship of her sister Tennessee Celeste Claflin (1845–1923), who quickly learned to arrange séances for Victoria, and the ability of a brother to act the role of a doctor, led to a traveling Claflin family medicine and fortune-telling show. At fifteen Victoria married Dr. Canning Woodhull, by whom she had two children. They were divorced in 1864 after several years of separation during which the sisters continued to travel about the Midwest engaging in various enterprises. In 1866 Victoria met and may have married the dashing Colonel James H. Blood of St. Louis, but she continued to use the name Woodhull.

In 1868 (moved by a vision of Demosthenes, Victoria claimed), the sisters traveled to New York City, where they met the recently widowed Cornelius Vanderbilt, who was interested in spiritualism. He set them up in a stock-brokerage firm, Woodhull, Claflin & Company, which opened in January 1870 and, in part through its novelty and in larger part owing to the sisters' native shrewdness, was quite successful. With their considerable profits they founded in 1870 *Woodhull and Claflin's Weekly*, a women's-rights and reform magazine that espoused a single moral standard for men and women, free love, legalized prostitution, dress reform, tax reform, and a variety of other causes. Much of each issue was written by Stephen Pearl Andrews, promoter of the utopian social system he called

"Pantarchy"; Andrews and Colonel Blood were the principal editors. Victoria Woodhull expounded her version of Andrews's ideas in a series of articles in the *New York Herald* in 1870 that were collected in *Origin, Tendencies and Principles of Government*, 1871.

Victoria's ardent speeches on woman suffrage, notably in January 1871 before the House Judiciary Committee, won her at least tentative acceptance by woman-suffrage leaders, who until then had been put off by her newspaper and her reputation. Invited into the National Woman Suffrage Association by Susan B. Anthony, she soon became a rival for leadership. She was repudiated over the proposal to form a new political party. In May 1872 she held a convention of an "Equal Rights" party nonetheless and accepted its nomination for president; the abolitionist and former slave Frederick Douglass was put on the ticket as her running mate, but he refused to take part in the campaign.

By mid–1872 Victoria Woodhull's troubles had begun to mount. Dr. Woodhull reappeared and took up residence with her and Colonel Blood, thus providing rich new material for her enemies. No longer enjoying the backing of Commodore Vanderbilt, she was forced to suspend publication of her *Weekly* that summer (it had lately published the first English-language version of the Communist Manifesto to appear in America). She was caricatured in a novel by Harriet Beecher Stowe.

She responded to critics of her morals by hurling back charges of her own. She learned of an alleged liaison between the highly respected Henry Ward Beecher of Plymouth Church in Brooklyn and a parishioner, the wife of Theodore Tilton, an editor with whom Victoria may have had an affair. On November 2, 1872, she printed a special issue of the *Weekly* containing the entire story of the Beecher-Tilton affair. Upon the urging of Anthony Comstock she and her sister were promptly jailed under a statute forbidding the passage of obscene materials through the mail.

After seven months of litigation they were acquitted of the charge. At the time the scandal was of national interest. In 1877, reportedly with money provided by William Vanderbilt to prevent their testifying in a court test of the late Commodore's will, the sisters moved to England. Victoria continued to lecture, write books and pamphlets, and work for charities; after a marriage to John B. Martin, a wealthy English banker, in October 1883, she was eventually received by London society. (Tennessee was married in 1885 to Francis Cook and became Lady Cook in 1886.) She wrote *Stirpiculture, or the Scientific Propagation of the Human Race*, 1888, *Garden of Eden: Allegorical Meaning Revealed*, 1889, *The Human Body the Temple of God*, with her sister, 1890, and *Humanitarian Money: The Unsolved Riddle*, 1892. From 1892 to 1901 she published with her daughter, Zula Maud Woodhull, the *Humanitarian* magazine devoted to eugenics. Although Victoria returned on occasion to the United States, she lived in England until her death at Bredon's Norton, Tewkesbury, Worcestershire, on June 10, 1927.

Woolley, Mary Emma 1863–1947 educator

Born on July 13, 1863, in South Norwalk, Connecticut, Mary Woolley grew up in Meriden, Connecticut, and from the age of eight in Pawtucket, Rhode Island. She attended private and public schools and in 1884 graduated from Wheaton Seminary (now College) in Norton, Massachusetts. She taught at the seminary in 1885–1886 and 1887–1890. A European trip in 1890 stimulated her ambition for further education, and in 1891 she was first among the initial seven women admitted to Brown University. She was one of the first two to graduate, in 1894, and she remained an additional year to take a master's degree in history. She became an instructor in Biblical history and literature at Wellesley College in 1895 and advanced to associate professor in 1896 and to professor in 1899.

Early in 1900 Woolley was chosen president of Mount Holyoke College to succeed Elizabeth Storrs Mead, and after a tour of Great Britain, during which she studied women's educational practices and problems, she assumed her new office in January

1901. Under her strong leadership the academic standards of the college were raised remarkably. Improved salaries and benefits attracted a larger and better qualified faculty (their number doubled between 1901 and 1911); elective courses multiplied while the line was held against such nonacademic subjects as home economics; and the graduate program was greatly expanded. The social atmosphere of the school matured, particularly with the adoption of a measure of student self-government in 1922. In 1914 the required housekeeping chores that had been a Mount Holyoke feature since Mary Lyon's time were abolished. The physical plant of the college grew by 16 major buildings during her 36-year tenure, and the endowment increased tenfold, to nearly $5 million.

The two principal causes outside Mount Holyoke that attracted Woolley's support were woman suffrage and peace. She helped found the National College Women's Equal Suffrage League in 1908 and was a vice-president of the American Peace Society from 1907 to 1913. She also served on the China Christian Education Commission that toured that country in 1921–1922, was a vice-chairman of the American Civil Liberties Union, was president of the American Association of University Women in 1927–1933, was active in the Institute of Pacific Relations, and in 1932 was the only woman appointed by President Herbert Hoover to the American delegation to the Geneva Conference on Reduction and Limitation of Armaments.

She retired as president of Mount Holyoke in 1937. Because of her strong disagreement with the trustees' choice of a man to succeed her, she never returned to the campus. She remained active in various organizations, notably the National Woman's party, until her death in Westport, New York, on September 5, 1947.

Woolsey, Sarah Chauncey 1835–1905 writer of children's novels

Born in Cleveland on January 29, 1835, Sarah Woolsey enjoyed a vigorous girlhood and early displayed a love for reading and writing stories. She was educated in local private schools and at the Select Family School for Young Ladies in Hanover, New Hampshire. In 1855 she moved with her family to New Haven, Connecticut (her uncle, Theodore Dwight Woolsey, was president of Yale). During the Civil War she was active in hospital work. In 1870, after her father's death, the family settled in Newport, Rhode Island. By that time Sarah Woolsey had already published a few magazine articles, and, in part through the influence of her close friend Helen Hunt (Jackson), she then began to write in earnest.

Her first book, a collection of stories for girls, appeared as *The New-Year's Bargain* under the pseudonym "Susan Coolidge" in 1871. She used that name thereafter. Subsequent books included *What Katy Did*, a novel for girls inspired by her own childhood and the first of a highly popular series, 1872, *What Katy did at School*, 1873, *Mischief's Thanksgiving*, 1874, *Nine Little Goslings*, 1875, *For Summer Afternoons*, 1876, *Eyebright*, 1879, *A Guernsey Lily*, 1880, *Cross Patch*, 1881, *A Round Dozen*, 1883, *A Little Country Girl*, 1885, *What Katy Did Next*, 1886, *Clover*, 1888, *Just Sixteen*, 1889, *In the High Valley*, 1891, *The Barberry Bush*, 1893, *Not Quite Eighteen*, 1894, and *An Old Convent School in Paris and Other Papers*, 1895. The good-natured mischief and high-spirited heroines of her books set them apart from much literature intended for girls of the day and helped them retain their popularity for decades.

She also published three volumes of poetry, *Verses*, 1880, *A Few More Verses*, 1889, and *Last Verses*, published posthumously in 1906; brought out editions of *The Autobiography and Correspondence of Mrs. Delany*, 1879, *The Diary and Letters of Frances Burney, Mme. d'Arblay*, 1880, and *Letters of Jane Austen*, 1892; and translated Théophile Gautier's *My Household of Pets*, 1882. Sarah Woolsey died in Newport, Rhode Island, on April 9, 1905.

Woolson, Constance Fenimore 1840–1894 writer

Born on March 5, 1840, in Claremont, New Hampshire, Constance Woolson, a grand-niece on her mother's side of James Fenimore Cooper, grew up in Cleveland, Ohio. She attended private schools in Cleveland and in 1858 graduated from Mme. Chegaray's School in New York City. During the Civil War she engaged in hospital work. Following her father's death in 1869 she accompanied her mother on travels through the East and South, and in 1870 she began submitting travel sketches and stories to *Harper's*, *Putnam's*, *Lippincott's*, *Atlantic Monthly*, and other magazines. *Castle Nowhere: Lake-Country Sketches*, 1875, collected several of her local-color stories written somewhat in the manner of Bret Harte. During the later 1870s she spent much of her time in Florida and the Carolinas, which became the scenes of her best stories.

In 1879 she traveled to Europe, where she remained for the rest of her life, wintering usually in Florence and Venice, summering in Germany and Switzerland, visiting Greece and Egypt, and making extended stays in England in 1883–1886 and 1890–1892. Her novels, serialized in *Harper's* before publication in book form, included *Anne*, 1882, *For the Major*, 1883, *East Angels*, 1886, *Jupiter Lights*, 1889, and *Horace Chase*, 1894; all were set in faithfully detailed locales, and they exhibited a progressive tendency toward a psychological subtlety suggestive of the writing of her close friend, Henry James. She also published a collection of short stories as *Rodman the Keeper: Southern Sketches*, 1886. After a lengthy period of ill health she died on January 24, 1894, following a fall (perhaps intentional) from a window in her Venice apartment.

The Front Yard, and Other Italian Stories, 1895, and *Dorothy, and Other Italian Stories*, 1896, and a volume of travel sketches, *Mentone, Cairo and Corfu*, 1896, appeared posthumously.

Workman, Fanny Bullock 1859–1925 explorer and mountain climber

Born in Worcester, Massachusetts, on January 8, 1859, Fanny Bullock was the daughter of a prominent Republican politician who served as governor of Massachusetts in 1866–1868. She was educated in private schools in New York City, Paris, and Dresden. In June 1881 she married Dr. William H. Workman, a Worcester physician. They began vacationing in Europe in 1886, and from 1889, when Dr. Workman retired for his health, they lived in Europe for nine years. From gallery- and opera-going Mrs. Bullock Workman (as she preferred to be called) turned gradually to climbing and exploring. Together they traveled through several Mediterranean and Near Eastern countries. They took up bicycling and logged thousands of miles in Algeria, Spain, Ceylon, Java, Sumatra, Cochin China (now Vietnam), and India.

Their bicycle journeys provided the substance for several jointly written books, including *Algerian Memories*, 1895, *Sketches Awheel in Modern Iberia*, 1897, and *Through Town and Jungle*, 1904. In 1899 they made the first of seven journeys into the largely unexplored Karakorum range of the Himalaya Mountains. In subsequent expeditions in 1902, 1903, 1906, 1908, 1911, and 1912 they mapped, photographed, and made detailed scientific observations of snow and ice conditions, glacier structures and movements, meteorological data, and physiological responses to altitude. In 1903 she climbed the 21,000-foot Koser Gunga to set a record altitude for women, and in 1906 she bettered it with a 23,300-foot climb to the penultimate peak of Nun Kun. (When Annie Smith Peck lodged a rival claim in 1908, Mrs. Bullock Workman dispatched a team of French engineers who disproved Peck's estimate of 24,000 feet for her Huascarán peak.)

The Workmans explored the Biafo, Chogo Lungma, Hispar, Siachen, Kalberg, and other great glaciers, some as the first westerners to set foot on them. They described their explorations in *In the Ice World of Himálaya*, 1900, *Ice-bound Heights of the Mustagh*, 1908, *Peaks and Glaciers of Nun Kun*, 1909, *The Call of the Snowy Hispar*, 1910, and *Two Summers in the Ice Wilds of Eastern Karakorum*, 1917. Mrs. Bullock Workman also contributed articles to *Harper's*, *Putnam's*, and other magazines. She was the recipient of medals from several European geographic societies, a fellow of the Royal Geographic Society, a member of the Royal Asiatic Society, and reportedly the first American woman to lecture at the Sorbonne. She died in Cannes, France, on January 22, 1925.

Wright, Frances 1795–1852 reformer

Born in Dundee, Scotland, on September 6, 1795, Frances Wright was the daughter of a well-to-do merchant and political radical who had circulated the works of Thomas Paine. Her parents died and left her and a sister a fortune when she was two, and they were reared in London and Devon by conservative relatives. At twenty-one she returned to Scotland to live with a great-uncle, a professor of philosophy at Glasgow College. There she read widely and wrote some youthful romantic verse and *A Few Days in Athens*, 1822, a novelistic sketch of a disciple of Epicurus that outlined the materialistic philosophy to which she adhered throughout her life. In August 1818, in preference to a suggested European grand tour, she sailed with her sister for America for a two-year visit, during which her play *Altorf*, on the subject of Swiss independence, was produced in New York City.

The enthusiasm of her highly laudatory and widely read *Views of Society and Manners in America*, published in England in 1821, won her the friendship of the Marquis de Lafayette, whom she visited in France in 1821. She timed her return to New York on a second trip in 1824 to coincide with his triumphal tour of the country and followed him on his entire journey. She joined him in visits with Thomas Jefferson and James Madison. Slavery was discussed, and they approved in general of her plan for gradual emancipation through purchase and colonization.

In 1825 Wright published *A Plan for the Gradual Abolition of Slavery in the United States without Danger of Loss to the Citizens of the South*, which urged Congress to set aside tracts of land for the purpose. In December 1825, by way of demonstrating her plan, she invested a large part of her fortune in a 640-acre tract in western Tennessee (near present-day Memphis) that she called Nashoba. Slaves were purchased in 1825 and established at the Nashoba community with the promise of eventual freedom. The colony got off to a poor start from which it never recovered.

During Frances Wright's absence in 1827 owing to ill health, a scandal broke over charges of free love; on her return to Nashoba in company with Frances Trollope in January 1828 she found a ruin. After publishing a widely reprinted newspaper article defending her idea she left Nashoba for Robert Dale Owen's socialist community at New Harmony, Indiana. In 1830 she returned to arrange for the emancipation of the Nashoba slaves and their colonization in Haiti.

She helped edit Owen's *New Harmony Gazette* and took to the lecture platform, an activity then considered scandalous for a woman. Her *Course of Popular Lectures* (1829 and 1836) attacked religion, church influence in politics, and authoritarian education and defended equal rights for women and the replacement of legal marriage by a union based on moral obligation. In 1829 she settled in New York City, where with Owen she published the *Free Enquirer* and led the free-thinking movement, calling for liberalized divorce laws, birth control, free education run by the state, and the political organization of the working classes. She lectured regularly in her "Hall of Science," a converted church on Broome Street. Her educational proposals, outlined in her *Address on the State of the Public Mind*, 1829, won respectable support, but others of her ideas (notably birth control) continued to feed hysterical attacks on her in newspapers and from pulpits. She assisted in the formation of the Association for the Protection of Industry and for the Promotion of National Education, a pioneer workingmen's organization, in the summer of 1829.

In 1830 she sailed to France with her failing sister, who died a short time later. In July 1831 she married Guillaume Sylvan Casimir Phiquepal D'Arusmont, a physician she had first met at New Harmony, and she remained with him in Paris until 1835. In that year they returned to the United States and settled in Cincinnati. In 1836 and 1838 she took to the platform in support of the Democratic party and in particular of President Andrew Jackson's attack on the Bank of the United States. Her own lecture courses attracted little attention, however. Over the next dozen years she traveled frequently between the United States and France. She and her husband were divorced in 1850. She died in Cincinnati on December 13, 1852.

Wright, Laura Maria Sheldon 1809–1886 missionary

Born on July 10, 1809, in St. Johnsbury, Vermont, Laura Sheldon grew up there and from the age of seven in nearby Barnet. From an early age she was a playmate of local Native American children, among whom she began holding prayer meetings at ten. After completing her formal education in local schools she became a schoolteacher in Barnet and Newbury. In January 1833 she married the Reverend Asher Wright, a missionary to the Seneca Indians in western New York. Taking up her husband's work at the Buffalo Creek reservation, she soon mastered the Seneca language. Over the years she became a respected and then a much loved figure among Indians. Using a Seneca alphabet devised by her husband, she began teaching the children to read and write from a series of schoolbooks she produced, including a primer printed in 1836, a speller in 1842, and a bilingual journal that appeared regularly between 1841 and 1850.

The Wrights labored to help the Senecas make the difficult transition from a hunting culture to a settled agrarian one, a task greatly complicated by the loss of Buffalo Creek reservation to the encroachment of land developers from the growing city of Buffalo.

The extreme hardships, including starvation and epidemic disease, that followed upon the Senecas' removal to the Cattaraugus reservation — the Wrights' mission moved there in 1845 — left scores of Seneca children orphans. Laura Wright took many of them into her home and in 1854 prevailed upon Philip E. Thomas, a wealthy Quaker merchant of Baltimore, to establish the Thomas Asylum for Orphan and Destitute Indian Children (later the Thomas Indian School), of which the Wrights served thereafter as co-directors. Laura Wright, known among the Senecas as "Auntie Wright," performed countless acts of charity and gentle leadership, always respecting Seneca customs and working when possible through her insights into Seneca psychology. From her husband's death in 1875 she lived in the home of Nicholson H. Parker (of the distinguished Seneca family that also produced General Ely S. Parker). She died at the Parker home, near Iroquois, New York, on January 21, 1886.

Wright, Mickey 1935– golfer

Born in San Diego, California, on February 14, 1935, Mary Kathryn Wright began playing golf when she was nine. At seventeen, in 1952, she won the U.S. Golfing Association junior girls' championship. She attended Stanford University for one year, 1953–1954, before deciding to devote full time to golf. She was the amateur winner of the U.S. Women's Open tournament in 1954 before turning professional later in the year. She advanced rapidly to the fore and in 1958 won the Ladies Professional Golf Association championship tournament and the U.S. Women's Open, the latter with a four-round total of 290 that broke Mildred Didrikson Zaharias's record. She bettered that record by three strokes in winning the Open again in 1959.

She won the LPGA title again in 1960 and 1961 and in the latter year scored an unprecedented slam in winning the Open and the Titleholders' tournaments as well. She won the Titleholders' again in 1962 and her fourth LPGA title in 1963. She was the recipient of the Vare Trophy, for best yearlong average on the LPGA tour, in 1960, 1961, 1962, 1963, and 1964; her 1963 average was a record 72.81, and she lowered that in 1964 to 72.46. In 1963 she won a record 13 tournaments on the LPGA tour. In 1964 she won the Open again and finished the year in first place for all-time money winnings at $176,994. In that year she also shot an LPGA record round of 62. In 1963 and 1964 she was voted Female Athlete of the Year by the Associated Press. She withdrew from competition for a time in 1965 but returned and was soon again among the top contenders on the tour. She remained the LPGA's top total money winner until passed by Kathy Whitworth in 1969, by which time her total earnings had topped $268,000. Probably the most powerful hitter on the tour, Mickey Wright was capable of drives of upwards of 300 yards. She was named to the LPGA Hall of Fame in 1964, the World Golf Hall of Fame in 1976, and the International Women's Sports Hall of Fame in 1981.

Wright, Patience Lovell 1725–1786 sculptor

Born in Bordentown, New Jersey, in 1725, Patience Lovell was of a prosperous Quaker farm family. In March 1748 she married Joseph Wright, a Philadelphia cooper. Little is known of her life from then until 1769, when she was left a widow with five children. She had from childhood been artistically inclined; she began modeling in wax, and within a short time she had created a traveling waxwork exhibit featuring remarkably skillful portraits of well known public figures.

In February 1772 she sailed to England, where, in part through Benjamin Franklin's help, she soon created a new exhibit of actors, political figures, nobles, and others that became highly popular. The attraction of her work lay partly in its novelty (she preceded Madame Tussaud by 30 years), partly in its skill, and partly in her own blunt, eccentric personality. (She was said to have addressed the King and Queen as "George" and "Charlotte.") During the Revolutionary War she opened her London home to American prisoners of war and corresponded frequently with Franklin in Paris, although there seems to be little evidence for the later belief that she passed on to him military intelligence gleaned from her contacts in London society. She may also have corresponded with members of the Continental Congress, perhaps, according to one legend, concealing her letters in wax figures consigned to her sister in Philadelphia.

In 1780 she went to Paris to open a wax museum, but found little opportunity. She died in London on March 23, 1786. The painter, wax modeler, and diemaker Joseph Wright (1756–1793) was her son.

Wu, Chien-Shiung 1912– physicist

Born on May 31, 1912, in Liuho, Chiangsu Province, China, Chien-Shiung Wu was the daughter of a school principal who encouraged her in acquiring an education. She graduated from the National Central University in Nanking in 1936 and then traveled to the United States to pursue graduate studies in physics at the University of California at Berkeley. She studied under Ernest O. Lawrence and in 1940 was awarded a Ph.D. She taught at Smith College and at Princeton University before joining the staff of the Division of War Research at Columbia University in March 1944. There her work concerned radiation detection.

After the end of World War II she remained at Columbia as a research assistant. She advanced to associate professor of physics in 1952 and to full professor in 1957. She was naturalized in 1954. In 1956 she was asked by Tsung-Dao Lee, a Columbia colleague, and Chen Ning Yang, of Princeton's Institute for Advanced Study, to conduct an experimental test of their revolutionary proposal that for certain interactions of subatomic particles, those governed by the "weak" force, the long accepted principle of conservation of parity does not hold. (The principle states essentially that nature is impartial with respect to right- and left-handedness.) Heading a group of experimenters from the National Bureau of Standards, Wu determined in 1957 that in the beta-decay of cobalt–60, electrons are emitted more frequently in one direction than the other, thus confirming the Lee-Yang hypothesis. For her work she was given the Research Corporation Award in 1958 and elected to the National Academy of Sciences. (Lee and Yang won the 1957 Nobel Prize for their work.) In 1963, with two Columbia colleagues, she obtained experimental confirmation for a theoretical law of conservation of vector current in beta decay that had been proposed in 1958 by Murray Gell-Mann and Richard P. Feynman.

Other honors accorded her included the woman of the year award from the American Association of University Women in 1962 and the Comstock Award of the National Academy of Sciences in 1964. She was named scientist of the year by *Industrial Research Magazine* in 1974. She received the National Medal of Science and the Tom Bonner Prize of the American Physical Society, both in 1975, and the Wolf Prize in Physics, 1978. In 1975 she served as president of the American Physical Society. Considered one of the premier experimental physicists in the world, Wu retired from her professorship at Columbia in 1981.

Wylie, Elinor Morton Hoyt 1885–1928 poet and novelist

Elinor Wylie

Born on September 7, 1885, in Somerville, New Jersey, Elinor Hoyt grew up from the age of two in Rosemont, a Philadelphia suburb, and from twelve in Washington, D.C., where her father served as assistant U.S. attorney general and later as solicitor general. She attended private schools and in 1904 graduated from the Holton-Arms School in Washington. In 1905 she was married to the scion of a socially prominent navy family; she left him in December 1910 and eloped to England with Horace Wylie, a Washington lawyer 17 years her senior, whose wife refused him a divorce. The scandal was widely publicized. At the outbreak of World War I they returned to the United States and lived in Boston and then in Augusta, Georgia. They were married in August 1916.

In 1919 they moved back to Washington, D.C. There Elinor Wylie met a number of literary figures engaged in war-related work — William Rose Benét, Edmund Wilson, Sinclair Lewis, John Dos Passos, and others — and was emboldened to submit some of her poems for publication. (In 1912 her mother had had a few printed privately and anonymously in London under the title *Incidental Numbers*.) In 1921 a volume of her poems was issued commercially as *Nets to Catch the Wind*, which was warmly received by critics and the public. Technically skillful, sensuous, drawing upon both the Metaphysical and the Romantic poets for imagery and diction, her poems struck a responsive chord in a general readership that more experimental poets missed. With the success of the book she moved to New York City, and, aided by her striking beauty and her air of easy elegance, became a leading figure in literary society. She and Wylie were divorced in 1923, and in October of that year she married William Rose Benét.

In the few years that remained to her she produced a remarkable quantity of work. Subsequent books included *Black Armour*, poems, 1923, *Jennifer Lorn*, a novel, 1923, *The Venetian Glass Nephew*, a novel, 1925, *The Orphan Angel*, a novel, 1926, *Trivial Breath*, poems, 1928, *Mr. Hodge and Mr. Hazard*, a novel, 1928, and *Angels and Earthly Creatures*, poems, 1929. Her novels in particular exhibited her gift for fantasy; *The Orphan Angel*, for example, imagined the later life of Percy Bysshe Shelley if he had been saved from drowning and had been brought to America. She summered frequently at the MacDowell Colony in New Hampshire and in England. She died in New York City on December 16, 1928. *Her Collected Poems*, edited by Benét, appeared in 1932 and her *Collected Prose* in 1933.

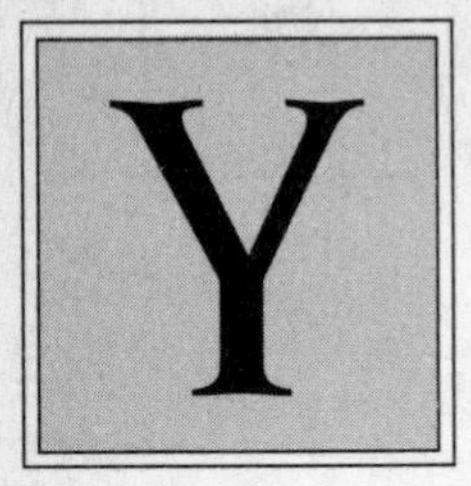

Yale, Caroline Ardelia 1848–1933 educator

Born on September 29, 1848, in Charlotte, Vermont, Caroline Yale grew up there and from the age of ten in Williston, Vermont. She was educated, with the constant encouragement of her parents, at home, by tutors, and in Williston schools, and in 1866–1868 she attended Mount Holyoke Seminary (later College). She taught in schools in Brandon and then Williston, Vermont, until 1870, when she joined the staff of the Clarke Institution for Deaf Mutes (from 1896 the Clarke School for the Deaf) in Northampton, Massachusetts. In 1873 she became associate principal, and in 1886 she succeeded the ailing Harriet B. Rogers as principal.

In all Yale gave 63 years of single-minded devotion to the school and its pupils. In 1882 she began work with a fellow teacher to develop a more detailed and accurate system of phonetic symbols to replace Alexander Melville Bell's "Visible Speech." The resulting "Northampton Vowel and Consonant Charts," explained in her pamphlet *Formation and Development of Elementary English Sounds*, 1892, became the most widely used system in America. In 1889 she established a teacher training department at Clarke, which by the end of her life had sent teachers to schools for the deaf in 31 states and 9 foreign countries.

Her championship of the teaching of speech to the deaf was of such effect that by 1933 all but 2 of the some 200 schools for the deaf in America employed the oral method. She also introduced pioneering classes in manual skills and programs of athletics for deaf children at the Clarke School. In 1890 she helped organize the American Association to Promote the Teaching of Speech to the Deaf, of which she was for many years a director. She also served for 25 years on the Northampton School Committee. She retired as principal of the Clarke School in 1922 but continued to direct the teacher training program until her death. In 1931 she published an autobiography, *Years of Building: Memories of a Pioneer in a Special Field of Education*. Caroline Yale died in Northampton, Massachusetts, on July 2, 1933.

Yalow, Rosalyn Sussman 1921– medical physicist

Born in the Bronx, New York City, on July 19, 1921, Rosalyn Sussman attended public schools and graduated with honors from Hunter College in 1941. She pursued graduate studies at the University of Illinois, where she served also as a teaching fellow in physics in the College of Engineering, and in 1945 received a Ph.D. in physics. During that time, in June 1943, she married A. Aaron Yalow, a fellow physics student. From 1946 to 1950 she lectured on physics at Hunter College. From 1947 she was also a consultant in nuclear physics at the Veterans Administration hospital in the Bronx, where research was being conducted on the medical applications of radioactive materials, and in 1950 she became physicist and assistant head of the radioisotope service at the hospital. There, working in collaboration with Dr. Solomon A. Berson, Yalow investigated a number of methods of using radioactive isotopes to analyze physiological systems. Radioactive iodine, for example, was explored as a tool in the diagnosis and treatment of thyroid disorders.

They devoted several years to refining an entirely new analytic technique they called radioimmunoassay, known simply as RIA. The technique combined the use of radioactive isotopes to "tag" certain hormones or proteins with a sophisticated analytical method based on the stimulation of antibodies and antigenic reactions. Through RIA highly precise measurements of previously undetectable concentrations of hormones, proteins, or other substances present in a sample became possible. The first practical medical result of the new technique came in 1959, when Yalow and Berson discovered that, contrary to common belief, adult diabetics do not always suffer an insufficiency of insulin in the blood; researchers were thus stimulated to seek some unknown factor blocking the action of the insulin. They had earlier confirmed their controversial discovery that therapeutic insulin, commonly obtained from animals was capable of producing an antigenic reaction in the human body and thus being rendered useless. RIA was subsequently applied to other problems of hormone assay, to screen blood in blood banks for hepatitis virus, to assay the effective dosage levels of drugs and antibiotics, to detect suspected but difficult to isolate foreign substances in the blood, and in many other fields.

Yalow was named acting chief of the radioisotope service at the Bronx VA hospital in 1968 and head of the RIA reference laboratory in 1969; she served as chief of the nuclear medicine service from 1970 to 1980. She was a VA senior medical investigator from 1972 to 1992 and was named director of the new Solomon A. Berson Research Laboratory (Dr. Berson had died in 1972) in 1973. She served at the same time as research professor in the department of medicine at Mt. Sinai School of Medicine from 1968 to 1974 and as distinguished service professor from 1974 to 1979. From 1986 she was the Solomon A. Berson distinguished professor at large at Mt. Sinai.. She was awarded the Albert Lasker Prize for Basic Medical Research in 1976, becoming the first woman so honored, and in 1977 she received a half-share of the Nobel Prize for Physiology or Medicine (the other half was shared by Andrew V. Schally and Roger Guillemin, both of whom had used RIA in their research on brain hormones). She was the second woman, after Gerty T. Cori, to win that prize. She was coeditor of the *Hormone and Metabolic Research* journal and author of a great many professional papers, articles, and notes. From 1966 she was a member of the President's Study Group on Careers for Women. Yalow was a professor at large at Albert Einstein College of Medicine from 1979 to 1985, and at the Montefiore Hospital and Medical Center from 1979 to 1985, where she also chairedf the department of clinical science from 1980 to 1985. She was awarded the National Medal of Science in 1988.

Yaw, Ellen Beach 1868–1947 opera singer

Born in Boston, New York, on September 14, 1868, Ellen Yaw attended school in Hamburg and a business institute in Springville, New York. At fourteen she moved to Morris, Minnesota, possibly with her widowed mother. She worked as a secretary to a lawyer and gave shorthand lessons at night to finance voice lessons, which she began in Minneapolis and continued later in Boston and New York City. She made perhaps her first public appearance as a singer in a concert in Brooklyn in November 1888. In 1894, by which time she and her mother had moved to southern California, she made her first national tour in order to raise money for European study. In promoting the tour her manager relied heavily on her ability to sing notes as high as E above high C.

In 1895 Yaw made a European tour, and in January 1896 she appeared at Carnegie Hall in New York. In November 1899 she opened at the Savoy Theatre, London, in *The Rose of Persia*, the soprano role in which had been written especially for her by Sir Arthur Sullivan. The comic opera was a great success, running for more than 200 performances, and it won Ellen Yaw a patroness who sponsored her study with Mathilde Marchesi in Paris. She sang at the Opéra-Comique while in Paris, and after her three-year period of intensive study there she appeared in Nice, Rome, Switzerland, and England. She also gave a concert for the shah of Persia. She made her grand opera debut in *Lucia di Lammermoor* in Rome in 1907 and sang that opera at the Metropolitan Opera House in New York in 1908.

She continued her successful concert tours of Europe until 1912 and her American tours until 1931. Known widely as "Lark Ellen," she delighted critics and audiences with the richness and beauty of her voice even more than with her range. In 1931 she retired to an estate in West Covina, California, where in 1934 she opened the Lark Ellen Bowl. She gave recitals and concerts for charity until 1946, notably her annual affairs for the benefit of the Los Angeles Newsboys Home, which was renamed the Lark Ellen Home for Boys in her honor. Ellen Yaw died in West Covina, California, on September 9, 1947.

Young, Ella Flagg 1845–1918 educator

Born on January 15, 1845, in Buffalo, New York, Ella Flagg grew up there and from 1858 in Chicago. She attended public schools and in 1862 graduated from the Chicago Normal School. She began teaching in a primary school that year and in 1865 was named principal of the new practice school of the Chicago Normal School. In 1868 she married William Young, a local merchant who died the next year. In 1871 she resigned her principalship and resumed classroom teaching in a high school. In 1875 she became principal of a grammar school, and in 1887 she was appointed assistant superintendent of Chicago schools. In that post she worked to improve teacher training and to include teachers in the development of administrative policies.

In 1895 Young began studying part-time under John Dewey at the University of Chicago, and on her resignation as assistant superintendent in 1899, following upon a reversal of her liberal policies, she was appointed an associate professor of pedagogy under Dewey. She received a Ph.D. degree from the University of Chicago in 1900 and was advanced to full professor. Her dissertation was published in 1900 as *Isolation in the School*, the first of her three volumes in the University of Chicago Contributions to Education series she wrote with Dewey; her other two were *Ethics in the School*, 1902, and *Some Types of Modern Educational Theory*, 1902.

Young left the university in 1904, shortly after Dewey did, and in 1905 she was named principal of the Chicago Normal School (a second school of that name, later Chicago Teachers College, now Chicago State University). In 1909 she was appointed superintendent of Chicago schools, becoming the first woman to head the school system of a major city in the United States. She again made the improvement of teacher training, the recognition of teachers' professional status, and the broadening of their responsibilities the major policy goals of her office. She also expanded the curricula of the schools to include vocational and physical training. In 1910, aided by Margaret Haley of the Chicago Teachers' Federation, she was elected president of the National Education Association; she was the first woman to hold that post.

In 1913 she defused a cabal within the Board of Education that planned to block her reappointment as superintendent by resigning. She resumed the post with the assurance that she would be reappointed, but when, in December, she was not, she resigned again. A public protest led by Jane Addams and others forced the resignation of four board members, and the reconstituted board reappointed Young. She resigned permanently in 1915. She was active in the woman suffrage movement, and in 1917 she became chairman of the Woman's Liberty Loan Committee. She died in Washington, D.C., on October 26, 1918.

Zaharias, Mildred Ella Didrikson 1914–1956 athlete

Born in Port Arthur, Texas, on June 26, 1914, Mildred Didrikson was the daughter of Norwegian immigrant parents. She grew up in Beaumont, Texas, where she starred on the girls' basketball team in high school. In high school and later as an employee of the Employers Casualty Company of Dallas, which fielded a championship amateur basketball team, she was chosen to the All-American teams in 1930, 1931, and 1932. In July 1932, at the women's national track and field tournament held by the Amateur Athletic Union in Evanston, Illinois, she entered eight of the ten events and won five of them: the 80-meter hurdles, the shotput, the broad jump, the baseball throw, and the javelin throw. Her personal score exceeded that of the second-place team.

In the Olympic Games of 1932 at Los Angeles she won two gold medals, setting new world records of 143′ 3¹¹⁄₁₆″ in the javelin throw (bettering the old mark by nearly 11 feet) and 11.7 seconds in the 80-meter hurdles. Her record-breaking mark in the high jump was disallowed because of objections to her then-unorthodox western roll. Shortly after the Olympics she turned professional and began giving athletic exhibitions throughout the country. She excelled in swimming, baseball (she played an exhibition with the touring House of David team and pitched for the St. Louis Cardinals), and billiards. For a time she toured in vaudeville.

In 1935 Didrikson took up golf and, regaining her status as an amateur, soon became the leading woman golfer in the United States. Her amateur status was revoked in 1936, and she toured as a pro for a time. In December 1938 she married wrestler George Zaharias and settled in Beverly Hills, California. In 1940 she won the Western and Texas Open golf tournaments. Her amateur status was restored in 1944, and that year she won the Western Open again. She became the first three-time winner of the Western in 1945. In 1946 she won the National Women's Amateur title. In that year she also became the first three-time winner of the Associated Press poll of woman athlete of the year (she had won in 1932 and 1945); she was to win again in 1947, 1950, and 1954. In 1947 she won 17 straight golf titles, including the British Women's Amateur, of which she was the first U.S. winner. She turned pro again in 1948 and won that year's U.S. Open and continued to win most of the tournaments in which she played. In 1950 she was voted in an Associated Press poll the outstanding woman athlete of the century. She won the U.S. Open again in 1950. She was the leading money-winner on the women's golf tour in 1948, 1949, 1950, and 1951. By 1952 it was obvious that she was very ill, and the next year she underwent an operation for cancer. She appeared to have recovered when she won the women's U.S. Open (for the third time) and the All-American Open in 1954. But she was operated on once again in 1956 and died that year in Galveston, Texas, on September 27. Her autobiography, *This Life I've Led*, had appeared in 1955.

Zakrzewska, Marie Elizabeth 1829–1902 physician

Born in Berlin on September 6, 1829, Marie Zakrzewska was the daughter of a member of the Polish gentry who had been retired from the Prussian army. She attended school until she was fourteen, when her father decided she had had enough education. She had early developed a strong interest in medicine when she had accompanied her mother to a school for midwives at the Charité Hospital in Berlin. At twenty she was admitted to the school; she became a teaching assistant in her second year, and she graduated in 1851. In 1852 she was appointed chief midwife and professor in the school, but staff opposition to her forced her to resign after six months.

In 1853 Zakrzewska emigrated to the United States to seek further training and a freer atmosphere. After a year in New York City, during which she supported herself by knitting, she met Dr. Elizabeth Blackwell, who helped her master English and secured her admission to the medical school of Western Reserve University in Cleveland, from which

Dr. Emily Blackwell had just graduated. Marie Zakrzewska received her M.D. degree in March 1856 and returned to New York, where, after failing to find a landlord who would rent office space to a woman physician, she opened her practice in Dr. Blackwell's quarters. She helped raise funds for Blackwell's projected New York Infirmary for Women and Children, which opened in May 1857, and she served as resident physician and general manager there for two years.

In 1859 Zakrzewska accepted the posts of professor of obstetrics and diseases of women and children and resident physician of a planned hospital at the New England Female Medical College in Boston. She held the posts for three years, resigning in 1862 as the result of profound disagreement with the college's founder, Samuel Gregory, who wished the college to be little more than a training course for midwives. (He had founded it because he found the idea of male doctors attending childbirth to be morally repugnant.)

On her resignation Gregory dissolved the small hospital she had developed. With the private support of several board members and trustees of the college she founded the New England Hospital for Women and Children in July 1862. From the outset the hospital was devoted to clinical care and to the clinical training of women physicians and nurses. Zakrzewska served as resident physician for a year, as attending physician from 1863 to 1887, and as advisory physician thereafter. She maintained high standards in the training courses and contributed greatly thereby to the eventual general acceptance of women physicians. In addition she maintained a growing private practice throughout Boston. She was also a supporter of the woman suffrage cause and a member of the New England Women's Club. She retired in 1899 and died in Jamaica Plain (now part of Boston) on May 12, 1902.

Zane, Betty 1766?–1831? frontier heroine

Born about 1766, probably in Hardy County (although possibly in Berkeley County) in the part of Virginia that is now West Virginia, Elizabeth Zane later lived in the town of Wheeling, which was founded in 1769 by her older brothers Ebenezer, Jonathan, and Silas. In September 1782, according to legend, she had just returned from Philadelphia, where she had been attending school, when the settlement was attacked by Indians. All the inhabitants crowded into Fort Henry but did not have time to secure a supply of powder from the magazine in Colonel Ebenezer Zane's fortified house some 40 or 50 yards from the fort.

When the powder in the fort ran dangerously low, Betty Zane volunteered to fetch more from her brother's house. To objections that a man could run faster, she is supposed to have replied "You have not one man to spare; a woman will not be missed in the defense of the fort" and "'Tis better a maid than a man should die." The gates were unbarred and she dashed for the house. The attackers, amazed and perhaps amused, shouted "Squaw, squaw," and did not fire. When she reappeared from the house with a supply of powder, however, they realized what she was about and opened fire. Although her clothes were pierced, no bullet struck her, and she regained the fort safely. The powder she brought enabled the fort to hold out until relief arrived. The tale is not well attested and is the subject of conflicting testimony, but it is nonetheless fixed in legend.

It was first published in *Chronicles of Border Warfare*, 1831, by Alexander S. Withers and was later the central incident in the novel *Betty Zane*, 1903, by Zane Grey, a descendant of the subject's. Little is known of Betty Zane's later life. She married and moved to Martins Ferry, Ohio, where she died about 1831.

Zeisler, Fannie Bloomfield 1863–1927 pianist

Born on July 16, 1863, in Bielitz, Austrian Silesia, Fannie Blumenfeld came with her mother and brothers to the United States in 1867 and joined her father, who had preceded them, in Appleton, Wisconsin. From 1869 she grew up in Chicago. She is said to have taken her first piano lessons from her brother Maurice (later a well known philologist and Sanskritist); later she studied with Bernhard Ziehn and from 1874 with Carl Wolfsohn. She made her public performing debut in February 1875 in one of Wolfsohn's Beethoven Society concerts. With the encouragement of the Russian pianist Annette Essipoff, who heard her in Chicago in 1877, she traveled to Vienna in 1878 to study under Theodor Leschetizky. She returned to Chicago in 1883, by which time she had anglicized her name to Bloomfield.

She gave her first full concert there in April 1884 and in January 1885 made her New York debut. From 1884 she was on the faculty of the School of Lyric and Dramatic Art in Chicago. In October 1885 she married Sigmund Zeisler, a lawyer; their home became a center of cultural and intellectual life in Chicago. While caring for her family and overseeing the work of her students she slowly built her concert career. During 1888–1889 she again studied with Leschetizky in Vienna. Her first European tour took place in 1893, when she appeared in Berlin, Leipzig, Dresden, and Vienna before illness forced her to return home. She toured Germany and Austria again in the fall of 1894, and by the end of that tour she was acknowledged one of the foremost concert pianists in the world. She combined flawless technique with a fiery and powerful expressiveness that enabled her to render the classical and Romantic masterworks with entire authority.

Subsequent European tours occurred in 1898, when she appeared mainly in England, in 1902, when she appeared in Germany, Austria, Switzerland, Denmark, and Paris (she was a great success at the Concerts Lamoureux, where her playing of the Saint-Saëns C-minor concerto won over an initially hostile claque), in 1911–1912, when she toured most of western Europe, and in 1914. She toured the United States annually, except for the 1905–1906 season, when illness kept her home, and from 1891 she appeared with Theodore Thomas and the Chicago Symphony Orchestra annually for 19 seasons. Her final public performance took place in February 1925 in Chicago, when she marked 50 years on the concert stage by playing the little Beethoven Andante Favori she had begun with in 1875 and concertos by Chopin and Schumann. She died in Chicago on August 20, 1927.

Index